THE CLASSIC
ENCYCLOPEDIA OF THE DOG.

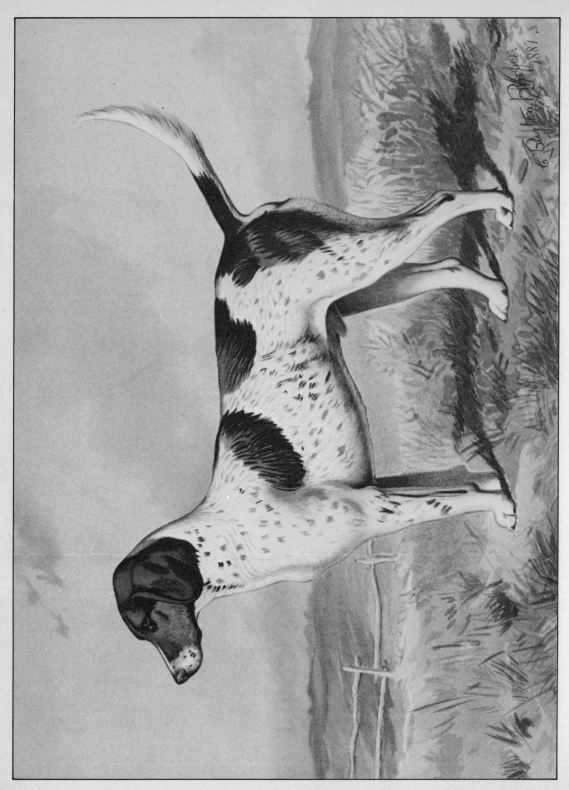

FOXHOUND.

THE CLASSIC
ENCYCLOPEDIA
OF THE DOG.

BY

VERO SHAW, B.A. CANTAB.,

Assisted by the Leading Breeders of the Day.

WITH AN APPENDIX ON

CANINE MEDICINE AND SURGERY,

BY W. GORDON STABLES, C.M., M.D., R.N.

WITH A NEW FOREWORD BY
HERM DAVID

BONANZA BOOKS

NEW YORK

ORIGINALLY PUBLISHED IN 1879-81 AS *THE ILLUSTRATED BOOK OF THE DOG*.

This 1984 edition is published by Bonanza Books,
distributed by Crown Publishers, Inc., One Park Avenue,
New York, New York 10016.

Manufactured in the United States of America

Library of Congress Cataloging in Publication Data

Shaw, Vero.
The classic encyclopedia of the dog.

Reprint. The illustrated book of the dog. Originally
published: London ; New York : Cassell, Petter, Galpin,
1879-1881.
Includes index.
1. Dogs.   2. Dog breeds.   3. Dogs—Diseases.
I. Stables, Gordon, 1840–1910.   II. Title.
SF426.S53   1984   636.7   84–2980
ISBN 0–517–43282–X

h   g   f   e   d   c   b   a

The publisher would like to acknowledge, with
gratitude, the assistance of Clifford Hubbard, dog book
specialist, of Aberystwyth, Wales, in researching
information on the author, Vero Shaw.

CAUTIONARY NOTICE

This book was originally published in 1879–81, and offers extensive suggestions for the handling and care of dogs commonly accepted at that time. Although there is value and interest in the long, vivid descriptions, the veterinarian advice in the book can not be substituted for modern methods of veterinary medicine.

Furthermore, as it pertains to human medical needs—as in the case of rabies and other diseases—the information is thoroughly outdated and potentially harmful. The reader should consult his or her physician or other modern medical authorities.

𝕿𝖔

THE REVEREND GRENVILLE FRODSHAM HODSON,

OF NORTH PETHERTON, BRIDGWATER,

𝕿𝖍𝖎𝖘 𝖂𝖔𝖗𝖐 𝖎𝖘 𝕯𝖊𝖉𝖎𝖈𝖆𝖙𝖊𝖉,

AS AN ACKNOWLEDGMENT OF THE BENEFIT DERIVED

FROM HIS TEACHING,

BY HIS AFFECTIONATE NEPHEW,

THE AUTHOR.

LA BELLE SAUVAGE YARD,
1881.

CONTENTS.

CANINE MEDICINE AND SURGERY.

LIST OF ILLUSTRATIONS.

—◆—

PLATES.*

DRAWINGS ON WOOD.

Note: The names and owners of the dogs portrayed in the Plates can be found on page 665.

FOREWORD

Perhaps it will be best to start with a bit of explanation. Editors have their ways. Like the rest of us, they are prone to leave their marks. Writers consider title tampering, when it is irresponsible, a not too sophisticated form of graffiti. That was my suspicion when I first discovered that the title this great book had proudly carried for over a century had been replaced. But, on reflection, I realized that time, truth, and technology, and not editorial caprice, were responsible.

This work, under its original title, *The Illustrated Book of the Dog,* was an immediate classic upon publication one hundred five years ago—and it has been increasingly appreciated ever since. Author Vero Shaw had had illustrious, immediate predecessors as authors of English dog books, among them Blaine, Hamilton, Jesse, Richardson, Walsh, and Youatt. But none was so sumptuously published. Except for some of Walsh's works, all were published personal pontifications. Shaw's work was collected expertise.

In 1879–1881, a book as profusely and as well illustrated as this was both a publishing rarity and a triumph. Its state-of-the-printing-art portraits of dogs were indeed something to be proclaimed in its title. Now, we have a world awash in photographic and electronic images. We have laser scanning for color photoengravings, closely followed by even more remarkable laser printing. An illustrated book is, now, a nonevent. But, a classic reintroduced, particularly one dealing with mankind's most devoted, most absorbing, even most essential, animal friends can, or should, be a publishing event.

"Encyclopedia" rather accurately describes what *The Illustrated Book of the Dog* was and has been. It is a gathering of the best knowledge of its time and place on its subject—not a conventional, signed work by an individual as this book has been universally catalogued.

And, it is not just sales puffery to call this a "classic." For those who could find copies to consult, it has offered guidance, as well as hand-crafted beauty, for all of its years. This traditionalist concedes that what the editors have done with the title is reasonable, accurate, and more illuminating than the original.

The new title is the entire extent of the editorial change. Except for that and this introduction and biographical notes, all text remains as it was.

It was a confluence of fortunate but fleeting factors in publishing that made Vero Shaw's *Illustrated Book of the Dog* a notable achievement as a popular art form and an authoritative contemporary contribution to the study of dogs. It is still authoritative, but now, chiefly as a stimulating opportunity to look back at the dogs, their breeders, and exhibitors during the very early years of organized dog affairs and competitions.

Thanks to its collective expertise, its propitious timing, and to the quality and quantity of its text-enhancing illustrations, this work strongly influenced the directions of dog breeding in its time, and for decades thereafter. Some British predecessors, starting with Topsell in 1604, had illustrated breeds that were known in England, but none nearly as well, as accurately, or as completely as Shaw.

It was—and remains—impossible to convey what a breed should look like in a written standard. Words alone cannot do that. Without faithful pictures of good examples of the breeds, or opportunities to view and study the animals, it was, and is, impossible to breed toward uniformity. How else to keep the Mastiffs from becoming St. Bernards and vice versa?

Today, we have unlimited opportunities to see what the various breeds should look like. Dog shows are within reasonable reach of almost everyone in Westernized societies and there are illustrated dog books and specialized periodicals beyond count. One hundred five years ago, in the United Kingdom, however, dog shows were few, and not all could travel to them. In North America, they were fledgling, marginal, generally inaccessible events. *The Illustrated Book of the Dog* filled a need of its time. For overseas purchasers and breeders (including those in the United States and Canada) it was an invaluable guide. It is still valuable, but now for its beauty, and because it offers treasured guidance from the past.

It can also happily serve, with certain understandings, as a guide to the breeds. Of the seventy breeds covered, there are many that are presently under-appreciated only because they haven't been publicized. For example, all of the smaller spaniels are closely related. Very recently, the Sussex Spaniel almost became extinct. In the United States, the American Cocker Spaniel is favored over the Sussex by more than 5,500 to 1. Not even the most ardent of Cocker enthusiasts would contend their breed is 5,500 times better than its near cousin. That is the extreme example.

The American Kennel Club registers dogs from approximately 130 breeds. Just fifteen of those enjoy over seventy percent of the public's patronage! That shouldn't be, but is.

This book is an excellent place to explore for deserving, very worthwhile breeds. But, be aware that the world's registries embrace over 200 breeds, each with its attractive features. If you don't find your breed here, keep looking. For everyone who wants a dog, there is a specialized breed that will please.

One further, essential caution: Be amused, if you choose, by the quaint veterinary advice, but don't follow it unless you have a modern veterinarian's endorsement.

Those who would know how to breed more effectively, to judge more knowledgeably, or to understand better what the breeds were originally meant to be, will appreciate the new availability of the wisdom collected in this book.

The dogs here described and depicted were the first to be registered and the ones most bred from. In professional parlance, they were our "foundation stock." This reintroduction of Shaw's compilation affords activists in seventy popular breeds opportunities to experience the concepts of the foundation breeders and, if they choose, to reevaluate their own breeding objectives.

In recent decades, *The Illustrated Book of the Dog* has become increasingly rare. Only a few have had opportunities to study and enjoy it. In the years since 1879, interest in pure-bred dogs has increased at least a thousandfold. Meanwhile, surviving copies of the book have been sought, bought, and stripped of their prints by dealers in such. Thus, supply has decreased, while the demand has been multiplying. Recently, offers for intact copies have been approaching $500.

In 1879–1881, interest in pure-bred dogs was a maturing excitement. The people of the United Kingdom were nearly as united in their admiration of the dog as they were of Queen and Empire. Those were England's glory days. Britannia was managing to stay out of Europe's wars. She had a firm and expanding grasp on much of the world's sources of wealth. Even her middle class was doing rather well. Together, the middle class and the wealthy formed a ready audience for ambitious publishing ventures. When Cassell, Petter, Galpin & Company, the original publishers of this book, appraised the market potential for their expensive project, the signs were highly favorable.

Books represented education, and in a class-oriented society, education—or the appearance of education—was a prerequisite to status. In Victorian England, status seeking—sometimes genteel—was an institutionalized fetish. Then, as now, some too busy to study sought culture through purchase. Fine and highly decorated bindings were highly favored—particularly by those buying more for display than information.

Publishers had a long-established sales device available which enabled them to develop profit insurance, and even collect some of their capital expenditure in advance. We see a variation now in television merchandising: "Order the first volume of this series. Then, each month you will receive another volume in the mail. You can . . ." In the nineteenth century one bought books like Shaw's as a subscriber to a series, with no return privileges. When the last "serial" was in hand the patron would send the lot off to his own bookbinder. That explains the considerable variation encountered in bindings and pagination. *The Illustrated Book of the Dog* was first issued that way, extending from 1879 into 1881. The publisher's two later editions were issued in gilt-decorated and illustrated cloth bindings.

As we entered the closing third of the nineteenth century, trains had replaced horses as the mode of transportation over distance. Not only could they move people faster and more comfortably, they also could transport heavy goods from place to place. They were erasing centuries of isolation and provincialism. Steam power was making possible what could not have been contemplated a half-century earlier. Science and its potentialities excited all of the literate world. The British referred to animal breeding as a "science," and considered themselves (and still do) the world's greatest practitioners. Actually, the science of genetics is almost exclusively a twentieth century development. But, despite some hard-fixed misconceptions, English and other agriculturally oriented societies had developed animal breeding to an art form. Ironically, the transportation that had breeched so many political, sociological, and commercial barriers erased the isolation responsible for the development of most of the world's best-known breeds of dogs.

The people of the United Kingdom's class-structured society were conditioned to value and patronize the tastes of their "betters"—in direct proportion to the station of the tastemakers. And, at the top, Queen-Empress Victoria made considerable public display of her own dogs, consented to be royal patroness of the Kennel Club and even did some limited breeding. That was the ultimate endorsement of pure-bred dogs. (Pekingese were introduced to the Western world in 1860 when the Duke of Wellington presented Victoria with one of five seized in the looting of the Chinese Summer Palace. That got them the attention they needed to survive and prosper.)

Printing technologies were advancing rapidly. It was possible, at great expense, to print in full color. But photoengraving was still about a decade and-a-half into the future. Most illustrations had to be laboriously hand carved from hard woods. Works were signed by both the artists and the engravers. The engravers would soon be technologically displaced, but the skills of those illustrative engravers were at or nearing their peak in 1879–81.

Dog clubs were forming, crowds were attending the metropolitan dog shows. A tiny but growing dog export industry was developing. For a dog book on a grand scale there was a profit-promising potential audience. Printing technologies were newly capable of quality impressions in quantity, while illustration was still the province of artisans. In Shaw, the publishers had found a man skilled in organization who had a bent for writing and the necessary editorial contacts. He knew dogs, and was respected by the United Kingdom's dog activists.

The publishers were anxious to display and exploit their advancing technology.

It was, indeed, a confluence of favorable factors that made this fine book possible.

New York City, 1984   HERM DAVID

VERO-KEMBALL SHAW

THE RIGHT TALENT IN THE RIGHT PLACE AT THE RIGHT TIME

The author of this book has been something of a mystery to contemporary researchers. My friend Clifford L. B. Hubbard of Aberystwyth, Wales, offered to help in the hunt for clues about the man's life. In a preliminary report, this most assiduous of researchers in dog lore said: "I am amazed that so little is known of so important a personage." Hubbard, however, persisted and unearthed much information which, in turn, led to other sources. American Kennel Club Librarian Roberta Vesley and Newark Free Public Library staffers also savored and joined our challenge. They, also, provided key facts.

The most salient facts known about Vero Shaw are proclaimed by catalogue cards in libraries across the world. They list the books and pamphlets he authored after this, his first; none was a comparable success. Shaw's talents were as compiler, an elicitor of literary contributions and expertise from the right people. He went on writing books for another forty-three years—but they are memorable only because of his association with *The Illustrated Book of the Dog* (the original title of this book.)

For Captain Vero-Kemball Shaw, Bulldogs were the breed of choice. He bred, owned, exhibited, and judged them. As a founder of the British Bulldog Club, he would have been one of the formulators of the modern Bulldog, the breed that has since, as a reflection of British doughtiness, become a national symbol.

The full-page illustration of Bulldogs in this book includes Smasher, a dog Shaw had sold before publication. Hubbard found, as well, that Shaw also owned Sepoy in 1874, the grandsire of a celebrated winner, Don Pedro.

Available records are not definitive about when and for how long, but Shaw served, at one time, as kennel editor of the British periodical, *The Stockkeeper,* and, after that, in the same capacity for its prestigious rival, *The Field*.

Presumably such a service would have given Shaw contacts with the contributors whose expertise was necessary to essay so ambitious a work as *The Illustrated Book of the Dog*. The publisher would have required the availability of extensive, high-quality contacts before adventuring into the ambitious and costly project. Although he is recorded here as author, this work is largely a stitching together by Shaw of contributions from many enthusiasts and authorities. His supporting cast, carefully credited, gave this work comprehensiveness and authenticity. It is dog history by the history makers.

Shaw is recorded as either the author or coauthor of eleven books—some of them brief pamphlets—in addition to rather prolific contributions to periodicals. In 1883, *The Illustrated Book of the Dog* appeared in bound form—almost coinciding with issuance of the last of the original issue serial numbers to subscribers. A second bound edition was issued, undated, in the nineties.

Shaw next wrote, or rather compiled, the *1883 National Dog Club Stud Book*. One might conjecture that it was during this period that he worked on *The Field*. Dr. John Henry Walsh, the indomitable "Stonehenge," was then its editor.

Walsh had masterminded formation of the National Dog Club's brief challenge to The Kennel Club. That was probably viewed as treason by members of the exclusive, private Kennel Club which still regulates pure-bred dog affairs in the United Kingdom. Men of Shaw's achievements were usually invited to Kennel Club membership. However, his name does not appear in its records. Involvement with the National Club may well have cost Shaw his invitation.

Also, in 1883, a most interesting variation of *The Illustrated Book of the Dog* appeared on the scene. Published from Leipzig and London, edited, revised and supplemented by Richard von Schniederberg, it was titled *Das Illustrirte Buch von Hunde.* Added was a new chapter, "Der Deutsche Vostehunde," with six extra engravings. This version won the state exposition medal at Berlin. The extra chapter was also offered separately, in wrappers. There was a Vienna edition the following year.

Then, between 1884 and 1891, there was a gap in Shaw's book writing for which we have not found an explanation. He subsequently returned to the ranks as a coauthor, with W.L.A. Coutts, of *Notes for the Brookfield Stud*.

Shaw was a major contributor to the 1894 version of W.C.A. Blew's *Light Horses: Their Breeds and Management*. It was "Livestock Handbook No. 2."

His *Dogs for Hot Climates* (1895) was written with Captain Matthew Horace Hayes, whose *Points of the Horse* remains the definitive work on the subject. Hayes was an Army veterinarian with much service in India and elsewhere in the Empire. Along with Marey, Stillman, and Muybridge, he was a pioneer researcher into the dynamics of animal locomotion. It is easy to visualize the two Army men, of equal rank, passing the months in discussion, debating the finer points of dogs and horses, while stationed at some remote outpost in India or Egypt.

How to Choose a Dog first appeared in 1897. Only eighty-one pages, it was little more than a pamphlet. *How to Choose a Dog* was a good selling title. Beginning sometime in 1922, one of the puppy press publishers picked it up. He kept it going for many years by inserting limited updatings after each press run had sold out.

The following year, 1898, Shaw's *Don'ts: Instruction What to Avoid in Buying, Managing, Feeding, and Exhibiting Dogs* [sic] was offered. Only thirty-four pages, it was a "Stockkeeper Handbook." Then, in 1899, came *British Horses Illustrated,* published along the lines of Shaw's initial, successful encyclopedic format.

There followed for Shaw another apparent publishing gap, this time of ten years. It ended in 1909 with his *Encyclopedia of the Stable,* which had a second, undated edition. That fixed Shaw's final format. Both his *Encyclopedia of Poultry* and *Encyclopedia of the Kennel* were published in 1913—on the eve of World War I. After that, the old soldier seems to have "just faded away." We have been unable, even with the valued assistance of the British Museum, to find further trace of him.

H.D.

CHAPTER I.

HISTORICAL AND LITERARY.

S in former works relating to dogs but small attention has been devoted by the authors to the modes of classification adopted by the earlier writers on the subject, a brief notice of the principal cannot but be of interest. As to later works, in several encyclopædias there has been an attempt made to classify the different varieties, but such classification has, so far as our observation carries us, invariably been founded on the structural development of the different breeds alone, and not unfrequently on comparison with the characteristics of other animals, little or no attention having been paid to the various temperaments and capabilities of the several breeds. Visitors to the great shows of the present day, on the contrary, must be struck by the extreme simplicity of the arrangement of the catalogues, which invariably divide the candidates into two divisions, namely, one for sporting, and one for non-sporting dogs. In our opinion this is an ample distinction, for all practical purposes; since in the present day, in consequence of dogs being so much better understood than they formerly were, the uses and capabilities of each breed are well appreciated by those at all interested in them. Moreover, the large increase in the number of breeds (owing to the manufacture of so many new varieties of late years) has rendered an elaborate classification undesirable, as being likely to complicate instead of facilitating the task of distinguishing between the various breeds.

The majority of the earlier writers on the dog, however, adopt different classifications in the lists of dogs published by them, and these, being of some considerable historical interest, we propose recapitulating; whilst due attention shall be given to the scientific division of Cuvier, in which the structural development of the dog is compared with that of other mammals.

Before turning our attention to the various works on the dog which have from time to time appeared in our own language, we may mention that in the earlier part of the Christian era only two races of dogs out of the sixteen or seventeen known to the ancients, are stated to have been recognised by them as hunting dogs. These were Greyhounds, and dogs hunting by scent. Arrian, however, also called the younger Xenophon, who wrote in the year A.D. 130, affirms that dogs hunting by sight and not by scent were quite unknown in the time of Xenophon the elder. At the same time Arrian, in his work above alluded to, most accurately describes our modern Greyhound; and the anonymous translator of this writer, who has been the means of rendering his works so popular, fairly shows the dog to be of Celtic origin.

The earliest work on dogs in English is a MS. in the British Museum, entitled the "Mayster of Game," and is written by Edmund de Langley. This work was published in the fourteenth century, and deals principally with hunting subjects, though frequent allusion is made to dogs therein.

The earliest *printed* work in the English language in which the various breeds of dogs then in existence are referred to, is the "Book of Field Sports," written by Dame Juliana Berners, Prioress of Sopwell Nunnery, in Hertfordshire. This lady, who was born about the end of the fourteenth century, thus expresses herself in the above work :—"Thyse ben the names of houndes, fyrste there is a Grehoun, a Bastard, a Mengrell, a Mastif, a Lemor, a Spanyel, Raches, Kenettys, Teroures, Butchers Houndes, Dunghyll dogges, Tryndeltaylles, and Pryckeryd currys, and smalle ladyes poppees that bere aweye the flees." From this catalogue it would appear that the list of dogs which came under Miss Berners' notice was a very limited one. It is, however, an important one; inasmuch as it shows that many of the breeds of dogs then in existence have retained at least their names until the present time, in spite of the vast increase in number of breeds.

The next work from which we are able to quote is a short treatise on English dogs, originally written in Latin, by Dr. John Caius, physician to Queen Elizabeth, and published in 1576. There was, however, also a translation of the work in old English, which we quote as more clearly showing the ideas of the time. According to Dr. Caius—

All Englishe dogges be eyther of
$$\begin{cases} \text{A gentle kind, serving the game.} \\ \text{A homely kind, apt for sundry necessary uses.} \\ \text{A currish kind, meet for many toyes.} \end{cases}$$

The first of these three classes is divided by Dr. Caius into two sections—viz., Venatici, which were used for the purpose of hunting beasts; and Aucupatorii, which served in the pursuit of fowl. The Venatici are treated by this author as follows :—

Dogges serving y pastime of hunting beastes are divided into
$$\begin{cases} \text{Leverarius, or Harriers.} \\ \text{Terrarius, or Terrars.} \\ \text{Sanguinarius, or Bloodhounds.} \\ \text{Agaseus, or Gazehounds.} \\ \text{Leporarius, or Grehounds.} \\ \text{Lorarius, or Lyemmer.} \\ \text{Vertigus, or Tumbler.} \\ \text{Canis furax, or Stealer.} \end{cases}$$

The next section of Dr. Caius's work is taken up by the dogs used for pursuing fowl, viz., Aucupatorii, which consisted of—

Dogs used for fowling.
$$\begin{cases} \text{Index, or Setter.} \\ \text{Aquaticus, or Spaniell.} \end{cases}$$

Section three is entirely devoted to the Spaniell Gentle, or Comforter. And Section four consists merely of—

| Canis Pastoralis, or the Shepherd's Dogge. The Mastive, or Bandogge, called Canis Villaticus, or Carbenarius. | which hath sundry names derived from sundry circumstances, as | The Keeper's or Watchman's. The Butcher's Dogge. The Messinger's or Carrier's. The Mooner. The Water Drawer. The Tinker's Curr. The Fencer. |

In the sixth section are the—

Admonitor, or Wapp.
Vernerpator, or Turnespet.
Saltator, or Dauncer.

The varieties of dogs contained in these six sections prove that there was at all events a considerable increase in the number of the breeds of dogs between Dr. Caius's time and that of Dame Berners. The former, however, is extremely vague and rambling in many of his statements concerning the dogs he describes in his work ; but the value to be attached to that will scarcely be diminished by this fault on his part, when it is remembered that Dr. Caius's work is the first book published in the English language which solely confines itself to the various breeds of dogs, and the manner of hunting them.

Shakespeare seems to have been a student of Dame Juliana Berners' work, for in *King Lear*, Act III., scene 6, the following lines occur :—

" Be thy mouth or black or white,
Tooth that poisons, if it bite.
Mastiff, greyhound, mongrel grim,
Hound or spaniel, brach or lym,
Or bobtail tike, or trundle tail,
Tom will make them weep and wail ;
For, with throwing thus my head,
Dogs leap the hatch, and all are fled."

Linnæus, in his classification of animals, enumerates the following breeds of dogs :—

Canis Familiaris, or Faithful Dog.
Canis Domesticus, or Shepherd's Dog.
Canis Pomeranus, or Pomeranian.
    (The above being the Chien Loup, or Wolf-dog of Buffon.)
Canis Sibiricus, or Siberian Dog.
Canis Islandicus, or Iceland Dog.
Canis Aquaticus Major, or great Water Dog (Grand Barbet).
Canis Aquaticus Minor, or lesser Water Dog.
Canis Brevipilis Pyrame.
Canis Parvus Melitans, or little Maltese Dog.
Canis Extrarius, or ⎫ Spaniel.
Canis Hyspanicus ⎭
Canis Pilosus, or Hairy Maltese Dog.
Canis Leoninus, or Lion Dog.
    (This was a small dog, having long hair on the fore-part of the body like a lion, the hinder part only growing short hair.)
Canis Variegatus, or Little Danish Dog.
Canis Hybridus, or Bastard Pug Dog, also called Roquet.
Canis Fricator, or Pug Dog.
Canis Molossus, or Bulldog.

Canis Anglicus, sometime Bellicosus, or Mastiff.
    (The above is the Canis Mastious of Ray).
Canis Sagax, or German Hound.
Canis Gallicus, Hound.
    (Also C. G. Venatorius, or sagacious Hunting Dog.)
Canis Scoticus, Bloodhound.
Canis Avicularis, Pointer.
Canis Aquatilis, Barbet (see above).
Canis Cursorius, Greyhound.
Canis Hibernicus, Irish Hound.
Canis Turcicus, Turkish Hound.
Canis Graius, Scotch Hunting Dog.
Graius Hirsatus, rough Scotch Hunting Dog.
Canis Italicus, Italian Greyhound.
Canis Orientalis, Persian Greyhound.
Canis Egyptius, Hairless Greyhound.
Canis Laniaris, Lurcher.
Canis Fuillus, Boarhound.
Canis Vertigus, Turnspit.
Canis Americanus, the Ala.
Canis Antarcticus, New Holland Dog.

Gervase Markham and Nicholas Cox, in the works they publish, allude chiefly to sporting dogs and their functions, at the same time making the smallest allusion to such varieties as did not enter into their sports. The writings of these authors cannot therefore be considered as standard works on the dog, nor do they apparently profess to be so.

Since the time of Linnæus several of the above varieties have apparently ceased to exist, while others have become amalgamated with each other, but it is still evident that many breeds alluded to by the Swedish naturalist are the originators of similar varieties in existence at the present day.

In Daniel's "Book of Rural Sports," published in the early part of the present century a subdivision of British dogs into the three following sections appears :—A. The most generous kinds ; B. Farm Dogs ; C. Mongrels. Of these the former is again subdivided into three subdivisions—viz., (1) Dogs of chase ; (2) Fowlers ; (3) Lap-dogs ; in fact, the classification of Dr. Caius is exactly carried out by the writer.

Daniel's work also reproduces a very curious genealogical table of the different races of dogs which Buffon drew up, in which all are described as originating from the Sheep-dog. This theory scarcely demands contradiction ; but we append the table, which is of considerable interest as representing the ideas of that great naturalist.

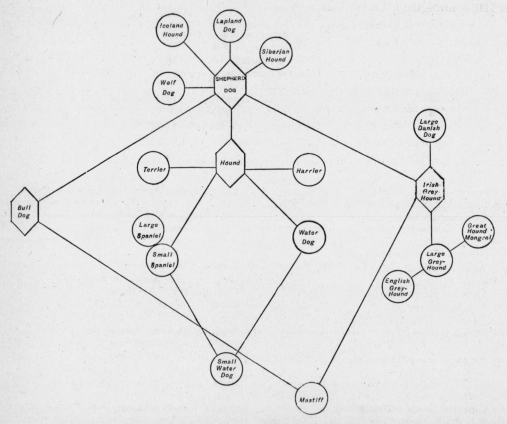

FIG. 1.—BUFFON'S GENEALOGICAL TABLE OF THE DIFFERENT RACES OF DOGS.

The arrangement adopted by Cuvier is regulated, as we have said before, chiefly by the structural development of the various breeds. He divides the canine world into three groups—namely, Matins, Spaniels, and Dogues. In considering the first group—Matins—he observes that the anatomical character of the division are—head more or less elongated, with the parietal or side bones gradually drawing towards each other. In this category he includes the Dingo or New Holland Dog, the Molossus, the Danish Dog, the lesser Danish or Dalmatian Dog, Scotch and Irish Greyhounds, Italian Greyhound, and the Boarhound.

Spaniels, or the second group, have the head only moderately elongated, and the parietal bones do not approach each other, but swell out so as to enlarge the cerebral cavity. In this division, in addition to the various breeds of Spaniels, there are included New-foundlands, Alpine Spaniels (this breed is described as partaking of the appearance both of a Newfoundland and Mastiff, and no doubt belonged to the St. Bernard species, from the stories related concerning their rescue of benighted travellers), the Hound, the Sheep-dog, and the Wolfhound.

The third division—Dogues—comprised those breeds in which the muzzle is more or less shortened, the skull high, the frontal sinuses considerable, and the lower jaw extends beyond the upper. In this group Cuvier includes the Bulldog and the Mastiff; but it certainly appears that the Mastiff is considerably out of place amongst a class of dogs whose leading characteristic is being underhung; in addition to which the Molossus, or Mastiff, is included by him in the first group.

Bewick's work is chiefly valuable on account of the engravings contained in it, as the letter-press so closely follows the *dicta* of former writers. The illustrations, however, render this book highly interesting.

Having now enumerated most if not all of the earlier writers of importance upon the dog, and the divisions created by them, and having already expressed the opinion that for present practical purposes the division of sporting dogs from their non-sporting relations is sufficient, we may now proceed to the practical details of our subject, adhering in this work to the divisions adopted by the leading show committees in the arrangement of their catalogues.

CHAPTER II.

KENNELS AND KENNELING.

"ANY place is good enough for a dog," is a venerable aphorism easy of quotation and capable of frequent application by those uninitiated in the management of dogs; but it is nevertheless wholly without foundation in fact, as those who have attempted to kennel valuable stock in unfitting quarters have discovered to their cost. There are many breeds which are totally unadapted for confinement in towns—at all events in numbers exceeding one or two. Dogs are not, like poultry and pigeons, pets whose natural tendencies can be rendered subservient to the will and desire of their masters. No amount of artificial feeding and attention can, in the case of many varieties, adequately supply the want of unlimited exercise, which is especially essential in the case of growing puppies, whose eventual success on the show-bench or in the field will greatly depend upon the development of bone and muscle, and the symmetry of a clean and well-proportioned body. In all breeds, the more exercise obtained the better it is for the dog; but in the case of certain varieties, especially ladies' toy-dogs, free exercise is not the absolute necessity which renders the successful breeding of the larger varieties an impossibility in crowded neighbourhoods. We do not for one moment doubt or deny that excellent specimens have been born and bred in the hearts of great cities, but these must be regarded as simply the rare exceptions which make manifest the rule. Nothing but the strictest attention to cleanliness can possibly be looked to as a means of successfully combating the diseases which are for ever lurking in the precincts of crowded kennels; and it is well-nigh hopeless to expect dogs to be clean either in person or habits, where a sufficient amount of exercise is denied to them. As an instance, one of the largest and most experienced breeders of the larger breeds of dogs in the neighbourhood of London, not long since had his entire kennel of puppies and young dogs swept off within the space of a few days. On inquiring into the cause of this calamity, we were informed that the disease had the appearance of typhoid fever, which we were not surprised to hear, having a lively recollection of the state of the kennels on a previous visit to them.

All dogs, but more especially puppies, suffer more or less from being chained up. Not only does the collar almost invariably leave an unsightly ring in the hair on the neck, and thereby considerably affect the dog's beauty, but the frequent struggling at the chain drags the shoulders out of all shape, and affects the proper development of that part of the body. Any one, therefore, who wishes to rear fine animals, but more particularly if he proposes to gain reputation as a successful breeder or exhibitor of canine stock, should, before embarking on such an enterprise, well consider the means at his disposal for comfortably and at the same time economically housing the dogs by whose instrumentality he trusts to arrive at the desired goal. We use the word economically in the last sentence advisedly; for any person who starts by investing a large sum of money in elaborate kennels is doing what all practical people will consider a very rash action. Many a young beginner in dog-breeding has retired in disgust from some disappointment or other circumstance, just at the moment when, had he persevered, victory was within his grasp : what use, then, is the elaborate range of kennels which he has erected ? The stock can be sold, perhaps at a profit, or without much loss ; but the outlay upon the buildings can never be recouped ; and the disgust with which the owner contemplates his ill-success is heightened by the loss entailed. We propose, therefore, to suggest expedients, the majority of which we have seen in use, by which dogs can be warmly and comfortably housed at a comparatively nominal sum, though we must of course also describe a higher class of kennel architecture and fittings.

Unfortunately some owners are compelled, from want of space, to keep their dogs chained up, instead of in yards where they can be loose. In such instances, as also in the case of watch-dogs, it is very desirable that the kennels provided should be of a slightly different construction from those generally met with. In the latter the fault lies in the opening being placed in the front, so that both wind and rain are able to reach a dog, even though he is crouched at the back of his kennel. A great improvement is gained by the opening being made in one side, as this gives the dog an opportunity of getting out of the way of such

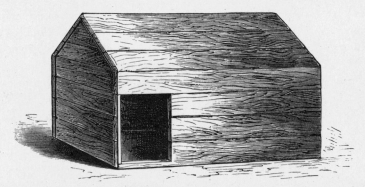

FIG. 2.—KENNEL, WITH SIDE ENTRANCE.

inconveniences, and the benefit he derives from the extra protection must be obvious to every one. Fig. 2 gives an exact representation of an improved kennel such as we suggest; and if dogs must be kept on the chain, we strongly recommend that this style of kennel be adopted. It is also the best pattern that can be adopted for all detached kennels, whether the inmate be confined or at liberty during the day ; and may be given as our model of a kennel for any dog sleeping or kept in a back-yard. The next best is an ordinary kennel, or even simple barrel, arranged with face towards the wall, as described further on.

All out-door kennels in which dogs are destined to sleep should be raised from the ground, for double reasons, as the damp would rot the floor of the kennel and also give the dog cold. A couple of pieces of three-inch quartering placed underneath, or even some bricks, serve this purpose in every way. It is not good to chain a dog to his kennel, for if he is a powerful animal he may drag it from its position. A stout piece of quartering or a post should therefore be buried from a foot or so in the ground, and the chain fastened to the piece which is above the surface. A staple is not so good a fastening for the chain to be fixed to as a screw ring, the latter not being nearly so likely to become loosened by the constant jerks it will receive.

The simplest and most economical arrangement for a regular kennel is a stable, if such accommodation is to be obtained ; and the addition of a dry and secure stable-yard attached to the same is a considerable further advantage. The means by which the various stalls can be turned into almost unexceptionable kennels are various and simple, but perhaps that shown in Fig. 3 is as useful and effective as any. It will be seen from the diagram that all required to convert an empty stall into an excellent kennel for a dog or dogs of any size are a few strips of wood and some extra strong wire netting. It is always well to line the lower half of the front (marked A in the figure) with wire, as well as the upper, as it prevents any possibility of the dog gnawing his way out. The upper half (B) is better fronted with wire only, as it enables visitors to see the dogs more easily. The cross-beam (C) should be of considerable strength, as great pressure is often put against it by the dogs if they endeavour to escape. Of course, in the case of the larger breeds, or destructive specimens of the smaller

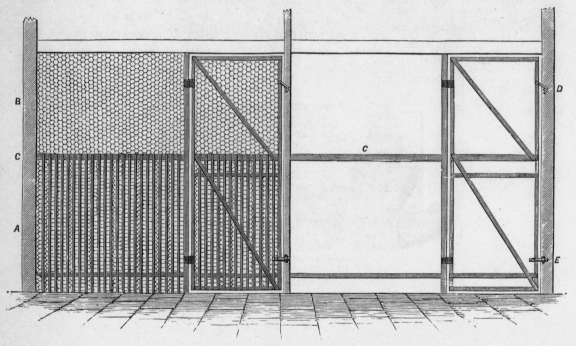

FIG. 3.—STABLE FITTED UP AS A DOG-KENNEL.

varieties, it will be necessary to substitute iron rails for the wire and wood work; but personal experience has taught us that the additional expense of iron rails is in the vast majority of cases quite unnecessary. We have kept scores of dogs, chiefly Bull-dogs and Bull-terriers, in the above sort of kennel, and have never known one to eat out of them. Due attention must, however, be paid to two things—(1) get wire of *extra* strength and thickness, and (2) be sure your doors come well down to the ground.

Whilst on the subject of doors, attention should be directed to a most important feature in their construction: *always have two fastenings on each door.* If there is only one, it is liable to come unfastened in the night, either through the instrumentality of the traditional cat, or the carelessness of the feeder; and the result is a serious disturbance, and perhaps a free fight in the kennel. Nothing seems to exasperate dogs when in confinement more than to witness a kennel companion roaming about the premises alone, and we have suffered severely from dogs breaking loose of a night. The best description of fastening by far is a bolt for the lower half of the door (see E), and a hook catch on the upper. It is a good plan to fix the latter in such a position that when it falls into the staple to close the door it is on a downward slant, as shown in the cut at D. This will prevent it from coming unfastened easily. The above system of fastening doors applies to all sorts of kennels with equal importance.

Having arranged the front of such kennel (as shown in Fig. 3) to his satisfaction, the beginner has little more to do ; for when a wooden bench has been erected in one corner, about eighteen inches from the ground, for the dog to sleep on, and the sides and back well lime-washed, the quondam stall is quite ready for the reception of its canine lodger. The lime-washing is most essential, if the dog's health and general comfort are to be considered ; when properly done, it not only renders the kennel clean and tidy in appearance, but has the effect of destroying the innumerable insects which are sure to infest the abode of every sort of dog, unless very stringent measures are taken for their extermination.

We much prefer such *portable* benches as that shown in Fig. 4, the back and one side of the bench being carried up for a foot or more. This prevents the dogs from injuring their coats against the whitened wall when turning round in their beds. The bench, being quite

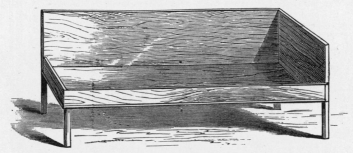

FIG. 4.— PORTABLE BENCH.

detached from the wall, is also far less likely to harbour vermin ; and finally, whenever occasion requires, it can be taken into the open air and thoroughly scrubbed with some disinfectant, which effectually disposes of any that may have gained a lodgment. Such benches are also very handy for placing about wherever required.

A gentle slope of the floor is highly desirable, as a drain-pipe can easily be run under the ground in front of the kennels, by which the water is enabled to run off, thereby increasing the salubrity of the establishment. In the case of the larger varieties of dogs, this arrangement becomes almost a matter of necessity, and the trifling outlay it involves most amply repays a breeder by the increased comfort it affords his pets, as well as by the effect it has upon the appearance of his kennel.

A good simple form of in-door kennel having been now described, attention may be drawn to special out-door erections of a very similar character, which we have proved by experience to be admirably adapted for those varieties which are of a hardy constitution, or even for those of more delicate nature, when they are not required to be in first-class show condition. The reason of the remark *apropos* of show condition will be understood by those who read the chapter on showing dogs, so need not be gone into further here. Such a form of kennel may be erected against a garden or any other wall, and consists of a series of compartments which closely resemble the stalls of a stable, and possessing a front of wooden or iron railings, as described in Fig. 3. We can vouch for the many good qualities of this kind of kennel, having erected many for the accommodation of our own stock ; and the dogs always seemed to do well in them, except when in delicate health, when naturally they were removed into warmer quarters. The size we built each stall in our kennels was ten feet deep by eight feet wide, and the dogs which inhabited them were Bulldogs and Bull-terriers, of from thirty-five to fifty pounds weight. We mention this, as it is desirable to explain to inexperienced readers as nearly as possible what arrangements were made, so as to enable them to judge for themselves of what size to erect their kennels; as, of course, this depends upon the variety of dog they propose keeping as well as upon the accommodation at hand. The stalls should be covered in by a lean to roof for at least three-quarters of their depth from the wall, as wet ground is one of the worst things possible for a dog to stand on for long ; and a wooden bench at the back of each must be provided. There is no occasion for this bench to be raised as high from the ground as the one alluded to in the description of the in-door kennel, for in the present instance the dog is not expected to sleep on it, at all events in cold weather. Three pieces of board each a foot wide and a yard long firmly nailed crossways on a couple of pieces of three-inch quartering forms an admirable bench of this description. The roof should be of weather boarding, covered over with the best felt, well

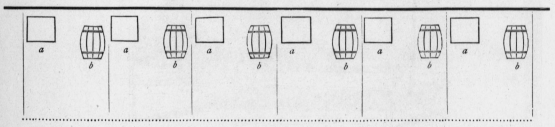

FIG. 5.—RANGE OF KENNELS.

tarred and sprinkled with coarse sand or gravel. Corrugated iron roofing is most objectionable, for in the summer the extent to which it attracts the sun renders the life of the unfortunate creature underneath it simply intolerable ; and most other roofings cost a considerable sum of money, which, as we have said before, it would be bad policy for a beginner to expend. Whilst upon this subject, however, we may remark that a tile roof well "pointed" is by far superior to all others, and in appearance it is certainly second to none. Under this description of roofing an owner may rest assured that his pets are as cool in summer and warm in winter as they can possibly be without the aid of artificial heat, which of course cannot be applied to out-door kennels. Thatch is cool in summer and warm in winter also, but it affords such a welcome retreat for all sorts of vermin that its adoption cannot be recommended.

The knotty subject of sleeping accommodation for dogs up to at least fifty pounds weight in such a range of kennels is easily settled, if the master of the establishment is not too ambitious in his views. A common petroleum barrel, which can be obtained in numbers of almost any oilman, with a hole cut in one end, forms a most admirable kennel for dogs inhabiting these stalls. It is highly desirable that the barrel should be purified from the effluvia of the petroleum to as great an extent as possible, and this is easily managed by placing a handful of lighted straw inside after the hole has been cut to admit the dog. This will ignite any petroleum which may be left in it, and when this is accomplished a thorough rinsing out, followed by a stand in the fresh air for a day, renders it fit for any dog's reception. If any extra effect be required, the barrels can be painted the colour which their owner most admires, and it may be added that they can easily be kept in their place by bricks or wedges of wood. The arrangement of the whole range of stalls will be readily seen from Fig. 5, where *a a* represent the low benches, placed at the back a few inches from the wall and partition; and *b b* are the barrels for sleeping in, placed with the *face* towards the back wall, and about two feet from it. A barrel thus placed with the face towards the wall makes a very good substitute for the more costly kennel shown in Fig. 2, as the wall in front of the entrance will keep the rain or wind from driving in.

This sort of kennel can also be so constructed that in winter or inclement weather wooden

VIEW OF KENNELS AT GLEN-TANA.

fronts, each containing a glazed window, can be fitted in front of the outside rails. These, if the yards are covered over all the way, make first-rate enclosed sheds for puppies or delicate dogs. A communication can easily be made with the next kennel, if empty, and the dogs can thus get a run in the open air, the wooden front not being of course attached to it. By this arrangement an owner can have all or part of his kennel open to the air as he pleases.

Where space and means permit, it is of course possible to erect more complete and specially-adapted accommodation. By the permission of the owner, and the kind assistance of Mr. George Truefitt, of Bloomsbury Square, the architect under whose superintendence were erected not only the kennels but all the other buildings at the shooting-lodge, we are enabled to give a view and ground-plan of the kennels erected for Mr. W. Cunliffe Brooks, M.P., in the forest of Glen-Tana, Aberdeenshire. It is built for stag-hounds, setters, and pointers, and is one of the most complete and compact examples we have met with of a gentleman's kennel for a good team of sporting dogs.

The references underneath the plan will explain the principal details of the Glen-Tana kennels, which are very fortunate in regard to position. This is not a small matter when it is a question of selecting a site, and of keeping working dogs in the highest health and condition. To attain this result, "kennels require," to quote from a note received with the view from Mr. Cunliffe Brooks, "plenty of air, yet shelter; plenty of sun, yet shade." These

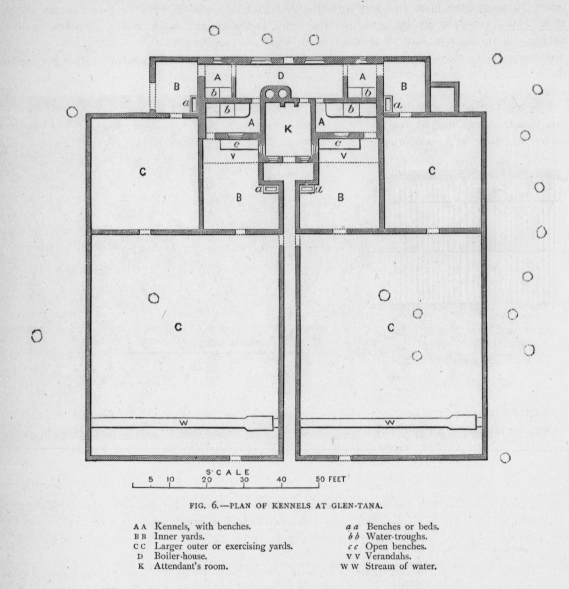

FIG. 6.—PLAN OF KENNELS AT GLEN-TANA.

A A	Kennels, with benches.	a a	Benches or beds.
B B	Inner yards.	b b	Water-troughs.
C C	Larger outer or exercising yards.	c c	Open benches.
D	Boiler-house.	v v	Verandahs.
K	Attendant's room.	w w	Stream of water.

kennels are built on the crest of a small hill, and have some old trees in the outer yards, as well as surrounding them, the position of these being shown by the dotted circles. They are also supplied with clear *running water;* not only are the streams at w w thus supplied, but the troughs *a a* in the inner yards are also filled with water *constantly* flowing, to which fact the owner very much attributes the good health and condition of his dogs.

It will be seen that in these kennels are comprised four separate sets of apartments, each containing an inner kennel (A), furnished with beds (*b b*), an inner open yard (B) with a water-trough (*a*), two of which have open benches (*c c*) under verandahs (V V), and larger or outer yards (C C) for exercise. The boiler or cooking-house (D), which is furnished with two coppers or boilers, is so situated as to communicate directly with all four kennels ; and here the dogs when brought home at night can be washed and attended to, and then put in their respective kennels without being taken into the open air. A sleeping-room for the attendant is also in the centre of all, at K. The yard-walls are built with masonry to a certain height, above that are iron railings, not spiked at the top, but with curled ends, as shown in the perspective view. This view necessarily shows the kennel buildings with the intervening portions of the yard-walls removed, the front of the picture representing the .dotted line shown in the plan in front of the verandahs (V V).

It has just been remarked that the railings of the Glen-Tana kennels are curved at the top, and this may suggest remark on a rather important matter. Many a good dog has been spiked in trying to leap pointed railings, which are very dangerous unless carried to a greater

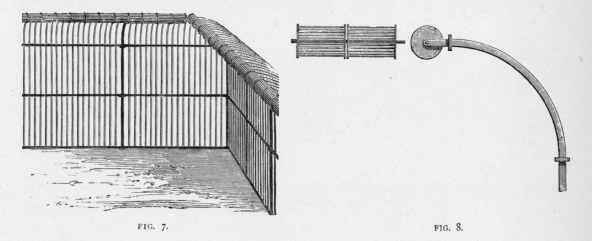

FIG. 7.   FIG. 8.

height than is usual or necessary. The railings should, therefore, be either carried up (if spiked) to a good height, or curved at the top in some way. In Figs. 7 and 8 is illustrated an admirable pattern of railing which is in use at the Paris *Jardin d'Acclimatation*, and in some other places on the Continent, and the only objection to which is its expense. The figures given will explain the construction, and show how the whole railing is curved in at the top towards the yards, while stronger railings at proper intervals support short lengths of a revolving cylinder. If a dog reaches the cylinder it yields to his weight at once, and he falls back into the yard. We have never seen this kind of railing used in England, but the idea seems to us worth importation. If properly made, as the bulk of the railing might be made light, the expense need not be greater than that of the ordinary spike railing, if so much.

Probably the most complete and extensive range of kenneling in existence is the Home for Lost Dogs at York Road, Battersea, London. Scarcely any of our readers, if indeed any, can require such a range of buildings as this ; but wherever accommodation has to be provided for any large number of dogs, and money is not more than usually plentiful, a careful study of the view and plan on page 15 will amply repay the trouble it entails. The large central building contains sixteen stalls or kennels under cover inside, and there is an outside yard shared between every two or three kennels. Good, wide, and not too high benches run along both the

sides of each, making ten or twelve feet of benching in each stall, and over every door communicating with the outside yards is a ventilator, which can be open or closed at pleasure.   In
the centre of each yard is a post for the convenience of the dogs, which without some such
provision (too often forgotten) will sometimes refuse to relieve the wants of nature ; and there
are both inside and out large troughs filled with water.

A capital feature in the general arrangement of this establishment is the facility with which
a dog can be removed from one kennel to another : the middle passage can be used, instead of
the keeper being obliged to lead him through the midst of the other dogs, which is always a
dangerous and bad plan.   In addition to the sixteen kennels alluded to above, there are other
large sheds with yards attached, an isolated hospital, and range of kennels for small dogs and
puppies, large numbers of the latter being born on the premises every year.   The kennels for the
small varieties are on the right hand of the diagrams, and the only difference in them is that
they are smaller, and the yards are partially covered over to protect the occupants from the
inclemency of the weather.   The boiling-house is close to the entrance of the main kennels, and
there is a loft over it for the storage of biscuits and other necessaries.

We are indebted to the courtesy of Mr. Thomas Scorborio, the manager of the Dog's Home,
for some details as to the statistics and management of the Home, which cannot fail to be of
interest.   The large dogs are fed twice a day upon Spratt's Patent Dog Biscuits and boiled tripe ;
the smaller varieties getting stewed beast's heads and boiled rice, and crushed Spratt's biscuits ; the
puppies, in addition, being supplied with milk.   The kennels and yards are washed out daily during
the summer months with a solution of " Heal's Creosoted Carbolic Soap," which Mr. Scorborio has
found by experience an excellent disinfectant and destroyer of vermin.   The average number
of dogs received per week is about six hundred, and the worthless ones are detained in the
Home three days before they are destroyed by poison.   The more valuable specimens are kept
until claimed by their owners, or disposed of by sale, which can be effected any time after they
have been three days in the Home.   Each dog, on his arrival at the Home, has a collar with
a brass number on put round his neck, and his fate is recorded in a book kept for the purpose,
so that he can be traced if necessary.   The average quantity of biscuits used per week is ten
hundredweight, and of flesh about eight hundredweight ; the cost of food of all sorts amounting
to nearly £15 a week, and the other expenses to at least as much more.   It will be thus
seen that the Dog's Home incurs heavy expenses, and it cannot recoup much from the sale of
dogs, the minimum price asked being five shillings.   The cost of the freehold was £1,500, and
the erection of the kennels and paving the yards came to nearly £2,500.

The subject of flooring kennels is one which is perpetually cropping up in canine discussions ;
and as a rule the supporters of the various principles are very stubborn in their convictions, and
slow of conversion to any other.   Asphalte, brick, cement, and even slate, have each and all their
supporters ; and we will endeavour to point out the objections which appear to our mind to exist
in the case of three of the above.   In the first place, asphalte is liable to get soft and spongy in
hot weather, and becomes very slippery when down for a long time.   This may not be much
of an objection to the dog, but might cause a nasty fall to any person entering the yard
incautiously.   For these reasons we deem asphalte objectionable, though we learn that Lord
Wolverton has had Claridge's patent asphalte laid down on the floor of his celebrated bloodhound kennels at Iwerne Minster.   Brick is sure to work up in time, and the urine must
sooner or later work into the cracks between the bricks, and tend to render the floor foul when
it should be sweet and clean.   Slates are apt to crack and chip.   There only remains for us
cement, which we are strongly of opinion is the best flooring by far.   Exception has been taken

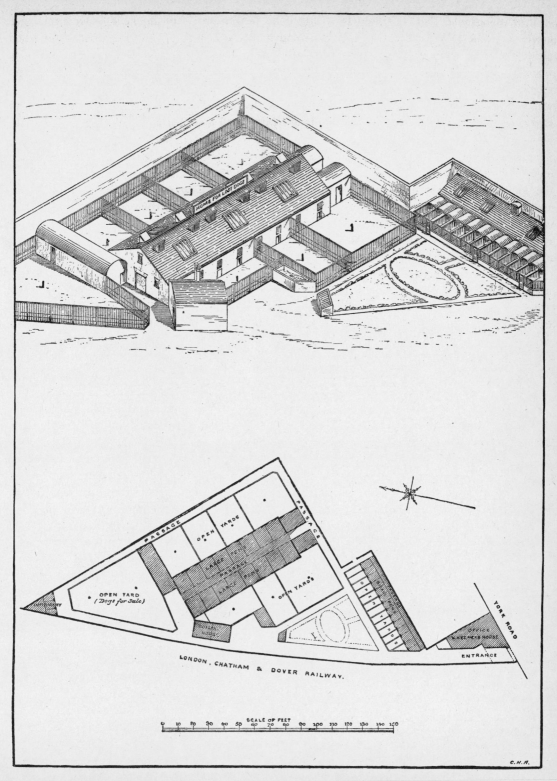

VIEW AND PLAN OF THE BATTERSEA HOME FOR LOST DOGS.

to it on the ground that it is cold to a dog if he lies or stands much on it. Our experience, however, teaches us that if a low, portable, wooden bench such as we have described is furnished, no dog will, when lying down out of his barrel, select any sort of floor in preference to his wooden couch, except in warm weather, when cement will do him no harm. This form of flooring, too, is so easily washed and scrubbed down that its merits cannot fail to be appreciated by those who give it a fair trial; and it is economical to a degree, for though the cement in itself is an expensive item, a little of it goes such a long way that all apprehension of extravagance rapidly wears off.

A sprinkling of sawdust over the floors of every sort of kennel is a great advantage, as it not only tends to improve the appearance of the establishment, but renders the task of cleaning the kennels more easy and efficient. Many breeders object to the use of sawdust in their establishments, on the ground that, when the dogs drag their food about, a quantity of sawdust adheres to it and gets swallowed by the dogs. We never found any ill effects arise from this ourselves, and question whether there is any probability of such occurring unless a large quantity of sawdust were laid down, which is quite unnecessary, a light sprinkling being quite sufficient.

All kennels should be thoroughly washed out at least once a week, and in the warm months some sort of disinfectant is required to clear away offensive odours. Several excellent disinfectants are objectionable for leaving a most unpleasant smell behind them; and on the whole nothing surpasses Condy's fluid for kennel use. A dilution of this preparation effectually purifies every nook and cranny, and its presence is not perceptible to the olfactory organs like carbolic acid, which is, however, a valuable disinfectant. A new patent preparation called Sanitas has been tried at some leading shows, and its success at them is pronounced; we have, however, had no personal experience of its merits in kennels.

It is sometimes considered desirable to warm kennels where delicate dogs are confined during the winter nights. If gas can be laid on nothing surpasses a small gas stove; but where this cannot be procured great advantage can be derived from the use of a mineral-oil stove, which emits no smell, and is not dangerous if kept out of the reach of the dogs. Should they overturn it, however, there is a risk of disaster from the inflammable nature of the mineral oil; and the greatest care should therefore be bestowed upon thoroughly ensuring security in this respect.

CHAPTER III.

GENERAL MANAGEMENT OF DOGS.

HAVING got his dog comfortably housed, the next duty of the owner is to see to the internal arrangement and comfort of his kennels. Suitable benches have been provided, but as yet no allusion has been made to the bedding which should be supplied on them. Hay has been recommended, but there is a particular and great objection to it, on account of its so easily working into the coat of a long-haired dog. From an economical point of view also it is far less preferable than straw, which as a bedding for all sorts of dogs is unsurpassed. We have found wheaten straw superior to oaten when it can be obtained, as it lasts longer, and is more comfortable for the dogs to lie on.

Many breeders of the larger and hardier varieties seldom, if ever, give their dogs anything to lie upon but bare boards, either from motives of economy, or in the belief that bedding is injurious to their coats. The latter objection is certainly a fallacy, as considerably more harm is likely to befall a dog's appearance if he is deprived of a warm and comfortable bed, than if he is snugly benched and a good night's rest ensured. The wooden bench shown in Fig. 4 should always be provided with the ledge round the front side, so as to prevent the straw falling off, which it is very apt to do when the dog makes himself comfortable in bed or leaps from it on to the ground.

Many persons are partial to pine shavings for bedding, and we have used them satisfactorily ourselves when straw has been unprocurable. The chief virtue of shavings appears to lie in the amount of turpentine which is contained in them ; and it has been stated that no fleas or other vermin can exist in a kennel where shavings are constantly in use as bedding material. This opinion is at least exaggerated, for we have found that fleas are to some extent proof against these shavings, though no doubt the odour of the turpentine is very distasteful to them. Of course, in the case of large kennels in neighbourhoods where straw is very dear and shavings cheap, it would be impossible to ignore the advantages of the latter; but they seem to break up and get dusty so soon, besides being hard and uncomfortable to the dogs, that we cannot recommend them to be supplied to show dogs, at all events on the eve of an exhibition. Some breeders, again, use sawdust on their dogs' sleeping benches ; but this practice is a thoroughly bad one. Such bedding gets into the ears and eyes of the dogs lying on it, and causes them great annoyance, if not absolute suffering. In addition to this, the trouble of getting sawdust out of their coats is very considerable. It is, no doubt, very good for the floor of the kennel, but has no recommendation whatsoever as an article of bedding.

Some dogs require a renewal of their bedding much oftener than others, but on no account should it be left in longer than a week ; and before the clean straw is placed on the bench, the latter should be thoroughly well cleansed, and, if necessary, scrubbed out with a hard brush.

During the hot summer months bedding is quite an unnecessary luxury for most breeds, even when their kennels are out of doors. In fact, very few dogs will consent to lie on straw if the weather is very warm, and will rid themselves of it if supplied them by scratching it outside their kennel. Under any circumstances dog owners should be most careful to see that the bedding is clean and dry, for nothing injures the gloss on a dog's coat more than a bed of frowsy, damp straw. It is also found that the animal is very likely to be attacked with rheumatism if his bench is in an unhealthy state.

FEEDING.

There is no doubt that a great deal of a dog's goodness goes in at the mouth. By this we mean that a well-nourished young dog is certain to turn out a better animal than one whose wants in this respect have been neglected. The great secrets in feeding are—firstly, wholesome food; and secondly, variety in diet. We do not, certainly, advocate the feeding of dogs wholly upon meat; such a diet is most injudicious, as it heats them, and in the case of sporting dogs injures their nose. Twice or three times a week, however, we do recommend meat to be given, in addition to the meal or biscuits which form the staple portion of the daily meal. Unsound, maggoty meat, such as we have seen supplied in more than one kennel, is sure to affect health sooner or later, and dogs will thrive better on a small quantity of sound food than upon an unlimited supply of bad quality. By a proper arrangement with his butcher, an owner can generally be supplied with the right sort of animal food upon really reasonable terms.

A great subject of discussion amongst breeders is how many times a day dogs should be fed. In the case of old dogs, we consider once a day quite enough, if they are given as much as they can eat then. In such a case the evening is the best time for feeding, for many reasons; especially as it allows the dogs to be put by comfortably for the night, and they will generally go to sleep quietly after feeding. Puppies, however, require food more frequently, and one or two extra meals should be supplied them.

The meat biscuits which are so largely used in most kennels form excellent diet, and can be given dry or soaked. If crushed up and steeped in boiling gravy, very few dogs will refuse them even at first, and after a time all get to like them. The chief objection to meat biscuits is, that so much depends upon the quality of meat contained in them; for if it is bad it is worse than useless as food for dogs. There are, however, good houses which supply biscuits whose quality is in all points above suspicion, and from experience gained in our own kennels we can say with certainty that such biscuits are both wholesome and nutritious. Another good food as a basis of diet is coarse oatmeal, which should be thoroughly well boiled, or it will disarrange the dog's stomach. Stale bread and ship biscuit, if not weevily, are used for changes in diet with good results, but naturally the meat portion of the food is that upon which most depends. Sheeps' heads, horse-flesh, bullocks' tripes, paunches, and liver, are all excellent additions to the meal and biscuit. We recommend that the meal be boiled in the liquor in which the heads and horse-flesh have been previously cooked, and the flesh chopped up and added to it in more or less quantity, as the dog's condition requires. The biscuits which already contain meat can be soaked, and the tripe and paunches mixed with them.

Rice is a great deal given in some kennels, but its fat-producing properties are so far in excess of its bone and muscle-producing constituents, that except as an occasional change, we do not recommend it for general use. Pearl-barley is superior to rice in every way, and we have got flesh on many a sickly dog with this food combined with scraps. Boiled potatoes, if crushed and mixed with gravy, are also a good change.

Liver is a food which dogs are very fond of, and it is a first-rate addition when the bowels are at all confined. It costs considerably more than the other meats we have mentioned, and this, in addition to its powers as an aperient, prevents its constant use in a kennel. Paunches we do not attach much importance to as either strengthening or fattening food; but though the nourishment contained in them is small in comparison, they are liked by the dogs, and are serviceable as a cooling diet if given now and then. In all cases they should be thoroughly well washed and scalded before being given, as in many cases they contain parasites, which must be destroyed lest they injure the dog's internal organs.

From remarks which have gone before it will be seen that variety in diet is not a very difficult matter, even in a large kennel, as we have biscuits in two forms, dry and soaked, and meal boiled in soup as the staple, without reckoning the supply of horse-flesh which would remain after some had been added to the other food. Horses suitable for slaughtering can usually be bought for from one pound to thirty shillings, and there is always something to come back from the hide and bones after the dogs have done with the latter. If *boiled as soon as killed*, the flesh will keep sweet for a long time; but in large kennels it is wonderful how soon it can be disposed of.

It will be seen that more or less cooking is necessary. For one or two dogs a large saucepan will suffice, which may be fitted over an atmospheric gas-burner, if the supply is convenient. When more than this is required, very good iron boilers can be bought of most ironmongers for a few shillings, and fixed in the corner of the shed or any outhouse, by which the offensive smell of the cooking is kept away from the dwelling-house. Only in large kennels will more than this be required: for them it will generally be found cheapest in the end to have a regular boiler-house, or at least a couple of boilers regularly fixed, as in wash-houses, which should for convenience be fitted with supply and draw-off taps. The boiler, of any sort, should be placed so as to give most ready access to all parts of the establishment.

Bones from which most of the meat is scraped should be frequently supplied, but care must be taken to keep the dogs apart whilst they are gnawing them, or a fight will be the consequence. Not only do bones amuse the dog for hours, but they benefit the teeth considerably, and help to strengthen the jaws. Large bones are preferable, as small ones may be bolted whole and stick in the throat.

Having enumerated so many varieties of food which are all more or less wholesome, a supposititious dietary table may not be out of place. We will assume that arrangements have been made by which a certain supply of sheep's-heads and tripes can be obtained; and that biscuits or meal are on the premises. On Sunday, then, the bill of fare may be dry, crushed biscuits, *followed* by some of the bones of the sheep's-heads. (If they are given at the same time the biscuits will not be touched, and the dogs not have enough food.) On Monday and Friday the liquor in which the heads were boiled may be given, mixed with meal, green vegetables, and a *little* tripe. Tuesday and Thursday biscuit can be given dry; whilst Wednesday's dinner may be the meat of the heads, with a little dry biscuit; and on Saturday rice, stale bread, or pearl-barley, can be boiled up with paunch or liver. Such a scale as this is of course only suitable for dogs that have a good amount of exercise, and where this is not the case, the amount of animal food should be reduced with discretion; the scheme being only given as affording an idea of the method in which the many ingredients at command may be turned to account in affording a varied diet. It is always useful to have some sort of plan to go by, though some dogs will often require a particular regimen.

Dogs that are "bad doers" require special treatment, and should be offered more tempting diet in small quantities two or three times a day. If a large dish full of food is placed before a dog who feeds badly, it is very apt to sicken him, and make him refuse to eat at all; whereas a little given him from his master's hand will most likely be swallowed eagerly. Cows' udder, well boiled, if given to delicate dogs, is almost always eagerly devoured, and certainly helps to put flesh on their bones. With regard to the feeding of light-fleshed dogs, the late Mr. Samuel Handley of Manchester once gave us a hint which has often proved valuable. His advice was to get some bullocks' "throttles" or gullets, and having chopped them up small, to boil with pearl-barley, and add a few currants. This is a very fattening food, and much liked.

When soft food is given it is very desirable that some boiled vegetable should be mixed with it, as this purifies the blood and keeps the bowels in good condition. Cabbage, brocoli, turnip-tops, and, when they can be got, young nettles are the best and easiest cooked, and one or other should be supplied at least twice a week. When, however, these cannot be procured, it is necessary to resort to other means, and try what mild physic will do instead. Get equal *weights* each of milk of sulphur and magnesia (this will give rather more magnesia than sulphur), and either mix it up with the soft food, or rub up with a little milk, and give it to the dogs. We prefer the latter plan, as many dogs do not like it in their dinner, and eat less in consequence. The dose is a tea-spoonful for a fifty-pound dog, and if mixed with milk it

FIG. 9.—FEEDING TROUGH.

should be of the consistency of cream. It is a good plan to give a dose of the above all round once a week in summer, and twice a month in winter ; and even if the vegetables are not given this is often enough, unless individual dogs may be disarranged in their bowels and require a mild aperient. This is also the best remedy we know for eruptions on the skin when they are caused by bad blood, and should then be given every day for a week, and after that alternate days until the dogs get better.

Some authorities recommend that dogs should be fed from off the ground, but we consider this a thoroughly bad plan. The best feeding vessels for single dogs are round tin baking-tins, which can be bought at any ironmonger's. By using these each dog can be given his portion, and the tin afterwards removed and washed out ready for the next day. These vessels are, however, inappropriate for the use of a number of puppies, or, in fact, any dogs when a number are fed together, and the best trough then is such a one as is illustrated in Fig. 9. It is too heavy to overturn, and the dogs cannot so easily steal each other's share, owing to the divisions.

A constant supply of fresh water is most important. The value of attention to this point can hardly be over-estimated, for though a dog will drink almost anything, he is sure to be upset by bad water sooner or later. Every owner should satisfy himself that his water-troughs are thoroughly emptied and rinsed out each morning, for they are apt to get slimy round the edges and bottom if let stand too long, the consequence being that the water is polluted before it gets to the dogs. The best sort of drinking vessel is a simple earthenware open spittoon, as shown in Fig. 10 ; these can be easily washed out, and from their shape are very difficult to overturn. In the case of large breeds, for which these vessels would hold an insufficient supply, we strongly recommend an enamelled iron trough similar in shape to the feeding-trough shown in Fig. 9.

Having thus described the feeding of dogs where considerable numbers are kept, and which consequently require regular business arrangements to be made, a few lines may be devoted to the requirements of those who only keep one or two dogs in-doors. Inexperienced persons often inquire how to feed their pets, and the first question generally is, whether scraps from the table injure the health. From what has gone before, it may be gleaned that scraps given *with judgment* are a very beneficial diet. The main thing, never to be lost sight of, is that the supply of meat given a dog must greatly depend upon the life he leads; and in the case of dogs kept in-doors, the amount of exercise they get is usually in one extreme or the other. The household pet is either the constant companion of the members of his master's family in their walks, and thereby, between one and the other, gets a good deal of exercise; or he is a petted little toy which is considered too delicate to leave the fireside, and so gets scarcely any running about at all. In the former of these cases, a moderate amount of meat is decidedly beneficial; in the latter, *the less he gets the better.* From one-quarter to one-third of meat is sufficient for most in-door dogs, and the rest of his

FIG. 10.—DRINKING VESSEL.

food should consist of bread-crumbs, vegetables, crushed-up potatoes, pie-crust, &c., &c., with a little gravy added. Bones now and then should be given to gnaw, but too much meat must not be left on them, and if an additional meal is required nothing can surpass dry biscuits. A dog will always eat when he is hungry, and tender-hearted mistresses should console themselves, if they see their dog leaving a portion of his food, by the conviction that a little wholesome diet is better for their pet than a bounteous fare of unsuitable materials. Dogs cannot speak when their food disagrees with them, and the life of many a little pampered toy is rendered a burden to him by the injudicious feeding of an over-indulgent master or mistress. Instead of getting a run in the open air, he is doomed to a life of unnatural inertness, and his stomach is periodically crammed with the richest and most unwholesome food which could possibly be selected for him. How can it be wondered at, then, that toy-dogs extend to such unnatural dimensions, that their teeth decay, that their bodies break out into sores, and their ears canker: causing them to become objects of disgust to all who have the misfortune to be associated with them? Whereas, had the same dogs been fed judiciously on plainer scraps from the table, and their drink been pure water, the abominations of cream, milk, "tit-bits," &c., being eschewed, they would have been lively and handsome companions for any lady in her walks, and a gratification to those to whom they belong.

EXERCISE.

We have implied that a good and daily amount of exercise is most essential to the general health of all dogs. Some varieties can exist for a certain time without proper attention in this respect, but in the majority of breeds a liberal allowance of out-door exercise must be provided if they are to be kept in *real* health and spirits. Dogs and bitches kept for breeding purposes cannot have too much open air under judicious management, and the health and future excellence of young stock is greatly affected by the liberty they obtain. The means by which the necessary amount of exercise is given the dogs must necessarily depend on the situation of the kennels and the space and time at their owners' disposal. If the establishment is in the country the task of exercising the dogs is a very easy one, the adjacent meadows offering every facility. But in towns the case is different, and means have to be devised by which comparative liberty can be obtained without risk to the dogs and annoyance to the neighbours. Under all circumstances a covered-in run is a very desirable addition to a range of kennels, for then the dogs can be exercised in all weathers, and an admirable run for young puppies formed. Unfortunately few breeders can afford the space that such an erection would occupy ; but we allude to it, lest the merits of an empty barn might be overlooked when exercising comes to be considered. In the case of dogs whose temperaments are peaceful, no difficulty will be found in taking them out for an hour or two's run in the morning, when few people and conveyances are about ; and this, with a daily turn of greater or less extent in the kennel yard, will suffice for most animals. The sporting varieties will, of course, require more exercise and special treatment, which will be gone into in the chapter on breaking.

It is not good to let dogs be exposed too long to a hot summer's sun ; for lying about in it is sure to disarrange their health, and render them dull and languid. Where they are let run in yards a plentiful supply of water should always be within reach, and this should be kept in a shady corner *out of the sun's rays*, which heat it and render it unfit for the dogs to drink. Sometimes an awning may be of great benefit.

In many establishments one or two good dogs are kept in-doors, which are forbidden to roam about in the garden on account of the injury they would cause there. It may be required to exercise them thoroughly, and if so the owner has to resort to artificial means, using a ball, or a cat-skin tied at the end of a fishing-rod or long cane, and dangled before them. In the first case, if the dog will fetch and carry, a great amount of exercise can be gone through at the cost of a comparatively trifling exertion on the part of the owner, who has only to keep on throwing away the ball for the dog to run after. Half an hour or so a day of such violent exercise will keep most dogs in good health, but it is particularly desirable that all their leisure time should not be passed in-doors before a fire, as nothing tends to demoralise a dog more than want of *fresh air*. No house is quite destitute of a yard of some sort, where a kennel can be fixed up for the dog's reception during some part of the day. Fuller description of the method of exercising by means of a skin and long cane will be given in the article on Bull-terriers, as it is a form of excitement more peculiarly adaptable to vermin dogs, partly from their disposition to worry a ball if given one to play with, and partly because less spirited dogs soon get tired of jumping at a thing they cannot reach.

GROOMING.

A great deal in a dog's appearance depends upon whether his owner has him well groomed or not. This most useful operation has probably never been resorted to by scores of exhibitors, who on showing their dogs are surprised to find that they compare unfavourably with others in the condition of their coats. Grooming, to be effective, must be constant and thorough. A casual overhauling with a dirty brush once in two or three months does not at all represent our views on the subject ; but it is very hard to convince some kennelmen of the benefit proper grooming can bestow on the dogs' coats. Latterly attention has been directed to this matter, and the result has been the appearance of several appliances which are more or less effective as aids to the canine toilet. Conspicuous amongst inventions which are really service-able is the *hair-glove*, and no breeder of smooth-coated dogs should be without some of these in his kennel. In the case of the long-haired varieties a coarse comb and dandy-brush are about all that are necessary. Very hard brushes, as a rule, are best avoided; they may do no harm to a thoroughly healthy coat, but the skin even of a healthy dog is peculiarly susceptible of irritation, and any undue stimulus may start him scratching till he is almost raw. A hard brush may therefore inflame some pustule on the skin, and before the injury is discovered a dog may have disfigured himself for months to come. A hard short-bristled brush, if constantly used, is also liable to remove more hair than is necessary, and thereby injures the dog's appearance.

Many dogs are very fidgety when they are being groomed, and throw themselves about in a manner which renders the operation a tedious one. There is no remedy for this but patience, and after a dog once becomes accustomed to his morning's grooming, he soon gets to like it, and seems to look forward to the luxury. It is always desirable to chain him up when grooming is carried on, in case he breaks away and gets into mischief. The *modus operandi* is very simple, but we have always found it best to let the dog lie down, and do as much of his legs as possible *first*. The reason of this is that during the grooming of his legs a dog very often lies down and fidgets about, and in this way gets his coat all covered with sawdust or whatever may be laid on the floor of the kennel. This is not so annoying when his back and sides have yet to be groomed, and he can return to his bench neat and tidy. The legs should be thoroughly rubbed with the brush or hair-glove, care being taken to pass the hand in the direction the coat runs, or instead of benefiting the coat it will be injured by being made rougher than it was before. Attention should then be directed to the head and ears; the back must next be done, and the proceedings terminate by brushing out the tail. Under ordinary circumstances the hair-glove is sufficient for smooth-coated dogs, but its bristles are neither long nor stout enough to penetrate the jackets of the long-haired varieties. When the latter have to be dealt with a dandy-brush will usually suffice, the comb only being resorted to when the coat is knotted and tangled up. In using the comb the operator should be as gentle as he can, for if he drags tufts of hair out he hurts the dog and injures his appearance. A thorough combing-out is an excellent practice before a dog is washed, as it helps to remove all superfluous hairs, but when the coat is wet it is always more or less tangled, and should not be combed. As we have said before, *systematic* grooming is at the bottom of many a dog's blooming condition, and no morning should go by without strict attention being paid to his toilet. Careful grooming also assists greatly in the destruction of fleas and other vermin, and renders the coat sweet and clean.

We may remark that these hints on grooming refer solely to general management, and no allusion is made here to any special attention show dogs may require in the course of their preparation for exhibition, as such will be fully gone into in the chapter on exhibiting. A good rub over with a large dry chamois leather after the brushing out is completed is an ex-cellent termination to the grooming, but in ordinary cases is not so essential as the brush or hair-glove.

WASHING.

No very great skill is required, under ordinary circumstances, to wash a dog, providing the necessary appliances are at hand. If the weather is warm, and the dog of a hardy constitution, the chances of his catching cold are very small, but in cold weather the chief difficulty is to get him dry before replacing him in his kennel. It should be borne in mind that almost all dogs strongly object to being washed, and are prepared to make an effort to escape at a moment's notice. If they succeed in doing so the result is usually disastrous; for, in addition to wetting everything in the house, a dog invariably, if he can, goes outside to roll, and if he does so, has to be washed over again. If his collar is worn during his ablutions, it is very likely to stain his neck, as it probably requires a wash itself, and the best plan is to have a clean leather strap handy to put on your dogs whilst they are being washed, and which is reserved for this purpose only. Some people maintain that they can hold a dog by the scruff of the neck when they are washing him, but their grasp when he is covered with soap must be very precarious.

In some cases, where a number of dogs have to be washed, and the object is more to cleanse their skins than to get them up for show purposes, no tub is used, but they are merely stood over the drain grating in the kennel, and some water poured over them; the soap is then applied, their coats rinsed out with cold water, and they are dried and sent back to their kennels. This is an unnecessarily untidy and unsatisfactory course, as, if a tub is used, there need be hardly any water spilt, and the washing can be far more thoroughly carried out. The best sort of tub is one about three feet wide across the top, and some fifteen to eighteen inches high at the sides. One end of a large barrel sawn through makes an admirable tub, and care should be taken to have a hole in the bottom, in which a cork is fitted, as by this means the dirty water can be let run off without making an unnecessary mess in the kennel. We always had our own washing-bath placed on trestles over the drain near the water-tap in the kennel. One end of an india-rubber tube was placed on the nose of the tap, and the other hung over the side of the tub; by this plan only the hot water had to be brought in pails, and any amount of cold was at the kennelman's disposal when he required it. As soon as the water was done with the cork was removed and the dirty water poured into the drain, not a tea-cupful being spilt about the kennel, and the tub was ready for the second dog by the time the first was dried.

The ordinary appliances necessary for washing a dog are, in addition to the tub, a large sponge, an empty jam-pot or other small vessel, a lump of soap (white curd for choice), and something to dry him with. We shall allude to washing for show purposes later on. Stand the dog up in the tub, which should be three parts full of moderately hot water, to which a little soda may be added, and wet his coat *thoroughly* through; this can be done by baling the water over him by means of the jam-pot above alluded to. When he is saturated with the water, commence by soaping his face and head, and get this completed and washed out before you go on to his body, legs, and tail, in the order named. Take care that the soap is well rubbed in, but be careful to let as little as possible reach his eyes. The head once done with, the rest is tolerably easy work in the case of most dogs; but it is always well to be prepared for efforts to escape being made. When he is well lathered all over his body and legs, and the soap thoroughly rubbed into his skin, the jam-pot must be again resorted to to remove the soap by baling the water over him. Finally, before lifting him out of the tub, it is well to give the dog a douche of cold water, as it not only cleanses his jacket of the soap, but diminishes the chances of his taking cold. Our arrangement of the india-rubber tube referred to above was here particularly serviceable, as the cold stream could be so readily applied to any part of the body.

When removed from his tub a dog is always anxious to shake himself, and rub himself on the ground; to the first proceeding there is not much objection, but the disadvantages of the latter are obvious. Before lifting him out of the tub, he should be partially dried by means of the sponge, and the towels will complete this part of the operation. When there is no fear of his taking cold, the dog can be returned to his kennel, where it is desirable that some clean straw should be provided for him.

Dogs kept in the house should be washed once every week or ten days; those out of doors about every three weeks or a month in summer, and less frequently in the cold weather. Washing is not so necessary where grooming is strictly attended to, but an occasional bath benefits a dog considerably. Many persons use brown or soft soap, but in breeds which show white this is objectionable, as it causes the coat to appear yellow after being used.

VERMIN.

If not properly attended to in the way of grooming and washing, all dogs are sure to be pestered with vermin. The remedies for clearing them of such torments are very numerous, but we have found the most ordinary means the most effective. Fleas can generally be got rid of by rubbing the dog thoroughly over with oil, from the tip of his nose to the end of his tail, and then washing him in water to which a little Condy's fluid or solution of permanganate of potash has been added. The oil should be left on three or four hours, and if thoroughly applied completely settles the fleas. Carbolic acid in the water and carbolic soap are also efficacious, but a too constant application of such remedies is apt to injure the dog's coat. Quassia chips are an excellent remedy in mild cases. Get two or three ounces from a chemist, and steep in boiling water; let them remain in it for some hours, and then drain off the liquor into the water in which the dog is to be washed.

Lice are very troublesome, and often will not yield to the above remedies. White precipitate powder will invariably destroy them, but must be used very cautiously, or it will poison the dogs. It should be applied dry to the coat, as if wet there is danger of the dog being poisoned by absorbing it into his skin. The patient should be securely muzzled, as a small dose in the mouth is sure to act fatally. The powder must be well brushed out with a dry brush in one or two hours, and care must be taken that the dog does not get wet.

Ticks are frequently found on the bodies of dogs which have been neglected, and are most troublesome to cure. They burrow into the skin, and hold on most pertinaciously. White precipitate powder has generally to be resorted to in order to get rid of them, and should be applied as stated above.

If the benches and bedding are not periodically cleaned and removed, vermin of some sort or other are sure to make their appearance in the kennels with disastrous results. The only remedy is a thorough purification; the walls and partitions must be at once white or lime washed, and the floor, benches, and iron-work well scrubbed, a good proportion of carbolic acid or Condy's fluid being added to the water used for the purpose. If discovered in time, and stringent measures are taken for their extermination, vermin soon disappear, but when allowed time to settle down they soon spread all over the building and occupy every crack in it. No time therefore should be lost in meeting their first appearance. On the other hand, vermin are sometimes confounded with effects arising from heated blood; and whenever a dog seems uneasy, an owner should make thorough examination, and satisfy himself that it is really vermin which cause the irritation.

Vermin will very seldom appear in dogs which are well groomed, but they must occasionally be communicated by means of dogs met in the streets, and especially at shows. An inspection of all dogs on their return from exhibitions will therefore be oftentimes profitable, as by discovering the presence of insects in good time a check on their advance can be made.

CLEANLINESS IN THE HOUSE.

Whether a dog is an acquisition or not as a household companion very much depends upon his habits of cleanliness; for nothing can be more offensive than an indoor pet upon whose behaviour no reliance can be placed. In the case of an old dog accustomed to live outside, and who has not been taught in his youth, we fear the inculcation of cleanly habits will be a difficult matter. The whip is the only remedy which can be applied, and its application should be neither light nor meagre. With puppies the matter is usually far simpler, and they soon acquire good manners if once convinced that punishment is the certain result of dirty habits. Before the whip is resorted to, the offender should always be taken to the place where the *faux pas* occurred, and the enormity of his conduct pointed out to him in stern but not passionate tones. A sound whipping should next be immediately followed by his expulsion from the room, and on his return from out of doors no further notice need be taken of his offence against good manners. After a few repetitions of this treatment the dog will understand what he is punished for, and will gradually learn to avail himself of the opportunities provided by his periodical runs outside. Some resort to the system of spreading pepper on the place where he misbehaved, and rubbing the dog's nose in it, and this is often effective in obstinate cases, but is an unnecessary severity in teaching young dogs. The opportunities for runs outside already alluded to, it need hardly be said, must be regularly given; and it must never be forgotten that a dog cannot, like most animals, void his urine by one act, but is obliged to expel it in small portions and by many separate efforts: much suffering may be caused by forgetting this. Indoor pets should always be allowed a run the last thing at night, and several outings during the day; else they cannot be expected to be clean, and it is cruelty to punish a dog for what he cannot help. Experience has taught us one thing, which is, that one *thorough* whipping does more good and less harm to a dog than a series of minor corrections. He remembers it far longer, and in his heart knows he deserved it for something or other, even if he has not learnt what the actual offence is; but if he is always being scolded and slightly punished, his master soon appears in the light of a persecutor, and the dog becomes either permanently cowed, or perhaps turns savage, and thereby unfitted for an indoor companion.

DOG BITES AND RABIES.

So many accidents occur in kennels from dog bites that attention may be directed to one or two simple precautions to be attended to if one has the misfortune to be bitten. The application of lunar caustic is universally recommended; but if this or any other remedy is used it should be applied to the wound *at once* and *thoroughly*. It is no use touching the outside of a bite with a little caustic; the stick must be well worked *into* the wound, and will cause considerable pain and subsequent inflammation. Often, however, this remedy is not at hand—though a stick of caustic is a useful appendage to any kennel—and other means have to be adopted. A very common practice is to plunge the injured part in hot salt and water, and keep it there for some minutes; and this is supposed to draw the poison (if any) out of the wound. Mr. Thomas Scorborio, manager of the Dogs' Home at Battersea, informs us of a remedy which he invariably causes to be applied to any of his attendants who are bitten badly. It consists of a large poultice of carbonate of soda, made into a *paste* with water and applied to the wound on a piece of linen. It should be kept on the wound about two hours, wetting the cloth with cold water every few minutes to keep the poultice moist. The thousands of stray dogs—by far the most dangerous class—which have passed through Mr. Scorborio's hands render any application which receives his support valuable ; and we may add that we have his authority for stating that an undoubtedly rabid dog bit an acquaintance of his, who at once applied a carbonate-of-soda poultice, and lived for years afterwards without suffering any ill effects. A celebrated veterinary surgeon at Bath also states that he has tried this remedy (with, so far, no failure) in many cases of bites from rabid dogs. It is unnecessary for us to go into the subject of hydrophobia here, or allude to the various recoveries which have been said to follow the treatment of alleged cases by the administration of curare, the Birling or other cures ; but, from what has been published, the benefit of prolonged and often-repeated Turkish or vapour baths should not be overlooked by any who have had the misfortune to be bitten.

One word is, however, necessary in defence of the dog. Many are annually mistaken for mad, and literally hunted to death by ignorant people, to whom the cry of "mad dog" is equivalent to positive proof that the animal is infected with rabies. Without under-rating the fearful dangers that may arise from a real case of this disease, we would at the same time caution owners not to hurriedly destroy every animal that behaves in a suspicious manner, if only for the reason that it is very desirable to know how many cases of genuine rabies really do occur. An owner, whenever an animal gives cause for suspicion, should secure it in a quiet place from which escape is impossible, and where it will not be disturbed. It is very possible the quiet may soothe the excited nervous system, and cure the eccentric behaviour which first caused suspicion. Meantime, of course, the dog should not be handled unless absolutely necessary, and ought to be carefully watched, that the development of every symptom may be noted ; it need hardly be said that competent opinion should be sought at an early stage. We need only observe here that rabid dogs often drink water greedily, contrary to the popular belief. The principal early symptoms of genuine rabies are a shrinking from light and a desire to hide in corners ; a propensity to gnaw and worry objects within reach, and to swallow bits of stick, buttons, hair, filth, &c. ; a disinclination to come when called ; and often a scared and wild appearance without apparent cause. The last sign is, however, valueless as regards a dog which has been hunted in the inhuman manner too common.

CHAPTER IV.

EXHIBITING, BUYING, AND SELLING.

ANY owner who has confidence enough in the merits of his dogs to desire to show them must bear in mind that excellence in symmetry and formation will probably be thrown away if condition is bad. For exhibition purposes condition is everything. A first-class specimen, however grand he may be in many points, if his eye is dull and listless and his coat ragged, cannot fail to suffer from comparison with a dog who, though perhaps inferior in some points, is lively and vivacious, thereby showing himself off to the best advantage when he is in the ring before the judges. The latter should—even if they do not always—judge a dog as he is before them, not reckoning what his performances have been or what merit he may develop with age. In getting up a dog for exhibition, therefore, an owner should try and make him look his best, never losing sight of the purposes for which the breed exists, and trying to bring his pet into the ring not only looking well, but fit to do his duty. A sporting dog looks ludicrous when he appears fat and flabby, and displays to every one how utterly incapable he would be of doing half a day's work. A bulldog or bull-terrier loaded with flesh instead of muscle is a sorry sight; and a black and tan or a toy terrier with a ragged staring coat cannot hope to be "in it" when competing for the prize of beauty with others of the same breed whose jackets shine like satin.

Experience can only be bought by practice, but here is a notable fact for the benefit of beginners: viz., that the most consistently successful exhibitors of late years have been those whose dogs have been shown in the best condition. We were once profoundly impressed by a hint given us by a deceased friend whose opinion in certain breeds was law. "Thoo'l have to learn, lad, hoo ta' show tha' dags," was all he said; we marked, learned, and profited by his suggestion, and never knowingly sent a dog off to a show who had not something in the way of condition to recommend him. To attain this desired end is difficult, merely from the fact that different dogs require different treatment; by following certain rules, however, great progress can be made, and if due attention is paid to feeding, exercising, and grooming, the most delicate dogs can be vastly improved in both health and appearance.

To begin with, it is always bad for an owner to place too much reliance on his kennel-man. An experienced person is no doubt an acquisition in any establishment, but the master will surely rue the day when he lets absolute control over his dogs slip from his grasp. A servant is very apt to consider himself of greater importance than he really is, unless his master keeps him up to his work, and supervises the daily routine of work as far as he can. Many masters profess to be above the task of looking after their own interests, and leave their kennels entirely under the control of their men. Such individuals cannot care much for the honour of winning a prize, as whatever *kudos* there is gained must rest with their deputy, and it is notorious that they generally suffer in the long-run by their blind confidence. We always had a slate hanging up in the kennel, and wrote any orders there were to be given on it; the consequence was that there was no excuse for them not being attended to, and the dogs flourished accordingly.

In getting a dog up for show, his comfort should be particularly looked after in every way.

See that his bed is comfortable and clean for him after his return from the unusual amount of exercise which should at this time be given him. The operation of grooming too should be more thoroughly carried out than under ordinary circumstances, and if his jacket is well rubbed down day by day with a chamois leather the gloss on it will be increased. In consequence of the greater exercise he takes a little more meat can be given him, but there is always a chance of his blood getting heated, and his skin breaking out in consequence into sores, or the hair coming off. Internal as well as external remedies must be at once resorted to if there are any indications of this misfortune befalling him. Let the dog, in such a case, be given a daily dose of the sulphur and magnesia mixture which has been alluded to in Chap. III., and give him sloppy food for a time. As regards a lotion for external application, the following, for which we are indebted to Mr. Hugh Dalziel, is highly efficacious:—

Carbolic acid	...	...	...	½ oz.
Glycerine	...	...	...	½ oz.
Laudanum	...	...	...	1 oz.
Carbonate of soda	...	...	...	1 dram.
Water	...	...	...	1½ pints.

This lotion should be dabbed very lightly indeed on the sores with a sponge, or wrung out of a piece of lint on to them frequently during the day, and it is marvellous how rapidly it dries up the raw places, and frees the dog from all irritation. If meat proves too heating, *bread-and-butter* is an excellent addition to a dog's daily allowance of food, and we have tried it with marked success in the case of several bad-constitutioned dogs. Let the butter be sound and good, and the bread not too new, however, or this diet may not succeed as well as the owner could wish. Cow's udder, if well boiled, is much relished by all dogs, and in getting up a light-fleshed dog upon whom a little bulk is wanted is simply invaluable, as its fat-producing properties are very high.

Cod-liver oil is most efficacious in its effects on dogs. A tablespoonful once or twice a day after food generally succeeds in putting flesh rapidly on a fifty-pound dog. This dose must be increased or diminished according to the size of the animal, and the effect it has on his condition. Suitable cod-liver oil can generally be obtained from saddlers or leather dressers, who use it in their trade. This is very much cheaper than what is obtained from chemists, and the only difference is that it is supplied unrefined.

In the case of many smooth-haired breeds, where the smoothness and brilliancy of their coats go a long way to ensure success in exhibition, it is desirable to keep them clothed for some time previous to the date of the show. Dog clothing is of various sorts, shapes, and materials; but the best for ordinary indoor purposes are plain white calico for summer wear, and ordinary fawn-coloured—but not too thick—horse clothing, to be used in winter or cold weather. These should be taken off when out of doors if the weather is fine, but if it rains many exhibitors employ thin macintosh sheets when exercising their pets. As regards the best make, we very much incline to the pattern which buckles in front, and to which a breast-cloth can be added. When the clothing is so constructed as to pull over the head like a stocking it is sure to ruffle up the dog's coat, and furthermore the same clothing cannot be made to fit various dogs so easily as the pattern which buckles in front. Fig. 11 exactly represents a pattern of exhibition clothing, which in workmanship and design we consider perfection, and which we arrived at after much study and many trials. For a long time we stood alone in various of its details, especially as regards fillet-strings and embroidered crest; but of late many others have copied our example.

From the design it will be observed that the strap A can be buckled in front of the chest, before the breast-cloth is attached to the clothing by buckles at B B. In very warm weather the breast-cloth may be dispensed with; but on journeys, or in cold draughty shows, one must bear in mind that it is desirable to protect the lungs of a dog as much as possible; the breast-cloth should therefore be worn in such instances. A slit, C, in the part of the clothing at the top of the neck, should always be provided for the ring of the collar to come through, as in leading a

FIG. 11.—DOG CLOTHING.

dog, or when he is tied up, the clothing should not be able to work out of its place if the dog struggles.

In sending a dog to a show, be sure his chain has *two* swivels on it, or else there is every chance of his being strangled before he gets home. If there is only one swivel it is apt to get choked with straw, and thereby cease to act; it then twists up and chokes the unhappy dog attached to the chain. There is an excellent chain manufactured expressly for show purposes, a sketch of which is given on the next page (Fig. 12), and which is made of various strengths, so as to suit any breed of dogs. It will be seen that there are not only two swivels, but a spring hook at each end and three rings in the chain, so that it can be shortened to any suitable length.

Washing has been so thoroughly gone into already that there is not much room for further observations here, beyond drawing the attention of our readers to the great necessity of always now getting the dog *perfectly dry* before letting him go back to his kennel. The best time to wash a dog for a show is the evening before he leaves home, and he can be then secured for the night without much chance of his soiling his jacket; but be sure to have abundance of fresh and clean straw for him to roll himself on, or he will be sure to stain himself, and all the labour of washing has to be gone through again, possibly under difficulties as regards time and place. Hand rubbing is most efficacious as a means of both drying and flattening down the coat; and after the process of drying is partially accomplished with a sponge and towel, we strongly recommend, in the case of smooth-haired dogs, that the operation be completed by rubbing the hands over the coat in the direction the hair runs. This may seem, and is, a tedious operation; but the dog's appearance is wonderfully improved by it. A little blue is often added to the water in which white dogs are washed, but it must be very little; and for our own part we rarely went beyond the use of the ordinary blue-mottled white soap, as, if good of its sort, this contains quite enough blue for all practical purposes. Loaf sugar is supposed by some to add brilliancy to the coat if put in the tub; but though we tried it, there were no adequate results to be perceived. In the case of the hard or wire-haired breeds, where a stiff, harsh coat is wanted, the addition of a little *alum*

FIG. 12.—DOUBLE-SWIVEL DOG-CHAIN.

in the water has a beneficial effect, and this should not be lost sight of by exhibitors of these varieties.

The delicate subject of trimming must be approached with caution, as any unwary expression regarding the various processes may be taken far more seriously than is desired. That many—in fact most—breeds of dogs can be vastly improved by various minor operations is admitted universally, and it is well known to most exhibitors that artifices are continually being resorted to which might, if detected, lead to the disqualification of the dog if he were awarded a prize. Long-haired dogs are plucked—*i.e.* bad or superfluous hair removed. Terriers are stained, shaved, and singed. Tails are shaved and resined. Curly coats which should be flat are ironed out; flat coats which should be curly have the tongs applied. White noses sometimes have lunar caustic (nitrate of silver) applied to them; and it may be well to remark that this can be easily detected by applying cyanide of potassium: care must, however, be taken with this drug, as it is a most deadly poison, and a very little allowed to get inside the mouth would kill the dog. Unsightly patches are dyed, and drooping ears gummed. All these and other artifices have been resorted to, and are often passed over by judges, who either do not possess the perception to detect the fault, or lack the moral courage to face the uproar a disqualification would bring about. How far the more trifling of such practices are recognised or permitted it is hard to say; but, trimming, or "faking," as it is popularly termed, is always a risky as well as an undesirable operation, and should be suppressed. In certain breeds mutilation is universal: such as docking the tail of a fox-terrier or spaniel, rounding the ears of a hound, or cropping those of a bull or English terrier. There are, however, operations performed on dogs, the only motive for which is the remedy of some fault which it possesses. For instance, a badly-carried ear is often " improved " by the application of a knife when the puppy is young; or a tail which is carried up over the back is operated on by having some of the refractory joints so severed that it cannot be raised. Filing the teeth when they are irregular or malformed is also practised, and there can be no doubt that this is illegal, for prompt disqualification is the certain result of detection. Many artifices to which the various breeds may be especially liable will be mentioned in connection with those breeds, and it is therefore unnecessary to go into them at length in the present instance.

Another improvement is more legitimate. A few drops of oil rubbed into the palms of the hand and applied to the coat has an improving effect upon it. Care must be taken to prevent the oil showing too palpably, and only a few drops must be used, or the coat will be greasy and sticky.

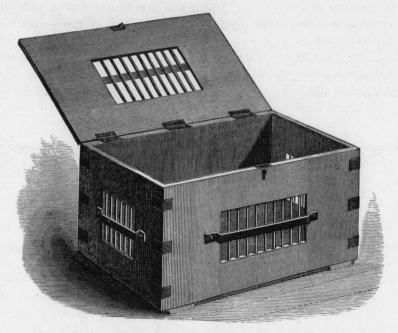

FIG. 13.—TRAVELLING BOX FOR DOGS.

It is always best to send dogs on a journey securely confined in a box or basket, though in the case of large dark-coloured breeds the necessity for doing so is not so decided as when delicate or white dogs have to be considered. Their chain can be let hang loose, so that when the lid is opened there will be less chance of their escaping. Of the two arrangements, a square-sided basket is preferable when the dogs are not of a destructive disposition, as it allows more air to reach its occupant. The use of a box must be resorted to, however, when powerful and violent dogs are to be sent off, or they will eat their way out in an incredibly short time. The box or basket should be large enough for the dog to stand up and turn himself round comfortably in, and should always be provided with a lock and key and two strong handles. When the owner does not accompany his dog on a journey to a show it is a good plan to tie the key securely to one of the handles, so that the dog can be at once liberated. A couple of straps and buckles, in addition to the lock, are desirable, as they secure the box if the lock gives way, and save too heavy a strain falling on it.

An illustration of a good dog's travelling box is given in Fig. 13, where the iron gratings used for ventilation are clearly shown. These should be in each side, the front, and lid, the back and floor only being boarded. The latter should have holes bored in it for obvious reasons. Care should be taken to ensure the ventilation gratings being sufficiently large for their object, and they should each have a bent iron fender outside, so as to prevent any other packages being placed close alongside them in the van, by which the circulation of air would be impeded. A couple of strips of two or three inch batten should be nailed on the bottom to keep the box off the ground, as if left on a damp floor it would soon decay otherwise. It is not desirable to send more than one dog in each box, unless they are known to be peaceably inclined, for they are liable to fight and seriously hurt each other, though many boxes are so made that they can be divided into two or more compartments by sliding partitions. Some clean straw should of course be placed at the bottom of the basket or box; and if a long journey is contemplated, a little soaked biscuit or bread may be thrown in, but no water, as it would only get spilled and be of no use. If there is a long stoppage on the road and any one is accompanying the dogs, the boxes can be opened and a drink given them; but this is a merciful action which is too often neglected in the master's anxiety to see after his own comforts.

The direction should always be clearly affixed to the box, and it is highly desirable that not only the time of the train's departure, but also the date, be inscribed on the label thus :—

LIVE DOG.—Forward at once.

To *JOHN JONES, Esq.,*

Blank House,

Blanktown,

Per G.W.R.   *Near* OXFORD.

3rd JUNE, 1879.   By 9.30 Train, a.m.

The insertion of the date seems to convey even to the minds of railway officials that a little energy is necessary, and diminishes the chances of the dog being left behind. Never use one of the dirty draughty dens called dog boxes by railway authorities. They are a disgrace to railway organisation, and if a dog travels in one he is most likely to catch an illness in the shape of a cold, influenza, or mange.

If an owner accompanies his dog to a show he should provide himself with a few trifling articles to assist in the final toilet: a chamois leather, scissors, hair-brush, and hair-glove are all useful, and a spare chain and staple or two are often handy. Some chalk for white dogs, powdered resin for tails, and a little oil for the coats very frequently form part of this portion of the luggage, but considerable risk is involved in their application by inexperienced hands; disqualification succeeds detection, and it is not a part of our business to assist exhibitors in their efforts to deceive the judges, who suffer enough from the art of the "faker" as it is.

Great discontent prevails amongst exhibitors with reference to the exorbitant charge made by railway companies for the insurance of live stock. Five per cent. is the modest request they make, and this is of course too high to be frequently paid. A reduction on this prohibitory charge could not fail to be remunerative to the companies; and surely, where threepence is charged for effecting an insurance on a human life for a thousand pounds, fifty sovereigns is too high for that of a dog.

JUDGING.

Not many shows can afford the expense of engaging a sufficient number of judges to enable each class to be judged by a gentleman who is qualified to do so, and there are very few judges who are able to deal fairly by all breeds. The unfortunate result of this is that many varieties are unsatisfactorily placed time after time, or else certain dogs are constantly found in the same positions, from the fact of the same judges being always selected for the duty. It is unduly hard upon any good young dog to make his first appearance before a judge who has frequently awarded high honours to other dogs in the same class, and who must feel considerable diffidence in over-looking them when a stranger appears. Judges are only mortal after all, and their ideas cannot fail to become so moulded to the form of a dog they have once admired, that the order in which many dogs will be placed at our leading shows is often correctly anticipated before the event comes off; so much so, that many exhibitors reserve young dogs until they can first bring them out under a gentleman whose judgment is unbiased in favour of a certain animal, to whose good points he has already paid substantial recognition. This could be remedied by occasionally varying the monotony which seems at present to inspire the committees in the distribution of their judges' duties. A change seems now to be made in the judges every three or four years, which period represents the average length of time a dog can be shown. If, therefore, a new judge once places first a good specimen which appears simultaneously with him, that dog stands an excellent chance of remaining at the top of the tree during his show career, to the detriment of another's chance of success. The latter should, in justice, have an opportunity given him for success under different opinions, and if he fails to win, then the honour gained by his conqueror is doubly increased.

Point judging is strongly advocated by a large section of breeders, who aver that if a certain number of points be awarded to each property, and the dogs judged by this standard, fewer errors and complaints would arise. Whilst admitting that a standard is most essential for each breed, and that the relative value of each numerical point in the standard is made clearer by being awarded a numerical value, we cannot express any sympathy with those in favour of point judging. The impracticability of consistently awarding the identical number of marks to each dog is so obvious that it is impossible to adopt the system, and the time wasted over the calculations is enormous. The Bull-dog Club, which at its origin ostentatiously included point judging in its programme, has been obliged to abandon the idea as unsatisfactory; and it may fairly be taken that the system is unpalatable to the majority of exhibitors throughout the kingdom. An especial objection is, that when dogs are judged by points, one notoriously defective in one portion of its anatomy can be awarded a prize, whereas under any other system he could not succeed.

At some shows the judges have been given catalogues instead of the judging books so commonly used; and this seems to be a rational action when adopted by committees who permit exhibitors to lead their dogs into the ring. The absurdity of playing at secresy, as carried on by committees who use the blank books and yet permit the presence of exhibitors in the ring, is so conspicuous to all but themselves, that criticising such proceedings is like crushing a butterfly on a wheel; but there are signs that some day authorities will have firmness enough to stand by their judges, and openly defend their integrity, without admitting a possibility of their acting unfairly, which half-and-half precautions most certainly imply. Nothing can be more suggestive of collusion between judges and exhibitors than the exclusion of the Press from shows where the judging is held in private. Almost unbounded confidence is placed in judges by exhibitors, but when the latter are absent they cannot help wishing to know how things go on ; and there is always something repugnant to Englishmen when things are done in a corner.

BUYING AND SELLING.

There are few breeders who do not at one time or another desire to dispose of some of their surplus stock, and these very often object to offer their property openly for sale, as they object to be included in the category of dog dealers, as they term it. This is hardly a fair view of the case (though a sapient Bow Street magistrate, in his wisdom, has laid it down that any one selling a dog or owning a stud dog is a dealer in point of law), for a man may dispose of a great many puppies or full-grown dogs before he can come into competition with professional dealers. An advertisement in the sporting journals which refers to any breed of dogs of a known strain will always receive replies, and if the price asked is not too high business can generally be done. Naturally, with unknown persons there is more difficulty in effecting a sale, but there is always a market for good animals. It is undesirable to keep puppies too long if profit is to be considered. Not only does their care involve considerable time and expense after they are first weaned, but they look better then than they do subsequently, and so frequently command a relatively better price. At about seven months old most young dogs are very ugly, and are almost unsaleable : they have all the gawkiness of hobble-de-hoy-hood, and certainly are uninteresting. Many breeders, therefore, have two weedings out in their kennels : one when the puppies are first weaned, and the second after they have begun to " make up," as it is termed ; this takes place when the dogs are about a year old. At the latter age it is generally pretty easy to tell what a dog is going to turn out, so intending purchasers can judge better than they are able to do earlier in the puppies' career.

In advertising a dog for sale it is best to give notice that he can be seen by appointment, or will be sent on approval at buyer's risk and cost, on the purchase money being deposited in the hands of some respectable third party. A sight of the dog is desired by many purchasers, and obviates the risk of future disagreements relative to the animal's merits. A limited time should be named for the dog to be returned, as many quarrels have been the result of one sent on approval being kept a long time. Cases have been known where a stud dog has been sent on approval and subsequently returned as unsatisfactory, after having been surreptitiously used for breeding purposes by the pretended purchaser. It therefore behoves sellers to be on their guard, and no valuable dogs should be sent alone to unknown or unreliable people. In all cases it is desirable for advertisers to be as concise in their remarks on the dog's merits as possible. Little good can come from flattering allusions to a dog's value from the man who wants to dispose of him ; and persons have been known to exaggerate a dog's good qualities to such an extent that subsequent disagreements have arisen between the purchaser and seller.

Buyers should on all occasions endeavour to learn something about the person from whom they purchase their dogs, for it is the height of rashness to accept the assurances of every one who has a dog to dispose of. The worse a dog is the more he is cracked up to unknowing purchasers by certain dealers. A guarantee from a breeder whose name stands high, on the other hand, is always valuable, for it is not probable that he would mar his good name for the sake of gaining a few pounds. Dogs can often be bought for very low prices at shows, and a person who contemplates an investment in dog-flesh can do worse than claim a dog off the bench. Misrepresentation is here less likely to be resorted to, and elementary tricks of the trade, which might be successfully practised on beginners, are pretty sure to be avoided where so many experts have an opportunity for examining the dog. It is well to make certain that a dog is in health, and at a show a veterinary surgeon can have very good opportunities for examining him quietly on the buyer's behalf. One thing to be guarded against by purchasers is, to see they do not get old played-out dogs or barren bitches palmed off on them. A dog's age and state of health can usually be seen, but in the case of a bitch purchased for breeding purposes the difficulty is very much greater. A person who contemplates buying a dog need not convey any suspicions of the seller's honesty to the latter in an offensive manner, but he is failing to do himself justice if, when he does not know the seller, he does not satisfy himself that the dog has not been manipulated so as to improve his appearance.

A system of dealing—for it is no better—by what may be termed "gushing letter writing" is sometimes resorted to when new exhibitors appear on the scene. The novice receives a letter couched in the most friendly terms from an individual he may perhaps have never heard of, who informs him that as he appears to be going in for showing dogs, the writer is prepared to offer him the well-known prize-winner so-and-so. Frequently the party addressed, feeling flattered by the attention, falls a victim, and becomes the possessor of some second-rate specimen whose late owner has a better at home. Exhibitors should therefore beware of dogs thus forced on them, and should remember that there is no necessity for so acting in the case of *really good dogs*, for which there is always a market.

The exportation of dogs from this country is now carried on to a large extent, America and Germany being our best customers. The rapidly increasing interest in all field sports in these countries has caused them to invest heavily in sporting dogs of our best and most famous strains; but as yet they have paid but slender attention to our non-sporting classes. A good opening for the disposal of first-class dogs may therefore be looked for from these quarters; and as we have had some experience in sending off dogs on long sea journeys, perhaps a few hints may not be out of place here. In the first place, it may be noted that as some lines of steamers refuse to carry dogs on any terms, all arrangements should be made by the owner with the company's agents some time before the proposed date of the dog's departure, so as to avoid all risk of disappointment at the last minute. The best form of package for a dog who is about to go on a voyage is a strong box, well clamped with iron at the corners, and standing on two pieces of quartering. The door should be at the front, so as to enable the box to be cleaned out easily, and should be of iron gratings to let in light and air. A canvas blind can be tacked above the door when the dog gets on board, and this can be let down in cold or wet weather. A few holes should be bored with a centre-bit in the floor, and also high up at the back, for ventilation and sanitary purposes. Great care must be taken to have secure fastenings on the box, and the dog should always have a chain and collar on when he is at sea. An arrangement can be made with the ship's butcher to look after him, and the promise of a *douceur* from his new owner on the dog's safe arrival will generally ensure his being well attended to on the voyage. It is desirable that whoever is entrusted with the dog be requested to give him a run on deck when practicable, and dose him if his bowels get confined. Some ordinary black draught can be supplied for this purpose, and will meet every ordinary want.

CHAPTER V.

TECHNICAL TERMS.

So much ambiguity seems to exist amongst the uninitiated as regards the technical terms which are applied to the various portions of a dog's anatomy, that before proceeding to describe the points which it is desirable to look for in the respective breeds, it may be as well if the leading terms are clearly laid before our readers. With a view to facilitate the task of description the subjoined figure has been prepared, and will materially aid us in our endeavours to explain matters :—

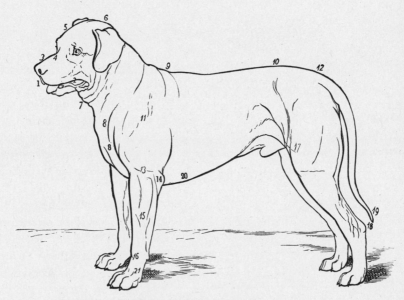

FIG. 14.—DIAGRAM OF DOG. .

REFERENCES.

1. Nose.
2. Flews or Chaps.
3. Nasal Bone.
4. Stop.
5. Skull.
6. Occiput.
7. Dewlap (where such exists).
8. Brisket.
9. Top of shoulder - blades, or "shoulder."
10. Top of Hip-joint.
11. Shoulder-blade, or scapula.
12. Rump-bone.
13. Arm.
14. Elbow.
15. Fore-arm.
16. Knee.
17. Stifle-joint.
18. Hocks.
19. Tail, stern, brush, or flag (the term used depends upon the breed).
20. Chest.
21. Pasterns.

Apple-headed.—This term implies that the skull is round instead of flat on the top.

Blaze.—A white mark up the face.

Brisket (No. 8).—The part of the body in front of the chest.

Brush.—One of the terms used for the tail; generally applied to Sheep-dogs.

Butterfly-nose.—A spotted nose.

Button-ear.—An ear which falls over in front, concealing the inside, as in Fox-terriers. (See Fig. 15.)

FIG. 15.—BUTTON-EAR.

Cat-foot.—A short, round foot, with the knuckles high and well developed. (See Fig. 16.)

Chest (No. 20).—The chest of a dog is not what many people speak of as breast, or chest, but extends underneath him, from the brisket to the belly.

Cobby.—Well ribbed up; short and compact in proportion.

FIG. 16.—CAT-FOOT.

Couplings.—The length or space between the tops of the shoulder-blades and tops of the hip-joints, or huckle-bones. The term denotes the proportionate length of a dog, which is accordingly spoken of as long or short "in the couplings."

Cow-hocked.—The hocks turning inwards. (See Fig. 17.)

Dewlap (No. 7).—Pendulous skin under the throat.

Dew-claw.—An extra claw, found occasionally on the legs of all breeds, but especially the St. Bernard.

Dish-faced.—This term describes a dog whose nasal bone is higher at the nose than at the stop—a feature not unfrequently seen in Pointers.

FIG. 17.—COW-HOCKS.

Dudley-nose.—A flesh-coloured nose.

Elbow (No. 14).—The joint at top of the fore-arm.

Elbows Out.—This term almost describes itself, but will be understood instantly from Fig. 18. Bull-dogs and Dachshunds are desired with elbows so shaped, but it may occur as a fault through weakness.

Feather.—The fringe of hair on the back of some breeds' legs—notably Setters, Spaniels, and Sheep-dogs.

Flag.—A term for the tail applied to Setters.

FIG. 18.—ELBOWS OUT.

Flews (No. 2).—The chaps, or overhanging lips of the upper jaw. The term is chiefly applied to hounds or other deep-mouthed dogs.

Fore-arm (No. 15).—This makes the principal length of the fore-leg, and extends from elbow to pastern.

Frill.—The projecting fringe of hair on the chest of some dogs, and especially of the Collie.

Hare-foot.—A long, narrow foot, carried forward. (See Fig. 19.)

Haw.—The red inside eye-lid, usually hidden, but specially prominent in Bloodhounds.

Height.—The height of a dog is measured at the shoulder, bending the head gently down. The proper method is to stand the dog on level ground close by a wall, and to lay a flat rule across his shoulders horizontally so as to touch the wall; then measure to the point touched by the rule. Some people "tape" from the centre between the shoulders to the ground; but this plan obviously adds to the real height of the dog, and is practically a fraud.

FIG. 19.—HARE-FOOT.

Hocks (No. 18).—The hock-joints.

Huckle-bones (No. 10).—Tops of the hip-joints. The space between these and the tops of the shoulders is called the couplings.

Knee (No. 16).—The joint attaching the fore pasterns and fore arm.

Leather.—The skin of the ear.

Occiput (No. 6).—The prominent bone at the back or top of the skull; particularly prominent in Bloodhounds.

Overshot.—The upper teeth projecting beyond the lower. This fault in excess makes a dog pig-jawed, which see.

Pastern (No. 21).—The lowest section of the leg, below the knee or hock respectively.

FIG. 20.—PIG-JAW.

Pig-jawed. — The upper jaw protruding over the lower, so that the upper incisor teeth are in advance of the lower, an exaggeration of an overshot-jaw. (See Fig. 20.)

Pily.—A peculiar quality of coat found in some dogs, which show on examination a short woolly jacket next the skin, out of which springs the longer coat which is visible. This short woolly coat is "pily." When an ordinary coat is described as pily, it means that it is soft and woolly, instead of hard, which in such cases is of course a fault.

Rose-ear.—An ear of which the tip turns backward and downward, so as to disclose the inside burr of the ear. (See Fig. 21.)

FIG. 21.—ROSE-EAR.

Septum.—The division between the nostrils.

Shoulders (No. 9).—The top of the shoulder-blades, the point at which the height of a dog is measured

Skull (No. 5).—This is formed by the frontal, parietal, and occipital bones.

Splay-foot.—The foot spread out flat and awkwardly. (See Fig. 22.)

Stern.—The tail.

Stifle-joint (No. 17).—The hip-joint.

FIG. 22.—SPLAY-FOOT.

Stop (No. 4).—The indentation between the skull and the nasal bone, near the eyes. This feature is strongly developed in Bull-dogs, Pugs, and Short-faced Spaniels, and considerably so in many other dogs.

Tulip-ear.—An upright or prick ear.

Undershot.—The lower incisor teeth projecting beyond the upper, as in Bulldogs. (See Fig. 23.)

FIG. 23.—UNDERSHOT.

CHAPTER VI.

THE MASTIFF.

THE Mastiff occupies an undoubtedly high position in the canine world; and there are not wanting many of its partisans who solemnly avow that there exist unmistakable proofs of its being *par excellence* the national dog of the country. With this somewhat ambitious boast we confess ourselves unable to agree, for reasons which can be gone into hereafter; but there can be no possible difference of opinion as regards the extreme antiquity of the breed, mention having been frequently made of it by many of the earliest classic writers. Considerable confusion appears to have existed formerly between this dog and the Bulldog, for the descriptions we find in various writers of the Molossus—a name which was conferred upon this breed in consequence of its supposed origin in Molossis in Greece—coincide very often with those we discover elsewhere of the Bulldog. According to Edmund de Langley, in his MS., "The Mayster of Game," published in the fourteenth century, two distinct breeds of dogs, the Molossus and the Alaunt, were in existence. The former appears to have been reserved for the guardianship of persons and property, whilst the latter, described by him as a *short-headed* dog, pugnacious, and gifted with an inclination to hang on to anything attacked by it, was used for baiting the bull. Linnæus, in the classification which he has drawn up, on the other hand describes the Bulldog as coming under the classification of Canis Molossus, whilst the Mastiff is in the next section under the title of Canis Anglicus, also called Canis Bellicosus, and by Ray, Canis Mastivus. Dr. Caius, physician to Queen Elizabeth (and, by the way, one of the founders of Caius College, Cambridge), in his book published about A.D. 1570, describes but one dog which can in any degree be made to resemble either the Mastiff or the Bulldog. This he alludes to under the name of Mastive or Bandogge, and a portion of his description is as follows:—"An huge dogge, stubborne, eager, burthenous of body, and therefore of but little swiftness, terrible and fearful to behold, and more fearse and fell than any Arcadian cur." This description, indefinite as it is, would seem to apply almost as well to the Bulldog as to the Mastiff: first on account of direct allusion being made to "Archadien curres," which must be taken as referring to the Molossus or Mastiff of Edmund de Langley, whose work is made use of most freely by Caius; and, secondly, from the description he gives of the animal's character, and the remarks he makes a little further on concerning the creatures one of them had been known to overcome in single combat for the especial edification of the "Frenche King." But still, from the fact of no separate allusion having been made by Caius to another variety of the dog which in any way resembled the one in question, we are driven back upon the supposition that about this period the distinction between the Molossus and the Alaunt, or the Canis Molossus and the Canis Anglicus, had nearly died out, probably from carelessness in the breeding of the two varieties, and that the breeds were so nearly amalgamated as to be with difficulty separated, a task which Dr. Caius does not appear to have attempted.

With the view of giving our readers an idea of what a real Molossus was like in appearance, we copy, in Figs. 24 and 25, two representations from an illustrated work in the British Museum,

MASTIFF.

entitled "Icones Animalium," by J. F. Riedel. It cannot be said on behalf of these illustrations that they in some points much resembled a modern Mastiff, nor were they possibly intended to be more than a rough outline of what the Molossus was in days gone by. There are, however, many characteristics of the Mastiff in this Molossus, and dogs of this variety were undoubtedly the progenitors of our modern Mastiff.

Assuming therefore that there is some foundation for this theory, is it not most probable that persons finding themselves in possession of a huge dog gifted with the savage disposition described by Dr. Caius should be desirous of improving him into an animal a little more deserving of their attention and esteem? If this were the case, by selecting suitable specimens to breed from they had it in their power to produce a large-framed loud-voiced dog, specially adapted for the guardianship of dwellings, or a smaller animal suitable in every degree for baiting bulls, a use to which the larger variety could hardly be put on account of his great size.

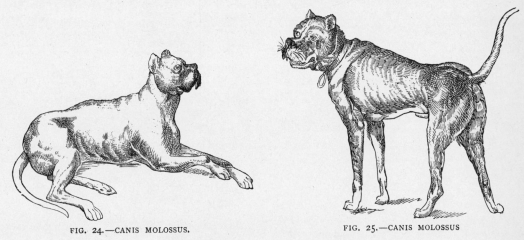

FIG. 24.—CANIS MOLOSSUS.   FIG. 25.—CANIS MOLOSSUS

(*Both figures copied from "Icones Animalium."*)

There are not wanting others who, with a show of justice, contend that the now-almost extinct Irish Wolfhound—a dog combining something of the appearance of the Mastiff with that of the rough Greyhound—was the original dog sought after by the Romans, and whose prowess was sung of by their poets. Leaving this point, however, as one incapable of solution, we shall here assume that the Bulldog and Mastiff had much of common paternity, if they did not diverge from one common ancestor; the Mastiff being the larger and coarser variety, and the Bulldog the sturdier, lesser, and more active; but both admirably suited for the work to which they were put.

According to many eminent breeders of Mastiffs with whom we have had conversation, the Lyme Hall breed is considered the purest and most valuable strain of blood in the kingdom; but owing to the jealousy with which it has always been guarded by the Legh family, to which it belongs, the general public have been unable to judge of its merits by either personal observation or experience. We ourselves are of the opinion that the value of the strain must be consider-ably less than it is usually estimated at, since the breed must have greatly deteriorated by in-breeding. Nothing, however, could be more remote from our object than any wish to cast a slur on the Lyme Hall breed. Judiciously crossed with dogs of other strains, this blood has very frequently been the means of resuscitating a failing line, and has largely contributed towards the existence of the splendid animal now accepted as the *beau idéal* of the English Mastiff.

The sire of Mr. Lukey's Governor was of Lyme Hall origin; and such dogs as Mr. Hanbury's Rajah and Prince, Bill George's Tiger, Mr. Wallace's Turk, and Mrs. Rawlinson's Countess, have the same blood flowing in their veins. It must, however, be added that innumerable disputes have from time to time occurred between various breeders concerning certain specimens of the Mastiff who are credited by their owners with Lyme Hall blood; and it is patent to the most casual observer that many of the dogs which appear at shows as laying claim to the above pedigree must either be entered wrongly by their masters, or else be very imperfect specimens of the famous Legh strain.

The famous Turk, just alluded to, was undoubtedly the champion of his day; and the highest-priced dog ever exhibited deserves more than a passing notice in this work. Five hundred pounds was the enormous sum paid for him in the earlier part of his career; and as his pedigree includes the names of many of the most famous Mastiffs produced, we give it at length as a valuable reference for intending Mastiff breeders. We also give an illustration, the drawing for which was made in 1874, when the dog was seven years old.

PEDIGREE OF MISS AGLIONBY'S TURK, BORN 1867.

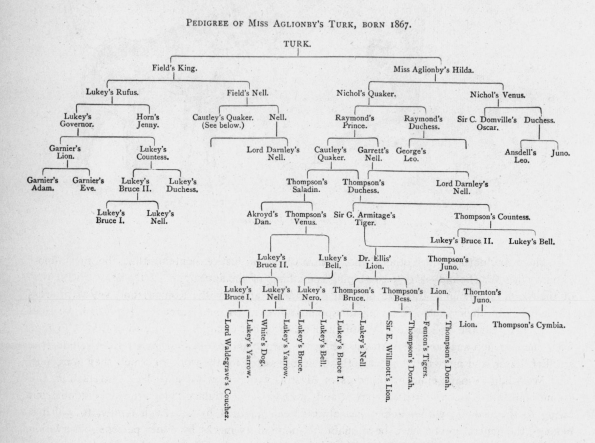

An excellent engraving of a Mastiff, and which we also reproduce, appeared in the *Sportsman's Repository*, edited by John Scott, and published in London 1820. This dog would unquestionably fail to take a prize at one of our modern shows; but still the portrait is valuable, if only for the conclusions it enables us to draw concerning the advance made upon the Molossus by later Mastiff breeders in the earlier part of this century. From the

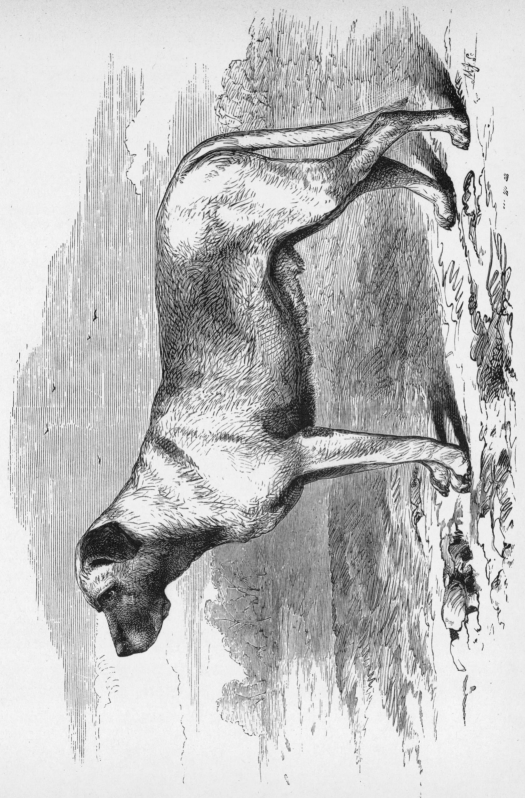

MR. WALLACE'S TURK.

engraving it would clearly appear that the dogs of those earlier days had at least better legs and feet than our modern specimens : that is to say, if the artist who depicted the dog in question is to be trusted.

Foremost amongst the names of celebrated Mastiff breeders appears that of Mr. T. H. V. Lukey ; who, nearly half a century ago, first turned his attention to the breeding of this dog, and whose strain on all sides has been most eagerly sought after by breeders and exhibitors alike. Closely following the name of Mr. Lukey are those of Capt. Garnier, Lord Darnley, Rev. J.

MASTIFF IN 1820, AS DEPICTED IN THE "SPORTSMAN'S REPOSITORY."

Rowe, Miss Aglionby, Mrs. Rawlinson, Mr. E. Field, Bill George of Kensal New Town, Miss Hales, The Rev. J. W. Mellor, Messrs. A. S. de Fivas, John Hartley, Octavius Green, T. W. Allen, J. Parkinson, J. Morris, C. T. Harris, and E. Nichols of Brook Green. One or two of these have had to overcome great difficulties in want of space, since care and experience alone cannot in the long run contend successfully against want of fresh air and exercise, and this breed of all others requires the utmost attention in its early days, so as to enable it to grapple successfully against the tendency to become cow-hocked. The blemish in question, in fact, appears to be considerably on the increase amongst Mastiffs of the present day, if those which appear at shows fairly represent the breed. Mr. Edgar Hanbury, of Highworth, Wilts, has bred some splendid dogs—Prince, by Lukey's Governor, Rajah, and his son Wolsey (the subject of our coloured plate) being conspicuous amongst the number. Mr. H. D. Kingdon, of Wilhayne, Colyton, Devon, lays claim to the possession of the pure Lyme Hall blood : but the inferiority of such of his strain as have come beneath our notice is so conspicuous when compared with the specimens of the gentlemen alluded to above, who undoubtedly do possess it, that we are impressed with the belief that if Mr. Kingdon's dogs are really more than "reputed" Lyme Hall Mastiffs, they signally fail to represent the type in a manner worthy of so valuable a strain.

About the year 1872 several gentlemen interested in the breeding and exhibiting of this class of dog banded together with the object of founding the present Mastiff Club. The principal aim of this Society was the improvement of the breed up to a standard of excellence agreed upon by the members, and show committees were to be invited to co-operate with the Club in their endeavours to benefit the Mastiff according to their ability. Unfortunately, considerable dissatisfaction was caused by some most arbitrary rules, one of which was to the effect that the members pledged themselves to exhibit at no dog show where others than members of the Mastiff Club officiated as judges of this variety. The result of this suicidal policy was an utter lack of support from breeders, and the exhibition held under their auspices in connection with the Northampton show of 1876 was only productive of four entries ; an almost similar *fiasco* occurring at Bristol in the autumn of 1877. Great exception has also been taken to the appearance of several dogs which have been exhibited by certain of the members ; and though we are not able to state positively what is the exact standard aimed at by the Club, we are, from the specimens shown by them, in a position to form an opinion concerning their type, which is not at all in harmony with that held by the members of the Mastiff Club.

Before leaving the subject of famous Mastiff exhibitors, it might be as well to add the names of some of those best known dogs from whom our future champions are destined to spring, and who themselves have been the heroes of many a hard-fought fight. Amongst them may be named Governor, Tiger, King, Lion, Turk, Nell, Quaker, Beauty, Rajah, Kay's Empress, Queen, Monarch, Punch, Granby, Bowness, Argus, Lottie, Nero, Countess, The Shah, Colonel, Wolsey, Cardinal, Mr. Banbury's Princess, Mab, and many others.

POINTS OF THE MASTIFF.

The following detailed description and valuation of the several principal points or characteristics of this breed will be found in accordance with the opinions of the majority, if not all, of the most prominent breeders, exhibitors, and owners of Mastiffs.

General Appearance, Size, and Symmetry.—In this we have to consider the special duties of the Mastiff in the present day. He is no longer a savage kept to bait "the bull, the bear, and the lion," as history (somewhat doubtful in its accuracy as to the last-named animal) informs us he was ; nor the mere drudge of the butcher, to keep his wild and doomed cattle in the shambles, and fight for him when required ; nor even the mere chained slave—the ban-dog of the country house—whose bay, however welcome to those who approached near home, must have had an awful sameness in it to the poor brute who, night after night, month by month, and year after year, listened to the echoes of his own dismal howl as he bayed the moon, or hoarsely barked warning and defiance to all who approached with predatory aim.

Now, although there are still enough and to spare of the ban-dog sort, who are by their owners called Mastiffs, and may no doubt lay claim to possession of a fair portion of Mastiff blood, they are impure, and suffer so from the cruelty of close confinement that they lose even the characteristics of the breed, which a kinder and more judicious treatment would develop, both in physical proportion and dignity of manner, and which are essential features of a Mastiff of the present day.

The Mastiff always has been the special guard of man's person and property; and the qualities demanded to fill that position of trust are: size, to impress with fear; the symmetry of well-proportioned parts evidencing a combination of strength and activity; a disposition watchful and keen, but confident in its own strength; dignified and calm, save the warning bark, which fills every echo within its reach with its full tones, so unlike the yelping of the noisy cur.

As he is now also more used as a companion and personal guard than at any time in his history, his general appearance becomes more important; for nothing looks worse than a poor shambling, weak-loined, cow-hocked dog. Therefore he must have size to give him a commanding appearance; a well-knit, compact frame, which gives symmetry; and the perfect condition shown in the firm flesh, clean and bright coat; while the superior feeding, grooming, and general care bestowed upon him now adds greatly to his beauty; and all combined make him the useful guard and ornament he is.

The *Head* is, in the Mastiff, even more than in most other dogs, a most prominent feature; and a dog with a bad head is at once condemned. The head is decidedly large, even in proportion to the immense carcase, although it does not now present the great contrast to the body to be seen in old prints, modern breeders having improved the dog in body from a gaunt and wolf-like to a square-built, massive animal. The head should be broad across the skull; the brow should be flat and not abrupt; the eyebrows rather prominent; the muzzle should be a medium length, cut off square, broad rather than deep; the lips should be full, but not so hanging as in the Bloodhound; and the teeth, which should be white and strong, ought to meet as level as possible. Many good specimens are slightly undershot, which is however a decided blemish. Whilst on this point we may refer to some remarks once made by the Rev. G. F. Hodson, after he had judged this breed at the Alexandra Palace. On that occasion, Mr. Hodson, who had most properly turned out of the ring all the cow-hocked and undershot specimens, remarked that he was convinced good Mastiffs were to be had without these defects, and he was determined not to be a party to the awarding of prizes to dogs so malformed. Subsequent events have proved the soundness of his decision.

The *Eye* should be a medium size; it is generally a light brown or hazel. A deeply sunken eye is objectionable, as it gives a sullen look; and if the haw is shown, it creates a suspicion of Bloodhound cross.

The *Ears* should be small, smooth, thin, and pendent; and if black, as the mask should also be, it adds to the dog's beauty.

The *Neck* should be strong, muscular, and of fair length, and having no dewlap on the throat.

The *Chest, Back, and Loin.*—The chest should be deep and moderately wide, but not so much so in proportion as his congener the Bulldog, or it is apt to throw the elbows out. The back should be very strong, broad, and with strong muscles running along each side of the spine—those should be especially so connecting the back ribs with the hind-quarters. The loin is thereby broadened and strengthened; and this most desirable point is also gained by having the ribs well set back. Some strains show a tendency to a tucked-up flank, which is one of the worst faults a Mastiff can possess. Both chest and loins should measure well, the latter not quite a third less than the former, and about equal to the dog's height at shoulder.

Legs and Feet.—Strong and straight legs are an absolute necessity, and it is a point in which many excellent dogs fail. The fore-legs are not so often crooked as the hind-legs; but many good puppies give way at the ankle, and have to be destroyed. Therefore, the greatest care has to be taken in rearing this breed; and no Mastiff should ever be chained if it is desired to exhibit him. Cow-hocks are also common, and a great eyesore, and this state is almost always accompanied with more or less wasting of the muscles of the hams, which gives a thin, almost wedge-like appearance to the hind-quarters. Some judges, we believe several members of the Mastiff Club included, consider dew-claws no disqualification; they are, however, most unsightly appendages which should not be encouraged.

The *Colour.*—The recognised colours are brindle and fawn, and the latter at present holds the highest place in popular favour. When the fawn is bright, and the mask a decided black, with an entire freedom from white, the effect is very pleasing. Some of the fawns run into red, which is not so desirable, and such as are of that colour are generally coarse in coat. The brindles are of various shades.

The *Coat* should be fine, short, and even, except along the shoulder, back, and tail, where it is stronger and longer.

The *Tail* should be of great length, strong at the root, and gradually lessening, but not tapered as a Pointer's is.

We are indebted to the courtesy of Mr. W. K. Taunton, the well-known and successful Mastiff breeder, for the following paper on mastiff breeding:—

"The following is what I consider a Mastiff ought to be, and what I should endeavour to breed for:—The head should be large and massive, skull perfectly flat and very wide across, the forehead well wrinkled, with a depression up the centre, a good stop, the eyes small, of a light brown or hazel colour, and set very wide apart; the muzzle short and very broad, with a square, blunt finish; lips loose, and a certain amount of flews, but not to the same extent as in the Bloodhound; the teeth level; ears small, set on high, and carried close to the head; neck muscular, free from throatiness; chest deep, good shoulders, body rather long with large girth, well-rounded ribs, wide strong loins, broad thighs showing plenty of muscle, fore legs perfectly straight with immense bone; feet round and close; tail tapering, not too long, and carried low. The dog should be compact and well knit together, and be the picture of muscular power and symmetry, with an open, honest countenance.

"I consider 30 to 31 inches a fair average height for a dog, but should prefer one 32 or 33, provided the extra height is accompanied by a *proportionate increase in bone and size throughout.* The increase in the size of a dog standing 32 inches over one 30 inches should be far greater in proportion than the increase in size of one 30 inches over one 28 inches. Size in a Mastiff is a great desideratum, but *not mere height alone.* Bitches generally stand two to three inches lower. I like a fine coat.

"It cannot be denied that the colour most admired at the present day is fawn with black muzzle and ears, the black commencing just below the eye. At the same time, I cannot help thinking the brindle would become somewhat more popular if better specimens of this colour were more frequently exhibited. I do not recollect to have seen an illustration of a brindle in any book or paper with the exception of Mr. Lukey's Wallace, and I do not hesitate to say that a very large number of the public do not recognise a Mastiff when of this colour. This is a fact I think to be regretted, because most of the oldest breeders and best authorities are agreed that the brindle was the original and is the true colour of the Mastiff, and, in the opinion of some judges, many of the finest specimens of the breed have been of this colour; in addition to which, it must be admitted that most, or at least many, of our best and purest fawns are descended from brindled ancestors. I would, therefore, impress upon breeders the advisability of not neglecting this colour too much, and allowing it to die out, feeling sure that, sooner or later, it will be well to have recourse to it to cross with fawn, in order to preserve the black muzzle so much admired, and without which, I fancy, the fawn will lose much of its attraction.

"It may be taken as a fact, that the female, in breeding, whether it be in the case of horses, cattle, or dogs, is quite as important an element as the male, and if it be wished to improve, or even to keep up without deterioration any breed, it will be necessary to pay quite as much if not even

MRS. RAWLINSON'S COUNTESS.

more attention to the quality of the dam as to that of the sire. This seems to me to be a fact too much overlooked by the committees of the various shows which are ostensibly held with a view to improve the various breeds of dogs. Yet it is but seldom that separate classes are provided for bitches; and exhibitors knowing full well that these have a poor chance of winning when in competition with dogs, it is but seldom really good specimens are to be seen. Many seem to be under the impression that in order to become successful Mastiff breeders all they have to do is to obtain a bitch of some sort—good, bad, or indifferent, but if the sire be a prize winner, so much the better. They then look through the prize list to discover the dog that has won the greatest number of prizes; and in due course, without ever considering whether they are likely to suit one another or not, send their bitch to this dog, and then anxiously await the arrival of the future champions. Such a plan, I need scarcely say, can but lead to disappointment ninety-nine times out of a hundred. Although there may be a litter of puppies, they will, in all probability, not repay the cost and trouble of rearing them. Good bitches are at all times scarce, and are not to be had for a mere trifle, although, of course, occasionally bargains are to be met with in these as in everything else; but it should be remembered that low-priced articles are frequently the dearest in the end.

"In selecting a bitch, particular attention should be paid to her breeding; the pedigree should be scanned carefully, to make sure she is well bred not only on the sire's but also on the dam's side, and that their ancestors, again, are descended from blood of undoubted purity. Having satisfied yourself on this point, see that the bitch is well made throughout, and likely to prove a good brood bitch; long in the body and great width across the loins. If there be any blemish, ascertain, if possible, if it be the result of accident or bad rearing, or hereditary. The new purchase having arrived home, study her carefully; not with a view to discover her good points, which will probably be apparent enough, but in order to find in what respect she is deficient. It is, in my opinion, far better to breed from a well-made bitch with a pedigree on which you can rely, but which for some reason may be an animal not capable of winning prizes, than from a bitch, perfect in appearance and winner of several first prizes, but of whose pedigree you know nothing, or as to the correctness of which you are in doubt; for it is like groping about in the dark to find out what blood will best suit her.

"The next step is to endeavour to find out the dog most likely to suit your bitch. Never mind whether he be a champion or not. Unless the bitch be very much in-bred, I would advocate selecting a dog that has a good deal of the same blood in him; and I like, if possible, to see some of his stock, taking care at the same time to ascertain what sort of bitches they are from, as this would be some assistance in forming a judgment as to whether he would be likely to suit your bitch. Endeavour to select a dog good in those points where the bitch is deficient; and if there be any special fault I wish to breed out, I should select a sire *coming from a strain* where this fault does not appear, or, if anything, from a strain slightly faulty in the opposite direction. What I mean is this: supposing I had a bitch deficient in head but with good body, &c., the simple fact of putting her to a perfect-headed dog would not necessarily have the desired effect of obtaining good-headed puppies, and especially so if the dog come from a strain not noted for its good heads; but if I could secure the services of a moderate-headed dog, provided I were satisfied he came from a *family* known to be good in this particular point, I should be more sanguine of success, although it would very probably be requisite to put a daughter of this pair to a good-headed dog of the same blood as the sire before I attained what I wanted.

"The aim of the breeder should be to breed animals as nearly perfect in all points as possible, and I should consider it a great error to breed with a view to perfection in one or perhaps two points to the neglect of all others. A Mastiff with the grandest head in the world is useless unless he has a body and legs in accordance. Neither should a breeder be bigoted as regards one particular strain, for some of the best results have been attained by crossing various strains; but this requires care and judgment, and must not be attempted in a haphazard sort of way.

"The most common faults which I notice in many Mastiffs are—want of breadth in muzzle, want of bone, deficiency in size (I mean body, &c., not height), over-large ears, together with bad legs and cow-hocks; these latter, however, being most frequently caused by want of exercise and bad rearing, and I believe that many, in their over-anxiety to have puppies of heavy weight, are too apt to overload the body to the detriment of the legs. So long as they have plenty of nourishing food and are in good health, it is an error to get Mastiff puppies too fat when young; this can be done later on.

"Size, bone, good shape, and correct skull, may be best obtained by the aid of such a dog as Mr. Green's champion Monarch, one of the largest, and at the same time, best made dogs that at the moment occurs to me. Against these advantages may be placed the probability of not obtaining from him the breadth of muzzle, so much looked for by judges of the present day; and this defect I would endeavour to remedy by putting bitches from him to such a dog as Rajah or one of his descendants, such as Wolsey, or The Shah. A happy result of such a course was to be seen in Mr. Fletcher's Lady Love, first prize at the Alexandra Palace Show of 1879; she being by the Shah, out of Norma by Monarch, and not only good in head and muzzle, but also in bone, body, loins, &c. To take another example from a different type, size and bone may undoubtedly be obtained from Big Ben, inherited, I believe, on his dam's side, from the Duke of Devonshire's strain. Many of Big Ben's immediate descendants, however, do not please me in other points, being, in my opinion, bad in skull, coarse in coat, and in many cases weak behind. To these objections I consider my dog Cardinal merely an exception; but at the same time I think excellent results may be looked for in combining Big Ben's blood with that of King's descendants, either through Turk or Rajah. This latter dog (Rajah) has, undoubtedly, done much to improve the head in many Mastiffs. Many of his descendants, however, are considerably undershot; and although I am not prepared to carry my objections to this as far as some, still I would endeavour to avoid it, as I see no advantage in it.

"If two bitches were offered to me for breeding, one with a good head but deficient in length of body and width of loins, and the other good in body but with inferior head, I would select the latter, believing that I should be more likely to obtain the improvement in the head through a suitable sire, than to add the other points. Of course I am speaking of two animals of equal pedigree. It will be gathered from what I have said, that having a bitch with good head, and deficient in other points, I should go to a well-made dog like Monarch; whilst on the other hand, good-made bitches I would put to such dogs as Rajah if young (Rajah is now nine years old); or Wolsey, or The Shah (where, however, we are likely to get that dog's fault in skull as well as want of mask). I have never seen any of the Lyme Hall, or so-called dogs, but if they resemble the dogs which are selected at shows as being the correct type by certain authorities, I do not fancy I should admire them.

"One thing, I think, some make a mistake in, is in not persevering in a certain cross, but having mated a dog and bitch together—say for instance Rajah and a Monarch bitch—and not at once getting what they want, they throw it up in disgust; whereas, if they would only try the bitches from such a cross again with the sire's blood, the result may be found just what is wanted.

"As regards in-breeding, it is difficult for me to give an opinion, for, in the first place, I have not yet had an opportunity of trying it myself, and if I turn to the stud-book to see how it has answered with others, I am met with this difficulty—viz., that I know instances in which the numbers of certain well-known sires—such as Turk for example—have slipped in somehow after the name, although it is not known what Turk is the ancestor, or anything respecting his breeding. To what extent this has been done I know not, and it may be that where in-breeding has apparently been carried to some extent, the ancestors are not related. However, I am of opinion that in-breeding, if judiciously carried out, proves beneficial, and I am about trying it. I base this opinion on one or two instances where it has undoubtedly been carried out advantageously, and on some promising litters of puppies from my dog, where the parents are half brothers and sisters, having a very considerable quantity of the same blood both on their sire's and dam's sides."

As regards the subjects for illustration, Wolsey is a dark brindle dog, bred by Mr. Edgar Hanbury of Eastrop Grange, Highworth, Wilts. He was born in 1873, and is by Hanbury's Rajah out of Queen by Druid, out of Phyllis by Wolf, out of Phœbe by Lukey's Governor. Rajah by Griffin out of Phyllis. Griffin by Hanbury's Prince out of Rowe's Nell by Rufus, out of Field's Nell by Governor. Amongst the numerous prizes which Wolsey has won are first and special cups, Birmingham, 1875; first, Crystal Palace, Bristol, and Brighton, as well as champion prize and cup at Birmingham, 1876; Alexandra Palace champion prize, and Agricultural Hall, Islington, champion prize, 1877; Crystal Palace champion prize, 1878. Latterly, this grand dog, the flattest-headed mastiff of his day, has suffered from an affection of the muscles in his loins, and has, we believe, retired from the show-bench with his well deserved honours thick upon him. Exception has been taken to a so-called "sour" expression of countenance, but this proceeds chiefly from his colour, and a rather deeply-sunken eye. As regards his temper, we have handled him frequently and always found him most amiable. It will be seen that Mr. Hanbury resorted to in-breeding in his production. His father and mother were out of the same bitch, Phyllis, whilst on his father's side he is still more closely allied to the blood of Mr. Lukey's Governor. Wolsey's measurements are—Weight, 136lbs.; length, from tip of nose to stop, 4 inches; stop to occiput, 9 inches; length of back, from shoulders to setting on of tail, 31 inches; girth of muzzle, 20½ inches; girth of skull, 29½ inches; girth of neck, 27 inches; girth of body, from shoulders round brisket, 41¼ inches; girth of body, from shoulders behind forearms, 43 inches; girth round loins, 32½ inches; girth of hind legs round stifle-joint, 21 inches; girth of forearm, 3 inches; below elbow, 10 inches; girth round pastern, 7¼ inches; height at shoulder, 30¼ inches; height, elbow to ground, 16¼ inches; height, top of loins to ground, 30⅜ inches; height, hock to ground, 9½ inches; length of tail, 21 inches.

Mrs. Rawlinson's Countess, an engraving of which is given on page 49, is a fawn coloured bitch, and an excellent specimen of the Mastiff. She was bred by Mr. Morris of Oswestry, and was whelped in 1872. Her pedigree shows that she is by Sultan out of Flora, a pure-bred bitch of the highly-prized Lyme Hall strain; Sultan by Turk out of Duchess, by Quaker out of Venus. Her chief performances are—first, Crystal Palace and Manchester, 1873; first, Dublin, and divided champion prize, Darlington, 1876; and first prize, Hanover, 1879. Her measurements are as follows:—Tip of nose to stop, 3½ inches; stop to occipital bone, 6 inches; length of back, 29½ inches; girth of muzzle, 17 inches; girth of skull, 25½ inches; girth of neck, 23 inches; girth round chest behind fore-legs, 42 inches; girth round stifle, 19 inches; girth of arm, 11 inches; girth round pastern, 6½ inches; height at shoulders, 31½ inches; height at elbows, 18½ inches; height at loins, 31½ inches; height at hock, 9½ inches; length of tail, 20½ inches.

SCALE OF POINTS FOR MASTIFFS.

	Value.
Head, muzzle, eyes, and ears	15
Neck, chest, back, loin, and stern	15
Legs and feet	10
Coat and colour	5
General appearance	5
Total	50

CHAPTER VII.

THE ST. BERNARD.

AMONGST the great diversity, both physical and mental—in size, character, and adaptability to our various requirements, taste, or mere whims and fancies—which the canine family offer to the philo-kuon, the dog of St. Bernard stands out in bold relief by his picturesque arrangement of colours, but still more by his immense size and grand proportions. His *tout ensemble* offers a strongly-marked contrast—weighing, as he often does, 150 to 160 pounds—to his diminutive brother the black-and-tan toy Terrier, who with his more sober tints sometimes fails to turn the scale at two pounds, and whose fragile form appeals for protection, instead of acting, as his giant relative does, the *rôle* of protector. A greater weight than even 160 pounds may have been obtained in isolated instances, but this was probably when the dog was in a very fat condition. When we consider the above two distinct and now pure breeds, distant in many respects from each other as can well be imagined, it almost staggers the belief in the common origin of the domesticated dog; but like many other facts that present difficulties at first sight, this also disappears or is greatly lessened by reflection.

We have, most of us, to consider in dealing with difficulties of this kind, that our personal experiences of the changes which take place in animal forms, by careful selection and other influences, is, by the necessity of our existence, limited. Yet how rapid the descent from the all-but perfect form of the pure-bred dog to the graceless and unshapely mongrel, where the animal is left to stalk uncared for at a time when the greatest watchfulness is required, must be patent to all. On the other hand, although improvement is always comparatively slow, none of us who have taken any interest in, or closely watched the progress of the breed under consideration, can have failed to mark the steady improvement which has taken place. Their faults have been eliminated, and desired qualities developed, under the patient care and intelligent skill of the breeder; so that could Mr. Macdona's Tell or Mr. J. Murchison's equally fortunate import Thor revisit the scenes of their victories, they would meet with numbers of their progeny even superior to themselves. We have simply to remember these facts, as occurring in a very short space of time, to prove how wonderfully plastic the dog is in the hands of man, and how amenable to surrounding and often accidental influences. And to remember also that from time immemorial he has been subject to man, will reconcile us to the fact that the tiny Toy and the gigantic St. Bernard are indeed of the same race and family.

It is not, however, to his physical excellence, his stately form, superbly grand and beautiful exterior, alone, that the St. Bernard owes his present position as first favourite with such numbers. The work in which he has been engaged for centuries has surrounded him with almost a religious halo in the popular mind. Here, where he has been naturalised, his gentle manners and the benevolent and magnanimous character which his countenance expresses and his conduct endorses, fully sustain the prestige with which he was introduced to us. Stories of the intelligence displayed by the St. Bernard in his search for benighted travellers are as well authenticated as they are widely known, and would simply become irksome by repetition, and we therefore forbear from inflicting them upon our readers.

In more than one leading book on the dog, the Rev. J. C. Macdona of Cheadle is credited —if not directly, at least by inference—with the honour of having first introduced the St. Bernard dog into this country some twelve or fifteen years ago. As far as our memory carries us, how-ever, the popular lecturer, the late Mr. Albert Smith, had some considerable time previous to that date done much to familiarise his friends and audiences with this noble breed. In making this statement, we do not wish it to be for one moment understood that we are desirous of depriving Mr. Macdona of the well-deserved glory due to him for his successful visits to the Hospice of St. Bernard, nor are we at all certain even that the dogs brought to this country by Mr. Smith were actually the first that ever reached our shores. Owing to the misfortune that befel the monks by the loss of their original strain—to which attention will be drawn hereafter—it is quite possible that dogs as purely bred as those now in the Hospice, and displaying all the St. Bernard characteristics, can be found in the neighbouring valleys close at hand. In support of this theory we may mention the name, presently quoted, of M. H. Schumacher, of Berne, Switzerland, from whose kennels were obtained those two grand specimens Thor and Miss Hales' Jura, and also the smooth-coated Monarque, who was, whilst in the flesh, the king of his class, winning at all the important shows throughout the country. At the international dog show in Paris, 1878, we had the pleasure of seeing from M. Schumacher's kennels one of the finest specimens of the smooth-coated variety ever exhibited. Although the gentleman named is the best known in England of any foreign breeder, there are many others of less fame, and by more than one noble family the breed has been kept up from which the Hospice itself has at times recouped the losses attendant on the charitable but most dangerous work in which these dogs are used. We are uncertain whether Mr. Albert Smith obtained his dogs from the Hospice, or from one of the outside sources to which we have referred. Little indeed in the way of particulars have we been able to glean of his dogs, for it must not be lost sight of that in Mr. Albert Smith's day dog shows were quite in their infancy, and many good specimens of every breed were destined never to emerge from the semi-obscurity of a purely local reputation. The precise date of the importation of this highly-popular variety of dog is, however, a matter of secondary importance, for their firm establishment in this country is now an indisputable fact, as their presence in large numbers at our leading shows proves. The Rev. J. Cumming Macdona's Tell—the first he ever exhibited—created such a furore amongst the visitors to the exhibition where he appeared, that other gentlemen were not slow in following his owner's example. Amongst these was Mr. J. H. Murchison, whose name appears most strangely to have been entirely overlooked by writers on the breed, but who deserves lasting credit in connection with these dogs, if only for the benefit he conferred upon them by the importation of Thor and Jura into this country. The result of an alliance between these was Mr. Armitage's grand dog Oscar; and Thor has further distinguished himself by begetting the champions Hector, Shah, and Dagmar, from Mr. Gresham's Abbess, as well as Simplon and many other most excellent specimens of the breed from various other females. As in the case with Sheep-dogs, both rough and smooth specimens frequently appear in the same litter; and we cannot help noticing as one of the most remarkable instances of good fortune or good judgment in breeding, the three dogs just referred to of Mr. F. Gresham. Abbess, smooth-coated, threw him in one litter by Thor, rough-coated, or the smooth-coated champion Shah, the rough-coated champion Hector, and one of the best rough bitches ever seen—Dagmar—now unfortunately dead. Since Mr. Macdona's disposal of the majority of his dogs, Mr. F. Gresham has been left in undisputed possession of the field, and his wonderful collection of St. Bernards, at Shefford, near Bedford, cannot be rivalled in any part of the world. In addition to Monk and Abbess, both great prize winners—and the latter we believe the best St. Bernard for some time before the public—Mr. Gresham has a grand young dog in Cyprus, sired by Monk, and several others only second to his cracks. At the present time there appears a chance of the public often seeing Mr. Macdona once more amongst the list of prize winners with his grandly-framed dog Bayard. Mr. J. Russell, M.D., has also some uncommonly fine specimens ; whilst Mr. W. A. Joyce, of Tulse Hill, certainly should make his mark as a breeder in rough bitches with his magnificent trio—Queen Bertha, Queen Bess, and Queen Mab. Among other notabilities of the present we must not omit Mr. A. C. Armitage's grand dog Oscar, Dr. Russell's Mentor and Cadwallader, Mr. S. W. Smith's Barry, Dr. D. E. Seton's Moltke, H.R.H. the Prince of Wales's Hope, H.S.H. Prince Albert Solms' Courage, Mr. Youile's Simplon, and Mr. De Mourier's Chang ; and among the finest bitches we may enumerate Messrs. Gresham and Tatham's Abbess, Augusta, and Gruyère, Mr. Tinker's Mab, the late Miss Aglionby's Jura, and Dr. Russell's Muren.

The origin of this dog is a matter of great uncertainty, and the monks of St. Bernard are themselves unable to throw any light upon the matter. Beyond pointing out to their visitors the portrait of Bernard de Meuthon, in which he is accompanied by a dog possessing many Bloodhound characteristics, they seem to be incapable of giving any information on the subject. The value of any reliable data, even if such existed, would however be sensibly diminished from the fact that in the early part of this century the breed nearly died out, and the monks were compelled to re-cross the few remaining dogs they had left in their possession with others which they obtained from outside the Hospice. According to one eminent authority, a cross with the Newfoundland was first tried by the monks in their dilemma, but was subsequently abandoned when it failed to succeed. Other good authorities, as will presently be seen, and apparently with reason, attribute more to this cross ; and to it we are most probably indebted for the existence of Mr. Macdona's Meuthon, a black-and-tanned dog, something after the stamp of a Thibet Mastiff, and a considerable winner in his day. This was doubtless more on account of his ample proportions than of his colour, which would keep him in the background in the present time. Another writer gives it as his opinion that the blood of the Pyrenean Wolf-hound was introduced at this later time into the breed, and still remains there. The tendency to a lanky, wolf-like form, with lightish frame and tucked-up flanks, combined with a light tapering muzzle, which crops out in undoubtedly well-bred litters, lends some strength to this theory ; but mere conjectures, based on hearsay evidence, can have but little effect on the future of the St. Bernard, who has for ten years occupied the proud position of the most eagerly-sought-after large dog of the day, and whose popularity, instead of diminishing, is decidedly on the increase, if steadily-increasing entries at shows are to be cited as authorities.

The most authoritative and probable account of the origin of the *modern* St. Bernard is that derived from M. Schumacher; and we are gratified, considering the great interest of the question, that the Rev. J. Cumming Macdona, of Cheadle Rectory, Cheshire, whose great services to this breed in days of yore have been duly chronicled above, has been kind enough to forward us the narrative of this gentleman, who is the greatest authority abroad on this class of dog. His views and statements are contained in a long letter, dated Holligen, 29th of August, 1867, and we are glad to be in a position to make the following extracts from it :—

"According to the tradition of the holy fathers of the great Saint Bernard, their race descends from the crossing of a bitch (a Bulldog species) of Denmark and a Mastiff (Shepherd's dog) of the Pyrenees. The descendants of this crossing, who have inherited from the Danish dog its extraordinary size and bodily strength of the one part, and from the Pyrenean Mastiff the intelligence, the exquisite sense of smell, and at the same time the faithfulness and sagacity, of the other part, have acquired in the space of five centuries so glorious a notoriety throughout Europe that they well merit the name of a distinct race for themselves.

"In winter the service of the male dogs (the females are employed or engaged only at the last extremity) is regulated as follows :—Two dogs, one old and one young, travel over every morning the route on the Italian side of the mountain towards Aosta. Two more make the voyage on the Swiss side towards Martigny, to a distance of about nine miles from the Hospice. They all go just to the last cabins of refuge that have been constructed for the benefit of travellers. Even when the snow has fallen during the night the dogs find their way surely and correctly, and do not deviate from the beaten way a yard. The marks of their feet leave a track which is easy for travellers to follow as far as the Hospice. Two dogs are made to go over the same road together, so if one perishes it is replaced by another —a young one, who is instructed and trained by the survey dog, of which he is the pupil. When the dogs arrive at the cabins of refuge they enter them to see if there are any travellers seeking shelter there, in which case they entice them to follow. If they find any travellers who have succumbed to the cold, the dogs try to revive them by imparting warmth in licking their hands and face, which not seldom produces the desired effect. If these means are inefficient, they return in all speed to the Hospice, where they know how to make themselves understood. . . . The monks immediately set out, well provided with means of recovery.

"In 1812 a terrible snow-storm took place, and the aid of the monks and dogs was so constantly required, that even the female dogs, the most feeble animals, were called into requisition, and perished. There were a sufficient number of males left, but not a single female. How was the breed to be kept·up? The monks resolved to obtain some females of the Newfoundland breed, celebrated for their strength, and accustomed to a cold climate. This idea turned out useless when put in practice, because the young dogs had long hair. In winter this long hair so collected the snow that the poor beasts succumbed under its weight, and perished. The monks then tried crossing one of their own dogs with the offspring of the cross breed, with their short stubby hair. At last this plan succeeded. From that bastard female dog they have reconstituted the race of dogs that are now at the Hospice. These dogs, notwithstanding their cross with the Newfoundland, have the same valour and courage as the ancient race, because, by an intelligent and systematic choice, they rear for service and reproduction only the pups who approach the nearest, by their exterior form and appearance, to the original and fatherly race. Those that proved themselves unable to sustain the work, or who, from their long hair, were disabled, were either given as *souvenirs* to friends of the Hospice, or else sold. Of such are those that have been sold to M. de Pourtalès, at Mettlin, near Berne, and to M. Rougemont, at Loewenberg, near Morat. These dogs come directly from the Hospice, where they are not fit for work on account of their long hair, but are distinguished by their colossal size and excellent qualities. They always retain in the Hospice the finest dogs, and train them for service ; those who do not possess all the marks of genuine breed are given away or sold, because among the number they still find some pups with long hair, who thus reveal their motherly ancestry.

"It is now some ten years since it could be read in many of the papers that a Mr. Essig, of Leonberg, had presented to the Hospice a couple of dogs of the celebrated Leonberg

ST. BERNARD.

breed, which is extraordinarily large and handsome. His intention was laudable and worthy of acknowledgment. But these dogs shared the same fate as those of Newfoundland some fifty years previous. Their long hair was their ruin; they perished; and at present there does not exist in the Hospice a single trace of these beautiful dogs of Leonberg.

"As already said, the Count of Rougemont, at Loewenberg, near Morat, possessed a couple of superb dogs, which were presented to him from the Hospice, because they were not good enough for the work on account of their long hair. These dogs were very large and very handsome; the colour of their coats was a red-brown, and they had white spots on their feet, their necks, their breasts, and their noses (? muzzle). They were on the paternal side of the ancient Bernardine race, and on the maternal side of the Newfoundland race. Several litters of pups were reared from this couple, which were given away and sold, and thus became spread about. In 1854 the female dog gave birth, among others, to a little pup of wretched appearance, spotted white and brown, which was not at all valued by the owner. This wretched-looking little pup was sold as a miserable abortion to Mr. Klopfenstein, of Neunegg, who trained it with care and attention. It prospered marvellously, and, growing up, attained a striking likeness to Barry, the most beautiful specimen of the ancient unmixed race, which is now preserved in the museum at Berne. Its resemblance was so remarkable in regard to external appearance and colour of its hair, that when I saw the dog for the first time I resolved to obtain it at whatever sacrifice.

"I bought, then, this dog in 1855, it being a year old, and called it Barry, on account of its striking resemblance to its illustrious ancestor. I entrusted it to Baron Judd, at Glockenthal, near Thun, and both of us reared some young dogs during many years, but without success. Never could we get young dogs resembling the original race, until 1863, when a pup was born from the bitch Weyerman, of Interlaken, of which Barry was the father. This pup, named Sultan, which was the image of Barry, came into my possession.

"I bred from Sultan without success until I received a bitch from Saint Galles whose father had been one of the St. Bernard dogs. This bitch, named Diana, with Sultan, produced such beautiful pups, that at last I saw my end achieved. At the second birth were two, male and female, so surpassingly fine that I resolved in silence to present them as a gift to the Hospice, in the belief that these dogs, habituated now to the fourth generation to a temperate climate, well selected from generation to generation, would invigorate and regenerate the ancient race with the descendants of its proper blood. The gift was accepted. I took them when they were seven years old, in January, 1866, to Martigny, where some of the old brothers pass the winter. The oldest of the monks received me with this exclamation: '*Mais, mon Dieu, c'est comme le vieux Barry!*' (Why, it is exactly like the old Barry!). I asked him which Barry he alluded to. 'Why,' said he, 'to the one that is stuffed at Berne;' and then he continued to relate that in the year 1815 he had himself taken Barry, then living, on foot to Berne, where he was killed and stuffed. The old man wept with joy, and said, without ceasing: '*Ça donnera Barry, le vrai vieux Barry; que je suis heureux!*' (This is Barry, the genuine old Barry, how happy I am!). There are at the present time (1867) at the Hospice some young pups of Barry that promise well, and which will be, according to all appearances, still finer and larger than Barry himself."

Thus far M. Schumacher, a gentleman whom St. Bernard breeders regard, apparently with justice, as the re-founder of their favourite race. His views being so universally respected, his information on the subject is especially valuable. We therefore attach considerable importance to his remarks on colour. The puppy Barry, it will be seen, was descended from parents marked with white, and he in his turn showed great resemblance to the old Barry of 1815. It is also clear, if this account is to be received as a correct statement of facts, that the extremely long hair of the English "rough-coated" dogs is foreign to the breed as kept up at the Hospice, being due entirely to the Newfoundland cross, and rigorously excluded by the monks, who cultivate a short, or rather we should call it a *medium*-coated dog. This fact is so far corroborated by the excellent engraving, by the celebrated German artist Specht, of the Hospice St. Bernards, where we have a medium, or rather short coat, while the immense development of bone is clearly seen, and white is included in the colour. In all respects, in fact, the noble animal portrayed by Specht is precisely that described by Schumacher. It is plain, in brief, if we follow Schumacher, that the long coat of modern English specimens, while due to the same blood, has been developed apart from all accepted rules of Hospice breeding, and by cultivating that very Newfoundland element in the strain which the monks persistently endeavour to eliminate or keep down. This much, we say, is clear, but at the same time it does not follow that the magnificent "rough coated" St. Bernard, as we have become familiarised with him at English shows, is an undesirable type to keep up. Those who have seen it in perfection will probably think the contrary ; and having endeavoured to establish the facts, as far as they can be ascertained, we can see no reason to run counter to the public judgment, though it seems desirable to make clear that the extremely long-haired dogs are not the type cultivated at the Hospice, and will probably, after a few more generations of selection, be no longer procurable from that source.

Mr. Fred. Gresham has kindly supplied the following as his opinion concerning some controverted points :—

"The question as to whether the white markings should be considered as a *sine quâ non* with the St. Bernard or not having been largely canvassed lately by the admirers of the breed, I am happy to give my views on the subject, and my reasons for arriving at them. That the monks place considerably more value on those dogs that have the white muzzle and line through pole and collar, there is not a shadow of a doubt, the fact having been handed down to us by our greatest authorities on the dog. In addition to which, gentlemen who have visited the Hospice for the express purpose of acquiring information on the St. Bernard, have been given to understand that the monks do not consider one perfect without them.

"In a conversation lately held with Mr. Neville Wyatt, a gentleman greatly interested in the breed, and who had then only just returned from Mount St. Bernard, where he had been for the purpose of consulting with the monks about the marking and also dew-claws, Mr. Wyatt said that he was given distinctly to understand that the dogs possessing the white markings were *greatly preferred*, but that if the markings could not be obtained, a dog would not be discarded from their kennels. He also said that he particularly noticed that almost every one, if not all the dogs he saw there, had a *considerable* amount of white, thus proving that the correct markings were being aimed at, and carrying out my opinion that too much white is preferable to too little.

"As regards dew-claws on the hind legs, the Rev. C. Bowling, of Houghton Rectory, Bedfordshire, when visiting the Hospice, was informed by one of the monks that they were considered of the utmost importance. Mr. Wyatt also said they were greatly esteemed if they could be got, and *double* if possible. The most successful breeders in England have obtained dew-claws fully developed, the exception being to find one puppy in a litter without them ;

ST. BERNARDS OF THE HOSPICE.

therefore, why wish to dispense with them ? The monks acknowledge that they do not object to the hind feet of the St. Bernard being slightly turned out, as it gives greater resistance to the snow. My experience is that the more fully developed the dew-claws, the more the feet are out-turned, the dew-claws forming a part of the foot, and giving six toes to cover the ground instead of four.

"In breeding, it is always advisable to choose a sire particularly good in those points in which the dam is deficient. A young sire should be put to an aged dam, and *vice versâ*. It is not desirable to breed from relations, except in cases where the animals are very strong and healthy; but at the same time an experienced breeder may in-breed to advantage, but it requires caution. The rough and the smooth St. Bernard may be crossed together, and the progeny, as a rule, are either decidedly rough or decidedly smooth. In my opinion the introduction of the rough blood tends to improve the stamina and size of the smooth. The most important thing is to select high-class sires and well-bred dams.

"In temper I have always found the St. Bernard most kind and affectionate, and am of opinion that it is not natural to the breed to be savage. Not one in my own kennel has ever shown the slightest ill-temper to strangers. As a matter of fact, I consider them superior to Newfoundlands in docility and obedience, and their affection for children is a remarkable trait in their disposition."

On referring again to Specht's admirable drawing of the Hospice St. Bernards, it will be seen how exactly the dog in the foreground answers to Mr. Gresham's description as regards the carriage of the hind feet, which are distinctly turned out; and it appears to us indisputable that the remark is founded in reason. A St. Bernard should certainly not be "cow-hocked" in the ordinary application of the phrase, but there is in many fine specimens this inclination to turn their hind feet out, which naturally draws their hocks apparently together. This is however not considered a blemish by many leading judges, especially as the presence of the dew-claws tends to the development, and this peculiar formation obviously adds to the power of the dog in walking over snow. In regard to other points, it is needless to say that with but few exceptions such gaunt-looking specimens as we have before referred to do not appear at great gatherings of the clans. Occasionally those who have bought pups on the strength of pedigree only, and with but little knowledge of their qualities, exhibit them, which is ample proof that many such are whelped; but it is the interest of breeders to eliminate this stamp of dog, and many are consequently put down.

As regards our illustrations, Bayard, the property of the Rev. J. Cumming Macdona, is a handsome medium length rough-coated orange-and-white dog. He was born in 1877, and bred by Mr. King in 1877, being by Bosco out of Juno by Wonder out of Juno by Thor, Bosco by Bruno out of Silverhorn by Thor. His chief performances are, first prize Crystal Palace and first prize Chesterfield, 1878. Bayard's weight is 150 lbs., and his measurements are—Tip of nose to stop, $4\frac{1}{4}$ inches; stop to occipital bone, $8\frac{1}{2}$ inches; shoulder-blades to setting on of tail, $31\frac{1}{2}$ inches; girth of muzzle in front of eyes, $16\frac{1}{2}$ inches; girth of skull, 25 inches; girth of neck, 25 inches; girth of brisket in front of fore-arms, 45 inches; girth round chest behind fore-arms, 40 inches; girth round loins, 34 inches; girth of hind-leg at stifle, $16\frac{1}{4}$ inches; girth of arm three inches below elbow, 12 inches; girth of fore-arm, $8\frac{1}{2}$ inches; girth round pasterns, 8 inches; height at shoulders, $32\frac{1}{2}$ inches; height at elbows, $16\frac{1}{2}$ inches; height at loins, $32\frac{1}{2}$ inches; height at back, $9\frac{1}{2}$ inches; length of tail, 28 inches.

Barry, the property of G. W. Petter, Esq., has never been exhibited, and is of a more rough-coated type.   He is by Mentor (2444) out of Dagmar (5350), the latter being by Thor out of the subject of the next paragraph.   It is interesting to trace his pedigree, the earlier links supplying strong collateral evidence of the correctness of M. Schumacher's account, quoted above.   Mentor is by Hope out of Hedwig by Alp out of Hospice, Hope again being by Tell out of Hospice. Hospice was bred by the monks of St. Bernard; and her pedigree is given as by "Barry (descended from OLD BARRY) out of Juno;" Barry being by *Souldan* out of *Diane*.   These are quite evidently M. Schumacher's Sultan and Diana.   Alp again is out of Hedwig; and Hedwig was bred by Mr. Schindler out of Diane.   Still, again, Thor is by Leo by "Souldan" (Sultan), thus again tracing to Old Barry through the dogs described by M. Schumacher.

Abbess, the property of F. Gresham, Esq., is (or perhaps more correctly speaking, *has* been) the best St. Bernard bitch of her day.   She is a smooth-coated brindle-and-white, and was born in 1870, being bred by her owner.   Her pedigree is—by Leo out of Bernie, by the Rev. J. Cumming Macdona's Bernard out of Bernardine, imported by Mr. Hooper.   Abbess's chief performances are—first Birmingham, 1872; first Birmingham, 1873; first Hull, 1874; first Dublin, first Maidstone, first Birmingham, 1876; first and cup, Bath; first Chesterfield, and champion prize Alexandra Palace, 1877.   The weight of Abbess is 150 lbs., and her measurements are :—Stop to nose, $4\frac{1}{2}$ inches; stop to occipital bone, $6\frac{1}{2}$ inches; length of back, 32 inches; girth of muzzle in front of eyes, $16\frac{3}{4}$ inches; girth of skull, 27 inches; girth of neck, 29 inches; girth of brisket in front of fore-arms, 42 inches; girth of chest behind fore-arms, 41 inches; girth of loins, 34 inches; girth of hind-leg round stifle, 19 inches; girth of arm three inches below elbow, 10 inches; girth of fore-arm, $7\frac{1}{2}$ inches; girth of pastern, $6\frac{1}{2}$ inches; height of shoulders, $30\frac{1}{2}$ inches; height at elbow, 16 inches; height at loins, 30 inches; height at hock, $7\frac{1}{2}$ inches; length of tail, 25 inches.

The following are the points of the St. Bernard :—

Head.—The head is large, square, and massive; the face not too long but square at the muzzle, with flew approaching that of the Bloodhound, but not so heavy.   The stop distinct, showing off the the great height of brow and occipital protuberance, which is specially marked.   Ears of medium size, carried close to the cheeks.   Eyes, dark, bold, and intelligent, sometimes showing the haw, in that respect also partially resembling the Bloodhound.

Neck and Shoulders.—The neck is lengthy, slightly arched on the top, with well-developed dewlap, sloping shoulders, and wide chest.

Legs, Feet, and Dew-claws.—Legs straight, with large feet, and *double* dew-claws if possible, but at least single.   The more fully developed the dew-claws the more inclined the dog is to turn his hind feet out, the dew-claws in such cases making one or two extra toes.   The monks do not object so much to this, as it gives greater resistance to the snow, but the feet are turned out without being cow-hocked.

General Appearance.—Its appearance is showy and gay, giving the observer an impression that the dog is possessed of intelligence, strength, and activity, in a marked degree.

Colour.—Orange-tawny or red is most fashionable with the public.   Many breeders prefer a brindle either dark-red or grey, particularly if tiger-marked, which gives a very showy appearance when relieved by the white markings.   The latter are delineated as follows—the muzzle white, with white line running up poll to neck, which should be encircled by a white collar, white chest, feet, and tip of tail.   These markings are very much valued by the monks, as representing the scapula, chasuble, and other vestments peculiar to the order.

Temperament.—In temperament, if carefully and properly reared, they are mild and affectionate,

ROUGH COATED ST. BERNARDS.

more so than almost any other class of dog; easily taught, and obedient to the slightest command of their masters.

Coat.—In the rough-haired, the coat is shaggy but flat in texture in order to resist the snow; and in the smooth, close and hound-like.

SCALE OF POINTS FOR ST. BERNARDS.

	Value.
Head	10
Neck and shoulders	5
Legs and feet	10
Dew-claws	5
General appearance and colour	10
Coat	5
Temper	5
Total	50

CHAPTER VIII.

THE NEWFOUNDLAND DOG.

THE dog of which we have now to treat is one of the oldest favourites with the British public. He was chosen as a companion and guard from among the classes of dogs we may describe as representing the major canines, when the Mastiff's popularity was for years in abeyance, and the noble Bloodhound's grand qualities as a detective police above the reach of bribery were for a time eclipsed by the novel glare of Peel's blue-liveried peace preserver. His hunting qualities were ignored by all but a few favoured sportsmen who, knowing his worth, used him, and thereby preserved him ; and long before the St. Bernard, with all his excellences, was known in England except to the learned and the travelled, the Newfoundland, with his grand appearance, noble mien, and majestic bearing, had taken possession of popular fancy. As a proof that he still holds it, we are quite certain that there are more Newfoundlands, or dogs so called, kept as guards and big pet dogs in this country by the general public, outside of those who are *au fait* in canine matters, than of any other breed of corresponding size.

If we are right in this, it may be asked why then are Newfoundland classes so sparsely filled in comparison with the classes set apart for those other breeds to which we have alluded ? To this we can only reply that in dogs, as in other things, dame Fashion exercises the same extensive sway. We have no doubt, as the proverb assures us, that "every dog has his day." The Newfoundland's day, as the great feature of our leading shows, is yet to come, and we must recognise the fact that the at-present dethroned monarch has a powerful rival in the picturesquely-marked St. Bernard, who has for the present displaced him. It has also to be remembered that, Newfoundland owners being comparatively unskilled in caniological points, it has generally happened that there have been one or more super-excellent dogs going the rounds of the shows, against whom mediocre ones stand no chance of getting a prize, and they have consequently been frightened away.

As a companion dog the Newfoundland answers every purpose. As a rule he is docile, and always sagacious and faithful to his master, but a terror to tramps and evil-doers, and therefore one of the best watch-dogs that can be kept about a country house. His colossal size strikes awe to the hearts of the vagabond and prowler, and his fine discriminating intelligence soon distinguishes the friendly visitor, and bids him welcome. As a retriever he is unexcelled, although too heavy for field work ; but he has done great service in producing for us our modern unequalled and justly-admired breed of flat and wavy-coated field Retrievers.

It is, however, in the water that this semi-aquatic dog is to be seen in all his glory. No sea is too rough for him to venture in. It is a fine sight to witness one of these intrepid swimmers buffeting the waves, carrying life and safety to the perishing, a work to which the Newfoundland seems to take instinctively, and in the performance of which he at once shows his high courage and benevolence of disposition, appearing to take pride in the display. We consider the qualities of the Newfoundland as a means of saving life

NEWFOUNDLAND.

have not been sufficiently utilised around our coasts; nothing is easier than to train him by means of an effigy to bring drowning people out of the water, and one or two would prove of great value at our bathing stations and in connection with our lifeboats. Water trials for these dogs have been tried at Maidstone and Portsmouth, but from various causes they proved unsuccessful. Such trials, however, if judiciously carried out, would, we are sure, prove both interesting and useful. The idea of instituting such contests originated with Mr. Hugh Dalziel, and it is to be regretted it has not met with the support it deserves. There is no dog that earlier displays intelligence, and his education may be commenced almost as soon as he leaves his dam. A Newfoundland's instinct for fetching and carrying is soon exhibited in his manner of playing with bones, pieces of wood, a ball, or anything he can pick up. He is continually running about with one or other of these things in his mouth, indulging in all sorts of antics, throwing his plaything up and catching it, hiding it when tired, to be brought out again when the spirit of play returns to him.

To take advantage of these natural propensities, and develop them, is the easy task of the judicious teacher. In doing so it is well to keep to one article—a piece of wood, round which some cloth is tied to make it soft to the mouth, and prevent it hurting the teeth, at the same time that it assists in bringing him up tender-mouthed, a most important point to be gained, and one which the use of a hard material in early lessons makes almost impossible of subsequent attainment. The lessons are easily imparted with a little patience and perseverance. This is the *modus operandi :*—Take the object in your hand, and having called the pup to you, show it him, gently shaking it before him, when he will at once want to take it in his mouth. Instead of letting him take it from your hand, throw it, when his attention is on it, a few yards away; he will be sure to scamper after it, when your next part is to coax him back to you, as his natural inclination will be to stop and play with it. If he does not come to you, go to him, and, taking hold of the ball with one hand, with the other very gently lead him back to where you threw it from, and then, with as little force as possible, take it away, place it on the ground, do not allow him to touch it, but pat him and praise him; in a few minutes repeat the operation, and continue until he gets tired of it, at the first signs of which stop the lesson. If this is repeated twice a day the puppy will soon be perfect, and will like the lessons all the better if at the end of each you reward him with some tit-bit. You must then gradually extend the lesson out of doors, throwing the ball into grass, or elsewhere, that he may have to seek for it; and go on until he will "seek" at the commanding use of that word, with a wave of the hand to guide him in the direction in which you have previously hidden the ball. These should be strictly private lessons, as the presence of any other man or dog will distract the pupil's attention, and spoil all. Lessons in the water are taught on the same plan; and diving by using a bone, or other white substance that will sink, beginning by at first dropping it into very shallow clear water. We have seen a dog trained in the manner we have briefly described (he was a fine pup, son of imported parents), so that at six months old he would go back two miles and fetch an article which he had not seen hidden; and he was so tender-mouthed that we have seen him carry a winged crow a mile without hurting him—no easy task when the temper of the crow and the strength of his bill are considered.

Of the dogs imported of late years we cannot speak very highly, none of them being equal to our home-bred specimens; and we look for improvement by careful breeding with these, rather than from the introduction of blood from abroad. An exception may be found in Moldau, a dog imported by Mr. Richard Lord from Hanover. In frame this dog is a grand specimen, but he is blemished by showing white on his feet and chest. We may, however, with marked advantage exchange blood with our American friends, if, as we are informed, fine specimens exist in the United States, where dog shows are now popular, and this breed is being carefully cultivated.

Mr. William Coats, of North Shields, one of the most successful breeders of this variety, and certainly an ardent admirer of the Newfoundland, has kindly supplied us with the following notes on breeding this class of dog:—

"In breeding I must have a powerfully well-built bitch, with plenty of bone and a good coat. Her ears must sit close to her head, which was the characteristic of Leo's mother. His father I did not like so well: he was a great lanky dog, but had a very grand head. Whilst on the subject of colour, I can truly say that I have never seen a *pure-bred* Newfoundland with a *jet*-black coat. I have made the acquaintance of some pretty dogs which have been jet-black; but the veriest mongrel has generally the blackest coat. Under any circumstances the coat must be *flat* and straight. As to size—if you ask any practical breeder of Newfoundlands what he thinks of your puppy, he will almost invariably say in his criticism, 'he doubts whether he is going to be big enough.' Some writers endeavour to write down all large Newfoundlands, simply because they are ignorant of what the breed should be, or are interested in the success of mongrels who are not big.

"With respect to breeding, I do not hold with some authorities in their respect for in-breeding. When I have not a dog of my own sufficiently far removed in blood, I always seek the most powerfully-built dog of the breed I can find elsewhere. The strains I like best are those of Robinson's Carlo, and Windle's Don; and these have provided most of the blood on the dog's side which I now possess. I always try to produce them as big as I can in *stature* and *bone*, with a head and tail resembling those painted by Landseer.

"As regards my experience of the habits and temperament of the breed, I can safely say that I have never had a bad or cross-tempered one; all have been of the most docile character. All Newfoundlands love water, and take to it naturally. Living, as I do, near the sea, my dogs have every opportunity of obeying their natural instinct. When they were missing we generally found them at the sea or river side, or else they came home dripping wet, their jackets telling where they had been."

To Mr. T. Loader Browne, of Chard, we are indebted for the following valuable notes, which his position as an authority renders highly interesting :—

"No doubt there is a great difficulty in breeding dogs up to anything like a perfect standard; and I think this is particularly the case with Newfoundlands, where size is a leading feature. It is comparatively easy to breed tolerably perfect small dogs; but he is fortunate who obtains one first-class large one out of thirty. My idea of a Newfoundland is that he cannot be too large in size, if he be symmetrical; but I would not sacrifice any recognised point to size, much less favour a long-backed, weak-loined animal that cannot turn quickly in the water. My reason for advocating large size is that, viewing him as a water dog, capable of saving life, his extra size and proportionate strength give him greater facility in buoying up and landing a drowning person. Any one, in such a case, would rather see a very large dog, say 33 inches at the shoulder, coming to his rescue, than a smaller one of 27 inches. Also, he makes a nobler companion, and a more powerful and efficient guard, whilst as a show dog he is certainly grander and more imposing on the bench. I know some judges do not insist on extraordinary size, and support their opinion by stating that he is not found so in his native country; but this appears of little weight, as it merely arises from careless breeding; and granting he is more useful for being large, there is no reason why he should not be increased in size, just as other prize stock has been improved within the last half-century. As to colour, the rusty-dun shade is very objectionable, and detracts much from the beauty of the dog; and without going so far as some in saying it arises from a cross with the St. Bernard, I cannot agree with those who maintain it is a sign of pure breeding. No doubt there are many dogs of this colour in Newfoundland, but there are also others of a glossy black. I have reason to believe there is no great care shown in breeding them, but that they vary a great deal in size, colour, and coat; so that every imported dog must not be considered to represent the true breed, which could only be the case if the islanders made a *spécialité* of their dogs, as the Jersey men do of their cows, not allowing any other breed to be imported into the island—not of course that this would be worth the trouble of doing. I think the coat should be of a glossy jet-black colour, and composed of rather coarse, not silky hair, long, straight, shaggy, and dense, but without much under-coat. It is astonishing how quickly this description of coat will dry, as compared with one that is curly; on account of the oily, glossy nature of the hair, very little water can remain in the coat, and that on the surface drips off and nearly disappears with the usual shake.

"The following are some of the defects frequently met with in breeding, but which certainly may be lessened and nearly eradicated by careful mating of the parents, of course never selecting both where the same defect exists, or it will undoubtedly appear in an exaggerated form in their progeny. Where there is a weak point in one of the parents, choose the other where this point is exceptionally strong:—

"Weakness of loin and shortness of the back ribs, both highly objectionable, and generally acknowledged to be a failing of this breed.

"The muzzle being too short, giving the dog a pug-faced appearance; in other cases too long and snipy. It should be a happy medium, with the mouth large and capacious, and teeth level, giving him facility to lay hold of and retain anything floating.

"Neck too short. It should be a fair length, with immense development of muscle; this is required to enable him to keep the object he is bringing to shore well out of the water.

"The ears too large. They should be rather small and lie close to the head, acting as valves to keep the water out of the orifices.

"The eye showing the haw, or under eyelid, leading in some cases to a suspicion of a St. Bernard cross. The eye should be deeply set, and not too large. I prefer colour to be dark hazel, but many good dogs have them rather a lighter shade.

"The tail with a twist or curl occurring in the last joints of the vertebræ, also carried generally too high; it should be gently curved and carried low.

"White colour in patches. A very small spot may be passed over on the chest, and some celebrated dogs have had more than a splash on the foot; but it should not be, and the less there is the better.

"Crooked legs and out at elbows I have found, even when breeding from parents perfect in these points; caused, I believe, by mating a very young bitch with an old dog. If possible, never breed from a bitch under two years, or, better, two and a half years old, the dog to be not more than five, or six at most. If the bitch be five, let the dog be two or three years old.

" The head has generally from twenty to twenty-five points out of the hundred assigned to it, and rightly so, as it is one of the chief characteristics of the breed. It should be essentially an open countenance, full of true dignity and benevolence.

"The Newfoundland has an immense development of brain, and a first-class education is not thrown away on him; he is an apt scholar, but, like some clever boys, at times rather stubborn; still, firmness and kindness will always carry the point. It is surprising to notice the change in his expression after becoming the frequent companion of his master; always intelligent, he now looks half humanised, and, other things being equal, this is a great advantage to him on the show-bench, and is pretty sure to turn the scale in his favour.

" It is much to be regretted that the attempts made in 1876, at Maidstone and Portsmouth, to carry out 'water trials' or 'life-saving contests' have not been repeated, as with good management they would have become most interesting and useful, and no doubt have been the means of many dogs being more carefully trained for this service, and winning the medals of the Royal Humane Society. I trust the day will soon come when a thoroughly well-trained Newfoundland will be attached to all the chief 'preventive stations' round the coast. He not only would be ready to rescue life from drowning, but his great intelligence and observation could be enlisted in many ways to further the objects for which the service is instituted. His scent and sight are wonderfully keen, and his curiosity unbounded; and, after due training, I would back him to drop to brandy and tobacco as truly as any Setter would to grouse or partridge."

It will here be seen that though Mr. Browne and Mr. Coats are at one on the question of size, they differ concerning colour. For our own part we are of opinion that a rusty tinge is far from objectionable; in fact, we rather like it.

In describing the points of these dogs we will take first, as we place first, that feature which generally first strikes the eye and impresses the mind.

The *Head*.—This should be large, broad, and rather flat on the skull, with the occipital bone well pronounced. The forehead is bold, but there is no decided stop; the jaws of medium length, and cut off abruptly. Without being tight-skinned, there should be no decided wrinkles or loose-folding skin such as we have in the Bulldog, Bloodhound, and the Thibet Mastiff, and no deep flews. The nostrils are large and wide, and the whole face is clean—that is, covered with short hair only.

The *Eye* is rather small and deep-set, varying in colour, but generally a shade of brown; it should never be bloodshot—that is, showing the haw or conjunctiva, as seen in the Bloodhound and some St. Bernards.

The *Ear* should be small. Nathaniel Hawthorne, the American writer, describes it as "a small and mouse-like ear." It should lie close, and be covered with a short velvety coat, with longer hair at the edges.

The *Neck* is generally rather short, and the great abundance of thick hair standing out from it adds to that an appearance of its being more so than it really is. It is an object with breeders to improve the dog by increasing the length; it should be thick and muscular, swelling gradually towards the attachment to the shoulders.

The *Chest and Body*.—The chest should be both deep and wide, and the ribs round, with the back broad and muscular, with strong loins. This formation is of great importance to a dog whose work is for the most part in the water, enabling him to float with ease.

The *Legs* should be large of bone, well clothed with muscle, and the fore ones quite straight, the elbows well let down ; the hind ones short from the hock, the height being got by the length from there to hip, which is more than in most other breeds. Both legs are feathered to the foot, although the hair is not long.

The *Feet* are of great importance, as they are his paddles, and consequently must be broad and flat. The vulgar opinion that this dog is web-footed, it may be as well to observe here, has no other foundation in fact than that the toes of all dogs are connected by a skinny membrane, but it does not extend to the point of the toes, as in web-footed birds. The broad, flat, and rather thin foot is of the greatest use in swimming, worked as they are by powerful legs, but for travel on hard roads they are decidedly against him, and he is apt to get footsore, although he is, from his immense bulk, but a slow traveller.

Coat and Colour.—The coat is long, shaggy, and very thick and flat, naturally coarse looking, harsh, and dry, an appearance partly due to his frequent sea-baths ; but those that are carefully tended and constantly groomed are glossy and softer. The coat is very wet-resisting, which enables him to remain long in water without harm.

The colour, as we have already observed, is often of a rusty hue, which, although not so fashionable as the jet-black, is the natural colour of the pure race, and therefore should be no whit against the dog in competition, but on the contrary, in his favour.

The *Tail* should be of good length and very powerful, as he uses it as a rudder ; it should be carried with a sweep downwards, ending in an upward curl similar to that of the Sheepdog, but much more thickly covered with hair, which is quite bushy.

Symmetry and General Appearance.—The general appearance of a good specimen impresses the observer with the dog's size, strength, and activity ; a weak loin, cow-hocks, or elbows out of the straight line with the body, give an awkward appearance, a shuffling gait, and destroy all symmetry.

Leo, whom we have chosen for our illustration, is without exception the most superb specimen of the breed we have seen. It is objected to him that his coat is of a brownish tinge, which it unquestionably is, and no doubt a jet glossy black is more pleasing to the eye, but this rustiness of coat is a characteristic frequently seen in dogs native to the island. In this opinion we are supported by the valuable and weighty evidence of no less an authority than Mr. William Lort, the experienced and justly-esteemed judge, who lived some years in Newfoundland, and assures us that a rusty coat is quite a common feature of these dogs, especially those of the purest race. Leo was bred by Mr. William Coats in 1872, and is by Windle's Don out of Meg of Maldon, by Bruno out of Robinson's Meg by Carlo, by Nero out of Bella, by Nero out of Gipsy. The following are his chief performances :—First, Darlington ; first, Nottingham ; first, Hull—1875. Darlington, champion prize ; Birmingham, first prize—1876. Edinburgh, first prize ; Wolverhampton, first prize ; Bath, first prize and cup ; Agricultural Hall, first prize ; Manchester, first prize ; Birmingham, first prize ; Alexandra Palace, first prize—1877. First, Alexandra Palace ; first, Birmingham ; first, Bristol ; first, Crystal Palace ; first, Oxford ; first, Wolverhampton—1878. He weighs 149 lbs., and his measurements are—From nose to stop, 5 inches ; from stop to occipital bone, $7\frac{3}{4}$ inches ; length of back, 34 inches ; girth of muzzle in front of eyes, $14\frac{1}{2}$ inches ; girth of skull, $26\frac{1}{2}$ inches ; girth of neck, 30 inches ; girth of brisket in front of fore-legs, 45 inches ; girth of chest behind fore-legs, 42 inches ; girth round loins, 38 inches ; girth round hind-leg at stifle, 22 inches ; girth of arm three inches below elbow, 11 inches ; girth of fore-arm, 9 inches ; girth of pasterns, 8 inches ; height at shoulders, 32 inches ; height at elbow,

17½ inches; height at loins, 32¼ inches; height at hocks, 8½ inches; length of tail, 24 inches. Mr. Coats sold Leo to Mr. Mapplebeck, of Birmingham, who, after winning many prizes with him, eventually disposed of him to Mr. S. W. Wildman, of Bingley, Yorkshire, who owns him at the present time.

Among Leo's more prominent rivals we may mention Mrs. Cunliffe Lee's Jet, Dr. Gordon Stables' Theodore Nero, whose praises have been said or sung too often to need repetition, and Mr. George Raper's Brewer. Mr. Lord's Cabot is also a good specimen, although rather small. Mr. Howard Mapplebeck had several fine bitches, so that from his late collection and those of a few other breeders we may look for an increase in the number of exhibits of dogs really up to show form. Amongst other excellent specimens are Mr. T. Loader Browne's Nora Creina, and Monarch; the latter a winner both on the bench and at water-trials.

SCALE OF POINTS FOR NEWFOUNDLANDS.

	Value.
Head	10
Neck, chest, back, and loin	15
Legs and feet	10
Coat and colour	5
Tail	5
Symmetry and general appearance	5
	—
Total	50

THE LANDSEER NEWFOUNDLAND.

Another class of dog which its admirers stoutly pronounce to be a pure-bred Newfoundland is the large black-and-white dog so often seen in this country. Opinions differ very considerably, however, regarding the merits of this dog's claim to be Newfoundland, and the best-informed authorities with whom we have an opportunity of discussing the subject are unanimous in pronouncing the species to have been originally a splendid mongrel, possessing in its structure many prominent Newfoundland points, but deficient in some important characteristics of the pure breed.

The painting by the late Sir Edwin Landseer of "A Distinguished Member of the Humane Society," though magnificent as a work of art, has undoubtedly done much to—if we may use the term—corrupt the public mind upon the subject of the Newfoundland. A vast number of people, without troubling themselves to inquire into the matter, have associated the black-and-white dog with the correct type of the Newfoundland, utterly regardless of the fact that Sir Edwin may have selected this colour as brighter and more suitable for the object he had in view.

How this large black-and-white dog, or Landseer Newfoundland as it is now termed, ever came into existence is hard to explain, but it is impossible to doubt for an instant that it partakes largely of the character of the pure-bred Newfoundland. It is certainly true that in the island of Newfoundland itself many black-and-white dogs are to be found, but they apparently have no stronger claims to be considered pure Newfoundlands than any large-sized mongrel in this country has to be styled a Mastiff. Admirers of the black-and-white dog endeavour to believe that the colour of a Newfoundland is immaterial, and hence that their favourites are of the same variety as the black, but in doing so they neglect to notice several other points of distinction between the two breeds. In the first place the head of the Newfoundland generally is larger and more solid than that of his parti-coloured relation, whilst the latter is slacker in his loins, and the tendency to curl in his coat is more frequent. Of course, in some instances magnificent specimens of the black-and-white dog—such as Mr. Evans's Dick—have been shown, and these can

THE LANDSEER NEWFOUNDLAND "DICK."

compare in almost every respect most favourably with the black variety. In many cases however they would, possibly on account of the prejudice which exists against their colour, stand but little chance of success in open competition, so the committees of some leading shows have instituted a class for Newfoundlands other than black, which we venture to predict will soon be largely patronised.

As a companion this dog is highly appreciated, and his markings certainly render him handsomer than the black dog; whilst for utility, devotion to his master, and gentleness of disposition, he is not inferior to the variety from whence he undoubtedly sprung.

By far the best specimen of the Landseer Newfoundland we are acquainted with is Mr.

Evans's Dick above mentioned, who has won prizes at every show where there has been a class for dogs of this breed. He is by Vass's Neptune by Evans's Nell, and was bred by his owner in 1871. In 1876 he won first at the Crystal Palace under the name of Castro, and first and cup at Maidstone under the name of Dick. In 1877 he won first at the Alexandra Palace and Agricultural Hall, and in 1878 again first at the Alexandra Palace. His weight is 139 pounds, and his measurements are as follows:—Length of nose to stop, 5 inches; length, stop to occiput, 7 inches; length of back, 30½ inches; round muzzle in front of eyes, 14½ inches; round skull, 24½ inches; round neck, 24 inches; round brisket in front of forearms, 41 inches; round chest behind forearms, 41 inches; girth of loins, 31½ inches; girth of hind leg at stifle, 20½ inches; girth of arm 3 inches below elbow, 10½ inches; girth of forearm, 8¼ inches; girth of pastern, 5½ inches; height at shoulders, 30½ inches; height at elbows, 15¼ inches; height at loins, 28½ inches; height at hock, 7¼ inches; length of tail, 22 inches.

The standard and scale of points for judging this variety are the same as in the Newfoundland, due attention, of course, being made for the beauty and regularity of the markings.

CHAPTER IX.

THE SHEEP-DOG.

THE Sheep-dog holds a very high place among our domestic dogs, to which his great usefulness and high intelligence fully entitle him. He has also had the honour of being considered by no less an authority than the great naturalist Buffon the origin of all our other varieties of dogs. Although this opinion of Buffon's is not now accepted by many, it is not without considerable show of reason, for none of our domestic varieties approach so near in form to the wild dog of India and Australia, and to the more closely-allied species of the Canidæ. This is, of course, much more marked in the rough working dogs, although these are not so handsome in the eyes of show-dog men. The latter, as a rule, know little practically of the work required from Collies in moorland districts, and prefer a glossy thin-coated dog that a Scotch mist would drench to the skin in half an hour, to the rough tyke that wears a coarse coat of wet-resisting hair, with its under-jacket as close and thick as the wool on the sheep he tends· These are the dogs that are light and sinewy in build, with long neck and head, ears certain to be more or less pricked, the belly a bit tucked up, and the hind-quarters sloping back to the well-let-down and sickle-shaped hocks, indicative of speed, and with a general outline, as his lithe frame and shaggy coat are seen looming through the mist, not at all unlike that of the wolf.

Speculation on the origin of this dog, as of most other breeds, is, however, profitless. We can only say that second to dogs used in the chase—as we must suppose man to have hunted wild animals for food before he advanced so far on the road to civilisation as to keep flocks and herds—the Sheep-dog must have been one of the earliest to come under man's dominion and form part of his home stock. Consequently we find in the history of Job the following direct allusion to the Sheep-dog: "But now they who are younger than I have me in derision, whose fathers I would have disdained to set with *the dogs of my flock*." This is however no proof that our Sheep-dogs are allied to or at all resemble the dogs that Job and his contemporary flock-masters owned. In countries where the wolf is common and the lion not unknown, their penchant for mutton had to be guarded against, and for such use it is probable that a more powerful and fiercer dog was employed than our modern Collie. Indeed this is the case at the present day; and in Thibet the large rough black-and-tan Mastiffs of the country are used to guard the flocks and herds. At the Paris exhibition of dogs, 1878, a prize was awarded to a dog used in the Pyrenees district as unlike our breed of Sheep-dogs as it is possible to conceive. It was coarse, ungainly, slow, with a long matted coat, which on a Scotch mountain in the winter, with its snows and alternating frosts and thaws, would get so clogged with balls of snow that the dog would not be able to move with the alacrity necessary to get round a flock of black-faced sheep. Moreover, it would so soon tire him that he would be practically useless for hard work.

Well-authenticated stories relating to the sagacity of the Sheep-dog—or Collie, as the breed is styled in the North—would occupy a larger space than is at our disposal to bestow; but all who are best acquainted with him unite in attributing to a well-trained Sheep-dog almost human intelligence. The narratives which have appeared in so many publications, and which tell of his wonderful devotion to his master cannot, too, be disbelieved by those who have had so many opportunities as we ourselves have encountered, of seeing the obedience with which he regards not only the voice, but even the slightest gesture of his owner when they are at work together upon the hills. Doubtless the fact of his Collie having been the almost inseparable companion of his daily existence since it was old enough to accompany him about, has tended to increase the natural intelligence of the shepherd's dog to a very great extent; but still there must have been a very superior instinct born in the dog to enable him to, as it were, anticipate his master's wishes and act accordingly.

There has been an attempt made by one or two writers in *The Live Stock Journal*—which devotes no inconsiderable portion of its pages to canine matters—to designate this dog the Highland Collie, but there was an utter absence of any reasoning in justification of claiming for the Highlands of Scotland the honour of being the peculiar home of the Collie. We are rather disposed to think that the pastoral dales of the Lowlands of Scotland and the North of England have had more to do with breeding the dog to his present high state of perfection as a shepherd than the North Highlands, where the more peaceful occupation of stock-farming did not so early take the place of petty warfare and the chase, which formed the chief employment. We may here observe that the system of breeding these dogs by shepherds has been altogether independent of consideration of pedigree, which, no doubt, has given rise to the very considerable diversity of colour and coat which we find among true-bred Collies. Rough and smooth are mated, the result being pups of each kind and intermediate, the first consideration with the shepherd being to produce a useful and intelligent dog, that will take naturally to his work and be easily rendered amenable to discipline. With this view the sire selected is always one known to be clever, considerations of outward appearance being made greatly subservient to that. We would not however be understood to say that the Scotch shepherd is heedless of the good appearance of his dog; he has generally an eye for a "bonny dowg," and if he can add that Glen or Rover is "as guid as he's bonny," depend upon it he is proud of his dog, and there is a friendship between them which money will not part.

There exists a difference of opinion as to the relative merits of the rough and smooth for hill work. Very heavily-coated dogs, such as is demanded for exhibition purposes, would soon lose a portion of their jacket in rough work; and for winter a long-haired dog has the disadvantage that in travelling through snow it attaches to his coat in constantly-increasing lumps, which heavily handicap him. This the smooth-coated dog escapes, and although the rough dog would appear the better protected against the cold, the smooth does not suffer much in that respect, nature supplying him with an increased jacket as the winter approaches.

Collies, like other dogs, differ individually in temperament, but it is not too much to say that most of them are shy, reserved, and sometimes dangerous, to strangers. Indeed, we have personally known not a few that not only would permit no liberties to be taken with them, but were of a treacherous disposition, sneaking round and snapping without warning; especially suspicious are they of strangers approaching their homes, and no more alert watch-dog exists than the Collie. They are, however, always amenable to the voice of their master, and under his command, and to those in whom they once place confidence they are for ever faithful. There is no breed of dog with such a wise look as the Collie; the heavy responsibilities that rest on him give him a sedate and sonsie or taking look, and his whole appearance is so engaging that it is no wonder he is such a general favourite with the public, and especially with ladies.

No better description in such few words has ever been written of the Collie than that given by the poet Burns, which we quote, premising, for the benefit of those readers who do not understand the Scottish dialect, that "gash" means wise;" "sheugh" is a ditch; "sonsie" means engaging; "baws'nt," marked with a streak of white like a badger; "touzie," shaggy; and "gaucie," large and flowing.

> " He was a gash and faithfu' tyke
> As ever lap a sheugh or dike,
> His honest, sonsie, baws'nt face,
> Aye gat him friends in ilka place.
> His breast was white, his touzie back
> Weel clad wi' coat o' glossy black ;
> His gaucie tail, wi' upward curl,
> Hung ower his hurdies wi' a swirl."

Unfortunately, owing either to carelessness on the side of the breeders, or a desire on their part to render the dogs they breed for sale, not for work, the services of the black-and-tan Gordon Setter have been called into requisition in many cases. The result, as might have been anticipated, has been to gain a possible increase of beauty in colouring and coat, at the cost of a decided loss in that intelligence which so clearly is the characteristic of a Sheep-dog pure and simple. Traces of this decided bar sinister can be plainly seen in many of the show-dogs now on the bench ; and those who really know what a Collie is, are horrified when they see a southern county judge, who cannot be expected to know more of the breed than what he has picked up at dog shows, giving first prize to a dog with a Settery head, second to one with legs feathered down to his feet, and third to a specimen without the slightest under-coat to enable him to resist the rain, when there are present in the class unnoticed dogs possessed of genuine Collie properties. Such eccentricities of genius so often occur that it is a matter of small surprise that the breed, fashionable as it is, should be so thoroughly misunderstood. The injury to the real Sheep-dog, too, is very great ; for persons who are ignorant of what a Collie should be, and think they are purchasing one when they pay a long figure for a second-rate Gordon Setter, get disgusted when they discover their purchase's lack of intelligence, and give up the breed to try their fortunes with another· Only a short time back we were requested by a friend to call and see a "magnificent Collie" he had recently " picked up" in a town not a hundred miles from Bristol; we did so, and although he was unfortunately not at home, his wife was in, and would be glad to see us. She was accompanied into the room by a black-and-tan rough-coated dog, of which we took no particular notice at first, but after a few minutes' conversation, expressed a wish to see the new purchase, when to our horror we were informed that the Settery mongrel before us was the animal upon whose merits we were expected to pass a favourable opinion. At last the reason for the purchase came out : the dog had been placed first at a show by a well-known judge—who should have known better—and our friend, in consequence, in his ignorance, was persuaded into giving £20 for a wretch not worth as many shillings as a Collie. Indignation followed the expression of our opinion, and fortune was tempted a second time at a show, on this occasion under a late lamented judge who knew his work. "Tak yon brute out," was the only notice taken of the "magnificent" creature, who, on his return home, was promptly given away, the fortunate recipient being the local postman, in whose hands he is likely to remain until a keeper's bullet—the dog is an inveterate poacher—puts an end to his existence. We should not have inflicted this narrative upon our readers but that it tends to prove to those ignorant of dog-show judging, that because a dog wins a first prize he is at all of necessity a good one.

We are fortunate enough to be enabled to lay before our readers the opinions of two gentlemen who are in our judgment, and in that of many others also, without a doubt two of the best Collie judges now living—we allude to Mr. S. E. Shirley, M.P., and Mr. W. W. Thomson of Morden, Surrey. Both these gentlemen are well known everywhere as breeders, and the successes of their kennels on the bench are accomplished facts. Before, however, giving their opinions, we wish to warn intending purchasers against investing in a dog which is marked by deep or mahogany-coloured tan. This is an almost certain indication of Setter taint, the tan of a true Collie being of a very pale shade. According to the opinion of Mr. Shirley—

"The *Head* of a Collie should be long and narrow; ears set high on the head, not dropping like a Fox-terrier's, but semi-erect, and in the case of a good specimen as small as possible.

"*Mouth* should be level. Unlevelness need not absolutely disqualify, though it must tend *greatly* against a dog, as an overshot mouth not only conveys a false idea of the length of a dog's head, but prevents him holding a sheep properly if required to do so." (This malformation is, according to Mr. Shirley's experience, far from uncommon in Collies.)

"*Coat* thick, *but not woolly.*

"*Colour* should be for choice black and pale tan, black, tan, and white, or red with black points, though there are some good black specimens to be seen about." (Some six years ago, when in Ross-shire, Mr. Shirley came across a strain of excellent black Sheep-dogs.)

"*General Symmetry* should be fairly light, a wide chest or heavy short neck being a bad defect, for one wants activity in a Collie.

"The *Tail* is a matter of importance, for though it has been stated in works upon the dog that this may be carried on the back when the dog is excited, still it is a fault, and a serious one, when such is the case."

Mr. Thomson says—

"Collies are divided into roughs and smooths, the former generally carrying off the palm for beauty. As far as build, shape, and colour are concerned the two are exactly alike, and one description will answer for both. They only differ in coat, the rough breed having a very thick rough jacket, in fact, a double coat, the under one being sealskin-like in both colour and texture, while the other is coarse and hard. The smooth dog has a short coat, almost as close as a Pointer's, but denser and harder; his legs are free of hair; except that on the hocks it is often longer and denser than on the body. The rough species carry a considerable amount of feather on the hocks, but from the hocks to the heels the legs should be quite clean. Down the back of the front legs there should also be plenty of feather, which in the working Collie is very dense, whilst in the drawing-room pet constant brushing renders it soft and long, as in the Setter. For working purposes one is equal to the other; in the North of England rough Collies seem preferred, whilst with the Southern drovers the smooth variety appears to be the most popular, many drovers being of the opinion that the smooth stand more work than the rough-coated are capable of, the long jackets of the latter getting heavy with mud and wet, causing them to tire.

"As a thing of beauty the rough Collie is favourite, especially with ladies, his long coat being more admired than the sober, business-like jacket of his *confrère*.

"The Scotch Collie should be strongly built, but lithe and active, giving one the idea of great pace.

" *Shoulders* well set back, not loaded.

" *Chest* deep, with room for his lungs to play freely.

" *Back* broad and muscular.

" *Fore legs* strong and straight, but not heavy, and well under his body.

" *Hocks* good "sickle-shaped," and free of feather down to the heel.

" *Head* long and sharp, but not snipy in the muzzle, or domed in the skull.

" *Ears* small, and semi-erect.

" *Colour* black-and-tan, black-white-and-tan, black and white, sable, grey, &c.

"There is one strain of smooth Collie which calls for particular attention, and that is the variety called sometimes the Welsh Collie, and at others the Highland 'heeler.' In colour this dog is a peculiar sort of greyish hue, to which the terms 'harlequin,' 'plum-pudding,' 'tortoise shell,' are all applied. He is usually found with one eye (sometimes both) 'wall-eyed,' or 'China-eyed,' which is a great additional attraction on the show bench, whilst there exists amongst many shepherds a belief that this sort of eye never loses its sight, which superstition, if it were true, would naturally greatly increase the value of a China-eyed dog in their eyes. A rough-coated dog of this colour is very rare, by far the best shown of late years being Mr. Brackenbury's Scott."

On reading the above opinions it will be observed that, curiously enough, both Mr. Shirley and Mr. Thomson have omitted to make any allusion to the feet of a Collie, which we consider one of the most essential points in the dog: they should be small and rather round.

It is also desirable further to describe the coat. The coat of a Sheep-dog (whether the animal is of the rough or smooth variety) is a matter of considerable importance, for a dog with a thin, sparse jacket would be unable to do his work on the moors. Mr. Thomson in his remarks speaks of the double coat as the correct style, and this we fully endorse. The under coat should, as that gentleman alleges, resemble sealskin, the damp-resisting properties of which ensures the dog being saved from the inclemency of the weather to a great extent. The longer or outer coat should be harsh and wear-resisting to the touch, not fine and thin, as in a Setter. Dogs possessing the latter cross invariably suffer from the cold and rain. The smooth-coated dog only differs in that his outer coat is shorter, stiffer, and denser than in his long-haired companions, and thus the absence of length is compensated for by additional thickness.

Mr. Shirley has also given us a scale of points as he apportions them, which will be very useful as showing the precise value he attaches to one point in comparison with another.

	Value.
Head	15
Ears	10
Coat	15
Chest	10
Shoulders	10
Loin	15
Feet	5
Legs	10
Colour	5
Tail	5
Total	100

As regards the breeding of Sheep-dogs, a well-known authority on the subject, who prefers to let his identity remain concealed, gives us the following hints, which, although briefly expressed, will be found of importance :—

"Avoid mating flat or prick-eared Collies, as the progeny is almost sure to come one or the other. An exception may be made to this rule when you *know* the ancestors to have been really good specimens of the breed ; there is a very great chance of the puppies throwing back to them, and not inheriting their parents' faults. I am always reluctant to mate rough Collies with smooth ones. Though you may do so, and get good puppies of each variety, you can never be certain of your expectations being realised when breeding from their progeny. Avoid heavy-headed, *flat*-eared Collies. Though both are objectionable, I would rather breed from a good-headed prick-eared one than a good-headed flat-eared one. Under-coat I always have been, and always will be, a great stickler for; in fact, I never breed from a dog with no under-coat, or an open top-coat.

"Colour is, in my judgment, a minor consideration, provided the leading points—such as shape, coat, head, and ears—are right. Collies throw back in this respect in the most extraordinary way, and in one litter you often get three or four different colours."

With regard to the animals selected for illustration, the rough-coated specimen is Mr. Shirley's Hornpipe, bred by him in 1876 by Trefoil from Kit by Malcolm, Trefoil by Twig out of Bess by Rattler. Her chief performances are: first Manchester, first Darlington, first Bristol, first Alexandra Palace, 1877 ; first Crystal Palace, 1878 ; Champion prize Alexandra Palace, 1879. We have not been able to obtain her measurements.

Yarrow, Mr. Thomson's smooth-coated bitch, is also an unusually good one, but is without a pedigree, having been imported into this country by Mr. Hugh Dalziel. Mr. Thomson pronounces her to be the best worker on sheep in his kennel, but an inveterate poacher. A peculiar trait in her character is referred to thus by her owner ; we give his own words :—"This same bitch when having whelps, will, as they get old enough to eat, sneak off like a wolf or fox, and on her return she will disgorge rabbits, eggs, &c., for the delectation of her young." Her chief performances are : first Chesterfield, 1877 ; first and cup Hanover, 1879. The measurements of Yarrow are as follows: —Tip of nose to stop, $3\frac{5}{8}$ inches ; stop to occiput, $4\frac{1}{2}$ inches ; length of back, 19 inches ; girth of muzzle, 10 inches ; girth of skull, 15 inches ; girth of neck, $14\frac{1}{2}$ inches ; girth of brisket, 26 inches ; girth round shoulders, 25 inches ; girth of loins, 21 inches ; girth of hind leg at stifle-joint, 11 inches ; girth of fore-arm, 6 inches ; girth round pastern, 4 inches ; height at top shoulders, 20 inches ; height at elbows, $10\frac{1}{2}$; height at loins, 20 inches ; height at hock, 6 inches ; length of tail, $14\frac{1}{2}$.

Amongst the best dogs of the day are Mr. Ashwin's Cocksie, although his ears are not quite perfect ; Mr. Thomson's Hero, Marcus, and Bess ; Mr. Bissell's Cockie, the sire of Cocksie ; Mrs. Skinner's Vero, the best dog out, only rather silky in coat, and usually shown like an alderman ; and last, but not least, Mr. Shirley's Trefoil, Hornpipe, and Hulakin.

In smooth-coated dogs there is only Mr. Thomson's Guelt, also imported by Mr. Hugh Dalziel (descended from Crichton's dog, who was hung with his master for sheep-stealing) that we can call to recollection as being above the ordinary run, whilst the same gentleman's Yarrow, together with Mr. Swinburne's Lassie, and Mr. James Fawdry's, late Mr. Mapplebeck's, Fan, compose a trio of bitches which combined cannot be beat.

SCALE OF POINTS FOR JUDGING SHEEP-DOGS.

Head	10
Chest and shoulders	5
Body	5
Loin and tail	5
Legs and feet	5
Colour	5
Coat	10
General appearance	5
Total ... ..., ...	50

THE BOB-TAILED SHEEP-DOG.

This variety has little in common with the Collie dog as described above, and is a rare companion for people in the higher classes of society, as his homely and rugged exterior place his claims to aristocratic patronage beneath those of the ordinary Collie. In appearance he is of a far stouter and coarser build than his cousins, the Scotch and Welsh Sheep-dogs, and his coat is usually long, shaggy, and inclined to curl. This last feature is a defect, but in this variety only a minor one. His face is shaggy, if not devoid of long hair, as in the Collie, and his colour is usually grizzle. The skull is round and muzzle truncated, with the couplings short and square. The chief feature in the breed, however, is the almost absence of tail, which is of the shortest possible dimensions. A theory has been started that this is the result of constant generations of Sheep-dogs with docked tails having been bred together; but this appears incredible to us. Should this reasoning be correct, we may shortly expect to produce English Terriers with ready cropped ears, or Fox-terriers and Spaniels with naturally docked tails. Another theory is that this breed has been crossed with the Bull-dog, and hence the natural singularity in its caudal appendage. We cannot however receive this suggestion with more favour than the former, as so large a cross of Bull would inevitably render the dog too "hard" in mouth, and give the breed a tendency to worry stock, which would be very undesirable in a drover's dog. However, whatever may be the reason for this development, the variety exists, and, as a working dog, has no superior.

Mr. R. J. Lloyd Price, of Rhiwlas, has owned some of the best specimens we have seen, his old Bob being a very large prize-winner at our shows. He says of them that "They come principally from the Lake Country, and are not adapted for penning or driving, but are best for escorting sheep along the roads, where they often show their cleverness by running over the backs of a closely-packed flock of sheep, and getting in front to turn them, when they cannot pass by the side. They are even better adapted for rough wear and tear than the long-haired sort, their coat being of a sort of door-mat texture. The bob-tail I believe to have arisen from the fact that a tax used to be imposed on all dogs with a tail, and a long course of breeding from dogs with the tails cut off has produced these results." It will be seen from the latter remarks that Mr. Price has faith in the theory given above, though we cannot admit our own is very great. His allusion, too, to the bob-tailed dog running over the backs of sheep has, to a certain extent, surprised us. We know the practice is a common one amongst Sheep-dogs, but should have considered the breed in question of too heavy a build to resort to such means of heading his sheep.

The original type of the bob-tailed Sheep-dog is uncertain. The best we have met with have generally been in Devon, where at Exeter and other shows in the county we have seen them in fair numbers, and in quality what we consider perfection. The animals are said to be very intelligent, and everlasting workers ; but although picturesque, they appear slow, and have not that bright knowing look that distinguishes the Collie. The colours are black and white, or grizzle, with more or less of distinct white patches. It is, however, singular that a very similar variety appears to be known in Scotland, where it also is sometimes termed the " Rough-coated " Collie, from the shagginess of its jacket. In a letter which appeared in the *Live Stock Journal* of Nov. 15th, 1878, Mr. Gordon James Phillips, of Glenlivet, described this variety as follows :—

" The origin of the rough-coated Collie is more difficult to trace back to its native wilds than any other dog that we know. It forms a small minority among shepherds' dogs, and it is seldom, if ever, seen pure-bred in the north of Scotland. Nature, however, has given it marks which cannot be effaced, which help to unravel the mystery which envelops its nativity. These are its shaggy coat, the thickness of its skin, and the formation of its limbs. The thick skin and the shaggy coat point unmistakably to its being the native of a cold climate; while the short powerful limbs point as powerfully to its being the native of a mountainous country. Glancing for a moment at other animals that are natives of Scotland, and marking the resemblance between them and the rough-coated Collie, we are inclined to think that it also is Scotch. Take, for example, Highland cattle and Highland horses. They have the rough coat, the short thick limbs, and the thick skin, and in their own characters the same amount of endurance. The only plausible argument against the Collie being Scotch is its scarcity in Scotland. This may be accounted for, however, when we take into consideration the fact that the black-and-tan Collie is better adapted than the rough-coated Collie for the ordinary work about small farms, such as driving in and out cattle, sitting beside a few sheep, and so on. It is also more easily trained for work of this sort. This would naturally make the black-and-tan Collie a greater favourite with farmers than its rough-coated neighbour. Within the last few years, however, sheep have become more valuable, and the rough-coated Collie has again become fashionable, shepherds preferring it for its endurance of cold and fatigue, and its ability as a driver. Shepherds also affirm that for sheep it is, on the whole, the best dog.

" The animal itself is about the size of an ordinary Collie, but a good deal deeper chested. As already mentioned, it is thicker in the skin ; it is also flatter in the forehead. Altogether, the head would be somewhat repulsive looking, if it were not relieved by the beautiful dark-brown eyes. Its greatest peculiarity in form is in the tail, which is simply a stump, generally from six to nine inches in length. That the animal is of Scotch origin, owing to its resemblance to other Scotch animals, is apparent, if we compare it with the Scotch Terrier, which it resembles very much in colour—a dark grey. At all events, the black-and-tan Collie, now common throughout Scotland, would be much more at home in the southern part of the island than in the north. It cannot endure the same amount of cold. In winter it has a great inclination to get near the fire, and is generally shivering, whereas the rough-coated Collie seldom draws to the fire, but seems to be at home among the drift and snow. It is finely adapted for hill climbing, owing to the strength of its limbs and the depth of its chest. Shepherds have an idea, which, on the whole, is not a bad one, that it was intended by nature to be specially a sheep-dog, owing to its short tail, which does not let it turn so swiftly as it would otherwise do, if gifted with the long tail of its brother Collie. To understand this it is necessary to know that when shepherds send a dog to hunt sheep they desire it to take a wide circle round, not to dash in

SHEEP DOGS.

amongst them. The black-and-tan Collie must be trained to do this, but the rough-coated one must make a wide sweep, owing to the stump. Perhaps better proofs exist of its being specially a sheep-dog, when we consider its aptitude for driving. Shepherds state that they can safely trust 200 or 300 sheep to the sagacity of this valuable dog, which does not hurry or push, but drives them as coolly and as cautiously as if its master were present. Another proof is that it will not follow game. The black-and-tan Collie, if it sees a hare, will dart away after

A SCOTCH BOB-TAILED SHEEP-DOG.

it at its utmost speed. Most dogs will do so; but it is different with the rough-coated Collie. If a hare start up amongst its feet, it will simply look after it with a scared-like look, and then move on its way again."

It will be obvious that Mr. Phillips in the above remarks uses the word "rough-coated" in a sense different to that in which it is usually applied to the Collie. We reproduce the engraving of a "rough-coated," bob-tailed "Collie," as described by him, and without pledging ourselves to any particular details of his statement, can testify to having seen dogs precisely resembling that here portrayed. The strong resemblance in many points of the English bob-tailed dog is too striking to be accidental, and it is hardly likely that there were two original types; but whether the northern or southern type was that original cannot now be decided. Perhaps, seeing the north country undoubtedly produced or perfected the other and better-known type of Sheep-dog, while Mr. Lloyd Price also traces the animal to the Lake district, the probability may be rather in favour of a general northern origin, whatever the precise locality may be.

The disposition of several rough bob-tailed Sheep-dogs we have met with has differed considerably from that of the Collie, being mild and affectionate.

It is impossible to give any standard for judging this variety. General appearance, tail, strength, and shagginess without too much length of coat, should be taken into consideration.

The Sheep-dog is capable of nearly anything in the way of herding or attending to stock; and the stories told of his intelligence almost surpass belief. Nothing has done more to illustrate the Collie's value than the institution of the Sheep-dog trials, which were first inaugurated at Bala by Mr. R. J. Lloyd Price. This gentleman further gave Londoners a treat by bringing a flock of 100 wild Welsh sheep up to the Alexandra Palace in 1876. Here three sheep were picked out of the flock (which was folded in a remote corner of the park), and were carried to the field of operations on the side of the hill. They were then liberated, and the dog whose turn it was to work them was required to pen them in a small fold situated in the middle of the green bounded by the racecourse. The only assistance the dog received was from his master, who was, however, forbidden to touch the sheep under penalty of disqualification. Those acquainted with sheep will fully appreciate the difficulties of the task thus set the shepherd and his dog, for wild Welsh sheep are very unlike their civilised brothers met with nearer towns. But—to quote from the account published at the time in the *Live Stock Journal:*—"Some of the dogs were so well trained that many spectators expressed the utmost astonishment at the intelligence they displayed. Some of them lie down before the sheep, so as to let them recover their equanimity; then they get up quietly, move a step forward, and lie down again; this they repeat over and over again, producing a corresponding step of the sheep towards the entrance of the pen, and finally they fairly drive them in, almost unconsciously to themselves."

This long and careful training is not conducted by any set rules. The best-trained Collies have *lived* with their masters from puppyhood, and learnt to associate with sheep from their earliest years. The inherited habits of generations also predispose the sagacious animals to the performance of the duties required of them; and old experienced dogs, with whom they are at first always worked, further assist in the process.

CHAPTER X.

THE BULL-DOG.

ALLUSION having been made to the great antiquity of the Bull-dog in the chapter on the Mastiff, it will be unnecessary for us to recapitulate in the present instance what we said before concerning the claims of rival breeds to be regarded as the most ancient variety of British dog. Few, however, can be found who refuse to award the Bull-dog the honour of being considered our *national dog*, for no variety of the canine species is so universally identified, both at home and abroad, with Great Britain, as the subject of the present article. Bull-dog pluck and endurance are qualifications eagerly cherished by Englishmen of all classes; and it would be manifestly unjust to deprive this dog of the title which has been so universally awarded him.

No breed of dog has provoked more discussion than the subject of this chapter, and in no canine controversy has party feeling run so high, and so many uncomplimentary epistles been exchanged. The result, however, of the angry battle of words has been so far a gain to the breed as to cause a perceptible increase in the number and quality of the exhibits at the principal shows, and, in the year 1875, it was the means of inducing several breeders to unite, and form the New Bull-dog Club, which has drawn up the scale of points now received by the vast majority of breeders throughout the country, whether members of the Club or not. Now that there seems to be some sort of unanimity between the various schools, the variety bids fair to prosper; and though from its excitable temperament the Bull-dog is not likely, in spite of its many high claims upon public favour, to be a general pet, it is gratifying to all lovers of this our national dog when they find it slowly, though surely, emerging from the hands of the residuum of the canine world, and taking its proper place in the kennels of a superior class of breeders and exhibitors. The gain to the dog will, we believe, be immense, for in the unhappy position into which it had fallen the Bull-dog had but slender opportunities of proving to the world that its intelligence was at least equal to that of the average run of dog. Chained up for weeks and months in damp cellars or dark confined hutches in miserable alleys, what chance had the poor brute of developing even that ordinary degree of sagacity which is expected to be found in an animal endued with sight and instinct? What possibility could there be that a creature so treated could beget offspring inheriting any of the better mental qualities which are naturally present in the Bull-dog, and which are developed in many dogs now before the public, whose lot has been cast in happier places than the habitation of a low scoundrel whose blow preceded his command, and who only noticed his wretched companion when desirous of participating with him in some revolting piece of cruelty, in which the dog, through his indomitable courage, was destined to take a conspicuous part? How the Bull-dog ever came to be so nearly monopolised by this class of individual is capable of explanation by the theory that when bull-baiting ceased to be a fashionable recreation in this country, yet before it was absolutely prohibited by law, the sport was carried on by the lower classes, and the dog naturally came into their possession, there to remain until the efforts that were periodically made to extricate it should at last succeed.

The antiquity of this breed is indisputable, mention being made of it by Edmond de Langley, in his work, the "Mayster of Game," the MS. of which we have consulted in the British Museum. It is there alluded to by him under the title of Alaunt, and is subdivided by him into three classes; but perhaps it may be as well to give the description as contained in the "Mayster of Game:"—

"Alaunt is a maner and natre of houndes, and the good Alauntz ben the which men clepyn Alauntz gentil. Other there byn that men clepyn Alauntz ventreres. Other byn Alauntz of the bocherie. Thei that ben gentile shuld be made and shape as a greyhounde, evyn of alle thinges, sauf of the heved, the whiche shuld be greet and *short*." After some further remarks, this same dog is said to gladly "renne and bite the hors." "Also thei renne at oxen and at sheep, at swyne, and to alle othere beestis, or to men, or to othere houndes, for men hav seyn Alauntz sle her maystir;" and, furthermore, they are described as being "more sturdy than eny other maner of houndes."

The second class of this dog is thus noticed:—"That other nature of Alauntz is clepid ventreres, almost thei bene shapon as a greyhounde of ful shap, thei hav grete hedes, and greet lippes, and greet eeris. And with such men helpeth hem at the baityng of a boole, and atte huntynge of a wilde boor. Thei holde fast of here nature . . . ."

The third division:—"The Alauntz of the bocherie is soch as ye may alle day see in good tounes that byn called greet bochers houndis. Thei byn good for the baytyng of the bulle and huntyng of the wilde boore, whedir it be w^t greihoundis at the tryste w^t rennyng houndis at abbay with inne the coverte."

Whatever distinction there may have been between the above three varieties of Alaunt in the days of Edmund de Langley, and though the anonymous writer on the works of Arrian describes these as above, and only attributes to the first two varieties an admixture of pure Celtic blood, it appears to us that the Alaunt is without a doubt the parent strain from which the present Bull-dog is descended; and although the Mastiff is alluded to by Edmund de Langley in his work, in addition to the three varieties of Alauntz, we can still discover no cause for altering our previously expressed opinion (see chapter on Mastiffs) that the Bull-dog and Mastiff originally sprang from the same origin—viz., the Mastive or Bandogge, which is alluded to in Dr. Caius' book, and has been before quoted in this work on the article on Mastiffs. Before leaving the subject of the "Mayster of Game" we desire to impress upon our readers three items contained in the extracts we have quoted: first, the dog was *short*-faced; secondly, he was used to bait the bull; and thirdly, when he attacked it or other animals he *hung on*. The first and third of these characteristics are present to a remarkable extent in the Bull-dog of the present day.

In the work of Dr. Caius, written in the reign of Queen Elizabeth, mention is made of the Mastive or Bandogge, as being a dog "stubborne, eagre, burthenous of body (and therefore but of little swiftness), terrible and feareful to behold," and which "alone, and wythout anye help at al, he pulled down first an huge beare, then a parde, and last of al a lyon, each after other before the Frenche King in one day." This description of Caius's, relating as it does to the Mastive, which has already been alluded to in the "Mayster of Game" as a peaceable dog, only tends to strengthen our previous conviction that the two breeds, Alaunt and Mastiff, had by some means or other become amalgamated, only to be again separated by the later breeders to suit the requirements of the times in the manner we have before suggested.

In the later works on the dog, mention of the Bull-dog is frequently occurring, and all writers are unanimous in their praises of the dog's courage and boldness in attack. The matter of size has provoked more discussion than any other feature in connection with this dog—one party holding out for a great, lumbering, long-faced dog, nearly as big as the bull itself, and destitute of any pretences to symmetry in its appearance; the other side advocate the claims of a large-skulled dog, of medium size—forty to fifty pounds—with the short head described by Edmund de Langley in the "Mayster of Game." As regards the respective merits of the two dogs there can, in an unprejudiced mind, be no hesitation in accepting the latter as the correct type. In the first place, supposing bull-baiting were again in vogue, what could be the use of using a large dog for the work when a small one can do it as well if not better? secondly, even assuming for the moment that a hundred years ago or more the Bull-dog was the coarse-looking creature some of its admirers say it was, is this breed to be the only one in which no refinement is ever to appear? We do not hold with improving a breed off the face of the earth, and have no sympathy with those who attempt to do so; but if we could by any surgical operation bring ourselves to look upon some specimens we see at shows as representing the correct type, we should gladly avail ourselves of any opportunity for refining and improving the breed.

Again, in baiting the bull the dogs usually approached him crawling along the ground on their bellies, and the result would be that a large dog would stand a much greater chance of falling a victim to his antagonist's horns. In this opinion we are supported by written authority as well as by all the gentlemen who have had personal experience of bull-baiting with whom we have conversed on the subject. Amongst these is Mr. Leare, of Sunbury-on-Thames, who, though born in the first year of the present century, still puts to shame many of his juniors when handling the rod or gun, and who, in his youth, was present at bull-baitings innumerable. According to this gentleman, a bull was rarely slaughtered in Devonshire—for this is Mr. Leare's native county—in former times without being first subjected to the ordeal of baiting by dogs in every respect resembling the Bull-dog as hereafter described:—The weight was between forty pounds and fifty pounds, a larger one being suspected—no doubt correctly—of having a Mastiff cross; and a short _retroussé_ nose was eagerly sought after as enabling the dog to breathe when hanging on to the nose of the bull.

During the last century it was the almost invariable custom to bait a bull before slaughtering him; and it was not solely on account of the "sport" entailed that this proceeding was in vogue, for there was a prevailing opinion that the flesh of a bull which had been baited was improved in quality by the exertions which he had to put forth in defending himself from his canine assailant. Whether this theory was correct or not we decline to decide; but very much the same idea is in existence in the present day as regards hares, many people being of the opinion that the flesh of a coursed hare is far superior to that of one which has been shot.

Some difference of opinion has risen, too, as regards the length of face in this breed, a statement having appeared in print to the effect that the nose should not be too short, and rather implying that a medium length from the skull to the tip of the nose was desirable. Such heresy against the accepted opinions of all recognised authorities could only emanate from the pens of those either completely ignorant of the subject upon which they were writing, or else in possession of a strain which differed materially from the British Bull-dog, under whatever designation they might appear.

Attempts have also been made to improve the breed of Bull-dogs existent in the country by the addition of a so-called Spanish cross. What was the precise advantage to be derived from the introduction of the blood of a Spanish Bull-dog we are at a loss to conjecture, as the animal selected for resuscitating our national dog was the notorious Toro, a red-brindled dog, with cropped ears, weighing some 90 lbs., and displaying many indications of a Mastiff cross. From what we have heard from various sources it appears that Toro, in spite of the assertion in the Kennel Club Stud Book to the effect that both his parents were pure-bred Spanish Bull-dogs, is supposed by many of his admirers to be descended from some English Bull-dogs which were exported from this country to Spain several years ago. Now, assuming for the sake of argument that both these theories can be correct, we still fail to discover from the appearance of Toro how he could possibly be of service in improving the Bull-dog as it now exists in this country, the main object of successful exhibitors being to eliminate all traces of the Mastiff in their dogs, as such would tend to place great obstacles in their success under a competent judge. That Toro may possibly be a perfect specimen of the Spanish Bull-dog we will not attempt to deny, for we consider the breed apocryphal, but we unhesitatingly assert that the introduction of his blood into our English kennels must inevitably be attended by the most pernicious consequences, and it is to be hoped that breeders will adhere to the blood that our ancestors possessed, without being led astray by the wiles of the charmers, charm they never so wisely.

In the year 1874 Mr. Theodore Bassett, the well-known Fox-terrier judge, astonished the Bull-dog world by importing an "African" Bull-dog, and exhibiting him at our shows. This dog, Leon by name, had, like Toro, been deprived of his ears, and though superior to the latter in every Bull-dog characteristic, was very soon after his first appearance relegated, by the good sense of his master, to the foreign dog class, where his fine proportions have been fully recognised, as his many successes testify.

Having thus warned our readers against attempting to improve the Bull-dog by a foreign cross, it behoves us to likewise put them on their guard against the great, coarse, lumbering-looking dogs sometimes met with at shows. These animals, though possibly in themselves showing little trace of Mastiff blood to the uninitiated, cannot deceive a practical breeder, and the result of an alliance between one of them and a young inexperienced admirer's brood bitch will almost invariably be years of disappointment on the show bench, coupled with vain endeavours at home to rid the strain of the noxious taint brought in by the injudicious selection of the founder of the stud.

The Bull-dog has undoubtedly suffered considerably from his association with the lower classes of the community; and amongst other undesirable practices which have crept in in connection with the breed is the abominable mutilation resorted to by some breeders in order to shorten the length of the upper jaw, and turn the nose well up. In their endeavours to attain the above object the operators in the first instance sever the middle and two side lip-strings which connect the upper lip of the dog with the gum; when this is satisfactorily accomplished, a sort of small wooden block, hollowed so as to fit the face, is applied to the outside of the upper jaw in front, and being smartly hit with a mallet, has the effect of compressing the bone and cartilage of the nose as desired. Naturally the operation has to be performed when the unfortunate puppies are of an early age, and the bones and muscles of their faces are soft and susceptible of compression. An instrument technically termed the "Jacks" is then applied, and has the effect of causing the mutilated parts to remain in their new and abnormal position. No words can express our repugnance at the horrible cruelty thus inflicted upon the unhappy puppies by the wretches who wantonly inflict such torture upon them, and no judge should award either prizes or commendations to a Bull-dog until he has perfectly satisfied himself that the dog has been spared the mutilation of "faking," as the operation is designated by the initiated. Unfortunately the detection of offenders is sometimes a matter of difficulty, and those credited with originating the practice have passed to the silent land beyond the reach of human laws; but considerable aid might be lent to honest exhibitors in their endeavours to stamp out this abominable scandal, if show committees were to appoint a really qualified veterinary inspector who understood the anatomy of a dog, and whose decision was to be final. As a case in point: when the Bull-dogs Bumble and Alexander were disqualified by the veterinary inspector at the Crystal Palace Show of 1876, the Committee of the Kennel Club actually permitted a further inspection to be made by another surgeon, who held no position in connection with the show, the result being that both dogs were by him pronounced "honest," and had their prizes restored them. Whether Bumble and Alexander were mutilated or not need not be the subject of discussion here; but we maintain that direct encouragement was unwittingly given to dishonest breeders by the Committee not supporting their own veterinary surgeon in the opinion he pronounced.

Amongst the best known owners, breeders, and exhibitors of the correct type of Bull-dog since the Birmingham Show of 1860 may be mentioned the names of Mr. J. Hinks, of Birmingham; the Lamphiers, father and son; Messrs. H. Brown, Stockdale; J. Percival, W. Macdonald, Jesse Oswell, H. Layton, P. Rust, Billy Shaw, J. Henshall, W. Page, R. Fulton, W. H. Tyser, R. Ll. Price, S. E. Shirley, M.P., G. A. Dawes of West Bromwich (in *many*, but not all instances), J. W. Berrie, T. H. Joyce, W. G. Mayhew, Egerton Cutler, Vero Shaw, G. Raper, W. St. John Smyth, H. F. Prockter, T. Meager, J. Turnham, C. E. Bartlett, E. T. Hughes, R. Nichols, W. W. Roger, Capt. Holdsworth, T. Verrinder, Sir William Verner, Bart., T. Alexander, R. Turton, the Duke of Hamilton (in *some* cases), and many others. All the above have either shown or bred first-class specimens of the breed, amongst which may be mentioned—King Dick, Dan, Michael (who was eaten during the siege of Paris), Romany, Punch, Beeswing, Bowler, Young Duke, Meg, Gipsy Queen, Maggie Lauder, Dido, Master Gully, Acrobat, Page's Bill, King, Nell, Smasher, Prince, Alexander, Baby, Billy, Gambler, Noble, Nettle, Sancho Panza, Slenderman, Sir Anthony, Brutus, Rose, Donald, Alexander, and the famous Sheffield Crib.

Mr. George Raper, of Stockton-on-Tees, has kindly supplied us with the following notes on this breed :—

"The properties of the Bull-dog have been divided into some eighty or ninety points. To the late Jacob Lamphier, in conclave with friends who, like himself, made the Bull-dog an especial study, we are indebted for a most carefully compiled list of properties and points, which are as follows :—

" 1. *The Ears.*—(1) Size: should be small. (2) Thinness. (3) Situation: they should be on the top of the head. (4) Carriage: they should be either "rose," "button," or "tulip" ears. The "rose" ear folds at the back; the tip laps over outwards, exposing part of the inside. The "button" ear only differs from the "rose" in the falling of the tip, which laps over in front, hiding the interior completely. The "tulip" ear is nearly erect; it is the least desirable form.

" 2. *The Skull* (exclusive of property No. 4).—(1) Size: should be large. (2) Height: this should be great. (3) Prominence of the cheeks: they should extend well beyond the eyes. (4) Shortness (*i e.*, breadth in comparison to length). (5) Shape of forehead: it should be well wrinkled, and not prominent, as in the "King Charles" Spaniel.

" 3. *The Eyes.*—(1) Colour; should be as nearly black as possible. (2) Shape of the opening of the lids: should be quite round. (3) Size; should be moderate. (4) Position: they should be quite in front of the head, as far from the ear and as near to the nose as possible—very far apart, but not so far as to interfere with point 3 of the second property, and neither prominent nor deeply set in the head. (5) Direction of the corners: they should be at right angles to a line drawn down the centre of the face.

"4. *The Stop* (this is an indentation between the eyes).—(1) Depth. (2) Breadth. (3) Length: it should extend some considerable distance up the head.

"5. *The Face.*—(1) Shortness, measured from the front of the cheek bone to the end of the nose: this point cannot be carried to too great an excess. (2) Wrinkles: these should be deep, and close together. (3) Shape: the muzzle should turn upwards.

"6. *The Chop.*—(1) Breadth. (2) Depth. (3) The covering of the teeth: these should be perfect.

"7. *The Nose.*—(1) Size: should be large. (2) Should be black. (3) Width of nostrils.

"8. *The Termination of the Jaws.*—(1) Breadth: should be as great as possible. (2) Relative position: the lower jaw should project considerably in advance of the upper, so that the nose is very much set back, but not to such an extent as to interfere with point 2 of the sixth property. (3) Shape of the lower jaw: this should turn upwards.

"9. *The Neck.*—(1) Length: this should be moderate. (2) Thickness: should be considerable. (3) Shape: it should be well arched at the back. (4) Wrinkles and dewlap.

"10. *The Chest.*—(1) Width: this should be very great. (2) Shape: it should be deep and round.

"11. *The Body* (exclusive of Property No. 10).—(1) Shortness of back. (2) Width acoss back: this should be very great at the shoulders, and the spine should rise at the loins, falling again very much towards the stern, and forming an elegant arch. The ribs should be well rounded.

"12. *The Stern.*—(1) Fineness. (2) Length: this should be moderate. (3) Shape: a slight crook is no objection, but a screwed or knotted stern is a deformity. (4) Carriage: this should be downwards; the dog should not be able to raise it above the level of his back. (5) Situation this should be low down at the insertion.

"13. *The Fore-legs.*—(1) Stoutness: they should be very thick in the calves. (2) Shape: rather bowed. (3) Length: they should be short, more so than the hind legs, but not so short as to make the back appear long. (4) Width apart.

"14. *The Hind-legs* (including stifles).—(1) Length: should be moderate, but greater than that of the fore-legs, so as to elevate the loins. (2) Position: the hocks should approach each other, which involves the turning out of the stifles. (3) Roundness of the stifle.

"15. *The Fore-feet* (including pasterns).—(1) Shape: they should be moderately round, but well split up between the toes. (2) Prominence of the knuckles. (3) Position: they should be straight—that is, neither turned outwards nor inwards. (4) Straightness of the pastern. (5) Size: they should be rather small.

"16. *The Hind-feet.*—(1) Shape: they are not expected to be so round as the fore-feet, but they should not be long like a terrier's; they should be well split up between the toes. (2) Prominence of the knuckles. (3) Position: they should be turned outwards. (4) Straightness of the pasterns. (5) Size: they should be rather small.

"17. *The Coat.*—(1) Fineness. (2) Shortness. (3) Closeness.

"18. *The Colour.*—(1) Uniformity: the colour should be "whole" (that is, unmixed with white), unless the dog be all white, which is, in that case, considered a "whole" colour. (2) Tint: this should be either red, red-smut (that is, red with black muzzle), fawn or fawn-smut, fallow or fallow-smut, brindled, white, or pied with any of those colours. (3) Brilliancy and purity.

"19. *General Appearance, Proportion, Carriage, and Size.*—(1) Proportion: no property should be so much in excess as to destroy the general symmetry of the dog. (2) The general appearance of the dog (that is, the impression that he makes as a whole on the eye of the judge). (3) Carriage: the dog should roll in his gait. He generally runs rather sideways. His hind-legs should not be lifted high as he runs, so that his hind-feet seem to skim the ground (4) Size: from about 20 lbs. to 60 lbs.

"Authorities differ regarding the origin of the Bull-dog, but we may safely aver that the demand produced the supply, and as the favourite sport of James I. of England had its rise, reached its zenith, and declined, so the animals best suited for the purpose of bull-baiting were

MR. MEAGER'S BULL-DOG BISMARCK.

fostered in these islands, which now claim them as indigenous; but, the time arriving when the village cry of "No bull, no parson!" became fainter and fainter, as our civilisation increased, so the Bull-dog of our ancestors has degenerated or improved (as the taste of our readers may suggest) into an animal to be pampered and petted and carefully bred for points, to be admired by his owner, or to compete for honours on the show-bench of our many exhibitions. As the field trials for our sporting dogs have done much to encourage the improvement of their mental qualities, which were beginning to be neglected in the pursuit of symmetry of form for show purposes, so without the field day for the Bull-dog the qualities for which he was famous are fast disappearing, under the blighting influence of this enlightened age. His service to the butchers in catching and throwing down cattle—which he formerly did with surprisingly apparent ease, by seizing an ox by the nose, and either holding him perfectly still or throwing him on to his side at his master's command—is now out of date, with his more distant performances of baiting the bull, the lion in the Tower of London, and, in 1825, the lion at Warwick.

"The purpose for which the dog was formerly bred having disappeared, the admirers of the breed, being at a loss for a common object, have cultivated a variety of specimens, according to the taste—or perhaps, more correctly speaking, according to the accident—by which they attached themselves to this noble dog, whose character combines all the qualities his more distinguished owner can boast, and many which his less fortunate hater or admirer might well aspire to imitate.

"It is not my province here to narrate the many acts of intelligence and faithfulness performed by this oft-maligned section of the friend of man, although they would compare most favourably with those of any of the more esteemed.

"It is generally acknowledged that of all breeds none are more liable to deterioration than the Bull-dog. In a litter you seldom find more than one specimen up to the mark when arrived at maturity. This breed of dogs varies very much in appearance, and even now, but more especially a few years ago, the types in different parts of the country were very marked.

"The Birmingham district has long been noted for its Bull-dogs. The marked defects of its specimens are that they want greater depth from the nose to the bottom jaw, many being so thin as to approach what is termed in the fancy "monkey-faced." Many are also wanting in length and width of under-jaw, and with few exceptions they are greatly in want of larger noses.

"Nottingham is another district where this breed has been fostered, and here again you find a marked difference of type. Generally they have good limbs and body, good skull and large eyes, but many are spoiled by a "tulip" ear, and are, moreover, inclined to be "frog-faced"— a great defect. The types of the London dogs vary considerably.

"In breeding it will therefore be seen that much depends upon the selection of a suitable sire for the bitch intended to be bred from. Most of our best specimens are undoubtedly in-bred. No doubt Percival's Toss holds prior claims, he being the grandsire of the celebrated dog King Dick, whose pedigree shows close in-breeding; nevertheless it is an undisputed fact that he can claim near relationship to the greater majority of the prize-takers of the present day.

"Were I breeding for size I should select a large roomy bitch and put her to a high quality dog, for I have almost invariably found the dog stamp the quality of the puppies. Experience has taught me that you cannot obtain the points you breed for from the first cross, but must breed in once, at least, to secure the improvement you seek. I am certainly an advocate for judicious in-breeding, believing it to be the much wiser plan to breed from reliable and good blood than to admit questionable blood into your strain."

Having endeavoured to enumerate the leading exhibitors, past and present, and some of their best-known dogs, we will pass on to the formation of the Bull-dog.

The *skull* of the Bull-dog is essentially one of the chief characteristics of the breed. It should be of as great a circumference as possible (19 inches in a dog and 17½ inches in a bitch is a fair estimate for a dog of 50 lbs. and a bitch of 45 lbs. weight), square in shape, broad in front, not wedge-shaped, and carrying a quantity of loose skin, which should lie in a number of heavy wrinkles over the head and face.

The *jaws* are peculiar in formation, as the lower jaw projects a considerable distance beyond the upper, and has, in addition, an upward turn in front

The *tusks*, or canine teeth, should be wide apart, and it is desirable that the front teeth should be regular, though this feature is absent in many of our best dogs.

The *upper jaw* is, as above stated, considerably shorter than the lower, and both should display unmistakable signs of strength.

The *lips*, termed "chop" by the initiated, should be very loose and heavy, and of considerable circumference.

The *nose*, which must lay well back, in fact be as *retroussé* as it is possible to imagine, must be broad, large, moist, and perfectly black—a parti or flesh coloured nose (technically-called "Dudley") being in the opinion of many good judges an absolute disqualification in competition.

The *eyes* should be large, but not too full or goggle, soft, round, and dark in colour, set as far apart as possible, and at right angles to an imaginary line drawn the centre of the skull—an oblique or "Chinaman's" eye is a decided blemish.

The *stop*, or indentation between the eyes, should be both wide and deep, extending up the skull in a deep furrow for a considerable distance (when this formation is present the skull is said to be "broken up"), and if this feature is absent it gives the dog's head an appearance of roundness which is highly undesirable, and he is termed "apple-headed" in consequence.

The *ears* should be small, and "rose" shaped—*i.e.*, laying back so that the inside burr is visible. They are set on wide apart at the *corners* of the skull; if set on too much at the top the skull is narrow, and if too low down the sides the head is rounded, and therefore it is most desirable that the ears should be set on well at the corners of the skull. The thinner they are, too, the better. According to the Bull-dog Club a tulip (prick) and button ear are admissible, but no judge could, if in his senses, pass a dog with a tulip ear; and, for our own part, a button ear would go greatly against a dog.

The *cheek bumps* at the base of the jaws should be clearly defined in a three-year-old dog; but as this feature is only to be satisfactorily obtained by age and maturity, though it should always be present to a certain extent, too much importance should not be attached to this point in a very young dog.

The *neck* must be muscular, slightly curved, and provided with a heavy double dewlap.

The *shoulders* sloping and strong, firmly set on, and very muscular.

The *chest* must be as *wide* and *deep* as possible, so as to give (in conjunction with the rounded fore-ribs) plenty of space for the heart and lungs to act in.

The *fore legs*, which are much shorter than the hind, should be very powerful and straight, though the large amount of muscle on the outside is liable to convey the impression that the dog is bow-legged, which he should not be. They should be turned out at the shoulders, so that the body can swing between them when in motion.

The *fore feet* should be straight at the pasterns, large, moderately round, with the toes well split up, arched, and rather splayed out.

The *body* should be very deep at the chest and must be of considerable girth, with round ribs, and has the appearance of being on an incline, which arises from the fore-legs being shorter than the hinder, and also from the peculiar formation of the back, which, in addition to being extremely short, rises from the shoulders to the loins and then slopes down to the stern, thus producing the "*roach*" or "*wheel*" back which is essentially present in a good Bull-dog.

The *loins* are powerful, well arched, and tucked up: a "cobby" body is undesirable in this breed.

The *stern* or tail, which must be set on low, must be short and very fine. A break or knot near the base is approved of, as it renders getting his tail up impossible, and a ring, or a crooked tail, is sought after by many breeders.

The *hind legs*, as before stated, should be higher than the front ones, and they should turn well *out* at the stifles and feet, which causes the hocks to turn inwards, which is imperative, for a Bull-dog should be "cow-hocked" and *not* go wide behind. The feet are in shape longer than the front ones, and more compact.

Almost any *colour* is admissible in a Bull-dog except black, or black-and-tan. Blue is undesirable; and perhaps the following classification of colours represents their respective values in the eyes of breeders:—Brindle-and-white, brindle, white, fallow or fawn smut (fallow or fawn with black muzzle), fallow or fawn pied, red, and, lastly, the blue-ticked dog; but where so much latitude is allowed, the colour of a Bull-dog must be left out in judging specimens, except in cases of equal merit, when a judge must naturally be guided by any special weakness he may entertain towards one particular colour.

The *coat* is short and close, and if brushed the wrong way extremely harsh, though on being smoothed down it is soft and silky to the touch.

The *walk* or *action* of the Bull-dog is almost indescribable in its ungainliness. We ourselves, though glorying in our admiration of the breed, cannot but admit that its paces are the incarnation of all that is clumsy. His short and immensely powerful body swings between the Bull-dog's out-turned shoulders, his high hind legs appear to be pushing his chest out between his fore legs, whilst the peculiar formation of his stifles and hocks scarcely permit him to raise his hind feet off the ground, and the result is an action which partakes of the elements of a rush, a shuffle, and an amble, without fairly representing either.

In *temper* the Bulldog will bear comparison with any breed of dog. To his master especially, and those he knows, he is amiable, loving, and obedient, but he will not usually make friends with strangers all at once, and invariably, if ill-treated, proceeds to resent the injuries inflicted on him in hot haste. If properly brought up, and not teased or irritated, a pure Bull-dog is both a noble-looking and enjoyable companion, but when once roused to action by cruelty his indomitable pluck and reckless disregard of physical suffering renders him a most formidable antagonist to man or beast.

The *general appearance* of a Bull-dog is that of a comparatively small dog very heavy for his size, of immense power, and great squareness of head, whether looked at from in front or profile, with the body gradually tapering off towards the stern; in fact, a first glance at a Bull-dog stamps him as the possessor of a combination of strength and activity unmet with in any other dog.

Weight, about fifty pounds for a dog and forty-five pounds for a bitch. Of course there are many first-rate specimens of considerably less weight than the above, and a few heavier; but most of the best dogs scale between forty-two and forty-eight pounds when in show form, and not too fat.

In regard to the dogs chosen for illustration in this work, Smasher is by Master Gully out of Nettle by Sir Anthony by Sheffield Crib; Master Gully by Briton out of Kitt, Briton by Saxon out of Duchess. He has won first Bristol, 1876; first Edinburgh, first Blaydon-on-Tyne, first Darlington, first Alexandra Palace, 1877. In 1878 he was not shown. In 1879 he has won first and medal Dublin, first Wolverhampton, first Hanover. His measurements have not been received by us complete, but a few of them are as follows: Girth of muzzle, 14½ inches; girth of skull, 21½ inches; girth of neck, 20 inches; weight, 43 lbs.

Doon Brae, the second subject of illustration, is without doubt the best dog under 40 lbs. now alive, and we question if, at his weight, his equal has ever been seen. He was bred by

BULL DOGS.

his owner, Captain Holdsworth, in 1876; and is by Sir Anthony out of Polly, by Vero Shaw's Sixpence out of Whiskey by Fulton's Falstaff out of Nosegay; Sir Anthony by Sheffield Crib out of Meg, by Old King Dick out of Old Nell, by Old Dan. Crib's pedigree is disputed, and therefore we do not give it. He has won first Bristol, first Crystal Palace, and first Alexandra Palace, 1878; and first Alexandra Palace, 1879. The measurements of Doon Brae are: Tip of nose to stop, 1 inch; stop to occiput, 5 inches; length of back, 15½ inches; girth of muzzle, 12 inches; girth of skull, 19¾ inches; girth of neck, 17½ inches; girth of brisket, 32½ inches; girth of chest, 28 inches; girth of loins, 20½ inches; girth of hind-leg at stifle-joint, 11½ inches; girth of fore-arm, 7¼ inches; girth of knee, 5 inches; girth of pastern, 4¼ inches; height at shoulders, 17½ inches; height at elbows, 8½ inches; height at top of loins, 18 inches; height, hock to ground, 5 inches; length of stern, 7¼ inches.

Mr. T. Meager's Bismarck, of whom we give a woodcut, is a very typical specimen of the breed. He won first in the small-weight class at the Bull-dog Club's show in 1876, at the Alexandra Palace, and, like Doon Brae, is under 40 lbs.

Subjoined is the scale of points as drawn up by the New Bull-dog Club in 1875. They are based on the well-known Philo-kuon scale, and received the support of the leading breeders and exhibitors at the time when they were first published:—

Points.	Details for consideration of Judge.	Distribution of 100 marks for total individual points.
General appearance	Symmetrical formation; shape, make, style, action, and finish	10
Skull ...	Size, height, breadth, and squareness of skull; shape, flatness, and wrinkles of forehead ...	15
Stop ...	Depth, breadth, and extent	5
Eyes ...	Position, shape, size, and colour	5
Ears ...	Position, size, shape, carriage, thinness	5
Face ...	Shortness, breadth, and wrinkles of face; breadth, bluntness, squareness, and upward turn of muzzle; position, breadth, size, and backward inclination of top of nose; size, width, blackness of, and cleft between, nostrils	5
Chop ...	Size and complete covering of front teeth	5
Mouth ..	Width and squareness of jaws, projection and upward turn of lower jaw; size and condition of teeth, and if the six lower front teeth are in an even row	5
Chest & neck	Length, thickness, arching, and dewlap of neck; width, depth, and roundness of chest ...	5
Shoulders ...	Size, breadth, and muscle	5
Body ...	Capacity, depth, and thickness of brisket; roundness of ribs	5
Back roach	Shortness, width at shoulders; and height, strength and arch at loins	5
Tail	Fineness, shortness, shape, position, and carriage	5
Fore legs and feet ...	Stoutness, shortness, and straightness of legs, development of calves and outward turn of elbows; straightness and strength of ankles, roundness, size, and position of feet, compactness of toes, height and prominence of knuckles	5
Hind legs and feet ...	Stoutness, length, and size of legs, development of muscles, strength, shape, and position of hocks and stifles, formation of feet and toes as in fore legs and feet	5
Size ...	Approaching 50lb.	5
Coat	Fineness, shortness, evenness, and closeness of coat; uniformity, purity, and brilliancy of colour	5
	Total for perfection in all points	100
	Judge's Net Totals	

Whilst thoroughly agreeing with the above scale as one by which Bull-dogs can be most satisfactorily judged, we propose adding another embodying our own ideas, being of the opinion that a standard of 50 points is more easy of application to this and every breed.

SCALE FOR JUDGING BULL-DOGS.

	Value.
Skull, size, and shape	10
Head and face	10
Neck, chest, and shoulders	10
Body	5
Legs, feet, and tail	10
General appearance	5
Total	50

CHAPTER XI.

THE DALMATIAN OR COACH-DOG.

IN spite of the meagreness, in point of numbers, of the entries in the Dalmatian classes at most shows, few breeds attract more attention, simply we believe on account of the peculiarity of the markings, which are indispensable to success on the bench. It is so seldom that a really well-marked dog is seen following a carriage, that those unacquainted with the few really good ones which appear at shows invariably express great surprise and admiration at the regularity and brilliancy of their colouring. Of the antecedents of the Dalmatian it is extremely hard to speak with certainty, but it appears that the breed has altered but little since it was first illustrated in Bewick's book on natural history, for in it appears an engraving of a dog who would be able to hold his own in high-class competition in the present day, and whose markings are sufficiently well developed to satisfy the most exacting of judges. Indeed, the almost geometrical exactness with which the spots are represented by Bewick impresses us with the idea that imagination greatly assisted nature in producing what he thought ought to be; his ideal, however exaggerated, is at the same time a standard worth breeding up to in that most important feature in this dog, the brilliancy and regularity of his markings. In former times it was the invariable custom to remove the ears by cropping, as is the case in the present day with Bull and English Terriers; and in many cases the whole flap of the ear was cut off entirely, exposing the cavity, as was the custom of the time to deal with Pugs, making the dog, to our modern notion, hideous, and laying him open to attacks of inflammation and canker in one of his most delicate organs, which frequently ended in deafness; but this barbarous and utterly useless practice at last died out, and the dog now appears as nature formed him. One decided argument to be used against the use of the cropping-knife in the case of Dalmatians is that the *colour and shape of the ear* are matters of some considerable importance. A heavily-marked or badly-formed ear would, of course, tell against a dog in competition, and when these are manipulated by cropping it is impossible to decide how they would have naturally appeared.

A change has come over the opinions of breeders of late as regards which other breed of dog the Dalmatian most resembles; a little time back it was the Bull-terrier, and now it is the modern Pointer which claims the honour. We cannot ourselves see any similarity between the former and the Dalmatian, as the heads are so totally distinct in shape and character, but our readers can have the opportunity of comparing these two breeds without difficulty, as they appear in the same illustration in this work.

A very general, but erroneous, impression is prevalent that the Dalmatian is a dog which is devoid of intelligence, and incapable of being employed in any other manner than following a carriage, or accompanying its master's horses at exercise. In its native land it certainly has been used in the field, and though we have never ourselves seen one thus employed, we can give no reason for doubting that, if carefully broken, the Dalmatian would be found a useful companion in a day amongst the heather, as from his similarity in shape and build to a large-sized Pointer, he should be well qualified to undergo the fatigue of a hard day's shooting.

Some few years back, when the Holborn Amphitheatre was open, there was a wonderfully clever troupe of performing dogs amongst the attractions there. Amongst these was a rather good Dalmatian, who was entrusted with the *rôle* of clown, and it was really surprising to see the intelligence he displayed in burlesquing the tricks of the other members of the troupe. For instance, the Poodles and other dogs would run up to a gate and leap it, then the Dalmatian, apparently influenced by the example of his human prototype, would run round the ring two or three times, barking loudly as if to attract attention, walk slowly up to the gate, and then scramble under it, amidst roars of laughter from the audience, who evidently sympathised with him in his performance. We can also render personal testimony to the general intelligence and docility of the Dalmatian. Although his love for the stable and the companionship of the horse is his constant and ruling passion, and one but rarely developed to the same extent in any other breed, he is capable of showing and exercising in a strong degree personal attachment to his master; and many of them are most excellent guards. As such they are peculiarly adapted to run with the business vans and parcels-delivery carts of our tradesmen, to which they would at once prove an ornament and a protection infinitely superior in both respects to the enormities in dog-flesh they allow their men to carry about with them. The idea—and it is a correct one—is gradually gaining ground that a well-bred and handsome dog is generally superior to mongrels in the execution of the duties they are chosen for, and one of our objects in writing this book is to strengthen and spread this healthy notion, the practical outcome of which brings credit to the country. We are at a loss to discover any valid reason for the existence of mongrels in a country where the supply of pure-bred dogs of every breed is practically unlimited.

The chief physical characteristic of the breed is the marking. The body of the dog is white, and its head, ears, body, tail, and legs should be covered with round spots about the size of a halfpenny, either black or liver in colour. In many specimens the muzzle and legs are marked with spots of both colours, and this is considered no disfigurement, in fact some judges rather prefer it as giving a gayer appearance to the dog. A very common fault is a black half-face, or a black ear, and these are decided blemishes, as is the lack of spots on the tail; and here it is that many good specimens fail in competition. Another point which should not be lost sight of in judging or buying a Dalmatian is the feet and legs. One requires these dogs for hard work, and it is impossible that a dog possessing weak legs and badly-formed feet can endure the fatigue of following a carriage for several hours a day.

Captain, the property of Mr. J. Fawdry, is the dog we have selected for illustration, as he is indisputably the best specimen now before the public. He made his *début* at the third Kennel Club Show held at the Crystal Palace in 1873 as Traviser, winning first prize, and on leaving his then owner and breeder's (Mr. Chas. Lewis Boyce) kennels, he was re-christened by his new owner, Mr. Oldham of Manchester, Uhlan, his name again being changed to Captain; but his merits were and are too genuine to be affected by a capricious and foolish change of title, and under each he has continued to hold his position as the best Dalmatian of his time, having won almost every prize of importance for which he has since competed. Captain is of illustrious parentage, being of the strain of those old and successful breeders, Mr. R. Hale of Brierley Hill, and Mr. H. Hale of Burton-on-Trent, the former of whom won with Noble, one of Captain's progenitors, at Birmingham Show in 1862. He is by Boyce's Carlo out of his Vic, by Mr. Hale's Noble, and his measurements are as follows: Nose to stop, $3\frac{1}{2}$ inches; stop to occiput, 5 inches; length of back, 21 inches; girth of forearm, 7 inches; girth of knee, 5 inches; girth of pastern, $4\frac{1}{2}$ inches; height at shoulders, 22 inches; height at elbow, 12 inches; height at loins, 20 inches; height at hock, $5\frac{1}{2}$ inches; length of tail, $12\frac{1}{2}$ inches.

BULL TERRIER.

DALMATIAN.

Before this dog's appearance, Mr. R. L. Price of Rhiwlas swept the bench with his champion Crib, who is also of Hale's blood, but age and infirmity prevented the old hero ever competing with a fair chance of success with Mr. Fawdry's grand specimen. But he also must, we fear, give way to younger aspirants, being at the time we write in his tenth year; and among the juniors that have as yet come under our notice is Mr. R. Ll. Price's Tom Crib, son of champion Crib. There are, however, a great number of these dogs kept in various parts of the kingdom which are not sent to dog shows, and among them we frequently observe specimens of great worth. Some years ago many excellent Dalmatians were to be met with in that part of the Black Country, as it is called, embracing West Bromwich, Swan Village, Dudley, Brierley Hill, &c. In the town of Banbury, too, we remember to have met with them in fair numbers and good quality, and at Kendal there is generally a good show of them; but nowhere in England are they to be seen in such numbers as in a radius of a few miles from the Crystal Palace, where they are not only numerous, but in many cases much above the average in good points. In a few instances we have noticed fair specimens of the tri-coloured variety, so rarely found good.

The *Head* of the Dalmatian should be wide and flat, blunt at the muzzle, and tight-lipped; nose black.

Ears rather small, V-shaped, and very fine. If these are well spotted, great beauty is added to the dog's appearance.

Eyes dark, and inclined to be small.

Neck arched and light, tapering on to powerful and sloping shoulders.

Chest deep, and rather broad.

Body round in ribs, and well ribbed up behind.

Fore legs straight and very muscular; plenty of bone is essential in this breed, so as to enable a dog to stand the wear and tear he has to encounter on the hard roads he is compelled to traverse.

Feet round, with the toes arched and well split up; pads round, firm, and elastic.

Hind legs muscular, with clean hocks placed near the ground, as in the Bull-dog.

Tail tapering from the root, and carried as a Pointer's: this must be well spotted.

Colour and Markings.—Well spotted all over with either black or liver-coloured spots, or both. These should *not* intermingle, and should be of the size of a sixpence to a halfpenny.

Coat is short, close, and fine.

General Appearance is that of a strong muscular dog, capable of enduring considerable fatigue, and possessing a fair amount of speed.

The scale of points by which these dogs should be judged is as follows:—

	Value.
General appearance	10
Colour, markings, and coat	25
Neck, chest, and body	5
Head, including ears and eyes	5
Legs, feet, and tail	5
Total	50

CHAPTER XII.

THE BULL-TERRIER.

No breed of dog is at present making such a rapid advance in public favour as the modern and improved Bull-terrier, and its well-deserved popularity seems far more likely to be permanent than that of other breeds which have in turn been taken up only to be dismissed by their owners when their lack of intelligence, cowardice, or general inutility, has proved them to be unworthy of the patronage bestowed upon them. The breed as it now exists is comparatively of recent manufacture, and is indisputably the result of judicious selection from and with the well-known Bull *and* Terrier of the Midland counties. This dog, in its turn, was brought into existence by crossing the Bull-dog with the white English Terrier, and was produced in the first instance by the supporters and lovers of dog-fighting, who wished to obtain a longer and more punishing head than that possessed by a pure Bull-dog. This latter cross, in the first instance, produced a sullen-looking, thick-skulled dog, showing slight indications of symmetry in his composition, but still admirably adapted for the purpose for which he was called into existence. How the present show Bull-terrier arose from such a dog is more or less the subject of conjecture, for no trustworthy particulars of its origin are obtainable from the part of the country where it first appeared; but there is little cause to differ from the general impression, that many of the larger-sized show specimens have Greyhound blood in their veins, whilst the smaller breed is more closely allied with the English Terrier than is desirable.

We ourselves have been applied to by a gentleman whose name is well known in the coursing world, for permission to cross some of his Greyhound bitches with the Bull-terriers Tarquin and Sallust. The object of this was his desire to instil stamina and pluck into his breed, which he fancied was degenerating in these qualifications, and need not be gone into here, though it will, with his permission, be noticed in the chapter on Greyhounds. The result of the first Bull-terrier cross, in each instance, was a large-framed, though light-boned and rather narrow-chested dog, with, for a Bull-terrier, very snipy jaws, and possessing the peculiar *action* of the Greyhound in a marked degree. The difficulty of breeding out the last point alluded to struck us the moment we saw the animals move; and the original introducers of this blood into the Bull-terrier—if there are such persons in existence—deserve considerable credit for their perseverance in their endeavours. However, not having the slightest desire to experimentalise in the matter, we are unable to give further information as regards the cross, so far as it affects the Bull-terrier, beyond the fact that the dog puppies were at once destroyed by their owner, the females alone being retained by him for the purpose of working out his experiment.

One of the earliest records we can find of the Bull-terrier is in one of the editions of Blaine's "Rural Sports," in which allusion is made to the breed in the following words :—
"A large breed of English Terriers has of late sprung up, most of which are rough-coated, but a few others are smooth. These, by being crossed with the Bull-dog, have gained undaunted courage in attacking the higher order of vermin—as the badger, &c."

In the "Naturalists' Library," too, by Sir William Jardine, published in 1843, the breed is thus alluded to :—" In England the cross of Terriers is perceptible in sheep and cattle dogs, but most of all in the breed called Bull-terriers, because it is formed of these two varieties, and constitutes the most determined and savage race known."

From all recognised accounts the ancestors of the modern Bull-terrier must have been a rough-and-ready race, and the illustration overleaf is useful in conveying an idea to our readers of what the creatures were like. In the dog situated in the lower portion of the plate may be found the type of a really half-bred dog, showing perhaps rather more bull, especially about the flews, than was permitted in even those days of careless breeding, but still displaying some Terrier characteristics. The two dogs on the top of the steps very much resemble the Bull and Terrier still used for fighting purposes in the Midland Counties, but in form and colour they are as unlike a modern show Bull-terrier as it is possible to imagine.

To the late Mr. James Hinks, of Worcester Street, Birmingham, is due the credit of bringing the breed before the notice of the public in its later and more desirable form, and with his well-known Old Madman and Puss he farmed our leading shows for a long period. After a time, Mr. J. F. Godfree, of Birmingham, appeared in the field. His celebrated Young Victor fairly monopolised the prizes at the great exhibitions for many a day ; and on his death his mantle fell upon his son Tarquin, for some considerable time our own property, whose portrait will appear in due course amongst the coloured plates. Almost all the leading breeders of the day have dipped deeply into Hinks' Old Victor strain, whilst that of Mr. Godfree is equally well patronised ; and it is an undoubted fact that the breeding of Bull-terriers is now a much easier task than it was some time back, as the offspring of dogs belonging to the above strains are more similar in type and uniform in general appearance than is the case with those whose ancestors are of less fashionable blood.

The Bull-terrier varies in size from five pounds weight up to fifty, and thus admirers of the breed have the opportunity of selecting a dog whose size is adapted for the work or kennel accommodation at hand, which is no small recommendation in the case of those whose out-door space is limited. Though his extreme docility and intelligence render this breed of dog eminently qualified for an in-door pet, few varieties require more genuine hard work and out-door exercise to get them into show condition, as the muscles which should be so plainly visible on the fore and hind quarters of a dog in perfect trim become relaxed and flabby if his proper amount of exercise is curtailed. Many exhibitors residing in towns, and who are unable to spare sufficient time to run their dogs in the country, have adopted the expedient of making them chase a ball about their gardens for an hour or two a day, or else by hanging a piece of cat-skin on a wall, or at the end of a stick, and keeping it out of the dog's reach they cause their Terrier to exercise himself in his unceasing endeavours to obtain possession of the treasure by jumping up at it. These methods of exercising a dog in a small space may perhaps be novel to readers who are unacquainted with the devices to which many successful breeders and exhibitors are compelled to resort, in their endeavours to compete with others whose opportunities for bringing their dogs fit and well to the post are more extensive.

A very silly prejudice exists against the Bull-terrier on account of his alleged in-variable ferocity of temper and irresistible inclination to fight with all other dogs that come within his reach ; thus many would-be supporters of the breed have held aloof from it in consequence of the reports they have heard concerning him. That there is a slight founda-tion for these detractions we cannot deny, but after a pretty considerable experience of Bull-terriers we unhesitatingly affirm that the prejudice against his temper is grossly exaggerated ;

no breed of dog, if properly brought up and kindly treated, is more susceptible of affection towards his master, and docility and intelligence are properties which are highly developed in a Bull-terrier. Naturally a dog which may be said to be a born gladiator possesses a greater amount of courage and tenacity in his attack than animals of a gentler temperament, and a firm temper is often required to keep them in thorough discipline; but as a gentleman's companion in town or country, the Bull-terrier is unapproached by any other breed of dog. He is handsome to look at, affectionate, clean in the house, and very tricky; an excellent water dog, and, though it may be discredited by some people, we are convinced that his nose is equal to that of many dogs used in the field, though his impetuous disposition would render it a difficult matter to keep him under the severe control so essential in a field dog. As a retriever he is naturally hard-mouthed, but no breed can more easily be taught to fetch and carry on land and water, and this is, doubtless a source of amusement to many owners. It is, however, for his indomitable courage (unsurpassed even by the Bull-dog) that the Bull-terrier is so highly prized by many—for, though usually mute like the Bull-dog, his system of attack is different from that of the latter, inasmuch as, instead of hanging on to his antagonist, the Bull-terrier tears him all over; and his pluck is so great that he is able to endure an enormous amount of punishment, whilst in his turn he is mangling his foe with his powerful jaws. During more recent years, and since the retirement from the show arena of Mr. S. E. Shirley, M.P., Mr. R. J. Lloyd-Price, Mr. Godfree, and the late Mr. Hinks, the majority of the Bull-terrier prizes have come down south through the kennels of Mr. Loveys of London, Mr. Pfeil of Sutton, Mr. Alfred George of Kensal New Town (whose capital little dog Spring is well worthy of the honours he has won), Mr. Tredennick of St. Austell, Cornwall (whose grand little Bertie will long be remembered as being both good and game), and ourselves; whilst the Midland prestige has been fairly maintained by Messrs. Roocroft of Bolton, Miller of Walsall, and R. J. Hartley of Altrincham. The latter gentleman, who is a most enthusiastic lover and supporter of the breed, owns two magnificent specimens in Magnet and Violet. Authorities differ on the merits of these two famous bitches, but we most unhesitatingly give our allegiance to the former, whose sole fault is being a little light in bone. The condition, too, in which Mr. Hartley's dogs are exhibited is a model for the imitation of all Bull-terrier breeders.

Before passing on to a detailed description of the points of a Bull-terrier, a few lines should be devoted to the subject of colour. It must appear an arbitrary rule to decide that a dog of this breed should, if of any use as a show dog, be pure white; but a moment's reflection must show that there is a motive for this decision. The difficulty of eradicating the undesirable traces of Bull in his face, body, and limbs, is tremendous; and it is solely by practically adopting the theory of the survival of the fittest that a satisfactory result can be obtained. Why only white dogs were selected in the first instance we could never discover; but of this we are convinced by experience, namely, that the introduction of a heavily-marked dog into a strain of Bull-terriers has a decided tendency to cause a throw back to Bull characteristics, and this can only be attributed to the fact that the colours other than white have been less carefully bred than the more fashionable colour. We are quite prepared to admit that there are many excellent dogs of a colour other than white, but we maintain that these, though in themselves good specimens, are undesirable for breeding purposes, and should be avoided, though many of them are the offspring of highly-bred pure white dogs, themselves successful competitors at our best shows. It is a painful fact that in most litters there even now appear one or more "marked" puppies; but the danger in permitting these to be used to

ORIGINAL BULL AND TERRIER CROSS.

any extent for breeding purposes would be that very soon countless good-looking marked dogs would be shown all over the country. These being used for stud purposes would, from their markings most likely beget a still larger proportion of marked stock, and contaminate the breed we have now brought to something like the desired perfection. In short, before a breed of brindled or coloured Bull-terriers can be fairly established, several years will have to be devoted by their admirers to them, in order that they may stand on an equal footing with their white brethren as regards uniformity of shape and reliability in breeding. Young Victor, late the property of Mr. Godfree, proves the truth of this theory; though disfigured by a patch on his eye, no dog could have been more successful on the bench, and few had better opportunities of distinguishing themselves at the stud. That he could beget good stock is indisputable; but the result of his triumphs was the introduction of a class for Bull-terriers " other than white" at a Crystal Palace show, and the subsequent appearance at other exhibitions of a number of thick, heavy-headed wretches, whose introduction into a good strain of the breed would jeopardise its prospects for many a day.

No breed of dog owes more to condition on the show-bench than does the Bull-terrier. A dog of this variety exhibited in bad order has little chance of beating an inferior specimen, even under a first-class judge; and where the awards are in the hands of inexperienced judges, his chances of success would be absolutely *nil*. The fact of the intensely brilliant white so often seen in the coats of dogs at the different shows being frequently the result of art, in the application of powdered chalk, is indisputable. However, detection and subsequent disqualification often follow in the wake of such practices, and should do so, especially as—unless the dog is suffering from some irritation of the skin—a resort to powder is quite unnecessary. In cases where the skin is inflamed by heat of the blood, the application of powdered chalk may be excusable; but adopters of this method of concealment should be particularly careful to brush it thoroughly out of the coat before the dog is led into the judging-ring, or they may find their specimen disqualified. Personally, we cannot too strongly advocate the showing of dogs honestly and fairly. Prizes won by means of foul play must, in the long run, cause more feelings of remorse in the mind of the exhibitor than they do those of triumph in the moment of victory; and we have proved by personal experience that a dog in good condition, and properly washed, can win unfaked if he is good enough. Our own system of washing show Bull-terriers is very simple, though it takes time. The dog is placed standing up in a large shallow tub half filled with warm water, and is in the first instance thoroughly wetted by the water being poured over him with a bowl or saucer. Next comes the application of the soap—the sort we invariably use is the common blue and *white* (not *yellow*) mottled—and the part first operated on is the head. When this is thoroughly soaped and rinsed, the body and legs are treated in like manner, and finally the first stage of his ablutions is completed with the aid of several *clean* towels. The second part of the operation consists in rubbing him perfectly dry with bare hands, by smoothing the hair down over and over again, in the right direction, until there is no more moisture left on it. The dog is then put on a clean straw bed, and if looked after to see that he does not get out of his kennel will in the course of a couple of hours be as white as snow, and his jacket will shine like silver. The greatest care must be taken in putting on the collar after the washing is completed, as collars often get soiled inside, and if so, will inevitably blacken the dog's neck.

Preparatory to the above, however, it is always most desirable to remove the superfluous hairs from a dog's ears and muzzle before he is shown, as this operation tends to smarten him up considerably. The *inside* only of the ears are operated on, and the hairs are removed by either careful clipping or shaving. This operation however requires the assistance of both art and experience, and therefore no tyro should attempt it without the assistance of some one who is an authority on the subject. The grotesque appearance of Old Puss in the champion class at the Agricultural Hall show of 1877 should be a warning to youthful owners against turning their 'prentice hands to such delicate operations. In her case the poor wretch had the hair shaved off the *back* of her ears; and her comical appearance caused roars of laughter amongst the breeders present. The removal of the long "smellers" from the muzzle, however, is an easy matter if the dog is not inclined to bite. If he is, it is generally a good plan to get a friend to perform the operation, care being taken, however, only to remove the smellers and *long* eyebrows, nothing more. Having given the above hints upon getting up Bull-terriers for show purposes, we have nothing further to add before passing on to a description of this breed, beyond again impressing on our readers the great importance of *muscular development* in this breed. They must recollect they are showing the gladiator of the canine race, and a fighting dog should, in our opinion, be exhibited thoroughly trained; that is, muscular and light in flesh. Hard work and good wholesome food will alone put on muscle and take off fat; and the more a Bull-terrier gets of either the happier he is.

It frequently happens in showing Bull-terriers that medicine has to be given to reduce the weight in the small sizes a pound or two, in order to qualify them for a certain class. The best physic to use under such circumstances is either ordinary black-draught, or buckthorn and castor-oil. As a rule we always postponed physicking until the week before the show, hoping that exercise would reduce the dog, and medicine could be avoided. Again, if a dog is weakened by aperients too long before a show there is a great chance of his losing muscle, which would be greatly against him on the bench. If you have a dog very near the required weight, feed him lightly the night before the show, and give him one drink of water. The last thing let him have a good dose of buckthorn and oil, and don't feed him or give him a drink until he is judged, when he will probably have lost half a pound weight, if previously in good condition.

It would now be as well to go through the points of this variety, and we will begin as usual with

The Head, which should be flat, wide between the ears, and wedge-shaped; that is, tapering from the sides of the head to the nose; no stop or indentation between the eyes is permissible, and the cheek-bones should not be visible.

The Teeth should be powerful and perfectly regular—an undershot or overhung mouth being very objectionable—and the lips thin and tight; that is, only just sufficient to cover the teeth, and not pendulous, as in the case of the Bull-dog.

The Nose, large, quite black, and damp, with the nostrils well developed.

The Eyes must be small, and very black. As regards shape, the oblong is preferable to the round eye.

The Ears are almost invariably cropped, and should stand perfectly upright. This cutting of the ears is now almost reduced to a science, and no inexperienced persons should attempt it, as if improperly manipulated, what is intended as both an ornament and a convenience to the dog becomes an unsightly disfigurement.

The Neck should be moderately long and arched, free from all traces of dewlap, and strongly set upon the shoulders.

The Shoulders, slanting and very muscular, set firmly on the chest, which should be wide.

The Fore legs should be moderately high and *perfectly straight*, and the dog must stand well *on* them, for they do not, as in the case of the Bull-dog, turn outwards at the shoulders.

Feet, moderately long and compact, with the toes well arched.

Body, deep at chest, and well ribbed up.

Hind legs, long and very muscular, with hocks straight, and near the ground.

Coat, short, and rather harsh to the touch.

Colour, white.

Tail or *Stern* fine, set on low, and not carried up, but as straight out from the back as possible.

In general appearance the Bull-terrier is a symmetrical-looking dog, apparently gifted with great strength and activity, and of a lively and determined disposition.

In spite of the popularity of the breed, it is a lamentable fact that its progress towards

NELSON, SMALL-SIZED BULL-TERRIER, LATE THE PROPERTY OF MR. S. E. SHIRLEY, M.P.

perfection is at present very slow. It has not had fair-play at the hands of show committees, and with its kinsmen—the Black-and-tan and White English Terriers—usually has to put up with a judge who is engaged for other classes and takes these as an addition to his other labours. Thus we see, show after show, dogs gaining prizes in these classes which do not show one atom of *Terrier* character in their composition, being great, lumbering, heavy-lipped, phlegmatical, cow-faced wretches, with no vivacity or "go" in them. These are just the dogs to be avoided by a Terrier breeder, and their success is highly prejudicial to the breeds. Naturally the breed suffers, and unless some one with private influence gets justice done to it, the Bull-terrier will drift back to the mongrel state it emerged from when it was first fortunate enough to receive the patronage of powerful friends. As a proof of the unsatisfactory state the breed is in at present, we have been unable to find a small dog possessing sufficient merit to entitle it to a place in our list of illustrations, and we are therefore thrown back upon a portrait of Nelson, late the property of Mr. S. E. Shirley, M.P. This dog was a really first-rate specimen of the small-sized Bull-terrier, and showed merit enough to deserve a place in any work on the dog ; and it is the more to be regretted that, in spite of the increase of breeders, the quality of the breed, especially the small ones, has not improved in proportion, as it unquestionably should have done.

A real Bull-terrier of 16 pounds weight will do all a Fox-terrier of 20 pounds weight can do, and then, if necessary, kill the Fox-terrier ninety times out of a hundred. Yet the Fox-terrier exhibitors have it nearly all their own way in electing judges, and getting special prizes awarded them, merely because, being a more numerous variety, they have more powerful friends at Court, and are not required to show the courage and resolution, lacking which, a Bull-terrier would be absolutely worthless.

Tarquin, the subject of our illustration, was bred by Mr. Charles Louis Boyce of Birmingham, in 1873, and was purchased from him by us in 1876. He is a pure white dog, weighing about 45 pounds, and is by Young Victor out of Puss, by Gambler out of Young Puss; Young Victor, by Old Victor out of Steel's Puss; Gambler, by Turk out of Kit, dam of Old Madman; Turk, by Rebel out of Fly. Tarquin has taken the following prizes: First Wolverhampton, first Northampton, first Birmingham, 1874; champion Nottingham, first Birmingham, first Alexandra Palace, 1875; first Cork, first Wolverhampton, first and special cup Maidstone, first Darlington, first Stockton-on-Tees, and champion Crystal Palace, 1876; first Edinburgh, first and cup Swindon, first Blaydon-on-Tyne, first Darlington, first Alexandra Palace, and champion Agricultural Hall, 1877; first Wolverhampton, 1878. His measurements are—Nose to stop, 3¾ inches; stop to occiput, 5¼ inches; length from occiput to root of tail, 30¾ inches; girth of skull, 18 inches; girth of muzzle, 12¼ inches; girth of chest, 26¼ inches; girth of loins, 22 inches; girth of forearm, 6¾ inches; girth of pastern, 4 inches; hock to ground, 5 inches; height at shoulders, 18½ inches.

Nelson was born in the year 1866, and was bred by the well-known Joe Willock. He weighed under 16 lbs., and was by Stokes's Bill out of Willock's Julia. He won first Birmingham, 1868; champion prize Crystal Palace, 1871, 1872, 1873; first prize Manchester, 1870; first and cup Dublin, 1872; first Glasgow, 1873.

Before leaving this engaging breed of dog we wish once more to urge upon intending breeders the value of kindness towards their pets. Do not be frightened at him, don't knock him about, or ill-use him, and no dog will treat his master with greater love and respect than will the game, handsome, intelligent, and lovable Bull-terrier.

SCALE FOR JUDGING BULL-TERRIERS.

	Value.
Head	15
Body and chest	10
Feet and legs	8
Stern	2
Colour	10
General appearance	5
	—
	50

CHAPTER XIII.

BLACK-AND-TAN TERRIERS.

HAVING disposed of the Bull-terrier, which is, as we have said, admittedly the result of a cross between the Bull-dog and the English Terrier, we now come to the Terrier family pure and simple. Whatever the Terrier may have been in days gone by, and whatever opinion may have been entertained of his merits by our fathers, there can be no doubt that the number of his friends in the present day are legion. The varieties of modern Terriers are so numerous, and the size of the dogs so various, that a Terrier of some breed or other is seldom absent from a country house. Large or small, smooth-coated or rough, useful or ornamental, as the case may be, it would indeed be singular if the varieties of Terrier were not highly popular in this dog-loving country.

The Black-and-tan Terrier must be ranked as one of our oldest varieties, for we find mention of a dog resembling him in many particulars in the works of several earlier writers. It is only reasonable to suppose, however, from the specimens whose portraits we occasionally come across, that in days gone by less attention was paid to colour and markings than to their utility as companion and vermin dogs. The formation of head, too, was very different to what we find it in the present day, the skull being then much heavier-looking and shorter than modern breeders affect ; but it must be remembered that, shows not having been established, and many popular breeds of the present day not being in existence, all that was necessary to breed for was a light dog, suitable for killing vermin and following his owner in his rambles. One thing is certain, however, and that is, that in older Black-and-tans there was more of the tan present in the coat, and it was far lighter in colour than it is now. The fancy markings, too, such as pencilled toes, thumb-marks, and kissing-spots, to which reference will be made later on, were conspicuous by their absence.

As regards the original uses to which the Terrier was placed, the name is in itself a sufficient index. Even now-a-days there are very few that will not go to earth after a fashion : it seems to come natural to them. Dr. Caius, in his book on dogs before alluded to, includes the " Terrar " in his list of sporting dogs, for the obvious reason, apparently, that it came under the category of dogs which " rouse the beast." The following are the worthy Doctor's exact remarks on the breed " of the dog called a Terrar, in Latine, *Terrarius.*"

" Another sort there is that hunteth the fox and the badger only, whom we call Terrars, they (after the manner and custom of ferrets in searching for coneys) creep into the ground, and by that means make afraid, nip and bite the fox and the badger in such sort that either they tear them in pieces with their teeth being in the earth, or else hail and pull them perforce out of their lurking angles, dark dungeons, and close caves, or, at least, through conceived fear, drive them out of their hollow harbours, insomuch that they are compelled to prepare speedy flight, and being desirous of the next (albeit not the safest) refuge are otherwise taken and entrapped with snares and nets laid on holes to the same purpose. But these be the least in that kind called Sagax."

It would thus seem that a Terrier's work three hundred years ago was very much the same as it is now, this class of dog acting as a bolter when animals went to ground on being chased. It is very remarkable, however, that the attribute of pluck and endurance varies considerably in the different varieties of Terrier pure and simple, the rough-coated ones being generally decidedly gamer and hardier than their smooth-haired relations. Formerly there was but little regard paid to colour and markings, and the general outline of the dog was less graceful than it is in the present day. A fair idea of what the ancient Black-and-tan Terrier was like may be gathered from the accompanying spirited woodcut, where the dogs appear not only of a very indifferent colour but also far heavier and coarser as well as thicker in the head than would now be tolerated.

Though one of the most beautiful breeds, the Black-and-tan Terrier is, nevertheless, one of the most neglected at the present time. A reason for the lack of patronage bestowed upon him by the general public is hard to discover, for his many good qualities are so palpably in excess of any shortcomings which may be alleged against him, that it is a matter of surprise to numbers of his admirers that he should be neglected as he is by lovers of the dog. The fact of his being so exceedingly difficult a dog to breed up to show form may have deterred would-be exhibitors from attempting to gain celebrity as breeders under his auspices.

As a vermin dog the modern variety can only reach mediocrity, for though gifted with sufficient pluck and endurance to enable him to hold his own with most breeds at ratting, he ceases to be of any material service when badgers or foxes are introduced. We do not desire to claim any virtues for a breed which we believe do not fairly belong to it, and, therefore, greatly though we admire the Black-and-tan Terrier, and appreciate his good qualities, we candidly confess, from experience, that as a rule he is inferior in sustained courage to most breeds of Terrier. As a companion or house-dog he is unrivalled, for though invariably on the alert indoors, and always ready to give tongue on the approach of a stranger by day or night, his temper is such that he can be trusted to roam at large without the slightest fear of his attempting to injure man or beast.

Owners of Black-and-tan Terriers experience great difficulty in keeping their coats in good order and their skin free from scurf and dandriff. In highly-bred show specimens of the breed this liability to skin disease seems to be more fully marked, and condition is very often the cause of a good specimen going down in competition with dogs of inferior quality. We believe heat of blood, the result of want of exercise accompanied with over-feeding, is responsible for many such cases, and cannot do better than suggest periodical doses of the sulphur and magnesia powder which is referred to on page 20. If an outward dressing is desirable, we have invariably tried the following very simple remedy with complete success:—

> Two parts hogs' lard.
> One part pine tar.
> One part sulphur.

This mixture must be well stirred together, and then thoroughly rubbed into the dog's skin. It has the effect of bringing off a great deal of hair, so that the dog is unable to appear at a show for perhaps five or six weeks. Two or at the most three applications at an interval of four or five days, accompanied by the administration of the sulphur and magnesia internally, has never in our experience failed to produce a cure.

Amongst the few really successful breeders and judges of this variety the name of the late Mr. Samuel Handley of Pendleton, Manchester, will always stand conspicuously first. To this gentleman's judgment and perseverance we are undoubtedly indebted for most of the beautiful

OLD-FASHIONED ENGLISH TERRIERS.

specimens of the breed to be seen at every great show. His celebrated Saff was almost invincible in her day, and her blood runs in the veins of many present champions. It is probably due to the great prestige attached to Mr. Handley's kennel that the absurd sobriquet of "Manchester Terrier" has been applied to the breed, a compliment which he himself informed us, not long before his death in 1878, he thought a very doubtful one, as he considered the name of Black-and-tan quite honourable enough, while, as a matter of fact, Birmingham produced quite as many good specimens as were bred in Cottonopolis.

Mr. J. H. Murchison and the Rev. J. W. Mellor have shown some excellent specimens, as have Mr. Tom B. Swinburne of Darlington, the late Mr. J. Martin of Salford, and Mr. J. H. Mather of Oldham; but up to the summer of 1877, when he dispersed his kennel, Mr. Henry Lacy of Hebden Bridge, Yorkshire, was recognised as the head of the exhibitors in this variety. His Belcher, General, Ruby, Rara, and the toy Pepita, were each and all magnificent specimens, and were usually shown in that pink of condition which is so essential to success in the Black-and-tan. Mr. Howard Mapplebeck, of Knowle, near Birmingham, had also a good bitch in Queen III., picked up by him at a low figure at Edinburgh show, 1877. Mr. George Wilson, of Huddersfield, will always be remembered as a breeder, and so will the names of Ribchester, Stellfox, Tatham, Roocroft, and Clarke.

One objection to showing in the Black-and-tan classes is the manipulation to which some unprincipled exhibitors subject their dogs in the shape of dyeing and staining various portions of the body when the colouring is deficient. The places most usually operated on are immediately behind the ears, and on the back and the thighs, where the hair should be perfectly black, but where there frequently appear a number of tan hairs, which would militate against the dog's success. In the case of the back of the thighs, when a dog is "breeched," i.e., shows tan, the undesirable coloured and superfluous hair is sometimes removed by plucking, but this should be always easy to detect if proper vigilance is exercised by the would-be purchaser of the dog.

The points of the Black-and-tan Terrier are as follow:—

Head.—Long, flat, and narrow, level and wedge-shaped, with the cheek bones invisible, with tapering, tightly-lipped jaws, and level teeth.

Nose.—Black.

Eyes.—Very small, sparkling, and intensely black, the oblong shape preferable.

Ears.—Are invariably cropped for show purposes, and should, of course, stand perfectly upright. Purchasers should, however, when examining a dog, satisfy themselves that the upright carriage of the ears of the specimen before them has not been obtained by the application of gum, so as to enable a dog, which usually carries one ear faultily, to carry it correctly whilst being scrutinised by a possible buyer.

Neck.—Slight, and free from throatiness, gradually increasing in size as it nears the shoulders, which should be sloping, and display powers of speed.

Chest.—Narrow, but deep.

Body.—Short and rather ribbed up, with powerful loin.

Legs.—Must be quite straight, set on well under the dog, and of fair length.

Feet.—Long, with arched and black toes. Whilst upon this point, we may draw attention to the fact that one authority in his work describes them as round. This is a most decided error, and must have been an oversight, as there can be no two opinions on the subject.

Tail.—Long, thin, and carried straight out.

Colour.—Jet-black and deep red-tan, distributed over the body as follows:—On the head the muzzle is tanned to the nose, which, with the nasal bone, is jet-black. There is also a bright spot on each cheek and above each eye, the under jaw and throat are tanned, and the hair *inside* the ear is of the same colour. The fore-legs tanned up to the knee, with black lines (pencil-marks) up each toe, and a black mark (thumb-mark) above the foot. Inside the hind-legs, and under the tail also tanned, and so is the vent, but only sufficiently to be easily covered by the tail. In all cases the black should not run into the tan, or *vice versâ*, but the division between the two colours should be well defined, and a "warm" or deep tan is essential, a "clayey" (light tanned) coloured dog being useless for exhibition purposes. The smallest spot of white is an absolute disqualification, so particular notice must be taken to see that no dishonest staining has taken place. The chest is by far the most likely place for it to appear.

Weight.—From 7 to 20 lbs.

General Appearance is of no little importance in this variety, as the dog should present the appearance of speed and activity in preference to strength and endurance, which are qualities he does not affect to any extent.

Mr. Tom B. Swinburne, of Darlington, has kindly given us his views as follows :—" My ideas of points of Black-and-tans are, first, that too much has been allowed for long heads. That is, though I would like a good long head I would not let that sway other bad points, such as breeching, and badly carried and thick tails, but would insist on having real *Terrier* points, such as good shape, legs and feet, tail and body, which should stand on the legs, and not bowed at shoulders, whilst they should be of good colour, a point much overlooked, especially in the smaller sizes. As to breeding, of course I should go for good blood in the first place, and would not breed from very large speci-mens, and would try to avoid breeding from dogs badly breeched, the most difficult thing to attain, especially in getting good coloured ones, as a good rich-tanned dog, as a rule, carries a certain amount of breeching. Too much care cannot be taken in rearing, and puppies are better sent into the country to run, as no breed of dogs require so much attention to their coats, being so subject to mange, and I hold that a dog well reared, and whose blood is kept healthy in his puppydom, very seldom develops skin diseases afterwards."

The dog selected for illustration is Salford, late our own property, who was bred by Mr. Clark in 1876. He is by Barlow's Duke out of Clark's Whiskey by Tiny, by Ribchester's Colonel out of Stellfox's Madam ; Duke out of Duchess by Tatham's Neptune out of Roocroft's Duchess by Prince Charlie by Colonel. He has won first Alexandra Palace, 1877 ; first Wolverhampton, 1878 ; first and cup Belfast, 1879. His measurements are—Nose to stop, 2¾ inches ; stop to occiput, 4¼ inches ; length of back, 14 inches ; girth of muzzle, 7 inches ; girth of skull, 12½ inches ; girth of brisket, 20½ inches ; girth of shoulders, 19 inches ; girth at loins, 13 inches ; girth of forearm, 4½ inches ; girth of pastern, 3 inches ; height at shoulders, 16 inches ; height at elbows, 8 inches ; hock to ground, 4¼ inches ; weight, 19 lbs.

SCALE OF POINTS FOR BLACK-AND-TANS.

	Value.
Head (including jaws, nose, eyes, and ears)	10
Legs	5
Feet	5
Body	5
Colour and markings	15
General appearance (including Terrier quality)	10
	—
Total	50

ENGLISH TERRIERS.

CHAPTER XIV.

WHITE ENGLISH TERRIERS.

THE difference in appearance between the white English Terrier and the Black-and-tan is very slight, but the obstacles in the way of a breeder's success in the two breeds are very different. In the former variety colour and markings have to be studied to a great degree, whilst in the white English Terrier the correct shape and action of a Terrier are very hard to obtain. It is naturally easier to breed a pure white dog from white parents than it is to breed correctly-marked and well-tanned puppies from almost perfect black-and-tans. The latter, however, breed much nearer the correct Terrier shape than do white English Terriers, and this is on account of the Italian Greyhound taint which runs in so many strains. One authority expresses an opinion that all white English Terriers show traces of an admixture of Italian Greyhound blood, but we cannot allow this to be the case, having both owned and seen specimens which do not show any symptoms of the cross. So little encouragement is, however, shown to breeders in their efforts to improve the variety, that the classes which appear at our shows are naturally meagre; but we are of opinion that if better known this Terrier would quickly rival the Black-and-tan in the estimation of the public. The intense brilliancy of their jackets contrasts so beautifully with surrounding objects, and their temperaments are so vivacious and affectionate, that they deserve to be more fully known and appreciated; and this, we trust, will some day be the case.

Mr. White, of Clapham, first brought the breed into the qualified prominence it now enjoys, as he was a large winner in these classes at the earlier shows. His dogs, however, would not pass muster in the present day, as many leading Terrier points were conspicuous by their absence, the Italian Greyhound apparently having been largely drawn upon in their production. Midland-county breeders next turned their attention to the variety, and the late Mr. James Hinks, of Worcester Street, Birmingham, showed and disposed of many first-class specimens. The late Mr. James Martin, also of Salford, Manchester, was very successful with his Joe, Gem, and Pink, but we always objected to them, the former especially, on account of the Italian blood he showed. Mr. S. E. Shirley, M.P., the Rev. J. W. Mellor, and Mr. J. H. Murchison, also showed some good ones years ago, as did Mr. Skidmore, of Nantwich, and Mr. George Stables, of Manchester, the latter's Viper being a very first-rate specimen, though possessed of a most savage temper. The latter dog not only did himself credit on the show bench, but gained additional honour by begetting the famous bitch Sylph, who was in her time the undoubted champion of this breed, and gained her breeder, Mr. Roocroft, many first prizes.

It is to the enterprise and judgment of the latter that we are indebted for the improvement of the white English Terrier, and the name of James Roocroft, of Bolton, occupies a similar position in this breed to that of the late Mr. Samuel Handley in Black-and-tans. Mr. Roocroft writes as follows concerning his earlier recollections of the breed in his neighbourhood:—

"The first good one I remember appeared, I believe, at the first Belle Vue show, Manchester. She was a deaf bitch, but her origin I know nothing about. This was about sixteen years since. The following year brought out the champion Tim, then shown by old Bill Pearson, and which some time afterwards came into my possession, and from which dog I produced the strain that I have been so very successful with since I first brought them out. I consider Tim was not only the first champion specimen, but the best Terrier we ever had, and was really the foundation of good Terriers. As regards the points of Terriers I think that by the conversations we have had together I have told you all I know. I may say that among others Tim was sire to Swindell's Gem, out of a bitch he picked up in Manchester, and which showed in a marked manner a cross of the Snap-dog breed, and you remember all his strain showed the same, more or less. He (Tim) was, as I have remarked, the best Terrier I ever saw, and champion for years; in fact, up to the time of his death, which occurred about three years ago (1876)."

The breed being of so modern an origin, we can find little to add to its history that could interest our readers. We will therefore proceed to offer a few hints on the breeding of this variety, which have been picked up in conversation with various admirers of the breed. It being so universally acknowledged that many strains show traces of Italian Greyhound or Snap (rabbit-coursing dog) blood, every endeavour should be taken to eradicate the evil. Not only does the dog suffer as a Terrier in its appearance, but the peculiar action in the fore-feet, which Italian Greyhounds show so conspicuously, is very much against it. These specimens we should mate with as light (*i.e.*, lightly built) a Bull-terrier as we could procure, and having destroyed the dog puppies, reserve the bitches for subsequent re-crossing with the best white English stud dog we could procure. In attempting this process, it should be borne in mind that there is very small probability of a breeder obtaining his desire in the first cross, and more probably the third or fourth will get him what he wants. Considerable care must therefore be taken in the next cross; and though much must depend upon circumstances, we would suggest resorting to the services of a sire of the same strain as the father of the latter puppies. Any dogs saved from this litter may, of course, be used to bitches of remote blood, when there will usually be plenty of offspring left to found and perpetuate a strain of well-bred white English Terriers.

In appearance this dog should closely resemble the Black-and-tan, so a full description of its structural development is unnecessary. Its colour is an intensely brilliant white, and its eyes very black and sparkling—the oblique shape being preferred. Spots of red, tan, or brindle, frequently appear on puppies, sometimes weeks after they are born. These chiefly show behind the ears or on the neck, and are, of course, a disfigurement to a dog which should be pure white. These are occasionally cut out when the puppies are young, and a wide collar is often used, when this breed is shown, to conceal these blemishes. Many good specimens, too, are deaf, and though some judges profess not to object to this infirmity, we consider it very much against a dog's chance of success, as a deaf dog is a sorry companion either at home or abroad. It is believed that nearly all *purely* white animals are deaf, and if so the present variety is only redeemed from the infirmity by the nose, or a few scattered, and so invisible, hairs.

The dog we have selected for illustration is Mr. Alfred Benjamin's Silvio. He was first shown by his breeder, Mr. James Roocroft, at Bath in 1877. We were judge upon that occasion, and gave him first in one of the best classes we ever saw. Subsequently we purchased him from Mr. Roocroft, and afterwards re-sold him to Mr. Benjamin. He is certainly, if well shown, the best specimen we ever saw, but absence of condition has often caused him a defeat. He was born in 1876, and is by Joe out of Sylph by Viper, and has won first Bath, Agricultural Hall, Darlington, and Alexandra Palace, 1877; first Wolverhampton, 1878. His measurements are—Nose to stop, 3 inches; stop to occiput, 4½ inches; length of back, 15 inches; girth of muzzle, 7 inches; girth of skull, 12 inches; girth of brisket, 19 inches; girth round shoulders, 19½ inches; girth of loin, 16 inches; girth of forearm, 3¾ inches; girth of pastern, 3 inches; height at shoulders, 18 inches; height at loin, 18½; weight, 19 lbs.

SCALE FOR JUDGING WHITE ENGLISH TERRIERS.

	Value.
Head, including jaws, nose, ears, and eyes	10
Legs	5
Feet	5
Body	5
Colour	10
General appearance	10
Action	5
Total	50

CHAPTER XV.

THE DANDIE DINMONT.

THE celebrity which this excellent Terrier well maintains he owes to Sir Walter Scott; the unenviable notoriety he has had undeservedly to submit to he owes to some of his injudicious friends.

Had the fact been frankly accepted that whatever he may now be he had no existence before the present century—and, like most, if not all, of our recognised breeds of the present day, sprang from mongrelism, or the produce of two different breeds, as we now use that word—we should have heard less nonsense about the absolute purity of some specimens that have been so much written up. The fact is that not a single dog living can, without a break in his pedigree, be traced back to the dogs owned by Davidson, although we have no doubt—and, indeed, there is a strong chain of evidence in favour of the supposition—that several strains in particular, and we may say the majority of those shown now-a-days, inherit a large percentage of the blood of the original Charlieshope Terriers. Sir Walter Scott, in his inimitable delineations of Scottish character, sketched to the life the burly Liddesdale yeoman, under the *nom de guerre* of Dandie Dinmont; and the rough, uncouth, but warm-hearted and generous farmer and sportsman, with his game little Terrier, are now, and will be whilst the English language is read, familiar to all who appreciate the genius of Scott. When "Guy Mannering" was published, and read with such avidity by our fathers, Dandie Dinmont and his pepper-and-mustard Terriers became public favourites, a strong desire to possess one of the breed of dogs that had so suddenly been made famous was very general, and in consequence specimens were widely distributed. No doubt those sent out by Mr. Davidson himself (the original of Scott's Dandie Dinmont) were genuine; but as time wore on the demand increased, receiving an immense impetus from the establishment of dog shows some eighteen years ago, these having thus raised the popularity of dogs in general; and this demand has had to be supplied principally from the pastoral dales whence the breed first sprung, and where it had been kept up with more or less of purity, although with no pretensions, so far as we can find, of recorded pedigrees.

Indeed, it appears a reasonable supposition that, so long as a dog was known to have some of the blood of the original Tarr and Pepper, the sole progenitors of the breed, and accorded in form, character, and aptitude for their special work with the dogs of Davidson, which must have been personally known to many of them, our friends of sporting proclivities across the Border would not inquire too curiously into pedigree. Probably they were warned off in some cases by a dread, not without cause, that they might suffer, like the Barber of Seville, for their "impertinent curiosity," by finding that their dogs had a somewhat different paternity from what they would have desired.

We do not thus express ourselves in disparagement of a dog for whose genuine good qualities we entertain an enthusiastic admiration. But from a desire to look the facts of the case in the face, and, admitting most heartily not only that there is "something in blood," but that there is "a great deal in blood," we would, rather than strain a pedigree beyond its bearing power, take the opposite line, and like

> " The grand old gardener and his wife,
> Smile at the claims of long descent."

Quite a fallacious idea appears to us to be entertained by the quibblers for "absolute purity." An unstained lineage is unquestionably an important consideration for a breeder, without which he can with no degree of certainty calculate on the character of expected produce; but neither the judge in the ring, nor the sportsman in the field with the dog, has any concern with that. The former has to consider whether the dog shows the characteristics of the breed as settled by recognised authorities, however he may have become possessed of them; and if the latter finds his dog in outward form a Dandie, and one duly "entered wi' rattans, stoats, and weasels, tods, and brocks," and who never flinches, but will "face ony thing wi' a hairy skin on't," he will be quite satisfied, although the dog may have a bar sinister on his escutcheon. Or, again, to quote Scott, he may be a veritable "Mishdegoat," as Herr Douster-swivel would pronounce it.

As regards the dogs "Dandie Dinmont" originally possessed, the Rev. J. Cuming Macdona in 1869 was the fortunate discoverer of a document in James Davidson's own handwriting, which ran thus—

" 1800.—Tuggin, from A. Armstrong, reddish and wiry; Tarr, reddish and wire-haired, a bitch; Pepper, shaggy and light, from Dr. Brown, of Borjenwood. The race of Dandies are bred from the two last.—J. D."

This document must be interesting to all lovers of this game little dog, as supporting Mr. Macdona's views that Tarr and Pepper were the progenitors of all the Dandies now in existence.

From considerable acquaintance with Dandie Dinmont Terriers, we have no hesitation in pronouncing them "dead game." They are, essentially, vermin dogs, and no more useful small dog can be kept about a country house if there are rats to be killed, a fox or an otter to be bolted a stoat, weasel, or marten to be destroyed, a badger or brock to be drawn from his "hollow harbour," or a rabbit to be hunted from his fastness in the thickest of whin bramble or bracken brake. He is all there, ever ready, eager, and equal to the fray, untiring, and up to the roughest work, but apt to show a little strong-headedness and to run riot when game is near and scent is strong, unless exceptionally well broken. At home he proves a good house-dog, and his quaint-ness and high intelligence render him a most lovable companion; affectionate to a degree, he is not given to quarrel; but once roused, he shows himself possessed of the very essence and spirit of Polonius's advice, and "bears himself so that his adversary must beware," for he can both take and give punishment, and in common parlance will "fight till all's blue." It is a curious feature in his method of fighting that a Dandie generally fights on his back, and tears and scratches at his opponent's throat literally with tooth and nail.

Those of his admirers who call the Dandie good-looking must have singular ideas of beauty; but, as the old proverb avoweth, "handsome is that handsome does," and in good deeds he excels; and his very pronounced character, the weird "auld farran" look of quaintness and intelligence, amply make up for beauty, whilst his rough-and-ready-for-anything look at once commends him to the sportsman.

To Mr. E. Bradshaw Smith the lovers of Dandies are indebted, he having, in the year 1841, founded a kennel of dogs by buying all he could of reputedly pure-bred dogs, which he has since kept select.

As to the constituent elements of the dog, the view we agree with is, that the Dandie is a cross between a rough hound, such as the Otterhound or Welsh Beagle and the old wire-haired Scotch Terrier. To the former he owes his large hound-like head, long hanging ears—which no other Terrier, except his relation the Bedlington, has—and also the hound carriage of stern and immense leg bone, whilst the mixture of hard and soft hair may be said to be equally derived from the two original breeds.

Few breeds have been the subject of so prolonged and acrimonious a correspondence, and, possibly, with the exception of the Bull-dog controversy, no dispute has been productive of so much ill-feeling. The result in each instance was identical, and the Dandie Dinmont controversy ended as did that concerning his elder brother, in the formation of a Club which was to settle the correct standard for judging the breed, and guard its interests generally. The two societies, however, started under widely different auspices; for whereas the Bull-dog Club was coldly looked upon at its outset, and received positive discouragement in quarters from which valuable assistance might reasonably have been expected, the Dandie Club was well supported from its first appearance. It blossomed into existence in 1876, under the presidency of Lord Melgund, and the vice-presidency of Mr. E. Bradshaw Smith, strengthened by the allegiance of the best known breeders and exhibitors, and aided by the experience of Messrs. Hugh Dalziel, Wardlaw Reid, and William Strachan, in the capacities of joint hon. secretaries.

A communication was addressed by the Club to the leading breeders of the Dandie Dinmont, requesting them each to draw up a scale of points which they considered suitable for judging the breed; and from these the standard of the Club was eventually selected. As a copy of these opinions is now laying before us, we propose giving some extracts from it for the benefit of such of our readers as have not had an opportunity for seeing the original. In the first place we will give the opinions of Mr. James Locke, of Selkirk, *in extenso*, having obtained that gentleman's permission to do so. These will be doubly valuable, as representing the ideas not only of the most successful exhibitor of recent date, but also those of a most frequent and highly respected judge of the breed, whose decisions are invariably well received by exhibitors.

MR. JAMES LOCKE'S DESCRIPTION OF A DANDIE DINMONT.

Head.—Skull round. Jaw long, tapering slightly towards the nose (which is *not* cut short like a Pointer's), with very strong teeth, level in front; on no account pig-jawed or undershot. Eyes large, full, and very expressive; colour brown. Ears pendulous, almond-shaped, set on low, and hanging close to the head, slightly feathered and not too large.

Body.—Very long. Chest full and well let down between the fore legs; ribs round; no slackness at loin, and back slightly arched. Neck very muscular.

Fore legs.—Short and muscular, well out at shoulder, consequently slightly bowed, with feet straight to the front.

Hind legs.—Very muscular and well spread.

Feet.—Not hare-footed; claws dark.

Stern.—Not set on too low, curving slightly upwards and never carried over the back, except in great excitement.

Coat.—This is of great importance. The hair on body must be hard and wiry, and plenty of it, with no tendency to curl ; on the head soft and silky, slightly curly, and very light in colour, being almost white. Jaw not too heavily.coated. Fore legs feathered with hair softer, shorter, and lighter in colour than that on the body. Hind legs no feather. Feet comparatively clean, but this depends much on exercise. Hair on stern of same texture as that on body—not bushy, but feathered, and thinning away towards the tip.

Colour.—Blue, mustard, or any combination of both. White is an objection, and is only allowed on the breast, and then to a very slight extent.

Height.—From nine to eleven inches, according to weight.

Weight.—From sixteen to twenty-two pounds ; from eighteen to twenty being the most desirable for work.

SCALE OF POINTS.

								Value.	
Head	...	...	...	...	...	...	...	10	
Ears	...	...	...	...	...	...	...	10	
Eyes	...	...	...	...	...	...	...	10	
								—	30
Body	...	...	...	...	...	...	...	15	
Legs and feet	...	...	...	...	...	...	...	10	
Coat	...	...	...	...	...	...	...	20	
Carriage of stern	...	...	...	...	...	...	...	10	
								—	55
General	...	...	...	...	...	...	...	15	
								—	
								100	

The above excellent description of the points of a Dandie Dinmont was followed pretty closely by the secretaries of the Club in the scale they submitted to the Society as the correct one for judging the breed by. The salient features of this were ultimately adopted by the Club as its standard ; and we propose giving it hereafter as the scale for universal adoption, as it differs but very slightly from the Club standard, and is in our opinion considerably more explicit and easy of comprehension.

The point in Mr. Locke's description which is most combated by other breeders is the expression "*not* cut short like a Pointer's" as applied to the muzzle. But as all the best opinions we have been able to collect (including that of Mr. Locke, as given above) agree that the jaws should *slightly* taper towards the nose, there does not appear to be much importance attached to the simile, which must be regarded as an unhappy one from either point of view.

Before giving the scale of points drawn up by Messrs. Dalziel, Reid, and Strachan, attention should be drawn to the most celebrated breeders and exhibitors of this excellent little dog. The list includes the names of Messrs. Taprell Hollands ; Rev. S. T. Mosse ; Paul Scott, of Jedburgh ; James Paterson, of Rutherford by Kelso ; Rev. J. C. Macdona ; Nicol Milne, of Faldonside by Selkirk ; Bradshaw Smith, Blackwood House, Ecclefechan ; James Richardson, of Dumfries ; P. S. Lang, Selkirk ; George Parker, Denholm, Roxburghshire ; William Pool, Dumfries ; W. Wardlaw Reid ; J. C. and W. Carrick, Carlisle ; J. H. Murchison and James Locke, Selkirk, immortalised by their connection with Peachem, Shamrock, Warlock II., Harry Bertram, Meg, Kilt, Melrose, Doctor, Sporran, Tib Mumps.

The standard drawn up by Messrs. Hugh Dalziel, W. Wardlaw Reid, and W. Strachan, to which we have alluded above, as the best description of a Dandie published, is as follows :—

"In forming an opinion of a dog's merits, the general appearance (by which is meant the impression which a dog makes as a whole on the eye of the judge) should be first considered. Secondly should be noticed the dog's size, shape, and make—*i.e.*, its proportions in the relation they bear to each other; no point should be so much in excess of the others as to destroy the general symmetry, and cause the dog to appear deformed, or interfere with its usefulness in the occupations for which it is specially adapted. Thirdly, the dog's style, carriage, gait, temperament, and each of its other points, should be considered separately.

"POINT 1.—*General Appearance.*—The general appearance of the Dandie Dinmont Terrier is that of a rough-coated, thick-set dog, very low on its legs, and having a body very flexible and long in proportion to its height, but broad, deep-chested, and compact. The head very large, with broad and well-domed skull, covered with light-coloured hair of a softer and more silky texture than that on the body. This hairy scalp very often gives the head an appearance of being disproportionate to the body, while such is not actually the case. Jaws long and slightly tapering to the nose, which must be large and always black; covered with shorter and slightly harder hair than on the body. Neck thick and muscular; shoulders low, and back slightly curved down behind them, with a corresponding arch of the loins, which are broad and strong. Ears pendulous, and bearing low. Legs short and very muscular. The Dandie carries in his countenance the appearance of great determination, strength, and activity, with a constant and vigilant eagerness to be busy. In brief, he is an embodiment of docility, courage, strength, intelligence, and alertness.

"POINT 2.—*The Head* should be very large, and rather heavy-looking in proportion to the dog's size. Skull broad between the ears, with a very gradual and slight taper towards the eyes. It should be long from back to front, with high forehead, and cranium conical and well domed, measuring about the same from the point of the eye to back of skull as it does between the base of ears, and round the largest part about a third more than the dog's height at the shoulder. The head should always be covered with soft silky hair, not curled, but slightly wavy, and not confined to a mere top-knot; it is also of a much lighter colour than that on the body. The cheeks, starting from the ears, proportionately broad with the skull, should, without any unsightly bulge, taper very gradually towards the muzzle, the muscles showing extraordinary development, more especially those that move the lower jaw. The head of the bitch, as in nearly every other breed of dogs, is comparatively smaller and lighter in proportion to that of the dog.

"POINT 3.—*The Muzzle* should be long, deep, and very powerful; very slightly tapering to the nose, which should be large, well-formed, well-spread over the muzzle, and always black. The muzzle should measure from the corner of the eye to the tip of the nose about three inches in length, or in proportion to length of skull as three is to five, and round, close in front of the eyes, about two and a half to three times its length. The muzzle should be thinly covered with short and hardish hair of rather darker colour than on the body; the top of muzzle should be nearly bare for about an inch from the black part of the nose, coming to a point towards the eye. A foxy or snipy muzzle is very objectionable. The jaws should be long and powerful, with very strong teeth perfectly level in front, the canines should fit well into each other, so as to give the greatest available holding and punishing power. A pig-jawed or under-shot mouth is very objectionable, though, as it occurs in the purest strains, it cannot be altogether considered a disqualification. The mouth should be very large, and the roof of it very dark, almost always black.

"POINT 4.—*The Eyes* should be wide apart, large, round, moderately full, very clear, bright,

BEDLINGTON TERRIER.   DANDIE DINMONT TERRIER.

and expressive of great intelligence, looking set, low, and well in front of forehead. Colour, a rich brown or hazel, yellowness being a great fault. Frequently they have a dark ring round the eye, the hair of which is rather short and of a downy nature. This dark shade, together with that (already referred to) down the centre of the nose, contrasts beautifully with the bright silvery top-knot, and imparts to them that gipsy, game, and genuine appearance which is an essential characteristic in the Dandie.

"POINT 5.—*The Ears* should be large and pendulous, from three and a half inches to four inches long, set far apart, well back, and rather low on the skull, hanging close to the cheeks like a Hound's or Beagle's, but a little more pointed or almond-shaped, *i.e.*, broad at the base, and tapering to a small rounded point. The taper should be all, or nearly all, on the back edge, the front edge hanging nearly straight down from its junction with the head to the tip. They ought to show a little shoulder at the base, which causes the tips of the ears to point a little forwards towards the jaw. They should be moderately thick and leathery, and covered with a short, soft, darker and brighter sort of hair than on the body, having a smooth velvety appearance showing no lint or silky hair, excepting in some cases a thin feather of lighter hair starting about an inch or so from the tip, and of the same colour and texture as the top-knot; this gives the top of the ear the appearance of a distinct point.

"POINT 6.—*The Neck* should be rather short, and very muscular, well-developed and strong, showing great power by being well set into the shoulder. The length of neck should average about one-third of its girth.

"POINT 7.—*The Body* should be very long and flexible, measuring from top of shoulders to root of tail about an inch or two over one and a half times the height of dog at shoulder. Chest well developed and broad, with brisket round and deep, being well let down between the fore legs. The back should be rather low at the shoulders, and slightly curved down behind them, with a corresponding arch, the rise commencing about two inches behind the shoulder-blade; over the loins, which should be higher than the shoulders, broad and strong, with a slight gradual droop from the top of loins to root of tail. Ribs well sprung and rounded, back and front, forming a good barrel. Both sides of spine should be well supplied with muscle; in fact, every part of the dog seems to be abundantly supplied with muscle, giving it great compactness.

"POINT 8.—*The Tail* (or stern) should be in length a little less than the height of the dog at the shoulder. It should be set on at the bottom of a gentle slope about two inches from top of loins, being rather thick at the root, getting very slightly thicker for about four inches, then tapering off to a fine point. It should be covered on the upper side with wiry hair, of darker colour and stronger nature than that on the body, while the under side is lighter and less wiry, with a little, nice, light feather, commencing about two inches from root, and from one inch to two inches long, getting shorter as it nears the tip, which is pointed. It should be carried gaily, or hound-like, slightly curved upward, but not directly curled over the back. N.B.—When not excited, nearly in a horizontal line, but otherwise hound-like.

"POINT 9.—*The Legs.* The fore legs should be very short in proportion to the dog's size, very stout, and set wide apart, thick, and straight, with immense muscular development in the forearm; this, with the ankles being very slightly turned inwards, makes the dog appear somewhat bandy-legged, but the leg-bones themselves should be stout and straight, and not curved. The feet should be well framed and broad, but not flat, standing firm, and well under the chest, with very little or no feather on the legs. Hind legs thick and strong, longer than the fore legs, well-spread, with a good bend in the hocks, the muscles of the thighs being very thick and well-developed; the feet are much smaller, with no feather or dew-claws. The toes rather short, not hare-footed. The claws black, and very strong. White claws, however, should not be a disqualification.

"POINT 10.—*Size.* Height from eight inches to twelve inches at top of shoulder, but never above twelve inches, even for a dog. Weight: Dogs, from 16 lb. to 24 lb.; bitches, from 14 lb. to 20 lb. The most desirable weight, 20 lb. for dogs and 16 lb. for bitches; but 24 lb. dogs are very useful to give bone, muscle, and stamina to the product of the smaller ones.

"POINT 11.—*The Coat.* This is a very important feature. The hair (about two inches long) along the top of the neck and upper part of body should be a mixture of about two-thirds rather hard (but not wiry), with one-third soft, linty (not silky) hair, which gives a sort of crisp feeling to the hand, and constitutes what old John Stoddart used to term 'a pily coat.' It becomes lighter in colour and finer in texture as it nears the lower part of the body and legs. The head is covered with hair of a longer, lighter, and much more silky texture, giving it a silvery appearance, but not so long as to hang completely over the eyes like a Skye or Poodle. The lighter in colour and softer the better.

"POINT 12.—*The Colour.* Either mustard or pepper, and their mixtures. Mustard is a reddish or sandy brown of various shades. Pepper is a bluish grey, either dark in shade, ranging from a dark bluish black to a slaty grey, or even a much paler or silvery grey; sometimes a combination of both, in which case the back is grey, while the legs, inside of ears, chest, and under side of tail, are mustard, verging on a pale red or fawn colour. No other colours admitted; and any white, even on chest, is objectionable.

"VALUE OF THE POINTS ACCORDING TO THE DALZIEL, REID, AND STRACHAN SCALE.

1.—General appearance	10
2.—Head	10
3.—Muzzle, jaws, and teeth	10
4.—Eyes	10
5.—Ears	5
6.—Neck and chest	5
7.—Body	15
8.—Tail	5
9.—Legs and feet	10
10.—Size and weight	5
11.—Coat	10
12.—Colour	5
Total	100 "

Doctor, the subject of our coloured plate, is the property of Mr. James Locke, of Selkirk, N.B. He has taken the first prize at Wolverhampton; first, Crystal Palace; first, Nottingham; first, Alexandra Palace, 1875; first, Darlington; first and cup, Birmingham, 1876; first, Manchester, 1877; first, Crystal Palace; first, Glasgow, 1878. His measurements are—Tip of nose to stop, 3¼ inches; stop to occiput, 5 inches; length of back, 17 inches; girth of muzzle, 8 inches; girth of skull, 14 inches; girth of brisket, 21½ inches; girth round shoulders, 20 inches; girth of loins, 16½ inches; girth of forearm, 5¾ inches; girth of pastern, 3½ inches; height at shoulders, 10¾ inches; height at elbow, 6¼ inches; height at loins, 12 inches; length of tail, 10 inches; weight, 21 lbs.

CHAPTER XVI.

THE IRISH TERRIER.

THE Irish Terrier is a marvellous instance of the improvement which the steady and combined perseverance of breeders can bring about in a variety of dog in the space of a few years. A decade ago the breed was practically unknown, and now the Irish Terrier class is one of the interesting features of our greatest shows. Like other breeds, it had to be known to be appreciated at its proper value; and like other breeds, when it once gained a fair footing amongst "doggy" men, supporters sprung up on all sides. With the Irish Terrier it is essentially the fact that "handsome is as handsome does," for though valuing the breed for the position it has gained as a vermin dog, we are fain to admit that in personal attractions it is not equal to many other varieties. A good, game, hard dog, his workmanlike jacket and somewhat plain outline are in themselves likely to escape the observation of any but an ardent dog-lover; but there is a spirit within the dog which, when discovered, must make him friends wherever he goes. The improvement to which allusion has been already made is mainly due to the energy and perseverance of a very few gentlemen; and as most of the future prize dogs of this breed may reasonably be expected to spring from the best-known winners which have been recently exhibited, we propose, before going into the characteristics and description of the breed, to give a brief summary of the best dogs up to the present time, and the several positions they have occupied in the leading prize-lists.

At Belfast in June, 1875, an Irish Terrier Club was for the first time spoken of, but nothing came of it. Before this time a discussion upon the points of the breed had been going on in the *Live Stock Journal*, and in July, 1875, an illustration was given of two of Dr. Mark's dogs. The illustration, however, does not represent the modern type of Irish Terriers at all; they look like Scotch Terriers with a few drops of Irish blood in them. They have long hair all over the head and neck, and it actually parts down the centre; what could be more Scotch? The picture is worth preserving as showing what the head of an Irish Terrier should not be. A correspondent, writing at the time, described this picture in the following words:—"The very look of them is enough to convince any fair-thinking man that Scotch blood is in their composition. We will take, for instance, the dog at the left-hand side, which I find is the splendid game bitch Kate. Look at the head and face of this dog; if Scotch blood is not stamped on it then I know nothing. Look at the long hair on the forehead, with the vein or equal division in the centre. Look again at the long hair on the muzzle and under the jaw, and if, as I say, this does not denote the Scotch cross, and a good deal of it, then I know nothing about the points which constitute an Irish Terrier. The surest sign of Scotch blood in a rough Terrier is the length of hair on forehead. Another thing which goes to prove the Scotch cross is the vein or furrow running up the centre of the forehead. This is not to be met with in Irish Terriers."

At Belfast, in July, 1875, appeared the best lot of Irish Terriers brought together up to that date. Mr. D. O'Connell was represented with Slasher, a capital stamp of a hard, wiry-coated, working Terrier, said to be a pure old white Irish Terrier, a splendid field and water dog. Newtownards, September, 1875, saw Mr. Morton's Fly to the fore, with Sport (under his new name, Celt) second. In the *Live Stock Journal*, August 20th, 1875, had already appeared an engraving, which is reproduced in this work, of Sport, then the property of Mr. George Jamison. This portrait was hailed with delight on all sides as representing the genuine true-bred Irish Terrier; and so it does. It may be remarked that this dog was shown often, only again and again to be beaten by curs that had no right to be

DR. MARK'S KATE AND BADGER.

in the same show with him; in fact, wherever Sport was shown in a dog class, until 1878, when Sporter appeared in the field, there was no dog he should have been put second to; and Mr. Jamison must be congratulated on his pluck in sticking so well to his colours in spite of constant disappointments. At Lisburn, in 1876, Sport was second to the late Banshee (who died a champion after a singularly lucky and successful show career, and also the property of Mr. George Jamison at that time). Banshee was then only a youngster of thirteen months, and not only gained the first prize but cup as well.

At Dublin, in March, 1876, took place the show over which such a commotion was after-wards raised. The variety was more than charming, it was ridiculous; reports say there was no attempt at type in particular, no style; long legs, short legs, hard coats, soft coats, thick short skulls, and long lean ones; all were there. "Long, low, and useful dogs" were held up for admiration. Long and useful, if you like, but never *low* for an Irish

Terrier. No pride nor genuine interest was yet taken in the dog (we, of course, except one or two veteran breeders who still pluckily continued), nobody yet bothered themselves about age, breeder, or pedigree. Boxer, the first prize dog, was entered "breeder, owner, pedigree unknown." That is too deliciously Irish, his own breeder not knowing his pedigree. Another exhibitor entered his as "Shaughraun, breeder one of the famous Limerick night

MR. JAMISON'S SPORT.

watch. Pedigree too long to give, but inquisitive people can inquire at the watch-house here, and most likely they will be told." We quote this to prove the nature of many earlier pedigrees.

To come to later days, when many of the best dogs of the present time, such as Sporter, Moya Doolan, Dr. Carey's Sport, and Colleen Dhas, were well before the public, we find at Belfast, in June, 1878, Mr. Despard's Tanner (afterwards 1st Birmingham) took 1st, 2nd going to old Sport, and 3rd to W. Graham's Sporter. In bitches Kate was 1st, and Moya Doolan 2nd. In September, 1878, at Newtownards, the opinions of experts are encouraging. "It is a pleasure to look along the benches at recent shows. The eye has not the same chance it had in former years of being offended, the majority of the weeds having disappeared." Mr. Graham won, with Sporter, the champion cup for the best dog or bitch exhibited. In open dogs Parnell and Tanner II. were 1st and 2nd, both since dead. In the bitches Moya Doolan beat Colleen Dhas. At Birmingham, in December, 1878, Tanner was 1st and Fly 2nd. Fly had no right to her place; and it was characteristic of the judging that Spuds was quite passed over. In December, 1878, at the Alexandra Palace, Fly (the 2nd prize winner at Birmingham) was 1st, and Spuds 2nd, Paddy II. commended, and Moya Doolan not noticed. The pent-up feelings of the Irish Terrier breeders now burst forth, and first took shape in a petition, which was to be presented to the Kennel Club, praying them in future to appoint them special judges, or, failing that, to let the same gentlemen that had wire-haired Fox-terriers also judge Irish Terriers. This latter was a good proposition, which we herewith recommend to the attention of dog-show committees; they will then get judged by a *terrier* man, and that will be a move towards satisfactory decisions. However, seeing the support which the petition promised to receive, the question was raised, Why not establish a Club at once? In a week or two the club numbered fifty, nearly half of which were Englishmen. Even so soon Irish Terrier Club was one of the greatest successes in dog clubs on record, and since that time the number and interest in it have gone on increasing. At the Irish Kennel Club Show, Dublin, in April, 1879, Spuds and Moya Doolan were 1st and 2nd in champion class; Tanner II. and Paddy II. were 1st and 2nd in open dogs; and Sting, still a puppy, made her first appearance, and won in open bitches, beating Rags and Kathleen. Gaelic was very highly commended, this being his first appearance. At the Alexandra Palace, in July, 1879, Gaelic was put over Sporter and Erin, and a new bitch over Moya Doolan.

Thus far we have endeavoured to trace the history of the Irish Terrier proper during the last few years, and now we venture to lay before our readers the experience of, and opinions on, the breed of Mr. George R. Krehl, the enthusiastic English Vice-president of the Irish Terrier Club. This gentleman, who at great personal trouble has in the kindest possible way collected for us the extracts and opinions of the most trustworthy authorities, and interwoven them with his own, writes as follows:—

"The Irish Terrier is a true and distinct breed indigenous to Ireland, and no man can trace its origin, which is lost in antiquity. Mr. Ridgway, of Waterford, whose name is familiar in Irish Terrier circles from having drawn up the first code of points, states that they have been known in Ireland 'as long as that country has been an island, and I ground my faith in their age and purity on the fact that there exist *old manuscripts in Irish* mentioning the existence of the breed at a very remote period.' In old pictures representing scenes of Irish life, an Irish Terrier or two are often to be descried. Ballymena and County Wicklow may almost claim to be the birthplaces of the breed. Most of the best specimens hail from Ballymena and the neighbourhood, where Mr. Thomas Erwin, of Irish Setter fame, boasts an extensive experience of this breed, and has always kept a few of the right old working sort for sporting purposes; and 'in County Wicklow,' Mr. Merry says, 'it is well known that the pure breed of Irish Terriers have been carefully kept distinct and highly prized for more than a century.' Mr. E. F. Despard, whose name is well known in Irish Terrier circles as a very successful breeder and exhibitor, claims an acquaintance of over 40 years with the breed. Mr. George Jamison, too, has known and kept them many years, and up till a little while ago had won more prizes than all the rest of the Breeders put together. I mention these proofs of the age of the breed to show those who have lately come to admire them that it is not a made up, composite, or mushroom breed. They are part of Ireland's national economy, and are worthily embodied in the Sportsman's toast—'Irish women, Irish horses, and Irish dogs' (which means, Irish *terriers*, setters, and spaniels).

"One's first acquaintance with this 'Pre-historic Terrier' is apt to be disappointing (except to a really 'doggy' *terrier* man), that is, because there is no meretricious flash about them; but there is that about them which you learn to like, they grow upon you. They supply the want so often expressed for 'a smart-looking dog with something in him.' There is that about their rough-and-ready appearance which can only be described as genuine terrier, or more emphatically '*tarrier-character*.' They are *facile princeps* the sportsman's terrier, and having never yet been made fashion's darlings still retain in all its purity their instinctive love of hard work. Their characters do not suit them for ladies' pets, but render them the best dogs out for the man that loves his gun and quiet sport.

"Amongst those wise old fellows that one comes across in the country, who like a dog with something in him and a 'terrier' of course, the Irishman is prime favourite. And they know what they are about, those old fellows, and are sportsmen, too, in their own sort of way, when the sun has gone down. This reminds me of a discreditable fact in the history of Irish Terriers, that were not always only 'the poor man's sentinel,' but oftentimes something more, when by the aid of their marvellous noses and long legs they, when the shades of night had fallen, provided the pot with that which gave forth the savoury smell and imparted a flavour to the 'spuds.' This, however, if it injured their moral principles, certainly sustained their love and capability for rabbiting. In olden times, too, the larger sizes were bred and used for fighting, and there is still a dash of the old fighting blood in their descendants. They dearly love a mill, and though it would be calumny to say they are quarrelsome, yet it must be admitted that the male portion of the breed are perhaps a little too ready to resent any attempt at interfering with their coats; but are they not *Irish*, and when did an Irishman shirk a shindy? My dog Sporter is very true to character in this respect. Small dogs, or even those of his own size, he never deigns to notice; but if some large specimen of the genus *canis* approaches him, putting on 'side' and airs, Sporter immediately stiffens up visibly, his tail assumes a defiant angle above the horizontal, his ears are cocked forward alertly, and there is an ominous twitching of his upper lips which says as plain as looks can speak, 'Lave me alone, ye spalpeen.' Should his warning not be accepted, a scrimmage ensues, which I speedily terminate by whipping him up under my arm by his tail and marching him off. *En passant*, I recommend this as a very effectual and safe manner of putting a stop to a canine *mêlée*. 'Hitting off' Irish Terriers when fighting I have found useless; they think the pain comes from their opponent, and this only serves to rouse them to fresh efforts.

Now although they have always been Ireland's national terrier, yet it must be admitted, and it is only too patent, that for many years the breed had been much neglected; allowed to 'grow wild,' in fact, and left too much in the hands of one class. I cast no reflection on 'the foinest pisintry in Europe' when I say that, knowing nothing of dog-shows, they bred to no standard and kept their dogs for work; and if they thought a cross with neighbour Micky's dog would improve their own in that quality they did not stop to inquire about pedigree. In this manner the breed depreciated, and Scotch and other blood crept in to the injury of the pure breed; but, fortunately, when the tide in their favour set in the genuine breeder found plenty of pure, unadulterated material to commence upon.

"I cannot with accuracy give the date when Irish Terriers first made their advent upon the show-bench. I believe it was some time about 1870. At Dublin, in 1873, Mr. J. O'Connor's bitch Daisy won one of the first prizes given for the breed. Speaking of the breed at Newtownards Show, in 1874, where a class was given for 'Irish Rough Terriers,' the reporter says: 'We were much struck with the Irish Rough Terriers, a "varmint" looking lot of beggars, which well deserve a corner at any of our shows. They quite repaid our visit, by the way, and "widened" our experience of the genus terrier. A Dubliner present said "he'd loike to see ere a dog that 'ud bate thim." The pick was acknowledged to be Mr. Morton's "Fly," the first prize bitch. She is a compactly-built, hard-haired, yellow terrier, about 18 lbs., with a face speaking kindliness, wisdom, and pluck.' The 'Fly' here spoken of had a very successful show career, and was the first one of the breed that earned the title 'Champion.' She was also a remarkably game bitch, and I will allude to her later when I discuss the qualities of the breed. At Dublin, in October, 1874, it is said there were a few good ones in the class. At Lisburn, in May, 1875, the dog Stinger, about which there has been so much discussion, won. It is beyond a doubt that Stinger was not of the present recognised type, he was long-backed and short-legged; a dark blue grizzle-coloured back, tan legs, and white turned-out feet; in fact, full of Scotch blood. His head and the texture of his coat were his only redeeming points. There were a better sort in the class than Stinger, and if, as I believe, Old Sport was there, he unhesitatingly should have won.

"The Irish Terrier is a very intelligent dog and most lively and amusing companion. He is equally suitable for town and country. He is a mine of fun for a country ramble, putting up everything he comes across; and there is no better terrier than a well-broken Irish for a quiet ramble round the fields with your gun. Mr. Despard aptly describes him as 'the poor man's sentinel, the farmer's friend, and generally the gentleman's favourite,' they are such merry, rough-and-ready looking fellows, and the dash of the 'devil' they all carry in their bearing makes them very attractive to terrier lovers.

"Mr. Erwin says, 'There are some strains of them that will hunt stubble, or, indeed, any kind of field or marsh, quartering their ground like a Setter or Pointer, and, moreover, standing on their game in their own style. When a lad I had a dog of this breed, over which I have shot as many as nine couple of snipe, and have been home in good time for school at ten o'clock A.M. There was little time for missing on the part of either of us, and the dog did not make a single mistake. The colour I like best is a yellowish-red.'

"Irish Terriers are not quarrelsome, but can and will take their own part if set upon, the size of the aggressor no object. Ballymena having sent more Terriers to the show-bench than any other locality that I know of, and this breed of dog having been a favourite here since I remember dogs, I have had a good opportunity of studying them, and think more highly of them the longer I know them. Their great merit lies in the following qualities :—

"*Pluck.*—Irish Terriers are remarkably good-tempered, and can be implicitly relied upon with children; they have this peculiarity, that they often appear shy and timid, but their true nature soon flashes out on occasion. Some of the pluckiest I have owned have had this peculiarity of appearing often timid, such as the late Tanner, Sporter, Banshee, Belle, &c. It is almost superfluous to speak of Irish Terriers' pluck; they are the Bull-terriers of the sister isle, fear is unknown to them; they are not only plucky as a breed, but individually. It is their fear-nothing natures that make them so suitable for use against the larger vermin. There are too many instances of their pluck on record to enumerate

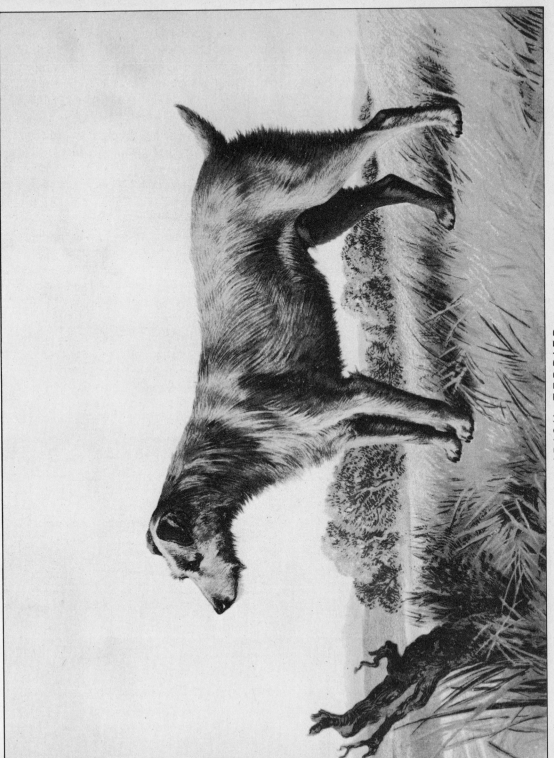

IRISH TERRIER.

them. Mr. W. Graham, writing in the *Live Stock Journal*, says: 'In disposition the Irish Terrier is very tractable, steady at work, and easily kept under command, compared with other breeds possessing the same amount of courage; I am sorry to say they are kept by some parties for fighting purposes. I once went to purchase pups, when the owner insisted upon me seeing the dam, a champion bitch (the Fly already spoken of), draw the badger before taking away my purchase; and I know a prize dog lately killed a badger before his hold could be removed. Again, I know a bitch puppy under nine months that killed the first cat she ever saw, and in a very short time.' Mr. Galloway writes: 'My Irish Terrier bitch (Eily O'Connor, by Sporter) jumped into the river Logan to retrieve in the month of January last, at which time the river was half frozen over, when my Retriever refused point-blank to go, although he saw the duck drop, and the said Retriever boasts of England's best blood by sire and dam.'

"*Rabbiting.*—Looking at them as workmen, rabbiting must first be mentioned. This is their special function, and there are few things I can imagine so enjoyable as a day's ferreting with a couple of Irish Terriers. Rely upon it, their quick noses never make a mistake; they never pass a burrow where a bunny lies, nor do they stop a second at an empty one; and once the ferret in, bolt the rabbit ever so rapidly, he'll not escape the attention of the wild Irishman waiting outside for him. It is marvellous the pace these dogs go; their action represents the level sweep of a thorough-bred, and their powerful hind legs propel them forward at an enormous rate. It is only when one sees them at full speed that one can understand the necessity for insisting upon their peculiar build. Hunting in the furze, they fear nothing, but boldly push in through brambles, pricks, &c., that would make a thin-skinned dog yell out with pain. At this work they are superior to the conventional Spaniel, who works too slowly and carefully, and his long, thick coat holds him often enough; but the short, hard jacket of the red Paddies is no impediment, and they work about with a dash and fervour enjoyable to witness. Again, see them working hedgerows; how assiduously and well! You would never want to use another breed.

"*Stamina.*—They will bear any amount of hard work and rough usage; constitution appears to never trouble them, they can give most breeds points for stamina. Mr. Graham says: 'As I work all my Terriers with ferrets, and require a good game dog, also a constitutionally strong one to work in winter for a whole day, and probably sit for hours in frost and cold should the ferrets lodge, I find no breed suits me nearly so well as Irish Terriers. They are more hardy, require less care, and are more free from disease than any other Terrier with which I am acquainted.'

"*Badger.*—At badger the Irish Terrier is not to be touched. No punishment frights them off, they will hold on till death.

"*Foxes.*—With regard to foxes, a well-known breeder writes: 'I have experience of five packs of Fox-hounds, and not one Terrier of any breed is kept in either kennel. When the varmint is earthed, some persons detach themselves from the crowd, and run to the nearest house where lives an Irish Terrier. They need not be trained nor specially bred; they will do the work if Irish Terriers proper, without tuition. In the winter of 1874, in the county Louth, I was at the killing of five foxes. From the meet, at 9 A.M., until 3 P.M. there were three of them earthed, and these were unearthed by two different Irish Terriers, one 10 lbs. and the other 27 lbs. weight. The pack was owned by Viscount Massareene and Ferrard." I prefer to give these quotations, as they contain facts and not general remarks.

"*Otters.*—Here the Irish Terrier is in his element, and all his qualities are brought into play—love of the water, nose, pluck, and stamina.   I quote an authority on this subject, Mr. Robert Dunscombe of Mount Desert, who says : 'I have had the pleasure of hunting two different packs of Otter-hounds, the former belonging to Mr. Johnson of Hermitage, and the latter to the Earl of Bandon of Castle Bernard, with both of which packs *pure-bred* Irish Terriers were used.   I owned one, called Dandy, who would go to ground, challenge and bolt the largest otter out of any sewer, no matter how long or how wet.   He, poor fellow, was poisoned by accident.   This dog ran with Mr. Johnson's hounds, which were sold some years since. My present Terrier "Jessie," a pure Irish-bred one, of a light yellow colour, was given to me by a poor countryman, and her equal I never saw anywhere.   She has bolted otters innumerable, and has always shown extraordinary gameness. I may mention as a proof of her pluck that during a capital hunt with Lord Bandon's hounds some weeks since, while the otter was being pressed from place to place by the hounds, Jessie, winding him under a bush, dived under water and laid hold of him ; after a severe struggle she came to the surface half drowned, being badly bitten across the loins.   The otter when killed weighed 20 lbs.'

"*Water.*—I had Sporter and Moya Doolan hunting the creeks in the marsh-land in Essex for water-rats ; and it was a pretty sight to see them, one each side, working the banks, uttering no sound, only showing their excitement by their agitated sterns.   As the rats dropped into the water, the dogs dived in after them.   The Irish Terrier is as fond of the water and takes it as readily as a Newfoundland, and one enthusiastic owner claims a forty-five minutes' swim for a dog of this breed belonging to him.

"*Rats.*—Irish Terriers deserve no praise for their ratting qualities ; it is pure instinct with them, they cannot help it, they rat as naturally as a bird flies.   My Banshee II. killed her first rat with her milk teeth when she was only 12 weeks old.   The following extract of a letter from Mr. Ridgway speaks for their ratting capabilities and intelligence : 'An incident which I think speaks volumes for the sagacity and wisdom of the old Irish Terrier breed, was written to me lately by a gentleman residing in the County Antrim (north of Ireland, where, I may add, I believe some very fine specimens exist, from all I hear), and it was regarding the performance of a bitch of this breed, named Jess, in his possession.   On one occasion we were boring a bank for the purpose of bolting rats, and at one place a rat bolted.   Jess, as usual, had him almost before he cleared his hole.   Then came another and another, so fast that the work was getting too hot for Jess, when a happy thought seemed to strike her ; and while in the act of killing a very big one, she leaned down her shoulder against the hole, and let them out one by one, until she had killed eighteen rats.   That Irish Terriers kill neatly I cannot say ; they kill not wisely, but too well.   Your little Black-and-tan shakes the life out of the rat ; but the Irish Terrier's jaw is so powerful, he doesn't need to shake, but crunches them into purgatory.   They always impress me with the idea that the game is not big enough for them, and they put too much energy in it.'

"I consulted with Mr. Geo. Jamison, and the following scale of points on the whole fairly represents the opinions of us both :—

"*Head.*—Long ; skull flat, and rather narrow between ears, getting slightly narrower towards the eye ; free from wrinkle.   Stop hardly visible, except in the profile.   The jaw must be strong and muscular, but not too full in the cheek, and of a good punishing length, but not so fine as a white English Terrier's.   There should be a slight falling away below the eye, so as not to have a Greyhound appearance.

"*Teeth.*—Should be strong and level.

"*Lips.*—Not so tight as a bull-terrier's, but well-fitting, showing through hair their black lining.

"*Nose.*—Must be black.

"*Eyes.*—A dark hazel colour, small, not prominent, and full of life, fire, and intelligence.

"*Ears.*—Small and V-shaped, of moderate thickness, set well up on the head, and dropping forward closely to the cheek. The ear must be free of fringe, and the hair thereon shorter and generally darker in colour than the body. Until some decided action be taken against it, we are afraid cropping will prevail, for it undoubtedly imparts a smart appearance to a dog, thus giving it an unfair and unnatural advantage over an uncropped dog. In the days when Irish Terriers were used as fighting dogs, it was reasonable and advisable to crop them; but now that they are used only as working Terriers, we should not deprive them of the protection nature has given them, and which they must so sorely stand in need of when under earth or in the water. A cropped dog should not be qualified to score any points for ears. Good ears must be bred for. Hair on face, of same description as on body, but short (about a quarter of an inch long), in appearance almost smooth, and straight. A slight beard is the only longish hair (and it is only long in comparison with the rest) that is permissible, and that is characteristic.

"*Neck.*—Should be of a fair length, and gradually widening towards the shoulders, well carried, and free of throatiness.

"*Shoulders and Chest.*—Shoulders must be fine, long, and sloping well into the back; the chest deep and muscular, but neither full nor wide.

"*Back and Loin.*—Body moderately long; back should be strong and straight, with no appearance of slackness behind the shoulders; the loin broad and powerful, and slightly arched, ribs well sprung, and well ribbed back.

"*The Hind Quarters.*—Well under the dog; should be strong and muscular, the thighs powerful, hocks near the ground, stifles not much bent.

"*Stern.*—Invariably docked; should be free of fringe or feather, set on pretty high, carried gaily, but not over the back, or curled.

"*Feet and Legs.*—Feet should be strong, tolerably round, and moderately small; toes arched, and neither turned out nor in; black toe-nails are preferable and desirable. Legs moderately long, well set from the shoulders, perfectly straight, with plenty of bone and muscle; the elbows working freely clear of the sides, pasterns short and straight, hardly noticeable. Both fore and hind legs should be moved straight forward when travelling; the stifles not turned outwards, the legs free of feather, and covered, like the head, with a hard texture of coat—as body, but not so long.

"*Coat.*— Hard and wiry, free of softness or silkiness, not so long as to hide the outlines of the body, particularly in the hind quarters, straight and flat, no shagginess, and free of lock or curl.

"*Colour.*—Must be 'whole-coloured,' the most preferable being bright red, next yellow, wheaten, and grey. White objectionable. It often appears on chest and feet; it is more objectionable on the latter than on chest, as a speck of white on chest is frequently to be seen in all self-coloured breeds.

"*Size and Symmetry.*—Weight in show condition, from 16 to 24 lbs.—say 16 to 22 for bitches and 18 to 24 for dogs. The most desirable weight is 22 lbs. or under, which is a nice stylish and useful size. The dog must present a gay, lively, and active appearance; lots of substance, at same time free of clumsiness, as speed and endurance, as well as power, are very essential. There must be a 'racing build' about the Irish Terrier.

"*Disqualifying Points.*—Nose white, cherry, or spotted to any considerable extent; mouth much undershot or cankered; colour brindle or very much white; coat much curly or very soft.

MR. GEORGE KREHL'S POINTS FOR JUDGING IRISH TERRIERS.

Head	15
Ears ... ..., ...	5
Neck	5
Shoulders and chest	10
Back, loin, and stern (including general make of body)	15
Hind quarters	5
Feet and legs	15
Coat	15
Colour	10
Size	5
Total	100 "

The subject of our coloured plate is the well-known and very successful dog Sporter, the property of Mr. George R. Krehl. This dog was formerly the property of Messrs. Despard and Graham. Amongst his chief performances are: 1st, Dublin; 1st and cup, Newtownards; 1st, Londonderry, 1878. He measures, from nose to stop, $2\frac{3}{4}$ inches; from stop to occiput, $4\frac{1}{4}$ inches; length of back, $14\frac{1}{2}$ inches; girth of muzzle, 10 inches; girth of skull, 13 inches; girth of neck, 12 inches; girth round brisket, 22 inches; girth round shoulders, 25 inches; girth of loins, $15\frac{1}{2}$ inches; girth of thigh, 10 inches; girth of forearm, $5\frac{1}{2}$ inches; girth of pastern, $3\frac{1}{2}$ inches; height at shoulders, 16 inches; height at elbows, 9 inches; height at loins, 16 inches; height, hock to ground, $4\frac{3}{4}$ inches. His age is about 4 years, and his weight 22 lbs.

The following scale agrees in all points with Mr. Krehl's enumeration—reduced, however, to simpler form, in accordance with the plan adopted throughout this work:—

POINTS OF IRISH TERRIERS.

Head and ears	10
Coat and colour	10
Legs and feet	10
Back and loin	5
Hind quarters and stern	5
Shoulders, neck, and chest	10
Total	50

CHAPTER XVII.

THE SCOTCH TERRIER.

THIS interesting breed of dog is supposed by very many of its admirers to have been the progenitor of the Irish Terrier, and is considered by them to have been introduced into the sister isle by emigrants from Scotland, who were accompanied to so their new residence by their faithful canine companions, who were destined to found the race of Irish Terriers. That there is ground for this impression we willingly admit, and as the head in certain characteristics approaches the Irish Terrier, we pass from one to the other, so that our readers may have a fair opportunity of comparing the two varieties. As the Scotch Terrier is so little known in the southern portion of these islands, and a class for this variety is a very uncommon institution at any shows, we consider ourselves fortunate in being able to lay the views of Mr. James B. Morrison before our readers. This gentleman has on several occasions judged the Scotch Terrier, and his knowledge of and connection with the breed has extended over several years. Mr. Morrison writes :—

"Every dog has his day, and, thanks to the continued efforts of a few admirers of the Hard-haired Scotch Terrier, there is every likelihood of 'Scottie' being better known and more appreciated, both by authorities on canine affairs and the public generally, than he has been since the advent of dog-shows.

"The designation *hard-haired* Scotch Terrier implies the existence of softer haired varieties, and these we find in the Skye and Dandie Dinmont. Fanciers of these two terriers can, no doubt, recognise their favourites in fusty books of 'ye olden time;' and without denying them the satisfaction of an inconceivable antiquity, it requires no great stretch of imagination to suppose, that at a time considerably posterior to the Cambrian period, the three varieties mentioned might have appeared under our present heading, having had a common origin, just as the short hard-haired, and longer and softer coated, together with the bob-tailed variety of Sheep-dog, are believed to have sprung from the same stock.

"It is more than likely that the subject of this chapter was the original Terrier of Scotland, from the fact that the hard, short coat could not have been produced from the Skye or any other longer haired variety, without the presence of a smooth-coated dog; and we know that, with the exception of the Blue Paul—a dog about forty-five pounds weight, bred at Kirkintilloch, which has come and almost gone within the last century and a half—there was no smooth-coated species indigenous to the Highlands, or Islands of Scotland, or even known to Lowlanders as a Scotch dog. It may be advanced that the hard, short coat is the result of judicious selection, but against this theory stands the fact, that in the Scotch Terrier era these dogs were used exclusively for work, and the great object in breeding was to produce an intelligent, plucky terrier, of a useful size, with a long powerful jaw, broad deep chest, and strong loins; colour, length of coat, carriage, &c., being secondary considerations—a course followed in certain quarters to this day. Such a specimen as 'The Shipwrecked Poodle,' which has become quite historical in the canine world, and who was blamed for the introduction of the silky-coated Skye, might, on the other hand, if crossed with the Scotch Terrier, produce a dog not unlike the modern Skye.

"In ferreting out the origin of the Scotch Terrier, we are reminded of the greater antiquity claimed for an inventive Scion of the Macleods for his clan over the Macgregors. Macgregor approached the ante-diluvian period as nearly as the Macleods' credulity, and his own connection with the Auld Kirk would permit; however, his opponent settled the matter to his own satisfaction at least, with the query, 'Did you'll ever know a Macleod that had not a poat of her own?' Whether or not the Macleod saved from the wreck of nature a brace of Scotch Terriers in 'her poat,' is 'not proven,' but they were known, and better known than they are to-day, at a time when we were indebted to ballad-singers for rescuing our own history from oblivion. The best Scotch Terrier authorities of our day are the more veteran of our Highland crofters and keepers, men who, unfortunately, were *compelled* to keep these terriers for the extermination of vermin, or, at least, to enable them to hold their own. We learn from this source that they were found in considerable numbers all over the islands and the mainland in the North-west of Scotland in the beginning of the present century.

"This is a terrier peculiarly adapted for the work cut out for him, in unearthing such vermin as the fox, otter, badger, wild cat, &c., than which the gamekeeper and farmer have not more indefatigable poachers to contend against.

"Dealing with such ticklish customers in their strongholds among the rocks, boulders, and cairns, or burrows, is no light task, but in the Scotch Terrier we have the assistance of an able and ever-willing ally, who, having a remarkable nose, gives tongue at once on the scent, following it up to the lair with spirit, where he works silently in on belly or side, if need be, till close upon the enemy, when outsiders can hear that the real work has begun.

"When he has heavy mettle to deal with, unless assisted by a pack, who rarely allow the foe to die from home, he compels the varmint to bolt for a reckoning outside; if the struggle is severe or protracted, the terrier who has borne the brunt may be seen coming panting to the open air for breathing space, bringing with him evidence of the severity of the combat; however, the sounds of war are too much for him, and indifferent to the kindly attentions of his master, he returns to the charge the embodiment of determination and excitement.

"Many a gallant little dog has found his grave in the maze of these cairns, the result of the encounter in many cases turning out to be a Cadmean victory, where a terrier either loses himself in the labyrinth of passages and crannies, or jumps over the ledge of a rock which he cannot ascend again, when he is entirely out of his master's reach. In some instances food can be thrown in to him from day to day until the boulders are removed or blasted, but this is not always practicable; if in a burrow, a few hours may suffice to dig him out if within call at all, although numbers are buried alive, paying for their temerity with their life.

"Working dogs are best studied in the field, being out of their element at the end of a yard and a half of chain on a show-bench; and a day spent on the Highlands with a keeper and his gang of terriers is fraught with interest and instruction to an admirer of the hardy tyke.

"When off duty—unlike the shambling drawing-room terrier out for an airing—he is sprightly, vigorous and gay, full of life and activity, the slightest attention paid him occasioning the most demonstrative delight; no day is too long for him; he is naturally mild-tempered and under ordinary circumstances not quarrelsome, although able to hold his own in an 'emergency;' he is a wonderful follower, even in puppyhood, a very valuable qualification when introduced to city life.

"The comparative scarcity of vermin in the Highlands shows how effectually the Scotch Terrier has done his work, and the recent neglect of this hardy little mountaineer may be attributed to the very fact that he has in a great measure outlived his occupation.

"While advocating the judging of working dogs by their performances in the field principally, it is necessary to erect a general standard of excellence for awards in the ring, and this can best be arrived at by a careful study of the points necessary to enable each breed to fill in the most efficient manner the sphere it has to occupy. I give the following description of the general appearance and points of the Hard-haired Scotch Terrier from dogs acknowledged to be good specimens by veteran breeders, whose testimony being the outcome of personal experience is entitled to be considered of the highest value; these points have also been adopted by the present generation of Scotch Terrier fanciers as correct:—

POINTS OF THE SCOTCH TERRIER.

"The *General Appearance* is that of a thick-set, compact, short-coated terrier, standing about 9½ inches high, with body long in comparison, and averaging 16lbs. or 17lbs. weight for dogs, and 2lbs. less for bitches; with ears and tail uncut. Although in reality no higher at shoulder than the Skye or Dandie Dinmont, it has a leggier appearance, from the fact that the coat is much shorter than in these two varieties. The head is carried pretty high, showing an intelligent, cheery face.

"The *Temperament.*—An incessant restlessness and perpetual motion, accompanied by an eager look, asking plainly for the word of command; a muscular form, fitting him for the most arduous work; and sagacity, intelligence, and courage to make the most of the situation, qualify the Scotch Terrier for the rôle of 'friend of the family,' or 'companion in arms'—*amicus humani generis*—in a sense unsurpassed by any other dog, large or small.

"The *Head* is longish and bold rather than round, and is full between the eyes; it is free from long, soft, or woolly hair, or top-knot, and is smaller in the bitch than in the dog.

"The *Muzzle* is a most important point, and should be long and very powerful, tapering slightly to the nose, which should be well formed, well spread over the muzzle, and invariably black; there must be no approach to snipishness; the teeth should be perfectly level in front, neither being under or over shot, canines fitting well together. A mouth off the level should not altogether disqualify, as this fault is often met with in the very best blood; however, it must always be considered very objectionable. The roof of the mouth is almost invariably black.

"The *Eyes* are very small, well sunk in the head, dark hazel, bright and expressive, with heavy eyebrows.

"The *Ears* are very small and free from long hair, feather, or fringe; in fact, as a rule, rather bare of hair; they are either carried erect, or semi-erect, the latter preferred for a workman—never drop-eared and never cut.

"The *Neck* is short, thick, and very muscular, well set between the shoulders, and showing great power.

"The *Chest* and *Body*.—The body gives an impression of great strength, being a combination of little else than bone and muscle. The chest is broad and deep; the ribs flat —a wonderful provision of nature, indispensable to a dog often compelled to force its way into burrows and dens on its side; the back broad; the loins broad and very strong; this is a feature calling for special attention, as a dog in any degree weak in the hind quarters lacks one of the main points in this breed, and should on no account be used as a stud dog. The body is covered with a dense, hard, wet-resisting coat about two inches long.

"The *Legs*.—Fore legs are short and straight, with immense bone for a dog of this size; elbows in same plane as shoulder-joints and not outside, the forearm being particularly muscular; the hind legs are also strong, the thighs being well developed and thick, the hocks well bent and never straight. The feet are small and firmly padded to resist the stony, broken ground, with strong nails generally black. Although free from feathering, the legs and feet are well covered with hair to the very toes.

"The *Tail* should not exceed 7 or 8 inches; it is covered with the same quality and length of hair as the body, is carried with a slight bend, and should not be docked.

"The *Colour* is various shades of grey, or grizzle and brindle, the most desirable colour being red brindle with black muzzle and ear-tips."

From the above it appears that the Scotch Terrier, like his Irish relative, may be reckoned "dead game;" his temperament, however, is more vivacious than the somewhat stolid Irishman. Mr. Morrison has so thoroughly described the variety that we consider further remarks on the points unnecessary, and therefore adopt the above as a true description of the breed, merely giving a table by which the variety can be judged.

SCALE OF POINTS FOR JUDGING SCOTCH TERRIERS.

Skull, shape, &c.	5
Muzzle and teeth	10
Eyes and ears	5
Neck	5
Body	5
Feet and legs	5
Coat	10
General appearance, temper	5
	——
	50

SKYE TERRIERS.

CHAPTER XVIII.

THE SKYE TERRIER.

THE Skye Terrier has certainly not improved its position in the canine world from the writings of its supporters : on the contrary, like its relative the Dandie Dinmont, it has suffered greatly from the intervention of fond though misguided friends. Many who have taken part from time to time in the various controversies which have arisen concerning the breed have certainly proved themselves masters of the subject upon which they wrote ; but the majority unfortunately appear to have devoted more energy to personal recrimination than to the Skye Terrier on whose behalf they rushed into print. However, all parties seem to agree upon two important points —viz., the antiquity and the utility of the breed ; and the real point at issue appears to be the distinction admirers of this game little dog have drawn between the type usually most successful at our shows, and the type met with in various parts of Scotland.

Before committing ourselves to any opinion on this important subject of dispute, it is desirable that our readers should be clearly informed what the duties of a Skye Terrier really are. It has been argued that he is *par excellence* the vermin dog of his country ; but this is naturally enough distasteful to, and contradicted by, the lovers of the Dandie Dinmont. Enough has, however, been proved by his supporters to convince all who are interested in but do not know the Skye that he is certainly a game, hardy little dog, sagacious in hunting, and death on all vermin. His suitability for going to earth, too, is beyond all question, and his constitution and formation must specially adapt him for the climate of his native country. A dog possessing so many recommendations must naturally be popular in the localities where he is mostly found ; and therefore it is a matter of small surprise that he is so largely patronised by keepers and sportsmen in a small way who reside in the northern portion of our island.

All being therefore agreed upon his duties, it is only natural that there should exist many differences of opinion on matters of detail—one party contending for one type of dog, and others for an animal different in many important points. The greatest diversity of opinion, however, appears to exist between those called upon to officiate as judges on the one hand, and the owners of types which as a rule are unsuccessful competitors at our shows, on the other. The former as a rule award their substantial support to long low dogs, with plenty of good long harsh coat, who are admittedly handsome specimens of the breed to which they claim to belong. Owners of what they are pleased to style the "genuine Skye Terrier," on the contrary, often object in no measured terms to the prizes being awarded such dogs, and with some show of reason point exultingly to the class of dogs commonly met with in Scotland, whose jackets, though certainly harsh and weather-resisting, do not approach in length and beauty those of their more favoured rivals. Here we confess we are unable to follow the latter's reasoning, and we cannot bring ourselves to believe that the promoters of such a theory have given due consideration to the facts of the case as it stands before them. They appear to us to have quite lost sight of the natural improvement which care and attention, combined with superior diet and warm housing, is likely to bring about in the coats of the show dogs they are wont to decry. We willingly grant that the working Skye Terrier is usually provided with an extremely weather-resisting coat, and that in some instances dogs of this breed have been awarded prizes who have certainly had jackets of a very soft and silky texture—jackets, in fact, which would incapacitate them from working for a whole day amongst whins or brackens in a Scotch mist, and which are entirely opposed to the requirements of the best judges of the breed. Nevertheless, it must be borne in mind that the majority of our principal prize-winners are dogs which have been carefully prepared for the show-bench, and are bred from parents who themselves had existed in more luxurious homes than the rough cottage of a Scottish keeper; added to which it should be remembered that exhibitors must have, from the earliest existence of shows, selected dogs to breed from which were supposed to be likely to develop beauty and improve the appearance of the race. Short rough coats are naturally harsher than long ones, but their wet-resisting capacity is more or less a matter of question when a comparison between the two has to be drawn. It is, nevertheless, as unfair to judge the show Skye Terrier by the standard by which the working dog is judged, as it would be to draw comparisons between a prize Colley and a shepherd's trusty tyke. Circumstances alter cases, even when dogs have to be considered; and freedom from exposure, combined with careful grooming, must tend towards a growth of coat which it is impossible for a less-cared-for dog to develop.

Another feature of difference which we have observed is the great length of body which the majority of show dogs attain; and here another diversity of opinion exists between the extreme supporters of the two types. We have ourselves been warned by a Scotch keeper against favouring Skyes which, as he expressed it, "run to back;" since he argued that a long dog finds more difficulty in his underground manœuvres than a short one does. This reasoning we ineffectually ventured to convince him was opposed to that law of Nature, which has ordained that so many animals which inhabit earths should be low and long. For our own part, however, we unhesitatingly adhere to the claims of a long-bodied Skye, and believe our opinion is shared by nine-tenths of the breeders of this variety of dog.

The Skye Terrier as a companion has few rivals. Though generally speaking of a peaceful disposition, he will not shirk an encounter, and if thoroughly aroused, defends himself most gamely against a larger dog. He is not impetuous, as so many dogs which possess Bull blood are known to be, but is always on the alert and ready for business. This renders him an especially useful dog for guarding dwellings of a night, as his vigilance is extreme, and he can be depended on to warn the inmates of the approach of strangers. It is however in rabbiting or in the pursuit of vermin that the merits of a Skye are most thoroughly displayed. Game to excess, he seldom lets his keenness get the better of discretion, and the intelligence he evinces in watching an earth where ferrets are working is unrivalled. No day seems too long for Skyes, and the way they work amongst brakes and thorns is incredible to those who have not seen them so employed.

The origin of the breed is lost in obscurity, but it doubtless has been the subject of certain crosses at remote periods. The Rev. J. Cumming Macdona, of Cheadle Rectory, Cheshire, tells us of a celebrated strain of Skyes belonging to Lady Macdonald, which was known to be descended from white dogs which were wrecked on the coast from a Spanish ship. These white dogs were probably of Maltese extraction, and this may possibly account for the undesirable silkiness of texture of coat, to which we have already alluded, in some dogs now before the public. The wreck, however, took place nearly three hundred years ago, and therefore it is not unlikely that the traces of so undesirable a cross have been obliterated. It is nevertheless a fact that for many generations certain strains have been most jealously guarded by their owners, and that several of our winners have descended from them, though in not a few instances foreign blood has been introduced into the latter's veins.

Certain writers on the subject of Skye Terriers credit the breed with a love of solitude, and a desire to hide themselves from the approach of strangers, by crouching under hedges and in ditches or drains. We question whether this is not more from a fondness for sport than solitude, for the Skye is a born sportsman, and is quite sharp enough to know without much teaching that there is more chance of encountering vermin single-handed by keeping quiet in a corner than by ostentatiously laying siege to the beast in his own quarters. Others who have laid their views before the public draw attention to many ramifications of the breed under various denominations. Amongst the latter, the terms Mogstads, Drynocks, and Camusennaries, are applied, with a result which we venture to think would bewilder the majority of Skye breeders. The most rational view to take, when considering any such subdivisions, is to regard them all as different strains of the same variety, each of which strain has been the subject of such pride to its possessor, that he has, by following certain rules of breeding, so moulded the original dog that certain slight differences are manifest in the appearance when they are compared with other equally pure strains. The very support which is given to such different families of Skyes—and it may here be remarked that many of their supporters belong to the number of those who are the bitterest enemies of the "show Skye"—is a powerful argument in favour of the latter being a true Skye, which has been improved by the judicious selection of mates into the handsome animal it is. Skyes, at least working Skyes, are not the things of beauty some of their admirers would make us believe. They are essentially useful members of society, and as such can afford to look down upon less favoured breeds.

There are admittedly two distinct varieties of Skye, namely, the Prick-eared Skye, and the Drop-eared Skye. There are, in our opinion, other essential differences between the breeds. In some instances they have been paired together, and have produced good offspring; but, as a rule, the cross is not a very judicious one. Amongst the different characteristics of the two varieties are the length of back, which is, as a rule, longer in the drop-eared variety. The coats are, or ought to be, the same, though it has often struck us forcibly that the drop-eared ones are more inclined to be soft and silky in texture than their relatives.

Before entering into a description of the breed, it is right that some allusion should be made to the Skye Terrier Clubs. Both societies were formed for the avowed protection of the true type of Skye, and at the outset their lists of members contained the names of many well-known writers on the breed. However, neither one nor the other has come to the front in the manner that the Dandie Dinmont Club has done, and we are not aware if either exists at the present day, as no reports of their movements have appeared for many months.

As regards the points of the breed, our idea of the *beau idéal* of a Skye Terrier is as follows :—

Head.—Long, with a broad flat skull, stout punishing muzzle, with powerful jaws and strong, perfectly level teeth. It is a decided fault in a Skye to be either pig-jawed or undershot. The skull is rather narrow between the ears, which are set on high, and it gradually widens towards the eyes.

The *Ears*, which, as we have before stated, should be rather on the top of the head in the case of a drop-eared dog, should fall close to the side of the skull, and not stand away from it; whilst in the prick-eared variety they must stand perfectly upright, as a falling or badly-carried ear is a great blemish. In the latter variety there is frequently a fringe of hair running up the sides, and terminating in a small tuft at the top, which gives them rather a top-heavy appearance.

The *Eyes*, which are certainly a great point in a Skye, as their intelligent appearance is remarkable, should be brown, and larger in size than in most terriers. This does not imply that they should be prominent, as if they were the dog would be more liable to accident when working underground.

Neck.—Long, powerful, and well coated with hair, especially on the upper surface. Shoulders sloping and powerful.

Fore legs.—Very short and muscular, well set on under the dog's body.

Chest.—Very deep, but not wide.

Body.—As long as possible, and well ribbed up, wide at ribs, and flat in the back.

Hind legs.—Straight and short, and muscular.

Stern.—Carried low.

Colour.—Grey, grizzle, blue, silver-grey, and yellow or mustard colour.

Coat.—As hard, flat, and weather-resisting as it can possibly be got. Naturally both varieties should, like other rough-coated dogs, have an under-jacket, short and weather-proof, with which to effectually keep the snow and mist from penetrating their skins.

The *General Appearance* is essentially that of a workman. The Skye is a long, low, well-knit little customer, with a good hard jacket, an intelligent but determined expression of countenance, and showing symptoms of a strong constitution, which would enable him to go almost anywhere, do almost anything, and rough it with his master in any climate.

With regard to what we have alluded to as the working type of Skye—to which category Mr. A. M. Shaw's Flora undoubtedly belongs—we have received the following notes from her owner :—

"I object very much to a woolly or a curly coat such as Skyes are represented to have by certain writers on the dog. An animal with such a coat could not be a pure Skye. The outside coat should be straight or *slightly* wavy, and the hairs anything but woolly : in fact, coarse but glossy ; the underneath coat soft and thick, and not coarse as in the outer." (This corresponds with Mr. W. W. Thomson's description of the under-jacket of the Sheep-dog in a former chapter.) " Personally I am opposed to the long-coated type, as I consider the long jacket to be a result of some impure cross to which the breed has been subjected. As regards the carriage of the tail, which is a point that I have frequently heard debated, I can confidently assert that the best Skyes I have come across were in the habit of carrying their tails high, except when being bullied for wrong-doing, or when their consciences have smitten them. Personally I can see little distinction between the two varieties, with the exception of the ears ; and this being so, can imagine no reason why Drop-ears and Prick-ears should not be judged in the same class. As regards the tufts of hair which so many judges consider to be indispensable adjuncts to the tips of a prick-eared dog's ears, I can only say that I have met many excellent specimens of undoubtedly correct pedigree whose ears have in no way differed from the drop-eared variety except in the carriage. My ideas have been gathered from what I have picked up in the North, and also from noted Skye breeders, including General Macdonald of Braelangwell (himself a Skyeman), who bred my Flora and other undoubtedly good specimens of the breed."

From a desire to give our readers every opportunity of judging for themselves between the merits of the two varieties—the show type and the working type—we have decided to give illustrations of each in this work. The dogs selected for the coloured plates are Mr.

Mark Gretton's Champion Sam and Mr. James Locke's Perkie; whilst the dog for the wood-cut is Mr. Alexander M. Shaw's Flora, which is as good-looking a specimen of the working type as we have met with for some time.

Sam is drop-eared, and was pupped 30th of August, 1873, and weighs 20 pounds; he is by Bowman's Tartar, out of Mr. Mark Gretton's Skye, and was whelped in 1873. Amongst his chief performances are—First Darlington, first Nottingham, and third Manchester, 1875; first Birmingham, 1876; first Carlisle, second Agricultural Hall, second Darlington, first Burton-on-Trent, second Alexandra Palace, second Manchester, first Birmingham, 1877; first Birmingham, first Bristol, first Burton-on-Trent, first Chesterfield, second Darlington, and extra Wolverhampton, 1879. He measures as follows :—From nose to stop, 3 inches; from

MR. A. M. SHAW'S FLORA.

stop to occipital bone, 5½ inches; length of back, 16 inches; girth of muzzle, 8 inches; girth of skull, 13½ inches; girth of neck, 13 inches; girth round brisket, 21 inches; girth of chest behind forearms, 18 inches; girth of loins, 14 inches; girth of thigh, 7 inches; girth of forearm, 5½ inches; girth of pastern, 4 inches; height at shoulders, 10 inches; height at elbows, 5½ inches; height at loins, 10½ inches; height at hock, 3½ inches; length of tail, without hair, 10 inches; with hair, 15 inches.

Perkie, the bitch selected for illustration of the prick-eared Skye, is the property of Mr. James Locke, of Selkirk, N.B. Her pedigree is not known, and as she was only born in 1877 she has not yet been much seen on the show-bench. She has, however, proved her claim to be considered a good specimen by taking first prize at Glasgow in 1878. Perkie's measurements are—Length from nose to stop, 3 inches; from stop to occiput, 5½ inches; length of back, 16 inches; girth of muzzle, 7½ inches; girth of skull, 12¼ inches; girth of neck, 11 inches; girth round chest, 17 inches; girth of thigh, 9 inches; girth of forearm, 5 inches; height at shoulders, 9 inches; height at elbows, 5½ inches; height at hock, 3½ inches; length of tail, 8 inches.

Flora, the specimen whom we have chosen to represent the working type of Skye, is the property of Mr. Alexander M. Shaw, of Chipping Barnet, Herts. She was bred by General Macdonald, of Braelangwell, by Fortrose, Rossshire, N.B., and is an excellent representative of his famous strain. As Mr. Shaw does not show, Flora has never appeared on the bench; but even had she done so, it is not probable that her success would have been conspicuous, as she is confessedly of a different type to that which finds favour with the majority of the judges. Flora's measurements are—From nose to stop, 2¼ inches; from stop to occiput, 3¼ inches; length of back, 17 inches; girth of muzzle, 8½ inches; girth of skull, 12 inches; girth of neck, 11 inches; girth round brisket, 17 inches; girth round chest, 16 inches; girth round loins, 15 inches; girth of thigh, 8½ inches; girth of forearm, 4 inches; girth of pastern, 2¾ inches; height at shoulders, 10½ inches; height at elbows, 5½ inches; height at loins, 10½ inches; height at hocks, 3½ inches; length of tail, 8½ inches.

SCALE OF POINTS FOR JUDGING SKYES.

	Value.
Skull, formation and strength of jaw	5
Eyes and ears	5
Teeth	5
Length of back	10
Legs and feet	5
Coat	15
General appearance	5
	—
	50

THE ABERDEENSHIRE TERRIER.

This breed of dog is considered by many competent judges to be merely a sub-variety of the prick-eared Skye. It is to our mind, however, clear that the Aberdeenshire Terrier and the Scotch Terrier are identical animals, possessed of but very slight structural differences. It may appear inconsistent in us to express a difference of opinion with those who recognise various families of Skye Terriers under the various names alluded to in the last chapter, and yet notice the Aberdeenshire Terrier separately here; but between the two cases there is this distinction—that many persons affirm that an Aberdeenshire Terrier is a breed distinct from both the Scotch Terrier proper and the prick-eared Skye. For our own parts, we fail to see any such distinction as could justify their being classed in different varieties or judged by different scales of points; we therefore shall apply to this breed the standard by which the Scotch Terrier was to be judged, as we are of opinion that an undesirable confusion would thereby be avoided.

CHAPTER XIX.

THE BEDLINGTON TERRIER.

A DOG which has made vast advances towards improvement of type of late years is the Bedlington Terrier. Like the Irish Terrier, some few years back it was practically unknown, and, like the Irish Terrier, its existence on the bench is in a great measure due to the correspondence and support it received in newspaper columns. A few ardent dog-lovers, amongst whom the late Mr. Samuel Handley was eminently conspicuous, being struck by this dog's gameness and love of sport, determined to bring the merits of the Bedlington Terrier before the public, and having interested many persons by their letters on the breed, were at last successful in getting them classes at most of the principal shows.

Unfortunately the support of the public at large has not hitherto extended much beyond affording prizes for Bedlingtons, and Geordie, the miner, is still almost alone in the possession of the breed. It is quite true that several north-country amateurs have patronised this dog, but it has only been in a lukewarm sort of way; and the majority of the southern exhibitors who took it up have quickly abandoned the Bedlington in favour of other breeds. This is almost unexplainable, for its merits as a companion and a vermin dog rank very high. Some are certainly rather short in their tempers, but so it is in every breed, and we have met with scores of Bedlingtons who will compare in temper with any variety. The more natural deduction to be drawn from the want of support which has been accorded this breed is that it is not an easy thing to get hold of a good strain of Bedlingtons without great expenditure of time and money. Miners are not able to show their dogs often, and even if they did so, are devoted enough to them to decline to let them go on any terms. An admirer of the breed, therefore, who purposes going in for it to any extent, will have to search the Newcastle and Blaydon districts thoroughly before he is likely to get together a stud of dogs which will do him credit. A Norfolk gentleman who had invested largely in the breed some time back, and who was pretty successful in his show operations, told us that though he had got together a nice strain of dogs, yet the difficulties he found put in the way of his obtaining crosses had determined him to give it up. He most sensibly remarked that it was useless to commence the foundation of a new strain without a dash of one or two of the best old blood in it, and as he could not be positive that this would be obtainable at the time he wanted it he did not care to risk a probable failure at the end of one or two years' breeding operations.

Though the breed may not be so popular as others with "doggy" men throughout the country, it is nevertheless certain that in its own district its merits meet with due recognition. In Newcastle and its environs almost every man has a "poop," and that "poop" is certain almost to be a Bedlington. In the company of his trusty tyke, the miner when off duty is supremely happy. They hunt or poach together, fight together, sleep together, and not unfrequently drink together; it is no uncommon sight to enter the tap-room of a north-country public-house and see as many dogs as men in the room, and all apparently equally interested in the evening's proceedings. The greatest insult which can be put upon such a master is a reflection upon his dog's appearance or gameness; and as for illtreating them, a stranger had better injure "Geordie" than hurt his dog. "If thau poonch' ma dog, 'arl poonch thee" is proof of the miner's love for his Bedlington, and is no uncommon threat in the neighbourhoods where this breed is mostly found.

The quality of the Bedlingtons now shown is undoubtedly superior to that of some years back, when at the most six or eight fairish specimens could be got from home to contend at our shows. The earliest supporter of the breed was the late Mr. Thomas J. Pickett, of New-castle-on-Tyne, whose Tyneside and Tynedale were almost invincible in their day at the principal canine exhibitions. Mr. Pickett gained such a name for the excellence of his dogs that he was christened by his acquaintances the Duke of Bedlington. He died, however, in 1877, and since then the head of Bedlington affairs has been the Bedlington Terrier Club. It is, we believe, in a great manner due to the energy of the Bedlington Terrier Club that the popularity of the breed has been kept up of late years. For this society did not stick at expense, and boldly sent their dogs to the leading shows, thus keeping them well before the public for the time being.

As regards the origin of the breed, and its various crosses, considerable discussion has arisen from time to time in the columns of the *Live Stock Journal*. For instance, Mr. Thos. J. Pickett, writing to that paper in November, 1875, gives some evidence concerning his connection with the breed in the following words:—

"Whilst a schoolboy, I recollect one day wandering through the woods of the Brandling estate of Gosforth, in the county of Northumberland, gathering primroses, where I met a woodman named David Edgar, who was accompanied by a northern counties Fox Terrier, and who gave me a whelp got by his celebrated dog Pepper. This whelp was the first of the breed I ever possessed. Being an ardent admirer of this description of dog, I followed up the breed, and have seen as many of them as most people, and also seen them tested. . . . . I have in my possession the original copy of Tyneside's pedigree, dated 1839, signed by the late Mr. Joseph Aynsley, who was one of the first breeders of this class of dog, and who also acted as judge at the first Bedlington show; and quote the following as a description of what a northern counties Fox Terrier should be, viz. :—

"'*Colour.*—Liver, sandy, blue black, or tan.

"'*Shape.*—The jaw rather long and small, but muscular; the head high and narrow, with a silky tuft on the top; the hair rather wiry on the back; the eyes small and rather sunk; the ears long and hanging close to the cheek, and slightly feathered at the tip; the neck long and muscular, rising well from the shoulder; the chest deep, but narrow; the body well proportioned, and the ribs flat; the legs must be long in proportion to the body, the thinner the hips are the better; the tail small and tapering, and slightly feathered. Altogether they are a lathy-made dog.'"

In the same number of the *Live Stock Journal* the following letter from an authority on the breed appears, and must be read with interest as expressing his views:—

"The Bedlington Terrier should be broad in the nostril, with a flesh-coloured nose, hazel eyes, long narrow head; smooth in the face, much resembling the ferret; the head surmounted with a silky tuft, large ear, rather narrow at the tips, slightly feathered round the edge, and lying close to the face; long in the back; rather coarse in the tail; cleanish and not too high in the leg; wiry in the coat; and weighing from 18 lbs. to 20 lbs. They were rather sleepy-looking dogs, but when shown were game and keen as any ferret.

"I and all old fanciers prefer the *Livers*, which are the proper species, and were all the vogue in former times; and in a conversation I had at one of the late exhibitions, with one of the old breeders of this variety of Terrier, relative to the blues, which are more commonly seen, and are all the fancy now, he said, when breeding them many years ago, he generally got one blue to six or seven livers in each litter; and when asked what was done with the blues, he acknowledged that they all got a watery grave, as they were not the right colour, and were not in the fashion as they now are; which was perfectly the case, as we would not rear any of them.

"About thirty or forty years ago I remember well people crossing these Terriers with the Bull-terrier, in order that they might stand more wear and tear for fighting purposes, which were *then* so extensively sought. A few years after that they again crossed them with our Poodle dogs, so as to get linty-haired Terriers, which are now so often seen, and even winning prizes (for Bedlingtons) at all our leading exhibitions; and when you look at them you will see they resemble very much the apple head of the Poodle, and upon placing your hand over the skull, you will find their bumps as large as any Bull-terrier. I have frequently seen those dogs when tried; they might kill from four to half a dozen rats well enough, but when it came to taking hold of the eighth or ninth, they seemed so excited they tossed up in the air and appeared to be almost red hot. When asked to face the badger, they will go very fierce at first, but as soon as they come in contact with 'Broc,' they are generally seen to come faster backwards than they went in, which was not the case with our real Bedlingtons, as the more you gave them of any vermin, the keener and cooler they appeared to turn; and when taken to the badger, they would never refuse, at least going five or six times, and always staying a considerable length of time, which is very seldom the case with dogs that are now called Bedlington Terriers.

"P.S.—You will see I am speaking of the livers when mentioning the flesh nose, as all your readers will be aware that a blue has a black nose."

In August, 1877, Mr. A. N. Dodds, of North Shields, who had been for some time taking a considerable part in a correspondence which had been going on, published the following table of points and description of the breed, which was certainly the most elaborate published up to that time. Mr. Dodds writes as follows:—

"From the following it will be seen that I have divided the points into three—head, body, colour, and tail. I contend that a good body is just as essential as a good head, and just as difficult to breed. I contend also that, under present circumstances, hard blue or liver hair is just as difficult to breed good as either. I am also well aware that as soon as they can be bred true to colour and hardness (then and not till then) the scale of points can be modified. It will also be seen that I have thrown in 'the tail,' thus giving preference to head and body properties. Some of the 'head' properties are seldom, if ever, seen in such perfection as I give them, but I am laying down general rules, which I hope may be easily understood.

"*Skull.*—Narrow, parallel, and well rounded; entirely free from flatness, and not receding, but extra high at occiput, and covered with a nice silky tuft.

"*Jaw.*—Long, tapering, and sharp; as little dent as possible between the eyes, no 'dish,' so as to form a line, if possible, from the nose-end along the joint of the skull to the occiput. The lips close-fitting, and no flew.

"*Nose.*—Large, broad and well-angled, the more acute the better. Blues have black noses, livers, linties, sandies, have flesh-coloured.

"*Teeth.*—Pincher or over a little.

"*Ears.*—Large, well forward, flat to the cheek, and pointed, thinly covered and well tipped with fine silk.

"*Legs.*—Tall, not wide apart, straight, stout, square set, very high behind, good sized feet.

"*Tail.*—Short, thick at root, tapering and scimitar-shaped, feathered on lower side.

"*Neck and Shoulders.*—Neck long, deep at the base; shoulders flat.

"*Body.*—Short coupled, flat ribs and deep, not wide in chest, well-arched back, and well 'clicked-up' loins, light quarters.

"*Hair.*—Hard and wiry, standing up, but not curled, each individual hair having its own twist, as if it had been slightly singed, and about an inch long.

"*Colour.*—Deep blue, deep brown, usually called 'liver,' linty, resembling loose flax, silkies of both blue and liver shade, and the commoner colours of blue-and-tan and liver-and-tan.

"VALUE OF PROPERTIES.

Head—
Skull	...	...	...	...	...	...	...	...	7
Jaw	...	...	...	...	...	...	...	...	7
Nose	...	...	...	...	...	...	...	...	6
Teeth	...	...	...	...	...	...	...	...	6
Ears	...	...	...	...	...	...	...	...	7
								—	33

Body—
Neck and shoulders	...	...	..	...	...	...	5		
Chest	...	...	...	...	..	...	...	...	8
Short couples	...	...	.	..	...	...	...	8	
Arched loins	...	...	...	...	...	...	...	8	
Legs	...	...	...	...	...	...	...	..	5
								—	31
Tail	...	...	...	...	...	...	...	...	5
Colour	...	...	...	...	...	...	...	...	8
Hair	...	...	...	...	...	...	...	...	20
								—	33
								—	
								100."	

Finally, we have ourselves been favoured by Mr. G. S. Waterson, of Bedlington, with the following description, which he considers a proper one of the breed, and which opinion is shared by the leading Bedlington Terrier men in his part.

"The Bedlington Terrier should be rather long and small in the jaw, but withal muscular; the head high and narrow, and crowned with a tuft of silky hair of lighter colour than the body; the eyes must be small, round, and rather sunk, and dull until excited, then they are piercing; the ears are filbert-shaped, long, and hang close to the cheek, free of long hair, but slightly feathered at the tips; the neck is long and slender, but muscular; the body well proportioned, slender, and deep-chested; the toes must be well arched; legs straight, and rather long in proportion to the height, but not to any marked extent ; the tail varies from eight to twelve inches in length, is small and tapering, and free from feather. The best, and indeed only true colours are liver or sandy—in either case the nose must be of a dark-brown flesh-colour ; or, secondly, a black-blue, with the nose black.''

On reading the above opinions of such well-known authorities, it will be observed that for the most part the liver colour is preferred by them to the blue which is now so fashionable. Whether the former shade has become rarer from a change of tastes on the part of Bedlington breeders, or whether it is merely a coincidence that so few good liver-coloured specimens happen to be shown just at present, we are unable to say ; but the fact remains, that of late high-class blue Bedlingtons outnumber the good liver ones in the proportion of about fifty to one. The only really first-rater of the latter colour which we can call to our mind as figuring prominently at recent exhibitions is Mr. William Norris's Elswick Lass, which is an admirable Bedlington, and considered by several competent judges to be the best out. It is remarkable, however, that ten years ago the blue colour was not only unfashionable but positively unpopular, one of the earliest writers on the breed describing the shade of the coat as "very much like dressed flax." There were, and had been, nevertheless, many good specimens of the darker colour which kept pushing themselves forward as well-shaped Bedlingtons, and it is noticeable that the mother of the celebrated Piper, the property of Mr. Ainsley, was a blue-black bitch, but possessing a light-coloured top-knot. Both Piper and his mother Phœbe were considerably lighter in weight and smaller in stature than the dogs of the present day, the former only scaling about 15 pounds, and the latter weighing one pound less. These dogs existed about sixty years ago (viz., in 1820), when Phœbe was left by her then owner, Mr. J. Howe, with Mr. E. Coates at Bedlington vicarage. Piper himself is referred to by one of his admirers as being of the good "old-fashioned liver colour." With regard to the gameness of Piper, we may refer to some of his doings which appeared in a sporting paper in 1870, and which are extracted by one of its correspondents from a document signed Joseph Ainsley :—

"With regard to the doings of Piper, it would take a volume to contain them ; but I may mention that he was set on a badger at eight months old, and from that time until he was fourteen years old was constantly at work, more or less, with badgers, foxes, foulmarts, otters, and other vermin. He drew a badger after he was fourteen years old, when he was toothless and nearly blind, after several other Terriers failed."

Piper's pedigree having been so much discussed, we are of opinion that a reproduction of it here may be of interest. The table given beneath is the work of Mr. Wm. Clark, who has been at considerable trouble in tracing the pedigree of his dog Scamp, who, as will be seen, is a descendant of the famous Piper.

" PEDIGREE OF BEDLINGTON TERRIERS FROM 1792 TO 1873.

"William Clark's Scamp, father of the celebrated prize Terriers Tearem and Tyne ; Scamp by Joice's Piper, and out of Clark's Daisy ; Piper by Robert Hoy's Rock ; Daisy by John Curley's Scamp, Piper and Daisy both out of Clark's Meg ; Meg by Clark's Billy, and out of Clark's Wasp ; Billy by Will Cowney's Billy, and out of Wasp, also ; Cowney's Billy, by James Maughan's Bussal, and out of a bitch of William Weatherburn's ; Wasp by Baglee's Viper, and out his bitch, Daisy ; Daisy by the Moor House Dog, Viper ; Viper was out of Thompson's Nimble, and got by Thompson's Old Tip ; Nimble was got by Tip, and out of Baglee's Nimble ;

Nimble was got by Joseph Aynsley's Young Piper and out of James Anderson's Meg; Meg was out of Jean, sister to Young Piper, and got by Robert Bell's Tugg, of Wingate; Tugg was got by Robert Dixon's Dusty, of Longhorsley, and out of John Thompson's Music of the same place; Young Piper, by James Anderson's Old Piper and out of Mr. Coats's Phœbe; Old Piper by Robert Cowan's Peachem, of Nock Law, and out of C. Dixon's Phœbe; Peachem by Cowan's Burdett, and out of David Moffat's Bitch; Dixon's Phœbe, by Sherwood's Matchem, and out of John Dodd's Phœbe, both of Longhorsley; Matchem by Edward Donkin's Pincher, and out of Mr. Wardle's Bitch of Framlington; Dodd's Phœbe, by Doncan's Old Peachem and out of Andrew Evan's Vixen, of Thropton; Vixen by the Miller's Dog, of Felton, and out of Carr's Bitch, of Felton Hall; Coats's Phœbe, by the Rennington Dog, and out of Andrew Riddle's Wasp, of Framlington; Wasp, out of Wm. Wardle's Bitch, and got by Wm. Turnbull's Pincher, of Holy Stone; Pincher, by Donkin's Old Peachem, and out of Turnbull's Venom; Venom, out of Turnbull's Fan, by Miles's Matchem, of Netherwitton; Matchem, by Squire Trevelyan's Old Flint. It will be 90 years since Flint was pupped.

"N.B.—Andrew Riddle's Wasp and the Rennington Dog were brother and sister.

(Signed)   WM. CLARK."

Another writer alludes to the gameness of the breed, and its eagerness in the pursuit of vermin, in the following anecdote :—

"A fox was run to ground near Edlingham, and a mason there had two of these Terriers, father and son. The younger dog (about twelve months old) was put into the hole to try him, but could not kill the fox. Although advised not to do so, the man put in the old dog also, which, not being able to reach the fox, actually seized and killed the young dog, and then reached and killed the fox."

Such instances certainly prove the gameness of this handsome and very interesting breed of dog, and are worth repeating, as they may be the means of inducing sportsmen who appreciate the merits of a good working Terrier to give the breed a trial. The Bedlington has very erroneously been given the character of a savage, headstrong dog, and one which is likely to get his owner into trouble if allowed to follow him in his walks. All those, however, who know the breed well, and with whom we have spoken on the subject, are unanimous in denying the accuracy of this statement, which they affirm is quite destitute of foundation in fact.

As regards the origin of the breed, there are of course numerous theories, all more or less practicable, but none which is universally accepted as correct. For our own part we are of the opinion that both the Dandie Dinmont and the Otter-hound have been pressed into the service at one time or another. We consider ourselves strengthened in our support of the belief in a Dandie Dinmont cross by the knowledge that formerly the breed was shorter on the leg than it is now, as latterly the pitmen found the short-legged dog too slow for coursing rabbits. One anonymous writer has given his opinion that in the earlier part of the century the length of a Bedlington from tip of nose to tip of tail averaged about thirty-six inches, whilst his height was about ten inches. Without, perhaps, going the length of this, it is an accepted fact that the breed has been of recent years bred higher in the leg than it was formerly.

Amongst the most prominent men and dogs in the Bedlington world, the name of the late Mr. T. J. Pickett of Newcastle-upon-Tyne will always be conspicuously first. No man in his lifetime was more enthusiastic and unfailing in his support of the breed, and the doings of his Tyneside, Tynedale, and Tearem, will never be forgotten. Col. Cowen, too, of Blaydon-on-Tyne, has justly gained for himself great credit as a judge. Other well-known exhibitors are Messrs. Carrick of Carlisle, T. Stoddart of Blaydon-on-Tyne, the Rev. H. Turner of Norwich, Mr. Christopher Cornforth, Mr. W. Norris, Mr. W. J. Donkin, and the Bedlington Terrier Club, all of whom are, or have been, in possession of excellent specimens of the correct type of Bedlington Terrier.

The *Skull* of a Bedlington should be narrow, and conical in shape, with a tuft of silky hair on the summit, and no stop.

The *Muzzle* is straight, rather long and tapering, not blunt, and with tight lips, with a large nose, varying in colour, as the livers have light and the blues dark noses.

The *Jaws* are punishing, and are on no account to be underhung, but rather inclined to be "pig-jawed," or overhung.

Ears.—Rather large and fine, fringed with silky hair, and hanging perfectly flat to the head.

Neck.—Long.

Chest.—Narrow, with rather straight shoulders.

Body.—Short and arched in back, well ribbed up, and flat-sided.

Legs.—Long and very straight, well placed under the body, and on good-sized feet.

Tail.—Rather short, and feathered slightly.

Coat.—Hard and weather-resisting on body, with a soft tuft on head, as in the Dandie. Here it may be observed that unprincipled exhibitors often pluck their dogs' heads round this tuft of hair, to prevent its dimensions exceeding the orthodox size. Indications of this manipulation should be sought for by judges or intending purchasers, as a too large top-knot is a blemish in a Bedlington.

Colour.—Blue, liver, linty or sandy, in the different shades of each.

General Appearance.—A sharp, keen, active dog, fast when extended, and capable of being roused very easily.

The dog we have selected for the coloured plate is Dr. Lamond Hemming's Geordie—a dog of excellent appearance, his head especially being first-rate, though his experience of dog shows is limited to Bristol of 1879, where he succeeded in obtaining second prize. His measurements are—Nose to stop, 3¼ inches; stop to occiput, 5 inches; length of back, 17 inches; girth of skull, 14 inches; girth of neck, 12 inches; girth round chest, 20 inches; girth of loins, 17½ inches; girth of thigh, 9 inches; girth of forearm, 5½ inches; girth of pastern, 3½ inches; height at shoulders, 15 inches; height at elbows, 8 inches; height at loins, 16 inches; height at hocks, 5 inches; length of tail, 12 inches; weight, 24 lbs.; age, 18 months.

SCALE OF POINTS FOR JUDGING BEDLINGTONS.

Skull, shape, &c.	5
Muzzle and jaws	10
Ears	5
Neck and chest	5
Body, arch loins, flat ribs	10
Legs and feet	5
Coat	5
General appearance	5

Total 50

CHAPTER XX.

THE AIREDALE TERRIER.

VERY many of our readers who are acquainted with the old Yorkshire Waterside Terrier will possibly fail to recognise him under his new denomination—the Airedale Terrier. The change has been brought about since the institution of classes for the breeds at north country shows, as so much confusion was found to be caused amongst the exhibitors if the breed was not distinguished by some definite title. The existence of a dog resembling the Airedale Terrier has ever been a subject for astonishment to individuals in the southern part of the country, and a by no means insignificant mare's nest was discovered when the breed was brought for the first time beneath the notice of some of the least cautious of them, who strutted, and crowed a welcome to what they imagined to be a "new" breed of dog, discovered by themselves. An excuse may, however, be made for these much-ridiculed persons, as really in its own neighbourhood the breed has only of late years come to be considered worthy of practical and intelligent support. It existed certainly, and had existed for years and years, but the ownership of the majority of specimens rested in the hands of those who had little time, money, or inclination, to devote themselves to the science of breeding. Still, the breed grew and prospered, mainly owing to the exertions of a few unprejudiced practical persons, whose mode of progress will be alluded to hereafter. Before, however, going into the points and descriptions which have been so kindly afforded us by Mr. Reginald Knight of Chappel Allerton near Leeds, we may say that it has been our desire to lay the opinions, not only of Mr. Knight, but also of other successful breeders and exhibitors, before our readers. With this object, we requested Mr. Knight to oblige us by communicating with certain gentlemen, which he most kindly consented to do, and in addition provided us with the following notes, including his own experiences of the pluck and utility of the breed, which we gladly reproduce *in extenso*.

"This breed was originally bred from a cross between one of the old rough-coated Scotch Terriers and Bull-terrier. What I mean by the old Scotch Terrier is a dog weighing from 12 lbs. to 22 lbs., with a bluish-grey back and tanned legs, with a very hard and coarse coat. This cross, of course, did not produce a large dog, neither had the animal a very keen nose, so it was then crossed with Otter-hound, thus producing a large, ungainly animal, with big 'falling' ears, and very soft coat. This was then crossed and re-crossed, first with the original cross, and then with Bull-terrier, to produce a good terrier ear and good feet. This again was crossed with Otter-hound, the offspring not showing so much hound, neither having such a soft coat, but possessing a good nose for hunting, and a fondness for water as well as great gameness, both from the Bull blood as well as from the hound. Then this was crossed with Bull again, and then the offspring crossed and re-crossed with the terrier till it was brought up to the present standard. I ought to say that if you go to a show now you will find that fully two-thirds of the dogs in the Airedale Terrier class are dogs of ungainly appearance, with big hound ears and narrow long heads, also flat-sided and very badly built behind, as well as with a great weakness about the pasterns, causing the joint to give, and thus pressing the foot out sideways. Also take half a dozen men who say they have a good Airedale over 50 lbs. weight, and make them show their dogs, and you will find that five of them are fully three-quarters Otter-hound.

"This breed was originally started from twenty to forty years ago by working men about Leeds, Shipley, Otley, Bingley, although many gentlemen had them, and in all the towns and villages in the valley of the Aire, hence the name 'Airedale.' They were used by them for water-side hunting after rats, water-hens, ducks, and in fact, anything that might turn up. They are also used for poaching hares and rabbits, the gates in the field being quietly netted, and the dog then sent in to 'seek up.' He would hunt the entire field over without ever a whimper, if properly trained to it. If broken to the gun they are one of the best sporting dogs out, as they will hunt, retrieve, and set and carry either 'fur or feather' without hardly a mark, and yet, if told, will chase and kill and almost catch anything. I need not tell you how game they are, as many of them have been known to stand up for an hour and forty minutes to Bull-terriers. Thunder when only twelve months old was killing his first rat, and a bystander was not satisfied with the style, and said he had a dog that would eat Thunder and the rats too. He brought it out (Thunder then weighed about 45 lbs., and had never fought or seen anything before); it was a white Bull-terrier, with marks about the head, chest, and fore-legs; it weighed 36 lbs., and had never been beaten. He slipped it at Thunder, who would not meet it, but stood for it; it simply worried him for the first round, also the second and third, all being done in half an hour, at the fourth Thunder got his hold low down on the throat, and you heard the breast-bone go with a 'crack.' Thunder was choked off, and the Bull-terrier died in two hours, of internal bleeding. Yet Airedales will never start fighting, and pass any dog in the street. As they are a dog that is constantly exposed to water and the weather, and always ready for any work—hence their first name 'Working Terriers'—particular attention must be paid to the coat. The hair ought to be *hard* in texture, and broken or rough. It is a great deal harder to the feel than it really looks, being a good admixture of hard, bristly, and soft hair. You will not find many of the large dogs with really hard coats, because such a lot have been spoilt with the cross of Otter-hound as to the coat, but they are improving them every year. I might say a little more about their gameness and obedience. Thunder, after having first seen a live rat thrown over the rails of the new Leeds bridge at the bottom of Briggate, over the Aire, on being told to 'fetch it,' jumped over into the river after it, a distance of from 40 to 50 feet: and will go into the heaviest sea after a wounded gull. He will, if in a room with a fire in, if told to 'put it out,' rush at the fire, and scatter all over the room with his mouth and feet the whole of the burning coal and red-hot cinders, and has only once burnt himself with it, and that was with a very deep and narrow grate. They make first-rate 'night dogs,' and all mine will tell me at night by a low growl whether a man is anywhere near. I had an Airedale about six years ago that we used to keep in a two-stall stable with two horses, and we had occasion to send a new lad about eighteen years old for some rugs at night, and he thought, he said, he would look how the horses were, so he opened the door and walked in, but he did not get out again so quickly. Directly he turned to go out the dog was at him, but fortunately he had the rugs, and put them up, the dog caught hold of one and pulled it away from him, and was preparing for another spring when it seemed to change its mind, and went and lay down by the door and watched him. Every time he moved it growled, so he stood there for about half an hour, and then we thought he was a long time bringing the rugs, and went to see what he was about, when we found all the doors open, and him standing in one corner, with a white face, and one rug in his hand, the dog lying on the other rug near the door watching him. We called the dog away, and let the man out, and they are, or at least they were, very good friends. I must just say in conclusion that Airedale Terriers can kill anything, and will do anything. They can be broken to the gun, and broken to ferrets; they can go out ratting, and will not touch a rat in the net, they will drive sheep and cattle like a Sheep-dog, fetch and carry like a Retriever, hunt like a Spaniel, and are as fond of water as a duck, and as game as obedient.

"If I were a 'fighting man' (in the dog line), I would not mind matching one in my

AIREDALE TERRIER, THUNDER.

kennels to fight any Terrier his own weight in England—or, in fact, any dog his own weight. For cat-worrying, badger-drawing, or, in fact, anything at which gameness and staying powers are required, this is the breed which excels.

"I give you a point table made up *entirely* from my own ideas, which I hope may be useful to you and appreciated by your readers:—

Head	10
Ears	8
Eyes	8 — 26
Body	20
Legs and feet	10
Coat (including colour)	20 — 50
Hind quarters	15
General appearance	9 — 24
Total	100"

We produce the above remarks of Mr. Reginald Knight, as from them, coming as they do from a practical man, our readers who are unacquainted with the breed will be able to see that the Airedale Terrier must certainly be placed amongst the front rank of those vermin Terriers which are, as a body, notorious for gameness and endurance. It was about the year 1875 that the Airedale Terrier began to appear at local shows in the neighbourhood of Leeds, and since then the numbers of the exhibits have steadily increased, until at last they usually form one of the strongest classes. As a matter of opinion, we differ slightly from Mr. Knight in one or two of the numerical values which he attaches to the different points; but we willingly give our allegiance to the following description, which Mr. Knight was considerate enough to lay before most of the leading admirers and judges of the breed on our behalf:—

"*Head.*—Flat, and of good width between the ears.

"*Muzzle.*—Long, and of good strength; the nose being black, the nostrils large, and the lips free from 'flews.'

"*Mouth.*—Level; teeth large and sound.

"*Eyes.*—Small, bright, and dark in colour.

"*Ears.*—Thin, and somewhat larger, in proportion to the size of the dog, than a Fox-terrier's; carried forward, like the latter's, but set on more towards the side of the head, and devoid of all long, silky hair.

"*Neck.*—Strong rather than neat, and free from dewlap and throatiness.

"*Shoulders.*—Well sloped.

"*Chest.*—Moderately deep, but not too wide.

"*Hind quarters.*—Square, and showing a good development of muscle. Thighs well bent.

"*Back.*—Of moderate length, with short and muscular loins.

"*Ribs.*—Well sprung and rounded, affording ample scope for the action of the lungs.

"*Legs.*—Straight, and well furnished with bone.

"*Feet.*—Round, and with no tendency to 'spread.'

"*Tail.*—Stout, and docked from 4 to 7 inches.

"*Coat.*—Broken or rough, and close and hard in texture.

"*Colour.*—A bluish-grey of various shades, from the occiput to root of tail; showing a 'saddle back' of same, also a slight indication on each cheek; rest of body a good tan, richer on feet, muzzle, and ears than elsewhere.

"*Weight.*—From 40 to 55 lbs. for dogs, and from 35 to 50 lbs. for bitches."

The following gentlemen have signed their names to the following statement:—

"I agree to the above standard, and will base my decisions on it.

"W. LORT, Fron Goch Hall, Dec. 9, 1879.

"J. PERCIVAL, Birmingham, Dec. 3, 1879.

"JOHN INMAN, Dec. 3, 1879.

"S. W. WILDMAN, Bingley, Dec. 9, 1879.

"JOHN FISHER, Dec. 3, 1879.

'EDWARD SANDELL, Dec., 1879.

"J. SPEED, Dec. 3, 1879.

"JOHN CROSLAND, Junr., Wakefield, Dec., 1879.

"CHARLES W. BRINSLEY, Dec. 10, 1879.

"T. KIRBY, Dec. 9, 1879.

"REGINALD KNIGHT, Chappel Allerton, Dec., 1879."

The standard having received the support and approval of the above and other judges and breeders, it is to be hoped that others will endeavour to reconcile their views to it, and that the Airedale Terrier will not suffer, as so many other Terriers have done, from a plethora of types, each judge at the same time advocating his own particular prejudices to the injury of the breed.

The dog we have selected for illustration is Mr. Knight's Thunder, a first-rate specimen of the breed according to the above standard, and one whose good qualities have been already referred to by his owner in a former part of this chapter. Thunder is aged 4 years, and weighs 52 pounds, and his measurements are:—Tip of nose to stop, $4\frac{1}{4}$ inches; stop to occiput, $5\frac{3}{4}$ inches; length of back, 20 inches; girth of muzzle, 12 inches; girth of skull, 18 inches; girth of neck, 16 inches; girth round brisket, 27 inches; girth round shoulders, $25\frac{1}{2}$ inches; girth of loin, $22\frac{1}{2}$ inches; girth of thigh, $16\frac{1}{2}$ inches; girth of forearm, $6\frac{3}{4}$ inches; girth round pastern, $4\frac{1}{8}$ inches; height at shoulders, $20\frac{1}{2}$ inches; height at elbows, 12 inches; height at loins, $20\frac{3}{4}$ inches; height at hock, 6 inches.

TABLE OF POINTS FOR JUDGING AIREDALE TERRIERS.

Head, including eyes	10
Ears	5
Muzzle and jaws	5
Body	10
Legs and feet	5
Coat	10
General appearance	5
Total	50

CHAPTER XXI.

THE YORKSHIRE TERRIER.

A NATION has been before now congratulated upon the non-possession of a history, and we are not at all sure in our own minds that the Yorkshire Terrier is not fortunate in finding itself in the same lucky category. So many breeds have been the subjects of acrimonious and narrow-minded disputes and petty quarrels, that a variety which has, comparatively speaking, been let alone, is certainly not to be commiserated with when it finds itself permitted to stand or fall on its own merits. Whatever the varieties of dog may have been which were called upon by breeders to combine and form the present beautiful Yorkshire Terrier, it is proved by results that the judgment of their earliest supporters was sound, and the trouble spent is amply repaid by the successful termination of their labours. There is no reference to be found in any of the earlier writers to a dog which resembles the modern Yorkshire Terrier, and we have, moreover, no recollection of ever having come across an admirer of the variety who claimed that the breed was anything but a manufactured article. It is surprising, therefore, when one comes to contemplate the immense amount of trouble that lovers of this remarkably beautiful dog must have been at to produce such good results. It is freely admitted by almost all writers on dogs that judicious selection of parents can produce almost anything in the shape of dog-flesh; but the difficulty always has been to get these productions to breed true, and obviate the inclination to throw back to some remote ancestor, which is so prevalent in all cross-bred creatures. The Yorkshire Terrier breeders seem to have overcome this obstacle by some means or the other, for though first-rate specimens are in this, as in other breeds, very difficult to obtain, there is an identity of type about the offspring of certain of the best strains which tends to prove that the breed is practically established amongst us, and may be looked upon as one of our national varieties of dogs.

The origin of the breed is most obscure; for its originators—Yorkshire-like—were discreet enough to hold their own counsel, and keep their secrets to themselves. Whether this reticence on their part has had the effect of stifling the inquiries of curious persons, or whether the merits of the breed have hitherto been sufficiently unappreciated by the public, we cannot pretend to say; but we are aware of no correspondence or particular interest having been taken on the subject of the Yorkshire Terrier's origin. In certain works on the dog however, deductions have been drawn which, no doubt, are more or less worthy of respect. The Black-and-tan Terrier, the Skye, and the Maltese, are all credited with the paternity of the Yorkshire Terrier. That the breed in question resembles the Skye in certain details is evident, but in many important points the two varieties vary widely. For instance, the back of the Yorkshire Terrier must be short and the back of a Skye Terrier long; so, as regards shape at least, the Yorkshireman cannot be accused of a great resemblance to his Northern neighbour. In our eyes the breed much more closely resembles the Maltese dog, save in colour; but there is no doubt but that some of our more typical breeds of Terrier have been also drawn upon for his production. Many persons who are ignorant on "doggy" subjects persistently confuse the Yorkshire with what they term the "Scotch Terrier"—thereby meaning the Skye, we presume. There is, however, no visible ground or reason ever given for their opinions, which are certainly based on error, and ignorance of the subject. Before leaving the subject of the Yorkshire Terrier's origin, it may be remarked that the puppies are born black in colour, as are Dandie Dinmonts, and do not obtain their proper shade of coat until they are some months old. Searchers after the truth may here discover some connection, which we ourselves confess we do not, between the Yorkshire and Dandie Dinmont Terriers, in consequence of this peculiarity in the young of both varieties.

Whatever the merits of an ordinary Yorkshire Terrier may be as a companion, it is not within the bounds of probability that many of the first-class show specimens are capable of much exertion out of doors, or attachment to their masters. The quality and extent of their coats must preclude them from venturing beyond the door-step in anything but the finest and dryest weather, whilst the additional disadvantage of being blinded by the hair which grows on their heads would render it impossible for them to pick their way about with any safety. The long hair on the forehead is, however, usually neatly plaited, save on state occasions, and much labour thereby saved the owner, though if left plaited too long without being undone it is liable to get broken and matted.

The most careful attention which can be devoted to any dog is demanded by this Terrier, as the fineness of his coat makes it peculiarly inclined to tangle up and get out of order. It being too long to derive any material benefit from the application of the hair glove which is mentioned in the chapters on kennel management, a long, though not too hard, bristled brush has to be resorted to instead. The best design of brush is the pattern called "balloon"-shaped brushes, whose bristles are not of equal length, those in the centre being longer than the outside ones. The advantage of this shape is that there are no sharp corners to irritate the dog's delicate skin; and it is easier to draw a round-surfaced brush through the coat, without causing injury to the hair and skin, than it is a flat one. Whilst referring to the delicate skin of this breed of dog, the unpleasant consequences arising from heated blood cannot be unnoticed. If a Yorkshire Terrier once commences scratching himself, and is not speedily and effectually prevented from continuing to do so, there will be very little chance of having him in show trim for a long time, for he will tear himself to pieces. To remedy this it is customary to tie up the feet in small bags of wash-leather, so that injury to the skin is not likely to be brought about if the animal scratches. It is, however, desirable to limit the cause of the evil as much as possible by providing suitable diet, which should be of a farinaceous and not heating quality. Milk biscuits, and bread steeped with vegetables in gravy, form an excellent food for toy dogs, and one upon which they will thrive wonderfully if at the same time properly looked after. Regular ablutions are also indispensable to their welfare and well-being, though we have been told by some exhibitors that they consider soap and water injure the texture and colour of the coat, and therefore they prefer to rely more upon careful and frequently-repeated grooming.

Considerable difference of opinion exists amongst its supporters as to the correct weight of a Yorkshire Terrier, as many specimens are to be found from 4 to 5 pounds up to 14 or 15, or even more. No distinct classes are usually made for this breed at the leading shows, which has doubtless in some way been responsible for this variety of opinion. As it is, the large dogs of the breed usually take their place in the class for "Rough-haired Toys other than Spaniels, Maltese, or Pomeranians," and the small ones find themselves relegated to the division for Rough-haired Toys under 7 lbs. weight. It is almost a pity that a regular class cannot be given them at every show of any importance, as their beauty would influence many to give the breed a trial; but, bearing in mind the smallness of the classes, committees are hardly to be blamed if they study their own convenience first. It is, however, we think, rather injurious to the Yorkshire Terrier to be so often shown in the same class as nondescript mongrels, which, though unsuccessful, come by association to be confused by the uninitiated with the genuine Yorkshiremen.

Before going into anything like a description of the Yorkshire Terrier, we may remark that at the present time it is usual to dock their tails and cut their ears. The desirability of such proceedings is more than questioned by certain authorities, but the writer is personally most decidedly in favour of the removal of the tail. It is certainly a thing to be proud of if a man succeeds in producing a dog with a perfectly-shaped and carried tail; but in the face of the enormities in caudal appendages which are frequently seen in pet dogs, it is certainly for the benefit of a breed if by custom a reduction of the offending member is permitted and encouraged. In the matter of ears the question stands on a different footing, as not being a fighting dog (though frequently of a snappish disposition towards human beings), there is no decided reason why the Yorkshire Terrier should lose his ears. The length too of the hair on his head usually conceals the ears, and it therefore seems that as regards any benefit to his appearance the dog's ears might as well be left on as removed. Again, a good ear being naturally harder to obtain than a bad one, a dog of this breed with an uncut, well-shaped ear is to be expected to beat one whose ears have been manipulated.

In showing and dealing in Yorkshire Terriers there are unfortunately many unfair advantages by which a cunning and unprincipled person can steal a march on youth or inexperience. The beautiful colour of the body is the most usual mark for the skill of the "faker," and a judge who knows his work, and is not afraid of doing his duty, has frequently to disqualify some of the competitors who appear before him. A common application is black-lead to the darker portion of the coat on the back, but this is easy of detection, and a white handkerchief will usually work out that mystery, to the discomfort of the owner if he is in attendance.

Mrs. M. A. Foster of Bradford, is, at the time of writing, *facile princeps* at the head of affairs in the Yorkshire Terrier line. It is marvellous to contemplate the success of this enthusiastic lady, and the condition in which she shows her pets is beyond all praise. Though her dogs are always good—she never showed a bad one—many of her successes are largely contributed to by the care she bestows upon them and their toilets. Mrs. Bligh Monk of Coley Park near Reading, Lady Giffard of Red Hill, and Miss Alderson of Leeds, are also exhibitors who have left their mark deeply on the list of successful competitors. Mr. Abraham Boulton, also, of Accrington, Messrs. W. Wilkinson, W. Eastwood, Alderson of Halifax, and Torr of Birmingham, have all done good service to all sizes of Yorkshire Terriers, by producing first-rate specimens of the breed. The dog we have selected to illustrate the Yorkshire Terrier is Mrs. M. A. Foster's very beautiful little Toy Smart, winner at the Alexandra Palace show of July, 1879. Unfortunately, as he has been sold, we are unable to get his measurements for insertion therewith.

With regard to the standard of a Yorkshire Terrier, it may truthfully be stated before going further, that the most essential points to be gained are coat and colour, as most of the other features shrink into insignificance before these two great *desiderata*. However

The *Skull* should be, as in all Terriers, long and gradually tapering towards the muzzle.

Eyes and Nose.—Small, dark, and sparkling, when visible, though they are usually hidden by the superabundance of hair on the head. Nose black.

Jaws must not be broad or heavy, but rather deficient in power, though fine in outline.

Ears.—Either cut or uncut, if the latter, fine, and semi-erect.

Body.—Short and compact, with rather wide chest, in comparison with his size (the two former points are important as differing from the Skye Terrier), and covered with silky hair

Legs.—Straight, placed under the body, and well feathered with silky hair.

Feet.—Long and feathered.

Tail.—Cut, and carried straight.

Coat.—Long, glossy, silky, and quite flat, not curly.

Colour.—On the head a beautiful golden tan, which gets much darker on the ears ; back a dark blue, inclined to silver, the latter colour extending over the other portions of the body, except the legs, which should be the same colour as the head—a golden tan.

General Appearance.—A pretty, fragile little dog, but one quite incapable of much out-door exercise, and of delicate constitution.

STANDARD FOR JUDGING YORKSHIRE TERRIERS.

	Value.
Head ...	3
Ears and eyes ...	2
Body ...	7
Legs and feet ...	3
Coat ..	15
Colour ...	20
	—
	50

CHAPTER XXII.

THE TOY TERRIER.

THE origin of the Toy Terrier is not hard to discover when the existence of such a variety as the English Black-and-tan Terrier is an acknowledged fact. In-breeding is certain, if carried too far, to stunt the growth of any animal, and this is, without any doubt, the means by which the modern Toy Terrier was first originated. In the rage for Lilliputian dimensions, however, many of those engaged in the production of the pigmy Terrier lost sight of the fact that in breeding from dogs of the same blood it was very desirable that healthy specimens should be selected to found the new race. There was quite sufficient probability of the offspring being delicate and sickly as it was, but the increased risk of producing delicate constitutions was unheeded by the earlier breeders, and no doubt accounts for many of the miserably wretched little dogs that are so often shown. A Toy Terrier is naturally a fragile little creature, and peculiarly susceptible of cold and chills. It should therefore be kept constantly clothed in winter, and an ornamental kennel or basket should be provided for it close to the fire. The shivering which is so perceptible in many Toys is due, we believe, to the Italian Greyhound cross which has been at one time or another introduced into their strain, and is not in itself a positive sign that the animal is suffering seriously from cold. This taint, however, as in the case of Bull-terriers or White English Terriers, is generally most noticeable in the action of the fore-legs—the peculiar "dancing," as it is termed in canine phraseology, being usually traceable for many generations.

Another unsightly disfigurement to which the vast majority of the breed is liable is the possession of a prominent forehead, or "apple head," which gives the dog the appearance of suffering from water on the brain. We believe we are correct in saying that many of the dogs so formed are sprung from parents and ancestors of about their own size, whilst the greater number of the flat, terrier-headed show specimens have been the result of the union of dogs superior in stature to themselves. This is the experience of more than one successful breeder; but, in the absence of any one person who has laid himself out to produce show specimens, a large number of trustworthy statistics are naturally not easy to be procured.

London deserves considerable credit for the production of these interesting little dogs, though what becomes of the vast majority of those which are annually disposed of by the Whitechapel and Clerkenwell breeders it is very difficult to tell. It may, however, be surmised that as the creatures are of so delicate a constitution, the absence of consideration and attention on the part of their owners is responsible for many an untimely end. In draughty rooms an excellent accommodation for a Toy Terrier is the glass-fronted show-box which we see at dog-shows, which has a wooden slide to slip down in front of the glass and protect it if taken out of doors. In the case of such boxes being used, it is imperative that due attention should be paid to their satisfactory ventilation. This can be secured by the presence of air-holes bored high up in the wooden back. The latter may or may not, as depends on their size, be protected by perforated zinc fastened over them. Special care must be taken, if zinc is used, to see that it is fixed in a workmanlike manner, as a sharp edge would be very likely to injure the dog.

The correct points and markings of the Toy are identical with those of the larger-sized Black-and-tan Terrier; only, as before mentioned, there is usually a great dearth of flat-headed Toys, the inclination to get apple-headed being a great hindrance to the breeder's success. Another disfigurement, and one to which the apple-headed ones are apparently more liable than the others, is a large, full, weeping eye, which is in every way opposed to the small, black, and bead-like eye so essential to a good Terrier. Again, in the Toys there is an increased difficulty in getting the correct shade of tan combined with the orthodox pencilling and thumb-marks. We know of more than one specimen otherwise capable of holding its own in any company but yet wanting in these points, and therefore unable to be shown with any certainty of success. We consider these markings to be a *sine quâ non* in a Terrier for showing, though there are many dogs most valuable for breeding purposes which have either no black at all on their feet and pasterns, or, on the other hand, show no signs of tan. In breeding from such specimens we recommend that the black-legged or heavily-marked ones should be preferred to those which are wanting in any pencilling, as the latter are usually pale and "clayey" in tan, and therefore unlikely to produce rich-coloured offspring. The darker ones are, on the other hand, very likely to beget puppies (if suitably mated) well marked, and with a rich, "warm-coloured" tan.

From the smallness of their size and their natural delicacy, Toy Terriers are difficult to rear, and the mother often succumbs when bringing puppies into the world. However, many long-headed breeders are prepared with artificial mothers in the shape of the domestic cat, who can usually be prevailed upon in any number to undertake the mother's duties to one or more puppies, and thus save any strain upon the latter's already reduced strength.

Amongst the best specimens of recent years have been Mr. Howard Mapplebeck's Belle, and Mr. Robert Fulton's (late) Lady Lucy. The latter was, in our opinion, when alive, the best-headed Toy we ever remember to have come across, and her untimely decease was a severe loss to the breed. Unfortunately Lady Lucy, like many others of her breed, succumbed to the effects of a chill, to which all these dogs are peculiarly liable, from the delicacy of their size, and the small amount of hair they usually possess. The latter infirmity is no doubt another of the ill effects of (we presume, in this case, the necessary abuse of) in-breeding, and very great difficulty is usually found by owners of toy dogs to keep them in good trim. A leading breeder, however, has informed us on several occasions that he has found excellent results follow the application of castor-oil to the skin, which he uses on all occasions, certainly with excellent results as regards his own stud, which is usually in a most satisfactory state of health. Amongst other good and successful Toys of late years may be mentioned Mr. Henry Lacy's Pepita, Mr. Abraham Boulton's Little Wonder, and a very fair one of Mrs. M. A. Foster's—by name, we believe, Linley. In the north of England we have sometimes come across Toy Terriers marked with white, who would otherwise have been good enough to win prizes anywhere. The white usually appeared on the chest, which is the most common place for it to appear in dogs, and was not considered a blemish for breeding purposes by the owners. In our opinion, though the disfigurement may be present in any litter, it is in-judicious to breed from dogs with white marks; and this idea is, we believe, endorsed by the majority of the London breeders of Toy Terriers.

The Toy Terrier we have chosen for our coloured illustration is Mr. Tom B. Swinburne's (of Darlington) Serpolette, by Ribchester's Trip out of Rose, and one of the best specimens seen for years. She was born in 1878, and weighs five pounds. Amongst her best perform-ances are first at Dundee, and first Birmingham, 1879, and she has won many other prizes about the country, but, from her youth, has been unable to take a part in many of the principal shows. Serpolette measures :—From nose to stop, 2 inches; from stop to occiput, 3 inches; length of back, 9½ inches; girth of muzzle, 5 inches; girth of skull, 8¾ inches; girth of neck, 7½ inches; girth round shoulders, 12½ inches; girth round loins, 9½ inches; girth round thigh, 6½ inches; girth round arm, 2 inches; height at shoulders, 9½ inches; height at elbows, 6 inches; height at loins, 9 inches; height at hocks, 3 inches; length of tail, 5 inches.

SCALE OF POINTS FOR JUDGING TOY TERRIERS.

	Value.
Skull, flatness and shape	5
Eyes and ears	5
Body	5
Colour and marking	10
Smallness	20
General appearance	5
Total ...	50

CHAPTER XXIII.

TOY SPANIELS.

THE King Charles and Blenheim Spaniels are so closely allied as regards structural development, that the task of separating them, were it not for their colours, would be extremely difficult. The origin of the two breeds is undoubtedly obscure, but the credit of bringing these most beautiful little pets into popular notice unquestionably lies with His Majesty King Charles II., from which monarch the former variety derives its name.

It must not, however, be imagined that the *existence* of the breed is due to the exertions of its royal patron, for direct allusion is made to it by Dr. Caius in his work alluded to before, in which he clearly connects this variety with the Maltese dog, as the latter then existed; he describes them in the third section of his book as follows :—

" . . . . Of the delicate, neate, and pretty kind of dogges called the Spaniel gentle, or the comforter, in Latine Metitæus or Fotor."

"These dogges are little, pretty, proper, and fine, and sought for to satisfy the delicatenesse of daintie dames, and wanton women's wills. Instrumentes of folly for them to play and dally withall, to tryfle away the treasure of time . . . ." "These puppies, the smaller they be, th more pleasure they provoke, as more meete play-fellowes for mincing mistresses to beare in their bosoms . . . ."

From the above extracts it would appear that the Toy Spaniel did not stand high in the estimation of Dr. John Caius; though a few lines later on there is an attempt to prove that this dog was of some service in the world, since he gravely announces, "We find that these little dogs are good to assuage the sicknesse of the stomacke, being oftentimes thereunto applyed as a plaster preservative, or borne in the bosom of the diseased and weake person, which effect is performed by theyr moderate heate. Moreover, the disease and sicknesse chaungeth his place, and entreth (though it be not precisely marcked) into the dogge, which experience can testify, for these kinde of dogges sometimes fall sicke, and sometimes die, without any harme outwardly inforced, which is an argument that the disease of the gentleman or gentle-woman or ouner whatsoever, entreth into the dogge by the operation of heate intermingled and infected."

How any person in his senses could publish the above, and seriously intimate that he believes in his theory, we are at a loss to imagine. It suits us, however, to reproduce it, as showing that in the days of Queen Elizabeth ladies were in the habit of keeping Toy Spaniels about them; and from these no doubt the King Charles Spaniel was subsequently derived.

In the time of King Charles II., the Toy Spaniel may be said to have reached the zenith of its popularity; it was the pampered favourite of the king, and the position it held at court is alluded to in Pepys' Diary, where he states that the Spaniels had free access to all parts of Whitehall, even upon State occasions.

In the "Naturalist's Library," by Sir William Jardine, published in 1843, the only allusion made to Toy Spaniels is as follows :—

"KING CHARLES SPANIEL.

A beautiful breed, in general black-and-white, and presumed to be the parent of

THE COCKER,

who is usually black, and shorter in the back than the Spaniel. This appears to be the Gredin of Buffon. The Blenheim, Marlborough, or Pyrame of Buffon, is very similar to the above, but the black colour is relieved by fire-coloured spots above the eyes, and the same on the breast and feet ; the muzzle is fuller, and the back rather short. The Maltese dog (*Canis Melitæus*) the Bichon or Chien Bouffé of Buffon, is the most ancient of the small Spaniel races, being figured on Roman monuments and noticed by Strabo ; the muzzle is rounder, the hair very long, silky, and usually white, the stature very small, and only fit for ladies' lap-dogs."

From the above description it would almost appear that the modern Blenheim Spaniel was practically unknown in the year 1843 ; but it is incredible that such could be the case ; and we must therefore presume that the opinion of Sir William Jardine is not altogether reliable as

TOY SPANIELS. *From "Icones Animalium."*

regards the subject of *colour*, which in the present day is a matter of very considerable importance in judging Toy Spaniels. We are strengthened in this opinion by the following extract from the *Sportsman's Repository*, written by John Scott, and published in 1820, which states that, " Twenty years ago (*i.e.*, 1800) His Grace the Duke of Marlborough was reputed to possess the smallest and best breed of Cockers in Britain ; they were invariably red-and-white, with very long ears, short noses, and black eyes."

Before passing on to the points of the two breeds, regret must be expressed at the gross neglect which these beautiful and highly-interesting little pets have experienced at the hands of the public. In intelligence and natural vivacity they are so far in advance of other ladies' toys, that it seems incredible that they should for so long a time occupy an inferior position to the uninteresting and often quarrelsome Pug. A ladies' pet need not be condemned to a life-long existence in his mistress's boudoir ; and the extreme stupidity of the generality of Pugs when out of doors is rendered eminently conspicuous by the very different behaviour of a King Charles or Blenheim Spaniel. Doubtless the fact of a Spaniel possessing a long coat, which requires constant brushing to keep in good order, is an obstacle in the way of its popularity ; but the beauty of the dog amply repays any trouble bestowed upon it, and a little care and attention devoted to the toilet of a "Charlie" or Blenheim is certain to be repaid a hundred-fold by the improvement it invariably effects in the dog's appearance. As a matter of fact we have ourselves owned several Toy Spaniels, which, but for the delicacy of their coats, were capable of entering any brushwood. That they frequently attempted to do so in the course of country rambles their torn skins fully attested ; but the early repetition of the conduct bore testimony to the animal's love of sport and plucky temperament. Unfortunately, however, the long coat gets clogged with mud and matted by damp when out of doors in bad weather, and the task of washing her pet and making him comfortable is beneath the consideration of many lady owners, who only keep the creatures because they, when in health, gratify their eyes by their beauty ; their comfort being quite a secondary consideration with those whose duty it is to keep them comfortable. Such persons should most certainly eschew keeping Spaniels in favour of a pet of a more phlegmatic temperament, and one that takes its pleasure and its exercise in a more respectable though a sadder manner. There is so much life and "go" in King Charles or Blenheims, if they are in perfect health, and accustomed to regular exercise, that they splash themselves with mud to a far greater degree than a quieter dog. On the other hand, as a rule, no toy dog is in possession of so much intelligence, and so capable of being brought under command, and we know of more than one first-rate specimen which is in the habit of following its owner about London as quietly and safely as it would in a country lane.

A Toy Spaniel is in reality a toy only from force of circumstances, and we believe could be readily broken, and worked with the gun, though there would not be much chance of its standing a day's work, on account of its smallness of stature. Our opinions here are shared by the author of the *Sportsman's Repository* above alluded to, who remarks, "The very delicate and small, or 'carpet Spaniels,' have exquisite nose, and will hunt truly and pleasantly, but are neither fit for a long day nor a thorny covert." With so much, therefore, to recommend them, it is to be hoped that these most beautiful of all dogs may yet regain the position they once occupied, especially as his affectionate disposition renders a "Charlie" or a Blenheim doubly dear to his owner. An instance of the importance attached to his dogs (which were presumably Toy Spaniels) by King James II. lies in the fact that once, on his escape in a boat from a sinking ship, he insisted on putting back to the wreck to save his dogs, though no room could be found on board for several sailors, who were left behind and eventually drowned.

An essential distinction between the ancient and modern type of Toy Spaniel lies in the formation of the muzzle, as well as in colour. In days gone by it is undoubtedly a fact that the short *retroussé* noses now so fashionable were things unknown ; in fact, the first reference to them that we have come across is in the *Sportsman's Repository*, which we have already quoted. That some outside cross has been at one time or another resorted to in order to produce this we may be quite assured, but how it came about is another matter, and presents a difficulty in solution. For our own opinion we fancy a cross of Pug has played some important part in the change of shape in the skull of the Toy Spaniel. One thing is certain, that by reducing the length of nose, much of the animal's sense of smell must have been impaired, and it is therefore reasonable to suggest that if breeders of Toy Spaniels deliberately set to work to try and breed short-nosed dogs, they did so subsequently to the variety being withdrawn from an active participation in field sports.

The subject of colour is a different one entirely, and we can only suppose when discussing the merits of the King Charles that the partial disappearance of the black-tan-and-white dog, is the result of neglect, and not of any fixed determination on the part of admirers of the breed to exterminate a colour which is to many tastes the most beautiful Spaniel colour we have. That white is a perfectly legitimate colour in a King Charles Spaniel, a reference to old paintings will prove, and we are glad to find the authorities at some of our shows instituting a class for King Charles other than black-and-tan. Here (unfortunately we think) red dogs are allowed to compete at the present time, but we are of opinion that the proper place for the latter under any circumstances is the Blenheim class ; and a class for Blenheims other than red-and-white would, we believe, soon be well filled with entries. There is not the slightest desire on our part to under-rate the beauty or value of a red Spaniel, but we are profoundly of the opinion that red is essentially a Blenheim colour, and one which has no right to be seen in a King Charles, whose colour should be either black-and-tan, or black-tan-and-white. As we have before remarked, the introduction of white most certainly used to be considered legitimate in the case of Toy Spaniels; and no unprejudiced person who sees such beautiful specimens as Miss Violet Cameron's Conrad, and Mrs. Russell Earp's Tweedledee, can regret that efforts are being made to restore one of the most lovely varieties of colour which ever belonged to dogs. A decided use to which the red dogs have been put is to improve the colour of the tan markings in the black-and-tan dogs. This would either inevitably get paler (or to use a technical term, more "clayey") in colour than the "warm" or rich-shaded tan breeders like to see in them; or, in the second instance, the tan markings would disappear altogether, and the dogs would become totally black, which would naturally be an eyesore to their admirers. As a matter of fact, we know positively that many of our reputedly best and certainly most successful strains have been crossed with each other to such an extent, that more than one mother has been known to produce red-and-white and black-and-tans at one birth. In the face of such facts, under the present circumstances we do not think sufficient care can be taken by supporters of the breed to keep their strains pure; as sure and certain evil will be wrought in the present fashionable colours if care is not taken to breed for colour and markings. This, if no market can be found for black-tan-and-white Spaniels, must necessarily prove of the greatest injury to all the other colours, as the propagation of a variety without pecuniary support from the outside public is an enterprise which few breeders care to embark upon.

Whilst on the subject of breeding for colour, the following practical remarks of Mr. Joseph Nave, of Henrietta Street, Covent Garden, London, who is well known as a breeder and authority on Toy Spaniels, will be read with interest:—

"The colour of King Charles most liked now is black-and-tan, but there are a great many all tan (red), which in my experience arises from breeding from White-and-red Blenheim bitches with black-and-tan King Charles. I have a black-and-tan King Charles dog from parents of the same colour; thinking to obtain black-white-and-tan puppies, I put him to a red-and-white Blenheim bitch, and the result was a litter of four, all tan. I kept one of the red bitches, and put a black-and-tan King Charles dog to her, and the result was five black-and-tan puppies, with very bright tan. Therefore, I have come to the conclusion, if you want to breed puppies black with very bright tan, it is best to breed from a red bitch; but I have experienced that, if you keep breeding and in-breeding always from black-and-tan parents, the tan will gradually get out of them, and you may get several puppies all black, without any tan; and all-black King Charles are not liked at all. The original King Charles were black-and-white, with long noses, and very long ears. Through the introduction of the black-and-tan Japanese Spaniel—of which I know at present a very fine specimen, brought over by Sir John Hay—black-and-tan King Charles were produced; but through the Japanese they have lost a great deal in the length of ears, and gained the high skull, short nose, and underhung, which is the nature of the Japanese. The present tendency of King Charles is for long noses again, and larger ears; and we should be very glad to see a fresh importation of Japanese Spaniels, so as to revive the short nose again. It is my firm opinion that the origin of the present Pug dog is nothing but the common English fawn-coloured smooth-coated Terrier bitch crossed with a little jet-black Chinese Terrier, of which I also have seen some—they have the short nose and high head, and very curly tails. King Charles should not be too small, and need not weigh less than 10 lb.; if they are much smaller they lose many of the properties and the beautiful coats of the breed."

We are gratified to find that so great an authority as Mr. Joseph Nave coincides with our views on the Pug cross. Our conclusions were arrived at, singularly enough, without any previous conversation, and by his support of our theory we feel considerably fortified in it; and, as an experiment, intend to try a Japanese Pug cross with a Toy Spaniel on the earliest opportunity. Mr. Nave has, however, hit the nail on the head when he alludes to this cross being likely to decrease the length of ear in the King Charles or Blenheim, and we candidly admit that on this point we see breakers ahead which will be difficult to weather in safety. Nevertheless there is now such a tendency to long snipy muzzles, that something should be done to prevent these breeds degenerating into nondescripts which do not fairly represent either the ancient *or* modern type of Toy Spaniel.

The two illustrations appended of the older types most strongly support this view of the case. The reader's attention cannot fail to be directed to the, at present, uncommon combination of long muzzles and long ears in the smaller illustration, which is taken from *Icones Animalium*, by J. F. Riedel. The Spaniels here portrayed are in our opinion intended to be black-tan-and-white King Charles, though the absence of descriptive letterpress, and the inferior engraving of that period render this conviction more or less a matter of conjecture. The large full-page engraving is drawn from two German dogs of the present day, but is a perfect representation of the longer muzzle and magnificent ears which were at an earlier date fashionable in England, and are very likely to be preferred by most who do not live in the artificial atmosphere of shows.

We are also favoured with the following notes on the Blenheim from Mr. James W. Berrie, of Lower Tooting, Surrey, which we have much pleasure in reproducing :—

"Next to the old English Bulldog, of which Englishmen may so justly be proud, the Blenheim stands pre-eminently first. This exquisitely beautiful little dog should have a long silky coat of the pure 'ruby and pearl' colour, and it should possess all the distinguishing characteristics of the King Charles Spaniel, which was so called because of the esteem in which it was held by the 'Merry Monarch.'

"The modern Blenheim, from a phrenological point of view, possesses properties and organs more nearly resembling the human head than any other kind of dog. He has Individuality, Eventuality, Comparison, and Causality, very largely developed. That the Blenheim possesses Individuality is obvious to all who have studied the breed and character of the dog: he knows at a glance the *canine lover*, and is friendly in a moment; while the *dog hater* may try his best to win his favour in vain.

"It is generally admitted that the dog has memory, but this quality is most singularly developed in the Blenheim; he having been known to remember some of the most trivial circumstances in his history, which have long escaped the mind of his master. Many instances could be given to corroborate this statement, but one will suffice. Little Blossom" (one of Mrs. Berrie's pets) "was visiting a friend in the country with my wife, and on one occasion she killed a shrew, which my wife took from her and placed in a hole in the wall of a barn, quite out of her reach. Blossom did her best to get it by 'sitting up' and barking for it, but at last gave it up in despair. Years after, when she went to the

EARLY TYPE OF TOY SPANIELS.

TOY SPANIELS.

same place, she ran to the old barn, and, putting her fore-feet against the wall, she did her utmost to get up to have a peep at the place where the dead shrew had been laid six years before.

"Generosity is another property natural to the Blenheim. I have known instances where one has kept another supplied with food, when he was tied up and unable to obtain it for himself. This happened more than once with two puppies of my own breeding. 'Bloom,' being a mischievous fellow, was very often imprisoned under a crate; when hungry, he had only to make a whining kind of cry, and 'Petal' (the brother) would forthwith start off and bring him bread or anything in the way of comestibles that he could find.

"The Blenheim is an exceedingly difficult breed to rear, hence the scarcity of good specimens. They are liable to brain diseases, supposed to be caused by the unusually large size of the head in comparison with the body. We find intense excitement very injurious to them when young, sometimes causing fits, which, however, rarely prove fatal unless the subject is exceedingly delicate.

"The best food for rearing puppies (we think) is a little finely-minced meat, with plenty of soaked bread twice a day, alternated with a little Swiss milk and bread.

POINTS OF A BLENHEIM.

"The *Under-jaw* should be wide between the tusks, and well turned up; undershot, but not to show teeth.

The *Nose* should be black, wide and deep, and as short as possible, almost in a line with the eyes; the nostrils being large and open.

"The 'stop' is wide, and as deep as in a fine Bull-dog, but the nose should not recede as in that animal.

"*Eyes* as large as possible, perfectly black, wide apart, and at right angles with the line of the face. Weeping at the corners is owing to a defect in the lachrymal duct.

"*Head* should be very large and round, with a dome-like appearance at the top. The forehead should project well over the eyes, so as almost to touch the nose.

"*Ears* as long as possible, not curly; about eight inches in length from where they join the head. They must be low down on the side of the head, almost on a line with the ears.

"*Shape.*—Thick-set and cobby; chest deep and wide; strong legs; short back; arched neck. *Tail* carried gaily, but not over the back; it should be almost on a line with the back. Well cut up from chest to loin; the latter should be strong and as sturdy as possible.

"*Colour* should on no account be whole, but rich ruby red and pure pearly white. The white should form the ground, and the red should be in detached spots scattered over the body. The fore-legs and nose should be slightly 'ticked.' The ears and cheeks should be red, and a blaze of white up the forehead, in the centre of which should be a spot of red as large as a sixpence, called 'the spot.' The best marked dogs are those with well-defined red markings on the sides and back, and a 'splash' at the root of the tail. Some few good specimens are cinnamon and white, but this is not a desirable colour.

"*Coat* should be fine, silky, long, and as free from curl and mixture as possible.

"The *Chest, Feet,* and *Tail* should be well feathered, and also the back of the legs.

"*Weight* from six to twelve pounds, but the best specimens are from eight to ten pounds.

"The *Feet* should be small and well-knit together, with the toes strong and well made;

from between the toes should grow tufts of hair like feathers, giving the animal the appearance of walking on mats."

Amongst the most conspicuous breeders and owners who are in possession of the correct type of King Charles and Blenheims, the names of Mrs. Forder of Bow, Mrs. J. W. Berrie of Lower Tooting, and Mr. Joseph Nave of Henrietta Street, are most prominent. Mrs. Berrie certainly confines her attention to Blenheims only, but her collection, as a collection, is without a rival. The Earl and Bawbee are her two best dogs as we write; but owing to the experience and sound practical judgment of her husband (Mr. James W. Berrie) being so often of late called into requisition in the capacity of judge at the principal shows, only very few opportunities are offered her for exhibiting her pets. Mrs. Forder, on the other hand, is practically at the top of the tree with black-and-tan King Charles, her Young Jumbo being deservedly the present champion. The Bow kennel, however, has also some grand Blenheims, and of late years Mrs. Forder has been wonderfully successful with Lizzie, albeit that to some minds her markings were too pale in colour. At present one of the best youngsters out also hails from Mrs. Forder's stud: this is Bo-Peep, who will, we think, prove the bright particular star in the Blenheim world for some time to come. Mr. Nave is a breeder of both varieties, but his splendidly-shaped dog Covent Garden Charlie is too large in stature to please every judge, and this has prevented his winning at many shows. Mrs. M. A. Forster of Bradford does a great deal of winning in the North of England by the assistance of the Blenheim Duke of Bow, who is a purchase from Mrs. Forder's kennel; and Mrs. Bligh Monk, of Coley Park near Reading, has also had some good specimens. A few years back Miss Dawson, of Coldharbour Lane, London, was almost invincible with Old Jumbo, but age and infirmity at length drove the grand little dog off the bench; and on his deposition Young Jumbo sprang at once into first place. Mr. S. A. Julius, of Hastings, too, has several excellent Blenheims, many of his belonging to the old or long-faced, and now unfashionable, type. The above are our principal and most successful exhibitors, but there are many choice collections, and excellent, but solitary, specimens of Toy Spaniels which never appear in public, though it is to be hoped that in the interest of the breeds their owners will support the classes more substantially than they do at present. There are some beautiful specimens, too, of that most lovely of all colours, the black-tan-and-white King Charles, to be met with, but the key of the position in this variety is held by Miss Violet Cameron with her Conrad—one of the best-shaped dogs out—and Mrs. Russell Earp with Tweedledee.

Before proceeding to give the points of a Toy Spaniel, we may remark that it is an invariable rule to dock their tails—that is, to cut them about four inches short. Our ideas on the breed are as follows:—

The *Skull* of a Toy Spaniel should be round, with a short, upturned muzzle, and a decided "stop," or indentation, between the eyes.

The *Muzzle* must be short and rather square-shaped, with a black nose well turned back towards the skull.

The *Eyes* must, as in the Bulldog, be wide apart, and very full and prominent—dark in colour and lustrous.

The *Ears*, a most important feature in a Toy Spaniel, must be set on rather low and hang perfectly flat to the sides of the head. In addition to their own considerable length, they are provided with long silken hair, which in some specimens almost trails on the ground.

The *Nose* must be black.

The *Body* is cloddy and compact.

The *Legs* inclined to be short, and with the backs well coated with long silky hair, or "feather" as it is termed.

Feet, large and well covered with hair.

The *Coat* in both breeds must be long and silky; without curl, which is a fault.

Size, about 10 pounds, or a little more in a King Charles; but the Blenheims weigh rather less. It is not, therefore, desirable to have the King Charles much under 10 pounds weight.

Colour.—In the King Charles: black-and-tan or black-tan-and-white. Blenheims: red-and-white. In this breed a red spot on the forehead is esteemed a decided characteristic, and should always be looked for in good specimens, as its absence is a blemish.

General appearance is that of an intelligent nimble little dog, which combines activity with a daintiness peculiar to good breeding and aristocratic connections.

The dogs we have chosen to illustrate the breed in all four colours are—for the black-and-tan King Charles, Mr. Joseph Nave's Covent Garden Charlie, whose sire is Young Jumbo and dam Daisy—Age, 2 years and 9 months; weight, 16 lbs.; he measures from nose to stop, three-quarters of an inch; from stop to occiput, 4 inches; length of back, 14 inches; girth of muzzle, 7½ inches; girth of skull, 13 inches; girth of neck, 12 inches; girth round brisket, 18 inches; girth round shoulders, 18 inches; girth of loins, 15 inches; girth round forearm, 5 inches; girth round pastern, 3½ inches; height at shoulder, 15 inches; height at elbows, 7½ inches; height at loins, 14 inches; length of ears from tip to tip, 22 inches; feather on fore-legs, 6 inches.

In the black-tan-and-white King Charles, Miss Violet Cameron's Conrad, age about three years. His breeder and pedigree are unknown, as Conrad was purchased, when quite a puppy, from a dealer in London who had no certain pedigree with him. He is an own brother to Mrs. Russell Earp's well-known Tweedledee, and in fact the whole litter was one of unusual merit. Conrad measures:—From nose to stop, three-quarters of an inch; stop to occipital bone, 4 inches; length of back, 12½ inches; girth of muzzle, 5½ inches; girth of skull, 11 inches; girth of neck, 9½ inches; girth round brisket, 17 inches; girth round shoulders, 15 inches; girth round loins, 13¾ inches; girth of forearm, 4 inches; girth round pastern, 2¾ inches; height at shoulder, 10 inches; height at elbow, 5½ inches; height at loins, 10½ inches.

For the red Spaniel, Mr. Joseph Nave's Sepperl by Hillus out of the owner's Fanny (both black-and-tans). He is six years old, and weighs 15 lb.; measuring from nose to stop, 1 inch; from stop to occiput, 5 inches; length of back, 16 inches; girth of muzzle, 7 inches; girth of skull, 13 inches; girth of neck, 12 inches; girth of brisket, 18 inches; girth round chest, 18 inches; girth of loins, 15 inches; girth of forearm, 5 inches; girth of pastern, 4 inches; height at shoulder, 15 inches; height at elbow, 7½ inches; height at loins, 14 inches.

And for the red-and-white Blenheim, Mrs. J. W. Berrie's Bawbee, who is four years old, and weighs 10 lb. 2 oz. Bawbee measures from nose to stop, ¾ inch; from stop to occiput, 4 inches; length of back, 10 inches; girth of muzzle, 6 inches; girth of skull, 11½ inches; girth of neck, 12 inches; girth round brisket, 19 inches; girth round shoulders, 19 inches; girth of loins, 12½ inches; girth of forearm, 4½ inches; girth of pastern, 3 inches; height at shoulder, 12 inches; height at elbow, 5¾ inches; height at loins, 10½ inches.

SCALE OF POINTS FOR JUDGING TOY SPANIELS.

	Value.
Skull	5
Stop and squareness of jaw	5
Shortness of face	5
Ears	5
Body and legs	5
Coat, including colour	15
Size	5
General appearance	5
Total	50

Before leaving these beautiful and engaging breeds, we must once more impress upon our readers the importance of frequently brushing their coats with a not too hard "balloon" brush, such as recommended in Chapter XXI. If the blood becomes heated too, which will soon be discovered by the dog scratching, a course of sulphur and magnesia, as recommended on page 20, should be at once prescribed, but the doses must not be too strong, or the constitution of the Spaniel may be injured by them.

CHAPTER XXIV.

THE PUG.

THERE is considerable uncertainty in regard to the origin of this peculiar breed of dog, but there is a decided preponderance of opinion in favour of his being an offshoot, in some form or other, from the Bull-dog. There are several formations identical to the two breeds, which very much influence us in favour of this opinion, even if there were not in the present day the gravest suspicion for imagining that modern breeders in some instances have availed themselves of a Bull cross in hopes of improving their strain in certain qualities. Rightly or wrongly, the Dutch have had the credit from time immemorial of first introducing the breed into public favour. For our own part we can see no positive grounds for the absolute accuracy of this popular belief, which though referred to by more than one of the writers on the dog in the earlier part of the century, was evidently not even then unanimously accepted as an incontrovertible fact. The author of the " Sportsman's Repository," to which reference has been already made, remarked some sixty years ago that—

" The Pug Dog is generally styled the Dutch Pug, and it is taken for granted that the breed is indigenous to Holland, since, according to universal but dateless tradition, it was originally imported hither from that country. Pugs indeed are numerous throughout the Low Countries, and, we believe, most of the northern part of the Continent. There is yet an obscure but confident tradition, that Pugism had its origin in Muscovy; which, being granted, we may not have been wide of the mark in tracing in it the form of the Arctic dog. Another, and which we deem an inconsequent conjecture on this most important affair of origination, is the Pug being, according to certain sage conjecturists, a sample or first-class mongrel, the production of a commixture between the English Bulldog and the little Dane, a conjecture we feel inclined to define by the figure *hysteron-proteron*, or setting the cart before the horse. We hold the Pug to be of the elder house; and if at this perilous anti-parodial crisis we may venture at a secular parody, the motto of the illustrious race of Pugs ought to be, not we from Bulls, but Bulls from us."

As our readers may conjecture, we do not by any means agree with the latter observation of the writer, as we have, in a former portion of this work, already expressed very decided opinions on the antiquity of the Bull-dog. Again, from another point of view, we cannot see how the small-sized Pug can be taken to be the ancestor of the large-framed, big-boned, and determined dispositioned Bull-dog, which is an animal far more likely to originate a race than the somewhat stupid and uninteresting Pug. The origin of this latter word is difficult of discovery, but in many quarters it is believed to be derived from the word *pugnus*, a fist, whether because of the dog's shape or former size we are unable to conjecture.

For some time on the Continent, in France especially, Pugs went by the name of Carlins, owing to the black mask on their faces, which is a characteristic of the breed. The analogy between Carlins and masks lay in the fact that formerly there was a famous and very popular harlequin in France whose name was Carlin, and hence the appellation as applied to Pugs.

The Pugs of the present are popularly supposed to belong to either the Willoughby or the Morrison strain, which at one time were almost identical in shape, but of different colours. So many breeders have, however, either from motives of economy or curiosity, been in the habit of crossing the above two varieties with each other, that a pure-bred specimen of either strain is not an easy thing to come across. Hundreds are advertised, and sold, as genuine Willoughby or Morrison Pugs, which have no claim whatever to so grand a distinction. The chief difference between the two breeds is that the Morrison Pug is a richer colour, and not so heavily marked with black as the Willoughby strain. The latter blood frequently shows too much tracing, and is apt to be smutty in colour, which in a Pug should be as pure a fawn as can be procured, but relieved by black in the proper places. This was certainly the opinion of authorities early in the century, for we find the following description of a Pug in a work published many years ago :—

"A *yellow* colour of various shades, small and moderate size, round and fixed shape, full breast, short neck and legs, arched tail, round prominent eyeballs, bluff head, black muzzle, lightly pendulous ears, prominent inferior jaw, or underhung; and a grave, often savage, countenance."

The above may even now pass as a very good description of a Pug, and helps to assist the belief in the Bull cross, which we have before remarked probably exists in the Pug, but which it is undesirable to perpetuate. Upon one point we personally disagree with an expression used by the author of this description, and that is the term "short" as applied to the legs. This breed of dog most certainly should not be leggy, but a very short legged or "ferret-fronted" Pug is an abomination, and should be avoided. A serious fault in so many Pugs now before the public is snipiness of face, and another coarseness in ear. As a rule the orthodox markings are present in full force, and the carriage of tail is also, in most specimens exhibited, good. How to eradicate the evil of snipy faces is a serious difficulty without resorting again to a dash of Bull. But we hold that a cross with the long-coated Japanese Pug would be beneficial as regards shape, though as the majority of these animals do not represent our Pug in colour, there would be some labour in getting their offspring to breed correctly-marked Pugs, and there would always be a chance of their throwing back. Nevertheless far more difficult crosses have been successfully carried out, and we strongly recommend a cross with a black Japanese Pug to enterprising breeders of this variety of dog.

With reference to the Pug as it at present exists amongst us, it is pleasing to discover that, in spite of its rarity some fifty years ago, the Pug classes are now in the majority of instances usually well represented in point of numbers at all important shows. Yet there is a want of uniformity of type which proves that there is yet much to be done in the way of improvement of this breed. A very undesirable advance is being made in the size of several of the best-shaped dogs, and this is greatly to be regretted, as a ladies' pet dog of about thirty pounds weight is an anomaly which almost refutes itself. It is in many of the inferior large-sized specimens that the Bull cross is so plainly evident, and this has been most probably resorted to in the hopes that increased size of skull and a blunter muzzle would be procured. As a matter of fact, though these advantages may be gained, the results of the cross are frequently disfigured by being out at shoulders and by badly-carried tails, which are the two principal defects which a Bull cross is likely to bring about. Nor are such experiments likely to benefit the Bull-dog, for Pug blood is in its turn plainly visible in some of the breed, especially the fawn and fallow-smut ones, which one comes across. Another trace the Bull-dog often leaves behind it in the Pug is in the carriage of the ears, which often fall back, as is the case in the "rose" Bull-dog ear, and do not drop down the sides of the head as should be in the case of a Pug. The carriage of the ears is, however, a modern introduction into the scale of points of the breed, as up to a few years

HEAD OF PUG. (*From an old Engraving.*)

back Pugs used to be shown with their ears closely cropped, as in the case of the Dalmatian.

The method of cropping which was formerly adopted can be gathered from the subjoined woodcut of a famous Pug which existed many years ago. The dog may not perhaps come up to that degree of perfection which has been reached by such modern specimens as Mr. Lewis's Tooley, Mrs. Monck's Sambo and Darkie, Mrs. Kingsbury's Tip, or Mr. Nunn's Baron, but there are many good points in the formation of his skull which we should be glad to see oftener in the present day. The extreme width of his muzzle in proportion to the size of the skull is a point which must recommend itself to all breeders; and the eyes, though possibly not so soft as those of modern prize-winners, cannot fail to be admired on account of their size and shape.

As a rule the Pug is, though decidedly aristocratic in his behaviour, not a remarkably intelligent dog, and his place seems far more to be in his mistress's boudoir than following her about the streets or out of doors. He is usually phlegmatic in his temperament, and appears incapable of taking care of himself if surprised or frightened. Some specimens, and especially those who possess the Bull cross, are nevertheless snappish; and the majority of them are reluctant to make friends with strangers. Their owners they do know, but the devotion of a Pug is usually not nearly so pronounced as is that of most dogs. This breed, too, seems abnormally inclined to lay on flesh, and the spectacle of a Pug in a painful state of obesity is no uncommon sight. Many specimens of the breed, moreover, give utterance to the most unpleasant sounds in the throat, which is due to the shortness of the muzzle and a consequent difficulty in respiration. On this account they are objected to by many ladies, who naturally dislike being disturbed by the snorting, wheezing, and grunting of a dog on their lap. Many persons innocent on the subject of doggy matters consider it is a desirable feature in a Pug if its tongue hangs out of its mouth, and cannot be drawn in. This formation is certainly an abnormal one, resulting from paralysis of the tongue (to which many of the smaller breeds are very liable) and so far from being an acquisition, should be many points against the affected animal.

In the face of the tendency towards stoutness which is alluded to above, it is very desirable to diet and exercise a Pug properly. Fattening food, or that which is calculated to heat the blood, should be carefully eschewed; and a daily walk, when the weather is favourable, is almost indispensable if the animal is to be kept in health and condition. Vegetables should be chopped up and mixed with bread and gravy for his principal meal, and plain, not sweet, biscuits are excellent for a Pug between times.

With reference to the unpleasant grunting to which notice was drawn above it may be remarked that the breed is not as a rule a hardy one, and naturally any affection of the throat or bronchial tubes is certain to increase the severity of such sounds. Especial care must, therefore, be taken to keep Pugs out of a draught when in the house, and warm clothing is invariably adopted by careful owners when their pets go out of doors in cold or damp weather.

The points of a Pug are as follow :—

Head.—Large and massive, not too round or apple-headed, with a short blunt muzzle.

Eyes.—Large, brown, and prominent.

Ears.—Small, fine in texture, and falling close to the head—"button ears" in short.

Neck.—Short and full, with no dewlap.

Legs.—Of a fair length, straight, and set on well under the body ; with round feet, well split-up toes.

Body.—Short and cobby, wide in chest, and well ribbed up.

Tail.—Well turned up over the back, and tightly curled, with an inclination to lie on one or other side of the spine.

Colour and Markings.—This is a most important feature in a Pug. The principal colour should be a bright fawn, or its various shades from the "apricot" fawn down to a pale yellow tinge. The black markings, however, must be clearly defined, and the success of many a Pug depends upon the position and brilliancy of his black. The muzzle or mask must be jet-black, and the ears, wrinkles, and moles on cheeks should be as dark as possible ; there should also be a "thumb-mark," or dark spot, on the forehead, and a black trace down the back to the root of the tail. The toe-nails, too, should be quite black.

YORKSHIRE TERRIER.   ITALIAN GREYHOUND.   PUG.

Coat.—Fine and short.

General Appearance.—A compact and aristocratic little dog, with a large square head and weighing about 14—16 pounds.

The most prominent breeders of the present day are Mrs. Mayhew of Twickenham, Mrs Bligh Monk of Coley Park, Reading, Mr. Strugnell of London, Mr. J. Nunn of London, Mr Lewis of Bristol, Capt. Digby Boycott of London, Mr. H. G. Foster of Stockton-on-Tees, Mr. Wakely of London, Mr. C. Maule of Stockton-on-Tees, and Mr. Locke of London.

The dog we have selected for illustration is certainly one of the best we have ever seen, though his owner does not care to exhibit him. He is named Tip, and is the property of Mrs. Kingsbury of Cecil Street, Strand, London. Tip is aged $2\frac{1}{2}$ years, and weighs about 19 pounds. His measurements are as follows :—From nose to stop, 1 inch ; from stop to occiput, $4\frac{1}{4}$ inches ; length of back, $12\frac{3}{4}$ inches ; girth of muzzle, 7 inches ; girth of skull, 13 inches ; girth of neck, 14 inches ; girth round brisket, 20 inches ; girth round shoulders, 20 inches ; girth of loins, 16 inches ; girth of thigh, 8 inches ; girth of forearm, $4\frac{3}{4}$ inches ; girth of pastern, 3 inches ; height at shoulders, $12\frac{3}{4}$ inches ; height at elbows, $6\frac{3}{4}$ inches ; height at loins, 13 inches ; height at hock, $3\frac{1}{2}$ inches.

STANDARD FOR JUDGING PUGS.

	Value.
Skull	5
Muzzle	5
Eyes	5
Body	5
Legs	5
Tail	5
Colour and mask	15
General appearance	5
Total	50

CHAPTER XXV.

THE ITALIAN GREYHOUND.

WHERE the original Italian Greyhounds were produced is more or less a matter of conjecture ; but doubtless a more congenial climate than our own was mainly instrumental in the creation of this beautiful though fragile little dog. Italy and the South of France are generally accepted as their birthplace, but it is possible that the honour thus accredited to these parts of the Continent is unmerited by them.

However, whatever was the part of the world which they originally came from, Italian Greyhounds, as a breed, are now firmly established amongst us, unsuitable as the damp and fogs of the English climate are to their constitutions. Moreover, the variety seems to have existed in this country for many years, for, according to the "Sportsman's Repository," the Italian Greyhound was probably first imported into England in the time of King Charles I. who had a great admiration for this breed of dog. On the same authority we learn that though from their fragile frames Italian Greyhounds are unsuitable for coursing purposes, yet "Lord Orford, so renowned for his partiality to Greyhounds, and who for years together kept fifty couple of them, never parting with a single whelp untried, made experiment of the Italian cross, and it was said with some degree of success." This tends to prove that not only was the breed in existence, but that its merits were fully recognised years ago. What advantage, however, Lord Orford could expect to derive from crossing the Italian with our English Greyhound we confess ourselves to be at a loss to conjecture, as the constitution, bone, muscle, and stamina of the larger breed would, we imagine, most certainly be impaired by the introduction of Italian blood into it.

As may readily be conjectured by any who have seen specimens of the breed, the Italian Greyhound is one of the most delicate breeds of dog, and the possession of one entails a great expenditure of care and attention upon its owner. The extreme delicacy of its skin has always been the subject of special comment by those who have written on it; and some of the earlier contributors to our canine literature solemnly assert that if an Italian Greyhound is held by the tail in front of a strong light the skin of the sides is so fine and transparent that the intestines can be plainly seen beneath it. Such statements are naturally exaggerated, but are worth repetition as showing that the skins of these fascinating little dogs were always recognised as particularly fine and delicate. In the face of their constitutional weakness, Italian Greyhounds should be most carefully kept beyond the reach of damp and draughts, as a chill is certain destruction if not taken in time and promptly treated. Warm clothing, too, should always be worn out of doors unless on very fine days, and the food should be cooling and not calculated to heat the blood if the coat is to be kept on the dog.

There is also a great inclination on the part of Italian Greyhounds, as in other Toy dogs, to contract mange, blotch, and other skin diseases ; which, however, will be treated of in another portion of this work. In the meantime it may be suggested to owners of Toy dogs thus affected that an injudicious application of the nearest mange lotion is likely to be prejudicial to the latter's recovery; as many of the preparations so extensively advertised and widely used are far too powerful in their effects upon delicate skins and constitutions. We have ourselves known Toy dogs killed by injudicious treatment, in which such remedies as tar and carbolic acid were largely used. Both these remedies are decidedly beneficial in some instances; but for mild cases of skin disease in small dogs (smooth-haired breeds especially) we strongly advocate the use of glycerine as a preliminary application. Several cases have come before us of cures when the above remedy has been applied in conjunction with strict dieting, and the sulphur and magnesia remedy we have so often before recommended in the course of this work.

Probably on account of the difficulty in rearing the young ones when first born, Italian Greyhounds are by no means numerous in this country; and the classes for them at dog shows rarely fill very heavily. By far the best collection, taken as a whole, which we remember to have ever come across was at the dog show held in the Gymnasium, Edinburgh, in 1877. On this occasion the number and quality of the dogs present was far above the average, and the whole class were the subjects of unqualified praise from the judges, Messrs. William Lort and Hugh Dalziel. On making inquiries of gentlemen present who knew the locality better than we did, it was stated that the weakness of the Modern Athens in the doggy way was certainly Italian Greyhounds, and from the many excellent specimens which we came across afterwards in the town, we fully believe the statement to be a true one.

Amongst those most identified with this breed the name of Mr. W. Macdonald of Winchmore Hill, Middlesex, will always be conspicuous from the unparalleled successes of his almost perfect Italian Greyhound Molly, who was, we believe, never beaten, and certainly won at all the principal shows. Besides Molly Mr. Macdonald owned many good specimens, including Duke and Silvey. The names, also, of the Rev. J. W. Mellor, Mrs. Giltrap of Dublin, Miss Pim of Lisnargarvey, Ireland, and Mr. S. W. Wildman, are closely associated with good specimens of the breed, which we fancy has been latterly rather increasing its circle of supporters.

The points of an Italian Greyhound are essentially the same as those of its larger and more popular relative, the English Greyhound, which will be fully treated of in a later chapter; in the meantime the following may be taken as representing what is required in good specimens of the breed now under consideration.

Head.—As flat as possible, with tapering jaws. The former requisite, however, is almost an unknown feature to see in an Italian Greyhound.

Eyes.—Moderately full.

Ears.—Generally carried back as in the rose-ear, fine and thin.

Neck.—Rather long, slight, and arched.

Chest.—Deep and narrow, and shoulders slanting.

Body.—Rather raised, and tucked up at loins.

Legs.—Straight and slight.

Feet.—Round and cat-like; well arched.

Tail.—Very fine and thin.

Size.—About 5—7 lbs.

General appearance.—A fragile, delicate little dog, slender in outline, and one which seems susceptible of considerable speed if extended, were it capable of such exertion.

The specimen chosen for our coloured plate is Mr. S. W. Wildman's (late Mrs. Giltrap's) Romeo, a most beautiful little dog, weighing 5¾ pounds. Romeo measures from nose to stop, 2¼ inches; stop to occiput, 3 inches; length of back, 11 inches; girth of muzzle, 4 inches; girth of skull, 8 inches; girth of neck, 7 inches; girth of brisket, 12½ inches; girth of chest, 13¼ inches; girth of loins, 10½ inches; girth of forearm, 2¾ inches; height at shoulders, 11 inches; height at elbows, 6¼ inches; height at loins, 11½ inches; length of tail, 7 inches.

STANDARD OF POINTS FOR JUDGING ITALIAN GREYHOUNDS.

	Value.
Head	5
Neck	5
Shoulders	5
Body	5
Size	15
Coat	10
General appearance	5
Total	50

CHAPTER XXVI.

THE POMERANIAN.

THE Pomeranian is admittedly one of the least interesting dogs in existence, and consequently his supporters are few and far between. He has not that delicate beauty of outline which belongs to the Toy class generally, and his unsuitability for field sports renders him perfectly useless as a sporting dog. The Pomeranian is certainly a foreign importation, but to what country the credit of his production is due is a matter of conjecture. Good specimens of the breed have appeared from time to time amongst us, which have been picked up in Germany, Belgium, France, and other parts of the Continent, but the dog appears to be claimed by no one nation in particular, though he certainly resembles the Esquimaux in outline. This breed is fairly popular in America under the title of Spitz dog, and we have seen a very good specimen imported into this country by a lady who had visited the United States.

As before observed, the virtues of the Pomeranian, whatever they may be, have failed to gain him many friends, and this is hardly to be wondered at when his good and bad qualities come to be weighed in the balance. Against a pretty coat, sharp and rather intelligent face, must be reckoned the snappish temper and lack of affection with which the Pomeranian is so generally credited. In fact, this breed looks far more intelligent than it really is, for it seems incapable of developing even an ordinary amount of instinct. As a guard to a house, however, if kept indoors, the Pomeranian is of some service, for his ears are keen, and an inclination to bark seems deeply rooted in the variety. On the other hand, though uncertain and treacherous in disposition, his courage is very much below the average, and a Pomeranian would sooner run than stand his ground any day. From this it may be surmised that as a vermin dog, which from his size and shape of head he might reasonably be expected to be, in some shape or other, a dog of this breed is worse than useless. Isolated specimens may on occasion do a little in the way of destroying rats, but we have seen many tried at all sorts of vermin, big and little, with the same result—an apparently irresistible inclination to get out of the pit as soon as possible, and leave their enemies to something which liked to kill them better. This experience is corroborated by almost every one who has seen the breed tried, and we do not believe any of their best friends take credit for a Pomeranian's gameness or resolution in attack.

With reference to the earlier history of the breed mention is made to it in a work entitled "Cynographia Britannica," by Sydenham Edwards, which was published in London in 1800, where we find that "the Pomeranian or Fox-dog" is thus described:—"He is of little value as a house-dog, being noisy, artful, and quarrelsome, cowardly, petulant, and deceitful, snappish, and dangerous to children, and in other respects without useful properties. He is very common in Holland, and there named Kees. . . . . . There is a peculiarity in his coat: his hair, particularly the ruff around his neck, is not formed of hairs that describe the line of beauty, or serpentine line, but is simply a semicircle, which by inclining the same way in large masses give him a very beautiful appearance.   Although his attachment is very weak, yet he is difficult to be stolen."

The same writer alludes to the colour in the following words :—"Of a pale fallow colour, lightest on the lower parts ; some are white, some black, but few spotted."

In the "Sportsman's Cabinet," published 1804, this breed is termed the Pomeranian or Wolf-dog, and the colour is referred to as being "mostly of a pale yellow or cream colour, and lightest in the lower parts ; some are white, some few black, and others, but very rarely, spotted."   The similarity of this description to the one given above renders it more than probable that the two were by the same hand, more especially as both works were pub- lished at so brief an interval.   According to the latter authority the following was the pleasing method of breaking Pomeranians to harness adopted in Kamtchatka :—"As soon as the puppies are able to see they are thrown into a dark pit, where they are shut up until they are thought able to undergo a trial.   They are then harnessed with other seasoned dogs to a sledge, with which they scamper away with all their might, being frightened by the light and by so many strange objects.   After their short trial they are again confined to their gloomy dungeon, and this practice is repeated until they are inured to the business of drawing, and are obedient to their driver.   From this moment begins their hard and miserable course, only alleviated by the short recreation the summer affords them.   As in this season they are of no service, nobody cares about them, but they enjoy a perfect liberty, which they principally employ in assuaging their hunger.   Their sole nutriment consists of fish, which they watch for all this time by the banks of the river, and which they catch with the greatest cunning and dexterity.   When they have plenty of this food, like the bears, they devour only the heads and leave the rest behind."   In the opinion of the latter writer the character of the dog is superior to that given him by Sydenham Edwards, assuming that the two authors are not identical.   In the "Sportsman's Cabinet" Pomeranians are said to possess an "instinctive sagacity of giving infallible notice when storms are approaching by scratching holes in the snow, and endeavouring to shelter themselves beneath it.   By these and many other good qualities the Kamtchadale dogs by far outbalance the casual mischiefs they do in their occasional petulance and perverseness."   Further on the writer remarks :— "He bites most severely, and always with greater vehemence in proportion as he is less resisted ; for he most sagaciously uses precautions with such animals as attempt to stand upon the defensive ; and is admitted to be instinctively a coward, as he never fights but when under the necessity of satisfying his hunger or making good his retreat."

In the "Naturalist's Library," edited by Sir William Jardine, Col. Charles Hamilton Smith, who is responsible for most of the canine information, remarks that "these dogs are white, white-and-brown, or buff."   Thus showing that the white colour was becoming more popular amongst us.   This latter is by far the favourite and most common colour in the present day ; though some authorities (with whom, however, we disagree) rather favour the fawn or lemon- coloured dogs.   It may, however, be taken as a rule that, whatever the colour is, the dog should be "whole" coloured, not pied, as patches are universally objected to in Pomeranians.

As regards shape the "Cynographia Britannica" says :—"Head broad towards neck and narrowing to the muzzle ; ears short, pointed, and erect ; about 18 inches high ; is dis- tinguished by his long, thick, and rather erect coat, forming a ruff around the neck, but short on the head and ears ; the tail large and bushy, curled in a ring on the rump ; instances are few of short-coated ones."   This description very closely resembles that of the modern

BLACK POMERANIAN.

Pomeranian, which certainly appears to have benefited less from the fostering influence of the attention of its admirers than any other breed.

Amongst the supporters of this breed may be mentioned the names of Mr. R. Oldham of Manchester, Mrs. Senden of Streatham, Mr. Enoch Hutton, Mr. Fawdry, and Mrs. Mayhew.

The dog we have selected is Mr. J. Fawdry's Charley, who has been successful at most of the principal shows throughout the country. He was born 1877, and scales 18 lbs. Charley's measurements are :—Nose to stop, 1¾ inches ; stop to top of skull, 3½ inches ; girth of forearm, 5 inches ; girth of pastern, 3¼ inches ; height at shoulders, 16 inches ; height at elbows, 10 inches ; height at loins, 15½ inches ; height at hock, 3½ inches.

The subjoined engraving, by a German artist, gives a most correct impression of a Pomeranian engaged in the congenial task of protecting his master's wagon. The black dog is to our mind an admirable specimen of the breed, and one which displays the chief characteristics of the Pomeranian to a marked extent.

The points of a Pomeranian are not numerous, and the dog may be described as follows :—

Skull.—Wide and flat and foxy-looking, tapering towards the muzzle, which is very fine.

Jaws.—Rather wide at base, but snipy towards nose.

Ears.—Fine and pricked.

Eyes.—Dark, not too full, and almond-shaped.

Chest.—Rather wide.

Body.—Short and cobby-looking.

Legs.—Stout, and placed well under the body.

Feet.—Round and small.

Coat.—Rather coarse, and very dense all over the body, especially on the lower side of the neck. It is long all over the body, but short on the head, with some feather on the forelegs.

Tail.—Bushy, and curled over the back.

Colour.—White or black. As before stated, some permit lemon or other shades, but the two former are certainly by far the most preferable. Parti-coloured dogs are much objected to.

General appearance.—An active, sharp-witted dog, capable of enduring fatigue, and giving every indication of hardiness and activity.

STANDARD OF POINTS FOR JUDGING POMERANIANS.

	Value.
Head, shape of skull	5
Muzzle	5
Ears	5
Body and legs	5
Coat	10
Colour	15
General appearance	5
Total	50

CHAPTER XXVII.

THE MALTESE DOG.

THE Maltese dog—terrier as it is sometimes erroneously described, for the creature has nothing of the terrier in its composition—is undoubtedly one of the most admired by ladies of all the varieties of Toy dog. The beautiful whiteness of a Maltese dog's coat is in itself a great attraction when the animal is carefully attended to by those who have it in charge, and the quality of the hair is so soft and silky that this variety is peculiarly adapted for the society of the gentler sex.

What the origin of the breed is cannot be positively ascertained, though it is only reasonable to believe it is similar in many respects to the *Canis Melitæus* of old writers, who, rightly or wrongly, ascribed to Malta the honour of possessing a national dog at the time of their writing. One is naturally puzzled to ascertain what this dog really was, and many consider that it was merely a long-haired, small-sized animal, whose services have of later years been largely drawn upon in the production of kindred strains, notably in the case of Toy Spaniels. Be this as it may, the antiquity of a dog in many essential respects resembling the modern Maltese is beyond a doubt, and a reference to the chapter on Skye Terriers will show our readers that certain strains of the northern dog are even now credited with a Maltese cross. In the face of such evidence it is only reasonable to suppose that the latter variety was recognised as an acquisition by the people of this country many years ago, though doubtless the original shape of the dog and its general appearance have been the subject of considerable modifications.

According to the "Naturalist's Library," the "Maltese Dog (*Canis Melitæus*), the Bichon or Chien Bouffé of Buffon, is the most ancient of the small Spaniel races, being figured on Roman monuments and mentioned by Strabo."

Dr. John Caius, more than three hundred years ago, thus alludes to the Maltese dogs in remarks which also refer to the Toy Spaniel or Fotor :—

" There is, besides those which wee have already delivered, another sort of gentle dogges in this our Englishe style, but exempted from the order of the residue. The dogges of this kinde doth Callimachus call Melitæers, of the Iseland Melita, in the Sea of Sicily (which at this day is named Malta, an Iseland in deede famous and renouned . . . .)."

By far the best modern strain of Maltese dogs traces back to the kennels of Mr. R. Mandeville of London, who from the years 1860 to 1870 practically swept the board at the shows held at Birmingham, Islington, Crystal Palace, and Cremorne Gardens. To this gentleman's Fido and Lilly we are indebted for many of the beautiful little dogs now in existence ; and the services which he rendered their pets should never, in common justice, be lost sight of by those who own Maltese dogs in the present day.

As an out-door companion a dog of this breed is inferior to many other varieties of Toy, both on account of its long, silky jacket, and rather delicate constitution ; the Maltese being

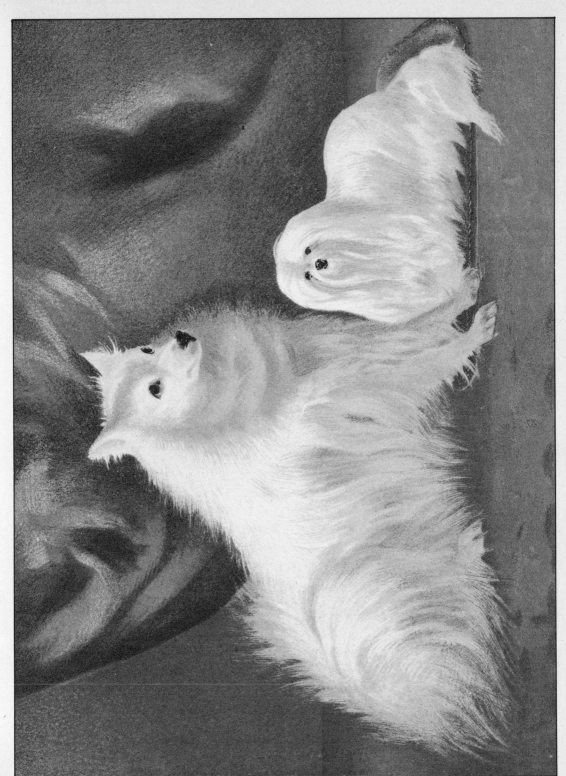

POMERANIAN DOG. MALTESE.

peculiarly susceptible of cold and chills. If affected by such causes, the eyes are frequently attacked, and the water running from them causes unsightly brown lines on the muzzle, which naturally detract greatly from the beauty of the dog. Being so densely coated with silky hair, which is both longer and finer than in any other variety of dog, the jacket of a Maltese is a particular source of trial to his attendant, and a very slight attack of skin disease (or rather an attack which in the majority of breeds would be hardly worth consideration) is very liable to remove his coat to an alarming extent. Constant attention with a soft brush, the balloon shape referred to on page 156, and coolness of blood, are the best preventives, for in such cases prevention is more than ever better than cure. Dieting in all small long-haired dogs must be most scrupulously attended to, and the daily supply of meat rigorously cut down to the smallest possible dimensions. Scraps of bread and vegetables well mixed up with gravy are the best items of diet, and now and then a little meat may be added, but for the welfare of the animal such excesses should be few and far between. As in the case of the Yorkshire Terrier, many owners encase the hind feet in wash-leather bags, which are supposed to have the effect of preventing the dog from scratching himself so much as to injure his coat, or raise the skin beneath it. The bags may doubtless be useful in this respect, but are on the other hand very liable, if worn too long, to injure the feet by keeping them too hot and close, and should therefore be used with caution. The Maltese too, like the Yorkshire Terrier, often appears with the hair down his skull neatly plaited, both in order to prevent it becoming matted and to enable the dog to see his way about with greater ease; and we know of more than one exhibitor who is in the habit of fastening back the ears when the animal is feeding, in order to prevent their dragging in the food and becoming soiled. Whether the latter precaution is a necessary one or not is naturally a matter of opinion, but cleanliness in jacket and purity of colour are very essential points in the success of a Maltese on the bench.

As a companion for in-doors the Maltese dog ranks highly in the estimation of its admirers; and certainly few prettier sights in dog-flesh can be imagined than a select collection of these taking little dogs, at home and uncontrolled in their mistress's boudoir. Unfortunately, the temper of a Maltese is often snappish, and the breed, in consequence, is not so popular as it would otherwise be with many who avowedly admire its beauty. Out of doors it is sharp and quick-witted, but yet its intelligence is far inferior to that of the King Charles or Blenheim Spaniel, which as intellectual Toys are *facile princeps* in the canine world.

Of late years the studs of Lady Giffard of Red Hill, and Mrs. Bligh Monk of Coley Park near Reading, have succeeded in winning the chief prizes at our leading shows. But at the time of writing the latter lady has almost ceased to exhibit in this class, thus leaving Lady Giffard practically at the head of affairs with her extraordinary good collection. This includes Hugh, who has taken premier honours at the Alexandra Palace and other principal shows. Mr. R. Mandeville of Southwark has been referred to before as virtually the founder of the modern Maltese, and in addition to the above the name of Mr. J. Jacobs of Oxford is conspicuous in connection with the breed.

With reference to the exhibition of Maltese, so very much depends on the washing they receive before going off to a show, that a few remarks, based on some hints received from a well-known exhibitor, may not be out of place, as they must apply equally well to all breeds of Toy dogs. In the first place it is well to be assured that the dog is not suffering from the effects of a cold when washing is determined upon; and, secondly, the greatest precautions must be taken to guard against his being chilled from not being properly dried. It is always, therefore, desirable to wash the dog before a fire, due care having been previously taken to see that his coat has been well brushed, and combed out with a coarse-toothed comb, which renders it less likely to become tangled and matted by the water. After the Maltese, or other Toy, has been well washed in a small tub of warm water, in which a very minute quantity of soda may be placed when the animal is undergoing his ablutions preparatory to state occasions, with a squeeze of the blue bag added as well under such circumstances, he should be taken out of the water and plunged in another tub of clean tepid water, to rinse all the soap-suds out of his jacket. When removed from this second bath, his attendant should most thoroughly dry him before the fire, care being taken to see that the interior of the ears, the feet, tail, and under the elbows, are as well dried as the body, or a heavy cold will be the most natural consequence of neglect in this respect. After the performances with the towels are completed, it is well to stand the dog in a clean open wicker basket before the fire, so that he can get thoroughly dry, without an opportunity being afforded him (which he would otherwise be sure to avail himself of) to rub himself on the carpet and soil his jacket. When well dried he can be combed and brushed.

Having thus alluded to the Maltese, we will proceed to give a description of the points which are now desired in a good specimen.

The *Skull* is rather wide, and appearing round from the position of the ears, and is covered with silky hair.

Muzzle, tapering towards the nose.

Nose and *Eyes*, black, the latter not so large and prominent as in the case of the Pug.

Ears, set on high, and well covered with long white, silky hair.

Body, deep in chest, well ribbed up with a level back.

Legs, short, and placed well under the body.

Tail, well feathered, and carried over the back in a curl.

Colour, a pure white: lemon markings being a disqualification. Many good specimens are touched on the ears with this colour, and suffer occasionally thereby.

Coat, long, soft, and silky, with no curl, which is a bad fault if present.

Size, from 5 to 7 pounds, or even more.

General Appearance.—A compact little dog, excitable when released from restraint, but palpably unfit for anything but an in-door existence.

The dog chosen to illustrate the Maltese dog is Hugh, property of Lady Giffard. He was bred by owner in 1875, and measures from nose to stop, 1 inch; from stop to top of skull, $2\frac{1}{2}$ inches; length of back, 8 inches; girth of muzzle, 4 inches; girth of skull, 9 inches; girth of neck, 7 inches; girth of brisket, $11\frac{1}{2}$ inches; girth round shoulders, 11 inches; girth of loins, 9 inches; girth of forearm, $2\frac{1}{2}$ inches; girth of pastern, $1\frac{3}{4}$ inches; height at shoulders, $7\frac{1}{2}$ inches; height at elbows, 4 inches; height at loins, $7\frac{1}{4}$ inches; length of tail, 5 inches; hair on tail, 7 inches; length of coat, 11 inches; length of ear with hair, $7\frac{1}{2}$ inches; weight, 4 lb. 10 ozs.

SCALE OF POINTS FOR JUDGING MALTESE.

	Value.
Skull, muzzle, and nose	5
Eyes	3
Ears	7
Body and legs	5
Tail	5
Coat	10
Colour	10
General appearance, size	5
	—
	50

CHAPTER XXVIII.

THE POODLE.

THE Poodle is one of the least understood and appreciated breeds of dog in this country. Of late years there has been a slight movement in his favour; but even in the present day his many powerful claims upon doggy people appear to have been greatly overlooked, though those who have devoted themselves to his study are loud in their praises of his sagacity and general utility, which a Poodle's antecedents certainly seem to fully entitle him to.

At present there are several distinct varieties of Poodle on the Continent, various parts of which are recognised as the home of the various types; but there seems to be but one opinion amongst naturalists as regards his origin, which, with a rather unusual unanimity of opinion, is alleged by writers on the breed to have been the *Canis Aquaticus*, or Water-spaniel of our forefathers.

In the "Sportsman's Cabinet," vol. i., which was published in London in 1803, the "Veteran Sportsman," by whom it is compiled, takes a so far different view of the case as to cause him to draw a distinction between the "Water-dog" and "Water-spaniel." In referring to the former the following are his own words:—"The particular breed of dog passing under this denomination differs materially from the former sort, distinguished by the appellation of Water-spaniel, which distinction will be more fully explained in the course of the work when we come to that head. The Water-dog, of which an exact representation is given from the life" [this represents an unshaved and rather short-headed Poodle in every particular], "is of so little general use that the breed is but little promoted, unless upon the sea-coast, and in such other situations as are most likely to render their qualifications and propensities of some utility. . . . . These dogs are exceedingly singular in their appearance, and most probably derive their origin from the Greenland dog, blended with some particular race of our own. . . . . Although these dogs are to be seen of almost all colours and equally well-bred, yet the jet-black with white feet stand highest in estimation; the most uniform in shape and make exceed in size the standard of mediocrity, and are strong in proportion to their formation. The head is rather round; the nose short; the ears broad, long, and pendulous; his eyes full, lively, and solicitously attracting; his neck thick and short; his shoulders broad; his legs straight; his hind-quarters round and firm; his pasterns strong, and dew-clawed; his fore-feet long, but round;" [sic] "with his hair adhering to the body in natural, elastic, short curls, neither loose, long, or shaggy; the former being considered indicative of constitutional strength, the latter of constitutional weakness or hereditary debility." . . . . "The Water-dog even in puppyhood displays an eager desire to be employed in offices of domestic amusement." The writer then proceeds to give full directions for teaching Poodles to retrieve, which it is needless to refer to here, as due allusion is made to such proceedings in the Newfoundland chapter, and in the present article in the course of Mr. T. H. Joyce's notes on the breed. Enough will have been gathered, however, from the above quotation to show that in the early part of the present century, and probably for some time before, there was a breed in these islands very similar to the modern and certainly improved Continental Poodle.

In the "Naturalist's Library" the following remarks occur, which prove the writer to be of a somewhat similar opinion to our own. Under the heading of "The Water-dog, *Canis Aquaticus*," we find that: "The Water-dog or Poodle of the Germans is in its most perfect state not a British race, but rose into favour first in Germany, and during the revolutionary wars was carried by the troops into France, and only in the latter campaigns became familiar to the British in Spain and the Netherlands. The coarser crisped-haired Water-dog was indeed long known to the middle classes of England, and to fishermen on the north-east coast, and professional water-fowl shooters; he was occasionally brought to the environs of London . . . . . . No dog is more intelligent or attached to his master; none like the Poodle can trace out and find lost property with more certainty and perseverance."

Poodles are on the Continent usually divided into at least four varieties, each of which is apparently descended from one common ancestor—the *Canis Aquaticus*—but which have become almost distinct from being crossed with other breeds and subsequently in-bred amongst themselves.

Mr. T. H. Joyce, an ardent admirer of the breed, kindly supplies us with the following information :—

"In England the Poodle proper is the least understood, and consequently the least appreciated, of almost any known breed of dog. Indeed, as a rule he is looked upon with a feeling approaching contempt, as a canine mountebank, amusing enough in his way, like a 'plum-pudding' trick horse in a circus, but of no practical use in real life. And yet in a great measure those very characteristics which render him first and foremost among canine performers are due to the simple fact that he is far superior in intelligence to his fellows, and capable of acquiring a greater variety of accomplishments, from walking about on his hind-legs with a parasol and petticoats, to retrieving on land or in water; while it should not be forgotten that so great an authority as Sir Edwin Landseer painted him as the type of wisdom in 'Laying down the Law.' In fact, in Germany, and indeed throughout a great portion of Northern Europe, he is looked upon as every whit as useful a companion as he is ornamental, and the appearance of a Poodle harnessed to a cart, or carrying his master's basket, is a very common one in the streets of Germany, Holland, and Belgium. He is also used for shooting purposes, as he is a capital water-dog, is easy to train either to retrieve or point. Opinions certainly differ with respect to his pointing abilities, though all acknowledge that his scent is exceedingly delicate. He is a steady and willing worker, moreover, and when well trained is extremely tractable; and it is this quality of extreme docility which makes him a most valuable dog in the house, as he is full of fun, ever ready for a romp with a child, to fetch his master's slippers, or to carry a note to some other member of the family, and patiently await and bring back the answer. He is also a capital watch-dog, and is never backward—perhaps indeed a little too anxious—to defend the interests or the person of his owner, for the thorough-bred Poodle, when not demoralised by too much coddling and over-feeding, is decidedly pugnacious, and is rarely averse to do battle with his own kind. A black Poodle in the possession of the writer has had many a tough fight with a Bull-terrier who is also a member of the family, and always comes off victor, while he never hesitates to attack a Newfoundland or St. Bernard twice his size should he feel himself in any way insulted.   Another of the writer's Poodles, this time of the white French breed, was sometimes wont to take a dislike to a passer-by in the street, and suddenly rising on his hind legs would dance round him, uttering a most menacing bark and showing a startling display of teeth, to the intense alarm and astonishment of his victim, whom, however, he was careful never to bite, apparently looking upon the whole matter as a practical joke.   Again, a third, of the large black German breed, was a little too officious in defending the house from visitors, and would keep people waiting outside the garden gate until a servant came to guarantee the good faith of the applicant for admission.   This gentleman had one frailty : he was addicted to pocket-picking, having been taught this doubtful accomplishment in his early youth ; and finally had to be sent away owing to his devotion to what the ' Artful Dodger ' would have called ' fogle-hunting.'

"Marvellous anecdotes, far too numerous to detail here, are told of the Poodle's faithfulness, affection, and versatile talent, ranging from the celebrated Munito, who in 1818 astonished all Paris by his clever card and arithmetical tricks, or the once well-known Paris Poodle of the Pont Neuf, who used to dirty the boots of passers-by in order that his master— a shoeblack—might have the benefit of cleaning them, to a white Poodle who, snubbed by his lady-love, committed suicide at Queenstown a few years since.   Like a child, however, he requires careful handling, for while he is very easily trained, he is exceptionally sensitive, and is far more efficiently taught when treated rather as a sensible being than as a mere quadrupedal automaton, and will learn twice as quickly if his master can make him understand the reason for performing his task.

"The history of the Poodle and the details of his lineage are somewhat obscure.   That he is of German origin there is no doubt, the name being identical in both languages—*Pudel*—and he there is ordinarily classed as the *Canis familiaris Aquaticus*, being very closely allied to the more crisp and curly-haired water-fowl dog well known to our sportsmen of the marshes. He assuredly dates his existence from some centuries since, for in various illuminated manuscripts of the sixteenth century, and notably in one depicting an episode in the life of Margaret of York, the third wife of Charles the Bold of Burgundy, and in another representing a family group of Maximilian of Austria and his wife and child (' The Abridged Chronicles of Burgundy') there is certainly the portrait of a shaven dog, which, allowing for the artistic shortcomings of that period, closely resembles the Poodle of the present day. Again, in Martin de Vos' picture of ' Tobit and his Dog,' which also dates from the 16th century, the faithful animal is an unmistakable shaven Poodle, while in two of the series of paintings of the story of ' Patient Griselda,' by Pinturicchio (1454—1513), in the National Gallery, a small shaven Poodle is conspicuous amongst the various spectators of Griselda's vicissitudes of fortune.   Thus, as far as ancestry goes, he is doubtless entitled to the numerous quarterings so valued by the Teutonic nobility.   Why, however, the Poodle should have been half-shaved from time immemorial is not clear, unless it be to imitate the Lion Dog (*Canis Leoninus*), of which a degenerate scion still exists, I believe, in Malta.   At the present day the Poodle is found throughout Europe from Amsterdam to Naples, where, completely shaven, he may be seen taking his siesta under the shadow of some friendly wall or doorway.   Poodles, however, considerably differ in the various countries.   Thus, in Eastern Germany and on the confines of Russia he is as a rule black, and the Russian Poodle proper should be lithe and agile ; while coming more into Central Germany the black Poodle seems to thicken in the legs and to shorten slightly in the muzzle, assuming more staid, sturdy, and aldermanic proportions. The white Poodle also presents marked variations, ranging from the great muscular fellow who draws a milk-cart in Antwerp and Brussels to his more slender French brother familiarly called *Mouton*, who is so constantly met with on the Paris boulevards. The size of the two breeds differs considerably, the larger one averaging some 30 or 40 lbs., while the smaller, generally known under the name of *Barbet*, only weighs about half that figure. Of the various breeds mentioned the Russian is the most valuable. As a rule he is highly intelligent, and is altogether a handsomer and more gracefully-formed dog, while his coat, being black, is free from that soiled appearance which is so great a drawback to the white breed. The hair of the various breeds is also somewhat different—that of the Russian being more wiry and less woolly than the French, who, from the texture of his coat, frequently merits his pastoral nickname. There is also a "sheep" Poodle in Germany, but his coat is long and pendent, in bunches something resembling those of the Musk Sheep, and presenting altogether a heavy and uncouth appearance. The Poodle appears to have been introduced into England during the Continental wars at the beginning of the century, although performing dogs were known previous to this era; but he was a favourite in France long before that date, and in a fashion plate of the time of Louis XVI. he is represented, shaven and shorn, begging hard for a biscuit from a child of the period.

"A word, to conclude, about training Poodles. In the first place, teach your dog when you give him his meal of biscuit, letting him have it piece by piece as every trick is performed; secondly, never attempt to teach him two new tricks at a time, and when instilling into him a new trick, let him always go through his old ones first; thirdly, *never be beaten by him*, If—as is frequently the case with young dogs—he declines to perform a trick, do not pass it over or let him go through something that he may like better, but when you see that he definitively refuses, tell him that he cannot eat without working, and put away his food for an hour or two. If he once sees he can tire you out you will have no further authority over him, while if you are firm he will not hold out long; and, once beaten, will not make a second attempt. It is, however, a bad plan to make a dog go through a trick, which he may apparently dislike, too many times during one lesson. A whip is of little use when training, as the dog will learn to associate his tasks with a thrashing, and go through them in that unwilling, cowed, tail-between-legs fashion which too often betrays the unthinking hastiness of a master, and is the chief reason why the Poodle has so often been dubbed a spiritless coward. The Poodle, properly treated, is a true and intelligent friend, and deserves more attention than is bestowed upon him by English fanciers.

"In selecting Poodles the chief points to be observed are:—

"1. *The Head.*—This should be broad, well developed, and carried high.

"2. *The Muzzle* in the French and Russian breeds should appear comparatively long when shaven, but in the German somewhat shorter and thicker, while the nose of the first-named should be a clear pink, and in the black breed the colour of jet. The roof of the mouth should also be black.

"3. *The Eyes* are a great criterion; they should be dark hazel, and clear, and look you straight in the face when spoken to; this in itself being no small test of the animal's intelligence and previous training.

"4. *The Ears* should be long, and thickly covered with long silky hair.

"5. *The Neck* should be well proportioned to the size of the animal, while the shoulders should be firm, but not too thickly set, the fore-legs being muscular, not too long, and perfectly straight.

GERMAN POODLES.

" 6. *The Chest and Body.*—The chest should be broad and fairly deep, while the loin should be muscular without being thick and ungainly, and well arched beneath.

" 7. *The Tail*, which is usually considerably docked in puppyhood, should be carried jauntily at about an angle of 45 degrees with his back. A drooping tail is a great disfigurement.

" 8. *The Colour* should be either pure white or pure black, though it is difficult to obtain the latter without a blemish of white on the chest.

" 9. *The Feet* should be slightly webbed, and when clipped the fingers should appear distinct and well-shapen.

" 10. *The Coat* of a Poodle differs considerably, ranging from the wiry horse-hair of the Russian to the curly wool of the French; or, again, to the long ringlets of the corded breed; so that it is difficult to lay down any general rule, save that the hair should be exceedingly thick and of a fine springy texture, which, while completely free from grease, should wear a well-groomed glossy aspect.

" If possible, it would be well to see him have a run, as there is a wavy snake-like motion imparted to the back of every well-bred Poodle, which decreases as age creeps on, when he becomes more staid and sober. Care should be taken in purchasing puppies not to part them too early from their mother, or to expose them to cold, as infantile Poodles are exceedingly delicate, and are rapidly carried off by an attack of bronchitis or pneumonia."

In the present day we find mention by numerous authorities of at least three or four different varieties of Poodle. Some writers, indeed, extend the number of distinct sorts to even more, but we confess that the difference between some of the varieties appears to us to be so subtle as to become hardly discernible. For our own part we feel strongly inclined, from conversations we have held with gentlemen interested in and acquainted with the breeding of Poodles, to divide that breed into but two distinct classes, viz., the curly-coated and the corded-coated Poodle. The former is most certainly the commoner variety, and may in its turn be sub-divided into two branches, viz., the large and the small sized, as the structural development of each sub-variety is essentially the same. Those Continental authorities, on the other hand, who add a third or medium-sized to the curly-coated variety, by doing so, in our opinion, open the door to difficulties in breeding which we think could easily be done away with. When the chief distinction between dogs of a similar type resolves itself merely into a matter of weight, it can hardly be successfully contended that the animals belong to different breeds, and if only for simplicity sake this slight distinction might be advantageously abolished in the interests of the breed. Such expressions as "Der grosse Pudel," " Der mittlere Pudel," and " Der kleine Pudel," look well on paper, but when these formidable adjectives are simply translated into large, middle-sized, and small, their value comes to be considerably discounted; and we do not believe that even those writers, who for their reputation's sake have to notice them, really believe in the desirability of such distinctions being perpetuated.

The large-sized Poodle is essentially a Continental sportsman's dog, and is by many of them considered in that capacity almost a paragon of perfection. He is quickly broken to gun, and can be taught anything in the way of tricks. His devotion to his master is beyond any question, and, as a descendant of the *Canis Aquaticus*, it may be surmised that he takes to water kindly. Under such circumstances it can hardly be surprising that the Poodle is a general favourite, and set great store by in countries where the good qualities of our English sporting dogs are either unknown, or the dogs themselves cannot be procured.

The small breed, on the other hand, though equally intelligent, are naturally enough inferior as sporting companions, and may therefore be considered more in the light of toy dogs, even on the Continent, than their larger relatives.

The corded Poodle is, however, a totally different dog in appearance to the curly-coated ones alluded to above. Though the structural development is the same, the vast difference in coat proves the distinction between the two varieties. Instead of the thick curly coat which is possessed by the large and small curly-coated dogs, the jacket of the corded Poodle appears at first sight to consist entirely of lengths of twisted cords or rope, which give the dog a most peculiar appearance. There is a complete line down the skull, neck, and back; the cords of hair hanging down and sometimes trailing on the ground from this line. The tail is also fully furnished with "cords," and the only parts exempt are the muzzle and feet. It is not often, however, that this variety is met with in this country, and the best collection we remember to have ever come across at English shows was at the Nottingham Canine Society's exhibition in 1875, when three or four excellent specimens faced the judges.

Herr R. Von Schmiedeberg, the great German authority on canine and sporting subjects, kindly writes to us as follows:—

"We distinguish two breeds of Poodles, one the woolly breed, or as we say, the *Schaaf Pudel*—sheep Poodle. The other is the *Schöner Pudel*—pedigree Poodle. The former has long woolly hair, which naturally forms little bunches, but which by combing becomes silky, and forms single hairs. The latter has its hair grown in long spirals, which sometimes touch the ground, even from the ears and tail. Some writers distinguish Poodles from each other on account of their size, but that is not correct. Poodles have all other peculiarities alike. Colour is either white or black, and sometimes brown, which is considered a bad one. White ones with black or brown patches appear also, but they are discarded. The long curly hair grows on the whole body, even on the muzzle and the legs. Frequently it is shaven, so that there is a sort of moustache growing round the nose; the feet are also shaven from below the knee.

"The first record we have of the breed is by Conrad Gessner in 1555, but it seems the ancients knew the breed, as *little* poodles are represented upon some monuments about the time of the Emperor Augustus, about A.D. 30."

The engraving which accompanies this chapter represents both the above-described varieties, one of which is trimmed in the manner described.

The following may be taken to represent the points of the Poodle:—

Skull high and well domed.

Muzzle short and rather blunt.

Eyes rather small and dark, but very intelligent.

Ears large, and lying flat to the head.

Body moderately long, with a deep chest.

Legs thick, and rather short.

Coat either very tightly curled, or corded as above described. In any case the jacket must be thick and dense.

Colour white or black. The latter is far rarer than white, and especially so in the case of the corded varieties. An excellent black-and-white pied specimen, called Domino, was exhibited at the Brighton dog show in 1879, but his peculiar markings apparently did not find favour with the judges, for he failed to secure a prize.

Tail, generally docked.

General Appearance.—An active and highly-intelligent dog, capable of great speed and exertion on land or in water.

N.B.—It is customary to shave curly-coated Poodles, at all events in the summer months, in a rather peculiar and quaint manner. The muzzle is shaven with the exception of a good-sized tuft of hair on either side of the nose, which corresponds with the moustache of a human being. The rest of the head, the neck, chest, fore-quarters, and fore-legs, are often left intact, the shaving commencing again two or three inches behind the fore-legs. This is not *always* the case, as it gives a heavy appearance to the dog, and many only clip to just above the elbow, with a bracelet of hair left on the pastern. This results in all the body being bare with the exception of a patch on the outside of each thigh, a little above and behind the stifle joint. The hind-legs are usually shaven down to an inch or two above the hocks, and a tuft is left on the end of the tail. All the feet are shaven. Of course corded Poodles are not subjected to this ordeal, their personal attractions being considered sufficiently powerful not to necessitate the assistance of art.

The following are the measurements of Mr. T. H. Joyce's Russian Poodle Posen. This dog is a male, weighing 31 lbs., and aged 3½ years. He measures from nose to stop, 3⅛ inches; stop to top of head, 4 inches; length of back, 17 inches; girth of muzzle, 9½ inches; girth of skull, 14 inches; girth of neck, 12½ inches; girth of brisket, 17 inches; girth of shoulders, 21 inches; girth of loins, 14 inches; girth of fore-arm, 5 inches; girth of pastern, 3¼ inches; height at shoulders, 20½ inches; height at elbows, 10⅝ inches; height at loins, 20⅛ inches; height at hock, 5½ inches.

STANDARD OF POINTS FOR JUDGING POODLES.

	Value.
Skull	5
Ears and eyes	5
Neck and body	5
Legs	5
Coat	15
Colour	10
General appearance	5
	50

THE TRUFFLE-DOG.

The Truffle-dog is nothing more or less than a bad small-sized Poodle, and is never, or very rarely, met with under the designation Truffle-dog. Its cultivation is due to the existence of truffles, which it is employed to discover when they are lying in the ground by the help of its acute nose. Any credit, therefore, attained by the Truffle-dog is certainly due to his better-bred relative the Poodle, as the main distinction between the two lies in the former being the leggier dog of the two, and therefore further remarks on the points of the Truffle-dog would be superfluous.

CHAPTER XXIX.

THE BLOODHOUND.

THOUGH the Bloodhound has lost much of his former utility, the breed is nevertheless one that is generally admired in the present day. The noble proportions of the dog, his magnificent head, and the knowledge of what he has been known to do, are each and all powerful agencies in his favour, and the usually brilliant colour of a Bloodhound is also an additional attraction. The uses to which this breed of dog was originally put in this country were the tracking of wounded beasts and the pursuit of malefactors. For either purpose their marvellously keen powers of scent admirably qualified them, and is alluded to by Dr. John Caius in the following words :—

"The greater sort which serve to hunt, having lippes of a large size, and eares of no small length, do not onely chase the beast whiles it lieth, but being dead also by any maner of casualtie, make recourse to the place where it lyeth, having on this point an assured and infallible guyde, namely, the sent and savour of the bloud sprinckled heere and there upon the ground. For whether the beast, beying wounded, doth notwithstanding enjoye life, and escapeth the handes of the huntesman, or whether the said beast, beying slayne, is conveyed clenly out of the parcke (so that there be some signification of bloud there), these dogges with no lesse facilitie and easinesse, their aviditie and greedinesse can disclose and betray the same by smelling, applying to their pursute agilitie and nimbleness without tediousnesse, for which consideration of a singular specialitie they deserved to be called Sanguinarii, or Bloudhounds. And albeit, perad-venture, it may chaunce (as whether it chaunceth sealdome or sometime I am ignorant) that a piece of flesh be subtily stolen and cuningly conveyed away with such provisos and precautions that all apparaunce of bloud is eyther prevented, excluded, or concealed, yet these kinde of dogges, by a certaine directione of an inward assured notyce and privy marcke, pursue the deede doers through rough long lanes, cruked reaches, and weary wayes, without wandring away out of the limites of the land whereon these desperate purloyners prepared their speedy passage. Yea, the natures of these dogges is such, and so effectuall is their foresight, that they can betray separate, and pycke them out from among an infinite multitude, creepe they never so farre into the thickest thronge; they will finde him out notwithstandyng he lye hidden in wylde woods, in close and overgrown groves, and lurcke in hollow holes apte to harbour such ungracious guestes. Moreover, although they should passe over the water, thinking thereby to avoyde the pursute of the houndes, yet will not these dogges give over their attempt, but presuming to swym through the streame perservere in their pursute, and when they be arrived and gotten the further bancke, they hunt up and downe, to and fro runne they, from place to place shift they, untill they have attained to that plot of grounde where they passed over."

According to the "Naturalist's Library," the Bloodhound was usually about twenty-eight inches high. The author of "Cynographia Britannica" gives the height as twenty-seven inches, and describes the dog as being—

BLOODHOUND.

"Of a strong, compact, and muscular form; the face rather narrow, stern, and intelligent; nostrils wide and large; lips pendulous; ears large, broad at the base, and narrowing to the tip; tail strong, but not bushy; voice extremely loud and sonorous. But what most distinguishes this kind is their uniform colour, a reddish-tan, gradually darkening on the upper part, with a mixture of black on the back, becoming lighter on the lower parts and extremities. One of the dogs I saw had a little white on the face, but this was not usual with that breed. Mr. Pennant mentions their having a black spot over each eye; this was not the case with either I made the drawing from."

Further on the same writer remarks of the Bloodhound:—

"There is no doubt he was originally the only dog used to trace game by the scent in this country. The manner of the ancient hunt was not all that is now practised; the game was found and surrounded in its haunts, when roused it was shot by the arrow or wounded by the spear; if in this state it escaped, the Bloodhound traced and the Mastiff or hunter killed it."

It will thus be seen that from the earliest records the greatest value has been attached to the keen scent possessed by a Bloodhound; but in the present day the dog is practically useless, such a thing as a pack of Bloodhounds being almost unknown. As a matter of fact, we believe that Lord Wolverton, at Iwerne Minster, has the only representative pack now in existence, and he certainly has some very creditable specimens of the breed, as his entries at the Alexandra Palace Show in July, 1879, fully testified. A marked difference, however, existed between Lord Wolverton's hounds and those of some other owners also present at the same show. His lordship's hounds were all placed on sound *legs*, which, on the other hand, carried plainer heads than their more luxurious neighbours—the latter being bred more for ornament than use, and the condition of many legs leaving much to be desired, though their *heads* were in many instances nearly perfection. This can, of course, be easily accounted for by the stress laid upon "taking" heads, and the disuse for the breed in the present day; but there can be no excuse for a judge tacitly encouraging infirm hounds by awarding the animals prizes. As the Rev. Grenville F. Hodson, who is a well-known judge of the breed, once remarked at a public dinner, "it is no use a hound having a good head or body if he has not the legs or feet to carry them."

On account of his marvellous scent the Bloodhound has from time immemorial been associated with the capture of escaped criminals. Dr. Caius, as shown above, and in fact the majority of earlier writers, have all alluded to this dog's success as a thief-taker, and his praises have been said or sung by every canine writer down to the present day. The natural consequence of so much adulation has been that the Bloodhound is credited with almost supernatural powers by many persons, and the simple exercise of its natural powers of scent by an ordinary dog under peculiar circumstances has been before now turned to the glory of the Bloodhound by ignorant folks. A case in point is the instance of a peculiarly revolting crime in the neighbourhood of Blackburn. A so-called Bloodhound was said to have been instrumental in tracking out the criminal, and bringing him to justice. As a matter of fact, the man was strongly suspected by the police authorities, and the dog (not a Bloodhound, by the way, but a mongrel) was brought into his house, where some portions of the body were concealed, and which the animal naturally enough detected. At the time this simple and very natural action on the part of the dog led to most extravagant stories being circulated about the extraordinary intelligence of this particular "Bloodhound," as ignorant people styled the beast. We do not, however, desire in the smallest degree to under-estimate the value of the Bloodhound, or cast reflections on his power of scent, which we believe to be of the highest. Unfortunately, his uses in the present day are not numerous in this country, and beyond in a few cases being serviceable as a guard about a house, the Bloodhound may be recognised as included in the ornamental but not useful category of dogs. The disposition of the Bloodhound is not by any means one upon which implicit reliance can be placed, and his size and immense power render him when roused a most formidable and dangerous antagonist.

From the writings of many old writers there appears to be small doubt that in early days there were more than one strain of dogs used for tracking purposes, and it is probably from an amalgamation of these that the modern Bloodhound originally sprang. Gervase Markham describes a Talbot, which no doubt is a relation of the Bloodhound, as a round, thick-headed dog, with a short nose—characteristics which certainly do not appear in modern Bloodhounds. A connection may be established between the present breed and other early varieties, if the subject of colour is studied, for a black race of hounds known as St. Huberts were formerly highly thought of, and it is very probable that from these the modern hound has derived the black saddle, which is so prized by breeders of this variety.

In the present day, though there are many more persons in possession of Bloodhounds than formerly, the breed cannot by any means be said to be widely popular. In days gone by there was considerable difficulty in obtaining pure-bred specimens, but even now that good whelps can readily be obtained at a comparatively trifling cost, the number of breeders seems to remain a very limited one. This neglect or apathy on the part of the public to support the Bloodhound no doubt arises in a great measure from the exaggerated stories which have been related concerning his ferocity. That the animal when roused is a formidable foe there can be no room for doubting; and his ferocity when on the track of an absconding ill-doer often cost the latter his existence when run down; in fact, as will be seen from the quotation given above, the hound in hunting was usually not permitted to break up the wounded animal, who was handed over to the tenderer mercies of a Mastiff or the huntsman. Be the uncertainty of a Bloodhound's temper as it may, we know of more than one specimen of the breed which is thoroughly under control, and of whom, in the presence of its owner, we should have no misgivings under any but the most exceptional circumstances. Kindness and firmness are, we believe, with this breed, as others, the royal road to successful management; and anybody who has visited shows cannot have failed to notice the perfect control which his mistress exercises over the champion Don and others of her kennel. Whether the confidence which Mrs. Humphries at present places in Don will ever be misplaced is more than can be foretold, but as far as can be seen, no animal could possibly be gentler in disposition, and obedient to his owner, than this famous hound.

The subject of colour is one upon which several conflicting opinions are brought to bear. All, however, seem to agree that white, if dispersed in large quantities over the body, is a decided blemish, if not absolute disqualification, on the show-bench. Some modern authorities even go the length of saying that any white at all—a snip on the forehead, a splash on the chest, or a spot on the foot—should prevent a dog from winning at an exhibition. Before, however, giving an opinion on such a subject, it would be well to look back and see what amount of white was allowed the ancient Bloodhound. According to Turberville, in his "Book of Hunting," the hounds showing white were preferred to several other colours which he gives.

This must certainly tend to prove that white was permissible if not actually a desirable addition to a dog's colour in the earlier days of canine literature. It is therefore hard to discover any sufficient reason for supporting modern authorities who advocate the disqualification of hounds which show traces of white. If marked too heavily great injury is certainly done the hound's appearance, and white legs, or a large patch on the chest, would very probably jeopardise his chance of winning a prize under most judges; but for our own part

CAPTAIN J. W. CLAYTON'S LUATH XI.

we are of opinion that slight indications of white should not stand between a Bloodhound and success on the show-bench.

Another point in colour upon which great stress is laid is the acquisition of the black saddle upon the back, the non-possession of which has caused more than one good dog the loss of prizes. A case in point is that of the magnificent Luath XI., the portrait of whose head appears in the subjoined woodcut. Luath XI., most unfortunately for himself and his master, is of a pale tan colour, and his legs are not of the best and straightest, or he must have proved invincible at every show. In spite, however, of his unfashionable colour, his services as a sire have been resorted to with the happiest results by many of the principal breeders of the day, and he is marvellously successful in transmitting his grandly-developed head characteristics to his offspring.

As stated above, the number of modern Bloodhound breeders and exhibitors is a very limited one, but amongst it the names of the following are the most conspicuous:—Lord Wolverton, who hunts a pack of Bloodhounds, but only occasionally exhibits; Mrs. Tinker, of Harborne, whose Dido is recognised as the champion bitch of the day; Mrs. Humphries, of Brixton, the owner of champion Don, who, though not perfect in head, is certainly the grandest exhibition hound as regards his body, legs, and feet. It may here be remarked that Don was selected by Lord Wolverton as a suitable cross for improving the working hounds in his lordship's kennel. Major Cowen, too, of Blaydon-on-Tyne, has exhibited many good ones, such as Druid, Dipton, and Draco. Captain Clayton's Luath XI. will always keep his owner's name in the memory of Bloodhound men; and the doings of the kennels of Messrs. Brough, Bird, Auld, and Mark Beaufoy, will speak for themselves of the quality of the occupants. In 1879 Mr. L. G. Morell of Pangbourne was remarkably successful, and his splendid Rollo won him many prizes most deservedly, thereby adding to the repute of his already famous strain. From the appearance of some young hounds shown since then, old Rollo's sons and daughters bid fair to keep their sire's name before the public long after he takes his departure from the bench. Previous to the successes of Mr. Morell, Dr. Reynolds Ray of Dulwich was the principal exhibitor of first-rate stock, his Baron, Roswell, and Baroness, doing him good service. Before Dr. Ray, Mr. Holford's Regent and Matchless were considered the best out, and were undoubtedly fine specimens of the breed. Dr. Forbes Winslow, too, shows Belle, a grand-headed, well-peaked bitch, who does her owner credit in the ring.

Having thus briefly alluded to the most famous Bloodhound breeders and their hounds, we may pass on to a description of the breed as it is now recognised, and begin as usual by

The *Head*, which is undoubtedly the most remarkable feature in this variety. The skull should be narrow and domed, very long, with the occipital bone terminating in a high peak at the back. It is also covered with thin, loose skin.

The *Jaws* long and narrow, the flews of the upper being very long and pendulous, thin in texture, and extending below the lower one.

The *Nose* large and black, with the nostrils well developed.

The *Eyes* rather small and deeply sunk, of a light brown colour, and showing the haw, or inside red lining.

The *Ears* must be set on low, and should be as long and fine in texture as possible. As regards length, they should meet in front of the nose, and the more they lap over the better.

The *Neck* is rather long, and is furnished with a heavy dewlap.

Shoulders rather slanting.

Body moderately wide at chest, with powerful loins.

Fore-legs set on straight, and very powerful.

Feet round and compact. Many specimens exhibited fail here either from bad rearing or other causes; the pasterns get crooked and the feet splayed, which certainly should disqualify a hound in competition.

Stern rather coarse, long, and carried gaily.

Colour.—The best and most popular is a deep tan, with a black saddle on the back. The tan in many specimens varies in deepness, and in some the black of the back is flecked with tan, which, though not a disqualification, is undesirable. The presence of white we have already alluded to above.

Coat, short and close.

General Appearance.—A wonderfully intelligent and powerful dog, not ferocious-looking, and one that seems incapable of great speed, though apparently full of stamina.

The dog we have selected for illustration as the subject of the coloured plate is Mrs. Humphries' Champion Don, to which reference has been already made. Don was bred in 1875, and is by Dr. Ray's Roswell out of Flora by Rufus out of Hilda, his breeder being Mr. W. Marshall. Don has won, amongst other prizes, 1st Manchester, 1st Bristol, 1st Alexandra Palace, 1877; 1st Bristol, 1878; 1st Hanover, and gold medal Dundee, 1879. He measures from tip of nose to stop, 5 inches; from stop to occiput, 8 inches; length of back, 29 inches; girth of muzzle, 14 inches; girth of skull, 21½ inches; girth of neck, 24 inches; girth round brisket, 38 inches; girth round chest, 35 inches; girth of loins, 29¾ inches; girth of thigh, 18 inches; girth of forearm, 8¾ inches; girth of pastern, 5½ inches; height at shoulders, 28 inches; height at elbows, 15 inches; height at loins, 29 inches; length of stern, 18 inches; age, 5 years; weight, 99 lbs.

Luath XI. belongs to Capt. J. W. Clayton, of 14, Portman Square, and was bred by the Rev. G. Straton in 1874, by Luath X. out of Bran VIII. As before stated, his head is exceptionally good; but his colour being too pale, Luath XI. has not been as successful on the bench as his grand outlines would suggest.

SCALE OF POINTS FOR JUDGING BLOODHOUNDS.	*Value.*
Head	10
Ears and eyes	5
Flews and dewlap	5
Body and chest	5
Legs and feet	10
Colour	5
Coat	5
General appearance	5
	50

CHAPTER XXX.

THE IRISH WOLFHOUND.

BY GEORGE A. GRAHAM, DURSLEY.

IT is with a certain amount of diffidence that this essay is entered upon, as there is a widely-spread impression that the breed to be treated of is extinct. That we are in possession of the breed in its original integrity is not pretended ; at the same time it is confidently believed that there are strains now existing tracing back, more or less clearly, to the original breed ; and it also appears to be tolerably certain that our modern Deerhound is descended from that noble animal, and gives us a very fair idea of what he was, though undoubtedly considerably his inferior in size and power. Had it not been for these facts, the courage to write this chapter might have been wanting ; but they appear to be so clear to the writer, that he can proceed, with the feeling that most of his readers will perceive that he is amply justified in undertaking a history and description of this very magnificent example of the canine race— that, indeed, may be said to have been its *king*.

There have been several very interesting and clever essays written on this subject. Two of the ablest and most valuable were written by Mr. A. McNeill of Colonsay, in 1838, and Mr. H. D. Richardson, in 1841. These treat exclusively of the Irish Wolfhound, though in Mr. McNeill's case it is more to show the identity of the breed with the modern Deerhound that he writes. Richardson, on the other hand, proceeds to show us that, though undeniably of the same stamp, the Irish dog was far superior in size and power, and that from him is descended, in these later days, the modern Deerhound. Both these authors have shown considerable ability and ingenuity in their arguments, and no one can deny that they are worthy of every consideration. Richardson would appear to be in error on some points, but in the main his ideas would certainly appear to be reasonable and correct. That Richardson was highly qualified to offer a sound and most valuable opinion on the subject is proved by the very admirable manner in which he has treated of and described almost every known breed of dog, whether British or foreign. That we have in the Deerhound the modern representative of the old Irish Wolfdog is patent. Of less stature, less robust, and of slimmer form, the main characteristics of the breed remain ; and in very exceptional instances specimens occur which throw back to and resemble in a marked manner the old stock from which they have sprung. It is not probable that our remote ancestors arrived at any very high standard as to quality or looks. Strength, stature, and fleetness were the points most carefully cultivated—at any rate, as regards those breeds used in the capture of large and fierce game. It is somewhat remarkable that whilst we have accounts of all the noticeable breeds from a remote period, including the Irish Wolfdog, we do not find any allusion to the Deerhound, save in writings of a comparatively recent date, which would in a measure justify us in supposing that the Deerhound is the modern representative of that superb animal.

It is a matter of history that this dog was well known to and highly prized by the

Romans, who, we are led to understand, frequently used him in their combats in the arena, for which his great size, strength, and activity, eminently fitted him. It has always been a moot point whether the Irish Wolfdog was, strictly speaking, a Greyhound, or was of a more robust form, approaching the Mastiff. Let us, then, proceed to investigate the question.

Richardson tells us that "Pliny relates a combat in which the dogs of Epirus bore a part. He describes them as much taller than Mastiffs, and of Greyhound form, detailing an account of their contests with a lion and an elephant." This, he thinks, suffices to establish the identity of the Irish Wolfdog with the far-famed dogs of Epirus!

Strabo describes a large and powerful Greyhound as having been in use among the Celtic and Pictish nations, and as being held in such high estimation by them as to have been imported into Gaul for the purposes of the chase.

Silius describes a large and powerful Greyhound as having been imported into Ireland by the Belgæ, thus identifying the Irish Wolfdog with the celebrated Belgic dog of antiquity, which we read of in so many places as having been brought to Rome for the combats of the amphitheatre.

Sir James Warr, in his "Antiquities of Ireland," thus writes regarding the Irish Wolfdog about 1630 (?):—"I must here take notice of those hounds which, from their hunting of wolves, are commonly called Wolfdogs—being creatures of great size and strength, and of a fine shape," &c.

Warr also gives as a frontispiece to his book an allegorical representation of a passage from the Venerable Bede, in which two dogs are introduced bearing a very strong resemblance to the Irish Wolfdog or Scottish Deerdog, in those days doubtless the same animal. The Venerable Bede was born 672, died 735.

We are informed by two very eminent authorities—the Venerable Bede and the Scottish historian Major—that Scotland was peopled from Ireland. We know that by the early writers Scotland was styled Scotia Minor, and Ireland Scotia Major, and it is scarcely necessary to make any remark as to the native languages of the primitive inhabitants of the two countries. The colonisation therefore of Scotland from Ireland under the conduct of Reuda being admitted, can we suppose that the colonists would omit taking with them specimens of such a noble and gallant dog, and one that must prove so serviceable to their emigrant masters, and that, too, at a period when men depended upon the chase for their subsistence? True, this is but an inference, but is it not to be received as a fact when we find that powerful and noble dog, the Highland Deerhound, a *tall* rough Greyhound, to have been known in Scotland since its colonisation? Formerly it *was* called the Wolfdog, but with change of occupation came change of name. In Ireland wolves were certainly in existence longer than in Scotland, but when these animals ceased to exist in the former country, the Wolfdogs became gradually lost. Not so in Scotland, where abundant employment remained for them even after the days of wolf-hunting were over. The *red deer* still remained, and useful as had these superb dogs proved as Wolfdogs, they became perhaps even more valuable as Deerhounds.

Richardson then goes on to show us, from Ossian's poems, that such dogs appertained to the chieftains regarding whose prowess, &c., he sings; but the writer does not apprehend that any real value can be placed on Ossian's accounts *prior* to the date at which they professed to be issued in a collective form by Macpherson, viz., about 1770, as in the judgment of many persons competent to form a just opinion, those poems almost entirely owe their origin to the prolific brains of the supposititious translator. Ossian is supposed to have flourished in the third century.

In the ninth century the Welsh laws contained clauses entailing heavy penalties on any one found maiming or injuring the Irish Greyhound, or, as it was styled in the Code alluded to, "Canis graius Hibernicus," and a value was set upon them equal to more than double that set on the ordinary Greyhound.

"Camden," about 1568, says: "The Irish Wolfhound is similar in shape to a Greyhound, bigger than a Mastiff, and tractable as a Spaniel."

"Holinshed's," or rather Stainhurst's, description of Ireland, about 1560, contains this short account of the noble Wolfdog: "Ireland is stored of cows, excellent horses, of hawkes, fish, and fowle. They are not without wolves, and Greyhounds to hunt them bigger of bone and limb than a colt."

Gough, in his edition of "Camden," published 1789, has this passage on the Wolfhound: "Bishop affirmed that wolves still infested the wild and solitary mountains. Under the article of Greyhounds, Mr. Camden (writing probably about 1530–60) seems to place the Wolfhounds, which are remarkably large, and peculiar to this country."

In November, 1562, the Irish chieftain Shane O'Neill (possibly an ancestor of the Lords O'Neill, to be alluded to as owning Irish Wolfhounds later on) forwarded to Queen Elizabeth, through Robert Dudley Earl of Leicester, a present of two horses, two hawks, and two Irish Wolfdogs; and in 1585, Sir John Perrott, who was Deputy of Ireland from January, 1584, to July, 1588, sent to Sir Francis Walsingham, then Secretary of State in London, "a brace of good Wolfdogs, one black, one white." Later still, in 1608, we find that Irish Wolfhounds were sent from Ireland by Captain Desmond of Duncannon, to Gilbert Earl of Shrewsbury. When Sir Thomas Rowe was ambassador at the court of the Great Mogul, in the year 1615, that emperor desired him to send for some Irish Greyhounds as the most welcome present he could make him. The foregoing are from an article on the Irish Wolfhound, by Mr. Harting, that appeared in *Bailey's Magazine* for September, 1879.

Ware is one of the few old writers (1654) who has said anything on the Irish Wolfdog, and his words are scanty. "Although we have no wolves in England, yet it is certain we have had heretofore routs of them as they have at present in Ireland. In that country is bred a race of Greyhounds, which is fleet and strong, and bears a natural enmity to the wolf."

Evelyn, about 1660–70, says: "The Irish Wolfhound was a tall Greyhound, a stately creature indeed, and did beat a cruel Mastiff. The Bull-dogs did exceedingly well, but the Irish Wolfdog exceeded!" He was then describing the savage sports of the bear-garden.

Ray, about 1697, describing the Irish Greyhound, says: "The greatest dog I have yet seen, surpassing in size even the Molossus (Mastiff?) as regards shape of body and general character, similar in all respects to the common Greyhound; their use is to catch wolves."

The writer would remark in passing that there is but little doubt that the ordinary Greyhound of that date was a rough-coated dog.

Buffon, about 1750–60, speaks of these dogs as follows: "They are far larger than our largest Mâtins, and they are very rare in France. I have never seen but one, which seemed to me when sitting quite upright to be nearly five feet high, and to resemble in form the dog we call the Great Dane, but it differed from it greatly in the largeness of its size. It was quite white, and of a gentle and peaceable disposition."

From Goldsmith, about 1770, the following is extracted:—"The last variety, and the most wonderful of all that I shall mention, is the Great Irish Wolfdog, that may be considered as the first of the canine species. He is extremely beautiful and majestic in appearance, being the greatest of the dog kind to be seen in the world. The largest of those I have seen—and I have seen about a dozen—was about four feet high, or as tall as a calf of a year old. He was made extremely like a Greyhound, but more robust, and inclining to the figure of the French Mâtin or the Great Dane," &c.

Brooke, in his "Natural History" of 1772, states: "The Irish Wolfdog is, as 'Ray' affirms, the highest dog he had ever seen, he being much larger than a Mastiff dog, but more like a Greyhound in shape."

Smith, in his "History of Waterford" (1774), uses very similar words:—"The Irish Greyhound, though formerly abounding in this country, is likewise become nearly extinct. This dog is much taller than the Mastiff, but made more like a Greyhound."

Pennant (1776–81) informs us that the Irish Gre-hound—a variety once very frequent in Ireland, and used in the chase of the wolf, now very scarce—is a dog of great size and strength.

From Bewick (1792) we gather that "the Irish Greyhound is the largest of the dog kind, and its appearance the most beautiful. It is only to be found in Ireland, where it was formerly of great use in clearing that country from wolves. It is now extremely rare, and kept rather for show than use, being equally unserviceable for hunting the stag, the fox, or the hare. These dogs are about three feet high, generally of a white or cinnamon colour, and made somewhat like a Greyhound, but more robust. Their aspect is mild; their disposition peaceable; their strength is so great that in combat the Mastiff or Bull-dog is far from being equal to them. They mostly seize their antagonists by the back and shake them to death, which their great strength generally enables them to do." M. Buffon supposes the Great Danish dog to be only a variety of the Irish Greyhound. About this time (1794) certain dogs in the possession of the then Lord Altamont were put forward as being Irish Wolfdogs; but there appears to be no doubt whatever that these dogs were degenerate specimens of the Great Dane. Mr. Lambert, describing them to the Linnæan Society, stated that "they were the only ones in the kingdom; their hair was short and smooth, the colour brown-and-white and black-and-white." An engraving of one of these dogs is given in the "Encyclopædia Britannica" published in 1810, and it represents an under-bred Great Dane, of dull and mild appearance. Richardson at one time was in error regarding these dogs, for he accepted them as being true specimens of the Irish Wolfhound; but he was afterwards, from careful inquiry and research, quite disabused of any such idea, and concluded that the Irish Wolfhound was a rough Greyhound of gigantic stature and immense power.

To suppose that these dogs were Irish Wolfhounds was absurd to a degree, as that breed was known to be very scarce, whereas the Great Dane was (and is) to be met with in great numbers on the Continent.

The present Marquis of Sligo informed the writer about twelve years ago that he had often made inquiries from persons who had seen his father's dogs, and as far as their descriptions would enable one to judge, they rather resembled some of the German Boarhounds, being rather like powerful, shaggy Greyhounds, but a good deal larger. It is probable that the shagginess was a mistake, as Mr. Lambert distinctly states them to have been smooth.

E. Jesse tells us that the late Lord Derby purchased the portrait—in Mr. Lambert's possession—of one of Lord Altamont's dogs. Now, it is a well-ascertained fact that, in the face of this model (!), Lord Derby bred, as Irish Wolfdogs, a very powerful and robust dog of Deerhound character (!!), showing that he set small value on the picture as representing the *true* breed of Irish Wolfdog.

In the "Encyclopædia Britannica" of 1797 we are shown a drawing of the Irish Gre-hound, which represents a very thick-set, tall Greyhound, with a rough coat and massive head ; colour apparently brindle or black-and-white.

The "Sportsman's Cabinet"—a very valuable old book on dogs, of which there were but a limited number of copies published in 1803, and which is illustrated by very good engravings after drawings from life by Reinagle, a Royal Academician—says :—"The dogs of Greece, Denmark, Tartary, and Ireland, are the largest and strongest of their species. The Irish Greyhound is of very ancient race, and still to be found in some far remote parts of that kingdom, though they are said to be reduced even in their original climate. They are much larger than the Mastiff ; exceedingly ferocious when engaged." A remarkably spirited drawing is given of this dog, which, though faulty in some minor points, gives us an admirable idea of what this grand dog was.

Notwithstanding the undoubted resemblance of this sketch to a gigantic rough Greyhound of great power, the letterpress is continued to the effect that the dog is identical with the Great Dane—a totally different dog in appearance—which is manifestly absurd ; and on the letterpress we can accordingly put no great stress, though the *portrait* undoubtedly has a real value. E. Jesse coincides in this opinion, as when speaking of the "Sportsman's Cabinet" he says :— "It is a work more remarkable for the truth and fineness of its engravings than for the matter contained in it." It is a noticeable and remarkable fact that whilst this book professes to treat of every known variety of British dog, it does not make any mention whatever of the Scottish Deerhound.

A few extracts from this book are given that bear on the subject under consideration, though not taken from the chapter descriptive of the Irish Wolfhound or Greyhound.

"The Greyhound, large Danish dog, and Irish Greyhound, have, according to Buffon, exclusive of their likeness of figures and length of muzzle, a similitude of disposition."

"The peculiar irritability of the olifactory sensation seems by natural observation to depend more upon the largeness than the length of the nose, for the Greyhound, Danish dog, and Irish Greyhound, have evidently less power of scent than the Hound, Terrier, &c."

"The Bulldog and Irish Greyhound have their ears partly erect."

"The Great Danish dog, taken from thence to Ireland, the Ukraine, Tartary, Epirus, and Albania, has been changed into the Irish Greyhound, which is the largest of all dogs."

"The Greyhound and Irish Greyhound, Buffon goes on to say, have produced the mongrel Greyhound, also called the Greyhound with the wolf's hair "—in all probability the present Scotch Deerhound (?).

Dr. Scouler, reading a paper before the Dublin Geological Society in 1837, says :—"The Irish Wolfdog was a very distinct race from the Scotch Hound or Wolfdog, which resembled the Irish breed in size and courage, but differed from it by having a sharper muzzle and pendent ears."

McNeill, in his article on the Irish Wolfhound, written 1838, says :—"Whatever may have been the origin of the name, there is little doubt as to the antiquity of a species of dog in this country (Ireland) bearing a great resemblance in many points to the Greyhound of the present day, and passing under that name, though evidently a larger, nobler, and more courageous animal."

He goes on to argue that "from the rough and uncultivated state of the country, and the nature of the game that was then the object of the chase—viz., deer of all sorts, wolves, and foxes—that the dogs would be of a larger, fiercer, and more shaggy description than the Greyhounds of the present day."

From the "Museum of Animated Nature," published in 1842–45, the following account of the Irish Wolfdog is taken:—"In Scotland and Ireland there existed in very ancient times a noble breed of Greyhounds used for the chase of the wolf and deer, which appears to us to be the pure source of our present breed. It is quite as possible that the Mâtin is a modification of the ancient Greyhound of Europe—represented by the Irish Greyhound or Wolfdog—as that it is the source of that fine breed, as Buffon supposes. Few, we believe, of the old Irish Greyhound exist."

From the very interesting book entitled "Anecdotes of Dogs," by E. Jesse, published 1846, the following is gleaned:—

"The dog flourished at the time of early kings of Ireland, and, with harp and shamrock, is regarded as one of the national emblems of the country."

"The Irish Wolfdogs were formerly placed as the supporters of the arms of the ancient monarchs of Ireland. They were collared 'or,' with the motto, 'Gentle when stroked, fierce when provoked.'"

The well-known Mrs. S. C. Hall, wrote to Jesse the following interesting account of an Irish Wolfdog:—"When I was a child (probably 1812–15), I had a very close friendship with a genuine old Wolfdog, Bruno by name. He was the property of an old friend of my grandmother's, who claimed descent from the Irish kings. His name was O'Toole. His visits were my jubilees. There was the kind, dignified, old gentleman, and there was his tall gaunt dog, grey with age, and yet with me full of play. The O'Toole had three of these dogs. Bruno was rough—but not long-coated."

Richardson tells us that the late Sir W. Betham, Ulster King-at-Arms, an authority of very high importance on any subject connected with Irish antiquities, in communicating with Mr. Haffield, who read a paper on the Irish Wolfhound before the Dublin Natural History Society, about 1841, states as follows: "From the mention of the Wolfdogs in the old Irish stories and poems, and also from what I have heard from a very old person, long since dead, of his having seen them at the Neale, in the County of Mayo, the seat of Sir John Browne, ancestor to Lord Kilmaine, I have no doubt they were a gigantic Greyhound. My departed friend described them as being very gentle, and that Sir J. Browne allowed them to come into his dining-room, where they put their heads over the shoulders of those who sat at table; they were not smooth-skinned like our Greyhounds, but rough and curly-haired."

"The Irish poets call the Wolfdog 'cu,' and the common Greyhound 'gayer,' a marked distinction, the word 'cu' signifying a champion."

Some dogs were owned by the late Hamilton Rowan, of Merrion Square, Dublin, which were *erroneously* asserted to be Irish Wolfhounds. Regarding these dogs the following communication was kindly made to the writer by Mr. Betham, a son of Sir W. Betham before alluded to:—"My father was very intimate with the late Hamilton Rowan, who was the only man possessed of the breed (Irish Wolfhound), and who was so chary of it that he would never give away a dog pup without first castrating him. I have repeatedly seen the dogs with him when I was a boy, and heard him tell my father how he became possessed of them. He was in Paris about the time of the first French Revolution, and was given a dog and a bitch, and was told there that they were *Danish*. He then went to Denmark, thinking he would see more of the breed. When he got there he was told they were not Danish, but Irish, and were brought over by some one from Ireland—I forget whom. The dogs were of a very peculiar colour—a kind of brindle blue-and-white, sometimes all brindled, and sometimes a great deal of white with large irregular brindle patches, and were much given to weak eyes. They stood about 2 feet 4 or 6 inches at the shoulder, were smooth-haired, and were a most powerful dog. Hamilton Rowan was very proud of being the only possessor of the breed, and seldom went out without one or more accompanying him.

In a second letter he goes on to say :—"I can speak from personal knowledge, and from having often seen the dogs, that the true breed of Irish Wolfdogs are smooth-haired, not shaggy like the Scotch Deerhound. They were coarse-haired, like the Bloodhound. I am not acquainted with the German Boarhound (*i.e.,* Great Dane) ; very possibly they might have been somewhat similar to the Irish breed. Hamilton Rowan's dogs were very power-ful, and at the same time active dogs, with rather a sharp nose and shrill bark. My father used to say that when he dined at Hamilton Rowan's the dogs used to be in the parlour, and were so tall they could put their heads over the guests' shoulders when sitting at the table, though the dogs were standing on the floor."

Beyond the shadow of a doubt these dogs were simply Great Danes, as Mr. Rowan had evidently been told in Paris ; the description leaves no doubt on that head. Richardson tells us the fact was that Mr. Rowan owned some of the breed known as Great Danes, and he never by any chance called them by a wrong name. He also owned a *true* Wolfdog, and knew him to be such, calling him "the last of his race." This dog was a large rough Grey-hound of iron-grey colour. Mr. Rowan subsequently presented this dog to Lord Nugent. In corroboration of this fact the writer was informed by the late Sir John Power, who recollected Mr. Rowan and his dogs, and who would have reached man's estate at the time, and been well able to judge of them, being a thorough lover of the canine race, that Richardson's description of the true Wolfdog belonging to Mr. Rowan was right. Mr. Betham remembers the dogs only as a boy, and the distinction between the Danish dogs and the true old rough dog would hardly have struck him ; hence his misconception on the matter. Mr. Betham's account is only inserted and confuted to remove any impression that certain of Hamilton Rowan's dogs were aught but Great Danes, which has been erroneously otherwise concluded. Mr. Betham confesses, it will be seen, that he is not acquainted with the Great Dane or Boarhound, which are common and plentiful in all Continental countries ; he cannot, consequently, be considered a fair judge on the subject.

Youatt has this regarding the Irish Wolfdog :—" This animal is nearly extinct, or only to be met with at the mansions of one or two persons, by whom he is kept more for show than use, the wild animals which he seemed powerful enough to conquer having long disappeared from the kingdom. The beauty of his appearance and antiquity of his race are his only claims, as he disdains the chase of stag, fox, or hare, though he is ever ready to protect the person and property of his master. His size is various, some having attained the height of four feet. He is shaped like the Greyhound, but stouter."

Literature and the powers of depicting an animal in its correct form were in such a crude and immature stage amongst the nobility and gentry of the land at the periods when we have our first accounts of the Irish Wolfdog, that it is not in the least to be wondered at that the imperfect descriptions given of the breed by such persons as were equal to the task were allowed to go uncontradicted by the only people in whose hands the breed was likely to be. From the accounts we have, however, we can clearly and distinctly gather that the dog has always been of Greyhound shape, of gigantic stature, and great power, in fact, such a dog as a cross between the Great Dane and present Deerhound would produce, as to form and bulk, but of superior size.

Richardson, to further his views regarding the probable size of the ancient Irish Wolf-dog, tells us that certain canine skulls were found by Surgeon Wylde at Dunshauglin which were concluded to be those of the Irish Wolfdog; of these the largest was 11 inches in the bone, and from that fact he proceeds to argue that the living dog must have stood about 40 inches. To begin, he takes for his guide a Deerhound dog standing 29 inches, whose head measures 10 inches. To the 11-inch Irish Wolfhound skull he adds 3 inches for muzzle, hair, skin, and other tissues, thereby making the head of the living dog 14 inches; thus getting the height of 40 inches from it, as compared to the 29 inches from the 10-inch head. Here, however, he would appear to be in error, as 1½ or 2 inches at the most would be enough to allow for tissues, &c., making the head 12½ to 13 inches only, and so reducing the height to 36 inches; moreover, the measurement of 10 inches for the head of a 29-inch Deerhound is manifestly insufficient, as the writer can testify from ample experience. A Deerhound of that height should have a head of at least 11 inches; so, calculating on the same principles, the skulls would have been from dogs standing about 34 inches. This skull is stated to have been superior in size to the others, so if the argument was of any real worth, we can only gather from it that the dogs would have ranged from 31 to 34 inches in height, which is probable enough.

It is an incontestable fact that the domestic dog, when used for the pursuit of ferocious animals, should be larger and apparently more powerful than his quarry if he is expected to take and overcome him single-handed, as the fierce nature, roving habits, and food of the wild animal render him more than a match for his domesticated enemy, if of only equal size and stature. We know that the Russian Wolfhounds (certainly very soft-hearted dogs), though equal in stature to the wolf, will not attack him single-handed—and wisely too, for they would certainly be worsted in the combat. The Irish Wolfdog, being used for both the capture and despatch of the wolf, would necessarily have been of Greyhound conformation, besides being of enormous power. When caught, a heavy dog, such as a Mastiff, would be equal to the destruction of a wolf, but to obtain a dog with Greyhound speed and the strength of the Mastiff, it stands to reason that his stature should considerably exceed that of the Mastiff— one of our tallest as well as most powerful breeds. The usual height of the Mastiff is thirty inches; and, arguing as above, we may reasonably conclude that to obtain the requisite combination of speed and power, a height of at least thirty-three inches would have been reached, though we are told by several writers that he exceeded that height considerably.

In the New York *Country*, about May, 1878, it is written:—"It is absurd to give as a reason for the indifference and apathy through which such a breed has been allowed to die out or its perpetuity to be endangered, that in the extermination of his particular foe —the wolf—his occupation was gone. A noble animal of this character should never have been permitted to waste away while curs of the lowest degree are petted and pampered and carefully provided for. In this country particularly the Irish Wolfdog could be made of special service. Here he would find in the chase and extermination of the wolf a wide field for his prowess and courage. On the western bounds of civilisation he would be invaluable for the purposes of hunting, his keen sight and scent rendering him superior to many breeds now in use, and as a companion and friend of man his fidelity and devotion have never been called in question. All the testimony which comes down to us agrees as to his sagacity, courage, strength, speed, and size, although in this last point we perceive there is a difference of opinion. Even allowing that he attained a height of from thirty-two to thirty-five inches, he is taller than any breed now living, although the early accounts published of him state he was from three to four feet high."

For many months a spirited controversy and correspondence on the Irish Wolfhound was carried on in the *Live Stock Journal* by the writer and others, without, it is confidently thought, in any way disturbing the conclusions on the breed which the writer has, from careful and prolonged consideration of the subject, arrived at, and which will be set forth presently.

The question as to whether it is desirable to continue and thoroughly resuscitate this superb breed now that his occupation is gone is hardly worth entertaining.

Have not a dozen breeds—such as St. Bernards, Collies, &c.—been taken up, cherished, and improved to a marvellous degree? Why not, then, take such measures to recover the Irish Wolfdog in its original form? It can be done; the means are at hand if the *will* be only forthcoming. From the materials forthcoming in such specimens of the breed as are extant and the largest Deerhounds, with judicious crosses for size and power, there is little doubt that the breed can be restored to us in much of its original magnificence, and the noble canine giant—always held to be typical of Erin—would be worthily and faithfully represented.

As the Deerhound of the present day is to the ordinary Greyhound, so is the giant Irish Wolfhound to the Deerhound. An Irish paper, waxing enthusiastic on the subject, says, not long ago, regarding the Irish Wolfdog:—"This animal has become celebrated as the heraldic protector of our country. Fair Erin sits pensively beside her harp, the round tower stands near, and guarding all three, reclines the Wolfhound. Scotland's lions have been famed in story; England 'stole' one of them, say some, and joining him in company with the unicorn, committed to his trust the honour of Albion; but the unicorn is a beast which even Dr. Houghton has never seen, while we must go back to the antediluvian era to find lions in Great Britain. But the Wolfdog is no mythic beast in Ireland; he was and we trust will again be, included amongst the undoubted, exclusive, and most distinguished specimens of the Irish fauna."

In the British Museum there is a Grecian vase, some 450 B.C., on which Actæon is depicted surrounded by his dogs. Some of them would appear identical with what the Irish Wolfhound was, save, perhaps, in the matter of coat.

On some ancient frescoes at Easton Neston Hall, near Towcester, are depicted various hunting scenes. In one of these two vast dogs of Deerhound type are represented as seizing a boar, and these frescoes having been painted at a time when the Irish Wolfhound existed, may be looked upon as throwing considerable light on the real type of that breed. They are shown to be vast Deerhounds, with rough wiry coats, of a dark blue-grey colour; ears small and falling over.

It will be well now to state the conclusions at which the writer has arrived as to the general appearance and character of the Irish Wolfhound, after a prolonged, searching, and careful study of the subject.

Form.—That of a very tall, heavy, Scotch Deerhound, much more massive, and very majestic-looking; active and fast, perhaps somewhat less so than the present breed of Deerhound; neck thick in comparison to his form, and very muscular; body and frame lengthy.

Head.—Long, but not narrow, coming to a comparative point towards the nose; nose rather large, and head gradually getting broader from the same, *evenly* up to the back of the skull—not sharp up to the eyes, and then suddenly broad and lumpy, as is often the case with dogs bred between Greyhound and Mastiff.

Coat.—There can be little doubt that from the very nature of the work the dog was called upon to do this would be of a rough and probably somewhat shaggy nature, and to this end points the evidence gained from Arrian—second century—who leaves no doubt in our mind that the great Greyhound of his day was rough in coat; also from the ancient Irish harp, now preserved in Trinity College, Dublin, which is ornamented with a figure of the Irish Wolfhound, rough-coated. Sir J. Browne's dogs were rough and shaggy; Mr. O'Toole's dog was rough; also Hamilton Rowan's. The former Earls of Caledon owned Irish Wolfdogs, which were rough; added to which, in former days all Greyhounds were, we have every reason to believe, rough; certainly the larger varieties, as is now without exception the case. So it is with justice concluded that the coat was rough, hard and long all over body, head, legs, and tail; hair on head long, and rather softer than that on body, standing out boldly over eyes; beard under jaws being also very marked and wiry.

Colour.—Black, grey, brindle, red, and fawn, though white dogs were esteemed in former times, as is several times shown us—indeed, they were often preferred—but for beauty the dark colours should be cultivated.

Ears.—Small in proportion to size of head, and erect as in the smooth Greyhound. If dark in colour it is to be preferred.

The *Tail* should be carried with an upward curve only, and not be curled, as is the case with many Greyhounds.

Size.—We may safely deduce that the height of these dogs varied from 32 to 34 inches, and even 35 inches in the dogs, probably from 29 to 31 inches in the bitches. The other dimensions would naturally be about as follows for well-shaped and true-formed dogs. Girth of chest—Dogs, 38 to 44 inches; bitches, 32 to 34 inches. Weight in lbs.—Dogs, 115 to 140; bitches, 90 to 115. Girth of fore-arm—Dogs, 10 to 12 inches; bitches, $8\frac{1}{2}$ to 10 inches. Length of head—Dogs, $12\frac{1}{2}$ to 14 inches; bitches, 11 to 12 inches. Most modern authors and all practical lovers of the canine race whom the writer has consulted are agreed that the foregoing is the correct type of dog beyond question; and although some differ slightly as to the comparative bulk and power of the dog, the difference is small when dispassionately looked at.

To any one who has well considered the subject such conclusions are inevitable, and this impression has been manifestly handed down to us for generations.

Although several writers have incorrectly confounded the Great Dane with the Irish Wolfhound, yet it is probable that the two breeds were not infrequently crossed; indeed, it is possible that in foreign countries the Irish Wolfhound may have degenerated into the Great Dane and other varieties, as it has into the Deerhound with us. That such was the case Buffon does more than suggest. Major Garnier, who gave the subject considerable attention at one time, rather holds to this opinion, and says "that whilst the Highland Deerhound is the most correct type, the German Boarhound has best retained the size, though at the expense of character."

These facts may possibly have influenced erroneously the opinions of some of the naturalists of the latter end of the last century, and will also account for the fact of Lord Altamont's dogs having been put forward as Irish Wolfhounds, which they certainly were not.

The last wolf was supposed to have been killed in Ireland about 1710.

Richardson says:—"Though I have separated the Irish Wolfdog from the Highland Deerhound and the Scottish Greyhound, I have only done so partly in conformity with general opinion, that I have yet to correct, and partly because these dogs, though originally identical, are now unquestionably distinct in many particulars."

The former Earls of Caledon at one time owned a breed of Irish Wolfhounds, regarding which the present peer has obligingly collected the following particulars :—"The dog was in appearance between a Mastiff and Deerhound ; slighter and more active than the one, more massive and stronger than the other; as tall or taller than the tallest Deerhound ; rough but not long-coated ; fawn, grizzly, and dun in colour: some old men on the property have mentioned a mixture of white."

A breed was also owned by the Lords O'Neil, also by Lord Castletown ; but no information regarding them has been obtained, although a friend of the writer was presented, many years ago, with a bitch of the former breed which answered very much to the description given above of Lord Caledon's dogs.

In a very interesting letter from America, written to a gentleman residing in England, published in the *Live Stock Journal* some time ago, the writer says :—"I have felt an interest in the subject for over fifty years. My father often spoke of Lord Sligo's (Altamont's) breed of dogs, and doubted their being the genuine Irish Wolfdog. He had every opportunity of observing them himself, being much at Westport House during his youth." After making other observations, he goes on to say :—"The bone of the fore-leg is, I should say, the point that best distinguishes dogs of this class from all of the Greyhound class, whom in actual build they so much resemble. The massiveness of that bone is out of proportion altogether, and it certainly was not made for speed so much as for power and endurance. I think all the Scotch dogs that I have seen are deficient in this respect, and I attribute it to crossing with lighter-built breeds in order to obtain swiftness for deer-hunting. The epithet 'hairy-footed' in old Irish poems leaves no doubt as to the comparatively rough coat of the Irish Wolfdog."

That it is beyond reason that any dog should have stood 36 inches is not the case, as Lord Mount Edgcumbe has a picture of a dog taken life-size which measures 36 inches to the shoulder. The skeleton of this dog (apparently a Great Dane), which is also preserved, would corroborate this measurement. A picture was also painted for the Marquis of Hastings in 1803 by Clifford de Tomsan, which represents a dog standing 36 inches at shoulder—also apparently a Great Dane, of a buff-and-white colour. The picture measures $7\frac{1}{2}$ feet by $5\frac{1}{2}$ feet, so it will be seen the dog must of necessity have been gigantic. We have also had some enormous dogs "in the life" of late years. The great American dog exhibited to Her Majesty some eighteen years ago was said to stand 36 inches. Sir Roger Palmer's Sam was 34. Both were Boarhounds. Several of our Mastiffs have stood 33 and even 34 inches. The great dog brought from America by Mr. Butler, of New York, about four or five years ago, stood about the same height. He was a descendant of the dog shown to the Queen—also owned by Mr. Butler. On the Continent it is not uncommon to find dogs standing 33 and 34 inches, and a Boarhound has been brought to the writer's notice, belonging to a gentleman residing at Cologne, that was reported to stand 37 inches by a gentleman well accustomed to large dogs. The tallest dog the writer has actually measured stood $34\frac{1}{2}$ inches on the shoulder-blade—a giant indeed. With all these examples before us, and some of them within our reach, there is no reason why the Irish Wolfhound should not be restored to its original height of from 33 to 35 inches.

It is worthy of remark that whilst some people scout the very idea that the Deerhound is the descendant of the Irish Wolfhound, McNeill is proud to claim such descent for his favourite breed.

Major Garnier at one time turned his attention to Irish Wolfhounds, and produced one or two dogs of great size, but he was unable to carry his projects to an end, being suddenly ordered to the Cape. He was thoroughly convinced that the recovery of this breed in its pristine grandeur and magnificence was only a question of time if the would-be breeders were steadfast in their endeavours. He had laid down for himself certain rules in breeding, which are given:—

" 1. Quality is very much more dependent on the dam than on the sire.

" 2. Bone or size, on the contrary, is far more dependent on the sire.

" 3. Colour is almost wholly dependent on the sire.

" 4. The coat is almost wholly independent of the sire.

" 5. Muscular development and general form is chiefly dependent on the dam.

" 6. All these are modified by the fact that the purer bred will (other things being the same) influence the progeny more than the other.

" 7. Every decided cross increases the size by one or two inches. This is merely an opinion formed from my own experience and observation; but I have never seen it carried out far enough to make me certain in my own mind about it.

" 1, 2, 3, 4, and 5 I have not merely met with as the opinions of other people, but I have proved them incontestably myself. With regard to No. 1—'Quality'—I mean 'blood,' nervous development, vigour, energy, and character."

He concludes by saying:—"Anyhow, with Ulmer Boarhounds and Russian Wolfhounds (of course, in conjunction with the Deerhound and such of the Irish breed as are in existence) I believe it is quite possible to re-establish the old breed of Irish Greyhounds in all their former beauty and power. I should, however, be content with perfection of form and coat at 34 inches."

The writer is not prepared to coincide entirely with the above rules, but in the main he considers them correct, and such as can safely be adopted by breeders. The Foxhound, the Pointer, the Shorthorn, and many breeds of sheep and pigs, have been brought to their present excellence by judicious crossing; why should not the same principle be applied to the perfecting of the Irish Wolfhound?

About the year 1863 the writer took the Irish Wolfhound question up, and instituted very searching inquiries after any specimens of the breed. For some time he did not meet with much success; but about twelve years ago three distinct strains were brought to his notice—viz., those of the late Sir J. Power of Kilfane, the late Mr. Baker of Ballytobin, and Mr. Mahoney of Dromore—alas! now all believed to be lost, save some of the descendants of the first two strains, which are in the writer's and one or two other hands. Isolated specimens were also heard of. The Kilfane strain owed their origin to dogs bred by Richardson, about 1840, who not content with writing, actively set to work to discover the breed; from him Sir John Power had more than one specimen. Richardson obtained bitches from Mr. Carter of Bray (whose strain he mentions in his essay), and crossing these with a grand dog of great height, produced some remarkably fine dogs. It is also believed that this strain was descended from Hamilton Rowan's dog Bran, before mentioned. Of this strain also were the Ballytobin dogs. Mr. Baker was an enthusiast regarding all old Irish institutions, and having built himself a castle, he did all he could to increase the size of the deer in his park, also to restore to their original form the Irish Wolfdogs. To this end he procured the best specimens, wherever to be had, regardless of cost, and at his death, some twelve years ago, he left a kennel of really fine dogs. The pick of these—bequeathed to a friend—a bitch, eventually came into the possession of the writer, and from her and from dogs of the writer's own breeding his present strain has sprung. The strain of Mr. Mahoney was originally procured from Sir John Power, and Mr. Mahoney thus speaks of them :—

"The pedigree I had, but I do not think I could now find it. I remember that the grandsire or the great-grandsire was one of the last old Irish dogs which I have an idea belonged to the famous Hamilton Rowan ; but of this I am not certain. As wolves disappeared in Ireland the dogs gradually fell away also. They were expensive to keep, and from the fifteenth century the diet of the people gradually changed from being almost exclusively animal to being purely vegetable. Thus there was no food to preserve the size and power of the dogs. The race of red deer also became extinct, except in the mountains of Kerry, where a few wandered ; but under the care of Lord Kenmare and Mr. Herbert, and their successors, have developed into noble breeds without a cross. Thus there was no inducement to extenuate the old powerful dog into the swifter but sparer Deerhound, and the few specimens that remained preserved the original characteristics ; while in Scotland the cause that preserved the race from extinction tended to change its qualities and older heroic proportions into the modern Deerhound.

"My idea was that by selection, avoiding in-breeding, and proper feeding, the old characteristics might in some generations be somewhat recovered. The colours were dark brindle, bluish-grey, and fawn. The bitch was usually lower, and therefore looked stouter than the dog ; indeed, she was so in proportion. They were stouter than Deerhounds."

Lord Derby, grandfather of the present lord, bred Irish Wolfhounds of evidently much the same character as the strains just alluded to. One of them is thus described by a gentleman :—" She was a dark brindle brown, the coat of long wiry hair, the build heavier and head more massive than that of the Deerhound, the hair on the head thicker and lying flatter, and the ears rather larger, though lying close to the head." Some of her descendants were nearly black.

The writer has not only studied the subject carefully, but has bred extensively, with more or less success, though death and disease have hitherto robbed him of the finest specimens. Dogs have been bred approaching his ideal closely in looks, though wanting the required height and power ; also dogs of very great height, &c., which were somewhat wanting in character. Yet the very certain knowledge has been gained from these efforts that it is perfectly possible to breed the correct type of dog in the course of a few years—bar losses from death and disease. It has been the steadfast endeavour of the writer to get crosses from such dogs of acknowledged Irish Wolfhound blood as were to be found, in preference to simply crossing opposite breeds to effect the desired object.

The Irish Kennel Club was courageous enough to establish a class for the breed of Irish Wolfhounds at their show, April, 1879, and it is strenuously to be hoped that this step in the right direction will be followed on the part of other shows.

Scot, the subject of the illustration, was from a Kilfane sire out of a fine red bitch. He is a powerful dog of strong red colour, deficient in coat, notably on head, and loses much in appearance thereby. Taken on the whole, however, he gives a very fair idea of the breed as to form and bulk ; but instead of standing only 29½ inches, as he does, he should be at least 33 inches, and be enlarged in proportion. The blood can be traced back for forty years. His dimensions are:—Height, 29½ inches; girth of chest, 33½ inches; length of head, 12 inches; girth of head, 18¾ inches; fore-arm, 8½ inches; weight, 110 lbs., which will serve to show what the general conformation of the dog is, though the head is represented as somewhat too deep behind the eyes in the engraving.

A very sensible letter was published in the *Live Stock Journal*, in 1879, by a German gentleman, from which the following extracts will prove of interest:—"That the Irish

MR. GRAHAM'S IRISH WOLFHOUND "SCOT."

Wolfhound is a pure 'Windhound' [Greyhound] I believe as little as that it is a pure Dane. As opposed to the wolf the largest 'Windhound' is not strong enough, and the Dane, on account of its short fine hair, is too vulnerable. I think the Irish Wolfhound is the Scotch Deerhound with some blood from our modern large German Dogge [Boarhound?] to give him the necessary strength."

The writer has had painted, under his close superintendence and guidance, a portrait of an Irish Wolfhound of 35 inches, life-size, of a grey colour, and it presents to the vision a most striking and remarkable animal of a very majestic and beautiful appearance, far, far beyond any dog the writer has ever seen in grandeur of looks.

In concluding this article, the writer would express his astonishment that so noble and attractive a breed of dog should have found so few supporters. Of all dogs the monarch and the most majestic, shall he be allowed to drop from our supine grasp?

The above article being from the pen of so able an authority, must command attention from all classes of the community who are interested in dogs. As Mr. Graham remarks, it is astonishing that so noble and attractive a breed is so poorly supported by admirers of the canine race. A few enthusiastic breeders would rescue it from the position into which it has fallen; and from the success which is attending the efforts of those gentlemen who are now interesting themselves on its behalf, we are confident that a breed of Irish Wolfhounds could soon be produced, which, if not actually of the old original strain, would at least fairly represent the breed in modern times.

As Mr. Graham has not appended a scale of points to his remarks upon the breed, we venture to add one upon our own responsibility, merely remarking that it is our own conception, and is inserted here without an appeal to Mr. Graham, who is, at the time of writing, too far away to be communicated with.

SCALE OF POINTS FOR JUDGING IRISH WOLFHOUNDS.

	Value.
Skull—shape and length	10
Jaws	5
Shoulders	5
Body	5
Legs	5
Coat	10
Size	5
General appearance	5
	50

CHAPTER XXXI.

THE DEERHOUND.

BY G. A. GRAHAM, DURSLEY.

THE transition from the Irish Wolfhound to the Deerhound is easy and natural, as in the latter we unmistakably have the descendant of the former. The subject is, moreover, the more easily treated of, as we have many excellent specimens of the Deerhound before us. Indeed, the examples of the breed now scattered in considerable profusion throughout the land are far finer dogs than those of which much boast was made forty years ago.

The earliest records we have of the Deerhound as a distinct breed are, it is believed, given to us by Pennant, who, in his tour in 1769, says :—" I saw also at Castle Gordon a true Highland Greyhound, which has become very scarce. It was of a large size, strong, deep-chested, and covered with very long and rough hair. This kind was in great vogue in former days, and used in vast numbers at the magnificent stag-chases by the powerful chieftains."

Then Macpherson, in his professed translation of Ossian's poems (1773), gives testimony—worthless, no doubt, as regards the Irish Wolfhound, but having a decided value when the Deerhound is considered, as it was almost a certainty that he wrote his descriptions from the living animal. The following extracts will be found of interest :—" Fingal agreed to hunt in the Forest of Sledale, in company with the Sutherland chief his contemporary, for the purpose of trying the comparative merits of their dogs. Fingal brought his celebrated dog Bran to Sutherland, in order to compete with an equally famous dog belonging to the Sutherland chief, and the only one in the country supposed to be a match for him. The approaching contest between these fine animals created great interest. White-breasted Bran was superior to the whole of Fingal's other dogs, even to the 'surly strength of Luath ;' but the Sutherland dog—known by the full-sounding name of Phorp—was incomparably the best and most powerful dog that ever eyed a deer in his master's forests."

Phorp was black in colour, and his points are thus described :—

> " ' Two yellow feet such as Bran had,
> Two black eyes,
> And a white breast,
> A back narrow and fair,
> As required for hunting,
> And two erect ears of a dark red-brown.'

" Towards the close of the day, after some severe runs—which, however, still left the comparative merits of the two dogs a subject of hot dispute—Bran and Phorp were brought front to front to prove their courage ; and they were no sooner untied than they sprang at each other and fought desperately. Phorp seemed about to overcome Bran, when his master, the Sutherland chief, unwilling that either of them should be killed, called out—' Let each of us take away his dog.' Fingal objected to this, whereupon the Sutherland chief said with a taunt that it was now evident that the Fingalians did not possess a dog that could match with Phorp.

"Angered and mortified, Fingal immediately extended his 'venomous paw,' as it is called (for the tradition represents him as possessing supernatural power), and with one hand he seized Phorp by the neck, and with the other—which was a charmed and destructive one—he tore out the brave animal's heart. This adventure occurred at a place near the March, between the parishes of Clyne and Wildonan, still called 'Leck na Con' (the stone of the dogs), there having been placed a large stone on the spot where they fought. The ground over which Fingal and the Sutherland chief hunted that day is called 'Dirri-leck-Con.' Bran suffered so severely in the fight that he died in Glen Loth before leaving the forest, and was buried there; a huge cairn was heaped over him, which still remains, and is known by the name of 'Cairn Bran.'"

Our next authority is Bewick (1792). Having described the Irish Wolfhound, he then goes on to say:—"Next to this in size and strength is the Scottish Highland Greyhound or Wolfdog, which was formerly used by the chieftains of that country in their grand hunting parties. One of them, which we saw some years ago, was a large, powerful, fierce-looking dog; its ears were pendulous, and its eyes half hid in the hair; its body was strong and muscular, and covered with harsh, wiry, reddish hair, mixed with white."

The "Encyclopædia Britannica" (1797) says:—"The variety called the Highland Gre-hound, and now become very scarce, is of great size, strong, deep-chested, and covered with long rough hair. This kind was much esteemed in former days, and used in great numbers by the powerful chieftains in their magnificent hunting matches. It had as sagacious nostrils as the Bloodhound, and was as fierce."

There is no allusion to the Deerhound in the "Sportsman's Cabinet," published in 1803; and, curiously enough, but little information regarding him from the beginning of this century up to about 1838, when McNeill wrote regarding him and the Irish Wolfhound in Scrope's book. That the breed *was* kept up in some families will be presently shown— in one case it was claimed that it had been in the owner's family for at least one hundred years. However, be that as it may, we have few, if any, reliable accounts of this dog until McNeill wrote. That gentleman, writing in 1838, says:—"It is not a little remarkable that the species of dog which has been longest in use in this country for the purposes of the chase should be that which is least known to the present generation of naturalists and sportsmen."

Mr. McNeill takes exception to the crosses which had been resorted to by "Glengarry" and others for the purpose of giving increased vigour and size to a breed then rapidly degenerating; but there seems every reason to suppose that had it not been for these judicious crosses the breed would have been almost extinct: at any rate, it would still further have deteriorated. It is very evident, from the following description of Captain McNeill's Buskar, that the Deerhound of forty years ago was a very inferior animal in size and power to the Deerhound of the present day, though possibly he equalled him in courage and speed. Buskar was a sandy-coloured dog, with dark ears, which were nearly erect when excited. He stood 28 inches in height, girthed 32 inches round the chest, and weighed 85 lbs. The hair was hard, not very rough, wiry only on head and legs. He was pupped in 1832, and was looked upon as a remarkably staunch and useful dog. McNeill considered that the purest dogs of his time were sandy or fawn in colour, and hard coated, but he also tells us that "there are dogs in the Lochabar district which are dark in colour and have a softer coat."

From "Chambers's Information for the People," published in 1842, the following extract is taken:—"The Scottish Highland Greyhound will either hunt in packs or singly. He is an animal of great size and strength, and at the same time very swift of foot. In size he equals, if not excels, the Irish Greyhound. His head is long and the nose sharp; his ears short and somewhat pendulous at the tips; his eyes are brilliant and very penetrating, and half-concealed by the long crisp hair which covers his face and whole body. He is remarkable for the depth of his chest, and tapers gradually towards the loins, which are of great strength and very muscular; his back is slightly arched; his hind quarters are powerfully formed, and his limbs strong and straight. The possession of these combined qualities particularly fit him for long endurance in the chase. His usual colour is reddish sand-colour mixed with white; his tail is long and shaggy, which he carries high like the Staghound, although not quite so erect. He is a noble dog, and was used by the Scottish Highland chieftains in their great hunting parties, and is supposed to have descended in regular succession from the dogs of Ossian."

St. John, in his "Wild Sports of the Highlands," published in 1846, says:—"The breed of Deerhounds, which had nearly become extinct, or at any rate was very rare a few years ago, has now become comparatively plentiful in all the Highland districts, owing to the increased extent of the preserved forests and the trouble taken by the different proprietors and renters of mountain shootings, who have collected and bred this noble race of dogs, regardless of expense and difficulties. The prices given for a well-bred and tried dog of this kind are so large that it repays the cost and trouble of rearing him. Fifty guineas is not an unusual price for a first-rate dog, while from twenty to thirty are frequently given for a tolerable one."

"Started this morning at daybreak with Donald and Malcolm Mohr, as he is called (*Anglicé* Malcolm the Great, or Big Malcolm), who had brought his two Deerhounds Bran and Oscar, to show me how they could kill a stag. The dogs were perfect: Bran an immense but beautifully-made dog of a light colour, with black eyes and muzzle, his ears of a dark brown, soft and silky as a lady's hand, the rest of his coat being wiry and harsh, though not exactly rough and shaggy, like his comrade Oscar, who was long-haired and of a darker brindle colour, with sharp long muzzle, but the same soft ears as Bran, which, by-the-bye, is a distinctive mark of high breeding in these days."

The "Museum of Animated Nature," published in 1848—50, has the following:—"In Scotland and Ireland there existed in very ancient times a noble breed of Greyhound, used for the chase of the wolf and the deer, which appears to us to be the pure source of our present breed; it is quite as probable that the Mâtin is a modification of the ancient Greyhound of Europe, represented by the Irish Greyhound or Wolfdog, as that it is the source of that fine breed. Few, we believe, of the old Irish Greyhound exist. In Scotland the old Deerhound may still be met with, and though it exceeds the common Greyhound in size and strength, it is said to be below its ancient standard. With the extirpation of the wolf, the necessity of keeping up the breed to the highest perfection ceased. The hair is wiry, the chest remarkable for volume, and the limbs long and muscular."

Youatt furnishes us with this description of the Deerhound :—"The Highland Greyhound, or Deerhound, is the larger, stronger, and fiercer dog, and may readily be distinguished from the Lowland Scotch Greyhound by its pendulous and generally darker ears, and by the length of hair which almost covers his face. Many accounts have been given of the perfection of its scent, and it is said to have followed a wounded deer during two successive days. He is usually two inches taller than the Scotch Greyhound. The head is carried particularly high, and gives to the animal a noble appearance. The limbs are exceedingly muscular; his back beautifully arched. The tail is long and curved, but assumes the form of almost a straight line when he is much excited. The only fault these dogs have is their occasional ill-temper or ferocity; but this does not extend to the owner and his family."

Richardson, writing about 1848, gives the following regarding the Deerhound :—"The Highland Deerhound presents the general aspect of a Highland Greyhound, especially in all the points on which speed and power depend; but he is built more coarsely and altogether on a larger and more robust scale. The shoulder is also more elevated, the neck thicker, head and muzzle coarser, and the bone more massive. The Deerhound stands from twenty-eight to thirty inches in height at the shoulders; his coat is rough and the hair strong; colour usually iron-grey, sandy, yellow, or white; all colours should have the muzzle and tips of the ears black; a tuft or pencil of dark hair on the tip of the ear is a proof of high blood. This is a very powerful dog, equally staunch and faithful; and when the Scottish mountains swarmed with stags and roes, it was held in high estimation, as being capable of following the deer over surfaces too rough and fatiguing for the ordinary hounds of the low country. The general aspect of the Highland hound is commanding and fierce. His head is long, and muzzle rather sharp; his ears pendulous, but not long; his eyes large, keen, and penetrating, half concealed among the long, stiff, and bristly hair with which his face is covered; his body is very strong and muscular, deep-chested, tapering towards the loins, and his back slightly arched. His hind quarters are furnished with large prominent muscles, and his legs are long, strong-boned, and straight—a combination of qualities which gives him that speed and long endurance for which he is so eminently distinguished. This is the dog formerly used by the Highland chieftains of Scotland in their grand hunting parties, and is in all probability the same noble dog used in the time of Ossian."

The last author treating of the Deerhound that will be alluded to is "Idstone," who brought out his useful book on "The Dog," in the year 1872; but as a considerable portion of the information in the article on the Deerhound therein contained was furnished by the present writer, he will embody it in this treatise as he proceeds. At the same time a few extracts which he cannot lay claim to will not be out of place.

"Until within the last few years the breed was very scarce, for they were kept by the few men who owned the Scotch forests or wide wild tracts of deer-park in the less populated parts of England.

"The fault of the present day with Deerhounds is certainly the short body, the thick, and, as the ignorant consider, the necessarily strong jaw, and the open, loose, flat foot. In proportion to the weight, the foot 'goes,' or deteriorates, and the strain upon a Deerhound's foot at speed amongst stones and boulders, 'in view,' and roused to desperation, is greater than that imposed upon any other domesticated animal. No dog but the 'rough-footed Scot' could stand it.

"The Deerhound is one of the oldest breeds we have. I should be inclined to think that it is an *imported* breed. He is probably identical with the 'Strong Irish Grey-hound' mentioned as employed in the Earl of Mar's chase of the red deer, in 1618, by Taylor, in his 'Pennilesse Pilgrimage.'

The oldest strain known is, without doubt, that of the late Mr. Menzies, of Chesthill, on Loch Tay. It is claimed, with every just right, no doubt, that this strain has been in the hands of Mr. Menzies' ancestors for something like eighty to ninety years. Whether it still exists in its integrity the writer is unable to say decidedly; but he is under the impression that as a distinct strain it has disappeared, though there are several dogs in existence that inherit the blood, and that not very distantly. It was asserted that during the time the breed had been in the Menzies family it had only thrice been recruited from outside! Mr. Potter, M.P. for Rochdale, then residing at Pitnacree, Perthshire, had, in 1860, a dog, called Oscar, from Mr. Menzies, and subsequently a bitch, called Lufra, from him. From these many puppies were bred, and given away by him with a liberal hand. A bitch was given to the late Dr. Cox, of Manchester, and from her and Dr. Cox's Ross (by Duke of Devonshire's Roswell, out of Sir R. Peel's Brenda) was bred Buz, the property of Mr. R. Hood Wright, of Birkby Hall, Cark, Carnforth. From this bitch Mr. Wright bred, by a dog (Oscar) of the Duke of Sutherland's breed, his celebrated prize-taker Bevis. It may be here mentioned that Oscar was sold to Prince Albert Solms, of Braunfels, and went to Germany some years ago. The brother to Mr. Cox's Lufra was presented to Menotti Garibaldi, for hunting the mouflon in Sardinia. Oscar, Mr Potter's original Chesthill dog, was given to the late Lord Breadalbane; and descendants of Oscar and Lufra were presented by Mr. Potter to Mr. Cunliffe Brooks, M.P., who, it is believed, has the breed now—indeed, the finest dog at Balmoral lately was one of Mr. C. Brooks's breeding. Mr. Hickman, of Westfield, Selly Hill, near Birmingham, exhibited two brindle dogs at the last Birmingham Show, got by his celebrated Morni out of Garry, by Chesthill Ossian—Lufra. Garry is the property of Mr. Spencer Lucy, of Charlcote. Next to the Chesthill strain, the earliest that the writer knows of is that of Mr. Morrison, of Scalascraig, Glenelg. Mr. John Cameron, of Moy, a farmer residing near Fortwilliam, formerly in service with "Glengarry" as keeper, can remember this breed as far back as 1830. From Bran, a celebrated dog belonging to Mr. Morrison (by him given to McNiel of Colonsay, and afterwards presented by McNiel to Prince Albert), was descended Torrom, the grandsire of Gillespie's celebrated Torrom. The strain of McNiel of Colonsay was known about 1832, and from his strain many of our modern dogs claim descent. The late Mr. Bateson, of Cambusmere in Sutherlandshire, deceased early in 1879, became possessed of a brace of this breed about 1845, named Torrish and Morven. These dogs were sketched by Landseer, the original being now in the hands of Mr. Bateson's family; and he considered them at the time the finest Deerhounds he had ever seen. They were two magnificent dogs, both very rough and of great height and power : Morven reddish in colour, Torrish, darker greyish-brown ; Torrish the thickest and biggest in bone, Morven the highest. It is believed this dog left no progeny, though there is an old dog, belonging to the Marquis of Bristol, at Ickworth Park, who is descended in a straight line from his brother Torrish. This dog, Giaour, was bred by Mr. John Bateson, brother to the late Mr. Bateson of Cambusmere, and to him the writer is indebted for all the information regarding these dogs. The breed was entirely in his and his brother's hands from 1845 to the present time, so there can be no doubt regarding its authentic character. The McNiel strain was also owned by Mr. Meredith of Torrish, Sutherlandshire. From a bitch bred by Mr. McNiel, and owned by Mr. Meredith, the Duke of Sutherland's Loyal was bred. Loyal was the dam of the dog Oscar, purchased by Prince Solms, Mr. Cameron's (of Lochiel) Pirate being the sire. As far as can be ascertained, the McNiel dogs in their earliest form were a smaller dog than the present animal, and hardly so rough in the coat, not much exceeding in size the dog, now nearly extinct, that was known as the Scotch Greyhound.

Sir John McNiel was kind enough to furnish the writer, in 1868, with the following information about his breed in later times :—

"The largest and finest dog I ever bred or ever saw was my Oscar. His speed was such that in a straight run he was never beaten by any dog, rough or smooth ; and in his best running condition he weighed ninety-four pounds."

From this it will be seen that the McNiel strain had gained both in size and weight since the time Buskar was looked upon as such a wonder.

Another celebrated strain was owned by a Scottish nobleman up to within the last twenty-six years, since which period he has given them up ; but some of the blood has passed into other hands, and has been infused in and incorporated with our present strains. The following information furnished by him will be read with much interest :—

"I have never had in my possession a dog above 31 inches. Black Bran, so called to distinguish him from my famous Bran, stood 31 inches in height, and at eighteen months old measured 33½ inches round the chest. He was a first-rate dog. I have seen a dog 34 inches in height, but he was an ill-shaped and utterly useless animal. Sir St. George Gore's Gruim was, I believe, about 32 or 33 inches in height, well-shaped, and a very excellent dog. Gruim was about the year 1843-44, Black Bran about 1850-51, at their best. Bran (the famous) was 29 inches high, and measured 31½ inches round the chest. In shape he was long and low, and so evenly made that he looked much smaller than he really was. He was dark brown at the top of his head—something of the colour of a yell-hind ; ears coal black ; muzzle black, with a little patch in front of the under-jaw—something like the lips of a roe ; back, sides, quarters, and outside of legs yellowish-fawn-—deepening in winter time, when his coat was longer, into a sort of yellowish rusty-grey ; tail just tipped with white ; head quite smooth to behind the ears ; ears quite smooth and velvety ; coat over body and sides not very long, very harsh and wiry ; legs and feet quite smooth ; coat, in winter, about three inches long. Bran was at his best about 1844-45. He was entered to his first stag at nine months old (too early), and killed his last stag at nine years old. His greatest feat was the killing of two unwounded stags single-handed in about three-quarters of an hour. The first bore 10 points ; the second 11. The pure breed was at one time confined to a very few different kennels. I think my own, and those

DEERHOUND.

of Mr. McNiel, of Colonsay, the late Mr. Stewart Menzies, of Chesthill, and one or two others, were the only gentlemen's kennels in which it was preserved. There were also three or four large farmers in various parts of the country who knew the value of the true breed, and took great pains to preserve the pure strain ; but since the great increase of deer forests, in most of which the use of Deerhounds is strictly prohibited, the breeding of these dogs has been very much discontinued, and it is now exceedingly difficult to find one worth anything. Colonel Inge and Lord H. Bentinck have both got my blood. I do not like the Glengarry blood. It was spoilt many years ago by old Glengarry crossing his dogs with the Bloodhound."

The Marquis of Breadalbane, many years ago, owned a famous strain of Deerhounds. They were kept at the Black Mount Forest Lodge. As many as fifty or sixty were kept. A dog called King of the Forest was of extraordinary size. He was an ancestor of a well-known modern prize-taker, also of great size, called Torrom, bred and first exhibited by Mr. Cameron of Lochiel.

The late Sir St. George Gore owned some very fine Deerhounds ; one of his is stated to have stood 32 inches. A young dog shown by him at Birmingham, about thirteen years ago, stood nearly 31 inches, and weighed 105 lbs.; a remarkably fine, well-shaped dog, of a cream colour, but nearly smooth-coated. A bitch, Corrie, brindled, was also large, but poor in coat.

The strain of the late Lord H. Bentinck was very similar to Sir St. G. Gore's—indeed, they bred together for years, and the consequence was that Lord Henry's strain was sadly devoid of coat. A bitch he owned, called Ferret, of McNiel of Colonsay's breed, was smooth, and from her, in all probability, the want of coat was introduced ; indeed, in many of the older strains the coat would appear to have been decidedly indifferent, to say the least of it. Lord Henry's Fingal, considered by him to be one of his very best, was a large red dog, almost smooth. From a bitch of this breed, called Carrac, at one time owned by the writer, many of our best modern dogs are descended. At Lord Henry's death his dogs were sold at Edinburgh in 1871, realising by no means large prices.

Some extremely fine Deerhounds were owned many years ago by the late Duke of Leeds.

Mr. Campbell of Monzie, Perthshire, had a very pure breed of Deerhounds about fifteen or twenty years ago. "Lochiel," speaking of them, says :—"I doubt if any Deerhounds except Mr. Campbell's of Monzie are quite pure. There were very few of them left at his death. His was the best and purest blood in the North." From his dog Grumach Mr. Cameron's Pirate and Torrom were bred.

Lieutenant-Colonel Inge of Thorpe for many years bred Deerhounds of remarkably good descent ; but he ceased to do so about 1862, when he sent sixteen to be sold at Aldridge's. They fetched prices ranging from 15 to 60 guineas. His celebrated old dog Valiant was bought in at a large figure. They were all well-made dogs and well covered with rough hair, but were not remarkable for size. Colonel Inge had the honour of winning the first prize with Valiant at the first dog show ever held at Birmingham in 1861. He was a very rough brindle dog of lengthy make. Valiant's pedigree was given as by Lord Saltoun's famous Bran out of Seaforth's Vengeance, and he was presented to Colonel Inge when a puppy.

The late Mr. John Cole, for many years head keeper to Her Majesty the Queen at Windsor Park, owned several splendid Deerhounds, bred from Prince Albert's Hector of Monzie's breed, and a bitch of a strain he had brought from Chillingham. At his death the writer purchased three, amongst them the well-known and superb dog Keildar and his sister Hag, a bitch of great size and very good shape, but wanting in coat.

Now to touch on breeders of the present day.

The Duke of Sutherland owns good-looking and useful dogs, but they are small, and a doubt is expressed in some quarters as to their *true* breeding. Regarding some of those *formerly* in his possession there, however, can be no doubt.

Mr. Spencer Lucy of Charlcote has some of the strain of Menzies of Chesthill, as before-mentioned, and has been crossing with one or two well-known prize-takers—it is believed with satisfactory results.

Mr. Gillespie of Tulloch, Kingussie, should be mentioned here, being the breeder and owner of the far-famed Torrom. Though Mr. Gillespie was hardly to be considered a breeder of Deerhounds, yet this dog was such a notoriously good one that, in justice to the subject, notice of his breeder cannot be omitted.

Mr. Donald Cameron of Lochiel is well known to Deerhound lovers as the breeder of Pirate and the giant Torrom. These dogs were from a bitch, Loy, by Mr. Gillespie's Torrom, by Campbell of Monzie's Grumach.

Mr. H. Chaworth Musters is known widely as the owner of the above-mentioned Torrom, which was purchased from "Lochiel" by a Mr. Bowles when exhibited at the Birmingham show in 1869, he then being three years old. He was afterwards purchased by Mr. Musters, and has been extensively bred from, with varied success.

Mr. R. Hood Wright has also bred some very fair Deerhounds. He is mentioned before as having the strain of Menzies of Chesthill in his kennels.

The late Sydney Dobell owned a very capital breed of Deerhound, descended from a bitch presented to him by Flora Macdonald of Skye. These dogs have had much to do with some of the best dogs now extant. They were said to be of pure Glengarry breed.

The last, and perhaps the most successful, breeder to whom allusion will be made is Mr. Thomas Morse. The dogs bred by this gentleman have proved themselves most successful candidates for public favour, and have gone to the top of the tree so far as prize-taking is concerned, and no doubt, where opportunity has offered, have proved themselves as good and true as they unquestionably are good-looking. Amongst them, Mr. Hemming's Linda, Mr. Chinnery's Duke, and Mr. Hay's Rufus, may be mentioned. Mr. Morse decidedly owes much, if not all, of his success to his judicious use of that magnificent dog Keildar, and the produce have in many instances thrown to him in a marked manner, even so far as two generations off.

Before concluding this notice of breeders, the Hon. Mrs. Deane Morgan, living in Co. Wexford, Ireland, should be mentioned, who now has dogs descended from pure strains brought from Scotland many years ago. It is believed these are fine animals, of which their owner is remarkably proud. One was given by her to Mr. George Dennis, Her Majesty's Consul in Sicily, and is reported by him to be an extraordinarily fine and noble animal. Mr. Dennis has lately taken a very well-descended young bitch out to Sicily to mate with him.

Mr. George Cupples has also bred many good dogs, amongst them Spey, now the property of Mr. Morse—selected to illustrate this article. There are several other breeders of years gone by whom the writer had perhaps better mention by name, and though he personally knows but little of their strains, they were reckoned to be remarkably good ones—namely, Lord Seaforth, McDonald of Keppoch, McKenzie of Kintail, and General Ross of Glenmoidart.

It is now proposed to allude to a few of the largest "noted" dogs—before proceeding to describe generally the "cracks" of the breed—that have arisen during the last thirty-five years.

Sir St. George Gore's Gruim has already been noticed. He was said to stand 32 to 33 inches (?), and was a very well-shaped and excellent dog. He was at his prime about 1843-44.

Black Bran, a 31-inch dog, in reality a black brindle, was a remarkably good dog about 1850-51.

The Marquis of Breadalbane's King of the Forest was a dog of extraordinary size, being, it is supposed, 33 inches high. He was held to be a good dog.

An unusually fine dog, called Alder, was shown many times about 1863-67—the property of Mr. Beasley, bred, it was asserted, by Sir John McNiel of Colonsay—that stood about 31½ inches, and probably weighed 110 lbs. This was a very well-shaped dog, not too bulky, of a dark brindle colour; coat very hard. Unfortunately, this dog never got any descendants worthy of himself. He was a grand animal.

In later years we have Torrom, first shown at Birmingham by his breeder, Mr. Donald Cameron of Lochiel, in 1869, he then being three years old. He afterwards passed into the possession of Mr. H. Chaworth Musters, and won numerous prizes, being known as Champion Old Torrom. This dog, as far as could be ascertained, threw back to some ancestor of gigantic size—probably Lord Breadalbane's King of the Forest. He was an extraordinarily heavy dog for a Deerhound, and usually considered lumbersome, and found too much so for work by his owner, who got rid of him for this reason. His head was very massive, and his coat very full and soft; legs by no means straight—a weakness which many of his descendants have inherited. He was a medium brownish colour, faintly brindle, very long in make; ears very coarse, and tail of extreme length. He stood 31 inches, girthed 35, and weighed, *fat*, about 110 lbs.

His two sons — Monzie, out of Brenda, bred by and the property of Mr. Musters, and Young Torrom, out of Braie, bred by Mr. Hancock—are both dogs of great size, standing 31 inches and weighing about 105 lbs.; the former considerably the better dog of the two. The latter dog was exported to America some three years ago.

Of a different strain—going direct back to McNiel's dogs—we have Hector, the property of Mr. Dadley, head-keeper to the Marquis of Bristol—a splendid dog, of darkish brindle colour, good rough coat, and well-shaped, by Giaour, out of Hylda; height, 31 inches; girth, 35; weight, 105 lbs. A good dog with deer, and thoroughly well-bred— probably the best-bred dog now extant.

His two sons—Oscar, the property of Mr. Phillips, Croxton House, Boxford, a very fine symmetrical dog, of great length, rather pale-fawn brindle, out of Lufra, a bitch of small size and somewhat uncertain pedigree, standing 31 inches and weighing about 105 lbs.; and Sir Bors, the property of Lieutenant-Colonel Leyland, a dog of similar colour, out of Lufra also (a prior litter), a very grand dog in every way. He stands 31 inches, girths 35, and weighs 105 lbs.

To go on to a general notice of the cracks. First to be noticed is Mr. Gillespie's celebrated dog Torrom, which is here described in Mr. Gillespie's own words :—"He did not stand very high, but was remarkably well formed for strength and speed; his weight I do not know; colour steel-grey (what we call blue); coat long and silky, with an undergrowth of close downy hair of a darker shade; ears small, and darker in colour than body, with silver-grey dots and tipped with silver-grey silky hair; he also had a great deal of the same silver-grey silky hair on his face; tail long and straight, with half turned to one side when erect; legs very strong, but clean and beautifully formed; feet small, round, and cat-like; chest very deep and round; neck long, arched, and strong; head small, but with wonderful power of jaw (I have seen him break the shoulder of very many red deer stags with a single twist); back very strong and arched; loins of wonderful strength. Torrom was by Faust, a dog (I believe *the last*) that belonged to Mrs. McDonnell, wife of the late Glengarry, and was one of the finest-looking dogs I have seen; his dam was Garry, a bitch given to me by Gordon Cumming when he last started for Africa. On Cumming's return I gave him back the bitch, which I believe he afterwards sold to Sir St. George Gore. Torrom when little more than a year old proved himself the best dog at deer I ever saw or expect to see.

All dogs of any note at the present time can trace their descent back to this exceedingly grand specimen of the race. Mr. Campbell of Monzie's Greumah was a particularly nice dog, got by a fine dog belonging to General Ross of Glenmoidart, of the Keppoch strain, out of a Monzie bitch. He was the sire of Pirate and Torrom, bred by Mr. Cameron of Lochiel. Mr. Cameron writes thus regarding this fine dog:—"He was a magnificent dog, not so massive as his son (Champion Torrom), but more like a Deerhound. He was a strong-framed dog, with plenty of hair, of a blue-brindle colour. He was very like the dog you refer to as belonging to Mr. Gillespie."

Keildar, bred by the late Mr. Cole, head-keeper of Windsor Park, was one of the most elegant and aristocratic-looking Deerhounds ever seen. He was a dog of great length, and yet possessed great speed and power. He was in constant use in Windsor Park for stalking deer, and was very adept at his work. He showed high breeding and symmetry to a remarkable extent. His height was a full 30 inches, girth $33\frac{1}{2}$, and weight 95 lbs.; colour bluish-fawn, slightly brindled, the muzzle and ears being blue; coat rather soft in character and tolerably full. He was by a handsome dog (Oscar), belonging to Mr. Bridge, of the breed of McKenzie of Applecross. His descendants have made their mark by their size, high breeding, and good looks. Amongst them are the well-known Linda, which resembles her sire in an extraordinary degree, his son Rufus, and amongst his grandsons Hector and Duke, Mr. Phillips' Oscar and Lieut.-Colonel Leyland's Sir Bors being his great-grandsons. Mr. Field's Bran, own brother, same litter as Keildar, was only slightly his inferior, and in most ways a very similar dog. Amongst his descendants Morni is perhaps the most remarkable. Mr. Cyril Dobell—brother to Sydney—owned a capital dog of good size in Bevis, the sire of Linda's dam and other good dogs. He was a sandy dog of good coat, stood 30 inches, and weighed probably near 100 lbs., being rather short in make. Major Robertson's Oscar, a nice brindle dog of good coat, long made, bred by General Ross of Glenmoidart, stood about 29 inches, and was a well-made, handsome dog. From him were bred some good dogs out of Sydney Dobell's Maida, and he was the sire of Morni out of a bitch by Field's Bran, out of Carrac.

Mr. Hickman's Morni was a nice dog, of a greyish-brindle colour, coat somewhat soft. He stood 30 inches, girthed 34, and weighed about 98 lbs. Showed quality and breeding.

Pirate, the property of Cameron of Lochiel, and own brother to the celebrated Champion Old Torrom (Mr. Musters'), was a smaller, more compact, and far better-made dog than his gigantic brother. Very dark in colour—blue-brindle—he had a harder and more dense coat than Torrom, and was in every respect his superior. He stood about 29 inches, and was considered "perfect" at work by his owner. He got some very nice stock, but none, it is believed, proved large, though capital dogs for work.

Duke, at one time the property of Mr. Chinnery, winner of several first prizes, was a dark, grizzled, hard-coated dog—perhaps somewhat deficient in hair on head and legs—and a handsome, well-built dog, though somewhat light of bone. He stood 30 inches, and was a fairly lengthy dog.

Spey, the bitch selected for illustration, was bred by Mr. Cupples, and has been owned for many years by Mr. Morse, who has bred many very superior dogs from her. She is about 27 inches in height and of a lengthy frame. Coat very hard and good. Colour is shown in illustration. Duke was her son, and resembled her strongly in coat and colour. She is a well-descended bitch, of thoroughly good appearance.

Mr. Musters' Young Torrom, winner of an extraordinary number of prizes, is a much superior dog to his sire, Old Champion Torrom, but is considerably his inferior in size. He is a dark slate colour, with a lighter head, of not very taking expression, extremely long and strong in make ; coat soft and dense. A striking feature in this strain is their very long sweeping tail. His height is about 29½ inches.

Mr. Wright's Bevis, a darkish red-brown brindle dog of about 29 inches, is a thoroughly well-bred dog ; perhaps, excepting Hector, the best bred Deerhound out. His coat is very long and shaggy, and extends itself to his ears, very much to the detriment of his appearance. He is a compact, well-shaped dog.

Dr. Haddon has shown a handsome bitch, called Lufra, with a remarkably handsome head and good coat—which former feature she has transmitted to her son, by Young Torrom (Mr. Musters'), Roy by name. The bitch has no ascertained pedigree.

There are many other good and fine dogs scattered through the country which could be mentioned ; but as this is not a stud book, it is considered unnecessary to do so.

The Deerhound will now be closely described. As regards size many arguments are put forward. In former days when the red deer was coursed (as hares are) without having previously been wounded, the larger and more powerful the dog was, provided that the Greyhound's speed and activity were preserved, the more was he valued ; but in these degenerate days, when deer are usually brought to book without the aid of dogs or often even in their presence, an *animal* that can find and bay a wounded stag is considered to be all that is required. In some few cases the Deerhound proper is used, but this is being fast allowed to fall into disuse in the majority of cases. To run into and hold a full-grown stag, a large and strong dog is certainly required, and it was found that a dog averaging 29 to 30 inches was the correct animal. His girth should be great and chest deep—without being too flat-sided ; for a 30-inch dog, 34 inches should be the average. The fore-arm, below elbow, should measure 8½ inches, and the dog weigh from 95 to 105 lbs. Should the dog stand as much as 31 inches, as is sometimes the case, these dimensions would be slightly exceeded. He should be of lengthy make. The average for bitches, which are very much less than the dogs, would be as follows :— Height, 26 inches ; girth, 29 inches ; weight, 65 to 70 lbs. In figure and conformation this dog should closely approximate to the smooth Greyhound, allowance being made for his superior stature and bulk. The head should be long and lean, rather wider behind the ears, yet not suddenly widening ; neck long, strong, and arched ; body long ; back slightly curved upwards, descending towards tail ; legs very strong and straight ; feet round, well and firmly set ; quarters well-developed, and equal to propelling the animal with extreme velocity ; ears small, semi-erect, dark in colour, and smooth, though several strains—really good ones — show a hairy ear ; tail long and free from curl, having a curve towards the tip only. The general appearance should be striking, elegant, and aristocratic to a marked extent, and nobility of carriage is a very strong feature in the breed. The coat should be coarse and hard, full and dense on head, body, legs, and tail, without being "exaggerated;" that on the head should be softer in character than that on the body; the hair over eyes and under jaws being of greater length, and rather more wiry than that on the rest of the head. The well-covered head gives much "character," and adds vastly to the general beauty of this magnificent dog. The length of the hair should be from three to four inches. Some breeders hold that no Deerhound is worthy of notice unless he has a good rough head, with plenty of beard and coat generally.; also, that the purity of a smooth skulled dog is to be doubted. Here, however, they are at fault, as several of the best known dogs have had nearly smooth heads.

In colour the Deerhound varies much—from *nearly* black, through dark brindle, blue, light brindle, grey, fawn, and sandy, and cream of all shades, to pure white. Black-and-tan dogs of the breed have also been known. As a matter of taste, the darker colours, as iron-grey and brindle, are to be preferred; but many first-class specimens have been and are of a lighter colour. On a dark heath a light-coloured dog shows plainer.

These dogs are usually remarkably fine and graceful jumpers, and possessed of great activity. In the matter of speed they often equal the smooth Greyhound, but owing to their great size are unequal to making such quick turns as their smaller congener. The scenting powers are developed in a remarkable way, and many wonderful tales are told of the tracking powers of these dogs. When unsighted, they often recover for their masters "cold" stags by their unerring powers in this line.

They are bad swimmers, but occasionally will take the water, and never shrink from it when in pursuit of their quarry.

The Deerhound is justly considered a difficult dog to rear, and to a certain degree delicate, though some authors put him forward as being the "hardiest of the hardy." They also are not a long-lived dog.

It was supposed that the gradual dying out of the practice of coursing the red deer would soon put an end to the breeding of the Deerhound; but such, happily, is not the case. This dog, in reality, has wonderfully increased the last twenty years, and is now, comparatively speaking, common. His beauty, gentleness, power, and courage, have so recommended him as a pet and companion, and his appearance is so ornamental and graceful, that he is highly esteemed by all the gentle in the land; and the fear that the breed would become extinct has long since vanished.

The late Sir St. George Gore, a breeder of experience, was of opinion that the Deerhounds of the present day are far finer than they were thirty and forty years ago; also that a dog could not then be found to run at 85 lbs., whereas now the standard is from 90 to 100 lbs.

Since Lord Henry Bentinck's demise in 1871 no *large* kennels of Deerhounds remain. Formerly there were from twenty to sixty kept in several kennels; at the same time, many magnificent specimens *are* scattered broadcast through the land, as many as six or seven, or even more, being in the same hands, and it is probable that instead of having decreased in numbers it has increased considerably; where *one* person owned a Deerhound or two formerly twenty do so now. Lord Breadalbane, the Duke of Athol, Lord H. Bentinck, "Glengarry," and others, kept large kennels of these superb dogs, but they have all passed away now.

This article will hardly be considered complete unless some allusion be made to the much-vexed question of cross-breeding.

"Idstone" says:—"Many crosses have been adopted, as I have already observed, and one of the Deerhound and Mastiff has been used by the proprietor of a deer-pack in my immediate neighbourhood, where there is a fine herd of red and fallow deer. Though I prefer the Deerhound, it must be granted that whilst the breed was not procurable such a measure as manufacturing a dog for the work was meritorious. The best I have noticed of this description were produced by the skill and patience of Mr. Norwood, of the South-Western Railway, at Waterloo. I have never seen these hounds in action, but I have been assured that nothing can be finer than their work. They had the race-horse points, the long neck, the clean head, the bright intellectual eye, the long sloping shoulder, the muscular arms, the straight legs, the close well-knit feet, the wide muscular arched back and loins, the deep back ribs, the large girth, the *esprit*, the life, the activity which when controlled and schooled is essential to every domesticated animal."

It is a well-known fact that the late "Glengarry," finding the breed of Deerhound deteriorating, resorted to several crosses—amongst them the Cuban Bloodhound and Pyrenean Wolfdog; from the latter especially he gained much. He was at the time condemned loudly for thus contaminating the breed; but, in the writer's opinion, he acted with great good judgment, for he resuscitated his strain very completely, and from his so-crossed dogs have all our modern Deerhounds descended, all symptoms of any such cross having long been obliterated. Mr. Gillespie, the owner and breeder of *the* notorious Torrom, says:—"With regard to your remark about the Glengarry dogs not being pure, I too have often heard it; but my *experience* is that there were few, if any, better strains." His Torrom was the son of a true Glengarry dog. Of this breed also was the world-wide-famed Maida, Sir Walter Scott's devoted and constant companion; but he was the offspring of the first cross between Pyrenean Wolfdog and Highland Deerhound, the former being sire, the latter dam. He was a magnificent animal, of great size, power, and endurance, partaking mostly of the appearance of the dam, gaining somewhat in power, bulk, and height from the sire. He was of an iron-grey colour (according to Irving), and of gigantic size. He died at eleven years of age. From this very Maida many of our best modern dogs claim descent!

A gentleman who has had much experience in breeding Deerhounds for the last thirty years and upwards, and who has bred many grand dogs, says:—"My brother informs me that McNiel *went all over the world* to get dogs to breed from—to Albania amongst other places—and that his breed represents a breed he himself founded, and that prior to that there was no real existing breed of Deerhounds in Scotland (! !). I think that their extreme delicacy and the difficulty of rearing them, also the way in which they feel the cold in bad weather in October, indicate their foreign origin."

It is thought that there must have been some misapprehension on this matter, as, putting aside the existence of Morison of Scalascraig's breed in 1830 (McNiel's dating a few years later), as well as that of Menzies of Chesthill, asserted to date from 1780 or thereabouts, Lord Colonsay, then Sir J. McNiel, communicated with the writer about 1865 in the following terms:—"There seems to be no doubt that the Deerhound of the Celtic Highlands is of precisely the same race as the Irish hound sometimes called Wolfhound; and all attempts to get size or speed by crossing have, it is believed, failed, or only succeeded in giving size by destroying the characteristics of the race. I imported Wolfhounds from Russia of fair speed and large size, but silky-haired, with a view to cross them with the Deerhound, but the result was by no means satisfactory. The late Lord Breadalbane crossed with the Bloodhound, and produced some good Retrievers for his deer-stalking; but they were no longer Deerhounds. The Macedonian Dog—a very powerful, smooth dog—was also imported by a member of my family without any better results; and it is my conviction that the race of Deerhounds can be improved only by careful selection and crossing different strains of pure blood."

The above remarks were shown to a friend of the writer who had given a full trial to crossing for size, &c. He says:—"I do not agree with Sir J. McNiel in all he says I think with you that he did not continue his experiments far enough. Then, again, speed was the element he aimed at chiefly, and it is not to be expected he would retain that when crossing with a slower dog."

The writer has not the smallest doubt—looking at the grand dogs we now possess—that the various crosses tried have in most instances profited very much the breed, which had evidently fallen into a degenerate state forty to fifty years ago. He knows by experience that all trace of a cross disappears as a rule in the second or third generation, and the dog has *in every way* the appearance and characteristics of a Deerhound proper. The cross from Russian Wolfhound, judiciously used, has certainly imparted to the Deerhound a degree of quality and certain blood-like look that the breed was fast losing, to say nothing of the gain in the matter of symmetry that almost invariably accrues.

It is a most noticeable and curious fact that the purer the breed is the more marked is the disparity between the sexes in the Deerhound. Thus, if two *pure* bred dogs be used, the difference between the sexes will vary from four to six inches in height; whereas, if the female parent be cross-bred and of large size, the difference between the males and females of the litter will only be two inches, and, oddly enough, even if the bitch so bred shall vastly exceed the truer bred one in size, the dog puppies from her—by an equally fine dog—will generally in no way exceed in size those from the smaller but truer bred bitch.

That size can more surely be obtained through the sire than through the dam is a fact worth remembering.

It is much to be regretted that the pedigrees of the prominent specimens of this breed have not been retained, but there is little doubt but that most of our existing cracks can claim them as their progenitors. In future there will be no trouble on this head, as the very admirable stud-books established about 1870 will obviate this.

Before concluding this article, the writer would strongly impress on all readers the extreme desirability of retaining, by judicious care and cultivation, this, of all dogs (save his undoubted progenitor the Irish Wolfhound), the most beautiful and picturesque, as well as the most majestic and ornamental—an animal to be loved and valued, and treated as a friend, as he richly deserves to be in all but rare cases.

The accompanying engraving, which so faithfully represents some Deerhounds on the watch, is the work of the great German artist, Specht. Though the dogs do not quite come up to modern ideas of show form in every minute particular, the artistic arrangement of the group is to the life, and thoroughly conveys in all essential respects the character of the dog, and what a Deerhound should be.

The dog selected for the coloured plate is Mr. Morse's Spey, who may be taken as one of the best specimens of the breed in existence, though not shown. She was nearly twelve years old in January, 1880, when she scaled 73 lbs., and measured as follows:—From tip of nose to stop, 4½ inches; length from stop to occipital bone, 5¾ inches; girth of skull behind the eyes, 15 inches; girth of neck, 15 inches; girth round shoulders, 30 inches; girth of loins, 20¾ inches;

SCOTCH DEERHOUNDS.

girth of thigh, 16½ inches; girth of forearm, 7 inches; height at shoulders, 26 inches; height at elbows, 14½ inches; height at loins, 26 inches; height at hock, 7½ inches; length of tail, 22 inches. The above must be considered exceptionally good measurements when the advanced age of the dog comes to be considered.

An extremely good bitch, too, which came before the public in 1879, is Heather, the property of the Rev. Grenville F. Hodson, of North Petherton, Bridgwater, which gentleman is one of our oldest Deerhound breeders, and a recognised judge of the variety. Mr. Graham has, we believe, not seen Heather, and has therefore omitted her from the list he gives above.

As in the case of the Irish Wolfhound, Mr. Graham in his article did not append a scale of points. We therefore give the following on our own responsibility.

SCALE OF POINTS FOR JUDGING DEERHOUNDS.

	Value.
Skull	10
Neck	5
Body	10
Legs and feet	10
Coat	10
General appearance	5
Total	50

CHAPTER XXXII.

THE GREYHOUND.

OF all the breeds of dog which were held in high estimation by our forefathers, the Greyhound is undoubtedly the most popular in the present day. Its utility as a provider of the means of sport may certainly not be as extensive as it was formerly; but the Greyhound still exists in its old capacity of the courser's indispensable companion; and has not, like the Bloodhound, found its vocation gone. It must not, however, be imagined that even in former days the Greyhound was to be found in very large numbers throughout the country, for stringent laws were passed which prohibited those beneath a certain station in life possessing this breed of dog. Such an edict was published in the reign of King Canute, and severe penalties were inflicted upon those who set them at defiance.

This is by no means the first mention of the Greyhound, early as the date is, for the existence of dogs which hunted by sight and not by scent is mentioned by Arrian, who is also known by the name of the younger Xenophon. What the precise class of dog was to which he refers cannot now be discussed; but the fact remains undisputed that dogs existed in the second century which hunted by sight, and this is one of the characteristics of the modern Greyhound. From the frequent reference, moreover, to this class of dog in the writings of all sporting authors from the most remote periods, it is evident that Greyhounds were always the popular dog with sportsmen; and it is further noticeable that they were employed in the capture of animals other than hares in those days. The wolf and the wild boar were both hunted with Greyhounds, who must presumably have been both larger and more powerful dogs than those of the present day, or they would have been unable to have coped with such powerful foes. As a proof of the value set upon Greyhounds, it is remarkable that prior to the signing of Magna Charta by King John we learn that the destruction of a Greyhound was looked upon as an act "equally criminal with the murder of a fellow man." We are further informed that Greyhounds were "frequently taken in payment as money by the kings for the renewal of grants, and in the satisfaction of fines and forfeitures." One fine paid to King John in 1203 consisted of 500 marks, ten horses, and ten leashes of Greyhounds; another, seven years later, was one swift running horse and six Greyhounds.

One of the most ancient, and at the same time most hackneyed descriptions of a Greyhound is that given by Juliana Berners in "The Book of St. Albans," to which work reference has been made in the first chapter of this book. The doggrel, however, may be of interest to many who have not seen it *in extenso*, and we therefore give it at length for their edification :—

"THE PROPERTIES OF A GOOD GREHOUNDE.

"A grehounde shold be heeded lyke a snake,
   And neckyd like a drake;
   Footed lyke a catte,
   Tayllyd lyke a ratte;

Syded lyke a teme,
And chynyd lyke a beme.
The fyrst yere he must lerne to fede;
The second yere to felde him lede;
The thyrde yere he is felowe lyke;
The fourth yere there is none syke;
The fyfth yere he is good enough;
The syxte yere he shall hold the plough;
The seventh yere he woll avaylle
Grete bytches for to assaylle;
The eygthe yere licke ladyll;
The nynthe yere cartsadyll,
And when he is comyn to that yere
Have him to the tannere;
For the best hounde that ever bytche had
At nynthe yere he is full badde."

From this it appears that the fair authoress had no faith in breeding from very old sires, an opinion which is generally shared in the present day by practical men.

All writers on the breed seem to be unanimous in denouncing thick, heavy-headed dogs. Arrian describes Greyhounds as bad who "are heavy-headed . . . with a blunt instead of a pointed termination" (to the muzzle). In the "Mayster of Game," by Edmund de Langley, which has been before alluded to, it is said that "The Greihound should have a long hede and some dele grete . . . a good large mouth, and good sessours, the one again the other, so that the nether jaws passe not them above." This certainly is an important remark in connection with the breed, and one which should not be lost sight of, as it would seem to imply that an under-hung dog—or, in plain words, one possessing too much Bull blood—was objected to in the days of the writer. It is only natural, however, to conjecture that the Bull, or rather Bandog cross had not had a fair trial at that period, for, as we have before endeavoured to show, there can be little doubt that the Greyhounds were, several centuries ago, of necessity a stouter dog than the modern hound, and therefore the introduction of a Bull cross was scarcely necessary.

Dr. John Caius thus alludes to the "Grehounde" in his book:—

"There is another kind of dogge which for his incredible swiftness is called Leporarius or Grehounde, because the principall service of them dependeth and consisteth in starting and hunting the hare, which dogges likewyse are indued with no less strength than lightness in maintenance of the game, in serving the chase, in taking the bucke, the harte, the dowe, the foxe, and other beastes ordained for the game of hunting. . . . For it is a spare and bare kinde of dogge (of fleshe but not of bone); some are of a greater sorte, and some of a lesser, some are smooth skynned, and some are curled; the bigger are therefore appoynted to hunt the bigger beasts, and the smaller serve to hunt the smaller accordingly."

Dr. Caius also alludes to another variety of dog, the description of which contains several points which are identical with the peculiarities of the Greyhound. The following is the manner in which it is alluded to by Dr. John Caius:—

"This kinde of dogge, which pursueth by the eye, prevayleth little, or never a whit, by any benefite of the nose that is by smelling, but excelleth in perspicuitie and sharpnesse of sight altogether, by the vertue whereof, being singular and notable, it hunteth the foxe and the hare. . . . . Our countrymen call this dogge Agaseum, a Gazehounde, because the beames of his sight are so steadfastly settled and onmoveably fastened. These dogges are much and usually occupied in the northern parts of England more than in the southern, and in fealdy landes rather than in bushy and woody places. Horsemen use them more than footmen, to the intent that they might provoke their horses to a swift galloppe (wherwith they are more delighted than with the pray itselfe), and that they myght accustome theyr horse to leape over hedges and ditches without stoppe or stumble, without harme or hazzard, without doubt or daunger, and so escape with safegard of lyfe. . . . But if it fortune so at any time that this dogge take a wrong way, the master making some usuall signe and familiar token, he returneth forthwith, and taketh the right and ready trace, beginning his chace a fresh, and with a clear voyce, and a swift foot, followeth the game with as much courage and nimblenesse as he did at the first."

From these quotations it would certainly appear that in the time of Dr. Caius the dogs used for hare-hunting and for stag or deer hunting were different animals, the more powerful breed being styled Grehoundes and the smaller Gazehounds. It is also highly probable that, as the occupation of the former disappeared, the two varieties became amalgamated once again, and formed the corner-stone of the existence of the modern Greyhound.

The accompanying engraving is of interest as representing the different varieties of Grey-hounds collected in one group. The similarity of outline in the Deerhound, the Greyhound, the Persian, and the Italian Greyhounds, is so plainly shown that their relationship must strike the most casual observer. The resemblance of the foreign dogs to our English ones must, in addition, attach increased interest to the remarks of Arrian, who is before alluded to as having described dogs who hunted by sight and not by scent ; and it is only reasonable to presume, from the similarity of the varieties in the present day, that the type of dog then in existence was similar to that contained in the cut.

Apropos of the Greyhound being used for coursing animals other than hares, we are informed, upon the authority of the "Sportsman's Cabinet," that in 1591 Queen Elizabeth, when not personally disposed to hunt, used to witness the coursing of deer by Greyhounds from her residence. On one occasion "she witnessed from a turret at Cowdrey Park sixteen bucks, all having fair law, pulled down by Greyhounds upon the lawn one day after dinner." The same authority informs us that "the Isle of Dogs, now converted to the great purpose of a commercial reservoir for the West India shipping, derived its name from being the receptacle for the Grey-hounds and Spaniels of Edward III."

Naturally enough, there have from time to time been many crosses introduced into the Greyhound before it could be brought to the pitch of perfection which it has reached in the present day. Amongst the most enterprising breeders of these or earlier times may be mentioned the name of Lord Orford, who is thus alluded to in the "Sportsman's Cabinet" :—

"There were times when he was known to have fifty brace of Greyhounds ; and as it was a fixed rule never to part with a single whelp till he had a fair and substantial trial of his speed, he had evident chances (beyond almost any other individual) of having, amongst so great a number, a collection of very superior dogs ; but so intent was he upon this peculiar object of attainment, that he went further in every possible direction to obtain perfection, and introduced every experimental cross, from the English Lurcher to the Italian Greyhound. He had strongly indulged an idea of a successful cross with the Bulldog, which he could never be divested of ; and after having persevered (in opposition to every opinion) most patiently for seven removes, he found himself in the possession of the best Greyhounds ever yet known, giving the small

Italian.   Persian.   English Greyhound.   Deerhound.
                                    Siberian Wolfhound.

THE GREYHOUND FAMILY.

ear, the rat tail, and the skin almost without hair, together with that innate courage which the high-bred Greyhound should possess, retaining which instinctively, he would rather die than relinquish the chase.

"One defect this cross is admitted to have which the poacher would rather know to be a truth than the fair sportsman would come willingly forward to demonstrate. To the former it is a fact pretty well known that no dog has the sense of smelling in a more exquisite degree than the Bulldog; and, as they run mute, they, under certain crosses, best answer the midnight purposes of the poacher in driving hares to the wire or net. Greyhounds bred from this cross have therefore some tendency to run by the nose, which, if not immediately checked by the master, they will continue for miles, and become very destructive to the game in the neighbourhood where they are kept, if not under confinement or restraint."

The best of Lord Orford's strain were purchased by Col. Thornton on the death of their breeder, and thus found their way from Norfolk to Yorkshire. Here they did not seem to be able to sustain the reputation they had gained in their own country, for except upon "the low, flat countries below the wolds" their success was inferior to the expectations formed concerning them. However, we are told that "it was unanimously agreed by all the sportsmen present, that they ran with a great deal of energetic exertion, and always at the hare; that though beaten they did not go in, or exhibit any symptoms of lurching or waiting to kill." These qualifications—pluck and endurance—were no doubt the result of the Bull cross alluded to above, which Lord Orford had introduced into his strain some generations before. With reference to the compliment paid above to the Bulldog's sense of smell, we confess ourselves to be at variance with the writer, for, though the last to deny the Bulldog the possession of any scent at all, or to class him with many less intelligent breeds of dog, we do not, after considerable experience of the variety, consider his powers of scent are by any means of the highest order. The chief objections that we personally should expect to find in the Bulldog cross are, first, a deficiency of speed in the animals for several generations; and, secondly, the existence of Bull blood even in this diluted form would, we imagine, be very likely to make the puppies both hot-tempered and headstrong, which are most naturally undesirable characteristics in a Greyhound. Our own personal experience of the Bulldog cross is very limited, for it is confined to that of a gentleman interested in coursing, who, about the beginning of 1877, availed himself of the services of our Bull-terriers, Tarquin and Sallust, for some of his Greyhound bitches. He has not, unfortunately, granted us permission to divulge his name, as he desires the experiment to remain a secret until the progeny appears in public, if any ever do appear. He writes us, however, that so far he is "more than satisfied with the result," and that he considers the acquisition of what he terms "a new heart" will materially benefit his strain in days to come. The whelps we saw were only the result of first crosses, and for the most part resembled the Greyhound far more than the Bull-terrier side of their family, though a peculiarity in one of them—a daughter of Sallust, who himself was *perfectly* level-mouthed—was that she was undershot to an extent which we have rarely seen equalled in any class of dog.

Though the work of a modern Greyhound is not of so arduous a description as that of its ancestors, its staying powers are often sorely tried. Two essential qualifications are therefore necessary in a good Greyhound—we allude to stoutness and speed. Even if a dog be much faster than his antagonist, he will probably be beaten in his course if he lacks courage and stamina; and it is far better, therefore, to trust the stout than the speedy dog, though it is highly

GREYHOUND.

desirable, rare though the acquisition of both virtues is, that speed and stamina should be combined. A very fast dog from the slips is not usually a great stayer; and though he may lead his rival and score a few points in the earlier portion of the course, it is more than likely that he will die away all to nothing if the hare is a good one, and his opponent knows his work. Stoutness and stamina, although not identical, resemble each other in this respect, that they both depend upon the amount of courage possessed by the Greyhound; and therefore one of the chief characteristics of a good Greyhound is a sufficiently deep and wide chest. In an animal where speed is so essential, too great a width of chest would be detrimental to his success in the field; but a narrow-chested, shoulder-tied Greyhound would have equally poor chances of winning courses in any company. As in the racehorse, so in the Greyhound, as much space is required for the due exercise of the heart and lungs as will not detract from the animal's speed. The neck, too, is an essential point to a good Greyhound, which is often ·injured by the introduction of Bull blood. The comparative length which is required to help the dog to pick up his hare stands a very good chance of being obliterated by this cross of blood; for though the neck of a Bulldog may be moderately long in comparison with that animal's size, its length is far less than that of a Greyhound, and its girth is quite out of all proportion to it.

Before alluding to the principal modern breeders and exhibitors of this class of dog, it is necessary to allude to the difference of opinion which exists on the subject of the shape of a Greyhound's feet. Dame Juliana Berners was most decided in her views, as she emphatically laid it down that the Greyhound was to be "footed lyke a catte." This formation, however, has several enemies amongst later breeders, many of whom prefer the long or hare-shaped foot. In fact, more than one authority on Greyhounds has expressed himself unable to decide upon this subject; and a coursing man of some position remarked to us, "I think I like the cat foot best, but I have owned good dogs with hare feet." For our own part we are certainly in favour of the cat foot, though we should be loth to discard a dog in competition, if he were good in other points, merely because he did not possess this shaped foot—provided always that the hare feet were not splayed out, and were in good condition.

As the following chapter will be devoted to coursing, it will be only necessary, before passing on to a description of the modern Greyhound, to mention the names of some of the principal exhibitors on the bench, who may or may not be in the habit of using their dogs in the field as well. It is a somewhat remarkable fact that Greyhound classes rarely fill well in the south of England, though at several of the northern shows—Darlington, for instance—they are one of the chief features of the exhibition. This may be accounted for by the fact that coursing men do not care to show their dogs as a rule, and that the best performers, on their withdrawal from training, are valuable for stud purposes, and so never get into the possession of exhibitors who are not coursing men. There are, however, some grandly-shaped Grey-hounds shown in various parts of the country, and the only regret is that their number is so limited.

By far the most successful show-dog from the years 1873 to 1880 has been Lauderdale, who is the property of Mr. Tom Sharples. As this dog is the subject of our coloured plate, due attention will be paid to him and his performances later on. Mr. Tom Swinburne's Marigold, too, is a bitch who has done her owner good service on the bench, and Mr. Fawdry's Ada is another which is near the top of the tree. Sister Mary, Dreaded Falcon, Mr. Waddington's Doctor, Mr. Bearpark's Game Cock, Mr. Sharples' Queen Bertha, and Mr. J. H. Salter's Amethyst and Fair Rosa, have each and all of them made a reputation.

Most of the principal exhibitors and Greyhounds having thus been alluded to, a description of the points of the Greyhound must be given, as in the cases of other breeds. We will proceed by describing—

The *Head*.—Should be wide between the ears and flat at the top, with powerful jaws. The latter should not, however, be thick or coarse, but should, as regards appearance, seem light in substance, their strength depending on the muscles at the sides of the head.

Eyes.—Dark and bright.

Ears.—Small and fine.

Neck.—Long and muscular, but not coarse, thick, or clumsy.

Shoulders.—Sloping, and very muscular; loosely set on, so as to allow free play of the fore-legs.

Chest.—Deep, and rather wide.

Back.—Square and "beam-like," and rather long.

Loins.—Very powerful, with considerable muscular development.

Fore-legs.—Set well under the dog, and possessing plenty of bone.

Feet.—Round, well split up, and with strong soles.

Hind-legs.—Well bent at the hocks, and very muscular.

Stern.—Fine, long, and curved.

Colour.—Almost any colour is admissible in a Greyhound, but the most usual are black, red, white, brindle, fallow, fawn, blue, and the various mixtures of each.

The subject of our coloured plate is Mr. Tom Sharples' Lauderdale, whose measurements are as follows:—Nose, to the joining on of neck, 11½ inches; girth of skull, 15 inches; girth of snout 8 inches; length of neck, from joint to shoulders, 11⅛ inches; girth round neck, 15½ inches; length of back, 25½ inches; girth of foreleg, 6½ inches; girth of thigh, 10½ inches; girth of chest, 30½ inches; girth of loins, 21 inches; length of tail, 21½ inches; weight 67 lbs. Lauderdale was whelped 1869, and was bred by Mr. W. Lowry, by Ewesdale, out of Spendthrift; Ewesdale, by Larriston, out of Meg; Spendthrift, by Canaradzo, out of Speculation. Canaradzo, who won the Waterloo Cup in 1860, was by Beacon, out of Scotland Yet. Lauderdale died March 29, 1880, his death being a severe loss to Greyhound breeders throughout the country.

The following is the

SCALE OF POINTS FOR JUDGING GREYHOUNDS.

	Value.
Head—skull	5
Jaws and eyes and ears	5
Neck	5
Chest—depth and width	5
Body	10
Legs and feet	10
General appearance	10
	50

CHAPTER XXXIII.

COURSING.

GREYHOUNDS are a variety of dog which require particular care and attention to be bestowed upon them, if their owners desire them to appear to advantage either on the bench or in the field. The dogs themselves are so highly bred that their constitutions do not withstand disease or cold as those of other breeds, and the artificial life a Greyhound leads when he is undergoing a preparation for a coursing meeting naturally enough increases his innate weakness in this respect. It would be impossible in the present work to attempt to enter deeply into the subject of training for and running Greyhounds in stakes; but, nevertheless, a few observations on general management may not be out of place.

To begin with, it is essential that the kennels for Greyhounds should be larger and more airy than those of other dogs, as the breed is not one which at any time stands close confinement well. As in all kennels, draughts should be rigorously excluded. On his return from exercise a highly-bred Greyhound is particularly liable to take a chill, his skin being so fine that any draught is sure to affect him injuriously if exposed to it for long. Though several Greyhounds may be kennelled together without ill results accruing, they are by no means a peaceable class of dog, and fights have frequently occurred in the kennel which have led to bad results. It is well therefore to keep as few as possible together, and under any circumstances to avoid their being overcrowded, either on the benches, or in the yard which should always be attached to a Greyhound kennel. The floors of both the inner and outer kennels should be cemented, and kept thoroughly clean, as much of the dog's health during training will depend upon the comfort and attention he receives at home, and nothing is more likely to affect him injuriously than an existence in an atmosphere which is at all contaminated by the odour of excrements, which should be removed at once by the kennelman.

In the "Courser's Companion," by Thomas Thacker, which was published at Derby in 1834, much valuable advice is given on the subject of training and feeding Greyhounds. The training of dogs for public stakes has, since the date of Mr. Thacker's work, become a science, and few Greyhounds run at any of the principal meetings who have not been under the care of a professional trainer. The owner, however, who is in the habit of keeping a Greyhound or two about his premises, and occasionally enjoying a day's coursing when he opposes a neighbour's dogs, may learn much from remarks made by Mr. Thacker, whose work is still regarded as one of the best ever written upon the subject of coursing. In his preliminary observations on the training of Greyhounds, the author commences by drawing a comparison between the race-horse and the Greyhound. He argues that in the case of the former his energies when racing are restrained during the earlier portion of the race by the man on his back, who desires to husband the animal's resources for a supreme effort at the finish of the race. The Greyhound, on the contrary, when running is beyond the control of his master or any one else, and therefore in the vast majority of cases neglects to husband his strength in the slightest degree. "Therefore," says Mr. Thacker, "feeding becomes a matter of first-rate importance, only surpassed by the physical superiority of the dog himself. If you feed a dog with a sufficient quantity of nutritious food to make him superabundantly fat and fleshy, you are obliged to give a corresponding quantity of severe exercise to reduce him to a standard of health and fine muscular development, while you unload his chest of superfluous fatty matter in order to increase its capacity, and consequently improve his wind. In producing this fine state, and during the process required, the dog necessarily becomes dull and stiff in his joints, and he is (*pro tempore*) deprived of that essential quality—fire—which I have spoken of before.

"A Greyhound in tip-top condition should be all fire, animation, and sprightliness; his gaiety, expressed in the sparkle of his eyes and the bounding elasticity of his limbs, should be so refreshing to the beholder as to produce the idea that the excellences of the animal could be carried no further. A combination of the greatest strength from large muscular development should be united with the best state of the wind to produce what is called fine condition, and to attain this very desirable end the animation of the animal should not be depressed by undue exercise, which frequently deprives him of the acme of his speed as well as fire. . . . . Dogs as well as horses may be over-trained; too much exertion long persisted in appears to destroy the vigour of the animal by exhausting his powers.

"In order to provide for this combination of circumstances, and to prepare the dog for coursing in the finest possible state of condition, there is a variety of considerations to be taken into account; for each sportsman has his favourite system of feeding them, and the food given is of different sorts, affording different degrees of nutriment and of different degrees of digestibility, flesh and bone, gelatinous and farinaceous substances, and liquids with more or less nutritious matter contained in them. Some feed but once in a day, while others, to avoid over-distending the stomach and oppressing the organs of digestion, commit an error in the opposite extreme by giving only half a meal at a time, and that twice a day."

This latter system is decidedly disapproved of by the author, as being injurious to a healthy dog, mainly on the ground that in the dog digestion is carried on with great rapidity. Upon the subject of diet the author of the "Courser's Companion" is most decided in his advocacy of meat being supplied; in his own words, he says: "There are different sorts of condition—good, bad, and indifferent — and I am aware that many Greyhounds run, what is called *well*, under a regimen of gelatine and farina, their natural courage being such as induces them to do so without flesh. But this is no proof that the same dogs would not have *run better with it.* . . . You may gain fire by keeping a dog under restraint, but unless you give him sufficiently severe exercise for his wind and strength, that fire will be only like a flash in the pan; you will in fact lose fire in a two-fold manner. Flesh, being more nutritious and stimulating, imparts more fire to his temperament than weaker or less natural food, and by giving flesh in proper proportion you do not lose the fire imparted by restraint; for with flesh he does not require such severity of exercise to compress the fibres to a state of active and powerful capability as will deprive him of his fire. Flesh, however, possessing much nutriment and stimulus, if given too plentifully would require very strong exercise to prevent the blood being too rich, and must, therefore, be equally avoided as giving him too little or none; a moderate quantity in his daily meals instead of jelly food."

Arrian, who styled himself the younger Xenophon, wrote the following description of coursing as carried on by the ancients, which clearly proves the antiquity of this class of sport, and is published in Blane's "Cynegetica" in 1788:—"The most opulent and luxurious among the Gauls course in this manner. They send out good hare-finders early in the morning to those places where it is likely to find hares sitting, who send back word if they have found any, and what number. Then they go out themselves, and put them up, and lay in the dogs, themselves following on horseback. Whoever has good Greyhounds should never lay them in too near the hare, nor run more than two at a time. For, though the animal is very swift, and will oftentimes beat the dogs, yet when she is first started she is so terrified by the holloaing, and by the dogs being very close, that her heart is overcome by fear, and in the confusion very often the best sporting hares are killed without showing any diversion. She should therefore be suffered to run some distance from her form and re-collect her spirits, and then if she is a good sporting hare, she will lift up her ears, and stretch out with long rates from her feet, the dogs directing their course after her with great activity of limbs, as if they were leaping, and affording a spectacle worthy the trouble that must necessarily be employed in properly breeding and training these dogs.

"Those are the best hares that are found in open and exposed places; for, being bold they do not hide themselves, but seem as it were to challenge the dogs: these, when they are followed, do not immediately try to avoid the danger by running to woods and brakes, though they should happen to be near, but take over the open country; and when they are contending in swiftness with the Greyhounds, if the dogs which pursue them are not fleet, they moderate their own speed according as they are pressed. But if the dogs are very fleet, they then run as fast as they can; and when running in an open country, if they find themselves so pressed by a good dog that they perceive his shadow, they try to throw him beyond them by frequent turns, making for the woods or the nearest shelter they know of; and this is a sure sign that the hare is overmatched by the dog. . . . .

"It is proper sometimes to speak to the dogs, for they rejoice to hear the voice of their master, and it is a kind of encouragement to them to know that he is present. In the first course there is no objection to speaking to them as often as we choose; but in the second or third course, when they will probably be weakened, I do not think it right to call them too often by name, lest, by too eager a desire to please their master, they should exert themselves beyond their strength, and hurt their inside, which has been the destruction of many a good dog.

"If the dog has caught the hare, or otherwise behaved well, you should dismount and encourage him, for they love to be praised. If the dogs through fatigue let the hare escape, they will nevertheless approach with pleasure and caress their master.

"Those who have not good hare-finders go commonly out, a number in company on horseback; and coming to a likely place, when they happen to find a hare let the Greyhounds loose after her. But those who are more diligent after the sport go out on foot, and if any one accompanies them on horseback, it is his business to follow the dogs when they run. They beat about, being drawn up in a regular rank, and having proceeded in a direct line to a certain point, wheeling round, they turn about together towards the place from whence they set out by the same way they came, leaving, as far as possible, no likely place unexplored. If many dogs are taken out they should not be stationed promiscuously; for when the hare is started no one can refrain from slipping his own dog, each being desirous of seeing his own dog run. The hare, being confused and terrified by the noise and number of the dogs, will be taken without showing any sport, and the diversion, which is the chief object, will be spoiled. A person therefore should be appointed to take the command of the sport, and the Greyhounds being in slips two together, he should give these orders—'If the hare takes this way you loose yours, and no one else; if that way you yours,' and these orders should be punctually obeyed. The Gauls sometimes when coursing mix their finders with the Greyhounds, and whilst these try, the others are led by the hand at a little distance, taking care to lead the good dogs where the hare is most likely to come, that they may be let go when she runs off. . . . But by this method the course is irregular, and the hare, however stout she may be, is so much alarmed by the cry of the dogs, that if she is not a considerable way before, she is so confused that she will easily be caught. Therefore, whoever lets slip a good dog should not do it while she is astonished, but let her make her first ring before he looses him, unless he means to spoil the diversion. It is not right to loose the greyhounds at a young hare, which should be spared, and the finders if possible should be called off, which is very difficult, as they are not under good command, being eager through hunger; and so desirous are they of eating up what they catch, that it is hard to get them off even by beating them with sticks."

Coursing meetings in the present time are generally under the management of some of the numerous Clubs which are now in existence, and entries are usually confined to dogs entered or nominated by members of these associations. The Waterloo meeting, held at Altcar, near Liverpool, is the head of the list, as the Waterloo Cup, Purse, and Stakes, attract more attention than any coursing events throughout the country. To enter a dog for the Waterloo Cup, an owner who does not happen to be a member of the Club is compelled to apply for a nomination from one of those who do belong to it, and as the stake is but a sixty-four dog one, it frequently occurs that a good dog is unable to compete. Many members, however, who have no Greyhound in their opinion worth entering, return their nominations to the secretary, who in his turn places them at the disposal of the owners of promising dogs who do not happen to belong to members. In this way many outsiders are enabled to run their dogs, who would otherwise be unable to do so.

It occasionally happens in coursing Clubs that more members apply for nominations in a stake than the committee have at their disposal. In such instances it is customary to ballot for them, upon the understanding that those members who have been un-fortunate enough to be balloted out shall have a priority of claim in the next stake to be run for. On the other hand, in some cases it comes about that an insufficient number of nominations have been applied for, and therefore the committee of the Club would be unable to carry out their programme if some steps were not taken to meet the difficulty. It is therefore usual in such a case to ballot *in* nominators, and thus it is decided by lot who are to have the nominations not applied for. By this means members of the Club who have no dog they care to enter, are compelled to find a dog outside their own kennel to run for them, or failing this must pay the entrance money, so that no pecuniary loss can fall upon the committee in carrying out the meeting on account of stakes. It is not, of course, customary to grant more than one nomination to an individual member in a stake if by doing so others who belong to the Club are prevented from entering a dog; but this rule is not usually enforced in produce stakes.

Another difficulty which occasionally arises is the postponement of meetings from bad weather, or other causes. In such instances the stewards are empowered to postpone the meeting from day to day, or even fix some other date for it, as they may think fit. When this occurs the draw is usually void, though the nominator is responsible for the nomination which he has had allotted to him.

The National Coursing Club, which is composed of the representatives of the leading clubs throughout the kingdom, forms a Coursing Court of Appeal, and is regarded as the head of affairs in the Greyhound world. But before going briefly over the principal rules laid down by it, we will describe shortly the functionaries indispensable to a coursing meeting, taking the existence of a Club committee as a fact.

Of all connected with this sport, the office of *Judge* is the most important and unthankful, for on his shoulders rests the responsibility of delivering the verdict which may mean so much to thousands. A quick eye and a good memory are essential qualifications in a judge of coursing, and it is scarcely necessary, we think, to add that his integrity must be unimpeachable, and his strength of mind assured in addition, or he will most certainly be unfitted for the post he fills. His duties are to ride with the dogs, and calculate the points they score. He frequently also has to give the slipper orders when to slip, and he has to deliver his decision immediately the course is over to the flag steward, whose duty it is to see the red or white flag hoisted by the man told off for this special duty. The colour under which a dog runs is regulated by his position on the card, which is in two columns, the victory of the dogs on the left column being represented by the hoisting of the red flag, and those on the right by the white one. In the event of an undecided course taking place, the judge takes off his hat, as an intimation that he is not satisfied, and the dogs have to go into the slips again.

The post of *Slipper* is, if not as responsible, a more arduous one than that of judge, for it is his duty to slip the Greyhounds when told to do so by the judge or slip-steward. A considerable amount of skill and quickness of eye is required in the slipper, for an uneven or a jerky slip must ruin many a course. His duties, too, necessitate a great amount of physical exertion, as the slipper has to be on his legs all the day; and in addition, before he slips the dogs, has usually to run some little distance with them before the word is given to slip.

Beaters are almost indispensable at a coursing meeting, as without their assistance hares would not be found in many instances when wanted, or if found, she would probably face in the opposite direction to that which a good course required. It is most desirable, therefore, that the beaters know their work, and by keeping in their proper positions prevent the hare either facing to cover or to the dogs, which would most likely occur if she were frightened by injudicious beating.

The *Field Stewards*, under whose direction the operations in the field are conducted, have the unpleasant task of keeping the ground clear, and seeing that the beaters do their duty.

The following are the values of the six points in coursing:—

1. SPEED.—1, 2, or 3 points.
2. GO-BYE.—2, or if gained on the outer circle, 3 points.
3. TURN.—1 point.
4. WRENCH.—$\frac{1}{2}$ point.
5. KILL.—2 points at *most*; but points may be subtracted if the kill is not meritorious —in fact, a kill may count for nothing.
6. THE TRIP.—1 point.

Of these the *Go-bye* is where one dog starts a length behind the other, but passes him in a straight run, and gets a length in front.

A *Turn* is when the hare is turned at not less than a right angle from her course.

A *Wrench* is when the hare is turned at less than a right angle from her course.

A *Trip* is when the dog gets hold of the hare, but fails to kill her.

In calculating the number of points which are to be given for speed, the judge must take into consideration the start which one Greyhound may have lost from being badly slipped or from not sighting the hare. Also when the hare bends round in favour of the slower dog, it is customary to allow one dog a point for speed, and the other one point for first turn. It is also determined that speed alone shall not determine a course, except under very exceptional circumstances.

In event of a dog losing ground at the start from being badly slipped or not sighting the hare, the judge is to decide what allowance is to be made to him, on the principle that the foremost dog is not to begin to score until the second has had an opportunity of joining in the course. Again, too, when the hare favours one dog the latter's next point shall not be scored, or, at most, only half his point, at the discretion of the judge. And no Greyhound is to receive any allowance for any accident unless he is ridden over by his adversary's owner or the latter's servant.

A Greyhound loses the course at once if he refuses to follow the hare when slipped. But when he wilfully stands still in a course, and desists from the pursuit of the hare, no subsequent points he may make are allowed him. If in such an instance the points awarded him up to this point exactly equal his opponent's, the offending dog loses the course; but when one or both dogs are unable to continue the course, and stop with the hare in view, the course is decided by the number of points already awarded by the judge. Also, where a dog refuses to fence where the other fences, his future points shall not be counted in his favour unless he sticks in a meuse, when in such an event the course shall end from the time he stuck. If, however, the points are equal up to then, he loses his course.

Amongst the most stringent rules of the National Coursing Club are those which refer to the description of the entries; and the reason of such a policy must be obvious to all who give the subject a moment's consideration. It is especially provided that the name and colour of the dog and of his parents shall be clearly given, and in the case of produce stakes any distinguishing marks must also be given. A subscriber must also, if requested by the secretary, state in writing, before or during the meeting, the names and addresses of those who reared his puppies; and any puppy is liable to disqualification whose description does not tally with that given by the subscriber. No Greyhound is said to be a puppy which was whelped before the 1st of January of the year preceding the commencement of the season of running. A Sapling is a Greyhound whelped on or after the 1st of January of the same year in which the season of running has commenced. If the name of a Greyhound which has run in public has been changed, the subscriber must notify the change to the secretary, who shall place both the new and the old names on the card of the meeting. The penalty for neglect of this rule by the subscriber is disqualification of his dog.

In cases where a subscriber names a dog which is not his own property for a stake, and fails to add the word "Names" or letters "N. S." to his entry, the dog is disqualified. Any subscriber naming another's dog is compelled, if requested, to furnish the secretary with the *bonâ fide* owner's name. The draw is arranged by putting either the dogs' names or numbers which correspond with numbers which have been allotted them, into a hat, and drawing them out by hazard.

The order thus decided upon is maintained throughout the course, unless some untoward event should render it impossible; and the winning dogs in each succeeding course are run against each other until but one remains, which wins the stake, the last dog beaten by him being termed the "runner-up." Dogs must be taken to the slips in their proper turn, and if one is more than ten minutes behind time his antagonist is entitled to claim the course and run a bye. In event of both dogs being late, they are both liable to disqualification. Owners or servants are permitted to follow their dogs after handing them over to the charge of the slipper, but they must be careful not to interfere with that official in his duties, or to encourage their dogs by calling to them whilst they are running a course. In event of two dogs being of the same colour, they are each compelled to wear a distinguishing collar, this collar to correspond with the colour—red or white—under which they figure on the card. If one dog gets out of the slips, the slipper is not allowed to let the other go; and in case of the slips breaking, the slipper is rendered liable to a sovereign fine. This penalty is also incurred by any one who lets a Greyhound loose, and thereby enables it to join in a course which is being run. In event of this loose dog being the property of the same owner whose dog is running in the course, the latter will be disqualified, unless the owner can prove that he was unable to take the loose dog up after its last course. *Apropos* of this subject, it may be here remarked that many a grand Greyhound is very shy of being taken up when once slipped. Misterton, winner of the Waterloo Cup in 1879, is a case in point, and he certainly ruined his chances of success in the following year by—after he had won his course—having a second, and severe, single-handed one on his own account, before he could be caught, or "taken up."

A "no course" is distinguished from an undecided by the fact that the former arises from the course being either too short to try the dogs together, or by some accident occurring which brings about the same result. An undecided is where the judge considers the dogs' performances equal—in which case he takes off his hat, which he does not do in event of a no course taking place. A no course or an undecided may be run again immediately, or, if claimed on behalf of both dogs, before the next brace are put in the slips, or in any case for no course, if ordered by the judge. Otherwise it must be run after the next two courses, unless deferred until the next day. If it happens to be the last course of the day, a quarter of an hour shall be allowed the dogs after being taken up.

As regards dividing stakes, the latter are divided if the two last dogs left in belong to the same owner or his partner, or if one owner prevails upon the other to withdraw his dog for some consideration. On the other hand, if one dog meets with some accident, and has to be withdrawn, the other may be awarded the stake by the stewards. If two Greyhounds have each won a stake, and have to compete for a final prize, should one have run more courses than the other, the dog which has run the smaller number must run a bye or byes, to make his number up to the total of his antagonist, so that he may not possess any unfair advantage when they meet. In event of it being proved that either the judge or slipper is interested in the success of a Greyhound running at the meeting, the nominator of the dog forfeits his winnings, unless it can be proved by him that he was unaware of and no party to the offence. And, further, any nominator who gives or lends—or *offers* to give or lend—money or anything of value to the judge or slipper, is liable to be disqualified from running or entering Greyhounds in another's nomination where the National Coursing Club's rules are in force.

There is no difficulty in taking Greyhounds about the country if proper notice is given to the railway companies, as arrangements can always be made by which proper accommodation can be provided for the dogs and their attendant. It is always best for the latter to travel with his charges, not only to quiet them if excited, but also to protect them from injury by accident, or by the design of evil-doers. It is often unhappily true that attempts, and successful attempts too, have been made to hocus dogs, so as to prevent them winning their ties, and therefore due vigilance must be exercised by those who have them in charge, and the use of a muzzle is strongly recommended. In journeying, the dogs should be well and warmly clothed, and care must be taken to keep them out of draughts and wet, for when in a high state of training the Greyhound is more than ever susceptible of chills. Many a dog has "gone wrong" on arriving at the scene of action by the change in the water from what he has been accustomed to at home, and therefore it is not unusual to boil the water given him, so as to render any change of quality less liable to occur. Precautions should also be taken by which every chance is given the dog of being made comfortable as soon as he arrives at his new quarters, as if he is rendered restless by the unfamiliar surroundings, he will naturally be fagged when called upon for action in the morning. To obviate such chances, it is usual with the owners of valuable dogs entered for important stakes to send their Greyhounds and attendants into the immediate neighbourhood of the meeting some days before the event comes off, so that the dog may be thoroughly accustomed to his new quarters before he has to do his best. We firmly believe that another advantage is also gained by such a course, and that is benefit to the dog's health, and consequently an increase of vigour, from the change of air, which in lower animals, as in man, has often been known to work wonders on a jaded system. This being our opinion, we strongly advocate an early move, when this is possible, to the neighbourhood of the meeting.

Dogs that are to run should not be fed in the morning of the same day, or if they are, only a few ounces of some nutritious but easily-digested food should be allowed. During the interval between the courses it is often necessary to give a dog a restorative in order to recruit his strength, and in the majority of cases a little weak brandy-and-water will do all that is wanted, though different professional trainers each have their own especial nostrum for such emergencies. As, however, we are addressing those who are but amateurs in the coursing world, we again repeat that a small dose of brandy-and-water well diluted, is in our opinion a more judicious pick-me-up under such circumstances than a more elaborate or mysterious one.

The advantage to be gained from keeping the dogs warm after they have run a tie cannot be too strongly impressed upon all beginners, especially as in the excitement of the event all remembrance of the clothing may fade away. It is also as well to take the dogs under cover if such is possible; but under all circumstances a Greyhound should be well rubbed down before being again given into the hands of the slipper, as by this means the chances of stiffness are sensibly diminished. In addition to the warm clothing, and the waterproof clothing to be used in case of rain, it is desirable to take a spare chain and collar or two to the meeting; accidents often occur, and in the face of the stringent rules referred to above concerning dogs which have broken loose, it is always well to be on the safe side. When the dog is in the slips his attendant should be handy to take him up at the conclusion of the course, and have his clothing ready to put on at once. On the conclusion of the day the dog must be thoroughly rubbed down, fed, and made comfortable for the night, so as to be ready for the exertions of the next day. It is also customary on their return home at the termination of a meeting, for the Greyhounds to be mildly physicked and given a little rest, unless they should be wanted immediately for other engagements. Such a course tends to cool them after the excitement of running in public and amongst strange dogs, whilst the rest must be beneficial to them after the exertions they have undergone.

As regards the preparation which Greyhounds require for the description of coursing we have alluded to above, it may be briefly said to consist of two most important items—viz., proper food and sufficient, though judicious, exercise. As the amount of the former must usually depend in a great degree upon the latter, it will suit our purpose better to allude to exercise first, and defer any observations on feeding until that subject is completed. The quantity of exercise naturally enough varies when different constitutions and circumstances have to be considered, for some breeds of Greyhounds will get into condition with a far less amount of physical exertion than is required by others. The description of country which has to be gone over, also, must influence the trainer considerably, but under any circumstances all superfluous fat must be removed from the dog, and his wind must be improved by exercise. Many Greyhounds, if permitted to run loose, will of their own free will give themselves enough exercise to keep in good health and fair condition; these, as long as this fondness for running about remains, will not require more than a few gallops to get tolerably fit for the class of coursing in which they are likely to take part. On the other hand, many Greyhounds are lazy, and disinclined to exert themselves, and are therefore compelled to take exercise under the immediate supervision of their trainer, whoever he may be. Most practical persons are strongly in favour of giving their dogs a large amount of exercise on the high road, as it has the undoubted effect of hardening the feet. The best hour for this sort of exercise is, for two reasons, the early morning—first, because the roads are less likely to be crowded by carts or passengers; and, secondly, the heat of the day is avoided.

It is always most desirable to muzzle Greyhounds when at exercise, as there is then no chance of their injuring themselves by fighting, or by picking up poison or injurious food. Another advantage to be gained by following this rule is, that it goes a long way to prevent their killing sheep, which is a fault to which some Greyhounds are particularly prone. The use of clothing, when training is being carried on, is a matter for the consideration of the head of affairs; although heavy sheets are invariably used when gross and high-conditioned dogs have to be got into condition, it does not consequently follow that lighter-fleshed ones require the same treatment. When, however, Greyhounds are likely to be compelled to stand about after taking exercise, or preparatory to a course, it is most desirable that a cloth should be used to protect them from the chances of a chill, the effects of which may be very serious.

Some trainers like the Greyhounds they wish to get fit to run after a dog-cart for several miles a day, and this, in the case of certain dogs, may be a judicious system. It has, however, its disadvantages, foremost amongst them being that it is difficult for the trainer to keep his dogs in order if he has a horse to control as well. Another objection is that there is always the risk of the dogs being injured by the horse or wheels of the trap, and in fact, unless under exceptional circumstances, exercise directed by a man on foot is considered the most preferable. This latter system, if carried out under the control of a conscientious trainer who does not shirk a daily walk of several miles along the road at a steady pace, is sure to benefit the majority of Greyhounds, if accompanied by a periodical gallop on a field or common for the benefit of the animal's wind. A too frequent sight of a hare is apt to injure a dog as a courser, for many Greyhounds get cunning, and refuse to do their best if too often treated to a hare. It is, however, absolutely necessary that young dogs should know their work in time, and, as a rule, they are not slow in picking up what is required of them. This is the reverse sometimes, for many a Greyhound who has afterwards turned out to be a veritable flyer has, in his infancy, shown little of that thirst for blood which afterwards marked his career. Owners should not therefore be disheartened if their puppies do not at once take to their work with kindness, but should remember that time must be given them to improve their ways.

Many experienced persons advocate the running of a puppy at first in the company of an old dog, in the hopes that the latter will act as schoolmaster, and instruct his pupil in the path in which he should walk. For our own part, though we are well aware that many authorities differ from our opinion, we totally disapprove of this arrangement, as the chances of the puppy receiving much benefit from the example of the old dog are more than counterbalanced by the certainty that, unless a most exceptionally game dog, his heart will be broken by the superior power of his preceptor. If a puppy has the making of a good dog in him, his merit will surely display itself sooner or later without the assistance of an older dog; but, on the other hand, there should be every chance given to the dog's natural qualities appearing in a natural manner, without risking the chances of disheartening him by pitting him at too early an age against a better dog.

On his return from exercise the Greyhound should have his feet and legs carefully overlooked, in order to discover if any injury has been done them by thorns, stones, or strains. If necessary they may be washed, but as a rule, a careful rubbing down with a dry brush or glove will be all that is required to make him comfortable. On his return to the kennel, precautions must be taken to prevent him from taking cold when heated, and most particularly should he avoid all draughts and damp. Many a good dog has suddenly taken cold and been prevented from running, merely on account of the carelessness of a kennelman who has provided him with a damp bed, or injudiciously let him stand about unclothed or unprotected in a cold wind or rain.

Having thus briefly alluded to the exercising of the Greyhound, the important subject of food must come to be considered. Here there are, as on other points, a variety of opinions, some advocating an almost entirely farinaceous, others an equal liberal meat diet. It appears nevertheless that an amalgamation of both is more likely to benefit the dog, as so much depends upon what is the amount of his daily exercise and the purposes for which he is intended. Oatmeal *thoroughly* boiled is undoubtedly a good food as the staple commodity, and the addition of meat, and liquor in which meat has been boiled, can always be easily effected and proportioned out. Sheep's heads and large bones of all sorts form excellent occasional additions to the ordinary diet, and the frequent substitution of Indian meal for oatmeal is desirable. The latter meal has often an ill effect on the bowels of some dogs, and therefore must be discontinued if it is found to purge them too freely, and thus reduce their strength. As in other breeds, a periodical dose of cooling medicine must be given, and due attention must be paid to this subject three or four days previous to a course.

The hour of feeding and the number of meals a day, are also subjects which are eagerly discussed, and many practical breeders and trainers argue strongly in favour of a morning as well as an evening meal for the dogs when being trained. Though a few mouthfuls after exercise, like the traditional chip in the porridge, may do no harm if it does not do any good, we are decidedly of opinion that those authorities are right who argue in favour of one substantial meal a day. A bone may be given the dogs when in the kennel in the earlier part of the day, to amuse them and prevent *ennui* during the long hours which ensue between exercise and dinner, but we do not advocate a meal at that time.

As in the case of other dogs, Greyhounds do better when fed in the late afternoon, as their food can then be thoroughly digested before the morning's exercise, and if, as is frequently the case, they have given them the advantage of a gentle run in the evening, the process of digestion is materially benefited. A full stomach is equally antagonistic to comfort in dog and man when violent exercise has to be undergone, but a gentle walk some two or three hours after meal time is beneficial alike to both. With reference to the use of bones, where there are more than one Greyhound in each kennel when they are given out, the presence of an attendant is most desirable, to prevent the fighting which most naturally will ensue. Horseflesh, beef, and mutton, are each and all beneficial to the Greyhound when in training, the last-named more especially so in the case of delicately-constituted dogs who, when in hard work, refuse their food and require tempting. Pork and veal should be eschewed, as also those portions of the others which contain small bones, which are apt to injure the dogs who eat them.

Of modern Greyhounds Lord Lurgan's Master M'Grath has more especially immortalised himself by winning the Waterloo Cup three times, an unparalleled feat since the extension of the cup to a sixty-four dog stake. Opinions differ as to whether he would not have carried off the prize in four successive years, but his going amiss in the third rendered his defeat an easy matter, though he avenged himself twelve months later. Master M'Grath having been a dog so much above the average his pedigree may be of interest to our readers, so we produce it here *in extenso* for their benefit.

MASTER M'GRATH					
Dervock	St. Clair	Figaro	King Cob	Ion / Kate
			Frederica	Damon / Daffodil
		Black Fly	Marquis	Rocket / Stella
			Kirtles	Kouli Khan / Knavery
	Erin	Lightfoot	Sam	Hilcoolie / Old Whisky
			Empress	Bennett's Rocket / Easterby's Empress
		Jenny Lind	Scythian	Fox / Warwick
			Syren	Sadek / Sanctity
Lady Sarah	David	Motley	Sam	Traveller / Tippitywitchet
			Tollwife	King Cob / Matilda Gillespie
		Wanton	Senate	Sadek / Sanctity
			Coquette	Kouli Khan / Knavery
	Lady Watford	Larriston	Liddesdale	Bowhill / Lady Seymour
			Hannah	Buff / Catlowdie
		Consideration	Kentish Fire	King Cob / Knab
			Linnet	Easterby's Emperor / Old Linnet

The pedigree of Canaradzo, another famous dog, closely related to the subject of our coloured plate, may not be out of place. It is as follows:—

CANARADZO				
	Beacon	Bluelight	Monsoon	Colonel Smart
			Stave	Bugle Strawberry
		Frolic	Waterloo	Dusty Miller Exotic
			Clarinda	Cessnock Young Hornet
	Scotland Yet	Wigan	Drift	Driver Coquette
			Cutty Sark	Kirkland Cutty Sark
		Veto	Dux	Driver Duppy
			Tillside Lass	Draffin Old Tillside Lass

Having thus touched briefly upon the most prominent rules of coursing, we can conclude by assuring any of our readers who are desirous of pursuing this branch of sport, that the best way of finding out whether their hearts are likely to be in the pursuit or not, is to attend one or more of the principal coursing meetings. Personal observation and practical acquaintance with coursing do more to determine a man's mind either for or against the sport than volumes written on the subject; and furthermore many a useful hint is given by those in charge of Greyhounds on the field which a sharp observer is very apt to profit by in days to come.

CHAPTER XXXIV.

THE WHIPPET.

THE Whippet, or Snap Dog, as it is termed in several of the northern districts of the country, may scarcely be said to lay special claim to be considered a sporting dog, except in those parts of the country where it is most appreciated. The Whippet is essentially a local dog, and the breed is little valued beyond the limits of the northern counties. In these, however, this dog is held in high respect, and its merits as a provider of the means of sport are highly esteemed.

Unfortunately for the dog, the uses to which he is often placed have, naturally enough, done much to injure his reputation in the sight of many who would otherwise have regarded him with a favourable eye. So many scandals have arisen from time to time in connection with the quasi-sport of rabbit-coursing, that many who would otherwise have felt disposed to do their best to elevate the breed in popular estimation have reluctantly been compelled to discontinue their efforts on its behalf, on account of the unpleasant treatment they received from other admirers of the dog.

The special claims which the Whippet possesses to be classed in the present instance as a sporting dog are its strong structural resemblance to the modern Greyhound, and its association with rabbit-coursing and dog-racing. The latter, illegitimate *sports* though they may appear to the mind of a sportsman unacquainted with the localities where they are so eagerly pursued, cannot be disregarded when an unprejudiced view has to be taken of what constitutes sport in the minds of many of our fellow-countrymen. In answer to any doubts that might arise on the subject, the only reply that can be made with safety would be a visit to those districts where the inhabitants patronise rabbit-coursing, which visit, we believe, would convince the most sceptical opponent of the institution that at all events, when honestly carried out, the recreation may legitimately be described as sport.

The Whippet is undoubtedly a cross-bred dog which has been brought into existence to meet the exigencies of the sport with which it is associated. As will be seen from the remarks of Mr. Raper, later on, it is supposed that in days gone by the English Terrier pure and simple was good enough for what was wanted ; but as time advanced a faster dog was required for carrying out what was required of him. Undoubtedly the Greyhound was selected for the purpose of improving the strain of rabbit-coursers then in existence; and with good results, as improved records most plainly testify. The sport of rabbit-coursing has of later years given way to dog-racing, where no rabbits are required, the struggle for supremacy lying in the fleetness of the competitors ; and an element of cruelty has thus been undoubtedly avoided. However, we will proceed to give some notes upon the subject kindly afforded us by Mr. George Raper, of Stockton-on-Tees, which, as the writer is practically acquainted with the subject, will no doubt be of interest.

Mr. Raper says :—" Rabbit-coursing, once so popular a sport, has gradually waned. Some ten to twenty years ago it was all the rage amongst that class with which the Whippet dog is so closely associated. The dogs then used were of an entirely different stamp to the dogs of the present day—in fact, they were *Terriers proper.* The predominating colours were red and wheaten; many, too, were blue, with tan marking. These Terriers were very hard and game, and the best of dogs for cover work. They were, with very few exceptions, rough, having a hard and strong coat. They were of a medium length of leg—decidedly not leggy.

" With the gradual decay of rabbit-coursing, and the introduction of straight-out running (now the popular amusement), has disappeared the type of Terrier formerly used for the former sport. Now speed is the main object sought for; the main consideration is to get the greatest amount of speed in the least possible size; hence, to obtain speed, those interested in the breed have resorted to Italian and English Greyhound crosses. You know these dogs are now judged on the same scale as Greyhounds—in fact, many of them are so finely bred that they must strike the observant eye as being little else than a diminutive Greyhound; and not only in outline are they alike, but most of the smooth specimens are of the same colour as the Greyhound—we have whites, blacks, reds, fawns, brindles, and compounds from each.

" These dogs are very swift, and are entirely trained for speed, and to run straight. Many will stand on a mark until told to go, when they will make the best of their way to their owner, generally placed within a few yards of the winning post.

" No class of dog receives more care or attention; they are very carefully fed and attended to, and in many cases receive better food than their master or family. I knew an iron-worker, who only worked a day or two a week; he himself lived entirely on bread, but his dog, who was undergoing a preparation for a race, was fed upon mutton. Nearly every ironworker has his Whippet, and, if he hardly has a coat to his back, his dog must have a good sheet, and, moreover, be muzzled. You can fell Geordie if you like, but don't touch his dog.

" From the above notes you will observe that the dogs formerly used for rabbit-coursing were an entirely different stamp to the dog now used.

" I must not forget to mention that there are now many rough-haired Whippets, but they are built entirely upon the same lines as the smooth ones.

" The rules of rabbit-coursing differ very materially from Greyhound coursing; in the latter every wrench, turn, &c., counts so many points, whereas in rabbit-coursing these are reckoned of no account; the dog that kills the rabbit is declared the winner.

" Each dog runs on merit, but size is always taken into account. In Newcastle, Durham, and district, the general rule is to allow four yards per inch, according to the height of the dogs competing.

" Until lately the dogs had to pass under a standard, but it was found to be an unsatisfactory way of getting the correct height of a dog. Many a dog in reality 20 inches high would easily pass the standard at $18\frac{1}{2}$ inches. This he was trained to do, the usual plan being to place a needle in the top of the standard; when the dog passed under he pricked himself, this in time he learns to avoid by lowering himself. Now, the general rule is to have the dogs laid upon their sides, and measured from the shoulder-blade to the end of the foot.

" By far the most popular sport at the present day is dog-racing, or as it is termed, straight-out running.

" The usual distance of the race is 200 yards, the rule being to allow eight yards per inch, according to the size of the dogs.

"In Leeds, Sheffield, Manchester, and districts, the rules vary, the dogs there run according to weight. The distance of the race is generally the same as further north—viz., 200 yards. The rule is to allow 2½ yards per pound; therefore, the great object in these districts is to obtain as tall and light a dog as possible, whereas, in Newcastle and neighbourhood the object is to procure as speedy a dog as small as possible.

"Conditions of course vary in matches. These are arranged by mutual agreement."

From what has gone before, it will be seen that Whippets differ little from diminutive Greyhounds in their general outline, though the difference in speed, of course, is very considerable.

In training a Whippet for racing there is so far a difference between this and preparing a Greyhound, that the Greyhound trainer has to keep in view the importance of stamina as well as speed, whilst great pace is what is most required in a Whippet. The length of the courses over which dog-races are held, rarely exceed 200 or 250 yards, and as the track is level there are no natural obstacles to be overcome. Thus the work that a Whippet is called upon to do is of a far lighter character than that of his larger relative. Superfluous flesh must, however, be removed at any cost, or the dog could never go the pace which he would have to do to have a chance of success in racing. It is not, however, by any means desirable that he should be over-trained, or there will be a decrease in pace through weakness, and to obviate all chance of this a Whippet should be steadily worked to get off his flesh, and only occasionally indulged with a full-speed gallop—which if too often repeated would defeat the object for which it was given the dog.

The food which is given to this class of dog when in training is the best which the master can procure; and many a supporter of dog-racing goes without himself in order that his dog may have the dainties which he cannot afford to give them both. The quantity, however, is necessarily limited, the general maxim of the trainer in such cases being, "the best that can be got, but not too much of it."

It is most necessary that the dogs in the course of their preparation should be frequently schooled in the parts which they will have to play upon the day of the race, and taught to toe the line at starting in the correct and orthodox fashion.

As before stated, dog-races are conducted on the handicap principle; it must, therefore, be apparent how many temptations there are to induce a novice to be unsteady at the mark. When in their proper places each dog is held securely by his owner or attendant, and their attention is directed to a person near the judge's box, who waves some object in his hand and encourages them to run after him to secure it. All being ready, the starter fires a pistol, and those holding the dogs release their hold and let them start on their journey to the judge's box. To distinguish one dog from another it is customary to make each competitor wear a coloured collar, so that the judge can at once deliver his decision without assistance from the lookers on. It may be here remarked that each dog is allowed but one person to encourage him by waving an object in his hand as above described, and each of these must be ten or fifteen yards beyond the winning-line when the dogs reach it, so as to prevent any chance of an opponent's dog being interfered with. It is particularly enacted that the object which the runners—as the attendants at the winning-post are styled— wave to attract the dogs' attention shall not consist of anything alive; and usually that any one attempting to weigh or measure one dog in place of another shall be prohibited from all future competition for a greater or less period. The dog which was to be benefited, also, is liable to disqualification as well; and the soundness of this latter rule is beyond all question, as by its enforcement a direct check is placed upon all fraudulent transactions, since detection would depreciate the value of the dog.

It is usual to give the dogs a few mouthfuls of some strengthening food between the heats, and having this in view a slight increase in weight is allowed after the first heat is concluded, if the handicap is conducted on the weight and not the height principle. Finally, to prevent fraudulent ages being given to dogs, many committees, or perhaps it would be better to say promoters, of dog-racing meetings decline to receive the age of any dog unless the latter was registered before attaining the age of eight months, about which period he gets his second set of teeth.

Enough has now been written about this branch of sport to give our readers an idea of what it is, but nobody who has not been present at a meeting can by any means imagine what excitement the different ties create amongst the spectators, the majority of which invest heavily on the success of their selections. A visit to such a meeting will amply repay the curious should they be in the neighbourhood of a place where the sport is fostered; but if they do attend it may be suggested that they keep their eyes open and their pockets shut, as a novice has but a slender chance of making money at dog-racing before experience has been gained.

The points by which a Whippet can be judged may be described as identical with those of a Greyhound.

CHAPTER XXXV.

THE STAGHOUND.

WHATEVER differences may have originally existed between the Staghound and the Fox-hound—which will be described in the succeeding chapter—have been swept away by the progress of time. At the moment of writing there is no dissimilarity of shape or form, the only difference being one of size and weight. Though doubtless nearly related in days gone by, the two varieties are now bred entirely separate, as the proportions of a large-sized Stag-hound would render him unsuitable for foxhunting.

Though it is more than probable that foxhunting men of the day may laugh at the idea of the Staghound being the ancestor of the modern Foxhound, it is nevertheless a fact that in the earlier part of the century this was a common opinion. For instance, the author of the "Field Book," which was published by Effingham Wilson, Royal Exchange, London, in 1833, writes as follows of the Staghound :—

"It seems extremely probable that this large, strong, and bony hound was the primeval stock from which all the collateral branches of this race have descended, and that all deviations from the original stem have been the result of crosses and improvements during many centuries by those skilled in rearing and breeding dogs of the chase, and varied in strength and size according to the particular sport for which they are intended. At the present day [*i.e.*, 1833] there cannot be a doubt but that the practical breeder, by judicious crosses, can either enlarge or diminish the stature and strength of his pack in the course of three or four generations." The writer next proceeds to say that "the Staghounds exclusively devoted to that sport in the royal establishment of this country, it is well known, have been an improved cross between the old English Southern hound and the fleeter Foxhound grafted upon the Bloodhound."

Owing to the scarcity of deer in this country the sport of stag-hunting has almost ceased to exist, though there are several packs of Staghounds still left. The most prominent of these are Her Majesty's, Baron Rothschild's, and the Surrey, all of which, from the close proximity of their meets to the metropolis, are well supported. It is most customary to hunt a carted deer, as, with rare exceptions, none of the modern packs hunt countries where wild deer are to be found, and therefore ingenuity has to be resorted to to produce the means of sport. In such cases the deer is vanned on to the ground, and after it has been allowed a certain amount of law the hounds are laid on, and the sport, such as it is, is commenced. The deer, which, by the way, is generally denuded of its horns, as a rule runs little risk of losing its life, for when brought to bay it is protected by the huntsman and whips from the hounds, and is reserved for another run on some subsequent occasion.

A decided advantage which hunting a carted deer possesses over most other branches of sport is the certainty of finding some sort of sport unless the weather renders it impossible. The date and place of the meet being previously arranged, and the deer being always in confinement, there can be no chance of a blank day, as both the deer and hounds can be brought any distance to the meet. There seems, however, something scarcely sports-manlike in chasing a domesticated creature across a country, and this branch of sport has been in consequence sarcastically characterised as "calf-hunting" by its detractors. A rather peculiar feature in connection with hunting a carted deer is the different manner in which different deer run. Those who have been hunted several times are more or less certain to provide good sport, and on being liberated from the van make the most of the few minutes' law which is allowed them, and take a bold line across country. Others, on the other hand, act quite differently, and are practically useless for this purpose. It is, therefore, customary to name the deer, and if it is thought probable that an old favourite will be uncarted the meet is certain to be better attended than if an untried one is to be liberated, as the latter often decline to take country at all. With reference to the behaviour of Staghounds in days gone by, the writer of the "Field Book" above alluded to writes as follows:—

"In taking the deer according to annual custom, either for the royal hunt or for the fattening paddocks, a stag or a buck which has been previously fixed upon is ridden out of the herd by two or three of the keepers in succession, each of whom is closely followed by a hound, the young dogs only being kept in slips. As soon as the deer has been separated from his companions the dogs have the requisite signal given to them, and they immediately follow in pursuit . . . . . The dogs are so well trained, and are so soon made aware which buck is intended to be caught, that they seldom make a mistake even if the deer regains the herd after being driven from it, but press him through it till they have again separated him from it. It is well known that when a hard-pressed deer tries to rejoin his companions they endeavour to avoid and get away from him as much as possible, or try to drive him away with their horns."

It is not to be supposed at the time of writing that Staghounds are thus employed, or need all the above writer states be accepted as fact. Nevertheless, what he says is so far useful as showing the purposes to which the hounds were put in his day, and the opinion enter-tained by a certain class of sportsmen concerning them.

Hunting the wild deer is mostly confined to the south-west portion of this country, and differs mainly from the former sport in the fact that the deer in this case is an undomesticated animal, and not a poor paddock-fed pet, whose life is periodically tormented by being pursued across country by a troop of cockney sportsmen. The whereabouts of the deer is usually pointed out by those who know the locality and are acquainted with the animal's habits, and when found the hounds are laid on. In hunting the wild deer the animal, if brought to bay, in the majority of instances loses his life, no quarter being shown him, as in the case of the carted deer, for the former animal is considered legitimate game, and is promptly converted into venison.

There being so much similarity between the Staghound and the Deerhound our readers will be in a position to judge of the former's points and standard after perusing the article on the Foxhound in the succeeding chapter. The scale of points, moreover, which are given in the Foxhound chapter are equally applicable to the Staghound.

CHAPTER XXXVI.

THE FOXHOUND.

THE precise source from which the modern Foxhound has been obtained has been a subject of debate from almost time immemorial amongst sportsmen; but the existence of several types in bygone centuries renders it certain that the present hound is the result of the judicious crossing of early breeders. Gervase Markham, in "Countrey Contentments," published in 1631, plainly gives it as his opinion that in his day all the dogs used by sportsmen to assist them in the pursuit of the "stagge, the buck, the roe, the hare, the fox, the badger, the otter, the boar, the goat, and such like" were each and all of them "the same kinde of creatures, namely hounds." This opinion is certainly shared by sportsmen in the present day, as the expression "dog," applied to a Foxhound, would be considered rank heresy by hunting men, and would assuredly subject the user of it to ridicule and laughter. Gervase Markham proceeds to expatiate upon the various varieties of hound which existed in his day in the following language :—

"Now of these hounds there are divers kinds, as the Slow Hound, which is a large great dog, tall and heavy, and are bred for the most part in the best countries of this kingdome, as also in Cheshire and Lancashire and most woodland and mountanous countreys. Then the middle sized dog, which is more fit for the chase, being of a more nimble composure, and are bred in Worcestershire, Bedfordshire, and many other well-mixed soiles, where the champaigne and covert are of equal largenesse. Then the light, nimble, swift, slender dog, which is bred in the north parts of this kingdome, as Yorkshire, Cumberland, Northumberland, and many other plain champaigne countreys. . . . . . .

"These Hounds are of divers colours, and according to their colours so we elect them for the chase, as thus for example :—The white hound, or the white with black spots, or the white with some few liver spots, are the most principal best to compose your kennel of, and will indeed hunt any chase exceeding well, especially the hare, stagge, bucke, roe, or otter, for they will well endure both wood and waters; yet if you demand which is the best and most beautifull of all colours for the general kennell, then I answer the white with the blacke eares, and blacke spot at the setting on of the taile, and are ever found both of good scent and good condition. . . . . The griffeld, which are ever most commonly shaghaired, or any other colour, whether it be mixt or unmixt, so it be shaghaired, are the best verminers, and therefore are chosen to hunt the fox, badger, or other hot scent; they are also exceeding good and cunning finders, and therefore of huntsmen not thought amisse to have one or two couple in every kennell."

These remarks, whilst showing what were considered the best class of hound at the time, also go to prove what were the uses to which each variety was put. The reference to the northern hound as being the lightest and fastest breed of that day will probably be eagerly received by those authorities who maintain that the modern Foxhound is mainly the result of a cross between the northern hound and the ancient Greyhound. Mr. John Scott writes nearly 200 years after Gervase Markham in support of this theory, and in vindication of the judgment of those who introduced the Greyhound cross. "We do not," says Mr. Scott, "hear any complain among modern sportsmen, as among the ancients, of the excess of Greyhound form or qualities in the present Foxhound, or of a want of nose, steadiness, or stoutness. On the contrary, the best packs of this improved breed have found and killed more foxes in their seasons than any other and slower breeds could boast, running as long and desperate chases." A little further on, however, the writer is compelled to admit the unsuitability of too-lightly-bred hounds to heavy countries, over which more powerfully-built ones naturally show to greater advantage. It is only reasonable that a lightly-bred hound should be faster in what Gervase Markham terms a "champaigne country" than a heavy built one; but when further comparison between the merits of the two varieties has to be drawn, a vast difference of opinion soon arises. Gervase Markham, who certainly understood the subject upon which he wrote most thoroughly, thus delivers his opinions :—

"The shape of your hound must be according to the climate where he is bred, and according to the natural composition of his body; as thus, if you would choose a large, heavy, slow, true Talbot-like hound, you must choose him which hath a round, big, thick head, with a short nose uprising, and large open nostrels, which shows he is of a good and quick scent. His eares exceeding large, thin, and down hanging much lower than his chaps, and the flews of his upper lips almost ten inches lower than his nether chaps, which shows a merry, deep mouth and a loud ringer. His back strong and straight, yet rather rising than inwardly yeelding, which shows much toughness and endurance. His fillets would be thick and great, which approve a quick gathering up of his legs without paine; his huckle bones round and hidden, which shows he will not tyer; his thighs round, and his hams straight, which shows swiftnesse. His taile long, and big at the setting on and small downward, which shows a strong chine and a good winde. The haire under his belly hard and stiffe, which shows willingness and ability to endure labour in all weathers and in all places. His legs large and leane, which shows nimbleness in leaping or climing. His foot round, high-knuckled, and well clawed, with a dry, hard soale. The general composure of his body so just and even that no level may distinguish whether his hinder or fore part be the higher. . . . . If you will chuse a swift, light hound, then must his head be more slender and his nose more long, his eares and flews more shallow, his backe broad, his belly gaunt, his taille small, his joynts long, his foot round, and his general composure much more slender and Grayhound-like, and thus in the generallity for the most part all your Yorkshire hounds, whose vertues I can praise no further than for scent and swiftness. . . . . ."

He then proceeds to give some hints upon the crossing of the various strains of hounds, which, as they occupied the position of ancestors to our modern Foxhounds, may be briefly summarised. If a dog was required for what the writer termed "cunning hunting," a cross of the slowest and largest northern hounds with the fastest and lightest west-country ones was advocated. Hounds thus produced were supposed to be endowed with exactly the amount of pace which was required for those early days, which was a matter of paramount importance then, as a slow hound would probably lose the chase, whilst a too fast one would be liable to leave the huntsman behind. For "sweetnesse of cry" Markham advocates the division of the pack into large dogs with deep, solemn mouths, to act as bass voices, then a double number of roaring and loud-ringing mouths, which must "beare the counter tenor," and also some "hollow, plaine, sweete" voices, to make up the middle part of the cry. A few lines further on he alludes to the fact that for the most part the Shropshire and Worcestershire hounds were the loudest, and the Cheshire and Lancashire the deepest, in cry.

The support given to foxhunting has vastly increased since the days of Gervase Markham, and instead of the limited number of packs which existed in his time there are considerably over one hundred packs in England alone. The following is a complete list of the packs in the United Kingdom in 1880, with other details, condensed, by permission, from *The Rural Almanac*:—

ENGLAND.

Hunt.	No. of Couples.	Master.	Days a Week.
Albrighton	50	Mr. T. F. Boughey	4
Atherstone	54	Mr. W. E. Oakeley	4
Badsworth	59	Mr. C. B. E. Wright	4
Beaufort's, Duke of	75	Duke of Beaufort	5
Bedale	42	Major H. F. Dent	3
Belvoir	62	Duke of Rutland	5
Berkeley	61	Lord Fitzhardinge	4
Berkeley, Old	50	Mr. A. H. Longman	3
Berkshire, Old	47	Earl of Craven	3
Berks, South	60	Mr. John Hargreaves	4
Bicester and Warden Hill	60	Viscount Valentia	2
Bilsdale	10	Mr. Nicholas Spink	2
Blackmore Vale	55	Sir R. G. Glyn, Bart.	4
Blankney	50	Mr. H. Chaplin, M.P.	4
Blencathra	12½	Mr. John Crosier	3
Border	10	Messrs. Robson and Dodd	2
Braes of Derwent	22	Lieut.-Col. J. A. Cowen	2
Bramham Moor	50	Mr. George Lane Fox	4
Brocklesby	48	Earl of Yarborough	4
Burstow	25	Mr. Henry Kelsey	2
Burton	58	Mr. F. J. S Foljambe, M.P.	3
Cambridgeshire	45	Mr. Charles S. Lindsell	2
Cattistock	30	Mr. John Codrington	4
Cheshire, The	51	Capt. E. Park Yates	2
Cheshire, South	29	Mr. H. Reginald Corbet	2
Chiddingfold	30	Mr. C. B. Godman	2
Cleveland	28	Mr. J. Proud Yearby	2
Combe's, Mr.	30	Mr. Richd. H. Combe	2
Cornwall, North	17	Mr. Charles F. Pollard	2
Coryton's, Mr. W.	30	Mr. Wm. Coryton	2
Cotswold	50	Mr. A. Holme Sumner	3
Cotswold, North	35	Mr. Algernon Rushout	3
Cottesmore	65	Lord Carington	4
Coventry's, Earl of	55½	Earl of Coventry	6
Craven	48	Mr. E. R. Wemyss	4
Crawley and Horsham	50	Lt.-Col. A. M. Calvert	3
Cumberland	50	Sir W. Lawson, Bt., M.P. and Mr. H. C. Howard	3
Cunard's, Sir Bache	42	Sir Bache Cunard	3
Dartmoor	33	Admiral G. Parker	3

ENGLAND (*continued*).

Hunt.	No. of Couples.	Master.	Days a Week.
Devon, South	20	Mr. Augustus F. Ross	2
Dorset, South	30	Mr. C. J. Radclyffe	2
Dulverton	22	Mr. J. Froude Bellew	2
Durham, North	40	Mr. Anthony L. Maynard	3
Eden's, Sir Wm.	32	Sir Wm. Eden, Bart.	3
Eskdale	16	A Committee	2
Essex	50	A Committee	2
Essex, East	30	Lt.Col. Jelfe Sharpe	2
Essex Union	50	Mr. W. H. White	3
Essex and Suffolk	28½	Mr. B. C. Chaston	2
Ferrers's, Earl	25	Earl Ferrers	2
Fitzwilliam's, Earl	60	Earl Fitzwilliam	3
Fitzwilliam, The	60	Marquis of Huntly	4
Flint and Denbigh	34	Mr. H. R. Hughes and Major C. Rowley Conwy	2
Garth's, Mr.	60	Mr. T. C. Garth	4
Glamorganshire	26½	Mr. John Samuel Gibbon	2
Grafton's, Duke of	53	Duke of Grafton	3
Grove	50	Viscount Galway, M.P.	3
Haldon	23	Sir John Duntze, Bart., and Sir L. Palk, Bart.	2
H. H. (Hampshire)	53	Mr. H. W. Deacon	4
Hambledon	50	Mr. Walter Long	4
Haydon	17	Mr. A. J. B. Orde	2
Herefordshire, North	28	Col. Heywood	2
Herefordshire, South	30	Mr. J. Ranken	2
Hertfordshire	50	A Committee	4
Heythrop	60	Mr. Albert Brassey	4
Holderness	52	Mr. Arthur Wilson	4
Hursley	30	A Committee	2
Hurworth	30	Mr. James Cookson	2
Irthing Vale	17	Mr. Thomas Ramshay	2
Isle of Wight	40	Mr. B. T. Cotton	3
Johnstone's, Sir H.	28	Sir Harcourt Johnstone, Bart., M.P.	2
Kent, East	50	Mr. F. J. Mackenzie	3
Kent, West	60	Hon. Ralph Nevill	4
Lamerton	25	Mr. George Lobb	2
Leconfield's, Lord	55	Lord Leconfield	5
Ledbury	43	Mr. A. Knowles	3

Hunt.	No. of Couples.	Master.	Days a Week.
ENGLAND (continued).			
Llangibby and Chepstow...	32½	Mr. John Lawrence and Mr. Charles E. Lewis	2
Ludlow	28	Mr. C. W. Wicksted	2
Luttrell's, Mr. G. F.	24½	Mr. G. F. Luttrell	2
Meynell, The	50	Lord Waterpark	4
Middleton's, Lord	46½	Lord Middleton	4
Monmouthshire	47	Mr. F. C. Hanbury-Williams and Mr. J. A. Rolls	3
Morpeth	28	Mr. J. Blencowe Cookson	2
N. F. H. (New Forest)	50	Mr. G. A. E. Meyrick	3
Norfolk, West	46	Mr. Anthony Hamond	3
Northumberland and Berwickshire	49	Sir John Marjoribanks, Bart.	4
Notts, South	45	Mr. Launcelot Rolleston and Mr. P. H. Cooper	4
Oakley	56	A Committee	4
Oxfordshire, South	30	Earl of Macclesfield	2
Pembrokeshire	20	Mr. Chas. Hugh Allen	2
Pembrokeshire, South	27	Major Henry Leach	2
Penllergare	20	Mr. J. T. D. Llewelyn	2
Percy's, Earl	48½	Earl Percy	3
Portman's, Lord	49	Hon. W. H. B. Portman, M.P.	3
Portsmouth's, Earl of	60½	Earl of Portsmouth	4
Powell's, Mr. W. R. H.	32	Mr. W. R. H. Powell	2
Puckeridge	50	Mr. Robert Gosling	3
Pytchley	54	Mr. H. H. Langham	4
Pytchley, North	28	Earl Spencer	2
Quorn	55	Mr. John Coupland	5
Radnor, Earl of	42½	Earl of Radnor	3
Radnorshire and West Hereford	24	Lieut.-Col. R. H. Price	2
Rayer's, Mr.	32	Mr. W. C. Rayer	2
Rufford	50	Mr. Charles A. Egerton	4
Shrewsbury	30	Mr. R. L. Burton	2
Shropshire, North	29	Sir Vincent R. Corbet, Bt.	2
Sinnington	20	Mr. T. Parrington	2
Southdown	50	Mr. R. J. Streatfield	4
Southwold	54	Mr. F. Crowder	4
Staffordshire, North	60	Marquis of Stafford	3
Staffordshire, South	28	Major J. M. Browne	2
Stars of the West	21	Mr. Nicholas Snow	2
Stevenstone	33½	Lieut.-Col. the Hon. W. Trefusis	2
Suffolk	30	Mr. John Josselyn	3
Surrey, Old	43½	Mr. Edmund Byron	3
Surrey Union	43	Mr. J. B. Hankey	3
Sussex, East	30	Mr. Edward Frewen	2
Taunton Vale	25	Mr. Lionel Patton	2
Tedworth	50	Sir R. Graham, Bart.	4
Tickham	47	Mr. W. E. Rigden	3
Tivyside	26	Mr. J. R. Howell	2

Hunt.	No. of Couples.	Master.	Days a Week.
ENGLAND (continued).			
Tredegar's, Lord	27	Lord Tredegar	2
Tynedale	45	Mr. G. Fenwick	3
Ullswater	18	Mr. J. W. Marshall	3
United Pack	26½	Mr. J. Harris	2
Vale of Gwili	25	Mr. Ll. Lloyd Lloyd	2
Vale of Towy	17	Capt. M. P. Lloyd	2
Vale of White Horse	66	Mr. O. A. R. Hoare	4
Vine, The	42	Mr. W. W. B. Beach, M.P.	3
Warwickshire	60	Ld. Willoughby de Broke	4
Warwickshire, North	—	Mr. Richard Lant	3
Western	22	Mr. T. B. Bolitho	2
Whaddon Chase	40	Mr. W. Selby Lowndes	4
Wheatland	25	A Committee	2
Williams's, Mr. George	—	Mr. George Williams	3
Wilts, South and West	50	Lieut.-Col. W. Everett	4
Worcestershire	50	Mr. Frederick Ames	4
Wynn's, Sir W. W.	60	Sir W. W. Wynn, Bart.	3
York and Ainsty	—	Captain Slingsby	4
Zetland's, Earl of	56	Earl of Zetland	4
SCOTLAND.			
Berwickshire, North and East Lothian	40	Hon. R. B. Hamilton, M.P.	4
Buccleuch's, Duke of	54	Duke of Buccleuch	4
Dumfries-shire	30	Mr. John Johnstone	2
Eglinton's, Earl of	50	Earl of Eglinton and Winton	4
Fife	40	Col. Anstruther Thomson	3
Fife, West	22	Capt. G. C. Chepe	2
Forfarshire	32	Mr. P. A. W. Carnegie	2
Lanark and Renfrewshire	—	Col. Carrick Buchanan	2
Linlithgow and Stirlingshire	40	Major J. Wauchope	3
IRELAND.			
Carlow and Island	45	Mr. Robert Watson	3
Clonmult	20	Mr. Edmund Fitzgerald	2
Curraghmore	52½	Marquis of Waterford	4
Duhallow	50	Mr. S. Bruce	4
Galway County	47½	Mr. Burton R. P. Persse	4
Humble's, Sir J. Nugent	25	Sir J. Nugent Humble	2
Kildare	57	Mr. W. Forbes	4
Kilkenny	55	Colonel Chaplin	3
Limerick County	40	A Committee	3
Louth	35	Mr. W. de Salis Filgate	2
Meath	70	Mr. T. O. Trotter	5
Muskerry	31½	Capt. F. W. Wordley	2
Ormond and King's County	35½	Earl of Huntingdon	2
Queen's County	40	Mr. R. Hamilton Stubber	3
South Union	21	Mr. T. Walton Knolles	2
Tipperary	30	Capt. Macnaghten	2
United Hunt	50	A Committee	3
Westmeath	43	Mr. Montague Chapman	3
Wexford	45	Mr. D. V. Beatty	3

With regard to the kennelling accommodation which must be supplied for Foxhounds, and the management of the hounds themselves, no better authority can be quoted than the letters of Mr. Beckford, who, as far back as the year 1810, gave to the world opinions on the above subjects which have been regarded with respect ever since ; so much so, in fact, that they have formed the groundwork of a great many remarks on hounds which have never been credited to their real source. In the first place Mr. Beckford writes to a friend as follows on the subject of the kennel :—

" I would advise you to make it large enough at first, as an addition to it afterwards must spoil the appearance of it. I have been obliged to add to mine, which was built from a plan of my own, and intended, at first, for a pack of Beagles. As my feeding-yard is too small, I have endeavoured to remedy that defect as occasion required.

" I think two kennels absolutely necessary to the well-being of the hounds. When there is but one, it is seldom sweet ; and when cleaned out, the hounds, particularly in winter, suffer both whilst it is cleaning and as long as it remains wet afterwards. To be more clearly understood by you, I shall call one of these the hunting-kennel, by which I mean that kennel into which the hounds are drafted which are to hunt the next day. Used always to the same kennel, they will be drafted with little trouble ; they will answer to their names more readily, and you may count your hounds into the kennel with as much ease as a shepherd counts his sheep out of the fold.

" When the feeder first comes to the kennel in a morning, he should let out the hounds into the outer court ; at the same time opening the door of the hunting-kennel, lest want of rest, or bad weather, should incline them to go into it. The lodging-room should then be cleaned out, the doors and windows of it opened, the litter shaken up, and the whole kennel made sweet and clean before the hounds return to it again. The great court and the other kennels are not less to be attended to, nor should you pass over in silence any omission that is hurtful to your hounds.

" The floor of each lodging-room should be bricked, and sloped on both sides to run to the centre, with a gutter left to carry off the water, that when they are washed, they may be soon dry. If water should stand through any fault in the floor, it should be carefully mopped up ; for, as warmth is in the greatest degree necessary to hounds after work, so damps are equally prejudicial. You will think me, perhaps, too particular in these directions ; yet there can be no harm in your knowing what your servants ought to do ; as it is not impossible, but it may be sometimes necessary for you to see that it is done. In your military profession you are perfectly acquainted with the duty of a common soldier, and though you have no further business with the minutiæ of it, there is no doubt but you will still find the knowledge of them useful to you. Believe me, they may be useful here ; and you will pardon me, I hope, if I wish to see you a martinet in the kennel as well as in the field. Orders given without skill are seldom well obeyed, and where the master is either ignorant or inattentive, the servant will be idle.

" I also wish that, contrary to the usual practice in building kennels, you would have three doors—two in the front, and one in the back—the last to have a lattice-window in it, with a wooden shutter, which is constantly to be kept closed when the hounds are in, except in the summer, when it should be left open all the day. This door answers two very necessary purposes : it gives an opportunity of carrying out the straw when the lodging-room is cleaned, and as it is opposite to the window, will be a means to let in a thorough air, which will greatly contribute to the keeping of it sweet and wholesome. The other doors will be of use in drying the room, when the hounds are out, and as one is to be kept shut, and the other hooked back (allowing just room for a dog to pass), they are not liable to any objection. The great window in the centre should have a folding shutter, half, or the whole of which, may be shut at nights, according to the weather; and your kennels, by that means, may be kept warm or cool, just as you please to have them. The two great lodging-rooms are exactly alike, and as each has a court belonging to it, are distinct kennels, and are at the opposite ends of the building; in the centre of which is the boiling-house and feeding-yard, and on each side a lesser kennel, either for hounds that are drafted off, hounds that are sick or lame, or for any other purposes, as occasion may require. At the back of which, as they are but half the depth of the two great kennels, are places for coals, &c., for the use of the kennel. There is also a small building in the rear for hot bitches. The floors of the inner courts, like to those of the lodging-rooms, are bricked, and sloped to run to the centre, and a channel of water, brought in by a leaden pipe, runs through the middle of them. In the centre of each court is a well, large enough to dip a bucket to clean the kennels; this must be faced with stone, or it will be often out of repair. In the feeding-yard you must have a wooden cover.

"The benches, which must be open to let the urine through, should have hinges and hooks in the wall, that they may fold up, for the greater convenience of washing out the kennel; and they should be made as low as possible, that a tired hound may have no difficulty in jumping. Let me add, that the boiler should be of cast-iron.

"The rest of the kennel consists of a large court in front, which is also bricked, has a grass-court adjoining, and a little brook running through the middle of it. The earth is taken out of it, is thrown up into a mound, where the hounds in summer delight to sit. This court is planted round with trees, and has besides a lime-tree, and some horse-chestnut-trees near the middle of it, for the sake of shade. A high pale encloses the whole, part of which, to the height of about four feet, is close, the other open; the interstices are about two inches wide. The grass-court is pitched near the pale, to prevent the hounds from scratching out. If you cannot guess the intention of the posts I have in the court, they are to save the trees, to which the urinary salts are prejudicial. If they are at first backward in coming to them, bind some straw round the bottom, and rub it with galbanum. The brook in the grass-court may serve as a stew; your fish will be very safe.

"At the back of the kennel is a house, thatched and furzed up on both sides, big enough to contain at least a load of straw. Here should be a pit ready to receive the dung, and a gallows for the flesh. The gallows should have a thatched roof, and a circular board at the posts of it, to prevent vermin from climbing up.

"A stove, I believe, is made use of in some kennels; but where the feeder is a good one, a mop, properly used, will render it unnecessary. I have a little hay-rick in the grass-yard, which I think is of use to keep the hounds clean and fine in their coats; you will find them frequently rubbing themselves against it; the shade of it also is useful to them in summer. If ticks at any time should be troublesome in your kennel let the walls of it be well washed. If this does not destroy them, the walls should then be whitewashed.

"In the summer, when you do not hunt, one kennel will be sufficient; the other then may be for the young hounds, who should also have the grass court adjoining to it. It is best at that time of the year to keep them separate, and it prevents many accidents which otherwise might happen; nor should they be put together till the hunting season begins. If your hounds are very quarrelsome the feeder may sleep in a cot in the kennel adjoining; and if they are well chastised at the first quarrel, his voice will be sufficient to settle all their differences afterwards. Close to the door of the kennel let there be always a quantity of little switches, which three narrow boards nailed to one of the posts will easily contain.

"My kennel is close to the road-side, but it was unavoidable. This is the reason why my front pale is closed, and only the side ones open. It is a great fault; avoid it if you can, and your hounds will be the quieter.

"Upon looking over my letter I find I begin recommending, with Mr. Somervile, a high situation for the kennel, and afterwards talk of a brook running through the middle of it. I am afraid you will not be able to unite these two advantages, in which case there is no doubt that water should be preferred. The mound I have mentioned will answer all the purposes of an eminence. Besides, there should be movable stages on wheels for the hounds to lie upon. At any rate, however, let your soil be a dry one.

"You will think, perhaps, my lodging-rooms higher than is necessary. I know they are considerably higher than is usual, the intention of which is to give more air to the hounds; and I have not the least doubt but they are better for it. I will no longer persecute you with this unentertaining subject, but send you the plan of my own kennel, and take my leave of you."

It is customary for arrangements to be made by the master with neighbouring farmers and the occupiers of premises in the vicinity of the kennel, to "walk" young hounds from the time the latter leave their mothers, until they are old enough to be taken up and entered. On the subject of kennel management, feeding, and the subsequent entering of young hounds, Mr. Beckford has the following practical and judicious remarks:—

"If you find they take a dislike to any particular hound, the safest way will be to remove him, or it is very probable they will kill him at last. When a feeder hears the hounds quarrel in the kennel, he halloos to them, to stop them. He then goes in amongst them, and flogs every hound he can come near. How much more reasonable as well as more efficacious would it be were he to see which were the combatants before he speaks to them! Punishment would then fall, as it ought, on the guilty only. In all packs there are some hounds more quarrelsome than the rest, and it is to them we owe all the mischief that is done. If you find chastisement cannot quiet them, it may be prudent to break their holders; for since they are not necessary to them for the meat they have to eat, they are not likely to serve them in any good purpose.

"Young hounds should be fed twice a day, as they seldom take kindly at first to the kennel-meat, and the distemper is very apt to seize them at this time. It is better not to round them till they are thoroughly settled; nor should it be put off till the hot weather, for then they would bleed too much. If any of the dogs are thin over the back, or any more quarrelsome than the rest, it will be of use to cut them. I also spay such bitches as I think I shall not want to breed from; they are more useful, are stouter, and are always in better order. Besides, it is absolutely necessary if you hunt late in the spring, or your pack will be very short for want of it. It may be right to tell you that the latter operation does not always succeed; it will be necessary, therefore, to employ a skilful person, and one on whom you can depend; for if it is ill done, though they cannot have puppies, they will go to heat notwithstanding, of which I have known many instances; and that, I apprehend, would not answer at any rate.

"It without doubt is best, when you air your hounds, to take them out separately—the old ones one day, another day the young—but as I find your hounds are to have their whey at a distant dairy, on those days both old and young may be taken out together, observing only to take the young hounds in couples, when the old ones are along with them. Young hounds are always ready for any kind of mischief, and idleness might make even old ones too ready to join them in it. Besides, should they break off from the huntsman, the whipper-in is generally too ill-mounted at this season of the year easily to head them, to bring them back. Run no such risk. My hounds were near being spoiled by the mere accident of a horse's falling. The whipper-in was thrown from his horse. The horse ran away, and the whole pack followed him. A flock of sheep, which were at a little distance, took fright, began to run, and the hounds pursued them. The most vicious set on the rest, and several sheep were soon pulled down and killed. I mention this to show you what caution is necessary whilst the hounds are idle; for though the fall of the horse was not to be attributed to any fault of the man, yet had the old hounds been taken out by themselves, or had all the young ones been in couples, it is probable so common an accident would not have produced so extraordinary an event.

"It is now time to stoop them to a scent. You had better enter them at their own game—it will save you much trouble afterwards. Many dogs, I believe, like that scent best which they were first blooded to; but be that as it may, it is certainly most reasonable to use them to that which it is intended they should hunt. It may not be amiss, when they first begin to hunt, to put light collars on them. Young hounds may easily get out of their knowledge, and shy ones, after they have been much beaten, may not choose to return home. Collars, in that case, may prevent their being lost.

"You say you should like to see your young hounds run a trail scent. I have no doubt that you would be glad to see them run over an open down, where you could so easily observe their action and their speed. I do not think the doing of it once or twice could hurt your hounds, and yet, as a sportsman, I dare not recommend it to you. All that I shall say of it is that it is less bad than entering them at a hare. A cat is as good a trail as any; but on no account should any trail be used after your hounds are stooped to a scent.

"I know an old sportsman, a clergyman, who enters his young hounds first at a cat, which he drags along the ground for a mile or two, at the end of which he turns out a badger, first taking care to break his teeth. He takes out about two couple of old hounds along with the young ones to hold them on. He never enters his young hounds but at vermin: for he says, 'Train up a child in the way he should go, and when he is old he will not depart from it.'

"Such young hounds as are most riotous at first, generally speaking, I think, are best in the end. A gentleman in my neighbourhood was so thoroughly convinced of this, that he complained bitterly of a young Pointer to the person who gave it him, because he had done no mischief. However, meeting the same person some time after, he told him the dog he believed would prove a good one at last. 'How so,' replied his friend, 'it was but the other day that you said he was good for nothing.' 'True; but he has killed me nineteen turkeys since that.'

"Hounds, at their first entering, cannot be encouraged too much. When they become handy, love a scent, and begin to know what is right, it will be soon enough to chastise them for doing wrong, in which case one severe beating will save a deal of trouble. You should recommend to your whipper-in, when he flogs a hound, to make use of his voice as well as his whip, and let him remember that the smack of a whip is often as much use as the lash to one that has felt it. If any are very unsteady, it will not be amiss to send them out by themselves when the men go out to exercise their horses. If you have hares in plenty, let some be found sitting and turned out before them, and you will soon find the most riotous will not run after them. If they are to be made steady from deer, they should see them often, and they will not regard them; and if, after a probation of this kind, you turn out a cub before them, with some old hounds to lead them on, you may assure yourself they will not be unsteady long.

"I will now endeavour to describe what a good huntsman should be. He should be young, strong and active, bold and enterprising; fond of the diversion, and indefatigable in the pursuit of it; he should be sensible and good-tempered; he ought also to be sober; he should be exact, civil, and cleanly; he should be a good horseman and a good groom; his voice should be strong and clear, and he should have an eye so quick as to perceive which of his hounds carries the scent when all are running, and should have also an excellent ear, as always to distinguish the foremost hounds when he does not see them; he should be quiet, patient, and without conceit. Such are the excellences which constitute a good huntsman. He should not, however, be too fond of displaying them, till necessity calls them forth. He should let his hounds alone whilst they can hunt, and he should have genius to assist them when they cannot.

"With regard to the whipper-in, as you keep two of them—and no pack of Foxhounds is complete without—the first may be considered as a second huntsman, and should have nearly the same good qualities. It is necessary, besides, that he should be attentive and obedient to the huntsman, and as his horse will probably have most to do, the lighter he is the better; but if he is a good horseman, it will sufficiently overbalance such an objection. He must not be conceited. I had one formerly who, instead of stopping hounds as he ought, would try to kill a fox by himself. This fault is unpardonable; he should always maintain to the huntsman's halloo, and stop such hounds as divide from it. When stopped, he should get forward with them after the huntsman.

"You will perhaps find it more difficult to keep your whipper-in back than to get your huntsman forward—at least, I always have found it so. It is, however, necessary; nor will a good whipper-in leave a cover whilst a single hound remains in it. For this reason there should be two, one of which should be always forward with the huntsman. You cannot conceive the many ills that may happen to hounds that are left behind. I do not know that I can enumerate one-half of them; but this you may be certain of, that the keeping them together is the surest means to keep them steady. When left to themselves, they seldom refuse, I believe, any blood they can get; they acquire many bad habits; they become conceited (a terrible fault in any animal); and they learn to tye upon the scent (an unpardonable fault in a Foxhound). Besides this, they frequently get a trick of hunting by themselves, and they seldom are worth much afterwards. The lying out in the cold—perhaps the whole night—can do no good to their constitutions; nor will the being worried by Sheep-dogs or Mastiffs be of service to their bodies. All this, however, and much more, they are liable to. I believe I mentioned in my fourth letter that the straw-house door should be left open when any hounds are missing.

"A few riotous and determined hounds do a deal of mischief in a pack. Never, when you can avoid it, put them among the rest; let them be taken out by themselves and well chastised, and if you find them incorrigible, hang them. The common saying, 'Evil communications corrupt good manners,' holds good with regard to hounds; they are easily corrupted. The separating of the riotous ones from those which are steady answers many good purposes. It not only prevents the latter from getting the blood they should not, but it also prevents them from being overawed by the smacking of whips, which is too apt to obstruct drawing and going deep in cover. A couple of hounds which I received from a neighbour last year were hurtful to my pack. They had run with a pack of harriers; and, as I soon found, were never afterwards to be broken from hare. It was the beginning of the season; covers were thick, hares in plenty, and we seldom killed less than five or six in the morning. The pack at last got so much blood that they would hunt them as if they were designed to hunt nothing else. I parted with the two hounds; and the others, by proper management, are become as steady as they were before. You will remind me, perhaps, that they were draft-hounds. It is true, they were so; but they were three or four years' hunters—an age when they might be supposed to have known better. I advise you, unless a known good pack of hounds are to be disposed of, not to accept old hounds. I mention this to encourage the breeding of hounds, and as the likeliest means of getting a handsome, good, and steady pack. Though I give you this advice, it is true I have accepted draft-hounds myself, and some have been very good: but they were the gift of a friend, mentioned by me in a former letter; and, unless you meet with such another, old hounds will not prove worthy your acceptance—they never can be very good, and may bring vices along with them, to spoil your pack. If old hounds are unsteady, it may not be in your power to make them otherwise; and I can assure you from experience that an unsteady old hound will give you more trouble than all your young ones. The latter will at least stop; but an obstinate old hound will frequently run mute, if he finds he can run no other way. Besides, old hounds, that are unacquainted with your people, will not readily hunt for them as they ought; and such as were steady in their own pack may become unsteady in yours.

"You desire to know what kind of hound I would recommend. As you mention not for any particular chase or country, I understand you generally; and shall answer that I most approve of hounds of the middle size. I believe all animals of that description are strongest, and best able to endure fatigue. In the height as well as the colour of the hounds, most sportsmen have their prejudices; but in their shape at least, I think they must all agree. I know sportsmen who boldly affirm that a small hound will oftentimes beat a large one —that he will climb hills better, and go through cover quicker; whilst others are not less ready to assert that a large hound will make his way in any country, will get better through the dirt than a small one, and that no fence, however high, can stop him. You have now three opinions, and I advise you to adopt that which suits your country best. There is, however, a certain size best adapted for business, which I take to be that between the two extremes; and I will venture to say that such hounds will not suffer themselves to be disgraced in any country. Somerville, I find, is of the same opinion:—

> "'But here a mean
> Observe, nor the large hounds prefer, of size
> Gigantick; he in the thick-woven covert
> Painfully tugs, or in the thorny brake
> Torn and embarrassed bleeds. But if too small,
> The pigmy brood in every furrow swims;
> Moiled in the clogging clay, panting they lag
> Behind inglorious; or else shivering creep,
> Benumbed and faint, beneath the shelt'ring thorn.
> For hounds of middle size, active and strong,
> Will better answer all thy various ends,
> And crown thy pleasing labours with success.'

"I perfectly agree with you, that, to look well, they should be all nearly of a size; and I even think they should all look of the same family :—

> "'Facies non omnibus una,
> Nec diversa tamen, qualem decet esse sororum.'

If handsome withal, they are then perfect. With their being sizable, what Somerville says is so much in your own way that I shall send it to you :—

> "'As some brave captain, curious and exact,
> By his fixed standard forms in equal ranks
> His gay battalion, as one man they move
> Step after step, their size the same, their arms
> Far gleaming, dart the same united blaze :
> Reviewing generals his merit own ;
> How regular ! how just ! and all his cares
> Are well repaid, if mighty George approve.
> So model thou thy pack, if honour touch
> Thy gen'rous soul, and the world's just applause.'

"There are necessary points in the shape of a hound which ought always to be attended to by a sportsman; for if he is not of a perfect symmetry, he will neither run fast nor bear much work. He has much to undergo, and should have strength proportioned to it. Let his legs be straight as arrows; his feet round, and not too large; his chest deep, and back broad; his head small; his neck thin; his tail thick and brushy, if he carries it well, so much the better. This last point, however trifling it may appear to you, gave rise to a very odd question. A gentleman (not much acquainted with hounds), as we were hunting together the other day, said, 'I observe, sir, that some of your dogs' tails stand up and some hang down; pray, sir, which do you reckon the best hounds?' Such young hounds as are out at the elbows, and such as are weak from the knee to the foot, should never be taken into the pack.

"I find that I have mentioned a small head as one of the necessary points about a hound. You will please to understand it as relative to beauty only; for as to goodness, I believe large-headed hounds are no way inferior. Somerville, in his description of a perfect hound, makes no mention of the head, leaving the size of it to Phidias to determine; he therefore must have thought it of very little consequence. I send you his words.

> "'See there with count'nance blythe,
> And with a courtly grin, the fawning hound
> Salutes thee cow'ring, his wide op'ning nose
> Upwards he curls, and his large sloe-black eyes
> Melt in soft blandishments and humble joy ;
> His glossy skin, or yellow-pied or blue,
> In lights or shades by Nature's pencil drawn,
> Reflects the various tints ; his ears and legs
> Flecked here and there, in gay enamelled pride,
> Rival the speckled pard; his rush-grown tail
> O'er his broad back bends in an ample arch ;
> On shoulders clean, upright and firm he stands ;
> His round cat foot, straight hams, and wide-spread thighs,
> And his low-dropping chest, confess his speed,

His strength, his wind, or on the steepy hill,
Or far extended plain; in every part
So well proportioned, that the nicer skill
Of Phidias himself can't blame thy choice.
Of such compose thy pack.'

"The colour I think the least material of all; and I think with our friend Foote, that a good dog, like a good candidate, cannot be of a bad colour.

"A good feeder is an essential part of your establishment. Let him be young and active, and have the reputation, at least, of not disliking work; he should be good-tempered, for the sake of the animals entrusted to his care, and who, however they may be treated by him, cannot complain. He should be one who will strictly obey any orders you may give, as well with regard to the management as to the breeding of the hounds, and should not be solely under the direction of your huntsman. It is true I have seen it otherwise: I have known a pack of hounds belong, as it were, entirely to the huntsman, a stable of horses belong to the groom, whilst the master had little more power in the direction of either than a perfect stranger. This you will not suffer.

"I shall now take notice of that part of the management of hounds in the kennel which concerns the huntsman as well as the feeder. Your huntsman must always attend the feeding of the hounds, which should be drafted according to the condition they are in. In all packs some hounds will feed better than others; some there are that will do with less meat, and it requires a nice eye and great attention to keep them all in good flesh—it is what distinguishes a good kennel-huntsman, and has its merit. It is seldom, I think, that huntsmen give this particular all the attention it deserves; they feed their hounds in too great a hurry, and not often, I believe, take the trouble of casting their eye over them before they begin; and yet to distinguish, with any nicety, the order a pack of hounds are in, and the different degrees of it, is surely no easy task, and to be done well requires no small degree of circumspection. You had better not expect your huntsman to be very exact; where precision is required he will most probably fail.

"When I am present myself, I make several drafts. When my huntsman feeds them he calls them all over by their names, letting in each hound as he is called; it has its use—it uses them to their names, and teaches them to be obedient. Were it not for this, I should disapprove of it entirely, since it certainly requires more coolness and deliberation to distinguish with precision which are best entitled to precedence, than this method of feeding will admit of, and, unless flesh is in great plenty, those that are called in last may not have a taste of it. To prevent this inconvenience, such as are low in flesh had better, I think, be all drafted off into a separate kennel; by this means, the hounds that require flesh will have an equal share of it. If any are much poorer than the rest, they should be fed again—such hounds cannot be fed too often. If any in the pack are too fat, they should be drafted off, and not suffered to fill themselves; the others should eat what they will of the meat. The days my hounds have greens or sulphur, they generally are let in all together, and such as require flesh have it given to them afterwards. Having a good kennel-huntsman, it is not often I take this trouble; yet I seldom go into my kennel but I give myself the pleasure of seeing such hounds fed as appear to me to be in want of it. I have been told that in one kennel in particular the hounds are under such excellent management that they constantly are fed with the door of the feeding-yard open, and the rough nature of the Foxhound is changed into so much politeness that he waits at the door till he is invited in, and, what perhaps is not less extraordinary, he comes out again, whether he has satisfied his hunger or not, the moment he is desired— the effect of severe discipline. But since this is not absolutely necessary, and hounds may be good without it—and since I well know your other amusements will not permit you to attend to all this manœuvring—I would by no means wish you to give such power to your huntsman. The business would be injudiciously done, and most probably would not answer your expectations. The hound would be tormented *mal à propos*—an animal so little deserving it from our hands that I should be sorry to disturb his hours of repose by unnecessary severity. You will perceive it is a nice affair, and I assure you I know no huntsman who is equal to it. The gentleman who has carried this matter to its utmost perfection has attended to it regularly himself, has constantly acted on fixed principles, from which he has never deviated; and I believe has succeeded to the very utmost of his wishes. All hounds (and more especially young ones) should be called over often in the kennel, and most huntsmen practise this lesson as they feed their hounds. They flog them while they feed them, and if they have not always a bellyful one way, they seldom fail to have it the other. It is not, however, my intention to oppose so general a practice, in which there may be some utility; I shall only observe that it should be used with discretion, lest the whip should fall heavily in the kennel on such as never deserved it in the field.

"My hounds are generally fed about eleven o'clock; and if I am present myself I take the same opportunity to make my draft for the next day's hunting. I seldom, when I can help it, leave this to my huntsman; though it is necessary he should be present when the draft is made, that he may know what hounds he has out.

"It is a bad custom to use hounds to the boiling-house, as it is apt to make them nice, and may prevent them from ever eating the kennel-meat. What they have should always be given them in the feeding-yard, and for the same reason, though it should be flesh, it is better it should have some meal mixed with it.

"If your hounds are low in flesh and have far to go to cover, they may all have a little thin lap again in the evening; but this should never be done if you hunt early. Hounds, I think, should be sharp-set before hunting; they run the better for it."

So much having been quoted from the work of the greatest and most practical writer upon the management of Foxhounds which the world has hitherto produced, any additional remarks of our own would be superfluous. We therefore now conclude this article on Foxhounds by giving a simple scale of points, after which we pass on to a class of dogs which renders material assistance to hunting men when their fox has gone to earth.

SCALE OF POINTS FOR JUDGING FOXHOUNDS.

	Value.
Head and throat	10
Chest	5
Body and loins	10
Legs and feet	15
Stern	5
General appearance	5
	50

CHAPTER XXXVII.

THE FOX-TERRIER.

IT is an indisputable fact that since the year 1875 the number of Fox-terriers exhibited at our shows has steadily increased. The breed having much to recommend it in the way of appearance, and not being of the impetuous disposition which is so characteristic of the modern Bull-terrier, there is no wonder that it should have become fashionable, amongst the fair sex especially.

Unfortunately, at its first appearance, almost anything in the shape of a Terrier which was hound-marked, and which had its tail removed, was received by the uninitiated as a Fox-terrier. Dog shows have, however, taught people differently, and the worst class of dog which used to be palmed off as a Fox-terrier has almost disappeared. It is nevertheless by no means to be taken for granted that the breed has shaken down into one regular even type. There are at least two principal schools of breeders, holding entirely antagonistic views concerning the class of dog which they want to see produced, and these two schools are in their turn subdivided into a number of smaller factions, who differ in certain details from the party to which they claim to belong.

Before proceeding to trace out the history of the modern Fox-terrier, and remark upon the differences of opinion which exist between his main supporters, we propose giving the remarks of several gentlemen who, being recognised authorities, have kindly given us the result of their researches. Foremost is Mr. J. A. Doyle, of Crickhowell, whose kindness in supplying us with so much valuable information requires our most cordial acknowledgment.

The antiquity and the precise origin of the modern Fox-terrier are involved in considerable obscurity, and I cannot pretend to do more than to point out a few scattered facts bearing on the subject. But before I approach that question it would be well to brush away certain fallacies on this matter which have, I believe, exercised a very deleterious effect on the breed of Fox-terriers. We are often told that the Fox-terrier is not a pure breed at all, but a manufacture—a compound of divers elements. Now, there is just enough of truth in this theory to make it dangerous. It is true enough that a large proportion of the dogs whom we see on the show benches, many of them more or less true Fox-terriers in outward appearance, are produced by ingenious, or more often by lucky crosses. It is probably true that the very best of them are not wholly free from alien crosses of Beagle and Bull-terrier. But I feel sure that a careful analysis and investigation of pedigrees will prove that the best Fox-terriers are those which for many generations have been bred from dogs of one definite type, and in whose pedigrees there is as little alloy as possible. To work out this in full would oblige me to anticipate what will come in more fittingly when I proceed to sketch the various families into which Fox-terriers are divided.

Whether the Fox-terrier was in his origin a cross-bred or made-up dog is another question, and a far harder one to answer. But even if he be so, that fact does not take him out of the category of pure breeds. What is the modern Pointer but a development of the old Spanish Pointer by judicious infusions of Foxhound blood? What is the Setter but a gradual development of the Field Spaniel by crosses calculated to give size and ranging power? Where are we to find a certainly pure breed of dog, excepting perhaps the Bull-dog and Mastiff? Yet who would deny the claim of the Laverack Setter or the Sefton Pointer to be now a pure, distinct, and unmanufactured breed? I make just the same claim for the modern Belvoir Terriers, and for others that can trace back to strains with a definite and well-established type. The purity of blood may not be of so high a degree, but it is the same in kind.

One argument often used by those who contend that the Fox-terrier is a manufactured dog is the extreme diversity of type, which baffles the efforts of breeders. To my mind this simply proves that there are an immense number of dogs about outwardly resembling Fox-terriers, but without any hereditary claim to the name, and incapable of transmitting even that amount of resemblance which they themselves possess. That breeders should fail, as long as they work with such materials, is but natural. I see no reason to think that if breeders will cultivate hereditary purity of type, and carefully exclude all impure blood, however tempting its immediate results may be, they will find more diversity in Fox-terriers than in any other kind of stock. Another cause of diversity, no doubt, is the system, or rather the no-system, on which Fox-terriers have been bred. So many are bred, and they are in so many hands, and multiply so rapidly, that impure blood has great opportunities of circulating. Moreover, no breed of animal has ever attained a high degree of uniformity and fixity of type, except through the operations of a few breeders, who have worked steadily and patiently from generation to generation with a definite goal in view. No one has yet done for Fox-terriers what two generations of Booths did for Shorthorns; what Edward Laverack did for Setters. They have for the most part been bred by men who had no real knowledge of the material with which they were working, and no aim beyond an immediate result. Even those who have bred carefully, have kept the control of their materials in their own hands for many generations together. Can we wonder that the result has not been wholly satisfactory?

The precise antiquity of the Fox-terrier is, as I have said, a question somewhat hard to solve. There is not, as far as I know, any definite evidence of the existence of the present breed earlier than the memory of men yet living. At the same time there is ample evidence for the existence of Terriers used for the same purposes as the modern Fox-terrier, and it is far from improbable that some of them closely resembled the present breed. For the early existence of Terriers we have the often-quoted evidence of Dr. Keys, or as he preferred to call himself, after the fashion of the day, Caius. In his great work on dogs, already alluded to, he describes *Terrarii*, small dogs used for chasing the lesser kinds of vermin and pursuing them underground. But of the shape and appearance of these dogs, and whether they were rough or smooth, he tells us nothing. Later writers who deal with field sports throw but little light on the subject. They occasionally refer to Terriers and their work, but none give us any idea of the external characteristics of the breed. One writer, indeed, tells us that a cross between a Mastiff and a Beagle makes an excellent Terrier! Another writer, somewhat later, describes the Terrier as a kind of mongrel Greyhound. It is, however, clear that the Terrier was well recognised as a sporting dog. Thus Gilpin, in his description of the New Forest, gives an account, evidently taken from some contemporary writer, of an eccentric Hampshire squire, in the seventeenth century, whose hall was inhabited by his hounds, Spaniels, and Terriers; and by the manner in which the last are spoken of, it is clear that they were part of a country gentleman's sporting establishment. There is even more definite evidence that in the last century

Terriers were bred with some care. In a memoir of the well-known Yorkshire squire, Colonel Thornton, who flourished in the latter half of the century, and whose tastes embraced every department of sport, we read of a Terrier belonging to him called Pitch, "from whom are descended most of the white Terriers in this kingdom." It is furthermore recorded that the Colonel paid special attention to his breed of Terriers. In the sporting works of the early part of the century we begin to find more definite and detailed accounts of the Terrier. The author of "The Sportsman's Cabinet" gives a minute account of the peculiarities and working capacities of the Terrier. There were, he tells us, two breeds; the one wire-haired, larger, more powerful, and harder bitten; the other smooth-haired and smaller, with more style. The former, he tells us, were white, with spots, the latter black-and-tan; the latter colour apparently predominating. An accompanying print represents two Terriers at work, one light coloured, the other dark, both prick-eared. The same writer tells us that it was customary to take out two Terriers with a pack of hounds, a larger and a smaller one—the latter as an ultimate resort, if the earth were too narrow to admit the bigger dog. That even at this time Terriers were bred with some care and that certain strains were highly valued, is shown by the recorded fact that a litter of seven pups was sold for twenty-one guineas—a good price even in these days—and that a full-grown dog on one occasion fetched twenty guineas. The real truth I imagine to be, that there was no one definite and well-established type of Terrier throughout the kingdom, but that here and there some squire or huntsman, who chanced to be an enthusiast on the point, cherished a particular strain, and to a certain extent developed a type for himself. Many a manor-house and farmstead in Devonshire and Yorkshire we may be sure had its three brace of Terriers, as well deserving of immortality as the heroes of Charlieshope, though not as fortunate in their historian. Pictures, unhappily, do not throw much light on the matter. In old engravings we sometimes meet with a pair of rough-looking mongrels as the companions of a huntsman or earth-stopper, but, unhappily, excepting the one to which I referred above, none give a sufficiently detailed idea to be of any value for the history of the breed. One exception indeed there is, and that a somewhat curious one: a picture at Vienna by Hamilton, a Dutch painter who lived early in the last century, contains a composition of fruit and flowers, with a white wire-haired Terrier in the foreground. The dog has all the characteristics of the modern show Terrier, with the one exception of a pink nose. He has apparently a good hard coat, and perfect drop ears. The shape of his head, the expression of his face, and his whole attitude and outline, are thoroughly characteristic and Terrier-like. The similarity is the more remarkable since there is, as we shall see, pretty good evidence that the modern wire-haired Terrier is the result of a distinct and well-ascertained cross in recent times. Hamilton ranks among Dutch painters; his name, however, suggests an English connection, and I certainly have never met with a Terrier, either in the paintings of Snyders or any of his countrymen.

As to the modern Fox-terrier, his history has been very clearly set forth in two articles published some while ago in the late *Country* newspaper, by a well-known writer, under the sobriquet of "Peeping Tom." He tells us, on the authority of Mr. Gibson, one of the best-known breeders of Terriers, that nearly forty years ago there were dogs in the Midlands possessing all the characteristics of the modern show Terrier. I may add that I have myself heard Mr. Gibson make the same statement. I may further illustrate this by mentioning that two old hunting men made, quite independently, the same criticism on a well-known modern show Terrier—*i.e.*, that she was exactly the same stamp as they remembered in their boyhood. The bitch in question was Vexer, by Venture, out of Fussy, all names well known in show annals. Now, it may be impossible to trace the origin of the modern show Terrier to these dogs in each particular instance. But when we know that a well-recognised breed existed some forty years ago, and that dogs are now found possessing precisely the same characteristics, it is hardly too much to assume that the breed has gone on in direct succession. It is worth notice that many of these old Terriers were black-and-tan. The sire of Old Trap, for example, was a black-and-tan dog; yet, I have been assured on good authority, a true Fox-terrier. I have certainly found, myself, that breeding closely to the Old Trap blood is apt to produce heavy markings. Mr. Gibson also once told me that he had got a litter of black-and-tan pups by Trap out of a white bitch. Indeed, I have little doubt that any enthusiast who took the trouble might, if he cared, re-establish the old black-and-tan breed by careful selection. But, of course, as every one knows, the white dog is the most easily seen, and therefore far the best for cover shooting and general purposes, and so, by the process of "survival of the fittest," he has extinguished the old black-and-tan type. The writer in the journal to whom I before referred mentions a picture of one of these black-and-tan dogs, in which he is represented as a thorough Terrier, according to modern notions, in every respect save colour. The tradition of his exploits with a badger has also survived. I may mention that I have actually seen a black-and-tan Terrier in the flesh to whom the same description would apply. He, I was assured, came from a distinct black-and-tan strain now almost extinct.

I may mention one fact, as illustrating strongly to my mind the connection between the modern show Terrier and the kennel Terrier of twenty or thirty years ago. Every one who is familiar with modern show Terriers knows Mr. Burbidge's Fan. A more thorough Terrier, in expression and general appearance, it would be impossible to find. Her pedigree goes back for several generations through well-recognised lines, chiefly to the kennel Terriers of the Grove hounds. Yet, except Old Jock, who, as is well known, was bred at the Rufford kennels, there is not a single show dog in her pedigree. This, I think, makes pretty strongly for my view that the modern show Fox-terrier (when good) owes his origin, not, as some would have us believe, to ingeniously-welded crosses of Bull-terrier, Beagle, &c., but to the old kennel Terrier of thirty years back. No doubt fair imitations of Terriers may be produced by the "manufacturing" process, but no man can hope to breed from them with success unless he expects the laws of Nature to be suspended for his special benefit.

I will now pass from the region of speculation to that of actual fact, and deal with the show Terrier as we have known him during the last ten or twelve years—in fact, since shows became an institution. Before going into details, however, it may be as well to say a few words as to the general character of show Terriers and the changes which they have undergone. At the outset of dog shows the prize winners were simply the best-looking kennel Terriers. The Grove contributed Old Jock and Grove Nettle, the Oakley Old Trap, and the Quorn Psyche. Very soon, however, the demand outran the supply. Fox-terriers became the fashion, and suffered accordingly. People were found ready to give £30 or £40, and even more, for actual or possible prize-winners, and pups with any pretence to merit were bought up greedily. The result was that the market was speedily filled with dogs who had no claim whatever to the title of Fox-terriers. This soon made itself felt on the show benches. Dogs either far too fine, or light of bone, or far too heavy for work, won prizes, and multiplied their kind. A well-marked head was regarded as a far more important point than such trifles as feet and coat. All definiteness of type was lost. One year toys reigned supreme, next season giants had their day. The true Terrier seemed in danger of extinction, and was probably only preserved by one or two persons who went on breeding the right type patiently with very little immediate reward.

It would be, perhaps, rather perilous to go into details as to the modern show dogs, but few will deny that the last few years have seen a considerable improvement. Not only are most of our prize-winners genuine working Terriers, in appearance and character, but they also most of them derive their good qualities from certain definite and well-established strains. We may therefore reasonably hope that breeders are at length on the right tack, and that we may look for a marked improvement during the next few years.

I propose now to take a survey of the leading families of show Terriers. But before I do so I must say a word about two or three special groups of Terriers somewhat antecedent to show days. First of all, there is one type which has contributed something, though not a great deal, to our stock of prize-winners. This is the old Cheshire or Shropshire Terrier. By far the most important strain of this sort was that belonging to Domville Poole, a well-known Shropshire squire. His kennel was in its prime some five-and-thirty years ago. Where he obtained his original blood from I have never been able to learn. They were bred with great care, and had at one time reached such uniformity of type that, as I was told by a friend of Mr. Poole's, a stranger often failed to distinguish one dog from another. This ought to be at once a warning and an encouragement to modern breeders. At one time Mr. Poole had about twenty couples of them, and was painted with his pack around him. At a later period, within my own memory, they had been reduced to about half a dozen, partly from their pugnacity and frequent deadly battles, partly, as Mr. Poole himself believed, from too persistent adherence to his own blood. Their pluck was most severely tested, and if a young one fell short in that respect, he was soon sentenced to the horse-pond. This pluck was undoubtedly originally obtained from a Bull-dog source, and I suspect occasionally replenished in the same fashion, and as a natural consequence, pink noses and prick and tulip ears found their way in. At the same time Mr. Poole always endeavoured to keep out those features; in fact, he tried to get his dogs with as much as possible of the exterior of pure Fox-terriers and the internal temper and character of the Bull-terrier. I do not know whether any of his Terriers ever ran with hounds. If they did I should think they must often have been too savage for their work, and inclined to close with and murder their fox, instead of snapping at and bolting it. And I would here remark that the Bull-terrier cross affects the whole temper and character as much as his external appearance. It does not, as far as my experience goes, affect a dog's nose, as might be expected; indeed, some of the keenest hunters I have known have been dogs with a strong Bull cross. *But it tends to make him mute instead of noisy, and more quarrelsome than belongs to the true Fox-terrier's character. Nor is the pluck of a Bull-terrier and a Fox-terrier wholly identical.* The former is stoically indifferent to pain: the latter feels punishment, yet returns to the charge again from sheer keenness and love of sport.

The Cheshire Terriers (or Shropshire, for the sorts were identical), were perhaps best known to the world through the kennel of Mr. Stevenson of Chester, whose blood was mainly obtained from Mr. Poole. In the early days he won a few prizes, but for the most part contented himself with breeding game useful dogs, for which he always found a ready market. Champion Tartar, whom I shall speak of again, was of his blood, and the late Mr. Arrowsmith, who won a good many prizes at Yorkshire shows, built up his kennel from a bitch of Mr. Stevenson's breed. Another well-known Shropshire kennel was Lord Hill's. His dogs were, I think, rather smaller and neater than Mr. Poole's, but of the same stamp. In former days I owned a Shropshire Terrier bred by Mr. Stevenson from Mr. Poole's blood, and he might serve as a good type of the sort. He weighed just 15 lb. when in good condition, and though he showed a little Bull in the head, was not otherwise deficient in Terrier character.

For his temper and mode of work he was a thorough Terrier, except that he was rather more teachable than is usual. His Bull-terrier descent showed itself chiefly in the extreme fineness of his ears. I have often seen him come out of a gorse covert with his ears raining blood, yet always ready for another go-in. One noticeable feature about these dogs was the almost entire absence of black-and-tan markings. I myself have seen a good many, and never saw one so marked. One I have seen with that sort of dark brindle which we sometimes find in the Belvoir blood, but as a rule if they were marked at all it was with a light lemon-tan. I do not know whether Lille, who for many years reigned supreme at Birmingham, had any Shropshire blood in her, but her appearance certainly suggested it. I well remember a Shropshire friend of mine pointing her out to me at Birmingham as the stamp that he had been brought up to admire.

The best known, however, of these dogs, and the only one that left his mark definitely among show Terriers, was old Tartar. He was bred by Mr. Stevenson, from Mr. Poole's blood (indeed, he was on his sire's side half brother to my old dog, whom I described). After winning some prizes he passed into the hands of Mr. Wootton for £40, a price which in those days created universal astonishment. Subsequently he was bought by the Hon. T. W. Fitzwilliam, who at that time also owned Jock. Tartar had a brilliant show career, and succeeded one year at Birmingham in beating his hitherto invincible kennel companion, Jock. Tartar was a short, thick-set dog, rather broad in chest, with extraordinary legs and feet, and wonderful muscle everywhere. At the same time he unquestionably showed Bull, not only in his head, but also in his loins and thighs, where the muscle stood out in bosses, a feature never found in the true Terrier. At the stud he was chiefly notable as the sire of Tyke and Trumps, both begotten from daughters of Jock. The former was the offspring of that good bitch, Nectar, and was in point of gameness a worthy son of Tartar. As a show dog he was fairly successful, and his name is to be found in more than one good pedigree. Tartar's chief claim to fame as a sire, however, rests on Tyke. As with his father, disputes ran high over him, and even in the very zenith of his show career he was roundly denounced by some as a Bull-terrier. Unlike his sire, he was a dog of remarkable style and quality, though it could not be denied that his fine coat, the build of his hind-quarters, and a patch on one cheek, which admirers called hound-tan, and enemies brindle, bewrayed his origin. He in his turn begot that sterling good bitch, Natty, and a very neat dog, Little Jim, in whom his sire's good and bad characteristics seemed to be intensified. Another fair son of Tyke was Mr. Procter's Tester. Indeed, it is probable that Tyke had a brilliant career before him as a sire, when he met with an untimely end in a fight, not long after he had become the property of Mr. Gibson of Brokenhurst at the long price of £120.

To sum up, I should say that looking at the many good qualities of the Shropshire blood, especially of the Tartar family, there is no objection to a slight infusion of it. But it needs to be handled gingerly, and a second cross of it would be almost sure to bring out objectionable peculiarities.

I now come to an important branch of my subject, the consideration, namely, of what I may for convenience call the Midland Terriers, from whom, as I believe, our best show blood is derived. The three packs with which this sort has been specially connected are the Belvoir, the Grove, and Lord Middleton's. An admirable account of these was given in the *Country* by the writer to whom I have before referred. Two of these packs, the Grove and Lord Middleton's, had for their huntsmen members of the Morgan family, a race as prolific in huntsmen as the Napiers have been in soldiers. Consequently there have been, I believe, frequent exchanges of Terrier blood between the two kennels. The kennel, however, which has specially made a point of its

Terriers is the Belvoir. Their pedigrees can be traced back in a direct line for more than thirty years, and though of course it would be impossible to get a detailed account of all the links, it is clear that there were dogs among them who would have held their own well in modern shows. As to their working capacities it is needless to dwell on them. The very fact of a particular strain being kept and cherished by more than one huntsman is evidence enough of its merits on that point. At the same time, I have my doubts whether they have been kept absolutely free from all introduction of Bull-terrier blood. At least I know that some twelve years ago prick-ears and pink noses were not wholly unknown among them; and I have been told that such traits do even now make their appearance occasionally. Besides these three packs, there are others that have had good Terriers. The Brocklesby had, I believe, some; and their Tartar deserves special mention as the grandsire of that good dog Jester II. Beers too, the Duke of Grafton's huntsman, specially prided himself on his Terriers, and had some good ones, partly, I believe, of the Belvoir blood. As an evidence of the value of the blood, especially for working purposes, I have been assured on good authority that he could always get £10 for a young dog, entered to work, before the present rage for Fox-terriers. Another who paid special attention to his Terriers was Whitmore, the Hon. Mark Rolle's huntsman. He, like Beers, got some of his blood from the Grove; and his Grip, so bred, was the sire of Foiler, and, through him, the ancestor of many of our best Terriers.

Just as thoroughbred horses are often grouped into three families, headed by the Derby Arabian, the Byerley Turk, and the Godolphin Arabian—the Shem, Ham, and Japhet of the Turf, as they have been called—so we may conveniently classify Fox-terriers under the families of Jock, Trap, and Belvoir Joe. That, at least, will practically include nearly all of any note. Other strains there are, notably that of Old Foiler, which have been of value, but they are almost extinct in the male line, and the division I propose will certainly include nineteen-twentieths of the really good dogs. First, if not in merit at least in the widespread nature of his influence, comes Old Jock. My own recollections of the old dog date from his declining days; but I can well believe what I have often heard alleged, that he has never had a superior, and scarcely an equal. My own impression, based on the recollection of what he was when I saw him in his wane at Birmingham show in 1867 is that Buffett, Bloom, Olive, and perhaps Hornet and Fussy, are the only Terriers since that could have held their own with him. At the stud he can hardly be said to have got anything of the same class as himself; still, he had a goodly list of winners among his progeny, and his blood has come out with wonderful success through his daughters. In fact, Jock bitches have been to Terrier breeders what Touchstone mares have been to the breeders of racehorses. The best, perhaps, of Jock's, as a show dog, was his namesake, Jock II., the Birmingham winner in 1872. He was a son of that grand bitch, Grove Nettle; at least, he was said to be so. I have heard, however, doubts thrown on this, and certainly Jock II.'s utter failure as a stud dog throws some suspicion on his pedigree. Another good son of Jock was Vassal, who won at Birmingham in 1866. His chief claim to celebrity as a stud dog rested on Gadfly. Gadfly was himself far from a show dog; but he begot a good many winners, including that most unworthy recipient of high honours, Rivet. Gadfly, I should add, was an undoubted son of Grove Nettle, so it can be no matter for surprise that his name often occurs in a good pedigree. Vassal's dam was, I believe, of unknown pedigree; but I have been told by one who knew her that she was a rather weedy bitch, deficient in coat, with a good deal of English Terrier character. This may account for certain objectionable peculiarities that have from time to time shown themselves in the descendants of Gadfly—prick-ears and fine coats among them. One special merit of the Gadfly blood is its great gameness. Indeed, though Jock himself bore a doubtful character in this respect, his descendants have been as a rule conspicuous for pluck. The son on whom old Jock's mantle really fell, at least as a sire, was Jester. His dam, Cottingham Nettle, was herself said to be a daughter of Old Jock. This, if true, strikingly illustrates the capacity of the blood to bear in-breeding, a capacity of which I shall have more to say hereafter. Jester himself was never shown, owing to an accident, and I should hardly imagine that he had the style and quality needful for a show dog. His fame as a stud dog was established by his two daughters, Satire and XL. Satire was, as I have said, out of a bitch of Mr. Stevenson's blood, and, besides winning many prizes, she was the dam of good ones. XL was seldom shown; but most good judges are agreed in placing her among the best ever seen. She was begotten from a bitch by old Tyrant, dam by Jock, and as Tyrant himself was a grandson of Jock, this is a pretty good comment on the lengths to which in-breeding may safely be carried. XL herself, whether from ill-luck or injudicious mating, never bred anything of any conspicuous merit. Of Jester's sons, by far the most noted was Jester II., from a bitch combining the Brocklesby and Lord Middleton's blood. His Terrier-like character, marred by a coarse head and ill-carried ears, is too fresh in the memory of the public to need description. As a stud dog, his best success has been with that sterling good bitch Akely Nettle. Her dam was a granddaughter of Old Jester, another illustration of the aptitude of the blood for in-breeding.

There is yet another son of Jock's that deserves mention, Mr. Shirley's Jack, a Birmingham winner in 1867. He passed into Mr. Gibson's hands, but was unluckily lost before he had time to prove his full merits as a sire. His memory, however, was preserved at Brokenhurst, by his daughter Judy, the dam of Moss, from whom are descended a host of good dogs, including Buffett and Bloomer, and thus, through two lines, Bloom.

Passing to Jock's daughters, unquestionably the most distinguished of them was Nectar. She was a genuine daughter—and the only one by Jock—of Grove Nettle. She was, however, a good deal lighter than her dam, and would hardly have had substance enough to satisfy most judges now-a-days. Still she would always have stood high. She was, in her turn, the dam of several good though of no first-class dogs. A more distinguished daughter of old Jock, at least as a matron, was Cottingham Nettle, the dam, by different dogs, of Jester, Willie, and Brokenhurst Nettle; the latter, in her turn, the dam of Flinger, Flasher, Brokenhurst Sting, and Boxer. Besides these we shall, in the course of our genealogical survey, come across other successful daughters of Old Jock. I have already noticed the special fitness of this blood for in-breeding, and I will mention a few more instances. Tyrant was out of a Jock bitch. His son, Sam, was also out of a Jock bitch. Sam's three best children, setting aside Venture—Myrtle, Willie, and Tickler—were all out of Jock bitches. Again, Nectar, when put to Tyke, produced young Tyke, a dog of remarkable quality; while to Tyrant she produced Nina and Lill, both prize winners. Lill, in turn, was put to Gadfly, a grandson of Jock, and also related to her through Grove Nettle, and produced Derby Nectar, a bitch of considerable merit. I may add that I myself owned a full sister to Derby Nectar, who, when put to Young Tyke, produced Gamester, a dog that has done remarkably well over in America, both as a show dog and a sire. It is noticeable, too, that both Gamester and his own brother, who was drowned on the voyage, were dogs of remarkable bone and strong coat, indeed rather coarse in general character, and with plenty of pluck; albeit their dam was a light, delicate bitch. I shall return to the whole subject of in-breeding further on.

As to the external peculiarities of the Jock blood, they are almost always full of Terrier character, and have plenty of substance, with good coats, legs, and feet. They are not always very good in shoulder, their ears are apt to be carried rather high, and their heads have not the beautiful cleanness characteristic of the Foiler and Belvoir blood, and are apt to get coarse with age.

I now come to a line of blood even more valuable, in my opinion, than the Jock strain, that, namely, of Old Trap. Trap himself was but seldom shown, and was consequently not very well known to the public. His sire was a black-and-tan dog, undoubtedly; I believe one of the old black-and-tan stock to which I before referred. Trap has been described to me by an M.F.H., in whose possession he at one time lived and worked. He was a compact, well-made dog, just the right size, with a lean head, and with plenty of bone. His one marked defect was a fine coat, which a good deal interfered with his work. There is certainly a tendency to this defect in one of the families descended from him—that of Tyrant—notably in the Chance branch of it. At the same time, I am not sure whether this may not have come in on the dam's side. Trap's most noted son, undoubtedly, was Tyrant, out of an own sister to Vassal. His lot was unluckily cast in the days when a well-marked head and a generally "graceful" appearance went for more than sterling working points, and though he was fairly successful on the show-bench, his merits were certainly not fully recognised. In build he was a regular "big little 'un," low on the leg, with great substance, and length in the right place. As a stud dog he was pre-eminently successful, but for some reason his sons and daughters were hardly equally so in reproducing the family good qualities. There seems to have been a certain tendency in the blood to grow big and coarse, and deficient in compactness and Terrier character. The best, probably, of Tyrant's sons was Bitters, a dog of something the same stamp as his sire, immensely powerful yet very compact. Unluckily his dam brought in an undoubted infusion of Bull-terrier, and, as a consequence, Bitters, although he has had great opportunities both with Mr. Gibson and Mr. Burbidge, has failed to keep up the character of the family. The best, perhaps, of his stock was Boxer, a big coarse dog, but the sire of several good ones. Pre-eminent amongst these was Bloomer, a neat little bitch herself, who has earned immortality as the dam of Bloom. Another well-known son of Tyrant was Old Chance. His dam appears to have been by a Grove dog out of a Belvoir bitch. There can be little doubt, however, that Old Chance inherited some Bull or English Terrier blood, as shown in the length of his head and the fineness of his coat. These and kindred faults were transmitted to many of his descendants, more especially of the male sex, though at the same time he figures among the ancestors of more than one good dog. A far more successful son of Old Tyrant at the stud was Sam, who, as we have seen, got a second infusion of Jock blood through his dam. Sam's history was a somewhat curious one. He was a low, coarse dog, with plenty of substance and working character, but with nothing in his looks which promised a great career. Accordingly, when he was stolen, early in life, his owner took but little pains to recover him. In the meantime, however, Tickler and that grand bitch Myrtle had come out as show winners, and had proved the value of the blood. Accordingly, there was a hue and cry after their sire, and he was with some difficulty unearthed. In his after career he begot a number of good Terriers, though none quite equal to Myrtle. His best son was Venture, whose dam was got by Hopcroft's Trap, a comparatively unknown dog, but an own brother to Tyrant. As might be expected from his double cross of Trap, Venture was a thick-set, stiff dog, not as long in head as most of the Tyrants, and rather wide in chest. His career was cut short by an apoplectic fit, before he had begotten a son worthy to fill his own place, so his fame rests chiefly on his daughters. Of these the best were Vanity from Cottingham Nettle, and Patch and Vexer from Fussy, who was herself full of Trap blood. Vanity and Vexer have both inherited their sire's wide chest, a defect much less noticeable in Patch. Another good son of Sam was Willie out of Cottingham Nettle, to whom I have already referred. As a stud dog he has rather disappointed expectation, his stock running too large.

Harking back to Old Trap, we come to one of his sons, who, I am disposed to think, has done even more permanent good than Tyrant—namely, Pickle. Pickle himself was never, I believe, either shown or advertised at the stud, and consequently had but little opportunity of getting show Terriers, as his services were practically confined to the bitches of that very successful breeder, Mr. Turner of Leicester. Pickle has been described to me as a thick-set dog with extraordinary bone. I have not been able to ascertain his dam's exact pedigree, but there is, I believe, little doubt that she was a pure-bred Belvoir Terrier. His best hit was in getting Artful out of Vene, a daughter of old Trap. Artful, as might have been expected from this breeding, was a thick-set dog of great substance. He was again crossed with Tricksy, a direct descendant of Trap through Chance and Tyrant, and begot Rambler, who has immortalised himself as the sire of Mr. Burbidge's Nettle. The former bitch was, in the opinion of some good judges, the best that ever stood on a show bench. That her expression and outline were those of a thorough Terrier could not be doubted, but her open feet and wide chest were serious drawbacks. The stud reputation of Rambler seems likely to be sustained by his grandson, Pickle II., got by an own brother to Nettle, from that grand bitch Olive. Pickle's deformed feet would alone have served to debar him from a show career, but such stock as Volo, Daisy, and Deacon Nettle, have already given him a high place at the stud.

There are yet one or two other sons of Trap who require notice. One of these was Ragman, from a bitch of no note, and, I believe, no pedigree. Ragman himself was a big coarse dog. By far his most creditable performance was getting Fussy from a daughter of Hopcroft's Trap—a decided case of in-breeding. Fussy herself, barring her somewhat thick shoulders, was almost faultless, and her Terrier expression was perfect. I well remember seeing her when between seven and eight years old, at Birmingham, showing all the life and fire of a young one, and with scarcely a trace of age in her contour. Ragman was also credited with the parentage of Spot, the sire of Vandal, a good workman-like dog, though somewhat coarse. I imagine, however, that Vandal's antecedents were not such as to make his pedigree a matter of great certainty.

There is yet another branch of the Trap blood which it would be high treason to omit, though I confess that I approach its merits and failings with fear and trembling, I refer to Bounce and his son Buffer. Over the merits and defects of the latter controversy has waxed as fierce as the Stud Book warfare over the Blacklock blood. Bounce himself I never saw, and except Buffer and a dog of some merit named Bismarck, I am not aware that he has left any noteworthy stock.

Buffer's dam, too, was not known to fame, but I confess, though I am not one of Buffer's thoroughgoing detractors, I have always suspected an infusion of Beagle blood somewhere. In general character the Buffers have little in common with the rest of the Traps, and seem to have struck out a new and well-defined type for themselves. Strong coats, long heads, good shoulders, and excellent legs and feet, are the main characteristics of the blood, while these merits are too often counterbalanced by heavy dead-looking ears and a sour expression. First, of course, among his sons comes Buffett, of whom I have already expressed my high opinion. Indeed, but for a tendency, and that not very pronounced, to the family type of ear, it is hard to find a fault with him. One drawback to his success has been a delicate constitution. Whence this is inherited it is hard to say. Indeed, altogether, Buffett is rather a violation of the laws of breeding. No dog ever showed more style and quality. Yet that is not the pre-eminent characteristic of the Buffer blood, while as for Buffett's dam, Frolic, a more plebeian-looking matron could not be found in a day's march. Be that as it may, Buffett has certainly transmitted his own style to his son Vulcan, from a bitch of old kennel blood. At the same time the family failings of head and ears have reappeared. Buffett's other distinguished son, Buff, is a far more characteristic representative of the blood, with immense bone and a decidedly plain head and ears. Any defects in the dog himself, however, were more than made up for by his progeny, when at the Alexandra Palace Show of 1878 he burst on the world as the sire of the three best bitch puppies that ever found their way into one class. The merits of the trio, Deacon Ruby, Bloom, and Blossom, are too well known to need comment. Another good son of Buffer is Nimrod, who, like Buff, shows all the characteristics of the family. In spite of his deserved successes on the show bench, even his admirers must admit that he has so far been a most disappointing dog at the stud. As yet Buffer's daughters have failed to rival their brothers, either on the show bench or the stud, with the one conspicuous exception of Dainty, the dam of Dorcas. My own general verdict on the Buffer blood is that, like that of Tartar, it has decided merits, but that it must be handled with very great care, and sparingly used. Its worst feature, in my opinion, is the extraordinary tenacity of its defects. The faults of other strains—the fine coats of the Tykes, the wide chests of the Traps, the open feet of so many of the Belvoir Terriers, and the weak hocks and crouching quarters of the Foilers—may all be eliminated by careful crossing, but the heavy ears and sour expression of the Buffers seem to reappear unexpectedly after we had hoped that they were completely eradicated. Still, the admirers of Buffer may console themselves with the reflection that as long as they can point to dogs like Buffett, Dorcas, Bloom, Buff, Vulcan, Nimrod, and Gripper, the blood is not likely to lose its popularity.

There is yet one more alleged subdivision of the Trap family to be considered, though its claims to the title are very doubtful. Hornet entered on public life as a son of Trap and Grove Nettle, though I have found very few breeders who accepted the pedigree as authentic. What Hornet's real origin was is, I imagine, a question never very likely to be solved. The merits of the dog himself were undoubted. Indeed, for a combination of substance and strength compressed into a small compass it would be difficult to name his superior. As might be supposed, however, the rumours about his ancestry rather militated against his popularity with breeders, and his untimely death, the result, I believe, of dumb madness, prevented him from showing such merit as he may have possessed as a sire. Still, he got one or two fair dogs; and it must be borne in mind that he was the sire of Moss and Brokenhurst Nettle, who perhaps did more than any other two bitches to establish the fame of the Brokenhurst kennel. Nor must it ever be forgotten that Bloom has three crosses of Hornet blood.

Setting aside the Buffers, who, as I have said, seem to have struck out a line for themselves, the characteristics of the Trap blood are a compact rather square build, with good Terrier-like heads, seldom long, except in the Chance family, small ears, strong loins and quarters, with sterns well or indeed in some cases rather too gaily carried, and especially good legs and feet. Their worst fault is a marked tendency to be broad in the chest, a fault especially found, I am inclined to think, in the bitches—at least Nettle, Myrtle, Vanity, and Vexer, who are otherwise among the best of them, were none of them good in that point. The Tyrant branch of the family are, I think, not always good in coat, while the descendants of Pickle, on the other hand, have generally coats of the very best type, close and hard, appearing fine to the eye, but deep and dense when handled.

I had almost forgotten to say anything of the daughters of old Trap, though the omission would not have been a serious one. Mr. Turner's Vene, the dam of Artful, was probably the best of them. Another good one was Riot, who occurs in more than one good pedigree—Nimrod's, I think, among the number. But for some reason Trap did not contribute nearly as large a supply of successful matrons as his rival, Jock. It is hardly needful to say that some years ago an immense number of Terriers laid claim to Jock and Trap as ancestors, whose claims to the title were of an exceedingly shadowy character.

I now come to the third and last of what I have treated as the three great families, that descended from Belvoir Joe. Four or five years ago the merits of this blood were known to comparatively few persons, and no one would have imagined that it was likely to assume equal importance with either Trap or Jock. There can be no better evidence of its merits than the extraordinary rapidity with which it has made headway, and asserted itself against formidable rivals. I have already touched upon the history of the Belvoir Terriers; and the best and fullest account of them is to be found in the articles by " Peeping Tom," to which I before referred. The representative of the Belvoir strain through whom the blood is specially connected with the present race of show dogs is Belvoir Joe, though at the same time there are are one or two less-known members of the family who occasionally appear in modern pedigrees. Belvoir Joe himself was got by Trimmer, a dog from the Grove, and his dam was also out of a bitch of Grove blood. Belvoir Joe himself was I believe never shown, and I have met but few people who knew him. I believe, however, that he was a coarse and rather large dog. From Belvoir Venom, whose title indicates her origin, he begot three sons, Jock, Grip, and Viper, all of whom left some fair stock, especially Belvoir Jock. Belvoir Joe's real success however, was achieved by his union with two bitches of Mr. Branston's, Vic and Nettle. I have never been able to learn any particulars about Vic, beyond the fact that she was all white, and extraordinarily game, and that she was believed to be of the Belvoir blood. Nettle was her daughter, by a small dog, supposed to be a son of Old Trap. From Vic Belvoir Joe begat Belgrave Joe, and from Nettle Mr. Turner's Old Nettle, and it is to these two that the Belvoir blood owes all its present celebrity. The latter is the dam of Mr. Burbidge's Nettle, of whom I before spoke, and of her brother, Tyrant, and thus is the ancestress of Pickle II. In addition to this, Nettle, when put to Brokenhurst Joe, a son of Belgrave Joe, and consequently closely related to herself, bred that good bitch, Needle, the Alexandra Palace winner in 1877. Belgrave Joe himself is so little known to the public, except by name, that it may not be amiss to say a few words about him. He is a dog of some 18 or 19 pounds weight, rather high on the leg, with a grand Terrier coat, and a head only equalled, in my opinion, by his daughter Olive. Unlike many of the Belvoir dogs, he has excellent feet, and there is none of that weakness behind which is often found in the family. My acquaintance with him only dates from his old age; but even now, in I believe his tenth or eleventh year, he could hold his own, I imagine, with most show dogs of the day. As most of his stock are still in their prime, it is needless to dwell upon them. The best evidence of his merits was perhaps to be found at the Kennel Club Show in the summer of 1879, where four out of the six winners in open classes were begotten by his two sons, Brokenhurst Joe and Beppo; while in one of the other classes his son Tom was disqualified for being over-weight, after being placed first by the judges. The capacity of the blood for bearing in-breeding is sufficiently shown by Tom, whose maternal granddam was the offspring of Belvoir Jock and Mr. Turner's Nettle, and also by the success which Pickle II. has had in connection with bitches of the Belvoir Joe blood, in the cases of Deacon Nettle, Daisy.

and Discord. Besides their Terrier-like character, general symmetry, and good coats, the family is noticeable for the great beauty of its heads and necks. Their main defect, and a serious one, is their weak, open feet. Too many of them, too, are narrow and light in the thighs, with a tendency to be cow-hocked. In both these points the Trap blood is a good corrective, and it is, indeed, to this cross that the Belvoir strain owes its best successes.

It might be thought that I had overlooked two important strains, those of Foiler and Turk, the former an undoubted, the latter an alleged, son of Grip. Considering the great value of the Foiler blood, such an omission would be little short of a crime. Foiler, however, so far owes his successes to his daughter, and consequently it is scarcely necessary in a classi-fication of strains to give him a place among the great families. Foiler himself was bred by Whitmore, of whom I before spoke. His sire, Grip, was got by Grove Willie, a Terrier of pure Grove blood, and the son of *a* Grove Nettle, but whether of *the* celebrated Grove Nettle is, I believe, doubtful. Grip's dam was a bitch of old Devonshire blood, descended from dogs belonging to the Rev. John Russell. Grip himself has been described to me as a square-built workman-like dog, full of Terrier character. His son Foiler was also out of a bitch of Mr. Russell's blood. Of this blood I have been unable to ascertain any details, but I strongly suspect that it possessed very marked characteristics of its own, and that it is to this that the Foiler blood owes certain peculiarities which distinguish it from any other strain. Old Foiler himself, like Tyrant, fell upon evil times, when a real working Terrier met with very little appreciation, and there is little doubt that in these days he would have won much higher honours than ever fell to his share. At the stud, too, his career was cut short, like that of Mr. Gibson's other noted sires, Tyke and Venture, by his untimely death. Still he had made good use of his opportunities, and besides begetting Dorcas, he had by his repeated unions with Moss laid the foundation of a whole host of winners. His only two sons of any repute were Flinger and Flasher, two fair but not pre-eminently good dogs. Neither of them, as far as I know, has left any noteworthy stock behind, probably from lack of opportunity. There are, I believe, one or two sons or grandsons of Foiler, from Belvoir bitches, still in existence, so it is not impossible that the strain may again be resuscitated in the male line. To judge from present appearances, however, it is through Folly and Frolic, the dams of Bloomer and Buffett, that Foiler will be best known to posterity. The main characteristics of the blood are very strong coats, narrow chests, and good shoulders, with a peculiar type of head, long and fox-like, but not in the least snipy. Another peculiarity of the blood is its tendency to throw out dew-claws on the hind feet. Indeed, I have seen a puppy closely in-bred to old Foiler who was furnished with a double set of these appendages! The defect of the blood is its tendency to drooping quarters and low-set sterns, and consequently to an awkward crouch-ing carriage. In this point the Trap blood is, as in the case of the Belvoir Terriers, a valuable corrective. There is another peculiarity about the Foiler blood which makes it, when judiciously handled, specially valuable to breeders, and that is the extraordinary persistence with which the leading features of the family assert themselves, and the power which it has of swamping and annihilating inferior lines. Bloom and her sister Blossom are, to my mind, striking examples of this. I well remember looking at them at the Alexandra Palace Show, where they first appeared, with a friend, who remarked on the entire absence of likeness either to the Buffer or Bitters families, which were the two principal elements in their pedigree. The difficulty was at once solved when we remembered that they were descended on both sides from Foiler, whose best points were strikingly reproduced. Thus, if a breeder only gets a concentration of old Foiler blood, he is at least pretty sure that he will get a fixed and definite type.

The claims of Turk to be a son of old Grip are, I believe, much more doubtful. Turk himself will be doubtless remembered by many as a square-built, workmanlike dog, a trifle coarse and large. This character was faithfully reproduced in his stock, almost all of whom were somewhat coarse about the head. From this charge I must except Saracen, a dog whose failings are certainly not on the side of coarseness. The Turk blood at one time seemed likely to take a high place, but though it has had good opportunities it has failed to produce any one dog of great merit, and I question whether it is ever likely to figure prominently in prize lists.

And, now, some one will probably ask, Do you intend to pass over the greatest of all show Terriers—the dog whose prizes alone made up an income that many a rising barrister might envy—the invincible Rattler? Certainly, to make no mention of Rattler would be to ignore a most conspicuous figure in the world of Fox-terriers. Still, my survey has hitherto included not so much celebrated dogs, as those strains of blood which have produced, and may in future be expected to produce, high-class Terriers; and, much as I admire Rattler himself, I can hardly find a place for him in that classification. However, his many victories and his real merits deserve mention, and I can at the same time deal with his great-grand-father, who, like himself, at one time held a high place in show records, Champion Trimmer. Trimmer himself was a dog who at least made no false claim to high pedigree, as it was pretty well known that his sire and dam were accidentally picked up, and were animals of no great merit. Trimmer himself was a neat wiry little dog, equally undeserving, in my opinion, of the prizes he won and of the undiscriminating abuse heaped upon him. His brother, Crack, was a dog of much the same stamp. Trimmer himself never, as far as I know, begot anything of much merit; but two of his descendants took a very high position indeed among show dogs. One of these was Mr. Bassett's Tip, by Burnham's Trimmer, a compact square-built dog, at one time of very great merit, but with a broad chest and a somewhat thick head, two faults which increased terribly with advancing years. And I may here remark that, as far as my experience goes, nothing more conspicuously distinguishes a really well-bred Terrier from a specious-looking mongrel than the durability of the former's good qualities, and especially of the outline of the head. A dog with Bull-terrier in him may have a good head at eighteen months or two years old, but two years later the objectionable characteristics will show themselves. A true Terrier, like Belgrave Joe, Dorcas, or Fussy, is almost as good at eight years old as in his (or her) best days. Trimmer's other noted descendant was Rattler by Fox, a son of Trimmer II., whose dam was that good bitch Vene, to whom I referred when speaking of her sire, Trap. I have never heard any particulars of Fox, or of any of Rattler's ancestors on the dam's side, so I think we may safely set Rattler down as the one distinguished member of an otherwise unknown house. Whether he really stood out among his contemporaries as far as was often thought may be questioned. Certainly, he did not impress one with that high-bred look and that Terrier-like dash and fire of expression which we see elsewhere. Still, when he was criticised in detail it was hard to find any faults beyond a slight tendency to a wheel back, and a somewhat soft and listless expression—the latter doubtless increased by a life spent for the most part either in railway trains or on show-benches. At the same time I cannot but look upon Rattler's unprecedented success as somewhat of a misfortune for the interests of Fox-terriers. Possessing, as I have said, no hereditary type, he utterly failed to transmit any to his progeny. Numbers of people set to work with the idea that they had only to breed from this universal conqueror to get good Terriers, and the failure which almost invariably ensued was set down as illustrative of the so-called "lottery of breeding."

I do not pretend in these remarks to have gone exhaustively through the whole range of show winners. I have, doubtless, omitted some good dogs within the families which I have mentioned, and some few, such as Lancer, lie outside of them. What I have sought to do is to show the lines on which Fox-terrier breeding has hitherto gone, and especially to give young breeders some definite idea of the materials with which they are working, and of the results which they may expect. To a beginner the pedigrees of his dogs are too often but an unmeaning list of names. I have endeavoured to clothe the dry bones of the Kennel Club Stud-book with a certain amount of life and individuality.

I now pass on to what is sometimes regarded and unhappily treated as a distinct breed, though it should really be looked on as a sub-division of Fox-terriers—the wire-haired Terrier. I have already mentioned the grounds I have for thinking that the wire-haired Terrier was known in the last century. I may add that I have reason to think that there was, till lately, a definite breed of white rough-haired Terriers, not unlike the Dandie or Bedlington in build and character, but rather harder in coat. It is easy to see that such a breed might, by crossing, or even by accidental variation, produce Terriers closely resembling the regular wire-haired breed. There was also in Shropshire a well-known breed of wire-haired Terriers, black-and-tan, on very short legs, weighing about ten or twelve pounds, with long punishing heads and extraordinary working powers. So too, one used to meet with sandy-coloured Terriers of no very well-authenticated strain, but closely resembling the present breed of Irish Terrier. It is clear that, from either of these varieties crossed with the smooth Fox-terrier, a wire-haired strain might be easily developed. As a matter of fact, I believe that the present race of show wire-haired Terriers do, to a great extent, owe their origin to a well-recorded cross of the kind. On this point I shall avail myself of some notes kindly communicated to me by the gentleman to whom I have before referred as writing under the signature of "Peeping Tom." He tells me that a certain Mr. Thornton, a Yorkshire squire living near Pickering, had a breed of wire-haired Terriers, tan in colour, with a black stripe down the back. He describes them as about 16 lbs. weight, with grand Terrier heads and drop-ears, in fact, in every respect, except colour, the model of the show wire-haired Terrier. One of these dogs, crossed with a smooth-haired Fox-terrier, produced a strain of white wire-haired Terriers. Of these the most famous was Kendal's Old Tip, a kennel terrier belonging to the Grimington hounds. He was a white dog with one marked ear, 16 lbs. weight, and is still known as an extraordinary workman. From him came one of the very best wire-haired Terriers ever seen, Carrick's Venture, and there has been scarcely a prize-winner since that has not inherited a strain of his blood. Another noted Yorkshire strain of wire-haired Terriers, so my informant tells me, belonged to the Cleveland hounds, and as he does not say that they were produced by a similar process of crossing, it is not unlikely that they may have been an old-established breed, though perhaps originally the result of a cross. Among the wire-haired Terriers of the present day, two stand out conspicuous, Thorn and Gorse. The former was bred from parents of unknown pedigree, but of Terrier-like appearance and remarkable working powers. Gorse's ancestry I have been unable to trace with any clearness. The besetting fault of modern wire-haired Terriers undoubtedly lies in their coat. The coat should be short, hard, and dense, and feeling, as the name implies, like a wire brush. Instead of that, it is too often long, soft, and open. Such a coat does not offer half the protection against wet given by a fairly good smooth coat. The latter throws off the rain, the former absorbs it, and becomes, after a hard day, like so much sloppy seaweed.

There seems to be also a great tendency on the part of modern wire-haired Terriers to be overgrown and leggy, and to lose all uniformity of type. In fact, they give me the idea of a breed produced by recent crossing, which, without care, would break up again into its original elements. Were I a breeder of these dogs I should be strongly inclined to try to refresh their merits by dipping into the original fountain-head, and to re-combine the

MR. THEODORE BASSETT'S FOX-TERRIER "BROKENHURST STING."

smooth Terrier, selecting a good hard-coated strain, such as that of Foiler, with either the original Yorkshire stock described above, or, if that could not be recovered, with a good Irish Terrier. By an Irish Terrier I mean a genuine Terrier of working dimensions, not one of the 24 lb. monstrosities that too often disgrace the name.

So far I have been concerned with the method according to which Terriers have been and ought to be produced. I now come to what many will consider probably a more practical question—what a Terrier should be. Obviously he must have good legs and feet, the former straight, clean, muscular, and not too fleshy; the latter close, round, and well braced up. The straightness of the legs should be tested rather by looking at the inside than outside, as a very muscular swelling fore-arm, which is an undoubted merit, may give an appearance of crookedness outside, when there is no real malformation. The chest should be deep and narrow; if wide, the dog's power of going to earth is lessened without any proportionate increase of power. Moreover, in nine cases out of ten a wide chest means bad action. On the other hand, if the chest be narrow, it must be deep to give space for the heart and lungs, as well as slope for the shoulders. The shoulders should be thin, long, and well laid back, the two last-named points being even more important than the first. The middle should be neither flat-sided on the one hand, nor tub-shaped on the other, but the ribs should spring well from the spine, and descend with an oval sweep. The back-ribs should be deep, and the dog should be well ribbed up. At the same time, I would rather have a dog a trifle deficient here, provided he had plenty of liberty and hind-leg action than have him too short in the quarters. The stern should be set on fairly high, and gaily carried, though of course not like a Pug's. In this point, indeed, a Foxhound is a good model, and if fashion allowed us to show Terriers with their tails unmutilated, the likeness in this respect would be complete. The thighs should be long and muscular, and the hocks well let down. This, indeed, is a more important point than is often supposed. Strong, well-formed hocks are no doubt important, but I would rather have somewhat weaker hocks well let down, than good ones with a long interval between them and the ground. Lastly, the dog should stand square and true on his feet.

Of the coat I have already spoken. It should be dense, abundant, and hard, fine to the eye, and thick to the hand. A strong feather on the thighs, and a thick stern are desirable, as sure accompaniments of a good coat, and symptoms of a hardy constitution. On no account should the belly and the under-side of the thighs be bare.

It is clear, however that a dog may have all these points, and yet not be up to the standard of merit required in a show Terrier. Here comes in what I have called secondary qualities. In the first place, besides being truly shaped, the dog must have that indescribable look of style and high breeding usually known as quality. The neck should be of moderate length and thickness, slightly arched, and sloping gracefully into the shoulders. I now come to that important point—the head. In calling this a secondary point I do not in the least mean to detract from its value. A good head is essential to beauty, and is also a requisite symptom of pure breeding. But provided that the jaw be strong enough that is all we require for mere working purposes, and therefore the head fairly falls under the class of what I have called secondary points. A few years ago an idea prevailed—now I think happily on the wane, though not yet wholly exploded—that length was the great thing to be aimed at in a Terrier's head. Now, where length can be got without any sacrifice of Terrier character or expression, as in Dorcas, and still more in Olive or Belgrave Joe, no doubt we have the perfection of a head. But the real point is the shape and expression of the head, and length is too often obtained at the expense of these. A long straight head, going down like a wedge, is an infallible symptom of affinity to the Bull-terrier or his first cousin the English Terrier. It is noteworthy that in certain strains, notably that of Old Chance, a short thick head is found alternating with an abnormally long one, the Bull-terrier cross manifesting itself sometimes in one form, sometimes the other. Those who care to push this inquiry further will find some interesting speculations on the subject of length of head in domestic animals in the writings of Mr. Darwin. The right type of head is more easily illustrated than described; and a walk round the benches at a big show with a competent critic will do more to instruct a beginner on this point than pages of writing. The jaw, of course, should be strong, and the teeth level. A slightly undershot mouth is no practical hindrance to a dog's work; but it is an infallible sign of a Bulldog cross, and as such very properly puts its owner out of competition. The head should be cleanly chiselled out below the eye, and the eye itself should be small and keen-looking, and on no account projecting. The eyes should be rather wide apart, and the forehead proportionately broad, and not conical like a Setter's. The ears should be small, triangular, and not too thin. They should not be set too high on the head, though that is better than their hanging helplessly from the neck. While on the subject of ears, I may mention to young readers that they never need fret themselves as to a puppy's mode of carrying its ears. I have known more than one case where the ears were never quite properly carried till the dog was in his second year. With bitches the first litter of pups often proves a turning-point. Lastly, I come to that all-important feature—Terrier character. The true Fox-terrier has a look of dash and vivacity which marks him off from almost all other breeds. A friend of mine, no inexperienced judge, goes so far as to say that at a show you can always tell the well-bred dogs by watching which wag their tails on the bench. Undoubtedly a cheerful temper and a gay lively carriage are essential features of the breed. Many a well-made dog has a stiff, wooden look, and from such I should be very loth to breed.

As to kennel management and the like, I do not know that there is anything in the Fox-terrier that requires special notice. It may not be amiss, however, to give a few words of advice to young breeders, and perhaps I cannot begin better than by describing the method in which such too often set to work. Our would-be exhibitor sees a bitch whose appearance pleases him. Her pedigree contains the names of a few well-known dogs. Without considering whether there is a likelihood of her reproducing her own qualities, whether those qualities are really obtained by descent, and sufficiently stereotyped in the family to ensure reproduction, he purchases her, and sets to work to breed from her. A dog is selected, possibly simply because he writes Champion before his name, possibly (if the breeder be exceptionally far-seeing) because he appears likely to correct the faults of the bitch, regardless of the fact that each of them inherits, though each does not display, precisely the same faults. He singles out and keeps the best puppy; the rest are scattered to the winds. The pup is perverse enough to obey the laws of Nature, and to grow up with the defects which his sire and dam owe to a common ancestor. The bitch is condemned as worthless for breeding, and the aspirant either gives up the attempt, or, if unusually persevering, tries another experiment on precisely the same principles. What, I may be asked, should he have done? Now, no paper instructions, nothing but care, patience, and experience, often dearly bought, will enable a man to breed any sort of stock successfully. Still, there are a few plain rules, by observing which a breeder will at least diminish his chances of failure at the outset. In the first place, what an animal reproduces is not primarily its own individual peculiarities, but the peculiarities of its family. If it is in-bred—that is, if the sire and dam possess the same hereditary type—then it is almost sure to reproduce that type. If it is cross-bred—that is, if it combines more than one hereditary type, it will probably, though not certainly, reproduce the oldest and most fixed. If it be an amalgam of a number of strains, it may reproduce anything. These remarks, of course, only take into account the influence of one parent. That influence may reign paramount, or it may be modified or wholly destroyed by the influence of the other parent. If both the parents be of the same hereditary type, and that a well-defined one, then and then only he may be pretty sure of the result. If they differ, we may get either one type or the other, or possibly, a new variety, differing from either of the parent types. In pure breeding then—*i.e*, breeding from animals of the same type, and who derive that type from a common stock—lies our only hope of certainty. Here and there of course it is necessary to cross to get rid of certain positive defects, but the process is a perilous one, and should be undertaken with caution. These are but trite maxims, yet few people obey them in practice.

Having then established the principle that there must be a sufficient degree of similarity and of common descent to ensure uniformity, we have to face the question of selecting and mating the individual specimens. And here I believe that an error is often made by breeders who have risen a degree above the practices which I described at the outset. A favourite notion is that we should correct the defects of one parent by the excessive merits of the other. Now, in details this may be true enough. If we have large ears on one side we must try to diminish the liability by getting small ears on the other; so with legs and feet and coat, and with peculiarities of temper. But it is a fatal error to couple two animals of widely different type, as a big leggy dog with a neat compact bitch, or a light shelly bitch with a coarse thick-set dog. Modify your type gradually by careful selection. No valuable breed of animals was ever yet produced, as far as I know, at one bound by the combination of widely differing sorts.

As to the question of in-breeding, my own view on the subject is, never be afraid of in-breeding, and never in-breed except when it is necessary. Use the most suitable dog. If two dogs be equally suitable, choose that one who is least nearly related. Without a certain amount of in-breeding it is impossible, as I have said before, to ensure certainty of type. With reference to the precise degree of in-breeding that may be permitted, it is impossible to lay down a general rule. The whole question was well discussed in some articles which appeared several years ago in the *Live Stock Journal*. The writer there clearly pointed out the reason why in-breeding has in domestic animals been sometimes attended with disastrous results. Almost every animal has certain morbid tendencies, and once any morbid tendency has established itself in a family, every consanguineous union of course tends to double it. In some animals the very process which fits them for the use of man is, in itself, the creation of a morbid tendency. The fattening properties of the Leicester sheep and the Shorthorn ox are obtained by a certain exaggeration of one part of the system—the consequent disturbance of the healthy harmony of the whole. In wild animals, the process of "struggle for existence" constantly tends to preserve that harmony and to redress any violation of it. Hence, among wild animals in-breeding is carried to great lengths with impunity. In all kinds of dogs used for field sports, artificial selection has, on the whole, adopted and perpetuated the same characteristics that Nature preserves in wild animals. Hence the extent to which in-breeding may be safely carried, as in the Laverack Setters. At the same time there are in all strains certain inherent defects, and the inevitable tendency of in-breeding is to enhance these defects; hence, if we in-breed closely, we must select those specimens who are most free from the family failings. In dogs, I am strongly of opinion that shyness is a result to be feared from too close breeding. It is hardly needful to say that this shyness, which is a fatal fault in a show dog, and a serious drawback to his working and companionable qualities, is wholly different from timidity. One of the very best working Terriers I have ever known is so shy as to be absolutely wretched in a crowded street or at a show. She is the offspring of very near relations, and in her case in-breeding has not produced any bad effects in the way of weediness or constitutional weakness.

There is one more point to be noticed in the management of the brood bitch—that is, the age at which it is desirable to breed from her. While I believe that a bitch does not reach her prime till she is over two years old, I never should object to put a bitch of ten or eleven months old to the dog if the season of the year were suitable. I have known good pups so bred, and in many cases the process is beneficial to the bitch's temper and appearance, and also, I think, to the next litter. To let a bitch remain a maiden beyond her second heat is, in my opinion, dangerous, as likely to make her a shy breeder hereafter. I need hardly say that March, April, and May are the best months for puppies to come in ; September and October the worst. Indeed, it is only under exceptional circumstances that I should ever breed an autumn litter.

It may perhaps be well to supplement these generalities by some more detailed advice. If any one wishes to establish a kennel of Fox-terriers in the easiest and least expensive way, I should recommend him to set about it as follows :—Let him get two bitches of good blood, and free from positive defects. The better-looking they are doubtless the better his chance, but let him be sure they are healthy and game. It is difficult to assign exactly the different share which each parent has in influencing the offspring, and I am inclined to think that most of the theories which have been put forward on this point rest on no solid basis. But this much may be taken for granted, that temper and constitution are largely determined by the mother, and that if we would have healthy offspring we must have a healthy dam. Let the breeder, then, give these bitches a fair chance, mating them carefully, and discarding none of their pups till he is sure they are worthless. Even then, if he can, he will do well to keep his eye on them. Every pup we breed is the result of an experiment from which something may be learnt, and in this respect one's failures may be the stepping-stones to future success. Suppose, for example, that there is one good bitch in a litter, while the rest have all bad shoulders. If the breeder keeps sight of these he will know that he must be on his guard against that fault in breeding from their sister. If, as is too often the case, he troubles himself about nothing beyond the individual animal, he will be astonished at the appearance in the next generation of a fault from which both parents are free. By such a system as I have indicated a breeder will get a thorough familiarity with the hereditary peculiarities of all his stock—he will, in a word, know the material with which he his working.

Having thus started our inexperienced breeder on his career, it may be well to say a few words about the management of his young stock. There are some people who tell us that they can infallibly pick out the best puppy of a litter. If a breeder can learn the art, "happy man be his dole." For my part I am content to keep all that do not show any very pronounced defect, in the belief, based on experience, that the least promising of the litter may often be the one prize in it. The only defects in my opinion that justify one in actually condemning a puppy are a fine coat and very large ears. Crooked legs may come straight, an undershot jaw may grow level (at least up to four or five months old), and a big overgrown puppy will sometimes stop growing with extraordinary suddenness, while a small weedy one, especially a bitch, will occasionally thicken and furnish wonderfully when well on in her second year. One bit of advice I would give every breeder, to keep a careful record of his pups, and to write down at the time of weaning or earlier his opinion of their merits. This will be the best means of testing his own powers of judging their promise.

As to rearing pups, my own belief is, that when reared in numbers they should be walked out at farmhouses and cottages. A number of pups kept together must either suffer from want of exercise or else constantly lead one another into mischief. Moreover, if distemper gets among them it runs through the whole lot, and probably disorders the older dogs. Pups kept out at walk get more liberty, their intelligence is more developed, and they are more likely to be cured of any tendency to molest sheep and poultry. No doubt when kenneled up their objection to restraint gives some trouble, but this is a slight set off against the advantages on the other side.

Entering young Terriers to the work is happily not a matter of much difficulty. If a pup is well bred he very soon learns his work in the company of an older dog. At the same time I have known dogs who showed no interest whatever in their work at first, who would simply play with a rat and run foolishly backwards and forwards outside a cover, but who nevertheless, when once the destructive impulse had asserted itself, proved thorough workmen.

With reference to feeding Fox-terriers I would only remark that I have never myself found the plan answer of putting their food before them and requiring them to eat it at once, and then removing what is left. Whether from their excitable temper or from any other cause, I know not, but few Terriers will eat their rations straight off. My own plan is to feed about four or five in the afternoon, and to remove their food either before night or the first thing in the morning. In preparing for show the special point to notice is to be careful that the dog gets no chill in washing; if he does his coat will stare and look dry. Some dogs, indeed, if well brushed with a glove, and hand-rubbed, and abundantly supplied with clean straw, need no washing. If they must be washed do not use common soap, but either some of the specially prepared dog soaps or, better still, yolk of egg.

The only artificial processes needed with Terriers are the removal of dew-claws and the docking of the tail. The removal of dew-claws is a real advantage, as they are apt to catch in rough cover or among stones, and to tear. It is as well to remove them at about three weeks old, though it can be done without much pain a good deal later. The amputation of the tail is, in my opinion, a senseless fashion. At the same time it causes little pain, even in an adult dog. This, too, should be done early—at a fortnight old or so. The tail may be either severed with the fore-finger and thumb or with a sharp pair of scissors. The only thing to be borne in mind is that it is better to take too little than too much. If it is necessary to shorten the tail of a full-grown dog the hair should be turned back: this can be best done by an india-rubber ring. If the hair does not grow over nicely, it can be drawn to a point, and either tied or glued. If this is done all trace of the operation will be lost in a few weeks.

Lastly, and it is well to end with so solemn an injunction, remember the fate of Tyke, and never kennel two dogs—males I mean—together.

Mr. Doyle having expressed his views so fully on the subject of Fox-terriers, and his judgment being deferred to by most modern breeders, it is not necessary, we think, to go much further into the subject; however, there is another gentleman, Mr. F. Redmond, of London, who is well known as a successful breeder and exhibitor, who has kindly given us his opinions, which we should like to lay before our readers. Mr. Redmond writes :—

"The points of greatest importance in the Fox-terrier are head and ears, legs and feet, neck and shoulders, back, loin and hind-quarters, smartness, activity, size, and terrier character.

"*Head.*—The skull should be flat and moderately narrow; broader between the ears and gradually tapering to the eyes, free from wrinkle. But little slope or indentation between the eyes should be visible, except in profile. The jaw should be clean cut, rather long, powerful and muscular, with little if any fulness or bulging out at the cheeks. There is a very slight falling away below the eyes, but this must be very gradual, and not to such an extent as to give a snipy or wedgy appearance.

"The *lips* should be fairly tight, without any superfluous skin.

"The *nose* must be quite black.

"The *eyes* should be small, not set too wide apart, neither too much sunk in skull or protruding, dark rimmed, full of fire, life, and intelligence.

"The *teeth* should be strong and level, the incisors of the upper jaw just closing over the under ones.

"The *ears*, a point to which great value has always been attached, should be V-shaped, moderately small, of good serviceable thickness, to stand work in hedge-row and covert, and must be carried forward, flat and close to the cheek.

"The *neck* should be of fair length, clean and muscular, gracefully set into the shoulders, from which it should gradually taper to the head.

"The *shoulders* should be fine at the points, long, and sloping well back, and the chest deep, if anything rather narrow than broad. Shoulders and chest have latterly rightly received greater attention at the hands of judges, much to the improvement of the breed; heavy-shouldered or broad-chested dogs are useless as Fox-terriers.

"*Back and loin.*—Back should be straight and strong, the ribs well sprung, the loin strong, wide and square, the back ribs deep; the loin may be in the smallest degree arched, but there must not be the slightest approach to wheel-back.

"The *hind-quarters* must be very strong, and wide when viewed from behind, the thighs showing plenty of muscle, being long as well as large, stifles slightly bent, the hocks straight, and the bone from hock to heel short and strong.

"The *stern* should be set on rather high, and carried gaily, but should not be raised beyond a right angle with the back; it should, if anything, be a trifle coarse.

"*Legs and feet.*—A point of extreme value, and one to which the greatest attention must be given. The elbows must be well let down, and in a straight line with the body, the fore-legs, viewed in any direction, must be as straight as gun-barrels, with upright and powerful pasterns; they must be strong in bone, and clothed regularly with muscle from elbow to foot, giving a most solid and unbroken appearance; the feet should be round and cat-like, very compact, toes short and only moderately arched, the sole as hard as adamant; the foot should neither turn in or out, but if any deviation it should turn in; there should be no dew-claws behind.

"The *coat* should be smooth, harsh in texture, very close and abundant—a jacket to protect the wearer from all weathers.

"*Colour.*—White should predominate. Brindle, fallow, liver, or red markings are objectionable.

"*Size.*—The Fox-terrier must neither be leggy or too near the ground, neither must he be cloddy, but should have plenty of liberty and galloping power, with good bone and substance, fair speed and endurance being essentially requisite for his legitimate calling. Seventeen pounds in hard working condition is a fair average weight, but this may vary a pound or so either way—make and shape, good shoulders and chest, being a far more certain criterion in this respect than actual weight.

"The following points of the Fox-terrier have met with general endorsement, and are, I think, incapable of improvement :—

Head and ears ...	...	...	...	...	...	...	15
Neck	...	...	...	...	...	...	5
Shoulders and chest	...	...	...	...	...	...	15
Back and loin ...	...	...	...	...	...	...	10
Hind-quarters ...	...	...	...	...	...	...	5
Stern	...	...	...	...	...	...	5
Legs and feet ...	...	...	...	...	...	...	20
Coat	...	...	...	...	...	...	10
Symmetry and character ...	...	...	...	...	...	...	15
							100

"*Disqualifying points.*—White, cherry, or spotted to a considerable extent with either of these colours. Mouth much undershot or much overshot. Ears rose, prick or tulip."

Having thus given the views of two thoroughly practical breeders on the subject of Fox-terriers, we should ourselves like to say a few words on two subjects which are often debated by supporters of the breed. The first relates to the coat, and the second to the size of the dog. In the course of the many controversies which have arisen from time to time concerning Fox-terriers, it has been pretty obvious that the supporters of the hard weather-resisting kind of coat have out-argued those who adhere to a silky jacket. The former have, in our opinion, quite successfully contended that a fine soft coat is perfectly useless in the case of a dog who, like the Fox-terrier, is supposed to be essentially a vermin destroyer, as a hard day in wet brushwood, or exposure to any sort of cold, would be more likely to knock up a soft-coated dog than it could one who was clothed in a harder jacket.

In the matter of size, however, we fear that opinions never will become reconciled. Almost all who have taken prominent parts in the discussion appear to have agreed that a dog who is too large to go to earth is practically useless as a Fox-terrier, but, unfortunately, the very gentlemen who argue thus have found themselves unable to agree upon the precise size which renders a dog unqualified for his work. At present, at shows, where classes are divided by size, the usual division is for dogs of 18 lbs. and upwards, dogs of under 18 lbs., bitches of 17 lbs. and upwards, and bitches under 17 lbs. This arrangement might surely be expected to meet the views of both parties, but hitherto it has failed to do so, apparently on the grounds that the more given, the more is expected. Certain authorities argue that a dog of 20 lbs. or upwards in weight, who is narrow in chest, can go to earth more easily than a wide-chested dog of 18 lbs. or less. The truth of this few will question, but still, in our opinion, it fails to affect the point at issue very materially. Unquestionably a Fox terrier should be able to go to earth, and it is only common sense to see that a breed of small dogs are more likely to, as a race, go to earth with ease and comfort, than a family of giants. There may be several individual exceptions to this rule, but as a rule it must hold good, and therefore we do not see why a premium should be given to the producers of a type of dog which is likely to be useless in the field for the purposes for which it is required.

Though our own opinion is that the most desirable weight for a Fox-terrier dog should be a maximum 17 lbs., and for a bitch 16 lbs., there are, as we have said before, many authorities who differ from us in this respect; but we fancy most practical men will be found to take our side in this matter.

Mr. J. H. Murchison, writing to the *Live Stock Journal* on the 1st of August, 1879, says :—

FOX TERRIERS.

"When in former times I exhibited with considerable success Trimmer, Bellona, Bitters, Lancer, Vandal, Pincers, and others, varying from 15 lbs. to 17 lbs. each, disappointed exhibitors raised an outcry against them because they said they were 'too small,' 'mere toys,' &c. Larger and coarser dogs then came to the front, and a new generation of judges regarded them with favour, till the encouragement they met with has ended in the official acknowledgment of the large dogs by special classes being provided for them. It may be true that several of the dogs I have alluded to above would have been better with a little stronger bone, but they were about the proper size for Fox-terriers. When, however, we look at weight we should take size into consideration. A dog may not be so large as another, and yet weigh more from having more bone and muscle. Another important point as regards the practical use of the Fox-terrier is height: he should not exceed thirteen to fourteen inches at shoulder."

Mr. W. J. Tredennick, of St. Austell, Cornwall, also writes :—

"On the point of size a Terrier that scales 18 lbs. in ordinary condition will certainly disappoint its owner if he uses it for fox or badger, and even at 16 lbs. it must be built on good lines, having a narrow chest to be able to perform its duties without being laid up a distance from its quarry. It is not impossible—as I believe some imagine—to get the 16-lb. Terrier without its being a Toy."

Mr. Edward Ker supports these two gentlemen in the following words :—

"A fox is an animal which, with his large pricked ears, lengthy limbs, dense fur, and handsome brush, covers a deal of ground, and has the appearance of being about the size of a small-sized Scotch Collie. But if you carefully pick him to pieces you will see that deducting the head, legs, and brush, leaves a mere shadow of a body. He is both very narrow and very shallow in his chest; his neck at the base of the skull is about the thickest part of him; his shoulders are exceedingly oblique, and, standing in front of him, you will notice his chest is so narrow that his fore-legs nearly touch each other. If you will then feel him all over you will find that there is not a particle of stiffness about him; he seems to sink to the touch, and be a mere bag of bones in a skin. Wherever these vermin—the fox, otter, badger, polecat, or stoat—can get their head and fore-paws, their bodies will follow. The biggest dog fox ever was seen can go up a six-inch pipe, and what is more, I witnessed a badger weighing 35 lbs. (one of the largest I ever saw) pass through a six-inch pipe."

On the other side Mr. Robert Vicary occupies a prominent position. He commences most practically by giving a list of Terriers who have distinguished themselves running to hounds, whose weights vary from 17 lbs. to 20½ lbs. Of course such dogs are capable of travelling fast enough to keep up with the pack, and have not to be carried in panniers as is the practice in certain hunts where very small Terriers are used. The Rev. John Russell, whose practical experience on hunting is unlimited, is also a supporter of Mr. Vicary, for he says : "The weights of Fox-terriers should not be under 17 lbs. nor over 20 lbs." Jack Morgan writes from the Grove kennel, "Fox-terriers should not be less than 18 lbs.—Grove Nettle was 18 lbs., Grove Trimmer 19 lbs." This was in working condition. In spite, however, of such authorities differing from us, we must adhere to our formerly-expressed opinion, and maintain that the best weight is 17 lbs. for a dog, and 16 lbs. for a bitch Fox-terrier.

Nevertheless, with a view to lay before our readers a record of the measurements of some of the best Fox-Terriers of recent times, we reproduce from the columns of the *Live Stock Journal* a table which was expressly compiled for the benefit of its readers, with the explanatory diagram by which it was accompanied :—

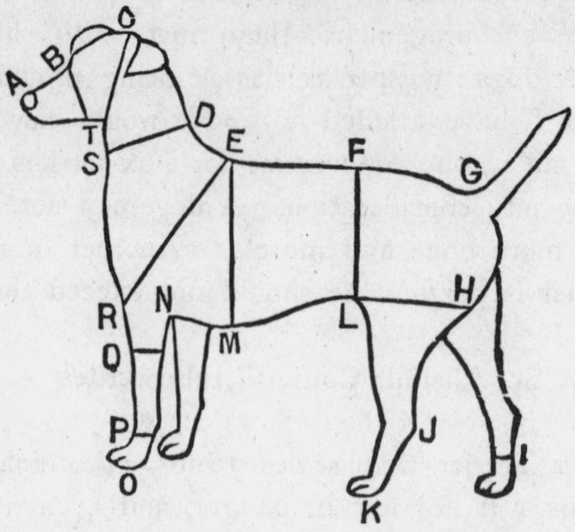

	Bitters,	Bufter.	Diver.	Flinger.	Jester.	Jester II.	General.	Yorick.	Sarcogen.	Speculation.	Nimrod.	Varmint.	Tip.	Scamp.	Saxon.	Rattler	Average.
A to B	3¼	3	3	3	2½	2⅞	2⅝	2¾	3	3	3¼	3¼	2⅞	2¾	2½	2¾	2¾
B to C	3¾	4½	3½	4¼			4	4½	5	4¾	3⅞	4	4⅛	4½	4¼	4½	4⅝
C to E	6	6½	5½				5½	{20½	6		6	6½	6½	6		5½	5¾
E to G	11¾	12½	13	12	13	13	13		14 6/8		12	14½	14½			13⅝	13½
Round B T	8	7½	7¼	8	7	7	8½	7¼	7⅝	8	7½	7	7	7½	7	7	7½
" C T	12	13	12½	13¼	13¼	13	12	11½	13	13¼	12¼	12	11¾	12½	12½	12½	12⅞
" S D	11½	13	12½	12	12¾	13	13	11	13	12¼	10¾	12¼	12	12	12½	13	12⅝
" E M	19	20	21½	20	21	21¼	20	19½	21½	20½	18¾	21	20¾	19¼	20	21	20½
" E R	21¾		23	20¼	21¼	20	20½	21½	20	20	20	23	23	20	20	21¾	20¾
" F L	14¾	17	18½	17¼	16⅛	16	16	18¾	19¾		14¾	18½	17			16½	16¼ to 18½
" L H	10¼	10	11¾		9½	9¾		10½			10	11¼	11			11¼	
																	should be
" Q	4⅝	4½	5	5	4½	4½	4⅝	4½	5¼	5	4½	5⅛	5	5¼	5	4¾	5
" P		3	3⅛	3⅛	3⅛	3⅛	3⅛	3	3½	3¼	3	3⅓	3⅛		3½	3½	3¼
E to Ground		14	14½	13½			14¼	14½			13¾	14¼	13¼	13½		15	14¼
J to "	4	4½	5	4	4⅛	4¼	4	3¾	4½	4½	4	4	4	4	4	4⅓	4⅛
	lbs.	lbs.	lbs.	lbs.			lbs.	lbs.	lbs.	lbs.	lbs.	lbs.	lbs.	lbs.	lbs.	lbs.	lbs.
Weight	8	17	22	19½			20	18	22½	21	17	19½	19	17	17½	19¾	17 to 20

The subject of pluck is one which seems to be but imperfectly understood by the vast majority of those who have not studied this breed with care. One often hears a youthful owner expatiating upon the pluck and courage of his Fox-terrier, and compare his capacity in this direction with that of a Bull-terrier. Nothing could be more absurd than this, for the latter *is*, but a Fox-terrier is *not*, essentially a "hard" dog. A Fox-terrier is required to go to earth after his quarry, and, if he can, to bolt him. If not, by barking he is enabled to direct the operations of the diggers-out. A Bull-terrier, on the contrary, would creep up to his quarry, and, if necessary, take his death without a murmur ; much to the disgust of those whose object was sport, and not the murder of a plucky dog, or a game chase in an earth without a soul to see fair-play to either.

"Terrier quality," or "Terrier character," is the last point upon which we propose to touch, and it is a most essential one when Fox-terriers have got to be considered. It is an almost indescribable characteristic which a Fox-terrier possesses, and which is certainly obliterated by the taint of Bull, so often seen in modern Fox-terriers. Mr. Theodore Bassett, who is certainly one of the most popular judges of the day, writes as follows upon this subject :—

"Of course a dog with *no* Terrier characteristic cannot be a Terrier; and, therefore, as a Fox-terrier could not win. But, query, should a dog with a superabundance of what is termed 'character,' even though at the same time he is possessed of positive deformities, beat an animal far better made in almost every point that may not have quite the same amount of 'Terrier expression,' but which for all that is a real Terrier? If White English Terrier expression is a drawback, what then about Bulldog properties. Surely White English Terrier is 'Terrier expression,' and surely Bulldog is the reverse; and yet it is a well-known fact that some judges go mad at the one and quietly ignore the other. My own opinion is that either may exist in a very good though by no means perfect dog; and that certainly of the two the White English Terrier type is far preferable, belonging as it does to the *genus* Terrier."

Having thus gone through the points of the modern Fox-terrier, we will briefly allude to the most notable breeders and exhibitors of the day. The number of exhibitors and supporters of the breed is legion, but prominent amongst them the names of the following gentlemen appear conspicuous :—Messrs. F. Burbidge, of Hunton Bridge, Watford; J. H. Murchison, of Sydenham; Mr. Theodore Bassett, Mr. Russell Earp, Mr. F. Redmond, of London; Mr. W. Allison, of Thirsk; Mr. H. Gibson, of Lymington; J. A. Doyle, of North Wales; R. White, of Sheffield; W. J. Hyde, of Battle; H. Champion, of Retford; J. C. Tinne, of Lymington; A. H. Clarke, of Nottingham; J. Terry, W. Hulse, and Wooton, of the same town; the Hon. T. Fitzwilliam; Mr. R. B. Lee, of Kendal, and others, have all owned some good smooth-haired ones; whilst some excellent wire-haired Fox-terriers have been exhibited by Messrs. S. E. Shirley, W. Tredennick, Harding Cox, W. M. Graham, J. H. Petler, Hayward Field, and L. Hogg.

The dogs which we have selected for illustration in the coloured plate are : first, Mr. J. W. Hyde's Buffet, who was bred by Mr. H. Gibson of Lymington, in 1872, by Buffer, out of Frolic, by Foiler; Buffer by Marquis of Huntly's Bounce, out of Trinket. He won second prize Crystal Palace and champion Nottingham, 1873; champion Wolverhampton and second Hull, 1874; champion prize Wolverhampton and champion prize Brighton, 1875; champion prize Bath, first prize Birmingham, champion prize and Fox-terrier Club challenge cup Alexandra Palace, 1876; Birmingham champion prize, Crystal Palace champion prize, Alexandra Palace champion prize, and Fox-terrier Club challenge cup, 1877; and champion Crystal Palace, 1880.

The next, Mr. F. Burbidge's Bloom, bred by owner from Bluff, out of Bloomer, winner of first prize and Fox-terrier Club challenge cup, and first and medal Dublin, 1879.

The Wire-haired Terrier is Mr. S. E. Shirley's Bristles, a wonderful good bitch, bred by Mr. J. Thorebeck, of Darlington, in 1877, by Crib, out of Wasp, by Spark. She has taken first Boro'bridge, champion Newtonards, first Whitby, and second Alexandra Palace, in 1878; and first Brighton, second Alexandra Palace, and first Birmingham, 1879.

Brokenhurst Sting, the property of Mr. Theodore Bassett, which is represented in the engraving, was, like Buffet, bred by Mr. H. Gibson; he was whelped in 1877, and is by Brokenhurst Joe, out of Brokenhurst Nettle. He won first and extra prize in the Puppy class at Crystal Palace in 1878.

We have been unable to procure the measurements of the dogs illustrated on the coloured plate, but Mr. Theodore Bassett has kindly forwarded us the following measurements of Broken-hurst Sting. Length from tip of nose to stop, 2¾ inches; length from stop to occiput, 4½ inches; length of back, 13 inches; girth of fore-arm, 4¾ inches; girth of pastern, 3⅛ inches; height at shoulders, 15 inches; height at elbows, 7⅞ inches; height at loins, 15 inches; height at hock, 4½ inches. Weight, 16½ lbs.

According to our rule we append scale of points to be used in judging this breed.

SCALE OF POINTS FOR JUDGING FOX-TERRIERS.

	Value.
Head and ears	10
Shoulders	5
Body	10
Legs and feet	10
Coat	5
Size	5
General appearance	5
Total	50

CHAPTER XXXVIII.

THE HARRIER.

THERE can be very little doubt that the modern Harrier owes his origin to the same sources which produced the Foxhound; and the points of difference in the structural developments of the two breeds are so very slight that the standard which applies to Foxhounds consequently will be equally useful when Harriers have to be judged. The size is the chief material difference between the two breeds, and the pace which they can travel of course is not the same, as the animals hunted differ from each other in so many respects.

That hare-hunting is an ancient pursuit is amply proved from the number of early writers who have borne testimony to the fact; and amongst those who have given us descriptions of the art, the name of Xenophon is eminently conspicuous. As more than one of the writers who have drawn largely upon his work for early information have observed, the knowledge Xenophon possessed of the habits of the hare was certainly considerable, and accurate to an almost unparalleled extent. We therefore propose in the first instance quoting some extracts from his writings, a full translation of which appear in William Blane's "Cynegetica," which was published in London so far back as 1788. In the form in which we reproduce them, Xenophon's remarks will be made to appear in a series of continuous paragraphs. This is simply for convenience sake, and it must not be supposed that his entire work is given, for condensation has had to be largely resorted to in order to confine his ideas within a reasonable limit. Xenophon remarks that—

"The trail of a hare is long during the winter, on account of the length of the nights, and in the summer short, for the contrary reason. In the winter there is no scent early in the morning, when there is either a hoar frost or ice; for the hoar frost, by its proper force collecting the warm particles, contains them in itself, and the ice condenses them. When this happens, the dogs with delicate noses" (literally, "the dogs whose noses are tender") "cannot touch before the sun dispels them. Then the dogs can smell, and the trail yields a scent as it evaporates.

"The scent of a hare going to her form lasts longer than that of her course when pursued. When she goes to her form she goes slowly, often stopping; but her course when pursued is performed running: therefore the ground is saturated with one, and not filled with the other. The scent is always stronger in woody places than in open ones, for there, sometimes running and sometimes sitting, she is touched by many things. The trail of the hare is the path she takes going to her seat" (or "form"), "which in cold weather will generally be in sheltered places, and, in hot, in shady places. When she sits, the lower parts of her joints are covered by her belly; her forelegs are most commonly close together and extended, resting her chin on the extremity of her feet; her ears are extended over her shoulders, and her hair is well adapted for a covering, being thick and soft. When she wakes she winks her eyelids, but when she sleeps she keeps them continuously open without motion, having her eyes fixed. She moves her nostrils frequently when sleeping, but less often when awake. Their eyesight is by no means sharp, for their eyes project, and their eyelids are short, and not sufficient to protect the ball, on which account their eyesight is weak and indistinct. When she is pursued, the fear of the dogs and hunters takes away her presence of mind, on which account she often runs unknowingly against many things, and sometimes falls into the nets. If she ran straight forward, these things would seldom happen to her; but running a ring, and loving the places where she was bred and has fed, she is taken.

"The accoutrements of the dogs consist in a collar, a leading leather thong, and a surcingle to guard the body. They should never be taken out to hunt unless they eat their food heartily, for if they do not, it is a sure sign they are not healthy. They should never be suffered to hunt foxes, as that does them the greatest damage. The places of hunting should frequently be changed, that the dogs may be thoroughly acquainted with the nature of hunting: and it is necessary to go out early in the morning, that the trail may not be gone. Those who go out late deprive the dogs of the chance of finding a hare, and themselves of the sport: neither will scent, by reason of its nature, continue in all weather.

"If the dog picks the trail out straight forward from the works the hare has been making, he should slip another, and as these persist in the trail he should loose the rest, one after another, without great intervals, and should follow himself, but not too closely, encouraging the dogs by their names, but not too vehemently, lest they should be too eager before the proper time. When the hounds are near the hare, they discover it to the huntsman by shaking violently not only their tails but their whole bodies, by rushing on in a warlike manner, by trying to surpass each other in speed, by running eagerly together, by now crowding close and then dispersing, and then again running on, till at length they come to the seat of the hare, and run in upon her. She immediately jumps up and flies, the dogs pursuing her in full cry, those who follow crying out, 'Haloo, dogs!' and the huntsman, wrapping his coat round his hand, and carrying his pole, should follow the dogs, taking care to keep behind the hare, and not to head her, which is unsportsmanlike. The hare, running off, and soon being out of sight, generally comes back again to the place where she was found —the huntsman calling to the person at the nets, 'To him, boy! to him, boy!' and he signifies whether she is taken or not.

"When the scent is very strong, the hounds rush upon it leaping, crowding together, and stooping down: but while they thus persist in the scent close together, the huntsman must restrain himself, and not follow the dogs too near, lest through emulation they should overrun the scent.

"The best time for breeding dogs is in the winter, when the labours of the chase are over—the quiet of that season, and the approach of spring, being most likely to contribute to form a generous race, for that time of the year agrees best with the growth of dogs. The puppies, when they are whelped, should be left with their mother, and not put to another bitch. The care of others is not so good for their growth; the milk, and even the breath, of the mother, is better for them, and her caresses more endearing. When the puppies can run about, they should have milk for the first year, and nothing else, for the filling them with too heavy food will distort their legs, fill their bodies with diseases, and hurt their inside. The bitch puppies should first be taken out to hunt at eight months old, and the dogs at ten; but do not let them loose during the trail, but, keeping them tied in long leather slips, suffer them to follow the dogs that are trailing, letting them also go over the scent."

From these remarks of Xenophon it is clearly shown that hare-hunting was carried on in his days in *something* of the same fashion as in more recent times. It certainly would be contrary to a modern sportsman's ideas to use a net in which it is hoped to drive the hare, and the appearance of the huntsman in the field with his coat over his arm, and carrying a long pole, would also provoke considerable astonishment in these more enlightened days. Again, Xenophon's remarks upon breeding, in which he advocates breeding in the winter season, on account of hunting operations being over, clearly tend to prove that at the time he wrote it was customary to hunt earlier in the year than modern masters do. However, there is so much good sense in all he says that the quotation from his work must surely be read with interest, if not with actual benefit, by those who take an interest in and support the science of hare-hunting.

For more modern experiences of the art we are again driven to the writings of that great authority whom we have already quoted—Mr. Peter Beckford, whose letters have been freely made use of by the editor of the "Sportsman's Cabinet," from which we quote the following :—

"As the trail of a hare lays both partially and imperfectly in proportion to the length of time elapsed since she went to her seat, so is the difficulty of finding increased in proportion to the late or early hour at which the hounds are thrown off; hence it is that the attendance upon different packs, under the denomination of hare-finders, so very little known or required at that time, are now become so truly and unavoidably instrumental to the sport of the day. Although the services of these people are always welcome to the anxious and expectant sportsman, yet it is admitted by every judicious and competent observer, they are exceedingly prejudicial to the good order and regular discipline of hounds; for having occasionally such assistance, they become habitually indolent and progressively wild; the game being so frequently and easily found for them, they become individually and conjunctively indifferent to the trouble of finding it for themselves. Those who are accustomed to have their hares found sitting, know the hare-finders as well as they know the huntsman, and will not only upon sight set off to meet him, but have their heads eternally thrown up in the air in expectation of a view hollaa!

" Packs of harriers well managed, and regularly disciplined, should be quietly brought up to the place of meeting, and when thrown off a general silence should prevail, that every hound may be permitted to do his work. Those well bred and properly broke seldom stand in need of assistance. Officious intrusions frequently do more harm than good ; nothing requires greater judgment, or nicer observation in speaking to a hound, than to know the critical moment when a word is wanting. Young sportsmen, like young hounds, are too much accustomed to babbling when newly entered, and often by frivolous questions, or obtrusive conversation, attract the attention of the hounds, and ensure the silent curse of or public reproach of the huntsman, as well as the contemptuous indifference of every experienced sportsman present upon such occasions.

" Those who keep harriers vary considerably in their modes of hunting them; but the humane and liberal-minded never deviate from the consistency and strict impartiality of the chase. If a hare is found sitting, and the hounds too near at hand, they should be immediately (and as it were accidentally) drawn off to prevent her being chopped in her form ; the hare should then be silently walked up by the individual who found her, or knows where she is seated, that she may be permitted to go off without alarm at her own pace. The hounds should then be drawn quietly over the spot from whence she started, where being permitted to come calmly and unexpectedly upon the scent, they then go away with it in a style of uniformity, constituting what may be candidly considered the consistency of the chase.

"Much noise and clamour are directly contrary to the systematic principles of hare-hunting, which is to be calm, perfectly quiet, and to let the hounds alone; few hounds are so good, none better, than many town packs who have no professed huntsman engaged to hunt them. If they have no one to assist them, it must, at the same time, be remembered they have no one to interrupt them, which in this kind of hunting is still more material; though

MR. CHURCHILL LANGDON'S HARRIER, "COUNTESS."

there is one fault such hounds must of necessity be guilty of, that is, running back to heel. Hounds are naturally fond on scent, and if they are foiled and disappointed in carrying it forward, they of course turn and endeavour to hunt it back: hounds left to themselves soon repeat this to a fault, and, it is to be observed, almost the only one they have.

"Although it is upon the broad scale of universality certainly best to let the hounds alone, thereby giving as much scope as possible to their natural instinct, yet in this particular instance it is necessary to check it mildly; for as it is an almost invariable rule in every kind of hunting to make the head good, they should be encouraged to try forward first; which may always be done without taking them off their noses, or the least prejudice to their hunting. If trying forward should not succeed, they may be permitted to try back, which they will at all times be ready enough to do; for they are always perfectly sensible how far they brought the scent, know where they left it, and are eagerly anxious to recover it. Much at this moment depends upon the temper, patience, and skill of the huntsman, who should be attached to the sport and indefatigable in the pursuit of it; he should be sensible, good-tempered, sober, exact, and cleanly, a good groom, and an excellent horseman; his voice should be strong and clear, with an eye so quick as to perceive which of his hounds carry the scent when all are running, and where they throw up; as well as an ear so excellent, as always to distinguish the leading hounds when he does not see them. Such are the qualities that constitute perfection in a huntsman; he should not, however, be too fond of displaying them, till called forth by necessity; it being a peculiar and distinguishing trait in his province to let the hounds alone whilst they can hunt, and strenuously to assist them when they cannot.

" It has been before observed, that when a hare is found, she cannot be permitted to steal away too silently before the hounds; her own extreme timidity frequently occasions her heading, and the pack are so repeatedly liable to overrun the scent. The huntsman, by not pressing too close upon the hounds himself, will keep the company at a proper distance also, and when they are thus left to a proper and free use of their own faculties, they are but little likely to over-run it much." Mr. Beckford, whose judgment and celebrity is so universally known and so frequently mentioned, has something so applicable and truly just in almost every page upon this subject, that it is impossible to resist the temptation of quoting a few occasional passages where the intentional purport is so emphatically expressed.

" High-bred, spirited Harriers should never be too much pressed upon by horsemen in the chase, or too much encouraged at a check; for their natural eagerness in the former, and their disappointment in the latter, will, at such a time, frequently carry them wide of the scent beyond a possibility of recovery, and this should, of course, be guarded against as much as circumstances will permit. On high-roads and footpaths a too hasty reliance must not be made; but when a hit is made on either side, the hounds cannot be encouraged too much. A hare generally describes a circle as she runs, larger or lesser in extent according to her own strength and the nature of the country she is hunted in. In enclosures intersected with small coverts, those circles are so small that it is an almost constant puzzle to the hounds.

" A hare will, it is well known, after running a path some considerable distance, make a double, and then stop till the hounds have passed her; she will then steal away secretly, and return the same way she came. This is the most arduous trial for hounds; it is so hot a foil that, in the best packs, there are not many hounds that can hunt it; those who can should be attended to, and an endeavour made to hit her off where she breaks her foil, which she will soon do when she thinks herself secure, except it is in covert, when the scent lies bad, and then she sometimes absolutely seems to hunt the hounds. In a favourable day for hunting, hounds seldom give up the scent at head; if they do, there is generally a palpable reason for it; and this, those who hunt the hounds should be careful to observe, as by it alone they will be the better qualified to make their cast. If the huntsman be of a superior description, he will attend as he goes not only to his hounds (minutely observing which have the lead and what scent they carry), but also to the various circumstances attendant upon sudden changes of the weather and difference of soil. He will also be mindful of the distance she keeps before the hounds, recollect her former doubles, and the point she principally makes to.

" It should be the peculiar care of every huntsman to prevent, as much as possible, his hounds from chopping hares in their forms; huntsmen are, in general, too fond of getting blood at any rate, and when hounds are used to it, it is surprising to see how anxious they are to find opportunities. In many instances a hare must be very wild or very nimble to escape them. Mr. Beckford remembers, in a furzy country, his hounds to have chopped three hares in one morning; for it is the nature of those animals either to leap up and steal away before the hounds come near them, or else to lie close, till they put their very noses upon them. Hedges also are dangerous in this respect, particularly if the huntsman beats the hedge himself, which is too much the practice; the hounds in such case are always upon the watch, and a hare must be exceeding lucky to escape them all. The best way to prevent it is to have the hedge well beaten at some distance before the hounds.

"Old dogs should never be warded to old or enfeebled bitches; such extreme should be avoided; when there is age on one side there should be youth on the other; and this experience seems with justice to have been decided in favour of the masculine gender. Both sire and dam should be healthy, or there can be no great probability of a healthy offspring. If a hound who in other respects be excellent, and a well-founded favourite, should be a little inclined to skirting, with too much dash in his disposition, such dog should be crossed with a close-tongued, thorough-line hunting bitch, from both which an admirable hit may probably ensue. The great and most substantial reason for not breeding from either a skirting-hound or a babbler is that they are too often seen to acquire one or the other, by imitation or practice, and it may be better not to render it natural by propagating habitual defects with the blood.

"Where it can be so managed, puppies are best produced in the spring months; late whelps thrive in an equal degree; at least, they all require the best walks and the greater attention. Bitches should not be permitted to hunt in the advanced stages of gestation: it frequently debilitates the puppies, and sometimes proves fatal to the bitch herself; nor is it altogether prudent to leave them in the kennel when the time of parturition is approaching. A bitch having many puppies (of whose future excellence great expectation is formed) may have them occasionally preserved by transferring a part to any other bitch happening to be in a similar state at the same time. This particular race seems to prove, upon the general scale, more prolific than most of the species, having sometimes an extraordinary number; they have been known to bring forth fifteen, and even sixteen, all alive.

"When breeding from a favourite sort, it is matter of convenience if another bitch can be warded at or about the same time; by which the whole of both litters (if required) can be saved. At this period the bitches should be amply furnished with flesh, and by no means stinted in milk. The whelps should not be taken away till they are very well able to take care of themselves: they will soon learn to lap by example, and the mother will be the sooner relieved. When the puppies are taken away, the bitches should have each three doses of physic, that no humours may be produced by the absorption of the milk. The distemper makes such a dreadful havoc amongst young hounds that too much attention cannot be bestowed upon its counteraction. Numbers of young hounds perish at their walks under the effects of disease, and this probably happens from the little care taken of them upon such occasions.

"You ask how many hounds a pack of Harriers should consist of, and what kind of hound is best suited to that diversion. You should never exceed twenty couple in the field·

it might be difficult to get a greater number to run well together, and a pack of Harriers cannot be complete if they do not. Your other question is not easily answered. The hounds I think most likely to show you sport are between the large, slow-hunting Harrier and the little Fox Beagle: the former are too dull, too heavy, and too slow, the latter too lively, too light, and too fleet. The first species, it is true, have most excellent noses, and I make no doubt will kill their game at last, if the day be long enough: but you know the days are short in winter, and it is bad hunting in the dark. The others, on the contrary, are all alive, but every cold blast affects them; and if your country be deep and wet, it is not impossible that some of them may be drowned.

"My hounds were a cross of both these kinds, in which it was my endeavour to get as much bone and strength in as small a compass as possible. It was a difficult undertaking. I bred many years, and an infinity of hounds, before I could get what I wanted. I at last had the pleasure to see them very handsome, small yet bony. They ran remarkably well together, ran fast enough, had all the alacrity that you could desire, and would hunt the coldest scent. When they were thus perfect, I did as many others do—I parted with them."

There can be no doubt that all the writings of Mr. Beckford are those of not only a practical man, but of an enthusiast. He is accepted by sportsmen as *the* authority on fox and hare hunting even in the present day, which is a period of ninety-eight years since the first edition of his work appeared in 1782. This speaks volumes for the conservative pro-clivities of masters of hounds and hunting men in general, though doubtless much credit—if any credit there be—for the absence of any great change is due to the natural instincts of the animals hunted having undergone but slight alteration. Beckford had, by the way, a contemporaneous brother-writer on sporting, and particularly hunting, subjects, of equal merit in another way. This was William Somerville the poet, whose position as bard of the sporting world much resembles that occupied by Dibdin in nautical circles, as *the* only recognised poet of his admirers.

In spite of the popularity of fox-hunting the number of packs of Harriers throughout the country is steadily on the increase. This is not to be at all wondered at when the love of sport for which Englishmen are so noted, and the comparative cheapness of hare-hunting, come to be considered. We use the expression "comparative" advisedly, as even a pack of Harriers is an expensive luxury to indulge in, though naturally a far lighter tax upon the Master's resources than a pack of Foxhounds would be.

Amongst the principal packs in the country are the Anglesey, the Master of which is Capt. Rayner; the Earl of Pembroke's; The Trafford, Master Sir Humphrey de Trafford; Sir Harvey Bateson's, Pendle Forest, a rattling pack of half-bred Fox-hounds, whose Master is Colonel Starkie; The Taunton Vale; Easton Park, Master Duke of Hamilton; and the Cotswold, of which Sir Francis C. Ford, Bart., is Master and huntsman. The number of couples in these packs is on the average about eighteen, and they hunt two or three days a week. The usual height of a Harrier is from 17 to 20 inches; if much higher than that a strong cross of Foxhound is probably present in the strain.

It is, however, notorious that many packs of Harriers are nothing more or less than half-bred or dwarf Foxhounds, and therefore a dash of this blood can hardly be looked upon with extreme disfavour, though it should not be encouraged, as it is likely to cause the breed to become too big and fast for the purposes for which they are required.

It is as a dwarf Southern Hound that the Harrier should be most properly regarded, and therefore he shows a somewhat coarser head and more throat than the modern Foxhound. A Harrier has also a far better nose than a Foxhound, but this naturally enough does not necessitate a structural difference. One peculiarity, however, which distinguishes a Harrier from a Foxhound is the recognition of blue-mottle as a correct colour for the breed. The other hound colours are also met with in Harriers, but blue-mottle is considered a disqualification in the case of any hound but a Harrier, as it is thought to be a certain test of Harrier blood, and therefore inadmissible in a Foxhound.

The worst feature in modern Harriers, which is derived from the Foxhound cross, is that gained from the insane craze for *pace*, which in the minds of so many Masters is essential in a Harrier. Harriers which are too much gifted with pace, often lose all, or, at all events, almost all, their great powers of scent, and instead of hunting their hare, fairly run her to a standstill. This is greatly deplored by lovers of the old style of hare-hunting, who were accustomed to pride themselves on the cleverness, not the speed, of their pack. And it should therefore be borne in mind by Masters of Harriers that, though a certain amount of Foxhound blood may be permissible in their pack, still their hounds are really descendants of the old Southern Hound, which was by no means a fast animal.

The subject of illustration in our woodcut is Countess, a badger-pied bitch, and the property of Mr. Churchill Langdon. Countess measures from tip of nose to stop, 3½ inches; from stop to occiput, 4½ inches; length of back, 19 inches; girth of thigh, 11 inches; girth of fore-arm, 5½ inches; girth of pastern, 4 inches; height at shoulders, 19¾ inches; height at elbows, 11½ inches; height at loins, 19 inches; height at hock, 5¾ inches; length of stern, 13 inches; weight, 37 lbs.; age, 2 years, 2 months.

As mentioned before, the structural resemblance between the Foxhound and Harrier is so marked that the standard for each is identical in every point.

CHAPTER XXXIX.

THE BEAGLE.

In "Cynographia Britannica" the following allusion is made to the Beagle:—

"Of the hound tribe the Beagle is the least, and is only used for the purpose of hare-hunting. Their method of finding is very similar to the Harrier, but they are far inferior in point of swiftness; yet to those sportsmen who hunt in a dry and enclosed country, where the coverts are not too large and strong, and who delight in unravelling the intricate mazes of the doubling hare, more than in the death, they afford no inconsiderable degree of amusement.

"When the atmosphere is a little hazy, and the scent low, they catch it better than the taller dogs, spending their tongues freely in treble or tenor, and though more soft yet not less melodious than the Harrier. But as most sportsmen prefer the faster and stronger dogs, these are by no means in such repute as formerly, a complete cry or pack of them being very rarely seen. They are now (A.D. 1800) chiefly kept as finders to the Greyhounds in coursing, which purpose they answer extremely well, hence they are frequently called Finders.

"The varieties are generally distinguished by the parts where they are bred, as the Southern Beagle, bearing a strong resemblance to the slow, deep-mouthed Southern Hound, but much smaller; the Northern Beagle which is lighter formed, with shorter ears, and swifter. A cross between these two is esteemed preferable to either.

"The Southern Beagles are smooth-haired, with long ears, and generally so loosely formed that they cannot for a continuance be hunted in a heavy country without being crippled. Besides which they have frequently some very great faults in a hound, as crooked legs, tailing or lagging behind when they begin to tire, or are too small.

"The Northern, which are commonly wire-haired, straight-limbed, and better formed in their shoulders and haunches, endure bad weather and long exercise with less inconvenience than the Southern. They hunt hedge-rows, thread the brakes, and runset" (i. e., follows the hare through the mews or opening in the hedges which she passes backwards and forwards through) "with the hare with great spirit, but it is evident to the most common observer that neither of them are calculated to bear much fatigue.

"Beagles, like other hounds, are of various colours, and preferred as the fancy of the owner dictates. In height about twelve inches, and are hunted and treated in the same manner as the Harrier.

"The term Beagle has been indiscriminately used by many for the Harrier and the Beagle but it is now wholly confined to the latter. They are seldom crossed with others unless to diminish their size, and are apt to challenge any scent when hot, even that of birds."

Three years later, in 1803, some very interesting remarks on the breed appeared in the "Sportsman's Cabinet," which are valuable as showing that the Beagle is essentially the same dog now as it was then. The writer in the "Sportsman's Cabinet" appears to have the modern prejudice against Beagles, for he commences his remarks as follows:—

"Previous to the present improved state of hunting and polish of field sports, packs of Beagles were frequently seen in the possession of gentlemen whose age or infirmities prevented their enjoyment of sport of a different description. But in proportion to the gradational improvements made in the different kinds of hounds (according to the different chases which they were intened to pursue) the former attachment to Beagles has been observed to decline.

"They are the smallest of the hound race used in this country, are exquisite in their scent of the hare, and indefatigably vigilant in their pursuit of her. This slow kind of hunting was admirably adapted to age and the feminine gender. It could be enjoyed by ladies of the greatest timidity, as well as gentlemen labouring under infirmity, to both of whom it was a consolation that if they were occasionally a little way behind, there was barely a possibility of their being thrown out. A pack of this description was perfectly accommodating to the neighbouring rustics—the major part of those not being possessed of horses found it a matter of no great difficulty to be up well with them on foot. The spirit of emulation seemed formerly to be who should produce the greatest degree of merit in the smallest compass, and packs were to be seen in different parts of the most diminutive description.

"Amongst professed amateurs every effort was made to attain perfection, and these indefatigable endeavours were generally attended with success. Beagles were almost uniformly so well matched that they did not exceed ten or eleven inches in height, and so carefully selected in respect to speed that whenever they were running they might be covered with a sheet—and this alone is the predominant trait of celebrity in packs of Hounds or Beagles, whether great or small. These, though slow, are incredibly destructive; for if the scent lays well, the hare has very little chance of escape, and this to the object of pursuit must prove a lingering as well as a certain death; for although in the early part of the chase they can never get near enough to the hare to press her, yet they are in general fatal, if even three or four hours in killing.

"The numerous and diversified crosses in the different breeds of both Beagles and Hounds, according to the views, wishes, and inclinations of those who keep them, have so complicated and variegated that particular part of the species that a volume might be produced in describing the various sorts and sizes as thought best adapted to the soil and surface for which they are bred and intended to hunt, from the old, heavy, deep-tongued, dew-lapped, Southern Hound of Lancashire (where the huntsman with his long pole follows on foot) to the fleetest-bred Northern Harriers of the present day, who kill their game in a burst of half an hour or forty minutes, with a degree of rapidity but little inferior to coursing.

"Beagles, in the sporting acceptation of the term, are not to be considered synonymous with Harriers, to whom, although they possess precisely the same properties, they are very much inferior in size. That some adequate idea may be formed of the original Beagle, the following ludicrous transaction is introduced from the most indisputable authority.

"The late Colonel Hardy had once a collection of this diminutive tribe, amounting to ten or twelve couples, which were always carried to and from the field of glory in a large pair of panniers slung across a horse. Small as they were, and insignificant as they would now seem, they could invariably keep a hare at all her shifts to escape them, and finally worry, or rather tease her to death. The catastrophe attending this curious pack was of a very singular description, for a small barn having been for some time appropriated to the purpose of a kennel, was one night broke open, and every hound, as well as the panniers, stolen; nor could the most diligent search ever discover the least trace of the robbers or their sporting appendage."

Originally there were several varieties of Beagles, and even now-a-days the difference between many of the packs is very obvious. This difference, at the present time, is certainly chiefly one of size, for the Beagles used for the purpose of being followed on foot would naturally be too fast if above a certain height. Formerly the two distinct breeds of Beagle were the Rough and the Smooth. The rough-coated Beagle was more frequently met with in Wales than in other parts of the country, though it has now almost disappeared from amongst us, being only rarely met with, and then in out-of-the-way places for the most part.

One of the keenest admirers of the smooth-haired Beagle was King George IV., who, when Prince of Wales, used to hunt with this class of dog; and his Royal Highness's dwarf pack was an institution on Brighton Downs. These dwarf Beagles are, however, almost useless except for following on foot, and run considerable risk of losing their lives by being drowned in the ditches in wet weather. Nevertheless, their superior powers of scent are conspicuous over the larger hounds, more especially when the atmosphere is close, as they run nearer the ground than the latter.

According to Blaine, the earlier varieties varied from the "deep-flewed diminutive type of the old Southern hound to the fleet and elegant Foxhound Beagle; to which we may add the pigmy breed called 'Lapdog Beagles.'"

It is not given to every one to be the happy possessor of broad acres where, in spinney furze or briery brake, or from the tussocks of the uplands, pussy can be dislodged from her seat to give play to the Liliputian hound, and afford hunters the pleasure of a display of the amazing powers of scent possessed by the Beagle.

There are, however, in England few localities where there is not common land, or, lacking that advantage, farmers too strongly imbued with the genuine English love of sport to interpret too closely the law of trespass when a cry of Beagles, with its followers, are in the case. Even in such districts there may be no ground game preserved, and the master of the musical pack may be in consequence compelled to hunt them on a drag. Here, the choice of articles that will challenge the olfactories of our little hound, and lead them to pursue a Will-o'-the-wisp they can never overtake, is so plethoric as to puzzle. A portion of dead rabbit or hare—the skin of a newly killed one is perhaps best—a red herring, or oil of aniseed, may be used. The two former must be dragged along the grass by a string. In using aniseed the powder may be resorted to, and the runner should let it out with regularity from a tin similar to that used in the drill sowing of seeds, or, what is better, the man who is sent on to make the drag should rub the soles of his boots with the essential oil of aniseed, and for economy this should be diluted with plain olive oil. It is of course necessary that the application of this should be frequently renewed, and at intervals, when the smell is strong on the boots, the man should tread around so that the hounds may occasionally dwell on the scent, and, whilst giving tongue in melodious tones, also give time for the sportsman following their windings to make up lost ground.

The following mixture is, perhaps, the best to make a drag for Beagles of an artificial character—it is extremely lasting, and the hounds take it up with great readiness. It consists of half an ounce of oil of aniseed, a quarter of an ounce of essential oil of valerian, and an ounce and a quarter of castor oil, mixed.

With reference to the relation of Beagle to modern Fox-terrier, Markham, in dealing with the diversities of the hounds of his time, after referring to and describing the large slow hounds of the west countries, the middle-sized and more swift, or nimble, as he puts it, hounds of the counties of Worcester, Bedford, &c., where the woods and plains were of about equal extent; the still more light, nimble, swift, and slender hounds of Yorkshire and the north, comes at last to the "little Beagle" of curious scent. And here we desire our readers to dwell carefully on what follows, for we consider it throws a great deal of light on the origin of our modern Fox-terrier, and strongly supports the opinion we have long held that our Fox-terriers have a large infusion of Beagle blood in them.

Markham, who was a practical sportsman, says:—"The white hound, or the white with black spots, are the most principal and best to compose your kennel of, and will indeed hunt any chase exceeding well . . . yet if you demand which is the best and most beautiful of all colours for the general kennel, then I answer, *the white with the black ears and the black spot at the setting on of the tail.*" The italics are ours, but we point to the description and ask, Does it not paint with considerable accuracy the Fox-terrier of to-day? Certainly, as far as colour and markings go, it leaves nothing to be desired; and, on the general argument, we may point to the fact as being strongly in favour of our view that a still older writer, Dr. Caius, in his treatise on "English Dogges," classes the Bloodhound, the Harrier, and the Terrier together, and omits all mention of the Beagle by that name.

Now the Beagle was known and had been described under that name as a dog native to Britain by Roman historians ten centuries and more before the time of Caius, which makes his silence on Beagles, whilst he classifies the Terrier with the Hound, still more remarkable; and is surely at least strongly suggestive that the Terrier he wrote of was the small hound formerly, then, and now, called a Beagle.

Again, Markham says:—"The grizzled, which are ever most commonly shag-haired, or any other colour, whether it be mixed or unmixed so it be shag-haired, are the best varminers, and therefore are chosen to hunt the *Fox, Badger*, or other hot scent—they also are exceeding good and cunning finders; and, therefore, of huntsmen not thought amiss to have one or a couple in every kennel."

Surely, so far as that description goes, it applies to the wire-haired Fox-terrier of to-day—it describes his special work, for now, as then, he is the dog *par excellence* for the fox, badger, otter, and all other animals we include under the term vermin.

The grizzled or grey-coloured patches—for we do not understand Markham to mean that the whole body was of that colour—are still characteristic of Fox-terriers, especially the rough-coated ones, and the very common description, used as a mark of merit, "hound-tan markings," surely suggests a hound origin for this Terrier; and it must be acknowledged that the various shades of tan, the badger-pie, hare-pie, &c., met with in hounds also appear in Fox-terriers, and to what hound can we ascribe the origin of these peculiarities if not to the Beagle, that dog being also of the size most likely to suit for crossing with the Terrier to produce dogs fit for fox, otter, or badger bolting or drawing.

It is not in colour alone that the Beagle asserts itself in the Fox-terrier—the very shape and make of many purely-bred ones (so-called) proclaim their descent—and in formation of head, and length of ears, pups of the best strains constantly show a throw-back to the Beagle. In the present day the wire-haired Beagle is limited in numbers, but still to be met with in Devon, Wales, and some few other localities—packs or cry of the smooth variety are plentiful—some used regularly for hare hunting, others, as already said, to hunt a drag. They vary greatly in size, from ten inches up to sixteen inches in height, according to the country they are to hunt, and the fancy of the master.

One or a couple of small Beagles prove excellent assistants to the gun in covert and hedge-row shooting, when a dog is not required to hunt mute—indeed, with some of them, the game they are on may be distinguished by the peculiar tone of their voice as they announce a find. The troublesome characteristic of Beagles, as dogs to shoot over, is their inveterate propensity to chase.

One of the most remarkable little packs of Beagles which ever came beneath our notice was shown by Mr. G. H. Nutt, of Maidstone, at the Alexandra Palace show of 1877. During the progress of the exhibition Mr. Nutt treated his friends to a glimpse of his pigmy pack at work, for he ran them a short drag in the grounds, much to the delight of many lady visitors to the palace. Mr. Nutt has since informed us that he has been compelled to give up his pets, as the difficulties he had to encounter in his breeding operations, from the small size of the bitches, fairly tired him out. As he somewhat pathetically remarked, "they had hardly the strength to produce their young, and when they succeeded in doing so, were usually too weak to bring them up." Of course this difficulty need not appear in larger-sized packs (Mr. Nutt's being remarkably small, and, as he expressed it, "only fit for ladies to run after").

In the present day the average height of the working pack is about 14½ inches, which, though small in comparison to the size of a Foxhound or Harrier, is sufficiently large for the purposes for which they are required.

As regards a standard of points for judging this breed, we cannot do better than refer our readers to that given in the Foxhound chapter; as the Beagle, with the exception of its size, can be satisfactorily judged by the scale used in the case of Foxhounds.

CHAPTER XL.

THE DACHSHUND.

WITH the exception of the modern Fox-terrier, it is doubtful if the institution of shows has done so much for any breed of dog as it has for the subject of this chapter. The quaint shape and peculiar appearance of the Dachshund rendered him from the first a conspicuous object on the bench, and no doubt greatly influenced many breeders to take up the breed. His admirers for the most part speak very highly of the Dachshund; but few breeds suffer oftener from the attacks of detractors, who affirm that the terms Dachshund and canine inutility are almost synonymous terms. For our own part, though we do not consider the Dachshund by any means to be the paragon of perfection which he is stated to be in some quarters, we willingly credit him with being a good useful working dog in his own country. Conversations which we have held on several occasions with German sportsmen have convinced us that this breed is largely used in the pursuit of wounded game, and his rather slow rate of progress makes a Dachshund more especially valuable, as it enables the sportsmen on foot to keep up with him with greater facility.

The name Dachshund conveys to many people the idea that this breed was produced for the purpose of destroying badgers only, and for no other object. As a matter of fact we believe that though many Dachshunds are " hard " enough to attack anything breathing, they are not as a rule so well adapted for such sanguinary employment as for the more peaceable and less painful task of tracking wounded animals, or beating coverts like an English Terrier. As a matter of fact, we know of an English gentleman, who prides himself upon the " hardness " of his dogs, who went in largely for Dachshunds. Six months' experience of the breed convinced him that they were unsuited for the work they were expected to go through in his kennels, and he finally abandoned them in favour of Bull and Wire-haired Terriers.

As will be seen from what appears below, there are at least two very distinct types of Dachshund; and the Rev. G. F. Lovell, of Oxford, who is admittedly an English authority on the breed, actually adds a third class to the number. The Toy class which he describes is, we really think, an objectionable ramification of the other two branches, for on the Continent we have seen toys of either type, and have always considered them weeds. The two chief distinctions are the *hound* and *terrier* type, both of which are fully alluded to below; but it is worthy of remark here that in this country, singular to relate, the former type is supported by the South Country school of breeders for the most part, whilst the Terrier stamp of dog finds admirers in the North.

Mr. John Fisher, of Carrshead Farm, is at the head of the northern Dachshund world, well seconded by Mr. Enoch Hutton, of Pudsey, near Leeds, who has kindly given us a detailed description of the points of the breed as they appear good in his eyes. In the South the Rev. G. F. Lovell reigns supreme, having for his lieutenant Mr. Everett Millais, of London, though the latter gentleman has devoted more of his affection to Bassets than Dachshunds, as will be seen in the succeeding chapter. We, therefore, consider ourselves especially fortunate in being able to give the opinions of three of these gentlemen; for though not unanimous in their estimates of the points, the views of each party are thoroughly sustained therein. We also propose introducing several engravings, mostly derived from foreign sources, descriptive of the breed, as, from its rapid progress in public estimation, we are of opinion that the Dachshund will soon be one of the most popular dogs in this country.

In the first place we will begin by quoting from the notes kindly supplied us by the Rev. G. F. Lovell, of St. Edmund's Hall, Oxford, who writes as follows:—

"Though the origin of the dog generally is lost in obscurity, yet the Dachshund can claim a very long pedigree; for a dog resembling it is found on the monument of Thothmes III., who reigned over Egypt more than 2,000 years B.C., and at whose court the inscriptions state he was a favourite; and a breed of similar appearance has been discovered by Dr. Haughton on early Assyrian sculptures. No doubt further research would bring to light other notices of the same kind, but these show that the abnormal shape of the fore-legs is not due to disease, as has been supposed by some who have not studied these dogs.

"This peculiarity is more commonly found than is generally imagined. Besides the Basset, both rough and smooth, and the Dachshund of France, it is apparent in an Indian breed, in the Swedish Beagle, in the Spaniel of Hungary and Transylvania, and almost certainly in the old English Bloodhound, though judges, setting Shakespeare at nought, are trying to get rid of it as a deformity.

"It has been asserted by a popular writer—'Snapshot'—that the Dachshund was not known in Germany until after the French Revolution, having been introduced by the French *émigrés*; but however this may be, most of our dogs of this breed have come from there, and it is the head-quarters of the race. Yet the Germans have in this, as in other cases, taken little pains to preserve the purity of the race, and mongrels abound among them.

"They may be divided into three varieties:—the Hound, the Terrier, and the Toy, though, of course, these are crossed with one another. The first of these is more generally recognised in the south of England, the second in the north. The third breed, which seems chiefly to come from Hanover and the adjacent countries, is distinguished by its snipy jaw, broad flat head, and small size. It has never found acceptance with judges, who prefer a dog that looks good for work.

"Dismissing this last, then, we find two distinct types, easily distinguished. The Terrier—which I shall pass over in few words, as I believe the hound-character to be the nearer to the original breed—is a hardy dog, with broad flat skull, short ears, often twisted, higher on the leg and shorter in body than the hound; his stern is also not so long as the other variety. The Dachshund proper, as it would seem from old engravings, was a hound in miniature; so he appears in Du Fouilloux for his Basset *à jambes torses* is clearly not the modern Basset, which has been developed from the ancient badger-digging dog of the sixteenth century (just as in Germany itself a large Dachshund is used as a tufter). No one would think of putting a modern Basset to dig out a badger or fox, so that either the badger or the Basset must have altered, and evidently the latter.

"I shall refrain in the following notes from criticising the opinions of others who have written, often very well, on their pet breed, but will merely give the conclusions which I have come to after having read everything I could find, having kept and bred these dogs for some years, and having taken notes of some hundreds of specimens.

"The head of the hound is long and narrow; the skull conical, with the protuberance strongly marked, though I have never seen it actually peaked as in the Bloodhound; no stop; the jaw long and very strong; the teeth long, the canines curved; the eyes of medium size and somewhat deeply set; ears long, fine, set on somewhat low, and farther back than in any other breed; the nose in a red dog should be flesh-coloured, but this is to be considered only when the competition is very close; the skin over the head not too tight, the forehead being wrinkled when the dog is excited; while the flews should be moderate in quantity, but not coarse.

DACHSHUNDS, FROM "LA VENERIE."

"The neck is neither so long as to give an appearance of weakness, nor so short as to be clumsy; there should be a certain amount of throatiness.

"The chest is broad and deep; the ribs well sprung, the back ribs being very short; the shoulders should be extremely muscular and very supple, the chest being let down between them; the loin is light and well arched; the muscles of the hind-quarters should have immense development.

"The fore-legs are very thick and muscular, bending in so that the knees nearly touch, and then again turning out, so that a line dropped from the outside of the shoulder will fall just outside the feet; the hind-legs are not so thick, and many good dogs are cow-hocked. They are much longer than the fore-legs. Almost all good Dachshunds either have dew-claws, or it will be found that they have been removed.

"The fore-feet are exceedingly thick and large, the sole being hard and horny; the stern is long, tapering gradually to the tip, it is rough underneath, and is carried straight with a downward curve near the end, but when the dog is excited gaily over the back; the coat must be short, fine, and as thick and close as possible; the skin very thick and extremely loose. The two original colours were the same as in the Bloodhound—red and black-and-tan—but from a long continuance of careless breeding they are found of all colours; but colour in the present state of the breed should count for very little if other points be all there. In height the Dachshund ought not to exceed 10 inches at the shoulder, and a dog of that height, and 40 or

DACHSHUNDS, FROM "LA VENERIE."

42 inches long, should weigh 20 lbs., the bitches being lighter than the dogs. At the same time many of our very best specimens are a little more than this both in size and weight. The prevailing faults in this breed are too great thickness of skull, combined with ears short and badly placed; the jaw is very weak—in fact, not one dog in ten has a good level mouth, while many have a lower jaw like an Italian Greyhound, and cannot crunch an ordinary chop-bone. Others get out at elbows from want of exercise or from weakness, while some have knees bent over, a great defect; the stern is often carried too high, or even over the back. There is one more hint which may be of service to exhibitors—Dachshunds are too often shown altogether out of condition: they require plenty of exercise and not too much to eat; their social qualities and their great intelligence make them pets in the house, but the points of the breed must be brought out by hard muscle, and it is impossible for a judge to give

points for a loin loaded with fat, or hind-quarters flabby from want of work. In character these dogs are very stubborn and headstrong, not standing the whip; from this cause, probably, arises the doubts which have been suggested as to their gameness, as, if corrected, they frequently lose temper and refuse to work, but when in sympathy with their master and once excited they will hesitate at nothing.

"I add the numerical value of the points of the Dachshund :—

Skull and eyes	15
Ears	10
Nose and muzzle	10
Body—throat, neck, shoulder, chest, loins, hind-quarters	25
Stern	10
Legs and feet	15
Colour	5
Skin and coat	10
	——
	100

"As to the use of points there is something to be said. First, they enable any one who has a dog to form some idea as to its worth; and secondly, when a judge has settled most of the dogs in the ring, either as not worthy of notice, or though not, on account of some great defect, fit for the prize, yet good enough for a commended or highly commended, he finds often he has three or four, or it may be half a dozen, dogs left in; it is then most satisfactory to compare the points of each specimen numerically, not necessarily in writing, to arrive at a right decision."

Mr. Enoch Hutton takes a widely different view of the case, as will be seen from the following description, kindly forwarded by him :—

"Very much has been written in the public papers—notably *The Live Stock Journal*—about the Dachshund, but not much to the purpose. It seemed to me that many persons who possessed a specimen (however moderate) of this interesting breed, although they had never bred a single one of the race, must needs 'rush into print,' without being able to help themselves, and give to the world *their* notion as to what an orthodox Dachshund should be; and their particular dog was held up as the correct model, which they advised all breeders to copy and aim at reproducing. Nor did it stop here: several persons who never even *owned* a specimen tried their hand at laying down the law of perfection in points, for the use and direction of breeders and judges.

"There were some few articles of relevant and reliable matter, emanating from the pens of one or two foreign writers of some experience—a few grains of wheat in bushels of chaff— but most of the articles were more calculated to mislead than to enlighten the reader.

"One of the pioneers of Dachshund lore in England was Mr. John Fisher, who has had much experience as a breeder and as a judge. Mr. Fisher's unrivalled old dog Feldmann was also the pioneer of his race on the show-bench in this country, in the days when even the judges had to be educated and enlightened as to the breed and utility of such an animal. I have myself heard a judge of some repute in the canine show-ring give it as his opinion that old Feldmann was '*nothing but a bad-bred bandy-legged Beagle!*'

"Now as to what a real Dachshund should or should not be like. He should be a *hound* in all hound-like points, the peculiarities of the breed only excepted—*i. e.*, he must have a hound's head set on a very long body on very short legs, and the fore legs must be very crooked or bandy without being much out at elbows or knuckling over at the knees, the *extreme length* from the nose-end to point of stem *should be* about *four times the height at shoulder*, and the animal should be massive, or, as some of us would say, clumsy and cloddy in appearance; in short, a big dog in small compass. The head should resemble somewhat that of a Foxhound, but must not be of so decided a type as seen in the Bloodhound.

" My plan is to reproduce the breed in its purity, and endeavour to get the best and purest blood possible to that end, but I will be no party to 'painting the lily.' It is difficult even in Germany to find really excellent specimens of the Dachshund which can be purchased, for the really pure breeds are mostly still in the hands of the nobility, and they do not care to part with even a puppy, except, perhaps, as a present occasionally to a relative or friend in their own sphere of life, or, may-be, a common specimen now and then to an inferior in position.

" The breed kept so select is preserved in its purity mostly, but in this, as in other breeds, unless the animals are properly cared for and kept up, there is no certainty of reproducing the breed *pure*. But the chances are that without such care the produce will be *mongrels*, with many of the characteristics of the breed doubtless, but still not the real thing ; and I aver that many, very many, of the Dachshunds which are imported into this country are not pure-bred. But yet with some people an *imported* animal *must* be correct and pure. Even where the pedigrees can be traced back for many generations without a single stain or cross on either side, it is impossible to breed *all* correct and good.

" For some time there has been a lot of noise respecting the style of *head* a Dachshund ought to have, some breeders making it appear that a " good head " makes a good dog, and with some judges who do not thoroughly understand the breed, a so-called " good head " has been an apology for the highest awards to otherwise badly-made dogs.

" According to the new modern fancy a 'good head' seems to mean a high-peaked skull and down face, with long ears, no matter how snipe-nosed and weak-jawed the animal may be, while the rest of his body may also be faulty—*i.e.*, it may be small and weak in bone, flat-ribbed, and short of muscle; and such a one is often allowed to rule the roast at our canine exhibitions.

" Now I wish to combat this erroneous idea, and as far as possible to write it down, if it may be ; and to do so, though late in the field, I will give my notions, with the rules and points by which I have been guided in my experience.

" A good head is an indispensable point with me, but there must be other grand qualities that must not be overlooked in a Dachshund; but to describe the breed properly it will be necessary to take point by point *seriatim*, and I will take the *head* first, allotting to it 25 points out of a possible 100 for perfection.

" 1. *Skull* (5 points) must be long and flat—*i.e.*, it should form a nearly straight line from the occipital bone to the nose point, and have very little stop ; and I prefer a moderate width of skull behind the ears, as I find a broad-headed dog has more courage than a narrow conical skulled one : the occipital bone should be well developed.

" 2. *Muzzle* (5 points) must be long and very strong, for the size of the dog ; the length from the lower corner of the eye to the nose-end in a 20 lb. dog should be 3 inches to 3¼ inches. The muzzle should be squarely cut, and broad at nose ; the under-jaw strong ; flews should be fairly developed, so as to cover the lower jaw, and rather more. The nose in black-and-tan dogs must be black; in red dogs it is often brown or flesh-coloured, but I must own a weakness for a red dog with a black nose and eyelashes, which is attained only by crossing reds with black-and-tans.

3. *Mouth* (5 points).—The front teeth must be perfectly even, and fit as close as a vice, so that a hair could not be drawn through when closed. The fangs—one in upper and two in lower jaw on each side—must be strong, sharp, and recurved, and all must be free from canker and disease (this I make a primary consideration whenever I purchase a dog of any breed, as being in my opinion the greatest safeguard against danger from the bite of a dog). I never saw a fine-bred dog of this kind underhung; I have seen pig-jawed ones sometimes, but never kept one; and either fault would effectually disqualify an otherwise good animal.

4. *Eyes* (5 points).—These always partake of the principal colour of the coat; they must be large and lustrous, and deeply set, and in expression should be soft and intelligent; and I like them to show the haw slightly.

5. *Ears* (5 points) must be thin, soft as velvet, and long enough to reach the end of the nose, or within a half an inch of it. In red dogs the ears are generally a shade darker in colour than

FROM "ICONES ANIMALIUM."

the rest of the body. They should be set on low, and should hang rather squarely with the front edges close to the cheeks, and not rise at the roots except slightly when the animal is excited, or at 'attention.'

"6. *Neck* (5 points) must be long, thick, and strong, with plenty of loose skin, but entirely free from goître or enlargement of the glands of the throat.

"7. *Chest* (5 points) must be very deep and wide, the brisket strong, and its point well up to the gullet. When the dog is standing, the chest should be within three inches of the ground.

"8. *Shoulders* (5 points) must be strong and heavy, and loosely fixed to the body.

"9. *Fore-legs* (5 points) must be very short and remarkably strong in bone, and must bend inwards from elbow to ankle, so that the latter nearly touch each other, but they must not knuckle over in front.

"10. *Fore-feet* (5 points) must be very large, splayed outwards, and be furnished with large and strong black or dark-brown claws. In some specimens the claws are often worn short from walking; but if very strong this is no detriment.

"11. *Ribs* (5 points) must be well sprung or rounded up from shoulder to loin; a flatness or hollow behind the shoulders is a defect, as it shows the animal has not sufficient room for his lungs to act properly.

"12. *Loin* (5 points) must be long and muscular and slightly arched, so that it is perceptibly higher than either shoulders or quarters.

TERRIER TYPE OF DACHSHUNDS.

"13. *Hind-quarters, hind legs and feet* (5 points). Thighs must be short and muscular, the legs fine and upright below the hock; *i. e.*, must not be sickle-hocked; hind feet smaller than fore ones; and the hind-quarters must not be higher than the shoulder.

"14. *Stern* (5 points) should be 9 to 12 inches in length, according to size of dog; must be thick at base, and also thicker again a couple of inches from the base, and gradually taper to a point; carried with a curve upward, but not slewed. The under-side of stern should be flat, and the hair should be parted and feather each side thereof sightly. A dog with a broad flat stern as described is a great rarity, and is held in very high estimation in Germany, where it is termed an 'Otter-tail.'

"15. *Bone* (5 points) must be large, and angular at points, according to the size of the animal.

"16. *Muscle* (5 points) must be large, hard, and particularly well developed and defined throughout.

"17. *Skin* (10 points) must be thick, yet soft to the touch, and remarkably elastic. No other breed of dog possesses the same elasticity of skin; the animal can nearly turn round in it when seized, or at will he can contract it by muscular action so tightly to the body that it is difficult to get even a pinch of it.

"18. *Coat* (5 points) must be short, hard, and bright, but it varies much in hardness according to whether the animal is kept in a kennel or in a warm drawing-room.

"19. *Colour* (5 points). The colours may be—(1) self-colours, *i. e.*, any shade of fallow, red, or fawn—the former preferred. (2) Bi-colours, *i. e.*, black-and-tan, liver-and-tan, or brown-and-tawny, as commonly seen in the Bloodhound. (3) Parti-colours:—tortoiseshell, or blue-and-tan grizzle with black spots (this colour is often accompanied by an odd, broken, or wall-eye). Hound-pied are very rare; but though they are not difficult to obtain, they are certainly not desirable. The best colours are fallow-red, black-and-tan, and brown or liver-and-tan, which is often the result of crossing the red and black-and-tans. I prefer brightish colour in black-and-tan for show purposes, and of these I like those with red 'stockings,' in preference to those with heavily-pencilled toes, which I consider partake more of the character of the Manchester Terrier than of the hound proper. Black-and-white I have seen, and have had one very good black one; but I am not very deeply impressed with the beauty of either.

"Having given my scale of points in detail, it will be seen that I have allotted them collectively thus :—

Head	25
Neck and chest	10
Fore legs and feet	15
Ribs and loin	10
Hind-quarters and stern	10
Bone and muscle	10
Skin, coat, and colour	20
	100

"I prefer the *self* and *bi-colours* free from white in chest, throat, and toes, but in the best of all strains these blemishes will often appear; and for a small spot on the chest I would deduct only one point; but for white toes I would deduct two points for each foot so marked; and a dog with white feet or legs, or with a spot or blaze on the head or face I would disqualify for the show bench, except in the parti-coloured class, although for working purposes it is no detriment whatever.

"For exhibition purposes I am a great stickler for colour and marking, as I consider it should be one object of breeders to make all animals as presentable as possible to the uninitiated public.

"I have awarded no points for size, as in Dachshunds we find that they vary considerably, some small specimens being frequently met with.

"These small ones may be equally pure, as regards breeding, with the large ones, and are often found models of perfection, and are certainly most fitted for ladies' pets, for which purpose the breed is unequalled for cleanliness and affection: 20 lbs. I look upon as the standard weight for a dog and 17 lbs. for a bitch; a couple of pounds either way may be allowed, but no Dachshund should reach anything like 25 lbs. If so, I should look for some impurity of blood, except in very old dogs, which often attain very great weights; and I do not object to a bitch weighing 20 lbs., but I certainly incline to the smaller weights.

"The bitches are generally much lighter in bone throughout than dogs, but at the same time they possess more *quality* or beauty than dogs, as is general with the female portion of animal as well as human nature. The large dogs are best for outdoor work; and I fancy that out of a pack of Dachshunds I could pick the best workmen by their conformation only. As to their ability, being hounds they are naturally most fitted for hunting, and possess extraordinary scenting powers, and may be trained to hunt anything, from a deer to a mouse.

"They do not possess great speed, yet they can get over the ground a good deal faster than a man cares to run; and being slow, they are not so apt to overrun the scent, while they do not so easily tire, but will follow their chase for many hours without a break.

"In Germany they are used to hunt the deer, roe, foxes, and badger; but in the south of that empire, particularly in the Black Forest, though they use the Dachshund to track the quarry, yet when it is too strong for them to kill, the sportsmen either use the rifle or a much stronger and larger breed of dog—generally a Boarhound, or cross-bred dog—for the finish.

"In the country they are used on a small scale for hunting both alone and with Beagles. One gentleman I know often hunts fur with about six couple, and many times have I seen the staunch and true little hounds, when they come across a dry stone fence—which abound in West Yorkshire—and which had been taken by a hare, work round, seek the nearest gap, and pick up the scent on the other side, a ten or twelve miles run seeming good fun to them.

"In covert shooting they are equal to any Spaniel, and when it is very close and thick, are superior, owing to their large fore feet and powerfully built fore-quarters, though in briars their ears, head, and shoulders get severely scratched at times, and yet they seem to enjoy it thoroughly, and never flinch on that account.

"They can be broken to quarter their ground and work the game to the gun, if it be possible, and may also be taught to retrieve.

"In temper they are somewhat stubborn, and require great patience in breaking, but when once trained their great intelligence leaves nothing to be desired by the sportsman who admires the breed.

"In hunting they give mouth, but may not be so musical as the Foxhound and its congeners; but this I prefer in covert shooting, as I then know the whereabouts of the dogs.

GROUP OF DACHSHUNDS.

The large paws and strong crooked fore legs are admirably adapted for working underground, while the length of head and neck combined enable the dog effectually to protect his feet when the quarry is reached, be he badger or fox; and put a Dachshund to either he will give a good account of himself. I write of the working Dachshund.

"There are some specimens of the breed which have never been educated, or that have been kept merely as pets, which would not look at a mouse even, but are for all sporting purposes quite useless.

"The dog I mean, properly bred and trained, is capable of affording sport *ad libitum*, whether in the open or in the covert. For courage or pluck I will back them against any breed.

"Cats they do not stand on any ceremony with, and I will give an instance. Some time ago we were fearfully overrun with cats, some of which came from great distances after the chickens, and often carried off full-grown bantam fowls; and one summer afternoon my little bitch Vixen hunted a very large Tom to bay in a stone quarry in my grounds. The hole or fissure in the rock was scarcely large enough for a cat to turn in, and was about three yards to the far end, and sloping upwards. Such a customer in such a corner was not easy to dislodge, and not caring to risk Vixen's eyes at such terrible odds, I caught her, and sent for my black-and-tan brood bitch Maud, 18 lbs. weight, and turned her in. There was not much noise, but in a few seconds the bitch backed out, bringing the cat firmly gripped by the brisket, while the cat's claws and teeth were as firmly embedded in her head and face, which I fully expected to see well ripped up by his hind claws; but both rolled down to the bottom of the quarry, the cat quite dead, and the bitch none the worse save a few gashes on her head, the whole taking far less time than it does to relate it.

"To give another instance of their power of jaw. I have had a little bitch only 15 lbs. weight turn a hedgehog out of a drain, and grip the prickly ball heedless of the spikes, and crush it with as much ease seemingly as a Terrier does a rat, and make no bones, or rather leave no bones whole, about it; and I have never seen even a pup of a few months old attempt to open the soft parts out before commencing the work of destruction. Young ones will worry at a hedgehog, pull it about, and make a great noise; but a staunch dog, though he may grumble a bit at the spikes, does not mind them; nor when the affair is over is there any bleeding at the mouth, unless some of the points penetrate between the gum and the teeth.

"For memory they are second to no other breed; for an affront they take a lot of coaxing to gain their friendship—(two years ago my bitch Puzzle was troubled with rheumatics, and I applied a stimulating liniment; and for a whole twelve months afterwards she carefully kept the width of the room between us)—while, on the other hand, they never forget any little kindness, nor do they require to be reminded who are their friends.

"As another instance of their sagacity and retentive memory, some weeks previous to the show at Birmingham in 1876, where my bitch puppy Dora was entered, and only six months old, I was anxious to get a pair of her milk-teeth removed, and being very fast I did not like to venture on the operation myself, but took her to the shop of a dental friend, who removed them with very little trouble.

"I had forgotten all about the affair when I called at the same shop some twelve months afterwards. The little bitch was with me, but I missed her, and at last saw her skulking against a wall about forty yards away; and not being able to understand her movements, I called my friend, who immediately remarked, 'Why, it's the little dog I drew the teeth for, and she does not care for the operation.'

"They are excellent guards, and, being on such short legs, seem, from their nearness to the ground, to have a quicker sense of hearing, and I have frequently known them give the alarm some time before longer-legged dogs took any notice whatever of the sound.

"With dogs of their own variety they are generally very peaceable, and may easily be kept in bulk in kennels, but when they once quarrel they must be separated for ever as kennel companions, else one or other will be destroyed.

"With those of other breeds they are peculiar, never quarrelsome, and hardly ever are the first to begin a fight; but if attacked by a bigger dog they will not by any means hang back, and generally come off best, as they fight low, and work among their adversary's legs and throat; while a small dog, even if as big as themselves, they will often treat with supreme contempt.

"Festus was the foundation of my kennel of this breed, and is by Feldmann, out of an imported bitch of equal character. He was shown for two seasons only, is about seven years old, and scales 20 lbs. when in good condition; in colour a beautiful fallow-red. During this time he was the winner of forty-seven prizes and two cups, including two firsts and one cup at Birmingham, in 1875 and 1876."

Mr. Everett Millais, of Palace Gate, London, who has studied the breed most carefully, is entirely of Mr. Lovell's opinion on the question of head; and in answer to a question put to him by us with reference to his views on the subject, replies as follows:—

"What is a Dachshund?—A hound used on the Continent, more especially Germany, for the purpose of driving badgers and foxes from their underground lairs; also for the purpose of tracking and beating underwood above ground. Often and often am I asked whether I have seen so and so's hound, or if I will come and see one that another friend has imported. When I come home from the visit I think what money might have been saved if the purchaser had only gone to a Kennel Club show, paid his half-crown, and seen what constitutes a Dachshund.

"Of all people in this world John Bull abroad is the easiest to swindle. If he goes to Waterloo, bullets, &c., are imposed on him that never knew the battle-field. If to Germany, he is let in with some mongrel with crooked legs. Being an old breeder—and I may say a successful one, although I only showed one Dachshund in my life—I hope it will not be taken amiss if I say that 90 per cent. of the Dachshunds now seen in this city (of London) are no more the pure Dachshund they are represented to be than those mongrels in Paris that have the audacity to sign themselves Bull-terrier.

"There are certain breeders who, not having the courage to stick up for one legitimate type, excuse themselves by saying that there are two distinct types of Dachshunds—the Hound type and the Terrier type. This is a great and fatal mistake. That there are dogs, and alas, too many of them, with fine bone, Terrier sterns, Terrier heads, and light crooked legs, I will not deny; but, at the same time, I say that they are mongrels. They have got a root in this country, and it will always be my endeavour to eradicate it on every opportunity. The Dachshund proper is a hound, and a little beauty too. It is very easy to breed a Terrier from a hound, but it is impossible to breed a hound from a Terrier.

"The male Dachshund should weigh, when in proper condition, from 20 to 22 lbs.—certainly not more—and the female proportionately lighter. The head of the Dachshund should be conical, though not to such a marked degree as the Bloodhound. The ears are set on low, and hang like a hound's; they ought to reach some way over his nose. The Dachshund possesses a good flew, and a fair amount of jowl. His neck is extremely muscular, and should stand well out from the chest. The legs, which are one of the most important parts of a Dachshund, should come down from the chest, which is broad and massive, slope well towards one another till the ankle-joints nearly touch one another, the chest dropping down to the ankles. The fore-feet should, an inch from the chest, turn away from one another, and spread well out. On no account should the joints at the ankles have a forward bend, as it is unsightly, and shows a tendency to weakness.

"The stern is not carried over the back; this is a sure sign of the Terrier type. It is carried straight, with perhaps four inches elevation.

"A good hound should measure from 8½ to 10 inches in height, and from 36 to 38 inches in length. The skin should be loose all over the body, so that on grasping the hound you find you have a handful of skin. The hair should be hard, short, and glossy.

"Colour is an essential matter to the Dachshund. I myself care little whether it be red, black-and-tan, or chocolate-and-tan, but I will have a good colour. I do not care for white about the hound, for he is far better without it; but I would not disqualify him for having it were he otherwise good.

"In red dogs, and other than red, I much prefer red noses and eyes the colour of their coats, as I think it gives them a much more pleasing look.

"One sometimes sees a mottled species like a Collie with a wall eye. It looks very funny, but in my opinion it gets this from some other stock, not the hound."

Having thus given our readers the opinions of three leading English breeders upon the subject of Dachshunds, we will, before we attempt to sum up their ideas, give a list of points drawn up by some German breeders, which have been forwarded to us. This description was published at the time of the Hanover dog show, held in that city in 1879, and was much commented on when it first appeared. It is as follows:—

The principal qualities are—

1. *General appearance*, low and very long structure, overhanging and well-developed chest, legs very short, the fore-legs turned inwards at the knees, with the feet considerably bent out. The whole appearance is weasel-like; the tail is not much crooked, and is carried either straight or a little sloping. Hair close, short, and smooth; expression intelligent, attentive, and lively. Weight not over 10 kilos.

2. *Head* long and pointed towards the nose; forehead broad and flat; nose narrow; the lips hang over a little, and form a sort of fold in the corner of the mouth.

3. *Ears* of medium length, tolerably broad and round at the ends, placed high up and at the back of the head, so that the space between eye and ear appears considerably larger than with other hunting dogs; they are smooth and close, and droop with any shaking of the head.

4. *Eyes* not too large, round and clear, rather protruding, and very sharp in expression.

5. *Neck* long, flexible, broad, and strong.

6. *Back* very long, and broad in the hind parts.

7. *Breast* broad, ribs deep and very long, and back part of body higher than the front.

8. *Tail* of medium length, strong at the root, and gradually running to a short point, almost straight, occasionally with a small curve.

9. *Fore parts* much stronger than the hind, muscular shoulders, which are short; fore-quarter very short and strong, bending outwards, the knee inwards, and the feet again outwards.

DACHSHUNDS.

10. *Hind legs*—knuckles strong and muscular; lower extremities very short, and quite in comparison with the front legs.

11. *Fore feet* much stronger than the hind feet, broad, and the toes well closed; the nails strong, uneven, and particularly of a black colour, with a strong sole to the feet. The hind feet are smaller and rounder, the toes and nails shorter and straighter.

12. *Hair* short, close, and glossy, smooth and elastic, very short and fine on the ears;

ROUGH-COATED DACHSHUNDS.

coarser and longer on the lower part of the tail. The hair on the lower part of the body is also coarser.

13. *Colour* black, with tan on the head, neck, breast, legs, and under the tail; besides dark-brown, golden-brown, and hare-grey, with darker stripes on the back; as also ash-grey and silver-grey, with darker patches (*Tigerdachs*). The darker colours are mostly mixed with tan and with the lighter colours; the nails ought to be black, and the eyes dark. White is only to be endured in the shape of a stripe on the chest straight down.

14. *Teeth.*—Upper and lower teeth meet exactly; they must be strong in every respect.

These dogs may be considered as *faulty* which have a *compressed or conical head*, if the nose is too short or too narrow, if the lips are too long, *long* faltering ears, thin neck and narrow chest, if the front legs are not regularly bent, or if the *crookedness of the legs is so strong as not to carry the weight* of the body. Further, the feet, if they are not regularly formed ; if the hind legs are too long, and likewise the tail when too long and heavy and conspicuously crooked. With regard to colour, it is to be said that white as ground colour is also to be considered faulty, with the exception of what is mentioned before.

The task of attempting to decide where doctors have disagreed now falls upon our shoulders ; for, as will have been seen above, the opinions we have quoted fail very much to coincide with one another. It has been our desire, however, in each and every instance, where we think a reasonable ground for difference of opinion exists, to give each side a full chance of publicity, and therefore we have devoted considerable space to the breed now under discussion. For our own part we are certainly in favour of the type supported by Messrs. Lovell and Millais, not out of any feelings of insular prejudice, but because we consider that type—the *hound* type—has been proved to be in existence for centuries. In the two earlier cuts of Dachshunds which accompany this article, and which are taken from *La Venerie*, by Jacques du Fouilloux, we notice most unmistakably that the dogs depicted are of the high conical skull which Mr. Lovell and Mr. Millais so stoutly maintain is the correct formation. Later on we come to a small cut from that *Icones Animalium* which has already been drawn upon to assist us in the present work. Here a very similar type of dog to those shown in *La Venerie* is produced, and the favourable impression towards the hound type is thereby much increased in our opinion. In estimating such matters, also, we cannot help thinking it advisable to turn one's thoughts in the direction of the uses to which a breed is put. In so doing, our views concerning the hound type have been greatly strengthened from the reflection that, as we have already said, tracking game is the Dachshund's forte, not baiting savage vermin in the latter's native earth. One remark, too, of Mr. Millais's has struck us very forcibly. " It is very easy to breed a Terrier from a hound, but it is impossible to breed a hound from a Terrier." Without going the entire length of Mr. Millais as to the impossibility of the latter achievement in breeding, we readily accept its difficulty, and recognise the force of the argument he makes use of.

We are not, however, wholly at one with Mr. Millais in his sweeping condemnation of the Terrier type. We prefer the hound type of Dachshund as being in our opinion the older and the more characteristic of the two ; but in the face of what we have seen and heard, it is impossible to ignore the existence of the Terrier type, and the store set upon it in certain parts of its native country—Hanover to-wit. How this class of dog originated, except by crossing the hound type of Dachshund with a Terrier, we cannot tell ; but as it now exists it is impossible to decline to recognise it as a variety, though perhaps an undesirable one, of the breed. A satisfactory illustration of this class of dog will be seen in the engraving, and our readers who are ignorant of the different types will thereby be able to form their own opinions on the beauty of the Terrier type of dog.

Another point on which Mr. Everett Millais and Mr. Enoch Hutton break a lance is that of the colour of the red Dachshund's nose. Here, as in Germany, considerable difference of opinion exists ; but we personally feel no hesitation in offering our allegiance to the party which advocates red noses, as black noses in such cases look quite out of keeping with the colour.

There remains one description of Dachshund which has been quite overlooked by Messrs. Lovell, Millais, and Hutton, and which is rarely seen in this country, and that is the rough-coated variety, which will be found to be represented in the engraving on the preceding page. This breed, no doubt, is but a cross from the original variety, and is not valued in its native country by admirers of the breed.

From what has been said and written concerning the breed from time to time by various authorities, it will be seen that it is not only on the subject of type that their admirers differ. Enthusiasts, as we have before remarked, give this breed of dog credit for an amount of gameness which we scarcely think it fully deserves. It is no doubt true that instances of exceptionally game Dachshunds have come beneath the observation of gentlemen who have studied the breed, as in the cases Mr. Enoch Hutton quotes; but we are inclined to imagine that these are exceptions rather than invariable rules. As house-dogs Dachshunds are without superiors, as their voices are deep enough to awaken the heaviest sleeper, and their sense of hearing is very acute.

In consequence of the fast-increasing number of these dogs which appear at the principal dog shows, efforts have been made to gain additional classes for them, as they are usually divided according to *colour* only. Classes for Dachshunds black-and-tan, and Dachshunds other than black-and-tan, have been up to the time of writing (1880) the order of the day, and no doubt during the earlier stages of this variety's existence as a show dog were amply sufficient. As, however, so many specimens of either type appear, certain exhibitors have been trying to gain classes for each variety of their favourite dog, with apparently some chance of ultimate success. The efforts of these breeders, however, are not regarded with favour by the supporters of the hound type of Dachshund, who maintain that the Terrier type is a mongrel unworthy of support, and therefore advocate the institution of heavy weight and light weight classes, instead of a division of the types. How things will work it is impossible to foretell; but an indisputable fact in connection with the Dachshund is its fast-increasing popularity amongst us, and its admirers appear to spare no trouble or expense in importing the best blood into the country.

Having now come to the end of our notes on the Dachshund, we can but once more repeat that our sympathies lie with the class of dog so ably depicted by the Rev. G. F. Lovell; but under any circumstances we would caution breeders against crossing the two types together, as certain ruin will be caused to each thereby. In breeding, we may remark that liver-coloured puppies frequently appear when reds are bred together. This colour, though disliked for show purposes, is often very valuable for crossing when increased depth of colour is required, and therefore a liver-coloured brood bitch or two is often seen in breeders' kennels. Whilst on this subject of colour we may remark that we cordially endorse the views already given on the subject of white. It is most undesirable that white blazes on the head or chest should ever be seen, and white feet we regard almost as a disqualification. In Germany we have seen many of the breed marked similarly to hounds, but cannot recall any to memory which were black-and-tans or fallow-reds marked with white. As regards the black ones, Mr. Mackenzie, of Perth, in 1879, imported a very handsome dog of this colour who rejoices in the name of Gravedigger. This dog was a good winner in his own country, and has done his master good service in the land of his adoption, and we do not know of a better-coated one, his skin being everything that could be desired.

Amongst the leading Dachshund breeders and exhibitors of the day the names of the Rev. G. F. Lovell, Mr. John Fisher, Mr. Everett Millais, Mr. W. Arkwright, and Mr. Enoch Hutton, are the most prominent, the first-named gentleman having been the owner of what is still considered to have been the best Dachshund ever seen in this country. We allude to Pixie, a wonderful little bitch, whose untimely death alone prevented her appearing in our coloured plate. Mr. John Fisher's Feldmann was truly, as Mr. Hutton says, the pioneer of his variety in this country, and Mr. Hutton's Festus, whose portrait is in our coloured plate, is recognised as a grand specimen of his type.   Mr. Millais has not shown much, but has good dogs ; and Mr. Arkwright's Xaverl was for a long time champion of his breed.

The dogs selected for illustration in the coloured plate are—

Major Cooper's (of Pitsford Hall, Northampton) Waldmann, an extremely good specimen of the black-and-tan variety, who is a winner at some of our best shows.

The Rev. G. F. Lovell's Schlupferle. A handsome fallow-red, whose measurements are as follows :—Length from tip of nose to stop, 3 inches; from stop to occiput, 4¾ inches; length of back from top of shoulders to setting on of stern, 16 inches; girth of thigh, 9 inches; girth of fore-arm, 5 inches; girth of pastern, 3½ inches; height at shoulders, 12 inches; height at elbows, 6½ inches; height at loins, 13½ inches; height at hock, 4½ inches; length of stern, 11 inches; weight, 23 lbs.; age, 4 years 10 months.

Mr. Enoch Hutton's Festus, already alluded to by his owner in the notes with which he obliged us as above.

The large full-page illustration of Dachshunds at work is the production of a celebrated foreign artist, who is especially happy in conveying the expression of animals to paper.

Following our usual custom, we shall now append a scale of points for judging the breed, which we cheerfully admit are founded upon the scale afforded us by Mr. Lovell in the preceding portion of this chapter :—

STANDARD OF POINTS FOR JUDGING DACHSHUNDS.

	Value.
Skull and muzzle	10
Ears and eyes	5
Shoulders and chest	5
Loins	5
Fore legs and feet	5
Hind legs and feet	5
Colour and coat	5
General appearance, including skin	10
Total	50

CHAPTER XLI.

THE BASSET HOUND.

CLOSELY allied as it is to the Dachshund, the Basset Hound is, thanks both to the popularity of the former breed and the energy of its own admirers, beginning to take a firm root on English soil. Mr. Everett Millais, of Palace Gate, South Kensington, London, is an enthusiastic admirer of the variety, and has spared neither time nor money in his endeavours to do it justice. As he has kindly provided us with some valuable and practical information on the breed, we think it desirable that his remarks should appear in the earlier portions of the article, as he not only alludes to the introduction of the Basset Hound to the show bench of this country, but also supplements his remarks with dates :—

"That the Basset Français and the German Dachshund or Basset Allemand were originally from common ancestors I am not going to deny, but that the Basset Français has preserved more especially his individuality is undoubted ; inasmuch as while the Basset Français, a hound in every sense of the word, reproduces specimens of his own type, the Basset Allemand, or German Dachshund, gives birth to puppies of a hound and also a terrier type in the same litter. Of course this shows the infusion of foreign blood at some period or other, which I hope soon to see eradicated.

"That these two different breeds of Bassets are now quite distinct I am sure of. One has only to visit the Jardin d'Acclimatation to see them exhibited as such. In corroboration of my statement I quote a letter by that eminent French author, Mons. A. Pierre Pichot, editor of *La Revue Britannique*, member of the committees on French dog shows, and one of the directors of the Jardin d'Acclimatation :—

" ' *To the Editor of the " Live Stock Journal."*

" ' The Basset Hounds, which differ in almost every point from the Dachshund, are, on the contrary, of every colour and both rough and smooth, and of these there are still more numerous varieties than of the Dachshund, the Bassets having in my own opinion sprung from the different local breeds of large hounds, and therefore connected with the Vendée, Saintonge, Artois, and Normandy types.

" ' *December 3rd*, 1875.'

"I may here mention that the only Bassets yet exhibited in England have been of the Normandy type, *à poil*, and one of the Vendée type, a Basset Griffon. I have only lately received a letter from a gentleman in Wales who informs me that he has imported a leash of the latter hounds for rabbiting, and so I now hope to see an increase of them, as the only one I mention above is a dog belonging to Mr. de Landre Macdona—a very fine specimen, but deficient in leather.

"Concerning the first introduction of the breed into this country, my mind goes back to the Wolverhampton Dog Show, 1875, where my first Basset Français was to make his *début*. On my arrival I was directed to the Talbot Hotel, as being nearest to the Agricultural Hall. It was late when I got back to the hotel, after seeing my hound chained up under his appointed number, and having dined I descended to the smoking-room, where several gentlemen were taking their ease, and anarchy in the shape of dog-talk presided.

"One of the gentlemen commenced to talk to me, and the following remarks took place :—

"'Showing Terriers?' said one.

"'Bulls?' said another.

"'No,' I replied, 'a Basset.'

"'A what?'

"'A Basset,' I repeated.

"'What's he like,' said another, winking at the gentleman who sat next him.

"'Oh, he's about 4 feet long and 12 inches high.'

"At this announcement there was a general desire to see the wonderful animal. I replied that I had already taken him to the show, but that I would be only too delighted to show him to them in the morning.

"I merely mention this to prove that even the breed of the dog had scarcely reached the ears of those whose duties led them, before other people, in the way of hearing it.

"Great was the excitement that day in the canine world when the hound was led into the ring, and at night many were the cups emptied by those who had seen the breed often before, but couldn't exactly remember where.

"Amongst Dachshund fanciers the sensation he caused may be gathered from the various letters which appeared shortly after the Wolverhampton show, wherein my hound, weighing then between 50 and 60 lbs., was pronounced by Dachshund fanciers, from a reported description, to be an overgrown specimen of their particular hobby.

"These letters produced no results as to clearing up the doubts, so I determined to exhibit at the forthcoming Crystal Palace show not only my Basset Français, but also a Dachshund. With the Dachshund I got highly commended, and with the Basset Français first in the variety class. The following were the remarks on the hound by the *Live Stock Journal* after the show :—

"'Mr. Everett Millais's Model was likewise amongst the winners (foreign class). This exquisitely pretty little hound was greatly admired, and acknowledged by Dachshund fanciers to be a totally distinct variety.'

"It was here that the Earl of Onslow, now the largest proprietor of these hounds, first saw a Basset Français. Struck by the singular beauty of the hound (which is a rich tricolour) he procured a pair from France. These, however, being aged, he again procured a couple and a half from Comte Couteul (1876), viz., Fino, Nestor, and Finette. All these hounds are of the Normandy type.

"This year (1880) at the Crystal Palace the Basset Français class was entirely composed of the above type, either imported or bred from imported parents, with the exception of two, one of which was Mr. Macdona's Basset Griffon (Vendée type) which I have mentioned before, and the other a tricoloured nondescript; the Normandy type of hounds belonging to Lord Onslow and myself.

"As in Germany anything with crooked legs is called a Dachshund, so in France for the same reason 'the anything' is called a Chien Basset, for the simple reason that people do not know better. In England it is the same; the word Terrier is good enough for the whole race, whether pure or mongrel. The other day I smiled on hearing men, who ought to know better, describe a well-known Skye Terrier breeder's team in the Park as Dandie Dinmont pups!

"The word 'Basset' is such a large word, that to ask a French sportsman for a Basset would be precisely as putting the same question to him, substituting the word 'horse' for 'Basset.' You might want a cart-horse, a cob, a hack, a racehorse, &c.

"In like manner there are various breeds of Bassets.

"The word 'Basset,' which means a 'dwarf dog,' is applied to all short and crooked-legged dogs, and those which appear to have had an accident in their puppyhood.

"I know many authors put this defect down to rickets, but I believe that these animals have been, like the mole, provided by Nature to do a certain work, which could not be done by those on high and straight limbs.

"Bassets are divided into two distinct breeds—the Basset Français and the Basset Allemand, which is the German Dachshund. So let us put this latter aside without further ado.

"Now the Bassets Français are divided into two classes—the *Basset à poil ras* (smooth-coated), and the *Basset à poil dur*, more commonly known as the 'Basset Griffon.'

"Both the smooth-coated and the rough-coated varieties are divided into three classes, and are named after the crookedness, if one may so express it, of their fore-paws. The names are as follows:—The crooked-legged (*Basset à jambes torses*); the half crooked-legged (*Basset à jambes demi-torses*); the straight-legged (*Basset à jambes droites*).

"So as to make my readers more easily able to distinguish the difference between the *Basset à jambes torses* and the *Basset à jambes droites*, more frequently known as the 'petit chien courant,' let me refer them to the two engravings, reproduced from a well-known French book on dogs used for sport, 'Chiens de Chasse.'

"The first engraving is that of the heavy *Basset à jambes torses*. Mark the high conical head, heavy flews, pendulous ears, and deep-set eyes. There is but one mistake in this drawing, and that is that the chest is not properly developed. It should come down straight to the ankle joints. A small ball may be observed, attached to the hinder hound's neck. This is a 'grelot,' and is put on for the purpose of letting the sportsman know where his hound is when in cover, but not on game.

"The second engraving is that of a couple of *Bassets à jambes droites*. The reader will see at once that the flews have disappeared, and that the hound is of a much lighter build than the *Basset à jambes torses*.

"Now the variety of these names is very confusing, and for sporting purposes the intending purchaser must exercise his own judgment when making a purchase. Should his ground be flat and easy to get over, then by all means have the long, low, heavy hound with crooked legs; but should it be of a stony and marshy description, with deep cuttings, &c., then one of the two latter. The rough-coated hounds are of course used for what might be called the hard work.

"The Basset, for its size, has more bone, perhaps, than nearly any other dog.

"The skull should be peaked like that of the Bloodhound, with the same dignity and expression, nose black (although some of my own have white about theirs), and well flewed. For the size of the hound, I think the teeth are extremely small. However, as they are not intended to destroy life, this is probably the reason.

"The ears should hang like the Bloodhound's, and are like the softest velvet drapery.

"The eyes are a deep brown, and are brimful of affection and intelligence. They are pretty deeply set, and should show a considerable haw. A Basset is one of those hounds incapable of having a wicked eye.

"The neck is long, but of great power; and in the *Basset à jambes torses* the flews extend very nearly down to the chest. The chest is more expansive in the Basset than even in the Bulldog, and should in the *Bassets à jambes torses* be not more than two inches from the ground. In the case of the *Basset à jambes demi-torses* and *jambes droites*, being generally lighter, their chests do not, of course, come so low.

"The shoulders are of great power, and terminate in the crooked feet of the Basset, which appear to be a mass of joints. The back and ribs are strong, and the former of great length. The stern is gaily carried like that of hounds in general, and when the hound is on the scent of game this portion of his body gets extremely animated, and tell me, in my own hounds, when they have struck a fresh or cold scent, and I even know when the foremost hound will give tongue.

"The hind-quarters are very strong and muscular, the muscles standing rigidly out down to the hocks.

BASSET À JAMBES TORSES.

"The skin is soft in the smooth-haired dogs, and like that of any other hound, but in the rough variety it is identical with that of the Otter-hound's.

"Colour, of course, is a matter of fancy, although I infinitely prefer the 'tricolour,' which has a tan head and black-and-white body.

"The Griffons generally are like the Otter-hounds in colouring.

"As to points, in a breed like this it is impossible, unless one had a class for every division. I hope, however, to see at the Kennel Show a class for the Basset Griffon, as well as for those of the *poil ras*.

"Bassets are used for tracking boar, wolves, deer, and turning them out of the woods and copses. They are likewise used for pheasant and general sporting purposes, where game is scarce. To use them in this country would be impossible, but I have done so in Scotland on the hill-sides, where avenues had been cut in the bracken, and very good sport was the result. Their affection is wonderful to their owner, but strangers they dislike. Their memory is wonderful. When at Lowestoft a friend, who lived in the next house, pushed my old dog from the door-step one day, to come in. Model deeply resented this, and never would allow 'that friend' in without growling, and turning up his bristles like a clothes-brush.

BASSET HOUNDS.

"I run mine as Beagles, and many people who have been with them infinitely prefer the sport, as they never run over a scent, and the pace, though a hard trot, is not too fast.

"Comte Couteul, from whom Lord Onslow and I got mine, writes the following in his book, 'History of the French Hounds':—

"'These Bassets have never been well known in England, though an eminent writer asserts to the contrary. It is only within the last four or five years that they have been spoken of as hounds for hunting, and even now they are very scarce in Great Britain.

"'At the first French dog show in Paris, 1863, many English visitors expressed their astonishment at this type of dog, which was so new to them, though the same general outline is reproduced in the Clumber and Turnspit breeds. In fact, though at the present time several English

BASSET À JAMBES DROITES.

sportsmen may have in their possession some French Bassets or German Dachshunds (this kind being much used in Germany for hunting the badger), it may be said that these hounds are as new to the English "veneur" as our own existing packs of Gascony and Saintonge hounds.'

"The Count further goes on to state that the reason of this is the absurd and selfish way that French masters of hounds have (up to the time of his writing) kept secret the fruits of their experience, or, as the Count himself describes it, 'hide their hounds like stolen treasures.'

Mr. Everett Millais having entered so thoroughly upon the subject of Basset Hounds, and being the recognised authority on the breed at present in the country, a very few lines from us will suffice to close the chapter referring to this class of dog. From the remarks of Mr. Millais few can doubt the high qualifications of the Basset for recognition as both a sporting and companionable dog, and from what we have learnt concerning him from other sources, we have no doubt but that his good character is a thoroughly well-deserved one. In appearance he is more showy than his relative the Dachshund, though it must be admitted against him that his greater size renders him a trifle less desirable as an indoor pet.

We can thoroughly endorse the above remarks concerning the affection of the Basset towards his master, and are convinced that there is a great future of popularity in store for this very engaging breed.

There is, however, almost the same difficulty before the Basset as a show dog, as there is in the case of his relative the Dachshund. We refer to the *two types*, the existence of which will always breed dissensions amongst exhibitors, unless one class is provided for Bassets à jambes torses, and another for Bassets à jambes droites. Believers in one type will find it very trying to be beaten by a dog of the (to them) distasteful shape, and may be disheartened,

MR. EVERETT MILLAIS'S BASSET HOUND "MODEL."

and therefore possibly retire from exhibiting in future. However, a defeat under such circumstances is not so serious a matter as it would be in the Dachshund classes, where many of the supporters of one type maintain that their dogs are the *only* true representatives of the breed, and specimens varying materially from them are mongrels. Amongst Basset breeders the existence of the two types is recognised; and though a preference may be shown for one of them by any breeder, he must bear in mind that his neighbour's dogs, though differing from his own in formation, may be equally pure Basset Hounds.

The illustration, by Mr. C. B. Barber, of Mr. Millais's splendid specimen Model, is, in our opinion, an exact representation of that well-known dog, whose name will never cease to be associated with the introduction of the breed into this country.

Model has won the following prizes amongst others: Twice first Crystal Palace, first Brighton, second Alexandra Palace, second Agricultural Hall, and third Darlington. Such performances, taking into consideration that he had to be shown in variety classes against dogs of all sorts of breeds, stamps Model as a remarkably successful competitor in the ring.

We append a table of weights and measurements of Mr. Everett Millais's Bassets, Model and Garenne, which he has kindly sent us for insertion.

	MODEL.	GARENNE.
Age	7½ yrs.	2½ yrs.
Weight	46 lbs.	28 lbs.
Height at shoulder	12 inches.	9½ inches.
Length from nose to set on of tail	32 ,,	29 ,,
,, of tail	11½ ,,	9 ,,
Girth of chest	25 ,,	20 ,,
,, of loin	21 ,,	16 ,,
,, of head	17 ,,	13 ,,
,, of fore-arm	6½ ,,	5 ,,
Length of head from occiput to tip of nose	9 ,,	8 ,,
Girth of muzzle midway between eyes and tip of nose	9½ ,,	7 ,,
Length of ears from tip to tip	19 ,,	17 ,,
Height from ground, fore-feet	2¾ ,,	2½ ,,

As regards a scale of points for judging Bassets, we are of opinion that the scale given in the preceding chapter on Dachshunds can be used with good results, and therefore refer our readers to that instead of repeating it here.

CHAPTER XLII.

THE OTTER-HOUND.

ALL writers on the dog, both ancient and modern, who in any way direct attention to the Otter-hound, are unanimous in fathering him on to the old Southern Hound. For our own part we can find no reasons for disagreeing with the opinions of those who have gone before us, though the difference in appearance between the modern Otter-hound and the ancient Southern Hound is very conspicuous as regards coat and colour. In his marking, all old pictures which we have come across portray the old Southern Hound as a coarse Stag or Fox hound, and certainly his similarity to these breeds is greater than it is to the Otter-hound, though the latter is, we believe, one of his descendants.

We have it on the authority of Youatt that it was the slowness of the Southern Hound which led to his falling into disrepute amongst huntsmen, who preferred short sharp bursts to a plodding day across country. Devonshire is popularly believed to have the honour of being the last county in England where a pack of these hounds was kept up; and after its dispersion a number of its members remained for years in the neighbourhood of a village called Aveton Gifford, which is situated in that county. As Devonshire now produces many good specimens of the Otter-hound, this may be regarded as lending additional strength to the theory that the Otter-hound is descended from the former breed.

The precise date of the introduction of the Southern Hound into this country it is impossible to ascertain, and even an approximate guess will be found a matter of difficulty, as no mention is made of this variety in the earliest references to the dogs of Britain. Shakespeare would appear to be alluding to this breed when he writes :—

> " My hounds are bred out of the Spartan kind
> So flewed, so sanded ; and their heads are hung
> With ears that sweep away the morning dew,
> Crook-kneed and dew-lapped like Thessalian bulls,
> Slow in pursuit, but matched in mouth like bells,
> Each unto each."

The allusion to the slowness of the hound alluded to by our national poet is to our minds a convincing proof that it was the Southern Hound which he had in view; and his reference to its Spartan origin would lead one to presume that its importation into this country was in his day an accepted fact.

Mr. W. Taplin, writing in the " Sportsman's Cabinet," in 1804, has, however, many good words to say for the Southern Hound, and stoutly maintains that although it was less frequently met with in the country than it had been, it was still in existence. To quote his own words, Mr. Taplin remarks—

" These hounds were once universally known and equally common in every part of the kingdom, and the breed were then much larger than those now to be found in the low and marshy parts of the country, where they are still in use for the purposes of the chase, although it has been said 'that the breed, which has been gradually declining, and its size studiously diminished, by a mixture of other kinds, in order to increase its speed, is now almost extinct.' The assertion of the author, however, savours much more of speculative conjecture than of experimental practice; for the present writer hunted the winter of 1775 in the neighbourhood of Manchester with each of the two packs supported by subscription in that town, one of which was denominated the Southern Hound."

Further on the same writer proceeds to remark that "the Southern (or old English Hound) is most undoubtedly the original real-bred Harrier of this country, and more particularly in those swampy parts where the chase is wished to be protracted without prolonging the distance."

In appearance the Southern Hound was a large majestic-looking dog, showing great power, with a long barrel, round ribs, and deep chest. His ears were long, and his voice very melodious, the prevailing colour being, as we have mentioned before, similar to that of the modern Foxhound.

That otter-hunting was conducted on very much the same principles in days gone by as it is in the year 1880, the following extract from Turberville's "Arte de Venerie" will clearly prove; and it is therefore only reasonable to surmise that although the hounds now in use are altered in many respects from the breed used then, the Southern Hound had begun to undergo that modification which has subsequently developed into the modern Otter-hound.

Turberville writes, in 1575 :—

"The otter is a beast well knowne; shee feedeth on fishe and lyeth neare unto ryvers, brookes, pooles, and fishe-ponds, or weares. Hir lying-in commonly is under the roots of trees, and sometimes I have seene them lying in a hollowe tree, foure or five foote above the grounde. Even as a foxe, polcat, wildecat, or badgerd will destroye a warren, so will the otter destroye all the fishe in your pondes, if she once have founde the waye to them. She dyveth and hunteth under the water after a wonderfull manner, so that no fishe can escape hir unlesse they be verie great and swift. A litter of otters will destroy you all the fishe in a ryver in two myles length. There is great cunning in the hunting of them, as shall be saide in the next chapter; and also it is possible to take them under the water, and by the ryver's side, both in traps and in snares, as you may take a hare with hare-pypes, or such like gynnes. They byte sore and venomously, and defende themselves stoutly. I will not speake much more of their nature, but onely that they are footed lyke a goose. I meane they have a webbe betweene theyr clawes, and have no heele, but onely a rounde ball under their soale of their foote, and their tracke is called the marke of an otter, as we say the slot of an hart. An otter abideth not much nor long in one place, but if she befrayed, or finde any fault (as they are very perfectly of smelling and hearing) they will forsake their couche and shifte a mile or two up or doune a river. The like will she do if she have once destroyed the store of fishe, and finde no plentie of feeding. From a pond garden or good store of fish pondes she wil not lightly be removed, as long as there is store of fish in them, for therein fishes are taken with more ease than in the rivers or greater waters; but inough of their natures.

"When a huntesman would hunte the otter, he should first send foure servants or varlets with bloodhounds, or such houndes as will draw in the game, and let him sende them two up the river, and two doune the river, the one couple of them on that one side, and the other on that other side of the water. And so you shal be sure to finde if there be an otter in the quarter: for an otter cannot long abide in the water, but muste come forth in the night to feede on grasse and herbes by the water's side. If any of theyr houndes finde of an otter, let the huntesman looke in the softe groundes and moyst places to see which way he bent the head, up or doune the river. And if he finde not the otter quickly, he may then judge that he is gone to couche somewhere further off from the water, for an otter will sometimes seeke his feede a myle (or little lesse) from his couche and place of reste. Commonly he will rather go up the river than doune, for goyng up the streame, the streame bringeth him sent of the fishes that are above him; and bearing his nose into the winde, he shall the sooner finde any faulte that is above him. Also you should make an assembly for the otter as you do for the harte; and it is a note to be observed, that all such chaces as you draw after, before you finde them, lodge them or herbor them, you shoulde make a solemne assembly to heare all reportes before you undertake to hunte them, and then he which hath found of an otter, or so drawen toward his couche that he can undertake to bryng you unto him, shall cause his houndes to be uncoupled, a bowshotte or twyane before he come to the place where he thinketh that the otter lieth. Because they may cast about a while untill they have cooled their bauling and hainsicke toyes, whiche all houndes do lightly use at the first uncoupling. Then the varlets of the kennell shall seeke by the riverside, and beate the bankes with their houndes untill someone of them chaunce upon the otter.

"Remember always to set out some upwards and some doune the streames, and every man his otter-speare or forked staffe in his hande. And if they perceyve where the otter cometh under water (as they may perceyve if they marke it well) then shall they watche to see if they can get to stand before him at some place where he would vent, and stryke him with theyr speare or staffe. And if they misse then shall they runne up or doune the streame as they see the otter bende, until they may at last give him a blowe. For if the houndes be good otter-houndes, and perfectly entered, they will come chaunting and trayling alongst by the riverside, and will beate every tree roote, every holme, every osier-bedde, and tuft of bullrushes; yea, sometimes also they will take the ryver and beate it like a water-spaniell, so that it shall not be possible for the otter to escape; but that eyther the houndes shall light upon him, or els some of the huntesmen shall strike him, and thus you may have excellent sporte and pastime in hunting of the otter, if the houndes be good, and that the rivers be not over great.

"Where the rivers be great, some use to have a lyne throwen overthwart the river, the whiche two of the huntesmen shall holde by eche ende, one on the one side of the river, and the other on that other. And let them holde the line so slacke that it may always be underneath the water. And if the otter come diving under the water, he shall of necessitie touche their line, and so they shall feele and know which way he is passed, the which shall make him be taken the sooner. An otter's skinne is very good furre, and his grease will make a medicine to make fishes turn up their bellies as if they were deade. A good otter-hound may prove an excellent good buck-hound, if he be not old before he be entered."

In modern days the pack of Otter-hounds hunted by Mr. J. C. Carrick of Carlisle is the leading one in the kingdom, and annually provides excellent sport for the members of the hunt. Mr. Carrick, who is a constant exhibitor at the principal shows, is in the habit of entering some of the members of his pack whenever there is a class for them, and with almost invariable success. His well-known dog Lottery, whose portrait we give, as portraying exactly what an Otter-hound should be in our opinion, was bred by his owner in 1876, and is in colour a fawn grizzle. He is by Lucifer out of Countess, and has won at Darlington and Birmingham on more than one occasion. Lottery measures as follows: Length of head, 10½ inches; girth of muzzle, 11 inches; girth of skull, 17 inches; girth round chest, 30 inches; height at shoulder, 24 inches; girth of forearm, 7 inches; length of stern, 17 inches; weight, 78 lbs.

MR. CARRICK'S OTTER-HOUND, "LOTTERY."

Many writers on dogs have described the modern Otter-hound as in appearance very closely resembling the Bloodhound. We fail to see the likeness except in the conical skull, and consider that the Otter-hound is a far thicker-made dog than the Bloodhound—at all events, we think he *appears* so. No doubt his rough jacket increases the cloddiness of his build, and depreciates from his naturally symmetrical outline, and for that very reason we dislike the comparison between the two hounds. In Otter-hounds

The Head is big, high, and rather broad.

The Eyes dark and intelligent.

The Ears thin, and hanging flat to the head.

The Shoulders sloping and very muscular.

The Body big, powerful, and well ribbed up.

The Legs very straight, heavily boned, and set on well under the dog.

The Feet large, to assist the dog in the water.

The Stern of a fair length, and carried gaily.

The Coat very hard, so as to keep off the wet as much as possible.

The Colour usually grizzle, or fawn grizzle.

SCALE OF POINTS FOR JUDGING OTTER-HOUNDS.

Head and eyes	10
Ears	5
Body and shoulders	10
Legs	5
Feet	5
Coat	10
General appearance, including colour	5
	50

CHAPTER XLIII.

BREAKING SPORTING DOGS.

FROM almost time immemorial dogs have been the chosen companions of mankind in their pursuit of game. Under any circumstances it was necessary to educate the dogs in the duties they were required to fulfil, and it is with this subject that we have now to deal. It is of course impossible to conjecture how the capacity of each breed for working game came to be displayed in the first instance, but the fact remains that from very early times indeed many breeds had each their respective duties in the field, as they have in the present day.

One of the earliest evidences of the fact that the art of training dogs is by no means a modern one will be found in the following curious agreement :—

" Ribbesford, Oct. 7th, 1685.

" I, John Harris, of Willdon, in the Parish of Hastlebury, in the County of Worcester, yeoman, for and in consideration of ten shillings of lawful English money this day received of Henry Herbert of Ribbesford, in the said county, esquire, and of thirty shillings more of like money by him promised to be hereafter pay'd me, doe hereby covenant and promise to and with the said Henry Herbert, his executors and administrators, that I will from the day of the date hereoff, untill the first day of March next, well and sufficiently mayntayne and keepe a Spanill bitch named Quaud, this day delivered into my custody by the said Henry Herbert, and will before the said first day of March next fully and effectually traine up and teach the said bitch to sitt partridges, pheasants, and other game, as well and exactly as the best sitting dogges usually sett the same. And the said bitch, so trayned and taught, shall and will delivere to the said Henry Herbert, or whom he shall appoint to receive her, att his house in Ribbesford aforesaid, on the first day of March next. And if at any time after the said bitch shall for want of use or practise, or otherwise, forgett to sett game as aforesaid, I will at my costes and charges mayntayne her for a month or longer, as often as need shall require, to trayne up and teach her to sett game as aforesaid, and shall and will fully and effectually teach her to sett game as well and exactly as it is above mentyon'd.

"Witnesse my hand and seale the day and year first above written,

" JOHN HARRIS, his **X** mark.

"Sealed and delivered in presence of,

" H. PAYNE, his **X** mark."

Gervase Markham, however, previously to this, had alluded in his work, "Hunger's Prevention, or the Art of Fowling," to the taking of partridges with the setting dog, in the following words :—

" The fourth and last way for the taking of partridges (and which indeed excelleth all the other for the excellency of the sport and the rarenesse of the art which is contained therein)

is the taking of them with the setting dogge, for in it there is a twofold pleasure, and a twofold art to be discovered, as first the pleasure and the art proceeding from the dogge, and is contained in this manner of ranging, hunting, and setting, and then the pleasure and art in the bird hunted. . . . . Being come into the fields or haunts where partridges doe frequent you shall there cast off your dogge, and by crying 'Hey-ret' or 'Hey-whir,' or such like words of encouragement, according to the custome of his own nature or education, give him leave to raunge or hunt, which as soone as hee beginneth to doe, you shall then cease from any more words, except any fault or mistaking enforce you, and then you shall use the words of correction or reprehension due for that purpose, and in all his hunting and labour you shall have great and speciall heede that hee never range too farre from you, but beate his ground justly and even, without casting about or flying now here and now there, and skipping many places, which the heate and mettall of many good doggs will make them do if they be not reprehended, and therefore when any such fault shall happen you shall call him in, and with the terror of your countenance so threaten him, that he shall not dare all that day after to doe the like. . . . . Now if in this ranging and hunting you chance to see your dogge to make a sudden stop, or to stand still, you shall then presently make in to him (for he hath set the partridge), and as soone as you come to him you shall bid him goe nearer, which if he doe you shall still say to him, 'Go nearer, go nearer,' but if you find hee is unwilling to goe or creepe nearer, but either lies still, or stands shaking of his taile, as who should say here they are under my nose, and with all, now and then looks backe upon you, as if he would tell you how near they are, then presently you shall cease from further urging of him. . . . . When you see how the covey lyeth, you shall then first charge the dogge to lye still, and then, drawing forth your net as you walke, having pricked downe one end to the ground. . . . ."

Upwards of a hundred years before the date of Gervase Markham's work, Dr. Caius refers in his book to the taking of birds in the net in the field, and distinctly alludes to the trained setting dogs used in the sport, which he classes with the Spaniel, and notices under the name of Index.

Having thus shown that the art of training sporting dogs is not entirely due to its modern exponents, though it has naturally been reduced to a science by them, we now lay before our readers the following hints from the pen of Mr. A. Fletcher, of Glenmarkie Lodge, Huntly, Aberdeenshire, N.B., whose experience in breaking is both practical and extensive.

"In training Pointers and Setters care must be taken to give the puppies every chance of starting them, and by careful handling and allowing them to see everything that will tend to make them hardy and not gun-shy, as it is the worst thing that could befall the puppy, as he cannot have too much pluck. Many a puppy is made gun-shy by being too much kept out of sight when being exercised, and not allowed his freedom to run about until five or six months old, when he can see everything for himself, and by that time he will be getting into trouble. But you may be sure he will be full of spirit, if he ever will have any.

"Begin at first to lead him with a chain and collar, which he will object to most decidedly; but hold on to him, and let him pull till he is tired out, when he very likely will think better of it, and follow you. If not, let him sleep a night over it and try him next day, and after a pull or two he will come pleasantly. By all means be kind to him at first, until you get thoroughly acquainted with his temper, and granting that his temper is not the best, it is probably only high courage, which is the best merit he can have for the breaker. Then, presuming you have a kennel of dogs, attach him to an old one. If your puppy is a dog, put him on with one of the opposite sex, which he will follow with after a little coaxing. The next and greatest in importance is the shooting over him, and by all means be careful at first by snapping a cap. If I have a few puppies, I take them all together, old dogs and all, and when all running loose fire off several caps; but don't take any notice of your puppies, rather run on with them as though something of importance was on hand. The old dogs will run on, and the young ones taking notice soon join in following their example; but were you to stand still the old dogs would all drop, and the puppy would very likely stand and look at them, and at last think 'matters are not right here, I shall be off.' At last, when he gets quite courageous, you must begin to teach him to drop to hand before going farther with the shooting, presuming you have added a little powder after they stood the cap trial. Take your pupil out, say after exercise, choosing a fine day and the ground dry, especially if a Pointer. With a thrash cord, say thirty or forty yards, lead him quietly, where no one is likely to be present but yourselves, to an old grass field, and put him down by hand, remain by him and keep him there. Should he rise, put him down again. Then step back, and see if he will remain. Should he advance, return and put him down again, and repeat until he remains at the spot. After a day or two at this, should he not take to it well, and after he knows what is wanted of him, use stronger means by giving a good cut with the whip. Then go to the end of the cord, should he lie till then; call him up, and if he does this well next time stop him half way. Then, when exercising, put your pupil on with a quiet, steady dog, who will drop well, and make them drop on the couples together. This he will not do at first, but will back off if he could; but the old dog keeps him steady. Go up to him and drop him, and he will watch the others, when he will soon become as expert as they are. Also use every day, when exercising along the road, your pistol with a little powder, and mind you drop your pupils every time, as by this time you will have got over their shyness, if they had any, so that they must drop to shot now. Should he at any time object to drop when out, next day put the cord on to him, and by a few sharp jerks make him drop at once, also come to your call when you want him, as there is really nothing will make a dog so obedient as the cord, and saves ever so much of the whip. But let the breaker bear in mind he is to do all this teaching by the gentlest means in his power, combined with firmness. Should he have to apply the cord often and sharp, he must speak gently all the time, so that the dog will come at once when told, and not frighten him at his end of the cord. Some are very headstrong to learn this, but when mastered are the most tractable. Be sure that collar and cord are strong; as once a dog finds he gets breaking away, he gives double the trouble, and is not to be depended on for a time, as often, when your dog is about half way from you on the cord, he thinks this is a chance to run away. Should your cord break, then you lose the battle. Breaking your pupil perfect in the drop is half the work done, as the dog is under your command then, and is now ready to be taken to a large grass field, or, if you have it, a large piece of dry, marshy ground, where you expect little game. By this time you ought to know thoroughly the temper of your dog, whether you will have to be gentle with, or have to keep a sharp eye on your pupil. Now, supposing he be of the former kind, let him range away at first of his own accord, and should he come across any game take no notice at first, but let him chase it; it will do him good, as after a few attempts he will see his folly, and it will at the same time give him the zest for his work which he will require, without which he will be nothing in the eyes of a good breaker. If of the latter sort and very plucky, keep a good eye on him, and should he be inclined to chase when he comes across game, give him a taste of the whip, as with him a stick in time saves nine. Now let him down, as you know which of the methods you will have to proceed on, and I hope you have a good stretch of ground before you. Let him go off by the words, 'hold up,' with a wave of the right hand. If a high-couraged one he will not have to be told twice, as you will have found by this time that his fondness for hunting has given you a little trouble at home before now. Let him have a good fling all by himself, to work off the steam before he settles down to your signals by hand, which you must try and get your pupil to understand and depend on as much as possible, which you will soon see he will look for. Therefore, let no one be with you to take up his or your attention at any time : rather stop your work for the day. Presuming by this time he is off to the right, be in no hurry to blow your whistle, as very likely he would not mind it, he is so full of work. Let him turn of himself, and when he does turn try to get him to cross you to the left. But very likely he will pay little attention until he has been down for a time ; he will likely repeat the same thing for the first few days until he knows what is intended to be done, when he will settle down steadily to you, when you will have a chance of getting him to work to your signals. Of course, all the time he has been down you have been giving a signal, when you could, by a wave of the hand, to make him cross backwards and forwards in front of you. I often find by sticking too close to a pattern in quartering at first, your dog will try to get behind you in crossing instead of thirty yards in front of you. This will try the breaker more than anything, as a rash word now would make your dog come to heel altogether. Should he cross behind you once or twice, when he comes next run forward yourself, and he will run up to see what is up. This will encourage him likewise, and will do no harm. As this is one of the most essential points in dog-breaking, great care must be taken with your pupil to quarter his ground thoroughly. It is only by perseverance —keeping at the work every day—that real masterpiece work in this part of the training can be done. Should your pupil get too keen, and be inclined to hunt for himself and not answer the call, drop him when he turns by hand ; go up to him, and I hope you have a few feet of check-cord in your pocket ; attach this to his collar, then take your whistle and blow it, also rating him with the words, 'Do you hear the call?' Repeat pulling the check-cord, you yourself going after the back, and making him follow you. You must now watch him for this, as you must have perfect obedience to the whistle.

"Now he should be ready to be shown game. If you have many to break, or not much game to show, take a steady old dog out with your young one, and let him get a point. I hope he is steady and stands in good style. Have your young one in your hand ; go quietly up, treading lightly, and give him a whiff of the delightful aroma. He may be very impatient at first, but very likely he may stand at once. Some will, others will not, until several days. However, persevere until he does. I myself never take an old dog, but it is the quicker plan. After you think you can depend on your pupil, leave the old dog at home, and give him a chance for himself. Let no attendant or anything be near you to take off his attention, and I hope he may stand his first point well. Should he not do so, mark down the first brace of birds you can for him. Now put on your check-cord when not far from them. Then bring him round and get near the cord when he winds them, allowing him to get well out from you, so that he thinks he is by himself. Should he be inclined to run in, give him a sharp jerk with the cord, and keep him there for a minute. Then walk gently up and pat him; then steady him, and go up with him to his birds, and I hope they will lie well to him. But do not keep him too long on his point at this time, as it is the first real one he has had to himself; two or three minutes will be quite enough. As soon as the birds rise drop him at once, say for five minutes, walk round him, still keeping him down. Don't allow him to sit on his haunches. Never allow half measures in anything after he should know better, that is the great secret and success in breaking, combined with good temper and patience in the breaker. After you have him so that you can depend on him, take your old dog again, which I hope is a good backer, so that your young one may get a lesson, as nothing is more beautiful than a dog to back well, and some are very difficult to teach, others doing it naturally. If the old dog is a kennel companion, so much the better; the young one will not be so jealous, as by this time he will have great confidence in himself. Let them both down, or if you like they can have a run separately to begin with, which will cool their heads before being down together. We now suppose they are both down; have a short cord on your young one, so that, should he require it, he can be pegged down. Should the old dog find first, get if possible betwixt him and the young one, and by any means stop him by holding up your hand, and using the word 'Yoho.' Keep him there by standing still. Advance yourself to the old dog, still keeping your eye on him and your hand up. Should he advance, as he likely will, go and put him to where he stood first and peg him down, or you may put him down without the peg for the first few times, retreating with your face to him. I only hope the weather is fine, if spring, and birds lying well, which will give you time for all this. Now spring your game, still keeping your young dog down; also the old dog for ten minutes if you like. Bid the old dog hold up till he looks where the birds have been, still keeping the young one down when he has seen there are no more left. Call up the young one, and start again. Now let the breaker take care that the old dog does not get all the points, as nothing will so soon discourage your young dog as making him perform all the backing. He will soon be going in the wake of the old dog, depending on him finding the game; only I hope your young one will prove, if not so sure in nose, fleeter of foot, which will give him a chance of a point now and again. Or, supposing you have two young ones, you will have a better chance of them getting equal points. Be sure to cast off one to the right, the other to the left, each time you have them down, as by teaching them this they go away free of each other, and don't run so jealous as I have often seen them let down together; and instead of who will find the birds, it is which will run the fastest, and go right into the covey and chase them, all through jealousy and high spirits. Don't whip for this, only rate them, as if you yourself were to blame for it, as they will only do so for the first turn or two. I once had a brace of lemon-and-white Setters I broke in 1871 that quartered their ground, one to the right, the other to the left, and each kept their own beat. I tried it for mere curiosity, and found it could be done easily. So much for patience and perseverance, always bearing in mind that there is a good understanding between you and your pupils by kindness if possible; and be with them at exercise and feeding-time if you can, so that they get well attached to you. But when necessary to apply the whip, let it be done firmly, and don't flinch from your duty; it will save your pupil from many smaller and larger beatings afterwards. Some are always whip-whipping; that of itself would spoil a dog. This mostly applies to high-couraged ones, but many of the wilder type give the most trouble, and must be left a good deal to the discretion of the breaker. As for instance, many a shy dog that will scarcely stand a look of the whip at the kennel, will in the field, for an act of disobedience, take a fair share of it, and rather improve him of his shyness than otherwise, always bearing in mind never to leave him until peace is made up between you. It is also essential that you keep at them every day, as they are quick to learn, and as soon forget when only half way with their work, and in the end much easier for yourself; for they quickly discern right from wrong, and who is their master. Nothing to my mind is more beautiful than a brace of dogs who quarter their ground thoroughly; this is only done by perseverance, and using the signals of waving the arm across you. But, to hark back when you throw off your brace of young ones. When they get their point, get up to them as quick as you can, and if not well up to backing by this time—or some will do so naturally—have an attendant, and let him go up to the dog who has the point, and go yourself to the one who backs, as he will require most attention from you at this time. Go behind him, and steady him. Should he not get into stiff, good form, advance a step with him until he gets a whiff of the game. Then keep him there if possible in his position. Let the attendant spring the game with the other dog. Then drop them, after a few minutes' sign to the attendant to go on with the dog to see if any are left, you still keeping your dog down until he is satisfied there are none left. Repeat this until you are perfect. Another thing: do not depend too much for some time on either of them, but keep a strict watch on both, as until the second season very few young ones are to be depended on. Should you not have had the luck to let them see many hares, be careful now when one gets up, or you may have a deal of trouble. If you cannot depend on them, take the first chance when you see her to shout at the top of your voice, 'Ware hare! ware chase!' and I hope you are not far from them; but stop them by any means, or else you may have to go back again in your work, and only let the one dog down. This would be awkward, for if once they get a beginning with fur they are difficult to stop; only you must apply the whip properly now, as this is the worst vice they could have, and nip it in the bud. I have departed a little here, as it is very necessary to instil this most essential point on the breaker—for what chance would one have with a dog that would chase even a few yards at a field trial, although some of the judges are not altogether consistent there, as I have been put out with a dog that only went a few yards, and the next brace chased out of the field and were not put out, although neither showed great merit to keep them in the hunt. Now I think the rules ought to be strict; and let every one have the same fair play for his money; and let it be binding that a chase of any sort be thrown out; as I think, now that so many are entering for field trials, we must look for a higher standard of work, and therefore stricter rules. I shall now give a list of words used for working the dogs:—'Go on'—hold up your arm, extending it to the right or left. 'Lie down!' 'Down charge!' or 'Down!'—holding up the hand on springing birds. 'Have a care!' ''Ware springing birds!'—leading him back to where he should have stood them, using the words 'Soho! steady!' On fur, 'Ware hare!' at the same time drop him and take him off the line of her. By attending to these simple rules, the young breaker will no doubt have little trouble, with perseverance, in turning out a good puppy."

The information contained in the above article is so practical and valuable, and likely to be of service to beginners, that we do not propose to add any further remarks to the present chapter. Any special features in the education and breaking of various breeds will be alluded to in the articles referring to those varieties.

CHAPTER XLIV.

THE ENGLISH SETTER.

WHATEVER the origin of the Setter may have been, there can be no possibility of a doubt but that he holds a position second to none in the canine world in the present day. The beauty of the dog's coat and the brilliancy of his colours, coupled with his use and intelligence in the field, cannot fail to make the Setter a favourite with all who really admire and love a good dog. Another important feature in connection with his popularity, and which has been no small support to it, is the amount of national jealousy and prejudice which has been from time to time imported into discussions on the breed, as, naturally enough, each variety finds keen supporters amongst its fellow-countrymen. To explain our meaning we must at once allude to the fact that in the present day Setters are divided into three distinct varieties—viz., the English Setter, the Irish Setter, and the Gordon Setter. This latter breed is recognised as the Scottish national Setter, its origin being traced to Gordon Castle, Aberdeenshire, and will, with its Irish relative, be fully alluded to presently. There was an old Welsh breed, too, of black-and-white Setters which is almost extinct, though frequently pathetically alluded to by veteran sportsman hailing from the Principality in question.

In various localities throughout the country families or strains of Setters from special lines adopted in breeding—doubtless with the object of producing the dog best suited to the country over which they were to be worked—assumed peculiarities distinguishing them from each other, and became known by special names, such as the kennels which became known for breeding good ones. The Earl of Carlisle has a strain, specimens of which have occasionally been shown, and which display strongly-marked Spaniel characteristics, and from the tendency to curl in the coat, the top-knot more or less developed, and their general shape, suggest their having been grafted on the Water Spaniel. In the Marquis of Bute's kennels in the west of Scotland there was long, and probably still is, a strain of black Setters, and numerous kennels of extent had strains specially their own with some distinguishing feature. The Beltons, famous in the northern counties, are a superb race, and form the great base of the now famous Laverack Setter, on which again is founded the majority of the great kennels so favourably known throughout the country, and which has an immense popularity with American sportsmen.

Whether any of the modern and present-day breeders have resorted to a Spaniel cross direct, we are not in a position to state, but that such might be done with advantage in some instances we do not doubt.

In spite, however, of the numerous families into which the Setter is now divided, there can be no doubt that the origin of each was the Spaniel, and it is a curious subject for contemplation that Spain (as will be seen in the chapter on Pointers) should have the credit of supplying us with the three breeds of sporting dogs—Spaniels, Setters, and Pointers —upon which we English so greatly pride ourselves. The credit of improving these dogs is of course our own, but it is impossible to claim any one of them as indigenous to this country, closely identified with it as they are at the time of writing.

Dr. John Caius alludes to the Setter in his work on "English Dogges" under the title of Index, and his classification of it with the Spaniel is a convincing proof of its identity with that animal at the period in which Dr. Caius wrote as follows :—

"Another sort of Dogges be there, serviceable for fowling, making no noise either with foote or with tounge, whiles they followe the game. These attend diligently vpon theyr Master and frame their conditions to such beckes, motions, and gestures, as it shall please him to exhibite and make, either going forward, drawing backeward, inclining to the right hand, or yealding toward the left, (In making mencion of fowles my meaning is of the Partridge and the Quaile) when he hath founde the byrde, he keepeth sure and fast silence, he stayeth his steppes and wil proceede no further, and with a close, couert, watching eye, layeth his belly to the grounde and so creepeth forward like a worme. When he approcheth neere to the place where the birde is, he layes him downe, and with a marcke of his pawes, betrayeth the place of the byrdes last abode, whereby it is supposed that this kinde of dogge is called *Index*, Setter, being in deede a name most consonant and agreeable to his quality. The place being knowne by the meanes of the dogge, the fowler immediatly openeth and spreedeth his net, intending to take them, which being done the dogge at the accustomed becke or vsuall signe of his Master ryseth vp by and by, and draweth neerer to the fowle that by his presence they might be the authors of their owne insnaring, and be ready intangled in the prepared net."

The above extract, though not throwing much light upon the appearance of the breed in the reign of Queen Elizabeth, nevertheless is a proof of its existence ; but the following remarks taken from Gervase Markham's "Hunger's Prevention, or the Art of Fowling," which was published in London in 1655, gives a considerable amount of information upon the dog's character and the uses to which it was then placed. Under the heading of "What a Setting Dog is" Gervase Markham writes :—

"Before I wade further into this discourse I show you what a setting dogge is. You shall then understand that a setting dogge is a certaine lusty land spaniell taught by nature to hunt the partridges before, and more then any other chase whatsoever, and that with all eagernesse and fiercenesse, running the fields over and over so lustily and busily as if there were no limit in his desire and furie ; yet so qualified and tempered with art and obedience, that when he is in the greatest and eagerest pursute, and seemes to be most wilde and frantike, that yet even then, one hem or sound of his master's voyce makes him presently stand, gaze about him, and looke in his master's face, taking all his directions from it whether to proceede, stand still, or retire. Nay, when he is come even to the very place where his prey is and hath as it were his nose over it, so that it seemes hee may take it up at his owne pleasure, yet is his temperance and obedience so made and framed by arte that presently even on a sudden he either stands still or falles downe flatte upon his belly, without daring once to open his mouth, or make any noyse or motion at all, till that his master come unto him and then proceedes in all things according to his directions and commandements."

This quotation might almost have been taken from a modern work on Setters, as it refers to a class of dog whose duties in the field appear to have little altered during the progress of time. There still seems to have been a considerable looseness in the classification of this breed of dog, and the barrier between the Setter and the Spaniel appears to have been unremoved at a much later time, and the name Setter only applied to dogs broken to set game, and not to those distinguishable by any structural difference in shape or build. In 1697 Nicholas Cox writes of the Setter in " The Gentleman's Recreation " in the following words :—

" The dog which you elect for setting must have a perfect and good scent, and be naturally addicted to the hunting of feathers ; and this dog may be either land spaniel, water spaniel, or mungrel of them both ; either the shallow-flewed hound, tumbler, lurcher, or small bastard mastiff. But there is none better than the land spaniel, being of a good and nimble size, rather small than gross, and of a courageous metal ; which tho' you cannot discern, being young yet, you may may very well know from a right breed, which have been known to be strong, lusty and nimble rangers, of active feet, wanton tails, and busie nostrils, whose tail was without weariness, their search without changeablenesse, and whom no delight did transport beyond fear or obedience."

With reference to the behaviour of this dog in the field, Nicholas Cox remarks as follows in his notes on training the setting dog :—

" You must teach him to come creeping to you with his belly and head close upon the ground, as far or as little away as you think fit. . . . . And this observe in his creeping to you, if he offer to raise his body or head you must not only thrust the rising part down, but threaten him with your angry voice, which if he seem to slight, then add a sharp jerk or two with a whipcord lash. . . . . If you walk abroad with him, and he take a fancy to range, even when he is most busie speak to him, and in the height of his pastime make him fall upon his belly and lie close, and after that make him come creeping to you."

Thus Nicholas Cox succeeds in clearly proving that late in the seventeenth century the Spaniel, or even a mongrel partaking of any breed, was used as a setting dog by British sportsmen. Things do not appear to have undergone any great alteration in the beginning of the next century, for in 1718 one Giles Jacobs produced a book called the " Compleat Sportsman " in which a good deal is said about the setting dog, and sporting in general. The " Compleat Sportsman," which was published in the Savoy, London, was dedicated to Sir Charles Keymis, of Keven-Mabley in the County of Glamorgan, Bart., and may be taken as having been a valuable handbook relating to the laws on sport and dogs at the time when it was written. Mr. Giles Jacobs, however, copies unblushingly from Nicholas Cox, without giving the latter any credit for what he has taken from his works, and the result is that the description of the setting dog which we have quoted above is reproduced in the " Compleat Sportsman." It is, therefore, only reasonable to infer that no change, or, at all events, any material change, had come over the dog during the interval which had expired since Nicholas Cox wrote, or it would have probably been alluded to by Giles Jacobs in his work.

It may here be mentioned in justice to the individual to whom the credit is due, that Robert Dudley, Duke of Northumberland, is supposed to have been the first person to train setting dogs in the manner which has since his time been universally adopted by his successors. His Grace lived about the year 1550, rather earlier than the date at which Dr. Caius wrote, but beyond casual references to him by subsequent writers, nothing is positively known of the system upon which he acted, though from the remarks made it is probable that his ideas were closely carried out by the Setter breakers who came after him.

The "Sportsman's Cabinet," in 1803, devotes a good deal of its space to the subject of Setters, which had evidently by that time taken their rank as a distinct breed of sporting dog. Whether, however, the author is quite correct or not in his assertion that "The dog passing under this denomination [Setter] is a species of Pointer originally produced by a commixture between the Spanish Pointer and the larger breed of English Spaniel," will always be a matter of discussion between persons interested in the breed, as many are to be found who deny the existence of the Pointer cross. This subject may, however, be abandoned for the present, as our desire is now to trace the existence of the English Setter from its first appearance down to modern periods, and at the same time draw what deductions we can from contemporary writers concerning its appearance and value as a sporting dog. Mr. W. Taplin, in the "Sportsman's Cabinet," proceeds to remark subsequently to the preceding quotation, that, "The sporting department of the Setter in the field precisely corresponds with the pursuits and propensities of the Pointer, but with this single variation, that admitting their olfactory sensations to be equally exquisite, and that one can discover and as expeditiously receive and enjoy the particles of scent (or, in other words, the effluvia of the game) as readily and at equal distance with the other, the difference of the sports in which they are individually employed renders it necessary that one should effect upon his legs what the other does by prostration upon the ground, in the very position from which the present appellation of the 'setting dog' is derived. And these are neither more nor less than the pure effect of sporting education; for as in shoooting with the Pointer the game is constantly expected to rise, so in the use of a setting dog and net the game is required to lie. . . . .

"Although the setting dog is in general used merely for the purpose of taking partridges with the draw-net, yet they are sometimes brought into occasional use with the gun, and are equally applicable to that appropriation, except in turnips, French wheat, standing clover, ling, furze, or other covert, where their sudden drop and point may not be so readily observed."

Personally we attach very great importance to the above extract, for two reasons: first, it is distinctly stated that up to that time Pointers were the fashionable, or rather the favourite, breed with sportsmen who amused themselves by shooting three-quarters of a century back; and, secondly, it gives us a good reason for the change which has come over the Setter's behaviour in the field of later years. It is, of course, perfectly well known that the modern Setter usually points his game standing up, as a Pointer does, and the abandonment of netting is unquestionably responsible for this alteration in the method of a Setter carrying out his work. Before, when the sportsman was anxious to net as many birds as he could, it was most essential that they should be as undisturbed as possible, and the presence of a dog would, of course, increase the chances of their being frightened away before the net was fixed for their capture. The chances of the dog being seen by the game were naturally lessened when he lay down, and this, no doubt, was the reason for his being broken to do so. Now things are much altered, and the sportsman only wants the whereabouts of the game to be indicated, so that he may walk them up. There is, however, a perfectly palpable tendency to crouch still observable in many of the best and highest bred Setters of the present day, which is unquestionably accounted for by the former habits of the breed, and the uses to which it was put.

From the following remarks of Mr. Taplin it will be seen that in the early years of this century the Setter was credited (as he is by many in the present day) with being naturally of a timid and nervous temperament, for he writes :—

"It has already been observed that the Setter is in possession of a constitutional timidity which induces him to dread the severity of correction, and, of course, to avoid the means of disgrace; fraught with this irritability their treatment in the field becomes matter of judicious discrimination. Dogs of this description, perpetually alive to the fear of giving offence and incurring bodily punishment, lay claim to every little tender attention as well at home as in the field. Warm, hasty, impetuous sportsmen contribute not unfrequently to their own mortification and disappointment, for many dogs of this disposition corrected in passion or beat with severity are so completely overwhelmed with distress or humiliated with fear that they almost insensibly sink at the feet, and can be prevailed on to hunt no more, or, what is sometimes the case, slink away home without the least chance whatever of being again induced to render further assistance in the sport of the day."

It is an undoubted fact that in the present day many Setters that would otherwise have been invaluable in the field are ruined in their breaking and subsequent education by the severe treatment they receive at the hands of those in whose power they are placed. We are decidedly of the opinion that were less stringent punishment inflicted for trifling offences upon the members of more than one well-known kennel, an even increased reputation would quickly be added to that which it already possesses.

Three years later than the date in which the "Sportsman's Cabinet" was published—viz., in 1806—there was a sale of Setters, the record of which has been handed down to the present day. The prices realised were for the period decidedly good, and as the kennel was the property of a rather famous individual in his way—Daniel Lambert, the historical fat man, who shortly before his death scaled fifty-two stone eleven pounds—and the list, moreover, is valuable as an index to the prices of sporting dogs seventy years ago, we reproduce it at length :—

Peg, a black Setter Bitch ...	...	...	...	...	41	guineas
Punch, a Setter Dog	...	...	...	...	26	„
Brush „	...	...	...	...	17	„
Bob „	...	...	...	...	20	„
Bell „	...	...	...	...	32	„
Bounce „	...	...	...	...	22	„
Sam „	...	...	...	...	26	„
Charlotte, a Pointer Bitch ...	...	...	...	...	22	„
Lucy „	...	...	...	...	12	„
Total	...	...	...	...	218	„

This gives an average which would make dog-breeding a successful commercial enterprise even in the present day; but it is a noticeable fact that the Setters fetched better prices than the Pointers, which must be taken as a proof that the breed was coming up into a higher position in public estimation, or possibly Mr. Lambert's kennel was stronger in Setters than in Pointers.

The date of introduction of the setting dog or Spaniel into this country is not clear. There is no special reference to him in the old forest laws of Canute, which guarded against the keeping of Greyhounds except under stringent conditions of maiming the animals or keeping them at a distance of ten miles from a royal forest, and even Mastiffs kept by farmers and others for the protection of their dwellings had to lose three claws, which was called "expeditating." Spaniels are, however, specially mentioned in a statute anterior to the time of Caius, and the dogs then regarded by the law were Mastiffs, Hounds, Spaniels, and Tumblers. And in a statute of James I. it is provided that no person shall be deemed qualified to keep setting dogs who is not possessed of an inheritance of the value of £10 per annum, a lease for life of £30 per annum, or who is worth £200 per annum, unless he be the son of a baron or knight or heir-apparent to an esquire.

The changed character of the sport of fowling when netting gradually gave way before the increasing use of guns, until it became finally entirely superseded, did no doubt act powerfully in modifying the Setter, and the plastic nature of the dog has been ever since taken advantage of to alter and improve him to suit the constant changes in the conditions of sport. As a factor in the conversion of the ancient Spaniel into the modern Setter, Blaine throws out the suggestion that a cross with one of the *celeres* or swift-footed dogs was resorted to, and that the Pointer is probably a cross between the Spaniel and one or other of the *pugnaces*. To produce the Setter by such a cross, we had in this country the Greyhound and the swift light hound, at one time peculiar to Yorkshire, Cumberland, Northumberland, and probably other northern counties. There were other varieties of the *celeres*, no doubt, but the two mentioned would in our view be the most likely to approve themselves to practical sportsmen. In the absence of proof of such a cross having been resorted to with a special purpose, we content ourselves with pointing out the great reasonableness of Blaine's theory. Granted that the cross was adopted, it is not to be supposed that it was adhered to, but the produce would be bred to the parent strain, the characteristics of which it was purposed should preponderate, and that would be, in this instance, the Spaniel.

It may be argued that the cross with the light hound equally with that by the Greyhound would quite alter the style of hunting, destroy the natural tendency to index or set the game, and the latter cross, to a great extent, destroy the olfactory powers. We do not think such a result would follow, for even if in the first cross such were apparently developed, they would be unequally so in the several members of the litter; and good judgment in selecting the bitches kept for brood purposes, and wise mating with Spaniel dogs excelling in the qualities partially lost by the cross, would soon restore these in all their former fulness of development, whilst the desired modification of form and other characteristics was sufficiently preserved.

If the theory of the cross with either of those mentioned, or some other of the *celeres* available (but none of which, we are of opinion, would be so suitable to the object in view) be rejected, then we are thrown back on the theory of selection of individuals of the same variety; for all must admit that, changed as the modern Setter is from all portraits of him in pen, pencil, or by brush, as he existed even so late as the last century, he still in all essentials shows a strong alliance with the Spaniel family. It is not impossible in the production of the modern Setter that he arose from the roughest of Spaniels described by our earliest writers by means of selection alone. None of our domestic animals are so easily changed, and, as it were, moulded to the breeder's will, as the dog, and, in the case under consideration, the time has been more than ample to effect the change.

It is very improbable that we have a better Setter judge than Mr. William Lort, of Fron Goch Hall, Montgomeryshire, and his experience of the breed is practically unlimited. We are, therefore, glad to be able to lay before our readers Mr. Lort's views upon the pro-

DOGS AND PARTRIDGES. (*After Desportes.*)

bability, and also of the desirability, of the Pointer cross, which so many believe to be largely present in most strains of Setters. Mr. Lort writes thus:—

"As to the origin of the Setter, I am not so sure of the correctness of my old and valued friend, Mr. H. Herbert, when he says: 'There is no doubt whatever that the true Setter is a pure strain of unmixed Spaniel blood, the only improvement produced in the breed arising from its judicious cultivation,' &c., &c. I am quite sure that years ago, say from forty to fifty, it was no uncommon thing to get a dip of Pointer blood into the best kennels of Setters. Sometimes it answered well, and though for a generation or two it diminished the coat, not always though at the cost of appearance, it fined and strengthened the stern, giving life and motion to it, and what, whether rightly or wrongly, in early times was thought a good deal of—it rounded the foot.

"I know how shocked some of our modern breeders will be at the idea of their favourites having in their veins a drop of Pointer blood. It is well perhaps that it is not generally known how many fashionable strains have been vitiated with much more objectionable blood than that of the Pointer. I have seen Droppers [cross between a Pointer and Setter], yes, *and dogs bred from Droppers*, possessing exquisite powers of scent, lovely tempers, and great pace. I think there is reason to believe the Spaniel to be the foundation of our present Setter.

"As a case showing that it is possible for cross-bred dogs to breed true, I knew of a black Setter bitch three crosses from Pointer, belonging to Robert Warner, of Leicester Abbey. She was good herself, having all the qualities of a pure Setter, and, curious enough, she bred *well* from either a Setter or Pointer. Mr. Warner gave his keeper (who afterwards came into my service) a brace of black puppies, by a Pointer, of this bitch. They looked all over Pointers, they worked like Pointers, they were excellent Pointers, and were sold, when broken, at 40 gs.—a good price in those days. I myself had Setters from her, and they were good Setters, and showed all Setter characteristics."

A strong confirmation of Mr. Lort's theory is to be found in the subjoined engraving from a painting by the famous French artist, Alexander François Desportes. This great animal painter—born in 1661, and died in 1743—was elected a member of the French Royal Academy of Painting in 1699, and of its Council in 1704. For many years he occupied the Court position of historiographer of the chase, created expressly for him by Louis XIV.; and his pictures, which are very numerous, can hardly be surpassed for their fidelity to Nature. The engraving we reproduce from his pencil is entitled "Dogs and Partridges," and is valuable as distinctly showing that the Pointer had been crossed with the Spaniel before and during his time, and that the result was a dog very like our modern Setter.

It has been before shown that up to the end of the last century Pointers were the more favoured breed of dog by sportsmen, but of late years the Setter has made great progress in public popularity. This may be, to a certain extent, accounted for by the existence of the three varieties—English, Scotch, and Irish—to which allusion has been already made; but we feel inclined to believe that the natural toughness of this dog's constitution has more to do with the change that has taken place. The thickly-padded feet of the Setter unquestionably render him a preferable dog for all sorts of rough shooting, and on the moors he is far better able to withstand the broken ground and the hard work that has to be encountered than the Pointer, who is more easily fatigued. On the other hand, exception has been taken to the Setter that, though physically stronger than the Pointer, he is not able to work so long without water, and it may be mentioned that this theory was in existence at the time Taplin wrote, for he remarks, with reference to this, his favourite breed :—

"There is an erroneous opinion in circulation that it is a disadvantage to Setters, they cannot continue to hunt long without water; though it is perfectly well known to the most experienced sportsmen they can endure heat, thirst, and fatigue as well, if not better than Pointers; they are certainly more difficult to break, and when broke are most apt to run wild and unsteady if not frequently hunted."

Nearly twenty years later John Scott writes in the " Sportsman's Repository ":—

" Many sportsmen prefer the Setter to the Pointer for pheasant shooting, as more active and hardy, having so much of the quality of the Spaniel, and thence not flinching at the thickest coverts. On the moors, and for grouse shooting also, the preference of the Setter is decisive, for although he is said to require much water, and to be unable to endure heat and thirst like the Pointer, the former, from his constitutional activity and the hardness of his feet, is superior in a long day over a rough and uneven surface. From accident, or from that never-failing desire of shining by the intermixture of breeds, with little consideration of the end, Pointers have been crossed with Setters, and Setters with Pointers, but we have not seen any beneficial result. On the score of utility, the Setter can derive no improvement from such a cross ; and granting—which, however, is not proved—that the Pointer gains something in regard of usefulness, such advantage will be countervailed by an abatement of size, figure, and stateliness, on which account only, perhaps, he superseded the Setter in the affections of the sportsman. . . . .

" It has been disputed very uselessly whether the Setter or the Pointer have the most powerful nose ; but let a sportsman take a thorough good dog of either kind into the field, and he will no longer trouble himself with that dispute. Beyond a doubt, the Setter is the most useful gun dog of the two, but the Pointer is the largest, most stately and showy, and is admired for his rate, his high ranging, and steadiness. The Setter on his part may put in his claim, and more especially when of the pure breed, to his full share of the intelligence, sagacity, and affection for man, which shines so eminently and so delightfully in the Spaniel."

Such remarks as above would seem to betoken a very rapid advance on the part of the Setter in the estimation of sportsmen who used the gun, for it must be borne in mind that not twenty years before it would seem that this dog was only being gradually introduced into this branch of sport, having been more generally used in netting operations up to the commencement of this century. At the period of writing (1880) the Setter is certainly the more successful dog in the field, as his many triumphs in field trial competitions must amply prove. With reference to these trials it may be briefly mentioned that they were instituted by the Kennel Club, which is a Society originated about the year 1869 for the purpose of promoting the general improvement of dogs, dog shows, and dog trials. These latter are unquestionably decided proofs of a dog's capacity for work, and may be regarded as most successful institutions, having been largely patronised by the higher class of sportsmen, who have shown great interest in the trials, and who have in addition entered their dogs largely for competition. The rules for the guidance of field trials are very clearly laid down by the Kennel Club, and being likely to be appreciated by sportsmen who may be desirous of instituting such competitions in their own neighbourhood, a copy of them will be found below.

1. *Management of a Meeting.*—The management of a meeting shall be entrusted to a committee in conjunction with Field Stewards, the latter of whom shall be appointed by the committee before the time of running. The stewards shall decide any disputed question by a majority of those present, subject to an appeal to the committee. No steward shall vote during a meeting in any case relating to his own dogs.

2. *Election of Judges.*—The judge, or judges, shall be elected by the committee, and their names shall be announced as soon as possible after their election. When a judge, from ill-health or any other unexpected cause, is prevented attending a meeting or finishing it, the committee shall have the power of deciding what is to be done.

3. *Description of Entry.*—Every subscriber to a stake must name his dog at or before the draw, giving the names of the sire and dam of the dog entered, and also, in puppy stakes, the name of the dam's owner. The secretary shall publish on the card the names of those who are subscribers, but do not comply with these conditions. These nominations shall not be drawn, but must be paid for.

4. *Disqualification.*—For Puppy Stakes, the names, pedigrees, ages, colours, and distinguishing marks of the puppies shall be detailed in writing to the secretary of a meeting at the time of entry. Any puppy whose age, markings, and pedigree shall be proved not to correspond with the entry given shall be disqualified, and the whole of its stakes or winnings forfeited.

5. *Definition of Puppy.*—No dog is to be considered a puppy that was whelped before the 1st of January of the year preceding that of its competing.

6. *Payment of Stakes.*—All money due for nominations taken must be paid on or before the draw, whether the stake fill or not, and although from insufficient description or any other cause, the dogs named may be disqualified. No entry shall be valid unless the amount due for it has been paid in full. For all produce and other stakes where a forfeit is payable no declaration is necessary; the nonpayment of the remainder of the entry money at the time fixed for that purpose is to be considered a declaration of forfeit. The secretary is responsible for the entry money of all dogs whose names appear upon the card.

7. *Alteration of Name.*—If any subscriber should enter a dog by a different name from that in which it shall have last been known in public he shall give notice of the alteration to the secretary at the time of entry, and the secretary shall place on the card both the late and present name of the dog. If notice of the alteration be not given the dog shall be disqualified.

8. *Prefix of "N.S."*—Any subscriber taking an entry in a stake, and not prefixing the word "names" to a dog which is not his own property, shall forfeit that dog's chance of the stake. He shall likewise, if requested, deliver in writing to the secretary of the meeting the name of the *bonâ fide* owner of the dog named by him, and this communication is to be produced should any dispute arise in the matter.

9. *Death of Subscribers.*—The death of a subscriber shall only affect his nomination if it occur before the draw, in which case, subject to the exceptions stated below, it shall be void, whether the entries have been made or not, and any money received for forfeits or stakes shall be returned. If he has parted with all interest in the nominations, and dogs not his property are entered, paid for, and drawn in ignorance of his being no longer alive, such entries shall not subsequently be disturbed. When dogs who have been entered in produce stakes change owners with their engagements and with their forfeits paid, the new owner, if otherwise entitled to run them in these stakes, shall not be prevented from doing so by reason of the death of the former owner.

10. *Power to Refuse Entries.*—The committee or stewards of any meeting may reserve to themselves the right of refusing any entries they may think fit to exclude; and no person who has been proved to the satisfaction of the Committee of the Kennel Club to have misconducted himself in any way in connection with dogs, dog shows, or dog trials, will be allowed to compete in any trials that may be held under the Kennel Club Rules.

11. *The Draw.*—Immediately before the dogs are drawn at any meeting, and before nine o'clock on every subsequent evening during the continuance of such meeting, the time and place of putting down the first brace of dogs on the following morning shall be declared. A card or counter bearing a corresponding number shall be assigned to each entry. These numbered cards or counters shall then be placed together and drawn indiscriminately. This classification, once made, shall not be disturbed throughout the meeting, except for the purpose of guarding, or on account of byes. Dogs whose position on the card has been altered in consequence of guarding or of byes must return to their original position in the next round if guarding does not prevent it.

12.—The stakes shall be run in the order they are given in the programme, unless the whole of the competitors or their representatives in the various stakes may agree otherwise—in which case the order may be changed, with the consent of the Stewards or Committee.

13. *Guarding.*—When more than one nomination in a stake is taken in one name, the dogs, if *bonâ fide* the property of the same owner, shall be guarded throughout: this is always to be arranged, as far as possible, by bringing up dogs from below to meet those which are to be guarded. This guarding is not, however, to deprive any dog of a natural bye to which he may be entitled, either in the draw or in running through the stake.

14. *Byes.*—A natural bye shall be given to the lowest available dog in each round. No dog shall run a second such bye in any stake, unless it is unavoidable. When a dog is entitled to a bye, either natural or accidental, his owner or nominator may run any dog he pleases with him.

15. *Postponement of Meeting.*—A meeting appointed to take place on a certain day, may, if a majority of the Committee and Stewards (if appointed) consider the weather unfit, be postponed from day to day ; but if the running does not commence within the current week all nominations shall be void, and the expenses shall be paid by the subscribers, in proportion to the number of nominations taken by each. In the case of produce stakes, however, the original entries shall contine binding if the meeting is held at a later period of the season.

16. *Running in Order.*—Every dog must be brought up in its proper turn, without delay, under a penalty of £1. If absent for more than a quarter of an hour its opponent shall be entitled to claim the trial—and shall, in that case, run a bye. If both dogs be absent at the expiration of a quarter of an hour, the judge or judges shall have the power to disqualify both dogs, or to fine their owners any sum not exceeding £5 each.

17. *By whom a Dog is to be Hunted.*—An owner, his keeper, or deputy may hunt a dog, but it must be one or the other ; and, when once the dogs are down, an owner must not interfere with his dog if he has deputed another person to hunt him.

18. *Method of Hunting.*—The person hunting a dog may speak, whistle, and work him by hand, as he thinks proper ; but he can be called to order by the judges for making any unnecessary noise, and if he persists in doing so they can order the dog to be taken up, and he will be out of the stake. An opponent's dog may not be purposely interfered with or excited, or an appeal can be made to the judges ; and if the opponent's dog points game, the other dog is not to be drawn across him to take the point, but if not backing of his own accord, he must be brought round behind the other dog. Dogs must be hunted together, and their keepers must walk within a reasonable distance of one another. After a caution, the judge or judges may have the power to disqualify the dog whose keeper persists in neglecting this rule.

19. *Control of Dogs Competing.*—The control of all matters connected with the dogs under trial shall rest with the judge or judges of the meeting, assisted in cases of peculiar difficulties by the stewards.

20. *Wearing Collars.*—All dogs, when necessary, shall wear collars—the red for the highest dog on the card, whose place shall be on the left, the white for the lowest dog, whose place shall be on the right side.

21. *The Judge or Judges.*—The judge or judges shall be subject to the general rules which may be established by the Kennel Club for his or their guidance. At the termination of each trial, he or they shall immediately proclaim his or their decision, either by word of mouth, or by the exhibition of a colour corresponding with that worn by the winning dog. No recalling or reversing of that decision shall be afterwards given on any pretext whatever.

22. *Length of Trials.*—The length of a trial shall be determined by the judge or judges. When he or they are satisfied that decided superiority has been exhibited by one of the contending dogs the trial should end.

23. *Injuring a Dog.*—If any subscriber or his servant shall, wilfully or by carelessness, injure, or cause to be injured, an opponent's dog during a trial, the owner of the dog so injured shall (although the trial be given against him) be deemed the winner of it, or shall have the option of allowing the other dog to remain and run out the stake, and in such case shall be entitled to half its winnings, if any.

24. *"No Trials" and "Undecideds."*—A "no-trial" is when, by accident or some other unforeseen cause, the dogs are not tried together. An "undecided" trial is where the judge or judges consider the merit of the dogs equal. If either is then drawn the owners must at the time declare which dog remains in. A "no-trial" or an "undecided" may be run again immediately, or at such a time during the meeting as the judge or judges may direct. If it stand over until the next day it shall be the first trial run.

25. *Withdrawal of Dog.*—If a dog be withdrawn from a stake on the field, its owner, or some one having his authority, must at once give notice to the secretary or stewards. If the dog belong to either of these officials, the notice must be given to one of the others.

26. *Impugning the Judge.*—If any subscriber openly impugns the decision of the judge or judges on the ground, he shall forfeit not more than £5, or less than £2, at the discretion of the majority of the stewards.

27. *Stakes not Run Out, and Arrangements Made Thereon.*—When two dogs remain in for the deciding trial, the stakes shall be considered divided if they belong to the same owner, or to confederates ; and also if the owner of one of the two dogs induces the owner of the other to draw him for any consideration ; but if one of the two be drawn without consideration (from lameness, injury, or from any cause clearly affecting his chance of winning), the other may be declared the winner, the facts of the case being clearly proved to the satisfaction of the stewards. The same rule shall apply when more than two dogs remain in at the end of a stake which is not run out ; and in case of a division between three or more dogs, of which two or more belonging to the same owner, these latter shall be held to take equal shares of the total amount received by their owner in the division. The terms

of any arrangement to divide winnings, and the amount of any money given to induce the owner of a dog to draw him, must be declared to the secretary.

28. *Objections.*—An objection to a dog may be made to the secretary or to any one of the stewards of a meeting at any time within ten days of the last day of the meeting, upon the objector lodging in the hands of such steward or secretary the sum of £5, which shall be forfeited if the objection prove frivolous, or if he shall not bring the case before the next meeting of the Kennel Club Committee, or give notice to the secretary previous thereto of his intention to withdraw the objection. The owner of the dog objected to must deposit equally the sum of £5, and prove the correctness of his entry or case. All expenses in consequence of the objection shall be borne by the party against whom the decision is given. Should an objection be made which cannot at the time be substantiated or disproved, the dog may be allowed to compete under protest, the secretary or stewards retaining his winnings until the objection has been withdrawn, or heard and decided. If the dog objected to be disqualified, the amount to which he would otherwise have been entitled shall be divided equally among the dogs beaten by him, and if a piece of plate or prize has been added and won by him, only the dogs which he beat in the several rounds shall have a right to contend for it.

29. *Defaulters.*—No person shall be allowed to enter or run a dog in his own or any other person's name who is a defaulter for either stakes, forfeits, or bets in connection with field trials or dog shows, or for any money due under an arrangement for a division of winnings, or for penalties regularly imposed for the infraction of rules by the stewards of any meeting, or for any payment required by a decision of the Kennel Club, or for subscriptions due to any club entitled to acknowledgment by the Kennel Club. As regards bets, however, this rule shall only apply when a complaint is lodged with the secretary of the Kennel Club within six months after the bet becomes due. On receipt of such complaint the secretary shall give notice of the claim to the person against whom it is made, with a copy of this rule, and if he shall not pay the bet or appear before the next meeting of the Kennel Club and resist the claim successfully, he shall be considered a defaulter.

30. *Ineligible Persons.*—Any person who is proved to the satisfaction of the Kennel Club Committee to have been guilty of any fraudulent or discreditable conduct in connection with dogs, may, in addition to any pecuniary penalty to which he may be liable, be declared incapable of entering a dog in his own or any other person's name during any subsequent period that the club may decide upon.

31. *Unfitness to Compete.*—Should any dog be considered by the judges of a meeting unfit to compete by reason of being on "heat," or having any contagious disease, or any other cause which clearly interferes with the safety or chance of winning of his opponent, such dog shall be disqualified.

N.B.—In the foregoing rules the term "dog" is understoood to mean both sexes.

We are decidedly of the opinion that Field Trials have done much towards the improvement of sporting dogs, and hope to see them more extensively held all over the country. They have in some degree, if not perfectly, the merit of combining the element of public competition with those practical tests so desirable in judging of sporting dogs. In these field trials the Setters have hitherto managed to hold their own uncommonly well, and up to the year 1880 no Pointer has succeeded in winning the Grand Challenge Cup which is given by the Kennel Club to be run for annually by dogs belonging to its members. Any member may run any dog he chooses, either Pointer or Setter, and it was decided when the cup was first offered that it should become the property of any member who should be fortunate enough to win it three times, but not necessarily in succession or with the same dog. To the astonishment of the sporting world Mr. G. De Landre Macdona has accomplished the feat with Ranger, a black-and-white Setter, whose portrait and pedigree we give on the following pages. This grand dog, though not himself a perfect model of beauty, has by carrying off the Challenge Cup upon three occasions stamped himself as the Setter of the day, and has moreover shown what is behind him in the matter of pedigree by begetting many first-class specimens of the breed. As a matter of fact Ranger III., who is the subject of our coloured plate, is himself a grandson of the old dog, and we therefore add his pedigree to the table, as Ranger's is naturally included in it:—

PEDIGREE OF MR. G. DE LANDRE MACDONA'S ENGLISH SETTER DOG, RANGER III.

Whelped 8th March, 1877.

RANGER III.

A. Fletcher's Cora (whelped 5th June, '75, own sister to Macdona's Moll.

Henderson's Pride.

Ruby.

Blue Prince.

Juno.

Fred IV.

Belle.

Nellie.

Pride of the Border.

Dicken's Blue Dash

Old Blue Dash

Old Blue Dash—Dash II.

Laverack's Belle.

Belle II.Laverack's Dash II.

His Moll III.

Cora II.

Fred I.

Belle II.

Sting.

Cora II.

Cora.

Dash II.—Old Blue Dash.

Laverack's Sting.

Cora II.

Fred.

Rock.

Blair's Cora.

Regent.

Jet I. Regent.

Jet I.

Dash I. Belle.

Moll II.

Dash I.

Peg.

Rock.

Moll II.

Pilot.

Moll II.

Pilot.

Moll II.

Pilot.

Moll II.

Pilot.

Old Moll.

Ponto.

Old Moll.

Ponto.

Old Mo'l.

Ponto.

Old Moll.

Ponto.

Moll II.

Dash I.

Moll II.

Pilot.

Belle I.

Dash I.

Belle I.

Dash I.

Belle I.

Dash I.

Belle I.

Dash I.

Belle I.

Dash I.

Belle I.

Dash I.

Belle I.

Dash I.

Belle I.

Dash I.

Old Moll.

Ponto.

Descended from Ponto and Old Moll, see Pedigree of Dash II.

Macdona's Ranger II.

Macdona's Champion Ranger.

Macdona's Wonder.

Macdona's Judy.

Jones's Roll.

Lort's Kit.

Laverack's Rock.

Madge.

Sal.

His Flash.

Withington's Frank.

Peg. Garth's Major.

Rock.

Moll II.

Dash.

Moll II.

Pilot.

Belle I.

Dash I.

Old Moll.

Ponto.

Belle I.

Dash I.

Belle I.

Dash I.

Bishop's Major.

Bishop's Rose from Lord Sefton.

Dr. Bath's Moll.

Lord Barrington's Major.

Calver's Countess.

Paul Hackett's Rake.

His Grouse.

Calver's Nell.

Rake.

Bell.

Don.

Nell.

Hackett's Bess.

Rake.

Nell.

Bond's Don.

Bond's Nell.

Flash.

Myrtle.

Lad.

Ben.

Burdett's Brougham.

Gordon.

Nell.

Flash.

Myrtle.

Lad.

Bond's Don.

Bond's Don.

Nell.

Nell.

Flash.

Myrtle.

Lad.

Macdona's Quince II.

Jones's Quince I.

Lort's Dip,

Shot.

Darkie (Anglesey).

Jones's Madge.

Laverack's Rock.

Garth's Major.

Sal.

Withington's Frank.

Bishop's Major.

Lord Barrington's Major.

His Flash.

Bishop's Rose from Lord Sefton.

Dr. Bath's Moll.

Withington's Flash.

Withington's Frank.

Lort's Sall.

Garth's Major.

Withington's Flash.

Withington's Frank.

Bishop's Rose from Lord Sefton.

Bishop's Major.

Dr. Bath's Moll.

Lord Barrington's Major.

Peg.

Rock.

Moll II.

Dash.

Moll II.

Pilot.

Belle I.

Dash I.

Old Mo'l.

Ponto.

Belle I.

Dash I.

Belle I.

Dash I

Burdett's Brougham.

With reference to Ranger's marvellous behaviour in the field we extract the following from a report of the Field Trials which appeared in the *Live Stock Journal*, April 25th, 1879.   In alluding to Ranger the writer says:—

" He made what is so much to the public taste at these trials—a sensation point. When running down a large grass meadow with Darkie he rushed with marvellous speed to the bottom, against which appeared a large embankment.   The dog suddenly found

MR. MACDONA'S CHAMPION ENGLISH SETTER "RANGER."

himself hurled by the impetus of his going into the midst of a twelve-foot river that ran between the embankment and the grass field in which he was running.   The impetus with which he went threw him to the opposite side.   Crawling up the bank half dazed with the shock, he scented some birds, and immediately coming to life again, dropped. The birds then rising, he plunged back into the river, swam across, and shook himself in face of the judges and spectators.   Anything more unique or sensational in the matter of field trials has not been witnessed before, except when he won the all-aged stake at the Kennel Club Field Trials, when, rushing down the hill, he suddenly winded birds, and stopped, and the impetus of his going caused him to make a summersault in the air, when he landed on his back, and as stiff as starch.   His four legs were seen in the air, and his neck and head turned round in the direction where the birds were soon put up about a foot from his nose."

ENGLISH SETTER.

Ranger, in addition to his Challenge Cup triumphs, has won the following stakes:—Reynold Stakes, Shrewsbury, 1874; Champion Cup, Shrewsbury, 1874; Champion Cup, Shrewsbury, 1877; Shrewsbury Stakes, 1877; Hawkstone Stakes, Shrewsbury, 1873; East of England Stakes, Ipswich, 1873; Trehill Stakes, Devon and Cornwall, 1875. Such performances, even unaccompanied by the fact that he has won the Challenge Cup outright, stamp Ranger as undoubtedly the best dog of his breed which has hitherto appeared.

To recommend the Setter as a companion dog to the non-sporting philo-kuon may be to invite a sneer from many a knight of the trigger, but nevertheless there is much to be said in favour of these dogs in the character of mere companions. There is no more elegant dog than the Setter; the outlines of a well-formed specimen are eminently beautiful, and his every movement most graceful. The coat is beautifully soft and rich, the featherings especially being of a fine silky texture, and the colours and distribution of them generally striking and picturesque, as they are soft, refined, and lovely. In intelligence the Setter has few equals, so that he soon accommodates himself to circumstances, and is so easy of control that he readily becomes a companion that can be thoroughly trusted, for his intelligence is great, and he seems to think for himself, and make the pleasing of his owner his sole delight. In temper they are almost invariably reliable, and their affections become deep and lasting. And added to all these qualities there is an air of refinement and superiority about him, inherited from a long line of blue-blooded ancestors, that commends him to all.

Those who keep but a few Setters to shoot over themselves should never fail to make friends and constant companions of them; the mutual understanding and trust arising from this doubles the pleasure of the sportsman in the possession of his dogs, and adds greatly to his success in the field.

We had Mr. Macdona's Ranger with us whilst Mr. Barber was sketching him, and although we met as strangers we were soon friends, and parted we firmly believe with mutual regret. Never have we seen a dog who so readily accommodated himself to circumstances—he seemed at once to be as much at home in London as he is in the stubble or the heather, and took his seat in a hansom cab as naturally as though to the manner born.

One word of caution only in respect to keeping Setters as companions. We should always advise having them broken to game, although there may be no prospect of using them; because if unbroken dogs were bred from an unbroken line, whilst their beauty and general intelligence might be sustained, they would lose the aptitude for their natural work.

As stated at the commencement of this article, it is an unquestionable fact that, whatever the source was from which the modern English Setter sprung, there are several distinct families of the breed at present in existence. But even these are themselves offshoots of older types, which in their turn originated from the Setting dog, either by breeding and selection, or the judicious admixture of foreign blood. It may therefore be as well to draw attention to some of the most famous of the old breeds, as well as make allusion to the most fashionable of the modern ones, before proceeding further with the subject.

Reference has already been made to the old *Welsh Setter*, a breed now practically extinct, and whose loss is so greatly to be deplored that supreme efforts should be made to restore it, before all hopes of doing so are vain. Mr. William Lort, of Fron Goch Hall, Montgomeryshire, who has before been quoted in this chapter, has kindly given us some valuable information concerning this variety of Setter, which is in purport as follows:—The coat of the Welsh or Llanidloes Setter, or at all events of pure-bred ones, is as curly as the jacket of a Cotswold sheep, and not only is it curly, but it is hard in texture, and as unlike that of a modern fashionable Setter as it is possible to imagine. The colour is usually white, with occasionally a lemon-coloured patch or two about the head and ears. Many, however, are pure white, and it is unusual not to find several whelps in every litter possessed of one or two pearl eyes. Their heads are longer in proportion to their size, and not so refined-looking as those of the English Setter. Sterns are curly and clubbed, with no fringe on them, and the tail swells out in shape something like an otter's. This breed is more useful than any Spaniel, for it is smart, handy, with an excellent nose, and can find with tolerable certainty at the moderate pace it goes. It usually has the habit of beating close to you, and is not too fast, being particularly clever at cocks and snipe, which they are no more likely to miss than is a Spaniel. With so much to recommend them, we cannot help repeating that this is a breed well worth saving from extinction, especially as it is so hardy, and far less liable to disease than the modern fashionable dog. Some excellent specimens of this variety have been in the hands of Mr. Charles Beck, of Upton Priory, Macclesfield, and he said that they stood hard work and briary dingles, when he worked them in Wales, better than any breed he could procure.

There was also a *liver-and-white* strain of Setter which was well known in the North of England, especially in the Carlisle district. Though this dog was coarse and lumbering, it has been argued, and as often denied, that the famous Laverack blood is tinged with that of this variety. However, this will be more fully referred to almost immediately, when the Laveracks are touched upon.

Another famous strain of jet-black Welsh Setters is now lost and gone for ever. It was a blood that was to be found in many parts of the Principality, and as a strain was second to none. Unfortunately, though jealously guarded by its owners, their interest in it gradually lessened, and it finally has disappeared entirely.

The *Anglesea Setter*, as it was once called, did not spring, as might be supposed, from the island of that name, but from Beaudesert, the residence of the Marquis of Anglesea, where it was carefully treasured. They were in character a light, active, very narrow breed of dog, with no chest, though deep in ribs. They were rather leggy, and possessed the habit of standing with their fore-legs and feet close together. This breed of dog was constitutionally delicate, but as long as they stayed, showed great pace in the field. In colour they were mostly black - white - and - tan, and in coat, though not so smooth and flat as a modern Setter, the Angleseas were not nearly so curly as the Welshmen described above.

To arrive more rapidly at the leading strains in 1880, we now come to the magic name of Edward Laverack, a gentleman who has done more to bring this Setter in all his glory before the public than any other has ever done or is likely to do. Mr. Laverack, who was an ardent sportsman, for half a century was engaged in improving the English Setter, and with most flattering results. The corner-stone of his breeding-stud was a pair he first obtained from a clergyman named Harrison, who resided in the neighbourhood of Carlisle. That he conscientiously followed the principles of strict in-breeding is amply proved by a reference to the pedigree table of Ranger, where it will be observed that all Mr. Laverack's best blood is represented on the one side; and the success of his system is clearly demonstrated by the position his strain occupies in the estimation of modern Setter breeders. In short, most of the leading strains are either pure Laveracks, or else they partake largely of the Laverack blood.   The formation of the Laverack Setter, to quote his own words, is as follows :—

"Head long and light, not snake-headed or deep flewed, but a sufficiency of lip; remarkable for being very strong in the fore-quarters; chest, deep, *wide*, and ribs well sprung behind the shoulders, carrying the breadth of back to where the tail is set on; immensely strong across the loins; shoulders very slanting or oblique; particularly short from the shoulders to where the hind-quarters meet. A Setter should not rise or be too upright in the shoulder, but *level* and *broad;* tail well set on in a line with the back, *rather drooping*, scimitar-shaped, and with plenty of flag.   Legs remarkably short, and very short from hock to foot; feet close and compact, thighs particularly well bent or crooked, well placed and close under the body of the animal, not wide or straggling.

"Colour black, or blue-and-white ticked; coat, long, soft, and silky in texture; eyes, soft, mild, and intelligent, of a dark hazel colour; ears low set on and close to the head, giving a round development to the skull.   There is another variety of the same strain called the lemon-and-white Beltons, exactly the same breed and blood.   These are marked similar to the Blues, except being spotted all through with lemon-colour instead of blue, and precisely of the same form and characteristics; equally good, hardy, and enduring."

These words of Mr. Edward Laverack must surely be treasured by Setter breeders, and the only unsatisfactory part in them to our mind is the total absence of any allusion to liver-colour.   We cannot see how he can reconcile himself to ignore all reference to this liver-colour, since, in the following letter to Mr. Rothwell, an old friend and fellow-breeder, he distinctly admits that there is a strong dash of liver blood in the Laverack Setter. The letter referred to runs as follows :—

[Copy.]

" Broughall Cottage,
" Whitchurch,
" Shropshire

"DEAR ROTHWELL,
  "I am glad to hear your bitch has given birth; save me a Blue. All five are true bred, and all take after the sire, Blue Prince.   The liver-and-white will be quite as handsome and good as any.   He strains to Prince's sire, viz., Pride of the Border, a liver-and-white; he strains back for thirty years to a change of blood I once introduced—the pure old Edward Castle breed—County Cumberland liver-and-white, quite as pure and as good as the Blues.   You may have heard Withington speak of the handsomest Setter he ever saw, viz., Pilot; he was this colour, and a clipper.   Pride's dam was my old blue-and-white, with tan cheeks and eyebrows.   Why I reserved Pride was to breed back with him and my Blues.   He is invaluable, as by him I can carry on the breed. . . . . . I have a demand from America for more than I can sell, but they are the best, and I *guarantee* all I send *bred* by *me*. . . . . . .

" Yours truly,
"E. LAVERACK.

" *May 23rd*, 1874."

There is a possibility that Mr. Laverack, knowingly or otherwise, had introduced some of the blood of the liver-coloured Setters we have above alluded to as being in the neighbourhood of Carlisle.   This breed was not a popular one, we understand, and therefore it might not have been worth his while to make a special reference to it.   But be this as it may, one thing is very evident from the letter, and that is that Mr. Rothwell, who bred many dogs for Mr. Laverack himself, was unaware of any such a taint, or this letter would not have been written. Its present publication may be a consolation to breeders of this kind of dog, as the appearance of a liver-coloured whelp will convince an owner who has read these lines that it is not necessarily a bar-sinister in the pureness of its pedigree as a Laverack. There could in fact be a great deal said upon this subject of the liver colour, which Mr. Laverack here remarks upon as being likely to appear now and then in pure-bred dogs of his strain. A tendency to throw back is of course inevitable in every breed of animal, and it is greatly to be regretted that in his work Mr. Laverack threw no light upon the origin of his breed. In fact, in his description of the Setter, he only alludes, in referring to his own strain, to black, or blue, and lemon-ticked ones. This reticence on the part of Mr. Laverack would seem to imply that, though he did not attempt to deny the fact that there was liver blood somewhere in his strain, he was not particularly anxious that this should be generally known, and consequently kept even his *fidus achates*, Mr. Rothwell, in the dark about it until some puppies of the colour appeared in his breeding operations, when he hastened to assure the latter gentleman that such an event was by no means impossible.

It would appear, further, not only from the above letter, but from many others which passed between Messrs. Laverack and Rothwell, and which subsequently came into our hands, that the latter gentleman, who appears to have had the free use of any of Mr. Laverack's stud dogs, was in the habit of giving Mr. Laverack puppies as the latter required them; and also that the great breeder himself was kind enough to sell Miss Rothwell's whelps for her. We do not consider ourselves that there is any harm in such a thing being done; but the practice is unfortunate, inasmuch as it opens the door to ill-natured remarks on the pedigrees of dogs, and is a practical illustration of the dangers to which breeders are liable. What we particularly allude to is the chance that is run of the authenticity of pedigrees being disputed afterwards, if it could be proved that certain dogs were actually bred by Mr. Rothwell, and not by Mr. Laverack. We do not impute any deception to either of these gentlemen, but it is possible that persons who purchased pure-bred Laveracks from himself might describe them as bred by him, when in reality Mr. Rothwell deserved the honour.

Another and generally unknown fact in connection with the English Setter-breeding operations of Mr. Edward Laverack is beyond a doubt; and that is, that in the year 1874 he was practically "out of" his own blood. Whether the fatalities to which he so pathetically refers in the following correspondence were in any way accelerated by the excess of in-breeding to which he had resorted we cannot say, but it would seem that for some years his stock had been dying off in a manner which was surprising to the great breeder himself, and caused him to draw upon the kennel of his friend Mr. Rothwell for dogs to supply his customers. The following extracts from some of Mr. Laverack's letters may be read with interest :—

> "Broughall Cottage,
> "Whitchurch,
> "Salop.
>
> "DEAR ROTHWELL,
> "I received your daughter's letter relative to the puppies. When old enough to take from mamma, place in a hamper, and send as directed above, and *advise* me *prior* in order I may send to station for them. Keep them till six weeks old. I shall be able to sell your daughter as many as you can spare; and when sold, will send either you or Miss Rothwell the money. . . . . .
> "Yours truly,
> "E. LAVERACK.
>
> "*June 17th, 1874.*"

" Broughall Cottage,
" Whitchurch,
" Salop.

" DEAR MR. ROTHWELL,

"I regret very much to inform you the three puppies you sent died a week ago in distemper, after rearing them all straight, and they really became beautiful, and showed a deal of quality. They were all three *bespoke* by an *American* at 15 guineas, to be sent in March. But what is still worse, I have lost *six more* dogs, *two brood* bitches 18 months old, which I refused to sell at fifty guineas apiece, and *four* more young dogs, all cut off in *distemper and fits.* All were the handsomest I ever bred or saw. Indeed, I am quite broken in spirits to think after all my trouble and expense (a life's), I fear I have or shall lose the breed, as I have only one old brood bitch left, I fear too old to breed. The only dog I have left except her is Prince. . . . . .

" Yours very truly,

" E. LAVERACK."

There is no date to the above letter, but the post-mark on the envelope is November 13th, 1874.

" Broughall,
" Whitchurch,
" Salop.

" DEAR ROTHWELL,

". . . . . . I am quite disheartened with the loss I have sustained—*nine.* Six were such as I never saw for beauty, and the three that came from you had greatly improved. I have only two old dogs left—viz., Prince and a lemon bitch, Cora. I have been here three years and only reared one dog out of 30. As I took this place apparently everything I could wish, and built an excellent kennel, and have a free range of fields, my dogs being cut off seems a fatality, as no expense is spared. . . . . . I will bring over several letters from America relative to dogs, and I think if I approve of your young ones I may perhaps get you a customer. . . . . .

" Yours most truly,

" E. LAVERACK.

" *March 24th,* 1875."

Such letters clearly show the difficulties under which Mr. Laverack laboured at the close of his career, and have no doubt been instrumental in earning the pure-bred Laverack Setter a reputation in certain quarters for being delicate and hard to rear. On the other hand, the success of crossing the Laverack blood with other strains is proved by the success of Ranger; and in our opinion there is a great probability of the English Setter deteriorating if modern breeders stick too closely to their own blood.

Amongst the number of great Setter breeders may be mentioned those of George Jones of Oscott, who was a great light at the first institution of dog shows, and showed Rap. Mr. Jones gloried in the Laverack blood, which he grafted on his own stock, and cheerfully acknowledged the benefits he received from it. The Brothers Withington, too, were great Setter men, and good friends to Mr. Laverack. They are said to have given the latter one hundred pounds for four unbroken puppies, which was then a very long price to give for dogs of such a tender age. Nor must the names of G. R. Rogerson and the Rev. Francis Adey be forgotten by lovers of the Setter. Mr. Statter, too, will always be remembered in connection with this breed. His great kennel is very near the top of the tree in Setter circles, and though its members are not all pure Laveracks, their owner sensibly admits that the more of this blood he gets the better pleased he is. Mr. R. Ll. Purcell-Llewellin, of Lincolnshire, is one of the greatest Laverack breeders of the day, and spares no trouble or expense in perfecting his strain. In consequence he has many grand specimens, though many breeders say that his bitches are better than his dogs. Lord Waterpark's handsome, heavily-flecked Setters, which appeared at a very early Glasgow dog-show, were, and have been, much admired. They are believed by many to be closely allied in blood to the original Laveracks, and their appearance certainly justifies the supposition.

The kennel of Mr. William Lort, now of Fron Goch Hall, Llanllugan, Montgomeryshire, is also one which must always be regarded with respect. To quote the words of Mr. Laverack himself:—

"Mr. Lort has also a beautiful and excellent breed of Setters, descended principally from the strain of the late Richard Withington, Ashfield House, Pendleton, Manchester, an old friend of mine, and who shot with me for many years in the Highlands. They are black-and-white and lemon-and-white; long, silky coats, hard enduring, and good rangers.

"Mr. Lort, from judging so constantly at dog shows, has given this fine strain but little chance, and they are not known as they ought to be; but from what I am told, and believe to be the case, there are no *better* . . . Setter breeders are under the greatest obligations to this gentleman for his unflagging endeavours to improve the Setter, and he spares no time, trouble, or expense."

Such praise from one who, like Mr. Edward Laverack, is the recognised father of the modern Setter, is a sufficient guarantee for the quality of Mr. Lort's strain, whilst his popularity as *facile princeps* the leading Setter authority now alive, is quite beyond a doubt. Mr. T. B. Bowers, of Woolton, near Liverpool, is also a noted Setter breeder, and glories in his admiration of the Laverack blood. Mr. John Shorthose, of Newcastle, whose grand bitch Novel is illustrated in this chapter, has several good specimens of the breed, and is a successful exhibitor at most of the leading shows. The great Shropshire kennel of Mr. Daintry Collins contains some of the best blood we have, being mostly pure-bred Laveracks. Sir Frederick Graham, too, has made his mark as a successful breeder; and both Lord Down and Mr. Barclay Field have been fortunate to produce successful Field Trial winners. Nor can the name of Mr. George Lowe's Tam o' Shanter be omitted from any list of the leading Setters and sires of the day.

Amongst the most prominent Setters of recent years the name of Rap will always be conspicuous. We believe that this dog was beaten in his day by Mr. Laverack's Prince, but he is generally credited with having been the best dog of the breed ever seen in public. A gentleman who knew him well when in his prime has kindly given us the following description of this great English Setter:—"Rap was a black-white-and-tan dog, with a most refined head, and very intelligent eyes. His ears were beautifully placed, and his long neck was well set into his back. His ribs were deep, his feet were good, and his legs as straight as gun-barrels; his hind-quarters were powerful; and last, but not least by any means, he had a well-carried, well-proportioned stern. His single fault, if fault there could be found in Rap, was that he was a trifle—just a trifle—high on his leg."

Mr. William Lort's Shot (1865) was another famous pure Laverack, and own brother to Sal, who was pronounced by Mr. Richard Withington to be the best bitch of the day. Mr. Laverack, however, who never saw either Shot or Sal, said Walter was the best Setter he had ever seen; they were by Withington's Frank, out of Flash. Nor must the merits of Quince II., Ranger's father, be overlooked, unlucky as this grand dog was in his owners, for he never seemed to be properly appreciated by those who had him in their possession. Quince II.

was sold for a few shillings, when worn out, at Aldridge's Repository in 1878, for the public never seemed to realise that very likely much of Ranger's excellence was inherited from his brave old sire. Count Wind'em, Countess Moll, and Countess Bear, are the bright particular stars of Mr. Llewellin's kennel, and the first-named is a great, big, useful-looking dog. Mr. James Fletcher's blue-ticked dog Rock, late Mr. S. E. Shirley's, has done a lot of winning, and Mr. Lort's own brother to him—Jock—is a successful sire, having fathered Belfast and other good ones. Milano, a black-tan-and-white (very little tan-and-white) dog, and Bandit, have done much to sustain the prestige of Mr. Bowers' kennel, and Mr. Shorthose's Novel has kept his name well before the public. Another English Setter who is, in our opinion, a very grand but unlucky dog, is Mr. J. Robinson's Emperor Fred; his chief fault is a want of spring in the ribs, but, with this exception, he is a Setter all over. Mr. T. B. Bowers, in addition to Bandit, is the fortunate possessor of an excellent bitch in Maid of Honour, who closely resembles the great dog in both colour and formation.

Having thus endeavoured to trace out the history of the English Setter from its earliest origin until the present day, and having drawn attention to many of the men who have done best for it, and many of the dogs who have done most to support the English Setter's reputation, there remains for us but very little more to say. Opinions on the Setter's merits must always be re-occurring when the large number of sportsmen is taken into consideration; and even in former days, as we have already shown, it was a debatable subject in sporting circles as to which was the better dog in the field—the Setter or the Pointer. For our own part we should prefer the Setter, but a good dog, like a good horse, is good under any circumstances. Mr. William Lort, in answer to a question, has written us as follows:—"I am often asked which is the better dog—the Pointer or the Setter. It is difficult to say. I keep and use both, and the only disadvantage I see in the Pointer is that on high, storm-swept hills he does sometimes, after a protracted lunch, shiver and shut up; but this is only on exceptionally wet and cold days. The Setter is undoubtedly the best dog we have for grouse-shooting, and this is beyond a doubt the poetry of all shooting.

"Now, as to the points of the English Setter, it is really difficult to give them in an understandable form—general appearance, or *tout ensemble*, goes for so much. The head ought to be long, and the eyes, which should match or be in keeping with the colour or complexion of the dog, should not be too wide apart, or placed in too deep a stop, or be separated by too much of a groove—all or any of these defects spoil the expression, a most important point in a Setter. The ears should not be set on too high or be carried too far from the head. The front part of the ear should not gape open so as to show the inside of the ear. The ear should not be Spaniel-like and large. The neck should be long and well set back into the shoulders. The chest should be deep, and the ribs carried well back towards the hips. N.B.—Some loose-loined, badly ribbed-up Setters go a great pace, but they are usually bad feeders, and not every-day workers. The stern should not be too long; it should be carried in a line with the back, and be straight, and be ornamented with a little pendant fringe. Nothing indicates mongrel blood in a Setter more than a defective stern. The forelegs should be straight, strong, and not too long; the hind ones should be muscular and well-bent. The feet should be round, and well supplied with hair between toes, not too far apart. The coat is affected by climate; the most approved is devoid of curl. The best colours are black-and-white, ticked, or blue Beltons, lemon-and-white, and lemon-ticked. Laverack preferred the blue Beltons; he thought them rather hardier than dogs of other colours."

Having thus given the ideas of the leading living authority upon Setters it only remains for us to give a short description of the principal points of the variety. They are as follows :—

The *Head*, moderately long, and not too heavy ; rather inclined to be narrow between the ears ; a dip below the eyes, and with the muzzle rather up-rising at the nose.

The *Nose* should be large and the nostrils spreading ; the colour, black or dark liver, dependent upon the colour of the dog himself.

The *Ears* not too heavy, set on low, and lying close to the head, not pricked up, and covered with a silky fringe.

MR. J. H. SHORTHOSE'S ENGLISH SETTER BITCH "NOVEL."

The *Eyes* large, bright, and intelligent ; nothing is so bad as a "pig-eyed" Setter.

The *Neck* long, curved, sloping, and well set on to the shoulders.

The *Shoulders* very muscular, and sloped.

The *Chest* deep.

The *Body*. Ribs rather round, wide at the shoulders, well ribbed-up and muscular ; loins a little arched.

The *Legs and Feet*. Legs not too long, *quite* straight, and feathered down to the ground ; feet well supplied with hair. In hind legs the stifles must be well bent, and the hocks and pasterns unusually strong.

The *Stern or Flag* not too long, and free from curl, and carried in a slight curve ; it should be well feathered.

The *Coat* is soft, silky, and free from all curl.

The *Colour*. Lemon-and-white, blue-and-white, orange-and-white, black-and-white, white, black, and liver-and-white. There are other colours, but they are seldom met with.

In *General Appearance* the Setter is a handsome though delicate-looking dog; in many instances increasing this appearance by a tendency to crouch and seem afraid. He, however, ought to give evidences of stamina, and should have a cut-and-come-again appearance in spite of seeming delicate.

The dog selected for illustration in our coloured plate is Mr. Macdona's Ranger III., a grandson of Old Ranger. This dog's pedigree has already been given, and, as he has been expatriated to Germany, it would be unfair to criticise his performances upon the bench.

The engravings of Ranger and Novel are, we consider, two excellent likenesses of the animals they represent. Ranger, also Mr. Macdona's, has already been done justice to above, and we can only add that he is as affectionate and obedient in private life as he is feared and formidable in the field. Mr. Shorthose's Novel was bred by Mr. T. B. Cockerton in 1877, and is by Blue Prince out of Flame, by Rall out of Countess, Blue Prince II. by Blue Prince out of Cora. She has won the following prizes:—Gateshead first and cup, Whitby first, Preston first, Kendal cup, Bishop Auckland champion, and Birmingham second prize, 1879; first Crystal Palace, first Darlington, 1880.

STANDARD OF POINTS FOR JUDGING ENGLISH SETTERS.

	Value.
Head	10
Eyes and ears	5
Shoulders and neck	5
Body and chest	10
Loins and stifles	5
Legs and feet	5
Coat and feather	5
General appearance	5
Total	50

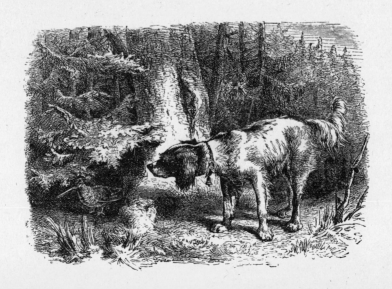

CHAPTER XLV.

THE RUSSIAN SETTER.

ANY book professing to refer to sporting dogs would, we think, be incomplete if no reference were made by the author to the Russian Setter. This breed of dog is unquestionably rarely met with in these islands, but some years ago his appearance made a considerable stir amongst all followers of the gun. It is certain, too, that his services were in some quarters called upon to improve the English Setter, and therefore, in spite of the dog's rarity in his pure state, it is desirable that he should be treated of in a chapter by himself, though necessarily the remarks concerning him will be very brief.

Mr. Joseph Lang, writing to the *Sporting Review* in 1841, and dating from No. 7, Haymarket, thus alludes to the Russian Setter :—

"In the season of 1839 I was asked for a week's shooting into Somersetshire by an old friend, whose science in everything connected with sporting is first-rate. Then, for the first time for many years, I had my English Setters beaten hollow. His breed was from pure Russian Setters crossed by an English Setter dog, which some years ago made a sensation in the sporting world from his extraordinary performances. . . . Although I could not but remark the excellence of my friend's dogs, yet it struck me, as I had shot over my own old favourite Setter (who had himself beat many good ones, and had never before been beaten) for eight years, that his nose could not have been right, for the Russians got three points to his one. I therefore resolved to try some others against them the next season, and having heard a gentleman, well known as an excellent judge, speak of a brace of extraordinary young dogs he had seen in the Yorkshire moors, with his recommendation I purchased them. I shot to them in August last, and their beauty and style of performance were spoken of in terms of high praise by a correspondent to a sporting paper. In September I took them into Somersetshire, fully anticipating that I should give the Russians the go-by, but I was again disappointed. I found from the wide ranging of my dogs, and the noise consequent upon their going so fast through the stubbles and turnips (particularly in the middle of the day when the sun was powerful and there was but little scent) that they constantly put up their birds out of distance, or, if they did get a point, that the game would rarely lie till we could get it. The Russians, on the contrary, being much closer rangers, quartering their ground steadily, heads and tails up, and possessing perfection of nose in extreme heat, wet, or cold, enabled us to bag double the head of game that mine did. Nor did they lose one solitary wounded bird ; whereas, with my own dogs I lost six brace the first two days of partridge shooting, most of them in standing corn.

"My friend having met with a severe accident while hunting last season, I determined to go to Scotland for the next three years. Seeing that my dogs were well calculated for grouse shooting, as they had been broken and shot to on the moors, and being aware of my anxiety to possess his breed of Russians, he very kindly offered to exchange them for mine, with a promise that I would reserve a pair of Russian puppies for him. . . . Since then I have hunted them in company of several dogs of high character, but nothing that I have yet seen could equal them. If not taken out for six months they are perfectly steady, which is a quality rarely to be met with. . . . I contend that for all kinds of shooting there is nothing equal to the Russian, or half-bred Russian Setter, in nose, sagacity, and every other necessary qualification that a dog ought to possess."

Mr. William Lort, to whom we applied for information concerning the breed, writes in reply about the Russian Setter:—

"Roughly speaking, in appearance this dog is rather like a big 'warm' Bedlington Terrier. There are two varieties of the breed, and curiously enough they are distinguished from each other by the difference in their colour. The dark-coloured ones are deep liver and are curly-coated. The light-coloured ones are fawn, with sometimes white toes and white on chest; sometimes the white extends to a collar on the neck. These latter are straight-coated, not curly like the dark ones. My recollection of this breed extends back some fifty years, and the last specimen I owned of it—a light-coloured one—I gave away to a friend who would not take a hundred pounds for it.

"Their noses never seem to be affected by a change of climate; hence their value in my eyes. I have worked them in September's sun and in January's snow, and they were equally good. They were some of the best dogs I ever had, and never varied; and under exceptional cases as regards the weather, we always had the Russians out. The only fault I found with them was the difficulty in getting new blood, for those we had showed evidences of scientific breeding, and a strict adherence to type. The fact that they were successfully crossed, to my knowledge, with English Setters, satisfies me that they are really Setters and not an allied breed. I may add that they are excellent water-dogs."

When a breed is so highly recommended by such sportsmen as the above, it seems marvellous that it has not been encouraged in a country like our own, which has been the nursery of sport for years. We cannot, therefore, express too strongly our conviction that the introduction of a dip of Russian blood would improve the working capacities of our English Setters. At all events, the experiment is well worth repeating, and we trust that Mr. Lort, or some other gentleman equally looked up to in the canine world, will set the example, and try to still further improve our breed of Setters. Unquestionably, the appearance of our dogs would suffer at first, but few sportsmen would regret the loss of good looks if an increase of working capacity was gained.

A scale of points is quite out of the question in treating of a breed of which so very little is known, and for a description of the Russian Setter we must take refuge under the ægis of Mr. William Lort.

CHAPTER XLVI.

THE GORDON SETTER.

THIS dog, which we have before alluded to as almost claiming to be the national Setter of Scotland, is one upon which a variety of opinions have been expressed. Its very origin is obscure, though all authorities agree in bestowing the honour of its production upon the Duke of Gordon, hence the name by which this breed is recognised in the present day. It is certain that in the early part of the century (about 1820) the then Marquis of Huntly, who was afterwards Duke of Gordon, possessed a strain of Setters which he was anxious to improve. The story runs that when looking around for a judicious cross the rumour reached his lordship that there was an extraordinarily clever Sheep-dog bitch belonging to a shepherd in the neighbourhood. This bitch had been taught to set birds by her owner, and her staunchness was said to be remarkable. On hearing of this wonderful bitch, the Marquis of Huntly is said to have immediately obtained her from the shepherd, and put her to one of his most successful sires. It is to this Collie bitch that many hold that the modern famous Gordon Setter owes its origin, and certainly the presumption seems a very fair one.

Whatever reliance, however, is to be placed in this alleged formation of the Gordon strain, the value of dogs from the Duke's kennel was far higher than of those coming from other quarters, and a genuine importation from Gordon Castle was always looked upon as possessing no impurity of blood. As a proof of this the following list of prices obtained at the Duke's sale in 1836 may be taken as conclusive, and the list is moreover valuable as showing the value of Gordon Setters at that time, as well as for another reason to which we shall hereafter make a reference :—

1. Duke, 5 years, black-and-tan	...	...	...	...	34 guineas.
2. Young Regent, 4 years, black-white-and-tan		...	...	72	„
3. Juno, 5 years, black-and-white	...	...	...	...	34	„
4. Satan, 2½ years, black	...	...	...	...	56	„
5. Crop, 3 years, black-and-white	...	...	...	...	60	„
6. Duchess, 11 months, black-and-white	...	...	...	37	„
7. Random, 10 months, red-and-white	...	...	...	35	„
8. Princess, 11 months, black-and-white	...	...	...	25	„
9. Bell, 11 months, black-and-white	...	...	...	...	34	„
Brace of Puppies, black-and-white...	...	...	...	30	„

417 gs.

Amongst the buyers at this historic sale were the Duke of Richmond, Lords Abercorn, Chesterfield, and Douglas, and Messrs. Martyn, Walker, and Robinson. The prices reached were certainly encouraging for the times, and it is questionable whether they would be headed at the break-up of any modern kennel. It is only reasonable, however, to suppose that this small

SETTERS IN 1805.

(*Facsimile of Coloured Plate by Sydenham Edwards.*)

The upper dog in the original is coloured black and pale tan.
The middle one red with white blaze up face.
The lower one white.

Showing apparently the three leading varieties as known at the present day.

number was not the entire stud, and that many other members of it were otherwise disposed of and dispersed throughout the country.

Having thus alluded to the reputed origin of this breed, and endeavoured to direct attention to its monetary value forty-four years ago, we find ourselves face to face with the burning question in connection with the Gordon Setter—its original colour. In every correspondence in connection with this breed, the writers who have addressed the sporting public through the Press have drawn attention to this subject; but still the matter has not, in the opinion of many, been finally settled. It would seem, however, from the colours given above, that by far the largest proportion of the Duke's dogs were wanting in any tan at all, and were simply black-and-white. On considering this, the question arises in our mind whether only those possessing tan were the descendants of the Sheep-dog cross which had been introduced into the strain some twelve years before the date of the sale. We learn from Gervase Markham's "Hunger's Prevention" that at the time of his writing his work, in the early part of the seventeenth century, "some had beene curious in observing of their (the Setting dog) colours as giving preheminence to the motley, the liver-hude, or the blacke and white spotted." It is, therefore, we may assume, within the bounds of probability that the original Gordon strain, before the introduction of the Collie cross, were descendants of the "blacke and white dogs" of Gervase Markham's time, and that, therefore, the now popular golden-tan of the Gordon Setter is in reality but a proof of a decided cross of Sheep-dog blood. The late Mr. Dixon, who wrote under the *nom de plume* of "The Druid," is positive in deciding that "originally the Gordon Setters were all black-and-tan, and Lord F. G. Halliburton's Sweep, Admiral Wemyss's Pilot, Major Douglas's Racket, Lord Breadalbane's Tom, and other great craftsmen of the breed of that colour. Now all the Setters in the Castle kennel are entirely black-white-and-tan, with a little tan on the toes, muzzle, root of the tail, and round the eyes. The late Duke of Gordon liked it: it was gayer, and not so difficult to back on the hill-side as the dark coloured . . . . . The composite colour was produced by using black-and-tan dogs to black-and-white bitches."

Mr. Laverack corroborates this statement of "The Druid's" to a very great extent, for he writes :—

"Two years after the decease of Alexander Duke of Gordon I went to Gordon Castle purposely to see the breed of Setters. In an interview with Jubb, the keeper, he showed me three black-tans, the only ones left, and which I thought nothing of. Some years after, when I rented on lease the Cabrach shootings, Banffshire, belonging to the Duke of Richmond, adjoining Glenfiddich, where his Grace shot, I often saw Jubb and his Setters; *then, and now, all the Gordon Castle Setters were black-white-and-tan*."

Here is the distinct evidence of a gentleman whose exertions in favour of Setters and whose knowledge of the breed are admitted by every person interested in canine matters; and from what he writes, and from what other equally eminent authorities have written, it is proved almost beyond contradiction that white is a permissible colour in the Gordon Castle kennel. From what "The Druid" has said, however, it would appear that the presence of white having been at one time considered by the head of the establishment to be an attraction, special efforts were made to retain it in the strain at the Castle, and that more of it is consequently to be found there than would otherwise have been the case. We confess ourselves to have a difficulty in explaining how the white could have been introduced into the Gordon Setter, assuming that they were originally black-and-tans only, otherwise than by the reputed Sheep-dog cross; and this we should have thought improbable, had it not been for the subjoined engraving from "Cynographia Britannica," as it was to our minds more likely that the tan was the colour then introduced into the original strain, the colour of which we were very much inclined to believe was black-and-white. But from this engraving, which was published in 1805, and a copy of which is in our possession, and in the original of which the colours of the dogs are clearly depicted, we are compelled to accept the existence of a black-and-tan Setter as a positive fact in 1805, *i.e.*, before the Gordon Castle kennel is mentioned in history. The topmost dog in the group is coloured a pale tan and black, and if not marked precisely in the same manner as a modern Gordon, is near enough to the breed in appearance to justify our belief that such a dog had much to do with the origin of our modern black-and-tan Setter.

One great authority, in writing on the alleged Sheep-dog cross, has questioned whether it would be probable that the Duke would stain his strain by a general introduction of Collie blood. This rather coincides with what we suggested with reference to the colours of the Gordon Setters at the famous sale; but we must venture to remark that what the then Duke thought fit to do, and what subsequent breeders have in their wisdom thought proper to attempt, are widely different things, and it is more than possible that the Collie-stained blood has been largely dipped into of later years. One thing is certain, and that is, that as modern fashion dictates, a Gordon Setter marked with white would not have much, if any, chance of success upon the show bench, as our present judges seem most hostile to it, and the tri-coloured dogs are very rarely seen at exhibitions.

Another much debatable point in connection with a Gordon Setter's colour is one which concerns his feet and legs. It must here be stated, for the benefit of those unacquainted with the dog, that his principal colour is black-and-tan (the question of white being for the time laid aside). The point at issue is whether there should be black traces, or "pencil marks," up his toes, as in the case of a black-and-tan Terrier. We have ourselves conversed with many of the eminent authorities of the day, and have almost been amused at the decided difference of opinion which exists amongst them on this question. Both parties, as far as we can judge, though not carrying their opinions far enough to desire the disqualification of a dog which does not represent their views in this respect, are most decided in their expressions as to what they think should be the case. Upholders of the "red-stockinged" dog object to pencilled toes as being, in the first instance, chance introductions, which if encouraged may come to be too highly thought of, and consequently lead to the degeneration of the breed, by being sought after to the neglect of other more essential points. On the other hand, those who advocate these fancy markings, with reason we consider, are wont to argue that any additional mark of beauty is a point to be gained by breeders, and they therefore claim that if other points are equal the pencilled-toed Gordon should be placed above his clean-legged rival.

It may be wondered that so much attention has been directed to the colour of the Gordon Setter; but it should be borne in mind that it is here where his chief difference from his English relative is to be found. The Gordon is far coarser in the head than the English Setter is found to be, his stern is shorter, and he is inclined to be a coarser dog all through. His ears particularly are inclined to show a want of quality; but, taken all over, point by point, there is little difference between the Gordon and the English

GORDON SETTER.

Setter save in coat and colour. In the former dog the jacket is not so fine as it is in his English relative, and his colour, as we have said before, is a black-and-tan. The shade of the black cannot be too deep or intense, and the tan must be as deep or "warm" in colour as it can be got. The dispersion of these colours for exhibition dogs should be as follows:—The tan should be on the fore-legs below the knee, on the feather on the fore-legs, on the throat, on the cheeks, inside the ears and over the eyes, on the belly, inside the thighs, and on the vent. The brilliancy of the tan in certain strains has been attributed to the introduction of Irish Setter blood; this cross, however, will be more fully alluded to in the succeeding article, but the reference to it is necessary, as it is a matter of importance to breeders of both varieties of Setter.

As a field dog the Gordon has both detractors and admirers. He is stigmatised by the former as an old man's dog, as they maintain that he can rarely do more than "potter about," and is always beaten by lunch-time. This latter opinion is certainly shared by most practical sportsmen; but many of these, even though admitting that he is only a half-day dog, at the same time gladly bear witness to his powers when he is at work. Undoubtedly the Gordon is a nervous dog, and here he is behind his English cousin; but it is claimed on his behalf that he does not possess that craving for water which knocks so many of the latter up. In nose a Gordon Setter excels, but this virtue is discounted by the want of endurance which has been already alluded to.

Amongst the most famous breeders and exhibitors of Gordon Setters of late years the names of the following gentlemen appear most prominently:—The Rev. Thomas Pearce, who bred Argyle II. from Lord Bolinbroke's Argyle out of breeder's Ruby; Mr. Sam Lang, of Bristol, celebrated especially as breeder of the champion Lang, afterwards sold to Mr. Coath; The Earl of Dudley; Mr. Josh Jobling, of Morpeth, who won the cup for Setters at the first dog show ever held, viz., at Newcastle in 1859, with his Gordon Setter Dandie, by Coward's Sam out of exhibitor's Nell; Messrs. Rogerson and Adye, who in turn showed Kent, a grand dog, and Premier, black-and-tan Setter, from 1863—1869; Mr. Barclay Field; the Marquis of Huntly; Mr. J. T. Richardson, whose name is identified with Duke; the Rev. W. Serjeantson; and the Rev. J. Cumming Macdona.

The black-and-tan Setter has unquestionably been crossed with the Irish, probably to improve the brilliancy of the tan. Hence the appearance in many litters of Gordons of liver-coloured whelps. It is also noticeable in the reputed pedigree of Old Kent, which we reproduce in this chapter, that the great-grandfather of that famous dog was a liver-and-tan dog belonging to Sir Matthew Ridley.

The similarity of this variety to the English Setter has already been alluded to, and therefore the description of the Gordon Setter need not necessarily be a long one. Speaking briefly:—

The *Skull*, and head generally, is very like that of the English, only that it is heavier.

The *Lips* and *Flews* are also heavier, and more like those of the Bloodhound than those of the kindred breed.

The *Nose* is rather coarse, and

The *General Formation* is altogether heavier than is the case with the English Setter.

The *Stern*, too, is shorter, though similar in shape.

The *texture of the coat* is not so fine as that of the English Setter.

The *Colour* is a deep raven black, and a rich mahogany "warm" tan.

In *General Appearance* the Gordon Setter is the heavy-looking specimen of his family, and the substantial amount of bone which he possesses makes him look a slow dog when compared with either the English or the Irish.

In spite of the similarity between the English and Gordon Setters, a different scale of points is necessary for adjudicating upon the merits of each breed, as the question of colour alone renders the English scale inapplicable to the Gordons. We, therefore, add a table, showing the numerical value of the points at the end of this chapter, as in other breeds.

The specimen of the Gordon Setter selected for illustration in our coloured plate is Blossom, late the property of Mr. Howard Mapplebeck, of Knowle, near Birmingham, but sold by him to Mr. J. S. Niven, M.B., London, Ontario, Canada. Mr. Niven has written us with reference to the dog:—"I have not had much luck with him here, as the Americans are all going in just now for big, heavy Gordons. I got first in Montreal with him, and also special for best Setter in the show. The old boy looks splendid now (March, 1880). I have some pups by Grouse out of a Duke bitch, but they are too big, and I am sure will never do the work that smaller dogs of the same class can do."

Blossom was bred by the Rev. J. Cumming Macdona, in 1872, and is by Shot, out of Bloom; Shot by Bruce, out of La Reine; Bruce by Bliss, out of Ruby; La Reine by Mr. Pearce's Kent, out of his Regent. The pedigree of Kent was always more or less obscure, but the following table appears in the "Kennel Club Stud Book," which is sufficient guarantee for its correctness:—

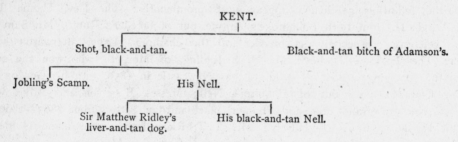

KENT.

Shot, black-and-tan.   Black-and-tan bitch of Adamson's.

Jobling's Scamp.   His Nell.

Sir Matthew Ridley's   His black-and-tan Nell.
liver-and-tan dog.

Blossom has in the course of his show career in this country performed as follows upon the bench:—1875, first Birmingham; 1877, first Agricultural Hall, first Bath, first Burton-on-Trent, first Manchester, first Alexandra Palace, first Edinburgh, first Bristol, first Swindon; 1878, first Birmingham, second Alexandra Palace, second Bristol, second Wolverhampton (champion class)—performances which prove how good a dog he undoubtedly is

SCALE OF POINTS FOR JUDGING GORDON SETTERS.

	Value.
Head, &c.	10
Shoulders and neck	5
Body and ribs	10
Feet and legs	5
Colour	10
Coat	5
General appearance	5
	50

CHAPTER XLVII.

THE IRISH SETTER.

THE origin of the Irish Setter is, like that of other breeds, buried in an obscurity from which it will never emerge, in spite of the many theories which have been propounded concerning it. The peculiarity of its colouring renders this dog distinct in itself, and it is more tnan possible that it is in some way descended from the liver-hued setting dog which is referred to by Gervase Markham in his " Hunger's Prevention."

As a matter of fact the earliest mention that we have been able to discover of any Setter peculiar to Ireland is in the " Sportsman's Cabinet," where, in the chapter on English Setters, direct allusion is made to this breed of dog in the following words :—

" The sporting gentlemen of Ireland are more partial to Setters than Pointers, and probably they are better adapted to that country. . . . The fields in many parts of Ireland are large, very rugged, and stony."

This clearly proves that at the beginning of this century the Setter, in some shape or other, was identified with the Emerald Isle. It is greatly to be regretted that no mention is made of the appearance of these dogs, as, if there had been anything of the kind, a good deal of light might have been thrown upon the Irish Setter as the breed at present exists. It is somewhat remarkable that in the cases both of the Irish Setter and the Gordon Setter so great a difference of opinion should exist among their supporters on the subject of colour. The controversy on the Gordon Setter question has already been done justice to ; but, on approaching the Irish Setter, we are met with almost identical difficulties. As in the Gordon so in the Irish, opinions are mainly divided on the question of white. Whether this colour is permissible in a pure-bred Irish Setter or not was, at one time, a very important feature in discussions on the breed, and we have of later years even heard it maintained that white marks should disqualify an Irish Setter in competition on the show bench.

Naturally, such extreme opinions as the above are shared by only a very limited number of breeders, as it is more than questionable whether any strain of Irish Setters is entirely free from white. Solitary specimens of the breed are, of course, prevalent in great numbers, but it can never be taken as a certainty in breeding that the offspring of pure bred dogs will themselves be of that colour wholly unmixed with white. A very large number of experienced breeders have written from time to time most strenuously in support of the introduction of white into the breed, and have given it not only as their opinion that the mixture of colours is more taking to the eye, but that it is a positive proof of purity in the breed. However, for our own part, we must confess that our affections lie in the direction of a whole coloured dog, and that we think the less white an Irish Setter has about him the handsomer he is. So much in modern times depends upon appearances, and there are so few opportunities for satisfactorily testing the merits of a show dog in the field, that the question of his beauty is of far greater importance than it was before the origin of canine exhibitions.

It must not, then, be thought that because the fashionable Irish Setter colour is a red, the red-and-white dog should not be encouraged; for, to begin with, the two coloured dogs of certain strains are just as likely to throw pure red puppies as the self-coloured dogs themselves, and, in addition, they are just as handy in the field. We, therefore, are strongly in favour of due encouragement being given to the red-and-whites by the committees of dog shows throughout the country.

Mr. Macdona certainly seems to share our opinions on this subject, for he writes as follows :—

"In Ireland, America, and Germany, at the great dog shows, there has grown up a strong inclination to mark the Irish Setter as an exclusively red dog, and to allow no white whatever to appear. This is all very well if it is thought desirable to establish it as a new breed and to frame modern rules for judging them, &c.; but some of the finest types of the old breed had a fair share of white on the face, neck, and feet.

"For endurance no Setter can compare with the Irish. They are as quick as lightning; but their pace never gets beyond their nose. True, unless they are extremely well-bred, they are so wilful and headstrong, that they require much breaking, and often to be broken a little every year, but when well-bred not much breaking is needed. (By-the-bye, I much prefer the American term "trained" to breaking, as it implies a much more rational treatment of dogs to train than break them.)

"The Irish Setter has certainly more dash and go than the Gordon, but for this reason he is the more headstrong, and therefore more difficult to control, and hence it may be his victories at field trials are as few and far between as the Gordon, even less, for I find only one Irish Setter a winner at field trials; this was my young dog, Plunket, in the spring of 1870, when he won, as a puppy, second in the Shrewsbury Stakes, and was immediately afterwards sold for £150, to Mr. Llewellin, considered a long price in those early days. Mr. Llewellin, I believe, sold him afterwards to an American for £300."

Another powerful argument in favour of the red-and-white colour is to be found in the illustration of the three Setters which has been given before and alluded to in the Gordon Setter chapter. The middle dog in the old plate is coloured red, with a distinct blaze of white up the face. This must prove that there was a red-and-white Setter in existence *somewhere* in 1805, as no artist such as Mr. Sydenham Edwards, who is responsible for what appears in "Cynographia Britannica," from which the illustration is taken, would be likely to invent a colour for a dog he was portraying. The dimensions of the blaze, too, are so considerable as to exceed the amount permitted by some opponents of white markings, who, though strongly objecting to the presence of any white at all, admit that they would not absolutely disqualify an otherwise good dog because he had a snip of white upon his head, chest, or feet. Having thus drawn full attention to the question of white in the Irish Setter, and given it as our opinion that, though the wholly blood-red is the more preferable, the parti-coloured dogs should not be discouraged, but rather the reverse, we will proceed to the discussion of another point in connection with the colour of the breed which has from time to time evoked considerable correspondence in the public press.

The desirability of a tinge of black along the back and around the edges of the ears has been keenly argued by several writers and experienced breeders supporting the introduction of these features, which they affirm is very frequently to be met with in many principal

IRISH SETTER.

strains of Irish Setters of undoubted purity. The vast majority of admirers of this dog, however, unite in deprecating such fancy markings, and their views, backed up by common sense, must certainly command respect.

Detractors of the Irish Setter are accustomed to make much capital out of the dog's headstrong nature, and no doubt there is a considerable foundation for their hostility to him. In comparison with the other breeds of Setter the Irishman is impetuous, and if not kept in constant work often requires re-breaking, and on this account has made many enemies of those sportsmen who, under other circumstances, would have gladly given him their best support. As it is, he must be constantly worked or he will soon be useless in the field; but if care has been taken with his education—and he is naturally a generous dog—an Irish Setter is no mean companion to the sportsman. He is active, intelligent, and possesses great pace, and is not at all of a jealous disposition. His constitution, too, is, as a rule, far superior to that of the Laverack, with which he has been often crossed. The advantage of this cross has been recognised by many eminent authorities, and even the great E. Laverack himself spoke of such an experiment as follows:—

"So highly do I value the true blood belonging to the Irish that I have visited Ireland four times for the express purpose of ascertaining where the pure blood was to be found, with a view of crossing them with my Beltons. I very much regret to say that, after all my troubles and efforts, I found that this fine and magnificent old breed had degenerated, owing to the carelessness and negligence of the Irish in not having kept it pure."

In our opinion, it was chiefly from a desire to improve and strengthen the constitution of his breed that Mr. Laverack was in favour of an Irish Setter cross; for it is more than probable that his practised eye was beginning to see traces of that delicacy of constitution which so injured his efforts later on. No finer cross for such a purpose could be possibly devised, for the hardy upstanding Irishman would most certainly correct the weakness of the Laverack in this respect. In spite of the disclaimer on the part of Mr. Laverack, it is almost beyond a doubt that some of the followers of his Setter have really crossed the Laveracks with the Irish, as unmistakable signs are often seen in so-called pure bred Laveracks. These dogs, for the most part, seem stronger in constitution than the others, though it is more than probable that the introduction of Irish blood has caused the Laveracks to be headstrong and hard to break. Mr. Laverack, in writing of a famous Setter of the former breed which he saw at Cockermouth Castle, alludes to the dog as follows:—"The most magnificent specimen of an Irish Setter I ever saw. This dog was very long in the head, particularly low, very oblique in his shoulders, wheeled or roached back, very deep and *broad* in the chest, remarkably wide behind the shoulders, and very short in the back and legs, more so than any Irish Setter I ever saw; he has an immense profusion of coat, with a tinge of black on the tip of his ears. I should have bred from this dog but for the following reason, and I think I was right: no one was ever able to break him, and his stock were frequently black."

This brings us to the consideration of another cross to which the Irish Setter has been subjected, though it is one which has almost certainly failed to improve this useful and handsome breed of dog. It is an unquestionable fact that Gordon Setter blood has been largely introduced into many strains of Irish Setter, and the result has been much injury to the latter breed. The presence of Gordon blood has, we have no doubt in our own mind, done much to impress upon certain breeders the importance of the black or deep-coloured fringe to the ears or trace down the back; but this is nevertheless, in our opinion, a decided fault, as being indicative of Gordon Setter blood. Another feature in this breed of dog, in which the Gordon cross is very wont to claim its presence, is in the ears, the heavy "saddle-flap" ear betokening the bar sinister beyond a doubt. What object the promoters of this most undesirable cross had in first attempting it, it is very hard to guess, and the success of their experiment is more than questionable, as it is probable that both breeds of Setter—the Gordon and the Irish—would suffer from its connection with the other; and what was meant to be an improvement would in reality turn out an injury to the breeds. There was, no doubt, a strong cross of Gordon blood in the dog which Mr. Laverack says he saw at Cockermouth Castle, which will account for that animal begetting black stock. Mr. Laverack himself admits that the introduction of black *is* a fault in the Irish Setter, though he frankly adds that, "notwithstanding this stain of black in the breed, the best and most perfectly-formed Irish Setters I have ever seen had this stain or taint of black, which I should never object to, although I am aware many of the most eminent Irish breeders state that they ought to be *without any tint of black whatever in their coats.* As far as I have seen and been informed, for general goodness and working properties, those possessing this tint of black have been quite as good, if not better, than those without it."

It is, in our mind, quite probable that, possibly at its first introduction into the sister isle, the Irish Setter was crossed with a black Setter; and the existence of both the black and red coloured dogs being clearly proved from the illustration given in a preceding chapter, we think it very probable that the cross was then a common one, and that the modern dogs throw back in many instances to their ancestors of the early portion of the century. But be this as it may, it is by no means uncommon for black puppies to appear in litters of Irish Setters the pedigree of which is irreproachable on paper.

One of the earliest Irish Setter celebrities on the bench was Carlo, who was owned by that great Setter enthusiast, Mr. Jones of Oscott; and when in the possession of this gentleman he won him many prizes. This dog showed what would now-a-days be considered unmistakable signs of a Gordon cross, for he had the black tips to his ears which are pronounced to be evidences of this taint in blood. The next great star of the Irish Setter bench was Captain Hutchinson's Bob, who was a whole-coloured red. It was reserved for Dr. Stone, of Coleraine, in Ireland, to bring out a greater champion, which he did in Dash, whose general contour was beyond criticism, though his colour was much objected to, as he showed a quantity of white upon his head, feet, and neck. This dog in time had to make way for Mr. Hilliard's Palmerston, who, since his first appearance on the show bench, reigned supreme until increasing age rendered his retirement compulsory. This grand dog had only the smallest snip of white upon his forehead, and was otherwise of a beautiful colour. His shape and symmetry were perfection, and his popularity with every judge is evident, as his many successes in every part of the country go far to prove. He died in the early part of the autumn of 1880, full of honours, and having attained the great age of eighteen years. The stock of this dog are generally of the highest merit, as are those of his relative, Dick, a splendidly-coloured dog, though cursed with a dreadful temper on the bench. We have often been assured, however, by those who have seen this latter dog at work, that when in the field he was amiability itself, and never attempted to injure either the sportsmen who shot over him, or the Setters who worked in his company.

As a field-trial dog the Irish Setter has not, as a breed, shone conspicuously, and very probably this is due to his headstrong nature and tendency to run riot. A brilliant exception to this rule, however, is to be found in the record of the doings of Mr. Macdona's Plunket, a grand workman, who was bred by the Rev. R. O'Callaghan, R.N., by Beauty, from his Grouse. His style of going at Shrewsbury was so far above the average that Mr. Purcell-Llewellyn gave the large sum of one hundred and fifty guineas for Plunket, and we believe never repented of his bargain.

The Marquis of Waterford's, Lord Rossmore's, Lord Lismore's, and Lord Dillon's strains have all been famous in bygone days; whilst amongst modern breeders and exhibitors, Mr. Hilliard (who showed Palmerston), Major Hutchinson, Dr. Kennedy (owner of Dick), Mr. Macdona, Mr. J. J. Gilltrap (who shows Garry Owen), Mr. Æneas Nuttal (owner of May-be), and the Rev. R. O'Callaghan (breeder of Plunket), are eminently conspicuous. First-rate specimens have been shown or bred by all these gentlemen, who have invariably adhered to the best type of Irish Setter, and have not been led into exhibiting indifferent specimens. At the time of writing (1880), Mr. Macdona is in the possession of some remarkably fine-coloured and promising young Irish Setters, which were successful at Bristol dog show, though only nine months old. The colour of one of them, Lady Roberts, is almost perfect, and her stock in years to come should be valuable on this account.

In appearance the Irish Setter differs somewhat from the English. His

Head should be longer and narrower.

Nose, deep-red or dark flesh-colour, to match his red jacket.

Eyes, brown and intelligent.

Ears, set on far back and low, light and feathered. A heavy "saddle-flap" ear is particularly suggestive of the Gordon cross, and is particularly to be avoided in an Irish Setter.

Flews, rather deep.

Neck, light and gracefully set on the shoulders, which should have a good slope.

Chest, deep and narrow.

Body, rather arched at loin and inclined to be flat-sided. Back ribs short, which tend to give a true Irish Setter a rather "tucked-up" appearance.

Fore-legs, very straight and well feathered—longer than in the English Setter.

Fore-feet, long, and not nearly so round as in the English Setter.

Hind-legs, bent at stifles, with strong hocks.

Stern, set on rather low and well feathered, particularly on the middle portion of it.

Colour, a deep blood-red. White is not liked in show dogs; but though undesirable, is not a proof of impure breeding. The colour of the feathering is paler than that of the body.

Coat, somewhat thinner than that of the English Setter, though coarser in texture.

General appearance in an Irish Setter goes for a good deal. A good specimen is the *beau idéal* of strength and activity. He should seem a trifle leggy; no doubt his tucked-up loins increase this appearance, which his extra length of leg naturally develops; and an Irish Setter should look all wire and whipcord. In fact he looks what he is, a thorough workman, and ready to gallop for ever.

The dog we have selected for illustration in our coloured plate as being typical of this famous breed is Grouse II., who is the property of the Rev. R. O'Callaghan, R.N., before alluded to as one of the great breeders of his national Setter. This bitch is by the old champion Palmerston out of Quail, and has been successful on the bench. In 1879, at Dublin show, she won first prize and silver medal and challenge cup. Palmerston, her sire, was by old Shot out of Cochrane's Kate ; Shot by Grouse out of Juno. Quail, the dam of Grouse, has no pedigree in the Stud Book, but she is credited with winning at Cork in the prize for red bitches. The selection of Grouse, we candidly admit, cost us much anxiety, as we were desirous to select a specimen who is regarded with favourable eyes by authorities who understand this dog, and it was upon the advice of several excellent judges that we asked permission of Mr. O'Callaghan to let his grand bitch be illustrated in this work. The study was executed by Mr. Breach under the owner's eye, and we have to thank both gentlemen for the pains they took to have the portrait of Grouse made characteristic of the breed.

Following up our rule, we append a scale of points for judging Irish Setters, in which it will be seen that we attach peculiar importance to general appearance.

STANDARD OF POINTS FOR JUDGING IRISH SETTERS.	Value.
Skull—formation of head and muzzle	5
Ears and eyes	5
Neck and shoulders and chest	5
Body, including loins	5
Legs and feet	5
Coat and feather	5
Colour	10
General appearance, including stern	10
	50

CHAPTER XLVIII.

THE SPANISH POINTER.

BEFORE commencing any remarks on the subject of the English Pointer it will be necessary to draw the attention of our readers to the dog from which our modern Pointers unquestionably sprung. Such was the subject of this chapter, from the crossing of whom with the Foxhound or Southern Hound—opinions vary on this subject—the Pointer as he now exists was originally produced.

SPANISH POINTER.

In "Cynographia Britannica," Sydenham Edwards writes thus of the Spanish Pointer in 1805 :—

"The Spanish Pointer is a heavy, loose-made dog, about twenty-two inches high, bearing no small resemblance to the slow Southern Hound. Head large, indented between the eyes; lips large and pendulous; ears thin, loose, and hanging down, of a moderate length; coat short and smooth; colour, dark-brown or liver-colour, liver-colour-and-white, red-and-white, black, black-and-white, sometimes tanned about the face and eyes, often thickly speckled with small spots on a white ground; the tail thin, smooth, and wiry; frequently dewclaws upon the hind-legs; the hind-feet often turning a little outwards.

"The Spanish Pointer was introduced into this country by a Portugal merchant at a very modern period, and was first used by an old reduced baron of the name of Bichell, who lived in Norfolk, and could shoot flying; indeed, he seems to have lived by his gun, as the game he killed was sold in the London market. This valuable acquisition from the

Continent was wholly unknown to our ancestors, together with the art of shooting flying, but so fond are we become of this most elegant of field sports that we now excel all others in the use of the gun and in the breeding and training of the dog.

"The Spanish Pointer possesses in a high degree the sense of scenting, so that he very rarely or never goes by his game when in pursuit of it; requires very little training to make him staunch, most of them standing the first time they meet with game, and it is no uncommon occurrence for puppies of three months old to stand at poultry, rabbits, and even cats. But as they grow old they are apt to get idle, and often go over their ground on a trot instead of galloping, and from their loose make and slowness of foot when hunted a few seasons soon tire, have recourse to cunning, and in company let the younger and fleeter dogs beat wide the fields, whilst they do little more than back them, or else make false points. They then become useless but for hunting singly with a sportsman who is not able or not inclined to follow the faster dogs. . . . . .

"There are other varieties of the Pointer, as the Russian, in size and form like the Spanish; coat not unlike a drover's dog, rough and shaggy, rough about the eyes, and bearded; colour like the Spanish, but often grizzle-and-white; they differ in some being more rough than others. This is probably a cross between the Spanish Pointer and the Barbet or rough water-dog. He has an excellent nose, sagacious, tractable, and easily made staunch; endures fatigue tolerably well; takes water readily, and is not incommoded by the most cold and wet weather."

In the illustration of Pointers which accompanies these remarks of Sydenham Edwards there appears a portrait of a rough-coated dog which is supposed to represent the Russian Pointer. This dog resembles in almost every point the pictures we have seen which purport to portray the Russian Setter of more recent times. It is, therefore, in our opinion, quite within the bounds of probability that the modern Russian Setter is very closely identified with the more ancient Russian Pointer. The remarks of Mr. William Lort upon the former dog, which appeared in a previous chapter, very nearly describe the dog written of by Sydenham Edwards, and certainly the latter's theory on the derivation of the breed appear to be possessed of reason. It is, however, more with the Spanish Pointer that we have to deal at present, for though practically extinct, his close connection with the modern dog entitles him to respect at our hands.

Mr. Taplin, writing of this dog in the early part of the present century, remarks that :— "Every trait upon record respecting their appearance in England is that they were in very early ages introduced from Spain, and that they were natives of that country from which their name was derived. The Spanish Pointer in shape, make, strength, seeming stupidity, and bodily tardiness, is a perfect specimen of the most consistent uniformity; well adapted in all these qualifications to the haughty, somniferous, majestic parade and dignity of the lofty Spaniard, but very inadequate to the life, spirit, agility, and impatient energy of the English sportsman. This race of dog in his natural and unimproved state is a mass of inactivity, as is evidently perceptible by his shape and make, in every point of which is displayed the very reverse of speed and action, objects so truly necessary in almost every sport of the field. The Pointer of this description is short in the head, broad in the forehead, wide in the nose, expansive in the nostrils, simply solicitous in aspect, heavy in the shoulders, short in the legs, almost circular in the form of the carcase, square upon the back, strong across the loins, and remarkably so in the hind-quarters. Although this breed, like the English Pointer (by the many collateral aids so much improved), are produced of various colours, yet the bold brown liver-and-white are the most predominant. These dogs, slow as they are, and accustomed to tire with quick work before the intended sport of the day is half over, are yet truly applicable to the purposes of those who are advanced in years, or, labouring under infirmities, feel themselves unable to get across a country in the way they could in former years. . . . .

"The Pointer we are now treating of, though exceedingly *slow*, must be generally admitted to be *sure;* indefatigable and minute in his researches, he is rarely seen to miss his game when game is to be found. . . . When a covey of birds is separated by repeated shots, and are afterwards found singly, the Pointer under description has opportunity to display his best ability, in most industriously recovering these scattered birds, the major part of which (if accompanied by a good shot) are generally picked up to a certainty. To the recovery of winged birds the patient perseverance of this dog is peculiarly adapted ; and for the sport of snipe-shooting alone they are entitled to the preference of every other."

No further description is necessary of a dog which, as we have before remarked, is practically extinct, as specimens which resemble the dog referred to by Edwards and Taplin are very rarely met with. It may, however, be worth considering if a cross between a good specimen, always provided that such can be procured, with a modern Pointer, might not improve the latter very considerably. Granted that the present dogs excel in strength and activity, is it still not worth experimenting with a dog concerning whose utility many former writers have spoken so very highly ? His nose is certainly a great feature in a Spanish Pointer, and though he is in the habit of knocking up, we think that if a little of his blood were infused into the veins of some of our field-trial Pointers in the present day they would stand a better chance of holding their own in competition with the Setter than they have hitherto succeeded in doing.

The illustration that is given herewith of the Spanish Pointer is particularly fortunate in portraying his square short head and deep flews to considerable advantage, and his heavy bone has also not been lost sight of by the artist. As in the case of the Russian Setter, it is unnecessary to append a scale of points for judging a breed which is very rarely to be met with. However, it should be borne in mind that depth and squareness of head and immense bone are characteristics of the Spanish Pointer which should never be lost sight of.

CHAPTER XLIX.

THE ENGLISH POINTER.

THERE are very few varieties of dog which owe more to the institution of dog shows than the modern Pointer does. Up to the commencement of canine exhibitions the majority of the admirers of this breed appear to have devoted the greater portion of their attention to breeding for sporting purposes, and to a certain extent seem to have ignored appearance. Now things are so far changed, by a wider knowledge of the Pointer having been extended to the public, that most breeders seem to regard good looks more favourably than formerly.

It must not, however, be thought that all those who bred Pointers were unimpressed with the desirability of producing a handsome dog, or that they were by any means indifferent to the symmetry of their strain, for many gentlemen have used great exertions to improve their dogs by every means in their power. The inauguration of dog shows, nevertheless, has done a great deal in the way of obtaining uniformity of appearance in the Pointer, though it must freely be confessed that more than one type is supported, and we may add that it is always likely to be so, by the various judges.

With reference to the appearance of this breed, it may, we think, be fairly taken for granted that it is the offspring of the old Spanish Pointer referred to in the preceding chapter, and the lighter variety of Foxhound, to which allusion has already been made in former pages. The introduction of the latter blood was unquestionably the result of a desire on the part of the Pointer's early breeders to increase the pace and stamina of the Spanish Pointer, for, as before observed, his *forte* was nose, not pace. The hounds selected for the purpose of crossing with this dog were, we consider most probable, chosen as light-formed as possible, and probably some attention was also paid to their colour, as breeders, no doubt, preferred to get their puppies well marked with white, as such are more easily seen at work than liver or dark coloured dogs. The precise period at which the Pointer was introduced into this country is, of course, unascertainable, as he is, as he at present exists, a manufactured breed, and consequently made his appearance gradually. That the introduction has been, comparatively speaking, of recent date, is, however, an almost palpable fact, as no mention is made of the Pointer in the earlier works on canine subjects. Dr. John Caius, for instance, though fully recognising the Spaniel and the Setter, makes no allusion to the Pointer, and this he most certainly would have done if the breed were in existence here in his time. He particularly alludes to the Spanish origin of the Spaniel ; and, as the earlier Pointers were unquestionably imported from that country, he would have remarked upon that fact at the same time beyond a doubt.

Gervase Markham, too, gives prominence to the Setting dog, but ignores the Pointer, and in fact it is only in the writings published towards the commencement of the present century that we find allusion to the latter. This is no doubt due to the fact that shooting was only becoming a popular recreation about this period, and this is clearly proved in the preceding chapter. Up to this time the Setter was the sportsman's dog, as his peculiar mode of working was found to be more of service when birds had to be driven cautiously into the nets that were spread out for their reception. The general introduction, therefore, of firearms into field sports may we think, be correctly taken as the final cause of the Pointer, and, no doubt, on his first appearance the Setter fell into temporary disuse, as it probably never struck our fathers for some considerable period that the Setter's abilities could be so easily moulded to suit the novel innovations introduced by the use of firearms as future events have testified.

However, about the period referred to ample mention is made of the improved Pointer; and Sydenham Edwards, writing in 1800, speaks of him in the following words:—

"The sportsman has improved the breed by selecting the lightest and gayest individuals, and by judicious crosses with the Foxhound to procure courage and fleetness. From the great attention thus paid has resulted the present elegant dog, of valuable and extensive properties, differing much from the original parent, but with some diminution of his instinctive powers. He may thus be described—light, strong, well formed, and very active; about twenty-two inches high; head, small and straight; lips and ears, small, short, and thin; coat, short and smooth, commonly spotted or flecked upon a white ground, sometimes wholly white; tail, thin and wiry, except when crossed with the Setter or Foxhound, then a little brushed.

"This dog possesses great gaiety and courage, travels in a grand manner, quarters his ground with great rapidity, and scents with acuteness, gallops with his haunches rather under him, his head and tail up; of strength to endure any fatigue, and an invincible spirit. But with these qualifications he has concomitant disadvantages; his high spirit and eagerness for the sport render him intractable and extremely difficult of education; his impatience in company subjects him to a desire to be foremost in the points, and not give time for the sportsman to come up; to run in upon the game particularly down wind; but if these faults can be overcome in training, if he can be made staunch in standing, drawing, and backing, and to stop at the voice or token of the hand, he is highly esteemed; and those who arrive at such perfection in this country bring amazing prices. . . .

"There is a circumstance worthy of notice in Pointers, that some of them have a deep fissure in the centre of the nose, which completely divides the nostrils. Such are termed *double-nosed*, and supposed to possess the power of scenting better than others. . . .

"The most judicious cross appears to have been with the Foxhound, and by this has been acquired speed and courage, power and perseverance, and its disadvantage, difficulty of training them to be staunch. I believe the celebrated Colonel Thornton first made this cross, and, from his producing excellent dogs, has been very generally followed."

There frequently occur now in modern litters of Pointers, puppies malformed by a "double nose," as described by Sydenham Edwards. We use the expression malformed advisedly, as, in our opinion, such a development is not only unsightly, but positively injurious to the animal's power of scent. In certain quarters we are aware of the existence of a lingering superstition to the effect that a "double-nosed" Pointer has superior scenting powers, but for our own part we cannot agree with the theory, and have never seen it proved in practice.

Apropos of the "amazing prices" which Sydenham Edwards dilates upon, reference may be made to the preceding chapter upon Setters, from which it will be seen that at the sale of Daniel Lambert's dogs the Pointers fetched lower prices than the Setters. On the other hand, in 1848, thirteen Pointers were sold by auction, and though only two of them had been shot over, the large total of 256 guineas was secured. The following is the catalogue:—

1.	Nelson, by Bounce out of Bloss	...	...	...	...	...	15 guineas.	
2.	Nell, by Bounce out of Bloss	...	...	...	...	...	16	„
3.	Drab, by Bounce out of Dido	...	...	...	...	...	13	„
4.	Buzz, by Bounce out of Mab	...	...	...	...	...	5	„
5.	Rake, by Rake out of Die	...	...	...	...	...	16	„
6.	Ben, by Don out of bitch by Rake	...	...	...	...	...	21	„
7.	Belle, by Don out of bitch by Rake	...	...	...	...	...	16	„
8.	Czar, by Don out of Sir R. Wilmott's bitch	...	...	...	...	17	„	
9.	Crack, by Don out of Sir R. Wilmott's bitch	...	...	...	...	17	„	
10.	Swap, by Duke out of Bloom	...	...	...	...	...	25	„
11.	Snake, by Duke out of Bloom	...	...	...	...	...	25	„
12.	Rock, by Rap out of bitch by Lord Mexborough's Romp	...	24	„				
13.	Bang, by Bounce out of Bess	...	...	...	...	...	46	„

256 guineas.

Lots 12 and 13 were shot over in England and Scotland; the others were well broke.

It may be remarked that Bloom, the dam of Swap and Snake, had previously been sold for 80 guineas.

Subsequently to the appearance of Sydenham Edwards's work, all the writers on canine subjects make special reference to the Pointer, and nearly all of them give special directions for his training. From the remarks which appear, it would seem that the large proportion of hound blood which then existed in the Pointer caused him to be very headstrong in the field, and completely changed the character of the old Spanish Pointer, whose extreme steadiness was one cause of his being so popular with sportsmen. According to the "Sportsman's Cabinet," it will be seen in the quotation given below, that the Pointer was supposed to have been imported from Spain about the year 1600, but, at the same time, it will be observed that no idea is given as regards the possible period when the Fox-hound cross was first instituted. It is, however, we should imagine, most highly probable that this was not resorted to until the use of firearms in the field became a custom, as when nets only were employed in the pursuit of winged game it is palpable that a slow hunting, keen-scented dog was more valuable to the sportsman than a fast and high-couraged one, who would naturally be more liable to flush the birds.

The ideas on the elementary education of the Pointer which were held by sportsmen in the early years of this century are thus expressed in the "Sportsman's Cabinet":—

"The Pointer, notwithstanding the beautiful uniformity of his frame, the docility of his disposition, and his almost unlimited utility, has been less noticed by naturalists than any other individuals of the species; hence it may be fairly inferred this particular breed was formerly unknown in Britain, and that the stock was originally of foreign extraction. A combination of circumstances tend to justify the predominant opinion that they were first introduced into this country from Spain (very little more than two centuries since), and that the heavy, awkward, slow, and somniferous appearance of the Spanish Pointer is nearly lost in what may be candidly considered the judicious crosses and improved breed of our own.

"It is no more than thirty or forty years since the breed of Pointers was nearly white, or most variegated with liver-coloured spots; except the celebrated stock of the then celebrated Duke of Kingston, whose breed of blacks were considered superior to all in the kingdom, and sold for immense sums after his death. But so great has been the constantly-increasing attachment to the sports of the field, particularly of the gun, that they have been since bred of every description, from a pure white, and flea-bitten blue or grey, to a complete liver colour or perfect black. After every experiment that can have been possibly made by the best judges and most energetic amateurs in respect to size, it seems at length a decided opinion with the majority, that when bred for every species of game and every diversity of country, both extremes are better avoided, and the line of mediocrity more advantageously adhered to; overgrown, fat, and heavy dogs very soon get weary in the hot and early part of the season; the smaller sort are likewise attended with inconvenience in hunting high turnips, heath, ling, and broom fields. . . . .

"The art of breaking Pointers was formerly considered a most difficult and mysterious concern, many of those denominated dog-breakers having nearly derived their sole subsistence from such employment; that charm, however, has been long since broken, and the simplicity of the process is now so generally known amongst sporting practitioners, that a tolerably well-bred Pointer puppy may have the groundwork of all his future perfections theoretically implanted in the parlour or kitchen of the dwelling-house before he once makes his appearance in the field. The instinctive impulse of this breed is frequently seen to display itself in subjects no more than three or four months old; where, in still and uninterrupted situations, puppies may be observed most earnestly standing at chickens, pigeons, and even sparrows upon the ground, by sight, before the olfactory powers can be supposed to have attained maturity to prompt a point by scent.

"When a whelp of this description has reached his sixth or seventh month, the process may be proceeded upon in the following way; and either a single dog, a brace, or more, may be managed with equal ease, in any convenient spot, room, or yard, at the same time, with no other assistance whatever than the alternate expression of 'To ho!'— 'Have a care!'—and 'Take heed!' (having the small field-whip in hand to impress attention and enforce obedience) although the most attractive meat is tossed before them in every direction. The commencement of the ceremony consists in throwing a piece of bread at some small distance before the dog, who, upon making his effort to obtain it, must be instantly checked by a quick exclamation of 'Have a care!' and the assistant terms alternately repeated, to keep him in a patient point of perseverance, till, having given ample proof of his obedience to the injunction, and stood time sufficient to demonstrate his comprehension of the restraint he must occasionally encounter, a vibrative, low-toned whistle, accompanied with a mild ejaculation of 'Hie on!' will prove the signal for proceeding, which the whole will quickly learn to obey; and it will be found by practice, that one or more may, at the very moment of seizing either the bread or the meat, be as instantly stopped and made to renew their point, by a repetition of either of the verbal cautions previously observed. Some there are who consider it a qualification in a Pointer to bring the game to foot when killed, and those who wish it, will find it easy of attainment, by teaching them to fetch and carry before they are at all accustomed to the field; it is a mode of being employed they are much delighted with, and never forget, but is attended by the chance of one inconvenience annexed to the experiment; if they become hard-mouthed, and take to breaking both flesh and feather, it is a fault, or rather crime, which generally becomes incorrigible, and is hardly ever obliterated without incessant trouble and much distressing severity. This circumstance, so naturally likely to occur, it is the more necessary to bring to memory, because punishment is at all times unpleasant to the humane and liberal-minded sportsman, who will coincide with the writer in opinion, that prudent prevention is preferable to the uncertainty of cure; and that a slight and salutary correction to-day, may sometimes render unnecessary the doubly and trebly enhanced deserts of to-morrow."

The above remarks are essentially practical, and show that considerable attention had been paid to the habits and breaking of the Pointer. Of a very different nature is the anecdote told of the worthy priest, in the following extract from the "Sportsman's Repository"—in fact, the story bears with it the impression that it was merely a playful invention of the author of the work, to excite the feelings of those responsible for the story of the staunchness of Juno and Pluto, when Mr. Gilpin was executing their likenesses; we therefore give the extract for what it is worth, merely observing that the story told of the price given for the Pointer Dash, and the conditions under which he was disposed of are, we believe, perfectly correctly referred to, as they are accepted as facts by other writers of that period, who themselves express no doubt of their veracity. The staunchness of Pluto and Juno is, of course, *possible;* but we should venture to suggest that the balance of *probability* lies in favour of it being slightly exaggerated. However, it is valuable as showing that, in the first place, breeders began to recognise the fact that too much Foxhound was undesirable in their Pointers, as it rendered them headstrong; and, in the second place, that the dogs had become more staunch, or any foundation for the story could not have existed.

"For something very extraordinary in the sporting way we must have recourse to the practice of Colonel Thornton, whose high and laudable ambition it has ever been, both to deviate from the common road and to excel; and he has undoubtedly so far succeeded as to raise a name which will go down with *éclat* to sporting posterity. We suppose that the Colonel himself meditated and carried into effect the crosses necessary to produce his famous Pointer, Dash, which is, as we have before observed, in all probability three-parts Foxhound. Dash, in his day, was held to be the Eclipse of Pointers, a character sanctioned by his high ranging over the moors, the vast expedition with which he cleared his ground, and the intuitive, heaven-born method, said to be almost incredible, in which he hunted inclosures for birds, which was by at once scenting and advancing upon them, without the previous labour imposed upon other Pointers, of quartering his ground: add to this, he was a most staunch and steady backer or seconder of other dogs. Dash was sold by Colonel Thornton to the late Sir Richard Symons for one hundred and sixty pounds' worth of champagne and burgundy, bought at the French ambassador's sale, a hogshead of claret, an elegant gun, and a Pointer; with the annexed stipulation that, if any accident should befall the dog, which might render him unfit for hunting, he was to be returned to the Colonel at the price of fifty guineas. This latter agreement actually took place: Dash had the misfortune to break his leg, and was returned to Colonel Thornton, who considered him in that state a great acquisition as a stallion.

"Exalted as was the reputation of Dash, it seems nearly impossible that he could have exceeded in point of steadiness the merit of a brace of other Pointers, the property also of Colonel Thornton, Pluto and Juno. Pluto has also been already cited as a famous deer hunter. It is recorded that this dog and bitch, being taken at a point, kept their point upwards of one hour and a quarter; namely, until the late celebrated Mr. Gilpin could take the sketch from which they were painted for their proprietor, an elegant engraving of which we find in Mr. Daniel's 'Rural Sports.'

" Many merry jokes have been passed in our hearing, by sportsmen, on the above account, with the view of promoting the cause of ridicule, comparing it with another still more marvellous and well known, given on the authority of a grave and most respectable member of the priesthood. For our parts we really believe both the possibility and probability of the staunchness of Pluto and Juno as just related ; and although Gilpin cannot be referred to, as having quitted—we hope for a better--this painting and plastering world, there are yet survivors to whose authority an appeal may be made. It remains to back the above story with the well-known one (but the repetition on this occasion will be pardoned) of the Rev. Theophilus Verity. On a certain Christmas Day this gentleman was riding his nag from his parish church, which was at considerable distance from his dwelling-house, and his way lay over the most private spot of a secluded and neglected heath. In the deepest recess of this wild he espied a Pointer by himself, standing at a covey of birds. He looked, admired, pondered on the wonderful and inscrutable instinct of the brute creation, blessed himself, and passed on. The cares and studies necessarily attendant upon his calling, however, soon expelled every vestige of this occurrence from his mind, until he was awakened to fresh admiration and benediction by a renewed and stupendous view of the same objects. Exactly on the above day twelve months, passing the same way, his second astonishment was far greater than the first ; for he saw, upon the self-same spot, the dog pointing at the birds in precisely the same attitude he had left both parties twelve months before ; with this difference, however, that they were then living and breathing, one party treacherously circumventing, the other apprehending ; whereas now they were in a state of skeleton, fit for a lecture in anatomy, and doubtless, as the reverend gentleman supposes, the partridges were held to their destiny by the well-proved and well-known power of fascination emitted from the eyes of the dog. Now, we particularly request that no light-minded person will attempt to make a joke of this, well convinced, as every rational man ought to be, that there are wonders of which, never having had the experience, he can have no adequate conception.''

This extract is also valuable as corroborative testimony that the introduction of the Foxhound cross was first due to the enterprise and judgment of Colonel Thornton ; as lovers of the modern Pointer will no doubt be glad to know to whom they are indebted for the improvement in their favourite breed, their later exertions having unquestionably been rendered more easy by the good he originally wrought upon this variety of dog. But, looking back to the year 1811—that is, eleven years after the publication of the account of the Pointer by Sydenham Edwards in " Cynographia Britannica," we find the following description of the Pointer given in the " Shooter's Guide," by B. Thomas, or rather, to give the author's correct name, by Thomas B. Johnson.

" The Pointer generally to be recommended is of the middle size, well made, active, light and strong. It will easily be perceived that a dog of this description will bear a vast deal of hunting ; whereas a small one, however good he may be, is by no means calculated for a piece of strong turnips or potatoes, strong and stiff stubbles, or mountains where the heath is strong and long. On the contrary, it is generally supposed that a large dog is much sooner tired by his own weight than one of the middle size, consequently the latter are in general to be preferred, and indeed I would by all means recommend them. But, at the same time,

I would not refuse a large dog for no other reason than his size, as, however large a dog may be, it often happens that he has strength according to his bulk. . . .

"With respect to colour, much may perhaps depend upon fancy—and no doubt there are very good dogs of all colours. However, those I would recommend are the liver or brown-and-white. A white dog is to be preferred on account of his good temper, and, being naturally less subject to disease than others, which arises from the predominancy of phlegm in his constitution. He has an excellent nose, is a curious hunter, is full of stratagems and cunning, and may be seen at a great distance. Pointers of a brown or liver colour are generally good ones, but they are certainly difficult to be seen at a great distance, particularly on a mountain, which gives the sportsman sometimes a vast deal of trouble. At the same time, a brown dog will bring you nearer the game, and is particularly useful when it will not lie well. Birds will suffer a brown dog to approach them much nearer than a white one, which arises solely from his colour approximating more nearly that of stubbles, &c., among which he hunts, and consequently renders him a less distinguished object.

"A dog of the lemon or red colour is generally of a giddy and impatient nature, as choler is found to be the most predominant humour in him. In fact, in general, white and brown, or these colours mixed, are to be preferred. If a dog has much white upon him, it is an indication of good temper."

The opinions of this writer certainly seem to be largely based upon conjecture, for as far as our own experience goes, we have no reason to agree with him that white, or nearly white dogs, are by any means better in constitution or temper than Pointers of any other shade. There is this much, however, to be said with reference to Thomas's theory, and in defence of any ideas he may have formed, that it must be borne in mind that there is every reason to believe that Foxhound blood was very largely contained in the veins of Pointers about that period, and consequently the lemon or red coloured dogs, to which he alludes, may possibly have been more nearly allied to the hound, therefore more headstrong than the livers, which partook more of the nature of the steady-going Spaniard. His ideas on the subject of colour are certainly sound, as far as they refer to the working of dogs in the field, for it is palpable that a white dog can be seen farther off than a liver-coloured one ; and also that the latter is less likely to disturb birds than a light-coloured one. His reasonings upon the amount of phlegm which he asserts to exist in the white dogs are merely conjectures on his part, and given as they are, unsupported by any practical reasons for the assertion, may safely be set aside when the question of colours is to be discussed. No reference to such advantages possessed by one colour over another is made in "Kunopædia," an excellent work on breaking the Pointer and the Spaniel, which was written by William Dobson, Esq., of Eden Hall, Cumberland, in 1814, and this, we are of opinion, would surely have been done if it were by any means a generally popular idea at that period that a white dog was constitutionally superior to a dark-coloured one.

The Foxhound cross has been resorted to by Irish sportsmen of the day for the purpose of increasing stamina, and giving a wet-resisting coat suitable to the moist climate of Ireland, and these results were well exemplified in specimens we saw exhibited at a Dublin show, bred and shown by a thorough sportsman — an appreciator of every branch, but whose specialities are hunting and shooting.

More than one later authority on Pointers has argued that the breed has been subjected

DOGS AND GAME, BY DESPORTES (ABOUT A.D. 1700),

SHOWING THE EARLY FOXHOUND AND POINTER CROSS IN FRANCE.

to crosses other than the Foxhound, and there are some who hold that both Greyhound and Bulldog blood have been introduced into it. This is, no doubt, a very probable circumstance, as on the face of it the Greyhound would have been quite as likely a cross to be attempted, in the first instance, as the Foxhound was, by breeders who were anxious to increase the pace of the old Spanish Pointer, and who were also bold enough to experimentalise in doing so. Though every credit is due to the men who are not weak enough to, upon all occasions, follow the beaten track with blind precipitancy, there can be little respect paid to the judgment of those who thought of adopting such a cross as a beneficial one in the case of Pointers. It must be remembered that the Greyhound is a dog which hunts by sight and not by scent, and therefore the introduction of his blood into the veins of a Spanish Pointer would unquestionably have the direct effect of injuring the grand nose of that breed of dog. A great addition of pace would most surely have been acquired, but the loss of nose when such a combination of blood was attempted must have been tremendous. A tendency to chase, too, must have been deeply instilled in the dispositions of the result of such a cross, and it is more than improbable that any breeder persevered for any length of time in his efforts to improve the Spanish Pointer by the help of the Greyhound.

The Bulldog cross can hardly be regarded in a more favourable light, for not only would it most certainly tend to injure the pace of any breed (the Bulldog probably being one of the slowest breeds of dog in existence); but it is well known amongst breeders that the fact of Bulldog blood being largely introduced into the veins of any other variety makes the animals possessing it both quarrelsome and headstrong. As we have before stated, the Bulldog pure and simple is, as a rule, a harmless, good-natured beast, long-suffering, and very slow to anger, but it is nevertheless certain that impure specimens differ very widely in temper from highly-bred Bulldogs. It is, however, probable that the Bull cross was introduced in certain instances upon the top of the Greyhound cross referred to in the last paragraph, and with the intention of increasing its staunchness and heart. But, still, until the Bull blood came by the lapse of time to be reduced to a minimum, we do not think the breed could be by any means improved by its presence in a Pointer's veins. Bulldogs have a "nose" beyond a doubt, but their warmest admirers do not pretend that they could, at any time, rival the Spanish Pointer in the possession of this important faculty; and therefore in giving it as our opinion that at one time or another Bulldog blood was introduced, we can only argue that it was either in the form of a counter experiment as a means to remedy the weaknesses of a Greyhound cross, or with a view to breed out to a very great extent. By this we mean that the breeders who have adopted it were very likely to have been influenced in their judgments by the knowledge that an important characteristic of the presence of Bull blood, even in the remotest degree, is to improve the courage of the animal possessing it. They may have, therefore, argued that by a series of judicious re-crossings, the slowness and obstinacy of the Bulldog, together with other objectionable features, could be obliterated, but that the indomitable spirit and heart of our national dog could be secured in some degree.

That the Pointer, as he now exists, does in many instances show signs of "softness," almost every one who is well acquainted with his nature will freely admit; and no higher authority can be quoted than Mr. William Lort, who remarked in the Setter article which has preceded this that often on an inclement day the Pointer will "shut up" after some hours' exposure to the weather. A dash of Bull might, therefore, have been considered by early breeders as very likely to remedy this evil, and we are very strongly impressed by the belief that formerly this dog's services were pretty largely resorted to by Pointer breeders of position and eminence.

There can be no sort of doubt, however, that it was the Foxhound to which the credit lay in improving the Spanish Pointer; and Colonel Thornton is entitled to every honour at the hands of modern breeders for what he did for their favourite dog at the close of last century. From the illustration which accompanies this article—and which is copied from an oil painting by the eminent French painter Desportes, already referred to in the chapter on Setters—a very good impression of what the early cross resembled can be gathered though the apparent lightness of bone, we must confess, surprises us. The Spanish Pointer was, we know, a heavy-boned, cumbersome dog, and the bone of a Foxhound has always been proverbial. It is therefore only reasonable to assume either that the *light*, fast Foxhound which was selected for the cross was, in reality, a very light-boned dog indeed, or that, at all events, the progenitors of the dogs depicted in this illustration answer to that description. But be this as it may, a very great disparity of weight exists amongst modern Pointers of the present day, many specimens exceeding seventy pounds in weight, and others not drawing the scale at anything near fifty pounds. Whether or no this is to be in any way accounted for by the heavier hound having been primarily introduced in some instances, and the lighter in others, we cannot say, this being purely a matter of conjecture for which no reliable data can be given; still, as so great a variety in sizes exists now-a-days, it is more than probable that the same differences in type appeared immediately after the Foxhound cross was tried, and that our illustration only represents the results arising from one of them.

Mr. William Lort has sent us the following notes on the breed from his point of view, and it may be remarked as a curious incident in connection with what his opinions on the subject are, that according to him the best strains of modern Pointers originated, like the Setters, in the North of England, or, at all events, came south from that part of the country. Mr. Lort, too, repeats the assertion that he made in the Setter article, in his comparison of the respective merits of Pointer and Setter; and on such a subject his opinion, from the position he occupies as a judge and breeder of both breeds, must be taken as ranking second to none.

"How often are we asked which we prefer, the Pointer or the Setter. Although a great authority says, 'at present the Pointer is regarded as a grouse dog,' we are inclined to credit the Setter with qualities which give him a prior claim to the Pointer for this sport. Rough, broken ground and stumpy heather try the feet and the courage of the Pointer, and the drizzle with which a deal of the Scotch grouse shooting is favoured tells sorely against the thin-coated Pointer, who, after a good soaking before luncheon, and an hour's shiver during lunch, is not unlikely to show a disinclination to gallop after lunch. The Pointer undoubtedly chills and stiffens sooner than the Setter. Then, on the other hand, the Setter shows exhaustion from heat and lack of water to an extent unknown in the Pointer.

"The Pointer has always had a slight pull over the Setter inasmuch as he is more easily broken, and when broken he is less likely to revert to an untutored state. In pace and nose there is very little to choose between well-bred specimens of either breed. The Pointer's work is in stubbles, grass, and roots, and he looks more at home there than in the wind-swept, mist-bathed hills, or the trying, treacherous peat-bogs of the lower moors.

"Mattingley, sixty years ago, and Webb Edge so lately as 1845, did for the Pointer, although to a less degree, what Laverack did for the Setter — Mattingley brought his Pointers from the North, as did Laverack his Setters; Webb Edge was less particular with his pedigrees than either of the other men, for while he used none, or very few, but his own sires, and those of the purest blood, he would now and then be tempted to buy and to keep a litter from a 'slashing bitch from the North.' At his sale (or rather that of his executors) in October, 1845, the best went to Prince Albert, Mr. Statter, Mr. Warner, and, I believe, the father of the present Mr. William Brailsford, and last, but by no means least, so far as result was concerned, the late George Moore of Appleby (with whom I judged at the first Birmingham show).

"Some writers on the Pointer have wrongly classed Webb Edge with the heavy brigade, such as Lord Derby, Lord Lichfield, Lord Sefton, Antrobus (Sir E.), and others; but he was with the flyers. His Pointers, in short, were the fleetest and best of their day.

"Between the introduction of the Mattingley blood and the sale at Strelley (Webb Edge's), there was a lull, a dark age as it, were, during which not much was done, and what was done was not recorded. Lord Kennedy, Osbaldeston, Sir R. Sutton, Sir R. Musgrave, Mr. Green, and Lord Sefton, did much to aid in bringing the breed down to the period of modern Pointer breeding. The Midland Counties received both the Mattingley blood and the best of the Webb Edge, and they retained it, and improved it. Staffordshire was for a long time noted for good Pointers, and we all know that of late years there has not been a better kennel than that of Mr. Whitehouse, of Ipsley, who may fairly claim to be the breeder of more good Pointers than any other man of his time. Pilkington, Brierley, Lloyd Price, the late Lord Berwick, all have owned dogs of undoubted quality, but they were seldom the breeders—they bought."

Unlike the Setter, there is no special or distinct breed of Pointer which is identified with any particular district of this country. The Irish even, though they possess their Setter, their Spaniel, their Terrier, and their Wolfhound, lay no claim to any particular variety of Pointer; on the contrary, the breed seems particularly ignored in the Emerald Isle. Scotland, too, has not done much towards improving this class of dog, but probably the inattention paid the Pointer in both these instances is greatly due to the nature of the country, for which the Setter is the better dog, as the ground is more broken and hilly than it is down south. Nor have, as far as we can see, many of the English breeders particularly identified themselves by their connection with any particular type. Some there are, however, who only pay their attention to dogs of about a certain weight, and attach little importance to animals who do not approach the scale which they consider to be the most correct one.

It is by weight alone that Pointers are divided at our modern dog shows, and no attention is paid to colour or other developments in the classification of these dogs. The most recent exhibitions, where a division of the classes have been made, have separated them as follows:—Dogs over 55 lbs.; bitches over 50 lbs.; dogs under 55 lbs.; bitches under 50 lbs. Supporters of the different sizes are often known to entertain very decided opinions on the merits of their different hobbies, and their various arguments are each entitled to respect when the uses for which the dog are required come to be considered. For old sportsmen the heavy dogs, partaking, as they do, largely of the character of the old Spanish Pointer, are chiefly to be recommended, as, from their greater weight, they are not so fast or so active in the field. On the other hand, there is a far greater development of pace to be found in the light-weights, and their staunchness in many instances is very slightly, if at all, inferior to the heavier animals. Active sportsmen are certain to enjoy the assistance of such companions in the field; but it is questionable if in many instances they may not be too much for the very people who attribute so much to the excellence of the Pointer; that is to say, if he is of the heavier, that is slower, type. It may, therefore, we are of opinion, be taken that the medium-sized Pointers are, as a rule, by far more valuable as sporting dogs than either of the extremes in weight, as they may be reasonably expected to combine pace and staunchness to an extent which is likely to commend itself to every sort of sportsman.

It is, we believe, a pretty generally admitted fact amongst sportsmen that modern Pointers are deficient in nose when compared with what they used to be; in other words, nose has been sacrificed by the almost insane importance which has been attached to pace. Breeders appear to have, in many instances, only had in view the production of an animal that can gallop, and thereby cover more ground than other dogs which might be brought against them; and nose has thereby suffered to a great extent.

Our Continental cousins, especially the Germans, have, however, viewed things in a very different light, for the Continental Pointers partake more fully of the nature of their Spanish ancestors than do the English. A leading German sportsman only recently remarked to us, that though he admired the English dogs (Pointers) they were too fast for the sport he wished to put them to, and that his experience taught him that the slow and staunch German Pointer was, in his part of the world, the more valuable dog. However, he added, that he hoped that the crosses he had in view between the two varieties, German and English, would improve both breeds, and render each more valuable for his purpose.

The German Pointer does not differ very materially from the English, save in his clumsiness. He is more throaty, certainly; but this is scarcely to be wondered at when his closer connection to the Spanish Pointer comes to be considered. The best specimens of this variety which we have seen at German dog shows, have been liver-and-white in colour, and the lower dog in the accompanying illustration may be taken as a very faithful representation of this class.

On comparing the three types of Pointer (Spanish, German, and English) which have been treated of in this work, our readers might almost be brought to style the three varieties as superlative, comparative, and positive, for they really represent these degrees to a remarkable extent. The superlative bulk of the original Spanish Pointer becomes greatly modified when the German branch of the family appears upon the scene, whilst the latter in his turn has to be at once refined if he is desired to be made anything like the English dog in shape.

In the accompanying engraving, the resemblance of the German Pointer to the Spanish is very apparent, especially in the fore-quarters, and it may be added that little pace could be expected to be found in either of these animals. Contrasted with the English Pointer, however, neither the German or Spanish members of the family are likely to suffer if strength is to be taken as any criterion of merit; but it is nevertheless notorious that their great bone has not had the effect of adding stamina to either breed.

Whether or no the German Pointer would be a desirable cross for our English dogs is a moot question at the present time. Personally we should be very much disposed to try it, if we had a strain of light-weight Pointers to work upon; and our desire to do so would be increased if we had the breeding of a field-trial winner before our eyes. At present, as we have said above, we consider that too much attention has been paid

GERMAN POINTERS.

to increasing the pace of a Pointer, and we believe that the time is not far off when this merit will play a secondary position to that of nose, as this has inevitably been the consequence of breeders sacrificing one property in an animal in their efforts to produce another feature of excellence. We do not wish it to be imagined for a moment that we by any means decry the acquisition of pace in a Pointer. A slow, pottering dog is enough to break an active man's heart we admit; but at the same time we reserve to ourselves the privilege of adding that a Pointer without a nose is as bad as one who is deficient in pace. In field trials a fast dog looks flash, and by his superior pace can cover more ground, and therefore increase his chance of finding birds. The natural result of this is that such a dog defeats his slower but surer companion, who keeps steadily plodding on throughout the trial, and would do so throughout the day without a fault, and probably would wear his gay companion down in half a day. That such a thing is done at every trial, a reference to the reports thereof will amply testify, and this, we trust, will have the effect in time of causing steps to be taken to remedy the evil. Field trials are such excellent institutions in themselves, if properly carried out, that every step should be promptly taken to prevent fashionable prejudices from doing any injury to the class of dog which is meant to be benefited thereby.

Allusion has been already made to the colours of the ancient Pointer, and the ideas of Mr. B. Thomas have been fully stated. In the present day, however, the markings of the Pointer have increased in variety, and now we may reckon upon finding good specimens in colour, black, white, lemon-and-white, orange-and-white, liver-and-white, and even an occasional all-lemon dog. The entire number of whole-coloured dogs is, however, a very limited one, and by far the most fashionable colours in the present day are the liver-and-white, lemon-and-white, and orange-and-white, which may be taken as favourites in the order named. Caprice is nevertheless chiefly responsible for the placing of one of these colours over another, and it is only of recent years that the liver-and-white dogs have re-occupied the position we have given them on the list. Personally we see little advantage in placing one colour over another, but we certainly prefer parti to whole coloured Pointers, and most strongly object to a lemon-and-white Pointer who carries a *black* nose upon his face. In our opinion this defect is simply a disqualification, though authorities of position, we know, differ from us on the point; but still we remain unconvinced, believing that the majority of Pointer breeders agree with us in this respect at least, and hold that a black nose is a decided blemish on this class of dog.

Whilst on the subject of colour it may be noted that many admirers of the liver or liver-and-white Pointer are accustomed to argue that he is in this point entitled to respect as more closely resembling the old Spanish Pointer than the lemon-and-white or orange-and-white. Still, when we take into consideration the crosses that have been admittedly introduced into the breed we cannot see that much is to be gained by this argument, even if it is strictly correct, which we have no means of proving.

The liver-and-white Pointers, however, had previously been the popular dog, and this certainly seems to support those who argue in favour of this colour. To Mr. Whitehouse, of Ipsley Court, the greatest credit is due in connection with lemon-and-whites, which is a breed he has succeeded in bringing to the highest pitch of perfection. His most famous dogs have been Hamlet and Rap, but an enumeration of all this gentleman's many first-class Pointers would be a task to any writer of a work on dogs which he could ill afford the space it would consume. Mr. Whitehouse is recognised as one of the leading judges of the breed with which his name has been so honourably identified, and the correctness of his decisions at the shows where he officiates is recognised by all.

In spite, nevertheless, of the popularity which the lemon-and-whites have attained, and the regard with which orange-and-whites are looked upon by many breeders, as well as the existence of blacks, livers, and other colours, the liver-and-whites appear to hold their own. Mr. W. Arkwright's Prude II. and Don Jose, Mr. R. J. Lloyd Price's Wagg, Belle, and Bow Bells, and the former's great rival, Mr. James Fletcher's Ponto, are all liver-and-white. Nor are these by any means the only first-rate specimens of this colour. Mr. Bartram, of Essex, has a grand specimen of the liver-and-white in Special, a very heavily-marked dog, and shot with liver ticks on the portions of his body which should be white. Many breeders admire this heavy marking, and certainly we can see no reason for decrying it, though it is uncommon on the show bench. In addition to Mr. Whitehouse, the following gentlemen have shown good lemon-and-whites: Mr. W. Arkwright (Prim and Primula), Mr. R. B. Lee (Miss Prim), and Mr. C. W. Brierley (General Prim).

As a companion the Pointer is confessedly inferior to his great rival the Setter, for, though there are exceptions to this as to every other rule, it is not for either his affection or intelligence in private life that the Pointer especially shines. As an indoor pet this dog is not the success he might be supposed to be, and his more homely jacket places him at a disadvantage with the Setter when the palm of beauty comes to be awarded. Having no luxuriantly silky coat, the Pointer looks to be what he in reality is—a workman— and as such he has succeeded in winning friends in every part of the country.

For years Devonshire has been the great home of the Pointer in England, and Mr. Francis, of Exeter, and Mr. S. Price, of Bow, Devon, have done much for gaining this southern county the reputation it bears so justly for the production of first-rate specimens of the breed. The latter has certainly gained immortality by breeding Wagg, a dog who in his day knew no rival, but who at the time of writing is beginning to show traces of that great destroyer—Time. Mr. E. C. Norrish, too, of Crediton, is rapidly making himself a name as an exhibitor of Pointers, and is in possession of a remarkably handsome brace of liver-and-whites in the persons of Digby and Revel, who began to win prizes in first-rate company when only a few months old. The credit of breeding these dogs, however, is due to Mr. R. Andrews, from whom Mr. Norrish obtained them.

Amongst older breeders the names of Mr. T. Statter, Mr. C. H. Mason, Lord Sefton, Lord Downe, and Mr. Garth, Q.C., appear most prominently, and their blood is eagerly treasured by breeders.

The dog we have chosen as the subject of illustration in our coloured plate is Wagg, who is the property of Mr. Richard J. Lloyd Price, of Rhiwlas. As remarked before, he was not bred by his present owner, but by Mr. Samuel Price, of Devonshire. Wagg was born March, 1871, and is by Champion Sancho out of Sappho, is liver-and-white in colour, weighs 65 lbs., and measures as follows:—Length of head, 10 inches; girth of muzzle, 10 inches; height at shoulder, 24 inches; girth of chest, 30 inches; girth of loin, 23 inches; girth of skull, 18 inches; girth of forearm, $7\frac{3}{4}$ inches.

The following list of his triumphs speak for his quality, and need no further comment— Field Trials: Field Trials divided Clinton Stakes at Devon, 1874. Shows:—1st Birmingham, 1874; 1st Crystal Palace; 1st and Cup Exeter; 1st Truro; 1st and Cup Nottingham; 1st and Cup for best Pointer in the whole show, Birmingham, 1875; 1st Crystal Palace; 1st Brighton; 2nd Exeter; and 1st and Cup for best Pointer in the whole show, Birmingham, 1876; Champion Prize, Birmingham; Champion Prize, Kennel Club Show, Alexandra Palace, 1877; 1st Kendal; 1st Oxford Show; Champion, Crystal Palace; 1st Cleckheaton; 1st and

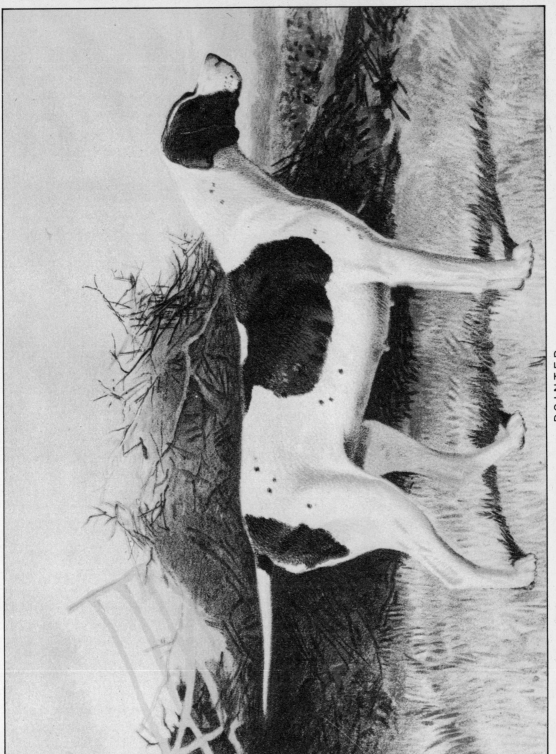

POINTER.

Cup for best Pointer in Show, Blaydon-on-Tyne; 1st Darlington; 1st Brighouse; 1st Great Horton; 1st Whitby; 1st Thornton; 1st Queensbury; 1st Bingley; 1st Skipton; 1st Todmorden, and Cup for best Sporting Dog; 1st Wakefield; 1st Farnworth; Champion Birmingham: Champion Kennel Club Show, Alexandra Palace; and Champion Kendal, 1878; 1st and Cup for best Sporting Dog in the Show, Wolverhampton; 1st and Cup for best Sporting Dog, Stockport, 1879; Champion Cup Irish Kennel Club Show, Dublin, April, 1879; 1st Epworth, 1879; 1st and Special Cup, Great International Dog Show, Hanover, Germany. 1879; 1st and Special Cup for the best Dog in all Classes of the Show, Ripon, June 10th, 1879; Champion Prize, Kennel Club Summer Show, Alexandra Palace, July,

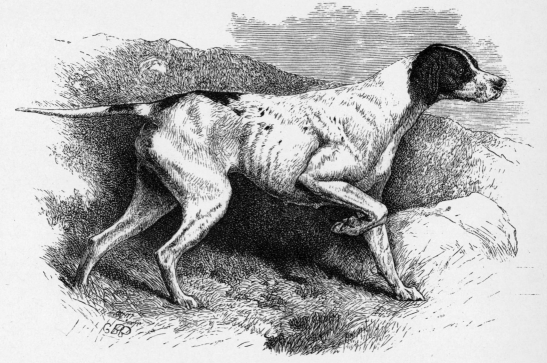

POINTER BITCH "BELLE," THE PROPERTY OF MR. R. J. LLOYD PRICE.

1879, and Cup for best Pointer in the whole Show; 1st and extra Cup for best Dog in the whole Show, Heckmondwike, 1879; 1st and Cup for best Sporting Dog, Cleckheaton, 1879; 1st Darlington, 1879; 1st and extra Cup, Brighouse, 1879; Hayley Hill, 1879, Special Cup for best Sporting Dog, a handsome Clock presented by Spratt's Patent; 1st Whitby; 1st Thornton, Bradford, Yorks; 1st Blackpool; 1st Keighley; 1st and Cup Woodsome, Huddersfield; 1st Halifax; 1st Armley; 1st Variety Class and Cup for best Dog in the field, Wortley; 1st and Cup, Todmorden; Champion Bishop Auckland; 1st Farnworth; 1st and Cup for best Pointer, K.C. Show, Brighton; Champion Birmingham, 1879; 1st and Cup Bradford 1880; 1st (Ehrenpreis) and Emperor's Cup for best Sporting Dog, Berlin, 1880; Champion Crystal Palace, 1880; 1st Thorne, 1880.

Belle, the subject of the engraving which accompanies this article, is also the property of Mr. Richard J. Lloyd Price. She was bred by Lord Henry Bentinck in 1870, and is by his Ranger out of Grouse. Belle weighs 55 lbs., and measures as follows:—Length of head, 9 inches; girth of muzzle, 8½ inches; girth of skull, 18 inches; height at shoulder, 24 inches; girth of chest, 28 inches; girth of loin, 21 inches; girth of forearm, 9 inches.

The following are amongst her performances, from which it will be seen that she, in the course of her illustrious career, has succeeded in lowering the colours of Mr. Purcell Llewellyn's Countess and Mr. Macdona's Champion Ranger:—County Stakes for All-Aged Bitches at Vaynol Field Trials, 1872, and with Judy of the Bangor Stakes for Pointer Braces at the same meeting. Won also the County Stakes for Aged Pointer Bitches, at the National Pointer and Setter Field Trials, held at Combermere, Shrewsbury, April 29th, 1873, and with her daughter Grecian Bend, won the Acton Reynald Stakes for Pointer Braces, at the same meeting; also at the Grouse Field Trials, 1873, second with Roman Fall, her son, in the Penllyn Stakes for Braces, August 13th, 1873, and 1st in the Rhiwlas Stakes for All-Aged Pointers and Setters, August 16th, beating Mr. Macdona's Ranger, Mr. Llewellyn's Countess and Flax, Mr. Statter's Rob Roy, and other celebrated animals, after which performance she was withdrawn from public competition and put to breeding purposes only. Appended are the points she made in the Rhiwlas Stakes, 1873, and County Stakes, Vaynol, 1872:—

RHIWLAS STAKES, 1873.

Name of Dog.	VALUE OF POINTS WHEN PERFECT.						
	30 Nose.	20 Pace and style of hunting.	20 Breaking.	15 Pointing (style and steadiness in)	10 Backing.	5 Drawing on game or roading.	100 Total value.
Belle	27½	20	20	15	10	5	97½
COUNTY STAKES, VAYNOL, 1872.							
Belle	30	20	20	15	10	5	100

FULL MARKS, *a feat only once accomplished, except by Belle.*

MEASUREMENTS OF BELLE, TAKEN MARCH 13, 1874.*

Round chest	2ft.	1½in.
Nose to root of tail	3	2¾
Height at shoulder	2	0
Head, skull-bone to nose	0	8
Round face, under eyes	0	10
Round thigh	1	3
Round loin	1	8
Round skull	1	3
Skull-bone to shoulder-blade	0	10

Whilst alluding to famous Pointers, and Drake especially, the pedigree of this great dog should not be omitted. We therefore give it, and also a short history of the crack, as they appear in Mr. R. J. Lloyd Price's Kennel List.

* These are taken from the Rhiwlas Kennel List, forwarded us by Mr. R. J. Lloyd Price.

DRAKE *was purchased at Sir R. Garth's sale, July 14th, 1874, for* 150 *Guineas. Died April 22nd,* 1877.

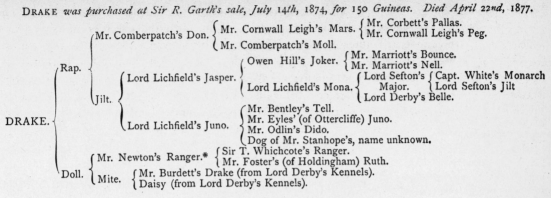

Drake's performances were:—1st prize, Puppy Stakes, Stafford Trials, 1868; 1st prize, All Aged Stakes, ditto, ditto; 1st Prize, Braces (with Mars), ditto, ditto; 1st prize, Champion Cup, ditto, 1869; 1st prize, Champion Cup, Shrewsbury Trials, 1870.—Drake was sire of the winners of the 1st, 2nd, and 3rd prizes, Puppy Stakes, Shrewsbury, 1874; also of the winner, Dandy Drake, and grandsire of second and third in 1878; also of Beau, Mallard, Romp, Lucky Sixpence, and Gipsy and Yellow Drakes, of Luck of Edenhall (winner of the Field Trial, Derby, 1879), and of Tick, in the Rhiwlas Kennels, as well as Lord Downe's Bang, Drake II., Mars, Grace, Jill, and Bounce; Lord Derby's Drake and Duchess; Lord Lichfield's Daisy; Mr. Barclay Field's Riot, and Mr. Price's Rose; Sir R. Garth's Mite II.; and many other Field Trial and Show Bench winners. Is also grandsire to Mr. Pilkington's Garnet and Faust; Mr. Barclay Field's Drake and Pride, and many others. We may here state that Faust was sold to America last year for the large sum of £450.

Considerable judgment is required in selecting a Pointer, for to no breed of dog is the axiom of "handsome is as handsome does" more applicable. Many of the very best Field Trial dogs of modern days having been singularly lacking in quality, additional importance has been given to the belief already in existence that in the matter of a

---

* Mr. Newton's Ranger, "Champion Pointer of England," awarded Prize at Leeds, July 16th; Birmingham, December 2nd, 1861; Preston, September 2nd, 1862; Ashburnham Hall, Chelsea, March 23rd; and Paris, May 4th, 1863.

Pointer good looks go for very little. Such is, however, by no means the case, and if the institution of dog shows has done nothing else, it has had the effect of improving the appearance of the modern Pointer very considerably. Until owners were in a position to be able to compare their dogs with those of their neighbours, naturally enough the sportsman was to a certain extent indifferent about his dog's appearance. When, however, it came to be a matter of winning credit for his kennel, a new aspect of affairs appeared, and Pointer men seemed to be particularly affected by the craze for improving the appearance of the breed, as before said. In selecting a Pointer a very great deal depends upon the nature of the circumstances under which he is to be worked, and the strength of the sportsman who wishes to use the dog. The small active dog is all very well if he is only intended to be shot over in a country where there is not much hard work to be gone through, and the big lumbering dog is also very serviceable under similar circumstances, or if the sportsman who proposes to work him is unable to undergo a vast amount of work or hardship. Judging, therefore, from the above remarks, it can be safely taken as a general maxim in Pointer judging that a good middle-sized dog is the best to select for general purposes of sport, yet it is by no means a wise proceeding to select an indifferent specimen of the middle-weight in preference to superior large or small sized Pointers. There are exceptions to every rule, but it is generally safer to trust in the undeveloped excellence of a good-looking dog than to rely upon coming across a diamond in the rough; so we will at once proceed to lay before our readers a description of what a Pointer should be like.

The *Head* should be rather wide between the ears, and of substantial appearance. It should not be in one straight line from occiput to nose; on the contrary, there should be a decided fall at the stop, which should be well developed, as also the occipital protuberance should be.

The *Muzzle* should be long, wide, and blunt.

The *Nose* must be large and moist, not black, but dark liver or flesh coloured. A black nose is an especial blemish in a lemon-and-white dog.

The *Jaws* should be powerful, with the teeth meeting evenly.

The *Lips* should be fairly well developed, but not to any great extent, as in the Bloodhound.

The *Eyes.*—The colour depends upon the colour of the dog, and are therefore either dark or light, as the case may be. They should be moderately well developed, as a pig-eyed Pointer is an abomination few can stand.

The *Ears* should hang flat to the sides of the head, and be soft and thin, low set on and long, may-be to reach the throat.

The *Neck* should be rather arched, and any dewlap is a serious fault.

The *Shoulders* moderately sloping, and well set up.

The *Chest* must not be too wide, as if so the dog's pace will be injured. It should be very deep.

The *Body* must be powerful-looking, and not too short, which is a fault, and well ribbed up. Loins particularly strong, and a little arched.

Fore-legs very strong and heavy in bone, and placed well under the body.

Fore-feet round and compact. Many authorities express admiration at the long hare-foot, but in our opinion there can be no question but that the cat-foot is infinitely preferable.

Hind-legs should be very muscular in thighs, with stifles turning out a little. Hocks powerful, and turning inwards very slightly, on account of the outward turn of the stifle joints.

The *Stern* short, and thick at root, but gradually tapering towards the tip. It must not be set on too low down, and should be carried straight out from the back.

The *Coat* should be soft, but at the same time weather-resisting.

Colour is a point which has been already discussed above. Though many judges prefer to ignore the question of colour, we are certainly of the opinion that liver-and-whites and lemon-and-whites are by far the most preferable on the show bench, if only on account of their beauty.

In *General Appearance* the Pointer should show every evidence of a combination of strength and refinement. A coarse-looking dog should be avoided, as also should a light-boned one, for reasons already given.

According to custom we append a

STANDARD OF POINTS FOR JUDGING POINTERS.

	Value.
Skull	5
Nose, ears, and eyes...	5
Neck and shoulders	5
Chest, depth and breadth	5
Body	5
Feet and legs	5
Coat	5
Stern	5
General apppearance...	10
	50

CHAPTER L.

THE RETRIEVER.

THE term Retriever is in itself sufficiently indicative of the duties which this breed of dog is called upon to carry out, and these duties can, it is universally admitted, be successfully performed by many varieties besides the one in question. In fact, the very creation of the Retriever proper, as he now exists, is comparatively speaking of but recent date. Up to the time of the introduction of this class of dog, sportsmen were compelled by force of circumstances to rely upon the services of their other sporting dogs, and the majority of the Pointers and Setters, and Spaniels, were broken to retrieve as well as to point the game. There are certainly many objections to this practice, as there is considerable difficulty in keeping Pointers and Setters who have been broken to retrieve their game steady in the field. The presence, therefore, of a well-broken Retriever is considered indispensable to a shooting party under most circumstances, and invariably so when beaters are employed.

In consequence probably of the recent introduction of the Retriever as a distinct variety into the dog family, there are numbers of very indifferent and unworthy specimens—to use a mild expression—of the breed to be found in all directions. These may, we think, reasonably be considered to be the results of some of the many experiments that no doubt have been made from time to time in breeding this sort of dog, which experiments in many cases have turned out disastrously for those whose fertile brains conceived the cross. At any rate, the almost countless number of black dogs which are seen in all parts of the country, and which are invariably styled Retrievers by those who are most interested in them, would cause it to be supposed that their owners, for the most part, are honestly under the belief that in doing so they are describing the animals correctly. It is not, however, only to sporting dogs alone that the art of retrieving game on land or in water is confined, for many breeds of dogs which are by no means identified with sport in popular estimation can be taught to do so easily by any one with patience enough to undertake their education. As a matter of fact, we have ourselves owned Bull-terriers which would do this retrieving business well enough; but still they always failed in one essential—mouth. The tenderness of a good Retriever's mouth has more than a great deal to do with his value as a workman, it is simply essential that he is not hard-mouthed, and does not injure fur or feather in carrying it in his jaws. In this respect a vast number of what would otherwise be very good Retrievers fail, and become worthless in the field, for a dog that mangles his game before he brings it in would be certain to gain but slender thanks for the assistance he lends a modern sportsman. In days gone by there was more importance attached to the loss of birds than there is now, when heavy bags are regarded as a matter of course, and therefore it was considered less a crime against a dog used as a Retriever if he pinched the game or broke its bones in bringing it in. Mouth, or rather the badness of its mouth, was the rock upon which the ancient Retriever split and came to ruin, and it is popularly believed that in the first instance a Spaniel was used to fill his place. The superiority of this dog over the older one was soon apparent, as it is certain that he long enjoyed the reputation of being regarded as invaluable at this kind of work. Things continued thus, and few changes or improvements were hazarded, though certain crosses were attempted by a few enthusiasts, until well on in the present century, when more attention came to be bestowed upon this breed of dog.

Up to the institution of dog shows most breeders seemed to follow the course of their own ideas in breeding—and Collie, Bull-dog, and even Hound blood was introduced by enterprising owners. When dog shows first began, however, it seemed to dawn upon sportsmen generally that a good-looking dog need not necessarily be an indifferent workman, and that more profit, if not pleasure, could be gained from the breeding of a handsome Retriever. The result has been that there is now a uniformity of type which was not long ago unknown, and the Retriever classes at every canine exhibition of importance present a very different aspect to that they showed at Birmingham in 1860. There has been also a decided improvement in the quality of Retrievers all over the country, which almost reconciles us to the presence of the countless mongrels alluded to above. It is now no uncommon thing to see fine upstanding specimens of the breed in places where in former times a cross-bred hard-mouthed dog was considered good enough to carry out all the duties which a well-trained Retriever is now expected to fulfil.

No breed of dog requires more careful handling than a Retriever, and his docility and intelligence should be beyond suspicion. It is in his power to mar a day's sport, or cause discomfiture to say the least, and therefore much responsibility rests with those who work him, though very frequently the dog is much hampered in his movements by the conduct of some sportsman present, who foolishly will interfere with the directions given him.

At present there are two distinct breeds of Retrievers in existence—one the flat or wavy coated, the other curly-coated ; the latter variety is divided by colour into black or liver. The wavy-coated dogs are also sometimes sandy, or even black-and-tan, but any colour but black is not regarded with favourable eyes by judges or breeders of the variety. Although there is not a very great amount of difference in structural development between the breeds, it will be better if we take them separately, and as the Wavies are certainly the greater favourites with the sporting public, to them shall be the place of honour, and we will begin with a description of

THE FLAT OR WAVY-COATED RETRIEVER.

This dog is admittedly a cross breed of very recent origin, and is popularly, and we believe correctly, believed to be a cross between the Setter and the Labrador dog. As in the case of Bull-terriers, the breed is now tolerably pure, and early crosses are seldom to be met with in the field or on the bench. Possibly it might be beneficial to the wavy-coated Retriever if some new blood were introduced into his veins, as it would appear probable, from the fact that the best strains are so few in number, that it will soon become weakened from the effects of in-breeding, and consequently a general and sudden recourse to either Setter or Labrador blood, or both, will have to be made by breeders, which will tend to affect the progress of this grand dog towards perfection. As matters stand, however, no breed has made more rapid strides in public estimation, and, thanks to the energy of his supporters, this has been thoroughly well deserved. Dr. Bond Moore, late of Wolverhampton, did much for the wavy-coated Retriever, and his breed of dogs was highly estimated. As a judge of the breed, too, Dr. Bond Moore was quite at the head of affairs, though he was on many occasions considered arbitrary in his decisions. As an instance, he has been known to disqualify a dog for having a few white hairs upon it, which, in the case of a cross-bred animal such as the Retriever is, was at the time considered by many an unnecessarily harsh action. Dr. Bond Moore was, we believe, influenced in pursuing this course by a determination to adhere to a type he had laid down, and feeling that he was dealing with a comparatively unknown breed, had made up his mind to give no encouragement to any but the correct type of dog. There can be little question but that his example influenced other judges, and possibly this may have done much towards the improvement which the variety has made since its first appearance on the bench.

Though undoubtedly of Setter extraction, the fashionable colour for the Wavy Retriever is black, and no others stand a chance at modern shows. In the earlier portion of its existence both black-and-tans and black-and-brindles were not disqualified, as it was argued that the former showed traces of the Gordon Setter, and the latter of its Labrador extraction; but now a dog showing traces of these colours would certainly be kept at home for breeding purposes only. As in other cross-bred varieties, extraordinary throw-backs very often happen in breeding Wavy-coated Retrievers, and a case which came beneath our own observation may be worth recording, as it, or rather they, appeared in the kennels of Dr. Bond Moore himself. It was at the Wolverhampton dog show of either 1876 or 1877 that Dr. Bond Moore, who was at that time practising in Wolverhampton, invited us to go over to his house and see his stud. We gladly availed ourselves of the opportunity placed in our way, and the more especially so as he told us he had some wonderfully promising young dogs at that time in his kennel. Mr. Hugh Dalziel, who was at that time editing part of a London sporting journal, accompanied us, and shared our astonishment at the sight of a brace of pale golden, almost liver, puppies amongst the number. In reply to our remarks, Dr. Bond Moore informed us that such appearances were, if not often, at all events occasionally met with, and that his experience taught him that the dogs of this colour were every bit as likely to breed puppies without a stain in colour as any dogs in his or other people's kennels. As a matter of fact the parents of these sandy-coloured whelps were black as jet; but we regret that we cannot call their names to recollection, though Mr. Dalziel, relying solely upon his memory, pronounces the dam to have been the famous Midnight. Dr. Bond Moore made us a present of one of the two puppies; but a chapter of accidents, finally terminating in its death we believe, prevented it ever reaching our kennels, greatly to our disappointment at the time, as we wished to try an experiment in crossing it with another breed, in the hopes of producing a further change of colour in its offspring.

The earliest specimen of this variety which can be regarded as something like up to high-class form was Wyndham, who was shown by Mr. R. Brailsford at Birmingham in 1860. He was rather a heavy-looking dog of the Labrador type; but was successful on the bench for some years, as he fairly divided the leading prizes with some of the best known curly-coated dogs of the day. Some three or four years later on, however, this dog had his colours lowered by another dog of the same name, and who very closely resembled him in appearance. The latter Wyndham was the property of Mr. T. Meyrick, M.P., of Pembroke, and he may be regarded as the corner-stone of some modern strains, and his services were largely resorted to by several influential breeders. Mr. S. E. Shirley, M.P., has owned some splendid specimens of the breed, and is at the time of writing at the head of affairs in the position of a successful breeder. His best dogs have been Paris, Lady Evelyn, Trace, Thorn, and Dusk, who is the subject of our coloured plate. A great merit in the dogs exhibited by Mr. Shirley is that they are almost invariably broken dogs and good workers, and this, naturally enough, adds a considerable amount to their pecuniary value. As a proof

FLAT-COATED RETRIEVER.

of the control under which his dogs are kept, Mr. Shirley, at the Brighton dog show of 1879, took off the bench his well-known Trace, and after making her follow him for some distance amongst the benches, sent her back to guard some articles he had left behind. We were witness to the steady way she went to work, and the little flurry with which she carried out her master's orders under certainly very trying circumstances. The Rev. W. Serjeantson and Messrs. Brewis have owned and shown good specimens, and Mr. E. G. Farquharson, too, of Blandford, has been a very successful breeder and exhibitor of Wavy-coated Retrievers, though, in our opinion, some of the dogs belonging to his kennel have shown too much of the Labrador in their formation to quite come up to our ideas; nor should the names of the Rev. T. Pearce and Major Allison be omitted from the list.

A Retriever should be big enough and powerful enough to do his work; but there is a limit to all things, and coarseness in a dog of this variety is certainly no exception to the rule. Opinions have, no doubt, differed greatly upon the question of size; but it is generally admitted that, in this respect, the Wavy-coated Retriever should err rather on the side of coarseness than on that of lightness. He must, in short, show power, for after a hard day's work he may at any moment be called upon to retrieve a wounded hare, and leap a gate or stone wall with it in his mouth. A little dog is practically useless, except for feather, and, as few owners care to keep a Retriever solely for recovering birds, are not looked upon with favour by sportsmen or by keepers. There is, moreover, one Labrador characteristic which is viewed with much distrust by breeders of the Wavy-coated Retriever, and that is in a most important organ, viz., the eye. The small sunken eye of the Newfoundland is just what is not wanted in the dog of whom we are treating, and by many breeders is looked upon with feelings of the utmost horror. In fact, the Setter's eye is by all considered as by far the most correct thing for a Retriever, and is encouraged where the beetling brows of the Newfoundland are decidedly objected to. A sullen-looking Retriever is almost sure to be hard to break, or headstrong, which, as we have before suggested, is fatal to all chances of his giving satisfaction in the field. Any indication of Bull blood is likewise most objectionable, as it is a sure and certain result of this cross that the dog possessing it is hard in mouth. All authorities do not agree, however, on this question, and when Dr. Bond Moore, in 1876 or 1877, threw out a bitch (we think, if memory serves us right, it was Mr. Thorpe Bartram's Nell) at Wolverhampton, because she was slightly—only slightly—underhung, great was the uproar his behaviour caused. Though, personally, we are quite of Dr. Moore's opinion that an undershot dog should be put out, because of the suspicion of Bull blood which this formation naturally creates, very many high opinions were given against it, though the matter was never thoroughly set at rest, but ended, as many others of a similar nature have done and will do again—in leaving things precisely where they first commenced.

There is a custom in connection with Retrievers, which, though it has been known by a few to exist for some time in certain quarters, yet requires attention in a work of this description. We allude to the practice of shortening their tails by the removal of a few of the joints; and this is done avowedly for the purpose of improving the carriage of the stern, and, admittedly, for no other purpose than for improving the appearance of the dog. It is not on account of the unnecessary pain which such an operation causes to the animal—for this is, in our opinion, very slight if the operation is performed skilfully and at an early age—that we feel it our duty to protest against the practice. In our opinion such "improvement" is little less than fraud upon the public who are not aware of its existence, and credit the animal operated upon with being handsomer than he really is. If these "improvements" were perfectly palpable, as they are when Spaniels' or Fox-terriers' tails are under consideration, and were either well-known trade practices, or for the benefit of the dog's comfort when at work, no exception could be taken to them; but as they are only for improving his beauty, and the existence of the custom is not by any means generally known, we are of opinion that it cannot be too strongly deprecated by all honest men. A proof of the extent to which it has been carried appeared in a letter to one of the leading sporting papers, in which the writer anonymously alluded to the fact of Retrievers' tails being shortened, and flippantly accused some leading breeders, whose names did not appear, of being guilty of such gross abuses, which the writer professed, honestly or otherwise, to think no sin at all. We have made allusion to the above letter, as it only tends to show how

MAJOR ALLISON'S RETRIEVER "SAILOR."

easy the consciences of some doggy men must be when writers are not ashamed to publicly support a fraud upon the unsuspecting public, and insinuate that they receive the countenance of leading breeders of a certain dog.

The dog we have selected for illustration in our coloured plate is Mr. S. E. Shirley's champion Dusk, who was bred by his owner, and whelped in June, 1877, being by Thorn out of Lady in Black by Paris; Thorn, bred by T. D. Hull, by Allison's Victor out of Hull's Young Bounce. The name of Victor, it may be here remarked, appears in the pedigree of most winning Retrievers. Paris was bred by Mr. Palmer, of Lyndhurst, Hants, in 1870, and was by an imported Labrador dog, Lion, out of Bess, who was an imported Labrador bitch.

An illustration is also given of Sailor, who was bred by the Rev. T. Pearce, and owned by Major Allison, to whom Victor also belonged.

The chief characteristics of the Wavy-coated Retriever should be as follows:—

The *Skull* broad and wide, flat, and with a ridge running down it. A rise over the eyes is greatly disliked, though there should be plenty of room in the skull for the brain to work in.

The *Muzzle* should be long, rather blunt, and the teeth white, regular, and powerful.

The *Jaws* should be very powerful, and free from lippiness.

The *Nose* black, large, and moist.

The *Eyes* of a good size, dark, gentle and intelligent looking.

The *Ears* should be small, set on low and well back. They should in all cases lie close to the head, and have no fringe of hair attached to them. A large Settery ear is much objected to by the majority of breeders.

The *Neck* must be long, or else the Retriever cannot stoop with ease to pick up his game or trail.

The *Shoulders* should be very sloping and extremely muscular.

The *Chest* rather wide, and certainly deep.

The *Body* muscular and well ribbed up.

The *Loins* should be deep and powerful, to enable the dog to do his work.

The *Fore Legs* quite straight, set on well under the body, and very muscular.

The *Feet* large but compact, well arched and with a good thick sole; hair between the toes.

The *Hind Legs* should have the stifles very muscular and well apart, and the hocks let down near to the ground.

The *Stern* well-feathered, and carried rather gaily.

The *Coat* should be very profuse, wavy and glossy, and of moderate length.

The *Colour* jet-black, any traces of white, brindle, tan, or rustiness, being particularly objected to.

According to custom we append—

STANDARD OF POINTS FOR JUDGING WAVY-COATED RETRIEVERS.

	Value.
Skull and muzzle	5
Ears and eyes	5
Neck	5
Shoulders	5
Chest and body	10
Loins	5
Legs and feet	5
General appearance, including colour and stern	10
	50

THE CURLY-COATED RETRIEVER.

There has been little light thrown upon the origin of the Curly-coated Retriever by writers who have treated of him, though most of them suggest that there is Irish Water Spaniel blood in his veins. Some, however, who make the assertion, throw doubts upon it almost in the same breath, and quote the opinion of Mr. McCarthy—a great authority on Irish Water Spaniels—who emphatically states that the latter breed will not bear crossing with any other. In spite, however, of the high authority of Mr. McCarthy, we are of the opinion that the Irish Water Spaniel has had something to do with the origin of the breed in question, and some of the earlier writers on the dog are decidedly of our opinion. Several of these state certain facts in connection with the Spaniel which might be read with interest by Retriever breeders, but none throw so much light upon the subject as the editor of the "Sportsman's Repository," who some sixty years ago held very much the same opinions as we do now. This writer had the advantage of succeeding Gervase Markham, Sydenham Edwards, W. Taplin, and

other eminent authors, and therefore must have benefited, in arriving at his judgment, by the
views which they expressed. It will be observed, however, that he is careful in alluding, in
the quotation which we give, to the Water Dog, not Water Spaniel; as the writer, John Scott,
in the "Sportsman's Repository" in 1820, gives an illustration of what he terms the Water
Dog, which he refers to in the following words:—

"The annexed plate presents the truest possible representation of the original Water
Dog of the opposite continent being long since adopted in this country, in some of the maritime
districts still preserved in a state of purity, but the breed more generally intermixed with the
Water Spaniel and the Newfoundland Dog. The size of this variety is between the Spaniel
and the Pointer. The original and prevailing colour on the Continent is black, with crisp
curly hair, black nose, white face, long black ears, the head and ears covered with black curly
hair, the feet and lower parts of the legs white. . . . . Without the softness of the Spaniel,
this breed, however, retains a great share of his native and peculiar properties, having equal
sagacity of nose, superior activity, and power and aptitude to learn those manœuvres and tricks
which render the dog either useful or amusing to man. . . . .

"There is this favourable peculiarity in the sporting dog, it should seem the natural
associate of man, that with some few exceptions he takes an equal interest in the diversions
of his master. This quality is most conspicuous in the Water Dog, which burns with inex-
tinguishable ardour in the pursuit, and which merely for the gratification of swimming after
and bringing to shore a bird that he is neither destined nor desires to taste, will risk his
life in the most dangerous abysses, or carry himself by repetitions of labour and fatigue to
the very verge of existence. . . . . There is one restraint which it is difficult to impose
upon the Water Dog—yet sometimes it is a necessary one—it is to prevent him from that rapid
start in the direction of the game the instant of the report of the gun, which he has watched with
the most tremulous anxiety. They may be indulged generally, but the dog should be also taught
to hold back whenever the gunner finds it expedient."

The above extract might apply almost equally to any breed of dog which is used for
retrieving game, but is chiefly valuable for the flat contradiction which it gives to the opinions
subsequently pronounced by McCarthy. It certainly does not allude directly to the Irish
Water Spaniel, which was then unknown as he now exists, as the breed which crossed with
the Newfoundland to produce the Water Dog, and it can hardly be surmised that the Irish
Water Spaniel was the breed to which he refers as the Water Dog, for the description which
he gives differs so totally from the Irish Water Spaniel. It may, however, be reasonably
argued that both breeds — the Curly-coated Retriever and the Irish Water Spaniel — are
descendants of this Water Dog of John Scott, or that they are both descended from a breed
which sprung from that original source; and this much we are disposed to concede, though
remaining firm in our first opinion that the Irish Water Spaniel is very largely concerned in
the production of the modern Curly-coated Retriever.

There is, however, another theory which many persons entertain in connection with the
Curly-coated Retriever, and that is to the effect that Poodle blood is largely present in his
veins. The latter dog is almost universally used in certain districts of the Continent by
sportsmen in the field, and efforts are being made in many quarters to introduce the Poodle
more generally into sporting circles in this country. The foreign dog alluded to above in
John Scott's remark upon the Water-dog was no doubt concerned in the production of the

Poodle, and thus a cross of Poodle in the Curly-coated Retriever of the present day would only be, in our opinion, a re-introduction of a dash of the old strain.

In spite of his very handsome appearance, the Curly-coated Retriever has steadily lost ground in popular estimation since the introduction of dog shows, and the subsequent rapid advance of the Wavy-coated breed. This is partly due, no doubt, to the prejudice against the Curlies for being less tender in the mouth than the Wavy-coated dogs; but this failing is not invariably the case, and numbers of Curly-coated Retrievers exist whose mouths are as tender as can be. There is another cause as well which should not be lost sight of, and that is that the Wavy dogs being some years ago more largely bred by the leading Retriever breeders who imported Labradors for the purpose, the public naturally followed suit, hence the Curly-coated variety gradually but surely lost its ground. With so much in the way of beauty and sagacity to recommend him it is a decided pity that the Curly-coated Retriever should be suffered to become extinct, an event which, taking into consideration the great dearth of good specimens, seems to be far from an unlikely one. In former days—that is at the first commencement of dog shows—the Curlies held their own right well against their Wavy-coated cousins; and it was not till 1863 that the classes for Retrievers were divided. The great Wyndham even, after his first appearance, lived to suffer defeat from Mr. Riley's Curly-coated dogs, Sam and Cato, who were the earliest champions of the latter breed. Subsequently, Mr. Gorse's pair of Jets—Jet and Jet II.— were for some time at the head of affairs. Later on, Dr. Morris of Rochdale carried nearly all before him with his beautiful dog and bitch, True and XL; and later still again, Mr. W. A. How's Toby, the subject of our coloured plate, was shown about the country with immense success. Mr. Samuel Matthew of Stowmarket, and also Mr. J. H. Salter, were the owners of a very handsome dog in King Coffee; and Mr. J. F. Staples Brown, of Brash- field, showed good specimens in Minor and Polly. Chicory, a very smart bitch, owned by Mr. Tom B. Swinburne, of Darlington, has been about the most successful specimen of the breed for the year 1880, and when shown in good condition this handsome bitch's coat is as good and curly as can be desired.

The most frequent faults, then, that are to be found with Curly-coated Retrievers of the present day are openness of coat and absence of curl, and also the presence of too much hair upon the face. It is of the utmost importance that the coat of this sort of dog should be in a series of tight curls all over his body, and even on his tail; but the face should be smooth, no curls appearing on it. It is here that so many of the breed are tampered with by unprincipled exhibitors or owners, for, in many instances, coats are subjected to the curling-irons, and the exuberance of superfluous curls corrected by shaving off the offending ringlets. It is, therefore, very advisable for intending purchasers, unless they know the vendor to be above such practices, to examine a dog of this description thoroughly before they con- clude the purchase, or a possible disappointment may be in store for them.

In colour, the vast majority of the Curly-coated Retrievers are jet-black, though occasionally a good liver-coloured one is seen at shows. Their appearance, however, is very rare except when classes are provided for Retrievers of any other colour but black, and these are seldom added to the prize lists of any but the largest shows. Livers are met with in litters bred from black parents, and are, therefore, in no way inferior in point of purity of blood; but popular opinion has always been in favour of the black dog, and appears likely to remain so. The best specimen of the breed of late before the public is Mr. L. MacKenzie's Garnet, who is a first- rate dog, and well-shaped enough to win in any company.

The specimen of the Curly-coated Retriever which we have selected for illustration is

Toby, the property of Mr. W. A. Howe, of Whitwick, Leicester. He was bred in 1873 by Mr. Colton, of Salford, and is by Hodgson's Sweep out of Colton's Nell by a dog of Lord Chesterfield's out of Jet, who was out of a prize bitch of Mr. Gorse's. Sweep was winner of first prize Manchester, 1866, and second Birmingham, 1867. Toby has won, amongst other prizes, first Nottingham and first Birmingham, 1874; first Henley, first Northampton, and champion prize, and cup for best Retriever in eight classes, Nottingham, 1875; first, Maidstone, first Brighton, and champion, Wolverhampton, 1876; first Carlisle, first Wolverhampton, first Bath, first Burton-on-Trent, first Bristol, and champion Darlington, 1877.

In many points there is but little difference between the Wavy-coated and the Curly-coated Retriever, though the former is the most massive of the two. In the Curlies

The *Head* is narrower, and the muzzle rather more snipy than in the Wavy dog, though the jaws must not be deficient in strength.

The *Coat* must be very curly on the body, legs, and tail; but the face must be quite smooth and only covered with short hair.

The *Stern* should be straight, and carried without any curl; thick at the base, and gradually tapering.

STANDARD OF POINTS FOR JUDGING CURLY-COATED RETRIEVERS.

	Value.
Skull	5
Muzzle	5
Eyes and ears	5
Neck	5
Shoulders	5
Body and loins	5
Legs and feet	5
Coat	10
General appearance	5
Total	50

THE NORFOLK RETRIEVER.

Attempts have been made in certain quarters to introduce the so-called Norfolk Retriever as a distinct breed. Although our own convictions are most decidedly against believing the Norfolk Retriever to be anything but a mongrel, related in some degree to the modern Retriever proper, we feel compelled, though reluctantly, to give it notice in these pages. It is claimed for this breed—which, by the way, we re-assert is in our opinion apocryphal—that it is peculiarly adapted for the pursuit of wild birds in the low-lying districts of Norfolk, and that few, if any other varieties of dog, could be found to endure the hard work equally well. For our own part we certainly believe that a Curly-coated Retriever would equal the Norfolk at this business; but, still, opinions differ, and the Norfolk may perhaps be better when at work than his looks foretell.

He is for the most part light liver in colour, and curly and coarse in coat; neck long, and shoulders sloping; head coarse and somewhat houndy; ears larger than either of the two former varieties; legs muscular, and his feet webbed.

The above is shortly a description we have received of the Norfolk Retriever, from which we should imagine that he is related in some degree to the Otter-hound or Irish Water Spaniel, or very possibly to both. He has Retriever blood in him, too, beyond a doubt, and he shows two bad Retriever faults in his jacket, viz., openness in curl, and a frequent indication

RETRIEVERS.

of a "saddle," *i.e.*, a patch of straight hair upon the back. No standard of points is necessary to be given for the purposes of judging this variety of dog, and many specimens of the canine race may be seen in all parts of the country who very closely resemble him, though no claim is made by their owners for them to the designation of Norfolk Retriever.

THE RUSSIAN RETRIEVER

Is seldom, if ever, used in this country as a sporting dog, though some specimens of the breed have appeared upon the show bench from time to time. It would seem, from the appearance he presents, that the Russian Retriever is somewhat allied to the Russian Setter described in a former chapter by Mr. William Lort. There is, however, far more coat on the Retriever, and this makes him perfectly useless in covert-shooting, whatever his value may be in his native land. Mr. E. B. Southwell showed a dog of this variety, named Czar, which was for some time a very successful competitor in the classes for foreign dogs at the leading shows; and another good specimen of the breed appeared at Dublin in 1880. This dog was shown by Capt. D. F. Allen, and gained second prize in the Variety class.

In appearance the Russian Retriever is square all over. He is square in muzzle and wide in skull, short-headed, and cloddy in body. His legs, however, are long, and here he closely resembles the Irish Water Spaniel. The chief peculiarity of the breed lies in the coat, which is long, very dense, and as often as not matted. This makes him unsuited to work in covert, and, in fact, we have never heard of one being employed in the field in this country with success.

CHAPTER LI.

THE SPANIEL.

THE antiquity of the Spaniel is an undisputed fact amongst sportsmen, for references to some varieties of this breed have been made in every work on canine subjects from the time of Edmund De Langley, in the "Maister of Game," down to the present day. This writer states most positively that the Spaniel came from Spain, and gives a description of the dog's appearance, and the uses to which he was put by sportsmen of his day. Dr. Caius, in the reign of Queen Elizabeth, draws attention to the Spaniel in the following words:—

"*Svch dogges as serue for fowling*, I thinke conuenient and requisite to place in this seconde Section of this treatise. These are also to bee reckoned and accounted in the number of the dogges which come of a gentle kind, and of those which serue for fowling.

There be two sortes
{ The first findeth game on the land.
The other findeth game on the water.

"Such as delight on the land, play their partes, eyther by swiftnesse of foote, or by often questing, to search out and to spying the byrde for further hope of aduantage, or else by some secrete signe and priuy token bewray the place where they fall.

The first kind of such serue
The seconde,
{ The Hauke,
{ The net, or traine.

"The first kinde haue no peculier names assigned vnto them, saue onely that they be denominated after the byrde which by naturall appointment he is alotted to take, for the which consideration.

Some be called Dogges,
{ For the Falcon
The Phesant
The Partridge
} and such like,

"The common sort of people call them by one generall word, namely Spaniells. As though these kinde of Dogges came originally and first of all out of Spaine. The most part of their skynnes are white, and if they be marcked with any spottes, they are commonly red, and somewhat great therewithall, the heares not growing in such thicknesse but that the mixture of them maye easely be perceaued. Othersome of them be reddishe and blackishe, but of that sorte there be but a very few. There is also at this day among vs a newe kinde of dogge brought out of Fraunce (for we Englishe men are maruaious greedy gaping gluttons after nouelties, and couetous covrorauntes of things that be seldom, rare, straunge, and hard to get.) And they bee speckled all ouer with white and black, which mingled colours incline to a marble blewe, which bewtifyeth their skinnes and affordeth a seemely show of comlynesse. These are called French dogges as is aboue declared already."

A peculiar feature in the remarks of Dr. Caius is that he appears to be in doubt whether or no there was more than one breed of Spaniels in the country. From the manner in which he speaks of "othersome of them" that were "reddishe and blackishe" it might be concluded that he was of the opinion that these were distinct varieties in themselves, but did not like to say so positively; though he had no hesitation in stating that a new variety was imported from France. Whilst alluding to the work which Dr. Caius wrote, we may add that he, in another portion of that work, describes the water Spaniel as another breed; but this will be remarked upon in the chapter on the water Spaniels, later on. The only classification which, it appears, was made between land Spaniels in the days of Dr. Caius was regulated by the work they were called upon to carry out, and the idea was prevalent for a considerable period that this was the only desirable method of distinguishing the classes from each other.

In "Icones Animalium" there are two illustrations of Spaniels given, one of the water Spaniel and the other of some small-sized dogs, not much bigger apparently than the modern Toy Spaniel, but displaying a distinct difference of type, as one is long-faced and the other decidedly short in muzzle. The latter illustration has been given in the chapter on Toy Spaniels, and the other will be found under water Spaniels, later on.

Nicholas Cox, writing in the "Gentleman's Recreation," in 1697, alludes to the value of the Spaniel as a sporting dog in the following words:—

"How necessary a thing a Spaniel is to falconry, and for those that delight in that noble recreation, keeping hawks for their pastime and pleasure, I think nobody need question, as well as to spring and retrieve a fowl being flown to the mark, and also divers other ways to help and assist falcons and goshawks. . . . It is necessary for several reasons to cut of the tip of a Spaniel's stern when it is a whelp. First, by doing so worms are prevented from breeding there; in the next place, if it be not cut he will be the less forward in pressing hastily into the covert after his game; besides this benefit, the dog appears more beautiful."

The custom of docking Spaniels' tails has been kept up until the present day, and in spite of the ill-advised proceedings that have been taken against persons detected in the act of removing dogs' tails, it appears likely to be continued. We cannot altogether agree with Nicholas Cox in his opinion that the beauty of a dog is improved by the removal of his tail, though we freely admit that, when a usage is established by custom, any new departure from it has the temporary effect of making the animal appear singular and possibly clumsy. Still, his remarks upon the benefit which this custom confers, in the comfort of a dog who has to work in brushwood, are recognised as perfectly correct by a vast majority of modern sportsmen. The same writer mentions that the land Spaniel can be trained as a setting-dog, and doubtless in his time the Setter was to all intents a Spaniel, as we have before attempted to prove in the Setter chapter. Nicholas Cox describes the land Spaniel as "being of a good and nimble size, rather small than gross, and of a courageous mettle, . . . lusty and nimble rangers, of active feet, wanton tails, and busie nostrils. Whose tail was without weariness, their search without changeableness, and whom no delight did transport beyond fear or obedience."

This high character given to the Spaniel appears to have been fully endorsed by other writers, all of whom are unanimous in declaring him to be the most useful dog to sportsmen. It must, not, however, be imagined that dogs were used in the field to anything like the extent that they came to be subsequently. Netting was the great means by which game was secured in the days Nicholas Cox wrote his work the "Gentleman's Recreation," and the major portion of it was taken up with hunting, fishing, and snaring of the different varieties of birds. He, however, seems to have laid himself out to give directions upon the breaking and working of several breeds of dog, and, as will be seen in a subsequent chapter, devoted considerable space to the working of what he termed the water-dog.

Sydenham Edwards, writing in 1801, in "Cynographia Britannica," gives an excellent description of the Spaniel, as well as a coloured plate containing four dogs. One of these is liver-and-white, another black-and-white, a third orange-and-white, and the last a sort of sandy liver. The only one that is standing up is the liver-and-white; it is represented as a long-bodied dog, with legs rather light in bone, and wide skull and hairy ears lying flat to the head. The tail is docked and is well feathered, but the feather on the legs is not very extensive, though the thighs are heavily breeched. The coat in two out of the four specimens is curly, but the dog referred to above is flat-coated except upon his back, chest, and loins, where there is a decided ripple. The whole-coloured dog is smooth-headed but very curly behind. In his remarks upon this breed Mr. Edwards states :—

"This was usually distinguished by the name of land Spaniel, in contra-distinction to water Spaniel, and may be divided into two kinds, the Springing, Hauking Spaniel, or Starter, and the Cocker, or Cocking Spaniel. The first was used for springing the game when falconry was amongst the prevalent sports of this island, and as it made one of the principal pursuits of our British ancestors, the chieftains maintained a considerable number of birds for the purpose. The discovery of the gun superseding the use of the falcon, the powers of the dog were directed to the new acquisition, but his fleetness, wildness, and courage in quest of game rendering him difficult to manage, a more useful kind was established, with shorter limbs and less speed. Yet some of the true Springers still remain about London, but are rarely found in any other part of the country. These are little different from the larger Spaniel or Setter, except in size; generally of a red or red-and-white colour; thinly-formed ears, rather short; long limbed; the coat wavy and silky; the tail somewhat bushy, and seldom cut.

"Differing from this is the Cocker, esteemed for his compact form, having the head round, nose short, ears long, and the larger the more admired, limbs short and strong, the coat more inclined to curl than the Springer's, and longer, particularly on the tail, which is commonly truncated. Colour—liver-and-white, red, red-and-white, black-and-white, all liver colour, and sometimes black with tanned legs and muzzle. . . . The term Cocker is taken from the Woodcock, which they are taught to hunt. . . .

"Spaniels are used as finders, or starters, to the Greyhound, and pursue the hare with the same impetuosity as they do birds. Their beautiful coats, their faithful dispositions, humble and insinuating manners, suavity, and obedience even to servility, procure them universal favour; but the gunner loves them for their intrinsic merit, bestows great pains on breaking them to the gun, and when properly broke or educated is amply repaid for their services, being indefatigable in their exertions, beating the coverts, brakes, and ditches in pursuit of game; their tails carried downwards, perpetually moving from side to side, and this motion, called feathering, becomes more rapid when they have caught the scent, eagerly following with frequent whimpers till it is disturbed, of which they give notice by repeated quests; nor should they open at any other time. Some sportsmen disapprove of their questing at all, as it spreads the alarm too far, therefore teach them to beat mute. As it is the nature of these dogs to put up all the game they find, good sportsmen are careful to keep them within gun-shot even if in cover, and if it is extensive, jingles or bells are put upon their collars, and the dog-call used if they beat too wide."

From these remarks it appears that the uses of the Spaniel in 1800 were very similar to those to which they are put in the present day; and a distinct advance had been made in the century which had elapsed since the time when Nicholas Cox delivered his remarks upon the breed. Now-a-days they are not used as finders for Greyhounds, but in many other respects there is little change in their mode of hunting.

W. Taplin, writing in the "Sportsman's Cabinet," in 1803, says that—

"The large Springing Spaniel, and diminutive Cocker, although they vary in size, differ but little in their qualifications, except that the former does not equal the latter in rapidity of action; nor do they seem to catch the scent so suddenly, or to enjoy it with the same ecstatic enthusiasm when found. . . . From the time they are thrown off in the field, as a proof of the pleasure they feel in being employed, the tail is in perpetual motion (which is termed feathering), upon the increasing vibration of which, the experienced sportsman well knows when he is getting nearer the object of attraction. . . . However Spaniels may be occasionally engaged in other sports, they are, in general, considered much more applicable to shooting in covert than to those pursuits in which the Pointer or Setter are more properly engaged. . . .

"The whole species are naturally inclined to voracity, but are capable of enduring very long abstinence, of which there are numerous well-authenticated instances upon record. The following is, perhaps, the most extraordinary fact of this description that has ever issued from the press. In 1789, when preparations were making at St. Paul's for the reception of his Majesty, a favourite Spaniel bitch followed its master up the dark stairs of the dome, when of a sudden it was missing, and both calling and whistling was of no effect. Nine weeks after this, wanting only two days, some glaziers were at work in the cathedral, and distinctly heard some faint sounds amongst the timbers by which the dome was supported, and thinking it might be some unfortunate human being, they tied a rope round a boy and let him down near to the place from whence the noise came. At the bottom he found a dog lying on its side, the skeleton of another dog, and an old shoe half-eaten." The rest of the story may be briefly told as follows—the bitch when lost was in whelp, and, no doubt, consumed her puppies when she brought them forth, and, possibly, also the remains of the other dog, who presumably had followed her into the cathedral. Her emaciated appearance, however, pointed to the extreme privations which she had undergone, a further proof of which was to be found in her weight, for when last scaled she drew twenty pounds, but when recovered the poor beast only weighed three pounds fourteen ounces.

In 1814 Mr. William Dobson, of Eden Hall, Cumberland, published a work on the breaking of Pointers and Spaniels. "Kunopædia," for that is the title, however, seemed to recognise the Spaniel as the Setter, as the former breed is not directly alluded to by the author. This would tend to prove that, subsequently to the writings of Sydenham Edwards and William Taplin, sportsmen of conservative tendencies still regarded the Spaniel and the

Setter as practically the same breed, though, on other hands, a decided difference was stated to exist between the two varieties.

In 1820 John Scott produced the "Sportsman's Repository," in which he re-copied the engraving of the Spaniel which appeared in William Taplin's work of 1803. This course leads us to believe that in outward appearance there had been but little alteration in the Spaniel during the twenty years which had passed over the breed. The dog which is illustrated is portrayed in the act of flushing a woodcock, and is apparently of a liver-and-white colour, with a long and rather lean head, and a palpable ripple in his coat. His stern, if shortened at all, has certainly had but a very small portion of it removed, and his legs, though nicely feathered, would be considered long if they belonged to a modern Spaniel. From the appearance we should say it was meant to represent a dog of about twenty-five pounds in weight, or perhaps a trifle more, and the inscription beneath the illustration consists merely of the one word "Springer," no further particulars being given. John Scott does not throw very much new light upon the subject of Spaniels, although he goes a little further into the description of their points than former writers appear to have thought necessary. He says :—

"Spaniels are generally rough-coated or long-flued, and in all probability such is one of their original characteristics, the smooth coats of some being the consequence of a cross in the breed. . . . . The true Spaniel is distinguished by the silkiness of his flue, his pendulous and fringed ear, clear eye, moist nose, and fringed tail. . . . . A cry of Spaniels is not at present thought so essential as in former days; indeed, many sportsmen of the present day, whether in shooting or hunting habitually attached to the Pointer and Hound, affect entirely to discard the babbling Spaniel. This, however, is too strong a prejudice, as the utility of the Spaniel is undoubted in thick and difficult coverts, copses and runs, where neither Pointer nor Setter can penetrate, nor, perhaps, even the large Springer, which partakes too much of their nature and size for such puzzling and thorny labours. The small Spaniels should yet have considerable substance and bone, and by no means be over-legged, and granting them true bred, a little harshness of the coat is no disadvantage, as such are more hardy and fearless of the thicket. The delicate and very small, or carpet Spaniels, have excellent nose, and will hunt truly and pleasantly; but are neither fit for a long day or thorny covert. The grand, or questing, quality of the Spaniel is well known, and his constant and bustling activity . . . . .

"The largest Springers were some years since, and probably may at present be, found in Sussex. The Cockers are supposed to have originated in a cross between the Springer and the small Water Spaniel, and are distinguished from the large Spaniel by a more compact, rounder, and shorter, head, deeper and more curly flew, and larger ears. The Spaniel colours are various—yellow, liver-coloured, red, brown, white, black-tan with tanned legs and muzzle— these last hues denote a Terrier cross. The Springer is often crossed and deteriorated by the Hound and Pointer. . . . . Twenty years ago His Grace the Duke of Marlborough was reported to possess the smallest and best breed of Cockers in Britain: they were invariably red-and-white, with very long ears, short noses, and black eyes."

So much for the opinions of Mr. John Scott, who appears to have derived many of his ideas from Taplin and Edwards. The latter quotation, however, gives one piece of information which we do not find in former writers, and that is, that bone and shortness of leg were recognised as desirable points to obtain in Spaniels. As John Scott attaches so much importance to these qualifications, we can quite understand the disfavour with which he regarded the Hound and Pointer cross, upon the undesirability of which he made some very stringent observations, which we did not consider it worth while to reproduce. As we have now come to a time when Spaniels appear to have been generally recognised by sportsmen as a totally distinct variety from the Setter, or rather we may more correctly put it that the Setter had become recognised as a variety by itself, and some idea has in addition been laid before our readers from the writings of earlier authors, and descriptions of the illustrations which their works contained, as to what the land Spaniel was like some sixty years ago, we may direct attention to a more recent date, 1845, when William Youatt wrote.

Youatt in his remarks upon dogs adopts the classification of Cuvier, and, to use his own expression, arranges the breeds—" According to the development of the frontal sinus and the cerebral cavity, or, in other words, the power of scent, and the degree of intelligence." Spaniels, according to this classification, come into the second division, and are in company with the Setter, Pointer, Hound, and Sheep Dog, whose heads should be moderately elongated, the parietal bones diverging from each other for a certain space as they rise upon the side of the head, thereby enlarging the cerebral cavity and the frontal sinus. Speaking generally of the Spaniel, Youatt lays down that his ears should be large and pendulous, and his coat of different lengths, according to the part of his body where it is situated, but longest on the ears, under the neck, behind the thighs, and on the tail. The list of Spaniels to which his book refers throws very little light upon any of the foremost modern breeds, for Youatt simply refers in general terms to the Cocker and the Springer and their duties. He also notices the King Charles Spaniel, the Blenheim, and the Norfolk, and black-and-tan Spaniel. The water Spaniel, however, has more space devoted to him than any of the other varieties of which he treats.

As the land Spaniel exists in the year 1880 in various different forms, it will be necessary to devote a separate chapter to each variety of the breed, some of which have been in existence for many years, although they have received but scant attention from early writers. We therefore propose to proceed to the description of the various breeds of land Spaniels after which the varieties of water Spaniels will be treated of in a chapter by themselves.

CHAPTER LII.

THE SUSSEX SPANIEL.

WHEN a writer on dogs finds himself face to face with the Spaniel family, he will be sure to find himself beset with a great difficulty when the place of honour has to be disposed of. For our own part we have been much perplexed by the rival claims of the Sussex, the Clumber, and the Black Spaniel, for each of these varieties have their thick-and-thin supporters, who are rather inclined to look disparagingly upon the Spaniels of other breeds. Breeders of the Clumber argue, and with some amount of reason, that the antiquity of their pet breed entitles it to great consideration, and add that the aristocratic associations of this breed of dog are solid proofs of the estimation with which it is regarded by the highest rank of sportsmen.

Supporters of the Black Spaniel, on the other side, maintain most stoutly that this variety to which they are devoting all their energies, is making such rapid strides towards perfection that it should be regarded as the most important member of the Spaniel family, and base their claims to pre-eminence for it on the ground that there are better Blacks now to be found than specimens of any other breed. This variety has certainly monopolised the prizes for Spaniels in the classes where Clumbers and Sussex are unable to compete, and certainly fine specimens of the breed have often appeared upon the bench—specimens which, indeed, for quality and for symmetry would rank second to no Spaniels in existence; but still we are of the opinion that the Sussex is the Spaniel which of all others should occupy the place of honour in a book on dogs. The beauty in outline of the Sussex is very great, and the colour, of a true "golden liver," is exceptional. Nor do his qualifications for regard end with these external points of elegance, for his value in covert shooting is gladly borne testimony to by those sportsmen who know the Sussex best and avail themselves of his services frequently.

Although this favourite breed of Spaniel has for many years occupied a high position in the estimation of sportsmen, there was some years ago a very great chance of its becoming extinct, as the kennels at Rosehill, Sussex—the birthplace, so to speak, of the breed—were depopulated by that dreadful canine scourge, dumb madness. About the year 1870, however, a few gentlemen, actuated by feelings of interest in the Sussex Spaniel, set themselves to work to rescue the breed from the annihilation which threatened it, and to their energy and devotion the present Sussex mainly owes its existence at the time of writing. It must not be supposed, however, that certain so-called Sussex Spaniels were not before the public previous to the action of these gentlemen; on the contrary, there were several animals about which laid claim to accurately represent the breed. The presence of these dogs, however, was injurious rather than beneficial to the pure-bred Sussex, for they did not fairly display his working capacities or the general beauty of his appearance. These impure specimens, moreover, were stumbling-blocks in the way of those who, as referred to above, had set themselves the self-imposed task of endeavouring to resuscitate the old Rosehill type, for their services were in many cases resorted to by breeders who were not familiar with their faults. They, therefore, crippled the action of these gentlemen, who knew the breed, and may be considered as responsible for many faults which are present in Sussex Spaniels of the present day.

As might have been supposed, in 1870 there were several types of Sussex Spaniel in existence—not that all were pure-bred, by any means; so perhaps it would be more proper if we said that there were several specimens of the breed in whose veins a large amount of the old Rosehill blood ran, but who bore the taint of foreign crosses in a small degree. It was, therefore, the task of these latter-day regenerators of the Sussex to select from these such animals as they could with some degree of safety mate with pure-bred specimens, and trust for good results. The efforts of these enthusiasts has certainly been crowned with the success it deserved, as we are now in the possession of a breed of Sussex Spaniels which is rapidly approaching that uniformity of type which its admirers have had in view for ten years past. At first, of course, many prizes had to go—for lack of better being present—to dogs which would not win when pure-bred Sussex were on the bench, and this accounts at once for a slight diversity of types in 1873 and for a few seasons after. The pure-bred ones being so hard to find, and in so few hands, could not be seen at every show, and the judges had to do the best they could with the materials they had before them. This was in itself unfortunate for those who had the interests of the breed at heart; but still they persevered, and though they, in many instances, differed in opinion, the various owners kept on showing at all the leading exhibitions until some decided opinions began to be entertained amongst exhibitors on the merits of the Sussex. As a sporting dog, all were agreed before the attempted revival of the breed took place, but upon his structural developments ideas differed, and do so still, in certain small details.

The names of two gentlemen—Mr. T. B. Bowers and Mr. A. W. Langdale—will always be identified with the movement in favour of the Sussex Spaniel; and though the ideas of these two gentlemen are not identical, they deserve equal credit for what they have done in the interests of this valuable breed of sporting dog, and we are convinced that their exertions in its favour have earned them the ungrudged thanks of those interested in the Sussex Spaniel. As we have been fortunate enough to secure the opinions of both these gentlemen, we propose producing them before adding any ideas of our own, and will therefore, without further delay, give the description forwarded to us by Mr. T. B. Bowers, of Hunt's Cross, Woolton, near Liverpool, which is as follows :—

"The Sussex Spaniel is beyond doubt one of the oldest branches of the Spaniel family; yet, strange to say, notwithstanding its beauty, and capacity for rough work, it has never been common, though greatly esteemed and at one time jealously guarded by its fortunate possessors, and certainly this was no more than its deserts, for no dog is more intelligent or affectionate than the pure Spaniel, and no Spaniel is more acceptable to a sportsman in a rough country than the Sussex. Doubtless, in modern coverts, where game abounds, where rides are cut, and which can be hunted in any direction to suit the guns, the silent Clumber will show more sport; but in dense woods and dingles, where one must really hunt up the game, and where the dogs penetrate a mass of jungle which a man cannot face, then the silent Clumber would not be so serviceable as the Sussex, which is also more active, and capable of greater endurance.

"In order to have the perfection of sport in a wild country, the best teams of Sussex

Spaniels were trained to hunt feather only, and I greatly suspect that these old strains were purer Spaniels than any we have now, for a great writer has said that Spaniels have been crossed with Beagles—hence their preference for fur to feather; and, indeed, in these days it almost sounds fabulous to be told that formerly Spaniels existed which could readily be taught to quest only for feather; yet such well-broken teams did exist in Sussex; and such dogs might be had now by careful breeding, and if breakers were encouraged to devote to Spaniel breaking that time of the year which is not required by the Pointers and Setters. But it might be well to remind any one who may desire to give the thing a trial that the Spaniels will in a great measure take their temper and disposition from the person with whom they are daily associated; so that to ensure success, a quiet, even-tempered man must be selected as breaker. Great attention also must be devoted to the breeding of the dogs, for it must be borne in mind how difficult it is to get rid of any faulty formation or habit when once it runs through the blood of a kennel; in fact, to get together a trustworthy team requires as much attention to their breeding and education as is devoted to Setters and Pointers.

"The Sussex Spaniel was so jealously guarded that from one cause or another (the celebrated Rosehill Spaniels were destroyed, owing to an outbreak of dumb madness) pure specimens became exceedingly rare, when, I believe, some who had specimens crossed them with other strains of Spaniels, and, being disappointed with the result, gave up the attempt to resuscitate their breed.

"In the year 1867 Mr. Thomas Burgess won first prize at Birmingham in each large-sized Spaniel class with Sam and Flora, two liver-coloured Spaniels with white markings, and their breeder, Mr. John Hopcroft, maintained that they were directly descended from an old Sussex breed. Their appearance and origin caused a lengthy discussion in the press, and it was conclusively proved that, even if Mr. Hopcroft's strain had once been Sussex pure, some cross had been introduced, hence the liver-and-white specimens Sam and Flora.

"Sussex Spaniels were also crossed with Water Spaniels, and again with the old breed of black Cocker, by which means it is understood Mr. Bullock produced his well-known black Spaniels Bob and Nellie (brother and sister), and these being mated together produced the liver-coloured George, which had so many attributes of the Sussex Spaniel.

"About this time (1872) a few lovers of the breed banded together, and obtained special classes at several shows. Birmingham followed suit in 1874, at which show the above-mentioned George was awarded second prize to Mr. Eddowes's Rufus. At this show I myself entered a protest against George, on the ground that, being the progeny of two black Spaniels, he could not be a Sussex Spaniel. The protest was disallowed, under the usual Birmingham regulation that, if possible, the decisions of the judges should resemble the laws of the Medes and Persians. However, the following year (1875) the same dog was exhibited at Birmingham under the same judges, and was passed unnoticed, since when he has been withdrawn from Sussex competitions.

"The chief prize-takers from this date down to the present time may, without egotism, be said to be my own Buckingham and Maude (of pure Rosehill blood); and the progeny of this pair—viz., Mr. Saxby's (afterwards Mr. Jacobs's, lately deceased) Bachelor, my (now Mr. Bates's) Lizzie, Rover III. (now Mr. Parkinson's), and my (now Mr. Gamon's) Max, and my (now Mr. Hawkins's) Duchess III.; Mr. Spurgin's Sydney and Major; Mr. Richardson's Buz, Beaver, and Beau; and the Rev. W. Shield's Bràs. In addition to these, which were all got by Buckingham or out of Maude, the most celebrated are Mr. A. W. Langdale's

Lawyer, Mr. Salter's Chance and Chloe, the Rev. W. Shield's Rex, Dr. S. W. D. Williams's Laurie, Mr. Arthur Arnold's Dash, Mr. Gamon's Guy, Mr. Green's Guess and Chloe, Mr. Brandreth's Beatrice and Baroness, and my own Bustle and Beryl.

"In order to set on record the value of Sussex Spaniels about this period, I give the prices obtained by myself for a draft of mine. Those sold were—Max, Rover III., Bustle, Bess, Duchess III., Lizzie, and Beatrice, and the total amount realised was 440 guineas. In Sussex, the best specimens may still be found in the neighbourhood of Hawkhurst, and notably at Squire Egerton's.

"In general appearance the Sussex Spaniel is lighter in build and higher on the leg than the Clumber.

"The *Head* should be a good length, but broad as well, so should not appear long.

"The *Ears* should not be large, and should be set on in front, rather above the level of the eyes; the feather on the ears should be straight and silky.

"The *Nostrils* should be very large, and the lower jaw rather recede.

"The *Eyes*, of a dark hazel colour, should be deep set; and the expression should be one of supreme intelligence.

"The *Neck* strong, and slightly arched.

"The *Body* long and deep, the ribs well sprung, the shoulders oblique, and the loins very broad.

"The *Legs* rather longer than a Clumber's, bony and muscular; the front ones as straight as possible, the hind ones very much curved at the stifles and hocks; the latter placed near the ground, similar to a cat's.

"The *Feet* large, round, and well furnished with short hair.

"The *Tail* should never, except under peculiar excitement, be carried above the level of the back. The correct carriage of the stern indicates purity of breed both in the Spaniel and the Setter sooner than any other point.

"The *Coat* (of a golden liver-colour) should be smooth and very dense, the feather should not be very long anywhere, and should on no account hang from the stern like a flag (as a Clumber's does), nor should it extend below the hocks.

"I am one who (for several reasons) does not believe in judging by points, but, for the benefit of those who do, I submit a code which I consider about right:—

POSITIVE POINTS.

" Head	10
Eyes	5
Ears	5
Neck	5
Body	15
Fore-legs	10
Hind-legs	15
Feet	10
Stern	5
Coat	10
General appearance	10
	—
Total positive points	100

NEGATIVE POINTS.

Light-coloured eyes or nose, or showing the hair	10
Ears with curly feather	10
Curly coat	10
Carriage of stern	20
A top-knot or any other colour or markings but golden-liver, with or without a white frill	50
Total negative points	100

"The subject of your illustration, Romp, winner of first prize Crystal Palace, 1880, is by Mr. S. W. Marchant's old Rover (the sire of Buckingham and Maude) out of Flirt, by a Rosehill dog out of my champion Bustle. Marchant's Rover was by Sir P. Micklethwaite's Dash out of Mr. Weston's Fanny, by Mr. S. W. Marchant's Rover II. out of his Duchess II."

Mr. A. W. Langdale writes:—

"There is a notion in Sussex, especially round Brighton, that liver-and-white is the orthodox Sussex Spaniel colour; but such an idea is ridiculed when we get further into the county. Old specimens are very bad to see, and worse to obtain. I have rambled all over Sussex and Kent in search of a *bonâ fide* specimen, and although I have been favoured with a view, have never yet been able to obtain one, and call it all my own. Of the use of the dog there is no doubt. He is a noisy, babbling sort, that will rouse a cock from the densest covert; and so natural does this babbling seem to the breed, that even when out at exercise if one gets off the high road into a meadow, that same moment, no matter how young, down go their heads, and out comes the music. The breed, since Sussex classes have been established, has brought out a number of different types, such as Bullock's George, Langdale's Lawyer, Salter's Chance, Spurgin's Bebb, and Pratt's General Prim, to say nothing of Max, Sweep, Rover III., Buckingham, Lady's-maid, Maude, &c. Now, of these, George, Chance, Lawyer, General Prim, Rover III., and Bebb, are as different in their respective points as it is possible to conceive. Buckingham (late Mat) is called pure, and claims his descent from Rosehill, the place, of all others, where this particular breed of Spaniel is worshipped. Taking him for a pure specimen, we cannot for one moment believe that Bebb, Lawyer, and George can be in the hunt. Lawyer is a most taking dog, and when he made his *début* he was lauded to the skies, as the report in the *Live Stock Journal* of July 4, 1874, when he was shown in the name of Nep, ran as follows:—'He appears to be good in all points, golden-liver in colour, with rare coat, good frill in front, and a head so characteristic of his breed that he must prove a very dangerous rival to Bebb when they meet in the ring.' So it was when, at the next show, Mr. Lort, after a long and deliberate look over the class, actually placed this dog over Buckingham—a dog decidedly dark in colour, and very Pointer-coated, but, as I have written before, said to be true-bred. Maude (his sister, same litter) is of much the same stamp, and if she were a little longer in the head I don't know of one to beat her. Max, though having liver-and-white blood in him, is decidedly the most typical dog of the day, and, barring the white star on Landseer's Spaniel and pheasant picture, is as like that worthy draughtsman's specimen as it is possible to be. I will now give you what I consider to be the proper points of a Sussex Spaniel. Taking the head first—it must be a large head, but not too narrow or long, yet not chumpy; in measurement I should for a dog say 8½ inches, a bitch half an inch less. The ears should be large, but not heavily feathered; no curl is admissible, and the shape of the ear is almost spoon-shaped, the mouth of the spoon at the top; they must be set low on the head. The eye is full, and always hazel-coloured. The nose liver-coloured and broad, not to say square. Fore-legs in many of the dogs I have been shown as pure bred are bowed, but why this should be I don't know. It will have the effect of making them slower at their work, and possibly that is desirable, but for appearance give me straight limbs. Let them be well feathered in the fore-legs, but not so below the hocks in the hind. The weight for a dog I put at 40 lbs., a bitch 35 lbs. His shape and make must be long, low, and heavy; his stern must be docked to about 10 in., and when at work should be carried below the level of the back. Toes and feet should be firm and compact, and well fringed between the former. Colour should be golden-liver—puce or a dead brown is decidedly objectionable—and the less white on the chest the better. Coat must be flat, not Pointer-coated nor yet Setter but just between the two; a slight wave is not unbecoming."

After so much has been said in favour of the Sussex Spaniel by the above two gentlemen, both of whom have worked so hard on its behalf, there can remain but little to be added by ourselves. The existence of a breed of Spaniels which was identified with the county of Sussex was known in the days of Taplin and Scott, and Youatt, in his book, makes the following observations anent this variety, for he says: "The largest and best breed of Springers is said to be in Sussex, and is much esteemed in the Wealds of that county." This is by far the handsomest compliment which has been paid the Sussex up to Youatt's time, and no doubt the writer meant what he said, for the inhabitants of Sussex undoubtedly set great store upon their breed of Spaniels.

As in other varieties of dogs, colour has been a fruitful cause for discussion amongst admirers of the Sussex Spaniel, and though specimens of the correct shade have appeared in public, and won prizes at great shows, there have been objections raised against them on the grounds that they were not pure Sussex; nor, indeed, were they such. The case of George, at Birmingham, which Mr. Bowers alludes to above, is a case in point, for here was a good liver-coloured dog, the offspring of black parents. It must not, therefore, be by any means taken for granted that a Spaniel is a pure-bred Sussex because his coat is of the desired colour. This should be a rich golden liver—which does not in the smallest degree resemble the liver of the Water Spaniel, which is more of a puce colour. The acquisition of the peculiar shade, so characteristic of the Sussex, is one of the chief points for a breeder to have in view, and without it no admirer of this variety would be quite satisfied. Unfortunately, owing to the many vicissitudes through which the breed has passed, and the numerous crosses which have, in consequence, been resorted to, there are a number of dogs to be met with who do not possess the proper shade of colour. Mention has, in fact, been made of dogs who, in many respects, resembled the true-bred Sussex, but who were disfigured by white markings, which would be fatal to their chances of success in competition, as breeders of this variety are singularly unanimous in their opinion upon the subject of colour.

As a workman, the Sussex lays strong claim upon the sportsman. Though not mute, they are not "babblers," and, in this respect, we must, with all due deference, differ from the opinion expressed above by Mr. A. W. Langdale, who describes him as a noisy babbling dog. The Sussex throws his tongue in covert, but that he is noisy few of his supporters will, we think, be brought to admit. As regards his staying powers there is no question, for, being lighter in the body, he is comparatively fresh when the heavier Clumber is beaten, and this is no small point in the favour of a Sussex. On the other hand, the dog is inclined to be headstrong, and a little sulky at times, though this can generally be got over by judicious handling. This variety can also be broken to retrieve with ease, and when he is so used his mouth is tender and he seldom injures the bird. With reference to his capacity for going to water, a well-known authority lately remarked to us "a Sussex is as good in water as he is on land."

With reference to this dog's unreliability in breeding truly, the pedigree of the well-known Sussex Spaniel Rex, which we give below, is a striking instance :—

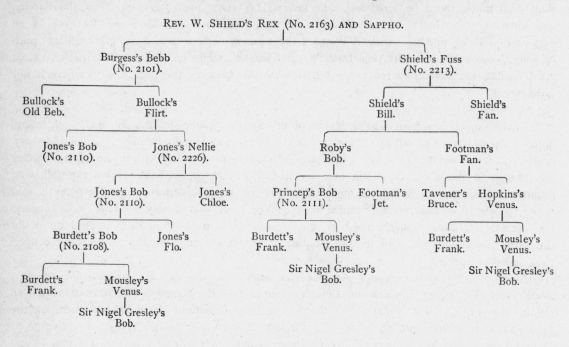

REV. W. SHIELD'S REX (No. 2163) AND SAPPHO.

Rex was a successful competitor in Sussex Spaniel classes, and yet his sister, Lena, was a liver-grey-and-tan, and was shown by Mr. A. W. Langdale, at Norwich, as a Norfolk Spaniel in 1874, upon which occasion she won first prize.

The dog we have selected for illustration is Mr. T. B. Bowers's Romp, which is alluded to by Mr. Bowers in his remarks upon the breed.

STANDARD OF POINTS FOR JUDGING SUSSEX SPANIELS.

	Value.
Skull	5
Eyes and nose	5
Ears	5
Neck and chest	5
Body	10
Feet and legs	5
Coat and colour	10
General appearance	5
	50

CHAPTER LIII.

THE CLUMBER SPANIEL.

THE next of the Spaniel family in order of merit is the Clumber Spaniel, whose long association with many of the highest families in the land has fairly entitled him to rank as the aristocrat of the tribe. The name by which he is known—Clumber—is unquestionably derived from the seat of the Duke of Newcastle, where the breed has flourished for years, and this has given rise to the impression amongst sportsmen that the Clumber Spaniel owes his existence and origin to some early member of that illustrious house. This is scarcely the fact, however, as we learn on the authority of Daniels that the breed was imported into this country by a Duke of Newcastle, who acquired them from the Duc de Nouailles many years ago. It is nevertheless equally certain that the breed was for a long time treasured at Clumber, and that it was extremely difficult for outsiders to gain possession of a specimen.

As regards his origin little can be said, as it is veiled in obscurity; but it may be remarked that certain authorities have argued in favour of there being a remote cross of the foreign Basset-hound in the Clumber Spaniel, though as far as our experience goes the supporters of this theory have hitherto failed to substantiate their statements by any appeal to facts. However, this theory has found its way into print, and may therefore be given merely as a theory which has been propounded, and without any intention on our part to support it. A great deal might be said on the antiquity of this variety by those who are disposed to attach importance to the possession of this attribute, for Edmund de Langley, who wrote in the fourteenth century, described the Spaniel as coming out of "Spayn," and being in colour white and tawny, with a large head and body. It therefore appears to us that it would require a very slight stretch of imagination to connect the ancient Spaniel alluded to by Edmund de Langley with the solemn-looking but patrician Clumber of the present day. Nor would this reasoning in any way detract from Daniels' statement that the strain of Clumber has originated from some dogs procured from the kennels of the Duc de Nouailles. On the contrary, it seems to be a support to it, as it is extremely likely that his dogs would resemble in many respects the breed that, according to the "Maister of Game," existed in Spain in the fourteenth century. Many authorities, no doubt correctly, connect the Clumber Spaniel with the old Setting-dog, who was included by Dr. Caius, in his Spaniel chapter, under the title of Index or Setter. In the present day, however, the duties of the Clumber Spaniel unquestionably lie more in the direction of covert-shooting than driving birds in the open, especially as both Setters and Pointers can readily be found who can manage the latter business far better than the short-legged Spaniel can.

In consequence of the jealousy with which the Clumber strain was formerly guarded by the Dukes of Newcastle, it was a difficult matter to procure a specimen years ago, and, therefore, indifferent Clumbers fetched very high prices when in the market. Of recent years, however, dogs of this variety can be more readily procured, and their value has sensibly diminished. In addition to the high value which their rarity placed upon the Clumbers, the fact of their being for years very much in-bred brought about the inevitable result, and signs of constitutional delicacy began to appear, which have remained characteristics of the breed ever since. It is not so much in the cases of the older dogs that this objection can be raised against the Clumbers, for a matured dog of this variety usually keeps hale and hearty to a ripe old age, and increases in sagacity and value as the years roll on. It is in their puppy-hood that young Clumbers are peculiarly susceptible to the ills to which puppyhood is especially heir. As a rule, they suffer terribly from the ravages of distemper, and most breeders of Clumbers are on thorns until their valuable stock have safely passed through this ordeal. Yellows or jaundice they also are very subject to, and if it appears in an aggravated form the malady is usually fatal to the invalid. In spite, however, of the difficulty experienced in rearing dogs of this description, the Clumber has always been a popular Spaniel with sportsmen, and his character fully entitles him to the respect which he has won himself from the highest in the land. Following on the Duke of Newcastle, the names of Earl Spencer, the Duke of Westminster, the Earl of Abingdon, the Duke of Norfolk, and the Duke of Portland, have all been identified at one time or another with kennels of this breed. The latter nobleman has at the present time a large and unusually strong kennel of Clumber Spaniels; but, as they do not appear often at dog shows, the public have but slender oppor-tunities of judging their merits, and comparing his Grace's dogs with those from better-known kennels. Mr. R. S. Holford, of Tetbury, formerly showed some excellent specimens of the breed, and Mr. Yeatman is also well known in connection with the ownership of many good dogs, nor must that old breeder, Mr. Foljambe, be omitted from the list.

In addition to his aristocratic associations, the Clumber Spaniel has much to recommend him to the general body of sportsmen, who, as a body, are more inclined to value a sporting dog on account of his own intrinsic merit than because he has been the recipient of patrician patronage. In covert shooting of a certain description the Clumber is almost unsurpassed by any breed, and a peculiarity in the breed is that the pure-bred ones, almost without exception, hunt mute, which enables them to draw close up to their game without disturbing it. On this account Clumbers are very frequently worked with bells attached to their collars, as by the help of these they can gradually drive the game forward, and the guns can more readily tell their whereabouts in the covert. These Spaniels can be worked in teams of any number upwards of one brace and a half, and when this practice is resorted to it has a singularly taking effect, in addition to which good sport is certain to be provided for the guns if any game is in the covert, as the Clumber beats his ground most thoroughly, being a very close worker. In working in teams they show but little jealousy, and single specimens can readily be broken to retrieve and take water, which naturally increases their value very consider-ably in the sportsman's eyes. The range of a Clumber should not exceed thirty yards, and they should be broken to down charge, or to return in a body when the shot is fired. It is not many sportsmen, however, who are in a position to work a team of Clumbers, as few kennels contain a sufficient number to enable them to do so, but, as will have been seen above, a single Clumber Spaniel is a valuable assistance to the sportsman engaged in covert shooting.

We have been furnished with the following notes by Mr. A. W. Langdale, who has devoted considerable attention to the Clumber as well as to the Sussex Spaniel, and has kindly sent us his ideas for publication :—

"This beautiful Spaniel is believed to be the oldest known breed of dog genus Spaniel,

FIELD SPANIELS.

and was preserved many years ago most strictly. The Duke of Newcastle's name has always been associated with the Clumber, as it was from this nobleman's estate the breed took the name. Through in-breeding a few years back they almost looked like disappearing, but now, I am glad to say, that in the Duke of Portland's, Lord Arthur Cecil's, Earl Spencer's, and many other sportsmen's kennels, may be found specimens as good as, if not better than, ever were. They are often used for covert shooting in teams of nine, and being naturally mute when at work are of great value, as they can work up close enough to a pheasant to almost clutch him.

'As regards the various points, of course the head comes foremost; this should be decidedly heavy and at least seventeen or eighteen inches round, with a deep stop and a flesh-coloured nose, a freckled jaw and lemon markings of such an even nature that you could not at first sight tell the off from the near side of the head. The lower jaw recedes, as in most Spaniels, so as to give the appearance of being anything but square. His fore-legs should be short, strong, and so put on that when, as is often the case, they descend or jump down steep banks or walls, they stand the shock it must give them from their weight; the feet must be large, but put together closer than those of his water brother. Length of body is a great point, but not less is the depth of his girth before and aft, so many specimens does one see nowadays with good fore-legs set on nice and low and the hind ones decidedly lofty. The ears should be squarer than those of the Sussex, and should not be feathered below the leather; the stern, when at work, is carried about level with the back, but when going to covert or at exercise you cannot see a prettier sight than their flags carried at about the same angle as a lancer's pennon on the slope. The coat should be thick and smooth—curl is decidedly objectionable—and, lastly, the colour should be white with lemon or very pale orange markings; the fewer of these about the body the better. Weight for dogs varies from 57 to 65 lbs., but the bitches run much lighter, the heaviest I ever saw scaled being my own Libnah, and she pulled down 50 lbs."

The *Head* should be large, long, and massive, flat at the top, and with a decided occipital protuberance.

The *Muzzle* wide and powerful looking. In this respect we differ from the views expressed above by Mr. A. W. Langdale.

The *Nose* large and flesh-coloured.

The *Eye* moderately large, light hazel coloured, and rather deeply set.

The *Neck* long though very powerful, and free from all throatiness.

The *Shoulders* very strong, which gives a Clumber a heavy appearance in front.

The *Ears* should be large in size, and rather long, lying close to the head, wide at the top, but not lobe-shaped like in the Sussex. They should be feathered slightly.

The *Body* should be very long and well ribbed up, with a deep chest.

The *Fore-legs* should be short, straight, well feathered, and immensely heavy in bone. In fact it is one of the chief characteristics of a Clumber to be exceptionally powerful in his fore-legs.

The *Fore-feet* should be large, moderately round, and well feathered like the fore-legs.

The *Loins* should be thick and powerful looking.

The *Hind-legs* short, not much bent, and heavy in bone.

The *Stern* set on low and carried downwards, and should be docked.

The *Colour* lemon-and-white throughout, the latter colour, of course, predominating. If a dog is marked as described by Mr. Langdale it is naturally an extra advantage to him in competition.

The *Coat* should be silky, but quite free from any curl, which is a most objectionable feature in a Clumber Spaniel's jacket. Though profuse the coat should not be too long, as it would interfere with a dog when at work in a covert.

In *General appearance* the Clumber is a slow heavy-looking dog, though his expression betokens intelligence, and he has a thoughtful look which cannot fail to attract.

The specimen we have selected for illustration in our coloured plate is Lapis, the property of Mr. T. B. Bowers, of Hunts Cross, Woolton, near Liverpool, though formerly owned by Mr. W. Arkwright, of Sutton Scarsdale, near Chesterfield. Lapis was bred by Mr. W. Arkwright in 1875, and measures as follows:—Length of head, from tip of nose to occiput, 10½ inches; girth of skull, 18½ inches; girth of chest, 29 inches; girth of loins, 25 inches; girth of fore-arm, 8 inches; weight, 60 lbs.; height at shoulder, 18 inches. During his career upon the show bench Lapis has been successful in carrying off the following prizes:—First and cup Chesterfield, 1876; second Agricultural Hall, Bristol, and Alexandra Palace, 1877; first Blaydon-on-Tyne, first Bristol, first Crystal Palace, and first Darlington, 1878; first Burton-on-Trent and first Darlington, 1879.

Following our usual custom we now conclude with

STANDARD OF POINTS FOR JUDGING CLUMBER SPANIELS.

	Value.
Head, skull, muzzle, and eyes...	10
Ears	5
Neck and shoulders ...	5
Chest	5
Body and loins	10
Legs and feet	5
Colour and coat	5
General appearance ...	5
	50

CHAPTER LIV.

BLACK SPANIELS.

THESE engaging dogs have of late years almost monopolised the classes provided at dog shows for Spaniels other than Sussex or Clumber, and their popularity is still increasing rapidly. As a beautiful dog, the Black Spaniel certainly ranks very highly, whilst as the companion of the sportsman he is invaluable. Opinions differ very considerably upon the purity of the breed, and even its most ardent admirers have in some instances been brought to affirm that the Black Spaniel is a mongrel; others are equally positive in their assertions that it is nothing of the sort, but that many specimens can trace an unbroken pedigree.

Mr. A. W. Langdale has written as follows :—

"This breed of Spaniels is most popular and highly prized, and has in the last few years been brought up to a standard of excellence such as has never before been arrived at. A team of black Springers, for so the large size of this breed are called, in their jet-coloured satin-like coats, on a bright winter's morning, on a snow-covered track, look lovely! I say the large size are called Springers, and this is so because of their peculiar movement among turnips, swedes, or mangolds, where, directly they get wind of fur or feather, they jump about from ruck to ruck in quite a different style to their Sussex or more sombre Clumber brethren. The blacks, as a rule, are not favourite dogs for covert shooting, as their colour behoves a sportsman to be very good-sighted or his pet may be made to suffer for his quarry. They are not so noisy or babbling as the Sussex, and I have seen some of the old-fashioned sort work up to their game with scarcely a note. Of late, to obtain smooth coats and shortness of leg, there has been a great deal of crossing between the Black and Sussex breeds; and I should say that, although it is not quite the thing, still it has undoubtedly had the desired effect, as seldom have there (if ever) been better Blacks before the public than have been shown at our recent exhibitions. I believe that Mr. Burdett first brought out the Black Spaniel, and it was from him that Mr. Phineas Bullock secured the cream of his world-wide known kennel. Amongst this team were such raven-coloured beauties as were the admiration of all breeders, and Mr. Bullock knew it, and kept his breed to himself. Old Bob, Flirt, and Nellie, to say nothing of Bruce, were indeed grand specimens—Nellie especially. By some of our most experienced judges this bitch was held up as the *beau idéal* of the Black Field Spaniel; she had a lovely head, ears, and eyes, and I quite endorse the opinion of the critics in saying I never saw her equal. Dr. W. W. Boulton had also a different strain, produced originally, I believe, from a liver-coloured bitch called Fern. However, this gentleman understood his work, and produced at different times such dogs as Beaver, my Lorne, Regent, Bruce *alias* Buccleugh, Beverlac, Runic, Brush, Black Prince, Blanchette, Pearl, &c., to say nothing of a grand team of black Cockers to be alluded to elsewhere. Dr. Boulton's dogs were, with few exceptions, straighter in the coat than those of his *confrère* Mr. Bullock, and so when they met each other in the judging ring it was always a very near squeak for either, the Doctor winning by the coat, but the other by the height and general symmetry. Dr. Spurgin, I myself, Mr. Handy, and Mr. Bonner, may be said to be amongst the principal breeders of Blacks of late years. Recently Mr. T. Jacobs, of Newton Abbot, has been most successful on the bench. Mr. Bowers seldom bred them, but always was a buyer of a good one. In speaking of Mr. Bonner, that gentleman keeps his dogs more for work in the fields than the show bench, and that is why we do not see him in the front rank as often as we should like. Blanche (one of the newly inter-liver-and-black cross) won for

MR. T. JACOBS'S BLACK SPANIEL, KAFFIR.

him at Birmingham, and claims my old dog Lawyer as her sire, the dam Flora being a Black. This same dog sired Gip, who did good service for Mr. Avery, of Southampton— in fact, as a stud dog I do not know his superior; he has immense power, and is a thoroughly symmetrical dog, and should be invaluable as a mate for shy bitches. The following are the principal points that should be looked to by an intending buyer:—Height at shoulder, 18½ inches; colour, whole black, no white; weight, 40 lbs.; ears, set low down and wavy; coat, smooth—a little wave is admissible, but both this and the ears must be free from curl; eyes, a dark hazel; stern, docked to about 10 inches, and carried low. The dog should be well feathered all round, but not below his hocks."

Following on the remarks of Mr. A. W. Langdale, the result of the experience of Mr. T. Jacobs, of Worlborough House, Newton Abbot, will be read with interest, as, at the present time, Mr. Jacobs's kennel is, *facile princeps*, at the head of affairs in the Black Spaniel world. Mr. Jacobs, it will be seen from his remarks, although so successful as an exhibitor, has not yet quite obtained what he wants, though from what we have seen and heard of his magnificent Kaffir, whose illustration accompanies this article, we are of the opinion that he must be very hard to please if he is in any way dissatisfied with this really typical dog. Mr. Jacobs writes as follows:—

" As a breeder and successful exhibitor of Spaniels, I freely give you, for the benefit of your readers, the little knowledge I have acquired in the art of breeding and rearing of that useful animal. What I write is not taken from books or former writers, but from my experiments and experience, confining myself chiefly to the present fashionable and handsome breed of Black Spaniel.

" Much has been written and said on the purity of the breed, deprecating the means I have adopted to produce them as calculated to alter a presumed type, and frequent missiles have been hurled at me and my dogs from behind the hedge. But where is the pure-bred Black Spaniel so much talked about? Proof of the existence of the pure-bred one (if ever there was one) has not been forthcoming; like most other sporting dogs, they are the result of different crosses.

' I have bred many times from the most noted dogs and bitches said to be the only pure strain of Black Spaniel, and have never known them to throw one even litter of blacks, always a mixture—liver, black, black-and-tan, liver-and-tan, black-and-white; some with long, some short, bodies and legs, curly, wavy, smooth, and all sizes and shapes.

" What does this indicate? Common-sense tells me, a cross with different types, varieties, and colours some time or other must have been introduced. I never can believe there ever was a distinct breed of Black Spaniel, nor do I believe that the Sussex is a distinct breed; it is true we can trace them back for many generations, like we do the Laverack Setter, but how were they derived in the first place?

" We may keep to one strain for many years, and, in time, call them a distinct breed, but what is the result? To preserve that strain we must be continually breeding in and in to one family, until we get them difficult to rear, weedy, and devoid of sense, when they become useless for the purpose they are required (I have noticed the latter fault showing itself in the Sussex). Therefore breeders have to resort to the crossing with another family, which may be of a different type or colour; by so doing you raise a great ' hubbub' and cry that your dogs are not pure. In spite of these cries I followed my own dictation; my great aim was to improve the breed of Spaniels. Purity of breed I had foremost in my mind, which I do not consider I sacrificed when I mated my black bitches with a liver-colour Sussex, the result of which was a decided improvement. Your readers may judge for themselves by having a look at Kaffir, Zulu, and Squaw, and noting their performances. I did not rest here, but thought there was still room for improvement, and by breeding these Blacks together, I have produced something that promises to eclipse everything I have yet seen. I am gradually creeping nearer the standard I have marked out for my beacon, viz.:—

" *Temperament.*—Pleasing temper I always look to first; never breed from a bad-tempered sporting dog, every sportsman knows what a nuisance they are.

" A *long body*, short legs, with plenty of bone and feather, a perfect smooth, satin-like coat, with no inclination to wave or curl, moderately long.

" *Ears*, covered with long silky hair (not ringlets), well set low down, and hung close to the cheek : small or narrow where they spring from the head, and large and lobe-shaped at the base, well furnished with hair on the inside leather.

" A *long head*, not snipy, or heavy like the Clumber ; dark, pleasing eye—a yellow eye denotes bad temper, therefore should be avoided.

" *Level mouth*, not pig-jawed or underhung, but I prefer the former fault to the latter, which prevails, I am sorry to see, in some of our present show dogs. Breeders should avoid these as stock dogs.

" A *long neck* slightly arched, well clothed with muscle ; strong across the loins.

" *Ribs*, well sprung, and barrel-shaped.

" *Belly*, well clothed with long hair, and not tucked up like the Greyhound (a common fault).

" *Broad chest*, well clothed with muscle and feather.

" *Feet*, round, cat-like, with a plentiful supply of hair between the toes.

" *Tail* carried in a line with the back.

" Many have argued with me that by mating black with liver-colour would throw the black puppies rusty or bad black ; but being a breeder of pigeons for many years, and knowing the fact that by mating a dun hen with a black cock, or *vice versâ*, you produce a much better black than by breeding two blacks together, I thought if this held good with pigeons, why should it not with dogs ? I therefore mated my Spaniels as before described ; the result is, I have never seen one bad black, and have bred more than a dozen litters in that way.

" I like to see my puppies grow like cucumbers, without a check, until they are over six months old. I often leave home for two or more days together, and on my return have exclaimed—How these puppies grow! When they have been neglected during my absence I should always discover it on my return, and, on inquiry, generally found their feeding has not been properly attended to. And now I will say a few words on feeding :—As soon as my puppies can lap milk they are supplied with it twice a day, at milking-time, from a herd of goats kept by me for the purpose. Never give cow's milk, without you want your puppies to grow backwards, have pot bellies, and be filled with worms. Years ago I used to lose 75 per cent. of the puppies I bred through this very cause ; now I rarely see one like it. As soon as the puppies can swallow solid food they are supplied with two meals a day—oatmeal, Indian meal, boiled with sheep's heads and scraps from the butcher's, and once a day with raw flesh. 'What! raw flesh?' said one of these clever writers to me one day, 'you will kill the lot of them.' I only laughed at him, as my experience has taught me different—it is their natural food. I have it chopped into mince-meat first, until they get their teeth developed, when it is given in larger pieces and quantities. When they arrive at the age of six or eight months they are fed almost entirely on it when it can be procured, and I ask any of your readers who have seen my dogs if ever they saw dogs shown in better condition, with coats always like satin. Well, friends, I will give you all a piece of advice, and let the cat out of the bag—the condition of my dogs is all due to raw flesh. Go and feed likewise, but don't over-do it. Feed at first with great caution if your dogs have not been accustomed to it, and then give them a certain quantity, not so much as they will eat ; oh dear no, you would make a pretty mess of them. Practice would soon teach you the proper quantity, which depends on the size and age of your dogs.

" Cleanliness I insist on. Every morning the kennels are all cleaned out, clean sawdust laid down on the floor, clean straw supplied for the benches, and any sickly puppies removed to the hospital; kennels once a month lime-washed with hot lime in which a little carbolic acid has been added. When dry, they have a daily run in an orchard of nearly two acres in extent. I rarely ever see deformed legs in my puppies; they are never chained until their bones are properly developed, and then only for training purposes, as they have large, roomy, well-ventilated kennels and sheds to run in should the weather be unfavourable for their out-door exercise. I seldom have any of my dogs washed; it is not necessary if they are regularly brushed with a dandy-brush.

"I always try to keep my puppies in the highest condition possible, never allow them to get thin and poor, so as to be prepared to meet that fatal malady—distemper. If visited with it when in condition above described, nine cases out of ten they will pull through it if properly nursed. Another piece of advice to your readers, and I have done, '*Be prepared*.'"

With reference to the breeding of the Black Spaniels from Sussex, which is alluded to by Mr. Jacobs, we may remark that the dog he used, though a good specimen of the latter breed, and a very successful dog too, had a bar sinister in his pedigree which might have in some degree influenced his stock. The dog to which we refer, and of whom Mr. Jacobs made much use, was the liver-coloured Bachelor, who was by Buckingham, late Mat, out of Peggie, by Babb out of Ruby, by Chance out of Pop, a black bitch by Joblin's Rags out of Floss. This, we think, may in some degree save the reputation of the Sussex Spaniel as regards his pretensions to purity of blood.

The illustration we give herewith is of Mr. Thomas Jacobs's famous Kaffir, and is a remarkably truthful representation of that excellent dog. Kaffir was unfortunately somewhat nervous when Mr. Barber was sketching him, and consequently there was a considerable difficulty in making him stand in the orthodox position. Mr. Barber therefore elected to draw him as he was, and hence the admirable likeness of the dog. Kaffir was bred in 1879 by his owner, Mr. Thomas Jacobs, of Worlborough House, Newton Abbot, and is by the Sussex Spaniel Bachelor, out of Smutty, by Lad o' Beverley out of Lass o' York; Bachelor by champion Buckingham out of Peggie. Amongst other triumphs Kaffir was first and cup for the best Spaniel shown at Birmingham in 1880.

In the face of the description given by Mr. Jacobs, it would be a work of supererogation on our part if we were to attempt to describe the points of this breed more fully, we therefore merely append a

STANDARD OF POINTS FOR JUDGING BLACK SPANIELS.

							Value.
Head and eyes ...	...	...	...	...	...	...	5
Jaws	...	...	...	...	...	...	5
Neck and shoulders	...	...	...	...	...	...	5
Body	...	...	...	...	...	...	10
Forelegs and feet	...	...	...	...	...	...	5
Loins and quarters	...	...	...	...	...	...	5
Hind legs and feet	...	...	...	...	...	...	5
Coat	...	...	...	...	...	...	5
General appearance	...	...	...	...	...	...	5
				Total ...	...	...	50

CHAPTER LV.

THE NORFOLK SPANIEL.

THE last variety of the Springer family which we shall treat of is the Norfolk Spaniel, which is a breed highly prized if met with pure, though there are, comparatively speaking, very few dogs of the variety which come under this category, as it has been very much crossed with other breeds of Spaniels. Interesting as the Norfolk Spaniel most undoubtedly is, there is not much in the way of pedigree for him to claim, though he is credited with having been for years a *protégé* of the Duke of Norfolk. Formerly he was much darker in colour than now-a-days, for he had usually a great deal of black about him. Now the colour mostly met with in dogs of this variety is liver-and-white, though good specimens of the black-and-white variety are often to be met with.

The Norfolk Spaniel does not hunt mute; on the contrary, he is disposed to throw his tongue when questing; but mute hunters have occasionally been known, though their appearance is very uncommon.

Youatt in his work gives his opinion regarding the origin of the Norfolk Spaniel, which may be taken for what it is worth by admirers of the breed, as he appears to have devoted but a very small portion of his time to the consideration of the Spaniel family. In speaking of the Springer, in 1845, he wrote:—

" From a cross with the Terrier a black-and-tan variety was procured, which was cultivated by the late Duke of Norfolk, and thence called the Norfolk Spaniel. It is larger than the common Springer, and stauncher and stouter. It often forms a strong individual attachment, and is unhappy and pines away when separated from its master. It is more ill-tempered than the common Springer, and if not well broken in is often exceedingly obstinate."

The above is the only theory which we can discover of the origin of the Norfolk Spaniel, who unfortunately appears to have fallen into disrepute since the Blacks began to appear in numbers. However, in the present day black-and-tan is by no means recognised as the correct colour for a Norfolk Spaniel. On the contrary, this dog is, when found pure, most usually a liver-and-white, the white spots being heavily flecked with liver, which gives him a very handsome and showy appearance. A blaze of white up the forehead adds a great deal to his beauty, and a white tip to his tail, which, as in other breeds, should be docked short, is an additional attraction, though, of course, these may only be taken as fancy markings, and would merely count as such in competition.

The Norfolk Spaniel will be found no mean assistance to the sportsman in pursuit of water-fowl, for he will take water readily, and retrieves well—though hard in mouth. On land he is also a very handy dog, and will face the thickest coverts pluckily, and may therefore be taken as a valuable dog, whose breeding should be encouraged by sportsmen of all denominations. He is not mute.

In appearance the Norfolk Spaniel is inclined to be higher on the leg than either the Sussex or the Clumber; his head is lighter than the latter's, and he is, in short, finer all over. Although longer in his leg than these breeds he is much lighter in bone, and has been rather aptly described as a thick-made English Setter. The height of a Norfolk Spaniel is about nineteen inches, but owing to the frequent crosses which have been made between this breed and the Clumber and the Sussex, a great difference of height is perceptible in so-called perfectly pure-bred Norfolks. In the face of so many cross-bred Spaniels, which are spread about the country and styled Norfolks by their owners, there is a considerable difficulty in giving a description of what a Norfolk Spaniel should be, but the chief difference between a dog of this description and the Clumber has been given above. As regards a scale of points for judging the breed, the standard which is given for the Black Spaniel will apply almost as well to the Norfolk, as will be seen from the annexed.

STANDARD OF POINTS FOR JUDGING NORFOLK SPANIELS.

	Value.
Head	5
Ears and eyes	5
Body and chest	10
Legs and feet	5
Loins	5
Coat	5
Colour and markings...	5
General appearance	10
	50

CHAPTER LVI.

COCKER SPANIELS.

THESE engaging members of the Spaniel family are almost extinct as regards purity, but their working capacity has never failed them. As will be seen from Mr. Langdale's remarks, there is more than one family of the breed which has practically been lost sight of. A breed of black or black-and-tan Cockers certainly existed, and has been perpetuated down to recent years, proof of which can be found in the pedigrees which accompany this article. In the first instance we give that of Dr. W. W. Boulton's Regent, which is as follows :—

PEDIGREE OF DR. BOULTON'S REGENT (No. 2,162).

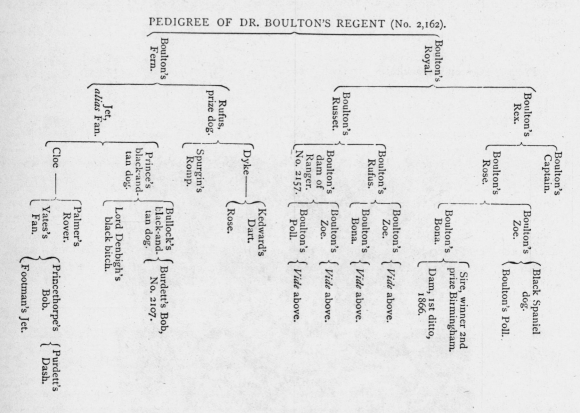

Mr. A. W. Langdale, who has long been an admirer of these valuable little dogs, has sent us the following for publication :—

" This breed of Spaniel is closely allied with Wales and Devonshire, and, I believe, more used in those parts than anywhere else. It is indeed rare, even in the adjoining country, to find Cocker Spaniels, but few people being apparently aware of their great value. Smaller than their brethren the Springers, they work in a totally different style ; and in a hedgerow, or copse, with a very thick underwood, are invaluable. They, like the Springers, are not noisy, but when they do give tongue it is of such a silvery note as to warm the ardent sportsman's blood. Dr. W. W. Boulton, as in other breeds, gave his mind to producing Cockers, and in his Rhea we saw a black Cocker of great merit ; she was bred by him in 1870, and was the offspring of those two good dogs, Captain and Rose. Rhea had rather a full eye, but a regular Cocker head and body : she was full of quality. Of late the big shows have left off giving classes for this splendid little dog, and it is to be deplored, as nothing tends to extinguish a breed sooner than their name not appearing in an important schedule. Cockers run into all sorts of colour, going from lemon-and-white, orange-and-white, and orange, most generally seen in Wales ; to the liver-and-white, liver-and-tan, and roan, generally seen south ; and the black-and-tan, of the north. Of this last colour, Mr. Burdett was the principal breeder ; and of the orange, perhaps the best seen on the bench was my Ladybird, bred by Mr. Lort, who was selected for illustration as a typical specimen. Their weight generally runs at about from four-and-twenty to seven-and-twenty pounds ; they are smooth-coated, free from top-knot, in fact a small cobby-made Spaniel. Of those shown at present I take Bessie II.—a liver-and-grey—to be the best specimen, but her pedigree is not a Cocker's proper, being by Bebb ex Smutt—Bebb, a liver-coloured dog, with a long winning list to his name ; and Smutt, I believe, a black-and-white."

From these remarks it will be seen that some of the best of modern Cockers have other than Cocker blood in their veins, but still many of the best specimens, Rhea to wit, has a long pedigree to be proud of. The following is her pedigree and performances :—

RHEA. Black Cocker Spaniel bitch, whelped May 8, 1870.	Captain (W. W. Boulton).		
	Rose (W. W. Boulton).	Zoe	Black Spaniel Dog. Poll—Old English Cocker.
		Bona	Bob, 2nd Birmingham, 1866. Nell, 1st Birmingham, 1866.

Rhea won first prize at Driffield ; second prize Manchester and Birmingham, 1871 ; first Thorne, first Driffield, second Kendal, and extra prize Crystal Palace, 1872 ; first prize, Manchester, first prize and cup Fakenham, second Birmingham, 1873 ; first prize and cup Northampton, first prize and cup Crystal Palace, first prize Manchester, first prize Darlington, and first prize Hull, 1874.

As so many Cockers are met with on all sides whose pedigrees are mixed up, and whose outlines differ considerably, a description of their points is scarcely possible ; but a reference to the former article on Blacks will, we think, be sufficient to give our readers the information they desire concerning these smaller dogs.

CHAPTER LVII.

THE WATER SPANIEL.

IN spite of the remarks made by Dr. Caius anent the Water Spaniel, there appears to be no mention made of him by subsequent writers for many years; and this fact is the more inexplicable when it is considered that allusions are made by several of them to the Water-dog, which, however, is also alluded to by some authors in addition to the Water Spaniel, as will be seen later on. The idea that has been forced upon us by the perusal of several of the earlier writers on canine

WATER-DOG, FROM "ICONES ANIMALIUM."

subjects is, that the Water-dog was a descendant of the Water Spaniel referred to by Dr. Caius in his "Englishe Dogges," and that he had become crossed with other breeds to such an extent that a great deal of his original identity was lost, and, generally speaking, dogs who were used for the pursuit of wild-fowl were designated Water-dogs. As will be seen from the accompanying illustration, which is taken from "Icones Animalium," by J. F. Riedel, there was, in his day, a Water-dog which very much resembled the Irish Water Spaniel of the present time, and there can be very little room left to doubt that this dog had much in common with the Water-dog. That the latter variety was largely used for sporting purposes is beyond all question, and Nicholas Cox, in his work, "The Gentleman's Recreation," devotes a considerable space to the Water-dog, and gives, in addition, a number of general rules to guide beginners in the act of breaking him; these we reproduce below.

The description which Nicholas Cox gives of water-dogs is as follows:—

" I shall begin with the best proportion of the Water-dog and, first, of his colour. Although some do attribute much to the colour, yet experience lets us know they are uncertain observations. To proceed, then, your dog may be of any colour and yet excellent, but choose him of long hair and curled, not loose and shagged ; his head must be round, his ears broad and hanging, his eyes full, lively, and quick. His nose very short, his lip hound-like, his chaps with a full set of strong teeth. His neck thick and short, his breast sharp, his shoulders broad. His forelegs straight, his chine square, his buttocks round, his belly gaunt, and his thighs brawny, &c.

"For the training this dog you cannot begin too soon with him, and therefore, as soon as he can lap, you must teach him to couch and lie down, not daring to stir from that posture without leave. Observe in his first teaching to let him eat nothing till he deserves it, and let him have no more teachers, feeders, cherishers, or correctors but one ; and do not alter that word you first use in his information, for the dog takes notice of the sound, not the language. When you have acquainted him with the word suitable to his lesson, you must teach him to know the word of reprehension. You must also use words of cherishing, to give him encouragement when he does well. There is also a word of advice, instructing him when he does amiss.

"Having made him understand these several words, you must next teach him to lead in a string or collar orderly, not running too forward nor hanging backward. After this you must teach him to come close to your heels without leading, for he must not range by any means unless it be to beat fowls from their covert, or to fetch the wounded. In the next place you must teach him to fetch or carry anything you throw out of your hands. And first try him with the glove, shaking it over his head and making him snap at it, and sometimes let him hold it in his mouth and strive to pull it from him. At last throw it a little way and let him worry it on the ground, and so, by degrees, make him bring it wherever you can throw it. If you use him to carry dead fowl it will not be amiss, for by that means he will not tear or bruise what fowl you shoot.

" Having perfected this lesson, drop something behind you which the dog does not see, and, being gone a little way from it, send him back to seek it by saying ' Back, I have lost.' If he seems amazed, point with your finger urging him to seek out, and leave him not till he hath done it. Then drop something at a greater distance, and make him find out that too, till you have brought him to go back a mile. Now you may train him for your gun, making him stalk after you, step by step, or else couch and lie close till you have shot.

" The last use of the Water-dog is in moulting time, when wild fowl cast their feathers and are unable to fly, which is between summer and autumn. At this time bring your dog to their coverts and hunt them out into the stream, and there with your nets surprise them, for at this time sheep will not drive more easily. Though some may object that this sickly time is unseasonable, yet, if they consider what excellent food these fowls will provide when crammed, the taking of them may be very excuseable."

From the directions he gives it certainly appears that Nicholas Cox had studied the art of breaking the Water-dog to retrieve, and valued him above all other breeds for this object. The description which he furnishes is not quite in accordance with our modern views ; for though he states that the jacket should be curly and not shaggy so as to get easily matted, he gives it as his opinion that the nose should be very short, which is a feature we do not care to find in the Water-dogs or Spaniels of the nineteenth century. On the whole, however, the Water-dog which Nicholas Cox describes must doubtless have been a serviceable companion to the sportsman of his day ; and if not quite of the modern type, he appears to have borne something of a resemblance to indifferent specimens of what is now the Water-dog *par excellence*, viz., the Irish Water Spaniel, a breed which has apparently monopolised the place made vacant by the retirement of the English Water Spaniel. There can be no doubt but that the original Water Spaniel was a cross between the Water-dog and the Land Spaniel. William Taplin, in 1803, says : " From the great similitude between some of these Cockers and the small Water-dog, both in figure and disposition, there is little doubt but they may have been produced originally by a cross between the Springing Spaniel and the latter." This opinion is confirmed by a statement made by the same writer later on, in which he says that, " The particular breed of dog passing under this denomination (Water-dog) differs materially from the smaller sort distinguished by the appellation of Water Spaniel. . . . These dogs are of different colours, though of the same shape and formation, and those who profess themselves connoisseurs in the art of canine discrimination go so far as to fix the criterion of superiority and excellence upon the colour itself in the following way. The perfect black is affirmed to be the best and hardiest, the least susceptible of fatigue, hunger, and danger ; the spotted, or pied, quickest of scent and sagacity ; and the liver-colour the most alert and expeditious in swimming. . . . The head is rather round ; the nose short ; the ears long, broad, and pendulous ; his eyes full, lively, and solicitously attracting ; his neck thick and short ; his shoulders broad ; his legs straight, his hind-quarters round and firm ; his pasterns strong and dew-clawed ; his fore-feet long, but round, with his hair adhering to his body in natural elastic short curls, neither loose, long, or shaggy, the former being considered indicative of constitutional strength, the latter of bodily weakness or hereditary debility."

As Taplin so carefully describes the Water-dog, to whom he devotes a considerable portion of his large work, the following quotation referring to the then method of water-fowl shooting with the Water-dog may be read with interest :—

" Amidst the various vacuities, clefts, and recesses, with which rocks abound, such are selected as, from their situation at certain angles, points, and prominences, hold forth the most promising prospect of success in the undertaking. In each of these, but not at a less distance than one quarter or a third of a mile from each other, huts are so curiously constructed with sods, inter-mixed with loam, marl, and other applicable articles, as to form when finished a seeming part of the rock itself. To each hut is a door, a shelf within for the convenience of depositing provisions and ammunition, as well as three circular openings of four inches diameter, to the right, left, and in the centre, for the discovery of the fowl in their approach, and the subsequent discharge of the gun when they fortunately happen to veer within shot. This sport (if to the more happy and enlightened part of the world it may be termed so) seems to require a much greater degree of patience and philosophy than any other recreation or amusement in which the dog and gun are individually or conjointly concerned. In this sequestered situation, remote from every human eye and association, accompanied only by his faithful dog, the adventurer takes his seat as near as can be to the very dawn of day, well knowing that every flattering prospect of his day's success depends much more upon the fluctuating favour of the elements than upon any energetic endeavours of his own.

" The gannet or Soland goose, and the larger kind of gull in all its varieties, are the principal objects to which he directs his attention, for the more probable procuration of which he silently continues seated, and most watchfully attentive to the apertures in the front and sides of his hut, through which he can perceive the approach of the game in whatever direction it may appear. The guns for use in this service are seldom shorter than from five to six feet in the barrel, and with swan-shot are destructive to a great distance ; upon their coming within reach of which the gunner has his choice of the apertures for the advantage of better aim, and in moderate weather is so expert at the practice that the deadly level is seldom made in vain. Upon the discharge of the gun, the earnestly sagacious and impatient animal instantly sallies from the hut, and in one moment, catching sight of the bird and the direction in which it is falling, he rushes with the most incredible fortitude and impetuosity, through and over every obstacle that can present itself, to the execution of his office. For whether the fowl falls dead amidst the infinite clefts, recesses, and vacuities of the rock, or, being only winged or wounded, and falling in the water, it is the distinguished property of this dog never to recede till he has performed his task, and brought the object of his mission to the hand of his master. In favourable weather, and on fortunate days, the quick succession of shots and rapid destruction of birds soon form an accumulation which bids fair to fill the huts."

Although further on in his work Taplin has an article upon the Water Spaniel, he gives precisely the same description of it as he did in an earlier portion of his work of the Water-dog. The illustrations, however, as our readers will observe, are widely different, and we give both so that they can compare them for themselves. His descriptions of the two breeds being so similar, there is very little worth referring to in Taplin's article on the Water Spaniel, though the reference he makes in the following passage to the dog's appearance in our opinion refers far more probably to the Water-dog than Water Spaniel as they are depicted in his book. He alludes to "the rough and awkward appearance," as well as to the "strong and unpleasant effluvia issuing from the shaggy coat," of the Water Spaniel. Now, there is nothing that we can see in the illustration which he gives of the Water Spaniel that would lead one to think that the breed was awkward in appearance, but the illustration of the Water-dog would certainly have that effect. It is, therefore, we think, more than likely that Taplin was a little confused in his ideas upon these breeds, as the fact that he gives a different illustration but an identical description for each breed shows he was to a certain extent at fault in his endeavour to dissociate the Water-dog from the Water Spaniel. We cannot help being of the opinion that at the time John Scott wrote there were two varieties of Water-dog, both of which were descended from the old variety alluded to under different titles by Caius and Nicholas Cox, and that these subsequently were united into one variety called the Water Spaniel. There can be to our own mind no sort of a doubt that the Water-dog or Water Spaniel was largely crossed with other breeds, and as the Land Spaniel or Springer was the most popular of all sporting dogs about the commencement, he was naturally selected for the cross.

John Scott strikes out with some original ideas of his own in the "Sportsman's Repository," for he says in his work :—

"We have two varieties of the Water-dog, the one so called, the other the Water Spaniel. We cannot give consent to the common conjectures on the origin of these two divisions of the species. It has been supposed that the Water-dog has been obtained in this country from a cross between the Arctic, or Greenland dog, and an English bitch, and the Water Spaniel from the union of the Springer, or Land Spaniel, and the Water-dog. We feel more inclined to the conjecture that both these varieties are of far longer standing than the above account would seem to indicate, and that we imported our Water as well as our Land Spaniels from the southern part of Europe, and our Water-dogs from the northern. It is certain that in Spain and Italy they have ever had distinct varieties of the Land and Water Spaniel, and also that on the opposite and more northern parts of the Continent they have Water-dogs like ours, which in truth have a foreign appearance."

What object the writer had in view is hard to discover, beyond showing that, in his opinion, the Water-dog had no trace of the Greenland dog in him, for he remarks, a little further on, after he has repeated his assertion that the Water-dog was not a British crossbred dog, that there is far more probability in the supposed origin of the Water Spaniel from the Springer and the Water-dog, the Water Spaniel wearing the face and ear and somewhat of the form and air of the Springer, together with the Water-dog's curly coat; so that, at any rate, there can be but little doubt but Water Spaniels might be manufactured by such a cross.

WATER-DOG (1803), FROM THE "SPORTSMAN'S CABINET."

These views have always been our own, as it seems to us to be the most natural course for breeders to pursue, if they were anxious to improve the Water-dog. Crossing with a Spaniel would be by far the most likely means to gain them what they wanted, as the questing propensities of the latter would add to the powers of the Water-dog, who, in his turn, would increase the size, and also improve the texture of the Spaniel's coat. In our opinion, the precise origin of the Water-dog is really a small matter of importance after all, though his existence at the commencement of the century is an unquestionable fact. Still, though the Water-dog does not appear in later years in the same form as he appeared then, we believe that he is represented in the Water Spaniel, and have, therefore, been at considerable trouble to describe him fully, as he deserves to be in his position of the founder of a breed. One fact is worth remarking upon in connection with the size of the Water Spaniel of 1820, and that was, we are told, "a medium between the Springer and the

Cocker, but perhaps with more general length than the latter, as we have observed that dogs with a reasonable length, swim with greater speed." These are the words of John Scott, who seems to have been at considerable pains to gather all the information he could about this variety of dog, of whom he speaks in terms of the highest praise.

Youatt, writing in 1845, alludes to two varieties of the Water Spaniel (the Water-dog is not alluded to by him except as a reference), both of which, he says, were popular with sportsmen, though the small breed was the better liked. He describes the dog as follows, and lays special importance on his compactness of form :—" His head is long, his face

WATER SPANIEL, FROM THE "SPORTSMAN'S CABINET."

smooth, and his limbs—more developed than those of the Springer—should be muscular, his carcase round, and his hair long and closely curled."

Youatt further on confirms the impressions of John Scott as regards the original importation into this country of the Water Spaniel, for he says "the Water Spaniel was originally from Spain, but the pure breed has been lost, and the present dog is probably descended from the large Water-dog and the English Setter." It must be remembered that in the very early part of the present century the Setter was in its infancy as a breed, and that the Spaniel was commoner, and more highly valued, and the more likely, therefore, to be adopted for the cross. As Youatt does not give his authority for the statement that the Water-dog was originally imported into the country, it may be taken as highly probable that he adopted the idea which had been previously published by Scott, who, it is very likely, in his turn, derived his ideas from Dr. Caius's work.

CHAPTER LVIII.

THE ENGLISH WATER SPANIEL.

UNFORTUNATELY the old English Water Spaniel has of late years practically ceased to exist as a breed, though isolated specimens are occasionally met with in out-of-the-way parts of the country. This is greatly to be deplored, as the extinction of any variety is generally deplored by naturalists, and the loss to sportsmen of so valuable a breed is a matter of considerable moment. We think it is very probable that the extra attention which Retrievers have been paid recently, has done a great deal towards injuring the position of the English Water Spaniel; but it is beyond a doubt, putting theory on one side, that the Irish Water Spaniel has, of late years, made ground in this country where his English relative has lost it. We do not mean it to be taken that the Irish Water Spaniel is in the position he should be, either here or in his own country, but it is a fact that he has not fared so badly, or sunk so low as the English Spaniel has done, and it is to be hoped that he never will find himself in so bad a condition.

The Water Spaniel, however, was at one time highly estimated in this country, where his many virtues were fully recognised by sportsmen who felt the want of a good dog in the pursuit of game. An admirable description of the Water Spaniel is given by Dr. John Caius in his " Englishe Dogges," and the worthy author devotes a considerable portion of his space to this breed. His description of it is as follows :—

"Of the Dogge called the water Spaniell, or finder,

"in Latine *Aquaticus seuinquisitor.*

"That kinde of dogge whose seruice is required in fowling vpon the water, partly through a naturall towardnesse, and partly by diligent teaching, is indued with that property. This sort is somewhat bigge, and of a measurable greatnesse, hauing long, rough, and curled heare, not obtayned by extraordinary trades, but giuen by natures appointment, yet neuerthelesse (friend *Gesner*) I have described and set him out in this maner, namely powlde and notted from the shoulders to the hindermost legges, and to the end of his tayle, which I did for use and customs cause, that beyng as it were made somewhat bare and naked, by shearing of such superfluitie of heare, they might atchiue the more lightnesse, and swiftnesse, and be lesse hindered in swymming, so troublesome and needelesse a burthen being shaken of. This kinde of dogge is properly called *Aquaticus*, a water spaniel because he frequenteth and hath vsual recourse to the water where all his game & exercise lyeth, namely, waterfowles, which are taken by the help & service of them, in their kind. And principally duckes and drakes, whereupon he is lykewise named a dogge for the ducke, because in that qualitie he is excellent. With these dogges also we fetch out of the water such fowle as be stounge to death by any venemous worme, we vse them also to bring vs our boultes and arrowes out of the water (missing our marcke) whereat we directed our leuell, which otherwise we should hardly recouer, and oftentimes the restore to vs our shaftes which we thought neuer to see, touche or handle againe, after they were lost, for which circumstaunces they are called *Inquisitores*, searchers, and finders. Although the ducke otherwhiles notably deceaueth both the dogge and the master, by dyuing vnder the water, and also by naturall subtilty, for if any man shall approche to the place where they builde, breede, and syt, the hennes go out of their neastes, offering themselues voluntarily to the hands, as it were, of such as draw nie their neastes. And a certaine weaknesse of their winges pretended, and infirmitie of their feete dissembled, they go so slowly and so leasurely, that to a mans thinking it were no masteryes to take them. By which deceiptfull tricke they doe as it were entyse and allure men to follow them, till they be drawne a long distaunce from theyr neastes, which being compassed by their prouident conning, or conning providence they cut of all incon-ueniences which might growe of their returne, by using many carefull and curious caucates, least theyr often haunting bewray ye place where the young ducklings be hatched. Great therefore is theyr desire, & earnest is theyr study to take heede, not only to theyr broode but also to themselues. For when they haue an ynkling that they are espied they hide themselves vnder turfes or sedges, wherewith they couer and shrowde themselues so closely and so craftely, that (notwithstanding the place where they lurke be found and perfectly perceaued) there they will harbour without harme, except the water spaniell by quicke smelling discouer theyr deceiptes."

The Doctor's allusion to the "long, rough and curled heare not obtayned by extra-ordinary trades," is proof positive that, even in the halcyon days of the sixteenth century, dogs were subjected to manipulation in order that their appearance might be improved; and that the custom of shaving off superfluous hair is not by any means the modern institution which some suppose it to be. The remarks which accompany the description given of the dog are useful in showing that even in those early days the qualities of the Water Spaniel were highly estimated by sportsmen, and that the dog was used to retrieve wounded birds in the times of the Good Queen Bess.

It may possibly appear to some of our readers that the above quotation from the writings of Dr. Caius might have appeared more appropriately in immediate juxtaposition with the ex-tracts we have selected from other writers who succeeded him. It, however, appeared to us that as the description given by Dr. Caius was the earliest which was published, it would be preferable to let it appear in the Water-Spaniel chapter, as our readers would then have a better opportunity for comparing his views with those of modern dog authorities. It cannot be maintained that the above description at all represents the accompanying illustration of the Water Spaniel, according to the views of the author of the "Sportsman's Cabinet;" but it must be remembered that modern opinions coincide much more nearly with the opinions of Dr. Caius than of the later writer, and we have before hinted that in our opinion the frequent crossing of the Water-dog and Spaniel is beyond all question.

In fact, the origin of the later English Water Spaniel may, we think, be very readily traced to the Water-dog and Spaniel, and the words of Youatt, which were quoted in the chapter on Water Spaniels, were no doubt meant to refer to this dog by the writer when he produced his work. As this theory seems to be generally accepted, it may be almost worth while suggesting that steps might be taken to resuscitate the breed, and, if a few fair specimens of the old type could be secured, we have no doubt that it could be done, and that it would be a profitable undertaking for the breeder. As in the case of other things, the loss of the English Water Spaniel has awakened sportsmen to a sense of his value, and regrets at his absence are often heard at dog shows, where the meagreness of the classes for Water Spaniels, other than Irish, almost invariably are a fruitful cause for discussion. In support of these views, we give the following notes from the pen of Mr. A. W. Langdale, who writes :—

" This old-fashioned favourite of both farmer and squire, whose appearance on the show bench is now so rare, that when he does come out of his shell he is passed over for what modern judges say is the correct thing, and our parti-coloured dog is left out in the cold. Colour has not all to do with it; feathering, make, and shape are things to be looked to, especially the former, as it would be impossible for the winners in late years at Birmingham, with all their wool and flew, to go through a day or night's work. To my idea, no Spaniel shows more sport than the English Water. He is artful, careful, and, above all, not too noisy ; slipped from the punt or shed it is long odds against the wounded mallard, so good are they in nose, and so unceasing are they in their endeavours to please. I give you a copy of what they wrote in 1846, so that your readers may learn that feather, whole colour, shortness of leg, and carriage of stern are not, if in other breeds, the essential qualities of an English Water Spaniel. Before, however, commencing, I may state that the subject of the quotation is Flush, a liver-coloured bitch, bred by H. G. Dawson, Esq., of Geldeston, Norfolk, about 1840, whose praises were thus sung in a sporting magazine :—' Her extraordinary prowess in recovering wounded game has been allowed by first-rate judges never to have been excelled, keeping directly on the line of the fallen bird in spite of whatever fresh game may arise before her, and ready to shake a rat to death in a minute, and bring a jack snipe alive the next. But besides this, what is prettier in look, merrier at work, and more even in temper, as much at home at the fireside as the brook, an equal favourite with lord or lady, than the Spaniel ? What more of one who hunts up his game with a dash and an earnestness, with a half-suppressed challenge, and a gradually increasing importance that makes shooting almost as exciting as hunting ? Of one who if he does occasionally, in his energy, sin against the strict letter and the law of the field, still errs on the right side, and who takes his correction so humbly, and then goes to work as if naught had happened ?'

"Young breeders and judges should have before them this fact, that colour should be a secondary matter with the English Water Spaniel, and the latter should never pass over a liver-and-white dog in favour of a whole-coloured liver, providing the liver-and-white is a well-made specimen of his breed. The weight again should not exceed forty pounds, and his height 19 in. ; his ears may be fairly long, and covered all over with curl, also the body, not the close curl of his Irish brother, but one somewhat looser and more straggly ; his head is broad and long, with a piercing eye ; his legs are well-feathered behind as well as in front, and there is no doubt that the feather which in a ticked dog comes out from each and every liver spot in front of the fore leg, has a great deal to do with his power of endurance in water. They may be called natural retrievers, as no dog is easier taught."

Very little need be added to Mr. A. W. Langdale's description of a now almost-extinct variety, which, though not absolutely lost beyond recall, is so scattered throughout the length and breadth of the land that great difficulty would be experienced by any enthusiasts who endeavoured to rescue it from obliteration. If, however, a few persevering persons were to take the matter up, we can only repeat what we have said before, when we expressed the opinion that the task would ultimately prove remunerative, and we should greatly like to see the attempt made if it were properly conducted.

Unlike the Irish Water Spaniel, the breed in question should have no top-knot, and a cross of blood may thus be detected easily. He is higher on the leg and larger in the foot than the land Spaniel, and, unlike his Irish cousin, the English Water Spaniel usually has his tail shortened considerably.

A comparison of Mr. A. W. Langdale's description with the illustration given in the preceding chapter, will tend to prove that the old English Water Spaniel, as portrayed in the illustration, was a different kind of dog to that of more recent years. In our opinion it is very probable that the first promoters of a cross between the Water-dog and Spaniel soon discovered that they were getting too open a coat in their dogs, and that the latter could not so well resist the cold and exposure to the wet as the more curly-coated varieties. To remedy this a more liberal infusion of Water-dog blood was no doubt subsequently introduced, and this may have occurred after the illustration which we reprint was published. Youatt's description, which we also referred to in the last chapter, certainly describes the coat of the Water Spaniel as being "closely curled," and this, we think, makes our view of the case still more probable. Later illustrations, too, which have appeared in earlier works on the dog, almost all depict the English Water Spaniel as being very curly in his coat, and showing more of the Water-dog character, and this is clearly discernible in his head, which is blunter and heavier than that of the early illustration which we have given of the Water Spaniel as existing early in the century.

In treating of this breed we have found it a matter of difficulty to draw up a scale which entirely meets our views, but after considerable reflection we have determined upon the following as a

STANDARD OF POINTS FOR JUDGING ENGLISH WATER SPANIELS.

	Value.
Head	5
Ears and eyes	5
Shoulder and chest	5
Body	10
Feet and legs	5
Loins	5
Coat	10
General appearance	5
Total	50

CHAPTER LIX.

THE IRISH WATER SPANIEL.

THE Irish Water Spaniel was at one time supposed to exist in two varieties, viz., the dog from the North of Ireland, and the dog from the South. The former was described as being short in ear, curly in coat, but bare in his legs, and generally liver-and-white. The latter possessed long ears, and a curly coat; his colour was deep liver, and, in fact, he resembled the dogs shown as Irish Water Spaniels in the present day far more closely than the first-mentioned variety. Whether or no the North-country Irish Water Spaniel was a pure and distinct variety it is very hard to say, for our own part we feel disposed to believe that he was not, and the fact of his colour being what it was said to be has much to do with the impressions we have formed. From the descriptions given of him, it is in our opinion more than probable that the Poodle had a large share in his production, and if this is the case the character of the dog as he now exists would undoubtedly be lost. The extreme shortness of his ears, moreover, is a difficulty which believers in the dog from the North of Ireland must find hard to get over, as a decided feature in the appearance of a pure-bred Irish Water Spaniel is the great length of his ears, which often measure upwards of two feet from tip to tip.

Mr. Justin M'Carthy's breed of Irish Water Spaniels was at one time the most widely known and highly treasured strain in existence, and, in fact, most of the best dogs of latter days are descendants of his famous kennel. Mr. M'Carthy contributed an article to the *Field* newspaper on the subject of the Irish Water Spaniel in general and his own strain in particular, which has been referred to by all subsequent writers, a summary of which is as follows :—The Irish Water Spaniel should be from twenty-one to twenty-two and a half inches high (seldom higher when pure-bred), head capacious, forehead prominent, with his muzzle and head from the eyes downward smooth ; ears from twenty-four to twenty-six inches from point to point. There should be a distinct top-knot on his head, which comes down his forehead in a peak. The body should be covered with crisp curls, and the tail round and stiff. The colour, a puce liver, with no white. In Mr. Justin M'Carthy's own words, "They will not stand a cross with any other breed ; the Spaniel, Setter, Newfoundland Dog, and Labrador Dog, &c., perfectly destroy coat, tail, ears, and symmetry, added to which the cross-bred dog is very difficult to dry. If any cross would answer, I should say the Bloodhound would give at least head and ears and nose." Mr. M'Carthy also adds, "It is essential for gentlemen purchasing puppies to see both sire and dam, as in this breed it is very easy to be imposed upon in a young one. The true breed has become very scarce, and, although very hardy when grown up, they are very delicate as puppies."

As in the case of the Irish Setter, a controversy has taken place with reference to the colour of the Irish Water Spaniel. At some of the earlier shows the judges undoubtedly awarded prizes to dogs with white upon them, and this brought out several angry letters from gentlemen who were of the opinion that white markings are disqualifications in a dog of this variety, as they are unfailing tests of impurity of blood. This seems to prove that there could have been little in common between the old North of Ireland Spaniel and the South of Ireland dog. It may be that the former had some of the old English Water Spaniel in his composition which his relative was deficient in, or that he was in reality a cross of the Spaniel formerly identified with the Southern districts of the Emerald Isle; but, whatever the truth of the case may be, one fact remains—and that is, that in the present day no Irish Water Spaniel who is disfigured with white markings can stand a chance of success in competing with the whole-coloured puce liver-coloured specimens. Patches of white upon the body, chest, or legs, and streaks up the face, are now looked upon as disqualifications in show competition, and care should be taken by intending purchasers to avoid all dogs so marked. It should be borne in mind that staining has been resorted to by unprincipled dealers in order to deceive their customers before concluding a deal. There is, however, a very great chance of many purely-bred sires and dams begetting puppies who show white markings, and it would be the height of folly for breeders or sportsmen to destroy such progeny merely because they were by reason of these white markings unlikely to win prizes on the show bench. A marked dog, if purely bred, is just as likely to produce whole-coloured stock as his or her relations who are self-coloured, and therefore it is always desirable to save all puppies, and give the "splashed" ones that chance of distinguishing themselves at the stud which from force of circumstances is denied them on the bench. If, after a good chance has been given them, it should still happen that their stock is marked with white, the case becomes altered, and no further use of their services would be made by experienced or careful breeders who had the reputation of their strain at heart.

We have been fortunate enough to obtain the following notes from the pen of Mr. J. S. Skidmore, of Nantwich, who is one of the leading and most successful breeders of the Irish Water Spaniel in the present day. The remarks made by Mr. Skidmore upon the breaking of this class of dog we most earnestly impress upon our readers, for personal observation has convinced us that hundreds of dogs of all breeds, who display a natural aptitude for retrieving, are annually ruined by injudicious treatment when they are young. Mr. Skidmore writes:—

"Much has been said, and much more written, about the Irish Water Spaniel. Some have called him hard-mouthed and headstrong, and consequently of no use in the field; whilst others have said that where a person only keeps one dog, and expects him to be a Jack of all trades, there is nothing like an Irish Water Spaniel. I incline to the latter opinion, as, when thoroughly trained, they will stand as steady as a Setter on game, retrieving the dead or wounded as tenderly as possible; whilst for wild-fowl retrieving I think it is admitted that they have no equal. Their coats being of an oily nature, are well adapted to resist the cold and wet, whilst their natural courage is such that they fearlessly dash into the water in the coldest weather. I admit that I have seen a number of them that have been hard-mouthed, but upon inquiry I have generally been able to attribute this failing to their defective education. Being very companionable dogs, full of fun and frolic, ever wishing to do something to please their master and show their abilities, they are often taught to carry anything that comes to hand—a stick or stone, for instance, being thrown repeatedly for the puppy to retrieve. If this is done, it will surely cause the dog to be hard-mouthed, but if he is allowed only to carry articles that are soft, such as a glove, a rabbit-skin stuffed with hay, or an air-ball, when he comes to be trained to retrieve game he will be tender-mouthed.

"There used to be three different strains or varieties of this breed. One, now, I believe almost lost, termed the Tweed Irish Water Spaniel, I have tried repeatedly to get information respecting the way it had been produced, but always failed to trace them further than about two generations. But from their appearance, close coat, sparseness of feather, and style of head, I always thought that there was a dash of Bloodhound in their veins, which was strengthened by the fact that when I have bred from them with dogs of the M'Carthy type they have often thrown pups with tan feet, cheeks, and vents. Their heads are, or were, conical, lips heavily flewed, ears set on Bloodhound-like, whilst they were all light in colour. The second variety, which, I believe, also is nearly extinct, were about twenty inches high, short-legged— which, by the way, were often crooked—longish-bodied, close-coated, feathered only at the back of the fore-legs, ears short and without feather, looking more like a bad specimen of a liver-coloured Retriever.

"The third is known as the M'Carthy or south country dog, the gentleman with whose name they stand associated having done much to bring the dog to perfection, and having succeeded in an admirable manner. At the same time, it must be admitted that the head of a good specimen of to-day is far before the coarse truncated muzzle which Mr. M'Carthy's dogs possessed, and which has only been got rid of within the last dozen years. I always thought it gave the dogs a morose and sullen appearance.

"It has been recently stated in the papers that he is at home when hunting coverts, but the opinion of the late Justin M'Carthy that they do not like strong thorny brakes, although they do not object to open coverts, coincides with my experience of them; for although their courage will make them dash into the roughest place, their ears, being heavily feathered, catch in the thorns to such an extent that I have seen them unable to extricate themselves; added to which, they are too big a dog for that work.

"The dogs of this breed stand usually about twenty-two or twenty-three inches high; bitches an inch or two inches lower. The head is capacious, giving plenty of brain room; the forehead is more raised than in most Spaniels.

"The *Face*, from the eyes downward, is perfectly smooth; a moustache shows Poodle blood.

"The *Eyes* should be a dark rich brown; not light gooseberry eyes, which are always accompanied by a coat which is yellow rusty-looking when in full feather.

"The *Ears* should be about eighteen inches in flesh—measuring across the head—and from twenty-four to twenty-six inches in hair, from point to point; but a very good specimen will exceed this. My Old Doctor, when shown at the Crystal Palace for the last time, measured thirty inches.

"The *Top-knot*, which is a characteristic feature of the dog, covers the top of the head, falling forward towards the face. But when the hair is lifted up, it should be found at its base to come down to a point above the eyes, instead of right across the forehead like that of a Poodle.

"The *Body* should be covered with close curls; but for several months before moulting time, the curls gradually fall together, until, if the coat is not attended to, it forms thick mats; whilst if a breeder is wise enough to shear these off, and the new coat is not properly developed, some ignoramus who sees him in this state will at once denounce him in the public press as 'not pure bred,' when a few months before he has been in perfect coat, and in two or three months will again be so.

"The *Fore-legs* should be straight, and well feathered all round. The feet of my dogs are very much smaller than we used to see; I got the small foot in my strain with the Old

IRISH WATER SPANIEL.

Duck cross. The hind-legs should be well bent in the stifle; hocks well let down, well feathered to the hocks, below that smooth in front, but feathered behind.

"The *Tail* is rather short and free from feather, thick at the root, and tapering to a sting; a dog with a feathered tail shows cross breeding somewhere.

"In *Build* they should be strong, not flat-sided, but ribs well sprung, with moderately deep chest, which should not be too wide or it will interfere with his speed in swimming.

"In *Colour* they should be a very dark *puce* liver, not a sandy-coloured liver, and free from white. I am not going so far as some who have written about the breed, and say that a dog with a little white on the chest or across a toe, or toes, is impure in breeding, for in nearly every litter there are some with a small white star, which must of necessity be as pure as their more fortunate brothers who were pupped clear of white."

There is not much that can be added to Mr. J. S. Skidmore's description of the breed, for he has, we think, contrived to lay his views before our readers with singular lucidity. We do not, however, much admire an extremely small foot in a dog whose duties compel him to pass a considerable portion of his time in the water. As far as our personal experience goes, a large dog—such as the Irish Water Spaniel really is—is benefited by large feet, which, acting as paddles when he swims, must naturally afford a greater resistance to the water than small ones could possibly do, and we therefore should prefer the larger foot, of course on the understanding that they are properly formed and clothed with hair. A peculiarity with regard to the coat may also be alluded to by us, and that is where it appears on the fore-legs. These should not only be well feathered on the back and sides, but should be abundantly provided with small crisp curls in front, which has the effect of causing them to appear very much stouter than they really are. In the case of the hind-legs, though smooth in front, they carry feather behind all the way down to the ground when the dog is in good coat; and these are points of importance which should not be lost sight of when the merits of Irish Water Spaniels have to be decided.

Amongst the best-known names in connection with this breed of dog those of the following gentlemen appear most prominently :—Mr. J. S. Skidmore, Nantwich; Mr. James Fletcher, Stoneclough; Mr. N. Morton, Ballymena; Captain E. Montressor, Bedford; Mr. W. B. Bridgett, Clapham; and the Rev. A. Willett.

The dog which we have selected for illustration as a typical specimen of the Irish Water Spaniel is (the now unfortunately late) Captain, who was the property of Mr. Hugh E. C. Beaver. Captain was never exhibited, as his owner, being devoted to travelling in foreign parts, had other uses for him. It may, however, be remarked that Captain accompanied his master twice round the world; and we have been assured by Mr. Beaver that there are sons and daughters of his old dog in almost every part of the globe. We can personally bear testimony to his grand colour, symmetry, and general quality, in addition to his good qualities in the field and his perfect behaviour in the house, all of which proved him to be in every respect worthy of representation in our pages as a thoroughly characteristic dog of his breed. Had Captain's lot been thrown in other places, we are confident that high honours would have been accorded him on the bench; but, as we have said before, his destiny lay in another direction. Unfortunately, we are unable to give his pedigree, for he came into Mr. Beaver's possession by chance and through the immediate agency of a Leadenhall Market dealer, just as his purchaser was on the eve of starting for a tour round the world.

Captain measured—Length of head, 8¼ inches; girth of muzzle, 8½ inches; girth of skull, 17 inches; girth of chest, 28 inches; girth of fore-leg, 7¾ inches; height at shoulder, 21 inches.

The following is the

STANDARD OF POINTS FOR JUDGING IRISH WATER SPANIELS.

	Value.
Head	5
Ears and eyes	5
Body and chest	10
Legs and feet	5
Loins	5
Coat	10
Colour	5
General apppearance...	5
	50

CHAPTER LX.

FOREIGN DOGS.

HAVING arrived at the conclusion of our remarks upon British dogs, we propose venturing to turn the attention of our readers to the consideration of foreign canine subjects. As almost everybody who has given the matter one moment's serious consideration must be aware, this country has gained for itself a reputation for its dogs which no other nation has hitherto attempted to question or dispute. It therefore has followed, in the natural course of events, that affairs in the canine world are in a more settled state in Great Britain than they are elsewhere, and consequently the types and standards of our various breeds have been more generally agreed upon than has been the case in other countries. That we have improved our breeds since dog shows have been matters of almost weekly occurrence, very few practical people can deny, and it is equally certain that field trials have also done much service, as they have been the direct means of bringing clever field dogs to the front. But not only have the varieties of dogs directly been benefited in the manner just alluded to, but they have also received indirect encouragement by the facilities placed before the public for comparing good dogs with bad. Foreign countries have not kept pace with us in such like matters, and consequently, even in the present day, considerable differences of opinion exist amongst Continental and other lovers of the dog upon many of their commonest breeds. Dog shows must, in the process of time, be the period long or short, have the effect of reducing the number of opposite types of every breed to a minimum, and still further must, sooner or later, assimilate the remaining ones to something approaching one definite standard. Few men would obstinately persist in exhibiting a class of dog which invariably found disfavour with the judges; and even if these authorities differ, as they often do, the voice of public opinion eventually steps in, and places one type above the other. However, of late our German cousins and our French allies have seriously taken the matter of canine exhibitions up, and much good has, we believe, already come from the exertions they have made. It would, nevertheless, be premature to discuss the question of Continental dog shows before a few more remarks have been passed upon the condition of canine matters in quarters of the world other than our own.

Before commencing, however, we must warn our readers that it should be borne in mind that many nations possess varieties of dogs which are practically unknown in this country, but which are peculiarly adapted to their native climes. From the Esquimaux dog of Greenland to the Dingo of Australia it is a very wide leap, and in his travels the lover of the dog will not only find much to interest and amuse, but also a great deal to surprise him. In short, we English must not parade the virtues of our native dogs too fully before the world until we feel assured that, under altered circumstances of climate and of fare, our tykes would do as well as those we secretly despise, simply because we do not properly appreciate their worth. Foreign sportsmen know for the most part what they require without much help from us, though we must fain confess that the exportation of English sporting dogs to France and

Germany has considerably increased of late; but this, we think, is greatly due to the institution of dog shows in these countries, and the belief that for looks, at least, the English dogs must carry off the palm. In discussing the comparative merits of English and German Pointers with a Continental authority at the Hanover dog show of 1879, he remarked to us: "Your English Pointers have too great pace for our work—at all events, to my idea it is so—and I shall try a cross between some staunch native dogs I own, with some I have imported from England, so as to get the best qualities of both." Such words might horrify Mr. Price or Mr. Whitehouse, who have done so much for English Pointers, but still they were used by a thorough sportsman, who knows a dog, and who was almost English Setter mad at the time he spoke, as he was determined to do wonders at some forthcoming field trials with some specimens of the latter breed which he had recently imported. We have merely alluded to the above conversation as tending to corroborate our own idea that, though the English may possess, as we have no hesitation in affirming they do, the best dogs in the world, taken collectively, it is quite possible for our crack breeds to be inferior to Continental dogs under the altered circumstances in which they find themselves placed.

We have before shown, in the course of what has gone before, that many of our principal varieties of dog have sprung from Continental sources, and that even of recent years the Dachshund and the Basset Hound have taken root amongst us, and therefore it is only reasonable that we from our abundance should in our turn supply our neighbours' canine wants. It is not with this subject, however, that we have now to deal, for we propose treating of the principal varieties of dog as best we can, and with every desire to do the breeds justice. The task which is set before us is, nevertheless, we regret to find, one which is beset with many difficulties, for the very reason which we have already alluded to—the variance of opinion which exists between Continental authorities upon many points. Dog shows have not yet had time to do their work, and bring about that concordance of ideas which all true lovers of the dog so cordially desire, and consequently, in many instances, our correspondence and conversations with eminent breeders have not been fruitful in the good results we anticipated that they would have been. Many a pitfall for the unwary has been dug by the dealers of every country (and it must be said that our own are not at all behind in this respect when selling dogs to foreigners), and the inferior specimens of every breed which are perpetually crossing the sea in every direction have only succeeded in making the natural obscurity which exists more thoroughly developed. A stranger desirous of purchasing dogs in a, to him, totally unknown country, can have but little chance of getting what he wants, if in the search of pure-bred stock, unless he has secured an introduction to some brother lover of the canine race who will help him in his search. Apocryphal breeds, too, have been sprung upon the world, which, though they find but little favour at home, have, by dint of the "writing up" which they have received in foreign sporting papers, been recognised abroad as pure and valuable varieties. Having, therefore, had so much to contend against ourselves in our search for information, which was certainly prosecuted under peculiarly favourable circumstances, we have only done our duty in warning our readers of the risks they run, and trust that our experiences may prove of service to them, in saving them from being taken in by what they hear from interested parties.

Allusion having been already made to foreign dog shows, we will endeavour to briefly sketch their method of procedure. In America, as in England, two, or at the most three judges officiate in a class, and in many instances single-handed judging is the order of the day. On the Continent all is different, for, with the exception of the classes for British dogs, which are usually added as special attractions, and which are judged by English judges, the decisions are entrusted to a jury of arbitrators, who appear to decide upon the merits of the respective dogs by a method peculiarly their own. For instance, at the great Hanover dog show of 1879, to which reference has been already made, the jury, consisting of a number of gentlemen, were in the habit of retiring into a small pavilion after they had seen the class, and of talking the matter over without the dogs before them. The precise object that could be gained by this we confess we cannot see, as in close competition it must be nearly impossible to sum up the merits of a number of dogs ; and no further opportunities were offered of seeing the competitors together. With this exception in the mode of judging, the English method of conducting shows has been pretty closely followed, and several other foreign exhibitions have subsequently been judged in the English style, and with, we think, happier results.

With the growth of foreign shows a better knowledge of foreign dogs must certainly be gained, as upon the occasion of every one, some good dog or other is certain to be brought back by at least one English visitor to the exhibition. An immediate effect of this is to increase the number of entries in the " Foreign Classes " at our shows, until one breed after another gets strong enough to have a class provided for itself alone. As matters now stand, there may be seen at leading shows, all huddled together in one class, Esquimaux dogs, Swedish Beagles, Chinese dogs of various breeds, Japanese Pugs, Persian Greyhounds, Dingoes, Thibet Mastiffs, Siberian Wolfhounds, and, up to very recently, Boarhounds or German Mastiffs, and French Basset Hounds. Other foreign breeds have also been shown, but not so frequently as the above ; and, in fact, the German Schweiss Hund and many varieties of French hounds are quite unknown to the majority of English dog-lovers, whilst to the mere frequenters of our shows their very names are unfamiliar. It will therefore be clearly seen that there is a great opening in the foreign classes for lovers of the dog who are possessed of enterprising temperaments, and who are gifted with a sufficient amount of shrewdness to enable them to resist the importunities of every foreign dealer who has a dog to sell a stranger, for which he knows there is no hopes of finding a customer in his native land. Purchasers, moreover, should be careful in importing specimens into this country, to satisfy themselves, if possible, that the animals selected are capable of producing offspring if it is desired to form a kennel. We know of several gentlemen who have been wofully disappointed in animals which they have brought from far-off countries at great trouble and expense. It may be stated that instances are believed to have occurred where animals, destined for the English market by their owners, have been previously subjected to operations with the object of preventing them from reproducing their species ; and this has doubtless been done in the hope that future deals may be transacted between the parties, as detection is in certain instances very difficult.

CHAPTER LXI.

THE ESQUIMAUX DOG.

THE various uses to which different foreign nations put their dogs altogether prohibit any attempts at classification of the breeds by us. We therefore purpose commencing with the canine inhabitants of the Northern latitudes, and select the Esquimaux Dog for consideration in this chapter.

It is an indisputable fact that this dog has been, almost from time immemorial, more intimately associated with the daily life of his master, during the greater portion of the year, than any other breed has been. It is therefore not surprising that, when specimens of the Esquimaux dog have appeared in this country they have attracted considerable attention. About 1876, Mr. Howard Mapplebeck, of Knowle, near Birmingham, was in the possession of a very good specimen in Zouave, but since that period other dogs of the variety have appeared who have put Zouave into the shade.

Considerable attention seems to have been directed to the Esquimaux dog early in this century, for Taplin, writing in 1803, in the "Sportsman's Cabinet," devotes a considerable portion of his space to his remarks upon this breed. We reproduce some portion of his article, as it will be found to be of considerable interest when read in conjunction with the views of Mr. Walter K. Taunton, who is now considered one of the highest modern authorities on uncommon varieties of foreign dogs.

Taplin writes thus of the "Greenland Dog":—

"The animal passing under this denomination is but little known in this country, and the only authentic particulars respecting their origin and ability seem to center in the productions of Captain Cooke and King, collaterally corroborated by various writers of somewhat less celebrity. This, and the Kamtschadale dog are said to vary but lightly in figure, strength, and appearance, though they differ a little upon the score of pliability and education. The Greenland dog has greatly the predominance of a wolfish aspect, and, at the first view, seems admirably calculated to excite the emotions of alarm. They are mostly much beyond the line of mediocrity in size, are usually white, with a black face, not unfrequently pyebald, rarely all brown, or black, but sometimes entirely white; they have sharp noses, hair thick and wavy, inclining to a twisty curl, short ears, and an oblique curvature in the tail; a discordant hoarseness in vociferating, which is more of a disquieted howl than an attempt to bark. These dogs sleep abroad, forming an excavated bed in the snow, from whence but merely the nose appears above it. They swim most admirably, and will hunt individually, or in a body, the Arctic fox, seals on the ice, and the Polar bear: in the latter of which they are used by the natives; they are universally admitted to be excessively fierce, and, in the manner of wolves, fly upon any of the few domestic animals which have been carried into that country. They are so instinctively courageous, and so invincibly persevering, that they will fight, even to death, among themselves; and it may be seriously considered a most fortunate circumstance for the inhabitants that canine madness, or hydrophobia, are neither of them ever known in regions of so much frigidity. Yet it is somewhat remarkable that in Sweden madness sometimes seizes the wolf, and the consequences are frequently dreadful; the symptoms are the same with those attendant upon the madness of a dog; fury sparkles in their eyes, a viscid ropy saliva drivels from the mouth, the tail is carried low, and they are always equally disposed to bite either man or beast; but as this disease happens mostly in the depth of winter, it cannot, of course, be attributed to the raging heat of the dog-days.

" It is by different writers considered singular that the race of European dogs show an antipathy as strong to the Kamtschatkan and American species as to the wolf itself. They never meet but the European dogs show all signs of dislike, will fall on and worry them; whilst the wolfish breed, with every mark of timidity, endeavours to avoid the others' rage. This aversion to the wolf is natural to the whole canine species; and it is a matter generally known, that a whelp who has never seen a wolf will, at first sight, tremble, and make to its master for protection; but an old dog will instantly attack it. It is well authenticated that the dogs of Kamtschatka are of wolfish descent, for wolves abound in that country, in all parts of Siberia, and even under the Arctic circle; their colour is black-and-white, they are strong and active, and are used for drawing sledges over the frozen snow. They are in size and shape little different from the large Russian Boor-dogs, and are held to be the best and most long-winded runners of all the dogs in Siberia. So incredibly great is their spirit, that they frequently dislocate their joints in drawing; and their hair is often tinged with red, from the extravasation of blood occasioned by violent exertions. The ordinary loading of four dogs amounts to five or six poods, and a single man can in this manner, in bad roads, go thirty or forty, but, in good roads, eighty to a hundred and forty versts in a day. The taste for dogs is as great here as it is for horses elsewhere, and considerable sums are not unfrequently expended in the purchase of them, and the elegance of their trappings.

" The natives of this peninsula always travel in sledges. The length of the body of the sledge is about four feet and a half, and the breadth one foot; it is made in the form of a crescent, of light tough wood, fastened together with wicker-work, and those of the principal people are elegantly stained with red and blue, the seat being covered with furs, or bear-skins. It has four legs, about two feet in height, resting on two flat long pieces of wood, of the breadth of five or six inches, which extend a foot beyond the body of the sledge at each end. These turn up before, something like a skate, and are shod with the bone of some sea animal. The carriage is ornamented at the fore part with tassels of coloured cloth and leather thongs. It has a cross-bar, to which the harness is joined; and links of iron or small bells are hanging to it, which, by the jingling, is supposed to encourage the dogs. They seldom carry more than one person at a time, who sits aside, with his feet on the sledge, having his baggage and provisions in a bundle behind him. The usual number of dogs employed in drawing this carriage is four, though they very lately have begun to use five. The reins being fastened to the collar, instead of the head, have no great command, and are, therefore, usually hung upon the sledge, the driver depending principally upon their obedience to his voice. Great care and attention are consequently used in training up the leader, which frequently becomes very valuable on account of his steadiness and docility, the sum of 40 roubles (or £10) being no unusual price for one of them. The driver has also a crooked stick, answering the purpose of both stick and reins, with which, by striking in the snow, he can regulate the speed of the dogs, or even stop them at pleasure. When they are inattentive to their duty, he often chastises them by throwing it at them. The dexterity of the drivers in picking this stick up again is very remarkable, and is the most difficult manœuvre in the exercise of their profession.

"The Greenlanders, though they derive such manifest advantages from the strength and activity of their dogs, are by no means kinder masters than the Kamtschatkans; they leave their dogs to provide for themselves upon mussels, berries, and whatever food they can pick up, unless after a large capture of seals, when they treat them with the blood and garbage. These people sometimes eat their dogs, and feed them for that purpose; they have their skins also for coverlets and for clothing, as well as to border and seam their habits; and from the intestines of the animals their finest thread is made. The Greenlanders fasten to their sledges from four to ten dogs, and they will with this carriage get over the ice, laden with their masters and five or six heavy seals, fifteen German or sixty English miles a day. Five of these dogs, that had escaped with their trappings, were found in Greenland, and brought to this country a few years since by one of our ships employed in the fishery. Of their expedition Captain King relates that a courier with despatches, drawn by them, performed a journey of 270 miles in four days; their fidelity, however, is not highly praised, and not seldom do they plague their masters with their malignant stratagems. The sledges are usually drawn by five dogs (though more are occasionally added when circumstances require it), and will readily carry three persons, with their baggage, fifty, or even sixty English miles a day. When the vehicle is drawn by five dogs, four of them are yoked two and two abreast; the odd one, who is placed before, acts as a leader, the reins being fastened to a collar round his neck, but which is of trifling service in their direction, as (before observed) the driver depending chiefly upon their obedience to his voice, by which alone, with the assisting flourish of his stick, he animates them to proceed. We are informed, by different writers upon this subject, that some nations, remote from the more polished and enlightened parts of the world, approve the canine species as food, and esteem a fat dog a proportional delicacy."

Twenty years later John Scott enlarges somewhat upon the views of Taplin, and adds to the halo of romance which enshrouded the Esquimaux dog by giving some curious views concerning his possible origin. We need hardly say that we do not go very far with him in his theories, or that the idea of the Pug cross is, in our opinion, simply ridiculous when seriously considered. However, it is only fair to let the author of the "Sportsman's Repository" give his views in his own words, which are—

"The Arctic or Greenland dog appears to be the indigenous wild dog of the hyperborean regions, unchanged with respect to his breed by human art, and abandoned during a part of the year to his native liberty. His upright ears, sharp muzzle, and shaggy coat, seem to denote a wolfish origin, whilst in his compact form, short quarter, and curled tail, he resembles the Dutch Pug. The origin of the breed may, with probability, be referred to a conjunction between the wolf, water-dog, and the native northern Pug."

Youatt, in his work, gives the following quotation from Captain Parry, the famous Arctic explorer, concerning the duties of these dogs. "A number of dogs, varying from six to twelve, are attached to each sledge by means of a single trace, but with no reins. An old and tried dog is placed as the leader, who, in their simple journeys, and when the chase is the object, steadily obeys the voice of the driver sitting in the front of the sledge, with a whip long enough to reach the leader. This whip, however, is used as seldom as possible; for these dogs, though tractable, are ferocious, and will endure little correction. When the whip is applied with severity on one, he falls upon and worries his neighbour, and he, in his turn, attacks a third, or the dogs double from side to side to avoid the whip, and the traces become entangled and the safety of the sledge endangered." Youatt remarks:—

"Each of these dogs will draw a weight of 120 pounds over the snow at the rate of seven or eight miles an hour. In summer many of these dogs are used as beasts of burden,

ESQUIMAUX DOG "SIR JOHN FRANKLIN," PROPERTY OF MR. W. K. TAUNTON.

and each carries from thirty to forty pounds. They are then much better kept than in the winter, for they have the remains of the whale and sea-calf which their masters disdain to eat. The majority, however, are sent adrift in the summer, and they live on the produce of the chase, or of their constant thievery. The exactness with which—the summer being passed— each returns to his master, is an admirable proof of sagacity, and frequently of attachment."

Youatt makes no allusion to the supposed wolfish origin of the Esquimaux dog, which is to be wondered at, as it had already been suggested by Scott that the wolf was, in some degree, responsible for the existence of the Esquimaux dog. It must, therefore, we think, be fairly taken that Youatt did not coincide in the theory, as, had he done so, he would assuredly have mentioned it. The quotation from Captain Parry's remarks is, we think, useful as a connecting link between the earlier and later portions of the century, and there certainly appears to have been but little change in the character of the Esquimaux dog.

With reference to the present state of the breed we are happy to be in a position to give our readers the views of Mr. Walter K. Taunton, of London, to whom we have already referred as a leading authority on foreign dogs, and whose unique collection of illustrious canine strangers has, we feel convinced, never been equalled by any in this country. Mr. Taunton writes as follows:—

"Of the various breeds of dogs inhabiting the North, the Esquimaux dog is the one best known to us, although, unfortunately, from the great difficulty in obtaining specimens of the breed, they are not often to be seen in this country. When, however, one does appear at an exhibition of dogs, it generally proves a centre of attraction to visitors, who seem fully to appreciate the opportunity of inspecting an animal of which they have frequently read, but rarely have the chance of seeing.

"There is probably no dog of such inestimable value to its owner as the Esquimaux is to the inhabitants of the Arctic regions. It would not be saying too much to say that without these dogs existence in these dreary parts would be impossible. Without them travelling would be altogether impracticable, whereas by their aid their owners are enabled to make journeys of many hundred miles. Several of these dogs are yoked to a sledge formed of boards lashed together with thongs made of deer-skin. A team of four dogs will draw, on a good track, a load of 300 or 400 lbs. a distance of thirty to thirty-five miles a day. Much depends upon the leader of the team to keep his unruly *confrères* in the proper track, the best-trained dog of the pack being always selected for this post. The hardships these animals have to undergo, and their power of endurance, is something marvellous. They are frequently treated most cruelly by their hard taskmasters, obedience being enforced by kicks and blows rather than by any attempt to attain the same end by kindness. The theory that the dog is a descendant of the wolf certainly seems to receive confirmation when we come to look at the dog of the Esquimaux breed and the wolf inhabiting the same part of the globe.

"It is a perfectly well-known fact that the wolf and the dog will breed freely together; and I have the authority of Mr. Bartlett, of the Zoological Gardens, for saying that the offspring of these animals will continue to breed—a fact which I have seen doubted by some writers. In the Esquimaux dog we have the exact type of head of the wolf; the pointed muzzle, the small erect rounded ear carried pointed forward, the treacherous expression of the eye, and the length of body, all tend to convey the idea that the Esquimaux dogs are little better than the breed of the wolf, domesticated and made subservient to man's requirements.

"By travellers these two animals have frequently been mistaken for one another, which can very readily be understood by any one who has had the opportunity of comparing the best specimens of the Esquimaux brought to this country with the Arctic wolf—lately among the valuable collection of animals belonging to the Zoological Society of London, but which is now unfortunately dead.

"The coat of this dog is perhaps the most striking characteristic of the breed: this consists of an outer coat which has the peculiarity of standing out erect, and is hard and stiff like bristles, and an under-coat, which is a beautiful soft fur. The puppies when whelped are perfectly smooth, with a glossy shiny coat like a black-and-tan terrier. The fore-legs, perfectly straight and without feather. Chest deep, rather than wide. The tail is a dense brush carried curled over the back, and in this respect, as well as size, the dog differs from the wolf, the latter being much the larger animal of the two, and not carrying the tail over the back. The average height I should take to be about 22 inches. They are to be found of various colours—pure white, black-and-white, grey, red, and other colours.

" As regards temper, I consider they will compare favourably with any other breed They are interesting companions, most affectionate, and not quarrelsome. The scarcity of bitches must necessarily make breeding Esquimaux a difficult thing, for I am unable to hear of any in this country except those I possess myself, which consist of a red bitch, Zoe, bred by one of the dogs in the Zoological Gardens, and two young ones of my own breeding by Sir John Franklin out of Zoe, from one of which I hope very shortly indeed to be able to breed. Since commencing to write this Zoe has given birth to her fourth litter of pups ; on each occasion she has whelped on the sixtieth day, and, singularly enough, the only litter I have bred from my Chinese bitch Chinese Puzzle was whelped at the end of the same time.

" In Lapland there is a breed of dogs considerably smaller than the Esquimaux, with a soft dense coat, pointed muzzle, erect ear, but much larger in proportion than that of the Esquimaux, and a closely-curled tail. They are rarely to be seen, and are obtained with difficulty. The best which has come under my notice was one exhibited at the Crystal Palace in 1880. There are dogs in Iceland much resembling this breed. I have lately seen a dog which might easily be mistaken for an inferior Esquimaux, but which, I was informed, had been brought from Sweden, where it is used in hunting the elk, keeping it at bay till the huntsman comes up.

"The Norwegian is a handsome dog about the size of a Collie, which, in some respects it resembles ; it wants the wolfish appearance of the Esquimaux, and unlike that dog, carries the ear, which is somewhat larger and more pointed, sometimes pointed forward, at other times thrown back, which the Esquimaux never does. The coat is thick and straight. I have seen them of different colours : my own dog Admiral being black mixed with grey, white chest, legs, and feet. I consider him the finest specimen I have seen at present : he was obtained for me direct from Norway by a friend who took considerable trouble to secure the best he could obtain. He was exhibited at the last Alexandra Palace show, where he was awarded a silver medal by the Rev. Grenville Hodson, and was afterwards placed first in the variety class at Margate by Mr. Lort, the only times he has been shown. He is an active, good-tempered dog, and very companionable, and the breed only wants to be introduced into this country, when I think it would very quickly become a favourite with the public."

When we read of the great services rendered to his master by the Esquimaux dog, we cannot help regretting the arbitrary and unnecessary law which prohibits the working of dogs in this country. We fully admit that the animals would be used differently to the manner in which the Esquimaux dogs are treated in their native land, but still even under the altered circumstances we fail to see why Englishmen should not be permitted to consult the dictates of their own discretion in this matter. Dogs of all sorts and sizes are used on the Continent to draw little carts, and they do not appear to dislike their tasks, or to suffer from ill-treatment. With such examples before us we are of opinion that the lot of many a dog would be made a happier one if he was allowed to make himself of service to his master, for then a number of animals who now rarely get a run would be assured of a good constitutional two or three times a week. Objections have been raised against the practice that dogs would be overworked, but this no more applies to dogs than it does to horses and the same steps which are now used to reduce the latter proceedings to a minimum might be applied when dogs are under consideration.

As Mr. Taunton has gone so thoroughly into the points and characteristics of the Esquimaux dog, we do not propose attempting to add anything to his description beyond an allusion to his grand specimen, Sir John Franklin, who is represented in the illustration which accompanies this article. He has been exhibited fifteen times, winning silver medal Alexandra Palace; first Cirencester and Farnworth; second Bristol and Brighton, 1879; silver medal Crystal Palace; first Waterloo, Margate, Dundee, and Birmingham, and second Manningtree, 1880; silver medal Alexandra Palace, and second Edinburgh, 1881.

In addition to Sir John Franklin, there are some other very good specimens of the Esquimaux dog in England, notably a couple imported by some members of the crew of the *Pandora*, exploring ship, and presented by them to the Zoological Gardens, Regent's Park, London.

AN "ALERT" SLEDGE PARTY EN ROUTE TO THE "DISCOVERY."

CHAPTER LXII.

THE SWEDISH BEAGLE.

FOLLOWING the Esquimaux and Norwegian dogs, the Swedish Beagle comes next under our consideration. Specimens of this variety are not commonly met with in Great Britain, and the subject of the accompanying illustration, Jerker, the property of Mr. Enoch Hutton, of Pudsey near Leeds, is the most successful dog of the breed which has appeared.

SWEDISH BEAGLE "JERKER," PROPERTY OF MR. ENOCH HUTTON.

Owing to their rarity in this country Swedish Beagles have excited little comment in the press, and we have found considerable difficulty in gaining much information concerning them. We have, however, been fortunate enough to meet with a Continental sportsman who professes to have had some slight acquaintance with them. This gentleman has informed us that as a rule they possess extremely good noses, and really render considerable assistance to their masters in their pursuit of game. Naturally enough they are not used for the same purposes as the English dog after whom they are christened.

The following description of a "Swedish Hare Hunt" is from the pen of Mr. Petter Niclas, of Göteborg, Sweden :—

"The number of sportsmen is generally limited to four or five guns, who, with two or three beaters and two to three couples of Beagles, early in the morning, whilst the scent is still fresh after the hares' nocturnal promenades, start off to some well-known hunting-ground. One couple of the hounds are then unleashed, and beaters and sportsmen make the woods ring with their holloas and shouts, to get 'puss' upon her legs. Ere long the hounds strike fresh scent, and off they are at full cry. The beaters then crouch down somewhere in the thicket, the guns each rushing to take up some well-known position along a pass, or crossing of some paths which the hares are known to traverse. The hare, as is well known, has the propensity of doubling or running in a circle, after returning to the very spot where she was started from her seat, and the sportsmen, therefore, have little difficulty on hunting-grounds where they know the small paths or roads of getting a shot at puss. As soon as a kill has been effected the hounds are called in, puss is butchered, and her 'principal parts'—heart, liver, head, &c.—divided between the hounds that have hunted her (which are now kept in), and a fresh couple, or three hounds, unleashed, when, a new hare being started, the game begins again. The excitement is often augmented by a sweepstake, which is pocketed by the lucky shot, and augmented by a fine for every miss. I know that seventeen head have been bagged during a forenoon's hunt. Of course, according to English ideas, it must be very wrong to pop puss over in the middle of a run; but in a thickly-wooded and rocky country like ours, it would be your only chance. A dram of brandy [Martel! * * *] after every kill is considered a very proper and necessary stimulant, and a preventive against envy, malice, and all uncharitableness."

In appearance the Swedish Beagle may be taken as somewhat closely representing a long-legged, straight-limbed Dachshund.

The *Head* is an amalgamation of the two types, Terrier and Hound, being rather wide between the ears, but still a trifle domed. The *Eyes* are soft and dark in colour. The *Muzzle* gradually tapering towards the nose. The *Ears* are very long, fine, and pendulous. The *Throat* is furnished with a double dewlap. The *Shoulders* slope towards the *Chest*, which is rather narrow. The *Fore-legs* should be placed well under the body, and should be straight, muscular, and show plenty of bone. The *Feet* are of good size, and well arched; with strong, substantial soles, so that they can stand hard work without becoming sore or tender. The *Body* is long and compact, being nicely rounded in the barrel, and well ribbed up at the loins, which should show signs of considerable strength. The *Hind-legs*, like the fore-legs, should be strong, and show plenty of bone, and be well bent at the hocks. The *Stern* is set on rather low, and is rarely carried up, as in the Foxhound. It is rather coarse, and should not taper very much towards the point. The *Coat* should be harsh, and weather-resisting, so as to enable the dog to resist the weather, which in his native country is unusually trying to man and beast. The *Colour* usually black and pale tan.

CHAPTER LXIII.

THE SCHWEISS-HUND.

IN commencing our remarks upon the German breeds of dog, we wish to take the earliest opportunity of informing our readers that, after having taken every opportunity of thoroughly going into the above question, we have decided upon only noticing four varieties in this portion of our work. The Dachshund has already been done ample justice to in former pages, as owing to his popularity in this country we elected to treat of him with the English breeds, and, therefore, we now only propose to mention the Schweiss-hund, the German Mastiff (or Boarhound), the Leonberg, and Berghund (mountain dog). The two latter breeds are unquestionably cross-breeds of modern manufacture, and will, therefore, be only referred to in the briefest possible manner, as they would not in fact deserve notice at all, but for the energetic manner in which they have been pushed forward as distinct varieties in certain interested quarters.

We will, however, commence our description of the German varieties of dog with the Schweiss-hund, who is, at the time of writing, the ideal hunting dog of Germany *par excellence.* Our first personal introduction to this breed was at the Hanover dog show of 1879, where a very strong class of Schweiss-hunds was exhibited, which enabled us to form a good idea of the points of the breed, and learn something of its merits from the mouths of experienced breeders. We were informed that this hound is chiefly used for the purposes of tracking wounded deer who have succeeded in escaping from the hunters, and we heard some marvellous stories concerning the power of scent possessed by the Schweiss-hund. For instance, M. U. Marais, one of the secretaries of the Hanover show, and himself an ardent sportsman, related to us the following adventure, which on the first blush seems incredible. It appears that he had wounded a stag one afternoon, but owing to the weather being very bad determined not to pursue the beast, and therefore returned home. About noon the next day it however cleared up, and he determined to try and hunt up the wounded animal, as he felt confident it was hard hit. According to custom he laid a Schweiss-hund on the track, and the dog at once took up the scent and led him up to where the stag lay dead. As this was twenty-two hours after he had wounded the stag, and rain had fallen heavily in the interim, the story appears to us little short of miraculous, but we have no reason to doubt the words of M. Marais, as he personally related the story to us when at Hanover.

The collection of Schweiss-hunds which we saw at Hanover seemed to us to be a remarkably level lot, and the uniformity of type struck us as being most unusual. The judging was carried on under the "jury" system to which we have already referred, and appeared to give the highest satisfaction, and the successful competitors were acknowledged to be first-rate specimens of the breed. Under such favourable circumstances we had exceptional opportunities for learning what a Schweiss-hund should be like, and were also fortunate in getting possession of a copy of the "official description," which we purpose giving below. The prevailing colour of the breed is red, and in many instances there is a black saddle, as in the case of the English Bloodhound. In stature the Schweiss-hund is much smaller than the latter breed, and in fact is not much larger than a smooth-coated sheep dog, only the German dog is considerably heavier in bone, and is, in addition, far more muscular in his body and limbs. They are undoubtedly hounds, and when they do take it into their heads to "bay the moon," there is no mistaking this fact.

The following is the official description of the breed to which we have already referred:—

General appearance; medium height, of strong and long structure, high in the back of head, tail rarely carried high, earnest expression of the face.

"*Head* of middling size, the upper part broad and flat, the forehead slightly wrinkled, the hind part of the head is moderately expressed. Nose broader than in other breeds of hounds, may be black or red. The bridge of the nose under the eyes is small or drawn in, almost arched. The eyebrows are considerably developed and protruding. Nose, round, and lips falling over in the corner of the mouth.

"*Ears* tolerably long, very broad, rounded at the ends, high, and equally set out, always lying close.

"*Eyes* clear, with energetic expression, no red observable.

"*Neck* long and strong, enlarging towards the chest.

"*Back* rather long, sunk behind the shoulders, hind part broad, and slightly vaulted and sloping.

"*Breast* wide, ribs deep and long, back gradually sloping up behind.

"*Tail* long, and well provided with hair.

"*Fore-legs* stronger than the hind-legs, shoulders sloping, very loose and movable; the muscles of the shoulders are well developed.

"*Hind-legs* moderately well developed, the lower parts not quite straight.

"*Feet* strong, round, and closed toes. Nails strong, uneven; the sole of the foot is strong and large.

"*Coat* close and full, smooth and elastic, almost glossy.

"*Colour* grey-brown, like the winter coat of deer; dark brown on muzzle, eyes, and tail, red-brown or red-yellow, or brown intermixed with black, and marked mostly with the darker colour; on the eyes, nose, and tail, as also with dark marks on the back."

Those dogs are considered as faulty which have a small high skull, narrow nose, running in the same dimension towards the forehead; if the ears are too long, too narrow, and too pointed; if the legs are bent, too short, or too thin, or strongly bent and too high carried tail; as also the structure, if not in correspondence with the different parts of the body. As regards colour, white, and also yellow marks, must be considered faulty.

CHAPTER LXIV.

THE GERMAN MASTIFF.

THE variety of which we now propose to treat has lately made a considerable advance in public estimation in this country, though under other names, as the designation which heads this chapter has only of late years been awarded it. However, as will be seen later on, the Great Dane was familiar to some early writers, and the kindred varieties of Ulmer Hound and Boarhound have both been patronised by British lovers of the dog. Lately, however, Herr Gustav Lang, of Stuttgart, who is one of the first German authorities on the breed, wrote to us the letter which we publish below, and informed us that the various German breeders had determined to classify the Boarhound, Ulmer Dog, and Great Dane, as one variety, which they proposed to term the German Mastiff. The wisdom of this change is very apparent, as the distinctions between these various breeds was, if any, of so slight a nature that mischief was being done by any attempts to disassociate them from each other. In fact, it was almost impossible to do so, as they were so generally bred together that, even assuming that the breeds had originally been distinct, the slight differences of type which had once existed had been completely obliterated by the commixture of blood.

The letter of Herr Gustav Lang to which we have referred is as follows :—

" As one of the judges, I had the honour to see you at the exhibition in Hanover, and I take the liberty of sending you a few lines bearing upon the dispute about the Irish Wolf-hound, which forms a pendant to our modern Deutscher Dogge or German Mastiff. The breed was formerly called Great Dane, Boarhound, or Ulmer dog, without any one being able at any of the German exhibitions to define the difference between these three races, because they are not distinct races which have been bred according to special ' points,' and formerly these dogs were not larger than they are to-day, the assumed size of 36 inches only being given in untrustworthy pictures. We have now agreed to abolish these various names, calling the breed *German Mastiffs*.

" The name ' Boarhound ' is not known in Germany. In boar-hunting every possible large ' mongrel ' was used. According to old paintings rough coats were preferred because they were less liable to injury than the smooth.

" It is greatly to be desired that a class should be established at German exhibitions for German Mastiffs, preferably near to the English Mastiffs."

Herr Gustav Lang's remarks upon the absurd statements of this dog's height should be carefully observed, as such an expression of opinion from such a high authority should convince all but the most sceptical that thirty-six inches is an all but impossible height for a dog to attain to. Specimens might appear of abnormal and phenomenal proportions, but dogs of a yard high will always be exceptions and not the rule, and readers should therefore proceed to disabuse their minds of the idea that they are likely to see a German Mastiff who stands thirty-six inches at the shoulder. Moreover, it cannot be alleged that early writers on the breed are responsible for representing this dog as attaining to a greater stature than he in reality does, and a case in point is Sydenham Edwards, who, writing in "Cynographia Britannica" in the year 1803, of the Dane, remarks that—

"The Dane is about twenty-eight inches high, some will reach thirty-one. In form he is between the Greyhound and Mastiff; head straight; muzzle rather pointed; ears short, half pendulous, usually cropped; eyes in some white, in others half white or yellow; chest deep; belly small; legs straight and strong; tail thin and wiry; colour sandy-red or pale fallow, with often a blaze of white on the face. A beautiful variety called the Harlequin Dane has a finely-marked coat, with large and small spots of black, grey, liver-colour, or sandy-red upon a white ground; the two former have often tan-coloured spots about the face and legs.

"The grand figure, bold muscular action, and elegant carriage of the Dane, would recommend him to notice had he no useful properties, and hence we find him honoured in adding to the pomp of the noble or wealthy, before whose carriage he trots or gallops in a fine style; not noisy, but of approved dignity becoming his intrepid character; he keeps his state in silence. That he is obliged to be muzzled to prevent his attacking his own species, or other domestic animals, adds much to the effect, as it supposes power and gives an idea of protection. . . . . . I certainly think that no equipage can have arrived at its acme of grandeur until a couple of Harlequin Danes precede the pomp. I do not know at what time he was introduced into England, nor whether he was ever used here for any but the above purpose. . . . . . Whether the Orientals use him in the hunt I do not know, but in the East they term him the Tiger Dog."

These remarks of Sydenham Edwards are accompanied by a coloured illustration which represents three Danes—viz., two Harlequins in recumbent positions, and one sandy-coloured one standing up. In the Harlequins the eyes are white or "china," whilst in the sandy-coloured one they are a pale yellow. Compared with the illustrations which accompany this article, the dogs pourtrayed by Edwards are light in bone and snipy in muzzle, but still their character and type much resemble the modern German Mastiff. The ears appear to have been partially removed, and the stern of the dog who is standing up is carried up, and shows a tendency to curl. It may be observed that probably some of this Harlequin Dane blood has found its way into the veins of our modern Dalmatians, though the latter are very much smaller in stature, especially as the Danes were used as carriage dogs as the Dalmatians are now; but this is a matter which hardly commands attention in the present chapter. A curious fact in connection with Sydenham Edwards' remarks, is the reference which he makes to the term Tiger Dog, by which he appears to have been of the opinion that possibly the Dane was used to hunt tigers. A more modern and, we think, feasible explanation, is to be found in the following extracts from a letter of Mr. Gustav Lang, whom we have already quoted, in which he says:—

"Referring to my notes on the German Mastiff, I add now a few remarks on the Tiger Dog, which only differs from it in colour. It is peculiar that we in German by 'Tiger' do not mean the colour of a tiger, but like a 'Tiger' horse, for example, which is white with small dark spots, as distinguished from the piebald horse. The large Tiger Dog has a ground-colour of white or silver-grey, with very *irregular* specks, as distinguished from the Dalmatian, which has its spots quite regular. These two breeds are essentially different from each other.

GERMAN MASTIFF DOG.

"Then, the large Tiger Dog has generally one or two blue or glass eyes, which gives them an unusual appearance. About fifty years ago these dogs were much in the fashion; especially when there are many of them together, their appearance is very pleasing and striking. They subsequently became very scarce, so that it was thought that they had died out. They are now coming again to the front, but they will only spread slowly, as there are many difficulties connected with their breeding. If Tiger Dogs only are bred together, the pups have generally too much white, so that it is necessary to take a black or a blue dog

HERR WUSTER'S TIGER GERMAN MASTIFF, "FLORA."

to give more colour. But of course the pups resulting from the first cross are not speckled in the desired way. From this cause it happens that dogs of the approved colour are much sought after, and fetch high prices."

This description exactly coincides with that given by Edwards of the Harlequin Dane, and it is therefore interesting to note the fact that the expression "Tiger Dog" has been so long used by admirers of the breed in connection with it. The illustration given by us of the beautiful bitch Flora is in every way an admirable likeness of a specimen of the breed recognised by German authorities as a representative German Mastiff of the "Tiger" colour, and was kindly forwarded to us by Herr Gustav Lang for publication.

The following remarks appeared in the *Live Stock Journal* with reference to the tiger-coloured German Mastiff, and may be read with interest, as Flora is referred to in them.

Some years ago this species of dog was very rarely met with, nor was there any demand for it, probably because it was supposed by many to have become extinct. It is therefore the more surprising that the collection of these handsome dogs at Elberfeld was so fine. They were much admired by the English visitors. The prize of honour was given to Nero, belonging to Mr. Fassbender. This beautiful animal was immediately bought by Mr. Wuster, jun., as a mate for Flora, already in his possession. Nero is large and elegantly shaped, while Flora is strong and beautiful.

Having already given the ideas of Sydenham Edwards and of Herr Gustav Lang, we will now lay before our readers a description of the German Mastiff from the pen of Herr R. von Schmiedeberg, editor of *Der Hund*, and a German sportsman of position.

"At the late Hanoverian dog show it was proved a fact that considerable progress has been made in the breeding of this class of dogs. Some years ago we still had the Ulmer Doggen, Hatzrüden Dänische Doggen (Danish Mastiffs), &c., but it has been impossible to settle with any clearness whether these were separate races. The fabulous race of Hatzrüden has often been mentioned. It is said that these have really been in existence, and are now produced fresh again, whilst following old pictures and Scripture. These dogs, which were almost only used for boar-hunting, were mostly rough-haired, and of a high and strong stature, and by no means animals of a decided pure class. The Parade Doggen, mostly owned and much thought of by the nobility in those days, can be as nearly as possible compared with the English and German Mastiff, but, with few exceptions, they would not now be suitable for shows, in consequence of not belonging to a distinct race.

"The Ulmer Doggen received their name in consequence of the very large Tiger Doggen having become so scarce. They are easily to be distinguished from the Dalmatiner (Dalmatian), which do not belong to the class of Mastiffs (Doggen) at all; the difference in these is, indeed, very considerable. The large Tiger Doggen in shows ought really to have a separate class, together with the German Mastiff or Deutsche Dogge. The latter denomination for these large and elegantly-built Doggen has soon been adopted everywhere, in contrast to the heavy English Mastiff, and the characteristic points of the breed are the following:—

"Figure high, elegant; head rather long; nose of medium length, thick—not pointed; lower jawbone to project only a little; point of nose, large, black (except with Tiger Doggen, where the same may be of flesh-colour, or spotted); lip trifling overhanging; ears placed high and pointed; eyes brown, not too light (except with Tiger Doggen, which often have glassy eyes); earnest and sharp look; neck pretty long and strong, without dewlap; chest broad and deep; back long and straight; toes closed; nails strong and long; thigh-bone muscular; knees deep, almost like a Greyhound; tail not too long, hardly to reach the hocks, and to be almost in a straight line with the back, never to be curly; the coat of the whole body, and particularly the tail, to be short and smooth; back-claws are allowed on the hind-feet if they are firm and not loose; colour bright black, wavy, yellow, blue, if possible without any marks, or, if striped, usually with glassy eyes.

"The best food for these Mastiffs is, without doubt, milk, soups of any kind, particularly of oatmeal, and, as an addition, raw, sound horseflesh, which latter the dogs of course prefer to everything, but must only be apportioned moderately. We need not mention that they must always have a good supply of fresh water. The colour of the German dog is quite a matter of taste, but those of one colour without any white marks are mostly preferred. The coat of the blue ones is frequently very soft and fine. The Tiger Doggen, sometimes with one or two glassy eyes, seem justly to come into fashion again. Several good specimens are still to be met with in Hamburg, and only last year there were still some to be seen at Ulm, as well as at Stuttgard. The foxy-coloured dogs are those which are least thought of."

This description of Herr von Schmiedeberg is by far the fullest and most detailed which we have seen, and we must heartily thank him for it. At the same time, we have it from other German authorities that, in their opinion, dew-claws on the hind legs are objected to most strongly, as being indication of a St. Bernard cross somewhere. It will be observed that Herr von Schmiede-berg lays great stress on the sort of dew-claws which he allows, and as these may appear in any breed, and do not in the least resemble the claws which are a *sine qua non* in St. Bernards, it may be fairly taken that both parties are at one with reference to this point.

With reference to the German Mastiff as it at present exists in this country, we can conclude as we commenced, by safely affirming that it is making rapid strides in popular favour, and lately many leading shows have offered prizes for the breed. English committees have, however, been slow to acknowledge the name of German Mastiff, and consequently confusion has arisen, which, until the donors of the prizes have the good sense to follow the example of our German friends, will always re-occur. A class for Boarhounds at present seems anomalous when no such breed exists upon the Continent; and German breeders naturally feel the slight which is put upon them, and rarely send their dogs over for competition against imported specimens. Nor have they hitherto received much encouragement to do so, for when His Serene Highness Prince Albert Solms of Braunfels entered his Hanoverian winner at the Alexandra Palace show in 1879, the grand dog was defeated by a far inferior specimen, simply through an error of judgment, but one which must have been extremely mortifying to his owner. The best specimens of the breed at present in this country are, to the best of our opinion, Lady Bismarck, the property of Mr. Charles Goas of Manchester, and Imperium and Libertas, who were imported direct from Herr Gustav Lang by Mr. James Davis, of Weymouth Street, London, as a present for his wife, to whom they still belong. Libertas, the female, though by far the better specimen, has never been exhibited; but Imperium, who has only been shown three times, has taken first prizes for his fair owner at Dublin and the Crystal Palace in 1880, and second at the Alexandra Palace in 1881. Lord Charles Kerr also owns what would be a good specimen, in Cæsar, but that the dog has dew-claws, which naturally are objected to in many quarters for the reasons given above; and, in addition, a portion of his tail has been removed, which also tells against him in competition with unmutilated specimens of the breed.

As Herr R. von Schmiedeberg has so thoroughly gone into the description of the points of the German Mastiff, any further allusion to them is unnecessary, and we therefore adopt his standard without reserve beyond the dew-claws, which we think objectionable, as evidences of impure blood. As a breed the German Mastiff is affectionate and docile, though some specimens are headstrong, as Sydenham Edwards observed, and inclined to attack other dogs and animals. Still, with so much in the way of appearance to recommend it, we trust that this grand variety of dog will go on as it promises to do, and yearly find increased favour amongst British *philo-kuons.*

CHAPTER LXV.

THE LEONBERG.

THIS variety of German dog, or rather commixture of various varieties which has been produced in Germany, has undoubtedly received more attention from the press than its merits entitle it to. We were at one time of the opinion that the Leonberg should not be noticed in any book upon dogs, but our views subsequently underwent a change, and we consequently introduce it, though more as a warning to purchasers than from any desire to laud the breed.

As a matter of fact, the Leonbergs which we have seen are little more or less than poor specimens of the St. Bernard breed, as they resemble the latter, though they lack their character. It is, moreover, an undoubted fact that dogs with Leonberg blood in their veins have been awarded prizes in St. Bernard classes, but this only goes to prove our conviction that the breed, as a pure one, is apocryphal, and can only base its merits on its approach in a greater or less degree to the St. Bernard, from whom it is descended. As stated above, the Leonberg has been greatly benefited by judicious puffing, and these friendly notices have not only been confined to this side of the Atlantic. As a case in point, the St. John's (Newfoundland) correspondent of the *Boston Traveller* wrote under date of August 20th, 1878, that—

"Last year a German friend of mine, Herr T. A. Verkruzen, a distinguished conchologist, brought here as a present three fine young dogs of the Leonberg breed, now pronounced to be the finest in the world, superior even to our own."

That is to say, to the Newfoundland, of whose blood the Leonberg partakes in addition to the St. Bernard and other breeds. The ingenuous correspondent of the *Boston Traveller* concluded his remarks on the Leonberg by stating that "they grow to be thirty to thirty-six inches in height, and are frequently over one hundred pounds in weight." This latter remark does not show its writer to be possessed of great canine knowledge, as for a dog of over thirty inches high one hundred pounds would not be a great weight, or even a reasonable one. However, his letter proves the existence of an effort to unfairly push this breed to the detriment of its progenitors.

Unfortunately for the Leonberg, Herr von Schmiedeberg, editor of the German sporting papers, *Der Hund* and *Der Waidmann*, wrote on November 25th, 1878, as follows :—

"A few months ago, two articles appeared in the *Live Stock Journal* under the the heading of "A New Breed of Dogs." Originally, I had seen these advertisements in the *Boston Traveller*, into which they had probably found their way through the management of a German who is interested in the sale of the new breed. The principal part of his eulogy is a translation of circulars sent round by Mr. Essig, the man who invented the name *Leonberg Dog*. I, therefore, consider myself perfectly justified in calling the articles an advertisement. Only in the opinion of their breeder, and a few low dealers, they are a valuable breed ; that is, every large dog they want to sell, is called a Leonberg. There is no reader of this paper who is

THE LEONBERG DOG.

not aware of the fact that it takes a long time to create a breed with peculiar points out of two other breeds, so that this new breed will propagate these peculiar points to the offspring. Now, Mr. Essig advertised his new breed directly after he had crossed a Newfoundland and a St. Bernard. I believe this was the origin; but two other dogs may have been chosen; that makes no difference, because the puppies found a ready sale by persons who wanted nothing but size and muscle. Some artists of fame—I am sorry to say—drew splendid pictures, ever so much idealised, and a few periodicals printed, and accompanied them with glowing descriptions. Essig was the lion of the day at once. He had calls from high-born and low-born persons; every one wanted those noble dogs, of which the papers related marvels. The demand exceeded the supply, and the consequence was, other large, ugly dogs, dogs of the Pyrenees, Wolf-dogs, and the common Watch-dogs of Wurtemberg, all these were mated together. So great was, at that time, the faith in Essig's proceedings, and so little were known the principles of breeding, that he himself dared to state publicly in advertisements and pamphlets, that his dogs had sprung from the above-mentioned breeds— and, this, in a couple of years or so! That state of things, when people believed in such humbug, has changed now-a-days. We have, at present, in Germany, four clubs, established for the purpose of breeding thoroughbred dogs. All these clubs—I am a member of three of them—do not countenance the Leonbergs any more; and, at our shows, we distribute these mongrels in the classes they resemble most, either into Newfoundlands, St. Bernards, Wolf-dogs, Shepherd-dogs, Setters, just as the case may be, even amongst the smooth-coated St. Bernards. My statements are proved not only by Essig himself, but even by the articles I am criticising. From them appears the origin of the different breeds, and also the want of given points for the new breed. For 'size' and 'long hair' are just as good as no points at all, especially when the texture of the hair is not defined, or when we read that 'some have split noses, others not.' The gentleman who carried the so-called Leonbergs to America, about which the article in Boston appeared, may have acted in good faith, just as other Germans did, before the Leonberg bubble exploded. But to me it looks suspicious, that the small landowner Essig is called a baron! True, a great many high personages own and owned Leonbergs; but this is no proof for their pure breeding or other qualities. Most of these gentlemen received them as presents from Mr. Essig, who knows full well how to make the mare go. Of course, a great many of his and similarly-bred dogs are striking and good-looking animals. But good looks are never a sign of any breed, and as it is, the *Leonberg is a cur.* I did not come forward sooner, because I expected some Englishman would set matters right, and because I am at present not used to the Queen's English. But friends of mine urged me not to be silent, saying, even, it was my duty to denounce the Leonberg humbug."

Subsequently Mr. Charles Goas, a German gentleman residing in Manchester, replied to Herr von Schmiedeberg, and from his letter we extract the following quotation:—

"About twenty-five years ago, Mr. Essig, of Leonberg, a small town in Wurtemberg, owned a pure bred St. Bernard dog and bitch of the same breed, which had been presented to him by the Superior of hospice of St. Bernard. About this time in an avalanche the whole of this grand breed perished in the fulfilment of their noble duty; and Mr. Essig, not like a humbug, as Herr von Schmiedeberg chooses to call him, but as a thorough gentleman, restored the two mentioned animals to the Superior of the hospice. He, therefore, is the man we have to thank that we have at the hospice still the original breed of St. Bernard dogs. But before giving up the dogs, he made the experiment of crossing them with his Newfoundlands, and not in a few years, but after a long time, succeeded in producing the present breed of Leonbergs. In all the important Continental shows they carried off the greatest honours. At the last great exhibition in Berlin the Leonbergs were awarded twelve prizes. In the Zoological Garden, in Paris, we find a grand specimen with the inscription on his cage, " Marko II., chien de Leonberg."

This communication drew a letter from a well-known German judge of high position, in which he wrote :—

" Reading in Mr. C. Goas's letter that in all the important Continental shows the Leonbergs carried off the greatest honours, and have taken at the last great exhibition of dogs at Berlin twelve prizes, I feel obliged as member of the Berlin Club, and as having been one of the judges at the last Berlin Show, to state that this is an error. Some years ago there had been a show at Berlin of a rather suspicious character, and Leonbergs did win prizes at that show; I don't know, but I think they did; but at the last Berlin Show, arranged by the Berlin Club, there was no class for Leonberg dogs, and they are excluded since the Hamburg show of 1876 as a class from all our leading shows, as well as from the shows which take place every year in Holland, for the single reason that the Leonbergs are not recognised here as a distinct breed. I know very well that Mr. Essig is of the opinion that there are no St. Bernards any more in existence, and that all dogs shown under this name are his breed. I don't think it is at all the question, if Mr. Essig did breed fine dogs under the name of Leonbergs or not, but simply if they deserve the name of a 'new breed.' Mr. Essig has himself not fixed the points of the breed; they represent a great variety of shape, colour, and texture, and Mr. Essig only tells us that his breed is the result of a cross between the St. Bernard, the Newfoundland, the Pyrenean dog, &c. There is no doubt that a great many valuable breeds have been created by crossing different breeds—as, for instance, the Retriever, the Bull-terrier, and even the Pointer; but the points of these breeds have been fixed, and they are inherited by the offspring. This is essential, and for sake of the purity of blood we must protest that any cross should have the right to be called a 'new breed,' as long as the points of the breed are not fixed, and as long as the proof is not given of the purity of blood, by the fact that the parents transfer as inheritance the same appearance, framed by certain points, to their offspring. Neither the one or the other *conditio sine qua non* is to be found among the Leonberg dogs bred by Mr. Essig, and called by him after the name of the town where they are born."

For our own part we unhesitatingly agree with the above remarks, and cannot regard the Leonberg as anything but a gigantic mongrel, who has been brought into existence merely on account of the rage for big dogs which has long been felt. The illustration which we publish gives a very fair idea of what the Leonberg dog really is like, and that is, in our opinion, an indifferent St. Bernard, by which it is to be hoped that lovers of the dog will not be led away.

HERR FRIEDRICH'S BERGHUND "MOULON."

CHAPTER LXVI.

THE BERGHUND.

AFTER the production of the Leonberg, and its temporary success from a pecuniary point of view, it was naturally improbable that other and opposition breeds would not appear. The production of the Berghund, or mountain dog of Germany, therefore, caused but a very small sensation in Continental canine circles.

This breed was fabricated by the well-known opposition (to Essig) dealer Friedrich, of Zuhna, in 1872, and owes its origin chiefly to Newfoundland blood. At the same time that Friedrich made this experiment, a Mr. Bergmann, in Waldheim, was making a similar trial, and both bred the same type of mongrel, which they sold to the public as a distinct breed.

Unlike the Leonberg, which appears to be very largely composed of St. Bernard blood, the Berghund shows more of the Newfoundland cross, though, as in the case of its rival, the character and dignity of the parent breed is almost obliterated by the adulteration which it has undergone. Nevertheless, in both instances large massive dogs have been produced, and it is most probable that the mixture of so many different breeds has had the effect of increasing the size and stamina of their descendants. Still, it is with the Berghund, as with the Leonberg, quite impossible to include it in the category of an accepted breed, and all efforts which may be made in certain quarters to receive them as such should be resisted.

We publish an illustration of Herr Friedrich's stud Berghund Moulon, which will give our readers an idea of the sort of animal which has been represented as being a distinct breed. The Newfoundland blood is so discernible in Moulon that no reference need be made to it; but we can assure our readers that the illustration we reproduce is from a likeness of a dog which is recognised in Germany as being typical of what some fondly but foolishly allude to as "the breed." It is, of course, impossible for us to give the points of either the Berghund or Leonberg, as these do not appear to have been decided upon by their originators. We therefore have decided to refrain from any further remarks upon them, and are content to rely on the illustrations which we publish to give our readers an idea of what these two mongrel "breeds" are like.

CHAPTER LXVII.

FRENCH BREEDS.

IT appears to us, when a comparison comes to be drawn between the merits of the German and French breeds of dog, that priority will usually be awarded to the latter. The French breeds certainly exceed the German ones in their numbers, though many of them, as will be seen hereafter, are merely offshoots of some older variety which is still in existence. Our neighbours across the Channel are also fortunate in the possession of at least three reliable works relating to canine subjects, for the writings of the Count de Couteulx, M. H. de la Blanchère, and Baron de Noirmont, are standard works which can be referred to without hesitation by those anxious to read of French breeds of dogs. The work of the Count de Couteulx is particularly interesting, and the graceful compliment which the author pays to English breeders and English dogs will, we are sure, be appreciated by all our countrymen who read his instructive writings.

With reference to the number of French breeds, it may be mentioned that the Count de Couteulx alludes to twelve different varieties, which were principally of the hound type, and which appear to have been known for centuries up to the time of the Revolution. M. de la Blanchère treats of no less than twenty varieties and sub-varieties of the canine race, which he tabulates as follows, at the same time giving the best English equivalent he can for each French designation :—

RACES FRANÇAISES.			RACES ANGLAISES.
Chiens d'Arrêt.	Braque		Pointer.
	Épagneul		Setter, Springer, Cocker, Clumber, Retriever.
	Griffon		Griffon.
	Caniche ou Barbet		Poodle.
	Dogue ou Mâtin		Mastiff, Bulldog.
	Levrier		Greyhound.
Chiens Courants.	Griffons au poil rude.	Griffons Vendéens.	
		Griffons de Bresse.	
		Chiens Gris de St. Louis.	
		Chiens Fauves des Ducs de Bretagne.	Otterhound (Chien à Loutre).
		Chiens des Ardennes ou St. Hubert.	Bloodhound (Vautrait).
		Chiens Greffiers du Roi.	Staghounds (Équipage de Cerf).
	Braques et Briquets.	Chiens Vendéens.	Foxhounds (Chiens à Renard).
		Chiens Poitevins.	Harrier (Chiens à Lièvre).
		Chiens Normands.	Beagle (Briquet).
		Chiens Gascons.	
		Chiens Saintongeois.	
		Chiens d'Artois.	
	Bassets et Terriers.	Basset à jambes droites.	Terrier.
		Basset à jambes torses.	Bull-terrier.
			Scotch Terrier (Terrier Griffon).

It is of course impossible to recognise the relationship which M. Blanchère claims for some of the French breeds with our own, but his list is an interesting one, and it is the most perfect table of the kind we have come across, and will be useful in assisting our readers to follow our remarks upon the various breeds. Unfortunately, some of the varieties which appear in the above table have ceased to exist, and others have so nearly reached the climax of extinction that any detailed notice of them is beyond our power. We will, however, do our utmost to follow out M. de la Blanchère's order, though it will, from motives of convenience, have to be slightly altered in the progress of our remarks. We desire, however, before we proceed to acknowledge the great obligations we are under to Mr. George R. Krehl, of Hanover Street, London, not only for the assistance he has afforded us, in procuring reliable information from foreign sportsmen of his acquaintance, but also for the kind way in which he has placed his idiomatic knowledge of French, and of French canine phraseology, at our disposal for the translation of difficult technical passages. Mr. Krehl has desired us to acknowledge his indebtedness for much of the information he has furnished us with to the works of the Count de Couteulx, M. de la Blanchère, and Baron de Noirmont, all of which have already been referred to. We will commence with the French Hounds in M. de la Blanchère's list, and place in the position of honour

The Vendéen Hound.

This breed, according to Count de Couteulx's opinion, is not a pure one, and he bases his arguments mainly on the fact that smooth and rough-coated whelps appear in the same litter,

WHITE VENDÉEN HOUND (POIL RAS).

as is the case with St. Bernards and Sheep-dogs in this country. There are, however, better reasons for considering the Vendéen Hound to be an offshoot of other breeds, for reliable information has been published concerning the crosses which originated the two varieties.

The smooth-coated (or poil ras) Vendéen Hounds, according to Couteulx, are descendants of the white St. Huberts, a famous race of white Bloodhounds, which, according to the Baron de Noirmont, existed in large numbers in the 15th century, an illustration of which we append. These white dogs were however less popular with the nobility than the black breed, simply because they were only suitable for the pursuit of deer, and were not adapted to general sporting purposes. Baron de Noirmont relates the story of a certain gentleman who had presented a dog of this breed, named Souillard, to the King (Louis XI.) who preferred the grey variety. Gaston de Lyon, Seneschal of Toulouse, who was in the king's suite, however, begged for Souillard to be given to the "wisest woman" in the kingdom—namely, to Madame de Beaujeau, who was a daughter of the king and a celebrated huntress. "I call you to order," said the king, "for having mentioned the wisest woman; you should have said the least foolish; for a wise woman—there is not such a thing in the world."

This dog, Souillard, subsequently came into the possession of the Seneschal of Normandy, and became the fountain head of the Greffiers du Roi, as will be seen in the chapter on that breed.

The smooth Vendéens (poil ras) should show breeding and quality in their heads.

The *Ears* should be long and pendent, and thin.

The *Chest* deep, and shoulders sloping slightly.

The *Legs* strong and hound-like.

The *Loins* powerful and deep.

The *Stern* rather coarse and houndy.

The *Coat* short and fine.

In temperament they are rather hot and quarrelsome, but lively and companionable. Their constitutions are delicate, rendering them short-lived, and they give tongue less than other breeds

VENDÉEN HOUND (GRIFFON).

of French Hounds. There are still some good packs of Vendéen Hounds (poil ras) to be met with in France, amongst the most famous of which are those of M. Baudry d'Asson, Fonteclose, près la Garnache (Vendée); M. Bailly du Pont, à la Châtaigneraie (Vendée); and M. J. de Lacharme, à Matoir (Saone-et-Loire).

The rough-coated Vendéen or Griffon is considered to be in all probability a cross between the Chien Bresse (treated of later) and the smooth Vendéen, which has been subsequently again crossed with the Chien Gris, or grey dog, and the fawn dogs of Brittany.

From the Chien Bresse the Griffon gets its nose and heavy dewlap, but his general appearance is rather commoned by the cross. From the Chien Gris, or Grey Dog, he takes his short loins, and his strength and stamina, and the mouse-grey ticks, which, in certain kennels of first-rate Griffons, used to be regarded as proofs of the highest lineage, and were eagerly prized. From the fawn dog of Brittany the Vendéen Griffon has derived the golden-wheaten tints, the peculiarity of certain hard-coated Vendéens, the origin of which is hard to discern. The colour is lemon-wheaten and white, grey or mouse-grey. He is of fair size, very powerful, sound in constitution, with good loins, and with powerful quarters, feet compact and hound-like. He is much sought after for hunting wolf and wild boar. Like the smooth dog, and perhaps more than him, he is headstrong and difficult to control, and this is a great fault which tells against him. There were, at one time, some gigantic Griffons to be found, but they were rarely met with, and their purity was doubtful.

HEAD OF GRIFFON DE LA VENDÉE.

The accompanying illustration is a faithful representation of the head of a Griffon Vendée, many good specimens of which breed are to be met with in the packs of the following gentlemen :—M. Josson de Bilhem, Château de Theil (Yonne) ; M. Léon Barré, à Issoudun (Indre) ; M. Millot, à Maulaix, près Fours (Nièvre).

Chiens Greffier du Roi.

The next variety of which we shall treat is the Chiens Greffier du Roi, which is, according to all the most eminent French authorities, descended from Souillard, the dog who was the hero of the story we alluded to in our description of the Vendéen Hound.

Souillard was not given to Madame de Beujeau, but was, at his eager solicitation, presented to the Grand Seneschal of Normandy, Jacque de Brézé, who was at that time an important member of her suite. He valued his new dog immensely, and eulogised him in the following words :—

" De son temps le meilleur et le mieux pourchassant."

Souillard was bred to an Italian Braque which belonged to the king's secretary (Greffier). The first result of this cross was an all-white dog with a fawn mark on his shoulder, which they called Greffier, from the former owner of the bitch. He was so excellent a hunter that few stags could escape him, and from thirteen pups bred from him (who were all as good as he) the once-famous race originated, which were much in vogue in the time of Francis I.

This king finding the Greffier rather wanting in size, reinforced it with a fawn hound named Miraud, which was given him by Admiral d'Annbault. Henry II. again crossed it with a white hound called Barraud, given him by the Queen of Scotland, Marie de Guise, mother of Mary Queen of Scots. From these successive crosses the breed was increased in strength and endurance, and became still more valuable in the eyes of its possessors, until Charles IX. designated them the true royal breed. It may be added that they did not admit into the royal packs any but white or fawn-and-white hounds.

A very good idea of the Chiens Greffiers du Roi may be gathered from the illustration which has already been given of the white Vendéen Hound, who is a near relation of the breed in question. As the points of the two varieties are also so similar, no detailed description of the Greffier is necessary, and we will pass on to the

Chien Gris de St. Louis,

Which is now extinct. It was originally imported by the French king St. Louis from Tartary. The breed was originally held in great estimation, but died out with the pack of Comte de Soissons in the reign of Henry IV.

Cheins Fauves des Ducs de Bretagne.

These dogs are of the same breed as Miraud, who is already alluded to as one of the progenitors of the Greffiers du Roi. They are described as being of medium size, and gifted with better constitutions than the Vendéen Hounds. As with many other breeds of French hounds, the Chiens Fauves des Ducs de Bretagne are better on deer than on other game, as, though their staunchness, nose, and gameness are undeniable, they are not thoroughly adapted for hunting in briars and underwood. They are headstrong, and hard to control. In colour they are generally fawn, and the brightest shade is most popular with sportsmen, who do not care for those marked with grey or black. The fawn dogs are the most popular breed in Lorraine, Nivernais, and Charolais, where they are used for hunting deer and boar in the forests. We have been unable to secure an illustration of this breed, but in appearance it resembles a rather short-coated Griffon Vendée. The principal packs of Chiens Fauves de Bretagne are owned by M. le Baron Halva du Fretay, au château de Vieux-châtel par Châteaulin (Finistère), M. F. Thérot, rue Saint-Pierre à Saint-Brieue (Côtes du Nord); and M. le Baron Sibuet, au château de Vireux, prés Rocroy (Ardennes).

Chien St. Hubert.

This is certainly one of the most famous of all the French varieties of dogs, and its antiquity is beyond a question, as it was a celebrated breed in the eighth century. At this period the St. Hubert was recognised by the name of the Dog of Flanders, and was divided into two breeds, viz., the black St. Hubert and the white. Reference has already been made to the above fact; but the origin of the breed may be traced to a famous Belgian breed, of which an early writer, Sirius Italicus, writes in the following terms, according to the Count Couteulx:—

"This Belgian dog follows the wild boars closely and cleverly; silently, and with his nose to the earth." This would seem to show that the progenitors of the breed were silent hunters, and therefore very different from their descendants. Blacks were decidedly the favourite colour, and the monks of the abbey of St. Hubert kept up this strain in honour of the memory of the founder of their order. In consequence of the preference for this colour it was the more common of the two; it may be said the blacks were marked with red (tan) on the eyebrows and feet. The St. Hubert was distinguishable by his long ears. His back was very muscular but rather long, and he was not high on the leg. He showed a well-developed dewlap, possessed a fine nose, and great stamina, but was very slow (from which it seems rather probable that the legs of the original hounds were not quite straight), and was, in addition, a keen and bold hunter. In spite of the preference which was popularly awarded to the black variety, we have it on the authority of a writer of the name of Salnove, that St. Hubert himself had two varieties, white and black, in the Ardennes. Nevertheless, the two earliest known packs (which existed in 1620, one of which belonged to the Cardinal de la Guise and the other to the Marquis de Souvray) were both made up of black-and-tan St. Huberts. These dogs were powerfully built but were very headstrong, quarrelsome amongst each other, and savage towards men, so had to be kept well under control; though, as the heroes of many a famous chase, their name is a household one amongst French sportsmen.

According to Count Couteulx the St. Huberts made their appearance in this country at the time of the Conquest, and again in the reign of James I., as some specimens of the breed were included in the present of dogs made to that monarch by the French king Henry IV. He adds that the breed has sadly degenerated on the Continent, but that good specimens can be found in England, though in many instances they have been crossed with the Mastiff. As a proof of the similarity or identity of the St. Hubert with our modern Bloodhound, it may be stated that the specimen selected for the illustration of the St. Hubert in Count Couteulx's work is Col. Cowen's Bloodhound Druid. The best packs of the St. Hubert which are in existence are those of M. L. Claverie, à Saint Sicaire, par la Roche-Chalais (Dordogne), and M. Piston d'Eauboune, au château de Fournil, près Mussidan (Dordogne).

Chien de Normandie.

There appears to have been no mention of this hound until the time of Louis XIV., but during his reign this king, who was anxious to improve the pace of his hounds, which had also it appears grown clumsy, introduced Normandy blood into his kennel. This action was literally the beginning of the end of the beautiful white Greffiers du Roi, who have been treated of above.

The hound of Normandy is from 24 to 28 inches in height, and usually tricolour, or orange-and-white in colour. The head, as will be seen in our illustration, is long, and the forehead has two large frontal bumps, and he has a large nose. His head is wrinkled, and he is heavily flewed. The eyes are full, and the haw shows well. Ears, thin, long, and velvety.

CHIEN DE NORMANDIE.

Shoulders rather heavy, but the body is strong and rather long. Loins deep and arched. Feet powerful and compact. Quarters drooping, and stern straight. This dog is adapted for the pursuit of all sorts of game, and is easily kept under control. Many packs of reputed Normandy hounds contain cross-bred members, but the following are amongst those which are considered by Continental authorities to be pure:—M. le Comte de Trébous, au château de Bérengeville, par la Commanderie (Eure); M. E. de la Broise, au château de Carantilly, par Marigny (Manche); and M. R. de Varin, à Gouneville-sur-Honfleur.

Chien de Gascogne.

This is a larger variety of hound, and a much heavier one than its kindred breeds. A Chien de Gascogne is chiefly remarkable for the extreme length of its ears, and for the amount

CHIEN DE GASCOGNE.

of haw its eyes display. It is very similar in many respects to the St. Hubert hound, from which it is descended, and many good specimens may be found in the south-east of France.

The following is the description, from the pen of Count Couteulx, of Major, the property of Baron de Ruble. Head expressive, body powerful and muscular, tail fine and well carried up. The following are some of the best packs of this variety of hound :—Le Baron de Ruble, au château de Bruka, par Aubiet (Gers); and M. J. Fourcade, au château de Caraman (Hérault).

Griffon De Bresse.

This is one of the most ancient breeds in France, and has for centuries been a favourite with sportsmen of all denominations. In appearance it closely resembles our English Otter-hound. Count de Couteulx, in his work, thus refers to the Griffon de Bresse and the above resemblance :—"In my opinion this variety is still to be found in a degenerated form in the Otterhounds of Lancaster, which have still much resemblance to the hounds of Bresse. Some Griffons, the issue of a cross between Bresse and Vendée Hounds, which I sent to Scotland to the master of a pack of Otterhounds, were found to have a complete analogy, except in colour, with the dogs that were already in his kennel."

There are still good specimens to be found in some of the packs of hounds which are located in Burgundy and Nivernais, where they are treated with great respect, as they are popularly believed to be descendants of the dogs alluded to by Arrian, who was naturally the first to direct attention to the shaggy and unkempt appearance of the breed. It may also be added that they were highly prized by the Romans and Gauls at the time when they were supposed to be the exclusive property of the Segusii, a people who took their name from their country, which was a district of Bresse. The Griffon de Bresse had a hard, bristly coat, and those which the ancient Greeks considered the most hideous were much esteemed in Gaul. The variety in question may be correctly taken as representing the primitive types of the old French breeds, and is beyond a question the founder of most of the rough-coated hounds of that country. As a proof of the value once set upon this breed it may be cited, on the authority of an old document of the ninth century, quoted by M. de Noirmont, that Heccard, Count of Autun, on his deathbed bequeathed, amongst his other most precious belongings, his dogs. These dogs he alluded to as Segusii, and from the conspicuous position assigned to them in his list of legacies, it is clearly proved that these dogs, which were described by Arrian in the eleventh century, and in the barbaric codes of the sixth and seventh centuries, were still an honoured race in the time of Louis the Debonnaire.

We regret that we have been unable to give an illustration of this breed, but the resemblance to our English Otterhound is, as before said, very marked.

Chien Saintongeois.

The above breed is tall yet lightly constructed, and authorities in Saintonge are generally of the opinion, according to Count Couteulx, that it is an "ameliorated" descendant between the white and black St. Hubert Hound. The only certain knowledge that we now have of the origin of this breed comes from a MS. preserved among the family papers of the Marquis de la Porte aux Loups. This states that at the time of the 1789 Revolution the last representatives of the Saintonge breed were a bitch, called Minerva, and two dogs, Melanthé and Fouiloux. After surviving the perils of that troublous time, they were presented by the Marquis to his nephew, Count de Légier, and became the progenitors of the new breed of

Saintonge, which has been subsequently much improved by judicious crosses. Some descendants of these dogs now exist in the kennels of the Vicomte de Saint Légier.

The following are the points of the old breed, which have however been greatly changed by the crossings to which the original strain was subjected. Colour, white with black spots, ears black, head marked with pale tan below the eyes. Height at shoulder about 28 inches. Lean head, with a slightly retroussé nose, or it may be rather said that this effect was given by the size and thickness of the nostrils. The flews were pendulous. Ears long and fine. The feet were hare-shaped. Powerful body, and sloping loins. The modern " improved " Saintonge, which goes by the name Virelade, is the result of a cross between the Gascogne and Saintonge Hounds, is generally not unlike its ancestors. They are large and characterised by a peculiarly aristocratic appearance. They are high at shoulder, but long and rather soft-looking. In colour they are black and white. The ears thin and pendulous, though fine, the quarters drooping, and stern long and well carried. They are hare-footed, but have plenty of substance. At the present time this is one of the most popular of all French breeds, and excellent specimens are to be found in the packs of the following gentlemen :—M. le Baron

CHIEN POITOU.

Joseph de Carayon-Latour, au château de Virelade, par Podensac (Gironde) ; M. le Vicomte de Chauteaubriant, au Courbat, par Genillé (Indre-et-Loire) ; M. A. Labadie, Société de Mios (Gironde).

Chien Poitou.

According to Count Couteulx most Continental authorities consider this breed to be a direct cross between the Normandy and Saintonge Hounds, which have been alluded to above. The Poitou Hounds are in colour tricolour for the most part, about 23 inches high, and full of quality. The head of this breed is lean, and his muzzle long, and rather Roman nosed. Ears moderately short, but very thin and velvety. In body they are narrow and somewhat flat-sided, though deep in chest. Their coat is coarse, and appears long for a smooth-coated dog. Their voice is musical, and power of scent extraordinary, for Count Couteulx gives them credit for being able to pick up a scent twenty-four hours old. As a rule, the Poitou Hounds are slow, but still they are fast enough for a winter's day wolf-hunting, and they are said to be able to follow a wolf from sun to sun without flagging. Count Couteulx remarks that he does not know of a more beautifully-shaped hound—and here we agree with him—or one more fitted for the chase ; but the great objection to the Chien Poitou is the difficulty found in rearing him, as, when young, he is extremely delicate.

PETITE RACE D'ARTOIS.

Chien d'Artois.

The antiquity of the above handsome old Picardy breed may be gathered from a letter written by Prince Charles Alexandre de Croy to the Prince of Wales, 8th of August, 1609, accompanying a present of a small pack of Chiens d'Artois. These hounds were in those days white, with fawn or grey markings; short muzzle and head; large in skull, with a full eye; ears flat and long; body compact and low; stern coarse and carried hound-like. Nowadays they are less strongly-built, and often have black markings, and are sometimes tricolour. In size they are as a rule from eighteen to twenty inches, but are conspicuous by their tremendous dewlap, exquisite nose, and great intelligence. They are hardy and strong constitutioned, with

HALF-BRED D'ARTOIS.

great stamina, although rather slow in the field. They are keen hunters, though inclined to riot. Unfortunately the old breed has been crossed with Normandy dogs and English Fox-hounds, though two or three pure packs are still in existence. Amongst the principal kennels of Chiens d'Artois are those of M. Paul Bernard, à Héry, par Seignelay (Yonne), and M. Delarue-Buisson, à Abbeville (Somme). In their glory the Chien d'Artois had the support of the aristocracy of Picardy, to whom they were invaluable in the chase as wolf-hounds, though subsequently they have degenerated into harriers, in which sport they now excel all other breeds of French hounds. It is, however, a peculiar trait in the character of this hound that he could never be taught to hunt foxes. There are now two varieties of Chiens d'Artois, the large and small, of which the latter is by far the most common. A grand specimen of the large size is Antigone, located in the Jardin d'Acclimatation in Paris.

Basset Hounds.

We have decided to add to the remarks which have already appeared on page 333 by publishing the following interesting notes, which are the result of the researches made by Mr. George R. Krehl, who has kindly sent them to us.

"A very excellent description, by Mr. E. Millais, has already appeared in an earlier part of this work; but the few supplementary notes that I have to offer may still be worth preserving if adding only a little to our present meagre stock of Basset lore. Bassets were until the seventeenth century described in French works as Chiens d'Artois; this appellation has since been exclusively retained for the noble Chiens courants d'Artois, which were in those times called Picardy Hounds. Du Fouilloux was the first French writer who spoke of them as Bassets, and he explains their ancient affix of Artois by giving us to understand that it was in effect from this province and the neighbouring country of Flanders that the breed of Bassets originally sprung. Sélincourt is at one with the authority quoted in attributing to them this origin. One recognises from that period, says the Baron de Noirmont, two varieties—the Bassets full-crooked, generally smooth-coated, and 'ayant double rangée de dents comme les loups;' and Bassets straight-legged with black and rough coats. Leverrier de la Couterie says that the straight-legged Bassets came from Flanders, and the crooked from Artois. He preferred the quicker Flamands, but found them 'mauvais crieurs et bricoleurs;' the Artesians, long bodied, and 'bien coiffés,' he found courageous and very enterprising *sub terra*. In going to earth it was noticed that the straight-legged had more dash, but the crooked stayed in longer. He concludes, though, by agreeing with Du Fouilloux that there were good and bad of both sorts.

"Though there are even at the present time several varieties of Bassets, yet I agree with Mr. Millais that English breeders would do well to confine themselves to the two popular types, viz., the smooth-coated Artesian and the rough Vendean Bassets. The latter is the Basset Griffon. He has straight but short legs; rough, hard coat, with a woolly undergrowth; colour iron-grey, or white with brown markings, or all white. They are powerfully built, not very long, and possess a speed which is extraordinary when one thinks of their shape. A Monsieur d'Incourt de Metz owns a pack of these hounds, that run down their hare easily in two or three hours. The Basset *par excellence*, though, is the beautiful smooth-coated tricolour of Artois, and this is the type with its rich and brilliant colouring of black, white, and golden tan, its noble Bloodhound-like head so full of solemn dignity, the long velvet-soft ears, the kind and pensive eye, the heavy folds of the throat, the strange fore-limbs, the quaint and mediæval appearance—this is the type, I say, that will stand first in the estimation of an intelligent dog-loving public. The type will always be associated with the name of Count le Couteulx de Canteleu, and all the Bassets at present (1881) in this country are descended from, or are direct importations from, his celebrated kennel. To this nobleman, inspired with a hereditary love of the chase and all its accessories, is due the credit of, in a manner, resuscitating this breed, which twenty-five years ago, by careless rearing and the freakish crosses that Continental sportsmen affect, had become well-nigh extinct. The Count has been kind enough to supply me with the particulars of that period. Observing the growing scarcity of good and pure tricolour Artesian Bassets, he set about to do for them what he had already accomplished for other ancient and moribund breeds of Gaul. He started to find a pair of true and pure specimens to revive the breed. After purchasing some thirty dogs, he at last acquired a grand dog, Fino (the first of the name), in Artois, and a lively bitch, Mignarde, in another part of the country. Their produce were true and level to their parentage, showing no signs of throwing back to *mésalliances;* the pups only differed in being more or less crooked, as is still the case in modern litters. The Count continues that he bred in and in to perfect the breed, and that his dogs were sturdy and vigorous enough to permit this means. Ten years later he endeavoured to find another stud-dog for new blood. His huntsman travelled the North of France through to find one, and the experiment made with a superb Basset that he bought in the Saumur having produced yellow pups, he destroyed them and continued to rely on his own strain. The Count, in his description of the breed, lays great stress upon the occipital protuberance, which he calls 'la bosse de chasse;' the head long, narrow and thin in the muzzle; the ears very long; the head of the dog being much heavier and stronger than the bitch's. He gives about four inches for the height of the crooked legs. Colour, tricolour, sometimes ticked with black spots. He goes on to say that some of them have more teeth than dogs usually have, and that many have the 'bec de lièvre'—*i.e.,* the lower jaw a little shorter than the upper. He states that two of the best bitches in his pack have this formation of the jaw. Of the dogs chosen for the coloured plate Jupiter shows most of the Bloodhound type of head; the bitch Pallas is but little short of perfection, and it was the eulogistic description of her qualities in *The Field,* when she won at Brussels, that induced the writer to find her out in France, and buy her and her mate, Jupiter. Fino de Paris, the third dog in the picture, is demi-torse; he is own brother to Mr. Millais's Model, which is full-torse. He was, until I purchased him from the Jardin d'Acclimatation, Paris, the stud-dug of Europe; and Count Couteulx considers him a 'particularly good and pure stud-dog, a perfect specimen of the breed, low on the legs, very strong, well-knit loins, and head typical of the breed, long and thin.' They are rare and very difficult to procure; they are also difficult to breed and rear, though when they do reach maturity they are as hardy as any of our breeds, the imported ones feeling the cold a little more perhaps. They are a peculiarly intelligent and interesting breed, with their *bizarre* aspect and deep-toned voices. There are now in England five grand specimens of the breed, which I fear (I hope the future will prove me wrong) will never be equalled, certainly never excelled, in this country: they are—Mr. Millais's Model, Lieutenant Monro's (late Lord Onslow's) Fino, and my Pallas, Fino de Paris, and Jupiter. I am sorry to notice in most of the home-bred specimens a tendency to lose size; this must be remedied; the size must be kept up. Your illustration depicts Pallas (first Brussels, 1880, and first Alexandra Palace, 1881), Fino de Paris (first Birmingham, 1880, and first Alexandra Palace, 1881), and Jupiter (first Dundee, 1880)."

CHAPTER LXVIII.

ASIATIC DOGS.

The Siberian Wolfhound.

UNFORTUNATELY, this most handsome variety of dog is seldom met with in Great Britain, though some beautiful specimens have appeared at some of the leading dog-shows. The Siberian Wolfhound partakes very much of the nature of the Scotch Deerhound, and in structure much resembles the latter. There is, however, a distinct dissimilarity in the coats of the two races, and the colours of the two breeds do not agree. In the first place the texture of the Siberian Wolfhound's coat is certainly finer than that of the Deerhound, and it is generally longer in addition, which gives the dog a more elegant appearance. Again, instead of the sombre jacket of the Scotch dog, we usually find in his Siberian prototype lemon-and-white to be the prevailing colour, though blue or stone-grey and white specimens of the variety also exist beyond a doubt. The accompanying engraving gives an admirable illustration of what these beautiful dogs are like, and we trust that the breed will soon become more generally known in this country. The best specimens which we have seen have belonged to the Rev. J. C. Macdona and Lady Emily Peel, whose Sandringham and Czar have never appeared on the show-bench without exciting universal admiration. As the formation of the Siberian Wolfhound so closely follows that of the Deerhound, we can confidently refer our readers to the chapter on the latter breed, which, with the exception of coat and colour, strictly applies to the Siberian Wolfhound.

The Persian Greyhound.

Is very rarely met with in England, and as it is not strikingly handsome or even taking in appearance there does not seem to be much probability of extreme popularity ever falling to the share of the Persian Greyhound. Like its relatives the English Greyhound, the Deerhound, and the Siberian Wolfhound, the Persian Greyhound hunts its prey by sight and not by scent. The variety in question is a smooth-coated dog extremely like our Greyhound, but is distinguished from him by the smallness of his size and the fact that the tail and ears of the Persian dog are feathered with silky hair. An illustration of this dog will be found on page 239, in the Greyhound family.

The Thibet Mastiff

Is very dissimilar in coat and colour to his English namesake, and in fact, to our mind, very much more resembles a sour-faced, heavy-eared Newfoundland. The skull is short, thick, and heavy; the eyes sunken, and the flews very heavy and deep. The above combination gives the dog a sullen, savage look, which makes strangers cautious in approaching a Thibet Mastiff. He is heavy in bone, powerful in body, and, as will be seen in our illustration, carries his tail well up over his back. The coat is rough and harsh, and not unlike that of

SIBERIAN WOLFHOUNDS.

THIBET MASTIFF.

a Newfoundland, whilst the prevailing colour is black-and-tan, the tan spots over the eyes being clearly defined in all good specimens.

Very few specimens of the breed have been met with in this country, and of these Siring, who is the property of H.R.H. the Prince of Wales, is by far the best.

The Rampur Dog.

This dog we believe made his first appearance in England on the return of H.R.H. the Prince of Wales from his Indian tour. At all events, we have no recollection of having seen any specimens of the Rampur Hound at our dog shows except at the Fakenham dog show of 1876, upon which occasion we acted as judge of the class in which they were entered. Only two appeared; one was of a mouse colour, the other spotted, a sort of pink-and-blue, somewhat similar to young "plum-pudding" coloured pigs. In appearance the Rampur dog somewhat resembles a small Deerhound, but his chief characteristic is the absence of hair, which leaves his body smooth. We have, however, been informed that since they have been in this country, a little hair has appeared upon these dogs.

The Indian Tailless Dog.

At the Fakenham show of 1876 a pair of Indian tailless dogs were exhibited by H.R.H. the Prince of Wales, but beyond exciting a certain amount of curiosity as novelties, they had little to recommend them. In appearance they resemble the Pomeranian, except that they have no tail, and are of a foxy colour; in fact, they are not unlike the latter animal, but they are heavier in bone, more stoutly built, and shorter in the body.

The Japanese Pug.

The Japanese Pug is not unlike our modern Toy Spaniels in general outline, for in his skull and retroussé nose he bears a great resemblance to these breeds. He is not, however, so heavily coated or feathered, and his almost invariable colour is black-and-white. In our opinion, the blood of the Japanese Pug has been introduced into the veins of many of the present King Charles Spaniels, and has been serviceable in assisting to reduce their length of nose. The subject of these remarks is a hardy and companionable little dog, and one which, if better known, would find a number of friends in this country. A very good specimen, named Tiny, was exhibited by Mr. Lindsay Hogg at the Alexandra Palace show, Jan., 1881, but being in the Toy Spaniel class, was most properly placed behind Miss Violet Cameron's champion King Charles, Conrad.

Chinese Dogs.

For the whole of the following remarks on the dogs of China, we are indebted to Mr. W. K. Taunton.

In China there are several breeds of dogs showing a marked difference from one another. The common dog of the country is not unlike a large, coarse Pomeranian, and is in all probability very closely related to the Esquimaux breed. The muzzle is pointed, ears erect, coat long, straight and rather coarse in texture, but with a soft furry undercoat, tail closely curled over the hip. The lips and tongue are black, which appears to be a peculiarity of most of the Chinese breeds. A dog with a black tongue or one spotted with black would lead me to suppose there had been a very recent cross of Chinese blood, for I am not aware that this colour is found in the tongues of dogs of any other country. I say a very recent cross, because I imagine the peculiarity would be lost in a generation or two. These dogs are seen in a variety of colours, but most commonly of a deep red, and most rarely of a jet-black. In this country they are generally known as the "edible dog of China," as they are used for eating by the inhabitants of China, but only by the poorer classes of the population, and very rarely if ever at all by the upper and middle classes. A gentleman who has lived several years in Hong Kong tells me they are only eaten when quite young, then only the forelegs and paws, and that the black dog is the favourite for the table. Archdeacon Gray, in his interesting book on China, also mentions this fact, and says that over the doors of restaurants in Canton patronised by mechanics and others, it is not an uncommon thing to see placards setting forth that the flesh of black dogs and cats can be served up at a moment's notice. He also gives the following translation of a bill of fare which may be of interest :—

Cat's flesh, one basin	...	...	...	...	...	10 cents.
Black cat's flesh, one small basin		...	...	...	...	5 cents.
Wine, one bottle	...	...	...	...	...	3 ,,
Wine, one small bottle	...	...	...	...	...	1½ ,,
Congee, one basin	...	...	...	...	...	2 cash
Ketchup one basin	...	...	...	...	...	3 ,,
Black dog's grease	...	...	...	...	...	1 tael, 4 cents
Black cat's eyes, one pair	...	...	...	...	...	4 ,,

All guests dining at this restaurant are requested to be punctual in their payment.

Packs of these dogs, I am told, are used in North China for hunting the wolf, and are often called the Chinese Wolf-dog.

In marked contrast to this breed is the Chinese *Crested Dog*, so called from having a crest of hair running along the top of the head from front to back. In addition to this the dog has a tuft of hair at the end of its tail, but otherwise, with the exception of a few scattered hairs round the head and muzzle and just above the feet, the dog is perfectly hairless, the skin being more or less mottled in some specimens. The one I have stands 16 in. high, and weighs 20 lbs.

There is another hairless dog said to come from China considerably smaller than the above, weighing about 8 or 10 lbs., and without any hair at all. The head is like the "apple-headed" Toy Terrier, with large bat ears standing out from the head, a very fine tail, and the skin of a uniform dark colour.

I will now endeavour to describe the subject of your illustration, which is certainly a singular specimen of the canine race. The head is more like that of a racoon than any other animal I

"CHINESE PUZZLE," THE PROPERTY OF MR. W. K. TAUNTON.

know of; the skin on forehead slightly wrinkled; small eye; flesh-coloured nose; tongue black; pricked ears; wide chest; short, thick neck; compact body; short, thick, but not bushy tail, carried somewhat high, with a slight curve, but not turned over the back; colour sandy red, the legs being rather deeper in colour than the body; toe-nails white, and dew-claws. The coat is short and thick, and was very soft, like the under-coat of the Esquimaux, but it appears to have got harsher lately, especially on the back. The inside of the ears, instead of being protected with hair—which is the case with most, if not all, pricked-eared dogs—is perfectly smooth. She has a peculiar gait when out, and has little or no idea of following, but when let loose at once starts off on her own account. I am unable to say what part of China she comes from, and only know she was brought direct from that country. When she was given to me I had some doubts as to her belonging to a distinct Chinese breed, never having seen any of the kind before; but I have since been told by a gentleman from China, as well by others who have seen her, that she is true breed, an opinion endorsed by Mr. Lort at the last Crystal Palace show. When first she arrived she acted more like a wild animal than anything else, retreating to the back of her cage and showing her teeth in a most determined manner. She is now, however, perfectly quiet with people as well as other dogs, and will allow puppies to play about with her without attempting to molest them. I have bred one litter from her, but the puppies died suddenly when between three and four months old.

In addition to the above, I am informed there are small breeds of Toy-dogs about Pekin which are kept as pets, one very much like Pugs, but I do not remember to have seen any of these myself; and another with some of the attributes of our Toy Spaniels, and very like the small Japanese breed of that kind. If I mistake not, two or three of these latter were exhibited at the last Brighton show, and, to the best of my recollection, these had the black tongue; but I would not like to speak positively on this point.

I may add that the height of Chinese Puzzle is 16 inches, weight 32 lbs., and that she won an extra silver medal, Crystal Palace, 1880, only time exhibited.

CHINESE CRESTED DOG.

CHAPTER LXIX.

AUSTRALIAN DOGS.

The Kangaroo Dog.

FOR the following remarks we are indebted to Mr. Hugh E. C. Beaver:—

"This dog is essentially Australian, in fact, may be called the national dog of Australia, as I think it is the only one upon which (until late years) an Australian prided himself. This was natural in the early days of the colonies, when everything was hard to get in the bush—flour at a premium, powder and shot not to be lavishly expended, and a sheep (the goose who was to lay the golden eggs by-and-by) not to be killed except in some dire emergency. Kangaroo were plentiful; too much so, as they ate as much grass as three sheep, and of course did not choose the worst. But they were good to eat, and a dog who was fast enough could kill them, and thus save both mutton and flour, not to talk about powder and shot. It was a common thing in the bush in the old times to hear the 'Boss' saying at meal times, 'Pitch into the kangaroo, boys, and spare the damper.' A good Kangaroo Dog, therefore, was often a perfect godsend to a struggling squatter.

"There is no doubt that the Kangaroo Dog is a thorough mongrel as far as the stud-book goes, but he has as great claims to notice as some other manufactured breeds which have sprung up of late years. At first he was no doubt a fast-running savage Collie (the only dogs taken out to Australia in the early days), afterwards crossed with either Greyhound or Deerhound, most likely both, but no one knows exactly. The Collie strain was very evident in the old class of dogs. I remember seeing in New South Wales Kangaroo Dogs with quite bushy tails. When I saw them they were quite past work, but the "old hands" used to say that they were better than the new style of dogs, because although not so fast they were more certain to kill, as they ran *by nose as well as sight*. In my time they had been improved vastly by crossing with Greyhound, and, in one case that I knew, with Mastiff; and they at that time reminded me extremely of the old country Lurcher, only larger. As a rule they were dark in colour, nearly black, with white hairs intermixed (what might be called grizzly); broken-haired, deep-chested, strongly but lightly built, and somewhere between the Greyhound and Deerhound in height and also in appearance. Of course there were other colours; I am only talking about the most usual. In my time they were *gaze-hounds*. I never saw one ever put his nose down, even when, in pursuit of a kangaroo, he had lost sight. They are hunted in very much the same style as the hare is coursed in this country, except that no slips are used. Two dogs are generally hunted together, the man riding with them by his side over the plains, or wherever he fancies he is likely to drop across the kangaroo. When viewed, the latter generally sit up watching for a time, the hunter going on quietly, trying, of course, to get as close as possible without disturbing them. This is seldom nearer than two to three hundred yards (sometimes much more where they have been hunted often). As soon as the kangaroo moves the man starts galloping, exciting and encouraging the dogs, and trying to point out the flying kangaroo to them. Then the dogs know well what is the matter, and will leap up into the air when the grass is long, endeavouring to sight what they know from experience is somewhere in the direction the man is pointing. As soon as they catch sight they are off exactly like Greyhounds when let slip.

"An old male kangaroo (called in the Colonies an 'old man') very seldom runs far before he 'bails up' (*Anglicé*, stops to show fight), which, by means of his long powerful hind legs, he is quite capable of doing. I have seen a kangaroo seize a dog with its fore-paws (which are almost like hands) and with one stroke of its hind-leg (upon which there is an immense centre claw) cut five ribs as clean as if it had been done with a knife. I may mention that we sewed the wound up, and by taking great care to keep the dog quiet for about a month, made a most successful cure, and killed many a kangaroo with his assistance afterwards. On the other hand, a young female kangaroo (which goes by the name of a flying doe) can go like the wind, and if the ground is at all down-hill it takes a really good dog to come on biting terms with her.

"Dogs vary very much in their style of killing; some, in fact, will not kill at all—only chase, and leave the important work of killing to either the other dog or perhaps to its master. The most approved style of killing, because the safest, is this. The dog runs up alongside the kangaroo, and generally makes a grab at his throat. I prefer a dog to go for the flank, as he only wants to trip the kangaroo up, as you may say, not to hold him. If he succeeds, the kangaroo generally falls, or, at any rate, staggers enough to give the dog a chance of getting him by the throat, and by turning his rump away from the kangaroo prevents any use of the hind legs, and then a few drags at the throat usually settle matters, as the kangaroo is not a very tough animal in the upper part of his body. A really good killer is not to be found every day, and is prized and talked about for many a mile round his owner's domicile. In the old times, especially in the broken country—I mean country heavily-timbered and cut up by gullies, ravines, and ranges—one often was unable to keep in sight of the chase, and, as of course the dogs did not give tongue, if you once lost sight of your dog you could not tell which way they might go. By-and-by you would very likely see the dog or dogs coming back to you with blood on them, showing that they had killed, but of course you could not tell where, and might hunt for weeks without finding your quarry. Of course this would not do, and so a dog was not considered really good that would not in such a case, when told to 'go back and show,' retrace his steps quietly in front of you until he came to the place where he had killed the kangaroo.

"The Kangaroo Dog is a capital companion, always ready to go any distance with you, and makes an excellent watch-dog; but they are not, I think, very amiable tempered—not exactly quarrelsome, but snappish—and they can give a most severe bite. They are rather fond of sheep worrying, too, however well-fed they may be; but I must say this for them, they very seldom do it at home. I have known them go twenty-five and thirty miles from the station and kill sheep when there were plenty close at home. They are certainly now a distinct breed, and certain strains are very famous, though of course no written record is kept of the different kennels, at least not to my knowledge. In the colonial dog shows they have of course a class for Kangaroo Dogs, and, I think, any one would say a noble-looking lot they are."

All we desire to add to the above interesting description of the Kangaroo Dog is, that it is from the pen of a thorough sportsman, and a genuine lover and judge of dogs, who has spent several years in the bush, and of whose practical knowledge we have not the slightest doubt. We therefore take this opportunity of expressing our obligations to Mr. Beaver for the valuable information he has afforded our readers and ourselves concerning the Kangaroo Dog and the Dingo.

The Dingo.

As in the case of the Kangaroo Dog, so with the Dingo, we have fallen back upon notes supplied us by gentlemen who have studied the variety. We will commence by giving a description of the Dingo from the pen of Mr. Hugh E. C. Beaver—an Irish Water Spaniel breeder, whose late dog, Captain, is the subject of our coloured plate—who gives us the Dingo from an Australian point of view.

" The Dingo, or as he is most usually called by colonists, 'the native dog,' is common to all parts of Australia alike, showing no difference in colour, formation, or habits, but varying

DINGO "LUPUS," THE PROPERTY OF MR. W. K. TAUNTON.

very much in size. In colour he is a red-brown on back and sides, getting darker towards the ridge of the back, in some cases showing almost a distinct dark line all down the back and tail. Head rather lofty, very wide between the ears, which are always pricked ; nose rather pointed, very powerful jaws, and far larger teeth than a dog of similar size would be expected to have. His tail is almost exactly like a fox's brush, having the same white tip, and is carried in the same way—never carried over his back in a curl, but floating loosely behind as he runs. I have seen in this country Dingoes with a curly tail, but it is not right, and shows at once that they have a cross of Collie in them. This, of course, they are liable to have, considering that no one is likely to bring a Dingo from the new country, far back in the interior, but would get one from somewhere near old settled districts, where you continually see crossbreeds with both Sheep-dogs and Kangaroo Hounds, and these are always considered the worst enemies to the sheep. The native dog is a pest to sheep-farmers, as he not only kills the sheep, but at the same time bites a great many more which almost always die from the effects. I have seen ten to twelve sheep dead in a sheep-yard in the morning, and forty or fifty more severely bitten, the work of two dogs. They bite with a snap, and if their hold gives go on to the next sheep, leaving generally a ghastly wound. They are very cunning. I remember once in Queensland a large yard which was divided into two parts—in one part a flock of weaners which had been shorn early to get rid of the grass-seed in the wool, and in the other division of the yard a flock of similar sheep unshorn with a heavy fleece. For three nights in succession two native dogs came into the yard where the woolly sheep were, and passed through into the adjoining yard, and killed the sheep with no wool on, leaving the woolly ones unharmed. They could not get into the shorn sheep-yard except through the woolly ones, but could see into it from the outside. The size of the Dingo depends entirely on the ease with which he can get food. The largest I ever saw were in Gippsland, Victoria, a county abounding at that time in kangaroo, wallabi, and many other smaller animals, and they also got a great quantity of fish left by the tide in rock-pools on the coast. In Gippsland, at that time, there were large herds of wild cattle; they came out on the open country from the timber to feed, and when they had young calves with them, I have often been amused at the cunning way in which the dogs would get one. They daren't attack them openly, because the mother would easily drive them off, so the two dogs (they nearly always go in pairs, dog and bitch; if you see more together it is generally the last litter of pups) go as near as they dare, and commence playing about together, chasing each other and rolling about like playful kittens. The stupid calves soon notice this, and want to go and see what it is, but are generally stopped by the old cow. I have seen this going on for hours, till at last a calf will get off unnoticed, and run up to the dogs; they are up in a moment, and have it by the throat; the rest of the cattle come charging down at once and drive the dogs away, but their end is gained, for if the unfortunate calf is not quite dead it does not live very long after, and the dogs sit down at a respectable distance and wait until the cattle go away, which must happen before long, then they proceed to eat the calf. These dogs were, I should think, often 25 and 26 inches high. In other parts of the colonies I have seen them very small, not more than 14 or 15 inches. This has been in parts where game is not plentiful, and where they have also to travel very long distances for water. When born they are very much like Collie pups, very thick fluffy wool on them of a deep chocolate colour, with the tiniest bit of white on the tip of the tail, hardly discernible. They are then very easy to domesticate, and will grow up and never want to go away, but they are never to be trusted; their nature makes them, *if out of your sight* (they will be quite good while you are with them), take to worrying sheep and killing fowls. A Mr. Lyall, a squatter near Melbourne, had two, I remember, who always followed him about, whether he was driving in the buggy or riding. He had them some years, but always kept a close eye on them. One day they gave him the slip, and went home to the station, and killed ten or twelve most valuable imported rams, quite close to the house-door. If taken old they never get tame. The blacks always have some of them in their camp just about half wild. They have a most melancholy howl. The true Dingo does not bark, but you will sometimes hear one howl, commencing with a sort of bark, but that is always in a place where you know there are cross-bred ones. They seem to me to be able to ventriloquise in a fashion, as it is often very hard to tell in what direction they are, and also how many of them there may be. If two dogs are howling you will often think there are six or seven in different directions. I have never known them attack a man, however hard pressed for food, although there *are* men to be met with in the bush who will narrate fearful stories of being chased by them, like a pack of wolves for miles, but there are *liars* everywhere. They will hunt a kangaroo for hours, sometimes I believe days, by sight and by smell until they tire it down. There used to be generally on stations a reward given for each tail brought in—it was, as a rule, half a pound of tobacco ; and immense quantities of poison (strychnine) is laid down for them. Hunted with a couple of Kangaroo Dogs, they give a fair run, and die very game—you never hear a whimper while they are being worried—they die fighting to the last."

Having thus given Mr. Beaver's ideas of the Dingo, we add those of Mr. W. K. Taunton, who is an authority on the subject of domesticated foreign dogs. The only point at which Mr. Beaver and Mr. Taunton appear to be at issue is in the carriage of the tail, and here Mr. Beaver's remarks appear to account for their difference of opinion.

Mr. Taunton writes :—

"The Dingo, or, as it is called by the natives, 'Warragal,' is the wild dog of Australia, in which country it causes great annoyance and loss to the inhabitants by the havoc it makes among their flocks. Large numbers are annually being destroyed, so that in some parts of the country they are now becoming scarce. Like most other wild dogs, the Dingo bears a considerable resemblance to the wolf, especially in head, which is wide between the ears ; the body is rather long, with a moderately short and thick coat and bushy tail, which, when the dog is in motion, is generally carried high and slightly curled, but not over the hip. The colour is almost invariably a reddish-brown ; white feet and a white tip to the tail are looked upon by some as typical of the breed. The Dingo stands about 22 inches at the shoulder, and is a strongly-made, very active dog, with powerful jaws, and teeth unusually large in proportion to the size of the dog. I see no reason why the Dingo should not become as domesticated as any other dog within a short space of time. Possibly it might take a generation or two before their innate wildness would be bred out, but much would of course depend under what conditions the puppies are reared. There is a general impression that these dogs are treacherous, and not to be trusted. I have owned two of this breed, and cannot say, as far as my experience goes, that I have found them so. My best specimen I gave to a friend in Paris, and I believe the dog is now located in the Jardin des Plantes. These dogs do not bark, but make a peculiar noise, which can scarcely be called howling. There are a handsome pair of Dingoes now in the Zoological Gardens which have lately bred, but the mother destroyed and must have eaten the puppies when they were a few days old. The same thing occurred only a few days before with the wild dog of Sumatra, a dog which is lower in the leg and more foxy in appearance than the Dingo."

The illustration which accompanies these remarks is that of Lupus, a Dingo belonging to Mr. Walter K. Taunton, the writer of the above. The chief fault in this Dingo is in the carriage of his tail, which is much too high.

CHAPTER LXX.

BREEDING, PUPPING, AND REARING.

"IT is surprising how soon a want of care, or care wrongly directed, leads to the degeneracy of a domestic race." Thus speaks Mr. Darwin in his "Descent of Man," and no practical breeder of any sort of stock can be found to disagree with him. No care and attention on the part of the owner and his servants can turn a badly-bred, ill-formed animal into a good one; and though it is impossible to bestow too much consideration on the treatment of the stock, all exertions on behalf of animals badly bred will be, as a rule, thrown away when they come before the judge. Years of anxiety go for nothing, if due attention is not paid not only to the health and strength, but also to the proper selection of the breeding stock. As in the articles on the various breeds full prominence has been given to the special points which must be studied in each individual variety, it is unnecessary here for us to go beyond a general outline of the management of what may be called the breeding materials.

It is wonderful to reflect upon the success which seems to attend the efforts of some of the most loosely-conducted establishments, and to see winner after winner turned out from a kennel where no rules of breeding are for a moment studied, and where the management is often left by the owner in the hands of a kennel-man whose knowledge of the breed is absolutely *nil*. Such success in the few instances in which it occurs is eventually unfortunate in its results, both to the breeders of the dogs themselves and also to many of the outside world, who, either to save themselves trouble, or through ignorance of the simplest principles of breeding, ignorantly rush for the services of the nearest prize-winner, utterly regardless as to whether he is likely to "nick" with the bitch they propose uniting with him, in shape, size, or pedigree. The result may be a temporary success, but is certain ultimate destruction of all type. Breeding *can* be regulated by rules and judicious selection, else how do we see so many breeds of dogs now in existence (which we can prove to have originated from a cross of two older varieties) keep on throwing puppies which consistently resemble their parents in every property, and whose difference from them only consists in minor insignificant and immaterial features? By rigidly adhering to an ideal type, and resisting all temptations to go from it, a breeder is certain in time to find himself in possession of the sort of dog he has, rightly or wrongly, determined on possessing; and then he is in a position to discover, from the success of his dogs, whether his exertions are to be repaid or not.

We must commence, then, by impressing upon all beginners, and many older hands, the desirability of adhering to *one type* if they want to make a name for themselves as amateur breeders. Of course, in the case of those who breed solely for the market it is right that they should produce good specimens of every recognised standard, so as to please buyers, whatever their own opinions may be; but as these remarks are not intended to be addressed to dealers, who are perfectly competent to manage their own business, but to amateurs, it is sufficient to point out the importance of adhering to one type. By breeding to one standard, we necessarily imply that no one should be induced to set up as a producer of canine stock until he has clearly made up his mind what sort of animal he wishes for. In the case of a beginner, there is generally an acquaintance at hand who possesses more or less experience in such matters, and who, if he be a real lover of the dog, will be glad to place his services at his young friend's disposal. The opinions of such an individual may not all be correct; but if he be fairly competent, and honest, he can always be useful to the beginner. It is a great assistance, too, in arriving at a correct opinion, if the uses for which the various breeds have been brought into existence are brought under consideration. It is no good breeding a dog, though he be ever so handsome-looking, if he is palpably unfit for the work he is supposed to perform if called upon; and, under a judge who knows his work, a flashy-looking dog often has to lower his colours to his more sober and workman-like neighbour, whose undoubted good properties have escaped the attention of the uninitiated.

Having decided upon the type which he himself desires to produce, a beginner should make it his next business to ascertain if his ideas in any way resemble the orthodox standard; if so, his labours are considerably diminished, as his object in breeding will be to obtain the services of such stud dogs as he particularly admires, and in whose pedigree he has satisfied himself there is no bar sinister. It is an indisputable fact that a well-bred dog is far more likely to beget stock resembling himself than a good-looking mongrel is. Again, in the case of the former, even if he fails to impress his own likeness on his progeny, there is a possibility, if not a fair amount of certainty, that the puppies will throw back to a well-bred ancestor of more or less elegant proportions; whilst with a dog whose pedigree is enveloped in mystery or something worse, there is a chance of the young ones displaying every conceivable type and temper.

The subject of in-breeding is one which has exercised the minds of breeders for many a day, and affords matter for a controversy which seems far from being brought to a termination. There can be no sort of doubt that, if carried to too great a length, in-breeding stunts the growth and weakens the intelligence and constitution of all dogs. This opinion is, we believe, unanimously received by all breeders of canine stock; though, in the case of game-cocks more than one authority has it that incestuously-bred birds are stouter, gamer, and more active than those whose parents are unrelated to each other. Observation has proved that the union of father with daughter and mother with son is far preferable, where dogs are concerned, to an alliance between brother and sister. Once in and twice out is, we believe, an excellent system if the crosses are judiciously selected, and the reasons for this appear to be as follows:— A breeder has a dog belonging to a strain which usually produces good-headed ones, but apt to be leggy and perhaps deficient in coat. He naturally wishes to remedy these defects, and in many instances selects as a mate a dog indifferent in head, but good in bone and in jacket; the result being most probably one fair puppy and several very indifferent ones which inherit the faults of both their sire and dam. On the other hand, however, had he exercised a little patience, and mated his dog with one of the same strain, thereby strengthening the probability of the puppies being in their turn likely to beget good-headed offspring when allied with another strain of blood, he would, in the course of a few years, have most probably got exactly the sort of dog he desired to obtain. We are perfectly aware that this argument may be said to cut both ways, and that those taking a contrary view of the case to our own may exclaim that the faults are just as likely to be perpetuated as the good properties; but we would observe that perpetual wandering from one blood to another *must* eventually produce specimens of uncertain type, whose services at the stud are perfectly useless from the fact that there is no fixed character in their breeding, and who are liable to throw puppies of every conceivable shape and make in the same litter. In short, in-breeding is, when judiciously carried out, absolutely essential to a breeder's success as a breeder, if such is to be maintained.

Finally, before closing our remarks upon the general subject of breeding, we wish to warn beginners that they are undertaking a tedious and very disappointing pursuit when they set up to be breeders of exhibition dogs. The best of calculations are often upset by accident or fate, and many a promising puppy falls a victim to the ills that puppyhood is peculiarly heir to. To have bred a first-rate dog of any breed is indeed a thing to be proud of, when it is considered how many scores of persons are expending time and money and judgment upon this very object. How few champions there are in the world is a statement which can be read in two ways—either there are so few that it should be an easy matter to add to their number ; or it may be construed as implying that a vast amount of labour is wasted in trying to produce what is in reality a matter of chance. To us there appears to be both truth and untruth in each opinion ; but the fact remains that champions have arisen, and will arise again, and are far more likely to be brought into existence when due attention is paid to the mates a breeder selects for his dogs.

Careful people invariably keep regular stud books referring to their breeding operations ; in these the date of birth (and if necessary of the purchase), colour, sex, weight, breeder, and performances of their stock, are registered. The visits of their own bitches, and of others to their stud dogs, are also entered ; as are the dates of sales, and the names and addresses of the purchasers. By this means ready and accurate information can be obtained concerning the history of any animal which may at one time or other pass through their hands.

THE STUD DOG.

A great deal of a breeder's success depends upon the state of health in which the stud dog is when he begets offspring ; for a delicate or unhealthy dog is more than likely to transmit his defects to his puppies, who are in consequence more difficult to rear, and of less value when they attain maturity. Considerable attention should therefore be paid to the comfort of a dog who is in the habit of receiving a large number of stud visits. He should, if possible, be well exercised morning and evening, either by a country walk, or a run round his owner's yard ; and his diet must be wholesome and liberal. A plunge in cold water materially assists in keeping a dog in vigorous condition, and in warm weather may be taken daily. It should be borne in mind, too, that it is always well to have your stud dogs look clean and tidy, both when out of doors and when in the kennels. Much depends upon the first impressions formed by the owner of a bitch who contemplates breeding from him, and many a dog is passed over whose services, had he been in better fettle, might have been resorted to. Care should be taken not to overtax the energies of a young sire by allowing him to receive too many stud visits ; the result of excesses in this way being both sickly offspring and his own ultimate failure at the stud. Fifteen or twenty bitches a year are quite enough for a dog not in his prime, and about twice the number for a dog in the full vigour of his strength. As a rule, dogs under eighteen months old are not likely to do themselves or their owners much good if bred from ; and availing one's self of the services of a very old dog is always risky. It is extremely hard to state an age at which a dog can be said to be " old " ; some retain the vigour of their youth up to ten years and more, whilst others get decrepit and break up at six or seven. So much depends upon constitution and careful attendance, that it is impossible to advise upon the age at which a stud dog ceases to be of use ; but breeders should see the dog for themselves, if they do not know him, and judge, from his appearance and condition, whether he is likely to suit their wishes.

On the arrival of a bitch for service, the owner of the stud dog should, unless time is a matter of consideration, fasten her up securely, and let her recover from the fatigues of her journey before the introduction takes place. A night's rest and a feed are very likely to assist nature's course, a bitch served immediately after a tiring journey being far more likely to miss conception than one who has rested and become a little accustomed to the place and those around her. Many bitches are very troublesome and restive when with the dog, and throw themselves about in a most violent manner; others are savage and morose, and if not carefully looked after are likely to fly at him and perhaps do some serious injury. In such cases the bitch must be held by the collar, but care should be taken that she does not get half suffocated by too tight a grasp being placed on it. The possibility of a fight taking place, or of the dog requiring some assistance, especially in the case of young bitches, make it undesirable that the pair should be left alone together for any length of time, much less after connection is terminated.

After union it is some time before the animals can be separated: twenty minutes is about the average, though, of course, this period is often exceeded or decreased in duration. After that the breeder must wait patiently for Nature to take its course, when the bitch should be kenneled by herself on straw, and kept as quiet as possible. It is desirable that a second visit should, if possible, be paid after an interval of thirty-six or forty-eight hours. The majority of the owners of stud dogs gladly consent to this arrangement, as it lessens the chances of the bitch proving barren, and also saves them trouble, and their dog from getting a bad name as a stock-getter.

A sire should be looked upon with suspicion if his services are in too great request, and the number of his receptions unlimited, as it is only reasonable to expect sickly offspring from a dog whose stud experiences are practically unrestricted. A very old dog, unless mated to a young and vigorous bitch, is more than likely to fail to beget stock at all: and if he succeeds in doing so, the puppies are very frequently of bad constitution and delicate in their earlier days. It is often the case that the services of a successful show dog are most eagerly sought after by breeders, and the merits of his *father* entirely overlooked; and this is certainly a fact which must puzzle all practical men when they reflect upon it. A sire of good pedigree, who can produce stock of superior quality to himself, is better worth patronising at a low fee than his successful son who has yet to prove himself the success at the stud which he is on the bench or in the field; especially as in the latter instance the sum charged for his services is sure to be a considerable one. Many of our champion dogs have turned out complete failures from a breeder's point of view; whilst their plainer-looking fathers or brothers have begotten offspring of a far better stamp, though with only half the chances of success. A golden rule in dog-breeding is, for the owner to satisfy himself that his bitch *really does* visit the dog he has selected for her. In many instances we know tricks to have been played upon owners who have sent their bitches to dogs at a distance; and we have ourselves been applied to for the services of a dog, standing at a low fee, by an owner of a stud dog, for a bitch sent up to the latter. Unfortunately, in ignorance of the fact, we granted his request, and only afterwards discovered what had occurred, and that the bitch, the name of whose owner we never ascertained, had been sent up to this gentleman's dog, and was not one of his own. The difference between the fees of the two dogs was three guineas; and as it was impossible for us to *prove* that the owner was not informed of what took place, we were unable to take steps in the matter, and our acquaintance still walks the streets an honest man. If the distance is too far to accompany the bitch or send one's man, it is a very good plan to get a friend in the neighbourhood of the stud dog's kennel to accompany her when she visits him, especially in dealing with strangers. Of course, in the case of owners whose characters are above suspicion these precautions are unnecessary; but it will always be a satisfaction to the proprietor of a stud dog to know that the bitch's visit has been witnessed by her owner or his nominee, especially if she should fail to be in pup. In event of the latter being the case, the usual practice is that the same bitch may visit the dog a second time gratuitously, or another of the same owner's at half price; but here again caution must be exercised on the part of the proprietor of the stud dog, for instances have occurred when puppies have been born dead, and he has been told there was no result from the union of the parents. Owners of stud dogs often do, and always should, provide the owners of bitches which have visited them with formal certificates of service; such documents are particularly useful in event of disputed pedigrees.

THE BROOD BITCH.

Young bitches often exhibit symptoms of an inclination to breed at the age of eight or nine months, but it is undesirable to place them at the stud until they have reached the age of at least eighteen months. The remarks we made above against the advisability of resorting to the services of too young a sire, apply with even greater force when a youthful bitch is under consideration. Stunted and puny puppies are almost sure to be produced from a young mother; and the injury they are likely to do her constitution is incalculable. It must be borne in mind that for weeks before birth her system is sorely taxed to provide them with nourishment, and after the shock of labour is gone through there is a further strain upon her until they are weaned.

The first symptom afforded by a bitch that she is likely to be soon ready for breeding purposes, is a desire on her part to romp and play with any dog she meets. This may possibly arise from merely exuberance of spirits, but it is always well to keep a close eye upon her as soon as any undue levity is observed in her conduct. It is most desirable to use every endeavour to keep the animal away from all risk of being got at by strange dogs; and when the matter is placed beyond doubt all former precautions should be doubled if possible. It must be remembered that there is not only a great risk of dogs getting into the place where the bitch is confined, but that she will probably be equally anxious to escape from her kennel, and some bitches have performed almost incredible feats in their endeavours to do so.

She should, if at a distance, be sent off to the kennels where the dog is standing a day or two after the earlier symptoms appear, so as to be in time. If despatched by public conveyance, it is imperative that she be securely confined in a box or basket from which escape is impossible. The transit of dogs has been more fully treated in the chapter on exhibiting, and need not be further alluded to here; but all breeders should be impressed with the absolute necessity of exercising the greatest vigilance when they have bitches by them under such circumstances. For at least a week after the bitch has visited the dog, the precautions for isolating her must not be relaxed, or all her owner's hopes may be marred by her forming a connection with a stranger.

The influence of a previous sire on a subsequent litter of puppies is a subject of the keenest discussion and interest amongst breeders, and a most interesting correspondence has taken place in the columns of the *Live Stock Journal* relating thereto. Some of the statements which have appeared from time to time in that journal upon this subject, and which have been substantiated by the names of writers whose position as breeders of various varieties of live stock is assured, are invested with a peculiar importance. But having carefully read and considered the matter, we find ourselves driven back on the supposition that although such occurrences undoubtedly have arisen, they are not by any means the matter-of-course events some of the correspondents of the *Live Stock Journal* consider them, and in more than one instance we have failed to satisfy ourselves that the influences imputed have regulated the course of events. In making this statement we attribute to the writers no desire to impose on public credulity, but we think they have too often forgotten the influence which surrounding objects exercise over the mind of a pregnant female. This opinion is shared by many breeders of live stock, and it is notorious that a celebrated breeder of black polled cattle had his premises and fences tarred, with the express object of assisting Nature in keeping the colour of his stock as deep as possible. It is, however, quite impossible for us to go at length into the subject, and it must therefore be dismissed with the remark that as many breeders firmly believe, from personal experience, that such a thing as past influence is possible, especially in the case of maiden bitches, due vigilance should be exercised in the thorough isolation of bitches when in season, or more than a temporary evil and disappointment may occur

PUPPING.

Having selected a proper mate for his bitch, and sent her to him, all anxiety is removed from an owner's mind for some time at least ; for during the first period of going with young, the bitch will require no special diet or attention. It may be here stated, for the benefit of the uninitiated, that the period of gestation amongst dogs is sixty-three days, and that this time is rarely exceeded unless something is wrong, though it sometimes occurs that the whelps make their appearance some days before they are expected. During this period the bitch should be allowed plenty of exercise, but during the latter portion of her pregnancy she is peculiarly liable to chills ; every care should therefore be taken to avoid any risk of her taking cold, and all washing operations and *violent* exercise must then be suspended. Our own experience has taught us that in the majority of instances it is almost impossible to tell whether or no the bitch is in whelp until the third or fourth week, and on many occasions we have known breeders to be in doubt for a much longer period ; in fact, on discussing with a very well-known Pointer exhibitor the accouchement of one of his exhibits during a show, he assured us that when she left home she had shown no traces of being in whelp, and as a matter of fact her time was not up until the following week.

A week or so before the date on which it is expected that she will whelp, the bitch should be installed in the quarters in which it is arranged the interesting event is to take place. The reason for this is that dogs must get used to a kennel before they will make themselves at home in it, and this feeling is peculiarly perceptible in the case of a bitch who has recently whelped ; for in many cases she will try and carry her puppies (greatly to the damage of the latter) back to her old quarters rather than let them remain in a kennel to which she is unaccustomed. Having got her reconciled to her change of abode, the *locale* of which should, if possible, be away from the other dogs, so as to let her have more quiet (but *warmth* and *absence of draught* are even more essential than isolation in such cases), and supposing the time of her whelping to be near at hand, it is desirable that the bitch should be provided with a diet of a more strengthening character than that which she has been in the habit of receiving. This need not consist entirely of meat or other heating foods, which can only tend to increase her discomfort in parturition, but may be made of scraps well boiled or stewed, with the addition of bread, meal, or rice, which in their turn will absorb the gravy or soup, and form, in conjunction with the scraps, when the latter are chopped up, a meal which is both wholesome and nutritious. A few days before the puppies make their appearance a considerable change is usually perceptible in the bitch ; the presence of milk can be detected, and a considerable enlargement of the stomach takes place. Her behaviour too, clearly indicates that she is uneasy and in pain, and in many instances the appetite entirely fails, and the bowels become confined. In the latter case a mild purgative of either castor, linseed, or sweet oil must be given. The first-named remedy is sometimes too powerful an aperient for a bitch in such a condition, as, in the more delicate breeds especially, it is apt to cause severe straining, which would injure the puppies. Before resorting, therefore, to castor-oil, an experimental dose of either linseed or sweet oil might be administered, which, if it succeed in acting on the bowels, will have satisfactorily accomplished the owner's object; and as the lubricating power of all three oils is essentially the same, the internal organs will be equally benefited by either medicine.

Two or three days before the puppies are due a good bed of straw should be provided, and this should not be changed till the whelps are at least a week old; for unnecessary attention will certainly worry the mother, and may cause her to destroy her offspring. The bed of straw should be placed on boards raised not higher than two or three inches from the ground; in fact, the bitch during the last few weeks of going in whelp should not be allowed the opportunity of leaping up and down on and off a high bench. On no account should the bed be placed on a cold stone or brick flooring; and even a carpet is objectionable, for the mother, in making her bed for the reception of her young, invariably removes all the bedding from underneath her, and piles it up at the sides in the shape of a nest. Her object in acting thus is to facilitate the operation of licking the puppies; as she will within a few hours of parturition have all her whelps thoroughly cleansed and freed from any offensive adherent matter, being during their earlier puppyhood most attentive to the personal cleanliness of her offspring. This would be impossible if she allowed them to lie on the straw, as the wet would soak into it and cause the bed to become foul.

The different temperaments and dispositions of various bitches become specially apparent as parturition approaches. Some will be impatient at the slightest intrusion on the solitude they evidently prefer, whilst others eagerly welcome the familiar voice of master or attendant, and seem to beg him to remain beside them in the time of suffering. A great deal must therefore be left to the judgment of those in charge of the bitch; but it should be borne in mind that, though an occasional visit is necessary even in the case of a most unsociably-disposed bitch, in order to see that nothing has gone wrong, still *too much* interference and fidgeting even with a quiet one is apt to render her feverish, and increase the difficulties of her situation. Under any circumstances a plentiful amount of cold water should always be placed near her, and beyond this she will, in the majority of instances, want nothing until the pups are born. Should she however become exhausted during labour, a little port wine may be given now and then. When safely delivered, some gruel should be given her, and she should be kept on this diet for the space of two or three days; it is strengthening and soothing to the internal organs, and can be made either with milk or water; the addition of a little gravy or beef tea is an excellent practice after the first two or three basins of gruel. The quantity of gruel should be unlimited, and very often she will devour a basinful every two or three hours for the first day; care, however, must be taken not to let it remain by her too long, so as to turn sour and disarrange the stomach, which it is very easy to do when a bitch has just whelped. It is always desirable to try and count the puppies when the mother is off the bed feeding, as it lets an owner know whether she eats her whelps or not; and if he misses puppies he must try and devise some way to stop the proceeding.

In event of a puppy dying, it must of course be removed at the first opportunity offering itself, and if this can be managed without the knowledge of the mother, so much the better; for we have known instances where a whole litter has been destroyed by a dam on the removal of one dead whelp from their midst; and, besides this, there is the danger of a bite from a bad-tempered bitch if she sees her family carried off. Opinions vary much as regards whether dogs can count or not; but our own belief is decidedly in favour of their being able to do so up to a certain number. This is a matter of considerable importance where puppies are concerned, for it is often necessary to remove some from the mother. Some bitches seem to take no notice of the diminished number of their family, whilst others appear frenzied by their bereavement, and, acting on a first impulse, have destroyed the remaining whelps, unless restrained from doing so. It being therefore certain that mothers are capable of discovering, by counting or otherwise, when any of their puppies have been removed in their absence, it behoves the breeder to be careful how he acts when such a course has to be adopted. If he carefully watches the bitch for half an hour or so on her re-introduction to her family, and sees that all is well, he need have no further care on that score; but should she become restless, and show signs of an inclination to destroy the remaining whelps, she must be closely guarded in order to prevent mischief. Some bitches are notorious for the habit they have of killing their puppies, and in such cases the only means to adopt is, in the absence of a foster-mother, to take the puppies in-doors, and keep them warmly wrapped up in a basket lined with flannel before a fire, and let the mother come and suckle them every two hours. Whilst with them she should be laid on her side, and gently held down so as to prevent her injuring them in any way.

Having alluded above to the subject of foster-mothers, we may express the opinion that, in the event of valuable puppies being expected, the acquisition of such an animal is very desirable. A bitch in whelp can often be obtained from the Dogs' Home, Battersea, for a few shillings, and if one is not to be obtained there in a suitable condition of pregnancy, Mr. Scorborio, the courteous and energetic manager of that institution can often put owners in the way of obtaining one at a very reasonable figure. Foster-mothers can also frequently be hired for a few weeks, if advertised for in the papers; and as a matter of fact we once obtained the services of seven at £1 each from one advertisement in the *Live Stock Journal.* The greatest precaution must however be exercised by owners, in order that no diseased or unhealthy bitch be received in the responsible position of wet-nurse to their puppies, for the danger of such an introduction can hardly be exaggerated; and therefore many persons rather shrink from investing in bitches of whose antecedents they are ignorant.

Aid from inexperienced persons when administered to a bitch in labour is almost sure to be attended with most unsatisfactory results, and we are simply re-echoing the opinion of the vast majority of practical breeders when we express the conviction that many of the so-called veterinary surgeons practising in this country know next to nothing of canine pathology. A man who may or may not have passed his examination at the Veterinary College, and professes to be an adept at physicking horses or doctoring cows, invariably considers himself quite qualified to attend upon dogs, and possibly in a few cases he may be so; but in most instances he knows less than the kennel-man does, and increases the ailing dog's difficulties by his injudicious treatment. "There is a man down the street who knows all about dogs," is a common saying when the owner is in a difficulty, and the man is sent for, generally turning out to be absolutely incompetent and grossly ignorant of what he professes to understand. For our own part we believe that doctoring their own dogs is an easy task for tolerably intelligent and fairly attentive owners, and experience has taught us that the list of drugs and remedies which are applicable to canine diseases is a very limited one indeed, and that an elaborate doggy pharmacopœia is a wholly unnecessary institution, which can only tend to complicate the difficulties which lie in the way of a beginner when he attempts to arrive at a correct diagnosis and treatment of his animal's ailments. In cases of protracted labour, where there are indications of internal complications, surgical aid must of course be rendered the bitch, provided really competent professional assistance can be obtained. All other is useless in such cases, and we must once again impress upon our readers the terrible danger and torture to which they subject their dogs by calling in the assistance of incompetent advisers. *Be convinced that your surgeon knows more than you do yourself*, is a golden rule for breeders to lay heed to.

In the event of the bitch being unable to pass her puppies after being in labour for some time, the application of crushed ice to the abdomen is frequently the means of enabling her to do so, as it has the effect of contracting the muscles of the womb, and thus assists in the expulsion of the whelps. Ergot is sometimes used in complicated cases as a uterine excitant, but should be resorted to only as an extreme measure, being, in the hands of inexperienced persons, a very dangerous medicine. Oiling the vagina is also in many cases a relief to the bitch. In some books we have seen it strongly recommended as a means of assisting protracted labour that the bitch should be immersed in a warm bath for a few minutes; this in ninety-nine cases out of a hundred involves two certain results—(1) almost instant relief to the dog, (2) DEATH. According to the theory propounded by Mayhew in his work on canine diseases, the application of warm water causes a relaxation of the muscles of the womb, whereas an exactly opposite effect is needed; thus the temporary relief from her suffering costs the poor beast her life, and her owner the mortification of having killed her by improper treatment. We know not of one only, but of scores of such instances occurring; and no doubt all breeders of experience are well acquainted with the ill effects of an injudicious bath to a bitch in labour.

Some curiosity on the part of a youthful breeder is natural enough where the first puppies of his own breeding are concerned; but he will be acting very foolishly indeed if he gives way to it. It cannot be any advantage to him to discover the sexes of the different whelps on the day of their birth, and all handling should be avoided unless it is thought desirable to remove some from the mother on account of the number being considered too many for her to bring up. It should be borne in mind that four or five strong, vigorous, well-nourished puppies are far more likely to turn out satisfactorily for their owner than eight or ten scantily-nourished ones; and it must be left to the good sense of the breeder to decide, from the condition of the bitch and the amount of milk she has secreted, how many she can do justice to without injuring herself. Five or six are enough for a moderate-sized bitch, and eight or ten for a large one. The extra ones can be destroyed if sickly, or placed under a foster-mother, if one can be got. In some instances puppies have been very successfully brought up by hand, through the immediate agency of a baby's feeding bottle; but before any one enters upon such an undertaking due consideration should be devoted to the magnitude of the task before him. Constant feeding is necessary, and the whelps require a great deal of warmth, patience, and attention. In circumstances like this the most valuable ally of all is to be found in the cook; if her hearty co-operation is obtained the chances are that the whelps will go on and prosper, for a snug corner for the basket on the kitchen hearth, and the constant supervision she can give them, is sure to benefit them very considerably.

About the ninth day the puppies begin to open their eyes, and very soon they commence crawling out of their nest and about the floor of the kennel; after which it is wonderful how fast they seem to grow and the strength they display. At two weeks old they will commence to eat bread-and-gravy, or bread-and-milk, if it is provided for them, though the latter is, we think, an objectionable diet, as it is apt to turn sour, and also, if cow's milk, to breed worms, to which young puppies are peculiarly liable. Goat's milk, however, we consider good for puppies, as it, according to our experience, does not increase the risk of worms. During this time the food given to the mother should be of a strengthening nature, so as to enable her to stand the strain on her constitution which her maternal duties involve, but care should be taken to prevent her bringing bones into her bed, as many instances have occurred of mothers severely biting their puppies who have attempted to take the bones from her. One or two gentle runs a day are now very necessary for the bitch, as exercise not only freshens her considerably, but gives her a chance of getting away from the persistent persecution which the puppies inflict upon her. At five weeks old the whelps may usually begin to be removed from their mother, and it is well to do this gradually, as they suffer less from the separation if this course is pursued; and by extending the intervals of the bitch's absence they can be almost entirely weaned without any ill effects to either themselves or their dam. The best method is to begin by removing the bitch for an hour or two in the warmest part of the day, so that the chance of the puppies catching cold is diminished. The periods of her absence can then be prolonged until she is only returned to them of a night, and finally ceases to visit them at all.

It frequently occurs that the teats of the bitch have been wounded by the teeth of the puppies when they suckle her; and inflammation, from the influx of milk, often arises when they are removed. Considerable relief can be obtained by rubbing some camphorated oil well over her stomach, and this can be repeated night and morning for some days, a mild dose of physic being administered when the puppies are finally removed. In the event, however, of the milk that she has secreted still bothering her, and her teats being so tender that drawing some off by ordinary milking is impossible recourse may be had to an ordinary soda-water bottle, heated with hot water, the mouth of which can be pressed over the inflamed teat. This has the effect of drawing some of the milk out, and thereby relieving the bitch of a great deal of pain. Or an ordinary breast-pump may be employed.

Having now given a brief sketch of the general treatment of a bitch when pupping, we will pass on to the future management of the whelps themselves.

REARING.

On the removal of the whelps from their mother, a very considerable change for the worse immediately takes place in their appearance, which is due mainly to the alteration in their diet and general mode of life. Instead of drawing a certain amount of sustenance from their dam at the cost of no trouble, they are now cast upon their own resources for a means of subsistence. The necessity of having to get up and hunt about for the dish which contains its food is a fact which it takes a puppy's mind a long time to master. Consequently the entire litter often passes many hungry hours during the night, although their food is within a few inches of their bed; and it is not until a happy thought strikes one of them that it might be a good plan if he got up and looked for something, that they all follow his example, and fall to as only hungry puppies can. Almost all puppies suffer greatly from worms, and immediately on their removal from their mother means should be taken to rid them of such torments. The presence of worms is certain when the stomachs of puppies swell and harden, but they frequently exist without developing such symptoms. It is therefore the safer plan to administer one or two doses of worm medicine all round, especial care being taken that their delicate mouths and throats are not injured in administering the remedy. The two best vermifuges are areca-nut and santonine. The latter, in its crystallised form, is an excellent remedy for worms in dogs, and about two grains in butter cannot be surpassed as a vermifuge for puppies of seven or eight weeks old, whose parents weigh from forty to sixty pounds weight. If too strong a dose is given, santonine has a tendency to affect the brain and cause fits, so precaution must be exercised in administering this medicine. The chief difficulty in the use of areca-nut lies in getting it freshly grated, as if allowed to become stale it loses its virtue as an anthelmintic. To avoid this the nut should be grated on an ordinary nutmeg-grater, and given immediately in butter or lard. The ordinary dose is two grains for every pound the dog weighs, but more than two drachms should never be given. Spratt's worm powders are also excellent remedies, if an owner has to clear his pets of these pests, and are easily procured of any chemist.

It is useless to resort to any remedy for worms in dogs unless the medicine is administered on an empty stomach. Small dogs should fast for at least twelve hours, and large powerful animals for twenty-four, before the medicine is administered. It is also desirable to prevent their drinking too much water during the period of their abstention, the object being to deprive the worms of all sorts of food, so that the anthelmintic may have a greater chance of success. Many persons give a dose of castor-oil the night before the vermifuge is given, and a second one two or three hours after if it has had no effect. As long as the purgative does not tax the dog's system too powerfully, these precautions materially assist the operation of the medicine; but judgment and caution must, of course, be exercised, and it would be foolish to adopt such vigorous treatment with a weakly puppy.

Crushed biscuits, oatmeal-porridge, and bread-and-gravy, with the addition of a little chopped meat and vegetables, are the best diet for puppies when first away from their mother, and the amount they can get through in the course of twenty-four hours is considerable. The greatest care must be taken to guard against the puppies (this, in fact, applies to any dogs, but to puppies especially) being given food which is *sour or decomposed*. A very fruitful and common cause of this has only lately come to our knowledge. We are indebted for the following information to Mr. F. Gresham, whose experience in feeding large dogs is very considerable. This gentleman has proved by experience that food cooked in a copper or other boiler is very apt to turn sour as soon as cooked, if allowed to stand and cool *in the vessel in which it has been prepared*. Care should therefore be taken to remove it, as soon as the culinary operations are completed, to a cool and clean receptacle, where it can remain until it is required for the dogs, or is returned to the boiler, to be added to other meals in course of preparation.

All draughts should be kept away from their kennel, which must be warm and dry, or the puppies will not spread and grow as they should do; and a run in a dry yard is imperative, if the weather is not too cold or damp. By keeping his puppies clean and dry, an owner considerably lessens the risk of distemper ravaging his kennels, for this fearful scourge is unquestionably amenable to sanitary arrangements, and except on very rare occasions, when its origin can usually be traced, is scarcely ever present in well-conducted establishments. In our own kennels we have never experienced a single case of distemper amongst puppies of our own breeding, and this has been under circumstances of great difficulty, where for over three years an average of nearly fifty dogs have been kept in confined spaces. A strict attention to cleanliness, fresh air, fresh water, sound food, combined with proper grooming and exercise, renders the presence of distemper well-nigh impossible, and if a breeder who attends to these matters has the misfortune to have it communicated to his stock (for distemper *is* contagious), he will find them the better able to resist its attacks if they have been previously well looked after.

Our own treatment in the few cases we had in cases of puppies we had bought (one or two of which sickened within the week) were thorough and absolute isolation in the first place, so as to preclude all possibility of contagion or infection in case of other diseases. We had a lumber-room attached to the house cleared for a hospital, and fitted with a gas stove; by this means a steady even temperature can be maintained night and day, and this is a most important feature in the treatment of distemper. All stuffiness in the air should be avoided, for it must be remembered that in this disease the nostrils become charged with a thick fluid which renders breathing very difficult. We invariably had the window open at the top, and with the gas stove aided by a thermometer kept the room at a steady temperature of 60 degrees. The only food given was beef-tea with some bread soaked in it, and the only medicine Rackham's distemper pills. Seeing is believing, and we believe these pills to be almost infallible in the treatment of distemper, never having lost a dog when using them, and knowing many breeders who share our opinion, we cannot resist alluding to them. When the graver symptoms begin to subside solid food can be administered, and the dog picks up wonderfully soon, though too premature an introduction to the cold outside is to be deprecated after his confinement so long in a warm temperature. A friend—we rather think it was Mr. R. Fulton, of Brockley—once told us of a food which he considered a capital change for dogs suffering from distemper, and this was a number of fresh haddocks' heads put into a pot and covered with water, to be boiled until the bones of the fish get soft and the water is almost entirely absorbed; this, when cold, forms a jelly, which is keenly appreciated by the invalids, and seems to do them good. Our friend's theory was that the phosphorus contained in the fish-bones assisted the medicine in curing the dog; but be this as it may, it is certain that no ill effects, but rather the contrary, resulted from giving it them.

Allusion having thus been made to the two greatest plagues of puppyhood—worms and distemper—there hardly remain more diseases to which they are peculiarly liable. Fits they certainly often suffer from, but these almost invariably are the result of worms, and will subside and disappear when the irritating cause of their presence is removed. Teething occasionally troubles them, but seldom to any great extent, for puppies do not usually shed their first teeth until nine months old, and then they are strong enough to bear the pain and annoyance the cutting of their new ones inflicts upon them. Should the puppies, however, appear to suffer from the swelling of their gums previous to the appearance of a tooth, it is well to lance the inflamed part, especially if the gum appears abnormally hard. Not only does this give immediate relief, but it helps the teeth to come up in a regular line, which in most varieties is most desirable.

The exercise and subsequent treatment of the whelps have been so thoroughly gone into in the chapters on general management and exercise, that no further allusion to them is requisite here.

CANINE MEDICINE AND SURGERY.

By W. GORDON STABLES, C.M., M.D., R.N.

—◆◇◆—

CHAPTER I.

INTRODUCTION—DIAGNOSIS—SOME SIMPLE REMEDIES.

IT has been the aim and object of the writer in the following pages to describe, in plain and simple language, the various diseases to which the dog is subject, their causes, their signs and symptoms—and the course these run—and the most rational method of conducting them to a successful termination.

By studying the probable causes of any given malady, we gain an insight into the laws that regulate the health of the animal, and good may thus be done, on the principle that prevention is better than cure. But it has not been deemed expedient to burden the reader with a description of the anatomy of any particular organ, further than is necessary for a clear understanding of the nature of the malady or accident; nor with more of physiology and pathology than is barely requisite to the elucidation of the plan of treatment adopted.

Throughout the treatise the classification of diseases is simple yet definite, the different ailments being arranged in groups under their proper headings: as, for example, the "Diseases of the Digestive Organs," "Skin Diseases," &c. &c. It is to be hoped it will thus form a work of ready reference which may be consulted in the case of any emergency almost without the aid of the index. Very nearly all if not quite all the numerous ailments that canine flesh is heir to will be found described at length. Those of a strictly surgical nature are grouped in a chapter by themselves. The diagnosis of the disease is given wherever necessary, that is, in all cases where there are two or more ailments which somewhat resemble each other though the treatment required may be different. It is an easy matter for any one who is in the habit of being among dogs to tell when one of them is ill, but often a difficult matter to tell what is the matter with him. The state of health is the dog's normal and natural condition, in which there is freedom from pain and sickness, and the proper performance of every vital function, without either dulness or irritability of temper.

As the natural standard of health varies somewhat in every dog, the owner of one is often better able at first to know when something is wrong than even a veterinary surgeon. The bright, clear eye of a healthy dog, the wet, cold, black nose, the active movements, the glossy coat, the excellent appetite, and the gaze, half saucy, half independent, but wholly loving, combine to form a picture which only the owners of dogs know how fully to appreciate. But nearly all this is altered in illness; and to treat a dog at haphazard, without first taking all possible pains to find out what is really the matter, is both careless and cruel.

Having come to the conclusion that a dog is ill, the first thing we must try to find out is, whether he is in any pain. For this purpose he should be examined carefully all over, beginning with the mouth, gently opening the jaws, feeling along the neck, down the spine, and down each limb, inside and outside; then, having laid him on his back, we ought to examine the chest and abdomen well, especially the latter, which should be gently kneaded. Sometimes a hardness will be found in the intestines, which, coupled with existing constipation, will be quite enough to account for the animal's illness, and the removal of this state of system is at least one step in the right direction. By such an examination, moreover, any swelling or tumour, bruise or fracture, will be readily discovered. The dog ought now be made to walk about a little, and talked to kindly, and his gait and manner noticed. Some dogs will almost speak to a person after their own fashion, that is, in sign language, and tell the whereabouts of their trouble.

Before prescribing for a dog, it is always best to have the whole history of the case, from the very first noticeable deviation from the straight line of health. We have various signs and symptoms afforded us, which—although the dog cannot express his feelings and sensations—generally guide us to a correct diagnosis of the case.

1. First let us take the *Coat* and *Skin*. A dry, staring coat is always a sign of illness, present or to come. The coat stares because the nervous system is in a low condition. Such an animal, if taken into even a moderately cold place, will most likely shiver. Now, this *shivering* is in itself important. It usually denotes a febrile condition of body, and it is generally seen at the commencement of most acute disorders; and if it amounts to an actual *rigor*, we may be prepared for inflammation of some important organ. Shiverings take place, again, when the inflammation has run on to suppuration. In continued fever these chills recur at intervals in the course of the illness.

The skin of an animal in perfect health—say the inside of a dog's thigh—ought to feel gently, genially warm and dry, without being hot. In the febrile condition, it is hot and dry, with a more frequent pulse than usual. A cold, clammy skin, on the other hand, with a feeble pulse, would indicate depression of the vital powers. Death-cold ears and legs are a sinking sign. The ears, again, may be too hot, indicating fever.

Elevation of temperature is more easily determined by the use of the clinical thermometer. Every one who keeps a large kennel of dogs should buy one, and it ought to be used in health as well as disease, so that changes may be more easily marked.

The colour of the skin is, of course, of great importance, often giving the first clue to liver mischief. White dogs, such as Maltese and Pomeranians, have a pretty pink skin, Yorkshire Terriers a bluish skin, while that of a jet-black dog ought to be very white. In jaundice this is altered to various shades of yellow. The skin of a dog in health ought to be soft, and pliant, and thin; in diseases of the skin it often gets thickened, and often scurfy.

2. The *Mucous Membranes.*—The appearance of these under various circumstances aid us materially in our diagnosis. Take that of the conjunctiva, for instance. The white of the eye of a dog should be like that of a well-boiled egg, with here and there, perhaps, a little capillary vessel making its appearance. In febrile disorders the eye is invariably injected. In jaundice it is a bright yellow. (N.B.—An injected eye without other symptoms must not make one think one's dog is ill; it is very often indeed injected in animals who sleep out of doors, and exercise will also redden the conjunctiva.)

The mucous membrane of the mouth ought to be of a pale pinkish hue. Pale gums in a white dog indicate debility.

3. *Mouth* and *Tongue.*—The tongue of a healthy dog should be of a beautiful pink colour, and soft and moist. A dry tongue, or a tongue covered with whitish saliva, is indicative of excitement of circulation. If the tongue is a darkish red, it shows that the mucous membrane of

the digestive canal is out of order. A brown tongue indicates a greater amount of inflammation of the mucous membranes.

Running of saliva at the mouth usually denotes some disturbance of the system. It is present in many inflammatory diseases of the chest and throat, especially if accompanied with nausea and sickness. It may, however—if there be no signs of inflammation—only indicate some disease of the teeth, and the mouth ought to be examined, for probably a bit of bone or wood may be found to have penetrated the gum, or got wedged between the teeth.

A foul mouth, with ulcerated gums and teeth covered with tartar, indicates indigestion, from errors in feeding, and must be seen to.

4. *The Pulse.*—The pulse in the dog in health is a firm, tense pulse. It gives you the idea of bounding life and spirits, a pulse that will not be repressed. Now, as to its frequency, this varies with the breed of the dog and with his age. In tiny dogs the pulse of the adult may be 100 and over, in the Mastiff and St. Bernard it should be about 80 or 85 beats to a minute. In young dogs it is very much more frequent, and in old animals it ranges from 60 to 80, according to the breed. The owner of a pet dog or dogs should make himself acquainted with their pulses, by frequently feeling them in health. The pulse is most easily felt on the upper part of the femoral artery, just about the middle of the inside of the thigh, near to where it joins the body.

Now it is sometimes very difficult to judge of the state of a small dog's health from the pulse with regard to fever or inflammation, so much so that we have to trust more to other signs and symptoms, but in large animals the state of the pulse often aids one materially in forming a diagnosis. Taking the state of the pulse, however, of any animal requires some considerable experience.

Two terms are very often confounded, even some medical men use them carelessly, namely, the *quick* pulse and the *frequent*. We cannot say that the terms are very happy ones, but only that they mean different states of the pulse. Thus, frequency of the pulse has reference to the rate of the pulse—to the number of beats in a minute; *quickness*, on the other hand, refers to the speed with which each individual beat does its work, each wave seeming to touch the finger but momentarily. In fever the pulse is more frequent, but it has not the force it has in health; in inflammation it has more force, and may or may not be more frequent.

Any transient frequency of the pulse might be caused by mere excitement, and unless other symptoms were present would not indicate fever.

By a *hard* pulse is meant a pulse small in volume but of considerable force. A *wiry* pulse is the same, only it is of still smaller volume.

A *soft* pulse means a pulse with plenty of volume but little force.

A hard pulse is met with in many inflammations; a hard, wiry, or thready pulse is often present during the first rigors of inflammation.

A soft pulse is indicative of general debility, and points to good nutriment and support, especially if it is not only soft but small withal. There are many other conditions of pulse, which need not be named here, those mentioned having reference principally to the state of the system.

5. *Breathing.*—The physical signs of chest disease are far too difficult for any but a professional to have a correct knowledge of. But there are certain symptoms of disease connected with the breathing, which every dog-owner would do well to make himself acquainted with. *Panting*, or quickened breathing, is present in many inflammations of the lungs, as well as in other diseases. If persistent it points to illness of some sort, but it may be brought

about by over-exertion or confinement in a close room, especially after a full meal. *Difficulty in breathing* is always a dangerous symptom. It is present in many diseases, in pneumonia and pleurisy, where we have other signs of inflammation to guide us to a correct diagnosis. The air-cells may be blocked up with exudation, or exudation into the pleura may be pressing on the lungs and impeding the breathing. The calibre of the bronchi or trachea, or larynx, may be narrowed by the products of inflammation, and cause dyspnœa. In these latter we should have the characteristic stridulous or whistling breathing. But from whatever cause dyspnœa may arise, it must always be looked upon as a very serious symptom indeed, for if the blood cannot be properly oxygenated, it is of course poisoned. *Snoring* is present in disease of the brain: it is called by medical men stertorous breathing. So long as the breathing is regular and comparatively easy, it is not a dangerous symptom. If, however, this is not the case, and the breathing is slow and laboured, and the animal cannot be roused, the case is bad indeed. Snoring in simple sleep is nothing to speak of, *but* it points to deranged digestive organs, and ought to be looked to. *Abdominal* breathing points to pleurisy or some other painful disease of the chest. *Thoracic* breathing again, when the abdomen does not partake of a share in the rise and fall, points to some mischief in the regions below the diaphragm. *Coughing* is either *dry* or *moist*. Whenever the discharge from the mucous membranes of the chest is abundant, it is moist. In the first stages of catarrh and bronchitis, while yet the membranes are merely roughened, the cough is dry; and in pleurisy, unconnected with bronchitis or pneumonia, it will continue dry. The cough of chronic laryngitis is harsh, that of croup a ringing cough. The cough of emphysema, again, is a soft, wheezy, voiceless kind of a cough, for the air-cells are enlarged, and have not the power properly to expel the air. Other dry coughs are caused by reflex action, indicating various diseases—teething, worms, indigestion, &c. &c.

6. The *secretions* in disease of an inflammatory nature are diminished, the urine, for instance, is scanty and high-coloured, there may be more or less of constipation, and the skin becomes dry and hot. The secretion of the inflamed surface, say of a mucous membrane as in bronchitis, or a serous membrane like the pleura, is at first dried, and afterwards increased and perverted.

7. The state of the *bowels* and *kidneys* should never be overlooked in disease, though a person should not jump to the conclusion that constipation and scanty urine alone determine the presence of fever without other symptoms. However, an abundance of pale urine proves directly that no fever is present.

8. *Loss of appetite* is usually, but not always, present in disease; hence the fallacy of believing that so long as a dog takes his food well he is all right. Dogs are like children, they will often eat when they really are not hungry; besides, in some diseases the appetite is either voracious, fickle, or depraved.

9. *Thirst* alone does not indicate fever; any large discharge, either from the intestines or the kidneys, induces it. In diuresis, and diabetes, and diarrhœa, there is thirst.

10. *Pain* does not, as some people imagine, always indicate inflammation. There are nervous pains, hysterical pains, and pains of a dozen different descriptions.

11. *Tenderness.*—This is an important point in our diagnosis, for the pain of inflammation is generally, almost invariably indeed, of a tender nature, that is, it is increased by pressure, and sometimes cannot be felt without pressure.

12. *Vomiting.*—A dog can vomit at will, or by merely eating a little grass or some rough leaf, such as that of vegetable marrow. The character of the vomit is often characteristic

of some organic or functional disorder, as the bilious yellow-looking matter dogs bring up of a morning when stomach and liver are out of order, or the vomit mixed with blood in cases of gastritis or gastric catarrh. Again, the vomiting in a case of impaction of the bowels, internal stricture, volvolus, &c., is of a most distressing character, and often the contents of the upper part of the bowels are brought up.

13. *Expression of the countenance.*—When the animal is in pain and suffering his face is pinched, he looks nervous and thin; even if he does not moan he appears by his countenance to think that he is being badly treated in some way. In dyspnœa, from whatever cause, there is a look of anxiety mingled with somewhat of terror, which is most touching to behold.

14. *Emaciation* is always a bad sign, but taken alone it is not diagnostic. It is very rapid, however, in many febrile disorders, such as distemper, for example. Emaciation, when coming on slowly, indicates mal-nutrition of the body in some way, some interference with the blood-making process.

15. *Obesity* is a disease to all intents and purposes, and is not a good sign in the old age of a dog (from 9 to 13 or 14 years). It must not be confounded with anasarca or general dropsy of the flesh. A fat dog feels firm, the flesh of a dropsical dog gives way to the fingers, *pits on pressure*.

16. *Position of body.*—In some inflammations this is very diagnostic. The wish to lie on the belly in disease of the liver, especially in some cold corner; the persistent standing or sitting up in cases of pneumonia; the arched back of inflammations in the abdominal regions (arched in order to release the muscles and prevent pressure on the painful parts); the pitiful appearance of a dog in rheumatism; the drooping jaw and half-paralysed body of a dog suffering from dumb rabies; the terrible unhappy-like ferocity of a rabid dog on the march; all tell their own tale, and speak volumes to the skilled veterinary surgeon. A slow gait is indicative of debility or old age, stiffness of rheumatism or old age; and the curious twitching or jerking movements of St. Vitus's Dance, need only be once seen to be remembered for evermore.

It will be observed that the medicines recommended in the treatment of the various diseases described in these pages are not only generally of the simplest kinds, but that the doses thereof are medium doses. There is no doubt that the older veterinary surgeons lost many valuable dogs from the harsh method in which they treated them. The same practice still obtains in many parts of the country, if not, indeed, in towns as well; and dogs are often cruelly slain by over-doses of emetics, and even *aloes*, administered by unskilled hands. There is no leaning towards homœopathy in this treatise, but this method of treatment, wrong though the premises be on which it is based, has at least one advantage: if an infinitesimal dose does no good, it can do no harm; it does not trammel Nature, nor throw obstacles in her way, but leaves the path clear so that she, unopposed, can go in and—cure.

Another thing which is claimed for the prescriptions is safety. Were the treatise intended solely for students, or the junior members of the veterinary profession, many remedies might be recommended, which, in the hands of an unprofessional person, would be like a razor in the grasp of an infant. Some medicines prescribed are, perhaps, new with regard to the practice of canine medicine; but they have been tried with success.

Much good may at times be done to sick dogs by administering even seemingly simple medicines, and these do all the more good if given in time, for little ailments if not seen to often lead to very serious mischief. It may be well here to give a few examples of the good that may be done by simple remedies.

Take, then, a case of simple fever. This is sometimes called *ephemeral* fever, because it is supposed only to last for about a day.* Towards evening the dog will seem dull and dispirited, and either refuse his food or eat lazily; his nose may not be hot, nor his eye injected, but under the thighs greater heat than usual will be felt; and, if the dog's owner has been in the habit of feeling his pulse in health, he will now find it is increased in frequency, and he will be sensible, too, of a greater heat than usual on the top of the head. Now what has to be done in this case is simplicity itself. First give a pill, compounded of from one-sixteenth of a grain of podophyllin for a Toy, up to half a grain or more for a St. Bernard or a dog of that size, mixed with from three to fifteen grains of extract of dandelion. This at once; then before sleeping-time give from a tea-spoonful up to six drachms of Mindererus spirit† in a little water, adding thereto from five drops to a tea-spoonful of sweet spirits of nitre. In the morning give a simple dose of castor-oil—from one tea-spoonful to one ounce. Exercise (moderate) and a non-stimulating diet will soon make matters straight.

Note.—In this treatise, wherever the words occur " dose from say two drachms to one ounce," the small dose has reference to a Toy dog, the large to one St. Bernard or Mastiff size.

Headache.—Dogs frequently suffer from headache. The symptoms are dulness, quietness, slight injection of the eye, and heat on the top of the head. Bathe the head for a quarter of an hour at the time with cold water. Give in the morning a dose of Epsom salts, with a little spirits of nitre. Give sulphur, a small dose, half a drachm to half an ounce, every second night; reduce the diet; and let the dog have abundance of fresh air.

In ordinary *Fits* all one has to do is to let the dog alone, and keep meddlesome people away. A whiff or two of chloroform or ether may at times cut short an attack.

Simple catarrh succumbs readily to a dose of Mindererus spirit at night, or to a dose of Dover's powder. Foment the forehead and nose frequently with hot water. Give Epsom salts with a little spirits of nitre in the morning, adding thereto from one to six grains of quinine.

Simple constipation is relieved by the bucket bath every morning, or a quarter of an hour's swim before breakfast. A piece of raw liver is a good aperient. Opening the bowels is not curing constipation. The cause must be sought for and removed. Plenty of exercise and a non-binding diet will do much good.

Bleeding from wounds.—Stopped by pressure, padding, cold water, or ice; if the blood is merely oozing, tincture of iron is infallible.

Pain.—Pain is inseparable from animal life, but much can be done to relieve it. No one except a professional man ought to handle such powerful narcotics as opium and its preparations, but there are other means which any one can apply. The warm bath (not hot) is an excellent remedy for little dogs. Then we have hot fomentations. These are used thus :— Have two pieces of flannel, each large enough to well cover the part. The flannel must be three or four ply. Wring each piece, time about, out of water as hot as the hand will bear it, and apply to the seat of pain; keep on for half an hour at a time. This is best suited for short-haired dogs. For long-haired there is nothing better than the bag of hot sand, or ironing with a flat iron, if there is no skin-tenderness.

Chloral is never to be given to produce sleep, or allay internal pain, without the orders of a skilled veterinary surgeon; *but* in cases of rheumatism, or great pain from injury, such as broken bones, &c., a little may be given. The dose is from five grains to twenty or thirty.

The hydropathic belt often does much good. It is used thus :—A bandage is to be wrung

---

* In the dog its usual duration is from one to five days.
† The solution of the acetate of ammonia.

out of cold water, and wound several times round the animal's body—the hair being previously wetted—and then covered with a dry bandage, or oiled silk may be placed over the wet bandage—however, it must be kept wet. This worn for a day or two is found useful in cases of chronic or sub-acute bowel disorder, whether diarrhœa or constipation. It is a good plan, too, to frequently give an injection of simple soap and water; in the latter complaint warm olive oil injected into the bowel, from one to four or five ounces, and allowed to remain in for twelve hours, or as long as it will stop, does good service in cases where hardened fæces block up the gut. From two drachms up to one ounce of Epsom salts, with a little olive oil, and from three ounces to a pint of weak starch water, is a capital simple enema.

Two grains of powdered alum to an ounce of water is a nice little wash for sore eyes. Drop a little in night and morning. Cold green tea infusion is another.

For lingering chronic cases of sore eyes, when the inflammation is not extensive, a very little powdered quinine is a good thing to blow in through a quill on them in the morning.

Tincture of arnica half an ounce, one ounce of brandy, and a tumblerful of cold water, makes a soothing wash for sprains or bruises from blows.

When the skin is not off, turpentine acts like a charm to a burn.

Quinine and cod-liver oil are capital restoratives when a dog is thin and out of sorts.

Examples might be multiplied, but enough has been said to prove that simple remedies are not always to be despised.

So valuable an animal as the dog deserves all the care and attention we can give him when ill. It is not possible to cure every case—would we could cure more—but in the very worst cases there is one thing that can always be done—we can alleviate suffering.

"How," says Sir Thomas, alluding to the *treatment* of disease, "are we to understand this familiar, and, at first view, almost presumptuous word? Do we propose to vamp and mend the animal machine when decayed, broken, or out of gear? According to the ordinary sense of those words, surely no. In urging upon medical students the indispensable necessity of anatomical knowledge, the question is sometimes put—What would be said of the discretion or sanity of him who, knowing nothing at all of its construction or working, should undertake to repair a damaged watch? However pertinent in one light the question may seem, it suggests a fallacious analogy. The mechanism which one man has devised and put together may be comprehended, imitated, and, when out of order, repaired by another man of like intellect and skill. But the animal body is the handiwork of Nature. Fashioned in obedience to unchanging laws imposed by the Creator, the processes of its formation can neither be clearly discerned by human intelligence, nor copied by human ingenuity. Through the natural laws thus ordained for its construction and maintenance, and not otherwise, can the imperfections, the hurts, the derangements, in one word the diseases, of that complex machine be rectified. One of the most wonderful and beneficent endowments of the body is its self-mending power. The art of healing implies indeed some insight, however imperfect, into the operation of the forces by which the body is built up and sustained, but it requires a clear perception also that through these forces, and through them only, may its flaws be sometimes remedied. The workings of these forces, the results of these laws, we can to a certain extent control and regulate. By removing hindrances to their effective and salutary operation, by arranging the conditions which yield the best means for their success, by thus fostering, assisting, and directing the allotted powers of Nature, we are able, not seldom—under Providence—to avert disaster, to mitigate suffering, to prolong life, to promote and conduct recovery, and, in a certain limited sense, to cure diseases."

CHAPTER II.

RULES FOR PRESCRIBING—CLASSIFICATION OF DRUGS—ADMINISTERING MEDICINES—
POISONS AND THEIR ANTIDOTES.

THE medicines or drugs used in treating the ailments of dogs need be but very few and simple. Blind faith should never be placed in medicine alone for the cure of any ailment. If we can, first and foremost, arrive at a correct knowledge of the nature of the disease which we propose to alleviate, there need not be much difficulty in prescribing *secundum artem;* but medicine alone is only half the battle, if even so much, for good nursing and attention to the laws of hygiene, combined with a judiciously-chosen diet, will often do more to cure a sick dog than any medicine that can be given. The following rules are worth remembering :—

1. In prescribing we should rather err on the side of giving too much than too little.

2. A harsh medicine should never be prescribed if a milder one will suffice.

3. The time at which medicines are given ought to be well considered, and the veterinary surgeon's orders in this respect strictly obeyed ; if a drug is ordered at bed-time, the dog should on no account be allowed his freedom that night after the administration of the dose.

4. Age must be considered as well as weight, and a young dog and a very old dog require smaller doses.

5. Mercury, strychnine in any form, arsenic, and some other medicines, require extreme caution in their administration.

6. Quack medicines should be avoided, for many and obvious reasons.

7. Never despair of a dog's restoration to health, he may begin to come round when least expected.

8. Cleanliness is most essential to sick dogs ; so is gentle warmth, and fresh air, and quiet.

9. Be very careful in dividing the doses, *i.e.*, never guess at the quantity, but always measure it.

10. One word as to the quality of the medicine prescribed. Expensive remedies, such as quinine, &c., are greatly adulterated. Get all articles, therefore, from a respectable chemist. The best are the cheapest. For example, never give to a dog—for how dainty and easily nauseated his stomach is we all know—the castor oil usually administered to horses, nor coarse cod liver oil, nor laudanum that has been made with methylated spirit, nor any other medicine one would not care to take one's self.

11. Do not force a dog with medicine, if he is going on well without it ; recovery must be slow to be safe.

Medicines are classed under the following heads :—

Antacids are medicines which correct acidity of stomach or system generally, by combining with the free acids and neutralising them. Remember (1) They palliate symptoms without removing the cause. (2) They debilitate, and ought to be prescribed along with some bitter tonic, and must not be continued for too long a time. (3) Their continued use might result in intestinal concretions. (4) They have a solvent power over fatty matters, hence their use in obesity. (5) If acid exists in the stomach, give soda or ammonia; if in the bowels, magnesia or lime; if in the urine or blood, the salts of potash and lithia.

Alteratives are medicines which tend gradually to restore a diseased organ to its proper state and tone. Some, such as mercury, exert their action on particular organs.

Anæsthetics.—Medicines which do away with pain by paralysing sensation, and are used either locally, as in the application of ether spray to a painful part, or generally, as in the exhibition of chloroform, either to relieve cough and spasm, or produce complete insensibility to enable us to perform an operation. They are to be used with great caution.

Anti-spasmodics.—A very useful class of medicines to counteract and allay the spasms of muscular action, and to relieve the nervous affections which give rise to them. It is evident that, as the causes of spasm are many and various, these must be sought for before we can prescribe; but, nevertheless, there are some medicines which exert a direct action on spasms, such as opium, brandy, chloroform, &c. Anti-spasmodics do not take long to act, and when we fail with one we must try another. Their action too, when induced, does not last long.

Anthelmintics.—Very valuable medicines, used either to kill internal parasites, vermicides —or to expel them, vermifuges.

Aperient medicines are also called purgatives, or cathartics, or evacuants, or laxatives, the latter acting very mildly. There is a difference in the action of different classes of aperients. Some simply increase the peristaltic motion of the bowels, and so hurry onwards, so to speak, their contents; others, by exciting the flow of mucous secretion, liquify the fœces, and wash them onward; and others, in addition to this, increase the flow of bile and pancreatic juice.

Our purgative medicines are among the most valuable we possess, and yet they are only too liable to be abused by the unskilled prescriber. They are often much more effective and less weakening, when combined with small doses of tonics, stimulants, or anodynes. Medicines of this class, that act slowly, are best given at night; others as salines in the morning.

Astringents are medicines which possess the power of contracting muscular tissue, and also of diminishing secretion. Applied to wounds or ulcers they not only coagulate albumen, and so in a manner tan the surface, but they constrict the calibre of the smaller blood-vessels.

Blisters. See *Epispastics.*

Diaphoretics are medicines that increase the flow of the natural perspiration. *Note.*—It is a mistake to say that dogs do not perspire.

Diuretics increase the secretion and promote the speedier discharge of urine.

Emetics.—Medicines given for the purpose of producing vomiting. Emetics should be administered to the dog with great caution, and not in very large doses. There are emetics that depress the system, such as tartar emetic; these should be avoided in cases of poisoning, because absorption takes place much more quickly when the vital energy is lowered; we should therefore prefer in such cases, sulphate of zinc or copper, all the more so in that their action is much quicker. Emetics, from the shock they give to the system, are often useful in cutting short fevers, but they must be given at the earliest stage.

Emmenagogues.—Medicines supposed to exert an influence in bringing the bitch in season. This should never be attempted: it is highly dangerous, and never of the least avail.

Emollients.—Under this heading we include remedies that, applied locally to the solid tissues, render them lax; they also lubricate and soften the tissues they are applied to, and defend them from the action of acrid matters, as poultices and fomentations. Demulcents also come under the same heading. These are given internally, and produce their effects on distant organs through the circulation—gum acacia for example, gruel, barley-water, liquorice extract, &c.

Epispastics.—Medicaments which, applied to the skin, produce temporary inflammation irritation, or vesication. They are called also vesicants, rubefacients, blisters, and counter-irritants. They are a most useful class of remedies when skilfully applied. Their uses are many, (1) they relieve inflammation of internal organs by drawing the blood to the surface. (2) Blisters may be used as general stimulants in some low forms of fever. But they are not to be used in inflammatory diseases, until the general excitement has been subdued by other means. (3) They are useful in dropsy of the pericardium, pleura, &c., in that they remove serum from the blood. (4) They are sometimes used to denude the skin, in order to introduce some medicine, such as morphia or strychnine, quickly into the blood by absorption. Before applying a blister to the dog, cut off closely or shave the hair from the part. Strong solution of ammonia is a good blister, applied by means of a woollen rag, covered over with oiled silk. It does its work quickly and well, and is to be preferred to cantharides if there is anything the matter with the urinary organs.

A slower and milder blister is the Emplastrum Cantharidis of the Pharmacopœia. It has to be kept on, however, for ten or twelve hours, and this with the dog cannot always be conveniently done. If it be tried, however, it must be covered well up, and the dog muzzled. A quicker and most effective cantharidine blister is the Liquor Epispasticus of the shops. The skin is to be painted with it four or five times if necessary. Then, as a rubefacient, we have turpentine poured over a piece of flannel, wrung out of very hot water, and applied to the skin. After a blister well rises, tap it, and dress with simple ointment.

Narcotics, including also Anodynes, and the so-called Hypnotics and Soporifics, ease pain, and also produce sleep. Those chiefly used in dog practice are Belladonna, Hyoscyamus, and Opium. Great caution is to be observed in their administration.

Sedatives must, as a rule, also be cautiously handled. They are in their nature calmatives to the system. They are employed in diseases where we have much nervous or vascular excitement, and the doses given must be in proportion to the degree of excitement. Under the same heading we include *anæsthetics*, those medicines the vapour of which, if inhaled, produces insensibility.

Stimulants are medicines which increase, though not permanently, the vital functions, and this is always followed by a corresponding depression. When given, therefore, in debility or exhaustion, the dose must be frequently repeated, until the body regains strength enough to be able to do without the stimulants.

Tonics.—Medicines which, given for some length of time, strengthen the vitality without producing any apparent excitement. If a horse on a journey becomes tired, he can be urged on either by applying the whip to him, or by stopping and giving him a feed of oats. The whip represents the stimulant, the oats the tonic. Now these remedies, although very powerful for good when judiciously administered, are just as powerful for evil when unskilfully prescribed. They are most useful in debility, and in cases where there is a want of tone in the secreting organs. They should, however, never be used when there is the least tendency to inflammation, or even irritation of the digestive canal, or when the secretions are vitiated. Before giving a dog a course of tonics, it is better to give some mild aperient, and one occasionally during the course. Quinine and arsenic are not only tonics, but they also counteract periodical fever, and are hence sometimes called *Febrifuges*.

ON ADMINISTERING MEDICINES.

A word now on the usual method of physicking dogs; premising, however, that the good to be obtained from the medicine a dog takes will depend, in a great measure, upon the regularity with which it is administered. The benefit most medicines effect is done little by little. Step by step the physician fights the enemy and drives him from his stronghold, but a step retrograde often enables the foe to bring up his reserves, and finally put the doctor to the rout.

A dog should never be treated roughly. Struggling with a sick animal often does him more harm than the medicine to be given can do good.

Medicines are prescribed in the form of either pill, bolus, mixture, or powder.

When giving a dog a pill or bolus, if a small dog, he may be held either on the administrator's knee, or on that of an assistant. The mouth is then gently but firmly opened with one hand, and the pill is thrust as far down as you can before being let go, the head being meanwhile held at an angle of 45° or thereabouts. Close the mouth at once thereafter, and give a slight tap under the chin to aid deglutition by taking the dog by surprise. See that the upper lips are folded under the teeth during the operation, thus protecting the fingers from being bitten, for the dog will hardly care to bite through his own lips to get at the hand. With a large dog the best plan is to back him up against the inner corner of a wall and get astride of him. Some dogs will positively refuse to have their mouths forced open by their owners, but will submit readily enough to the veterinary surgeon.

The least nauseating or bitter of fluid medicines can generally be given in the food, those, however, that have a bad taste, must be forcibly put over the throat. Hold the dog in the same position as in giving a bolus, only there is no necessity for opening the mouth so wide, although the head is to be held well back, gradually then, and *not too much at a time* pour the mixture over the front teeth down into the back part of the throat. When it is all down, giving the animal a morsel of meat, or anything tasty, will often prevent him from bringing it back again. This tendency to vomit is very strong in the dog, but may often be overcome by taking the animal out into the open air for a little while, after he has been drenched, and engaging his attention as much as possible, or by tying up his head for a time. Powders, if tasteless, are best mixed with the food, or if nauseous and bitter, and still not bulky, they may be given enclosed in a thin layer of beef, only do not let the dog see you preparing it. Or, they may be mixed in butter or lard, syrup or glycerine, and placed well back on the tongue, or, better still, well back against the roof of the mouth. Close the mouth for a little after placing it there, until you hear the act of deglutition performed.

Everybody who has had anything to do with the physicking of dogs knows how sly they often are, and how they will try to hoodwink one. Sometimes they will hold the medicine in their mouths for a considerable time, until they see a good chance of spitting it out. It is sometimes even necessary to hold the dog's nose until he swallows.

A better plan of drenching and a safer is to keep the mouth shut and form the lips into a funnel. Get an assistant to pour the medicine a little at a time into this funnel, and keep the mouth close, or mouth and nose shut until each mouthful is swallowed.

N.B.—In giving medicine to a dog, one must keep very cool, and on no account make a fuss, or any great display of bottles and preparations, or the poor animal may think some great evil is going to happen to him, and be obstreperous accordingly.

Medicines are sometimes administered by enema; in this case, it is well to oil both the anus and nozzle of the syringe, and to be exceedingly gentle ; it is a tender part, and we must therefore assure the animal we mean no harm.

Some powders may be rolled in greased tissue paper, and given in form of bolus. The paper must be thin, however.

POISONS AND THEIR ANTIDOTES.

Whether as the result of accident or by evil design, dogs are exceedingly liable to suffer from poisoning. Independently of either accident or design, the animal is sometimes poisoned by his owner unwisely administering to him drugs in too large doses. In most cases the great difficulty is to tell what kind of poison the animal has picked up. Prevention is certainly better than cure, and people cannot be too cautious in handling or using poisons where dogs or even cats are about. At the same time, the law for regulating the sale of poisons is far too loose. Poison is often put down to rats and mice, and in a form, too, which is usually just as palatable ·to the house-dog as to the vermin. There are so many ingenious traps now-a-days sold for the catching of mice and other vermin, that really the practice of poisoning rats should seldom be resorted to.

The symptoms of poisoning always appear very rapidly, and this combined with the urgency of the symptoms and the great distress of the animal, usually lead us to guess what has happened. In this chapter, those poisons only which are most likely to be swallowed by the dog are treated of, and the antidotes given.

Poisons are divided into three classes—the Irritant, the Narcotic, and the Narcotico-irritants.

The Irritant class give rise to great pain in the stomach and belly, which is often tense and swollen, while the vomited matters are often tinged with blood. The sickness and retching are very distressing ; so, too, at times is the diarrhœa.

The Narcotico, such as opium, morphia, &c., act upon the brain and spinal cord, causing drowsiness, giddiness, and stupor, accompanied at times by convulsions or paralysis.

The Narcotico-irritant give rise to intense thirst, great pain in the stomach, with vomiting and purging. Whenever it is suspected that a dog has swallowed poison, the first thing to do is to encourage vomiting by the mouth. We must get rid of all the poison we can as speedily as possible. Sulphate of zinc—dose, five to twenty grains in water or more—is one of the speediest emetics we have ; or sulphate of copper—dose, three to ten grains—is good. At the same time the dog must be well drenched with lukewarm water. When the stomach has been well washed out by the action of vomiting, give some of the antidotes recommended below.

Arsenic.—Keep up the vomiting by giving warm mucilaginous drinks, as gruel, barley-water, raw eggs beaten up with milk, lime - water and oil, lime - water and milk ; castor-oil, a large dose to carry off poison from the intestines. The hydrated sesquioxide of iron in large doses, from a half a teaspoonful to a dessert-spoonful, frequently repeated is uncertain. Afterwards give stimulants, brandy and full doses of opium, to get rid of the depression caused.

Phosphorus.—Keep up the vomiting, encouraging it in the same way as in arsenical poisoning. Avoid giving oil, because it is a solvent of phosphorus. The antidote is calcined magnesia in large doses.

Tartar Emetic.—Encourage the vomiting by giving large draughts of warm milk. Antidotes—strong tea, gallic acid, decoction of oak bark, tannic acid, powdered Peruvian bark.

Butter of Antimony.—Give magnesia in milk. Antidotes—same as for tartar emetic.

Nitrate of Silver.—Common salt. Give emetics, if vomiting not present.

Lead Salts.—Emetics. Milk and raw eggs. Sulphate of soda and sulphate of magnesia are antidotes.

Corrosive Sublimate.—Encourage the vomiting by diluents, as in arsenical poisoning. Raw eggs, being albuminous in a high degree, form the best antidote, or the gluten of wheat, as flour mixed with milk. Afterwards keep up the system. Give demulcent drinks, and a dose or two of morphia.

Strychnine and Nux Vomica.—Emetics, and the vomiting to be kept up. Antidotes—animal charcoal, olive oil; perfect rest and quiet; hydrate of chloral, to diminish the spasms; and a purgative enema.

Aconite.—Give emetics. Castor-oil; brandy in strong coffee.

Iodine and its compounds.—Encourage the vomiting. Plenty of gruel, and thin starch in full doses.

Opium and *Morphia.*—Sulphate of zinc as an emetic, or sulphate of copper. Strong coffee as a drench. Electric shocks to the spine.

Prussic Acid.—No known reliable antidote. Ammonia to the nostrils. Fresh air, and strong stimulating to chest.

Carbolic Acid.—It is not an uncommon thing for a dog that has been washed with too strong a lotion of carbolic acid, for some skin disease, or to kill vermin, to be seized with shivering and every symptom of depression, and die within an hour. Friction while the dog is in a warm bath, and the internal exhibition of plenty of brandy-and-water, with a few drops of laudanum, is all that can be thought of as likely to avert fatal consequences.

In all cases where life is quite despaired of it is best to let the animal pass away quietly, aided by drenching with large doses of hydrate of chloral in water.

In cases of poisoning the greatest difficulty to be contended with rests in the fact that it is difficult to know what a dog has swallowed, and there is, unfortunately, no universal antidote.

CHAPTER III.

DISEASES OF THE DIGESTIVE SYSTEM.

PROPERLY speaking, the first portion of the digestive canal is the mouth. As, however, the diseases of this region are described in another chapter, we shall for the present pass over this, merely mentioning the fact that mastication can hardly be said to be performed by the dog, who belongs by nature to the carnivorous animals. In mankind the due mingling of the food with the saliva is of the greatest importance in the economy of digestion. In the dog it is equally or almost equally so, but the food does not require to stop so long in the mouth, owing to the greater abundance of the salivary juices.

Now we shall be in a much better position to understand the diseases of the digestive canal if we first and foremost give our attention for a moment to a short description of the anatomical and physiological construction of the nutritive canal, and to the theory of digestion. Such description can hardly fail to be of interest to the majority of readers.

The first portion, then, of the canal to be considered, is that which, beginning at the mouth, ends at the upper or cardiac opening of the stomach. It is called the œsophagus or gullet; it lies directly behind the larynx and trachea or windpipe. The œsophagus is somewhat funnel-shaped; that is, it is very wide at the top, the upper portion being termed the pharynx. This is divided from the mouth by a movable curtain called the veil of the palate. In the dog the œsophagus is all along its course very dilatable, hence the immense masses of flesh and pieces of bones which the animal can swallow.

From the lips all the way to the anus the alimentary canal is lined by what is called mucous membrane. This is, in other words, a sort of inner skin, and while the outer or true skin secretes perspiration and sebaceous matter, this membrane secretes mucus.

This mucus keeps the membrane moist, and lubricates the mouth and gullet for the passage of food. In the mouth, nose, cheeks, palate, &c., this membrane is a plain secreting lining, it does not absorb to any appreciable extent. In those portions of the canal where it not only secretes but absorbs, we find it no longer a plain lining membrane, but corrugated, to give it a larger surface in less space.

In some parts of the mucous membrane, as the stomach for example, we find that not only is the surface studded with villi, which give it the appearance of the pile of velvet, but also with little pits or holes, the openings of numerous *culs de sac*, or minute mucous pouches called follicles. Now, each follicle and villus is supplied with its own little artery, vein, and nervelet, and the villi absorb while the follicles or pouches secrete.

In the animal body immensely large surfaces are required for the vast amount of fluids and juices that have to be secreted, so that Nature is in a manner cramped for room. Hence the economy of that wonderful *multum in parvo*, a secreting gland, the mechanism of which is not only very beautiful but very simple. If it were not for those little secreting pits or follicles in the stomach, the surface of that organ would have to be of immense size. A follicle, then, a pit or depression, is the very simplest form of secreting gland imaginable. A large number of these little pits, all opening into a common reservoir, and having attached to this a common duct to carry its secretion where it is needed, would give us a higher form of gland, where we would have a large extent of secreting surface at the expense of very little room. Now, let us go a step higher, and we find a gland, like the parotid for instance, which is formed thus :— Instead of little pouches, all opening into a common reservoir, as in a more simple gland, imagine innumerable little bags, each with a tiny pipe or stalk, and all those pipes or stalks opening into each other to form rather larger pipes, and going on joining others, until they finally form one large tube, which conveys the secretion to its destination, as the duct of the parotid conveys the saliva to the mouth.

But where, it may be asked, does the secretion come from ? Why, from the blood. And every little grape-like bag or pouch, the whole of which together unite to form that great conglomerate gland, the parotid, is surrounded by capillary arteries and veins. Now, all the little grapes, as it were, are united together by connective tissue, and imbedded, in the case of the parotid, in fat. If we can understand the construction of the parotid gland, we have *the key to every secreting gland in the body*—salivary glands, kidneys or urinary glands, testicles or semenary glands, and the great liver itself, the biliary gland, which, with its net-work of blood-vessels, &c., is the most complicated gland in the body. The appearance of a bunch of grapes gives one a good, though rough, example of the shape and mechanism of a large gland. The grapes themselves represent the single secreting glands or pouches, the small stalks their ducts, and the large or main stalk the final or efferent duct.

The alimentary canal may be compared throughout its whole length to a tube, wider at some parts than at others ; it has three coats, that is it is in reality three tubes one inside the other. Having already shortly mentioned the lining coat—the mucous membrane—it will suffice for our purpose at present to mention the muscular coat. The fibres, then, of this muscular coat are for the most part circular, that is they are in concentric rings, but in some portions of the canal they are transverse as well, as in the stomach ; the bearing of which will presently be seen.

Muscles and Muscular Contraction.—Muscle, in plain language, is flesh. Each muscle is composed of a bundle of fibres held together by connective tissue, which, if examined by tearing the fibres of a bit of raw meat asunder, we find not unlike cobwebs. It is this tissue, this cobwebby tissue, that binds all the different portions of the soft organs of the body together. Muscles are meant for motion. In addition to the blood-vessels which supply them with nutriment, they are supplied with nerves to enable them to contract. To contract means to draw together, to shorten. A muscle always contracts in its long axis. If one *wills* to contract his biceps, for example, he shortens it, and consequently thickens it ; and one tendon of the biceps muscle being situated in the forearm and the other in the shoulder, by contracting the biceps the forearm is either drawn up, or, if the hand is fixed in—say an iron ring in the ceiling—contraction or shortening of the biceps will draw the body upwards.

There is not a function of the body in which muscular contraction does not play an important part.

Now, as muscles always contract in relation to their long axis, if a tube is encircled by a muscle, the contraction of that muscle would evidently result in a narrowing of the diameter of the tube, and the contents of the tube would be forced onwards.

The muscles of the alimentary canal are presided over by nerves, over which the animal has little or no control. The mere contact of the food upon the lining membrane of a healthy digestive canal, however, is sufficient to cause alternate contractions and dilatations of the muscular coat thereof. In the stomach this contraction causes the food to be turned round and round, and up and down (there being both circular and transverse fibres in the coat of this organ) until every particle of it is in its turn brought into contact with the walls of that organ, and so receives and is mixed with the gastric secretions, that turn it into *chyme*.

In the intestines, where the muscular fibres are circular, contraction alternating with dilatation results in a creeping, worm-like (vermicular or peristaltic) motion, which not only mixes the food, but propels it along the canal towards the anus.

We see, then, that it is the contact of the food that excites the muscular contraction of the intestinal walls, and propulsion onwards of the bowel's contents. And this is one reason why we give soft, liquid, and non-stimulating food in a case of diarrhœa. Again, any druggist's apprentice knows that a dose of opium or its tincture (laudanum) will cure a case of simple diarrhœa, but for the life of him he could not explain why. The reason is that opium benumbs the nerves, puts them asleep nearly ; at all events renders them less able to act as conductors of animal electricity. They are less easily excited, therefore, by the contents of the intestine, and the vermicular motion is in a corresponding degree checked. But this is not all ; for, for the same reason, the secretions of the bowel do not flow so abundantly, and so the bowel's contents are rendered less fluid.

The œsophagus begins at the funnel-like pharynx, and ends at the stomach. In the dog it widens out again as it approaches the stomach, and is not only very dilatable, but remarkably muscular.

The next part of the alimentary canal which demands our attention is the stomach. It is a membranous and muscular bag or pouch. In the dog this is somewhat pear-shaped. The upper opening is called the œsophagal or cardiac, and the lower the pyloric. This latter is surrounded by a concentric band of muscular fibres, a strong ring in fact, which shuts up the lower orifice, until Nature requires it shall be opened.

The dog's stomach of course differs in size in different breeds, and, upon the whole, it is a very accommodating and capacious viscus, although it is very easily excited to the act of vomiting. There is one other peculiarity about a dog's stomach—the muscular fibres are partially under the control of the voluntary nerves. At all events, it is well known that the animal can vomit at will. This faculty is sometimes, though very rarely, met with in the human race.

The next portion of the digestive canal begins at the pylorus, and is continued to the anus. It is called the intestine, large and small. The small intestine comes first. It is divided into the *duodenum*, the *jejunum*, and the *ilium*. There is no special need for the reader to burden his memory with these names. They are quite arbitrary, and Chauveau's division, into the first, the fixed or duodenal portion, and the second, the free or floating portion, is better.

The small intestine is maintained in its position at one extremity by the stomach, at the other by the cæcum, and is fixed in the centre by what is called the great omentum, by butchers the apron, which is, in fact, a fold of the peritoneum.

The peritoneum is the largest serous sac in the body. Serous membranes are sacs or bags which line the closed cavities of the body. Neither their uses nor their positions in the body are difficult to understand. Serous membranes are beautifully designed by Nature to counteract the evil effects of friction. Wherever, then, in the human body two surfaces are opposed to each other, and rub or move against each other, we find a serous sac placed between them. Take a common articulation, for example, or joint. Here you have two surfaces which are opposed to each other, rub against each other, and, but for the interposition of this serous membrane, would become roughened and inflamed. The membrane itself is a *closed* bag, suited exactly to the size of the surfaces it is meant to intervene. The inside of this bag, which is of a fibrous nature, is very thin, and exceedingly smooth, and secretes a sort of lubricating mucus which makes it still more smooth.

Now, this serous bag, with its smooth well-lubricated inside, being firmly attached by its outsides, it is not the actual surface of the bones that move against each other, but the smooth inner sides of the serous sac. The intestines are guarded by a protecting bag of this sort, called the peritoneum, a portion of which envelops every organ beneath the diaphragm or midrif, as the liver, spleen, pancreas, kidneys, &c. The heart has a serous sac to itself, so have the lungs (two, in fact); wherever, in a word, there are two opposing surfaces and motion, a serous membrane intervenes to do away with the danger from friction.

Now, in the joints these membranes are termed synovial membranes, that around the heart the pericardium, and those around the lungs the pleuræ. They are subject to inflammation, these membranes, and when so inflamed they pour out a large quantity of serous fluid, which fills and swells out the sac, and constitutes a dropsy.

The internal surface of the small intestine is distinguished first by a number of longitudinal folds, which are unfolded when the gut is distended, and it is covered throughout its whole length with villi and follicles.

The villi are so numerous on some portions of the internal surface of the small intestine, that it presents the appearance of the pile on velvet.

Each villus, as in the stomach, is surrounded by a net-work of blood-vessels, and each villus *has its own absorbent vessel.*

The follicles are little sacs opening on the internal surface of the intestine, their use being to secrete.

Beneath the mucuous membrane of the duodenum, and opening on to its surface, are some small globular bodies (Brummer's Glands); also Lieberkühn's Glands, or simple follicles *in* the mucuous membrane, and which open on the free surface of the intestine. They are tube-like in shape, but microscopic in size.

The *solitary glands*, found chiefly in the large intestine, are bigger, and easily seen. They are round bodies, and around each is a circle of villi. Then we have what are called " Peyer's Patches," or " Peyer's Glands," which are simply a collection of the solitary glands. These patches of glands vary in number in the dog about from fifteen to twenty-five, and some are half an inch or more in diameter.

The large intestine is composed of the cæcum, a blind sac, opening into the intestine (said in ruminants to act as a reservoir for water). It is small in the dog, and somewhat twisted, yet it is sometimes the seat of inflammation. Next comes the colon; and, finally, the rectum, which ends with the anus or outer opening, surrounded by a circular muscle, the sphincter ani, which naturally is in a state of contraction.

The intestines of the dog are comparatively short, and the colon, indeed, is little more than a continuation of the small intestine.

And now, just a few words on digestion itself. When a dog is hungry, and sees his food, " his mouth waters." This is a common saying, and a true one; and the explanation is this: The glands which secrete the saliva are large in the dog—the submaxillary is larger even than the parotid—they are, moreover, easily excited by the imagination to secrete, and secrete largely too. When eating, this saliva speedily mixes with the food in the mouth, rendering the necessity for slow mastication null.

The next process of digestion is deglutition, or swallowing. I need hardly say, that with our canine friends this is not a very protracted one.

Received into the stomach, the real work of digestion begins. This is called by physiologists, *chimification*. The stomach keeps the food constantly in motion, so that every portion of it, in regular rotation, is brought into contact with the walls of the viscus, and is thus mixed with the secretions from the follicles—the gastric juice. This fluid is acid, and contains *pepsin*, which, with the acid, has the power of dissolving the albuminous, gelatinous, and saccharine portions of the food. Not, however, the oleaginous; that is reserved for lower down.

One thing with regard to this juice should be borne in mind, as it has a bearing on the feeding of dogs: the gastric juice can only dissolve a limited portion of food at a time. Any superabundance with which the animal may have gorged himself will ferment, and become a source of irritation to the nerves and stomach, and prevent the animal from enjoying good health or sound sleep; and it is a well-known fact that house-dogs that are sparingly fed always thrive best.

The food when dissolved and mixed with the gastric juice is called chyme, and escapes into the intestine through the pyloric opening.

And then begins the process of *chylification*, or intestinal digestion. The chyme, still kept in motion by the walls of the intestine, is mixed with the bile, the pancreatic juice, and the secretions from the follicles.

The bile from the liver saponifies the fatty portion of the food, and renders it fit for absorption by the intestinal villi. The pancreatic juice is somewhat similar to the saliva, and has similar functions, while at the same time it assists the liver in its duties.

The intestinal secretions, like the gastric, dissolve albuminous substances, and convert starch into sugar.

The good portion of the food converted into chyle is separated from that which is unfit to be made into blood, and taken up by the absorbents of the villi. The contents of the bowels are being continually whirled onwards by the alternate contraction and dilation of the circular muscular fibres that surround it, these muscles forming, so to speak, a sort of intestinal police force that are continually ordering them to "move on."

There are what we call lacteal vessels, rising from the intestine; these lacteals originate in the absorbents of the villi, which have sucked up—to use familiar language—the chyle from the food. And this milky-looking chyle is carried along through the mesenteric glands, and poured into a kind of reservoir which lies near the aorta, and which also receives the contents of another set of vessels, called the lymphatics, with which at present we have nothing to do. Upwards, then, from this reservoir of chyle there passes a larger vessel, named the thoracic duct. Right in front of the spine runs this duct, bearing along its nutritious load, until it comes to near the extremity of the jugular vein, and here it pours its contents into the blood. The reservoir for the chyle is, in the dog, very large. By a process of *endosmosis* there is also direct absorption of fluids through the walls of the stomach into the capillary vessels of the villi.

Let us now consider the ailments of this great canal.

1. *Dyspepsia.*

Dyspepsia, or indigestion, is one of the commonest of all diseases in non-sporting, and especially in pampered or petted dogs. Sporting dogs are like sporting men, they seldom want an appetite. They live hardy, healthy, active lives, are not often troubled with illness, and, if they do not get cut off by accident, they either live to a decent old age, or die in the prime of their lives, slain by some sthenic inflammation, or some other gentlemanly disorder. Seldom do they hang about for months with chronic ailments; their rule is to be ill for a day or two— then die.

But it must not be inferred that sporting dogs never suffer from dyspepsia. Unfortunately they do at times, although it is very often the fault of those who own them.

Pathology.—What has been already said on the subject of digestion will be quite sufficient to enable us to understand the pathology of dyspepsia. Some of the glandular secretions necessary to the proper assimilation of the food are either too scanty, over-abundant, or vitiated.

Dyspepsia is said to be of three different species—(1) Stomachic, when the gastric juices are at fault; (2) Duodenal, when the pancreas or liver err; and (3) Intestinal, when there is a want of proper absorbing power, and the muscular coats of the long portion of the alimentary canal are weak. As the same causes produce all three, and the treatment but little different, we include them all under the simple heading—dyspepsia.

Dyspepsia is generally considered a very simple ailment. It is a complaint that is so very apt to be pooh-poohed. "His stomach is out of order, nothing more," is the common observation. But dyspepsia, or in other words indigestion, is the forerunner of very many illnesses in the dog. It is often but the shadow of some coming evil, the prelude to some organic disease that in all probability will end his life. Happily, however, we can cure dyspepsia, and bar the way, by proper regimen, against its return, and thus keep at bay almost any disease that is not epizootic, and many that are.

Causes.—One cause of indigestion is improper feeding; want of proper exercise is another; and want of cleanliness a third. We have not far to look for others: irregularity in the time of feeding; and, in sporting dogs, too hard work soon tells a tale.

The errors in diet alluded to as the chief cause of indigestion are either the administration of improper and unwholesome food, or the giving of food in too great abundance. Food is given in too large quantities, and the dog enticed to eat under the mistaken notion that it will do him good. But no mistake could be more fatal to the animal's health and comfort. The power of the muscular coat of the stomach to properly mix and digest a meal is in indirect ratio to the size of that meal—if the meal is very large the power will be small, and *vice versâ*, because if the organ is overfilled it becomes stretched, and the muscular coat is thinner in consequence, and paralysed and weakened.

Too dainty food, on the other hand, has not the same power to excite the secretion of the gastric juices, nor the peristaltic action of the intestines, that a coarser diet possesses.

Over-work in the field, or over-exertion of any sort, depresses the nervous power, and in this way produces dyspepsia.

Prognosis.—If the ailment is taken early, and proper attention is paid to the orders of the veterinary surgeon who is consulted, nothing is more simple than to correct the digestion. Old-standing cases resist treatment, probably because some organic lesion has taken place. The liver or pancreas or spleen may have become the seat of disease.

The train of *symptoms* of the dyspepsia we usually see in the dog is the following: The dog has been ailing for some time, never very ill, and never really well. He never has very much appetite, or if he has it is a depraved and capricious one.

Perhaps he is fat; and when we inquire into the case and ask how he has been fed, it will usually be found that, especially if he be a lady's pet, he has had whatever he cared to eat.

But whether fat or lean, the dog will be found to be lazy, dull, and listless, and probably peevish and snappish—indication of irritability of the brain and nervous centres. The dog knows as well as any one that he is not well, and he cannot bear good wholesome food, but will eat beef or steak with a will. Dyspeptic dogs often have an irritability of the skin, at all events an unhealthy condition of coat. They suffer, too, from flatulence, sleep but badly, and seem troubled with nightmares, and as to their bowels, they may be bound one day and loose the next, and the stool itself is seldom a healthy one.

Vomiting and retching, especially in the morning, are by no means uncommon in dyspepsia.

Treatment.—If the case be one of severity, it will be better to begin the treatment by a dose of opening medicine, and as the liver is frequently at fault, nothing better can be given than a little podophyllin, nitrate of potash, and extract of taraxacum.

> ℞ Podophyll. ... ... gr ¹ ad gr. ½.
> Pot. nitrat. ... ... gr. iij. ad gr. x.
> Extr. tarax. ... ... gr. iij. ad gr. xv.
> Fᵗ· pil j. Misce.

Lower the diet for a day or two, and give twice a day from five to fifteen grains of the bicarbonate of potash in water, with from five to twenty grains of Gregory's powder. Give the most easily digested food, and give it on the principle of little and often. A milk diet alone may be tried. For *chronic* dyspepsia the treatment resolves itself very easily into the hygienic and the medicinal, and you may expect very little benefit from the latter if you do not attend to the former.

When a dog is ill and out of condition, one must either proceed with determination and energy to restore him to health, or let him run the risk of dying by some lingering illness, than which latter it would be far kinder to shoot him.

Begin the treatment of chronic indigestion, then, with a review of the dog's mode of life and feeding, and change it all if there is a chance of doing good. Insist upon the necessity of his being turned out first thing every morning, and of having a bath before his run and his breakfast, unless there be any disease present which might seem to contra-indicate the use of the douche.

Insist upon his being regularly washed, groomed, and kept sweet and clean, and housed in a pure kennel—not in a room, unless it be a large one, has no carpet, and has the window left fully open every night—likewise upon his having two hours' good romping or running exercise every day. Then as to his food, let his breakfast be a light one, and his dinner abundant, and of good substantial, digestible food. Give him a good proportion of flesh, not liver—liver should never be used for dogs unless now and then as a laxative. He is to have simply the two meals a day, and *nothing* between them. Give no sugar, no dainties, and bones most sparingly. Have his dish always filled with pure water, and washed out every morning, so that he may not swallow and sicken on his own saliva. See that he has no disease of the mouth, and has his teeth cleaned.

The late Mr. Mayhew, who was wise in hygienic matters, albeit his modes of treatment were sometimes questionable, deprecated the custom of starving dogs for one or two or even three days, as was often done by ignorant practitioners in order to make the animals "come to their stomach," as it was called. Such practice is but the cruellest and most ignorant barbarism, and the persons who make use of it ought to be summoned by the Society for the Prevention of Cruelty to Animals.

There are so many different varieties of dyspepsia, and the malady depends upon so many different causes, that it is difficult to recommend drugs. One thing is certain, however ; medicine alone will not cure a dog, although proper hygiene may. See that the bowels are kept regular; this a dip in the water every morning will generally effect. If they are much bound, gentle doses of sulphur or Youatt's Mixture should be given occasionally, or Gregory's Powder, but no rougher aperient; indeed, medicines of this class often do more harm than good. If the stools are clay-coloured, from two to eight or ten grains of extract of dandelion twice a day will do good, with a podophyllin pill once a week. The following is a safe and simple tonic pill, one to be given twice daily :—

$$\text{R}\!\!\!/\ \text{Sulph. Quinæ.} \quad \dots \quad \dots \quad \text{gr. } \tfrac{1}{4} \text{ ad gr. ij.}$$
$$\text{Sulph. Ferri.} \quad \dots \quad \dots \quad \text{gr. } \tfrac{1}{2} \text{ ad gr. vj.}$$
$$\text{Extr. Taraxac.} \quad \dots \quad \dots \quad \text{gr. iij. ad gr. x.}$$
$$\text{F}^{t\cdot}\ \text{pil. j.} \qquad\qquad\qquad \text{Misce.}$$

For small Toy dogs a little dinner pill may be given once a day, made of one grain and a half of pepsine, a grain of ginger, and half a grain of best Barbadoes aloes, and a little glycerine.

2. *Acute Gastritis.*

Acute gastritis, or inflammation of the stomach, is a very fatal and very painful disease in the dog, though happily somewhat rare.

It is supposed by most authorities to be a disorder that may originate as an idiopathic or primary disease, but it is more often the result of an irritant poison, or the administration by ignorant kennel-men of excessive doses of tartar emetic. It is doubtful, however, whether it *ever* presents itself as a primary disease. But supposing a case of acute gastritis to come before a veterinary practitioner, and granting that a chemical examination, or analysis of the matter vomited may prove that the animal has swallowed no metallic poison, or any well-known vegetable poison, how can he be sure that the symptoms have not been brought on by some animal irritant, or even some decomposed vegetable matter which the dog may have eaten?

The dog's stomach is so easily irritated, that an over-dose of an emetic, especially tartar emetic (which some people who use it for horses and dogs do not seem to know, *is a most virulent poison*) might induce gastritis.

Symptoms and Pathology.—The disease is the result of inflammation either of the mucous membrane of the stomach with its villi and follicles, or of the muscular coat itself of that viscus.

There is distressing vomiting, great thirst, high fever; the animal stretches himself on his belly in the very coolest corner he can find, panting, and in great pain. Enteritis generally accompanies bad cases; the ears are cold, and the limbs as well. Dark grumous blood may be vomited, or pure blood itself, from the rupture of some artery. And thus the poor dog may linger for some days in a most pitiful condition. Finally he is convulsed, and dies, or coma puts a milder termination to his sufferings.

Treatment of milder forms of gastritis—small doses of dilute hydrocyanic acid, in conjunction with opium, once in four hours, may do good, preceded by one to five ounces of olive oil in the form of enema.

$$\text{R}\!\!\!/.\ \text{Acid Hydrocyan. dil.} \dots \quad \text{m j. ad m v.}$$
$$\text{Tinct. Opii.} \dots \quad \dots \quad \text{m v. ad m xxx.}$$
$$\text{Aq.} \quad \dots \quad \dots \quad \text{ʒ ii. ad ʒ jv.}$$
$$\text{Misce et ft. haustus.}$$

The warm bath, and hot fomentations afterwards to the region of the stomach, may give relief, and the strength must be kept up by nutritive *enemata*—beef-tea mixed in cream. If the animal can drink, let him have plenty of milk or gruel, cooled by ice, the colder the better He must not drink much at a time, however.

When he is getting better nothing must be allowed to be eaten of a meaty or stimulating character for a time. The diet must be entirely farinaceous for some time to come; and if aperients are needed they must be of the very mildest description, or, better still, purgative clysters may be used.

3. Gastorrhœa.

Gastorrhœa, or Chronic Gastritis, or Stomach Catarrh, is a disease much more common than Acute Gastritis.

Causes.—The primary cause of this disorder, which is more commonly found in petted and pampered dogs, is bad feeding, which weakens the digestive powers; and the disease culminates probably from the animal having eaten some garbage which has disagreed with him, or probably from exposure to an amount of cold and wet to which he had been hitherto a stranger.

Pathology.—The disorder consists in a very irritable or sub-inflammatory condition of the mucous membrane of the stomach, combined with a congested state of the liver.

Symptoms.—Loss of appetite, quickened breathing, sighing, and restlessness, hot dry nose and mouth, and breath likewise hot; thirst, and frequent vomiting, or rather retching. What he does bring up is partly bile, partly frothy mucus. There is pain and tenderness in the abdominal region, and constipation. The vomit is often tinged with blood, so, likewise, are the stools. The pain seems to be most severe in the upper region of the abdomen, or epigastrium, and the vomiting rather increases than diminishes it. If the animal is not relieved prostration ensues, the pulse gets feeble and almost imperceptible, and death ensues.

Treatment.—The indications of treatment are twofold: to relieve pain, and subdue congestion. It would be well to get the bowels to act; but purgatives given by the mouth rather add to the mischief. Give, therefore, a castor-oil enema—

$$\text{R Olei Ricini ... ... } \mathrecal{3} \text{ ij. ad } \mathrecal{3} \text{ j.}$$
$$\text{Olei Oliv. ... ... } \mathrecal{3} \text{ iij. ad } \mathrecal{3} \text{ j.}$$
$$\text{Decoct. Avena ... } \mathrecal{3} \text{ ij. ad } \mathrecal{3} \text{ vj.}$$

Misce et ft. enema.

This will aid in relieving the liver. Place a large mustard poultice over the abdomen, and frequently foment with hot water. With small dogs the warm bath may be used with advantage.

To allay the irritation of the stomach we must trust to alkalies, and dilute hydrocyanic acid; small doses of bi-carbonate of potash, and from one to five drops of the acid every four hours. If the animal seems very low indeed, his strength must be kept up by injections of port wine and starch; and small quantities of diluted wine should be given by the mouth.

N.B.—If poisoning be suspected, the ejections ought to be kept and forwarded to an analytical chemist. The symptoms are very similar to those produced by some irritant poisons, although poisoning is more quickly fatal. However, when a person sees his dog ill—retching, and perhaps bringing blood up—he is very apt to jump to the conclusion that the animal has "picked up something."

Great care must be taken during convalescence, and nothing given that is in the least likely to disagree.

4. *Diarrhœa*.

Diarrhœa, or looseness of the bowels, or purging, is a very common disease among dogs of all ages and breeds. It is, nevertheless, more common among puppies about three or four months old, and among dogs who have reached the age of from seven to ten years.

The name, diarrhœa, is given by medical men to all cases where purging is the principal symptom, and when there exists no concomitant disease of any important organ, for diarrhœa is often symptomatic of other ailments.

Causes.—These are very numerous. In some weakly dogs exposure alone will produce it. The weather, too, has no doubt much to do with the production of diarrhœa. In most kennels it is more common in the months of July and August, although it often comes on in the very dead of winter. Puppies, if overfed, will often be seized with this troublesome complaint. A healthy puppy hardly ever knows when it has had enough, and it will, moreover, stuff itself with all sorts of garbage; acidity of the stomach follows, with vomiting of the ingesta, and diarrhœa succeeds, brought on by the acrid condition of the chyme, which finds its way into the duodenum. This stuff would in itself act as a purgative, but it does more, it abnormally excites the secretions of the whole alimentary canal, and a sort of subacute mucous inflammation is set up. The liver, too, becomes mixed up with the mischief, throws out a superabundance of bile, and thus aids in keeping up the diarrhœa.

Among other exciting causes, we find the eating of indigestible food, in even small quantities, drinking foul or tainted water, too much green food, raw paunches, foul kennels, and damp, draughty kennels.

Diagnosis.—It can hardly be mistaken for any other complaint, unless perhaps for dysentery. into which the diarrhœa often merges, or, more correctly speaking, dysentery often commences with an attack of diarrhœa. Now, many dog doctors tell us that if there be blood and mucus found in the stools, the case is one of dysentery "undoubtedly." It may be nothing of the kind, however, for we may often find small quantities of blood and mucus in simple diarrhœa. Neither are hard scybalous masses always found in dysentery. In dysentery there is always tenesmus, much straining, a dejected appearance of countenance, pain, and an anxious look about the eye, with frequent micturation, and a highly-coloured state of the urine.

Prognosis.—You can cure nineteen cases out of twenty if the animal is in the prime of life. If old there is less chance, and the diarrhœa of puppyhood is often very serious and fatal.

Symptoms.—The purging is, of course, the principal symptom, and the stools are either quite liquid or semi-fluid, bilious-looking, dirty-brown or clay coloured, or mixed with slimy mucus. In some cases they resemble dirty water. Sometimes, as already said, a little blood will be found in the dejection, owing to congestion of the mucous membrane from portal obstruction. In case there be blood in the stools, a careful examination is always necessary in order to ascertain the real state of the patient. Blood, it must be remembered, might come from piles or polypi, or it might be dysenteric, and proceed from ulceration of the rectum and colon. In the simplest form of diarrhœa, unless the disease continues for a long time, there will not be much wasting ; and the appetite will generally remain good but capricious.

In bilious diarrhœa, with large brown fluid stools and complete loss of appetite, there is much thirst, and, in a few days, the dog gets rather thin, although nothing like so rapidly as in the emaciation of distemper.

Treatment.—A case of simple diarrhœa should never be deemed unworthy of attention. Attack the disease at its commencement. A puppy that has once had a bad attack of this complaint will always be more or less subject to it, and, if he should happen to take distemper, ten to one it will be of the enteric form.

The treatment, then, will, it need hardly be said, depend upon the cause, but as it is generally caused by the presence in the intestine of some irritating matter, we can hardly err by administering a small dose of castor-oil, combining with it, if there be much pain—which you can tell by the animal's countenance—from five to twenty or thirty drops of laudanum, or of the solution of the muriate of morphia. This in itself will often suffice to cut short an attack. The oil is preferable to rhubarb, but the latter may be tried—the simple not the compound powder; dose, from ten grains to two drachms in bolus.

If the diarrhœa should continue next day, proceed cautiously—remember there is no great hurry, and a sudden check to diarrhœa is at times dangerous—to administer dog doses of the aromatic chalk and opium powder, or give the following medicine three times a day :—

> ℞ Pulv. Catechu. Co. ...   ... gr. iij. ad gr. xv.
> Pulv. Creta Arom. c. opio.   ... gr. v. ad gr. xxx.
>   Misce.

If the diarrhœa still continues good may accrue from a trial of the following mixture—

> ℞ Tinct. Opii.   ...   ... ♏ v. ad ♏ xxx.
> Acid Sulph. dil ...   ... ♏ ij. ad ♏ xv.
> Aquæ Camph. ...   ... ʒ ij. ad ʒ j.
> Fᵗ haustus.   Misce.

after every liquid motion, or, if the motions may not be observed, three times a day. If blood should appear in the stools give the following—

> ℞ Kino   ...   ... gr. j. ad gr. x.
> Pulv. Ipecac.   ... gr. ¼ ad gr. iij.
> Pulv. Opii.   ... gr. ⅛ ad gr. ij.
>   Misce.

This may be made into a bolus with any simple extract, and given three times a day. Williams recommends the hyposulphite of soda in cases where there is much fœtor. This seems to be a good plan, and, as there is no taste with the medicine, it may be dissolved in water and given in the food or drink. Dose, from two to ten grains. If there be much irritation of the rectum, with straining at stool, a compound lead and opium suppository may be introduced at night, after the dog has lain down.

The food is of importance. The diet should be changed, the food requires to be of a non-stimulating kind, no meat being allowed, but milk and bread, sago, or arrowroot, or rice, &c. The drink either pure water, with a pinch or two of chlorate and nitrate of potash in it, or barley-water if he will take it.

The dog's bed must be warm and clean, and free from draughts, and, in all cases of diarrhœa, one cannot be too particular with the cleanliness and disinfection of the kennels.

5. *Dysentery.*

This is a far more serious complaint in the dog. Pathologically, it consists of an inflammation, mostly chronic in the dog, of the colon and rectum, leading on to ulceration of the mucous membrane. It is generally considered by medical authorities that the inflammation takes place first in the solitary glands of the colon, and that the intervening mucous membrane gets inflamed, secretes largely, and is tender, and bleeds easily. After death we find abundant ulceration, and sympathetic inflammation of the mesenteric glands.

Symptoms.—Most troublesome and frequent stools, with great straining, the dejections are liquid, or liquid and scybalous, with mucus, and more or less of blood. There is also some manifestation of pain, an anxious appearance of countenance, loss of appetite—unless in very mild cases—frequent micturition, the water being scanty and high-coloured. The dog is usually dull and restless, and there is more or less of fever, with great thirst. If the anus be examined it will be found red, sore, and puffy. If the disease goes on to death the animal gets rapidly emaciated, pus appears in the stools, which become very offensive, the belly is tumid and tender, and soon the dog sinks exhausted and dies. Sometimes the disease assumes the chronic form, when there will be but little fever, but the pulse is frequent and weak, and the appetite sometimes ravenous. Nevertheless, the dog gets thin, the coat is harsh and dry, the tenesmus continues, and the stools are watery and highly fetid.

Diagnosis.—*See* diagnosis of diarrhœa.

Treatment.—Judicious diet is of great importance in the treatment of this disease. It must be very light, nutritious, and easily digestible, such as jellies, broths mixed with flour or fine white bread, bread-and-milk, cream, beef-tea, eggs, flour, porridge, &c., with an allowance of wine if deemed necessary. The drink may be pure water frequently changed, barley-water or other demulcent drinks.

The animal should be properly housed, and well protected from damp and cold, which in dogs very often produce the disease. Give a dose of castor-oil with a few drops, according to the dog's strength, of the liquid extract of opium; follow this up in about two hours with an enema or two of gruel, to assist its operation. Much good may be done by hot fomentations to the abdomen, and by linseed-meal poultices, in which a table-spoonful or two of mustard has been mixed, to the epigastrium, followed by a full dose of the liquid extract of opium.

This may be followed by from five grains to thirty of the trisnitrate of bismuth, in conjunction with from an eighth part of a grain to two grains of opium, thrice a day.

If the thirst be great, bicarbonate of potash, or chlorate of potash, and a little of the nitrate, should be added to the drinking water. Injections of gruel or starch, to which from twenty drops to a drachm of tincture of opium has been added, do good, and probably better still if a little good port wine is added to each.

When the disease has become chronic, our principal object is to sustain the animal's strength, and give the bowels all the rest we can. The mixture recommended for diarrhœa must be persisted in, and great fœtor of the dejections indicates the use of some deodoriser, as the hyposulphite of soda, with from twenty to sixty grains of wood charcoal, twice a day.

If there be much emaciation cod-liver oil must be given, combining its use with tonics, such as quinine and iron, in small doses.

The anus, if much inflamed, must be bathed frequently in warm water, and some cooling ointment smeared over it. This may be either cold cream or camphor ointment, or the common blue ointment may be sparingly used.

Bleeding is contra-indicated in this disease, so, too, is the exhibition of calomel and opium; a less heroic treatment, with good nursing, proper dieting, and clean kenneling will usually do more good.

A warm cloth bandage had better be worn for some time after the disorder has yielded to treatment and until the dog is fairly restored to health.

6. *Superpurgation.*

Superpurgation may either be a symptom of a badly-treated or neglected diarrhœa, or that of dysentery. A dog suffering from long-continued abdominal flux is a most miserable being indeed. The emaciation is extreme, the coat staring, the eye glassy and probably half closed, the flanks tucked in, and the poor dog shivers at the slightest breath of air.

It is often produced by the abuse of purgatives, especially of aloes.

The treatment consists in removing the cause, in taking the animal in out of the cold, and in judicious dieting, and the administration of astringent medicines, as recommended in diarrhœa.

Carbonate of ammonia may do good in these cases in doses of from two to five grains three or four times a day.

7. *Colic.*

Colic is a most distressing complaint, far from uncommon among the canine race, and not unattended with danger. By colic we must be understood to mean a non-inflammatory disease, usually termed "the gripes," or "tormina," due to an irregular and spasmodic action of the bowels.

Causes.—The disease may be caused by cold, parasites, or the passage of a calculus; but is more often the result of some indigestible matter irritating the small intestine or the colon.

Symptoms.—Great pain in the region of the abdomen, as evinced by the restlessness and distress of the animal, who frequently gives vent to piteous moans and cries. That there is nausea with colic no one will ever doubt who has seen a poor animal suffering from an attack of it. His wish is to lie quiet and take no food, although he will drink readily enough; also to lie quiet if the pain would permit him; this, however, comes on every now and again, causing the dog to jump up howling, and presently, when the pain in some measure subsides, to seek out another position and lie down again, his distress being piteous to behold. There is no sign of inflammation, however; the animal prefers to lie curled up, seemingly to relax the abdominal muscles, to relieve the tormina. During the attacks the breathing is quickened and the pulse accelerated, and the animal's countenance gives proof of the agony he is enduring. If the pains be not continuous, which they seldom are, the nose may continue throughout the attack cool and wet, and the eye remain uninjected. The bowels are nearly always constipated.

Diagnosis.—The pain of colic is relieved by pressure and friction; in inflammation, pressure cannot be borne. The pulse, too, is not of the inflammatory character. The suddenness of the attack is likewise a good clue.

Treatment.—The first indication of the treatment of colic, from whatever cause, is evidently to get the bowels to act, and thus effect the expulsion of offending matter. This offending matter may be either indigestible food, hardened fœces, or some irritating substance which the dog may have swallowed. A young dog, for example, but little over his puppyhood, had swallowed some lead paint, which gave rise to severe colic. This was relieved by cathartics, the warm bath, chloroform and opium, with simple aperients for some days to come. If the dog is otherwise apparently in good health, give the following:—Of castor-oil three parts, syrup of buckthorn two parts, and syrup of poppies one part (this is a prescription of Youatt's); followed immediately by an anodyne draught, such as—

$$\text{℞ Spirit. Ætheris.} \quad \dots \quad \dots \quad \text{ℳ x. ad ℥ ij.}$$
$$\text{Spirit. Chlorof.} \quad \dots \quad \dots \quad \text{ℳ v. ad ℳ xxx.}$$
$$\text{Sol. Mur. Morphiæ} \quad \dots \quad \text{ℳ iij. ad ℳ xx.}$$
$$\text{Aquæ Camph.} \quad \dots \quad \dots \quad \text{q. s.} \qquad \text{M.}$$
$$\text{F}^{\text{t}} \text{ haustus.}$$

The action of the purgative may be assisted by an enema of warm water, in which a little soap has been rubbed down.

In less urgent cases of colic, a simple dose of castor-oil will be found to answer quite as well, and the oil is to be followed by a dose of brandy in hot water.

If there be much drum-like swelling of the abdomen, hard rubbing will do good, likewise give a draught, such as —

R Sp. Æther.   ...   ...   ℥ x. ad ʒij.
Sodæ Bicarb.   ...   gr. x. ad ʒ j.
Ol. Carui.   ...   ...   ℥ j. ad ℥ x.
Tinct. Opii.   ..   ...   ℥ v. ad ℥ xxx.
Aq. Camph.   ...   ...   q. s.   M.

The tympanites may be further reduced, and great relief given by a turpentine and castor-oil enema—

R Olei Ricini   ...   ...   ʒ ij. ad ʒ j.
Olei Terebinth.   ...   ʒ j. ad ʒ vj.
Decoct. Avenæ.   ...   ʒ ij. ad ʒ x.
M.

8. Constipation.

Constipation, more commonly called costiveness, is a complaint we are often required to treat. It often occurs in the progress of other diseases, or as one of the symptoms of some other malady, such as inflammation, where the secretions are dried up. Nevertheless, it is just as often a separate ailment.

Perhaps no complaint to which our canine friends are liable is less understood by the non-professional dog doctor, and by dog owners themselves.

Causes.—Idiopathically considered constipation may arise from a variety of causes, but the principal of these will probably be found to be irregularity in the time of feeding, food of too dainty a nature, and want of exercise, leading to a weakened and torpid condition, or even atony of the muscular coat of the digestive canal.

Just as in the human being a sedentary life results in torpor of the liver and constipation, so is it with a dog that is continually lolling in the recumbent position. If we remember that it is the vermicular motion of the intestinal canal, caused by the contraction and dilatation of the muscular circular fibres, that causes the food to move onwards, and that this motion depends upon a healthy and vigorous condition of those fibres, it will readily be understood that any-thing that weakens the system generally, or debilitates the nerves, and lessens the quantity of iron in the blood, will produce constipation. If constipation is thus induced, from weakness in the coats of the intestine, *the exhibition of purgatives can only have a temporary effect in relieving the symptoms*, and is certain to be followed by reaction, and consequently by further weakness.

Youatt was never more correct in his life than when he says, "Many dogs have a dry constipated habit, often greatly increased by the bones on which they are fed. This favours the disposition to mange, &c. It produces indigestion, encourages worms, blackens the teeth, and causes fetid breath."

Symptoms.—The stools are hard, usually in large round balls, and defecation is accomplished with great difficulty, the animal having often to try several times before he succeeds in effecting the act, and this only after the most acute suffering. The fœces are generally covered with white mucus, showing the heat and semi-dry condition of the gut. The stool is sometimes so dry as to fall to pieces like so much oatmeal. In worse cases there is straining without the power to accomplish defecation, the stretched and attenuated rectum being quite unequal to the task of expelling its contents.

There is generally also a deficiency of bile in the motions, and, in addition to simple costiveness, we have more or less loss of appetite, with a too pale tongue, dulness, and sleepiness, with slight redness of the conjunctiva. Sometimes constipation alternates with diarrhœa, the food being improperly commingled with the gastric and other juices, ferments, spoils, and becomes, instead of healthy blood-producing chyme, an irritant purgative.

Treatment.—The treatment must of course have reference to the cause of the complaint, but, in all cases of habitual constipation, we must depend more upon hygienic treatment than upon the exhibition of medicines. Avoid purgatives—as a rule, at least, for to a certain extent mild doses of castor-oil, compound rhubarb pill, or olive-oil, will at first be necessary. Sometimes an enema will be required, if the medicine will not act; and there are cases in which it may be found necessary to break down a hard mass of compacted fæcal matter with the stalk of a small spoon before this can be injected.

Give the dog plenty of exercise and a swim daily (with a good run after the swim), or instead of the swim a bucket bath. This forms a capital natural purgative, for by the sudden immersion the blood is sent bounding inwards, and a renewed flow of the secretions is the happy result.

The use of the morning bucket bath, first thing after the animal has been turned out, is much to be recommended, but care must be taken to dry well down after it.

Regulate the diet. Give oatmeal, rather than flour or fine bread, as the staple of his diet, but a goodly allowance of meat is to be given as well, with occasionally cabbage or boiled liver, or even a portion of raw liver. Let the dog be as much as possible in the open air. There is nothing so good as plenty of exercise in the fields for this troublesome complaint. You may give a bolus before dinner, such as the following:—

$$\text{R Pil. rhei co.} \quad \ldots \quad \ldots \quad \text{gr. i. ad gr. v.}$$
$$\left.\begin{array}{l}\text{Pulv. ipecac.}\\ \text{Quinæ}\end{array}\right\} \ldots \quad \text{ā ā gr. } \tfrac{1}{4} \text{ ad gr. ij.}$$
$$\text{Ext. tarax.} \quad \ldots \quad \ldots \quad \text{gr. iij. ad gr. x.}$$
$$\text{M.}$$

Purified ox bile does an immense deal of good in old dogs with a tendency to constipation. The dose is from one to five grains. If there is a deficiency of bile in the stools, as known by their whitish colour, then give twice a day nitric acid dil., and juice of taraxacum, from three to fifteen drops of the former to half a teaspoonful up to two teaspoonfuls of the juice, in a little water.

The mildest of purgatives are to be given no longer than they are actually required. As soon as we can get the dog's bowels to act in a natural way—but not before—we may tone the dog up by giving cod-liver oil and quinine, or the phosphate of iron or zinc, in a pill.

9. *Impaction, and* 10. *Obstruction.*

This accident may occur either in the stomach or some portion of the intestinal canal. It is dangerous at the best, but if unskilfully treated is sure to end in death.

Impaction of the stomach in a dog is the result of overfeeding on some indigestible substance or other. It is a rare accident, from the simple fact that a dog can vomit so very easily. Some dogs have a craze for chewing old wood, a symptom of dyspepsia which should be seen to.

We usually have the history of cases of impaction to guide us, and the symptoms generally found are a swollen and somewhat tender stomach, some degree of fever with dulness, a hot nose, colicky pains, and constant efforts at vomiting without any result. In puppies you may even have convulsions. One case of stomach impaction was occasioned in a Mastiff by his swallowing shavings, another case by the dog gorging himself on uncooked bullock's lights. The distress of the latter was very great, until relieved, then great heat and pain in the stomach continued for many hours, which the animal endeavoured to relieve by licking snow constantly.

Treatment.—If the dog fails to relieve himself by natural means, an emetic must be given. The speediest is tartar emetic, from a quarter of a grain for a very small dog up to five grains for a large-sized Mastiff. An enema might do no harm afterwards; but do not give any purgative by the mouth for some time at least. Give the animal plenty of cold water to drink, and if much distress of stomach continues try the dilute hydrocyanic acid; dose, one to five drops.

Impaction in some portion of the Bowels.—A case of this kind occurred not long since in the practice of a country veterinary surgeon. There were dulness, loss of appetite, colicky pains, and obstinate constipation, but no fever at first. The case was treated so " heroically " that inflammation of the gut, ending in gangrene, was the result. The post-mortem revealed the cause of the mischief—namely, the firm impaction of the joint of a ham-bone in the small intestine. This case speaks for itself.

But impaction in the bowels of a dog may occur from other matters as well as from bones; pieces of half-chewed sticks may find their way into the intestine and cause obstruction. Again, gall-stones may cause occlusion of the gut, as well as intestinal concretions, formed perhaps of hair swallowed, and hardened fœces.

Intussusception, or invagination of the bowel, is the name given to that internal accident in which one portion of the bowel is received into the other. This will not only result in obstruction of the bowel, but of strangulation of the part itself and its blood-vessels, and consequent gangrene.

Volvulus.—By this term is meant that a loop of gut gets turned round, so to speak, on itself.

Now, both intussusception and volvulus, along with internal hernias of different kinds, and indeed occlusion of the bowel from concretions of any kind, must be looked upon as most dangerous and generally fatal accidents. They are, too, most difficult to diagnose. Post-mortem examination only can at times prove what the complaint has been. In the dog, the retching is so severe at times that the contents of a portion of the gut are brought up. In cases of this sort veterinary aid ought at once to be called in, for there is just a chance for the dog, as the case may be one of strangulated external hernia, which in a valuable animal ought to be submitted to operation.

It must be noted that in obstruction from intussusception, volvulus, invagination, or internal hernia, diaphragmatic or otherwise (the diaphragm, or midriff, is that thin muscular partition which separates or divides the contents of the chest from those of the abdomen, and a loop of gut sometimes breaks or forces its way through into the chest cavity, and becomes strangulated) in the accidents above mentioned the symptoms are both more sudden and more acute than those of simple or chronic obstruction of the bowels. Vomiting quickly ensues, and after a time may become feculent. There is also a tympanitic or blown-up condition of the bowel on the side in which the obstruction is, which contrasts markedly with the flattened appearance of the other. At times a tumour may be detected on the site of the accident. The disease, or accident, usually ends fatally in a few days.

The *treatment* of these cases must be carried on much upon the same principle as that for enteritis—by leeching to the abdomen and hot fomentations, and either calomel and opium by the mouth or the subcutaneous injection of morphia.

Now, if the obstruction to the bowels is caused by hardened fæces, impacted bones, &c., the symptoms will be altogether of a more chronic nature, and the obstinate constipation will be the most prominent of these, and the constitutional disturbance will not be of so severe a nature, nor will the vomiting be of a stercoraceous character, although it may finally become so ; and although the belly may become tympanitic, it does not do so so speedily as in a case of intussusception.

Treatment of chronic obstructions.—The first object is to relieve the bowel as speedily as may be, but no harsh measures are justifiable. The obstruction may be in the rectum : this must be explored, and if it be found filled with hardened fæces, these must be broken up, when a simple enema should be given, which may be followed by castor-oil. Keep the dog as quiet as possible, and administer occasionally a little beef-tea and brandy ; but give no solid food, unless eggs may so be termed.

Enemas ought to be thrown well up into the bowel by means of a long tube.

It should be remembered that purgatives should never be given rashly in any kind of obstruction.

Two interesting cases of intussusception which recently occurred may here be noticed. The dogs were Setters, both belonging to the same gentleman ; both had been running together, both fell ill about the same time, and both died within a short time of each other. The post-mortem revealed the cause of death. Now we usually call intussusception an accident, and so it is. Are we to look upon the cases of these two Setters, then, as a mere coincidence? The only cause that could be assigned was deducted from the fact that they were both seen drinking largely from a pond of putrid water. The poison of this water may have caused relaxation of the coats of the bowel—a condition favourable to intussusception—or may have produced cramp or spasm of a ring or two of the muscular coat, and hence the invagination.

11. *Hæmorrhoids.*

Hæmorrhoids, better known as piles, constitute a disease to which dogs are only too subject. They consist of small round painful tumours which form at the base of the rectum, sometimes inside the *sphincter ani* and at other times outside, originating in an abnormal state of the veins of the part, and consequent congestion and tumefaction of the subcutaneous areolar tissue.

Causes.—The rectum of the dog is not only predisposed by nature to piles, but the habits of the animal and his feeding have a great deal to do with their production. Remember, the dog's rectum is comparatively narrow, and is plentifully supplied with a network of blood-vessels, and by far the greatest portion of the venous blood is returned to the heart through the liver. Now, the liver of the dog is large, and, as we all know, is easily put out of order; when it is so, and the circulation in the portal system is sluggish, the veins of the rectum are apt to become congested. If, in addition to this, the bowels are constipated, the areolar tissue gets stretched and loose, irritation is set up, and piles result.

The habits, too, of dogs are likely to produce piles. They are so prone to pick up all sorts of filth—bits of greasy ropes, wood, leather, bones, &c.—which, being mostly indigestible, have to pass through a perhaps already congested rectum and anus, and cannot fail to produce piles by the tension they exert on the veins of the areolar tissue.

Feeding of a rough and careless kind is another fruitful source of the disorder. Some people labour under the idea that dogs can digest anything—and, indeed, the dog himself seems to fancy that the swallowing of any fancy tit-bit is the principal part of digestion; at all events, once down, he has nothing more to do with it. Want of regular exercise is another predisposing cause of piles, because it tends to render the liver sluggish. Constipation is an exciting cause, and the abuse of drastic purgatives, and there are many others which need not here be specified.

Symptoms.—The dog will generally, if not invariably, manifest some uneasiness which will draw the attention to the seat of mischief—perhaps a straddling gate and stiffness. Pain while sitting at stool should at once arouse suspicion, or he may be observed to frequently lick the regions under the tail, or sit down and trail the anus along the ground (although some healthy enough little dogs have a trick of this sort).

However, upon examination—which the animal does not always submit to with an easy grace—the anus will be found to have lost its usual healthy contracted appearance, it is puffy and swollen, and probably the piles may be seen protruding. There are seldom external piles without internal as well. There is always more or less pain, but if, however, the dog is firmly held, and the anus gently pulled open, you will not fail to see the congested mucous membrane. The stools, too, will often, especially if the dog be constipated, be found tinged with blood. Old dogs are more frequently troubled with piles than young ones.

Treatment.—This must, of course, be both local and constitutional. First and foremost we must see that the dog gets proper food, and also see that he gets a judicious amount of exercise. The food ought to be of a non-constipating nature, and contain a due amount of flesh. Boiled greens ought to be given once a week at least, and occasionally a piece of raw bullock's liver. Exercise is most essential. At the same time any bad habits he may have formed, such as eating wood, or even too much dog grass, must be corrected. Gentle purgatives may be required, just enough to keep the bowels moderately free, such as a little sulphur in the food, or a little castor-oil given the last thing at night. If he seem very dull, with a dry nose and little appetite, and vomits some yellow fluid sometimes of a morning, a ball, consisting of a little sulphur, with from five to fifteen grains of the extract of taraxacum, should be given every morning.

Locally.—Cleanliness of the parts and the frequent application of cold water cannot fail to do good, and we must also make use of some astringent injection. We have a good one in sulphate of zinc, three grains to two ounces of water, injected at night. An ointment will also be of great service, and ought to be not only well smeared on twice or oftener every day, but a little inserted into the rectum. The compound ointment of galls, with a double proportion of powdered opium, is very useful. Or the benzoated oxide of zinc ointment may be used, but if there be much tenderness the dog does not like it so well.

This treatment is simple but effective: it must not be forgotten that local treatment must go hand in hand with constitutional.

12. *Fistula in Ano.*

Fistula in ano, or anal fistula, is sometimes found in the dog as the result of long-neglected or badly-treated piles. Dogs who suffer from fistula are mostly those animals who have led inactive lives, been pampered, and overfed, and consequently whose portal system is out of order. Although it is by no means a common disease in the dog, still it is one of so painful and distressing a nature that it demands our best attention. From the natural movements of the bowel, and owing to the fact which the reader already knows, that the sphincter ani or muscle which closes the end of the rectum is naturally in a state of contraction, this disease is most difficult to heal, and only succumbs to surgical interference.

Treatment.—This painful disease very often requires an operation which need not be described here further than as the Scotch veterinary surgeon graphically described it, "cutting oot the grip." The treatment must be both local and constitutional. The constitutional treatment consists in giving the dog a fair allowance of wholesome food of a laxative nature, such as oatmeal porridge and milk, or oatmeal brose and sheep's-head broth. Be careful that he neither gets bones or dog-grass, nor those masses of wool which you often see adhering to a skinned (?) sheep's-head, and which many people do not take the trouble to remove, being under the impression that anything is good enough for a dog. Give the dog a moderate amount of healthful exercise, but do not overdo it ; and permit him to have a swim daily if he chooses. At the same time he will require some tonic, such as the following—

℞ Sulph. Zinci ⎫
Ext. Gentian ⎬ ā, ā, gr. j., ad gr. v.
Ext. Taraxac. ⎭ Fᵗ pil. j. M.

or from half a teaspoonful to a dessertspoonful of Parrish's Chemical Food, to be given twice a day.

Never allow the bowels to become constipated. If they can be kept easy by means of food so much the better, if not, an occasional gentle laxative will be required, such as castor oil or olive oil. But avoid aloes as you would poison. Keep the parts clean, always using a few drops of carbolic acid in the water you wash them with.

N.B.—The above constitutional treatment stands good in nearly all diseases of the rectum.

Local treatment.—If the fistula be a complete one, nothing but a surgical operation will do any good ; if a blind, external one, an attempt should be made to cure it. The gut ought to be syringed out every morning with cold water to give tone to it; and the fistula, about every second day, must be gently probed, the probe having been previously dipped in a solution of nitrate of silver (ten grains to the ounce). This is all that can be suggested ; and, after all, it must be confessed, that simple though the latter operation reads on paper, very few dogs will submit to it twice without a strenuous resistance.

Without the aid of the knife fistula in ano is only very slightly amenable to treatment.

13. *Other Diseases of the Rectum.*

The rectum in the dog is particularly liable to disease of different kinds, not to mention cancer, which shall be treated of under another heading. Abscesses often form around or near the anus, filled with pus of a peculiarly fetid odour. In these cases not only must the treatment be directed to the improvement of the general health, but as soon as fluctuation can be detected, the abscess is to be freely opened in the dependent position ; then after the matter has been evacuated, it may be treated as a simple ulcer. Great cleanliness must be observed, and washing frequently with water to which a few drops of strong solution (50 per cent.) of carbolic acid has been added. If the ulcer becomes indolent, it is to be brushed every morning with a ten-grains-to-the-ounce solution of nitrate of silver. Or it may be touched with a bit of blue-stone or nitric acid.

The rectum is subject not only to cancer, but to non-malignant tumours of other sorts, which sometimes require the use of the knife.

Polypi are to be treated by the ligature, and a surgeon must be applied to, as dilatation by a particular instrument is usually required, unless, indeed, they protrude, when it is easy to transfix the neck with a needle, and tie the two ends one at each side. Or the silken ligature may simply be tied tightly round the neck, when in a day or two the polypus will drop off. This treatment is preferable to that of excision by the knife, as in the latter operation there is apt to be considerable hæmorrhage. N.B.—A polypus must not be confounded with a pile, the *latter is broad at the base, the former has a neck.*

Prolapsus ani, or a coming down or falling out of the rectum, is occasionally met with in dogs of a weakly disposition; and if not understood, or improperly treated, it may end in gangrene, sloughing, and death. This protrusion of the rectum is caused at times by quantities of hardened fæces being retained in the rectum. The rectum is stretched, and loses tone; the muscular walls and mucuous membrane relax, and hence the liability to protrusion. At first the prolapsus only occurs during defecation; but latterly the rectum protrudes at any time, and is generally more or less inflamed and excoriated.

Treatment.—At first, along with the usual constitutional treatment, and the careful regu-lation of the bowels with the simplest laxatives, or by means of food, fresh air, and *gentle* exercise, it is advisable to employ cold water enemas containing three or four drops of the tincture of iron to an ounce. Not more than from half an ounce to three ounces should be injected, as it is meant to be retained. Do this three or four times a day. Or the sulphate of iron may do as well, two or three grains to an ounce of water.

Any loose, baggy portions of mucous membrane, or the remains of former piles, may be ligatured and allowed to drop off, after which the part may be touched with nitrate of silver or blue-stone.

The protruded portion of the gut is to be carefully returned before the injection is used.

14. *Enteritis.*

Enteritis, or inflammation of the bowels, is one of the most painful as well as dangerous diseases with which the canine race are afflicted, and unhappily it is far from rare.

Causes.—In nine cases out of ten it is the owner's own fault that his poor dog suffers from enteritis. The dog has been ill-treated in some way. Perhaps he has been over-pampered, over-fed, his constitution rendered weak—killed, in fact, by kindness. Or he may have been over-run, over-worked, or allowed to disport himself in the water too much, and afterwards exposed to cold.

Unwholesome food will also produce enteritis; and direct violence, as from kicks or blows. It may also proceed from the extension of inflammation from the stomach, and from over-doses of irritant poisons—the abuse of tartar emetic, for example. Again, neglected colics may end in inflammation, so may impaction of the bowel.

Or enteritis may have a constitutional origin, that is, it may arise from mange, or the poison of distemper; but from whatever cause it proceeds, its symptoms are unmistakable, and the disease, as a rule, very speedily fatal.

Pathology.—There is some dispute about the exact pathology of this disease among learned practitioners, some affirming that it is the muscular coat that is the seat of inflammation, others that it is the mucous. Probably both these coats are affected, but the mucous coat much more so than the muscular. Ulceration is often found in the bowel—just what one would naturally expect —and often gangrene.

Symptoms.—There are, to commence with, the usual symptoms of inflammatory fever. The disease is ushered in by rigors and general uneasiness, hot and dry mouth, hot breath, injected conjunctiva, scanty high-coloured urine, and hard frequent pulse. These symptoms are followed by those of pain—colicky pains, one might almost call them, for the pitiful, agonising cries are similar to those in a case of colic, although sharper and shorter. That the animal is in intense agony, and that the seat of pain is internal, no one who sees him can for a moment doubt. His face is expressive of the greatest anxiety; if standing, it is with fore and hind legs drawn well together, and back arched to relieve the tension of the abdominal muscles, while the tail is pressed down between the thighs. He looks mournfully in one's face, then perhaps round to his side, as if trying to indicate the very seat of his ailment. If lying, it is with belly on some cool spot, and in some dark or out-of-the-way corner.

The thirst is very urgent, the appetite of course entirely lost. The bowels are at first constipated, but gradually, from the effusion of serum into the bowel from the inflamed surfaces, the system is thrown open, and diarrhœa comes on, and this diarrhœa is generally the beginning of the end; the pulse gets thready, feeble, and sometimes imperceptible, breath gets cold and fetid, the belly swells, the pupils dilate, and the dog gradually sinks exhausted, and dies.

Manual examination reveals very great tenderness to the touch. This the author has *always* found, yet some authorities assure us that pressure is grateful to the animal.

Diagnosis.—Enteritis is sometimes mistaken for rabies, but there is the extreme nervousness of the latter disease to guide us. The attitude, too, is different in the two disorders; there is a difference in the bark, and, moreover, the absence of abdominal pain in rabies, and that peculiar speaking glance round to the side. From colic it is easily distinguishable, from the more gradual onset of enteritis, from the difference of the bark, and from there being pain on pressure in enteritis, whereas pressure gives relief in colic.

Treatment.—Our treatment must be to endeavour to subdue the inflammation, ease the pain, and at the same time give the bowels all the rest we can. The old treatment was to bleed till the pulse faltered, and repeat the bleeding, and the old vets. had no occasion certainly to grumble if their patients died.

Let the dog be kept as quiet as possible. Let opium be given in large doses. The tincture is the best, as it acts more quickly; the dose from twenty drops to a drachm, repeated if necessary every two or three hours. The bowels are not to be attempted to be opened by means of purgatives. The idea of expecting good to accrue from forcing matter through an inflamed bowel, and increasing its peristaltic motion, is very absurd indeed, and almost sinful, but as the lower part of the gut is frequently blocked up with hardened fæces, we must get rid of that. Use simply warm water, in which dissolve a little mild soap, and this throw up as far as possible, and as slowly and gently as possible.

Leeches may be employed in this disease: if they are they must be in quantity from ten for a little animal, up to thirty for a Mastiff. The belly being shaved, they are applied to the most tender spot. This only for strong dogs. Whether leeches are applied or not, hot fomentations must not be omitted, and the warm bath will be found to do good in the case of small dogs; with the larger breeds it is inconvenient.

If we have succeeded in subduing the inflammation, then after the lapse of a day or two, if the bowels are not naturally opened, you may give a dose of castor-oil. The drink is to be demulcent, and the return to solid food during convalescence very gradual.

It may be as well to say a word or two here about the disease called peritonitis.

Peritonitis, or inflammation of the serous sac which lines the abdominal cavity, is a disease to which dogs are but little subject. Even wounds, which in the horse and other animals result in inflammation of the peritoneum, in the dog heal kindly.

Causes.—It may occur from the extension of inflammation from other organs, or be the result of kicks, blows, or severe falls.

Peritonitis is seen both in an acute and chronic form, but more frequently in the latter. In the acute stage, after rigors and all the other symptoms of high fever, in which the dog conducts himself almost similarly to a case of enteritis, the abdomen, if examined, will be found swollen, tense, and tympanitic and excessively tender, not in any one spot, but all over. There is even more tenderness on pressure than in enteritis.

The diagnosis is at first difficult, but after a time lymph becomes effused into the sac, and there is then no doubt of the case.

The treatment is the same as that for enteritis, with which, indeed, it is often associated. Cases of acute peritonitis usually end in death. The chronic form may follow the acute, but is more often quite a distinct disease.

Symptoms.—There is little evidence of pain or even uneasiness, there is deterioration of the general health, and some tenderness on pressure, with frequent attacks of diarrhœa, but there is little else to lead to a proper diagnosis of the case until ascites or dropsy ensues. (See Dropsy.)

CHAPTER IV.

DISEASES OF THE RESPIRATORY ORGANS.

By the expression "respiratory organs" is meant, not only the lungs themselves, but the trachea or windpipe, the larynx or organ of voice, and the nares or nostrils. The trachea or windpipe descends downwards and backwards to the interior of the chest, where it divides into two large bronchi, one for each lung. The trachea is formed of a series of cartilaginous rings joined together by ligaments, and lined with mucous membrane. The bronchi are also lined with mucous membrane, and the lungs throughout their whole course. It is this membrane which is the seat of inflammation in severe catarrh or bronchitis.

No sooner have the bronchi entered the substance of the lungs than they commence giving off innumerable branches, forming smaller and smaller tubes, getting less and less until they end in what are termed the intercellular passages. If one looks at a leafless oak-tree it will give a very good idea of the division and subdivision of the bronchial tubes. The stem or trunk of the tree shall represent the windpipe, the larger branches the larger bronchi, the smaller the smaller, and the ultimate ramifications, or twigs of the branches, the intercellular passages, which are probably not more than one-fiftieth of an inch in diameter.

Now there are, opening into these inter-cellular passages, innumerable little four-sided cavities or depressions. These are called the *alveoli*, or air-cells. They are not larger than between one two-hundredth and one-seventieth of an inch; and it is all around these that the minute capillary or hair-like blood-vessels are spread. And not only the bronchi large and small, but the air-cells even, are lined with mucous membrane; this, being a secreting membrane, in health is always moist, the moisture or secretion enabling the membrane to throw off foreign matters from its surface, such as fine dust. When the vessels that supply this membrane become reddened and congested, the secretion is largely increased, as happens in bronchitis.

Spasmodic contraction of these air-cells constitutes asthma, while dilation of them constitutes the disease called emphysema or "broken wind."

The theory of respiration is very simple, and may be described in few words. The venous blood—that is, the vitiated blood returned from the various organs and tissues of the body—is pumped by the heart into the lungs, where, through the medium of myriads of capillaries, it is spread out around the air-cells to be revivified by the air which is breathed. This revivification is simply a chemical act. The oxygen of the air combines with the carbon (or carbonaceous matter or impurities) of the venous blood to form carbonic acid (CO_2), which is exhaled. The carbon is burned off, so to speak, and the blood is not only purified, but heated, and thus returned to the heart, to be re-distributed to every portion of the body. Respiration thus becomes not only the purifier of the blood, without which purification it would speedily produce death, but also a source of heat. Formerly it used to be considered the only source of heat in the body; now it is pretty well known that there is a union of oxygen with carbon and hydrogen, which takes place in the tissues themselves and evolves heat, and there are several other sources of heat which need not here be enumerated.

Let us now consider the diseases to which the lungs are subject, beginning with the most simple.

I. *Catarrh.*

Catarrh, sometimes called coryza, or, in common language, "a cold," is far from an unfrequent complaint in the dog.

Causes.—It is usually the result of neglect in some form or another. The kennel probably is leaky, or the dog has been left out to shiver in the rain, or has been sent into the water towards nightfall and allowed to go to kennel in his wet coat. Exposure to cold and wet when the dog is tired, and the system consequently weak, will be very apt to produce it.

Catarrh is very common among puppies; and dogs that are much confined to the house, and get but little exercise, are more liable to colds than rough out-of-door dogs.

Now this catarrh may seem a very simple matter to many, and no doubt it is, and it speedily yields to judicious treatment; but the results of a neglected cold are sometimes disastrous in the extreme, and one never knows where a cold may end.

Pathologically speaking, catarrh is a sub-acute inflammation of the mucous membrane of the naso-pharangeal passages. If it extends downwards into the lungs, and attacks the lining membrane of the air-passages it is called bronchitis. We know that the skin is one of the great emunctories of the body; if its secretions are suddenly checked by cold, deleterious matters are retained in the blood, which nature seeks outlet for through the medium of the mucous surfaces of the air-passages, upon which, therefore, an extra strain is put, and they become inflamed. More or less fever is bound to be the result, and on this theory either catarrh or bronchitis may be accounted for.

Symptoms.—In severe cases the dog or puppy exhibits unwonted lassitude, is more dull and sleepy than usual, has slight shiverings, and may-be loss of appetite or a capricious appetite. This is followed by running at the nose, and a slight discharge from the eyes, and if the conjunctiva is examined it will be found either redder or darker than usual, showing that it is injected. Sneezing is a frequent symptom, but unless the catarrh extends downwards there will not be any cough. The discharge from the nostrils will indicate the extent of the disorder; and the dryness of the nose and heat of the mouth the amount of fever.

Treatment.—By the tyro a common cold is often called distemper, and "cured" by a specific.

A simple cold is easily got rid of, but there is no reason why it should be utterly neglected, especially in valuable dogs, for this reason, *that it is apt to recur and will each time evince a greater downward tendency.*

Give the animal a dose of castor-oil when he is first observed to be ailing, and let him have a dry warm bed at night, and from two drachms to an ounce (according to the animal's size) of Mindererus spirit. Let him have plenty of water to drink, in which you may dissolve a teaspoonful of chlorate of potash and also a little nitre, or you can give a dose or two of nitre made into a bolus with soap and sulphur.

Next day give the following linctus thrice daily :—

℞ Syrup Scillæ   ...   ℳ v. ad ℳ xxx.
Tinct. Camph. Co. ...   ℳ x. ad ʒ j.
Syr. Papaveris   ...   ʒ ij. ad ʒ jv.
M.

If there be any hacking cough the neck may be fomented or rubbed frequently with a stimulating liniment ; the dog's muzzle and brow may also be fomented. Repeat the Mindererus spirit the second and third nights, and if there be much constipation repeat the oil ; but too much opening medicine is weakening. Do not confine the dog to the house, but let him have exercise and good wholesome food.

Ladies' pets may be made to inhale steam, or the vapour of iodine, if there be much running at the nose. If ozœna, or an offensive running, takes place, syringing will be required with warm water and a little Condy's Fluid or chloride of zinc.

The food ought for the first two or three days to be rather less in quantity and of a more stimulating quality.

This simple treatment, if persevered in, cannot fail to have the desired effect.

2. Bronchitis.

Bronchitis, or inflammation of the lining membrane of the bronchial tubes, may take place from an extension downwards to the mucous membrane of the lungs of a common catarrh, or it may come on as a distinct disease.

Sometimes only the larger bronchi are involved, sometimes the smaller ; and often both. The disease is very common in the human being, less so in the horse ; but, unfortunately, it is far from rare either in the dog or cat. It is a dangerous disorder in both the latter animals ; and what makes it all the more so is that it is generally either neglected entirely, or unskilfully treated.

Four different kinds of bronchitis really are known, namely : 1, the acute ; 2, the chronic ; 3, the symptomatic, when it is associated with some other disease ; and 4, the mechanical. It will be sufficient, however, to give a short description of the two first-named only.

Pathology.—There is at first a congested and dry condition of the mucous membrane of the bronchi, and consequent narrowing of their calibres, afterwards the moist stage sets in with increased secretion of mucous and muco-purulent matter.

Causes.—The same causes that produce a catarrh will produce bronchitis, which in ordinary parlance is simply a severe cold with cough.

Symptoms.—There is always more or less of fever, with fits of shivering and thirst, accompanied with dulness, a tired appearance, and loss of appetite. It will not be long before our attention is called to the state of the lungs. The breath is short, that is, the breathing is quickened, and the inspirations are evidently painful, and the breathing may be heard—the sound is called "the rhonchus," and is caused by the air passing through the dry or roughened pipes—when the first stage is past, and the secretion of mucus increased, this dry rhonchus is succeeded by moister sounds.

The most prominent symptom perhaps is the frequent cough. It is at first dry, ringing and evidently painful ; in a few days, however, or sooner, it softens, as we might say, and there is a discharge of frothy mucus with it, and, in the latter stages, of pus and ropy mucus. This is often swallowed by the dog ; and when a good deal of it is ejected it gives the animal great relief. Often the cough is most distressing, and there may be fits of shortness of breath. As additional symptoms we have a hot, dry mouth, and very probably constipation and high-coloured urine. Sometimes one of the bronchial tubes during the progress of the disease gets completely plugged by a piece of lymph or phlegm. The portion of lung thus cut off from all communication with the air gets collapsed, and finally condensed.

Diagnosis.—The peculiar character of the cough, the painful inspirations, the fever, and the physical signs, must guide us in our diagnosis.

Prognosis.—Generally favourable, unless in old dogs, in which debility soon becomes marked. A slight case can be cured in a few days; a more severe may last for weeks.

Treatment.—This is another of the many diseases our predecessors used to treat with lance or flemes.

Bleeding is never allowable in the bronchitis of the dog. Keep the patient in a comfortable, well-ventilated apartment, with free access in and out if the weather be dry. Let the bowels be freely acted upon to begin with; but no weakening discharge from the bowels must be *kept up*. After the bowels have been moved we should commence the exhibition of small doses of tartar emetic with squills and opium thrice a day. If the cough is very troublesome,

$$\begin{array}{lll} \text{R Tinct. scillæ} & \dots \quad \dots & \text{m v. ad m xxx.} \\ \text{Tinct. camph. co.} & \dots & \text{m x. ad \ 3 j.} \\ \text{Ant. pot. tart.} & \dots \quad \dots & \text{gr. } \frac{1}{16} \text{ ad gr. j.} \\ \text{Aq.} \quad \dots \quad \dots & \dots & \text{q. s.} \qquad \text{M.} \end{array}$$

we may give a full dose of opium every night as well.

In mild cases the treatment recommended for catarrh will succeed in bronchitis.

The inhalation of steam, either medicated or otherwise, often does much good if it can be managed.

Carbonate of ammonia may be tried; it often does good, the dose being from two grains to ten in camphor water, or even plain water.

The chronic form of bronchitis will always yield, if the dog is young, to careful feeding, moderate exercise, and the exhibition of cod-liver oil with a mild iron tonic. The exercise, however, must be moderate, and the dog kept from the water. A few drops, to a teaspoonful, of paregoric, given at night, will do good, and the bowels should be kept regular, and a simple laxative pill given now and then.

3. *Laryngitis.*

Laryngitis, or inflammation of the organ of voice, is a disease frequently met with in the dog, although more commonly in the chronic than in the acute form. The acute form may be present without any other disease, or may be accompanied with bronchitis or catarrh.

It is characterised by difficulty not only in breathing, but also in swallowing, although there is both thirst and fever. There is prolonged inspiration and a hoarse rasping cough, dry at first, but latterly getting moist. If the back part of the pharynx be looked at it will be found red and congested, and there will be a plenteous discharge of viscid saliva.

If there should be much effusion about the glottis or rima glottidis, the danger to life will be extreme, and only averted by the early performance of tracheotomy, which only a skilful veterinary surgeon may be trusted to perform. But unless the symptoms are very urgent the operation will not be required. Hot fomentations, however, ought to be very frequently applied, and the dog made to inhale medicated steam. Mustard poultices will also do good, and stimulating liniments or turpentine dressings.

Care must be taken when the inflammation has been got under, which we can tell by the diminution in the violence of the symptoms, to keep the animal's strength up with gruel, beef-tea, milk, eggs, &c., and perhaps wine will be wanted as well.

Open the bowels well at the commencement of the disease, give low diet for the first few days.

Give also in water thrice a day from five to ten grains each of the chlorate and nitrate of potash.

In the chronic form of laryngitis we have a loud, harsh, ringing, and evidently painful cough, easily induced by excitement, or rushing suddenly into the open air. There will also be heard a stridulous or kind of crowing sound with inspiration. The disease may run on to ulceration. The cough is often produced by the effort necessary to eat or drink. There is some little tenderness usually evinced on pressing the larynx between the finger and thumb, a symptom which, however, cannot be depended on, as dogs, if game, will frequently stand pain to a considerable extent without crying out, so long as they know no harm is meant them.

We have known a case of laryngitis produced mechanically in a large five-months-old Landseer pup. It was caused by the dog being lugged along the highway by a thin rope, which was passed round the neck.

It must not be forgotten that laryngeal cough is sometimes of a reflex character, depending on disease of another organ. At all events, in chronic laryngitis we nearly always find the dog in a low state of health, and frequently suffering from loss of appetite and indigestion.

Treatment.—The object of our treatment must be to relieve the symptoms and strengthen the general constitution. Sometimes, if there be much accumulation of mucus, an emetic may do good, and give much relief; this only in the latter or moist stage, however.

Mustard to the chest, lower part of the neck, and hot fomentations in short-haired dogs, with the flat iron frequently applied to both sides of the chest in long-haired animals.

The diet is to be rather sloppy at first; oatmeal-gruel, a little beef-tea and milk.

Take advantage of the animal's thirst to add to his drink a little of the chlorate of potash and a portion of nitre. In convalescence give tonics, such as quinine or barks, with a little iron and cod-liver oil. Blistering in obstinate cases may be had recourse to, but is seldom needed.

If the disease lasts very long, which it rarely does in dogs, and the cough will not yield to generous diet and oil, the iodide of potassium will do good, with a castor-oil purgative once in three or four days.

$$\text{R Pot. iod.} \ldots \qquad \ldots \qquad \text{gr. j. ad gr. v.}$$
$$\text{Ext. bellad.} \qquad \ldots \qquad \text{gr. } \tfrac{1}{16} \text{ ad gr. j.}$$
$$\left. \begin{array}{l} \text{Ext. gent.} \\ \text{Ext. tarax} \end{array} \right\} \ldots \quad \text{ā, ā, gr. ij. ad gr. v.}$$
$$\text{M.}$$
$$\text{Ft. pil. j.} \ldots \qquad \ldots \qquad \ldots \qquad \ldots \qquad \ldots \quad \text{ter die.}$$

The disease sometimes resists treatment for a long time. Stimulating liniments and occasional blisters (small) to the lower part of the neck often do good, and hot fomentations when the cough is prolonged and very troublesome. Daily inhalations of steam (medicated with tincture of iodine, one tablespoonful to a pint of water) do good, and all the more if combined with a course of iodide of potassium internally. Give also cod-liver oil if the dog be low in flesh.

The bowels must be kept regular with either occasional doses of castor oil or with Gregory's powder. If there seems to be much soreness of the throat, touch it daily by means of a probang and sponge with a solution of nitrate of silver, three or four grains to an ounce of water, or with equal parts of glycerine and tincture of iron.

Some practitioners find they do good in these cases by making the dog wear a wet compress of two or three bands of flannel, covered on the outside by oiled silk and leather, like a broad collar. This may be tried, but we ourselves have found more benefit from the treatment above recommended, and by attending in every way to the state of the general health. Arsenic and iron may be used in old standing cases, and likewise the douche or bucket bath, followed by immediate exercise.

4. *Croup*.

Croup in its true form is a very rare disease in the dog, although cases are occasionally met with, especially in pampered pet dogs.

Croup may be characterised as a sthenic inflammation of the larynx and trachea, accompanied by the exudation of false membranes, accompanied also by a fever which at first is inflammatory, but has a marked tendency to run on to the low form.

The *symptoms* are the high fever, the curious crowing inspirations, the violent fits of coughing, difficulty of breathing, and latterly the coughing of fibrinous patches of false membrane. It is only a disease of young and delicate animals that have been exposed to cold and wet, or any of the exciting causes of inflammation of the mucous membranes of the air passages. It may be a complication of pneumonia or bronchitis, and is nearly always fatal.

The *treatment* must first be directed to cutting short the attack. Bleeding must not be resorted to however, but the bowels should be freely opened with calomel and jalap—

> ℞ Calomel ... ... gr $\frac{1}{2}$ ad gr. v.
> Jalap ... ... gr. x. ad ʒ ij.
> In form of bolus.

After an emetic has been given (ipecacuanha will be best and safest : dose, from ten to thirty grains) blisters to the throat may do good, and the inhalation of steam, and also the warm bath—this latter is better suited to short-haired small dogs.

Liquor ammonia acetatis (Mindererus spirit) may also be given at night.

As soon as the fever assumes an asthenic, or low type, stimulants must be given (wine and brandy and beef-tea, and other easily-digested nourishment).

5. *Pleurisy*.

Pleurisy, or more properly speaking, *pleuritis*, is, as the name indicates, an inflammation of the pleuræ, either one or both.

To prevent friction against the walls of the chest and other surrounding surfaces, the lungs are enveloped as it were in two serous sacs, one for each. It would take up too much space to describe with any degree of minuteness the various windings of the pleuræ, suffice it for our purpose to know that while one side of each pleura is attached to the walls of the chest, the other surrounds the lung.

Pleurisy is generally confined to one side of the chest, and is often combined or complicated with pneumonia, or inflammation of the lung tissue itself.

Terminations.—The disease may end in resolution in mild cases if properly treated, or lymph may be exuded, and the inflamed sides of the sac may become adherent, or there may be large effusion of serum constituting what is called hydrothorax, or water in the chest. Again, pus may become the product of the inflammation.

Causes.—The disease is usually idiopathic. We have known the disease more than once brought on by allowing dogs to plunge into cold water when fatigued and heated. Sudden changes from heat to cold are very well borne by dogs, and do *not*, as a rule, produce inflammations ; but if the dog is both *fatigued* and *hungry*, while at the same time he is *hot* from running, it is dangerous, to say the least, to allow him to take to cold water.

Lying in damp, cold spots, or on brick or stone, and exposure to cold and damp while the feeding has been neglected, are the commonest causes of pleurisy.

Sometimes however, although rarely, pleurisy may be the result of direct violence from kicks or blows or stabs, and it may also be combined with pneumonia—a very dangerous complication of distemper.

Symptoms.—The disease always sets in with some degree of rigor or shivering, which, however, may pass unnoticed. The next symptom is uneasiness ; the dog keeps roaming about and pays frequent visits to his water-dish, his countenance is somewhat anxious, and his coat is staring. Then the breathing becomes affected ; from lying on his belly the animal will rise suddenly to his haunches, with neck well stretched out and panting, and it will be observed that the respiration is chiefly abdominal, the dog seeming to dread inspiration, which is short and painful, while expiration is longer and easier. The evident distress of the animal soon calls for manual examination. His pulse—if a large dog, for it is hardly worth while feeling the pulse of a toy—is hard, wiry, and quick.

The cough is peculiar : it is a *dry, harsh* cough, and combined with this you have all the other symptoms of inflammation, hot skin and nose, and restlessness, &c.

On passing the hand ever so lightly over the affected side, we will observe a quivering movement as if the dog dreaded being touched, and if we press in the intercostal space we will generally find the dog will evince signs of pain and tenderness.

If the ear be applied to the chest, over the seat of pain—generally the lower part of the lung—while yet there is no effusion, and the inside of the pleuræ are simply roughened, we can easily detect the friction sound, as it is called, a sort of a grating or rubbing noise, and with this there will be dulness on percussion. If effusion takes place into the cavity of the pleura we will no longer hear the friction sound, as the sides of the sac are not now close together, or if the disease ends in resolution the sound will disappear, and the dog will improve. In the case of effusion the symptoms of dyspnoea will be very marked (the dog persistently sitting on his hind-quarters or standing), and dulness on percussion—a prominent sign.

If the disease goes on to suppuration, this will generally be known by the dog having shiverings, while clammy sweats bedew the insides of the thighs.

Treatment.—We have to lessen pain, subdue the inflammation, and endeavour to restore the pleura to its wonted state of smoothness and simple moisture.

Pleurisy was another of those diseases which the older practitioners thought it impossible to subdue without bleeding. But if, as already hinted, the disorder generally attacks dogs when they are rather low than otherwise, it cannot be good practice surely to weaken them still further.

We commence our treatment, then, by giving a simple dose of opening medicine, say castor oil, and no lowering aperient.

Rest in this disease is of paramount importance ; the bed must be comfortable without being too warm, and it must be placed out of a draught, but plenty of fresh air is requisite.

Locally, we neither blister nor bleed now-a-days, especially in the case of small dogs, although a few leeches might be applied to the tender side of a large and powerful animal, such as a Mastiff or St. Bernard. However, it is probably best to be on the safe side, and trust to very large warm linseed-meal poultices, or better still, if the animal will lie down, to bags of heated sand. If the poultices cannot be kept on all night, a nice warm flannel roller ought to be well wound around the chest. In addition to the poultices, well foment four times a day with hot water.

Constitutionally, the animal must have plenty of clean cold water within easy reach of him. As to medicine, I know of nothing better than, first, tincture of opium, in full and repeated doses, to allay the pain; and, secondly, either the Mindererus spirit in water by itself, or the following:—

$\mathrecipe$ Liq. ammon. acet. ... ... ℥ ½ ad ℥ iij.
Tinct. aconit. ... ... ♏ j. ad ♏ x.
Aq. camph. ... ... q. s.
F^t haust. M.
Give four times a day.

We must act upon the kidney by means of nitrate of potash, which, combined with a little chlorate of potash, ought to be mixed in the drinking water, or if the urine is very scanty indeed, give occasionally a little tincture of colchicum, from five drops to a drachm.

If the disease goes on to effusion we must endeavour to promote its absorption by the iodide of potassium and colchicum, and sometimes a little calomel may be used as well.

The bowels ought to be regularly washed out with a simple enema, unless they are quite open. If there is much constipation, give in the morning a dose of Epsom salts, and a little cream of tartar.

The food must be restricted for the first few days, but if there be much weakness early resort must be had to strong unstimulating nutriment.

During convalescence the greatest care must be taken, for the disease is apt to recur, and recur again. Cod-liver oil and tonics must now be our sheet anchors. If there be but little appetite the bitter tonics are the best.

6. *Pneumonia.*

Pneumonia, or inflammation of the lung tissue itself, is a very serious and ofttimes fatal disease in the dog. Youatt, in his work on the dog, speaks of an epidemic form of pneumonia, and says that this form is usually fatal. The cases we usually see are sporadic, or are sometimes connected with distemper, which latter may be epidemic, or epizootic in other words.

Causes.—The causes of pneumonia are much the same as those of pleuritis, and are generally due to a chill of some sort, especially if gotten when the animal *is tired*, as from some unwonted exertion, and when he has been deprived of his usual food, and suffers in addition, perhaps, from the depressing effects of anxiety of mind. That they do so suffer no one nowadays who understands canine nature will think of doubting or denying.

"Some pathologists," Williams tells us, "conclude that pneumonia is a specific fever terminating in exudation into the lung tissue, just as the variole fever terminates in an eruption on the skin." Williams cannot agree with these pathologists, nor can we, for the inflammation of the lung substance is certainly a concomitant condition from the very commencement of the disease.

Pathology and Physical Signs.—Pathologists of the present day divide the disease into four different stages. The first stage, like all the others, is characterised by fever, the temperature of the dog's body being very elevated. This is the stage in which the lining membranes of the air-cells are simply inflamed and dry. The second stage is called the stage of engorgement, because the air-cells are filled now with exudation of bloody serum. If we were now to examine a piece of lung tissue we should find it externally of a dark unhealthy red colour, and on cutting into it we would find it spongy and filled with a reddish frothy serum, and where, as in the first stage, by putting the ear to the animal's side, we should merely hear slightly roughened breathing, you will now in the second stage be able to hear distinct *crepitation*—a sound somewhat similar to that produced by placing your tongue between the front teeth and drawing the air gently in over it, or the sound produced by rubbing a lock of hair between the finger and thumb close to the ear. Percussion, too, at first will elicit the usually resonant sound, but as the air-cells get engorged this will, of course, give place to dulness.

The third stage is called the stage of hepatisation or solidification. The lung is no longer spongy, neither will you any longer hear moist crepitation, but, instead of this, tubular breathing—that is, the sound of the air passing through the larger bronchi, and conveyed to your ear through the media of the solid parts of the inflamed lung. If the disease gets on to the fourth stage it will be that of purulent infiltration, where the tissue of the lung suppurates.

These, then, are the commonest physical signs in one of the worst cases. If, however, as generally happens under sensible treatment, the disease should not go on to the last stage, we shall find, along with a gradual abatement of fever and all bad symptoms, signs that the solidification of the lung is being absorbed, the air thus once more getting into it, and we, therefore, again hear the moist crepitation of the second stage.

Symptoms.—The disease is ushered in by restlessness, thirst, and some degree of rigor, which often escapes observation. It is seldom, therefore, until the animal is really ill, that any notice is taken of him. There is evidence of pain now, and the breathing is quickened and laborious. "The extended head," Youatt graphically tells us, "the protruded tongue, the anxious blood-shot eye, the painful heaving of the hot breath, the obstinacy with which the animal sits up hour after hour until his feet slip from under him, and the eye closes, and the head droops through extreme fatigue, *yet in a moment being aroused again by the feeling of instant suffocation*, are symptoms that cannot be mistaken." The italics are ours.

Add to these symptoms a disagreeable short cough, dry at first, but soon accompanied by the hacking up of pellets of rusty-coloured mucus. Extensive lung inflammation may go on to death without any cough at all. Unlike the breathing of pleurisy, where inspiration is short, painful, and interrupted, that in pneumonia has expiration longer, if anything, than inspiration. We generally have, in addition, constipation of the bowels, high-coloured urine, and perspiration on the internal parts of the thighs.

Pneumonia may often be complicated with pleurisy, or with bronchitis, or inflammation of the pericardium, the liver, or even the peritoneum itself, which latter is more rare. Again, fits are not infrequent in pneumonia, especially if it is occasioned by distemper. These fits are adynamic in their character, and depend on the anæmic condition of the blood, and should therefore never be treated by setons and such rough remedies.

Treatment.—Such heroic treatment as that by bleeding, mercurials, and antimony, cannot, in our opinion, be too highly condemned. A simple mode of treatment is better, and trusting largely to Nature unencumbered. Remove the patient, first and foremost, to a well-ventilated place, where he may be kept quiet, cool, and comfortable, and at the same time have plenty of fresh air. If a short-haired dog, he had better be dressed in an old blanket, and placed upon an ample bed of shavings or soft straw.

Let him have a dose of castor oil and buckthorn to open his bowels. Blisters will be of great benefit, the hair first being removed from the chest.*

* Cantharides oil, or glacial acetic acid.

They are to be well rubbed in, and washed off again with hot water after the effect is produced. The chest should then be delicately bandaged; and if the animal seems much worn-out by incessant sitting on his haunches, his chest ought to be supported by soft pillows.

If the case is a mild one we should omit the blister, trusting simply to hot fomentations, and turpentine, and mustard poultices.

Give the animal plenty of cold water to drink, in which a teaspoonful or two of the nitrate of potash has been dissolved. This for a large dog. The diet is to be light and rather low for the first two or three days; and a fever mixture is to be administered every four hours for the first day or two.

R Sol. ammon. acetat.   ...   ℥ Ss. ad ℥ jv.
Sp. æth. nitr. ...   ...   ℥½ ad ℥ jSs.
Tinct. bellad. ...   ...   ℥ v. ad ℥ j.
Aq. camph.   ...   ...   q. s.
      Fᵗ haustus   M.

Great care must be taken to support the system, and the slightest change noted. As soon as any change is observed in the pulse, and it loses its hardness, nutriment of the least irritating sort, but strong withal, must be administered; beef-tea, cream, and raw eggs, will be found of the greatest service. Along with this wine must be given; and its effects upon the pulse and system marked. These, indeed, must be our guides as to the quantity. To do any good at all it must be given with no sparing hand.

If the dog gets still weaker, brandy in water must be given instead of wine.

If the animal is in much pain, occasional small doses of hydrate of chloral—five grains to thirty grains in water—may be administered with advantage. If diarrhœa comes on during the course of the disease it is usually rather salutary than otherwise, and must not be suddenly checked. Give now a diuretic, say spirits of sweet nitre, five drops to a drachm, with from two to ten drops of colchicum wine in a little water, thrice a day.

In cases of very great prostration brandy and beaten eggs must be given repeatedly, and essence of beef. When signs of convalescence come about—when the eye gets brighter, and the breathing is less laboured, and the appetite begins to return—cod-liver oil and quinine, with occasional small doses of the chlorate of potash, will do immense good. Keep up the strength meanwhile; but take care not to overdo it in the matter of food.

In the first stages of this disease we have known small repeated doses of the tincture of aconite recommended; but cannot speak from experience. The dose is from two to ten drops in a little water every three hours.

Pouring turpentine on boiling water, and causing the animal to inhale it for fifteen minutes at a time every two or three hours, has been recommended by Dr. Skoda, of Vienna; and if a dog can be got to allow such an inhalation, it gives relief in the latter stages of pneumonia.

CHAPTER V.

DISEASES OF THE LIVER, SPLEEN, AND PANCREAS.

IN the human being the liver is the largest gland in the body, weighing, according to some authorities, from 1½ lb. up to 4½ lb.; according to others, from forty to fifty-five ounces. In the canine subject it is even larger in proportion, and probably also proportionately more important.

In man the liver has five lobes or portions, and in the dog we also find five principal lobes, in a depression in the middle lobe of which we find the gall bladder. This receptacle of bile ends in the ductus choledochus, or bile duct, which, along with the smaller efferent duct of the pancreas, enters the duodenum, at from one to five inches (according to the size of the dog) from the pyloric opening of the stomach.

The pancreas of the dog is much more elongated than that of the human being; it pours the principal portion of its contents into the duodenum, an inch or two beneath the opening of the bile duct.

The spleen of the dog deserves no special mention here. As to the enormous gland called the liver, its value in the animal economy can hardly be over-rated. All the blood of the body passes through it. The arterial blood that is distributed to other portions of the body, such as the head, the fore-legs and hind-legs, &c., having performed its life-giving functions, is taken up by the veins and carried back to the heart directly. Not so, however, with the blood that has been arterially distributed to the intestines. This does not go back at once to the heart; it is taken up by a series of capillary veins, which unite to form the portal vein, and this vein enters and is spread out in the tissue of the liver around the cells of that gland, and from this blood and by this gland, the liver, the bile is secreted, which is to perform such an important function in the process of digestion.

Now the bile ducts carry off this secretion, which has been either extracted from the blood or formed in the cells, from the blood of the portal veins; carry it off and pour it into the gall bladder, or reservoir for the bile; the blood itself is then taken up and returned into the inferior vena cava, and so sent on to the heart. We have seen water diverted from a river to form some distant mill-dam, and, after it had done its work for the mill, returned again by another channel. This gives us, in a rude fashion, some idea of the economy of the portal system.

We need not here discuss the question as to whether bile exists to a certain extent ready made in the blood, and is simply separated from it by the liver; or whether the hepatic cells positively manufacture the bile, although we incline to the former theory. Neither need we occupy space by describing the chemical constituents of this curious fluid. Suffice it for us to know that bile is the product of the liver, and is of the highest importance to digestion. It is a yellow oily-looking fluid, with an extremely bitter taste. It is essentially of a soapy nature, and its uses are supposed to be—(1), to destroy or neutralise the acidity of the chyme which has been derived from the gastric secretions; (2) to aid the pancreatic juice in rendering fatty matters into such a state of emulsion or suspension, as will permit of their being easily absorbed by the villi of the intestines, and (3) to act in some way as a natural purgative.

Dr. Flint tells us that the liver manufactures the glycocholate of soda *in the liver*, but *separates* cholestrine from the blood. Now, bear in mind that cholestrine is a poison which, if allowed to collect in the blood, would produce toxæmia. We can see the bearing of this upon our subject, when we remember that there are two kinds of jaundice; or, to put it in another way, we have jaundice as the result of bile re-absorbed into the blood from the gall-bladder, after having been secreted—this owing to some obstruction of the duct preventing the natural flow of the bile into the duodenum; or jaundice may be produced by some structural change in the liver itself, that organ lacking the power to extract the cholestrine from the blood, and hence the toxæmia, or blood-poisoning.

We have never seen a case of acute atrophy of the liver in the dog, leading to the complete or partial destruction of that organ, and consequent fatal toxæmia, although there is no reason to suppose that such does not occasionally take place. The symptoms would probably be great excitement, ending in delirium, and, soon after, fatally, in coma. There is little doubt, however, that any one unacquainted with disease would put such a case down as one of rabies. The dog would be killed if he did not die beforehand, with the usual results: proclamations by magistrates, confinement of all dogs for two calendar months, &c., &c.

The liver is of paramount importance to the animal, if we only limit its functions to two: the neutralisation of the over-abundance of gastric acids, and the saponification or emulsifying of fat. If the liver fails even to a small extent to separate cholestrine from the blood, just to that extent is the blood poisoned; nervous symptoms and depression ensue, the animal becomes peevish and excitable, and is not only more liable to many dangerous diseases, but becomes at the same time unfitted for properly performing his duties as the servant or companion of man. How many cases of temper in sporting dogs, how many of unthriftiness and bad condition, may not be attributed to this?

Failing in one of its other functions, think of the evils that may arise from the retention of acid in the blood. Will not the animal be more liable to take chills and inflammations of all sorts, if exposed to wet or damp, or inclement weather? Will he not be more liable to become the victim of kennel lameness and rheumatism, which is supposed to arise from lactic acidity of the blood?

The juices of the pancreas, which are poured into the duodenum, are intended to suspend or turn the fatty portions of the food into an emulsion of easy absorbency. In this it aids the liver. Those juices help to change starch into sugar, and thus aid the salivary glands.

As to the real uses of the spleen, probably the least said the better.

I. *Hepatitis.*

Hepatitis, or acute inflammation of the liver, is a disease which is happily not very prevalent in this country among dogs; but we have seen many cases of it in India and other hot countries, and dogs—especially the larger and long-haired breeds—often speedily fall victims to it if they are taken from England directly out to the Tropics. That the disease is sometimes associated with pleurisy, has been proved by *post-mortem* examination.

Causes.—Like most other inflammations, acute hepatitis may be produced by cold and damp, or bathing in chilly water after having been heated as in running, provided the liver has been weak and out of order beforehand. We should ever bear in mind that in cases where inflammation is the result of exposure to cold and wet, which ever organ of the body happens to be the weakest at the time of such exposure, will be sought out, and become the seat of disease. Thus the same causes may produce hepatitis in one dog, and rheumatism in a second, bronchitis in a third, and so on. Probably a good many of the cases of hepatitis we meet in this country are caused by blows or kicks. These would be the exciting causes, the primary being errors in diet and exercise.

Pathology.—The capsule of Glisson, or encasing membrane of the liver, may be the seat of inflammation, in which case symptoms of pain will be more manifest, and fever will run higher. Or the inflammation may—and more commonly is—confined to one or more portions of the substance of the liver itself. There will then be, first, simple darker redness of the organ, with turgescence of its vessels, afterwards exudation of lymph, which may end in suppuration and abscess, or be re-absorbed.

Symptoms.—As we should naturally expect, we will find all the symptoms of inflammatory fever, with some degree of swelling in the region of the liver and considerable pain and tenderness. This pain is often manifest when the dog gets up suddenly to seek the open air. He will frequently be found lying on his chest in dark corners, on cold stones perhaps, and panting. His eyes are heavy and dull, his coat stares; he is dull himself, is frequently sick, with loss of appetite and very high temperature of body. About the second or third day jaundice supervenes—the symptoms of which will be considered presently. Very highly-coloured and scanty urine is another symptom; and often there is considerable dyspnœa, especially indicative of inflammation of the upper portion of the liver.

The bowels are constipated, of the colour of clay, and of great and sour fetor.

The disease soon produces emaciation, and often dropsy of the belly.

Diagnosis.—The diagnosis is somewhat difficult. The tenderness and pain in the region of the liver, and the swelling as soon as it can be made out, will help us. The great fever and the recurrence of jaundice make us certain.

Treatment.—We must endeavour by every means in our power to subdue the fever, and get the disease to end in resolution. Bleeding, mercury, and emetics, are never requisite in a case of acute hepatitis. Many a good dog has been killed by such treatment. In this disease sickness is only far too easily produced, and the effects of the pressure of the diaphragm and abdominal muscles during vomiting upon an already inflamed liver, may be better imagined than described. Our treatment must be as mild and palliative as possible.

Unless, then, there is diarrhœa or dysentery present at the outset, as there might be if the disease were a complication of distemper, we must endeavour to relieve the portal system by alvine discharges.

R Aloes Barbad. ... ... gr. x. ad ℥ ii.
Extr. hyoscyam. ... ... gr. ij. ad gr. viii.
Fᵗ pil j. M.

This to be given at night, followed up in the morning by a dose of sulphate of soda and magnesia, with a little nitre.

Give from three to fifteen grains of Dover's powder thrice daily.

In very acute cases a large blister will be needed to the right side. Mustard poultices, hot fomentations, and a large linseed-meal poultice, will be sufficient in sub-acute cases; and a little mustard may well be added to the poultice.

When you have succeeded in subduing the symptoms, and if there be much yellowness of the skin, combined with constipation or scanty fœces, give the ipecacuanha and extract of taraxacum bolus thrice a day.

> ℞ Ipecac. pulv. ... ... gr. ½ ad gr. iij.
> Ext. taraxaci ... ... gr. iij. ad gr. xv.
> Fᵗ pil j. M.

The food, which was at first sloppy and non-stimulating, must now be made more nourishing; and good may be done by rubbing the abdomen with a strong stimulating liniment of ammonia, while a wet compress is to be applied around the belly, the coat having been previously wetted with water well acidulated with diluted nitro-hydrochloric acid, the compress being wrung through the same solution. Great care must be taken on recovery with the dog's diet; and moderate exercise only should at first be allowed, and tonics administered.

2. *Chronic Hepatitis.*

Chronic hepatitis may at times be the sequel of the former; but it is more often an independent disorder, and might with more propriety be termed congestion of the liver.

It is characterised by extreme dulness and lassitude on the part of the animal. He has little or no appetite, and is inclined to lie about, as much in dark quiet corners as anywhere else, and especially in the open air. There is fetor of breath, and general debility, the animal getting gradually emaciated, and the belly becoming more or less enlarged. The eyes seem dull; and there may, or may not, be jaundice. The bowels are torpid, and the urine scanty and high-coloured; and there is frequent vomiting, during which the animal usually manages to evacuate some green or yellow frothy matter. Sometimes, but rarely, there is tenderness to the touch in the seat of the liver, which may be considerably swollen.

Treatment.—The first thing to be done is to well open the bowels.

> ℞ Podophyll.* ... ... gr. 1/16 ad gr. j½.
> Ext. tarax. ... ... gr. v. ad gr. xx.
> Fᵗ pil. j. M.

> ℞ Sodæ sulph. ... ... ʒj. ad ℥iij.
> Ferri. sulph. ... ... gr. j ad gr. v.
> Decoc. tarax. ... ... ℥¼ ad ℥ij.
> Fᵗ haustus. M.

The pill, or bolus, is to be administered at night, and followed by the draught in the morning.

Continue this treatment on alternate days, giving meanwhile only the least irritating kinds of food; and while giving enough to eat, taking care not to overload the stomach. As soon as there are decided signs of improvement, we must begin to give something rather more tonic in action, and we have found the following medicine do much good given twice a day, morning and afternoon; or give the last dose in the evening and administer the pill, containing from an eighth of a grain to a grain of quinine, with three to fifteen grains of pulv. rhei. co. a little before dinner.

> ℞ Acid. nitr. dil. ... ... ♏ iij. ad ♏ xv.
> Succ. tarax. ... ... ♏ x. ad ʒ ij.
> Sp. æther. nitr. ... ... ♏ v. ad ʒ ½.
> Infus. gent. c. ... ... ʒ ij. ad ℥ j.
> Fᵗ haustus. M.

* Podophyllin is an extremely useful purgative, but it is somewhat difficult to define its exact dose. Its action should be watched, therefore; for some dogs will take two or three grains without being over-purged, in others of the same size half a grain will be enough.

When the urine is very scanty and red good will be done by giving from three to thirty grains of the benzoate of ammonia in water twice a day, morning and afternoon.

Never let the dog want for plenty of nice cold clean water, and if he should be at all thin he ought to wear a blanket whenever he goes out. A judicious amount of exercise must likewise be given, and a comfortable, airy place allowed to sleep in at night.

Friction with some stimulating liniment to the region of the abdomen, twice or thrice a day, might be tried with good results.

The more obscure diseases of the liver in the dog are far from easy to deal with; they often lead on to dropsy and death.

3. *Jaundice.*

Jaundice, called also *icterus*, and by kennel-men and the public generally known as "the yellows." We have been taught to consider jaundice as merely symptomatic of other disease or diseases, and, properly speaking, it is really nothing else; and we must be excused for treating it herein as a distinct disease, yet how often in our practice are we not obliged to treat symptoms where we can, as in many disorders, merely guess at their cause! And, after all, the term or name "jaundice" is a handy one.

There are a great many diseases of the liver which we have purposely avoided giving any description of, which dogs at times undoubtedly suffer from. We allude to cirrhosis, or hobnail-liver, cancer of the liver, fatty degeneration, atrophy, hypertrophy, softening of the liver, and some others. A detailed account of these and their pathology would, we think, only tend to confuse the general reader. At the same time, the knowledge of them which even the profession possesses is, it must be confessed, far from perfect. Such diseases when they occur—or perhaps, to put it more truthfully, when their existence is suspected—in the dog must be treated symptomatically.

Pathology of Jaundice.—Before attempting to treat a case of jaundice we must endeavour to ascertain its cause. We have already hinted that there are, as it were, two kinds of jaundice—the same, but different in their causes, and requiring somewhat different treatment. There is the jaundice arising from re-absorption of the bile, and the jaundice of suppression of bile; although Frierichs and some others seem to dispute the correctness of the theory embodied in the words "suppression of bile," still nearly all medical authorities are now agreed that the theory is a correct one.

Causes.—1. *Jaundice* from *obstruction* and re-absorption may be produced by some state of the gall-ducts, which cause a stoppage therein, as by (1) inflammation of the mucous membrane thereof caused by cold; (2) by pressure on the common duct by a tumour, a collection of fœces, &c. (3) The duct may be closed up by the passage of a gall-stone. (4) Enlargement or hypertrophy of the liver, congestion * of the liver, or cancer of that organ, may cause obstruction to the mechanical flow of the bile, and determine its re-absorption into the blood. (5) The common duct has been found choked by liver flukes, a parasite common to the livers of dogs and other animals.

Jaundice of *suppression*, or non-secretion of bile, may be produced from an impeded circulation through the gland from disease of some distant organ, or from some morbid change in the blood, or from enervation, or from all three combined. On the other hand, the ingredients of the bile may be present in the blood in such excess that the liver is unable to

---

* Dogs that are over-run and over-heated are subject to congestion of the liver, which may end in jaundice.

separate them. This set of causes may be tabulated (giving only those interesting to us of the canine world) as follows : (1) diseases of the heart, lungs, and nervous system ; (2) mental emotions such as fright, intense anxiety, grief ; (3), dyspepsia ; (4) snake bites (rare in *this* country) ; (5) epizootic jaundice.

By far the largest number of cases of jaundice are those caused by obstruction, and we can easily glean from the above remarks, that the treatment which would alleviate the jaundice of obstruction might have quite a deleterious effect upon the jaundice of suppression, and *vice versâ*. We may also see the reason why jaundice is considered such a sadly fatal disease by kennel-men, and even by masters of hounds, and why a head huntsman or whip may be quite successful in carrying out the cure of one case, and utterly fail—from using the same remedies—in another.

We now stand face to face with the question : How are we to tell the difference between the two forms ? We all know jaundice when we see it, and we all ought to know that, whatever be the colour of the skin of the dog, the sclerotic coat of the eye is bound to be yellow. We all know the symptoms of bile-poisoning, or jaundice, too : the loss of appetite, the confined bowels, the clay-coloured mucus-covered stools, the frequent vomiting often present, the dark and scanty urine, the dulness and apathy, with restlessness, of the animal, and his desire to lie in cool corners and the yellow tinge of the mucous membrane as well as the skin, and the glassy eye, with many other symptoms, too well known to all dog-keepers to need mention.

Now, Dr. Harley has been the originator of a very simple test, whereby we can tell in a few minutes whether the jaundice be that caused by obstruction or that caused by suppression.

Take about a dessert-spoonful of the dog's urine (which you must use your own judgment how to obtain ; place, for instance, a clean damp sponge at a spot where you think the animal will stale) ; put the urine in a small clean test-tube ; add a little bit of loaf sugar, rather bigger than a pea ; then add—very gently, to prevent admixture—about half a drachm of strong sulphuric acid. If at the place where the two liquors come into contact you observe a purple or scarlet line, then you have proof that all the bile acids are present in the blood—that the case, in fact, is one of re-absorption, or obstruction ; if on the contrary you have no such line formed, but simply browning of the bit of sugar, then is the case one of suppression.

Treatment.—If the jaundice is caused by obstruction, we think it must clearly be our object to, if possible, remove the cause, and at the same time to try to diminish the activity of the liver until this be accomplished. If the dog seems to be suffering much pain, hot fomentations and large poultices are to be applied to the region of the liver, after smearing the belly with belladonna liniment. Give also from four to ten or twenty grains of chloral hydrate, and repeat the dose if necessary, and afterwards, when the pain has somewhat abated, give either simply an aloes bolus to open the bowels, or, better still, give an aloes bolus at night, and a draught in the morning, containing sulphate of soda and sulphate of magnesia, from half a drachm to three drachms of each in water.

As emaciation very soon comes on from the want of the bile in the food, much good may often be done, and valuable dogs saved, by the administration every morning of purified ox-bile ; dose, from two grains to ten or fifteen, made into a pill, combined with from five to twenty grains of Barbadoes aloes, especially if the obstruction is of long standing.

Give light, nutritious, and easily-digested food, and the addition of a little nitre in the animal's drinking water will do good. Afterwards give tonics—iron and quinine best—and plenty of food and moderate exercise. In *jaundice* from *suppression* of bile, our treatment, of course, must be different. It must, however, be borne in mind that we must not weaken the digestion in any way. Our sheet-anchors here are purgatives, in order to stimulate the secretion of the bile. We may also use some of the mineral acids, the dilute nitric or nitro-hydrochloric with taraxacum. If the reader cares to try the effect of mercury in some form, he may do so, giving small doses of calomel combined with aloes, in the morning, for two or three days; but probably in this case

$$
\begin{array}{lll}
\text{℞ Calomel} & \text{... ...} & \text{gr. j. ad gr. v.} \\
\text{Aloes} & \text{... ...} & \text{gr. v. ad gr. xx.} \\
\text{Mucilag.} & \text{... ...} & \text{q. s.}
\end{array}
$$

F[t.] pil j.   M.

podophyllin will be found as effectual and less dangerous, especially if combined with small doses of rhubarb. Instead of the nitrate of potash in the dog's drink, the bicarbonate, a tea-spoonful or two, may be given with advantage.

The food should be light, and easily digested; boiled eggs, bread puddings, bread-and-butter with a little beef-tea, and a very little raw meat minced.

4. *Sluggish Liver.*

Dogs that are over-fed, and not *regularly* fed, who get but little exercise, and that at no stated time, are apt to suffer from irregularity in the performance of the functions of the liver so important to digestion and life. At one time there is activity of the liver, at another there is inactivity. The stools of a dog suffering thus may one day contain bile in abundance, and on another barely any; or one portion of the stool is hard and clayey, and the other shows evidence of bile admixture. The dog, too, suffers alternately from constipation and diarrhœa. He is dull, except when taken out for a romp, in which case the air seems to revive him, and for a time he is gay enough; but he is easily fatigued, and suffers afterwards from any unwonted exertion. His coat is not as it should be; his tongue is often whitish, or too dark a red; and his nose dry, either in whole or in part.

In a case like this we need never prescribe or give medicine, unless it be a simple occasional purgative of castor-oil or rhubarb or aloes. For unless we regulate the animal's food, his exercise, and habits of life, all the medicine in the world will fail to do good. Let this be done; and give him a bucket-bath every morning, rubbing the dog well down, and turning him out for a romp immediately thereafter. Then, after a week or so of this treatment, give some such gentle liver-exciting tonic as the following :—

$$
\begin{array}{lll}
\text{℞ Podophyll. ...} & \text{... ...} & \text{gr. } \tfrac{1}{16} \text{ ad gr. j.} \\
\text{Ext. hyoscy.} & \text{... ...} & \text{gr. j. ad gr. v.} \\
\text{Pulv. zingib. et pulv. rhei ...} & & \text{ā ā gr. ij ad gr. viij.} \\
\text{Ext. tarax.} & \text{... ...} & \text{gr. v. ad gr. xv.}
\end{array}
$$

F[t.] pil j.   M.

Give this every day at his dinner-time, and let him have no food except two meals a day. In a few weeks such treatment is sure to set him straight again, probably much to the joy of an over-indulgent master or mistress.

5. *The Ailments of the Spleen and Pancreas.*

The diagnosis of diseases of the liver is often very difficult; but still more so is that of the ailments of the spleen and pancreas, and especially of the spleen. That the lower animals suffer from those complaints is only too certain. Tumours of these organs may at times be distinctly felt; but the symptoms allied to the appearance of those tumours are by no means clearly defined, and they are generally associated with ailments of other organs. Fatty stools—that is, the appearance of oily matter on the fœces, which congeals on cooling—is pretty good evidence that the pancreas is at fault in some way.

Treatment.—Avoid mercurials. Give iodide of potassium, with some simple tonic extract such as gentian, and a little extract of taraxacum, twice or thrice daily, and an occasional simple aperient and diuretic. Pay particular attention to the health of the animal. Give moderate exercise and good food; and now and then quinine in small doses (one-eighth of a grain *ad* two grains), twice a day, for a fortnight at a time. This, and the daily morning bath, is calculated to restore the animal to health, if the disease be not complicated.

CHAPTER VI.

DISEASES OF THE URINARY ORGANS.

1. *Nephritis.*

NEPHRITIS, or inflammation of the kidney, in the dog is by no means a very common disease.

Causes of Nephritis.—First must be mentioned our old enemies, cold and damp, especially if it be applied directly to the loins, as in the case of a dog left to sit out of doors all night in the rain; a dog, that is, who is in a weak state of health, or whose blood is impoverished by bad feeding. Blows and kicks occasionally produce it; the presence of a stone in the pelvis of the kidney may give rise to it; so may many irritating medicines, such as copaiba, cubebs, turpentine, and cantharides, when given in too large doses.

Symptoms.—The disease is ushered in with shivering, staring of the coat, and a generally dejected appearance of the poor dog. We then have thirst and fever, with a hard pulse, if you care to examine it; and there is often sickness and vomiting. The animal is evidently in great pain; but there is less restlessness than we find in some inflammatory disorders— hepatitis, for instance. There is pain, and there is stiffness in the region of the loins, with some degree of tenderness on pressure. There is a frequent desire to micturate, and some- times suppression of urine; or the urine, if passed, is scanty, high-coloured, and may contain blood, or even pus. The bowels are constipated, and the belly probably tympanitic, and the testicles retracted, one or both. If the disease goes on favourably, there is gradual mitigation of all the symptoms; if not, and the retention of urine is not relieved, delirium may occur, succeeded by coma and death.

Diagnosis.—It is most commonly confounded with lumbago, but in the latter case we will have more tenderness on pressure and no sickness, and loss of appetite; nor in lumbago are the bowels necessarily constipated. It may also be mistaken for the pain of the passage of a calculus along the urethra to the bladder, but here the pain and distress of the dog is ever so much greater for the time. Injuries to the spine generally have a previous history.

Treatment.—We must try to give the kidneys all the rest we can, and endeavour to reduce the inflammation, and get rid of a portion at least of the urea of the blood by the bowel. This may be done by purgatives, podophyllin and jalap, or elaterium may be tried.

$$\text{R} \quad \begin{array}{lll} \text{Jalap resin.} & \dots & \text{gr. j. ad gr. v.} \\ \text{Podophyll.} & \dots & \text{gr. } \tfrac{1}{16} \text{ ad gr. iij.} \\ \text{Ext. hyoscy.} & \dots & \text{gr. ij. ad gr. viij.} \end{array}$$

Pil j.   M.

To be given every morning.

From two to fifteen grains of factitious Dover's Powder must be given twice a day, the dog being kept warm and dry and clean. Plenty of hot poppy fomentations must be applied to the loins (occasionally the flat iron may do good), and followed up by large linseed-meal and mustard poultices. Enemas of hot water (not too hot) often do good, and the vomiting and sickness may be relieved by giving occasional doses of dilute hydrocyanic acid, from one to five drops, and by applying mustard poultices to the region of the stomach.

If suppression of urine continue for several days, the loins may be frequently fomented with hot infusion of digitalis. This should be discontinued as soon as the dog can stale.

Two things we must here warn the reader against, the use of *diuretics* and *fly blisters*. Both are highly dangerous, although sometimes used.

Diet and *Drink*.—The diet must be low at first, low and sloppy; but we must look out for signs of weakness and prostration. Do not let the animal sink for want of nourishment, such as beef-tea, eggs, a little raw meat, and a little port wine; and lastly, cod-liver oil and tonics in convalescence. The drink may be water, or milk-and-water, or barley-water.

2. *Cystitis.*

Cystitis, or inflammation of the bladder, is happily rather rare in the dog, and we believe nine-tenths of the cases which we meet with can be traced to the effect either of cantharadine blisters, or to some other irritant medicine administered internally. Youatt tells us that he has sometimes seen the disease appear as an epizootic. Probably he refers to the disease among horses, and not dogs.

Symptoms.—Attention is first called to the dog from his uneasiness and generally excited condition. He pants, whines, and makes frequent efforts to pass his urine, which comes only in drops and driblets, while he cries out with the pain the effort gives him. His appetite fails him, he is feverish, and, if examined, the lower part of the belly will be found swollen and tender to the touch. Just after the dog has made a little water there is ease for a short time, but as soon as the urine collects the pain comes on again. Usually the bowels are affected, but they may simply be bound up, or there may be straining, and slight diarrhœa of a mucous character, sometimes stained with blood.

Diagnosis is comparatively easy if we attend to the symptoms just related. Difficulty of micturition is a symptom of calculus in the bladder, but in this disease it comes on more gradually, and there are no inflammatory signs.

Treatment.—Our object is to abate pain, calm the excitement, and combat inflammation. Hot fomentations of poppy-heads must be used not only to the loins, but more especially to the abdomen. If a small dog, a hot bath will be found to give great relief. In order to relieve pain and calm excitement, opium must be given in repeated small doses, and the bowels must on no account be neglected, but the rule is, not to give any irritant purgative like aloes or black draught. However useful such aperients may be in some disorders and inflammations, they simply mean death in this. Small doses of castor oil may be given if they seem to be needed.

Some practitioners recommend emetics. We fail to see any advantage in such treatment; but on the other hand, we see a danger in the practice from rupture of the bladder, especially if there be retention of the urine. If the opium seems to bind the bowels too much, we recommend hyoscyamus in its stead, or small doses of hydrate of chloral.

N.B.—Diuretics are to be avoided, but a little cooling mixture of Mindererus spirit, one drachm to six in camphor-water, may be given every four hours. If the water cannot be passed and the belly is swollen, with moaning and evident distress, a qualified veterinary surgeon should be called in, who will no doubt pass the elastic catheter. The use of the catheter should be followed up with nice hot poppy fomentations, and a large linseed-meal poultice to the region of the abdomen; and an opium pill may now work wonders, or the morphia suppository of the Pharmacopœia may be placed in the rectum.

Food and Drink.—Food must be light, tasty, and easily digested, but rather low, especially at first. Drink—demulcent linseed-tea, barley-water, &c.

Cystitis may sometimes be simulated, if not indeed produced, from the extension of inflammation of the prostate gland. Although abscess of the prostate gland, which surrounds the neck of the bladder, is rare, it is nearly always fatal, unless it can be speedily resolved. In prostatitis, as in cystitis, the morphia suppository will be found of great value.

3. *Retention of Urine.*

Frequent and ineffectual attempts to pass water are sometimes witnessed without the presence of actual inflammation. It may be caused by enlargement or some chronic disease of the prostate gland, stone in the bladder, &c. In this case the bladder must be relieved twice a day by the catheter, and an effort made to reduce the size of the prostate (if this be the cause), by the exhibition of iodine internally, with the external application of the officinal iodine ointment to the perinæum, as recommended by Williams.

If the retention is caused by debility, as in low cases of fever and distemper, the catheter must be used, and tonics, stimulants, and good food administered.

If caused by paralysis of the hind-quarters, the remedies suggested for that disease must be tried. We have seen retention of the urine caused by spasm at the neck of the bladder, in dogs who had been kept too long on the show bench and who would not urinate there. Here hot fomentations, the inhalation of chloroform, and finally the catheter, gave relief.

In obstruction in the urethra, or pipe, the catheter must again be our stand-by.

4. *Hæmaturia.*

Hæmaturia or bloody urine in the dog is sometimes met with. The urine has a peculiar smoky colour, or it may be very dark indeed. The blood, of course, will be altered if it comes from the kidney; if it comes from the bladder it may be bright red, and the first drops of urine passed may be clear, the blood only coming the third or fourth time the animal stales.

As bloody urine may be a symptom of disease of the kidney, or may be present in cystitis, or in calculus of the bladder, of course our treatment must be directed to the removal of the cause.

Astringent injections may be needed if there be very much arterial bleeding from the urethra or bladder, along with the application of cold.

5. *Stone in the Bladder.*

The symptoms are frequent straining while making urine, painful urination, occasional bleeding, and general irritation of the urinary organs and penis. The appetite is usually good, although the dog is worse at certain times than at others.

Treatment must be palliative; sometimes an operation is necessary, but unless the dog be very valuable indeed it were less cruel to destroy him.

The treatment likely to do most good is the careful regulation of the bowels, not only by occasional doses of the mildest aperients—Gregory's Powder in the morning, for instance—but by *moderate exercise* and the morning *douche*, and occasional washing to keep the skin clean and wholesome. The dog's kennel must be very clean and warm, and he ought to have all the fresh air possible to properly oxygenise the blood.

The food is a particular point: it must be wholesome and nutritious, but not stimulating. Avoid flesh, therefore, or give it only in very small quantities.

Small doses of hyoscyamus or opium given as a bolus, with *extractum taraxaci*, will ease the pain, or an opium and belladonna suppository will give relief. Some men recommend diuretics. We question their utility; but if the case is seen early, colchicum would very likely do good.

CHAPTER VII.

THE BLOOD AND BLOOD DISEASES.

IN the chapter on the diseases of the digestive organs we saw the manner in which the better part of the food taken into the stomach was reduced from food to chyme, changed from chyme to chyle, taken up by a series of vessels termed absorbents, and finally poured into the veins, there to mix with and be matured into blood.

Blood is that nutritive, life-giving fluid that courses through every portion of the animal system, and that sustains our bodies, and keeps them in health and heat. In appearance it is a reddish fluid, and about the consistency of milk.

It is of a reddish hue, but the blood drawn from an artery is of a bright vermilion colour, while that abstracted from a vein is more of a purplish tint. In the dog and all mammalia there are not only two sets of blood-vessels (the veins and arteries), but there are in reality two hearts. Both joined together are these two hearts, and communicating, and both covered with the same sac-like membrane called the pericardium, which is one of the large serous membranes of the body, and prevents the friction of the heart against the chest or surrounding structures.

The heart is a muscular and hollow vessel of somewhat oval form in the dog, similar, or nearly so, to that of a man. It rests on the upper part of the sternum or breast-bone. It is divided into four chambers—viz., two auricles (a right and a left), and two ventricles (also right and left).

The heart is constantly contracting and dilating, and this movement, which goes on until life is extinct, and which resembles the motions of a double force-pump, is sufficient to propel the blood through every artery and vein in the body. The arterial or pure life-giving blood leaves the heart by the great aorta, the largest blood-vessel in the body. No sooner, then, has the aorta started upwards a little way from the left ventricle than it begins to give off branches to the fore-quarters and head; then, passing backwards in the dog's body along the spine, it gives off branches to all the regions and organs of the abdomen, and finally bifurcates into two large branches, one for each hinder extremity. If we follow the course of one of these we shall find it continuing still to ramify and split up into branches, and each branch ramifying in its turn, until the whole ends in a network of capillaries or hair-like arteries, so small that we cannot prick the flesh with the finest needle without dividing some of them. The diameter of these capillaries is from $\frac{1}{2400}$ to $\frac{1}{1600}$ of an inch.

And in what do the capillaries end? They end by anastamosing with veins of their own size, capillary veins.

We thus trace the arteries down to their capillaries; to these capillaries the several arteries have carried oxygenated blood, and by means of this blood the system is nourished; but when the capillaries have done their work, and the effete matter has been taken up into the veins, the blood is no longer pure—it can no longer support life until it is taken back to the heart, and thence to the lungs to be purified. Where, then, the arteries end the veins begin, and as the course of the arteries was from the heart, so is the course of the veins towards that centre organ.

The veins, then, through the intermedium of the capillaries, having taken up the blood, commence the return journey, receiving tributary veins from all directions, and getting larger and fewer in number as they near the heart. The veins thus formed unite at last to form one large vessel, the vena cava, which pours the blood into the right auricle. The blood has not yet quite completed the circulation, however; for, be it remembered, it is still dark and impure blood, and unfit for the further nutrition of the body, until the effete matter with which it is loaded has been burned off in the lungs. For this reason and purpose it is received by the right ventricle from the right auricle, and by the former pumped into the lungs through the medium of the pulmonary artery; and here the same minute subdivision of arteries takes place that we noticed throughout the general circulation, the artery ending in capillaries, which are spread out around the air-cells of the lungs, and the blood in them absorbs oxygen, and gives off carbonic acid and water, which is exhaled. The capillaries of the pulmonary artery join those of the pulmonary veins, which, uniting and re-uniting, finally pour the purified blood into the left auricle, from which it descends to the ventricle of the same side, and so is once more pumped away to carry nutriment to every portion of the body. And thus the wheel of life goes round.

We usually speak of arterial blood being red, and venous blue or purple; but the reader will observe that in the lesser circulation, or that through the lungs, matters are simply reversed, for here it is the arteries that contain the dark blood, and the veins the red. In considering the circulation of the blood, there is one thing that cannot fail to strike any one who has some knowledge of mechanics. There are openings between the auricles and ventricles through which the blood has to pass. Well, on the contraction of this ventricle (say the left) necessary to send the blood with force in the aorta, why does it not just as easily flow back again into the auricle as go onward. To prevent this a valve is placed in the orifice between the two chambers, called the mitral valve, and this valve is so arranged that it opens to permit the blood to flow into the ventricle, but *closes as the ventricle contracts*, just as the air gets freely in through the lower opening of a pair of bellows, but cannot get out again.

Now this has an important bearing with regard to heart disease, for it sometimes happens that this valve—or any other valve in the heart, for that matter—becomes the subject of disease, gets either insufficient or thickened by deposit, so that it cannot close properly, and then at every contraction of the heart a portion of blood regurgitates, which forms one very serious kind of heart disease.

Another question that will doubtless present itself to the intelligent reader is: What power or force is it that sends the blood upwards and onwards through the veins, the contractile force of the left ventricle, which has pumped the blood through the arteries, being naturally to a great extent expended at the capillaries. There is a certain resiliency in the arteries themselves, which gives the blood in the venous capillaries a start, at all events, to begin with, but on the dilatation of the right ventricle it will naturally form a vacuum, and so, after the manner of a pump, it will suck the blood towards it. Again, the walls of the veins themselves have a certain contractility which aids the flow of the blood, and the action of surrounding muscles will also help the work. "But," it may be said, "this latter is a force that may act in both directions." True enough; but we find in the venous system a beautiful provision of Nature which determines the flow of the blood in the right direction only. This is accomplished by means of valves or little pockets, having their mouths pointed in the direction in which the blood is flowing. These valves are simply little pouches formed of the lining membrane of the veins themselves. Now it must be evident to every one that so long as the blood flows in one direction, these pockets will lie flat against the inside of the vein, and present no obstacle, but if any attempt is made by the blood to flow backwards, this would result in the opening of the valves, which would dam the way and prevent the retrograde flow.

The position of these valves in the veins of the forearm of a lean person can be distinctly perceived by performing a very simple experiment. The arm is bared, a handkerchief is tied tightly round it above the elbow, to stop the upward flow of blood. If the hand be then tightly clenched, and the eye cast along the distended veins, we see a series of little knots here and there. These represent the valves or pouches opened to prevent the backward flow of the blood.

Now, these valves themselves are sometimes the seat of disorder; from undue strain upon them they get dilated and ruptured, and are therefore not in a position to perform their duties. The veins themselves get elongated and tortuous, a state in which you frequently find them in the limbs of old London cab-horses, and, more rarely, in the limbs of dogs as well, such as Greyhounds.

Let us now say a few words about the blood itself and its component parts. Blood is composed of red particles, and a transparent fluid called the *liquor sanguinis*. If we allow blood that has been newly drawn from an animal to stand for some time in a basin, we will perceive that it resolves itself into two parts, viz., a red clot in the centre, not unlike a piece of raw liver, and a pale straw-coloured transparent fluid, which is all around and above it. The clear fluid is the serum of the blood, the clot is termed the *crassamentum*, this last consisting of the red corpuscles of the blood. These latter, which seen under the microscope look like small round discs or pieces of money, in the veins float along in *liquor sanguinis*. Chemically examined, the red corpuscles are found to consist of what is called *globulin*, and also of *hæmatin*. *Globulin* is somewhat akin to albumen, while the *hæmatin* it is which gives the colour to the blood. This *hæmatin* is a compound of carbon and *iron*. This latter fact gives medical men a hint which we are not slow to act upon; we know that in any animal in a low state of health the red blood corpuscles are too few, and we know that animals that breathe the largest amount of oxygen have the best and reddest blood—are the healthiest and happiest—hence we give to anæmic patients good nutritious food, and *iron* in some shape (that which is the most easily assimilated is the best) and recommend plenty of fresh air.

The principal uses of the red corpuscles are two. They take oxygen (the life-giver) from the air that is breathed, and they roll it away through the arteries to the capillaries; then they come back—rolling their way along the veins—laden with carbonic acid to the lungs, and there give up their charge, which is *exhaled*. Busy bees are those red corpuscles, clustering around the cell walls of the lungs, unloading their carbonic acid, and taking in oxygen with every breath we breathe, then hurrying off again to perform the work for which the great Author ordained them.

Not less important is the work which the *liquor sanguinis* has to perform in the system. The microscope reveals nothing of its composition, as it is *within* the body; but when the blood is drawn, and placed in a basin, we find that, as we have already said, it separates into clot and serum. This serum is a part of the *liquor sanguinis*; the other part is the fibrin, which, from the tendency its particles have to draw together or agglutinate, entangles the red corpuscles, and thus the clot is formed. The serum itself is found to consist of water and albumen, with various salts and other substances. It is from this albumen that the greater portion of the tissues supply their waste. We find, then, in the blood not only the materials of which the whole animal structure is built up, but those also which keep up the heat without which life would be impossible. And whence does the blood get its own supply? From the food eaten and from the air breathed: and this surely tells its own tale.

"The blood that circulates in our bodies," says Dr. Carpenter, "may be likened to a tidal river, rolling onwards through the centre of a large city, and supplying it with the water needed for the drink of its inhabitants, as well as that which is required for the various manufacturing and cleansing operations that are carried on within its walls. The same stream also receives the drainage of the town, and becomes charged accordingly with the products of animal and vegetable decomposition, and the refuse of all its manufactories; and, as the flow of the tide brings back a large proportion of what was carried down by the ebb, the waters speedily become so contaminated with offensive matters as to be unfit for use, unless means be provided for getting rid of these as fast as they are poured in. The perfection with which this requirement is fulfilled in the animal body, while it excites our admiration, should also excite us to imitation, so far as the art of man can hope to imitate the works of the Divine Artificer."

I. *Inflammation.*

What is inflammation? We know that the word is derived from the Latin *inflammare*—to set fire to, or to burn. This gives at least one of the symptoms of inflammation—namely, heat; and puts one in mind of the saying of old Celsus:—"Notæ inflammationis sunt quatuor, rubor et tumor, cum calore et dolore." *

Now let us take one of the simplest cases of external inflammation, and see how far this description of Celsus coincides with it. The case is not hypothetical; it recently occurred. A large dog, in jumping into a cart at Henley-on-Thames, missed footing, and was struck by the sharp edge of the front step just in the groin and a little on the abdomen. Nothing was observed for two days, when, the dog appearing to walk lame, he was examined, and there was found a very large, very tender *swelling*, hard in the centre, and getting gradually softer as it neared the surrounding or healthy tissue. Here we have two of Celsus's *notæ*: the *tumor cum dolore;* but there were also the other two—there was intense redness, deeper in the centre of the swelling and brighter towards the edge, and intense heat. Now these were the local symptoms; but combined with these we had

Inflammatory Fever.—Symptoms, to wit: at first one or two distinct rigors or shivering fits, soon succeeded by heat of all the surface of the skin; pulse (which can easily be felt in a large dog) hard, more full, and rather more rapid. Eyes rather injected, nose hot and dry, mouth and breath hot. Coat staring, bowels confined, bladder inactive, and urine scanty and red. The dog cared little to move, unless peremptorily called by his name; when, on seeing he was not really wanted, he dropped his head again dull and heavily, and with a moaning sigh. The appetite was gone, and all spirit seemed to have left him. The tongue paler than usual, and thirst great. Now the inflammation might have resolved or subsided under the treatment, which would have been looked upon as *the* favourable termination. It did not, however. Symptoms of pain and fever increased, and by-and-by distinct fluctuation (a bogging feeling) was felt in the tumour, clearly indicative of the presence of pus (matter). Now was the time to plunge the bistoury in, carefully, cautiously, but sufficiently deep withal. Matter escaped plentifully, and with it blood, to the great relief of the congestion, and in a few days the dog was well.

But had the wound not healed; had the pus continued to be discharged in abundance, then the weakness would have become great; frequent shiverings would have alternated with fits of feverish heat. These, of course, would be the symptoms of *hectic* fever.

---

* "The signs of inflammation are four—redness and swelling, with heat and pain."

Had the abscess not been opened at all, and had it not even burst of its own accord, mortification might have ensued—the part would in simple language have rotted out, and perhaps the patient gotten feebler and more feeble till he sank, and died of low fever.

Now in inflammations of internal organs we should have a fever or fevers of much the same character to guide us.

Pathologically considered, we may state in few words that the local *redness* is caused by the increased amount of blood in the capillaries. This redness momentarily disappears when pressed by the finger.

The *swelling* is caused partially by the greater volume of blood in the part, and partly by œdema—that is, by the oozing into the tissues surrounding the over-filled capillaries of a portion of serum, or blood itself, from rupture of the small vessels.

The *heat* is caused by the greater amount of oxidation going on in the part.

The *pain* may be of different kinds. This the poor animal cannot tell you of; he cannot describe his feelings, so he suffers in silence, or gives vent to cries, to howls, or to simple moans.

Tenderness on *pressure* is another symptom of inflammation, and one that at times is diagnostic.

Congestion is simply, so far as we are concerned, a kind of mild inflammation. In inflammation, say in the centre of a tumour, there is stagnation of the blood, perhaps rupture of some of the capillaries, and exudation of the *liquor sanguinis*. Around this we have active congestion, the blood is not quite stagnant, but the little vessels are very full of blood. Around this, again, there is what is called *determination*. Capillaries are still gorged, but there is rapid movement of the blood through them.

Treatment of Inflammation.—Our first endeavour ought to be to remove the cause, and to obtain resolution. Failing in this, suppuration would be the next best thing to be desired.

Our treatment, then, resolves itself into the local and constitutional. But all harsh and weakening measures are to be deprecated. The day has gone by when practitioners trusted to bleeding, leeching, large doses of tartar emetic, setons, and all such lowering remedies. Why, even in those cases which they managed to cure, the period of convalescence was necessarily very protracted.

In the case of a superficial injury to a dog's limb or other part of the body, if seen at once, our treatment must be directed to the *prevention* of inflammation. This cannot be better carried out than by the application of cold, either by cold water applied by means of linen rags, or by the india-rubber ice-bag. Care must be taken, however, not to *freeze* the part, else gangrene may occur. Or you may use the cooling lotion, or the arnica lotion, or a drachm of sugar of lead to a pint of soft water and a little spirit, or the vinegar lotion where there is much pain.

℞. Spirit. Mindereri ... ... ℥ ij.
Sp. vini rectific. ... ... ℥ iiij.
Aquæ camph. ... ... ℥ xv.
Fᵗ lotio. M.

℞. Arnicæ tinct. ... ... ℥ vj.
Aquæ ... ... ℥ x.
Fᵗ lotio. M.

℞. Acet. acid dil. . .. ℥ v.
Aquæ ... . ℥ xv.
Tinct. Opii ... ... ℥ j.
Fᵗ lotio. M.

N.B.—In using these lotions, mind the bruise is not to be covered closely up, but the rag dipped in one of them simply laid over it, the hair being first well damped. *Rest* must be enjoined, and the bowels are to be opened by a brisk purgative—Epsom salts and cream of tartar, or from ten grains to a drachm and a half of aloes. Thus we try to prevent local inflammation.

If, however, the inflammation has for the present gotten the upper hand, we try means to subdue it. First we endeavour to place the seat of inflammation (say a wounded or bruised paw in a dog) in the most favourable position for getting well, and try to keep it at rest. The inflammation having fairly set in, the application of cold would now be very wrong indeed. Fomentations (warm) and poultices must now be our sheet-anchors. We have already described the usual method of fomenting; a warm decoction of poppy-heads, or the old-wife's remedy, camomile flowers, is very soothing. After well fomenting, a nice large poultice ought to be used.

Thus we try to reduce the swelling, relieve the tension of the distended capillaries.

When the inflammation and pain have gone, cold water sponging will give great relief, and restore tone to the congested vessels.

The *constitutional treatment* of simple sthenic inflammatory fever. We must first give a brisk purgative. (We are talking of cases where there is no abdominal inflammation.) This does great good in many ways. Then three or four times a day diaphoretics and salines should be given; they reduce the pulse and bring to our aid both the kidneys and skin. Nitrate of potash and chlorate and citrate of potash may be used, and especially Mindererus spirit (liquor ammoniæ acetatis).

Opium is of great use in allaying pain and irritation, and should be given in full doses towards night.

Tincture of aconite we have not very much experience of in canine diseases; it deserves a trial, however, in simple sthenic inflammatory fever. It is anodyne and sedative, and, we might add, diaphoretic. In human practice it is used with success.

Rest is of great importance—rest in a well-ventilated, not too warm room, and the diet must be low. We must mark the change of pulse, however, and not forget that the system must be kept well up during convalescence.

2. *Congestion.*

This must not be confounded with inflammation, although it often is. It does, however, sometimes run on to inflammation. In congestion there is redness of a dark or even purple hue, serous exudation, and consequent swelling and pitting on pressure, but no elevation of temperature, and no pain. The œdematous state of the tissues may lead on to ulceration of the structures. The capillaries in congestion are turgid, the flow of blood slow, and there is sometimes rupture of the vessels.

Causes of Congestion.—These may be divided into two classes—(1) Those that act by preventing the return of the blood to the heart, damming it up in the blood-vessels, causing redness, exudation, &c.; and (2) those that act by directly enfeebling the blood-vessels of the part, as cold, &c. The cause will determine the treatment.

3. *Acute Rheumatism.*

This disease, one form of which is known by the name of chest founder, is very common among dogs, and is a most painful complaint, deserving our utmost sympathy and care.

Pathology.—We have long believed with many other professional men that rheumatism is the result, primarily, of a superabundance of free acid—most probably lactic—in the blood.

By injecting a solution of lactic acid and water into the peritoneum, Dr. Richardson succeeded in producing in the dog and cat not only endocarditis, with swelling and obstruction of the valves of the heart, by fibrinous bands, but well-marked inflammation of the joints, and inflammation of the sclerotic coat of the eye.

One peculiarity in the inflammation of rheumatism is its tendency to shift its seat, and this, too, not only from one joint to another, but to serous membranes in parts of the body more intimately connected with life itself. Thus, we find rheumatic fever often complicated with pericarditis and endocarditis, and sometimes even with pleurisy. Rheumatism uncomplicated is an inflammation of the fibrous sheathing of the joints and muscles ; any or many joints may be implicated, and we always have more or less of fever.

Causes.—Whatever may be the real pathology of this disease, its exciting causes are not far to seek. It is generally found in dogs that have been neglected, not only as to the comforts of their kennels, but as to their food. Also in dogs that are over-pampered and over-cared for, and by this means rendered constitutionally tender.

The disease is also hereditary ; and if a dog has one attack of rheumatism, either acute or chronic, it usually predisposes to another.

There are, to our knowledge, some kennels of sporting dogs in England that for many years have never been free from rheumatism in some form or other.

The proximate cause of rheumatism is exposure to damp and cold, or alternate heats and chills combined with damp. Probably the first generation of the evil is to be traced to the lungs themselves, and the diathesis may be acquired from alteration in the blood, owing to its not being properly purified in the process of respiration.

Symptoms.—In our own experience the disease—we mean acute, not chronic, rheumatism—does not come on suddenly ; for the first symptom, but one which unfortunately generally escapes observation, is a certain degree of stiffness in all the dog's motions, and a departure from his ordinary state of activity. If walking with his master he lags behind, or if in the field he is stiffish at first, although when he warms to his work this soon wears off, and there seems for a time nothing wrong with him. Again, especially if a large dog, after he has been lying down for some time he feels unable or unwilling to get up with his wonted ease. Perhaps he cries out, and he will have to go some distance before this pain and stiffness be shaken off. This may go on for a day or two, or even much longer, before any symptom of really acute rheumatism supervenes ; and all the while the blood is getting more and more poisoned with the acid.

At length acute or sub-acute inflammation of the ligaments, tendons, and aponeurosis of the muscles takes place, it may be in the shoulder, the leg or legs, the neck, the chest, or back, in any of these regions or in all combined. The dog now not only exhibits stiffness and pain, but he becomes restless and feverish ; he moves about anxiously, stopping at times and crying out, as if he had hurt himself ; or he seeks out a quiet corner, generally in under something, where he can lie unmolested.

Even in slight cases there is always more or less of fever. The nose is dry, the breath and mouth hot, and the tongue furred. The pulse, too, will be found hard, and increased in frequency, and the insides of the thighs hot, and often covered with perspiration. The dog's temper is bad, as a rule. He is peevish, at least, and often snarly. All he seems to wish is to be left alone.

On examination, the affected joints will be found more or less swollen, and exceedingly tender, and the swelling has this peculiarity, it is firm in its nature, and rarely, if ever, points to or runs on to suppuration.

There is a marked alteration in the urine, it is scanty and very high in colour, and if tested with litmus-paper it gives a strongly acid reaction. There are other alterations in the urine, which only a professional man can detect. The bowels are confined. Paralysis of the hind-quarters, either complete or partial, is not an unusual concomitant of acute rheumatism.

Diagnosis.—There is hardly any mistaking a case of rheumatism, but the lameness, fever, pain to the touch, and acidity of the urine, are sufficient to guide us.

Prognosis.—Favourable, as a rule, unless very much complicated. It will generally run its course in from two weeks to a month.

Treatment.—The treatment must be both constitutional and local.

Constitutionally, the indications of treatment are to allay the pain, and assuage the fever. We may fulfil the first indication by opium and belladonna in conjunction, as by a pill like the prescription—

$$℞ \text{ Opii pulv.} \quad \dots \quad \dots \quad \text{gr. } \tfrac{1}{2} \text{ ad gr. iij.}$$
$$\text{Ext. bellad.} \quad \dots \quad \dots \quad \text{gr. } \tfrac{1}{8} \text{ ad gr. ij.}$$
$$\text{Ext. tarax.} \quad \dots \quad \dots \quad \text{gr. v. ad gr. xv.}$$
$$\text{F}^t \text{ bolus.} \qquad \text{M.}$$

given every night, and if there seems to be very much distress give also from three to ten or fifteen grains of this powder—

$$℞ \left. \begin{array}{l} \text{Pulv. ipecac.} \\ \text{Pulv. opii} \end{array} \right\} \dots \quad \bar{a} \, \bar{a} \; ʒ \text{ ij.}$$
$$\text{Pulv. pot. nitr.} \dots \quad \dots \quad ʒ \text{ ij.}$$
$$\text{F}^t \text{ pulv.} \qquad \text{M.}$$

three or four times a day. Let the dog have a soft, warm, comfortable bed, with plenty of fresh air, but with freedom from draughts. Let his water, in which a teaspoonful or two of nitre should be mixed, be placed handy to him, and always kept fresh. And let him have from ten to thirty grains of nitre, with from five to fifteen grains of bicarbonate of potash, made into a bolus, with fat or any simple extract, or even mixed in water as a drench, three times a day. When the dog is first attacked his bowels ought to be cleared with a saline purgative, and afterwards kept open with from a drachm to four drachms of Epsom salts every morning, combined with three to ten drops of tincture of hyoscyamus, and five to twenty of dilute sulphuric acid. Sometimes from five drops to a drachm and a half of the tincture of colchicum may be added with advantage to the morning draught.

Food low at first, but we must take care not to allow the dog himself to get too low; if signs of weakness are exhibited, resort to beef-tea, mutton-broth, milk, or eggs.

Locally, in a case of really acute rheumatism, very little can be done. In small dogs, the warm bath may effect some good, but we must remember the difficulty we shall experience in getting the animal thoroughly dried again. Embrocations and stimulating liniments are better suited to chronic or sub-acute cases. Heat applied to the seat of pain by means of a common flat iron we have found do most good, or the use of bags of heated sand. After the acute stage is got over, you may begin with advantage to administer iodide of potassium and quinine three times a day, and the diet ought now to be more generous.

$$℞ \text{ Quinæ sulph.} \quad \dots \quad \dots \quad \text{gr. j. ad gr. ij.}$$
$$\text{Pot. iod.} \quad \dots \quad \dots \quad \text{gr. j. ad gr. v.}$$
$$\text{Ext. tarax.} \quad \dots \quad \dots \quad \text{q. s.}$$
$$\text{F}^t \text{. pil. ter die.}$$

4. *Chronic Rheumatism.*

This is a disease which is not very easily diagnosed in the dog. For we must not forget that dogs, especially sporting dogs, are liable to go lame from many other reasons besides rheumatism—sprains, for example, blows and falls, and myalgia and neuralgia. This myalgia is often seen in hounds and in Pointers that have been over-worked. It consists only in a partially inflamed state of some of the muscles, and a little rest puts it soon to rights.

Now dogs suffer at times from rheumatic gout, and have swellings about their joints, and even bones, that point significantly to a rheumatic diathesis. Such dogs should be carefully fed and not overworked, and their kennels or sleeping-places always kept warm and clean and dry. An occasional dose of castor-oil when needed will also do good, followed up by a fortnight's course of tonic medicine—iron and bark.

Chronic rheumatism is known by the name of chest founder and kennel lameness. It is very often situated in the shoulder—sub-scapular muscles or their tendons—and in the chest. It is common in the back and loins, when it is termed lumbago. It is less common in the hind-quarters, but the feet are often affected. There is usually some degree of swelling if it be in the limbs; there is little or no fever, though sometimes the appetite is lost; but the animal is stiff and lame, and cries out when you handle the tender part, and even when attempting to walk. But the disease is so well known that it is almost a waste of space to describe its symptoms.

Treatment.—Attend to the cleanliness, the dryness, and purity of the kennels; give the animals liable to kennel lameness a good warm bed, and abundance of it. Give the dogs their food regularly, and see that they are never allowed to lie out in the wet and cold. Regulate the bowels, and give tonics, or arsenic may do good. Cod-liver oil cannot fail to improve the animal's condition, unless he is gross. Avoid giving small animals sugar, or indeed dainties of any kind.

Locally.—The flat iron. Do not make it too hot, but just as hot as the animal can comfortably bear it. Pass the iron slowly along the affected part, and pass your hand after it to see it is not too hot. Do this three or four times a day, and always at least a quarter of an hour at a time. The bags of hot sand may also be tried. Another simple application in lumbago is common sulphur well dusted into the coat and allowed to remain in, a flannel roller being applied around the dog's body all night. It may, if desired, be brushed out in the morning and more dusted in again at night. Other local applications, which may be tried, are the liniments of opium, belladonna, or aconite. In some cases a blister does good, but a veterinary surgeon should first be consulted.

5. *Rickets.*

This is a disease which is far from uncommon in puppies.

Pathology.—The growth of bone in dogs is completed in from one year and a half up to two years and a half. During the period of its growth the bone may be acted upon either for good or for evil. From some error in the blood-making process, sufficient earthy salts may not be deposited, and ossification therefore retarded; the bones, if bones they can be called, will accordingly be unnaturally soft and yielding, and easily thrown out of plumb. The legs, especially, become bandy and crooked, and seldom or never get straight again.

Causes.—Improper food is one great cause; taking the puppy too soon from its dam, and supplying it with a diet unsuited to its digestion, will produce rickets. A weakly bitch, or one that has been over-suckled, will often have rickety pups. A damp or wet and unwholesome kennel, and the breathing of foul air, with little exercise in the warm sunshine, especially if combined with insufficient food, will be very likely to induce rickets in a puppy.

Symptoms.—The first symptom will be decline of the general health. The pup is not so lively as he ought to be, and suffers from indigestion, with occasional attacks of diarrhœa. The coat is not so nice as it ought to be; it is dirty and harsh and staring. At the same time there will be more or less tumefaction of the belly. Soon the bones begin to bend, especially the fore-legs, and there is no longer any doubt about the nature of the complaint, although ten to one the puppy has been previously treated for worms.

Now if the deformity has proceeded to any extent the case should not be taken in hand. Bandy-legged dogs ought not to be permitted to live ; and we merely mention rickets to show how the disease can be prevented, and cases that have not made any great advance cured.

You must give the puppy good wholesome nourishing food suited to his time of life ; his sleeping-berth ought to be dry and warm, and free from all bad smells, and he *must* have sufficient exercise and *sunshine.* Sunshine is a great vital restorative. A douche bath every morning will do good if the puppy can have a run immediately afterwards—not otherwise. Good milk with a little lime-water will do good, and beef-tea may be given with advantage.

The only medicine you need use is an occasional dose of castor-oil—say once a week, or when the dog is constipated. Parrish's syrup of the phosphates will help to strengthen the constitution, and, in conjunction with cod-liver oil, is sometimes wonderful in its action for good. We may support the bones by gutta-percha splints, but there is seldom need to do so, and the bones often straighten again of their own accord. Bone-meal does good in these cases.

6. *Obesity.*

Although a dog is much better to be plump than lean, over-fatness or obesity is really a disease, and not only so, but it tends to induce other diseases both of the heart and nervous centres, and the dogs who are very obese are likely some day to drop suddenly dead.

Prevention of obesity is certainly better than cure, but much can be done to restore the dog to a state of frame conducive to his comfort. Give a good wholesome diet with meat and soup, or Spratt cake with thirty per cent. of meat in it. Give no rice, potatoes, or any farinaceous food or vegetables, except oatmeal or stale bread. Give an occasional aperient and plenty of walking exercise, and not too warm or soft a bed at night. Avoid giving the dog anything sweet, especially sugar, which not only renders lap-dogs fat, but induces dyspepsia and causes premature decay of the teeth. The following medicine may also be given with advantage : From one to six grains of carbonate of ammonia, and from three to ten grains of carbonate of magnesia, made into a bolus with a little Castile soap and extract of taraxacum. This is to be given twice a day before meals. The bromide of ammonium might be tried.

7. *Goitre.*

Goitre is a word of Swiss origin. This disease is better known in this country as bronchocele, and consists of a painless swelling or enlargement of the thyroid gland, which flanks the larynx, or organ of voice. It is apt to arise in dogs of all ages, only in older dogs it comes on much more gradually than it does in puppies. In older dogs, too, it is seldom fatal to life, but it is often the death of pups.

The thyroid gland in a puppy enlarges very speedily. We have known it come on in a single night. Sometimes it goes away again just as suddenly, and may come again and again. We saw a case not long since which we have every reason to believe was induced mechanically. The animal, a young Spaniel, was sent to a show, where he was put on the chain for the first time in his life; next evening he had well-marked goitre.

The swelling is soft, and pliant and yielding; it would almost give one the notion it was blood.

It may cause difficulty of breathing, congestion of the brain, coma, and death. In old dogs the swelling is firmer.

Treatment.—A nourishing diet is necessary to begin with. The exhibition of cod-liver oil does a deal of good in most cases. Tonics and alteratives are also required. It is a good plan to change the tonic occasionally. The medicine likely to do most good is the iodide and bromide of potassium—from half a grain to five grains of each twice a day; and you can give at the same time iron and aloes, or the syrup of the iodide of iron, with a little glycerine.

Locally.—Shave the neck, and paint daily with tincture of iodine, or use the officinal ointment of iodine, which you can get at any chemist's shop. It must be well rubbed in, to do any good, every night and morning.

The dog must never be chained, but have plenty of freedom and exercise, and a bucket bath before his run of a morning.

8. *Diabetes Mellitus and Insipidus.*

This disease is classed by some practitioners among the disorders of the urinary organs; we prefer to treat it as a general or blood disease, considering the excessive urination as merely symptomatic.

Causes.—It is not easy to determine the real causes of diabetes mellitus in the dog, though we are half inclined to look upon it as a disease caused by nerve deterioration, which may be brought about in many ways; bad feeding and exposure to wet and damp in the kennel, or on the hill, especially if combined with too much excitement and over-work.

A very interesting account of a case of diabetus mellitus in a dog is given by Gamgee; and Williams tells us that in all the cases of this disease that have come under his notice, the animals have been fed for a long time upon boiled liver. And certainly no style of diet could be chosen for a dog more likely to produce disease of some sort than that of boiled liver daily.

Diabetes mellitus is that form of diabetes in which sugar may be detected in the urine. We believe this form of the disease is much more common among dogs than many of us are aware of.

Symptoms.—There is at first merely some slight illness combined with a little fever, but almost the earliest symptom that will attract attention will be the excessive diuresis, combined with inordinate thirst. The coat is harsh, and dry, and staring, the bowels constipated, the mouth hot and dry, and probably foul. Soon emaciation comes on, and the poor animal wastes rapidly away. Sometimes the appetite fails, but more often it is voracious, especially with regard to flesh meat. The dog is usually treated for worms, and the case made worse. The disease is a very fatal one, and if fairly set in can seldom be kept from running its course onwards to death. Death may take place from other and secondary diseases. Tumours form in the lungs, the liver becomes diseased, and the bowels seldom escape till the last.

Treatment.—We have found the treatment of diabetes exceedingly unsatisfactory. We have found the most benefit accrue from treating canine patients in the same way as we do human beings suffering similarly. We therefore do not hesitate to order the bran loaf if the animal is worth the trouble, and forbid the use of potatoes, rice, flour, oatmeal, and most vegetables, and feed mostly on flesh, and occasionally beef-tea and milk. We do not know, however, that we are quite justified in giving milk.

As to medicine, we must of course attend to the constipation, and occasional doses of Youatt's castor-oil mixture will be less weakening to the system than any other aperient. Give from half a grain up to three grains of opium (powdered), and the same quantity of quinine in a bit of Castile soap, twice or thrice daily. The iodo-bromide bolus recommended for goitre may also be found useful; it will at least moderate the symptoms, if it does not cure the disease. Then we have cod-liver oil and nux vomica to fall back upon, and also iron; but after all said and done, a diabetic dog is really of very little use.

9. *The Distemper.*

As the word Distemper simply means disease, it cannot be said that the name given to the ailment now under consideration is a very happy or instructive one, when we wish to denote a very serious form of ailment in the dog, resulting from the imbibition into the system, in some way or other, of a specific blood poison. The name, however, is so well known that no practitioner would care to alter it, at all events not in a treatise like the present.

Distemper is termed by the French *Le maladie des chiens*, which is certainly no improvement on our own name for the disorder. In Scotland it is designated by a much more expressive word; it is called the "snifters" in the South, and in some parts of the North the "snoughers," the *gh* having the sound of the Greek letter χ, or the *ch* in the Scotch "loch."

This distressing disease, with its symptoms and treatment, have only lately come to be thoroughly understood, or as thoroughly as any disease can be, by men who make it their business to become acquainted with the disorders of the lower animals. But, although more than a hundred years have elapsed since it was first imported into this country from France, a great amount of misunderstanding still prevails among a large section of dog-fanciers regarding its true nature and origin.

The fact is, the disease came to us with a bad name, for the French themselves deemed it incurable. In this country the old-fashioned plan of treatment was wont to be the usual rough remedies—emetics, purgatives, the seton, and the lancet.

Failing in this, specifics of all sorts were eagerly sought for and tried, and are unfortunately still believed in to a very great extent; and we cannot take up a sporting paper, or indeed a weekly journal of any sort, without coming across all manner of advertisements of so-called cures for distemper, distemper balls, and specifics, and other useless if not dangerous drugs. And the advertisers flourish. People believe in these nostrums, probably because it is their wish so to believe. They will not take the trouble to have the disease treated in a rational manner, because it is *so* handy just to give a dog a dose or two of medicine and have done with it.

"But," it may be asked, "is it not the case that hundreds of cases of distemper have been either cured or cut short by these specifics?" We do not think so, for ninety-five per cent. of all reputed cases are not distemper at all, but cases of simple catarrh or stomach-ache.

Definition.—Distemper is a specific catarrhal fever, the result of a peculiar poison circulating in the blood, and of the efforts of Nature to eliminate that poison. It occurs most frequently from infection or contagion, but *may* probably arise spontaneously.

Like all fevers arising from a specific contagion, or infective poison, distemper has a certain course to run, and in this disease Nature seems to attempt the elimination of the poison, through the secretions thrown out by the naso-pharyngeal mucous membrane.

Our chief difficulty in the treatment of distemper lies in the complications thereof. We may, and often do, have the organs of respiration attacked; we have sometimes congestion of the liver, or mucous inflammation of the bile ducts, or some lesion of the brain or nervous structures, combined with epilepsy, convulsions, or chorea. Distemper is also often complicated with severe disease of the bowels, and at times with an affection of the eyes.

Indeed, whatever important secreting organ happens to be the weak point in the dog, that organ will during distemper be sought out and determined to.

The disease has been compared by some eminent veterinary surgeons to measles in the human frame, and by others to typhoid fever. There is, however, in our opinion, a far greater analogy between distemper and measles than between it and typhoid. In the latter disease we have always diarrhœa, and sometimes hæmorrhage, and so we have at times in distemper; but in distemper such symptoms are to be looked upon more as complications than diagnostic. Again, in typhoid or enteric fever, we have always a change in the glands of Peyer; they are found swollen and ulcerated. Well, we have ulceration of the mucous membranes of the bowels in the muco-enteritis of distemper, but we question very much if ever the solitary glands, or glands of Peyer, have been found diseased.

Says Williams: "I can compare distemper to no human disease except measles, and the points of analogy are very great. In both diseases catarrhal symptoms are manifested; they are infectious diseases; they generally occur but once in a lifetime; they chiefly affect the young; in almost all cases of distemper there is some eruption or rash, and desquamation of the cuticle; catarrhal ophthalmia, bronchial and pulmonary inflammation, and dysentery, are complications of both diseases; and, finally, convulsions sometimes occur both at the commencement and during the progress of measles and of distemper."

"I am not aware, however," the author continues, "whether paralysis or chorea ever follows measles." Yes; paralysis is, although rarely, one of the sequelæ of measles, but we are not certain about chorea. We ourselves have never seen it succeed measles, but it is both possible and likely, as any disease that weakens the nervous system, and places the health below par, may induce chorea if there be a predisposition to it.

We have heard it said (though we have no reason to believe it) that distemper in the dog might sometimes arise from contact with the putrid emanations from typhoid patients. A dog, however, to our own knowledge contracted distemper a few days after he had been positively seen eating offal on a dunghill in the rear of a house afflicted with typhoid. But this proves nothing.

Instead of saying that distemper is contagious or infectious, it would be better, we think, to call it communicable from one dog to another, either through the medium of positive contact, or through the air itself.

We all know that distemper is communicable, but the doubtful question is: Can distemper arise spontaneously, as we have already hinted? It might. By the word "spontaneously," we do not mean "originating in the dog's blood or system;" for so long as he is kept clean, properly fed and attended to, he will not, cannot, have distemper, unless there has been actual contact in some way with contagion. There must be a seed of the poison, a disease-germ, and that germ, we submit, may occasionally, even now-a-days, come into existence in filthy, badly-ventilated, and badly-conditioned kennels. It is no explanation of the origin of a disease to tell us, as some authorities do, that it came from France, was imported to that country from Spain, and probably to Spain from Spanish America. That sends us across the Atlantic, but how much better are we? How did the disease originate in America? There are just the same chemical agencies at work now as there were 20,000 years ago ; and although we have no actual proof that a disease-germ may originate in our own land, and find soil congenial to propagation in the animal called a dog, still we have no proof at all that it cannot.

Fleming, we think, *does* believe in the spontaneity of certain diseases. Hunting, a shrewd man and close observer, does not. He defends his belief, or rather disbelief, by the following arguments :—(1) " That many dogs never have distemper at all." (Quite right ; some people manage as a rule *to so order it* that their dogs, seldom, if ever, contract the disease.) (2) " That one attack very rarely follows another, which is the opposite to what would obtain if cold could induce it." (But cold alone will not produce it. And again, dogs who have had the disease once, do not possess the same immunity from other attacks that people do who have once had small-pox.) (3) " That cases of distemper often arise in dogs that have not been exposed to the alleged causes." (We grant this, and these cases are doubtless the result of contagion alone.) (4) " That we know the disease is contagious, and therefore in the infected dog there must be a specific poison." (This we also admit.) And, lastly, that " previous to 1763 dogs were exposed to all the alleged causes, and yet never showed a sign of distemper." And this last statement is perhaps the strongest part of Mr. Hunting's argument.

Concerning one thing, at all events, there remains not the shadow of a doubt in the minds of any of us. Distemper is a highly contagious or communicable disease ; and as to the possibility or impossibility of its arising spontaneously in our kennels, it is better to err on the safe side, and protect our dogs from as many of the *alleged causes* as we can.

We know for a fact that dogs *may* have distemper more than once in a lifetime. The pathological reasons for this are expressed in beautiful language by Watson and Tyndall. Referring to the exanthematous diseases of the human frame, Watson compares the growth of a disorder of this nature to that of a vegetable in the field.

" We have," he says, " the visible and tangible seed, the manifest sowing, the hidden germination ; then the outward growth and efflorescence, the ripening, the mature seed-time, the reproduction manifold of the original specific germ—every stage in the process of development occupying a definite period of time. Lastly—for here the analogy, though weaker, does not wholly fail—we have the total or the partial, the final or the temporary exhaustion of the soil, even for a single crop for that particular substance. Sometimes (to continue the metaphor) the soil slowly regains the power to grow the same disorder ; we see this in the waning protective influence of distant bygone vaccination."

Tyndall holds the same idea. " A tree," he said, " or a grain crop requires for its existence an infinitesimal amount of mineral matter, without which, however rich the soil, it cannot grow. It is perfectly conceivable that a soil may contain this matter in such minute quantity that a single crop may exhaust it ; and this without prejudice to the capacity of the soil as regards other crops. Now may there not, prior to the sowing of the virus, be something analogous in the human system which a single crop of pustules entirely removes ? Some such change is certainly wrought, and I would rather express it in terms of matter than in terms of force. If after one attack of small-pox the system ever becomes receptive of a second, this would be equivalent to the restoration of the requisite mineral matter in the soil."

Causes of Distemper.—Whether it be that the distemper virus, the poison seedling of the disease, really originates in the kennel, or is the result of contact of one dog with another, or whether the poison floats to the kennel on the wings of the wind, or is carried there on a shoe or the point of a walking-stick, the following facts ought to be borne in mind. (1) Anything that debilitates the body or weakens the nervous system paves the way for the distemper poison.

(2) The healthier the dog, the more power does he possess to resist contagion. (3) When the disease is epizootic, it can often be kept at bay by proper attention to diet and exercise, frequent change of kennel straw, and by the use of disinfectants. (4) The predisposing causes which have come more immediately under our notice are debility, cold, damp, starvation, filthy kennels, unwholesome food, impure air, and grief.

The age at which dogs may take Distemper.—They may take distemper at any age, but the most common time of life is from the fifth till the eleventh or twelfth month.

Highly-bred dogs are, we believe, in some degree more liable to take distemper; at all events, the disease is generally more severe with them than with low-bred curs. Certain breeds of dogs, too, are apt to suffer from more severe complications than others—the Newfoundland and St. Bernard, for example.

Symptoms.—There is first and foremost a period of latency or of incubation, which may be longer or shorter according to circumstances, in which there is more or less of dulness and loss of appetite, and which glides gradually into a state of feverishness. The fever may be ushered in with chills and shivering. The nose now becomes hot and dry, the dog is restless and thirsty, and the conjunctivæ of the eye will be found to be considerably injected. Sometimes the bowels are at first constipated, but they are more usually irregular. Sneezing will also be frequent, and in some cases cough, dry and husky at first.

At the commencement there is but little exudation from the eyes and nose, but as the disease advances this symptom will become more marked, being clear at first. So, too, will another symptom which is partly diagnostic of the malady, namely, increased heat of the body, combined with a rapid falling off in flesh, sometimes, indeed, proceeding quickly on to positive emaciation.

As the disease creeps downwards and inwards along the air-passages, the chest gets more and more affected, the discharge of mucus and pus from the nostrils more abundant, and the cough loses its dry character, becoming moist. The discharge from the eyes is simply mucus and pus, but if not constantly dried away will gum the inflamed lids together; that from the nostrils is not only purulent, but often mixed with dark blood. The appetite is now clean gone; there is often vomiting and occasional attacks of diarrhœa.

Now in mild cases, and cases that have been carefully and scientifically treated from the first, we may look for some abatement of the symptoms about the fourteenth day. The fever gets less, inflammation decreases in the mucous passages, and appetite is restored, as one of the first signs of returning health. More often, however, the disease becomes complicated.

Diagnosis.—The diagnostic symptoms are the severe catarrh, combined with not only *fever*, but speedy *emaciation*. Simple catarrh may be, and doubtless is, often called distemper; but there will be no confusion if we remember that in a simple cold there is but little, if any, emaciation, and the disease is usually over and done with in a few days.

Complications of Distemper.—Although it seems Nature's wish in distemper to eliminate the poison through the mucous membranes of the naso-pharyngeal passages, many causes may combine to produce dangerous and often fatal complications. The first complication to be mentioned is one we often find in dogs that have been wrongly treated, and too much reduced in condition. We refer to extreme exhaustion, which sometimes carries the dog off as early as the second week.

Pneumonia, as we might easily imagine, is a very likely complication, and a very dangerous one. There is great distress in breathing, the animal panting rapidly. The countenance is anxious, the pulse small and frequent, and the extremities cold. The animal would fain sit up on his haunches, or even seek to get out into the fresh air; but sickness, weakness, and prostration, often forbid his movements. If the ear or stethoscope be applied to the chest, the characteristic signs of pneumonia will be heard ; these are sounds of moist crepitations, &c.

Bronchitis is probably the most common complication ; in fact, it is always present, except in very mild cases. The cough becomes more severe, and often comes on in tearing paroxysms, causing sickness and vomiting. The breathing is short and frequent, the mouth hot, and filled with viscid saliva, while very often the bowels are constipated.

Liver Disease.—If the liver becomes involved, we shall very soon have the jaundiced eye and the yellow skin. The jaundice may be caused by suppression from the distemper poison, or interfering with the proper secretion of the bile, or it may be caused by obstruction ; and this is the more common cause—owing to catarrhal inflammation of the lining membrane of the gall-duct, and consequent occlusion thereof from thickening and discharge.

Diarrhœa.—This is another very common complication. We have frequent purging, and, may-be, sickness and vomiting. The stools are at times thin, slimy, and watery; more often, however, they are about the consistency of gruel, and dark and very offensive. This diarrhœa, if not kept in check, may go on to *dysentery* itself, the fœces being tinged with mucus, pus, and blood. There will be also considerable tenesmus. The discharge of a quantity of pure blood is by no means a rare, though always dangerous, symptom. Attacks of colic and tympanites may occasionally be expected.

Fits of a convulsive character are frequent concomitants of distemper. The animal sometimes falls down howling in agony and pawing the ground, or he becomes insensible quite, and very much convulsed.

Epilepsy is sometimes seen in cases of distemper, owing, no doubt, to degeneration of the nerve centres, owing to blood-poisoning. Epileptic fits are violent while they last, and one may succeed another, until at last, getting feebler and feebler, the dog dies in one.

There are many other complications seen in distemper ; for instance, inflammation of the conjunctivæ and ulceration of the cornea, various skin complications, eruptions on the thinnest portions of the hide of the animal, and towards the end, when the dog is getting convalescent, eczematous eruptions about the rump and tail, &c., &c.

Erysipelas, or an inflammation resembling it, sometimes attacks the extremities.

Again, we may have as sequelæ both chorea and paralysis ; this latter, indeed, sometimes coming on even as a complication, and a very dangerous one too.

We have purposely avoided enlarging on these complications, as this would only tend to confuse the general reader, who is apt to look upon complications as symptomatic of distemper. Moreover, both complications and sequelæ are more fully treated of in other portions of the book.

Treatment of Distemper.—This consists firstly in doing all in our power to guide the specific catarrhal fever to a safe termination ; and secondly, in watching for and combating complications.

The older practitioners used to trust largely to the lancet, to strong purgatives, and to emetics. Knowing, as we now do, the true pathology of the disorder, we are not likely to follow their example. We have seen that distemper is really the effects of a specific poison, afloat in the circulation and generating more poison, which Nature does her best to eliminate ; and we have seen, too, that the naso-pharyngeal mucous membrane is the soil chosen by the poison-seed of distemper whereon to grow and flourish. As, then, the symptoms of catarrh are caused, not by irritation from without, but by irritation from within—by a poisonous *vis-a-tergo*, it is evident that our efforts must be directed to support Nature, and assist her to eliminate the poison.

What lesson are we going to learn from the fact that sheep-curs and hardy street dogs get over the distemper with so little trouble, while high-bred animals and indoor pets only too often fall victims to the disorder? Surely it is this: that in the former cases Nature has more power to do battle with the poison. And the following is our own experience, and probably the experience of most practitioners: Whenever we get a case of distemper in a hardy constitutioned dog—probably one of no particular breed—we find we can almost invariably bring the dog through it with little or no medicine, by simple nursing and supporting the animal's strength.

It is, in our opinion, a great mistake to begin the treatment by giving a strong emetic. Emetics are very seldom, if ever, needed. If we think that the dog has need to evacuate the contents of his stomach—which, seeing he has not eaten anything signifying for days, perhaps, is highly improbable—we must let him out to the grass: he will find his own emetic.

It is needless to caution the reader against the use of strong purgatives or cathartics, nor against the use of the lancet, or, as a rule, the seton; they are all lowering in their nature, and that is precisely what we want to avoid.

Let the treatment be simple and rational. Whenever we see a young dog ailing, losing appetite, exhibiting catarrhal symptoms, and getting thin, we should not lose an hour. If he be an indoor dog, find him a good bed in a clean, well-ventilated apartment, free from lumber and free from dirt. If it be summer, have all the windows out or opened; if winter, a little fire will be necessary, but have half the window opened at the same time; only take precautions against his lying in a draught. Fresh air in cases of distemper, and indeed in fevers of all kinds, cannot be too highly extolled.

The more rest the dog has the better; he must be kept free from excitement, and care must be taken to guard him against cold and wet when he goes out-of-doors to obey the calls of Nature. The most perfect cleanliness must be enjoined, and disinfectants used, either permanganate of potash, carbolic acid, or iodine. If the sick dog, on the other hand, be one of a kennel of dogs, then quarantine must be adopted. The hospital should be quite removed from the vicinity of all other dogs, and as soon as the animal is taken from the kennel, the latter should be thoroughly cleansed and disinfected, and the other dogs kept warm and dry, well-fed and moderately exercised.

Food and Drink in Distemper.—Our object is to support the system without deranging the stomach, therefore, for the first three or four days let the food be light and easily digested. In order to induce the animal to take it, it should be as palatable as possible. For small dogs, milk or cream, eggs, arrow-root, rice, and beef-tea, may be given. For larger dogs you cannot have anything better than milk-porridge.* At all events, the dog must if possible, be induced to eat; he must not be "horned" unless there be great emaciation; he must not over-eat, but what he gets must be good. If the appetite is quite gone, and he turns up his nose at everything, beef-tea, eggs, milk and sherry in small quantities must be frequently administered by the spoon.

When the dog comes to be very low indeed, brandy may be substituted for the sherry. It must be diluted with water, and the quantity to be given will depend not only on the size of the dog, but upon the *benefits that seem to accrue from it.* As to drink, dogs usually prefer clean cold water, and we cannot do harm by mixing therewith a little plain nitre.

Medicine in Distemper.—Begin by giving a simple dose of castor-oil; just enough and no more than will clear out the bowels by one or two motions. Drastic purgatives, and medi-

---

* Oatmeal porridge made with milk instead of water.

cines such as mercury, jalap, aloes, and podophyllyn, cannot be too highly condemned. By the administration of any such, we are merely bleeding the patient through the intestinal capillary system. Avoid them. For very small toy-dogs, such as Italian Greyhounds, Yorkshire Terriers, &c.; we should not recommend even oil itself, but *manna*—one drachm to two drachms dissolved in milk. By simply getting the bowels to act once or twice, we shall have done enough for the first day, and have only to make the dog comfortable for the night.

On the next day begin a mixture such as the following:—

> ℞ Sp. æther.   ...   ...   ℳ xxx. ad ʒ iij.
> Vin. antimonial.   ...   ℳ iij. ad ℳ 40.
> Mucilag. tragacanth. ...   ʒ ij. ad ʒ j.   M.
> Give this thrice daily.

If the cough be very troublesome, and the fever does not run very high, the following may be substituted for this on the second or third day:—

> ℞ Syr. scillæ   ...   ...   ℳ x. ad ℳ ʒ j.
> Tinct. hyoscyam.   ...   ℳ x. ad ℳ 40.
> Sp. æther. nitros.   ...   ℳ x. ad ʒ j.
> Aq. camph.   ...   ...   q. s.   M.

A few drops of dilute hydrochloric acid should be added to the dog's drink, and two teaspoonfuls (to a quart of water) of the chlorate of potash. This makes an excellent fever drink, especially if the dog can be got to take decoction of barley—barley-water, instead of plain cold water. Williams speaks highly of the good effects of the hyposulphite of soda, in doses of from two to six grains. We have not yet given it a trial, so cannot speak from experience. It may be given instead of the fever mixture.

If there be persistent sickness and vomiting, the medicine must be stopped for a time. Small boluses of ice frequently administered will do much good, and doses of dilute prussic acid, from one to four drops in a little water, will generally arrest the vomiting.

If constipation be present we must use no rough remedies to get rid of it. A little raw meat cut into small pieces—minced, in fact—or a small portion of raw liver may be given if there be little fever; if there be fever, we are to trust for a time to injections of plain soap-and-water. Diarrhœa, although often a troublesome symptom, is, it must be remembered, generally a salutary one. Unless, therefore, it becomes excessive, do not interfere; if it does, give the simple chalk mixture three times a day, but no longer than is needful. It is better that our whole plan of treatment should be gentle and simple, and only harm can accrue from hastily rushing from one remedy to another. Injury to the dog is sure to result from such a course.

On the other hand, specifics had better be avoided.

The discharge from the mouth and nose is to be wiped away with a soft rag, or, better still, some tow, which is afterwards to be buried. The forehead, eyes, and nose, may be fomented two or three times a day with moderately hot water with great advantage.

It is not judicious to wet long-haired dogs much, but short-haired may have the chest and throat well fomented several times a day, and well rubbed dry afterwards. Heat applied to the chests of long-haired dogs by means of a flat iron will also effect good.

Williams recommends hydrate of chloral at night. Hydrate of chloral, in our opinion, ought to be expunged from the Pharmacopæia.* Sometimes it may do good, but oftener evil, because brain symptoms are apt to follow its use, and also great nervous prostration.

The Complications of Distemper.—See under their proper headings. Some authorities make different kinds of distemper, such as head or brain distemper, nervous distemper, belly distemper, &c. &c. This classification, however, is calculated to make the general reader lose sight of the real symptoms and causes of the malady.

There is only one form of distemper, and the lesions of other organs are its complications.

Supposing no very severe complication to have arisen, you may begin, as soon as the fever abates and there is some show of depression, to give tonics. The following is an excellent one :—

> ℞ Quinæ ... ... gr. ¼ ad gr. iij.
> Pulv. rhei. ... ... gr. ij. ad gr. x.
> Ext. tarax. ... gr. iij. ad gr. xx.
> Ft. bolus. M.
> Give three times a day.

If there be much heat on the top of the head and brow, we usually substitute this—

> ℞ Bebeerin. sulph. ... ... gr. j. ad gr. v.
> Rosæ conf. ... ... q. s.
> Ft. bolus.

During convalescence good food, cod-liver oil, moderate exercise, fresh air, and protection from cold. These, with an occasional mild dose of castor-oil or rhubarb, are to be our sheet-anchors.

---

* Hydrate of chloral was at first in great vogue with the profession. It is now used almost solely for cases of muscular pain.

CHAPTER VIII.

DISEASES OF THE NERVOUS SYSTEM.

JUST as the arteries given off by the great aorta divide and subdivide, and go on dividing and subdividing, like the branches of a great oak-tree, until they end in the minutest capillaries, so minute that we cannot pierce the skin with the finest needle without thrusting the point of it through some one or more of the ultimate ramifications of the largest artery in the body, so also do the branches of the nerves that are given off by the brain or spinal cord subdivide, and re-and-re-subdivide, until they end in branches more hair-like and tiny than the capillaries themselves. More hair-like and tiny, because every capillary artery, or capillary vein, is supplied with its nervelet. Again, as every artery is supplied with nerves, so does every nerve receive blood from some artery.

If we dissect any portion of the body, say the fore-arm, and search for the principal nerve, we shall find it generally running alongside the principal vein and artery—a simple-looking, whitish cord, composed of some soft, fatty kind of matter, and not unlike a violin string; and yet that which you behold is one of the telegraph wires of life and mind.

Each nerve contains, bound up in one sheath, two kinds of fibres, just as a thread might be composed of silk and cotton. One set of fibres is called the motor, the other the sensory. When we *will* do a particular action, say to clench the fist, the impression, the will, the wish, or the command, is sent from the brain along the *motor* fibres to the flexor muscles of the hand; contraction is the result, the muscular fibres obey the order, shorten themselves, and the fist is clenched. The sensory fibres, on the other hand, convey impressions to the brain. If a dog bites one, he quickly draws away his hand; but, quick as was the motion, the impression of pain had first to be flashed upwards to the brain by the sensory fibres, and another impression, the *will*, to be sent back again along the motor fibres, before the person had the power to draw the hand away. Every nerve, then, is a kind of double lectric wire.

Now this set of nerves that we have just mentioned are called the nerves of voluntary motion and sensation, because the will has power over them. But there is one other set of nerves in the body, over which the mind has no direct power. These are called the involuntary nerves, or the nerves of organic life, and they are even more important than the voluntary nerves, because they regulate and keep going the inner wheels of life itself. They spring from a row of ganglia, or nerve-knots, that lie alongside the spine. These ganglia seem, in fact, a whole row of smaller nerve-centres, and they give their nerves to all the internal organs of the body, keep up the peristaltic motion of the bowels, and the beating of the heart itself. They are of all importance in the animal economy, and it is to a great extent this system of nerves that suffer, when an animal is ill for want of properly oxygenated blood, or from bad feeding, or any other cause which causes the health to deteriorate.

When we have said that the nerves of motion and sensation and the nerves of organic life are intimately connected, and that the one system cannot suffer without the other being affected, we have done all that space will permit, and must now describe a few of the more common disorders of the nervous system.

First, however, just one word on what is called *reflex* action, the simplest example of which probably is the act of deglutition. The throwing a morsel of food backward towards the pharynx by means of the tongue is a voluntary action, but when the morsel has reached the top part of the pharynx, and tickles or excites the lining membrane, the action of swallowing is no longer under our control, for the excitement is carried by one set of nerves to the top of the spinal cord, induces there a motor-power which is transmitted along another set of nerves to the muscles of the pharynx, and thus the act is completed, and would be even if the power of the brain were destroyed, as in apoplexy.

The diseases of the nervous system of the dog, as at present understood, are by no means numerous, comprehending only paralysis, fits, inflammation of the brain, chorea, and asthma. Some writers include rabies in the list of nervous ailments. It should not be so included. However much the nervous system may suffer in rabies (or hydrophobia), it is clearly a disorder depending upon a morbid condition of the blood, caused by a specific poison.

I. *Paralysis.*

If the diseases of the nervous system are difficult to treat, and even difficult of intelligible comprehension in the human being, much more so are they in the lower animals, who can neither speak nor tell their feelings. Our treatment of these ailments in the dog must often be, to a great extent, speculative and empirical. Nervous diseases are not yet understood by the medical profession; our theory of causation is often at fault. Could we even manage to ascertain the physical conditions in a diseased brain or spinal cord, it would remove at least a portion of our difficulties; but they are hidden away from us under their bony shields, and we can only guess at their state and condition from the symptoms in other parts of the body, and these are often most deceptive. We find one day a certain train of symptoms, which after death and dissection we attribute to a certain condition of the brain or spinal marrow; we find another day the same train of symptoms in another case, and, behold! a post-mortem reveals to us not the same, but quite a different alteration in the nerve-centres. Another difficulty is that we are often unable to tell whether the symptoms of interference with the natural functions of the nerves which we see before us are due to a lesion in the nerves themselves or their centres, or whether they are merely sympathetic, and dependent upon disease or disorder in some other part of the body.[1]

The *symptoms* of paralysis or loss of power in a limb or in any group of muscles are familiar to every one. In a paralysed limb there is either entire or partial loss of power. It may arise from pressure on the roots of the nerve, pressure by effusion or otherwise upon the spinal cord or brain itself, from a diseased or altered condition of the component parts of the great nerve-centres, and it may arise from constipation in the case of the hind-quarters. In cases of facial paralysis, one side of the face only is paralysed. The symptoms are caused by some pressure upon or disease of the seventh pair of nerves. In this case there will be difficulty of mastication on the paralysed side, and constant dribbling away of saliva from the pendant lips.

Paralysis is sometimes the result of a blow or injury to the spinal column, causing either the fracture or displacement of a bone, or simple congestion. These cases may prove speedily fatal or get slowly well, according to the extent of the injury.

Another cause of paralysis, which we sometimes see in puppies, is caused by the irritation of teething—about the fourth or sixth month—or indigestion, and want of sufficient exercise.

Here it may be one limb or all the limbs that are affected; this is an example of reflex paralysis. Probably there may be along with this irritation of the digestive organs and vomiting.

Paralysis is sometimes present in, or comes on in, the latter stages of distemper, and must be looked upon as a very bad and ominous sign, indicating, as it does, effusion about the spinal cord, or congestion of the same.

Paralysis of the tongue is likewise not uncommon, the tongue lolling out to one side, and giving a very unsightly appearance indeed.

Treatment.—In the paralysis of distemper, begin the treatment by giving a mild purgative. Castor-oil and buckthorn will in this case do as well as any other, three parts oil, two parts buckthorn syrup, and one part poppy syrup. See that the medicine has acted, if not it must be repeated, but do not forget that the dog is weak. Keep his strength well up, and begin the administration of iodide of potassium and belladonna, as in this prescription—

$$
\begin{aligned}
&\text{R Potass. iod. ... ... } && \text{gr. j. ad gr. v.} \\
&\text{Extr. belladonn. ... } && \text{gr. } \tfrac{1}{16} \text{ ad gr. ij.} \\
&\text{Extr. gentian.... } && \text{gr. iij. ad gr. x.} \\
&\text{F}^\text{t.} \text{ bolus.} && \text{M.} \\
&\qquad\qquad \text{Ter. die.}
\end{aligned}
$$

Continue this treatment for a week; if little improvement, the dose is to be slightly increased, and cod-liver oil given.

Sometimes nux vomica may be used, but it is of doubtful efficacy in this form of paralysis.

Local applications are of no use, for the simple reason that the muscles are not the seat of disorder. It is their misfortune, not their fault. However, gentle friction or shampooing with the warm hand will go far to maintain the nutrition of the limbs, and prevent ataxy or wasting.

We must not forget to mention that a sort of convulsive palsy is sometimes brought on by the incautious use of mercury. Here the treatment is the warm bath, good diet, and small doses of iodide of potassium.

Only in old-standing cases do we use nux vomica, and we do not care to continue its use longer than three weeks without intermission. Give from $\frac{1}{8}$ to 2 grains of the extract in a pill, continuing its use with good food and other tonics. We have seen paralysis produced by even a small dose of nux vomica given in a case of constipation. The animal had a strange susceptibility to this drug on a previous occasion while under the treatment of a London vet., being attacked in the same way from the same cause. The paralysis in both instances was cured by an emetic.

Remember that in all cases of paralysis the urine must be attended to, and if the bladder is paralysed the elastic catheter must be used.

Rest, good food, beef-tea, eggs, and sherry in bad cases, and an occasional aperient if needed; and let the dog's bed be comfortable and *dry;* that is, kept dry, as he may wet it.

For *reflex* paralysis.—If from constipation, a few doses of the castor-oil and buckthorn mixture, as prescribed by Youatt, will generally remove it. If it is not retained, give about half an hour before the next dose from 1 to 3 drops of dilute hydrocyanic acid, rubbed up with 5 to 15 grains of the trisnitrate of bismuth. See that the teeth are not loose or decayed, if they are they must be extracted.

If paralysis continues after the bowels have been well opened, give the iodide of potassium;

and if good has been done after a week or two, to complete the cure small doses of nux vomica, carefully watching its effects. Hot fomentations and stimulating liniments will also do good, and in odd cases blistering. In some cases a seton over the spine might be tried. If the dog has worms, they must be removed. In puppies, after the paralysis is gone, cod-liver oil will be sufficient in itself to restore tone to the system, with good food and exercise.

2. Chorea.

Chorea, or St. Vitus's Dance as it is more frequently called, is a very common sequence to distemper, especially if that disease has been badly treated.

Pathology.—The profession are not agreed as to what is the real cause of this extraordinary disease. Post-mortem examinations have sometimes revealed alterations in the brain or spinal cord, but just as often they have revealed nothing unusual. Some pathologists consider it a blood disease ; it may be so, but we prefer including it among the diseases of the nervous system.

Symptoms.—Either the whole or only a part of the body is affected, as the neck or one leg, or both, or one side of the body alone. It is merely a form of irregular palsy, and probably it depends greatly upon a lowered condition of the vital force, with impoverished blood. The movements of the limbs consist in a sort of twitching or shaking motion, easily increased by acting on the dog's mind, either through fear or kindness. There may be, and very often are, spasmodic twitchings of one side of the face, or the whole head may shake up and down. Sometimes, long after distemper is past and done with, and the dog well and strong, and able to do a day's work, twitchings to a slight degree will continue.

Treatment.—If our view of the pathology of the disease be right, the treatment must naturally resolve itself into trying in every way to improve the general health. We must give nutritious diet and milk. We must give the dog as much out-door exercise, walking, running, or romping, as he can take. And we may try the bucket bath every morning, only gently at first lest we give too great a shock.

Nux vomica may also be tried ; it sometimes does good. Sulphate of iron and arsenic often does good, especially if combined with cod-liver oil, in *chronic* cases, be it remembered, and not for some time after distemper. The nitrate of silver pill (one-sixteenth to half a grain made into a pill with bread crumb and administered thrice a day) we have occasionally found service-able. The bowels must be carefully attended to, but purge as seldom as possible. The treatment of this disease is, on the whole, far from satisfactory.

3. Fits and Epilepsy.

A dog's nerves being altogether finely strung, he is very liable, among other complaints, to have fits.

Epilepsy is by no means an uncommon disorder, especially in young high-bred dogs. Whether a dog before the fit comes on has any premonitory symptoms or not, similar to the *aura epileptica* in the human being, we cannot be positive, but from the peculiar way the dog stops suddenly for a moment, may-be in the middle of a run, stares a few seconds, as if in some dread fear of impending evil, and then cries out and drops convulsed in every limb, we are inclined to think he has.

A fit may be either transitory or severe. In the former case the animal soon recovers the use of his senses, and comes on again much the same. But more frequently, after some spasmodic champing of the jaw, the dog falls down, stiff as death at first, and with outstretched legs and arched back and neck (*opisthotonos*) ; then, in a few seconds, the convulsions come on in every limb, the dog foams at the mouth, sometimes the tongue is cut, urine or fæces, or both, pass involuntarily, and a strange vacant look about the eyes, if open, which they usually are. This is one fit, and, after a longer or shorter period, the dog gradually recovers, seems to wonder at first where he is, and what you have been doing to him, but he is soon himself again, and either gets up or falls asleep. It will be well indeed if he does not soon have another, and perhaps many more, until death itself ensues.

Causes of Fits.—Mal-nutrition is certainly the principal cause, although injuries to the spinal cord may produce them. There are, of course, many other lesions of the nervous system, that at all events have been blamed for producing fits. In young dogs, blood-poisoning from distemper often induces them; worms do so likewise, so does the irritation from teething and constipation. So, too, will any unusual excitement or exercise if the dog is suffering from general debility. You sometimes find them in a bitch that has been badly fed and over-suckled.

Treatment.—The treatment resolves itself into that during the fits, and that during the interval. The first is simple enough. We have only to take care the poor animal does not injure himself. A piece of short stick may be placed between the jaws, and little else can be done, except keeping meddlesome people at bay. You may use cold water to the head, but not to the body; no bucket douche. We have often seen dogs killed through it.

The treatment after the fit consists in keeping the poor animal quiet for a short time, and we must then set about at once and in earnest, if we would have the dog's life spared, to improve his general health. Have we been feeding him regularly? Are his bowels regularly opened? Has he enough exercise? Does he suffer from teething or worms? We must ask ourselves such questions as these, and when we find any seeming cause for the fits, endeavour to remove it.

Gentle purgatives will do good to begin with, but if carried too far they will do positive injury. The feeding must be generous. The exercise must be gentle. All sorts of excitement must be most carefully avoided. Bleeding, blistering, and setonising, are very useful, if one wishes *speedy death to the dog.*

Let the dog have plenty of animal food, and milk or butter-milk, and let him sleep out of doors well protected from the cold. The bucket-bath of a morning, which we have found do good in chorea, we here hesitate to use. Cod-liver oil can be highly recommended; and if the dog is recovering from distemper, quinine may be added. Bromide of potassium, half a grain to five grains, three times a day, conjoined with some bitter tonic, we have also known do good, but it must be given a long time.

If the dog has quite got over distemper, that is, if the feverish stage has passed, and weakness only remains, a pill like that which follows may be given thrice a day, and continued for some weeks.

℞ Ext. belladonn. ... ... gr. $\frac{1}{8}$ ad gr. ij.
Ext. gent. ... ...⎫
Ext. quass. ... ...⎭ ā ā gr. j. ad gr. v.
M.

Sulphate of zinc is also a good nervine tonic. From half a grain to five grains made into a pill with extract of quassia, and given three times a day for weeks, administering now and then a mild laxative.

4. *Asthma.*

Asthma, which was formerly looked upon as purely a lung disease, is now well known to be of nervous origin. The disorder literally consists in a spasmodic contraction of the muscular fibres of the bronchial walls, and in the dog is nearly always the result of reflex action.

The causes usually assigned by medical men and veterinary practitioners for the spasm, and consequent dyspnœa, are very many, such as hepatisation, or solidification of a portion of lung tissue, emphysema or air in the lung, disease of the diaphragm, nervous ailments, heart disease, &c. One or more of these disorders may be present certainly, but in the dog we are convinced it is nearly always produced from indigestion, brought about by over or irregular feeding, indulgence in the delicacies of the table, and want of proper exercise. Gastric disturbance is set up, the irritation is carried along the pneumo-gastric to the medulla oblongata, and reflected thence by motor filaments to the lungs.

Symptoms.—Although the animal may be as a rule a sufferer from shortness of breathing, and is often troubled with a dry, harsh cough, it is only at times that the paroxysmal fit comes on, and usually some time after a heavy meal. The dog may be observed previously to be more dull than usual, but the fit may come on without any warning whatever. There is difficulty of breathing, which gradually increases, until actual suffocation seems imminent. The fit wears off again as gradually as it came, ending with cough and a hacking sound; the spasm wears off, there is secretion of mucus from the lungs, and such relief that the poor animal usually falls asleep. During the fit the dog's body is cold, and his pulse feeble.

Dogs that are the subjects of asthma are not only apt to have dyspnœa on any exertion, but they are of a coarse habit of body altogether, and may be troubled with skin disease in some form. The coat is rough and dry, and, especially in old dogs, the hair comes off in patches about the loins and rump. The bowels are irregular, and the appetite not lost but depraved. The dog prefers dainties, and while refusing good wholesome food, he appears hungry enough when flesh is offered him. Combined with other symptoms, there may be piles and chronic bronchitis, either one or both.

Diagnosis.—The peculiar nature of the breathing, which is a struggle for breath, the anxiety of the countenance, the staring eye, and general distress, make the diagnosis simple even to the tyro.

Prognosis.—This is favourable if the dog is attended to after the first attack, and especially if he be a young dog. In old standing cases a cure is far from certain, not that death ever takes place during the actual fit, but asthma never goes on long without being complicated with other disorders that prove fatal in the long run.

Treatment.—1. In order to cut short the fit, recourse must first be had either to an emetic—common salt, or sulphate of zinc, or powdered ipecacuanha, if we have reason to believe that the dog has been gluttonising; if, on the other hand, he has been suffering previously from constipation, the rectum must be unloaded by means of a large enema or clyster of simply soap and water. Afterwards you may use either of the following draughts—

> ℞ Tinct. belladonn. ... ... ℳ v. ad ℳ xxx.
> Sp. chlorof. ... ... ℳ v. ad ℳ xx.
> Iod. potass. ... ... gr. v. ad gr. xx.
> Aq. camph. ... ... q. s.
> Ft. haustus. M.

> ℞ Sol. mur. morph. ⎫ ā, ā, ℳ v. ad ℳ xx.
> Sp. chlorof. ⎬
> Aq. camph. ... ... q. s.
> Ft. haust. M.

The latter may be repeated in half an hour if necessary. The effect of these may often be aided by giving the animal a few whiffs of chloroform, or by slowly igniting common match or nitre paper under or near to the dog's nose.

2. The treatment during the intervals between each fit is of the greatest importance. Should the dog's bowels be confined, or the stools any way unhealthy, we must, on the morning after, begin our treatment by administering a dose of castor oil. He must not be over-dosed, however, for aperients always increase the tendency to dyspepsia, if any such exist ; besides, they weaken an animal, and this must be avoided.

The compound rhubarb (or Gregory's) powder may be given once a day in doses of from ten to forty grains, made into a bolus with a little soft soap and a little of any simple extract.

Having regulated the bowels, we must trust in some measure to tonics, or tonics and alteratives combined, remembering however that medicine alone will not regenerate the dog to that state of health which will render asthmatic fits impossible. The animal must have (1) regular exercise, he must be taken out at the same time every morning, and have two hours at least of good romping or running daily. He must be kept in the open air as much as possible, and for this purpose the kennel should be out of doors in some sheltered situation. (2) Before he goes out every morning he must have a cold shower or bucket bath, and a rub down with a rough towel. (3) His diet must be altered *in toto*, and it must be diminished in quantity, but be upon the whole nourishing. (4) Any form of skin disease which the animal suffers from will be usually of an ekzematous kind—for its treatment *vide* article cn ekzema. (5) As to medicine: if the dog is much troubled with cough, some degree of chronic bronchitis is doubtless present, squills or ipecacuanha would give ease, or solution of morphia, or paregoric, but the latter two must not be given in too large doses. At the same time tonics may be given. As a rule small doses of quinine do good, or quinine with iron or cod-liver oil if the animal be thin, or any of the bitter tonics, the object being to increase the appetite, improve the blood, and get the dog into a better habit of body generally.

We mentioned alteratives ; we usually combine these with tonics, and have found most good come from the use of iodide of potassium and arsenic, the iodide to be given in conjunction with quinine—

R Iod. potass. ...	...	gr. $\frac{1}{2}$ ad gr. iij.
Quinæ ...	...	gr. $\frac{1}{8}$ ad gr. 1$\frac{1}{2}$.
Ext. bellad. ...	...	gr. $\frac{1}{16}$ ad gr. $\frac{1}{2}$.
Ext. tarax. ...	...	gr. iij. ad gr. x.
F^t pil. j.		M.

Ter die.

Give this for three weeks, after which change your tonic for a fortnight for some simple bolus—

R Zinci. sulph. ...	...	gr. $\frac{1}{2}$ ad gr. v.
Ext. tarax. ...	...	gr. iij. ad gr. x.
Ext. gentian. ...	...	gr. ij. ad gr. v.
F^t pil. j.		M.

Ter die.

Arsenic may be tried instead of the iodide in cases where there is any determination to the skin and ekzematous humours. The simple liquor arsenicalis is to be preferred. Full directions for its administration are laid down under the treatment for ekzema.

CHAPTER IX.

INTERNAL PARASITES.

THE importance of the study of helminthology (the science which discourses of internal parasites or worms) to the veterinary practitioner can scarcely be over-estimated. To the dog-fancier, the kennelman, and, indeed, to every one who possesses an animal of the canine species, the subject we have now to treat of is one of very great moment indeed. The amount of injury done annually, not only to our sporting dogs but to dogs of all breeds, and the amount of disease and death caused by internal parasites, is almost incalculable. Yet much of this mischief is preventible, and it is the duty of dog-fanciers and owners to do all they can to stay the evil.

Nor is it our dogs alone that suffer. That were bad enough, but many thousands of our precious sheep fall victims every year to diseases directly engendered from contact with the larvæ of the internal parasites of dogs. We wish we could say that the evil ended here, but we must go a step further, and state that hundreds of human beings die annually of that painful racking illness occasioned by hydatid tumours of the liver caused indirectly by our friend the dog.

There may be some of our readers to whom the subject of internal parasites may possess much interest, these we refer to the works of Dr. Cobbold, a gentleman whom we have to thank for many an hour's pleasant and profitable reading.

Says Leuchart, referring to the amount of irritation, congestion, and even inflammation, which parasites gives rise to in the human frame, "The most striking example of the truth of these statements is afforded by the trichinæ which, on their passage into the intestinal canal, induce a malignant enteritis, with the production of false membranes, and lead to appearances which have a great resemblance to typhus."

In a case of trichinosis, Leuchart has seen as many as 300,000 of these spiral worms in half an ounce of the flesh of a corpse!

This terrible disease is produced from eating the under-done flesh of such animals as swine that happen to give a lodgment to the trichinæ. But it is with the parasites of the dog we have more especially to do at present.

"Of the encysted parasites," says Leuchart, "the dog above all other animals supplies us with germs. It is the dog that favours the spread of Pentastomum denticulatum, Cysticercus tenuicollis, and echinicoccus, from the development within the nasal sinuses, of Pentastomum tænioides, and in its (the dog's) intestine of Tœnia marginata and Tœnia echinicoccus."

"But," adds Leuchart, "even the muscle trichinæ of men may in some cases be communicated from the dog to man."

Most canine surgeons make three different classes of worms found in the dog, namely, the round-worm, the tape-worm, and the maw-worm.

Now, these "maw-worms," which we are all so well accustomed to see crawling over the stools of dogs, are *not* a distinct species. They are nothing more or less than the "semi-inde pendent segments of two of the largest species of tape-worm which infests the dog—the Tœnia marginata and Tœnia serrata."

1. *Round-worms.*

The principal round-worm found in the dog is called the Ascaris marginata. Cobbold tells us that in our own English dogs it occurs in seventy out of a hundred. In the autopsical examination of 500 dogs, Dr. Krabbe of Copenhagen found round-worms in 122, while out of 144 dogs dissected at Vienna, 104 were found to contain this round-worm.

Symptoms.—Sometimes these are very alarming indeed, for the worm itself is occasionally seized with the mania for foreign travel, and finds its way into the throat or nostrils, causing the poor animal to become perfectly furious, and inducing such pain and agony that it is an act of charity to end its life.

The worms may also crawl into the stomach, and give rise to great irritation, but are usually dislodged therefrom by the act of vomiting.

Their usual habitat, however, is the small intestines, where they occasion great distress to their host. The appetite is always depraved and voracious. At times there is colic, with sickness and perhaps vomiting, and the bowels are alternately constipated or loose. The coat is harsh and staring, there usually is short dry cough from reflex irritation of the bronchial mucous membrane, a bad-smelling breath, and emaciation, or at least considerable poverty of flesh.

The disease is most common in puppies and in young dogs. The appearance of the ascaris in the dog's stools is, of course, *the* diagnostic symptom. No doubt the reader has seen them : about the length of ordinary earth-worms, but perfectly round, a palish pink colour, and tapering at both ends. The females are larger than the males.

Treatment of Round-worms.—We have cured many cases with areca-nut powder (betel-nut). Dose, ten grains to two drachms. We have also at our command calomel, in conjunction with jalap or scammony ; kamela, dose from fifteen grains to three drachms ; and turpentine, dose from twenty drops to a drachm and a half, beaten up with yolk of egg.

But areca-nut does better for tape-worm, so do some of the others that we have just mentioned ; and we cannot do better than trust to pure santonine for the expulsion of round-worms. The dose is from one grain for a Toy, up to six grains for a Mastiff. Mix it in a little butter, and stick it well back in the roof of the dog's mouth. He must have fasted previously for twelve hours, and had a dose of castor oil the day before. In four or five hours after he has swallowed the santonine, let him have a dose of either olive-oil or decoction of aloes. Dose, two drachms to two ounces or more. Repeat the treatment in five days.

The perfect cleanliness of the kennel is of paramount importance.

The animal's general health requires looking after, and he may be brought once more into good condition by proper food and a course of vegetable tonics. If wanted in show condition we have cod-liver oil to fall back upon, or extract of malt.

Nematode worms are sometimes found in the hearts of dogs, especially in India, where we have often seen dogs assisting the cows, adjutants, and blue-bottles, in the work of scavenging. The animals either die suddenly, or after a few hours of excruciating agony. The worm so found is called the Filaria immitis. There is, of course, no remedy for the disease induced by its presence in so vital an organ as the heart.

Sometimes, though very rarely, a nematode worm is found in the kidney of the dog, producing death from disintegration of that organ. It is called the giant strangle (Estrangylus gigas). It is shaped like the common round-worm, and in some animals, for instance the North American mink, this terrible parasite has, according to Cobbold, been found to exceed a yard in length, and equal one's little finger in thickness.

There is a round-worm which at times infests the dog's bladder, and may cause occlusion of the urethra; a whip-worm inhabiting the cæcum, another may occupy a position in the mucous membrane of the stomach, some infest the blood, and others the eye.

2. *Tæniæ or Tape-worms.*

Probably one of the commonest of cestodes or tape-worms, and one with which many of my readers are doubtless only too familiar, is the cucumerine (Tœnia cucumerinus).

This is a tape-worm of about fifteen inches in average length, although we have taken them from Newfoundland pups fully thirty inches in length. It is a semi-transparent entozoon, each segment is long compared to its breadth, and narrowed at both ends. Each joint has, when detached, an independent existence.

And here is a curious and noteworthy circumstance with regard to the propagation of tape-worms. These animals live for one portion of their existence, and in one state, in one animal, and for another in another. Indirectly, tape-worms are generated from eggs; that is the fully-developed tape-worm lays a number of eggs, each of which may contain one or many embryo entozoons; but this egg must first be swallowed by an intermediary bearer—by some small animal—where it is hatched, and where the embryos live as guests until their host happens to be swallowed by a larger animal, and in the body of this latter it is developed into the mature or complete tape-worm.

To give an example. A dog is infested with the common cucumerine we have just described; well, a segment or two escapes *ab ano* whilst the dog is lying among his straw. As this segment has a semi-independent existence it manages to crawl away up through and over the dog's coat, and as it moves it deposits or drops its eggs. Now, if this dog is not only infested with tape-worm but also with the Trichodectes latus, or common dog louse, probably some of these disgusting parasites will play the part of intermediary bearer or host to the embryo tape-worms, for they swallow the eggs which the entozoon has dropped, and in the body of the trichodectes the eggs are hatched, and little six-hooked embryo cucumerines are the result.

The dog louse, infested with the larvæ, may drop into the water dish, and thus be swallowed by other dogs; or it may be introduced into their bodies in several other ways we need not specify. But, getting there, it soon becomes developed into the perfect tape-worm.

We see, then, that without this intermediary bearer, the internal parasite—the tapeworm— would not be reproduced. This surely teaches us to keep our dogs' coats and their kennels clean, if we would save the poor animals much unnecessary suffering and pain.

Every one has heard of the gid in sheep, known in different parts of the country as the "sturdy," "vertigo," "staggers," "turnside," or the "whirls." Well, if the brain of an animal that has died of this disease be opened, there will be found therein what are called hydatids or cysts, little bladder-shaped objects. These are nothing more or less than small colonies of the larvæ of the very large tapeworm, called the Tœnia cœnurus. We have seen this parasite nearly two yards long, and repeatedly over one yard. Each gid hydatid is loaded, so to speak, with hundreds of tapeworm heads, growing from a common centre, and every head, if introduced into the dog's body, is capable of being developed into a tapeworm.

The dog often becomes infested with this parasite from eating sheeps' brains; and dogs thus afflicted and allowed to roam at pleasure over fields and hills where sheep are fed, sow the seeds of gid in our flocks to any extent. We know too well the great use of Collie dogs to the shepherd or grazier, to advise that dogs should not be employed as assistants, but surely it would be to their owner's advantage to see that they were kept in a state of health and cleanliness.

Says Cobbold: "The propagation of entozoa in general and of tapeworms in particular, is intimately connected with, and absolutely dependent upon, the promiscuous association of different kinds of animals; and as regards the production of parasitism amongst domesticated animals used as food, it is perfectly certain that the tapeworms of the dog play a most conspicuous part."

Striking language this from so great an authority, and affording much food for thought.

One of the commonest tape-worms of the dog is the Tœnia marginata. It grows to an immense length. The dog becomes infested from the sheep. The Tœnia echinococcus is another, very destructive to animal life in the larval state. The Tœnia serrata is the tape-worm most commonly found in our sporting dogs. The larva of this entozoon is found in the intestines of the rabbit and hare.

We must be content with merely mentioning another parasite, the Bothrocephalus latus or pit-headed broad tape-worm. If a dog is infested with these he may give it to mankind in the following way. He may, by bathing in a pond, impurify it, the eggs of the parasite may adhere to watercresses, which may be eaten by man; dogs may also infest celery, lettuce, endive, fruit, as strawberries, &c., &c., and thus the eggs be introduced into the stomach of the human subject.

Treatment.—We ought to endeavour to prevent as well as to cure.

We should never allow our dogs to eat the entrails of hares or rabbits.

Never allow them to be fed on raw sheep's intestines, nor the brains of sheep.

Never permit them to lounge around butchers' shops, nor eat offal of any kind.

Let their food be well cooked, and their skins and kennels kept scrupulously clean.

Dogs that are used for sheep and cattle ought, twice a year at least, to go under treatment for the expulsion of worms, whether they are infested or not; an anthelmintic would make sure, and could hardly hurt them.

For the expulsion of tapeworms we depend mostly on areca-nut. In order that the tapeworm should receive the full benefit of the remedy, we order a dose of castor oil the day before in the morning, and recommend no food to be given that day, except beef-tea or mutton-broth. The bowels are thus empty next morning, so that the parasite cannot shelter itself anywhere, and is therefore sure to be acted on by the drug.

Infusion of cusso is sometimes used as an anthelmintic, so is wormwood, and the liquid extract of male fern, and in America spigelia root and pumpkin seeds.

Ground glass is dangerous, and often ineffective. The best tonic to give in cases of worms is the extract of quassia.

℞ Extr. quassiæ ... ... gr. ij. ad gr. x.
    Extr. hyoscyam. ... ... gr. j. ad gr. v.
Fᵗ pil. j.   M.
Ter die.

The action of the quassia here is anthelmintic as well as tonic, and the hyoscyamus when continued for some time has a gentle action on the bowels, and being a narcotic, it is probably also an anthelmintic. We have the opinion that many narcotics are.

CHAPTER X.

DISEASES OF THE SKIN.

SKIN DISEASES in the dog constitute no inconsiderable proportion of all the ailments the animal is subject to.

It is only of late years, however, that much interest has been taken in this branch of canine medicine. If we look into the older works on dog diseases, we shall find very imperfect accounts of it indeed. More recently, Mayhew describes five different forms of skin diseases; but we cannot agree on the whole with the style of his treatment, and even he himself has frankly hinted that he was in a manner working in the dark.

It is only very lately, however, that the researches of such men as Fleming, Gruby, and Mr. Hunting, aided by the microscope and experiment, have enabled us to adopt a better and more useful classification, and really rational treatment. To Mr. Hunting's excellent paper on "Follicular Mange," indeed, we are indebted for present success in the cure of a class of most troublesome cases, which, in times gone by, we had often looked upon as beyond the power of medicine to remedy. To a great extent, too, we also follow his plan of treatment in other forms of cutaneous disease, modified or altered at times to the circumstances and constitution of the canine patient.

Before going on to describe a few of the most important cutaneous affections, let us take a brief glance at the skin itself, and see what is its structure, and what are its nature and functions.

The skin, with its appended hairs, is the outside protective covering of an animal's body. It is composed of two portions or layers. The outer, usually called the scarf skin, or, more refinedly speaking, the cuticle or epidermis, is devoid of feeling, as it is unsupplied with nerves which, along with the minute capillary blood-vessels, end in the inner or true skin. And it is this inner skin that secretes the outer, in several layers of nucleated cells, those cells nearest the true or sentient skin being rounded, those exposed to the air being flattened, and peeling off in dust or dandruff.

Under the epidermis lies the true skin, closely joined to the structures under it by areolar or connective tissue. The outer surface of the true skin is rather peculiar. It is not smooth, but is covered with minute elevations called papillæ. They increase the sensation of touch, many of them having very small nerves distributed through them; other papillæ have no nerves, but blood-vessels instead, and as they project some distance into the epidermis they are believed by physiologists to nourish it.

Now there are one or two things, both of interest and moment, to be noted about the cutis, or true skin.

Herein are situated the sweat-glands, also the oil-glands, and the hair-follicles. In man, and in many other animals, the sweat-glands are very tortuous; in the dog they are more simple, opening by a funnel-shaped aperture or pore externally in the epidermis. These are the glands which secrete the perspiration. In man, and also in the horse, there are two states of perspiration, viz., sensible or visible, and insensible or invisible perspiration. One or other of these states is always present, unless sweating has been temporarily checked by disease. In the dog, however, the sensible or visible perspiration is never present,* owing probably to the more open condition of the mouths of the pores, which permit the sweat to be evaporated as soon as secreted; and this has given rise to the erroneous notion that the dog is an animal who never sweats, or "sweats only with his mouth."

Perspiration has it uses, two of which it may be sufficient to mention here. First it carries off from the body matters which if retained would give rise to disease, as, for example, the poisonous acid which is supposed to occasion gout and rheumatism; and secondly, it cools the body when heated by the process of evaporation, with which most people are well acquainted.

The sebaceous or oil glands have a different office to perform. They secrete a fatty or oily matter, which, through their tiny ducts, is poured into the tube from which the hair grows, lubricating not only this passage, but creeping out and along the hair itself, down to its very end. The coat of the dog is thus protected from wet or moisture. In some dogs this secretion is more abundant than in others. It is especially so in the Newfoundland and in the Scottish Collie. It is also more abundant in health than in disease; its absence gives rise to the harsh, dry, staring coat we see in dogs that are suffering from illness.

The hair-follicles are the tubes in which the hairs grow. At the bottom of each tube is situated a small vascular papilla or elevation, and on this the hair is planted. A hair is simply a quill on a small scale, being supplied with nutrition and colouring-matter from the papilla on which it grows.

The thickness of the skin varies on different parts of the body. On the back, head, chest, and indeed on every portion requiring protection, it is thick; on the inside of the thighs and lower part of the abdomen it is much thinner, and to this arrangement may be attributed the fact that eruptions are much more common on the latter regions.

The principal use of the skin is to form a protective envelopment to the whole body, which, although permitting the free exit of the perspiration, is still proof against the absorption of many of the most virulent of poisons.

On the other hand, it must not be forgotten that the skin is to a certain extent an absorbent. It has been proved beyond question that the skin is even, in some measure, a respiratory organ, and this in itself should convince us of the value of keeping our animals as much as possible in the pure open air, and the danger of keeping them shut up in badly-ventilated kennels or apartments; for the skin is just as capable of absorbing deleterious as non-deleterious gases or matters from the atmosphere surrounding it. The absorbent power of the skin is retarded by the cuticle; it is the inner or true skin that is so highly absorbent, that we often introduce medicines such as morphia or belladonna through it into the system, having first removed the cuticle by blistering.

Having seen how delicately constructed the skin is, and how sentient, with its bundles of arteries, veins, and nerves, its delicate glands, its minute pores—over 2,000 to the square inch— and even its tiny muscular system, we need not wonder that it is very liable to disease in itself, and also, if its secretions be interfered with and checked, that it becomes the cause of disease in other organs of the body.

In this division of the treatise we shall content ourselves with describing

1. The more common non-contagious diseases.

---

* Except in cases of fever, when it is abundant on the inside of the thighs.

2. The commonest contagious diseases ;

3, and briefly, the external or hair parasites found on the dog.

N.B.—Having already mentioned that skin diseases form a large proportion of the ailments incidental to canine life, it may be as well, before describing their general symptoms and treatment, to state that they are seldom or never incurable, even in old dogs, and that the common notion of the disease getting into the blood is quite erroneous. We have known cases cured in six weeks which had lasted half that number of years.

I. NON-CONTAGIOUS DISEASES.

1. *Erythema.*

By the term erythema we mean that condition of redness with slight inflammation of the skin, the deeper tissues underneath not being involved.

Causes.—The causes are usually local and mechanical, although they may be constitutional, and the result of cold and wet. Damp and dirt and carelessness in grooming often produce *erythema simplex* in Poodle dogs, Newfoundlands, and in most long-coated dogs. The hair gets matted and felted, and under the matting the skin will be found red, inflamed, and in a most unhealthy condition, causing great uneasiness to the poor dog, either from pain or itching, or both alternating. We see it sometimes between the wrinkles of well-bred Pugs, Mastiffs, and Bulldogs, and also between the scrotum and inside of the thigh in Greyhounds and Foxhounds. Bad feeding in gross dogs, who get but little exercise, may be instanced as a constitutional cause of erythema.

Symptoms.—The symptoms are simple enough, so that any one may know the disease. They are much the same as those of chafe in the human being. There is at first simply redness, with very slight tumefaction, generally traceable to some local cause ; when the skin breaks there is discharge of serum, or in some bad cases pus ; the skin becomes thickened and sometimes cracks, and if the disease is situated in any part that the dog can reach with his tongue, his careful attentions thereto will speedily draw attention to it.

Treatment.—The treatment of erythema greatly depends upon the cause. If the dog has been improperly fed, and weighs more than he ought to, regular proper feeding, with plenty of exercise, cleanliness, a mild course of tonics, and the morning bath, will speedily put an end to the mischief.

Local causes must be removed ; rest for hounds, along with a tonic, may be prescribed. Before the animal starts on a run the chafe should be anointed ; after he returns it ought to be washed and dusted with oxide of zinc, starch, fuller's-earth, or the violet powder of nurseries. In erythema of the wrinkles of Pugs, &c., the same treatment will be found serviceable. In dogs where the disease has been produced by matting of the hair, the coat must be clipped—taking care to protect the animal from cold afterwards. When the clipping has been accomplished, washing the inflamed parts with mild soap and lukewarm soft water will do good ; then, if there is much inflammation, poultices will be required, or the simple lotion of lead, of arnica tincture, or of brandy-and-water, may be sufficient to effect a cure.

2. *Erysipelas.*

Erysipelas is a disease of a more dangerous nature. It depends upon a deeper-seated inflammation than does erythema ; for in erysipelas we have not only the skin, but the underlying tissues involved, and infiltration first of serum, latterly of unhealthy pus.

Causes.—It is more frequent in gross, plethoric, soft-fleshed dogs, in whom it is often the result of a sudden check to the perspiration from immersion, and subsequent exposure to the cold. It is caused also by falls and blows and from wounds. The worst case we remember was in a Greyhound. The poor animal had taken a sudden affection for a butcher's sausages, and had been wounded by the proper owner's knife.

Symptoms and Treatment.—The symptoms are great pain in the part, redness, and swelling, with constitutional disturbance, dry nose, injected eye, heat of skin, staring coat, and heightened pulse. The treatment must be both local and constitutional. It will be as well to begin with a gentle purge of castor oil. The diet must be light at first. We cannot do wrong to give plenty of milk, and either boiled rice or oatmeal porridge, according to the fancy of our patient, but no meat. We cannot speak from experience of the treatment in the dog of giving large doses of the tincture of iron three or four times a day, but have often seen the very best results from it in human practice, and think it deserves a fair trial in canine. Port wine and quinine, or the liquid extract of cinchona, we recommend to be given from the commencement. Dose of the latter, five to thirty drops three times a day.

The local treatment consists in the application of repeated hot fomentations of poppy-heads. In the intervals, the application of a lotion consisting of the diacetate of lead, and sesqui-carbonate of ammonia, one drachm each, laudanum half an ounce, and camphor water one pint, will do good; or gentle inunction with an ointment containing morphia may be tried. If pus should come to be formed, the earlier free incisions are made the better; and after the wounds are carefully fomented, a large charcoal poultice will greatly assist nature in completing the cure.

3. *Prurigo.*

We give the name of *Prurigo simplex* to an ailment in the dog which, in most cases, it must be confessed, is more of a symptom than a real disease. The dog is troubled with a constant and evidently distressing itching in many parts of the body, and there is very little to show for it. The skin may be found scurfy, and probably in some parts slightly thickened, and the hair or coat is usually not in good form.

Although it is well known that scratching in the dog is often a habit, and comes to be such a common one that the animal engages in the luxurious exercise when he is not thinking, still we always associate the disorder with some constitutional disturbance of the system. At all events, the habit is neither very polite nor agreeable, especially if the dog is a pet, and consequently it ought to be remedied.

No local treatment is required if there be little or no evidence of skin deterioration, but give tonics internally; carefully regulate the diet, which must be neither over-abundant nor over-stimulating. Insist upon plenty of exercise, and the daily use of the bucket-bath before a slight farinaceous breakfast. We never knew this treatment to fail, unless the dog is troubled either with *hæmorrhoids* or *worms*. This must in all cases of pruritis be ascertained and remedied.

4. *Ekzema.*

We had purposed describing a skin disease sometimes, though rarely, seen in the dog, and termed by medical men *lichen*, but as it resembles in many respects the disease at present under consideration, we refrain from doing so.

Ekzema—*synonyms:* Blotch or Surfeit, and *Red Mange.*—Of the two terms, blotch or surfeit, and red mange, we feel naturally inclined to give the former to the more simple kind or type of ekzema, retaining the latter name of red mange for the more virulent.

Of all cases of canine disorder that the veterinary surgeon is called upon to treat, none is more troublesome and less satisfactory than this same red mange. Till late years, the profession laboured under two mistakes concerning it: the first was that it was a contagious disorder, and the second that it could be cured by *specifics*. Practitioners know better nowadays, but the rage for so-called specifics is still rampant among the less well-informed dog fanciers, and consequently ekzema is a disease, or rather one of the diseases, on which dog quacks fatten.

Causes.—In the human being ekzema may arise from at least a dozen different causes, any one of which, or several combined, may produce the disease. In the dog—and the longer we live the more we are convinced of the truth of what we state—in the dog the disorder is nearly always the result of errors in diet and hygiene, producing debility and an impoverished state of the blood, combined with derangement of the whole system. Want of sufficient exercise is another common cause; want of cleanliness a third cause, to which may be added want of proper grooming, and a sluggish condition of the whole cuticular system. How can people who keep their kennels in a state of filth and foul air expect their dogs to be otherwise than mangy, especially if the only exercise the poor brutes get is a doleful walk up and down their own dirty yards, and their only bath the rain, which but tends to make matters worse?

Sudden alternations from heat to cold will tend to bring on the disorder in some dogs; so will grief. Although there are some who will pooh-pooh this latter cause as frivolous, it is none the less true.

Young dogs, and especially animals that have been much weakened by distemper, are prone to ekzema. The rapid growth, too, of puppies may cause a tendency to this form of skin disease. Mr. Hunting says feeding on dog cakes alone, or on oatmeal, often produces mange We do not quite agree with him, especially as regards the oatmeal, for we know of many healthy kennels where the animals are entirely fed upon oatmeal, and never have tasted flesh in their lives. Old gross dogs are very subject to it; the coat in some long-haired animals coming completely off, leaving the thickened, scarred, and unsightly skin quite naked and open to view. We have often known it form a very distressing sequela to distemper; in fact, any sudden lowering of the vital frame will produce the disorder.

Chronic ekzema is much more frequent about the time the animal is casting his coat.

Pathology.—Ekzema is a diseased condition of the skin, resulting from over-vascularity therein, more or less of tumefaction, and the exudation of serous matter, either alone, or combined with pus.

Diagnosis.—Ekzema is not dependent on a parasite either on or in the skin, consequently we have the microscope to guide us in our diagnosis. Otherwise we have the redness, the slight thickening, the exudation, desquamation, and the *itching*, for our guides.

Prognosis.—Should be guarded. It is a difficult disease to manage at the best, and it may return again and again, after being apparently perfectly cured. We have little doubt that some dogs acquire an ekzematous diathesis, and it is possible that in some cases the diathesis may be inherited.

Symptoms.—*Ekzema simplex* is the milder and more common form of the disorder, one of the earliest symptoms of which is the itchiness, as evinced by the animal scratching himself on every possible occasion. If on the back, or top of the shoulders, or probably the rump or tail, redness will be found, and the skin will not be so pliant as usual, small vesicles form, filled with serum or pus and serum; these, on breaking, form scabs, matting the hair together in lumps and patches, and these hairs are easily removed, leaving a wet exuding surface. Other parts of the body may be covered with dry furfuraceous scales, and again you may have larger solitary blebs or vesicles about the neck or behind the ears in long-haired dogs. In this form of ekzema there is but little if any constitutional disturbance; but an acute observer can easily see that the animal is not in perfect health. Sometimes a bare patch will speedily heal, appear scaly for a day or two, and then be seen to be covered with the young sprouting hairs.

Simple ekzema may, if not attended to, be speedily followed by the more acute or red mange of older writers. Here we have the same intense itching, or even more severe, accompanied by a greater amount of redness and inflammation, and at the same time constitutional disturbance. This form is well seen in some short-haired dogs, especially in the white Bull Terrier, where not only is the skin of a deep red, but even the hairs themselves change colour and die. The hairs fall off from the inflamed patches, which also give off a very offensive odour. The disease may become chronic and increase in severity. Not only is the chest, legs, scrotum, &c., affected, but the disorder extends upwards to the head and neck; the lips may be swollen, the ears affected, or the eyes bunged up.

The animal either loses all appetite, or it becomes fastidious; the whole alimentary canal also becomes affected, and the dog's stools are offensive and never of proper consistency. This state of affairs cannot continue long without producing great debility and loss of flesh, which may terminate in death itself.

There is another form of chronic ekzema which we have seen a good deal of in old dogs, and which sometimes indicates the beginning of the end, the up-break of the general system. It is more of the dry kind, there is abundant desquamation, great loss of hair, and a thickened hide. However, the appetite is generally good, sometimes even ravenous, and, bar the discomfort from the itching and probable want of sleep, the dog suffers little inconvenience.

We should not forget to mention that over-doses of mercury, and the incautious use of certain unguents, may produce a disease in every way resembling ekzema.

Treatment.—The treatment of a case of ekzema or red mange is by no means so easy as we could wish. Seeing, then, that for the most part red mange depends upon constitutional causes, we must at once set about correcting disordered functions, improving the blood and digestion, and giving tone to the whole system.

Our treatment must be both constitutional and local. We must attend especially to the organs of digestion. We cannot err by commencing our treatment with a moderate dose of opening medicine, to clear away offending matter. This simple aperient may be repeated occasionally—say once a week—and if diarrhœa be present, it may be checked by the addition of a little morphia, or dilute sulphuric acid, or any of the remedies suggested for the treatment of this complaint. Mr. Gamgee recommends the exhibition of the acetate of potash in this complaint. We have tried it, and have every reason to be satisfied with its effects, given in ten or fifteen-grain doses thrice a day for a small dog, up to forty for a large. The acetate of potash is an excellent derivation, being both diuretic and diaphoretic, but it must not be given in doses large enough to purge. Aperients are useful, but they are a class of medicines which are so often abused that we hesitate at times to recommend them. At the same time we may give a tonic pill like the following—

℞. Sulph. quinæ	...	...	gr. ½ ad gr. ij.
Sulph. ferri	...	...	gr. j. ad gr. v.
Ext. hyoscy.	...	...	gr. ½ ad gr. iij.
Ext. glyc.	...	...	q. s.
Fᵗ pil. j.		Ter die.	M.

After we have persevered for a week or two with this treatment, we may begin to give arsenic, but first let us say a word on

Diet in Ekzema.—We have only to remember that the blood is impoverished, and the strength below par. Whatever, therefore, the food used may be, it must be both nourishing and easy of digestion. Some alteration in the diet must necessarily be made, and if the appetite be lost, the dog may be coaxed to take extract of beef, soups, &c. *We must not lower*.

Exercise.—The dog cannot be too much in the open air, so long as he is kept dry and clean, but exercise must never be carried to the borders of fatigue.

We do not believe in beginning the exhibition of arsenic too soon. We prefer paying our first attentions to the digestive organs and state of the bowels. The form of exhibition which we have found suit as well as any is the tasteless Liquor Arsenicalis. It is easily administered. It ought to be given mixed with the food, as it ought to enter the blood with the chyle from the diet. It ought day by day to be gradually, not hurriedly, increased. Symptoms of loathing of food and redness of conjunctiva call for the cessation of its use for two or three days at least, when it is to be recommenced, at the same size of dose given when left off.

There are two things which seem to assist the arsenic, at least to go well with it : they are, iron in some form and cod-liver oil. The latter will be needed where there is much loss of flesh. A simple pill of sulphate of iron and extract of liquorice may be used. Dose of Liquor Arsenicalis, from one to six drops *ter die* to commence with, gradually increased to five to twenty drops.

Our local treatment is directed to keeping the animal clean, by occasionally washing him with lukewarm water and some very mild and non-irritating soap, such as Spratt's elegant preparation ; and allaying the itching and irritation. The latter we endeavour to accomplish by means of astringent lotions and ointments. Mild lotions of lead or zinc or even alum, patted frequently on the inflamed parts, will do great good. Sometimes they may also be beneficially painted with a weak solution of nitrate of silver—two grains to the ounce, and many other astringents may be tried ; or try a solution of carbonate of soda. Ointments sometimes irritate and mat the hair, become offensive, and do more harm than good ; in which cases their use is incompatible with perfect cleanliness. Mr. Erasmus Wilson, however, has solved this difficulty, and we cannot too highly recommend his benzoated oxide of zinc ointment, which any chemist can supply. This ointment must be plentifully employed, as one of its actions is to protect the inflamed surface. It does not prevent the use of heat-allaying lotions, however.

Briefly, then, what we have to remember in treating red mange is as follows :—(1) We must not begin the arsenic too soon. (2) Combine it with iron. (3) Stop it when it seems to be doing harm. (4) As little purging as you can possibly do with. (5) As little *washing*, and that of the mildest. N.B.—It is REST the skin wants. (6) Nourishing diet. (7) Exercise to be moderate ; and (8) Perfect cleanliness of the dog's food, his skin, kennel, and bed straw.

II.—CONTAGIOUS DISEASES.

1. *Mange Proper.*

We have sometimes wished that the word " mange " had never been invented. It is a word that really expresses little or nothing, and yet it is a dangerous word, because it confuses two diseases quite different in their causes, different in their symptoms, and altogether different in their treatment.

Yet the older writers made quite a hotch-potch both in describing the symptoms of and in the treatment of their so-called mange.

Just let us see for a moment what Youatt—a man deservedly honoured as an authority upon many other ailments of the horse and dog, though notably the horse—says about mange. He begins by confessing that mange is caused by various tribes of animalculæ burrowing under the skin, and he seems to favour the idea that these animalculæ, if placed on the skin of a healthy individual, will produce a form of *scabies*. Of this we shall speak presently. Then he says a mangy bitch will be liable to produce mangy puppies. If he had said an ekzematous bitch may produce ekzematous puppies he would not have been wrong; but as true mange depends upon a skin parasite, the puppies cannot catch the disease until after they are born. Presently he says, "Close confinement and salted food are frequent causes of mange." Again, this is not the true mange but ekzema, vulgarly called red mange. "The scabby mange," he goes on to say—and now he has clearly got on to ekzema, and the parasites have crawled away somewhere out of sight entirely—"the scabby mange is a frequent form which this disease assumes. It assumes a pustular and scabby form in the red mange, particularly in white-haired dogs, when there is much and painful inflammation." Again he says, "A peculiar eruption, termed surfeit, which resembles mange, is sometimes the consequence of exposure to cold after a hot, sultry day." Mr. Youatt is right here, reader; this form of ekzema will come on suddenly either in a child or delicate young dog, from any sudden lowering of vitality. Then he describes the symptoms of acute "mange" (ekzema) very well, and, with the exception of "bleeding" (just fancy bleeding a dog in ekzema) his internal and local treatment is rational till he comes to the tobacco dip. Tobacco is lowering and easily absorbed by a broken skin; but, to his credit be it told, he advises both this and mercurial preparations to be used but sparingly. And two other remarks he makes are well worthy of transcription—viz., the sentences, "A change in the mode of feeding will often be useful," and "The diarrhœa produced by mercury often has a fatal effect."

Mr. Youatt says, "Mr. Blaine had a favourite Setter who had virulent mange for five years." And no wonder, if dressings and dips were alone used, and the disease was all the time chronic ekzema.

Again, still on the subject of mange, and referring to the year 1843, Mr. Youatt speaks of it assuming a form or type having for its prominent symptoms "the sudden appearance of redness of the skin, and exudation from it, and actual sores attending the falling off of the hair, and an itching that seemed to be intolerable"—ekzema, of course, and not parasitical mange.

Now, if we bear in mind that the older writers on veterinary medicine were not by any means too well informed with regard to nerve pathology, we cannot wonder for a moment that these cases of intense itching which came before them should be put down to the action of parasites, especially when sometimes there was but little inflammation, or anything else seen on the skin to account for it; whereas the itching might have depended upon some form of ekzema, or it might have been altogether of a reflex character, depending on some distant source of irritation, probably worms in the bowels. No wonder, then, that in Mr. Youatt's cases, where there was that "intolerable itching, with very little to show for it," that "all unguents were thrown away upon them," and that "lotions of corrosive sublimate, decoction of bark, infusions of digitalis or tobacco effected but little good," and that "purgatives and iodide of potassium" did "generally succeed."

Mr. Mayhew, on the other hand, in his description of the various kinds of mange, is much nearer the mark, and his treatment is at least rational; still, even his classification could afford to be considerably more specific.

Mange proper.—As this disease is caused by parasites that either crawl upon the skin or burrow in under the cuticle, and is quite analogous to itch in the human being, we should much have preferred that name or scabies for the disease. However, in this case the *vox populi* must rule.

Like *scabies* in mankind, mange in the dog is due to the presence of one of two insects—either the Sarcoptes Canis or the Dermatodectes Canis. The mange caused by the former insect is more difficult to cure than that caused by the latter, for the simple reason that, as the name indicates, the sarcoptes burrows in the skin, while the latter confines its attentions to biting and holding on. Unlike ekzematous affections, mange proper is solely and entirely contagious, and one dog catches mange from another just as one human being may catch the itch from another. It is highly contagious, for hardly can a healthy dog lie on the spot where a mangy dog has recently reclined without being affected with the loathsome disease.

The disease is in this way greatly fostered by the railway companies, to whom great blame is attributable for the disgraceful condition of filth and contagion in which almost all of their dog-boots are kept. It is a well-known fact that these dirty dens are never disinfected, nor are they washed or cleaned out from one year's end to another—a state of affairs to which we have often endeavoured to call the attention of the sanitary authorities, but hitherto in vain. Both mange proper, then, and the disease called follicular mange, are again and again caught by healthy dogs from travelling in the railway boot. This statement, which I have unfortunately little difficulty in proving, ought to be a warning to the owners of valuable dogs not to permit their animals to be confined in that loathsome box, the boot.

The parasites that may drop or crawl from a dog on to the floor where he lies may live there for several days; it is well known that on man they will live for weeks, and, although they are not supposed to breed on man, still they excite an irritable disease which for a time is nearly as intolerable as itch itself.

We have said that mange is contagious, therefore the same causes which produce ekzema—such as low feeding, wet and dirty kennels, &c.—will not produce it; nevertheless, filth of all kinds seems to favour the reproductory powers of the parasites.

"The acari, or parasites," says Mr. Hunting, "are male and female, the latter rather larger. The females measure about $\frac{1}{80}$th of an inch in length, and $\frac{1}{112}$th in breadth."

The female runs for some time on the surface along with the males, which are said to be fewer in number, but we think this is doubtful. After cohabitation has taken place, the female acarus burrows into the skin, reappearing with her brood in about a fortnight, having apparently, from the number of her offspring, laid just one egg a day.

Symptoms.—The symptoms are very much like what they are in human itch; there are at first little red, round spots, on which, by-and-by, vesicles may be noticed, and these may be filled either with serum or with pus. The disease spreads, of course, as the acari extend their operations, and the itching, from the amount of attention the dog pays himself in the way of scratching, must be considerable. This scratching, however, not only increases the disease, by conveying the animalculæ to other regions of the body, but also considerably irritates the skin, so that scabs and sores are found; the hair gets matted with the matter, and soon falls off.

The regions of the body most commonly attacked are, in our experience, the head, chest, back, and extremities.

We have really no primary constitutional symptoms in this disorder, the disturbance of the dog's health being attributable to the extreme irritation, want of sleep and rest, and the effect upon the nervous system.

When the parasites have fairly gotten a hold all over the body, the poor animal is indeed in a sad plight.

Diagnosis.—A study of the symptoms, the gradual oncome of the disease, and the want at first of constitutional disturbance, greatly aid us in forming a correct diagnosis, which, however, is rather difficult ; but by a microscope of ordinary power we are enabled to see the acari.

Treatment.—The cure of any disease consists in removal of the cause. In the case of mange the cause is the acarus with which the poor animal is infested ; therefore the destruction of this parasite means the removal of the disease.

Now there are one or two things to be observed, if we would cure a case of mange speedily, and still with safety to the dog. If quite certain in our diagnosis we may ignore internal medicines entirely, and stick to topical, dressing the animal with some of the many acaricides which the Pharmacopœia furnish us with in numbers, and most of which will kill the parasites in from half a minute up to five or six hours. Our advice is to sacrifice time for the sake of safety. We must, before applying any dip or application, wash the dog in plain soap and luke-warm water, rubbing the animal well, but using no extra violence. This alone does good ; then dress. Select the parasiticide with care, remembering that the skin in many places is denuded of cuticle and will rapidly absorb any poisonous application. The green iodide of mercury ointment is a favourite with many, but only a portion of the dog's skin ought to be gone over at one dressing. The same ointment we have often used with effect diluted with one part of lard, and mixed with an equal bulk of compound sulphur ointment. The sulphur ointment itself, either compound or simple, is also an excellent remedy.

The application is to be allowed to remain on for three days, then the dog is to be washed and another dressing given ; but, as we have seen that the parasites (the females) burrow under the skin for some fourteen or sixteen days, five or six dressings and washings will be needed to perfect the cure.

Meanwhile, you must not forget that the animal's bedding is to be burned, and the kennel itself completely scoured out with a hot lye of soda and water ; afterwards the wood-work, &c., is to be carefully gone over with a mixture of pure carbolic acid dissolved in water—viz., a wineglassful to a pint.

We have still a word to say on the subject of mange. We have seen that it is a disease caused by a skin parasite, and therefore only local remedies are really needed to effect a perfect cure. But we have seen, also, that the disease is in the commencement rather difficult to diagnose, and that we who have microscopes are very glad to use them in order to make sure. The reader may not possess a microscope, consequently he may be in doubt whether he may not be treating a case of ekzema for one of mange. We see no harm, therefore, in recommending the use of internal remedies, as well, to make assurance doubly sure. Mild purgatives during the mange can do no harm ; neither, after a course of mild purgatives, can a course of *liquor arsenicalis* do any harm, and it may do good, especially if the animal is in a low state of health, for arsenic is one of the best nervo-tonics which we possess.

At some large kennels in America the following plan of curing mange is adopted. The animal is quarantined for a week or ten days in a warm room, the temperature of which is never allowed to fall under 70°, and during this time his skin is well wetted two or three times with *whale* oil, nothing else.

2. *Follicular Mange.*

For most of our information concerning the symptoms and treatment of this disease we are indebted to Mr. W. Hunting and Mr. Duguid; and what follows is indeed none other than an epitome of the former gentleman's very excellent and very complete paper on "Follicular Mange."*

It is somewhat remarkable that a microscopic animalcule, the Acarus Folliculorum, should exist in neglected hair-follicles of the human body without giving rise to any inconvenience, but that the same creature transferred to the dog should create a loathsome and often almost intractable disease. But such is indeed the case. The disease in the dog was first described by Gruby, who induced it by direct inoculation with the parasite from man.

"The *symptoms*," says Hunting, "of the disease are seldom seen in the first stages; they consist merely of circumscribed spots from which the hair falls, and upon which are noticeable a few small pimples. These patches extend rapidly, and fresh ones appear on other parts. Any portion of the skin may be affected, but the head, legs, belly, and sides, are usually the seat of the disease. The affected places are almost hairless, and what hair remains is easily pulled out; small pimples and pustules stud the surface, the latter varying in size from a pin's head to that of a pea. The confluence of the pustules, and the discharge of their contents, give rise to scabs; these crack and bleed, and so produce a most repulsive appearance. In white-haired dogs, the skin is red; in all it is extremely hot, and emits an unpleasant odour. The irritation does not excite much scratching, but the dog frequently shakes himself. More pain than itching seems to accompany the disease. In cases where the whole body is affected, loss of condition is most marked; and in cold weather the almost total loss of hair may cause death, if the animal be not kept in a warm place. This stage, too, is always accompanied by a ravenous appetite, due, probably, to the rapid loss of animal heat.

N.B.—The disease has been proved beyond dispute to be highly contagious, but not to such an extent as scabies.

Diagnosis.—The pustules, the heat of the skin, and the comparatively slight degree of itching, are nearly diagnostic. Puncturing one of the pustules, mixing its contents with a little water, and putting it under the microscope are, however, requisite in order to arrive at an indisputable diagnosis.

Treatment.—The following is the formula used by Hunting, and we may add it has proved very effectual in our own hands.

$$
\begin{aligned}
&\text{R. Creosotæ} && \ldots && \ldots && \text{℥ jv.}\\
&\text{Ol. oliv.} && \ldots && \ldots && \text{℥ vji.}\\
&\text{Sol. potassæ ..} && && \ldots && \text{℥ j.}
\end{aligned}
$$

Mix the creosote and the oil, then add the caustic solution.

* "With regard to the treatment of follicular scabies, the situation of the *dermodex* renders it almost inaccessible to parasiticidal remedies; the disease it engenders is therefore looked upon as extremely troublesome, and in the majority of cases almost beyond a cure. Often when it is believed to be extinguished, it re-appears in all its virulency in one or two months. Nevertheless, Zürn asserts that he has frequently succeeded with an ointment composed of one part of benzine to four of lard. Weiss recommends the inunction of essence of juniper. Zundel states that the balsam of Peru has often yielded good results when the malady has not been of too long duration; he has employed it dissolved in alcohol (one to thirty); he has likewise used the green ointment of mercury with success, as well as the nitrate of silver ointment. Hofer speaks highly of an ointment composed of carbolic acid, and Vogel prescribes a solution of caustic potash."—*Veterinary Sanitary Science and Police*, vol. ii. p. 458.

Dress the affected spots about twice a week, and allow longer intervals as soon as the skin becomes soft and tender. In cases where the whole body is affected, we adopt the plan of shaving the animal as soon as the skin is sufficiently smooth for the action of a razor; and in all cases it is good policy to shave about an inch of hair off the sound skin all round the diseased spots. This prevents the spread of the parasites. On a case I have now under treatment, and in which most of the skin was affected, I have tried clipping instead of shaving, and with good results. I fancy the absence of hair not only allows the dressing to act better, but injuriously affects the parasite. If this really be the case, may it not account for the difference in the symptoms caused by the parasite on man and on the dog?

Be careful to wash thoroughly and disinfect the kennels of dogs in follicular mange, and separate them from other dogs.

A cure requires from three to eight months, and even a longer time than this must be allowed for the growth of the hair.

III.—EXTERNAL PARASITES.

The external parasites found on the dog, with the exception of those already named, comprise only the flea, two kinds of dog lice, and the tick.

I. *The Flea.*

The flea, the *pulex irritans*, is by far the most common of hair parasites, although by no means the most dangerous and troublesome. They are most annoying pests, however, and often very difficult to get rid of; for not only must those actually on the animal himself be destroyed, but the animal's bed, the carpet, and everything, in fact, on which the dog may have lain for any length of time, must be thoroughly cleansed and disinfected.

In long-haired dogs these insects are principally to be found along the spine, in the neck, and behind the ears. Here, then, they exist in colonies, and lay most of their eggs, and lead altogether a very active life. They are generally found in pairs, the male and female, the latter being much the larger. The eggs, or nits, black and hard and numerous, will be found at no great distance, adhering to hairs. Warm weather, a too hot, foul kennel, and filth in general, are all favourable to the multiplication of these pests.

Fleas on dogs we believe are much more injurious than many people suppose; from the constant biting and irritation they render the dog nervous and excitable, and this, combined with the loss of sleep, often causes indigestion, loss of tone, and emaciation, and paves the way for the incoming of dangerous and perhaps fatal diseases.

By biting himself and scratching himself, the poor dog ofttimes so disfigures his skin that he is supposed to be suffering from mange, is taken to some so-called "dog doctor," is dressed—salivated if the dressing be mercurial, because the broken skin absorbs it so quickly—and so "cured" by being sent to his long home.

There are many ways of getting rid of fleas in the dog, but we shall only mention the most simple, and not the dangerous class of remedies.

We have found powdered flowers of *Pyrethrum roseum*, sometimes called Keating's insect powder, very effectual. The hair must be lifted up, and the powder blown in. Little pairs of bellows are sold for this purpose, but once empty, it is cheaper to buy the powder in bulk; or it may be introduced into the coat by means of an india-rubber puff-ball. Next morning the dog must be washed and have a good run, and the process will want repeating. If a dog is much troubled with fleas, the powder should be introduced out of doors, not in, as the insects are more often driven off than killed.

Olive oil or warm castor oil may be used. If so, we must thoroughly soak the animal's coat with the oil, and we have to take care he does not catch cold in the meantime. If we soak the dog at night, we can wash him next morning. This process also will want repeating.

Then there is a remedy which is better suited for long-haired dogs : we refer to the quassia wash. With this the dog's body must be thoroughly wetted, and he may then be turned out to shake himself and have a scamper.

There are many other remedies, but we think we have named sufficient. Mr. Gamgee recommends the oil of aniseed mixed with common oil. We have not tried it, but should think it would do good.

Carbolic acid and tobacco juice, to which we may add corrosive sublimate, are all fatal to flea life, but may destroy the dog as well.

Why is it that people find it so difficult to rid a dog of fleas? We may keep on poisoning the fleas and washing the dog, and a few days thereafter find he is as bad as ever. This is the reason : he gets a new stock of fleas from the place he lies in, and fleas are wonderfully prolific. The main point, then, is to give the dog a perfectly clean kennel. Change his bed from straw to pine shavings, sprinkled with a little turps, and thoroughly clean out and disinfect his kennel. We may also dust a little of the powdered pyrethrum flowers in the place where he lies. You will thus get to the very root of the evil.

2. Lice.

There are two species of these troublesome insects found upon the dog—the Trichodectes Latus and the Hæmatopinis Piliferous. The latter is far from common, the former being the one 've usually see.

The common dog louse is not unlike the head louse of mankind, but is not so large, more squarely built, and of a light-grey or straw colour. They are found occasionally on the bodies of all breeds of dogs, but mostly in long-haired animals like St. Bernards, Newfoundlands, &c., who have been allowed to roam about wherever they list, and sleep out on dirty straw. But lice do not seem to inconvenience those out-of-door dogs very much; but let an in-door or house dog catch a breed of the disgusting creatures, and you will find that they not only cause very great distress to the poor animal, but that they are very difficult indeed to eradicate.

On puppies, on the other hand, lice multiply very quickly indeed, and the agony the poor things suffer is sometimes really pitiful to see.

We have known a case of a black-and-tan English Terrier infested with lice, but, strange to say, in this case they turned out to be not dog lice, but the Trichodectes Equi, or horse louse, and it was afterwards found that this dog, which we bought from a coachman, was in the habit of sleeping every night on the back of one of the horses. They did not seem to give him any trouble, however, and were soon got rid of.

The lice are hatched from nits, which we find clinging in rows, and very tenaciously too, to the hairs. The insects themselves are more difficult to find, but they are in puppies sometimes in millions; in older dogs they are found about the back, the tail, the neck, behind the ears, and in the face, and congregate around the teats of bitches.

They *do*, contrary to the opinion of some, get upon human beings, and we have known them remain there for days and create great annoyance.

To destroy them we have tried several plans. Oil is very effectual, and has safety to recommend it. Another plan is dusting in ammoniated mercury, and brushing it out again in a couple of hours. N.B.—The dog must be muzzled all the time, as it is virulent poison. This is better for short than long-haired dogs. Common sweet oil is as good a cure as any ; and you may add a little oil of anise, and some sublimed sulphur, which will increase the effect.

The matted portions of a long-haired dog's coat must first be cut off with a scissors, for there the lice often lurk. One thing must not be forgotten—namely, that this dressing will not kill the nits, so that after a few days the dressing must be repeated, and so on three or four times. To do any good, the whole of the dog's coat must be drenched in the oil, and the dog washed with good dog soap and warm water twelve hours afterwards.

Hunting recommends, to kill lice and fleas, a solution of soft soap in spirits of wine, medicated with creosote in the proportion of one ounce to a pound of the soap. It is very effectual. You pour a portion of it along the spine, and down the legs and thighs; work it into a lather with warm water, and well work it all over the coat. Then wash clean, and give a bucket-bath of soft water.

Many other antiparasitics might be mentioned, but few are more effectual than those we have named, and few so free from danger.

3. *Ticks.*

We have noticed these disagreeable bloodsuckers only on the heads and bodies of sporting or Collie dogs, who had been boring for some time through coverts and thickets. They soon make themselves visible, as the body swells up with the blood they suck, until they resemble small soft warts, about as big as a pea. They belong to the natural family, *Ixodiadæ*.

Treatment.—If not very numerous, they should be cut off, and the part touched with a little turps. The sulphuret of calcium will also kill them, so will the more dangerous white precipitate, or even a strong solution of carbolic acid, which must be used sparingly, however.

CHAPTER XI.

DISEASES OF THE EYE AND ITS APPENDAGES.

THE eye of the dog is more spherical than that of the horse; it more nearly resembles in shape the human eye. It is situated in what is called the orbital cavity, which in the dog is destitute of an orbital arch, but has a ligament instead; and this is the reason that the eye of the dog is more easily displaced than that of man.

The eyelids, which are meant for the protection of the eye, we need not describe; but there is one membrane in the dog's eye not found in man's which does deserve to be noticed. It is called in medical parlance the *membrana nictitans;* in common language, the inner, under, or winking eyelid, and also the haw. It is situated on the inner portion of the eyeball, and the outer margin of it is usually of the same colour as the iris. This also is meant for the protection of the eye-ball, which it keeps clear from dust, and all extraneous matters. To do this, it shuts from within upwards and outwards. Its movement is a purely mechanical one, being caused by the retraction of the eyeball into the socket, which retraction simply pushes the membrane up. It is wholly or partially raised when the dog is asleep.

If we imagine a needle to be entered at the pupil, and carried right through, until the point emerged at the back part of the eyeball, what should we pierce?

Taking things in regular rotation, and not being too precise, we should first puncture a portion of the conjunctiva—transparent here and merely epidermal; but this conjunctiva is a mucous membrane which, joining the skin at the eyelids, lines the eyelids, and forms the external covering to every portion of the eye you can see in the living animal. Next to be pierced would be the cornea—a transparent membrane composed of three layers, and forming the covering to the front of the eye, joining which is the sclerotic coat, or the principal sheath of the eyeball.

Still going inwards, the needle would traverse the chambers, divided into the anterior and posterior, and which contain what is called the aqueous humour of the eye; the use of this being to retain the convexity of the cornea, the aqueous humour and the cornea combining to form a lens which refracts the light passing through it to the crystalline lens and retina. Now, situated between the anterior and posterior chambers is a diaphragm, just like that which is used in the tube of a photographic apparatus. This is called the iris, and the hole in the centre is termed the pupil. The iris in the human being may be blue, grey, or hazel; in the dog it is usually either a beautiful golden yellow, light or dark brown, or hazel, or nearly black. The iris, in fact, is simply a curtain with a hole in the centre, and the widening or narrowing of this opening is what is termed dilatation or contraction of the pupil. Its use is to regulate the amount of light required for correct vision. In the dog the pupil is circular, as in the human being.

Behind this the needle finds its way into the crystalline lens, held in position by the ciliary ligaments, which are simply a continuation of the choroid coat. The crystalline lens is a transparent body, and is enveloped in a transparent capsule, and its use is to bring the rays of light to a focus upon the retina. Now, once through the crystalline lens, the needle finds itself in the vitreous or glass-like body, or the vitreous humour which occupies the largest chamber of the eye; it consists of a kind of colourless jelly, more fluid than that which forms the crystalline lens, the use of it being to aid in the refraction of the rays of light. We need not describe what is called the hyaloid membrane. The needle next comes upon the most important structure of the eye—namely, the retina itself. The retina is simply the optic nerve spread out into a curtain at the inner and back part of the eyeball. This is the curtain on which the picture seen is painted by the light, developed as a photographer would say, and the impression being carried to the brain through the medium of the optic nerve and taken cognizance thereof, sight is the result.

Onward through the retina, and the needle pierces the choroid coat, and a very important coat this is. It is a thin and delicate membrane of a deep black hue, which lines the inner surface of the sclerotic coat, and its black colour is occasioned by the numbers of pigment cells which it contains.

Now, the use of this choroid coat is evidently to absorb the rays of light, which would otherwise be reflected, and disorder vision. The choroid, in fact, renders the principal cavity of the eye a dark chamber. Without it the picture on the retina would be indistinct. To use familiar language, then, the *sclerotic* coat is to the eye what the tin box is to the magic lantern—no portion of the apparatus itself, but only its box. Supposing a magic lantern built of china, it would not be of much use, because the rays would pass through; but if you lined that china box with black it would do well enough. The sclerotic may be called the china framework of this truly magic lantern, the eye, and the choroid coat is its black lining. Without the choroid coat the picture on the retina would be as hazy and indistinct as a positive photograph taken on glass before it is darkened with black varnish.

The last portion for the needle to transfix is the sclerotic coat—the strong, white, fibrous sheath which, as I have already told you, encloses the principal portion of the eye. It is largely supplied with nerves and blood-vessels, and to it are attached all the little elongated muscles that move the eye about in any direction the animal wishes.

Let us now pass on to the diseases of this delicate organ.

1. *Ophthalmia.*

This disease, which signifies an inflammation of the eye, is sometimes called *conjunctivitis.* For our own part, we prefer the simple term ophthalmia, for the disease is often more than merely an inflammation of the mucous membrane. The sclerotic may partake, and the areolar tissue of the eyelids always does.

Ophthalmia may be either traumatic—that is, it may be the result of injury either from blows or from foreign bodies, such as sand, particles of straw, or other foreign matters getting into the eye—or it may arise idiopathically, or be sympathetic with other diseases, such as distemper.

Perhaps this is the right place to mention that the eye of the dog, more perhaps than that of any other animal, sympathises with the disorders of the mucous membranes. Given a case of diarrhœa, for instance, or gastorrhœa. Examine the dog's eye, and you will find the capillaries congested, perhaps even the darker veins of the sclerotic shining through the conjunctiva. Even a disordered stomach will have the same effect, though in a less degree. The eyeball of a dog ought to be most beautifully white and pure, although it is not always so even in health, for healthful exercise will temporarily redden the eye.

Causes of ophthalmia.—The first to be mentioned are injuries. Generally speaking, in this case only one eye is inflamed. The worst case of this sort we remember was caused by a bit of chaff. A large dog he was, and, poor fellow, he had been blistered and bled and physicked to a great extent, but nobody had thought of examining the eye.

One common cause of ophthalmia is the dog's being allowed to sleep in a draught, or exposed to wet and cold, after having had violent exercise.

Symptoms.—The symptoms of ophthalmia may be either mild or severe; in the former case there is evident pain and intolerance of light, the eyes are closed or nearly so, and the eye-lids more or less swollen. There is, moreover, an increased flow of tears, and if the eyes are examined they will be found very red and inflamed. In simple cases there is but little constitutional disturbance, although the animal is duller than usual.

In traumatic ophthalmia, or that caused by injury of any sort, the inflammation is much more severe, and the discharge becomes as a rule puriform and abundant, and the eye is completely closed.

In more severe forms of idiopathic ophthalmia there is not only abundant secretion of tears at first, but the inflammation runs a speedy course. The eyelids here are much swollen and often glued together with pus. There is, moreover, much constitutional disturbance, with hot nose and mouth, constipation, and high-coloured urine. In some cases, as in distemper, after the eyes can be opened a film seems to be spread over the eye, which, being merely an exudation, gradually disappears as the eye gets well. It should not be cauterised, as this process might lead to disintegration of the cornea. Ulcers, too, are sometimes seen on the cornea, but these also soon heal under the mild treatment which we are about to propose.

Treatment.—In the milder cases of ophthalmia very little treatment will be required, beyond keeping the dog at rest for a few days in his kennel, on rather lower diet, and giving (unless the dog is very weak) a purgative each morning—an ordinary dose of Epsom salts. The only local remedy required will be a drop or two of the *vinum opii,* or a mild alum eye-wash, or a lotion of two grains of nitrate of silver to an ounce of distilled water.

In ophthalmia from a wound, blow, or injury, our object is to subdue the inflammation, and local treatment alone will be required. Be careful to examine the eye, and if any foreign matter is found it must be removed. It will usually be found adhering to the eye-lid internally, and a camel's-hair pencil will be the best instrument to use. Afterwards nature, aided by hot fomentations or astringent lotions, will complete the cure.

In more severe cases of ophthalmia we must set about without loss of time to endeavour to subdue the inflammation, in order to prevent ulceration or sloughing. It is not necessary to weaken the dog much, but begin with the same brisk purgative recommended in the more simple form of the disorder. We never bleed, but a small blister behind the ear often does good. Let the animal be kept in a darkened room, and apply over each eye a pledget of lint, which must be kept wet with decoction of poppy-heads, or a lotion of the wine of opium (*vinum opii*), one drachm to three ounces of water. To prevent the adhesion of the iris to the cornea, we employ the sulphate of atropia, four grains to one ounce of distilled water; one or two drops of this solution into each eye every morning or evening, if need be. The alum lotion ought to be used every hour. If spots or little ticks of ulceration appear on the cornea, use the nitrate of silver lotion, *four* grains to the ounce. If there is much restlessness at night, either tincture of henbane or chloral hydrate may be used. We prefer the former to opium, in doses from ten drops to a drachm or two drachms.

Give low diet at first, and afterwards—that is, as soon as the inflammation is subdued—keep the strength well up with beef-tea, soups, raw meat, and port wine.

Complete the cure with tonics, and that most invaluable adjunct cod-liver oil, or extract of malt for Toy dogs. Take care how you expose the dog for some weeks after, either to sun or cold or wet.

2. *Cataract.*

This is at times the result of blows, but often comes on without any apparent cause, and without inflammation, although it may supervene upon an attack of ophthalmia. There is generally dilatation of the pupil, and if closely examined, the lens usually has a striated appearance, the striæ either radiating from the centre or circumference.

In addition to this cataract, which is of a soft nature, we have what may be termed senile cataract—that milky bluish-white appearance of the crystalline lens which we see in all old dogs, but to a larger extent in animals that have been carelessly treated in life. We cannot expect to cure this species of cataract until the philosopher's stone is found; but by a better regulated diet, and plenty of exercise, with comfortable housing, we can usually check the tendency to degeneration of the lens, and prevent total blindness.

Treatment.—Try to find out if there has been any error in the feeding, and remedy it. Let the animal have abundant exercise, and a cold bath every morning; let him not be pampered or coddled, nor have too warm a bed. Let him have plenty of food and a larger supply of meat than usual, but avoid giving sugar. As to medicine, small doses of tincture of nux vomica may be given twice a day, and cod-liver oil most assuredly deserves a fair trial. You may change the tonic occasionally for a short course of quinine.

3. *Disease of the " Haw."*

The *membrana nictitans*, or inner eyelid, so useful in the canine economy for preventing dust, &c., from injuring the eye, is subject to enlargement or hypertrophy; it gets hardened, somewhat cartilaginous, and rolls outwards, thus giving not only an unsightly appearance to the eye, but considerab y annoying and inconveniencing the animal.

Spaniels, and some dogs that go to ground, are more subject to the disease than others, although general ill-health and bad treatment may induce it.

Treatment.—The congestion must first be got under by mild eye-lotions, while at the same time we endeavour to improve the dog's condition by keeping him clean, and feeding well and rationally. The enlarged portion of the membrane must then be got rid of by operation. This is simple enough, but must be done carefully. Either with a hooked needle or small arterial forceps, you seize the "haw," and dragging it forward, pare it with a fine-pointed surgical scissors. Continue the eye-wash until the inflammation is quite gone.

4. *Amaurosis.*

Amaurosis, or *gutta serena,* as it is often called, from the peculiar almost glass-like appearance of the eye, is a form of blindness or dimness of sight sometimes seen in the dog, and depending on a partially or completely paralysed state of the retina and optic nerve, which prevents the picture on the former being taken cognizance of or conveyed to the brain.

The eye is peculiarly clear and the pupil dilated, perhaps immovably so. The gait of the animal attracts attention: he staggers somewhat, and seems unable to avoid stumbling against objects in his way, while his expression seems meaningless.

Treatment.—As a rule, this is unsatisfactory. The strictest attention, however, must be paid to the general health and the feeding. If the disease seems induced by the presence of worms, they must be got rid of; if by foul mouth and decayed teeth, see to those. If the *gutta serena* follows violence to the head, in which case it is more often limited to one eye, put the animal on low diet, give a cooling aperient, and keep him strictly quiet for a time.

If amaurosis depends upon weakness, the remedies most likely to do good are tonics, such as the tincture of iron, to begin with, followed in a week by zinc, from half to four grains of the sulphate in a pill, with extract of dandelion. This is an excellent nervine tonic, but must be used for a month at least. A small blister behind each ear may also be tried, or a seton in the nape of the neck.

5. *Ulceration of the Eyelids.*

This is sometimes seen in dogs, and is generally associated with ekzema in other parts of the body. The edge of the eyelids are ulcerated and covered with matter, and usually a scurfy appearance, attended with loss of hair, extends for some distance around the eyes.

The *treatment* is that for ekzema, combined with the most perfect cleanliness. Wash the animal's eyes carefully every morning and evening with warm water and a sponge, to entirely remove offensive matter. An astringent eye-lotion is to be applied twice or thrice a day, and night and morning the eyelids are to be smeared with citrine ointment. If the ulcers seem unwilling to heal they must be touched with nitrate of silver solution, five or ten grains to the ounce. At the same time, the eyelashes are to be clipped as short as possible.

6. *Fistula Lachrymalis.*

At the inner canthus of each eye are two small openings through which, after moistening the eye, the tears pass downwards through the lachrymal ducts to the lachrymal sac, from which they find their way by a duct called nasal into the nostrils. When the nasal duct is obstructed in any way an abscess of the sac is the result, and if this is neglected it opens through the skin, and a fistula is the result. Whenever an abscess of this kind is observed, the dog ought at once to be taken to a skilled veterinary surgeon or medical man ; the treatment cannot be conducted safely by any one unacquainted with the anatomy of the parts.

7. *Dislocation of the Eyeball.*

This is an accident which, although by no means uncommon, is more likely to occur to such dogs as Pugs, Blenheims, or King Charles Spaniels, and is usually the result of injury caused in fighting with other dogs, or even in having a difference of opinion with the cat.

The eye must be returned to its socket in as careful a manner as possible. No undue force or pressure must be used. After the eye has been thoroughly cleansed by lukewarm water and a soft sponge of all dirt or grit, the eyelids must be held as widely apart as possible by an assistant, and gentle but firm pressure exerted on the eyeball (previously touched with olive oil) by the two thumbs and two forefingers of the operator. A slight rotatory motion may assist reduction. If it is found to be impossible to reduce the eye in this way, the outer corners of the eye will have to be divided with a lancet or scissors, but to no great extent. This will simplify matters, and the eye will easily slip home. One stitch or suture will be needed afterwards, and the wound will heal quickly, especially if a little *vinum opii* be used in lotion to soothe the pain.

CHAPTER XII.

DISEASES OF THE EAR.

IN drawing the reader's attention to the structure of the eye we endeavoured to show that that organ was nothing more nor less than a beautiful optical instrument designed by Nature, and perfect in its adaptation to vision. The ear, on the other hand, is a most wonderfully constructed acoustic instrument. Anything like a perfect description of the auditory apparatus space prevents us from giving, nor in a book like the present is it required; and we therefore beg to refer the reader, if very much interested in the subject, to any good work on comparative anatomy or physiology. Meanwhile, we will endeavour to render our description as concise and simple as possible.

We divide the organ of hearing, then, for convenience sake, into three portions—viz. (1) the external, (2) the middle, and (3) the internal ear. By the external ear is meant not only the outer portion or flap of the ear, which in the dog is either erect or drooping, but also the tube that leads down into the head, and into which we can thrust a probe or the finger. The outer portion, then, or flap, as we all know, varies in shape, not only in different animals but in different breeds of dogs. It is, properly speaking, a collector of sound, and in animals like the bat, for example, reflects the collected sound down into the meatus of the ear. Sound may in this instance be compared to running water; it flows against the flap of the ear, which stops its progress, and it thus flows in a backward current into the meatus. Now, the nearer any breed of dog approaches in descent to the wild dog, the more will his ear be pricked. We have only to instance the Yack dogs or Esquimaux.

Those dogs, too, will have pricked ears, or partially erect, who have to depend much upon their sense of hearing to enable them to perform their duties as the servants of mankind.

The organ of hearing proper is placed deeply down in the centre of the petrous portion of the temporal bone. The canal which leads from the outside to the middle ear is terminated by a thin skin or membrane which partitions it off, as it were, from the middle ear.

This membrane is, in other words, the parchment cover of the kettledrum of the ear. This membrane is elastic, and vibrates to every sound.

Now, if you were to put a needle through this membrane, the point of it would enter the tympanum or drum, or middle ear. Herein there is a little chain of bones which need not here be particularised further than to say they stretch from the membrane across the drum, one end being attached to this, and the other to the membrane dividing the drum from the internal or ear proper; and we will see the purpose of this chain presently. A tube opens into the drum. This is called the Eustachian tube. It is an air-pipe, and supplies the drum with air. It runs downwards and forwards, and opens into the back part of the throat. When we hold the nose and go through the motions of swallowing, we hear a crackling in the ears; this is caused by the air rushing up that tube and distending the drum of the ear. When this tube is closed partially, as when one has a cold, or permanently from inflammation, no air can get to this drum, the outer membrane cannot vibrate, and the person or dog becomes deaf.

This is a common cause of deafness, and quacks pretend to cure it by pouring stuff into the ear; the qualified surgeon, on the other hand, directs his attention to the tube itself, up which he passes a catheter, and thus restores communication with the drum, and consequently hearing.

The internal or real ear is composed of several curiously-shaped cavities, all communicating one with the other. The first of these is called the *vestibule*. This vestibule has a window (*fenestra ovalis*) opening into the drum. To the membrane covering this window is attached the inner end of the delicate chain of bones already mentioned. From the *vestibule* on one side go three semi-lunar canals, and on the other a curious-shaped cavity called the cochlea, the opening through which the auditory nerve descends. Now, the whole of the cavities of the internal ear are lined by a delicate membrane, and in this lining the auditory nerve ramifies and is spread out, and the cavities of this internal ear *are all filled with fluid*.

The physiology of hearing is simple enough. Sound, which is air in motion, passes down the meatus or external passage, and sets the drum to vibrate; the drum cannot vibrate without pulling the little chain of bones inside it, this being attached to the other membrane, which closes the aperture to the internal ear. This membrane likewise vibrates, and the motion is communicated to the water in the cavities, and thus, of course, to the nerves, which carry the sensation to the brain, and the brain takes cognizance thereof, and, being the thinking portion of the human frame, or the frame of a dog either, it—the brain—knows well from experience what the sound is, whether the report of a gun, the crack of a keeper's whip, or the whirring wings of a rising covey.

And now we get to the diseases of the ear; and we may premise that although these are apt to attack any portion of the organ of hearing, those of the external auditory canal are by far and away the most numerous, and next in point of frequency come diseases of the flap of the ear.

Like skin diseases, diseases of the ear constitute a large proportion of the canine practitioner's work. They are too often troublesome to heal, and not only that, but they are apt to recur.

1. *Chronic Otitis.*

Chronic otitis, called also chronic inflammation of the ear, or more commonly canker.

The term canker is rather objectionable, in that it tends to mislead the ignorant. As the word sounds so like cancer, the disease is often considered to be of a cancerous nature; and being deemed incurable, no notice at all is taken of it. The word canker really means an eating ulcer; and probably the word originated from that sort of disease we see on some esculent roots, as turnips, carrots, &c., caused by larval worms.

The word being so common, however, we are obliged to retain it.

Chronic otitis, or canker, really is an inflammation of the lining or secreting membrane of the external auditory canal, often extending to the outer surface of the tympanum itself.

Causes.—These are often very obscure; and considerable difference of opinion exists among authors on the subject. Youatt tells us that all water-dogs are subject to this disease. Mayhew seems to doubt this, and instances the case of a number of water-dogs that were kept for the purpose of retrieving wild fowl at the mouth of the Ex, none of which, although constantly in the water, ever suffered from canker.

But Youatt says, "When the whole body, except the head and ears, is surrounded by cold water, there will be an unusual determination of blood to those parts, and, consequently, distension of the vessels, and a predisposition to inflammation." At first blush this seems logical enough, but it will not bear dissection; for, first and foremost, is the water always cold? We have seen quite as many cases of canker in summer as in winter. Secondly, no matter how cold the water is, the animal keeps himself warm enough by his exertions, and his head is often under the water; and after being once well wetted, both his head and ears will be as cool, if not cooler, than any other part of the body. It is very necessary indeed we should form as correct a judgment as possible on the causes of a disease so distressing and so common as canker.

As to its relative frequency in different kinds of dogs, our own experience is as follows: long-haired dogs are more subject to the disease than short-haired; large dogs, such as the Newfoundland and St. Bernard, than small; water dogs, than dogs that do not take the water; and old dogs, than young. "A Newfoundland dog," says Youatt, "or Setter or Poodle that has been subject to canker, is often prevented from having a return of the disease by being kept from the water." And this is doubtless the case, because the animal is thus prevented from running the risk of catching cold. Among the most common causes of canker may be ranked cold, want of proper feeding, overfeeding, or injudicious feeding; sometimes, though rarely, by blows or falls. Anything which suddenly lowers the strength and vitality of a dog will predispose to canker.

Pathology.—The skin which lines the meatus or external auditory canal is exceedingly thin and delicate, and here, in addition to other glands, it is studded with wax glands, or, in anatomical phraseology, sebiparous glands. These secrete the cerumen, or wax, which is supposed to prevent the entrance of insects. (Other kinds of wax might rather tempt them, but the ear wax is bitter.) Now, the same causes which produce ekzema are liable to produce canker, and do we not often find the two diseases combined? There is first increased vascularity; the glands, waxy and otherwise, are stimulated to throw out more secretion than is usual. If this is expelled from the ear, well and good; if not, and there is any heat about the head from catarrh or simple fever, the black wax, mixed with perspiration, cakes and decays, producing redness and slight inflammation, and so the mischief is begun. From simple inflammation and extra flow of wax we by-and-by get superficial ulceration; then, instead of the discharge being dark-coloured, it becomes yellow—pus, in fact.

Symptoms and Diagnosis.—There is hardly any disease that canker can be mistaken for. We never know anything about the disease until the mischief has fairly begun, and the first symptom, or sign, rather, we see, is the poor animal shaking his head, generally to one side, for all the world as a dog does who has a flea in his lug. If we look into the ear now, you will—but not always, as the inflammation may be deep-seated—find a little redness. (N.B.— You must have a good light, and pull the ear well but gently asunder.) There is one thing, however, that you will not be slow in observing, and that is, a bad odour. This is diagnostic in itself. When the disease is a little farther advanced, by gently working the ear backwards and forwards, you will hear a crackling sound, and the dog will evince some signs either of pain or itchiness.

When the disease has fairly set in, the symptoms are running of pus, mingled with cerumen from the ear, frequent head-shakings, dulness, capricious appetite, and very often a low state of the general health.

Treatment.—On no single matter is our mind more fully made up than on this, that canker is often, we had almost said *always*, improperly treated, except by those vets. who make dog diseases a speciality. We are told the disease is most difficult to cure; true, because the worst part of the mischief is done before we see the case. We are told it is apt to recur; true, because the lining membrane of the meatus, by mistaken treatment, has been rendered a weakened part for life. If we want to treat a dog according to correct principles, we must not forget, to begin with, that the primary symptoms of canker point *to a constitutional aberration from the standard of health.*

Our advice, then, is, whenever you find a dog showing the first signs of canker, take the case in hand at once. Do not begin by pouring strong lotions into his ear. The ear is such a *very* tender organ, disease and inflammation are so easily induced therein, that harsh interference is positively sinful.

Begin by giving the dog a dose of some mild aperient, either simple castor oil, or, better still, from one to four drachms of Epsom salts, with a dust of quinine in it. Let the dog have good nourishing diet, but do not let him over-eat. Let him have green, well-boiled vegetables in his food to cool him, a nice warm bed, exercise, but not to heat him, and try to make him in every way comfortable. Then give him a tonic pill of sulphate of quinine, sulphate of iron, and dandelion extract.

Local treatment.—We all know the soothing effect of a nice hot fomentation. Why, the very dogs themselves do. See how gently they cleanse a sore with their warm tongues; see, again, how a dog with canker will wet the joint at his pastern and apply it to his ear. And so we say fomentation is all that is needed in the early stages. Place cotton wadding gently in each ear, lest one drop gets in to increase the irritation; then apply your fomentation to both sides of the ear at once, using four flannels or four woollen socks. A quarter of an hour will be long enough each time.

But if the dog has been neglected in the beginning, and the discharge allowed to increase, and probably become purulent, then our chance of resolving the inflammation has passed, and local applications are needed. The disease has now become chronic, and canker is fairly established.

In addition now to doing everything we can to establish the dog's health and keep him well up, avoid letting him go into the water, and avoid also all risk of letting him catch cold; and you must also use a lotion for the ear.

Previously to pouring in the lotion, be careful to wash out the matter from the dog's ears as gently as possible. Purchase half an ounce of the red salt called permanganate of potash, dissolve this in two pints of water, and pour as much of the solution into the warm water you use as will redden it.

We give several astringent lotions for canker. The first we should try is the infusion of green tea. It should be strong enough to resemble the colour of pale brandy, and if it is used lukewarm all the better. Then we have a lotion of dried alum, from one grain to five to an ounce of distilled water; or nitrate of silver, sulphate of copper, or sulphate of cadmium, which are used in the same proportions. Lastly, but not least, we have the liquor *plumbi subacetatis*, ten to twenty drops to an ounce of water, to which a little glycerine may be added, but greasy mixtures, should, we think, be avoided.

They are all of them good, and it is not a bad plan to change them occasionally, and stick most to that which seems to decrease the discharge. To prevent the animal shaking the head, and increasing the disease, it is better to confine the head in a canker-cap.

Let me, however, impress upon you that you are to look upon canker of the ear as a distressing symptom of ill-health, for it is seldom indeed unaccompanied by degeneracy of the constitution. You will often find arsenic and iron work wonders if steadily persevered in, as recommended in the article on ekzema.

2. *Inflammation of the Flap of the Ear.*

Under this head we include all diseases of the external ear.

First, then, we find the disease usually known by the name of external canker. It may exist as a separate disease, but it is far more commonly found as a concomitant of internal canker. It is more usual in long-eared dogs. The constant shaking of the head, from the irritation caused by internal canker, combined with the acridity of the discharge from the ear, often produces an inflamed condition of the flap, ending in ulceration, scurf, and thickening of the edges of the ear. The ulcerated surface is often situated near the inside border, but more commonly it is the edge of the ear or ears themselves that is the seat of this troublesome complaint, which the head shaking in which the animal persists in indulging never fails to aggravate. The flap becomes thickened, and splits, and a ragged, exceedingly unkindly edge is the result.

Cases of this class are usually deemed very difficult to cure, and the first of those that came under our own care we really found so; but recently we have been more easily and speedily successful. The treatment is as follows :—When the ear is buried in long hair, probably matted, have the latter removed with the scissors. Perfect cleanliness is the next thing to secure, and for this reason have the ear well though gently washed with warm water and a little mild soap. Then apply the ointment : simple benzoated oxide of zinc is generally all that is required, although at times the following prescription—

> ℞ Zinci. sulph. exsicat. ... ... ℥ ij.
> Unguent simp. ... ... ℥ j.　　M.

may be found better. It may be necessary, too, occasionally to touch the sores with blue-stone, or twenty-grain solution of nitrate of silver.

The canker-cap must imperatively be worn, and in order to give the ears a better chance of healing, we fold them back over the head, and bind them in that position.

The strictest regulations as to diet and exercise must be enforced, but the animal must be kept from the water, and not permitted to overheat himself.

As to the barbarous habit of cropping, adopted by the old vets. and some kennelmen of the present day, we never adopt it.

An occasional purgative will do good, and the ear or ears must be bathed before every application of the ointment, say twice a day.

Secondly, *abscesses* of the flap of the ear are by no means uncommon, and cause great pain and irritation. Sometimes these are accidental, being caused by blows from a rope or whip. They often go away of their own accord, stimulated only by the application of blue ointment. If they do not, they must be opened by a free incision ; for if only pricked the matter will form again, while setons do more harm than good. The incision, then, must be free, and afterwards a little lint is to be inserted, wetted in water to which a few drops of carbolic acid solution has been added. The cap may be worn, and the ear turned back, and as soon as suppuration is formed, the wound will heal if kept perfectly clean and softened by the zinc ointment.

Thirdly, we have, either combined with ulceration of the ear or without it, an *ekzematous* condition of the outside of the flap, and considerable thickening may sometimes be felt around the edges. The hair falls off, beginning at the tip of the ear and ascending, and as long as the disease lasts, a constant exfoliation of the dandruff goes on. Scurf of the ears is often accompanied by mange in other parts of the body.

Treatment.—Frequent washing, attention to diet, cleanliness, and exercise, the application of the compound sulphur ointment, or the green iodide, and the exhibition of arsenic internally. (*See* article on ekzema.)

3. *Deafness.*

Deafness in the dog may either be congenital or may come on at any period of the animal's life, and from many different causes. Perhaps the commonest of all causes is perforation of the tympanum, as the result of canker of the ear, or the accumulation of matter, or hypertrophy of the lining of the ear from the same disease.

Deafness may sometimes come on suddenly from catarrh, causing occlusion of the Eustachian tube, or from the metastasis of rheumatism. Obscure cases are no doubt often of a nervous character.

Treatment.—To begin with, deaf puppies ought to be destroyed. There is no more stupid nor useless animal in the world than a deaf dog. When the disease comes on gradually in old dogs, nothing can be done except improving the tone of the general health. If it is caused by canker, curing that disease will always relieve, if it does not actually cure, the deafness.

If it is of rheumatic origin the treatment must be directed to the removal of the cause. In all cases of deafness coming on suddenly, a careful examination of the ear should be made, and if inflammation is found, washing out of the meatus should be resorted to, and a lead lotion of half the strength of that used in canker afterwards dropped in twice a day. Several doses of opening medicine should then be given, letting one day intervene. The sulphate of soda with a little nitre will be best. Give also every night, for three or four nights, a dose of Mindererus spirit. If the deafness still continues, recourse must be had to the iodide of potassium, a course of which will often cure it when everything else fails.

> ℞ Pot. iodid.   ...   ...   gr. j. ad gr. v.
> Ferri et quinæ citr.   ...   gr. ij. ad gr. x.
> Aquæ   ...   ...   q. s.
> Fᵗ haustus.   M.
> Ter die.

In all diseases of the ear the general health of the animal should be attended to, and a course of tonics and cod-liver oil, with now and then a gentle aperient, never fail to do good.

CHAPTER XIII.

DISEASES OF THE MOUTH AND NASAL ORGANS.

THE mouth of the dog is beautifully adapted for the purpose Nature meant it to serve—namely, as a weapon both of defence and offence. It is very capacious, and is armed with strong incisors and powerful fangs, which latter are in some ·breeds—such as the Dachshund and Bull-dog—partially recurvent, like those of the shark, this recurvency enabling him to retain a firm hold of the prey he may have captured.

The dog, like the human being, is furnished during his lifetime with two sets of teeth. The first—the milk teeth—are all cut within a fortnight after the birth of the puppy. They are exceedingly beautiful and very fragile. They begin to fall out and be replaced in the following order : first the front teeth or incisors go (this in from a month to seven weeks), and soon after the second, third, and fourth molars fall out, and in a few months the other molars follow suit ; so that in from five to six or eight months the milk teeth are replaced by the permanent. These latter are forty-two in number, twenty-two occupying the lower and twenty the upper jaw. The following is the correct formula as given by the highest authorities :—

$$\text{Upper jaw—Incisors } 6 ; \text{ Fangs } 1-1 ; \text{ Molars } \left.\begin{array}{l} 6-6=20 \\ 7-7=22 \end{array}\right\} = 42.$$
$$\text{Lower jaw— } \quad\text{,, } \quad 6 ; \quad \text{,, } \quad 1-1 ; \quad \text{,, }$$

In most breeds of dogs the teeth are level ; that is, the incisors of the two jaws meet when the mouth is closed, so that you cannot insert your finger-nail behind either row. But some breeds of dogs are underhung, and in some the upper jaw projects. The four middle incisors $\frac{2}{2}$ are called the pincers, the next four $\frac{1-1}{1-1}$, at each side of these, the intermediates, and the last four flanking these $\frac{1-1}{1-1}$ the corners. The upper incisors are larger than the under, and the cutting or free edge of each incisor has on it—in the young dog—two or three little tubercles. The middle lobe or tubercle is the first to wear ; finally they all disappear. The fourth molars in the upper jaw and the fifth in the lower are the largest ; and notice, too, the cutting or free edge of these—they are not like those of an ox or human being, they are made to tear and rend, not to grind.

The teeth of the young dog, and indeed of any dog that has been properly cared for and correctly fed, are beautifully white and pearly ; one reason for this being that the crown or exposed portion of the tooth is covered with enamel, not *cementum*. Can we tell the age of a dog by looking at his teeth ? By no means correctly. The presence of the tubercles on the middle incisors would lead one to infer that the animal was under three years, but their absence would not prove that he was over three. The complete possession of all the permanent teeth in a puppy would prove that it was over six months old, but the absence of some of them would not prove him to be under. We have to remember, too, that the dog's teeth are very subject to disease and to different degrees of wear and tear, according to how he is fed and used. Neither by the teeth nor by the eyes can you tell a dog's age, although from the eyes you can generally tell whether or not a dog is aged. But there is no certain method of determining a dog's age from examination.

The gums of the dog are hard and solid to the touch, and firmly embrace each tooth, and more or less surround each separate tusk. The mucous membrane of both the gums and the inside of the cheek, as well as the hard palate or roof of the mouth, is generally patched with black and sometimes wholly black.

The soft palate, or curtain that guards the entrance to the gullet, is in the dog broad and short and has little or no uvula; the opening from the mouth into the pharynx and larynx is therefore capacious and freely admits either food or air; this latter being so extremely necessary to the animal after a hard run, when he wants to do a deal of breathing in a short time.

The tongue of the dog differs considerably from that of other animals. It is very long and soft, and extremely mobile. It is covered with long silky papillæ, which give it its peculiar smoothness, so different from the rough tongue of the cat, with its horny recurvent papillæ. Erectile tissue enters into the formation of the dog's tongue when the animal is heated or tired and enervated, the nerves lose much of their power over the organ, and it lolls from the mouth limp and flaccid; but even then it is not without its use, for all the glands that open into the mouth being for the time congested, there is a free flow of saliva, which trickles over the tongue and drops quite clear away from the coat, thus cooling the animal.

The lips in the dog are thin and pliant: sometimes tight, as in the Bull-terrier, sometimes flewed, long, and pendent, as in the Blood-hound. Externally the upper lip is grooved in the median line, and at the lower edge at the back parts is beautifully vandyked with long papillæ all along its free surface.

1. *General Treatment of the Teeth.*

We presume the dog is to a great extent happily free from what Burns well names "the deil o' a' diseases," toothache. Probably at times he does suffer in this way, but he says little about it. Loose and carious teeth are, however, of very frequent occurrence, often existing as one of the symptoms of either dyspepsia or intestinal worms, more especially in pampered pets, who are allowed to eat what and when they choose.

As a rule, puppies shed their milk-teeth without any trouble. Nevertheless, if any one has a litter of valuable pups he will be consulting his own interest by occasionally having a glance at their mouths. The milk-teeth, after getting loose, sometimes get fixed again. This is a matter that wants looking to, for the presence of milk-teeth often deflects and renders irregular the growing permanent teeth. Whenever, then, you find a milk-tooth loose, try to extract it; this can generally be done with the finger and thumb covered with the corner of a handkerchief. If, however, the tooth has been allowed to remain so long in the jaw as to become re-fixed, its extraction becomes rather more difficult, and requires instrumental assistance. Use what you like to aid you; a handy man can work with any kind of tools.

After extracting the tooth you may touch the gums with a solution of tincture of myrrh and water, equal parts. As your dog grows up, if you want him to retain his dental apparatus to a goodly old age, you must trust to regular and wholesome feeding, and never permit him to carry stones, nor to indulge in the filthy habit of chewing wood. For show dogs powdered charcoal should be used to clean the teeth, with a moderately hard brush, but tartar should never be allowed to remain on the teeth of any dog one values. It ought to be scraped off, or it will give rise to disease.

2. *Foul Mouth.*

There is a condition of the canine mouth very often seen to which we give the above name. The highest bred dogs are those most subject to it, and among these it is more frequently seen in household pets. The *symptoms* vary in degree, but in a well-marked case you will find your patient is generally somewhat surly and snappish, and on inquiry we will not be surprised to learn that he gets but little exercise—perhaps because he has become too fat to take it—that he gets what he likes to eat, everybody gives him tit-bits, and perhaps that he sleeps before the fire, or in a bed, or on the couch, and is restless at night, and often troubled with bad dreams. Examination of the mouth reveals, first, a very obnoxious breath, the gums are swollen, may be ulcerated at the edges, but at all events bleed with the slightest touch. Some of the teeth may be loose or decayed, but invariably even the sound ones are encrusted with tartar. Coupled with this, the dog generally has a capricious appetite and a *penchant* for dainties.

Treatment.—The treatment of such a case is very simple, when we can get the owner to act as our first-lieutenant, and see that our orders are obeyed. Cases of this kind are much better treated in hospital. Now, it used to be the custom of the older practitioners to commence the treatment of such cases by two or three days' wholesale starvation. This treatment is terribly cruel, and any one who should prescribe such should be punished by law. You ought to begin by thoroughly cleaning and scaling the teeth; this done, use a wash—water well reddened with permanganate of potash. The teeth are to be cleansed every morning with vinegar and water. The only medicine needful will be an aloetic aperient once or twice a week, and a dinner pill.

Quinæ sulph.	gr. $\frac{1}{4}$ ad gr. iij.	
Rhei ⎱	ā, ā, gr. ij. ad gr. v.	
Zingiber. ⎰		
Ext. tarax.	q. s.	M.

The feeding must be altered for the better. If the dog is fat and gross, meat, and especially sugar and fat, must be prohibited. Put him on oatmeal porridge and milk, or boiled Spratt cake, either alone or with a little sheep's-head broth. If lean and poor, an allowance of meat must be given, or the thirty per cent. Spratt cake, and also from a teaspoonful upwards of cod-liver oil twice a day. Let the drink be pure water or butter-milk. The bath—matutinal douche—does much good in cases of this kind, and two hours' good romping exercise every day must be strictly enjoined. Perseverance in such treatment, simple though it be, must prove successful after a time, unless the dog is very old.

3. *Canker Oris.*

Popularly called canker of the mouth, and, properly speaking, caries of the jaw, or at least the fangs of some of the molar teeth. It is called by some authorities dental gangrene.

Causes.—Generally either the result of age, or it has its origin in a neglected state of the teeth from improper feeding. The mischief generally begins in the neck of the tooth, *i.e.*, between the root and the crown.

Symptoms.—These are seldom noticed until the disease is pretty far advanced, and a swelling is formed on the dog's jaw beneath or over the carious tooth. This swelling discharges either pus and blood or thin sanious effusion. In either case the discharge is offensive. There is pain, as evinced by the unwillingness of the dog to have his mouth examined or the jaw touched.

If neglected you will have a nasty fungus-looking growth, easily made to bleed, and frequently bleeding of its own accord.

The only disease it is likely to be mistaken for is true cancer, but there will be an absence of the cachexia, and also the microscopic character of the discharge will be different.

Treatment.—Our attention must first be directed to the teeth, and any carious tooth or portion of a carious tooth must be extracted. This operation will probably have to be performed after the dog has been placed under the influence of an anæsthetic, and therefore he must be taken to a skilled vet., unless, indeed, he can be securely held, and his mouth kept open by aid of an assistant and any means at your command. The disease must then be treated on general principles. If there is proud flesh, blue-stone must be used, or the solid nitrate of silver. If only ulceration and fœtid discharge, use a wash of Condy's fluid (one drachm to three in a pint of water), or a weak solution of chloride of zinc (twelve grains to six ounces of water), and the alum and myrrh wash (ten grains of alum and a drachm of tincture of myrrh to one ounce of water) ought to be used several times a day, by means of a rag or bit of sponge tied to the end of a stick.

Attention must be paid to the general health, and especially to the state of the stomach. The feeding will depend upon condition of body; if thin and poor, the diet must be generous, and cod-liver oil given; if gross, the simplest of food only, but in all cases this must be soft, and no bones are to be allowed on any account. Give an occasional dose of oil, and administer one of the bitter tonics recommended in the treatment of dyspepsia.

4. *Inflammation of the Tongue.*

Glossitis, as we usually term it, is far from common, but is sometimes seen as the result of injury, such as from the cruel and vulgar practice of worming the tongue, or from bites; it may also arise from the exhibition of mercury by unskilled hands.

The symptoms are dulness and languor of the dog, injection of the conjunctivæ, shivering, and fever, increased flow of saliva, with thickening and swelling of the tongue, with pain to the touch; there is also more or less stiffness of the jaw.

Treatment.—An aperient must first be given, if the state of swelling will permit, then cooling lotions must be applied, such as vinegar and water or ice. If, however, the swelling is great, two incisions must be made on the under surface of the tongue, one at each side of the raphe, and deep enough to allow of the escape of pus or blood and serum, and the wounds afterwards treated *secundum artem;* in fact, as a rule, very little treatment will be required.

5. *Ptyalism.*

Ptyalism, or excessive secretion of the salivary glands, may be the result of the abuse of mercury, or it may arise from decayed teeth and foul mouth, or simply from some local irritation of the glands themselves.

Treatment.—If from the abuse of mercury, remove the cause and give a gentle aperient, and food of a light nutritious kind. The mouth, too, had better be plentifully rinsed out with cold water. If arising from decayed teeth, the treatment recommended for foul mouth will be indicated. If there be no apparent cause for the salivation, in all probability the animal is not thriving, and probably is losing flesh. Give a bitter tonic or dinner pill, see that the dog is well housed and properly fed, and rub in every morning and evening with some degree of friction under the jaws a stimulating liniment, such as strong hartshorn and oil.

6. *Blain.*

The word blain is generally used to designate a carbuncle or swelling of an unhealthy character under the tongue.

Causes.—Bad feeding, cold, or an impoverished and impure state of the blood.

Symptoms.—The disease comes on slowly; perhaps the first symptom discernible by the dog's owner will be an increased flow of saliva, often of a very fœtid order. When the mouth is examined, one or more carbunclous swellings will be found underneath the side of the tongue. When the disease is further advanced these swellings ulcerate, and unhealthy matter is discharged. If it be not cured the glands become affected, and a low form of fever is the result, to which the animal may finally succumb.

Treatment.—This is simple enough in all conscience, but it must at the same time be energetic. As soon as the carbuncles are seen, they should be pretty deeply lanced. The mouth is then to be frequently sponged out with the wash recommended for foul mouth, or that for canker oris, or diluted Condy's fluid may be used. Attention must be paid to the state of the bowels and system generally. Take the dog in hand, give an aperient, and follow up with bitter tonics. Food of an easily-digested kind must be plentifully allowed, and if the dog gets very low, beef-tea and good port wine must be given freely.

7. *Wounds of the Tongue.*

Wounds of or injuries to the tongue are best left to Nature, so long as they show a disposition to heal kindly; if not, they may be touched with a solution of nitrate of silver, five grains to the ounce, or the myrrh and alum wash may be used.

8. *Ulcerations of the Tongue or Gums.*

These may arise from many causes. Attention is to be paid to the general health; a change of diet is usually necessary, while, at the same time, the teeth should be examined, stumps removed, or any sharp spiculæ that might tend to wound the cheek or tongue removed. Touch the ulcers with caustic, either silver or blue-stone, and afterwards use the myrrh and alum wash. In superficial ulcers of the mucous membrane of cheeks, &c., a borax lotion will suffice.

9. *Nasal Gleet.*

Nasal gleet, or ozœna, is usually the result of cold, or the sequel to a common catarrh. There is a discharge of mucous or muco-purulent matter from the nostrils, sometimes tinged with blood, and generally of a fœtid odour.

The septum of the nose in long-continued cases is apt to be attacked, and even eaten through.

Treatment.—Careful regulation of diet, which is to be nourishing. Frequent bathing of the nostrils in hot water, succeeded immediately by complete syringing out of the nostrils with warm water, to which a little Condy's fluid has been added, and occasional mild injections of sulphate of zinc, will effect a cure, all the more speedily if Fowler's solution of arsenic and cod-liver oil are given internally.

CHAPTER XIV.

DISEASES OF THE GENITAL ORGANS.

DOGS are often the subjects of a kind of non-inflammatory gonorrhœa or gleet, which not only causes the animals themselves a good deal of distress, but also makes them offensive to their owners.

This discharge should never be neglected, for if so ulceration is apt to take place, and the whole of the organ to become the seat of loathsome disease.

Treatment.—Simple local treatment will give relief for a time, but only for a time. The dog's general health needs seeing to. Probably he is suffering from ekzema or some other form of mange, of which the gleet is merely concomitant; or the dog may be simply over-pampered and over-fed. General hygienic measures, if adopted, will be found better for the dog than any amount of medicine. However, a short course of *liquor arsenicalis* will do good; and if the dog is weak or debilitated, quinine, with an allowance of cod-liver oil, will soon pull him together. Meanwhile, the parts must be gently bathed three times a day with any of the lotions recommended for canker, pulling back the sheath of the organ for that purpose as far as possible.

Paraphymosis is a condition in which the penis, having been protruded, the glans refuses to retract again into the sheath. It thus becomes strangulated, and much swelling and great pain is the result.

Treatment.—We must endeavour first to reduce the swelling by cold water douches or lotions; if we succeed in this the glans will easily be returned. If not, an operation must be performed, and this can only be done by a skilled vet. It consists in dividing by longitudinal section that portion of the prepuce which is causing the stricture. Care must be taken not to cut too far. Lead lotion will require to be used afterwards, and probably a suture will be needed.

Cancer of the scrotum is a name given to a diseased state of the scrotum. It commences superficially, with some degree of redness and irritation of the skin; pustules form, and burst, and the matter forms a scab. On the removal of the scab, the skin is found to be moist and inflamed and tender. If the disease progresses the skin hardens, becomes corrugated, and ulcerates. The ulceration usually assumes a malignant character, and attacks the tissues lying underneath.

Causes.—Derangement of the general health is the usual cause; scratches or wounds may determine the ulceration in the first instance.

Treatment.—This must be both constitutional and local. If you see the animal before much mischief has been done, change the diet, and do everything in your power to re-establish him in good health. Meanwhile, brush the scrotum with a weak solution of nitrate of silver (four grains to an ounce of water), keep the parts very clean, and use the benzoated zinc ointment; or the green iodide of mercury ointment diluted with four parts of common lard may be applied twice or thrice daily.

Sometimes there is considerable hardening and thickening of the integument without ulceration: local treatment to such cases may be productive of mischief.

A course of iodide of potassium often does good in disease of the scrotum, having first put the dog into as good condition as possible by a short course—ten days to a fortnight—of *liquor arsenicalis* in his food, and the administration of a quinine bolus. Should the disease make progress, the only thing that can save the dog is the excision by the hands of a skilful vet. of every portion of diseased integument or tissue. Even this operation, however, is not always followed by success.

The genital organs of the female are subject to disease of different forms, the commonest being various forms of tumours within the vagina. These at times admit of excision, notably the *polypus ;* this is a hard, semi-solid, smooth, pear-shaped tumour, attached by a pedicle or stalk to the wall of the vagina. The tumour is supplied with blood-vessels, and is often extremely sensitive and tender. The *treatment* is removal. This must first be attempted by ligature. If possible, pass a strong silk thread round the neck of the tumour, and tie tightly : the polypus will drop off of its own accord in a day or two ; if this cannot be done, the tumour may be seized with a pair of forceps, and twisted several times round, which will cause strangulation of the neck of the tumour and subsequent dropping off; or, thirdly, the tumour may be removed by the wire canula, or torsion may be used, and the tumour twisted off. The after treatment consists in the injection of mildly-stimulating injections, such as alum, borax, or lead.

Ignorant practitioners, however, have more than once mistaken protrusion of a portion of the uterus for a tumour, and have performed a brutal operation, which could not fail to kill the unfortunate animal. It should be remembered that the womb is soft, and not vascular; nor does it glisten like the polypus, which latter can generally be felt to depend from a stalk.

Tumours having broad bases are sometimes found in the canine vagina. These do not admit of removal, and the general health of the bitch must be attended to.

Prolapse of the walls of the vagina or part of the uterus itself is not uncommon at special times in some weakly animals. The swollen parts must be carefully returned, and frequent injections of cold water used, to which a few drops of tincture of muriate of iron had better be added. Great cleanliness is needed, and quinine or some bitter tonic mixture should be given internally.

CHAPTER XIV.

ON ABSCESSES, DISLOCATIONS, FRACTURES, WOUNDS, SPRAINS, BRUISES, ETC.

ABSCESSES may be defined as matter or pus generated and collected in any of the glands or tissues of the body. They are met with in all regions of the body, and are sometimes small and sometimes very large. They are usually very painful, and in some situations may be highly dangerous, from the effects of their pressure on important parts.

The causes of abscess are numerous: the presence of some foreign body, as a thorn, may give rise to it, or the deposit of unhealthy matter from constitutional reasons. In dogs blows very frequently give rise to large abscesses.

The commonest kind of abscess is the acute or phlegmonous: there is swelling, a glazed and glittering appearance of the skin, which is considerably reddened, and there is great pain and tenderness, accompanied with heat, and the dog is more or less fevered. If let alone the abscess usually goes on to suppuration, fluctuation is felt, pointing occurs, and finally it bursts. Mammary abscess is common in the teats of a bitch, frequently occurring when there is milk in them that is not removed, as about the time she would have had pups had she been in whelp.

Treatment.—We first endeavour to prevent matter forming; if unable to do so, we take the earliest opportunity of evacuating the pus when formed, and afterwards heal up the wound.

The antiphlogistic treatment consists in the application of leeches and cold lotions, such as the following—

℞ Ammoniæ hydrochlor.	...	...	ʒ iij.	
Spirit. rectific. pur.	...	...	ʒ vj.	
Acid. acetic. dil.	...	...	ʒ j.	
Aquæ	...	...	...	ad ʒ v.
Fᵗ lotio.			M.	

and discutient applications, such as the tincture of iodine for chronic abscess. In order to promote the absorption of matter in a chronic abscess you may also use some mercurial ointment in the form of plaster; nothing is better than the blue-ointment of the shops.

When matter is formed, and the fluctuation is distinct while the pain continues, the abscess must be opened. For this purpose a bistoury or lancet may be used. The incision must be pretty free, and to prevent bagging of matter afterwards it must be made on the most depending part. The incision ought to be made parallel to the course of the vessels, and the matter allowed to drain out; much squeezing is bad. If there be much bleeding cold should be applied.

A poultice or water-dressing is next to be applied, and probably a bit of lint may have to be stuffed into the wound to secure healing from below. If there be the slightest tendency to bagging of matter, a counter opening must be made to secure free draining. It will be necessary to give the dog a dose or two of opening medicine at first, and if the discharge is very great to keep up his strength well, and afterwards to use a quinine tonic.

Dislocations of Bones.—By dislocation is meant the displacement from their normal position of the joint ends of bones. The signs of dislocation of a joint are, a change in the shape of it, the end of the bone being felt in a new position, and impaired motion and stiffness. This immobility of the joint and the absence of any grating sound, as of the ends of broken bones rubbing against each other, guide us in our diagnosis between fracture and dislocation, though it must be not forgotton that the two are sometimes combined.

Treatment.—Try by means as skilful as you possess to pull and work the joint back again into its proper position, while an assistant holds the socket of the joint firmly and steadily. It is the best plan, however, to call in skilled assistance. Do this at once, for the difficulty of effecting reduction increases every hour. Only a careful study of the anatomy of the dog enables one successfully to reduce dislocations, the assistance of a good veterinary surgeon should therefore be always called in.

After the bone has been returned to its place, let the dog have plenty of rest, and use cold lotions to the joint, to avert the danger of inflammation.

Fractures.—By a fracture surgeons mean the solution of continuity between some parts of a bone—a broken bone, in other words.

Fractures are called *simple* when the bone is only broken in one place, and there is no wound; compound or open when there is a wound as well as the fracture, and communicating therewith; and comminuted when the bone is smashed into several fragments.

The usual cause of a fracture is direct or indirect violence.

The diagnosis is generally simple enough. We have the disfigurement, the displacement, the preternatural *mobility*, and grating sounds, for our guides. If the fracture be an open one, the end of the bone often protrudes. We mentioned the mobility; this to the hands of the surgeon, remember, for the dog himself can rarely move the limb.

Treatment.—We have first and foremost to reduce the fracture—that is, to place the bones in their natural position; and secondly, we must so bandage or splint the bone as to prevent its getting out of place again, and thus enable it to unite without disfigurement.

Very little art suffices one to fulfil the first intention, but correct and successful splinting is more difficult to attain, owing to the restlessness of the dog's nature and the objection he generally evinces to all forms of bandaging. Happily, the fractures that are most easily set and reunited are just those that are commonest in the dog—namely, those of the long bones of either fore or hind legs. The splints used may be either wood or tin, or, better perhaps than either, because more easily shaped and moulded, gutta-percha—this latter is cut into slips, and placed in moderately hot water to soften it, the fractured limb is meanwhile set and covered with a layer or two of lint, to arm it against undue pressure. The slips of softened gutta-percha are next placed in position lengthwise, before and behind, and gently tied with tape. If a layer of starched bandage is now rolled round, all the splinting will be complete. We have been very successful in treating fractures with the starched bandage alone. Care must be taken, however, not to apply either splints or bandages too tightly, else stoppage of the circulation may be the result, and consequent inflammation or gangrene itself. Some little care and "can" is necessary in applying the starch bandage. After setting the limb, pad it well with lint, then apply two or three strips of strong brown paper dipped in the starch; over this goes the roller, well saturated with thick starch, over all the limb, including the joints, upper and lower. Remember it must go *very lightly* over the actual seat of injury, your object being to keep the parts in apposition without doing anything that is likely to excite inflammation. Put over all a temporary splint—say of tin—to be kept on until the starch dries, which will take fully thirty hours. If there be a wound, a trap can be cut in the bandage for the purpose of dressing.

Fracture of a rib or ribs is not an uncommon occurrence, and is to be treated by binding a broad flannel roller round the chest, but not too tightly, as this would give the animal great pain, as well as dyspnœa. Keep him confined and at rest, to give the fractured parts a chance of uniting.

Little constitutional treatment is required. Let the diet be low at first, and give an occasional dose of castor-oil.

Sprain.—This is an accident which is much more common than fracture. In jumping or running, some of the ligaments become stretched, and detached from their sheath; the result is lameness, great pain, and probably a considerable degree of heat and some swelling.

Treatment.—Rest for the injured limb is imperative. If there seem to be very great pain, either hot fomentations or the hot flat-iron will afford relief, especially if a dose or two of tincture of opium or chloral hydrate is given by the mouth. Afterwards treat the sprain with the arnica lotion. A dose of aperient medicine—sulphate of soda or magnesia—will usually be needed, and if the animal seem much distressed low diet is indicated.

Bruises are to be treated according to general principles. Little will as a rule be needed saving rest, hot fomentations of poppy-heads, and afterwards a free use of the arnica lotion.

Wounds.—The class of wounds we are most often called upon to treat are incised wounds, and the indications of treatment to be fulfilled are three: (1), the stopping of the bleeding; (2), cleansing the wound from foreign matter; and (3), securing coaptation. If the bleeding be from an artery, the open end must be seized by a pair of forceps, and twisted round seven or eight times; or it may be ligatured, but the first method is better in the dog. It is, however, but seldom that any one other than a vet. or medical man can use torsion; but pressure alone is often quite as successful, and can always and easily be applied. It must be kept up for an hour at least, if any good is to be obtained. If the bleeding be not arterial, exposure to the air may stop it; cold is the best styptic, applied either by ice or rags rung out of the coldest water procurable. The tincture of the perchloride of iron is a capital styptic but apt to irritate.

Everything of the nature of a foreign body must be searched for and carefully removed before the wound is bound up. The wound is then washed with cold water, and when the bleeding has stopped it should be gently sponged with a weak solution (1 to 50) of carbolic acid and water. The edges of the wound are then to be brought together, and in nearly every case one or more stitches will be necessary. A curved needle is the best to use, and silken thread or thin silver wire. The stitches are placed not too near the edges, so as to give them a firm hold; they are placed about half an inch apart, each stitch being tied and quite independent of the other. Some kind of simple dressing will be needed; cold water and lint with a bit of oiled silk and a loose bandage is best, but the dog must be kept muzzled or he will not fail to relieve himself of dressings, stitches, and all. The wound is to be dressed every morning and gently sponged, and touched over with the weak carbolic lotion. As soon as the wound is capable of holding together, the stitches must be removed.

Sore Feet.—Dogs that work much in the field or on roads, such as Setters and Sheep-dogs, are often the subjects of inflammation about the toes and feet. It is easily removed, if seen to at once—washing in hot water, the use of the arnica lotion, and a few days' rest, will generally suffice. In severer cases it may be necessary to poultice the dog's feet, and during the day to wrap them in rags wetted with weak solution of carbolic acid or chloride of zinc, three grains to an ounce of water.

Ulcerations around the Toe-nails.—This is a very painful and troublesome complaint to which dogs are sometimes subject. In some cases the nails loosen and fall off, or have to be removed. Great cleanliness is necessary to aid in healing it, and the use of astringent lotions; the sore places must occasionally be touched with strong solution of nitrate of silver. In chronic cases blue ointment will assist Nature. In all cases socks or shoes must be worn.

Warts are too well-known to need description. They occur on the lips and cheeks and on the eyelids, causing the poor animal great discomfort; they also occur on the prepuce or vagina.

Treatment.—Excision is the best and most radical cure. They are easily snipped off with a pair of surgical scissors, or dissected off with forceps and scalpel. If in broad patches, however, on the inside of the cheek or lips, it is preferable to touch them with potassa fusa, or the homœopathic remedy, thuya, may be tried.

Sometimes a dog has a tendency to the growth of warts; in these cases I have known much good done by a course of *liquor arsenicalis.*

Worming the Tongue.—We merely mention the operation in order to condemn it as a most brutal and useless act.

CHAPTER XVI.

ON RABIES AND HYDROPHOBIA.

HOWEVER interesting the study of canine rabies and hydrophobia may be to the medical practitioner and veterinary surgeon, it is nevertheless a subject on which one has but little pleasure in writing, for the saddening fact is ever present to our mind that all human efforts to cure the disease—either in mankind or in the dog—if once fairly established, have hitherto proved futile.

Two things, however, we have in our power to effect ; we can, by gaining a knowledge of the earlier symptoms of the disorder in the dog, prevent its extension in our kennels, and, in the case of wounds from the teeth of even a truly rabid animal, we can use means to be presently stated, which will render the advent of the terrible disease all but impossible.

Now, in attempting to give a short outline of the pathology of rabies in the dog, we are met at the very outset by two difficulties. The first is that the earliest symptoms, which after all are just those with which the public ought to be most familiar, are not by any means the same in every dog ; and the second is that, professionally, we know well how hard it is for any one, no matter how well educated, to learn to know the symptoms of a disease from mere printed words—a disease they may never have seen a case of. We can only try, therefore, to describe rabies as well as words can do it.

Firstly. What is rabies?—By rabies we mean that disorder in the lower animals commonly, but erroneously, called hydrophobia, the result of a specific poison, received traumatically or otherwise, which produces a certain train of symptoms usually, if not invariably, ending in death. The disease is most common in the dog, but is sometimes seen in the cat and others of our domesticated animals.

Secondly. Does rabies ever arise in the dog without the positive absorption of the poisonous matter from another animal?—It is our opinion, from all we have read and heard and seen, that the possibility of the spontaneity of rabies is placed beyond a doubt, although without question the grand majority of cases are the result of direct contagion.

Thirdly. The duration of the stage of incubation or latency of the disorder.—Rabies will most likely appear in the dog within forty days after the reception of the contagium. But the actual time, we should say, would depend on a variety of causes : as the state of health and temperament of the wounded dog, the stage of rabidity in the dog that bit him, the portion of the body injured, the amount of contagium inserted, and on the age—puppyhood seeming to favour an earlier development of the disease.

Fourthly. The causes of rabies.—It could serve no good purpose to enlarge on the various alleged causes of rabies, most of which have been over and over again proved to be merely hypothetical. Contagion is the only *proved* cause, and in cases where it arises spontaneously rabies is doubtless the result of a combination of causes.

Fifthly. The virus or contagium itself.—With regard to this we have only to ask the reader to bear in mind its extreme, we were going to say its almost indestructible virulence.

We may mention, however, but we do so reservedly, that while the poison is only latent in the dog, and the animal still apparently in his usual state of health, we do not think it very likely to be communicable to another dog. Our theory is that any specific poison, no matter what, received into the body, may, during the period of its latency, be compared to a seedling in the earth—the seedling is not the plant, the virus is not the disease, both must grow, both must ripen. In the matter of rabies, however, theories are nasty tools to handle.

The virulence of the contagium of rabies is indeed very great, and it can be communicated in many different ways, even from dried saliva—though this to a medical man seems nothing remarkable, although it may account for the way rabies has been known to break out periodically in some kennels where the former hounds had been all destroyed and the boards apparently properly washed and disinfected. One cannot be too cautious in handling a mad dog. Although, as a matter of duty, we have sucked a snake bite in another, we would be chary in doing the same office were the bite that of a mad dog. Two cases just occur to us, both proving how easily the contagium is transmitted. Both were related to us by Professor Pirrie, of Aberdeen, but whether they actually occurred in his own practice we are unable to say for certain. A lady was mending a rent in her dress caused by the teeth of her pet dog, not suspected of being rabid. She merely bit off the end of the thread, with hydrophobia as the result. In the other case, a gentleman was reclining on the sofa, when his dog affectionately licked his cheek. He, too, succumbed. In both cases there must have been slight cuticular abrasion.

Having, however, always the interests of our canine friends at heart, we cannot leave this part of our subject without informing the reader that, as regards bites from animals unmistakably rabid, it is believed by most authorities that not more than forty per cent. of the bitten succumb to hydrophobia, and nothing like so large a proportion if the wounds have been speedily and properly attended to—facts which ought to go far to allay excitement and panic. We are drifting into the subject of hydrophobia, however, which is not our present intention. But we may just add that in no case ought a suspected dog who has bitten any one to be destroyed at once; he should be kept under supervision until the question of rabies or not rabies be placed beyond a doubt.

Sixthly. The symptoms.—That the grossest ignorance with regard to the symptoms of canine rabies prevails, both among the police and the general public, is proved by the accounts we read almost every other week of so-called rabid dogs. The individual members of our excellent police force are not over-intelligent, the public are naturally easily alarmed, and it is just possible that, at the very moment some poor harmless though excited animal is being hounded and beaten to death, a *really mad*, albeit all unsuspected, dog may be trotting along on the other side of the way. We are well acquainted with a gentleman who was, partially at least, to blame for a recent Berkshire panic. The dog was his own, and was followed and destroyed by him. Now, we do not say that this dog may not have been rabid, but his master could not tell us, on inquiry, *one solitary reliable symptom of canine rabies.* And we could, if space permitted, give many more instances quite as instructive. The symptoms which are given us by the older writers on this subject of rabies are, in many respects, so different from those we see now-a-days, that either the writers themselves must have been careless in their annotations, or the disease must, in the lapse of time, have become altered in type; and this last supposition is by no means improbable.

We have more than once advocated the plan, first proposed, we believe, by Mr. Fleming, of having the usual symptoms of canine rabies printed on the back of every license, along with the advice that, on a dog exhibiting any two or three of these, he should be, not destroyed, but placed under supervision.

Dogs do not, as the public suppose, at once go rabid and bite. The disease is very much more gradual in its onset. Rabies in its first stage seems much more like an exaggerated form of nervous irritability than anything else. *A dog never looks wiser than when he is beginning to go mad.* Mind and body seem struggling for mastery. The animal has a melancholy but restless eye, a far-away, listless look. Any one accustomed to his ways can tell there is something wrong with him. He becomes restless, and strangely suspicious of everything and every one, save his master, to whom indeed he shows an exaggerated affection, and from whom he seems to plead for pity or help. He knows and feels he is ill, and cannot bear to be looked at by any other animal. There are moments, at this stage of the disease, when he seems a little delirious ; he will get up suddenly, and examine behind things, snap in the air, or make a rush at nothing at all, but even then a word from his master will bring him back to his senses, and to his master's feet.

Once more, contrary to popular opinion, *he does not fear water.* He is not hydrophobic (ὕδωρ, water, and φοβεω, to fear). He will drink so long as he can swallow, and when unable to imbibe he will dip his poor parched open mouth into the water up to the eyes, in hopes it may reach his throat. We say "parched mouth" on purpose, for it is nearly always so, although there is generally at first a viscid or ropy saliva. The word foam is most misleading ; foam can only be produced from healthy saliva, as when a dog is eating a biscuit, or running hard. At the later stages of the disease the tongue will be dry, and sometimes nearly black.

Food, at first, he may or may not refuse, but afterwards he has a strange desire to bite at and swallow all sorts of deleterious matter—sticks, stones, clay, bones, straw, cinders, glass, &c. This, we opine, is not from any depravation of appetite, but seemingly from an irrepressible itching of the gums, from irritation of the nerves, which itching he *must* chew or bite something to relieve.

Now, as long as he has the power to control himself, he will do so, and perhaps prefer to hide away in dark corners; but there comes the moment when the dread poison lashes him to pained and awful fury. He barks in his agony a hoarse, peculiar bark, as we would naturally expect, considering the inflamed and swollen condition of his larynx and pharynx. The very act of barking gives such pain that the bark itself ends in a mournful, stridulous howl.

The unhappy animal usually has a desire to escape, and rove the country, generally rushing straight onwards, turning aside to bite at nothing, but spending its fury on any one, or any animal especially, he may come in contact with. His whole appearance when on the march— his furious yet frightened eye, and pinched but serious features, and strange gait, if once seen are not easily forgotten.

The diagnosis is not difficult on the whole, yet there are many diseases which bear some resemblance to rabies. Two cases have lately come under our notice, neither of them rabies, but each presenting some peculiar features. One was a Scotch Terrier, and the history was simply this—He had been wounded by a cat which he killed on his master's lawn, and five days after fell ill. There was the same emaciation you see in rabies, occasional curious howlings, and *satyriasis*, as seen in his persistently licking the parts of the other dogs ; there was also more or less of nervousness, but there were no hallucinations, and the howl was not the *rabid* howl, and there was no attempt to bite, even while giving him medicine. He died, but we did not get the chance of a *post-mortem.*

The other case was that of a Newfoundland bitch of our own. In the morning she had been greatly startled by a black cat having been suddenly thrown on her while she was not looking. The fright was severe ; all day she evinced extreme uneasiness and restlessness, looked strange about the eyes, which were congested, and the flow of saliva was increased ; drank much, but would not eat. Took her to our bed-room for safety sake, as she cares only for us. At first slept a little, but evidently had bad dreams ; awoke, and till far into the morning saw things about the room, and kept constantly snapping at imaginary flies, &c., &c. She was quite well again in a day or two.

There is another type or form of rabies, to which the name of dumb madness, or tranquil madness, has been given to distinguish it from the furious rabies. It is characterised by a greater intensity of pharyngeal and laryngeal symptoms, and there is probably less brain mischief. There is dumbness—that is, an entire absence of the peculiar bark heard in the furious type ; there is, however, a strange, harsh noise of roughened windpipe. There is partial or complete paralysis of the elevator muscles of the lower jaw, abundance of saliva ; the creature has altogether a mournfully dejected look, a strange glitter in the eye from dilated pupil ; he prefers to keep away in a corner, and seems to have little inclination to bite, even if he could.

This form of rabies is often seen in kennels affected with the furious form, some of the animals dying from one type of the disease, others from the other.

Hydrophobia in Man.

Hydrophobia in the human being is always considered by competent authorities to be equivalent to, or, in fact, the same disease as rabies in the canine race, and always transmitted to him from the bite of a dog or some other rabid animal.

That one-half of the cases we hear of and read of are really and truly hydrophobia we do not for one moment believe.

We do not for one moment believe that any case of true hydrophobia ever occurred in the human subject as the sequence to a wound from an animal that was not rabid.

We *do* believe that there really are cases of a kind of spurious hydrophobia induced by fear, and of this nature we doubt not are those cases of the disease which are reported to have occurred after the bites of animals undeniably in good health.

We do firmly believe that there is no more danger to be apprehended from the bite of a healthy dog, or cat either, than there is from the scratch of a clean knife, and *not half so much* as there is from a stab with a rusty rail.

Symptoms of hydrophobia.—On the symptoms of true hydrophobia we have little need to dwell, and just as little inclination. After a period of incubation, varying in length with the temperament and idiosyncrasy of the individual, there is usually, though by no means invariably, some slight pain and tingling in the cicatrix of the wound, followed by shooting pains in the bitten limb. At the same time there will be nervous feelings, innate fear of something impending, restlessness, and indigestion. These premonitory symptoms are not always present ; but when they are, they to a certain extent resemble those from incipient *delirium tremens* from alcoholism. The more advanced symptoms are unhappily too well known to need description. If the reader is much interested in the subject, he will find a capital description of it in the first volume of Watson's " Practice of Physic," p. 589.

The most characteristic symptoms of the disease are the terrible spasms, and horrible fear of impending death, and the viscid saliva that clings to the mouth, and constricted throat. These spasms we have seen induced by the sound of one drop of water dropped from the medical attendant's finger into a saucer, and latterly by the very sight of fluid.

Before leaving this subject, we think it our duty to inform the reader that tingling and slight pain in the cicatrix of an old dog bite is *not uncommon*, and there is no reason to apprehend danger from this symptom alone. As a rather curious instance of the force of imagination, we may mention that last year, while writing an article on rabies for a London periodical, we felt a curious nervous sensation in some old cat-bites in the forefinger, and we could not help touching it occasionally; by afternoon this feeling had increased to pricking pains, although they were by no means constant, and only came on when we thought about the matter. Towards night they were worse, and being in rather low health, sleep was impossible. In the morning the upper cicatrix was inflamed and slightly swollen; and so matters continued for nearly a week, when, gradually abating, they finally ceased.

Diagnosis.—There is a species of dysphagia, or difficulty in swallowing, brought on some-times in the nervous and hysterical from seeing a hydrophobic case, or even from hearing or reading of one. This generally comes on rather suddenly, is unaccompanied by difficulty of breathing, and the absence of convulsions of the body. It may be cured by compelling the patient to drink. Tetanus or lock-jaw may be mistaken for hydrophobia; but in tetanus *the jaw is fixed*, while it is almost constantly in motion in the more certainly fatal disease. Again, the tetanic spasm is more continuous in its nature, and not induced by sights or sounds, and there is no fear of water, although the suffering is increased by the act of swallowing. Now, tetanus is just the disease that might be mistaken for hydrophobia, especially as a lacerated wound from the fangs of a dog might produce it.

In some forms of mania there is a dread of water; but a case of this kind could easily be diagnosed, because the maniac has hallucinations—he has lost his reasoning power; whereas in hydrophobia, although the patient may at times be "a little off his head," still the reason, the mind, and intellect, remain clear until the very last.

Treatment.—We must begin by frankly confessing that every one of the few cases of true hydrophobia which we have had the great pain to witness, have had but one ending—death. We are periodically hearing of certain specifics having been discovered, tried, and proved to be perfect remedies. We regret to say that such reports when weighed in the balance have invariably been found wanting. It would take pages of our space to even name the numerous medicinal agents that have been proposed and prescribed in vain. The older plan of treatment by large bleedings could but hasten death; opium, or chloroform, or chloral, even if they succeeded in allaying to a certain extent the irritation and pain of body and mind, could hardly be expected to eliminate or counteract the poison. In all probability, many years may yet elapse before a perfect antidote to the poison of rabies is discovered, and we can only hope for the happy end through earnest study in the combined science of medicine and chemistry, aided by skilful experiment and well-arranged observation. Meanwhile, if we cannot positively cure, we can do very much to prevent hydrophobia, and to keep it in check.

If an individual, then, is bitten by a dog or other animal which is undoubtedly or even presumably rabid, the local or preventive treatment should be gone about *as speedily as it possibly can be*. We have not been able to prove how soon the poison of the saliva becomes absorbed, although some writers tell us in less than five minutes, while others mention a very much longer time. We all know, however, the rapidity with which some of the salts of the metallic poisons can find their way from an abraded surface into the circulation and the secretions themselves.

Now, we have very little doubt, judging from all we have read and heard, and from the little we have seen of accidents from rabid dogs, that if proper measures are adopted within five minutes, or even a quarter of an hour, after a bite has been received, the absorption of the poison, and consequently the occurrence of hydrophobia, are rendered impossible.

Suction and cauterisation, then, are our sheet-anchors. The mucous membrane of the lips, it must be remembered, is a secreting, and not an absorbing membrane, so the danger of inoculation by the mouth is very small indeed, unless there is some slight abrasion, when poisoning might result, as in the case of the lady whose dress was torn by a rabid lap-dog. She sewed up the rent, and bit off the thread, thus bringing her lips into contact with the little saliva left on the dress ; hydrophobia, and we need hardly add death, was the result. But so slight is the danger of inoculation through the mucous membrane of the mouth, that if the bite is in a position which the individual himself cannot reach, a friend need hardly fear to perform the suction for him. The mouth of the sucker ought to be frequently rinsed with water, and the teeth ought to be used in nibbling the edges of the wound to secure a plentiful flow of blood. The sucking is to be kept up for a quarter of an hour, with short intervals of washing or laving the parts with warm water, or warm water with either a little salt in it, or some spirits, or a few drops of carbolic acid.

As soon, however, as cauterisation can be resorted to, it must take precedence. What we wish to obtain is the complete destruction of the poisonous matter in the wound, and the sloughing away of the adjacent portions of tissue, that may reasonably be supposed to have become imbued with the contagium.

Probably the best way of fulfilling these indications is either the use of the actual cautery— the hot iron—or any one of the three powerful caustics, nitrate of silver, potassa caustica, or carbolic acid.

As to the actual cautery, it has one advantage over the others, it is never far to seek ; a piece of strong wire, a nail, or anything in shape of a probe, can be heated to redness in a few moments in the fire, and its application only requires reasonable courage.

N.B.—It is better to err on the right side, and burn too much than too little, and, remember, the cautery must be of sufficient thickness to retain enough heat to do its work well. The wound had better be kept open for a few weeks by the application of some stimulating ointment. We have seen snake bites cauterised with a burning brand, and by gunpowder ; but this latter plan is not so easily adopted with a wound from a dog's tooth, owing to the greater amount of bleeding.

There is great difference of opinion among authorities regarding the relative value of the actual cautery as compared to caustics. Probably it is best to apply which ever comes first and readiest. Nitrate of silver, a small pencil of which can easily be carried in the pocket of any one who is constantly among dogs, is greatly extolled by Youatt. We have only to say that the pencils usually sold by chemists are too blunt, and not long enough. They will not go home, as it were, to the bottom of the wound, and it must be patent to everybody that to do any good the cauterisation must be deep and effectual. Potassa fusa is better, we think, than silver, but is deliquescent, and so is not so portable, unless prepared with guttapercha, as proposed by M. Robiquet. The carbolic acid is diluted with one part of spirits of wine, and a bit of lint or rag, well soaked in this, *probed* into the wound, and covered over with a pad or bandage, which must be kept on for three or four hours. Afterwards keep the wound open for some time, and frequently wash with a weak solution of carbolic acid.

The excision of the bitten part is recommended by some. After the part has been well washed and sucked for a short time, a small skewer is thrust into the wound, and you must manage, by means of two curved incisions, to cut the piece out without actually touching the skewer with the knife. This plan was first proposed, we believe, by Abernethy.

The second part of our preventive treatment might aim at the prevention of absorption by Lafosse's plan—which is at least feasible—of giving at intervals large quantities of water to drink, mixed with some brandy and ammonia. This may be kept up for days.

The third is the exhibition of blue-pill, or a mercurial in some form, to an extent which shall cause salivation. Whether this does any real good is of course extremely doubtful, but if the patient has been bitten by a really mad dog, no means that awakens even a glimmering of hope of preventing hydrophobia is to be despised.

Afterwards, the *mind* of the individual who has incurred the unfortunate accident must be quieted and rendered cheerful by the best means in our power. Some course of tonic or alterative medicine should be prescribed, with perhaps the frequent use of the Turkish or vapour bath. If these, however, have a tendency to cause the thoughts to dwell upon the recent injury, change of scene and residence, or travelling, must be ordered instead.

We must not, of course, forget to dose the dog as well as the bitten person. He ought to be put under veterinary supervision, and in no case destroyed. If he should really die rabid, the fact had better be kept a secret from his victim; but if he should live, and seem in good health, what a relief to be able to tell the bitten individual and his friends, "Well, such-and-such a dog isn't dead after all; so that is all right, and it is a pity we inflicted the pain of cauterising the bite." This, said in an off-hand sort of a way, would go far to prevent "mental hydrophobia," and tone the patient's mind up to a healthy standard.

The indications of treatment of a case of undoubted hydrophobia are two—viz., to endeavour, as far as possible, to ease pain and tranquillise the mind.

The most complete quietude, combined with absence of gloom, must be maintained in all the patient's surroundings. The attendants ought to be attentive, cheerful, but not officious. No muttering or whispering, either in the patient's room or in an adjoining room, must be permitted, and the fewer visitors, and the more absence of all seeming concern, the better. He ought, if possible, to be made believe he is suffering from quite a different disease.

The room should be darkened, without excluding the air, and any mirror or other glittering object had better be removed, or the poor patient so placed that he cannot perceive it.

The whole house is to be kept as quiet as possible; for we must not forget that distant noises, as of articles falling, as well as sudden draughts of air and the sound of fluids, induce the terrible paroxysms. If during the fits a tendency to bite is observable, the end of a stick rolled round with a soft rag and dipped in water may be placed in one side of the mouth. Who knows but this may give even great relief?—for we do not look upon the attempts to bite as characteristic of a wish to inflict injury, so much as a desire to relieve an excessive and unbearable itching in the gums.

The administration of the hydrate of chloral in repeated large doses, administered as an enema, affords, we think, the best chance of producing sleep and easing pain.

GENERAL INDEX.

CANINE MEDICINE AND SURGERY.

NOTES TO THE PLATES.

Following are the names and the owners of the dogs portrayed, from left to right, on the pages opposite: